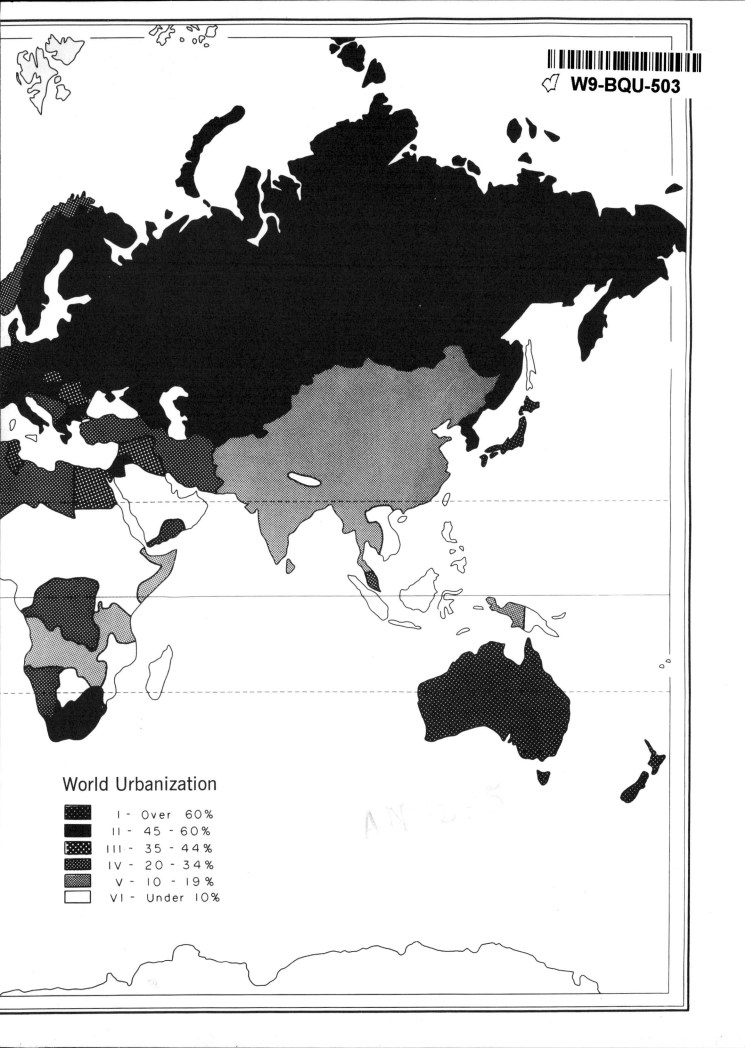

World Urbanization

- I – Over 60%
- II – 45 – 60%
- III – 35 – 44%
- IV – 20 – 34%
- V – 10 – 19%
- VI – Under 10%

THE GEOGRAPHY OF ECONOMIC SYSTEMS

Prentice-Hall, Inc., Englewood Cliffs, New Jersey

BRIAN J. L. BERRY

Irving B. Harris Professor of Urban Geography
The University of Chicago

EDGAR C. CONKLING

Chairman, Department of Geography
State University of New York at Buffalo

D. MICHAEL RAY

Professor, Carleton University
Ottawa, Ontario

THE
GEOGRAPHY
OF
ECONOMIC
SYSTEMS

Library of Congress Cataloging in Publication Data

BERRY, BRIAN JOE LOBLEY (date)
  The geography of economic systems.

  Includes bibliographies and index.
  1. Geography, Economic. I. Conkling, Edgar C.,
joint author. II. Ray, David Michael (date) joint
author. III. Title.
HF1025.B455 1976   330.9–04   75-15841
ISBN 0-13-351296-7

Printed in the United States of America

10 9 8 7 6 5 4 3 2

Cover: Computer-generated population density map of the
United States provided through the courtesy of the
Laboratory for Computer Graphics and Spatial Analysis,
Graduate School of Design, Harvard University.

PRENTICE-HALL INTERNATIONAL, INC., London
PRENTICE-HALL OF AUSTRALIA, PTY. LTD., Sydney
PRENTICE-HALL OF CANADA, LTD., Toronto
PRENTICE-HALL OF INDIA PRIVATE LIMITED, New Delhi
PRENTICE-HALL OF JAPAN, INC., Tokyo
PRENTICE-HALL OF SOUTHEAST ASIA (PTE.) LTD., Singapore

contents

Ours is a crisis-ridden age. Not only do war, famine, and pestilence continue to stalk the world, but new threats now are added to the apocalyptic challenge to our earlier hopes of a millennium in which there would be unparalleled prosperity for all. The energy crisis, environmental pollution, urban blight, and unemployment combined with high inflation afflict the industrial nations of West and East alike. The poorest countries, with scant resources, have descended into a new United Nations category known as the *Fourth World* to which some apply the World War I concept of *triage*—sorted out because they are beyond help and hope. The old Third World has become a more exclusive OPEC-led grouping limited to those nations with rich mineral or agricultural resources, who, organized politically into resource-producer cartels, are seeking to redress imbalances existing between them and the world's industrial powers and who now have the capability to threaten the bases of international trade and the growth and prosperity of the developed countries.

The extent of these problems may be magnified by the news media and given greater immediacy by the increasing sophistication with which national and international agencies quickly analyze trends and bring them to public attention. But there can be no doubt that they are as real as they are serious. Growth and economic efficiency in a competitive freely trading world no longer afford a sufficient basis for understanding the broad outlines of the geography of economic systems. We must add resource politics, the limits to growth, and the goals and methods of economic planning by sovereign nation-states as major concerns. And we must recognize the global pattern of interdependencies through which problems in one place are related to events in others. Indeed, the interdependencies are so complex that we must take them into account or suffer the likelihood that we will create new problems that are far worse than the ones we attempt to solve.

The need to understand spatial interdependencies has led us to examine them in a *systems* framework in this book. A *system* may be defined as an entity that functions as a whole because of the interdependence of its parts. And so we have adopted a strategy of first analyzing the parts in twelve *systematically* organized chapters, then exploring the different ways in which the parts come together in distinctive national entities within the world economy in twelve *regionally* organized chapters. Finally, we draw the threads together in a concluding chapter that looks at growth and its limits in a more general system theory framework.

The book begins with a review of the sequence of ideas in economic geography that are represented in one way or another in the text: commercial geography in the late nineteenth century, the environmentalist idea, the concept of areal differentiation, location theory, and the general systems theory approach, which embraces both the general idea of interdependency, and the specific behavioral idea of man's ability to produce and effect change. This leads directly into questions of value systems and the goals of national and regional economic planning. Five types of economic systems are identified, arising from the nature of decision making and the capability of national leaders to control and effect change: the laissez-faire market economy, the large-scale market-negotiated system of the modern industrial state, the welfare state, the socialist state, and the diverse group of Third and Fourth World economies that nonetheless share common traits and problems.

Chapters 2 and 3 deal with world population patterns and dynamics, with questions of world food supply, and with the complex of issues relating to the adequacy of global supplies of resources for an expanding population. The discussion makes it clear that the world has entered an era in which resources will count for more than ever before, in which conservation must gain a premium over consumption, and in which more attention may be paid to exploiting resources than to curbing pollution, in spite of both the short- and long-run costs that greater pollution will force us all to bear.

To understand the nature of costs and benefits, and the likely shifts in locational relationships that such changes will produce, we must understand some basic principles of economics and the processes by which land uses are determined, industrial locations are selected, trade takes place, and urban hierarchies shape the spatial organization of economic systems. The next nine chapters of the book are devoted to these building blocks. Chapter 4 explores how prices bring demands and supplies into balance, and it outlines the key elements of the geography of prices. Chapters

preface

5 and 6 deal with demand and supply. Chapter 7 is devoted to theories of land use, both urban and rural, Chapters 8 and 9 to industrial location, Chapters 10 and 11 to international trade, and Chapter 12 to local and interregional trade and urban hierarchies. The reader who has comprehended the materials to this point should have a working knowledge of the geographies of population and resources, and the principles that guide the location of economic activities, regional specialization and trade, and market centers.

To end a book on the geography of economic systems at this point would be to condemn it to incompleteness. The parts have to be put together in a systems framework. This is what is attempted in Chapters 13 through 24. Chapters 13 and 14 are the transition—the first deals with the regional concept (geography's basic integrating device) and with regional types within the international system. The second deals with the heartland-hinterland paradigm, a theory that explains the regional structure of the world economy. Chapters 15 through 18 analyze four of the world's urban-industrial heartland economies: Canada, where resources have been replaced by urbanization as the growth lever; the United Kingdom, whose position of world leadership has been replaced by the problems of adjustment to "mini" status on the margin of a United Europe; Japan, whose spiralling postwar growth has been spurred by technological initiatives; and the Soviet Union, whose urban-industrial transformation was planned and executed with the command structure and goals of a socialist state. Chapter 19 follows with a description of the Denison Model, which explains the differences in the postwar growth rates of these nations. In these four regional chapters, the nation-state is taken as a unit of analysis because of its continuing (and, indeed, increasing) saliency as a unit of economic organization and decision making in a world where autarky is on the increase. Each of the four cases was selected to illustrate a different regional type of political economy—dominantly laissez-faire Canada, welfare-state Britain, the large-scale organization of "Japan, Incorporated," and the directed socialist economy of the USSR. Chapters 20 through 23 repeat the process for a parallel set of resource-producing hinterland nations: the highly dualistic laissez-faire economies of the member-countries of the Central American Common Market; welfare-state New Zealand; Indonesia, where attempts are being made to break the dualism between traditional cultures and colonial "development islands" by large-scale organization of resource-oriented growth; and China, where Marxist planning in the Oriental mode is producing a new space-economy. Finally, Chapter 24 looks at the changing balance of heartland-hinterland power in the world economy, as produced by resource-producer cartels in the new Third World, and political revolutions in the Fourth World—two different forms of a continuing "revolution of the external proletariat." The questions that are raised are those of the changing status of regional groupings of national economies within the world economic order, that is, the changing geography of economic systems.

Questions of economic growth, its consequences, and its limits run throughout the book. These questions are isolated for special attention in Chapter 25. Different types of growth are analyzed, world heartland-hinterland differences are set into the context of industrial revolution and innovation diffusion, and the debate on the limits to growth is reviewed. Everett Hagen has suggested that in an anxious age the way to achieve popularity is either to relieve the anxiety that people feel or to feed it. Charles Reich's *The Greening of America* is an example of the former, arguing that a beautiful new society is coming into inevitable and effortless existence. But the authors of the Club of Rome's *The Limits to Growth* contend that unless we take very drastic, immediate, and rather unlikely steps the world faces a Malthusian catastrophe within a century. In our book, we favor neither of these extremes, presenting instead key theories, essential facts, and critical geographic problems faced by our economic systems, leaving it for the reader to decide whether industrialization has proceeded so far that civilization is trapped or whether new challenges will evoke fresh responses. Every culture and time has had its own image of the future with its hopes and expectations, its aspirations and ideals. Indeed, the Dutch sociologist Frederick L. Polak argued that the history of culture is the history of its image of the future and that "thinking about the future is not only the mightiest lever of progress but also the condition of survival." Economic geographers, caught up with other disciplines in the problems of our age, are beginning to turn their attention to their image of the future and to the contributions they wish to make to that future. The basis of their contribution is a better understanding of the geography of economic systems. It is to these ends that this book is offered.

a note to the teacher

If some of the foregoing sounds different from other books on economic geography, it represents our attempt to bridge a series of gulfs—between what we teach and how we approach our work as professional geographers, between what is fashionable and what are important heritages from our past, between fact and theory, economics and geography, and between systematic and regional, and macro- and micro-approaches to our subject matter. To accomplish this task of integration we have used systems ideas—ideas which are, after all, not new in geography. Geographers, more than any of the other social scientists, have always played a special integrative role and have frequently relied upon systems ideas. The cornerstones of system theory are concepts of organization, environment, interaction, hierarchy, and growth, and it is on these concepts that geographers have built most of what they know. Thus, this book contains much traditional economic geography as well as some that may be new. It is not the individual components of this book that may be different, but rather the integration of diverse ideas into a framework that bears directly on current critical problems.

We feel the materials could be used as readings to support a variety of lecture-course plans. As the book was being written, initial drafts were read and evaluated by many geographers in a wide range of colleges and universities, and their assessments were instrumental both in extensive rewriting of an original text and in the reorganization of the rewritten text into its present form. Several readers pointed out that they might not require their students to read all the chapters, but they welcomed the opportunity to have available an array of options from which they could judiciously select the combination that best matched their individual course designs. In this way, we tried to anticipate today's need for economic geography books that are different and up to date, but neither unfamiliar nor unduly constraining.

a note to the student

To aid you in studying the materials presented in this book, Judith Duncan has prepared a *Student Guide to the Geography of Economic Systems*, which is also available from Prentice-Hall, Inc. In Ms. Duncan's workbook, a hierarchy of learning goals is described, and the contents of each chapter of the book are analyzed in terms of these goals. Specific learning objectives are presented chapter-by-chapter, as are questions that test whether the objectives are being achieved. If you feel that you need something to help you study economic geography with your teacher's lectures, the textbook, and supplementary readings that may be assigned, the *Student Guide* may be what you need.

geographic
fundamentals

one

The field of economic geography is primarily concerned with ideas about the location of economic activity, the spatial organization and growth of economic systems, and man's use and abuse of the earth's resources. There has been a progressive accumulation of these ideas since the 1880s, when economic geography was first recognized as a separate field of study.

Before that time, the highly practical field of *commercial geography* provided knowledge to prospective merchants and governmental officials about the main products and exports of the principal regions of the world.

Along with the other modern social sciences, economic geography developed between 1880 and 1900 as an attempt to forge a more analytic, explanatory science than that provided by commercial geography. Until the early 1930s, a philosophy of *environmentalism* dominated the thinking of many of the intellectual leaders of the field. The following twenty-five years saw a variety of regional and topical approaches to the study of the *areal differentiation* of economic activities, accompanied by a growing concern for conservation and the wise management of the earth's resources. More recently, interest in spatial patterns has been generalized to include *locational analysis and dynamics of spatial systems.* Location theory, for many years developed by economists far beyond the limits of geography, has become an important part of economic geography and new quantitative methods of locational analysis are now widely used by researchers. The result is that the present discipline of economic geography is a complex mosaic of ideas and approaches.

A BRIEF HISTORY OF THE FIELD

To appreciate the accumulation of ideas in economic geography we should first look at earlier thinking, beginning with the waning of commercial geography as a field of study. This will provide some sense of the continuity and the change in the approaches and ideas of economic geographers.

the transition from commercial geography, 1880–1900

Commercial geography had grown up as the Western European nations expanded their trading relationships and empires across the globe and both merchants and governments needed well-organized information about the populations, regions, and resources of the world. One of the first textbooks in the field was written in the middle of the seventeenth century by the geographer Bernhardus Varenius to provide practical commercial information for Amsterdam merchants. Later on, other volumes were published: Patrick Gordon's *Geography Anatomized,* which had twenty editions in England between 1693 and 1728; William Guthrie's *New System of Modern Geography,* published in 1770 and revised through 1843; and Jedidiah Morse's

the changing nature of economic geography

1

Geography Made Easy. These books were the world's first financially rewarding educational publications.

Commercial geography reached its zenith in the work of a British scholar, G. G. Chisholm. In the first edition of his *Handbook of Commercial Geography* (London: Longmans, Green, 1889, p. iii), Chisholm said that the general purpose of commercial geography was to stimulate "an intellectual interest [in] the study of geographical facts relating to commerce." However, this kind of geography was little more than an inventory of production and trade statistics for different areas, and younger scholars demanded better explanation of the facts.

The transition from commercial to economic geography came after a German geographer, S. Götz, suggested a new analytic approach in his paper, "Die Aufgaben der Wirtschaftlichen Erdkunde," ["The Task of Economic Geography"] which appeared in the *Zeitschrift der Gesellschaft für Erdkunde zu Berlin* in 1882. The first article to use the term "economic geography" in the United States was published in 1888, and in 1900 one of America's outstanding early geographers, Ellen Churchill Semple, authored a major book with that title. World War I proved a great stimulus to the infant field; economic geographers were called upon to provide knowledge about sources of food and raw materials in the world, and for understanding of the economic problems of different countries. By the early 1920s the field was well established, and a special journal called *Economic Geography* appeared in 1925.

What was this new subject about? An economist, E. Robinson, wrote a hopeful prospectus in the early days of the new field:

. . . It seeks to ascertain and explain geographic division of labor . . . a unified scientific discipline connecting with classical economics through the doctrine of division of labor and comparative costs . . . it deals with principles rather than details; its method is in the main analytical rather than descriptive; and its controlling purpose is to establish scientific truth rather than to serve practical utility. ("Economic Geography," *Papers and Discussions of the American Economic Association,* 10, 1895, p. 247).

Hopes and realities, however, did not always match. The economic geographers of the early twentieth century found their links with economics to be rather more tenuous than Robinson thought they should be. Although the geographers were concerned with theory, their emphasis was upon specific "geographic principles":

Economic geography is the study of the different kinds of environments as they affect the different ways in which men get a living. (C. R. W. Dryer, *Elementary Economic Geography.* New York: American Book, 1916, p. 11).

[Economic geography is] . . . the study of the relation of economic activities to natural environment . . . (C. C. Colby, ed. *Source Book for the Economic Geography of North America.* Chicago: University of Chicago Press, 1921).

The peculiar contribution of economic geography is an understanding of the relation between natural environment and economic life in the various regions of the earth. (W. D. Jones and D. S. Whittlesey, *An Introduction to Economic Geography.* Chicago: University of Chicago Press, 1925, p. 3).

The field that the new economic geographers described was not closely related to economics, but instead a discipline whose ideas were consistent with the philosophies of *environmentalism* that dominated the social sciences as they emerged out of natural philosophy in the later nineteenth century.

origins of environmentalism

Environmentalist thinking had been present in Western thought at least from the time of the Greeks. In his *Traces on the Rhodian Shore* (University of California Press, 1967), Clarence Glacken reports how men have persistently asked three questions concerning the habitable earth and their relationship to it:

a. *The idea of a designed earth:*
   Is the earth, which is obviously a fit environment for man and other organic life, a purposefully made creation?

b. *The idea of environmental influence:*
   Have its climates, its relief, the configuration of its continents influenced the moral and social nature of its individuals, and have they had an influence in moulding the character and nature of human culture?

c. *The idea of man as a geographic agent:*
   In his long tenure on earth, in what manner has man changed it from its hypothetical pristine condition?

The idea of environmental influence had its origins in pharmaceutical lore, medicine, and weather observation; environmental factors were associated with the development of different groups of people and individuals in these environments. As early as the Middle Ages, ideas of environmental influence and adaptation were used to explain racial and cultural differences, whether in the writings of Europeans like St. Thomas Aquinas or in the work of Muslim scholars like Ibn Khaldun, and these ideas continued throughout the eighteenth century.

At the beginning of the eighteenth century, a German named Carl Ritter developed an approach to geography that emphasized the unity of man and nature. Every detailed observation, Ritter said, must be related to the general laws that govern the physical earth. The ultimate explanation of these laws, he felt, was that of divine purpose irrevocably working through human evolution towards divinely endowed ideal states.

Ritter's physical geography was carried (without the deism) to the United States in 1848 by Arnold Guyot, who became professor of geography and geology at Princeton. Guyot and Matthew Fontaine Maury, whose textbook on physical geography was a classic work in this country by 1875, did much to separate geography from geology as a university-level discipline in America—a consequence of the interest among physiographers in the influence of natural environment on mankind. The first North American university department of geography, established at the University of Chicago in 1903, stated as its purpose "to occupy the ground intermediate between geology and climatology on the one hand and history, sociology, political economy and biology on the other." It was in this kind of intellectual context that environmentalism became the dominating idea in early economic geography.

the environmentalist idea

The basic environmentalist idea was clearly expressed by the first president of the Association of American Geographers, William Morris Davis, in his 1906 presidential address: "Any statement is of geographic quality if it contains . . . some relation between an element of inorganic control and one of organic response." To Davis, human society was an organism that survived by adjustment to the physical environment; the nature of its growth was thus environmentally prescribed.

Davis was a tireless scholar who sought for many years to impose a uniform environmentalist concept on American geographic education. His viewpoint, as well as that of his contemporaries, such as Ellen Churchill Semple, Albert Perry Brigham, Ellsworth Huntington, and Griffith Taylor are best illustrated in the following quotation from Semple:

Man is a product of the earth's surface. This means not merely that he is a child of the earth, dust of her dust; but that the earth has mothered him, fed him, set him tasks, directed his thoughts, confronted him with difficulties that have strengthened his body and sharpened his wits, given him his problems of navigation or irrigation, and at the same time whispered hints of their solution. (Ellen Churchill Semple, *The Influences of Geographic Environment*. New York: Henry Holt, 1911, p. 1).

The environmentalist idea was so strong that when sociologist Pitirim A. Sorokin published his masterful review and critique, *Contemporary Sociological Theories Through the First Quarter of the Twentieth Century* (Harper & Row, 1928), he devoted one-sixth of his study to what he termed *The Geographical Theory:* "Almost since the beginning of man's history," he wrote, "it has been known that the characteristics, behavior, social organization, social processes and historical destiny of a society depend upon the geographical environment."

Among the phenomena, Sorokin noted that the environmentalists tried to explain by environmental differences were population distribution and density; housing types; road location; clothing; and the amount of wealth produced and owned by a society. A dominating belief was that all brilliant and wealthy civilizations of early times occurred in "favorable" natural environments, whereas "unfavorable" climates and inaccessible or isolated areas bred backwardness and savagery. The

location and nature of industry, business cycles and the rhythms of economic life, race, and physiological, social, and historical differences among societies were all also held to be environmentally determined. So were health; energy and efficiency; suicide; insanity; crime; birth; death, and marriage rates; religion, art, and literature; and the social and political organization of society.

The strongest hypotheses about civilization and climate were those of a geographer named Ellsworth Huntington who argued that climate is the decisive factor in health and physical and mental efficiency; and that since a civilization is the result of the energy, efficiency, intelligence and genius of the population, *ergo:* climate is the "mainspring" factor in the progress or regress of civilizations.

The economic geographies of the time faithfully followed the environmental dictum. The chapter headings of one small book illustrate the contemporary mode of thought: Influence of Climate, Influence of Vegetation, Influence of Animal Life, (R. N. Rudmose Brown, *The Principles of Economic Geography*. London: Pitman, 1920).

the waning of environmentalism

Even as environmentalism reached its height, geography was developing new ideas. Scholars such as Frederic Le Play, who developed the first scientific method for the study and analysis of social phenomena, had already correlated the character of places with the type of work, forms of property, types of family organization and other institutions and social processes. Le Play, however, emphasized the *mutual interdependence* of place, economy, and culture, rather than the single-factor causation of environment.

The idea of the interdependence of culture and nature was developed more fully by the French geographer, Vidal de la Blache, in his *Principles of Human Geography* (1926). According to Vidal

The dominant idea in all geographical progress is that of terrestrial unity. The conception of the earth as a whole, whose parts are coordinated, where phenomena follow a definite sequence and obey general laws to which particular cases are related.

What was emerging out of environmentalism was a concern in geography for ecology. Vidal thought that "every region is a domain where many dissimilar things, artificially brought together, have subsequently adapted themselves to a common existence" and in which "the influences of environment are seen only through masses of historical events which enshroud them." He also believed that the physical environment set limits or margins within which man was free to work, rather than controlling him directly.

The gradual change in thinking can be traced in the following series of quotations from successive editions of Bengtson and Van Royen's textbook *Economic Geography*. In 1935, the authors indicated that "differences in the natural environment not only affect the physical activities of man, but generally they also lead to fundamental differences in thoughts and ideals. . . . The Norwegians of today—strong, agile, alert, and serious—are in large measure the product of the environment which has fostered them." The next edition of the text (1942) makes certain adjustments. The first edition's "differences in environment *lead* to differences in activities" becomes "differences in productive activities *are often results of* differences in environment." Again, "the Norwegians of today—virile, agile, alert, and sincere—in large measure have been shaped as a regional group by the environment which has fostered them." The subtle change from before is noteworthy. Finally, in 1956, the authors indicated that "the physical environment does *not determine* the economic activity and the mode of life of man." Evidently some old dogs were willing to learn new tricks!

areal differentiation: 1930s–1960s

"The simple faith in the determining influence of natural environment has almost disappeared," wrote Jan Broek in "Discourses on Economic Geography" that appeared in *The Geographical Review* for 1941. As geographers extended their research they looked for new explanations in economics. W. H. Carter and R. E. Dodge for example, argued that economic geography "should analyze . . . universally applicable economic principles that underlie our whole industrial life" (*Economic Geography,* New York: Doubleday, Doran & Co., 1939, p. vi).

But widespread use of economic principles in economic geography did not come, except for some experimentation with industrial location analysis, and for O. E. Baker's uses of Ricardo's rent theories in his studies of land use. During the Depression and the New Deal many American economic geographers, such as J. Russell Smith, did become concerned about resources and the conservation of the environment, and some geographers moved into problem-solving roles in President Roosevelt's National Resources Planning Board and in the Tennessee Valley Authority. Although these involvements were to prove valuable later, the thrust of academic economic geography once again resembled that of the earlier commercial geography, however, and this approach persisted until the 1960s. To quote from the two most widely quoted recent textbook authors, economic geography was, once again

an inquiry into similarities, differences, and linkages within and between areas in the production, exchange, transfer, and consumption of goods and services. (Richard S. Thoman, "Economic Geography," *International Encyclopedia of the Social Sciences,* 6, New York: Macmillan, 1968, pp. 124–28).

Or

The study of the areal variation on the earth's surface in mans' activities related to producing, exchanging and consuming wealth. (J. W. Alexander, *Economic Geography.* Englewood Cliffs, N.J.: Prentice-Hall, 1963).

Some economic geographers organized their books by *regions* or *countries* and described their principal products and exports. Some authors dealt systematically with the spatial patterns of production and trade of particular *commodities.* Others organized their works around "*activity systems,*" such as primitive subsistence economies, commercial grain-livestock farming systems, industrial-urban complexes, which could be described in some jointly systematic-regional manner.

There were some changes over the years, too. Although the regionally oriented approaches dominated the 1940s, there was a gradual shift towards the topical plans; and with this shift came an increasing concern for the locations and spatial patterns of economic activities, and new attempts to provide explanation. Thus,

. . . proficiency in economic geography consists largely of the ability to develop hypotheses that provide satisfactory solutions to the problems presented by the locations of economic phenomena. (Harold McCarty and James Lindberg, *A Preface to Economic Geography.* Englewood Cliffs, N.J.: Prentice-Hall, 1966, p. 12).

However, the variety of phenomena and the increasing abundance of facts led others to despair of ever having a unified field of economic geography again. As the 1954 review of the field appearing in *American Geography: Inventory and Prospect* noted:

General economic geography [has] ceased to exist as a research specialty . . . More and more the scholar who claims penetration in his research thinks of himself as a specialist in land utilization, in resources, in manufacturing geography, in the geography of transportation, or some other special aspect, and he makes no pretense to competence in research in economic geography as a whole.

On the other hand, it was admitted that

There is a central theme, however, common to all the topical specialties within the general limits of economic geography. Economic geography has to do with the similarities and differences from place to place in the ways people make a living. The economic geographer is concerned with economic processes especially as manifested in particular places modified by the phenomena with which they are associated. (Raymond E. Murphy, "The Fields of Economic Geography," in *American Geography: Inventory and Prospect,* ed. P. E. James and C. F. Jones, Syracuse, N.Y.: Syracuse University Press, 1954, pp. 242–43).

post–1960: other approaches to economic geography

World War II, combined with the earlier experience of the New Deal, marked the beginning of new approaches to economic geography that helped resolve the dilemma of increasing disunity. Wartime military intelligence and economic planning required applied geographic studies in which inferences had to be drawn from limited data with the help of sound theory. The search for this theory began at the time when the social sciences were becoming increasingly interdisciplinary, when computer technology was revolutionizing quantitative analysis, and when governments were subsidizing research, particularly for planning- and policy-oriented studies. There were many suggestions and calls to action. Geographers rediscovered the classical economic theories of location of J. H. Von Thünen, Alfred Weber, Walter Christaller, and the newly translated (in 1954) work of August Lösch. At the same time an economist, Walter Isard, was sparking a renewed interest in the economics of location. Because he felt that both economics and geography had let the development and application of location theory fall into the gaps between them, he called for creation of a new discipline, *regional science.* Partly as a result of Isard's challenge, geographers' work became more highly analytic.

So pervasive and swift were the results that by 1968 Richard Thoman could write

. . . the past decade has marked the emergence of a new school of thought . . . This school has chosen an explicitly theoretical approach, emphasizing nomothetic research and depending . . . upon mathematic abstraction. ("Economic Geography," p. 124).

Parallel changes were taking place in other parts of the world, for example in the Soviet Union. At a 1955 Congress of the Soviet Geographic Society it was reported that

The Congress considers the main tasks of economic geographical research to be the study of the laws of the geographical distribution of production, the territorial division of labour, and the formation of economic regions, the economic evaluation of the natural laws and resources, the combined study of the geographical distribution of the branches of industry, agriculture, and transportation, and of regions on the basis of an integrated study of the geography of population. (O. A. Konstantinov, "Economic Geography," *Soviet Geography. Accomplishments and Tasks.* New York: American Geographical Society, 1962, p. 31).

An assessment of the changes was made by the U. S. National Academy of Sciences' National Research Council in a 1965 report entitled *The Science of Geography:*

Several traditional subfields of geography, including economic, urban and transportation geography, are not discussed . . . as they once might have been . . . It would appear that the three . . . subfields have been joined in a problem area which we entitle . . . location theory studies . . . The development, testing and refinement of location theory, related studies of the geographic organization of economic life, and of urban and transportation systems, have been fundamental. . . . The applicable body of theory includes . . . abstract concepts concerning spatial distributions and space relations. . . . Very recently a new synthesis has begun to emerge based upon: (1) the identity of spatial concepts and principles developed in (several) subfields of geography; and (2) emphasis upon the interaction of economic, urban and transportation phenomena in interdependent regional systems that are the material consequences of man's resource-converting

and space-adjusting techniques. *This emerging synthesis thus results from a concerted application of systems theory within geography* [italics ours].

Some commentaries have proceeded even further, emphasizing not only systems theory, but *normative* considerations, involving control of these systems to reach specific goals. Many geographers, both East and West, began to think of their discipline as

a science concerned with the laws of development of dynamic spatial systems formed on the earth's surface in the process of interaction of nature and society, and with control of these systems . . . the science dealing with the laws of development of geosystems and their control. (Y. G. Saushkin and A. M. Smirnov, "The Role of Lenin's Ideas in the Development of Theoretical Geography," *Vestnik Moskovskogo Universiteta, Geografiya,* no. 1, 1970, pp. 3–12).

economic geography emphasizes the need of *control* in the spatial allocation of our resources. It . . . (involves) . . . *geocybernetics,* the study of spatial organization. (Commission on College Geography, *A Systems Analytic Approach to Economic Geography.* Washington, D.C.: Association of American Geographers, 1968).

The widened role of government in the evolution of spatial systems, increasing concern for overcoming social and spatial inequalities, and the growing realization of the need to preserve environmental standards have all contributed to this growing awareness that the field must contribute to the clarification and solution of a widening range of public issues. This, in turn, has produced growing concern for the nature of decision making and a rising tide of studies now called *behavioral geography.*

GENERAL SYSTEM THEORY

fundamental notions

The crucial ingredient in this changing set of concerns is that of general system theory, supported by the techniques of systems analysis. What are systems and what are the essential viewpoints and principles of systems theory?

A system is simply an entity consisting of a set of interdependent and interacting parts that is separated from its surrounding environment by definable boundaries. Such systems may be real, or conceptual. *Real systems* are directly observable, such as river systems. *Conceptual systems* are abstracts from the real world, usually simplified to show key elements of structure and to highlight the interaction of significant variables. The boundaries of abstract systems separate the pertinent system variables from the "exogenous" or external variables. In real systems, the spatial boundaries of what appears to be an obvious entity are sometimes indistinct. The spatial boundaries of a cell, an organism, or a population are vague in that each unit is maintained by continual interaction with its environment. Because of this "openness" of all systems, the emphasis in this book is therefore on a *general systems approach* rather than on the definition of particular systems.

The study of systems reveals that there are principles and laws that may be formulated to apply to all systems. Identifying and formulating such principles and laws is the task of general system theory. The fundamental system principles deal with *organization, interaction, hierarchy* and *growth*. Although these principles are elaborated in the chapters ahead, some points should be noted here.

the systems approach to spatial organization

Geographers treat the world as organization in theories of land use, location, transportation, and trade. In the identification of urban and regional specialization, geographers are also concerned with interaction, and with hierarchies of interactions among hierarchies of locations, hierarchies being the basis of most spatial organization.

Expressing the same idea, Peter Haggett has remarked that the build-up of systems involves

movements, that [produce] the channels along which the movements occur, the *network,* structured around *nodes,* organized as a *hierarchy,* with the interstitial zones viewed as *surfaces.* (Peter Haggett, *Locational Analysis in Human Geography*. London: Edward Arnold, 1965, p. 18).

What Haggett is suggesting is that the characteristics of places are directly affected by the volume and nature of their interrelationships with other places. The economic geographer is therefore concerned with the attributes of accessibility, nodality, and geographic position. But the converse also is true: the attributes of places influence their interactions with other places. The most obvious examples involve the location of natural resources, such as fossil fuels. Favorable climate can enhance the attractiveness of areas for modern economic activities, for production and investment, and to new immigrants, and thus profoundly affect the interactions of areas with other places.

What is being suggested is that there is no simple or one-way relationship between the geographies of distribution and interaction. Rather, spatial structure and behavior are interdependent, each affecting the other. Furthermore, the interaction involves a hierarchy of scales, from small groups of people in limited regions to world commodity production, trade and consumption in a succession of types of regional organization and spatial interaction.

Hierarchy is so fundamental a concept of system organization and interaction that it must be isolated for special attention. As Arthur Koestler writes:

We cannot help interpreting nature as an organization of parts-within-parts, because all living matter, and all stable inorganic systems have a parts-within-parts architecture, which lends them articulation, coherence and stability. (*The Ghost in the Machine*. New York: Macmillan, 1967, pp. 82–83).

Hierarchy is related to the idea of thresholds, the minimum size or scale of organization necessary to undertake a function or perform an operation. Organizations typically undertake a variety of functions with differing thresholds. These may range from low-order functions with small thresholds provided to many small regions, to high-order functions with large thresholds provided to few large regions. The most carefully measured thresholds in economic systems are for retail functions; consequently the best developed theory of hierarchies is that relating to *central places,* that is to market towns and cities providing retail functions to surrounding market areas.

One of the consequences of system growth is the attainment of thresholds for higher-order activities and the possibility of greater functional specialization of subsystems. But economic geographers today are beginning to question seriously some of the other consequences of size and the question of limits to growth.

All open systems can grow and their absolute growth is characterized by acceleration followed by decelerating growth. Growth accelerates at first because of the advantages of size and economies of scale and because a growing system first draws on the most favorable elements of its environment. Growth later decelerates as less favorable elements must be utilized, weakening, diluting, or polluting the system. Furthermore, the growth of a system depends on maintaining satisfactory interrelationships among its components. The *allometries,* or proportionalities of the parts to the whole, thus become critical to the maintenance and even survival of the system. Of all aspects of general system theory, economic geographers, and social scientists in general, have done the least research on allometry and the types of balance needed to maintain viable systems. The concluding chapter on system growth and spatial dynamics will illustrate the meaning and application of allometry to the geography of economic systems.

ECONOMICS, GEOGRAPHY, AND ECONOMIC GEOGRAPHY

This discussion of the principles of general system theory should serve to indicate that the geography of economic systems is primarily concerned with identifying regional patterns as the explicit product of economic processes working over a variable earth's surface. Second, it is concerned with the consequences of size and the limits to growth of economic systems. To further discuss regional patterns, size, and growth of economic systems it is necessary to consider the ways in which these concerns relate to the broader disciplinary goals of geography and economics, and the ways in which these factors can be distinguished in various cultural and sociopolitical contexts.

disciplinary goals

Let us look at economics first. Most economists would agree today that the long-range goal of their discipline is to develop an understanding of precisely how the economic system operates. By this they mean the mechanisms of allocating resources, determining prices, distributing income, and promoting economic growth.

The goals of geography are similar. In order to understand precisely how spatial systems operate, the geographer is concerned with the use of resources, the determination of locations, patterning of space, and the growth of particular regions.

Economic geography, occupying the middle ground between these two disciplines, is concerned with analyzing the spatial aspects of economic systems.

In economics, economic theory represents the core of the discipline. The aim of the economic theorist is to develop economic models, using a relatively small number of variables to explain observed phenomena. The concepts and assumptions underlying such models were initially derived from casual observation and experience. Increasing sophistication and rigor however, have led to a growing concern with testing hypotheses using carefully selected data and elaborate statistical analysis. To an increasing extent, economists are striving for a theoretical-quantitative discipline that can reconcile abstract model-building with empirical analysis.

Economic geography has gone through a similar development. The aim of the location theorist is to build spatial models of economic systems using a relatively small number of variables to help explain the spatial distributions of production and consumption, the spatial interactions evidenced by data on communications and trade, and regional differences in growth and development. Although these geographic models are not as highly developed as those of modern economics, they do point the way to the emergence of theoretical-quantitative approaches that link a trinity comprising the abstract models of location theory, the empirical procedures of locational analysis, and the down-to-earth interest in spatial organization.

behavioral bases

The economic geographer's concerns begin at the individual level, for ultimately it is individual decisions and behavior that create spatial systems and that change them. Man is both a producer and a consumer, acting less on the basis of what the world is actually like than according to what he perceives it to be. As a producer, man's employment results in the creation of materials and services, and yields income. As a consumer, man has needs, and his values, embedded within a culture, translate these into wants for materials and services that he obtains with the income he earns. The free-enterprise economist might explain how equilibrium between demand and supply is maintained by price mechanisms, how resources are allocated, supplies provided, incomes generated out of the production cycle, and how demands

arise out of consumers' needs and values. To the geographer, however, the interesting questions involve regional specialization in production and how these relate to natural and economic resources, regional income differences, spatial variations in the numbers, needs, and values of consumers, and to the systems of communication, interaction, and trade that satisfy these needs. In other words, the basic concerns of economic geography remain with production, consumption, and trade. To develop these concerns, however, economic geographers must develop theoretical structures that can be applied to economic planning as well as individual and social need satisfactions.

issues of scale

The question of *scale,* one of the most fundamental in economic geography, arises out of the need to establish a bridge between the individual and society. For some individuals, the relationship between production and consumption is local and self-sustaining. For example, an individual in an isolated village in the Highlands of New Guinea may be part of a local, essentially closed and self-sustaining spatial system. On the other hand, the spatial domain of Western man has become that of a single worldwide system. Indeed, the world economic scene can be viewed as a complex network of flows of people, money, energy, goods, information, and ideas where changes in any single part of the spatial system will affect the whole. Between these two extremes of local and worldwide systems is a wide variety of types and scales of social groups and socio-economic systems, many of which will be discussed in later chapters.

sociocultural bases of traditional economies

This variety of socio-economic systems is, of course, a product of a long period of sociocultural evolution. Recently, American anthropologists have tried to develop a taxonomy of cultures that charts this evolutionary process. They argue that change has been expressed in two fundamental ways: (a) a steadily rising level of sociocultural development throughout human history, expressed in increasing economic and social control of the environment; and (b) progressively more complex development of organizational resources to permit larger and larger groups to work together to mutual advantage. Furthermore, they argue that up to the modern transformation of the world beginning in the Industrial Revolution, human social systems have evolved through four stages:

1. Hunting and gathering societies.
2. Semi-nomadic groups engaging in simple slash-burn agriculture without animal husbandry,
3. Settled villages of tropical agriculturalists with animal husbandry,
4. The larger-scale Eurasian plow agriculture dominated by urbanized central governments and complex forms of social stratification.

sociopolitical bases of modern economic systems

Fundamental transformations in these basic cultural systems occurred in the last three centuries as the result of a succession of industrial, political, and social revolutions. Consequently, it may be appropriate to describe world economic organization today in terms of five basic *sociopolitical systems,* case studies of each of which will be found later in the book:

1. *Free enterprise decentralized market-directed systems.* In such systems decisions are made by individuals, and groups of decisions interact in the market through the free interplay of forces of demand and supply. Economic and political power, vested in the claims of ownership and property, are widely dispersed and competitively exercised in such pluralistic societies. Collective or government action protects and supports the central institutions of the market and maintains the decentralization of power. These systems are found in North America, Western Europe, Australasia, and Japan, but because of recent trends in these areas, they are tending to change into either type 2 or type 3, discussed below.

2. *Organizational market-negotiated systems.* These have been a recent outgrowth of the decentralized free-enterprise systems in the West. Major developmental decisions are made by negotiation among large-scale autonomous organizations: voluntary associations, profit-oriented but not necessarily maximizers, countervailing and countervailed against, negotiating together and existing in a context of negotiated relationships. Decision making power is determined as a matter of policy or agreed upon by counterbalancing powers. Listing the characteristics, we obtain the following:

   (a) Organization of production by large corporations run for benefit of many stockholders. Labor negotiates wages through large-scale unions.

   (b) Consumption of end products partly determined by individual choice, and partly by governmental policy.

   (c) Collective power of organizations, collective power of the government, and free choice of individuals are all part of the system. A classic case is the current alliance in Japan among business, labor, and government in what is often called "Japan Incorporated."

3. *Redistributive welfare states.* In such states, the free-enterprise system has been modified by government action to reduce social and spatial inequities, to provide every citizen with minimum guarantees for material welfare—medical care, education, employment, housing and pensions—usually achieved through differential taxation and welfare payments. Throughout the world, but particularly in Western Europe, there has been a progressive increase in these welfare functions of society with an associated extension of more centralized decision making designed to make the market system satisfy social as well as traditional economic goals.

4. *Socialist economies.* This group consists of single-party political systems, state operation of nonagricultural industries, (in some, agriculture too), centralized direction of the economy (with experiments in decentralization), semi-industrialized production structures, per capita incomes more variable than in the West, and strong commitment to economic growth. This group includes the USSR, the Eastern European countries, China, Cuba, North Vietnam, and North Korea (although the latter countries share many features with type 5, discussed below). In particular, in such systems:

   (a) the *plan* rather than the free movement of market prices controls production, consumption, and distribution.

   (b) the essence of the plan is centralized decision making; the few decide for the many and the activities of the many are carried on under the directives of the few.

   (c) centralized action requires a complex apparatus for gathering basic data needed for decision making, for formulating goals and alternatives, and for enabling the feedback necessary to adapt processes and expectations to changing circumstances.

5. *Less developed economies.* This group is characterized by one-party governments or military dictatorships, political instability, with limited capacity for public administration, small public sectors, fragmentation of the economy along geographic and modern-versus-traditional lines, imperfection of markets and limited industrial development and continued predominance of agriculture, lower per capita product, and market dependence on foreign economic relations. This group comprises the nations of Central and South America, Africa (except South Africa), Asia except Japan and the socialist countries, and many small island economies.

continuing questions about spatial organization

In analyzing these sociopolitical systems, the economic geographer begins to ask the same questions about elements of spatial organization that repeat themselves within the systems, regardless of scale, as well as about those elements that differ between them. For example, he concerns himself with studies of the *locations* of centers of economic activity; trade *flows* to and from hierarchies of these centers and the transport *networks* over which the trade flows; patterns of *resource use; regions* of production and consumption; and the *spatial dynamics* of growth and decline. Another way of saying this is that the economic geographer is concerned with such spatial building blocks as *points of focus, lines and channels of movement,* and *areas of organization,* and with their changes. Instead of saying that he is concerned with the geography of economic systems, the economic geographer will often express the previous things in shorthand by saying he is concerned with analyzing the *space-economy.* As the Commission on College Geography said in 1968:

A systems analytic approach . . . frequently implies viewing the *space-economy* as points and lines (or sites and routes). The lines depicting the network of any system are in fact its *communications.* The state of the lines at any given moment reflects the amount of *information* in the system . . . the existence of power in some portions of the communications network is a form of information . . . and will switch it on or off. This is fundamentally a *decision-making* process.

It is with such issues that this book ultimately is concerned.

Before we can begin to analyze the economic-geographic logic of the space-economy, however, we must first consider population and resources, the basic ingredients in demand and supply. We will discuss these basic ingredients in the next two chapters.

RECOMMENDED READINGS

Chisholm, M., *Geography and Economics*. London: Bell, 1966.

Haggett, P., "Changing Concepts in Economic Geography," in *Frontiers of Geographical Teaching*, eds. R. J. Chorley and P. Haggett. London: Methuen, 1965.

McCarty, H., and J. B. Lindberg, *A Preface to Economic Geography*. Englewood Cliffs, N.J.: Prentice-Hall, 1966.

McNee, R. B., *A Primer on Economic Geography*. New York: Random House, 1971.

Solo, R. A., *Economic Organization and Social Systems*. Indianapolis: Bobbs-Merrill, 1967.

Thoman, R., "Economic Geography" in *International Encyclopedia of the Social Sciences*, ed. D. L. Sills. New York: Macmillan, 1968.

population: the prime variable

The focus of economic systems is man, who plays numerous roles: manager and organizer; laborer in the production and distribution of goods; and consumer of those goods. The organization of the world economic system and its growth and development, therefore, depend upon people. The successful operation of most economic enterprises requires a labor force and a market of some minimum size. But there are also upper limits to the size of a human population, since excessive numbers press on resources, creating strains in the system that reduce its effectiveness.

The size of a population influences economic systems in many ways. This may be seen by contrasting the path of economic development and the types of goods produced and traded by labor-short economies, such as those of Australia and Canada, and by labor-surplus economies, such as those of Taiwan and Hong Kong. The presence of an adequate labor supply is recognized as an important precondition for the locating of a new productive enterprise. Although it was often presumed in the past that wherever a large industrial plant might be sited it would inevitably attract the necessary workers, it has been found that labor is not completely mobile and that locational decisions are more prudently made on the basis of existing labor supplies. By the same token, regional and national economies may be retarded in their growth when too few people are available to permit adequate exploitation of opportunities. The opposite problem is more common today, however; in countries such as India, Egypt, and El Salvador, overpopulation inhibits economic development.

Yet there is more to the question than mere numbers of people. The particular qualities of human populations—education levels, age structure, the availability of crucial skills, the presence or absence of particular social attitudes—are also important. A critical dimension of this problem is the unevenness with which human populations (and population characteristics) are distributed in space, not only between countries but also within countries.

This chapter is therefore concerned with three main problems. The first has to do with the spatial distribution of populations. Where are particular kinds of people concentrated and why is the pattern so uneven? Clearly a number of material needs must be satisfied if people are to make the economic system work. They must have a physical environment suitable to sustain normal human life and they require raw materials and sources of energy. Knowing that these material conditions are also erratically distributed, we are then led to ask what relationship, if any, this uneven distribution may have to the patterns of human populations.

The second major problem of this chapter concerns population change. Several questions arise in this connection: What are the components of population change? What are the influences affecting the rise (or fall) in total numbers of people and their distribution in earth space? And what are the effects of population change, especially of population growth?

Table 2.1 World Distribution of Population by Continent

REGION	POPULATION (THOUSANDS)	PERCENT OF WORLD	DENSITY (POPULATION PER SQ. MI.)	ARABLE ACRES PER PERSON
World trade	3,707,232	—	70.7	0.97
Africa	375,713	10.1%	32.3	1.67
Asia (excluding USSR)	2,082,441	56.2	194.2	0.54
Europe (excluding USSR)	462,802	12.5	243.0	0.82
North & Central America	325,145	8.8	34.7	1.95
South America	196,149	5.3	28.5	0.92
Oceania	19,916	0.5	6.1	4.17
USSR	245,066	6.6	28.5	2.32

Sources: Encyclopaedia Britannica Book of the Year, 1973; Food and Agricultural Organization of the United Nations, Production Yearbook, 1969.

Because change does not take place in the same manner and at the same rate in all parts of the world, our third problem is to examine regional differences in population change and to learn what future population patterns are likely to result from these.

PRESENT DISTRIBUTION OF HUMAN POPULATIONS

Any attempt to analyze the spatial distribution of populations must take into account the physical limits of human habitation, based on the biological needs of man as an organism, as well as the physical opportunities for gaining a livelihood—the needs of man as an economic being. While these material considerations tend to set the basic framework, there are many social or cultural influences that importantly modify the fundamental pattern. Political organization and control, the policing and regulatory powers exercised by governments over the territories within their borders can affect directly or indirectly, birth and death rates, patterns of migration and settlement, and many other aspects of demography. Population distributions are influenced by still other kinds of group behavior, including the cohesive or divisive forces created by racial, linguistic, and religious affiliations, and the traditions associated with marriage and the family, and diets and hygiene. Other factors, such as level of education, may affect the mobility of populations and the rate of population growth and change.

Population distributions can be viewed on different scales of observation. At the macro level, comparisons can be made between countries or between the regions of individual nations. There are also important variations at the local level, especially within cities; this micro view of population will be discussed later (see Chapter 7). The emphasis in this chapter will be on international and interregional patterns.

numbers of people: world patterns

The study of population is essentially quantitative, because understanding population distributions and their associated problems requires a certain amount of measurement. The chief sources of population data are official records, especially those compiled by national governments and the United Nations. Unfortunately, the quality of such data varies, especially the data relating to less developed countries; for some countries in Africa, Asia, and Latin America there are no reliable statistics at all. Interpreting such data requires great caution, especially for temporal comparisons. For example, studies sponsored by the United Nations have disclosed that previous censuses in parts of Africa have suffered from under-enumeration; apparently the populations of some of these countries are much larger than had been suspected. Comparisons with past data are also complicated by boundary changes, such as the separation of Bangladesh from Pakistan. Moreover, censuses are insufficiently standardized, particularly with respect to data on population characteristics.

For these reasons we can usually make only the grossest comparisons, mainly on the international scale. From this broader perspective of totals for countries and aggregates for continents, many of the data errors tend to cancel each other.

population size

Despite the deficiencies in the data, it is clear from Table 2.1 that there are great disparities in population distribution among the continents. Asia contains more than half the world's people, excluding the Soviet Union, which has the third largest population of any nation. Europe, with the second largest population among the continents, has less than one-fourth as many people as Asia. Africa now has the third largest population and is gaining on the leaders. Oceania, which includes Australia, New Zealand, and the islands of the South Pacific has the smallest population. The Soviet Union, comprising 15 percent of the world's land area, is almost as large as all of North America; for this reason, and because it is partly in Europe and partly in Asia, it is usually listed separately.

A closer look at world population is given by Table 2.2, where the countries with the largest populations are

Table 2.2 Fifteen Countries with Largest Populations
(1972 Estimates)

COUNTRY (ACCORDING TO RANK SIZE)	POPULATION (THOUSANDS)	AREA (SQ. MI.)	DENSITY (POPULATION PER SQ. MI.)	PERCENT OF WORLD POPULATION
1 China	787,176	3,691,500	213.2	21.2%
2 India	547,950	1,261,810	434.3	14.8
3 USSR	245,066	8,600,340	28.5	6.6
4 United States	208,323	3,615,122	57.6	5.6
5 Indonesia	119,232	782,658	152.3	3.2
6 Japan	106,251	143,818	738.8	2.9
7 Brazil	98,854	3,286,470	30.1	2.7
8 Bangladesh	75,000	55,126	1,360.5	2.0
9 Nigeria	69,253	356,669	194.2	1.9
10 West Germany	61,281	95,979	638.5	1.7
11 Pakistan	60,000	366,041	193.0	1.6
12 United Kingdom	55,355	94,216	587.5	1.5
13 Italy	54,025	116,313	464.5	1.5
14 Mexico	52,641	761,600	69.1	1.4
15 France	51,487	210,038	245.1	1.4
	2,591,894			70.0

Source: Encyclopaedia Britannica Book of the Year, 1973

presented in rank order. Altogether, these fifteen nations account for more than two-thirds of the world total. As the table shows, one in every five persons lives in China and one in seven in India. Note that six of the nations in this list are Asian. Based on the data of these two tables it is clear that continental and national population totals do not give an accurate impression of crowding, one of the principal discussions in this chapter. There are wide areal variations among those countries having the largest populations (Table 2.2, column 2), and this becomes even more apparent when numbers of people are related to amounts of land (column 4). Note that the third and fourth most populous countries, the Soviet Union and the United States, have much lower densities than the others, a result of their very large total areas.

population density

The concept of density therefore provides some idea of the area that is available for human habitation. The simplest measure is *arithmetic density* (see Table 2.2): total numbers of people divided by total land area. Some of the greatest densities occur in tiny city-states, such as Monaco with 40,000 persons per square mile, the Vatican City with 3,000 persons per square mile, and island entities under 1,000 square miles, such as Hong Kong, which has 9,870 persons per square mile, and Singapore, which has 9,420. Excluding such cases, six of the sixteen most densely populated countries are European (see Table 2.3). The Netherlands and Belgium appear fourth and fifth on the list, and West Germany and the United Kingdom are not far below. Six Asiatic countries are also among the leaders: Bangladesh, Taiwan, South Korea, Japan, and Sri Lanka (Ceylon). It is important to note, however, that two of the largest populations, those of China and Pakistan, are missing from the high-density list. The Middle East is represented by Lebanon. Three countries from Middle America also rank high: Trinidad, Jamaica, and El Salvador. Observe that six of the

Table 2.3 Most Densely Populated Countries
(1972 Estimates)

COUNTRY (RANKED ACCORDING TO DENSITY)	DENSITY (POPULATION PER SQ. MI.)	AREA (SQ. MI.)
*1 Bangladesh	1,360.5	55,126
2 Taiwan	1,086,2	13,892
3 South Korea	872.3	38,022
4 Netherlands	835.0	15,892
5 Belgium	822.9	11,781
*6 Japan	738.8	143,818
*7 West Germany	638.5	95,979
*8 United Kingdom	587.5	94,216
9 Lebanon	538.2	3,950
10 Trinidad & Tobago	520.2	1,980
11 Sri Lanka (Ceylon)	501.8	25,332
*12 Italy	464.5	116,313
13 El Salvador	450.6	8,098
14 Jamaica	450.3	4,244
15 India	434.3	1,261,810
16 East Germany	408.0	41,768

*Also appears on list of countries with largest populations.

Source: Encyclopaedia Britannica Book of the Year, 1973

countries are island nations, including Japan, the United Kingdom, Sri Lanka, Trinidad, and Jamaica.

The extreme contrasts in arithmetic densities seem to suggest that some areas have a greater capacity to support human life than others. For broad areas, the Food and Agricultural Organization of the United Nations (FAO) has estimated the proportion of land available for each major type of use. From this it is possible to derive a measure of *physiological density*, which relates the size of a population to the amount of arable land available for its support. The last column of Table 2.1 shows physiological densities for the world as a whole and for each of the major continental areas. Note that at present there is just under one acre of crop land available for each person in the world. The table also shows that three-fourths of the world's population live in areas having less than this much land per person. In Asia, for example, the figure is approximately one-half acre. With its unusually high proportion of arable land, Europe is somewhat better off, yet European population densities are so great that each individual can call upon only four-fifths of an acre. South America's rapidly growing population has now also reached the point where each person has less than the world average of land available for his support.

Even this measure is not entirely satisfactory, since it does not take into account the quality of the crop land in each area. Africa, for example, has a per capita supply of arable land well above the world average; but in fact the productivity of African land is generally far below that of North America or Europe. Although Oceania appears to have a large amount of land per person, this sparsely populated region has only two percent of the world's arable acreage.

limits of world habitation

However they may be measured, density figures for continental or national areal units can be misleading, as Figure 2.1 illustrates. This map shows that population densities are rarely consistent throughout the territories of countries, and it also discloses many instances where major population concentrations cross national borders into neighboring countries. Although we are limited

mainly to national data for most quantitative comparisons of world population, we can examine why certain areas are heavily occupied and others are sparsely occupied.

Perhaps as much as three-fifths of the earth's land surface opposes human settlement, usually because these areas are physically unsuitable for agriculture. Figure 2.2 provides an overview of those regions that are too dry, too wet, too cold, or too mountainous for the ordinary forms of agriculture. As can be seen on the map, sometimes two or more of these negative conditions may coincide in a particular region. Note that few of the major world regions are entirely devoid of human beings. Within these broad nonarable areas are local variations that may permit agriculture, such as a supply of water or special soil conditions. Some of these regions may also acquire nonagricultural settlement, attracted by valuable mineral deposits, biotic resources, recreational facilities, or other special circumstances.

Because of excessive aridity, farming is virtually excluded from large parts of the world. The amount of moisture available to crops varies according to the area's evaporation rate or the season in which most of the precipitation falls. At least ten inches of annual rainfall are usually required in the middle latitudes, but thirty inches or more may be needed in the tropics to replace evaporation losses. Much of the earth can be classified as desert (under ten inches of rain per year) or steppeland (between ten and twenty or thirty inches), and these

Fig. 2.1 *World population*

Source: Alexander, Economic Geography *(Englewood Cliffs, N.J.: Prentice-Hall, 1963).*

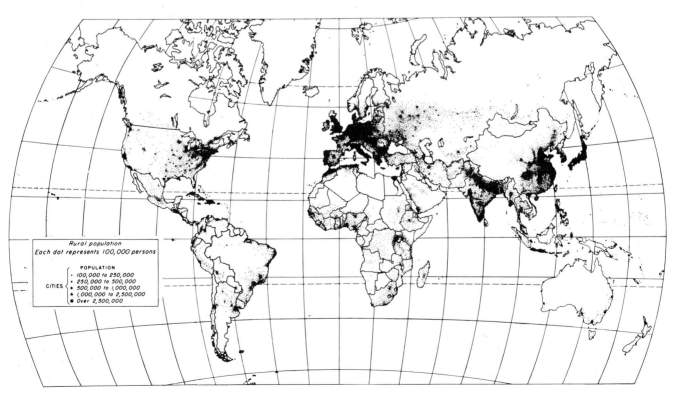

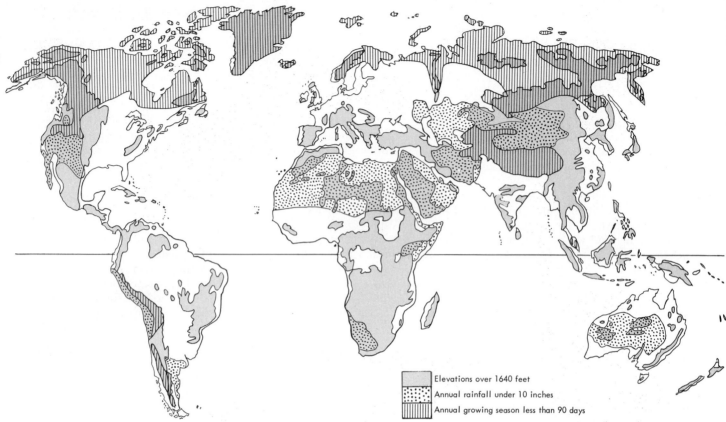

Fig. 2.2 *Limits of agricultural production. Much of the earth's land surface is too mountainous or too dry or has too short a growing season to support the usual forms of agriculture.*

areas are poorly suited for agriculture. Important exceptions occur when irrigated farming is possible, as in the case of "exotic" streams (such as the Nile or the Colorado) that rise in regions of high rainfall and pass through arid lands, or local springs or wells that permit the existence of oases in the desert. Even so, vast areas of the Sahara and other major deserts are either remote from any source of water or lack a true soil to relieve their inhospitable sandy or rocky surfaces. Although human habitation may occur in arid regions that offer valuable minerals, such as petroleum, nitrates, or metallic ores, the labor requirements of mining are usually minor and such settlement rarely has an important effect on population distribution.

Ironically, some large regions may only support a small population because they receive too much rainfall. The vast equatorial basins of the Amazon and Congo rivers, for example, are covered with a rain forest vegetation so dense that many persons have been led to propose that these lightly populated areas be resettled by surplus population from Asia. The accumulated evidence, however, rejects the possibility of productive agriculture in these areas, because of the poor quality of tropical rain forest soils. Heavy rainfall in every month throughout the year causes the soluble mineral plant food in the soil to be leached out by ground water and carried to depths beyond the reach of ordinary shallow-rooted food plants. Trees, however, remain unaffected by this problem; with their long taproots, the forest giants of the Amazon can easily reach these underground nutrients. Most equatorial areas are therefore lightly settled—fewer than two persons per square mile live in Amazonia, for example. Still, there are important exceptions. In some specially favored areas, local soil conditions permit successful farming despite heavy rainfall. With the aid of rich volcanic soils peculiarly suited to rice culture, the island of Java, for instance, is able to support some of the world's highest rural population densities (see Figs. 2.1 and 2.2). In other places, comparatively large numbers of people obtain a livelihood from tree crops such as rubber, bananas, and cacao.

Possibly the most serious limitation of all is excessive cold. Ice and snow permanently cover great areas near the poles and some of the higher mountains. Vast territories adjacent to these polar regions are likewise incapable of supporting the usual forms of agriculture because of temperature conditions. Most food plants require at least three months without frost to reach maturity and the boundary of agricultural production on this basis is customarily taken to be the limit of the 90-day growing season (see Fig. 2.2). The colder climates, however, do support some human habitation. Small populations are engaged in the exploitation of minerals and other local resources. Fishing provides a livelihood along the coasts of the northern continents, and forest products along the southern margins where temperatures are high enough to support useful vegetation.

Many mountainous areas cannot be farmed because some slopes are so steep that little or no soil can cling to them. Furthermore, since temperatures are reduced approximately three degrees with each additional one thousand feet of elevation, the higher slopes are too cold for farming. Even forestry, which may be practiced on the lower slopes, is precluded at upper elevations where temperatures are too low for trees to grow. Important exceptions occur in the tropics, where the moderate temperatures and relatively gentle slopes of highland basins often provide ideal farming conditions. Indeed, these are the preferred places for human habitation in tropical America, as Figure 2.1 shows. Some mountainous zones have rich mineral deposits, and mining may support a fair number of persons.

Areas unsuited to agriculture can often be used for grazing. With their sparse natural covering of grasses and herbaceous plants, the steppelands and the basins and upper slopes in some mountainous regions are much used for this purpose. Even reindeer are herded in the far north of Eurasia and Alaska; because such lands have a meager carrying capacity for grazing animals, they are able to provide support for only small populations.

We must also consider some nonphysical factors when we interpret the world population map, such as the length of settlement. Certain parts of Asia and the Middle East, for example, suffer rural overcrowding, despite the submarginal quality of much of the land and poor agricultural conditions in general. In these situations the increasing numbers of people over time have exhausted the capacity of their lands to support them. Another nonphysical condition that may explain the maladaptiveness of population densities to land capabilities is political control. This phenomenon may be illustrated by the case of underpopulated Australia, whose government excludes immigrants from the burgeoning lands of nearby Indonesia and southeast Asia.

It is also important to note that when human beings have a compelling reason to live in a negative area they manage to create their own artificial environments. Heating, air conditioning, desalinization of water, and drainage represent some of the expensive measures that modern technology has provided for residents of otherwise inhospitable surroundings. Some of the most artificial environments are found in great cities, which attain an economic momentum of their own and attract human settlement regardless of the inherent physical characteristics of the land.

the empty areas

Having noted the factors that limit human habitation, we may now examine some of those regions on the map (Fig. 2.1) that are essentially devoid of people. A nearly empty area in North America is the enormous arctic region, including the mainland areas of northern Alaska and Canada, plus Greenland and the Canadian Arctic Islands. Another sparsely settled area of North America comprises the dry lands of the west. Two virtually empty areas occur in South America: the tropical rainforests of Amazonia and the great deserts of the south—the Ata-

cama of Chile and Peru and the Patagonian region of Argentina.

Africa has three prominent empty areas: the vast Sahara Desert in the north, the tropical rainforests of equatorial Africa, and the Kalahari and Nabib deserts. Although the most populous of continents, Eurasia has two of the most extensive negative areas: the great polar fringes of the Soviet Union and Scandinavia, and the exceedingly arid deserts of Central Asia and their adjacent highlands. The continent with the largest percentage of unoccupied land of all those that are inhabited is Australia, with its so-called dead heart. Finally, Antarctica, with its vast ice sheet up to two miles thick, has no permanent human habitation at all.

the major population nodes

Where, then, is the world's population concentrated? Four great population nodes overshadow the rest. The three largest of these, all in Eurasia, have half a billion people or more each; together they comprise more than three-fifths of the total world population. The *East Asian node* leads them all. It includes the densely populated sections of eastern China, Korea, and Japan, each area occupying a middle-latitude location with generally favorable climatic conditions for agriculture. The inhabitants of this node are particularly concentrated within the great expanses of river flood plains and deltas on the Chinese mainland and the densely packed coastal plains and river valleys of mountainous Japan and Korea. These areas have an ancient history of habitation, representing the birthplace of one of the principal human races. In addition to length of settlement, the high population densities of these areas have occurred because of religious and cultural traditions that favor large families. High rural densities have been supported through intensive agriculture; but Japan's industrial economy enables her to sustain a population of more than half that of the United States on a group of mountainous islands having a combined land area less than that of Montana.

Second in size is the *South Asian node,* made up of most of India, Pakistan, and Bangladesh, plus the island of Sri Lanka (Ceylon) and parts of Burma. Here the greatest population densities are found in areas with a heavy monsoon rainfall. The only limit on the growing season of the South Asian node is the availability of water, since temperatures are high twelve months of the year. Exceedingly high rural densities, as well as the largest cities, are found in the river deltas and flood plains and along the coastal plains; but even the drier interior of the Indian peninsula bears large numbers of people. Despite the generally poor quality of soil—exhausted from several millenia of continuous use—agriculture remains the chief support of life, although persistently high birth rates threaten its ability to do so.

The third great population node is that of *Europe and the western Soviet Union.* This region enjoys one of the most reliable of all agricultural climates. With moderate temperatures, a dependable supply of rainfall well distributed throughout the year (except in the Mediterranean areas), and a long growing season, this region has the largest proportion of cultivated land area of all the continents and produces some of the world's highest crop yields. Despite its productivity, this region employs only a small proportion of its people in farming. Although other groups are engaged in exploiting the rich mineral and other natural resources, most people are in the manufacturing and service trades, resulting in a high degree of urbanization. This node, too, occupies a region of long settlement, dating at least to the end of the last ice age.

The population node of *Eastern North America,* large as it is, contains only one-fourth as many people as each of the three other major concentrations. This region includes the "megalopolis" of the Middle Atlantic seaboard of the United States with its westward extension into the Great Lakes regions of the Middle West and southern Ontario and Quebec, together with the associated rural populations of this important farming region. Although this region enjoys a temperate climate, its growing seasons are decidedly shorter than those of the other three population nodes. Important natural resources are found in this area, including coal, iron ore, natural gas and petroleum, and a variety of chemical raw materials. In contrast with the other three population nodes, this region has only a recent history of settlement and experienced its rapid growth mainly through immigration and natural increase during its formative period. As in Western Europe, agriculture in Eastern North America is very efficient and productive but occupies only a small percentage of the labor force. Most of the population is employed in secondary and tertiary activities.

lesser population clusters

In addition to these major concentrations, there are at least thirteen smaller clusters of population that appear on the world map. One of these is the *Los Angeles–Central Valley–San Francisco* area of California, until recently the fastest growing concentration in the United States. A prime attraction of this area has been its magnificent scenery and benign climate, but shortages of water and other environmental and economic problems have now begun to retard growth. Another of the smaller Anglo-American clusters is that of the *Vancouver* and the *Puget Sound–Fraser River* area of the Pacific Northwest and neighboring British Columbia, likewise a region of pleasant physical surroundings.

Mexico City and adjacent parts of the central plateau offer the most attractive climatic conditions in all of Mexico. Although agriculture is limited, this area has attracted the greater part of the country's population and has become the center of a rapidly growing industrial district. The valleys of the *Central American highlands,* as previously described, contain the greater part of the populations of those countries. Although too widely separated to be regarded as a distinct cluster, the islands of the Caribbean are among the most densely populated areas of the Western Hemisphere.

For the most part, the rapidly growing population of South America is concentrated at various points along the continental margins. Largest of these clusters is the district comprising the *Central Plateau and Northeast Coast of Brazil,* the leading industrial area of Latin America and one of the principal agricultural districts as well, despite numerous problems associated with supporting a burgeoning population. The *Rio de la Plata* district is the heart of Argentina's and Uruguay's populations; it contains most of the industry, and is the focus of commercial agriculture. *Middle Chile* is another area of particularly pleasant climatic conditions and productive agriculture and hence contains the majority of that country's people. Finally, in South America, there are the *Highland Basins of the Northern Andes,* extending from La Paz, Bolivia, northward through Peru, Ecuador, Colombia, and Venezuela. Again, this area provides the attractive conditions found in a similar environment in the Central American highlands.

One of the most unusual of all population concentrations is that which occupies the *Valley of the Lower Nile River in North Africa.* Here occurs one of the highest rural densities in the world concentrated within the narrow confines of the irrigated flood plain and delta of an exotic stream that flows from the humid East African highlands through one of the world's driest deserts (less than one inch of rainfall per year). The *Gulf of Guinea* of coastal West Africa supports large numbers of people, especially in the countries of Ghana and Nigeria, where subsistence agriculture is the main way of life. The cluster in *East Central Africa* is at least potentially overcrowded but, until recently, its population has been held in check by intertribal warfare. The other concentration of people in that continent is the *Republic of South Africa,* whose coastal belt has a benign Mediterranean climate and whose interior is rich with valuable mineral deposits, including gold, diamonds, coal, and iron. Finally, there is the population node that comprises *Eastern Australia and New Zealand.* Australia's people live mainly along the southeast coastal lowland, which, by contrast with the arid region to the west, is well watered, has moderate temperatures, and offers most of the country's agricultural potential.

within-country variations

Most of the population literature is devoted to comparisons among countries. As suggested earlier, the weakness of such an emphasis is that it assumes that each national territory is homogeneous in its internal population distribution, or at least that its population focuses upon a single node. These conditions are rarely met and most countries are very diverse internally. National figures, which are essentially statistical summaries and averages of local-area data, thus tend to mask many population differences, and we therefore need to examine the kinds of variations that occur within countries.

regional patterns

Every continent and nearly every country of any size shows substantial inequalities in population distribution. Even as small a nation as Belgium, with an overall density of 823 persons per square mile, has its lightly populated Ardennes uplands. And although the United Kingdom as a whole has a high density, certain regions contain few people, as, for example, central Wales, the Pennine uplands, and the Scottish Highlands. Still greater contrasts obtain in such countries as Brazil, with its large and active population in the São Paulo-Río de Janeiro region, its crowded rural northeast, and its virtually empty Amazonian north; or Canada, with its densely peopled Toronto-Golden Horseshoe district and its nearly vacant Arctic lands.

China, however, presents one of the best examples of regional variations in population densities. Despite a huge population of 787 million, China's overall population density is only 213 persons per square mile. This is lower than the densities of most of her neighbors in eastern and southern Asia and decidedly less than those of western European countries. Unevenly distributed, China's population is densest in the coastal and central provinces; indeed, most of the people are concentrated on about one-tenth of the cultivated land. Rural population attains an incredible density of 2,500 persons per square mile on the Chengtu Plain in Szechwan Province, while great areas in the western parts of the country remain nearly empty.

There are several reasons why the Chinese population failed to become more evenly distributed after its more than forty centuries of existence. One of these is the extreme variation in the physical capabilities of the land. The wide regional differences in soils, temperatures, and rainfall found in China have profoundly influenced the locational choices of this predominantly agricultural people. Even where opportunities seem to be present, however, the Chinese have been unusually reluctant to move, owing to their traditionally strong ties to family and village, to ancestor worship, and to regional language differences that severely limit communication. Finally there is the problem of extreme poverty that has been endemic in China for centuries. Lacking savings, being vulnerable to a variety of natural calamities, and having little assurance of bettering themselves elsewhere, the Chinese have preserved a remarkably stable population pattern. Communist control appears to have had little relative effect in redistributing population among provinces, although important shifts have occurred locally.

urbanism

The ultimate form of population concentration, of course, is that of the city. One of the most discussed demographic topics has been the continuing rush of people from the farms to cities and, more recently, from smaller urban places to larger ones. It has been esti-mated that by 1970 the urban population of the world had reached 37 percent of the total, considerably above the 28 percent of two decades earlier.

This gregariousness among human beings, however, is instinctive, and the survival of early man depended on it. Throughout known history, people have established cities for defense as well as for the various social and economic advantages of cooperative efforts. Both commerce and industry enjoy numerous savings from agglomeration within urban areas, as later chapters will show (Chapters 8 and 10). Cities perform many other important roles, too; for example, they serve as centers for administrative control, education and culture, and as points of convergence for transport routes.

The very large city is a phenomenon of modern times; indeed, the word "civilization" is derived from the Latin term for city. Primitive man's activities, providing an insufficient surplus of food, were unable to support a large non-food-producing population. Subsistence gathering, hunting and fishing, herding, and agriculture, supplying barely enough food for tribal members, are very extensive in their use of land; migratory peoples may require as much as two square miles to support each individual. Although the well-organized Romans were able to mobilize production to support sizeable populations, the skill was lost in Europe when the Roman legions vanished. The Chinese, however, were able to maintain large cities, as Marco Polo discovered, at a time when European urban centers remained small.

Modern urban growth developed as a result of three essential developments. The first was the agricultural revolution of the late eighteenth century, which, for the first time, allowed European farms to feed a large nonagricultural population. Farm yields increased because of improved cultivation methods, new crops, scientific breeding of both plants and animals, consolidation of land holdings, and better communications and transportation. Transmitted across the Atlantic, the agricultural revolution brought similar results to the United States, as demonstrated by the steady decline of agricultural employment as a percentage of the total labor force. In 1820 farm labor represented 72 percent of the gainfully employed, but by 1900 this had dropped to 37 percent; by 1970 it had reached the remarkably low figure of 4.5 percent.

The Industrial Revolution, beginning at about the same period, brought about the factory system, displacing cottage industry, and hastened the growth of large concentrations of people. Simultaneously, the communications revolution provided cheap, fast, and dependable transportation of food, industrial raw materials, and other goods required by an expanding urban population. These developments likewise served to expand the commercial hinterland for the products of these centers.

The ultimate result of the agricultural, industrial, and transportation revolutions has been the development of the great metropolis. London increased eightfold during the last century and a half to reach its

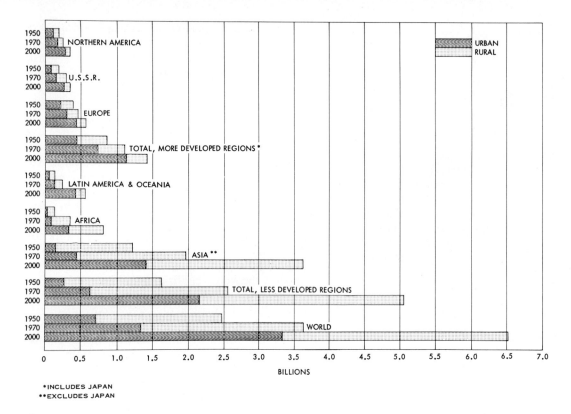

Fig. 2.3 *Urban and rural population (in millions) by major areas and world regions, 1950–2000*

Source: World Bank Group, Trends in Developing Countries *(Washington, D.C.: International Bank for Reconstruction and Development, 1971).*

present population of 7.4 million. During that same period, New York City expanded a hundredfold to reach a roughly comparable size, and similar rates of growth were experienced by a number of other major centers. In recent years the most dynamic growth of all has been that of Tokyo, Toronto, and São Paulo. Tokyo, for instance, doubled in size between 1940 and 1970 to become the world's largest city with 8,800,000 people, although according to United Nations estimates, Shanghai, China, may be even larger. Even these figures do not fully convey the true rate of growth, since much of the increase has been outside the officially designated limits of many principal centers. Thus Chicago's 3,367,000 people are more than equalled by the population now filling its nearby suburbs.

Degree of urbanization varies considerably from one part of the world to another, however, and with some notable exceptions has attained its highest levels in the most developed lands. Although census definitions of "urban population" differ markedly, certain international comparisons are possible (Fig. 2.3 and front endpapers). Taken as a group, the technically advanced countries had become two-thirds urbanized by 1970. Not only are most of the populations of these countries engaged in urban pursuits, but even the majority of those persons living in rural territory work at nonagricultural jobs.

Nevertheless, certain developed countries are more urbanized than others. Anglo-America is three-fourths urban, but only 56 percent of the Soviet Union's people live in urban places. Despite high per capita incomes, less than one-third of the Norwegian population is classified as urban. Not counting city-states such as Monaco and Singapore, one of the most urbanized lands of all is Australia, with an essentially suburban population of more than 83 percent—hardly the picture most people have of that vast land.

Urbanization also varies from one region to another within countries. A map of urbanism in the United States, for example, reveals that dense concentrations have grown up along each coast and on the shores of the Great Lakes (Fig. 2.4). Elsewhere in the country, urban centers tend to be smaller and more scattered. In the lightly settled, largely rural plains and Rocky Mountain states, most cities exist in semi-isolation.

There is a strong positive correlation between degree of urbanization and levels of economic development. Highly urbanized countries also rank high on a scale of technology that combines indexes of transportation, communications, energy production and consumption, national and per capita incomes, and foreign trade. Underdeveloped countries fall at the lower end of the scale of technology and tend to be decidedly less urban. As a whole, the underdeveloped nations are only one-fourth urbanized, whereas the technically advanced

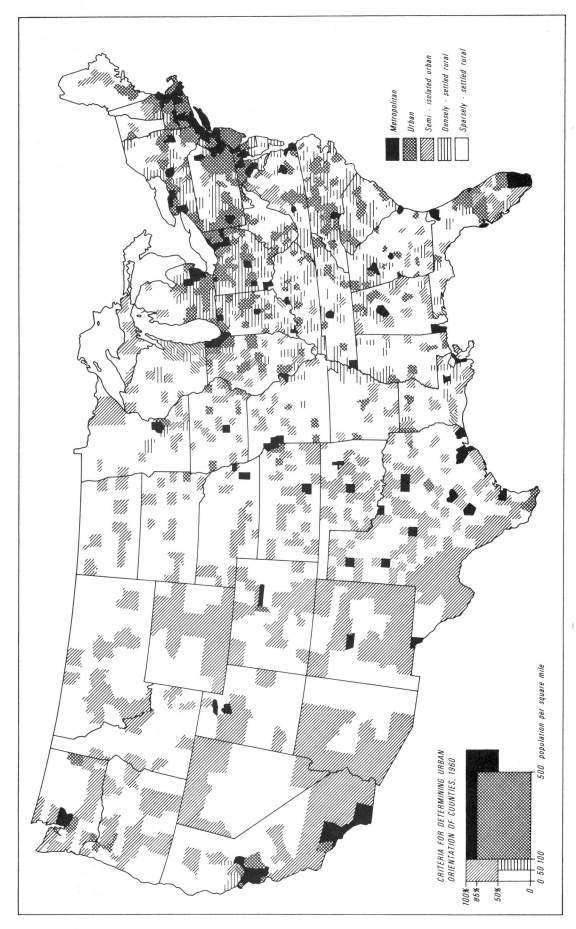

CRITERIA FOR DETERMINING URBAN
ORIENTATION OF COUNTIES, 1960

Metropolitan

Urban

Semi - isolated urban

Densely - settled rural

Sparsely - settled rural

Fig. 2.4 *Urbanization in the United States*

countries as a group are two-thirds urban (Fig. 2.4). In most underdeveloped nations, at least half the labor force is employed in agriculture, and many of those persons living in cities and towns go daily into the country to work in the fields.

The map in Figure 2.4 shows that some parts of the underdeveloped world are more rural than others. Some of the lowest percentages of urbanization are found in Asia. Nepal and Sikkim are among the lowest, with 3 and 4 percent respectively, while Viet Nam has only 10 percent of its population in cities. The very large populations of Indonesia, India, and Sri Lanka (Ceylon) range between 17 and 20 percent in urbanization. By contrast, another Asian country, technically-advanced Japan, has 72 percent of its population in urban places. Sub-Saharan and equatorial Africa also have particularly low levels of urbanization; for example, Malawi (5 percent), Central African Republic (7), Uganda (8), and Kenya (10). At the same time, the more developed Republic of South Africa has nearly half its population in cities.

Latin America, on the other hand, is more urbanized than either Asia or Africa. The least urbanization occurs in parts of Central America and the Caribbean, the Guianas, and certain Andean areas, where it ranges between 16 and 36 percent. Most of the remaining Latin American lands have at least 35 percent of their people in cities, and several (Mexico and Brazil, for example) are over 45 percent. The most advanced Latin nations, such as Argentina, Chile, Uruguay, and Venezuela, are more than 60 percent urbanized.

Although the populations of the underdeveloped and developing nations are thus mainly rural, some very large urban centers are to be found in certain of those countries. Calcutta, Bombay, Shanghai, and São Paulo, to name a few, are among the world's largest cities and all four are continuing to grow rapidly.

Only the most backward societies lack cities altogether. More commonly, an underdeveloped country will have one city that is far larger than all other urban places in the land. Examples of such "primate cities" are San José (Costa Rica), Asunción (Paraguay), Mexico City, Manila, Bangkok, Addis Ababa (Ethiopia), and Nairobi (Kenya). The primate city dominates the economically active parts of an underdeveloped country; but, when compared with cities in technically advanced lands, its functions tend to be severely limited. In addition to the usual commercial activities common to all urban places, a city of this type serves as a center for the country's political and social life. Manufacturing, transportation, and communications, however, are usually poorly developed, except in so far as they link demands of the developed world to the resources of the primate city's hinterland.

In view of the rapid pace of urbanization throughout the world, what can we expect from the future? Urbanization has already proceeded far in those countries currently high on the ladder of economic development; by the year 2000, four-fifths of their people will probably live in cities (Fig. 2.3). As a group, the under-

developed countries should increase their proportion of urban dwellers from one-fourth to nearly three-fifths, although Africa and Asia are expected to lag. By the end of this century there will still be only two out of every five Africans living in cities, and the percentage in Asia will be about the same. In Latin America, however, it is predicted that very nearly three-fourths of the population will have become urbanized.

As a natural consequence of this worldwide urbanization trend, the cities of the future can be expected to grow extremely large. Metropolitan Tokyo, for example, which now has about 22 million inhabitants, has been projected to reach 40 million by 2000! Many other great metropolises are expected to have coalesced to form additional conurbations and megalopolises by that date. The most severe urban problems are likely to occur in the larger cities of underdeveloped countries. Calcutta, already swollen with homeless migrants, will probably double and redouble its present 8 million inhabitants in the near future. No doubt, too, rural populations will continue to converge on the primate cities of Latin America.

POPULATION CHARACTERISTICS

Thus far, our discussion has been concerned only with spatial variations in numbers of people. Yet people differ from each other in many respects, and differ from place to place. Among these differences are a number of cultural, demographic, and economic characteristics that may affect the economic behavior of populations.

Although the components of population tend to differ most from one country or world region to another, important differences obtain between sections, between rural and urban areas, and even between small towns and large cities within countries. Some of the greatest distinctions of all are between peoples at different levels of economic development. To some degree, certain of these population traits are predictable, because they tend to be spatially associated with one another, either positively or negatively.

demographic traits

sex ratio

One way in which populations differ is in the proportion of males to females. This relationship, the sex ratio, is obtained by dividing the number of males by the number of females and multiplying by 100 to remove the decimal. High sex ratios, indicating proportionately larger numbers of males than females, are characteristic of newly settled areas. This is because men tend to be the most mobile members of the population, especially young men. With relatively larger numbers of women remaining behind, areas of heavy out-migration usually have low sex ratios. Furthermore, older, more stable areas have low sex ratios owing to the greater life expectancy of women. Thus the long-stable populations of Western Europe are typified by the low ratio of the United Kingdom (93.6), while the higher ratio of Australia (101.3) is representative of countries still receiving immigrants.

As time passes, the sex ratios of newer countries and regions undergo a gradual decrease. Throughout its earlier years the United States had proportionately large numbers of males owing to heavy immigration. In 1910 the sex ratio was 106.2, by 1940 it had fallen to 100.8, and by 1969 it was only 95.2. The lowest ratios of the United States are in New England, while the highest are in the West, especially Alaska, where the ratio is 132.3.

The proportion of men to women in a population can affect the labor force in many ways. Because women usually work outside the home to a lesser extent than men, a population that has an excess of females is likely to have a lower labor force participation rate. Areas having a surplus of males may be attractive to heavy industries, such as basic metals production, while areas with large numbers of females may draw industries such as textile manufacturing or garment making.

age composition

The number of people of different ages in a population varies with the stability of that population, as well as its growth rate and the quality of public health. The countries of Western Europe have relatively large numbers of old people, whereas the Central American countries have very few. The reverse is obviously true of the number of younger members of the population. In Sweden, for example, only 21 percent of the population is below the age of 15; but in Guatemala, 46 percent are in that age class, and in Honduras the proportion reaches 51 percent. This attribute is also affected by migration, since young adults are those most inclined to move. Consequently rural areas are likely to have proportionately greater numbers of the very old and the very young, while the cities have predominantly young and middle-aged adults.

other demographic traits

The marital composition of a population affects labor force participation rates, consumer behavior, and birth rates. The proportion of married people is, in turn, a function of the sex ratio, since any imbalance between the sexes reduces the marriage opportunities of a monogamous people. But this proportion is also influenced by social attitudes, as shown by the experience of India, where early marriage is customary, as opposed to that of Sweden, where marriage is often postponed.

cultural attributes

nationality and language

There are a great many population characteristics based on culture, and their effects can be considerable.

One of these is membership in particular linguistic or nationality groups, whose customs and traditions cause members to draw closer to one another and tend to reduce communication with outsiders. The in-group–out-group feelings thus engendered often influence economic and political behavior. This has been an endemic problem throughout the history of Europe, for instance, whose spatial distributions of innumerable linguistic and nationality groups are frequently reflected in the configuration of national boundaries.

Population differences of this type may be a divisive force that retards political and economic progress within a country. Even some of the smallest European countries have such problems, as seen by the rancorous disputes between the Flemish people of northern Belgium and the Walloons of the south. On the other hand, Switzerland appears to have achieved an accommodation among its German, French, Italian, and Romansch-speaking populations, probably aided by its loose, federal form of government.

In addition to the political and economic fragmentation resulting from these population differences, differences in birth rates, consumer behavior, and attitudes toward certain forms of employment influence the regional and national economy. Many French-Canadians, for example, favor the professions as a life work, while English-speaking Canadians tend toward commerce and industry. Serious communication problems between linguistic groups handicap the economic growth of certain less developed nations.

race

Although racial differences are physical, their main effects are cultural and social. Historically, racial discrimination has been expressed by dominance and subdominance, with the subjugated race becoming severely disadvantaged economically, politically, and socially. This in turn affects the population in terms of literacy, differences in birth and death rates, and age composition.

religion

The religious groupings of mankind frequently coincide with nationality and language. As the problems of Northern Ireland amply demonstrate, religious differences can seriously disrupt an economic system. In addition, birth rates tend to be related to religious beliefs and therefore contribute to spatial differences in population growth rates. Religion can influence the structure of production and consumption of nations and thus the content of their exports and imports (see Chapter 11).

literacy

The amount of education a population is able to provide its members has much to do with rates of economic development and growth. Literacy varies considerably throughout the world, with the highest illiteracy rates occurring in underdeveloped lands. For instance, 75 to 80 percent of Egypt's population is illiterate, while in Morocco the figure is between 80 and 90 percent. The lowest illiteracy rates are in the technically advanced lands of Anglo-America (0 to 3 percent), Oceania (0 to 2 percent), Northern Europe (0 to 1 percent) and Japan (0 to 2 percent).

economic variables

labor

As indicated earlier, the cultural and demographic traits of a population affect the structure, participation rates, and other qualities of the labor force. The nature of the labor force is at the same time a function of level of economic development. The participation rate is affected by the age composition of a population, as well as by marital status and prevailing attitudes toward women working outside the home. Among technically advanced countries of North America and Western Europe about 40 to 45 percent of the population participates in the labor force. In Japan, this percentage reaches 49 percent, and in the Communist countries of Eastern Europe the usual figure is between 52 and 54 percent, indicative of the degree to which centrally planned economies mobilize their populations. In the less developed countries the participation rate ranges between one-fifth and two-fifths of the population, although it is difficult to distinguish between the commercial labor force and that occupied in subsistence production.

Levels of economic development are apparent in the structure of the labor force in different areas. In the

Fig. 2.5 *Effects of economic development on the structure of the labor force. As a region rises in the scale of development, the proportion of its labor force engaged in primary activities steadily diminishes. The percentage employed in secondary activities increases until industrialization is essentially completed, at which time it begins a relative decline. The proportion in the services, both the tertiary or commoner types and the quaternary or more advanced control functions, consistently rises.*

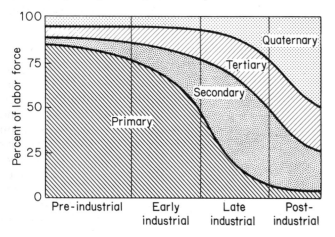

world as a whole, somewhat less than three-fifths of the labor force is engaged in primary production, mainly agriculture, while nearly one-fifth is employed in secondary activities, principally manufacturing. The tertiary activities—retailing, wholesaling, and various other services—account for the rest, amounting to a little over one-quarter of the labor force.

From one-half to as much as three-fourths of the workers in most underdeveloped countries are employed in farming. Only one-tenth to one-fifth are engaged in manufacturing, and tertiary employment represents from 15 to 25 percent. Agriculture, a minor employer in most technically advanced lands, falls as low as 4 to 5 percent in Britain and the United States but reaches as high as 16 percent in France, with its stable peasant population component. Manufacturing is a major source of employment, accounting for more than one-fourth of the total in the United States and about one-third in the United Kingdom and West Germany. The services account for more than two-fifths of all employment in countries such as France and Germany but reach 70 percent in the United States.

As a country passes through the various phases of economic development, the composition of its labor force seems to undergo the kinds of changes illustrated in Figure 2.5. During the preindustrial phase, primary activities engage the major part of its work force, while the secondary forms of production, mainly handicrafts, occupy relatively few people. The nonproductive occupations, providing only minor employment, can be separated into two parts. Retailing, wholesaling, and the other more ordinary tertiary activities may have a fair representation because of the inefficient marketing and the prevalence of personal and domestic service in some less developed countries; but there is very little call for the quaternary occupations, such as administration, higher education, and research.

The early industrial period, which corresponds to industrial revolution, accelerates the demand for workers in the secondary occupations. When manufacturing becomes firmly established, it requires an increasing proportion of the labor force; by the end of the phase, manufacturing becomes a major employer. Primary employment begins to decline as farm labor is used more efficiently. The tertiary and quaternary activities are as yet little affected, since services and administration are mainly provided from outside the region.

The late industrial stage, which began about 1920 in the United States, is accompanied by accelerating decline in agricultural employment, until ultimately it reaches a very low level. Manufacturing employment continues to grow, although at a declining rate as labor productivity rises; it finally attains its maximum by the end of the period. Meanwhile the tertiary activities are expanding very rapidly in order to satisfy the proliferating demands for supporting services for manufacturing and to supply the growing requirements of an increasingly prosperous population. Development of the quaternary sector (information-processing activities, research and development, and high order services) is delayed at the outset, but later expands more rapidly as the economy and society become increasingly complex.

Finally the society reaches the postindustrial phase, an event that occurred about 1960 in the United States and more recently in much of Western Europe and Japan. This era is characterized by a declining emphasis upon acquiring material goods and more of an interest in improving the quality of life. Primary employment falls to a virtual minimum, and a remarkably few farm workers are able to provide food and industrial raw materials for the remainder of the population. The industrial labor force begins to shrink with the advent of automation and a growing emphasis upon forms of production that require less labor and more capital. Tertiary employment, now more specialized than ever, begins to approach saturation; but the quaternary occupations continue their rapid expansion, acquiring an elaborate division of labor and supplying a whole new set of societal needs.

the spatial character of demand

One of the most important characteristics of a population is its income. This is a measure of the population's capacity to consume and hence its attractiveness as a market. Indirectly, income is also an indicator of the productivity of that population with income measures being the most frequently used indexes of economic development. Since this subject will be treated at some length in Chapter 13; here we merely consider the spatial variations of populations at different levels of income.

Some of the most extreme income differences appear at the international scale. At one end of the continuum is the United States, which in 1970 had a per capita gross domestic product of $4734. Canada and the countries of Western and Northern Europe follow closely with a per capita GDP between $1292 (Ireland) and $4055 (Sweden). At the other extreme are the less developed countries, comprising the majority of the world's population. The African nations typically have per capita GDP figures between $86 (Uganda) and $265 (Ghana), although technically advanced South Africa (at $864) is an important exception.

As usual, however, these national figures conceal wide internal variations. The United States maintains detailed information on personal income, a somewhat more appropriate measure than GDP but not so widely available internationally at this scale. For the country as a whole the per capita personal income was $4138 in 1971, but the northeastern part of the country was well above this level while the southeast was substantially below it. The highest incomes coincide with the North American manufacturing belt, including the Middle Atlantic, New England, and Northeastern states, plus a second, smaller region of high income centering upon California in the Southwest. Connecticut and New York lead the list of individual states with per capita incomes

of $5032 and $5021, respectively. The lowest figures were in the South, comprising the east south central, west south central, and south Atlantic states. Mississippi ($2766), Arkansas ($3036), and Alabama ($3050) were the lowest in the union. In all parts of the country the cities recorded per capita income figures above those of their regions.

One distinctive feature of income distribution in the United States is the degree to which regional differences are narrowing with time. In 1929, for example, the east south central states had per capita incomes averaging only 46 percent of the general level for the country. Since then those states have been increasing their incomes at a rate three-fourths again as high as that of the nation as a whole. On the other hand, in 1929 the Middle Atlantic states had incomes 147 percent above those of the nation, but they have subsequently progressed at only 70 percent of the national rate. New England incomes are also rising at a below-average rate, and some northern sections of that region are experiencing economic problems, especially peripherally located Maine.

POPULATION DYNAMICS

The previous section has shown that certain areas are favored for human habitation over others, producing extreme spatial variations in population densities. Although these disparities can be explained partly in terms of the physical limits to human occupancy, this still leaves questions as to how these population concentrations originated and the processes by which they continue to change. Two kinds of dynamic processes are usually considered to affect spatial distributions of human populations: migration and differential growth rates. Both have been active throughout man's existence on earth, but their relative importance has changed substantially in modern times.

human migrations

Migration is a permanent movement of human beings over a significant distance. In practice, however, the definitions of permanence and significant distance are both relative. The United Nations considers any change of residence of one year or more as migration, while a shorter stay is termed a visit. The United States Bureau of the Census applies the term *migration* only to persons whose move involves crossing a county line; but many students of population insist that any distance is significant, even a move to the apartment next door.

It is also useful to distinguish between internal and external migrations, especially when there is a question of relative freedom of movement. Internal migrations refer to movements within a single sovereign nation, while external migration applies to international moves. The latter can be further subdivided into intercontinental and intracontinental migrations, the intercontinental type tending to be the more permanent. The subject of migration is difficult to treat precisely, mostly because statistics are often inaccurate, particularly when no record is kept of "remigrations," that is, persons returning to their homelands.

the migration process

Viewed broadly, migration is similar to trade, with flows of people substituted for flows of merchandise. As in the case of commodity movements, there is an area supplying surplus populations, or at least providing some "push" that causes people to leave. At the other end is the area of demand in which there is either a population deficit or some other form of attraction or "pull." Between regions of supply and demand are various barriers that offer obstacles to the movement of people.

The trade analogy can be carried no further, however. Goods are passive, even though some are more transportable than others; but people are active agents, free to decide for themselves whether or not to migrate. There are important exceptions, however, and involuntary movements of people are not unusual. Many large population transfers have been effected by governments or other external agencies. Moreover, children and other dependents often have their migration decisions made for them.

WHY PEOPLE MIGRATE.   One approach to explaining migration is that of the classical economic model of factor mobility—the "factor" being labor. Several simplifying assumptions underly the model, one of these being that the migrants are economic men. This means that they are motivated to move by the desire to maximize their incomes and that they have a perfect knowledge of the opportunities for employment in each location and the wages that will be paid. Secondly, the model assumes that the workers are numerous and are identical in their skills, values, and needs. Finally, the model assumes no barriers to migration. Under these conditions a migration of labor will occur from Region *A* to Region *B* so long as *real wages* (wages expressed in terms of how much they will buy) are higher in *B* than in *A*. The expected final result of this model is a labor supply that is everywhere in equilibrium, with a job for every worker and all vacancies filled.

This focus upon economic reasons for migration finds some justification in both less developed and advanced countries. In India, for example, one study found that the decisions of individuals to move hinged largely on whether there were expectations of job opportunities in the new area. In another case, it was shown that 85 percent of the labor movements between regions of the United States were associated with changes in unemployment levels. In other words, people tend to migrate to those places where new jobs are opening up most rapidly in relation to the number of persons entering the labor force.

Even so, the "economic man" assumption of the classical model has limited applicability. People have other than economic motives for moving, and they rarely are able to decide with complete objectivity. Much rationalization is connected with most decisions to move, and knowledge about conditions at the other end of the journey is usually imperfect. In each case, the prospective migrant must weigh his perceptions of his **present** location against those of the proposed location. In this evaluative process, economic reasons therefore do not tell the whole story, and under certain conditions they do not even give the most important part.

Often the most compelling reasons for moving are of a cultural nature. Religion, for example, has been an important migration factor; throughout history many individuals and groups have moved to new places where they could practice their beliefs unhindered. Kinship, friendship, and linguistic and ethnic ties have also played important parts in decisions to migrate.

Cultural groups have tended to produce "streams" of migrations into particular places. During the American colonial period large numbers of German migrants settled in Pennsylvania, where they came to be called "Pennsylvania Dutch." The Mormons, in their highly organized westward movement, followed distinct paths and settled in certain selected areas. In Canada, the Finns chose to congregate at the head of Lake Superior and the Mennonites in southern Manitoba. In the Italian migrations to the Western Hemisphere, those from southern Italy went mainly to the United States while those from the north tended to go to the Rio de la Plata region of South America. Meanwhile, those migrants who changed their minds, or who perhaps decided to return home to marry or to retire, produced "counterstreams."

Finally, political considerations have been a prominent factor in decisions to migrate. Persons seeking relief from political persecution, expelled from their homelands because of unpopular beliefs, or fleeing because of war have traditionally formed an important stream of migrants to new lands. Governments have also engaged in forcibly resettling of large numbers of people or have sent sizable groups to colonize new areas.

In view of the many explanations for migrating, demographers have made various attempts to classify these reasons. Petersen's fivefold classification is widely used for this purpose, with each category of migration subdivided further as to whether it is "innovating" or "conservative." Migrants whose moves are innovating are undertaking a new way of life; those whose moves are conservative are preserving their accustomed way of life in their new surroundings.

1. *Primitive migration* describes the movements of peoples at a very low level of development in response to conditions of a physical environment over which they have little control. In its conservative form primitive migration is exemplified by the wanderings of the herdsmen of Central Asia, the subsistence farmers of Amazonia, or food gatherers in the Congo. The innovative form is indicated by the settling of Middle Eastern nomads into an urban way of life in Egypt or Syria.

2. *Forced migration* is the compulsory transfer of a people, usually by a political agency. The resettling of populations as a result of the westward shifting of the Polish borders was a conservative type of forced migration, while the African slave trade was an innovative type.

3. *Impelled migration* is similar in that migrants are under some form of duress, but it differs in that they retain some ability to decide whether or not to move. The flight of ancient Britons before the Saxon invaders was a conservative form of impelled migration, since those who chose not to escape to the security of the Welsh mountains had the option of remaining behind to be enslaved. Jewish victims of the Russian pogroms, who could have stayed at home under subjection, elected instead to leave their rural homeland to pursue urban trades in American cities.

4. Individual movements for economic betterment or mere adventure are referred to as *free migration*. The westward migrations of pioneer farmers in the United States and Canada were a conservative type of free migration, whereas migrations of modern Americans or Canadians leaving their cities for the farms, logging camps, or mines of Alaska or the Northwest Territories are innovating.

5. When large numbers of people participate in a *mass migration* they tend to submerge their individual motivations and may not even be fully informed of what to expect in their new settlements. Entire rural communities from the Westlandit region of southwestern Norway migrated to North America in this way. Some found opportunities to establish farms in their new environments, but others did not.

Migrations may also be classified according to the degree of governmental control they receive. Before World War I the United States government accepted virtually all immigrants; following the war, however, immigrants were admitted according to rigid quota systems that excluded some nationalities altogether. Thus a policy of "unrestricted" immigration was replaced by one of "selective" immigration.

Typologies of migrations have more than academic uses. In particular, they aid government policy makers in dealing with the numerous problems created by emigration or immigration. Such an analytical approach provides a better understanding of the kinds of pressures and motivations underlying the present trend, for example, of the movement of people from farms and small towns to the great metropolises.

BARRIERS TO MIGRATION. The question of why people move must be distinguished from how many actually do so. Often large numbers of people would like to move but are prevented from doing it because of three main types of barriers: distance, political restrictions, and those characteristics of potential migrants that reduce their mobility.

One of the most imposing barriers to migration is distance, which therefore serves as a leading variable in most analyses of the spatial distribution of migrants. Studies consistently show that most people move short distances and that the frequency of moves declines with an increase in distance from the original homelands of the migrants. In economic terms, migrants may find that

long-distance moves simply entail too much transport cost. Moreover, the "opportunity costs" of moving—the income that may be foregone at the old location—also must be taken into account.

There are also noneconomic reasons that discourage long-distance moves. For one thing, people's knowledge about other areas grows dimmer with increasing distance from home. Long-distance moves, especially to foreign countries, produce many personal disruptions owing to unfamiliar customs, language, and lack of family and community ties. This is sometimes referred to as a "psychic cost."

Because of the prominence of the distance factor in human migrations, gravity and potential models have frequently been used to study this subject (see Chapter 12). The basic hypotheses involved in this approach are, first, that the propensity to migrate from region i to region j is inversely related to the distance separating them (or, more commonly, the square of that distance), and secondly, that the number of persons moving to a particular point is directly proportional to the populations living at each end of the journey. In its simplest form, therefore, the relationship is given by the following familiar expression:

$$M_{ij} = \frac{P_i P_j}{d^2_{ij}} \cdot k$$

where M_{ij} = number of migrants moving from region i to region j.

P_i, P_j = size of population in regions i and j, respectively.

d = distance separating regions i and j.

k = a factor of proportionality.

In practice it is usual to adjust this model in several ways. It is necessary to make some kind of allowance in the formula for the nature of employment opportunities in the new place, which, as we have already seen, provides a better measure than population alone. There may also be the need to take into account intervening opportunities that may appear along the various routes of travel from the place of origin. Studies of labor migrations in Sweden, for example, have shown that proximity to other employment centers tends to syphon off sizable numbers of migrants from more distant places. Another variable that can be usefully added is some measure of the number of friends and relatives who may already have moved to the new location, persons who can be depended upon to give information about opportunities in that place, and perhaps even to provide food and shelter at first. Finally, it is common to allow for other possibly attractive qualities of the destination, such as a particularly benign climate. A recent study of migration among the 48 contiguous United States has confirmed the significance of these variables.

Because of the various influences of distance on migration, the areas nearest the prime sources of migrants have been found to fill up first. Migration may therefore take the form of a diffusion of people outward from an initial center. This has been confirmed by a number of studies conducted at local, regional, and international levels of observation.

Under certain circumstances, political barriers to migration can be especially compelling. In this respect migration resembles trade, since international movement presents more obstacles than internal movement. In the case of migration, however, this is a fairly recent development. National governments have closely controlled immigration and emigration only in this century. So far has this trend proceeded, in fact, that free international migration has virtually ended. Even the few lands still actively encouraging immigration have become increasingly selective. Australia, for example, solicits immigrants from most British Commonwealth and European countries, but excludes non-white immigrants from her overpopulated neighbors, such as Indonesia and the Philippines or India.

Except for the Communist countries, most modern countries do not restrict emigration. The Soviet Union, the states of Eastern Europe, China, and Cuba allow only a few people to emigrate. The Berlin Wall has improved East Germany's economy by preventing the emigration of her best trained young adults.

Another, and more subtle, barrier to migration is the imperfect mobility of populations who are otherwise free to move. Because young adults between the ages of fifteen and thirty are the most likely to migrate, the remaining population consists of the very young and the elderly. The more prosperous among the elderly, however, may retire to areas with warmer climates. Moreover, women are less likely to move than men. Studies have further suggested that persons staying at home tend to have poorer health than migrants in the same age groups. Migration tends to skim off at least some of the best educated, most intelligent, and most highly skilled members of a community. Among migrants of all types, moreover, it has been found that the least-skilled and poorest persons tend to move the shortest distances. Negro migrants from the southern United States tend to be exceptions to this rule, however, since many of these leave the southern rural environment altogether for both noneconomic and economic reasons.

Among the most binding ties to the home area, however, are the links between would-be migrants and their families and culture groups. This has been a strong deterrent to interregional migration in China, and has also operated to keep persons from leaving depressed areas such as Appalachia, the Ozarks, and South Wales. Migration is thus a selective force, disclosing important differences between those who move and those who do not.

Not only are some persons more likely to migrate than others but people are also more inclined to move at certain times than others. Migration is much greater during times when the business cycle is ebbing in the sending country and rising in the receiving country. Decisions to migrate are further affected by the life cycle of the individual. People are more inclined to move upon completion of their education, as they are entering the labor market, when they are retiring, or undergoing a change in marital status. More difficult to predict are such accidental events as expulsions from a community or a country. The colonizing of Georgia and southeastern Australia, for example, both occurred initially through the transporting abroad of British criminals.

regional effects of migration

The selectivity and timing of migrations have decided impacts on both supplying and receiving regions. In some cases these effects are almost as great as the magnitude of the movement itself.

DEMOGRAPHIC, SOCIAL, AND PSYCHOLOGICAL CONSEQUENCES. Intuitively one would expect the selectivity of migration to influence the population size of the areas at each end of the stream, but these effects are not as simple as might be supposed. Initially migration causes the total number of people in the supply region, A, to fall and that of the receiving area, B, to rise. This much is to be anticipated, but there are also secondary effects from selectivity. The birth rate in A is reduced by the loss of young adults, while that of B goes up for the same reason. Thus the selectivity of migration has accentuated A's loss and B's gain. In the end, however, the balance may become readjusted. The general levels of health in A may rise when population pressures are released and infant mortality rates fall. This, together with a rise in fertility rates, stimulates population growth in the source region. Meanwhile, the influx of immigrants to B accelerates the development of urbanization, which is normally attended by falling birth rates. The problem becomes further complicated in the special case where B is a region with a warm, sunny climate, such as Florida or Arizona, and the immigrants are elderly retirees instead of young adults. Here the effect is likely to be an increase in death rates in the receiving area simply because of the advanced age of the newcomers. We have earlier noted the effects of migration on sex ratios of both the sending and receiving regions.

Although emigrants tend to be the more physically healthy members of a source population, their mental health and emotional stability often range from the very best to the worst. The problems of adjustment to a new environment may contribute to increased incidence of crime, lawlessness, and the disintegration of families among migrant groups. Many of our urban problems appear to be generated by such stresses. At the same time, any cultural conflict may produce antagonisms between newcomers and the indigenous population of the region.

ECONOMIC CONSEQUENCES. A region that receives large numbers of immigrants may benefit economically in many ways, at least in the earlier stages of its development. This appears to have been true of the United States prior to the first World War, although not since that time. The influx of immigrants has been credited with increasing the growth rate of the country's total gross national product, and it may even have raised it in per capita terms. This may be attributed to the addition of large numbers of persons mainly of working-age who were healthy, possibly of better-than-average intelligence, skilled and conditioned to hard work. As they prospered, these persons provided a rapidly expanding market for goods of all kinds and especially those of the newly developing manufacturing industries. These conditions, in turn, created an attractive investment market for the European capital required for further expansion.

The economic effects upon those regions supplying migrants vary. For the technically advanced western European countries emigration to the New World provided temporary relief during downward swings of the business cycle. The large numbers of farmers moving to agriculturally rich lands in the Americas also supplied Europe with abundant new sources of foodstuffs at low prices. At the same time, the industrial nations gained rapidly expanding markets for their manufactured goods in these overseas areas.

For today's less developed countries and regions emigration is often detrimental, since the emigrants are the most enterprising, skilled, and highly educated members of the population. For the most part, these business leaders, and professionals not only receive their educations abroad, but they often elect to pursue their careers in advanced countries where the financial rewards and opportunities are greater than at home. Because the developing nations often desperately need such skills, this type of migration has perverse effects.

patterns of migration

With this basis, we next examine briefly the broad patterns of migration that have helped to give us the world distributions of population described earlier in this chapter. First we shall look at international migrations and then at some of the more recent internal population movements.

INTERNATIONAL.   The earliest human migrations were group movements of clans and tribes; individual movements and migration streams were to appear much later. These first primitive migrations were impelled mostly by climatic changes, or by calamities, such as hostile invaders. In view of the comparatively small number of inhabitants on the earth during the period of prehistory, it is paradoxical that one of the most probable reasons for early migrations was population pressure. It must be remembered, however, that primitive means of livelihood were (and still are) highly extensive in their use of land. With much land needed to support each human being, primitive folk had constantly to adjust their activities to an uncertain food supply. When their numbers increased to the point that their traditional lands became inadequate, migration to new areas became necessary. Routes of travel were dictated by the physical features of the landscape, such as mountain passes, ice bridges, wide plains, and valleys.

All primitive movements have been dwarfed, however, by modern migrations. Whereas the earlier migrations usually involved the encroachment of primitive peoples upon the lands of more advanced cultures, most modern migrations have reversed this process. It has been estimated that at least 60 million Europeans and Africans took part in the great migrations since A.D. 1500. These migrations began slowly. Although from 10 to 20 million African slaves were transported to the new lands, relatively few Europeans moved permanently prior to 1800, probably no more than 2.5 million in all.

During the nineteenth century, the European exodus increased, particularly after 1830, and reached a peak on the eve of World War I with an annual flow of 1.5 million. These persons were escaping rural overpopulation in Scandinavia, Ireland, Scotland, Germany, and Italy, as well as political upheavals, religious persecution (such as the Russian pogroms), and economic depressions. Many people came for the sake of adventure, of course, and most of the movements formed streams to particular locations. Of the total, about two-thirds went to the United States, but Canada and the other British Commonwealth countries attracted large numbers as well. South America received immigrants mainly from the Mediterranean lands.

INTRACONTINENTAL.   Familiar flow patterns were quickly altered by changes in national policy following World War I. The Great Depression reversed migration flows during the early 1930s when most western European countries actually experienced net gains, mostly from returnees. For a time the United States, Australia, New Zealand, Argentina, and Uruguay experienced net losses of migrants. Since that period the most significant population movements have occurred within continental areas.

Intra-European migrations have been particularly large since the beginning of World War II, the war itself being responsible for wholesale displacements of populations. Just prior to the war about 400,000 persons (mostly Jews) had escaped from Nazi Germany, while during the war the Germans imported 8 million foreigners as forced labor. In all, it is estimated that the Nazis uprooted more than 30 million persons. The postwar boundary changes produced large population changes, especially the westward expansion of the Slavic area at German expense. This resulted in the displacement of 11 million Germans and a very large exchange of populations between the Soviet Union and Poland along their new border. Another million Germans subsequently escaped from East Germany into West Germany. In all, 25 million or more people moved during the time of postwar settlement.

Among the prospering nations of postwar Europe a new pattern of population movement has emerged. Surplus labor from the southern Mediterranean, North Africa, and Asia Minor has streamed into labor-short Germany, France, Switzerland, and the Low Countries, while unwanted immigrants from Commonwealth countries in the Caribbean, Africa, and South Asia have poured into already overcrowded Britain. Among the countries of Africa and Asia there have likewise been very large migrations, mainly unrecorded, of peoples uprooted by food shortages, intertribal conflicts, and wars.

INTERNAL. Although international and internal migrations stem from the same basic causes, internal movements are of much greater magnitude today because they encounter fewer barriers. The two main types of internal migration, interregional and rural-urban, are both evident in the United States. Replacing the historically important westward movement, there has been a general exodus of people from the center to both coasts.

Between the censuses of 1960 and 1970 large numbers of people migrated to the three West Coast states, especially California, which is now the most populous of all. Texas, Colorado, Arizona, and Nevada also experienced net gains. During the same period, the East Coast states from New Jersey southward had similarly large influxes of people; Florida was the leading destination. New England's population failed to grow at the national rate.

Net out-migrations took place in each of the East North Central and West North Central states and in all but one of the East South Central States. These regions averted absolute losses only because births exceeded deaths during the decade. North and South Dakota and economically depressed areas in Appalachia actually had fewer people in 1970 than in 1960.

Although some of the largest increases occurred in states with unusual environmental attractions, it is important to note that these recent interregional migrations have at the same time been rural-urban movements. Rural-urban migrations are by no means peculiar to the United States nor are they a new phenomenon. In technologically advanced lands, most rural-urban migration results from a coincidence of agricultural innovation and industrial development. Changing rural land use patterns and increased productivity of farm labor have displaced large numbers of workers.

Through a combination of such developments the United States, which was a nation of farmers at its birth, now employs only some 5 percent of its work force in agriculture. Most of this change, however, had taken place prior to the 1960s. During the 1960–1970 period the majority of the inter-state migrants were moving from small urban places—hamlets, villages and small towns—to larger metropolitan areas.

One of the most significant postwar population developments in the United States has been the exodus of southern blacks, a combination of interregional and rural-urban migrations. Whereas the majority of American blacks had lived on southern farms in 1940, the majority are now urban dwellers outside the South. Three main streams of black migrations have been distinguished. One has had its source in the inner coastal plain and Piedmont areas of the Southeast and its terminus in the northeastern metropolises. A second stream of migrants has come mainly from the Mississippi delta and black belt regions of the states of Louisiana, Mississippi, and Alabama and settled in such urban centers of the East North Central states as Chicago, Detroit, and Cleveland. Migrants forming the third stream have originated mostly in southern Arkansas, northern Louisiana, and east Texas and have moved predominantly to Los Angeles, San Francisco, and Seattle. Massive as this movement has been, there is recent evidence that the flow is slowing and that counterstreams are beginning to appear.

Canada, too, has had important internal migrations, both interregional and rural-urban. Canada's interregional migrations have had two spatial components: east to west and hinterland to heartland. The east-west trend was especially prevalent until World War II, with the result that each province, with few exceptions, has had a net gain of people from every province to its east and lost population to every province to its west. At the same time, streams of migrants converged on the Ontario industrial belt from resource-oriented hinterland regions. Increasingly since the war, both immigration from abroad and internal migration have tended to follow these trends.

Other technically advanced countries have had similar internal migrations, both rural-urban and interregional. Italy, for example, has experienced a substantial flow of Calabrians, Sicilians, and others from the overpopulated and economically depressed rural south to the prosperous industrial cities of the north.

Large-scale internal migrations have likewise occurred in many less developed nations, particularly rural-urban movements. Indeed, taken as a whole, cities in the underdeveloped countries gained nearly 58 percent in population between 1960 and 1970. China has had an enormous influx of in-migrants to its cities, as has India, although in China this has been countered by Maoist preferences for the countryside. Some African cities are said to be gaining population at rates between 7 and 14 percent each year. The trend is strong in nearly all Latin American cities, too.

POPULATION GROWTH

Populations vary spatially through the process of "natural increase," that is, an excess of births over deaths. One region may accumulate larger numbers of people than another simply because its indigenous population is growing more rapidly. The world's population is now increasing at unprecedented rates, and the subject of growth has become one of the great public issues of today, just as was international migration earlier in this century.

1,600,000 years of population growth

It is believed that modern man's existence on the earth extends back at least 600,000 years and possibly as much as one million years prior to that. Quantitative information before A.D. 1650 must be estimated from circumstantial evidence based on what we know of

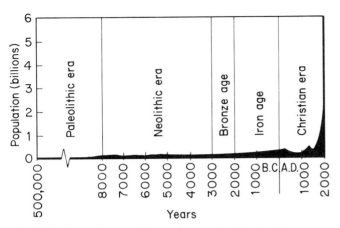

Fig. 2.6 *Growth of world population. Note that, after having gained but little during the thousands of years of early human life, population began a slow rise during Roman times, slipped backward during the Dark Ages, and began to rise again by the fourteenth century, when the bubonic plague brought a sharp but temporary decline. Since then population growth has accelerated rapidly.*

Source: After Population Bulletin, *vol. 18, no. 1.*

early men's livelihood and the capacity of the land to support primitive economies. From the evidence we have today, for example, we know that subsistence gathering and hunting and fishing require as much as two square miles per person. Agriculture, on the other hand, can support much denser populations. These estimates are supplemented by some scattered records of early communities and countries, particularly those of the Roman Empire, together with other archaeological evidence.

accelerating growth

Estimates of early populations, census data that have accumulated since, and projections of the future provide enough information to construct curves of world population growth like that shown in Figure 2.6. The main impression given by this diagram is its persistent upward trend, with the world's population reaching approximately 3.7 billion people in 1972. It is also clear that until modern times, population increased at a very low rate, with periods of actual decline. Only within the past 300 years—a tiny fraction of man's tenure on the earth—has world population grown at consistently high rates.

During the preagricultural era, before 8000 B.C., when man was using only rudimentary tools and weapons, not more than 5 million people inhabited the earth. Numbers increased to between 200 and 250 million by the beginning of the Christian era and possibly as many as 275 million by the end of the first millennium. During the next 300 years the population of Europe began to rise, and the world total is thought to have reached about 384 million by 1300.

The following century brought a series of plagues to Europe that reduced its population so drastically that world population declined. From 1400 to 1650, however, there was a rebirth of European civilization and an

energetic conquest of new lands by European peoples. Although Europe's population rose at more than twice the world rate during this period, it is probable that the indigenous population of the Americas was much reduced by the impact of European invasions. The population estimates of 1650 indicated a total of about 500 million. Within the next two centuries the world total rose much more rapidly, doubling to approximately 1 billion people by 1850. By 1930 the population reached 2 billion, and by 1970, 3.6 billion. This is a significant figure in view of the fact that the world contains about 3.6 billion acres of arable land. In other words, we have now passed the point where we have one acre of arable land per person.

nature of the population growth curve

The accelerating rate of growth has thus brought a nearly constant steepening of the population curve. In A.D. 1300, the annual rate of growth for the world as a whole was perhaps 0.11 or 0.12 percent, but between 1650 and 1750 it was probably nearer 0.3 percent. By the 1930s the annual rate had reached 1.0 percent, and currently it is about 1.9 percent. Another way of looking at this is to note the number of years it takes for the world's population to double. Between 8000 B.C. and A.D. 1650, for example, this doubling required 1,500 years; but the next doubling, between 1650 and 1850, took only 200 years. Eighty years later, in 1930, population had doubled again; and it is estimated that it will once again have doubled by the year 1975, a mere 45 years. It is probable that only 35 years will be needed for the next doubling. From this evidence, the population curve would be exponential; that is, the rate of increase is itself rising by some fairly constant percentage.

There is reason to believe, however, that the population growth curve is not quite so simple. If, instead of plotting world population on an arithmetic scale as in Figure 2.6 we use a double logarithmic scale (Fig. 2.7),

Fig. 2.7 *Technological revolutions and world population growth. Population growth for the past million years plotted on a log-log scale shows a series of surges, each associated with a technological revolution that has increased the earth's capacity to support human life.*

Source: After Deevey, "The Human Population." Copyright © 1960 *by* Scientific American, Inc. *All rights reserved.*

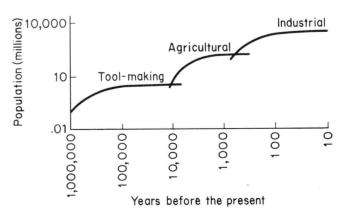

which emphasizes *rates* of change, we discover a number of details obscured in the previous diagram. We now find that there have apparently been three main surges of population growth rather than one, and that each appears to correspond with a technological breakthrough that has increased the capacity for the world economy to support more people. The developments that have fostered these bursts of population were the tool-making, agricultural, and industrial revolutions.

As we shall note in the next chapter, it is doubtful that population growth rates can continue to accelerate for long without exhausting food supplies and natural resources and polluting the environment. For this reason the present phase of population development may in the end be better described not by an ordinary exponential curve but by a logistic curve, one that eventually levels off and perhaps even declines. (This point is considered in Chapter 25.)

the mechanism of growth

What are the components of population growth? As in the case of migration, this is a matter of additions and subtractions. Whereas the net effect of migration is determined by balancing the numbers arriving in a region with those leaving, population growth (or decline) is measured by comparing the number of births with the number of deaths.

birth rates, death rates, and growth rates

Birth rates are commonly expressed in terms of yearly births per thousand people. For example, in 1970 the population of the United States was 207,960,000 at the midyear point, while the number of births was 3,718,000. Dividing the number of births by the population and multiplying by 1,000 gives a birth rate of 18.2 for the year. Similarly, the death rate of the United States in 1970 is obtained by dividing the number of deaths, 1,921,000, by the midyear population and multiplying by 1,000, resulting in a rate of 9.4. The growth rate for 1970 is then calculated by subtracting the death rate from the birth rate, yielding 8.8 persons per thousand population. It is more common, however, to express the growth rate as so many persons per hundred, which, in this case, would give 0.88 percent. This number is the *rate of natural increase,* since migration is excluded from the calculations. These 1970 figures for the United States, which are fairly typical of technically advanced nations, are well below the world rates. In 1969 the world birth rate was 34 per thousand, the death rate was 15, and the growth rate was 1.9 percent. Note that the growth rate can be increased either by a rise in the birth rate, a fall in the death rate, or vice versa.

Although these are the most common forms of birth, death, and growth rates, more refined measures are required for other analyses. The above *crude birth rate* is not as revealing as the *fertility rate,* which is the number of births in a given year per thousand women of childbearing age (15 to 49). Fertility rate is more meaningful for comparing anticipated changes in a young population having a large number of females with those in an older population with an excess of males. Fertility rates have been found to be higher in rural areas than urban ones, in lower classes than upper classes, and in blue-collar occupations than in the professions, although these differentials have diminished in technically advanced nations as levels of mass communication have risen.

Likewise the *crude death rate* does not give as much information as the *age-specific death rate,* defined as the number of deaths per thousand in a particular age group. The most widely used type of age-specific death rate is the *infant mortality rate,* which is the number of deaths in the first year of life per thousand live births. This is considered one of the most valuable indexes of social welfare and sanitation. A similar function is performed by measures of *life expectancy,* that is, the average age attained by the inhabitants of a given area.

events affecting population growth

Most primitive peoples tend to have birth rates approaching 50 per thousand, but these are generally balanced by similarly high death rates. Rates of natural increase (or decrease) remain low under these conditions, unless some event alters the birth or death rate and tips the balance.

Until modern times the death rate has been the more volatile of the two measures. The most dramatic effects on death rates have resulted from disease and pestilence, famine, and war. The bubonic plague (A.D. 1348 to 1350), for example, quickly reduced Europe's population by at least one quarter, while the London plague of 1665 eliminated from one-third to one-half of that city's population. In some places endemic diseases, such as malaria, have been almost as destructive.

In some parts of the world many of the deaths attributed to disease are merely the indirect effects of hunger and malnutrition, and the correlation between disease, hunger, and death rates is very high. In fact, periodic famine, caused by floods, droughts, insect plagues, and war was one of the earliest population controls. Between A.D. 10 and 1846, for example, Britain recorded approximately 200 famines. China is said to have had 1,828 famines between 108 B.C. and A.D. 1911, an average of about one per year. Nine to thirteen million Chinese died between 1869 and 1876 alone. Famines are by no means unknown in this present century. In all, the Soviet Union experienced from 5 to 10 million deaths between 1918 and 1922 and between 1932 and 1934. India lost from 2 to 4 million in 1943, and similarly large numbers of famine deaths occurred during Bangladesh's recent struggle for independence from Pakistan and during Biafra's struggle against Nigeria.

More noticeable, though, are the wartime deaths resulting directly from the fighting. Among some primitive peoples intertribal wars are a major and customary cause of death. The two world wars in this century reduced population throughout Europe.

Although famines, epidemics, and war tend to reduce birth rates by reducing the ability to conceive or by disrupting normal family life, it is the voluntary means of reducing births, that have produced the most pervasive and prolonged effects on population growth. While the main force of birth control has been felt only in modern times, all societies have traditional methods of limiting population growth: infanticide, sexual taboos, killing the sick and aged, or marriage restrictions. Abortion has been illegal in most modern countries except Japan and Scandinavia, but these restrictions are gradually being lifted, especially in the United States. Contraception, an ancient practice even mentioned in the Bible, is now becoming the most important technique for preventing births. The extent to which birth control is practiced, as well as the choice of methods, is influenced by knowledge and cost, within a framework of religion, customs, attitudes, technological development, and degree of urbanization.

population theory

It is clear from the steeply rising curve of world population that the balance between births and deaths has been seriously disturbed. This fundamental problem gave rise to various theories of population, the most famous of which was that of Thomas Malthus. The eighteenth century had been a period of much optimism concerning man's perfectibility, combined with the view that a large population was a source of national strength. By the end of the century, however, a reaction occurred. The Industrial Revolution in Britain had revealed the evils of the factory system, the period of economic growth had seen a rapid increase in population, and the appearance of bad times soon caused these numbers to appear excessive. A time of bad harvests, high food prices, and a great deal of human misery, provided the setting for Malthus's pessimistic pronouncement of 1798.

Malthus

Thomas R. Malthus was an English clergyman, historian, and economist, born in 1766 to the English landed gentry and liberally educated at Cambridge. His famous *Essay on Population,* intended originally as an answer to the Utopians, strongly expressed his view that it is not desirable for a population to expand indefinitely when there is no assurance that the means for supporting that population can be made to keep pace. In this essay Malthus concluded that population has a natural tendency to increase rapidly as long as food or "subsistence" is available. If unchecked, population will go on doubling itself every 25 years, that is, it will increase at a "geometric ratio" (2, 4, 8, 16, 32, etc.). At the same time, however, even under the most favorable circumstances, the food supply cannot be increased faster than in an "arithmetic ratio" (3, 6, 9, 12, 15, etc.). In this way the food supply is quickly overtaken and exceeded by the numbers of people to be fed.

Malthus believed that the ultimate check to population growth, as in the case of the lower animals, is exhaustion of the food supply at the point when the two growth curves cross. This ultimate check to population growth would, of course, cause death from starvation, but more usually either of two *immediate* checks can be expected to intervene. The first is the *preventative* check, resulting from man's ability to recognize the consequences of his behavior. This preventative check Malthus termed "moral restraint," by which he, being a good churchman, did not mean birth control. To Malthus, moral restraint meant postponement of marriage, "accompanied by strictly moral behaviour"—its purpose being to avoid having children before the parents are able to support them. The second kind of intervening influence consists of the *positive* checks: "All of those causes which tend in any way prematurely to shorten the duration of human life." These include "vice"— those misfortunes we bring upon ourselves, such as war and the various consequences of immoral behavior—and "misery"—unavoidable products of the laws of nature, especially plagues and famines. Note that the positive checks act to limit population growth by raising death rates, while the preventative checks accomplish this same result by reducing birth rates.

According to Malthus it is the lowest stratum of society that is most affected by positive checks. In mature societies these forces cause the population to rise and fall in a cyclical fashion. In times of prosperity, the population increases; but this in turn causes the price of labor to fall and the cost of living to rise. The ensuing hard times bring the Malthusian checks into play and the population decreases until once again the labor force is in balance with job opportunities. Prosperity then returns, bringing with it complacency and a repetition of the population growth cycle. Malthus indicated that this cycle is not confined to technically advanced lands but is seen even in tribal societies, where a population is subjected to a whole range of positive checks upon reaching the limit of subsistence.

According to Malthus, there is no lasting way out of this dilemma through charity or emigration, which can bring only temporary relief from population pressure. Malthus's proposed solution was the general adoption of "moral restraint," that is, postponement of marriage, together with mass education (including the teaching of population principles) and more respect and personal liberty for single women.

Malthus was enormously influential. His basic ideas had a pervasive effect not only on philosophical, economic, social, and political thought but on the physical sciences, legislation, and popular education. Out of Malthus's work grew a school of population study that, with modifications, persists today.

However, Malthus's population theory later fell into some disrepute as the populations of Western

European countries and colonies experienced accelerated growth during the nineteenth century while enjoying unprecedented improvements in their standards of living. This was taken as a direct refutation of Malthus, justified by his failing to recognize the important effects of the social, economic, and technological changes taking place during his time. Yet it has since become apparent that Malthus's perspective held a great deal of validity for the long run: today human populations do indeed threaten to increase to that point beyond which the world's resources can support them.

other population theories

As Malthus's predictions failed to be immediately realized in Western Europe, alternative theories were advanced in an effort to correct the deficiencies in the Malthusian thesis. Like Malthus, many theorists sought "natural laws" of population growth, but they tended to look more to the newly developing social sciences for these laws. Michael Sadler, for example, maintained that as population densities increase fertility rates will drop. Herbert Spencer suggested that the increasing complexity of modern life will divert human energies from procreation and cause a reduction in the capacity to produce children. And Corrado Gini claimed that population growth is directly related to the rise and fall of nations.

Population theorists have also proposed theses to substantiate their political and social ideas. For example, Karl Marx, who misinterpreted Malthus's writings, insisted that it was not overpopulation that produced poverty and hardship, but rather the failure of the economic system. Henry George maintained that his "single tax" system would provide land for everyone who needed food with the result that food productivity could be expanded indefinitely.

Among modern theorists, Alexander Carr-Saunders suggested that the rate of population growth is determined by man's perception of the densities that are economically desirable for a particular way of life. He tended to agree with Malthus's assessment of the trends of population growth and food supply, but he felt that other checks operated to limit population. Contemporary theorists disclaim any "natural law" of population growth but attribute differences in birth and death rates to social, economic, and physical conditions.

population growth and regional development

As we observed earlier, the rapid growth of Europe's population conformed to Malthus's predictions, but the remarkable increase in European prosperity did not. Moreover, he was unable to anticipate the effects that regional development might have on those forces determining the size of a population. Today there is a growing recognition of the close interrelationships between the processes of development or "modernization" on the one hand, and those of population growth on the other.

the European experience

The demographic history of modern Europe illustrates some of these relationships. Just prior to the Industrial Revolution, when death rates and birth rates were very high, population was fairly stable. Urban death rates were especially high, and city growth was made possible only by heavy in-migration. The unwholesome urban conditions responsible for such death rates resemble those of many Oriental cities today: uncertain food supply, contaminated water, inadequate housing, lack of sewage disposal, and poor medical service.

The Industrial Revolution that began in Britain during the second half of the eighteenth century had profound effects on both death and birth rates in Western Europe. The application of inanimate energy to mining and manufacturing greatly increased the total and per capita output of goods. The rising incomes that resulted from higher volume of production made possible the purchase of foods in larger quantities and higher quality. They also provided financial support for better sanitary practices and for medical research. Although these improvements in food supply and public health came gradually, their cumulative effect was to reduce death rates sharply and to make cities capable of maintaining their populations. Much of the rise in population in the succeeding two centuries can be attributed to this cause.

Related to these industrial developments and essential to them was the accompanying revolution in agricultural production. Previously British agriculture consisted mainly of subsistence farms providing very little surplus output for cash sale. Even the most productive rural areas were unable to produce sufficient food to support more than 15 to 20 percent of their populations in urban activities. Near the end of the eighteenth century, however, farmers began to breed higher quality livestock, introduce new crops, and develop farm techniques that increased the yields of traditional commodities. Thus, as the Industrial Revolution made large urban concentrations necessary, these developments in agriculture provided the necessary additional food. Increased productivity of farm labor also resulted in a surplus of manpower for the growing urban labor force.

Important innovations in transportation were related to these industrial and agricultural developments. The construction of roads, canals, and railways, and the invention of new types of vehicles, greatly expanded the areal range of distribution and collection. No longer was it necessary for communities, or even countries, to be self-sufficient in raw materials and foodstuffs. Hunger and famine caused by local crop failures were thus eliminated. Not only goods but also people and ideas circulated freely and over increasing distances, thereby accelerating the rate of scientific discovery, including those related to health.

As these events combined to bring about a steady decline in death rates, birth rates were also dropping, although at a slower rate. The Industrial Revolution influenced birth rates in a way not anticipated by Malthus. It did this first of all by concentrating people into towns and cities, where they no longer had the incentives for large families that they had had on the farm. At the same time, the decline in infant mortality removed an important incentive for large numbers of births. With this effective change in attitudes toward family size, the practice of contraception spread rapidly. Beginning among the upper income groups in urbanized areas contraception quickly diffused to lower levels of society and into rural areas. Malthus could not have foreseen this, and he would not have approved of it if he had.

To summarize, the many changes brought about by the revolutions in manufacturing, food production, and transportation acted first to produce a rapid increase in the Western European population as the positive checks of an uncertain food supply and endemic and epidemic diseases were removed. These conditions in turn stimulated the adoption of a new kind of preventative check, contraception. There was a decided lag in the appearance of this latter development, however, and its force was not entirely felt until this present century. Europe was spared from what might have been excessive population pressures by the large-scale migration of its surplus peoples to newly discovered lands of the Western and Southern hemispheres. These migrants in turn brought rich virgin lands into cultivation and shipped an ever increasing supply of grain and other commodities back to the markets of their former homelands. Thus as Western Europe has stabilized its population, and as these demographic trends have diffused throughout the lands settled by European peoples, the Malthusian trap seems to have been evaded by the technically advanced world, at least for the present. The real worry today is directed toward the less developed countries where rapidly growing populations threaten to corroborate Malthus's dread prophesy.

population growth in the underdeveloped world

It is believed that certain of the densely settled lands of eastern and southern Asia, especially China and India, had reached their optimum population densities centuries ago. The Chinese population had apparently fluctuated at a high level over a long time, despite being held down by war, plague, and famine. It had probably followed a cyclical pattern like that predicted by Malthus, rising in good times and falling in bad. This equilibrium was likely disturbed by the coming of colonial control by European powers, bringing a new burst of population growth in such areas as Indonesia and India. Colonial administrations reduced internecine fighting among native populations and introduced economic improvements, causing death rates to fall below the persistently high birth rates.

Following World War II, however, a population crisis occurred in most underdeveloped lands as a result of new techniques of public health, better food distribution, and the prevention of local wars. Unlike the gradual process by which death rates were reduced in the

present developed countries, which had to await a whole series of medical advances over a period of two centuries, today's less developed countries were able to import low-cost, highly effective death-control measures that were ready-made. Many primitive villages otherwise untouched by modernization have benefited from the most sophisticated medical technology. So successful have these programs been that crude death rates in some less developed countries are at least as low as those in the most advanced. Europe's death rate (1969), for example, is 10 per thousand and that of the United States is 9.6, while Mexico's death rate is only 9 and Costa Rica's is only 7.

Meanwhile, however, birth rates in those countries remain largely unchanged. (Fig. 2.8). Crude birth rates of 40 per thousand are typical, in undeveloped countries, with many being much higher. Burma, for example, has a birth rate of 50, while Honduras and the Dominican Republic both have rates of 49.

Since migration to other areas has largely been prohibited, populations have boomed, giving rise to the expression, "population explosion." Costa Rica has the highest growth rate of all; her annual increase of 3.8 percent is enough to double the population every eighteen years. Latin America as a whole is growing at the rate of 2.9 percent, while Asia is growing at a rate of 2 percent. This compares with a growth rate of 1 percent for the United States and only 0.8 percent for Europe as a whole. Indeed, the dividing line between technologically advanced and underdeveloped lands is often defined as the 2 percent growth rate. Even at their

Fig. 2.8 *Relationship between birth rates and level of development. Countries at higher levels of development tend to have the lowest birth rates. When development is measured by per capita GNP, as in this example, the nonindustrialized oil-producing nations such as Libya and Venezuela appear as exceptions to the rule.*

Source: The Limits to Growth: A Report for The Club of Rome's Project on the Predicament of Mankind by *Donella H. Meadows, Dennis L. Meadows, Jørgen Randers, William W. Behrens III. A Potomac Associates book published by Universe Books, New York, 1972, p. 112. Graphics by Potomac Assoc.*

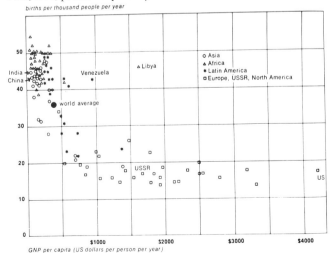

highest, growth rates in the advanced countries have never approached the present rates of the less developed world.

The already crowded lands of the Far East and West Africa have experienced the most immediate and obvious impacts of this growth. The less densely populated Latin American countries, however, are seriously affected also. Having achieved their independence from European powers a century or more earlier, they were free to begin the process of reducing their death rates sooner and have now progressed further in this respect. Consequently theirs are the highest *rates* of growth of all.

One important result of high growth rates is a very young age distribution. The proportion of dependent children in relation to the number of adults is exceedingly large in Costa Rica, for example, by comparison with that of Sweden (Fig. 2.9). In Honduras 51 percent of the population is under the age of 15; in Nicaragua the percentage is 48. In Europe the average is only 25 percent and in Sweden only 21 percent.

transition theory

From this discussion of population growth, it is apparent that countries experience a clearly defined *demographic transition* in the course of their development. Transition theory provides a tool for predicting future population changes of developing countries and a way

Fig. 2.9 *Comparison of age structures of Sweden and Costa Rica. Costa Rica's population, with large numbers in the dependent years, is typical of newly developing nations having high birth rates and low death rates. Sweden's population structure is representative of more developed countries, whose death rates and birth rates are both low, with the birth rates tending to fluctuate according to the business cycle.*

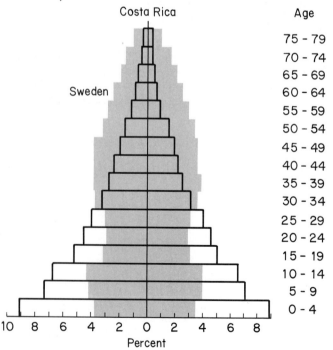

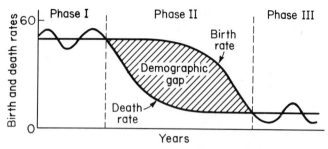

Fig. 2.10 *Transition theory. At the beginning of a country's development, the death rate tends to drop quickly while the birth rate remains high for some time. This creates a demographic gap or population explosion, until equilibrium is ultimately reestablished during the later stages of development.*

for anticipating their population problems. According to this theory, a country goes through three demographic phases as it develops (see Fig. 2.10).

In the first phase the population is relatively stable. It is kept in equilibrium by the combination of a high birth rate and a similarly high, but fluctuating, death rate. This describes preindustrial Europe, premodern China, and certain contemporary tribes in the rain forests of the Amazon and the Congo.

As soon as the development process commences, the country enters the second phase. With improved diets and standards of health the death rate drops, but the birth rate remains high throughout the earlier stages of the development process before it, too, begins to drop. This causes the two curves to diverge, producing what has been termed *the demographic gap*. This is the period of rapid population growth, or "population explosion." Much of Latin America and parts of Africa and southern and eastern Asia are at this stage.

Maturing of the economy brings urbanization, higher per capita incomes, and various social changes, all of which favor smaller families. This change in attitude lowers birth rates, which now approximate the low death rates. Note that in this final phase it is the birth rate that fluctuates about some mean, a response mainly to the business cycle (Fig. 2.10). The countries of Western Europe, Anglo-America, and Oceania, as well as Japan, have now reached this final stage of equilibrium.

Transition theory actually represents a generalization of the Western European experience. Increasingly, however, using the industrialized nations as a model for predicting the course of the less developed world is being brought into question. First of all, today's fertility rates are much higher in the underdeveloped countries than they were in premodern Europe. This is attributed to the religious beliefs, marriage customs, land tenure arrangements, and other cultural factors prevailing in many of the developing areas. Almost anyone will eagerly accept an innovation that will improve his health and increase his longevity, but attitudes toward marriage and the home are another matter.

Difficulties of applying transition theory today are also aggravated because the largest of the underdeveloped lands, especially India and China, are more densely populated than the preindustrial European countries. Other complications are caused by the different demographic histories of some of the currently developed countries; Germany, for example, reached population equilibrium much later than did France.

Despite these criticisms, certain aspects of transition theory still remain valid. First, the death rate always begins its decline before that of the birth rate, except perhaps in totalitarian regimes where individual choice is restricted. Second, changes in the death rate are the main determinant of population size in less developed lands, but fluctuations of the birth rate are the principal determinant in technically advanced societies.

developmental problems relating to demography

We have seen how the development process affects the patterns of population growth; but the reverse is also true. Population conditions can adversely affect production and delay economic growth. The difficulties of countries trying to achieve development can be greatly compounded by high growth rates, which create or aggravate problems of food distribution, agricultural productivity, income and education levels, and relations with neighboring countries.

Malthus particularly stressed the problem of providing sufficient food for a rapidly growing population. Evidence that most of the less developed countries are already failing to supply the daily nutritional needs of their people is to be seen in Figure 2.11, which indicates a fairly close relationship between daily per capita food energy (calories) and level of development as measured by per capita gross domestic product (GDP). Even so, the average member of an underdeveloped society spends a larger proportion of his income on food than does the

citizen of an advanced country. This relationship, termed *Engel's Law,* is illustrated by the case of Ghana, where half the family income is spent on food or that of Honduras where a family spends more than two-fifths of its income on food. Contrast these cases with Denmark, where less than one-fourth of income is spent on food, or with Canada, where the figure is approximately one-fifth.

Not only do most people in the less developed world receive less food per day, but they are more likely to suffer from dietary deficiencies. The poorer the population, the more dependent the people are upon starchy foods, such as grains and root crops. The essential "protective" foods, which are more costly, are generally lacking from the diets of the poorest peoples, as shown by the relationship between consumption of proteins (Fig. 2.12) and especially animal proteins (Fig. 2.13). Thus a

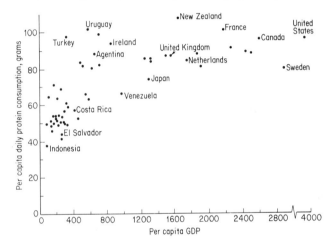

Fig. 2.12 *Relationship between per capita protein consumption and level of development.*

Sources: United Nations, Statistical Yearbook 1969 *and* Yearbook of National Account Statistics 1969 *(New York: United Nations, 1970).*

Fig. 2.13 *Relationship between per capita animal protein consumption and level of development.*

Sources: United Nations, Statistical Yearbook 1969 *and* Yearbook of National Account Statistics 1969 *(New York: United Nations, 1970).*

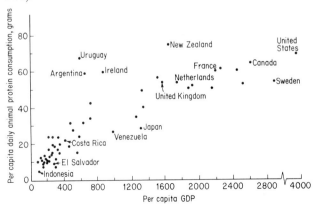

Fig. 2.11 *Relationship between per capita calorie consumption and level of development.*

Sources: United Nations, Statistical Yearbook 1969 *and* Yearbook of National Account Statistics 1969 *(New York: United Nations, 1970).*

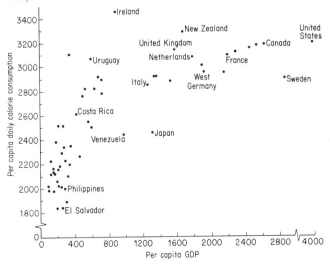

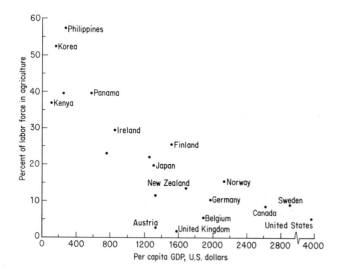

Fig. 2.14 *Relationship between percent of labor force in agriculture and level of development.*

Sources: United Nations, Statistical Yearbook 1969 *and* Yearbook of National Account Statistics 1969 *(New York: United Nations, 1970).*

rise in per capita income should be expected to bring a drop in the percentage of income spent on food, an increase in the total amount consumed (but only until an optimal level is reached), and a shift from cheaper starches to more expensive and nutritious foods, especially animal products ("indirect calories").

Despite the difficulty of feeding their growing populations, most underdeveloped countries employ a majority of their labor force in agriculture (Fig. 2.14). Much of this agriculture is of a very unproductive sort, however. Consider the plight of the Asian peasant on his plot of exhausted land, so tiny that it must all be devoted to grains and other foods for direct human consumption. In his poverty he is caught up in a vicious circle. Being unable to afford machinery, fertilizer, or improved seeds, he can only apply increased quantities of manpower in an effort to raise the level of output. He is thus motivated to have a large family, but this in turn merely means more mouths to feed. High rates of population growth in developing countries therefore tend both to reduce the quantity and quality of per capita food consumption and to affect adversely the conditions for producing that food.

Problems of employment are similarly related to population growth. In a mainly agricultural economy, rapid population increases overcrowd the available land. Manufacturing employment usually cannot be provided rapidly enough for the cities to absorb the growing labor force, especially since capital is so urgently needed in agriculture for feeding the additions to the population. The result is high unemployment, or *underemployment,* especially in rural areas where surplus workers remain with their families even though their labor is not really needed on the farm.

Overpopulation is sometimes defined in terms of income. A country or region is considered overpopulated

if per capita incomes would be substantially raised by a reduction in population size. Although this concept is difficult to measure, there is much evidence that developmental gains are being wiped out by population increases. In recent years, for example, India has seen her total gross national product rise but has then found that this must be divided among an even larger number of people than the year before. On the other hand, by means of a strenuous effort, Mexico has succeeded in raising total output so rapidly that it has more than compensated for a high rate of population growth.

One of the serious but little-noticed problems caused by high population growth rates in less developing lands is their effect on education. In some areas, particularly in Central America and the Caribbean, so many children are reaching school age that schools cannot be built or staffed fast enough to accommodate them. Compulsory education laws are thus of no practical significance and literacy rates in certain cases are actually falling. This, of course, reduces the quality of the labor force.

Another series of problems has to do with the political consequences of rapid population growth. If the population of one country is increasing faster than the populations of its neighbors, international relations may become strained. There is an ever-present temptation for an overcrowded country to seize the territory of less populous neighbors. For centuries the rice basket areas of the Mekong delta of Indochina have had to defend against the periodic incursions of more heavily populated nations to the north and west. History provides many instances of wars of conquest prompted by the desire for relief from population pressures.

population patterns of the future

The chief determinant of population distribution used to be migration, as we noted earlier, and this continued to be the case as long as the rapidly expanding European population moved to other continents. In many parts of the world internal migration remains an important force for population redistribution, but between countries the movement has been greatly reduced. Therefore the main agent of international population change has now become differential rates of growth. Although some countries have already achieved population stability, the majority have not, and this condition can be expected to give us a very different world by the end of the century.

It is important to have reliable forecasts of future population growth if we are to foresee danger spots and to devise a strategy for handling the problems these may bring. Unfortunately, population forecasting has been unsuccessful in the past, most of the earlier projections having been too conservative. For example, in 1942 the eminent demographer, Warren Thompson, listed six alternative projections for the United States population to the year 1980, each based on different assumptions about birth and death rates and migration. The highest of these projected a 1980 population of 187 million, a figure that was surpassed after the 1960 census. In 1949 Colin Clark forecast a world population of 3.5 billion by 1990, but that number had been exceeded before 1970. Better information and improved techniques are now available, however, and careful analyses of particular world regions should offer today's forecasts a greater probability of realization.

classifying countries according to population growth characteristics

Most regional analyses and population forecasts now rely to some degree on transition theory. The Population Division of the United Nations has developed a classification system that subdivides the second phase of demographic transition into three parts. It is important to know whether a country is just entering this critical period of rapid population expansion and thus has the major part of its population growth ahead of it, whether it is in the middle or most explosive part of the phase, or if it is about to conclude this part of the growth cycle.

Figure 2.15 illustrates this adaptation of transition theory. The crucial Phase II has been shaded to indicate the dimensions of the demographic gap and the UN subdivisions of this phase are designated with Arabic

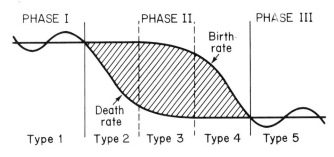

Fig. 2.15 *United Nations classification of countries according to population growth types. Phases I, II and III represent major stages in the demographic transition, while types one through five refer to classes of countries according to their demographic characteristics.*

numerals. Altogether five population growth types result. As the diagram shows, Type 1 countries have high birth rates and high, fluctuating death rates, giving a stable population with a growth rate generally under 1 percent. Although several densely populated countries had these characteristics during an earlier period, the combination is now rare. One of the few areas that could be classified as UN Type 1 today is an isolated portion of Central Africa.

Fig. 2.16 *World map of population growth types, 1970. From this map it is apparent that some of the world's most populous regions have entered or are about to enter the most explosive phases of the demographic transition.*

Source: United Nations, Demographic Yearbook.

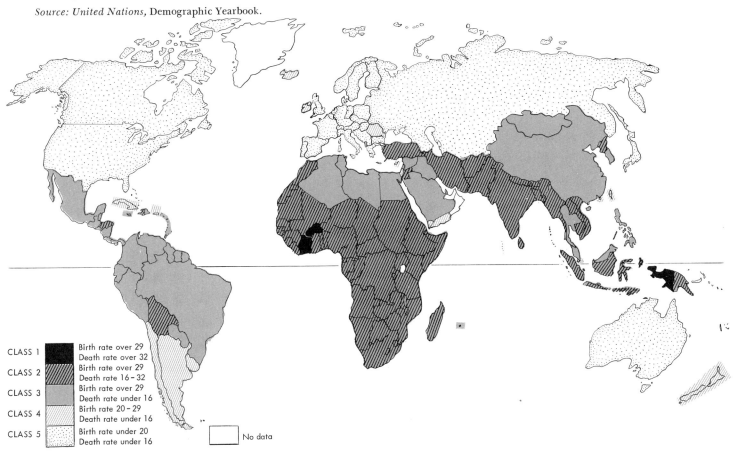

CLASS 1 — Birth rate over 29 / Death rate over 32
CLASS 2 — Birth rate over 29 / Death rate 16–32
CLASS 3 — Birth rate over 29 / Death rate under 16
CLASS 4 — Birth rate 20–29 / Death rate under 16
CLASS 5 — Birth rate under 20 / Death rate under 16

No data

Type 2 countries have high birth rates and high but declining death rates. The two curves are just beginning to diverge (Fig. 2.15), indicating the start of the expansionary Phase II of the demographic transition. Population growth is at a rate of at least 1.25 percent and climbing. Much of South Asia is at this stage, as are several parts of Africa.

Type 3 countries are in the midst of the most explosive part of Phase II, with high birth rates and fairly low death rates. This combination gives exceedingly high growth rates, often between 3 and 4 percent per year. Most of Middle America, Mexico and the tropical parts of South America, have these characteristics. Other areas of this type are found in the southern part of Africa and in portions of Southeast Asia.

The distinguishing marks of Type 4 countries are a declining birth rate and a fairly low death rate, resulting in a slackening in the growth rate. These countries are approaching population equilibrium. Examples are the southernmost countries of South America, especially Argentina and Uruguay with southern Europe having only recently emerged from this category.

With their low but fluctuating birth rates and low death rates, Type 5 countries are in what corresponds to the last phase of the demographic transition. Growth rates are usually not more than 1 percent and in many countries they are well below this level. Type 5 countries tend to differ from each other in the degree to which their birth rates fluctuate above and below the mean. The European countries experience far less varia-

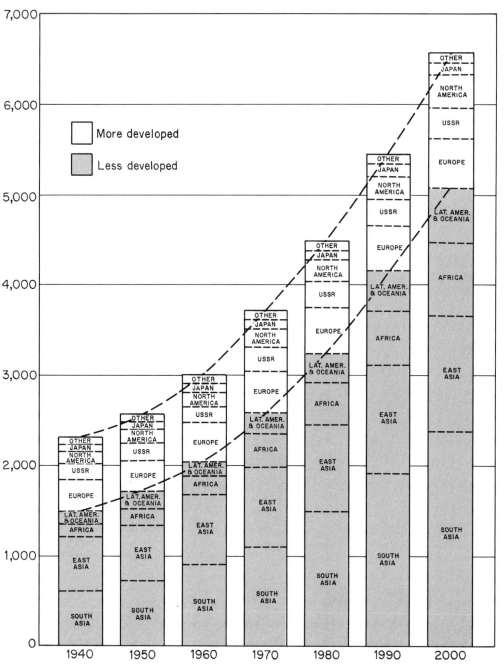

Fig. 2.17 *World population by regions, 1940–2000. The underdeveloped countries of Asia, Africa, and Latin America are expected to supply most of the additions to world population between now and the year 2000.*

Source: World Bank Group, Trends in Developing Countries *(Washingon, D.C.: International Bank for Reconstruction and Development, 1971).*

tion than do the more recently settled technically advanced lands. The map in Figure 2.16 shows how the countries of the world fit into this classification system.

population projections

Taking into account the present spatial distribution of population and allowing for regional variations in growth characteristics, what can we expect the world population map to look like in the year 2000? The United Nations Population Division has prepared a number of alternative projections, or *variants,* each with a different set of assumptions concerning birth, death, and fertility rates. A summary of the UN's *medium variant* projections appears in Table 2.4, and this information is graphed in Figure 2.17.

THE WORLD IN 2000. In the early 1970s, the world total stands at 3.7 billion people and, according to the UN's figures, the growth curve is to continue steepening (Fig. 2.17). At this rate, the world population would reach 6.5 billion at the end of the century, but some experts doubt that the total will attain that level by the year 2000. In view of the already overcrowded conditions in many of the less developed countries, these demographers expect the Malthusian model to operate, with famine and disease causing a tragic death rate. If we are to accept the UN's more optimistic predictions, however, we find that no region is expected to decline in absolute numbers. Even so, it seems probable that there will be decided changes in the relative sizes of the world's regions.

THE DEVELOPED COUNTRIES. The technically advanced lands are all classified according to the United Nations' Type 5, the nature of which is seen in their composite age structure (Fig. 2.18). Note the small pro-

portion of their populations under the age of 15, for example, as well as the large number of middle-aged and elderly. Particularly significant are the very nearly equal sizes of the populations in the age groups 0–4, 5–9, and 10–14. This forecasts only modest future growth of those populations. Comprising slightly more than one billion people in 1970, these populations are expected by the UN to reach a little less than 1.5 billion in 2000. Because the world total is expected to rise at a much faster rate, however, this means that the technically advanced nations will have a declining proportion of the total, a decrease from 30 percent to 22.3 percent (see Fig. 2.17 and Table 2.4).

Europe (excluding the USSR) currently has the most mature population, as the age structure of that region shows (Fig. 2.18). Only one-quarter of its population is below the age of 15, while an unusually large proportion, 11 percent, is 65 years or older. The continent's growth rate is now only 0.8 percent per year. According to the UN's projection, therefore, this region with the second largest population among the continents in the 1970s is to decline to only 8.7 percent of the total by 2000 (Table 2.4).

It is just recently that the Soviet Union has joined the group of Type 5 nations. The USSR's population has now stabilized, with an annual growth rate of 1 percent and a shrinking proportion in the youngest age categories (Fig. 2.18). Consequently, that country is projected to account for a declining percentage of the world's total by 2000. The age distribution of the Soviet Union's people is of special interest because it graphically illustrates the effects of one of Malthus's positive checks, in this case World War II. Note the unusually small percentage of population in the 50–54 age category, the group that would have fought in the war, and in the 25–29 category, the group that would have been born to participants in the war.

Table 2.4 World Population by Regions: Estimates and Projections, 1940–2000 (United Nations Median Variant)

(Population in millions in boldface, followed by percent of total in parentheses)

	1940	1950	1960	1970	1980	1990	2000
World total	**2,295**	**2,516**	**2,998**	**3,635**	**4,468**	**5,457**	**6,514**
More developed regions*	**821** (35.8)	**858** (34.1)	**976** (32.6)	**1,090** (30.0)	**1,210** (27.0)	**1,337** (24.5)	**1,453** (22.3)
Europe	**379** (16.5)	**392** (15.6)	**425** (14.2)	**462** (12.7)	**497** (11.1)	**533** (9.8)	**568** (8.7)
USSR	**195** (8.5)	**180** (7.1)	**214** (7.2)	**243** (6.7)	**270** (6.0)	**302** (5.5)	**330** (5.1)
Northern America	**144** (6.3)	**166** (6.6)	**199** (6.6)	**228** (6.3)	**261** (5.8)	**299** (5.5)	**333** (5.1)
Japan	**72** (3.1)	**83** (3.3)	**93** (3.1)	**103** (2.8)	**116** (2.6)	**125** (2.3)	**133** (2.0)
Others	**31** (1.4)	**37** (1.5)	**45** (1.5)	**54** (1.5)	**66** (1.5)	**78** (1.4)	**89** (1.4)
Less developed regions†	**1,474** (64.2)	**1,658** (65.9)	**2,022** (67.4)	**2,545** (70.0)	**3,258** (73.0)	**4,120** (75.5)	**5,061** (77.7)
South Asia	**610** (26.6)	**697** (27.7)	**865** (28.8)	**1,126** (31.0)	**1,486** (33.3)	**1,912** (35.0)	**2,354** (36.1)
East Asia	**563** (24.5)	**601** (23.9)	**701** (23.4)	**827** (22.7)	**979** (21.9)	**1,140** (20.9)	**1,291** (19.8)
Africa	**191** (8.3)	**222** (8.8)	**273** (9.1)	**344** (9.5)	**457** (10.2)	**616** (11.3)	**818** (12.6)
Latin America and Oceania	**110** (4.8)	**138** (5.5)	**183** (6.1)	**248** (6.8)	**336** (7.6)	**452** (8.3)	**598** (9.2)

*More developed regions include Europe, the USSR, Northern America, Japan, temperate South America, Australia, and New Zealand.
†Less developed regions include East Asia less Japan, South Asia, Africa, Latin America excluding temperate South America and Oceania less Australia and New Zealand.

Notes: The projections for the years 1980, 1990, and 2000 are the United Nations "Medium" Variant projections. These estimates and projections should not be taken as accurate to the nearest million; the figures are presented as taken directly from the sources cited.

Source: United Nations, *World Population Prospects, 1965–2000, as assessed in 1968,* ESA/P/WP.37.

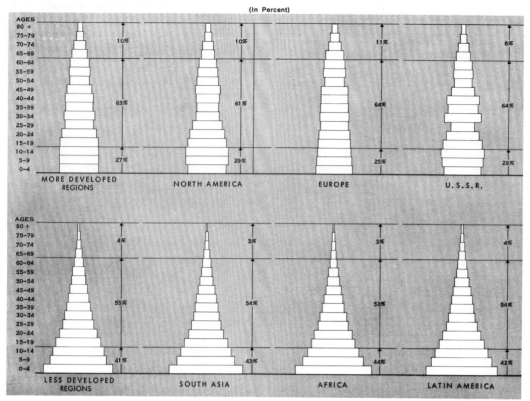

(In Percent)

Fig. 2.18 *Age structure of world population by selected regions, 1970. A comparison of the population structures of developed and underdeveloped regions helps explain the population projections upon which Fig. 2.17 was based.*

Source: World Bank Group, *Trends in Developing Countries* (Washington, D.C.: International Bank for Reconstruction and Development, 1971).

Fertility rates in Anglo-America are now at their lowest levels in history, although the large number of women in the childbearing ages yields an annual growth rate of 1.1 percent. Further decline in the growth rate is foretold by the reduced size of the youngest age groups (Fig. 2.18), and indeed the United Nations predicts that this region will have a slightly smaller proportion of the world total by 2000. Japan has similar growth characteristics, even though her rate of population growth has only recently been brought under control. Nevertheless the projected increase from a 1970 population of 103 million to 133 million at the end of the century will strain the space resources of that already crowded country.

THE LESS DEVELOPED COUNTRIES. There is a great variety in the growth characteristics of the less developed countries, but the composite pattern is one of rapid growth (Fig. 2.18). The "population pyramid" of this group is broad-based, owing to the fact that more than two-fifths of the people are under the age of 15, while only 4 percent or less are 65 years or older. If the UN medium projection holds, the total population of the less developed countries will go from 2.5 billion in 1970 to more than 5 billion at the end of the century, a doubling of their present numbers. By 2000, these countries will contain nearly four-fifths of the world's people.

The most serious problem area promises to be Asia, not just because of its high rate of growth but because of the vast size of the population to which those growth rates will be applied. Already comprising 54 percent of the world's population and grossly overcrowded in many areas, Asia's population is projected by the UN's medium variant to reach the astounding total of 3,645 billion people by 2000. This is very close to the present population of the entire world. Particular countries in Asia threaten to become trouble spots. One of these is the Philippines, a Type 3 country whose very young population is now doubling every twenty years; another is Malaysia, doubling every 23 years. But most formidable of all are the population giants of China, India, and Indonesia, Type 2 countries whose greatest period of growth lies just ahead.

Hardly less worrisome, however, are Africa and Latin America. Africa has particularly high birth rates and in many parts of the continent death rates are only now beginning to fall. Africa's age structure is exceedingly young (Fig. 2.18). If death rates are brought under control, explosive growth of the UN Type 3 variety will surely ensue, posing grave problems in a region where much of the population is already pressing the resources of the land.

As a whole, Latin America has the highest growth rates in the world. A very young population (Fig. 2.18), it doubles every 24 years. Virtually all the Caribbean and Central American countries, together with those in the tropical portions of South America, fall within the UN Type 3 classification. In 1940, only 110 million people lived south of the Rio Grande, but by 2000 the UN expects nearly 600 million to occupy that land. For the most part Latin American population densities are not so great as those of South Asia, East Asia, or West Africa, but the present growth rates could quickly change this. Indeed, certain spots are already over-crowded, especially in the islands of the Caribbean and in the small Central American country of El Salvador. Even those areas not yet experiencing physical crowding are encountering severe difficulties in their abilities to feed, educate, and employ the new additions to the population at fast enough rate.

In summary, the world's population is not only predicted to grow in total, but it is expected to undergo a considerable redistribution mainly because of dif-ferential rates of natural increase. The proportionate share of the technically advanced countries is to shrink, while that of the presently less developed lands is to grow. In short, the current rapid rate of world growth is concentrating the population in those areas least able to accommodate it. The severity of this problem will be discussed in the next chapter.

RECOMMENDED READINGS

Demko, George J., Harold M. Rose, and George A. Schnell, *Population Geography: A Reader*. New York: McGraw-Hill, 1970.

Hauser, Philip M., ed., *The Population Dilemma*. Englewood Cliffs, N. J.: Prentice-Hall, 1965.

Smith, Robert S., Frank T. deVyver, and William R. Allen, *Population Economics: Selected Essays of Joseph J. Spengler*. Durham, N. C.: Duke University Press, 1972.

Thompson, Warren S., and David J. Lewis, *Population Problems* (5th ed.). New York: McGraw-Hill, 1965.

Wrong, Dennis H., *Population and Society*. New York: Random House, 1965.

resources for a growing population

3

The population projections discussed in Chapter 2 are based on the assumption that there will be sufficient resources to support an enormous world population. There is already evidence that some of the most rapidly growing less developed countries will not have the means of subsistence to attain the population levels projected for the year 2000. But an even more compelling problem is whether there will be enough for *all* the world's citizens in the long run. In this chapter, therefore, we will consider the earth's capacity to provide for future generations.

So far our attention to natural conditions has focused mainly on their role in influencing the spatial distribution of people. We have already discussed, for instance, how the physical environment tends to set limits to human habitation by repelling man from those areas that are most hostile.

On the other hand, areas that contain important natural resources attract human habitation. Recent migrations, mainly internal, have been less affected by the locations of physical resources, however. Today, most migrants are seeking employment in the services or in manufacturing, both of which have become market-oriented in modern times, although as incomes have risen, the most rapid growth of markets has been in areas with superior climates and amenities. The relationships between rates of natural increase and physical conditions are possibly even more equivocal. Although under primitive conditions people may have multiplied most rapidly in those places where nature was most generous, this does not appear to be the case today when commodities are moved freely over long distances. Indeed, there appears to be a perverse tendency for those peoples with the most tenuous means of livelihood to increase most rapidly. Compare, for example, the high growth rates of Brazil's impoverished northeast with the low rates of natural increase in prosperous Sweden.

As we look to the future, however, the subject of natural resources begins to assume a more central and obvious role. In this connection there are several questions that must be answered: What kinds of resources shall we be needing and how much will be required? How much of each of these is available? How long can they be expected to last under present conditions and how can they be made to stretch further? Other questions regarding the distribution of resources may become increasingly important in the future: Who has these resources? Will their present owners always permit them to move as freely as in the past?

Concerning the first set of questions, the most crucial resources for future generations are those required for food production: soil and biotic resources. The problem has become more complex today and we must add another essential class, the minerals—including energy-giving minerals—which are needed today to produce and distribute food. Still a third class of resources includes such commonplace environmental necessities as air and water. This leads, then, into the matter of environmental quality, which is not just an aesthetic and psychological problem. A clear atmosphere and an adequate supply of pure water are required if the earth is to retain its capacity to produce food and, for that matter, if man is to preserve his ability to utilize what nature provides. In short, the problem of this chapter is whether man can achieve a self-sustaining balance between population and the earth's resources, one that will at the same time provide him with satisfactory conditions of life.

THE NATURE OF RESOURCES

The term *resource* refers to the supply of anything that is regarded as useful or necessary to man, a store upon which he can draw as he needs it. Here we distinguish between *human resources,* which include labor supplies as well as economically useful creations of man (or even man himself, in the sense of a supply of labor and other skills), and *natural resources,* which can be taken directly from the physical environment.

There is nothing absolute or constant about a resource. Indeed, it does not actually become a resource until it is conceived as such by man; moreover, what is classed as a resource changes as human perceptions of it change, or as new technology or rising prices make its exploitation feasible. Oil bubbling from the ground in Persia was a nuisance to some of the earlier inhabitants, but it is eagerly sought in modern Iran as a vital source of energy. Uranium was discarded as a waste product of Canada's radium mining operations during the 1930s, but since then the old mine tailings have been reworked to extract the newly valuable uranium ore that remains in them. The abundant but low-grade Lake Superior taconite ores were considered a resource only when the rich Mesabi iron deposits became exhausted.

At a given state of technology, the absolute supply of certain natural resources can be sustained at a given level or even increased. These are the *renewable resources,* those capable of replenishing themselves or being replenished by man. Most biotic resources, such as forests, animal populations, and fish, are of this type. Even soils can be made to recover from excessive use in some instances; indeed, many of the soils of Western Europe and Southeastern Asia are essentially manmade.

Resources that cannot regenerate are referred to as *nonrenewable resources.* Most minerals fall in this category. The concentration of mineral ores in economically exploitable quantities relies upon physical processes that normally require many thousands or even millions of years. Once a given deposit has been mined out, that resource for all practical purposes ceases to exist. Because the demand for minerals continues to accelerate with an advancing technology, there is a constant search for new deposits to replace the old. As a consequence, the total known world reserve of a particular mineral tends to rise and fall as new deposits are discovered or old ones exhausted.

Still another class of resources consists of those which do not ordinarily become exhausted but must be used as they appear or they are lost. These are the *flow resources,* such as running water, winds, ocean tides, and solar energy. Each of these represents a potential energy supply.

food resources

Ultimately, each type of resource is drawn upon to feed a relentlessly growing population. In much of the world today the results of this effort are discouraging. Indeed it is likely that there are between 1.5 and 2 billion hungry people in the world at this moment. A world map of nutrition in Figure 3.1 (p. 46) shows the coincidence between inadequate diet and low levels of economic development. What the map does not disclose, however, is the surprising amount of hunger (including malnutrition) that is widespread among the urban and rural poor of the technologically advanced countries, including the United States.

The effects of hunger and malnutrition on human beings are not fully understood as yet, but it is known that they do contribute to stunted physical growth, a lower resistence to disease, high childhood death rates, and arrested mental development. Studies of this problem in Latin America, for example, have identified malnutrition as either the main or contributing cause of 57 percent of all deaths between the ages of one to four. In Brazil, children in this age group account for four-fifths of *all* deaths. In the less developed world as a whole, according to estimates by the UN Food and Agriculture Organization, more than two-thirds of the present group of 800 million children will develop illnesses related to malnutrition. Upon reaching adulthood many of the survivors will remain mentally or physically handicapped to the extent that they will either be dependent upon society for their support or will be able to contribute little to it because of their reduced productivity. Thus hunger and malnutrition are clearly a serious drag on the economic development of impoverished nations.

It has been estimated variously that total world output of food must be increased at least by 50 percent within the next two decades merely to keep pace with population growth at current consumption levels. Obviously, then, much more food will have to be produced to raise the levels of per capita consumption as a stimulus to the development of poorer areas. With this in mind, therefore, let us examine the world's resources currently allocated to food production and those likely to be needed to fill expected future needs.

conventional sources of food supply

All types of food trace their origins to solar energy that has been captured by green plants through the process of photosynthesis. The plants are then consumed by herbivorous animals, which may be eaten by carnivorous animals, or human beings. In the sea the food chain commences with the phytoplankton, tiny one-

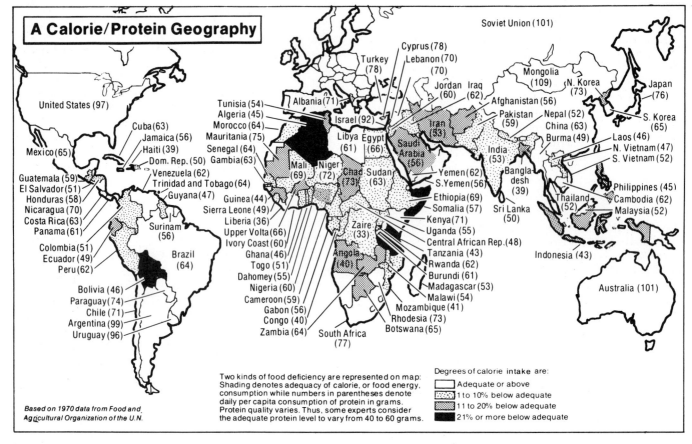

Fig. 3.1 *The geography of nutrition*

Source: © *1974 by The New York Times Company. Reprinted by permission.*

celled plants that are eaten by certain fish that are themselves eaten by larger ones. More than 99 percent of the world's food supply currently comes from agriculture, while a mere 0.7 percent is obtained from the sea.

AGRICULTURE. As we enter the last quarter of the twentieth century only 30 percent of the world land area is being used for the production of food and nearly two-thirds of this small proportion is devoted to permanent pasture, which characteristically yields a relatively meager output per acre (Table 3.1). This leaves less than 11 percent of the world's land surface for field and tree crops. Large portions of the total arable acreage are in Asia, North America, Africa, and the Soviet Union; but the figures can be misleading, since the productive capacity varies. A more revealing figure than that for total

Table 3.1   World Land Use in Million Acres and Arable Acres Per Person

Region	Total land (including water surface within each continent)	Percent	Arable land and land under permanent crops	Percent	Permanent meadows & pastures	Percent	Forested land	Percent	Other area	Percent	Arable acres per person*
World	33,432	100%	3,581	10.7%	6,416	19.2%	10,044	30.0%	13.391	40.1%	0.97
Europe (excluding USSR)	1,218	100	378	31.0	222	18.2	336	27.6	282	23.2	0.82
North & Central America	5,995	100	633	10.6	899	15.0	1,999	33.3	2,464	41.1	1.95
South America	4,398	100	180	4.1	741	16.8	2,241	51.0	1,236	28.1	0.92
Asia (excluding USSR)	6,712	100	1,113	16.6	1,048	15.6	1,289	19.2	3,262	48.6	0.54
Africa	7,463	100	626	8.4	1,460	19.6	1,796	24.0	3,581	48.0	1.67
Oceania	2,110	100	83	4.0	1,132	53.6	208	9.9	687	32.5	4.17
USSR	5,536	100	568	10.3	914	16.5	2,175	39.3	1,879	33.9	2.32

*Based on 1972 population estimates from *Encyclopaedia Britannica Book of the Year, 1973.*

Source: Food and Agricultural Organization of the United Nations, *Production Yearbook,* 1969.

arable acreage per continent is the amount of arable land per person (Table 3.1). On this basis Asia provides only one-half acre per person while North America provides nearly two acres per person. Since much of this land is of prime quality, North America has been a major surplus food supply area from the time of the first European settlement. Despite its small overall size, Europe has the largest proportion of its land area in crops of any region (31 percent), and this acreage is used intensively to contribute a substantial part of the world's food output. Oceania appears deceptively important according to the persons-per-acre measure, but it must be remembered that this region accounts for only 2 percent of the world's arable land.

A great variety of food crops is grown throughout the world, but a surprisingly few of these carry the main burden of feeding the human and animal populations. The overwhelming leaders are the grains, especially rice, wheat, and corn (in that order), even though all three are low in protein. These commodities are the staples of world food supply, having a multitude of uses and being eminently transportable. The world grain supply therefore provides a dependable barometer of the world food situation. There has been a steady increase in total output of grain since the end of World War II, but per capita production has risen only slightly. The rapid increase in population effectively cancelled the gain in total volume.

The pattern of the world grain trade discloses some ominous shifts in recent years (Figs. 3.2, 3.3, and 3.4). Although both South America and Asia were net exporters of grain prior to the war, both have become net importers since. Africa has never been important in world grain commerce, but the continent has been a net importer since 1950. The Soviet Union and Eastern Europe have barely produced enough for their own needs and in bad years they have been forced to import great quantities of grain. Western Europe's output, mainly wheat, has remained at a fairly constant high level, which, however, is not sufficient to care for the continent's needs. Oceania (mostly Australia) has relatively large surpluses of grain, but these represent but a small fraction of world output. Canada and the United States represent the modern bread basket of the world, and they are increasingly assuming the burden of supplying grain to countries whose production is failing to keep up with population growth. As Figure 3.5 indicates, many countries of the Far East and Latin America now have lower per capita food outputs than before the war. In short, the less developed countries are steadily losing the capacity to feed themselves, and are turning more and more to North America for help. But as the populations of those countries continue to increase at accelerating rates, it is doubtful that present food sources will be able to maintain the pace unless new measures are taken. What are the possibilities for this?

There are two main ways of increasing the volume of food production from agricultural sources: (1) expanding the cultivated area and (2) increasing the output per acre (yield). Nowadays, however, cultivating

Fig. 3.2 *World rice production and trade*

Source: Olof Jonasson, Atlas of the World Commodities (Stockholm: P. A. Norstedt & Söner, 1961).

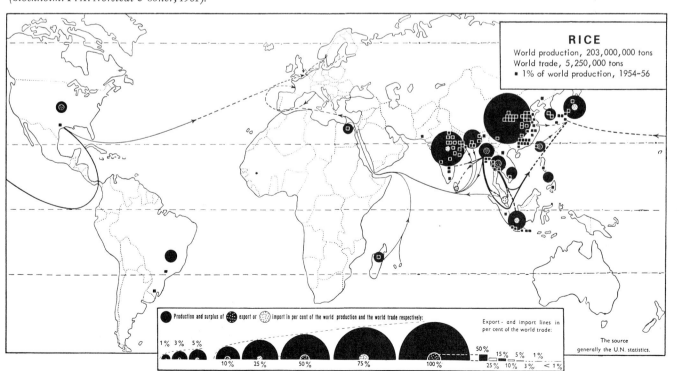

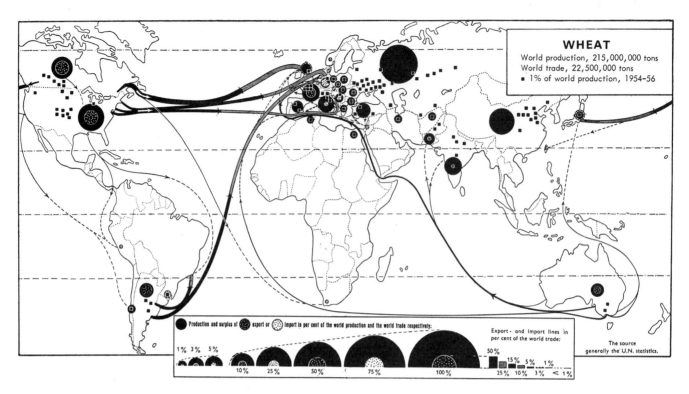

Fig. 3.3 *World wheat production and trade*

Source: Jonasson, Atlas of the World Commodities.

Fig 3.4 *World corn production and trade*

Source: Jonasson, Atlas of the World Commodities.

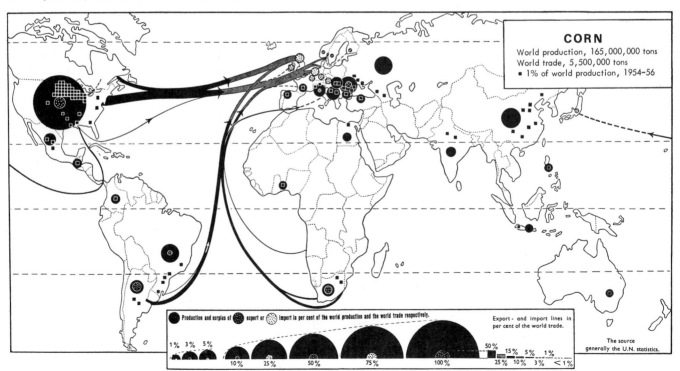

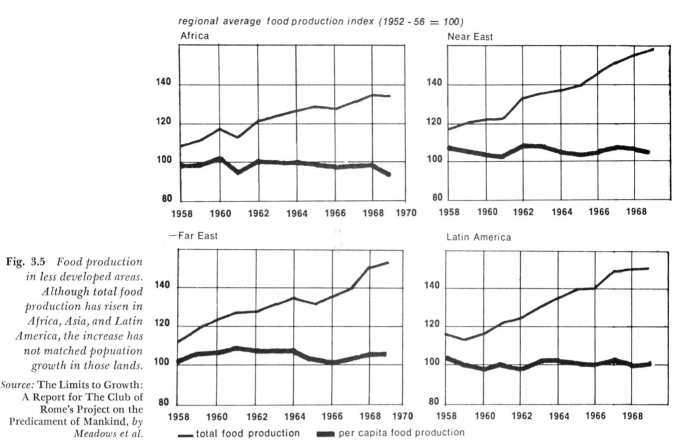

regional average food production index (1952 - 56 = 100)

Africa

Near East

—Far East

Latin America

Fig. 3.5 *Food production in less developed areas. Although total food production has risen in Africa, Asia, and Latin America, the increase has not matched popuation growth in those lands.*

Source: **The Limits to Growth: A Report for The Club of Rome's Project on the Predicament of Mankind,** *by Meadows et al.*

—— total food production ▬▬ per capita food production

more land has become a grossly inadequate solution to the mammoth problem. Superficially there would seem to be great possibilities for expanding the cultivated area, since at least twice the present total acreage in use has been classed as potentially arable. In fact, expert opinion is generally agreed that almost all the land that can be economically cultivated under present conditions is already in use, particularly in the less developed countries. There is very little possibility for expanding the arable areas of South Asia, much of East Asia, the Near East and North Africa, and parts of Latin America and Africa. Where such potential is present, there are formidable obstacles to development of these lands. What, then, is this potentially arable land like? What are the problems in bringing it under cultivation?

One obstacle is excessive aridity. One-fourth of the earth's land surface is classified as desert, with rainfall averaging less than 10 inches per year. Most of the unused potentially arable land of Asia is in this class. Only a small fraction of such land can be irrigated. One problem is that many deserts are covered either by shifting sands or by "desert pavement," stony surfaces devoid of any soil. At least as difficult is the problem of finding enough irrigation water in the right places. The principal areas of irrigated agriculture today are along "exotic streams," such as the Nile or the Colorado, which flow into desert lands out of humid mountainous regions. Most of the remaining irrigated districts make use of ground waters available through an unusual com-

bination of geological conditions linking such areas with rainy uplands. Besides being rather uncommon, artesian systems have an extremely slow rate of natural recharge. In many places, such as west Texas, water tables are falling precipitously. In addition, irrigation projects are expensive; they require dams, canals, soil preparation, road construction, and administration.

Aside from the virtually rainless desert areas, nearly one-third of the earth's surface is steppeland, with rainfall averaging between 10 and 20 inches per year. Because of high evaporation, such land is usually suitable only for grazing in tropical latitudes, but in the temperate areas commercial grain farming is often possible. The upper-latitude steppes have some of the world's best soils—excellent for wheat or grain sorghum—but the undependability of rainfall makes the farming of these areas highly uncertain. The tragic dust bowl conditions of the American plains during the 1930s and the failure of Premier Khrushchev's "virgin lands" project in the Soviet Union (see Chapter 18) dramatize the problems of relying on regions of this type for substantial additions to the world food supply.

A very large proportion of what is usually included in lands classified as "potentially arable" lies within the vast areas of tropical rain forest, such as the Amazon and Congo basins. The agricultural potential of these areas, however, is overrated (see Chapter 2).

At the other extreme are the great tundras of the far northern latitudes. With their frozen substrata, the earthen coverings of the tundra do not develop true soils. The only vegetation they are able to support consists of mosses, lichens, and scattered small shrubs, suitable only for exceedingly extensive forms of grazing.

The most promising approach to increasing the world food supply from agriculture is thus not to be found in the expansion of arable acreage, but in more intensive use of existing farmlands—applying more labor and capital in order to raise per acre yields. Recent advances in this direction in the technologically advanced lands of North America, Western Europe, and Japan point the way. Japan's experience holds particular hope for the less developed countries. During a 50-year period the Japanese were able to increase their arable acreage only 18 percent, but within that time average yields rose by two-thirds and total national farm output nearly doubled (see Chapter 17). It is technically possible to increase yields substantially in many of the less developed countries, but putting these techniques into actual practice poses great obstacles.

One of the surest ways of increasing yields is through greater use of commercial fertilizer. Farmers in technically advanced lands have relied heavily on massive applications of fertilizer in expanding the output of their lands, but the per acre use of fertilizer in less developed areas is estimated to average less than one-fifth that of advanced regions. The increased output to be obtained by using fertilizer in underdeveloped lands should not be overestimated, however. Fertilizer requires adequate moisture to function adequately, and some grains do not respond to fertilizer as well as others. For the underdeveloped countries there are the additional problems of providing adequate distribution for the fertilizer and supplying skilled personnel to train farmers in its use. Then, too, commercial fertilizer is expensive and the present world supply is not nearly great enough to accommodate this additional demand. Fertilizer production facilities require much capital to install and operate and they require much time for their development. Decided increases in yields usually result from the introduction of irrigation; but as we have seen above, there are only a certain selected number of areas where this is feasible, aside from the high capital requirements.

A great deal of public attention has been given to the so-called green revolution resulting from the breeding of new high-yielding plant strains and their introduction into less developed lands. This holds much promise for such areas, as shown by the remarkable yield increases in wheat in India and Pakistan following planting of new varieties in 1968, as well as similar results obtained with new types of rice in the Philippines and Sri Lanka. These programs have encountered resistance by the farmers, however, and in some instances have had to combat the conservative food habits of native populations. Moreover, they make heavy demands on the available fertilizer supply.

Mutiple cropping, the growing of two or more crops in succession within the same year, is another technique proposed for increasing food supply. It requires at least twice as much labor and greater amounts of fertilizer, however, as well as a decidedly higher order of farming skills. In addition, multiple cropping needs a long growing season. The best prospects are in tropical and subtropical regions, but ordinarily multiple cropping is already practiced in such regions. Nevertheless, the introduction of new seed varieties makes multiple cropping feasible in a larger number of places.

Other expedients that have raised output in the advanced lands include the use of pesticides and herbicides, but these are expensive and ecological problems are bringing such practices increasingly into question. Important benefits have also resulted from farm mechanization in developed countries; however, the poorer countries usually find this too costly, especially because they are often afflicted by small farms and fragmented fields. Improved methods of farm storage of grains and other commodities would also help to reduce the often sizable losses to insects and rodents encountered by farmers in underdeveloped countries, although again the problem of finding the capital for such modern facilities is a difficult one. Finally, there are the possibilities for improving the quality of livestock in underdeveloped lands. Although the upgrading of farm herds has already progressed in the less crowded lands of Latin America, livestock raising is an inefficient way to use scarce land in overpopulated countries of the Orient; and at present rates of population growth this may in time become true of certain Latin American countries as well.

A persistent question underlying the preceding discussion is that of time and cost. Enormous amounts of capital would be required to develop new acreages (recent costs for the world as a whole have averaged about $465 per acre), to build new fertilizer factories, and to distribute fertilizer and new seed varieties. Much time is needed to develop those new seeds and to train farmers and technicians in their use, but time is very short. How short it is can be seen in Figure 3.6, which compares the current projected needs of future arable land with its availability. Note that total arable acreage is projected to decline as urban populations expand. The solid line indicates the amount of land required at present levels of agricultural intensity, while the broken lines indicate the effects of increased output from higher levels of intensity. It is clear that increasing farm output in this way merely postpones the day when present land reserves are finally exhausted. Therefore, still other approaches to the food problem are needed to supplement these.

FOOD FROM THE SEA. The seas supply about one-fifth of the world's high-quality animal protein, and this source of food is particularly important to certain fishing nations such as Japan, the Soviet Union, Norway, and Iceland. Nevertheless, the 60 million metric tons of food obtained from the seas, lakes, and rivers provides less than 1 percent of the world's total food.

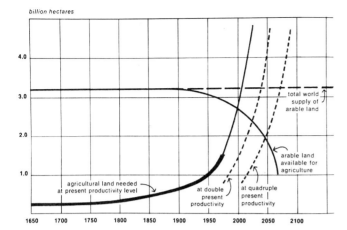

billion hectares

total world
supply of
arable land

arable land
available for
agriculture

agricultural land needed
at present productivity level

at double
present
productivity

at quadruple
present
productivity

1650 1700 1750 1800 1850 1900 1950 2000 2050 2100

Fig. 3.6 *Projections of arable land requirements and availability. Given currently projected rates of population growth and continued preempting of farm land for nonagricultural uses, even quantum increases in agricultural productivity are unlikely to provide an adequate world food supply through the next century.*

Source: Meadows et al., The Limits to Growth.

Moreover, many public statements overestimate the unused potential of food from the sea. Informed sources insist that the present catch cannot be increased by much more than 15 percent on a sustained-yield basis.

This last qualification provides the real problem, since overexploitation today means reduced catches in the future. Indeed, we have already seen stocks of many varieties of food fish virtually depleted. This is especially true of the more vulnerable species, such as salmon and whales. Overfishing is one of the results of the "open seas" principle, by which the world's oceans are treated as common property. This means that no one is responsible for maintaining the "fertility" of fishing grounds; in fact, the open seas concept results in intense competition among national fishing fleets, which develop increasingly sophisticated gear to capture larger quantities of diminishing stocks of fish. Another unfortunate paradox is the practice among less developed nations of exporting their catches instead of retaining this valuable protein to feed their own undernourished populations.

The seas thus contribute only a small part of the world's food needs, and it seems unlikely that conventional sea foods can be relied upon even to keep pace with the rate of world population growth. Can we then help to solve the food shortage by searching for unorthodox forms of food?

more radical methods of increasing the food supply

From time to time the Sunday supplements tell us of spectacular new scientific discoveries that will multiply the world's food supply limitlessly. Many such claims fall within the realm of science fiction, but some of them

merit serious attention, especially in view of the gravity of the situation that threatens.

PLANT SOURCES. One of the paradoxes of world agriculture is that some of the driest deserts are found next to enormous bodies of water; the salinity of these oceans or seas, however, precludes their use for irrigation. Although the technology of desalination is advanced enough to supply large quantities of drinking water, its costs are still too high for agricultural or industrial use (75¢ to $1.00 per thousand gallons). One solution that may prove feasible is the construction of very large multipurpose nuclear installations whose costs are largely borne by the sale of the electric power that is generated along with the production of fertilizer and desalinated water for adjacent farmland. While costs for such projects have not yet been sufficiently reduced to make them practical, some alternatives have been proposed. One of these is the breeding of food plants that tolerate salt water.

A second approach to the world food problem is to follow the traditional oriental practice of bypassing animals in the food chain. In other words, we would eat the products of the soil directly rather than first converting them into animal products. These "direct calories" are much more efficient in their use of the land since at best only 14 percent of the plant food value per acre reaches the meat eater. This would require radically altering the eating habits of most people, especially in the wealthier nations, but it might also reduce them to the same high-starch, low-protein diets that stunt the growth and dull the brains of many persons in the underdeveloped world.

Even this latter problem likely has its solution, however. Recent years have brought increasing success in the effort to develop high-protein foods from plants. The soybean has been the main focus of the search, and to some extent the cotton seed, both of which have already become important sources of nutritious animal feed. An acre of land can supply ten times as much protein in the form of soybeans as it can in the form of beef and at a much lower cost. The difficulty has been to make soybean products sufficiently palatable to human appetites. Imitation meats now being made commercially from an extruded soybean solution are good replicas in taste, consistency, and appearance of beef, pork, and veal. With the rising cost of beef, more and more of this inexpensive and nutritious product is now being used as an additive to ground meats and for other purposes.

Just as unusual are experiments with preparing high-protein human food from alfalfa leaves, forest leaves, pea vines, and roadside weeds. More radical yet, however, is the attempt to develop a palatable food from single-celled organisms cultured on petroleum. British Petroleum is already producing a high-protein animal feed of this type in a French factory, but making this into a food acceptable to human tastes is proving more difficult. Somewhat more success is being obtained from breeding new high-protein grains. Common grains are very low in protein; corn, for example, has less than 5 percent of low-quality protein. A new type of corn now being developed has yielded as much as 35 percent of good protein, about the equivalent of soybeans. Additionally, protein concentrates have been produced for use as additives in conventional milled grain products, although these have not as yet been well received by consumers in technically advanced lands. In India, however, fortified wheat is now being introduced into the diet of the poor, and fortified salt and even fortified tea are under consideration.

New sources of animal foods are also being explored. Tundra pastures now being used for a relatively limited amount of reindeer herding may be profitably grazed by future commercial herds of musk oxen, which would be sources both of meat and fiber; but this scheme can contribute relatively little to solving the world food problem because of the exceedingly low carrying capacity of tundra pastures. Commercial herding of wild antelopes and other herbivorous animals on the tropical savanna lands of Africa is also being explored. Meanwhile, the search for new low-cost and abundant feeds for cattle and other meat animals is being extended to such plant forms as aquatic weeds and cultured algae.

NOVEL SEA FOODS.   Concerted efforts are similarly being made to find ways of multiplying the food-producing potential of the seas. One widely publicized product is fish protein concentrate, a flour that is made by grinding up whole fish to use as an additive in low-protein diets. Not only is more of the fish used for food by this method, but it also makes possible the use of fish not now being caught for human consumption. Thus far, however, fish protein concentrate has not been well accepted by consumers.

Despite the sophisticated techniques that some of the world's fishing fleets now employ, commercial fishing is still not essentially very different from the activities of food gatherers and hunters. Modern fishing consists of merely seeking out what nature provides, with little or no provision for cultivating or replenishing the breeding stock. It seems logical, therefore, that fishing should attempt to follow the example of agriculture or animal husbandry and devise methods for commercial fish farming. Oriental rice farmers, for instance, have traditionally cultivated carp and other fish in their irrigation ditches, ponds, and flooded fields as a source of much-needed protein in their starch-filled diets. This example has been adopted by rice farmers in the lower Mississippi valley and delta, who are successfully producing edible crayfish as by-products of their rice growing, and are fish-farming catfish from ponds. Oyster farming has long been practiced in the brackish waters of Chesapeake Bay and elsewhere in the coastal waters of the United States. The possibilities are now being explored of adapting these techniques to the cultivation of other forms of sea life, such as lobsters, clams, and crabs. It has even been proposed that the fjords of Norway, British Columbia and Alaska, as well as other large bays, be fenced off from the open sea to serve as enclosures for the cultivation of high-quality food fish, and one such salmon-farming venture is now operating in Puget Sound. Among the difficulties confronting most of these proposals are high developmental costs and large outlays for fertilization and harvesting operations and warding off predators.

As in the case of agriculture, suggestions are also being put forward for shortcutting the food chain in the seas. Harvesting seaweed has already become a commercial reality along the coasts of Japan and the Canadian Maritime provinces. The seaweed finds a ready market in the food additive (ice cream stabilizer) and chemical industries. Much is being said also of the feasibility of harvesting plankton directly instead of concentrating on catching the fish that feed on it. Experiments have shown this to be an expensive operation, however, and the fishy taste of the product is distasteful to many consumers. Furthermore, it is possible that large-scale harvesting of plankton would merely deprive the food fish of their main source of sustenance.

SUMMARIZING THE PROBLEMS OF UNORTHODOX FOOD SOURCES.   Although we certainly need to search for new sources of food, we cannot rely upon these to solve the food problem. As we have seen, the main difficulties that must first be overcome are human acceptance, cost, and time.

Surprisingly, an important barrier encountered by those attempting to relieve world hunger is the extreme conservatism of people's eating habits. Some of the hungriest people are the most reluctant to accept foods that are novel to them. This is understandable in the case of fish protein concentrates and other high-protein food additives that taste bad, but it is harder to explain the negative attitudes toward foods generally consumed in most parts of the world. An extreme example of this was the reluctance of the rice-eating population of Kerala, India, to accept relief shipments of wheat during a famine.

Eating habits can be changed in the long run, of course, and the most grievous problems remain cost and time. Enormous capital outlays are required for developing new food sources, building facilities, providing equipment, manufacturing and distributing fertilizer, and training and paying technicians. These new techniques also require much experimentation and this takes much time. Meanwhile the world population grows at ever increasing rates.

Another problem that is usually overlooked is the increased demands that an expanding food production makes upon other resources, most of which are non-renewable. Minerals are needed for the manufacture of commercial fertilizers, for smelting the metals used in making farm machinery and transport equipment, for supplying fuels for mechanical energy both on the farm and off, and for the construction of buildings, roads, and other necessary facilities. What are the prospects for an adequate supply of these?

energy, minerals, and other earth resources

Soils can often be restored to fertility, plants and animal stocks can be replenished, and some barren wastes can be afforested; but a mineral deposit, once exhausted, is gone for ever. The rate at which non-renewable resources are being used is rising rapidly throughout the world and especially in the industrialized countries. The United States alone accounts for between one-third and one-half of the total world consumption of these resources; U.S. mineral usage increased tenfold (reckoned in constant dollars) during the first seventy years of this century while population was rising only 2.7 times.

Fewer than 6 percent of the world's people live in the United States, and American per capita consumption of resources is thus far greater than in any other country. In 1970, for example, the industrial output per person was $1600 as compared with a world average of only $230. The implications of this for future world resource use are suggested in Figure 3.7, which relates industrial output per person to levels of per capita resource use. The S-shaped curve indicates that resource use can be expected to rise steeply during the earlier stages of industrialization but eventually taper off at some high level. Note that United States' consumption of resources has now reached that leveling-off stage but that the rest of the world is just entering the steepest part of the curve. This implies that the rest of the world is likely to follow the path already taken by the United States in nonrenewable resource use, an ominous thought in view of the vast quantities that the world as a whole would ultimately require to attain the current American level of per capita production.

Fig. 3.7 *Per capita industrial output and resource use. With only 6 percent of the world's population, the United States currently consumes resources at a rate seven times the world average. If the rest of the world catches up with the United States level of consumption, following the path of the S-shaped curve in the diagram, massive quantities of raw materials will have to be found.*

Source: Meadows et al., The Limits to Growth.

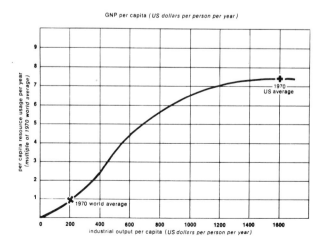

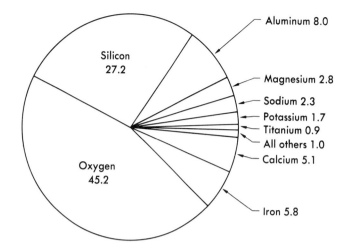

Fig. 3.8 *Elements in the earth's crust. Some of the most important industrial raw materials are included in the category, "All others," shown here to comprise only 1.0 percent of the earth's crust.*

Source: Brian J. Skinner, Earth Resources *(Englewood Cliffs, N.J.: Prentice-Hall, Inc., 1969).*

The important question to be addressed in the following pages, therefore, is whether or not there will be an adequate supply of these resources for a world consuming at the United States rate. The resources to be examined will be mainly of the nonrenewable kind, including the various minerals and energy sources; but attention will also be given to physical resources of the flow type, such as water, that are constantly being renewed by nature but are limited in total amount and subject to deterioration in quality as a result of human use.

reserves

Viewed in absolute terms eighty-eight known elements are found in the earth's crust in great tonnages. While some of these elements are indeed plentiful, others are relatively scarce (Fig. 3.8). These less abundant materials have become available to man only through the natural processes of concentration, which cause comparatively large amounts of each to occur in a few places. This is the basis for the usual concept of a *reserve*, which is defined as that part of a known natural supply of a raw material that can be exploited commercially with existing technology and under present economic conditions.

PROJECTED RESERVES. Considering the erratic, seemingly capricious way in which such concentrations have formed, what is the current state of world reserves of the principal resources? Our present knowledge of these is summarized in Table 3.2, which also indicates the projected life of each resource calculated in two ways. The *static index* gives the number of years remaining before the exhaustion of a resource, assuming no change in the current rate of consumption. Although

Table 3.2   Reserves, Projected Consumption, and Principal Producers and Consumers of Selected Nonrenewable Resources

RESOURCE	KNOWN GLOBAL RESERVES[a]	STATIC INDEX (YEARS)[b]	PROJECTED RATE OF GROWTH (% PER YEAR)[c]			EXPONENTIAL INDEX (YEARS)[d]	EXPONENTIAL INDEX CALCULATED USING 5 TIMES KNOWN RESERVES (YEARS)[e]
			HIGH	AVG.	LOW		
Aluminum	1.17×10^9 tons[j]	100	7.7	6.4	5.1	31	55
Chromium	7.75×10^8 tons	420	3.3	2.6	2.0	95	154
Coal	5×10^{12} tons	2300	5.3	4.1	3.0[k]	111	150
Cobalt	4.8×10^9 lbs.	110	2.0	1.5	1.0	60	148
Copper	308×10^6 tons	36	5.8	4.6	3.4	21	48
Gold	353×10^6 troy oz.	11	4.8	4.1	3.4[l]	9	29
Iron	1×10^{11} tons	240	2.3	1.8	1.3	93	173
Lead	91×10^6 tons	26	2.4	2.0	1.7	21	64
Manganese	8×10^8 tons	97	3.5	2.9	2.4	46	94
Mercury	3.34×10^6 flasks	13	3.1	2.6	2.2	13	41
Molybdenum	10.8×10^9 lbs.	79	5.0	4.5	4.0	34	65
Natural gas	1.14×10^{15} cu. ft.	38	5.5	4.7	3.9	22	49
Nickel	147×10^9 lbs.	150	4.0	3.4	2.8	53	96
Petroleum	455×10^9 bbls.	31	4.9	3.9	2.9	20	50
Platinum Group[m]	429×10^6 troy oz.	130	4.5	3.8	3.1	47	85
Silver	5.5×10^8 troy oz.	16	4.0	2.7	1.5	13	42
Tin	4.3×10^6 lg tons	17	2.3	1.1	0	15	61
Tungsten	2.9×10^9 lbs	40	2.9	2.5	2.1	28	72
Zinc	123×10^6 tons	23	3.3	2.9	2.5	18	50

[a]*Source:* US Bureau of Mines, *Mineral Facts and Problems, 1970* (Washington, D.C.: Government Printing Office, 1970).

[b]The number of years known global reserves will last at current global consumption. Calculated by dividing known reserves (col. 2) by the current annual consumption *(Mineral Facts and Problems, 1970).*

[c]*Source: Mineral Facts and Problems, 1970.*

[d]The number of years known global reserves will last with consumption growing exponentially at the average annual rate of growth. Calculated by the formula

$$\text{exponential index} = \frac{\ln((r \cdot s) + 1)}{r}$$

where r = average rate of growth from column 4
s = static index from column 3.

[e]The number of years that five times known global reserves will last with consumption growing exponentially at the average annual rate of growth. Calculated from the above formula with 5s in place of s.

[f]*Source: Mineral Facts and Problems, 1970.*

[g]*Source:* UN Department of Economic and Social Affairs, *Statistical Yearbook 1969* (New York: United Nations, 1970).

RESOURCE	COUNTRIES OR AREAS WITH HIGHEST RESERVES (% OF WORLD TOTAL)[f]		PRIME PRODUCERS (% OF WORLD TOTAL)[g]		PRIME CONSUMERS (% OF WORLD TOTAL)[h]		US CONSUMPTION AS % OF WORLD TOTAL[i]
Aluminum	Australia	(33)	Jamaica	(19)	US	(42)	42
	Guinea	(20)	Surinam	(12)	USSR	(12)	
	Jamaica	(10)					
Chromium	Rep. of S. Africa	(75)	USSR	(30)			19
			Turkey	(10)			
Coal	US	(32)	USSR	(20)			44
	USSR-China	(53)	US	(13)			
Cobalt	Rep. of Congo	(31)	Rep. of Congo	(51)			32
	Zambia	(16)					
Copper	US	(28)	US	(20)	US	(33)	33
	Chile	(19)	USSR	(15)	USSR	(13)	
			Zambia	(13)	Japan	(11)	
Gold	Rep. of S. Africa	(40)	Rep. of S. Africa	(77)			26
			Canada	(6)			
Iron	USSR	(33)	USSR	(25)	US	(28)	28
	S. America	(18)	US	(14)	USSR	(24)	
	Canada	(14)			W. Germany	(7)	
Lead	US	(39)	USSR	(13)	US	(25)	25
			Australia	(13)	USSR	(13)	
			Canada	(11)	W. Germany	(11)	
Manganese	Rep. of S. Africa	(38)	USSR	(34)			14
	USSR	(25)	Brazil	(13)			
			Rep. of S. Africa	(13)			
Mercury	Spain	(30)	Spain	(21)			24
	Italy	(21)	Italy	(21)			
			USSR	(18)			
Molybdenum	US	(58)	US	(64)			40
	USSR	(20)	Canada	(14)			
Natural gas	US	(25)	US	(58)			63
	USSR	(13)	USSR	(18)			
Nickel	Cuba	(25)	Canada	(42)			38
	New Caledonia	(22)	New Caledonia	(28)			
	USSR	(14)	USSR	(16)			
	Canada	(14)					
Petroleum	Saudi Arabia	(17)	US	(23)	US	(33)	33
	Kuwait	(15)	USSR	(16)	USSR	(12)	
					Japan	(6)	
Platinum Group[m]	Rep. of S. Africa	(47)	USSR	(59)			31
	USSR	(47)					
Silver	Communist countries	(36)	Canada	(20)	US	(26)	26
	US	(24)	Mexico	(17)	W. Germany	(11)	
			Peru	(16)			
Tin	Thailand	(33)	Malaysia	(41)	US	(24)	24
	Malaysia	(14)	Bolivia	(16)	Japan	(14)	
			Thailand	(13)			
Tungsten	China	(73)	China	(25)			22
			USSR	(19)			
			US	(14)			
Zinc	US	(27)	Canada	(23)	US	(26)	26
	Canada	(20)	USSR	(11)	Japan	(13)	
			US	(8)	USSR	(11)	

[h]Sources: *Yearbook of the American Bureau of Metal Statistics 1970* (York, Pa.: Maple Press, 1970).
World Petroleum Report (New York: Mona Palmer Publishing, 1968).
UN Economic Commission for Europe, *The World Market for Iron Ore* (New York: United Nations, 1968).
Mineral Facts and Problems, 1970.

[i]Source: *Mineral Facts and Problems, 1970.*

[j]Bauxite expressed in aluminum equivalent.

[k]US Bureau of Mines contingency forecasts, based on assumptions that coal will be used to synthesize gas and liquid fuels.

[l]Includes US Bureau of Mines estimates of gold demand for hoarding.

[m]The platinum group metals are platinum, palladium, iridium, osmium, rhodium, and ruthenium.

Additional sources:
P.T. Flawn, *Mineral Resources* (Skokie, Ill.: Rand McNally, 1966).
Metal Statistics (Somerset, N.J.: American Metal Market Company, 1970).
U.S. Bureau of Mines, *Commodity Data Summary* (Washington, D.C.: Government Printing Office, January 1971).

Adapted from: Meadows, *The Limits to Growth*, table 4, pp. 56-60.

this is the usual way of expressing projections of re- source usage, it overlooks the fact that the consumption of practically all resources is growing at an *increasing* rate. This is shown in the table under the heading "projected rate."

For many materials, the rate of consumption is rising more rapidly than the rate of population growth. Not only are more people consuming resources, but the average person is consuming larger quantities. A more realistic view of future prospects is thus given by the *exponential index*. Reckoned in this way, most of the known resources of the world will be used up well within the next century, and some of the more impor- tant ones will become exhausted within the next decade or two.

Can we expect new discoveries to solve this prob- lem for us? To assess the effects of this, the next column in Table 3.2 (the sixth column) has been calculated on the assumption that total reserves will increase fivefold. This quantum increase in reserve estimates, however, yields a remarkably short extension of reserve life be- cause the curve of resource usage is becoming increas- ingly steep. Even so, new discoveries of such magnitude are unlikely in most cases, since the greater part of the world has been intensively and systematically pros- pected for many years.

RESOURCE DEPLETION AND COST. Rarely, however, are natural resources totally exhausted; usually their extraction is abandoned as a result of accelerating costs and prices. This is already beginning to happen in certain critical cases, as, for example, mercury, whose price has increased sixfold in two decades, and lead, whose price has increased fourfold in thirty years. The effect of such cost increases is to slow the rate of use to the point at which exploitation virtually ceases and substitutes are sought.

Among the variables affecting the cost of exploit- ing a resource are quality and accessibility. In the case of a mineral resource, accessibility includes both the depth of deposits in the ground and distance from mar- kets. As exhaustion of a material approaches, reserves of increasingly poorer quality are pursued at greater depths and in more remote locations. In most instances, resource exhaustion in this economic sense is postponed by technological developments that retard the rate of cost increase.

SPATIAL DISTRIBUTION. Table 3.2 also demon- strates the unevenness with which most natural re- sources are distributed. This can be attributed to the physical processes by which they became concentrated in the first place. The table discloses numerous cases where a single country, or two or three, possesses a major share of the world total. The table also shows that the leading producers of a material are not always those with the largest reserves, since the most intensive production usually takes place in the most industrial- ized countries. Of the nineteen materials listed in the table, the United States leads the world in reserve holdings in only six cases, but it is the leading consumer in every instance.

A number of important implications can be seen in this combination of production and consumption patterns. However, let us first examine the present and projected status of the principal types of earth resources.

energy

Besides being the foundation of modern technology, mechanical energy is also indispensable for extracting and processing the other kinds of earth resources. Hu- man porters, hand laborers, and craftsmen still pre- dominate in much of the underdeveloped world, but this is no longer the case in technologically advanced countries. A century ago, for example, the United States depended upon human labor for 94 percent of its in- dustrial power; today a mere 8 percent comes from this source.

The energy with which man supplements his own is drawn from five storage banks, all ultimately related to the basic source, solar energy. The first of these to be used by man was the living-plant bank, which he tapped through the domestication of herbivorous draft animals and the burning of wood. Exploitation of the water-storage bank came next, followed by develop- ment of the fossil-fuel bank, consisting of decayed and buried plant remains in the form of coal, oil, and gas. More recently the nuclear-fuel bank has been drawn upon through the harnessing of the products of nuclear decay. In some localities, heat generated deep in the earth itself is being developed commercially to provide geothermal power, while in other places the power of ocean tides and direct solar energy are the subjects of experimentation.

The development and use of these stores of non- human energy are proceeding rapidly, especially in the technologically advanced lands, where each individual is able to draw upon a steadily increasing amount of energy-producing capacity. One way in which this growth can be measured is by the horsepower of the main "prime movers," that is, the means for harnessing energy, such as electric motors and steam and gasoline engines. Figure 3.9 shows that the total nonhuman energy capacity of the United States has more than doubled in almost every decade since 1870. Viewed in another way, the average resident of the United States could draw upon 0.4 horsepower in 1870, but in 1970 he had access to 100.6 horsepower. Today the United States consumes more than one-third of all the energy produced in the world. Its per capita rate of energy use is more than six times that of the world; and Canada is not far behind. Soviet Union is also a large user of energy, accounting for nearly 16 percent of the world total. On the other hand, the less developed coun- tries together consume only 15 percent of the world's energy, although they have three-fourths of the popu- lation. The relationship between energy consumption and per capita GNP is shown in Fig. 3.10. The world map of energy consumption (Fig. 3.11) lends further

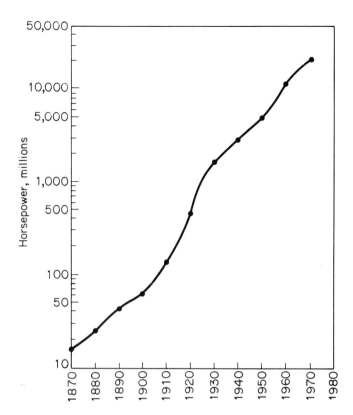

Fig. 3.9 *Total nonhuman energy of all prime movers, United States 1870–1970 (Horsepower). Capacity for mechanical energy use in the United States has doubled nearly every decade during the past century.*

Sources: Statistical Abstract of the United States, 1971 *(Washington, D.C.: U.S. Government Printing Office, 1971)* and Historical Statistics of the United States *(Washington, D.C.: U.S. Government Printing Office, 1960).*

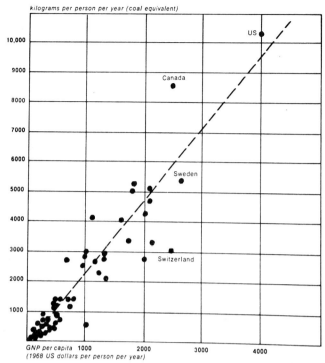

ENERGY CONSUMPTION AND GNP PER CAPITA

kilograms per person per year (coal equivalent)

GNP per capita
(1968 US dollars per person per year)

Fig. 3.10 *Energy consumption and per capita GNP. As countries rise in the scale of development, their per capita consumption of mechanical energy increases proportionately.*

Source: Meadows et al., The Limits to Growth.

Fig. 3.11 *World energy consumption per capita*

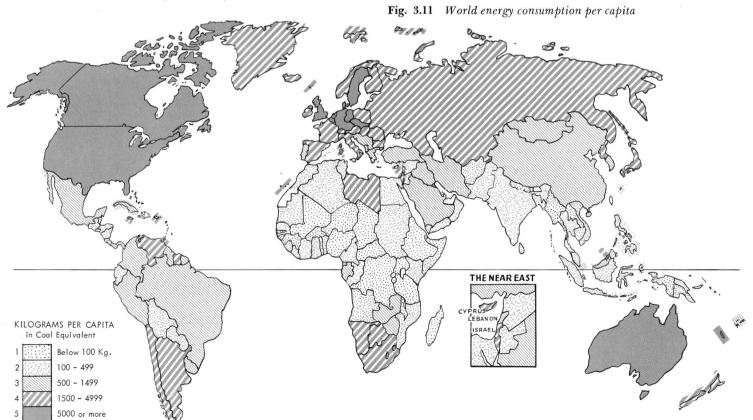

KILOGRAMS PER CAPITA
in Coal Equivalent

1   Below 100 Kg.
2   100 – 499
3   500 – 1499
4   1500 – 4999
5   5000 or more
6   Data not available

THE NEAR EAST

CYPRUS
LEBANON
ISRAEL

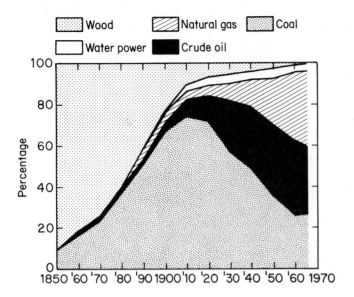

Fig. 3.12 *Percentage production of energy from various fuels and water power, U.S., 1850–1965. Wood, the most important source of energy a century ago, is little used for that purpose in the United States today. Its place has been taken mainly by the fossil fuels—first coal, then oil, and, more recently, natural gas.*

Source: Skinner, Earth Resources.

emphasis to these contrasts between countries at different levels of development.

Future energy needs are projected to climb steeply. It is estimated that during the last quarter of the twentieth century United States requirements will at least double and world needs will actually triple. Half of this projected rise is expected to result from increased per capita consumption, but the other half will be required by the increase in population.

During the past century there have been important shifts in the degree of reliance upon the different energy banks. In 1870, for example, draft animals provided the major part of the United States energy supply and these remained dominant until the end of the nineteenth century. At that time electricity came into general use, followed quickly by the internal combustion engine. This meant increasing dependence first upon the water-storage bank for electric power and then upon the fossil-fuel bank, which subsequently gained overwhelming dominance. There has been much change during this present century in the relative importance of the various fossil fuels, however (Fig. 3.12). Before 1910, coal had been the principal fossil fuel, but it has since been increasingly overshadowed by oil and gas. Today our soaring needs require us to turn to the remaining energy banks, especially nuclear power.

In view of the accelerating demand for mechanical energy, we need to ask just how good are our reserves in each of the principal energy-storage banks, where these reserves are located, and who has them. Considering our present heavy dependence upon fossil fuels,

let us examine first the problems of maintaining their future supply.

THE FOSSIL FUELS. Today the United States obtains approximately 95 percent of its energy from the fossil fuels, and this proportion is even greater in many other countries. This form of energy is derived from the fossil remains of plants and consists of the energy products of plant decay. These decay products are normally lost into the atmosphere by radiation, but under certain special conditions they may be trapped and stored. Most commonly this occurs in swamps and bogs, which may later become preserved and concentrated under the pressure of layers of rock. The resulting hydrocarbons assume the form of solids (coal), liquids (oil), and gases. Although these formed under ground in minute quantities each year, their total accumulation eventually became exceedingly great during the millions of years of the Carboniferous era (between 280 and 350 million years ago). Considering their slow rate of formation, the fossil fuels are essentially nonrenewable, which poses grave problems of future supply.

Coal is a solid fuel that has evolved from the burial, compaction, and aging of peat, a process that progressively increased its density and carbon content. As a result, the energy-giving qualities of coal vary with its age. There are hundreds of coal types, ranging in quality from anthracite (hard coal) and bituminous (soft coal) to lignite (brown coal). It is believed that all of the major coal basins of the world have now been found, but coal is nevertheless the most plentiful of the fossil fuels. The projected life of world reserves (Table 3.2, pp. 54–55) is 2,300 years as measured by the static index, but this is reduced to 111 years according to the exponential index. Final exhaustion of world coal reserves should be delayed somewhat by the fact that extraction, transportation, and use of coal is less convenient than oil and gas. For this reason the oil and gas reserves will be exhausted first, after which coal will increasingly be converted into liquid and gaseous fuels, thereby hastening its final end.

Figure 3.13 shows the wide spatial variation in the proportion of total energy supply that comes from coal. Note that very high percentages occur in Poland, the United Kingdom, West Germany, South Africa, and India, while the United States and the countries of Latin America rank much lower. One reason for this difference is the variation in relative size of coal reserves from one place to another (Fig. 3.14). Each of the above coal-using countries has comparatively large domestic stocks of this fuel. However, these variations also reflect the degree to which supplementary energy supplies are available. The United States, for example, has very large reserves of coal, but in addition it has had large supplies of the more convenient hydrocarbons, oil and gas. Perhaps 97 percent of the total world coal reserves are found in the Northern Hemisphere, especially in the United States, the Soviet Union (the greater part of which is in Siberia), and Europe (Figure 3.15). Nevertheless, sizable coal deposits are found

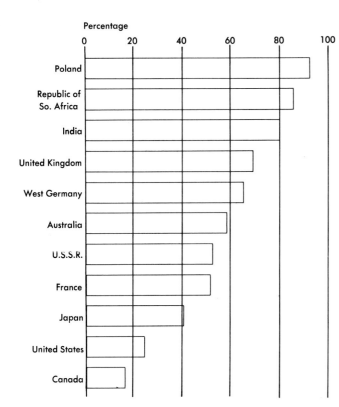

Percentage

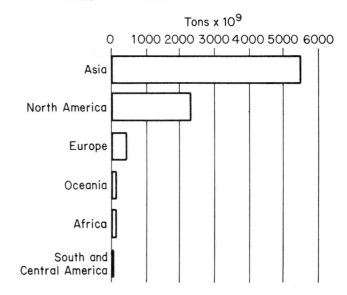

Fig. 3.13 *Percentage of total energy supplied by coal, selected countries, 1964. The extent to which a country relies upon coal for its mechanical energy depends partly upon the relative size of its coal reserves and partly on the availability of competing sources of energy.*

Source: Skinner, Earth Resources.

Fig. 3.14 *Distribution of recoverable coal reserves. Most of the world's coal reserves are in the Northern Hemisphere, especially the United States, the USSR, and China.*

Source: Skinner, Earth Resources.

Tons x 10^9

Fig. 3.15 *Coal: world production and trade. Not shown here is the very substantial intra-European coal trade.*

locally in such Southern Hemisphere countries as Australia and South Africa. The pattern of coal consumption is currently changing as world trade in coal (Fig. 3.15) increases, especially the metallurgical coking grades so much in demand for steel manufacture.

Petroleum is the most eagerly sought fossil fuel and it is consumed in ever-increasing quantities. Technically speaking, petroleum includes both crude oil (a liquid) and natural gas (mainly methane), which usually occur together. Oil and natural gas have common origins, both having been derived from decayed organic matter in ancient sea basins. Petroleum is a complex mixture of hydrocarbons—hydrogen and oxygen chemically combined in many ways. As a result there are numerous grades of petroleum, some light and others very heavy. The lighter grades are richer in gasoline and other valuable "fractions"; but modern refining technology has also made it possible to "crack" the heavy fractions into lighter forms. Petroleum differs from coal in that it migrates from the rocks in which it originated. It moves upward toward the surface and becomes caught in "traps," rock formations that act as barriers. There it accumulates in "pools," with the gas partly dissolved in the liquid and partly resting on top. Petroleum is also capable of lateral migration, sometimes moving many miles from its origin. As the lightest fraction, natural gas often migrates farther and may become entirely separated from the oil.

In both the liquid and gaseous forms, petroleum is highly prized as a fuel and as a raw material. It is generally preferred to coal because it is easier to transport and store, has a higher caloric content, and gives more nearly complete combustion. Virtually all the crude oil that is brought to the surface today is used. Not only does it provide gasoline, kerosene, jet fuel, lubricants, and fuel oil, but it is also the basis for hundreds of thousands of petrochemical products in direct competition with coal. Natural gas is similarly versatile. Modern urbanized and mechanized economies have thus become deeply dependent upon petroleum.

Even though petroleum and coal both originated as products of organic decay, they differ considerably in their spatial distribution. While the technically advanced countries have a major share of the world's coal, a select group of less developed countries possess the greater part of the petroleum reserves (Fig. 3.16). It was estimated in 1971 that 87 percent of the world's oil is in the Eastern Hemisphere and that somewhere between 55 percent and two-thirds of the total is held by the politically volatile countries of the Middle East. Not only are the Middle Eastern deposits vast, but the output per well is generally many times that in North America and costs of discovery, development, and production are decidedly lower. The Communist countries —the Soviet Union, Eastern Europe, and China—are estimated to have another 16 percent; Western Europe, despite important new finds, has only a minor percentage of the world total. This leaves a relatively small portion, 13 percent, for the Western Hemisphere countries. Much of this occurs along the Andean margins in

Fig. 3.16 *Crude oil: world production and trade. Only the largest fields and most important trade flows are shown here.*

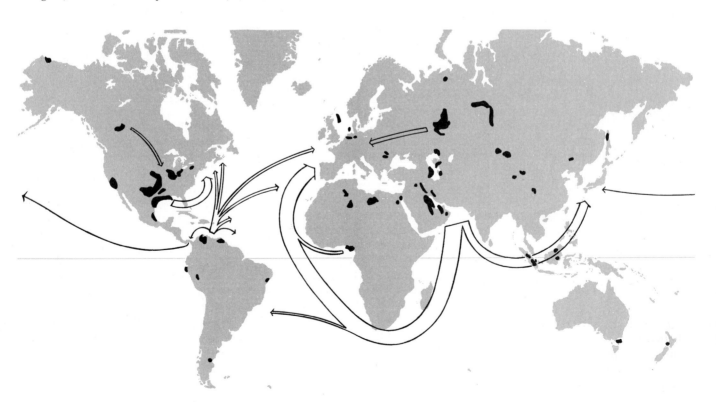

Fig. 3.17 *Natural gas: world production and trade*

South America. The United States is reckoned to have about half of the remaining reserves of the hemisphere, but its supply is dwindling rapidly despite the remarkable new finds in Alaska. Canada has a little less than 2 percent of the world's oil.

Predictably, however, it is the technologically advanced countries that consume most of the petroleum. Per capita consumption of oil in the United States is currently about eight times that of the world as a whole. The main supplier of petroleum to the world for a century following the drilling of its first well in 1859, the United States is now unable to meet its own needs. Demand is increasing at even faster rates in Western Europe and Japan, where the number of automobiles and trucks is rapidly growing.

In view of the great distances separating the principal regions of petroleum production and consumption, there is an enormous and rapidly growing international trade in oil (Fig. 3.16). Tankers from the oilfields of the Middle East, North and West Africa, and Venezuela form a steady stream to the oil-deficit countries of Western Europe and to Japan, the United States, and Canada. The international trade in natural gas is mainly of recent origin, although there have been pipeline shipments between adjacent countries for some time, as, for example, the Soviet Union's exports to Eastern and Southern Europe and American purchases from Canada and Mexico (Fig. 3.17). It has been more difficult and expensive, however, to transport gas between continents because of its great bulk. Today this problem is being solved by converting the gas to a liquid state by reducing its temperature to −259°F. Liquid natural gas (LNG) is very compact and can be

transported long distances in a tanker designed like a thermos bottle. Britain has been receiving North African gas in this form since 1964 (see Chapter 16), and the United States is beginning to import it also. Despite the efficiency of modern tanker operations, transport costs constitute the major part of the delivered cost of petroleum products. Such shipments are feasible from the Middle East only because oil is very cheap to produce there and because alternative sources cannot provide an adequate supply.

Another way in which technically advanced countries attempt to minimize their petroleum deficit is through more intensive exploitation of existing reserves and exploration for new ones. Thus, the United States still produces 21 percent of the world's oil despite dwindling resources, while the Middle East, with a major portion of world reserves produces only 29 percent of the total output (Fig. 3.16). New petroleum output in the United States is taking place mainly through horizontal and vertical expansion of existing fields. The only important new find in recent years is the discovery on the north slope of Alaska, the development of which will be delayed until the resolution of grave environmental issues that have emerged out of growing concern for the *quality* of growth alongside its quantity. Meanwhile, Canada is exploring for gas and oil hard in its Arctic regions. The Western European nations, concerned by their extreme dependence upon Middle Eastern petroleum, have engaged in an intensive and costly search for local reserves of gas and oil. Their efforts have been rewarded by important discoveries under the North Sea and on its neighboring shores, notable examples of which are Norway's rich

Ekofisk oilfield, Britain's Forties field, and the very large gas field in the Dutch province of Gronigen (see Chapter 16). Similarly, the Australians have their newly discovered Bass Strait deposits.

In each instance the increase in domestic supplies has resulted in a reduced dependence upon politically uncertain foreign supplies, as well as substantial savings in transport cost. Still, there is no indication that any of these countries is to receive more than short-run relief from a basic reliance upon African and Middle Eastern petroleum. It seems likely, therefore, that the future is to bring, if anything, an increased interdependence among the world's nations in the production and consumption of these fuels. What, then, is the world reserve situation?

Petroleum reserves are harder to assess than are coal reserves. Oil and gas pools are smaller and more difficult to locate and measure than the great, relatively continuous coal basins. However, the principal sedimentary basins suitable for the occurrence of petroleum are known and estimates are possible, even though there is considerable disagreement about how much lies under ground. According to Table 3.2, known oil reserves are projected to last 31 years at present rates of consumption and 20 years if consumption rates are to rise in the manner expected. Gas is calculated to last for another 38 years at present rates, but to be used up in 22 years at increasing rates of use. Recent finds should extend these times, but world demand is continuing to grow very rapidly. In 1970, for example, the increase amounted to 9.6 percent over the previous year. As we have seen, exploration and development are being hardpressed for both nationalistic and competitive reasons, but petroleum experts consider it unlikely that any new "Middle Easts" will occur to provide a quantum rise in world reserves. Since oil and gas are decidedly nonrenewable resources, where do we turn next for our highly prized fossil fuels?

There are other potential sources of fossil fuels that should postpone the ultimate exhaustion of this source of energy. Most important of these are the tar sands and oil shales, which may add as much as two-thirds to the world's fossil fuel stores. Tar sands contain large-molecule hydrocarbons like crude oil, which, however, do not migrate as do oil and gas. Instead, they adhere firmly to the sand grains. They are found in limited quantities in several parts of the world, but the most important known occurrence is in western Canada. The Athabaska tar sands of northern Alberta are 200 feet thick and extend over 30,000 square miles. Recovery of this resource is accomplished by mining the sands and then heating them with steam to cause the asphaltic hydrocarbons to flow.

Similarly, certain rock formations, known as oil shales, contain high concentrations of bituminous material that can be converted into valuable petroleum products. Vast reserves of these occur in the Rocky Mountains of the United States, extending over much of the states of Colorado, Utah, and Wyoming. These Green River shales can be made to yield from one-half to one-and-one-half barrels of oil per ton, and in total probably exceed the capacity of the country's conventional oil reserves. The tar sands are currently being developed, and pilot plants have proved the technical feasibility of mining oil shale; but both sources are very costly to exploit at present price levels. Nevertheless, they represent a potentially important supplement to future fossil fuel reserves. Even with these additions, however, the incredible rate at which world consumption is accelerating threatens exhaustion or at least severe shortages of petroleum early in the twenty-first century. Clearly, then, we shall have to turn increasingly to other forms of energy.

ELECTRICITY. Of the conventional forms of energy, electricity is currently experiencing the most rapid increase in demand, even greater than the demand for fossil fuels. Indeed, electric energy requirements are growing so fast that in many areas new generating capacity cannot be installed quickly enough to avoid power shortages during peak periods of use. Electricity has a number of special advantages that have given it this great popularity. First, its mobility has provided a new locational freedom for its users, especially for light industry. It is clean to use, although, as we shall see, generating electricity can create a great deal of dirt. It also can be used in precisely the quantities needed, unlike the big steam engines that supplied power for factories in earlier times.

Finally, electricity is exceedingly versatile, an ideal type of energy for an infinite variety of applications. In the United States more than one-fifth of the electricity is consumed by private households and commercial establishments; another quarter is used in transportation; and the rest goes into industry. In most other parts of the world the percentage allocated to manufacturing is much larger. Electric motors account for much of the industrial consumption, but great blocks of power are also required by electrometallurgical and electrochemical producers.

Electricity is difficult to categorize, since it is something of a hybrid. Consisting of a movement of electrons, it has many characteristics of a flow resource except that it is actually used up. Unlike other flow resources, electricity is hard to store and most of the output, except for transmission losses, is consumed as it is produced. It is easy to transmit over short distances, but long-range transmission entails higher costs and greater losses. The difficulty of storing electricity presents the power industry with serious problems of anticipating demand, which can vary seasonally, daily, and even hourly.

Electricity is distinctive also because it is a derived form of energy and not a primary source in itself. It is produced by generators powered by other, primary, energy forms. Thus the force of falling water drives turbines, which generate hydroelectricity. In the production of thermoelectricity, heat from the burning

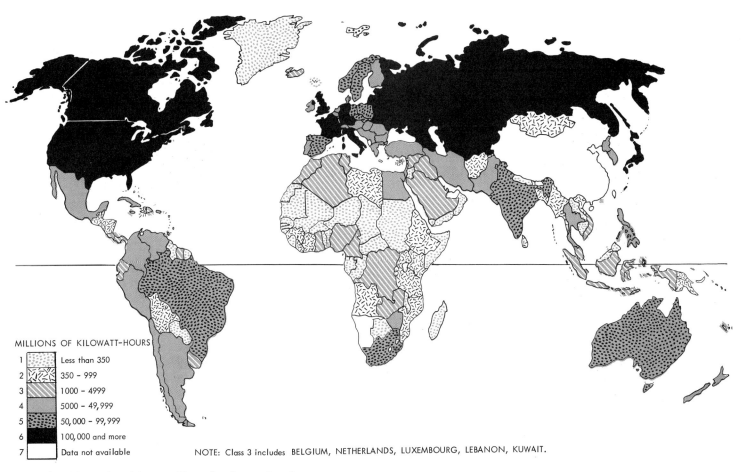

MILLIONS OF KILOWATT-HOURS

1	Less than 350
2	350 – 999
3	1000 – 4999
4	5000 – 49,999
5	50,000 – 99,999
6	100,000 and more
7	Data not available

NOTE: Class 3 includes BELGIUM, NETHERLANDS, LUXEMBOURG, LEBANON, KUWAIT.

Fig. 3.18 *Electricity: world production and trade*

of coal, oil, or gas is used to raise steam, which in turn drives the turbines. Generators may also be powered by internal combustion engines, which may burn either gasoline or diesel fuel. More recently, new types of primary power for generating electricity have been introduced. Two thermal sources—nuclear and geothermal energy—have become commercially feasible, while solar and tidal energy are still in the experimental stage.

There are wide variations throughout the world in the per capita consumption of electricity (Fig. 3.18) and also in the source of primary energy used to produce it. The technologically advanced countries use vast quantities of electricity in their industries and transportation and they are requiring ever greater amounts for household use. As a measure of development, however, the rate of electric energy consumption is not as reliable as the rate of use of total energy. For example, although the United States produces and uses one-third of the world's electricity, it does not have the highest per capita consumption among the technologically advanced nations. Canada's per capita electricity use is greater, and Norway consumes almost twice as much per person. Both Canada and Norway have small populations and very large hydroelectric potentials (Fig. 3.19). They have therefore succeeded in acquiring many

electrometallurgical and electrochemical firms, attracted by the abundance of cheap power. Both countries have exported important quantities of electricity, especially Norway, which obtains 99.6 percent of its electricity from falling water. Canada's hydroelectric potential is nearly used up, however, and the country now relies upon thermal sources—mainly coal and nuclear power —for nearly a quarter of its needs.

Other technically advanced nations with large hydroelectric potentials are Switzerland, which receives 95 percent from that source; Sweden, 72.2 percent; and New Zealand, 78.8 percent (Fig. 3.19). On the other hand, many other developed countries have little or no hydroelectricity: the Netherlands, Denmark, the United Kingdom, and West Germany, for example. Most of the larger advanced countries rely upon both thermal and hydroelectricity, especially the United States and the Soviet Union.

Among the poorer nations, per capita electricity consumption corresponds very well with other measures of development, such as per capita GNP. Indonesia uses only 14 kilowatt hours (kw-hr) of electricity per person (as against 7500 kw-hr per capita in the United States), Pakistan consumes only 43 kw-hr, and India 103. Higher in the scale of advancement, Mexico consumes 503, Argentina 850, and Venezuela 1057. In each of these

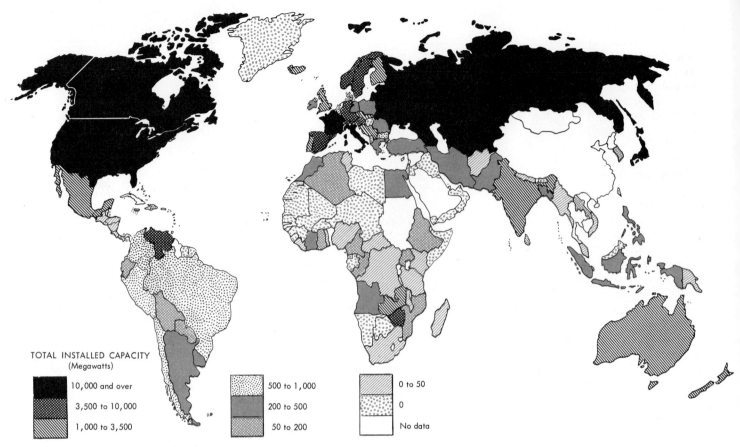

Fig. 3.19 *World hydroelectric power*

TOTAL INSTALLED CAPACITY
(Megawatts)

- 10,000 and over
- 3,500 to 10,000
- 1,000 to 3,500
- 500 to 1,000
- 200 to 500
- 50 to 200
- 0 to 50
- 0
- No data

countries, per capita electricity use is considerably lower than total energy consumption, much of which is used to operate motor vehicles and other transport equipment.

In many less developed countries a high proportion of the electricity is obtained from hydroelectric sources, often dams and generating facilities built with foreign aid funds. Egypt's great Aswan dam is the most notable example, but others are found in Brazil, Rhodesia, and Indonesia (Fig. 3.19). Since electricity is essential to the functioning of a modern economy, the difficulties encountered by less developed countries in building up their generating capacities are typical of their predicament generally. Electric power generation requires exceedingly high initial capital investments—about $4 of investment for each $1 of electric power output. Moreover, there are important economies of scale in power production, unit costs being markedly lower for the larger installations. Most underdeveloped economies are still too small to justify these efficient large plants.

Today increasing amounts of electric power are traded (Fig. 3.18). International trade is growing, particularly as power-surplus nations sell their excess supplies to power-short neighbors. Regional and national power grids have also been linked with those of adjacent countries in order to balance differing peak loads and to provide an extra reservoir in case of emergency. Norway has long supplied Sweden and Denmark with large quantities of surplus electric power. The British

and French national grids are now linked by a power cable under the English Channel, and similar grid interties exist among the EEC countries. France, Switzerland, and Italy, participate in a joint scheme for development and sharing of the hydroelectric resources of the Alps. The United States and Canada also exchange a great deal of electric power along their lengthy border.

Total world demand for electricity is growing much faster than either population or GNP, the pace being set by such vigorous economies as that of Japan, where power use increased by 11.3 percent in 1970 alone (see Chapter 17). The question that is now pressing is whether or not new capacity can be installed quickly enough in the advanced countries. A very long lead time is required for building new facilities. Already shortages are threatening, as evidenced by "brownouts" and "blackouts" of power in the densely populated northeastern United States. Delays in installing new generating capacity have been caused by citizens' concerns about environmental pollution (see below), but they have also resulted from shortages of conventional primary energy supplies.

The dwindling supply of fossil fuels, the main source of primary energy for electric power generation, has already been noted; but what are the prospects for hydroelectric supplies? Today the largest and most accessible sources of hydroelectricity in the advanced countries have been pretty well used up, especially in Western Europe and North America. The matter is quite different in the underdeveloped countries. Africa has 27 percent of the world's hydroelectric potential but only a tiny fraction of that has been harnessed. This is likewise true of Southeast Asia, which has 16 percent of the potential, and Latin America with 20 percent. In each of these continents the problems are lack of capital and lack of a present market for the power. Even so, the total hydroelectric capacity of the world is inadequate to supplant the waning supplies of fossil fuels.

Because it is a derived form, electrical energy can be obtained by tapping the less conventional energy storage banks of nature. One of the most promising of these is nuclear energy, which appears to be the only alternative source of power with a potential to satisfy the rising demand for electricity with our present technology. The power of the atom is harnessed in two ways: nuclear fission (the process used by the atomic bomb), and nuclear fusion (the hydrogen bomb method). The first of these entails the capture of energy released by the fissioning of radioactive elements. This process can be controlled to release steady amounts of heat energy for generating electricity. One pound of nuclear fuel can produce as much electric power as 5,900 barrels of oil. This fuel is uranium 235, a rare and costly element. Nuclear fusion, on the other hand, relies upon cheap and plentiful raw materials and the process is nearly pollution free. Fusion reaction is difficult to tame, however, and the technology for obtaining electric power from this source is progressing slowly. The forecast is that fusion will become a commercial reality by the end of this century.

Today, the world is turning to nuclear fission as quickly as problems of raising capital, resolving ecological issues, and perfecting engineering design will permit. In 1972 the United States had 23 nuclear power plants in operation and an additional 106 stations under construction or on order. It is now anticipated that 13 percent of the country's electric power will be supplied by nuclear energy in 1980 and that half of it will be from this source by 2000. Economic considerations increasingly favor atomic energy. In terms of energy output nuclear fuel is already cheaper than coal at the mine, and coal costs are expected to continue to rise.

Canada is stressing nuclear power for new generating capacity, especially in the province of Ontario, which has virtually exhausted its hydroelectric potential and is far from domestic coal supplies. Nuclear energy is also being emphasized in Europe, where the supplies of fossil fuels are diminishing and the costs increasing. The United Kingdom pioneered in developing commercial atomic power generation and as yet still leads the world in total atomic energy production (see Chapter 16). The EEC nations, especially France, are likewise turning to this source of power, as are West Germany, Sweden, Spain, and countries of eastern Europe. Although only 1 percent of the Soviet Union's present electric capacity is nuclear, plans call for a twentyfold increase in the next decade. Meanwhile, Japan has succeeded in becoming the third-ranking nation in nuclear power generation. For countries with small economies, however, nuclear power offers less promise. Because nuclear reactors must be very large to be economical, only the largest of the underdeveloped countries can use them. India, for example, has already begun to generate electricity in this manner.

Uranium is a scarce element—comprising only 0.00016 percent of the earth's crust—and high-grade ores of U-235 are severely limited in occurrence. In total reserves Canada, the United States, South Africa, and France lead the non-Communist world; Communist reserves are a closely guarded secret. The ore must be beneficiated by an intricate process before use, and at present the United States is practically the sole source of enriched uranium for the Western world. For the short term the best hope of conserving this resource is through the perfection of the "breeder" reactor, which uses a lower-grade of uranium that is relatively plentiful, especially in the United States. The answer for the longer term seems to be the harnessing of nuclear fusion.

Does this mean that all our energy problems will eventually be solved by atomic energy? This seems unlikely, since it cannot substitute for fossil fuels in several important applications. Moreover, our present nuclear fuels are nonrenewable also. It is prudent, then, to look to still other potential sources of energy. One of these is solar radiation, our largest undeveloped resource. Despite considerable research, however, the technology for commercial use of the direct rays of the sun appears to be far into the future. Another alternative is geothermal energy. Several countries have hot springs, geysers, and other underground supplies of hot water that can be easily tapped; but the occurrence of this resource is strictly local. Italy obtains about 2.5 percent of her electricity from this source, and New Zealand relies upon it for about 10 percent. Smaller quantities are utilized by Japan and the United States. Promising experiments are now under way to find ways of using earth heat in areas where there are no naturally occurring subterranean waters. A third unconventional source of energy is that of ocean tides, which may acquire some local significance. The Soviet Union has concluded some successful experiments at Murmansk and is now building two stations on the Black Sea.

AN ENERGY CRISIS?   Clearly, then, we have numerous options for maintaining the world's future energy supply. Although it is true that oil and natural gas reserves are steadily dwindling, final exhaustion is not immediately upon us. Meanwhile, there are large reserves of coal in many countries, including some of the most fuel-hungry nations; in addition, there are oil shales, tar sands, and other potential sources of liquid hydrocarbons. Despite eventual exhaustion of fossil fuels, a continuing supply of electrical energy appears assured through other sources.

If long-run prospects for global energy seem so optimistic, why do we hear so much about an impending energy crisis? Throughout the technologically advanced lands of Western Europe, North America, and Japan there is mounting concern for such a dread possibility. Are such fears founded? The answer is that there are likely to be energy crises in the short run and in particular places. Energy shortages have already begun to appear, resulting from the erratic distribution of energy resources and a complex of political, economic, social, cultural, and environmental considerations.

It is significant that one place where energy shortages threaten is the United States. In the past, talk of dwindling energy supplies was generally ignored by Presidents and populace alike; but today the evidence of imminent crisis is too insistent to be avoided longer. During each of the past few summers the increased use of air conditioners has contributed to electric power shortages in many large cities. In fact, power companies have mounted advertising compaigns urging their customers to save electricity. In many areas, natural gas has been rationed to industrial users while service has been denied to new applicants. During the winter of 1972–73 the first shortages of fuel oil appeared, and more severe shortages were avoided only because of an unusually mild winter. This was followed in the spring and summer by the country's first peacetime gasoline shortages, resulting in the closing of gasoline stations and rationing of supplies to customers. Taxi, bus, and truck fleet operators were unable to contract for wholesale supplies of fuel and had to patronize local service stations. Fuel prices began to climb. If more evidence of American vulnerability to energy-supply problems was needed, the Arab nations provided this during the winter of 1973–1974 with their oil boycott, which caused critical shortages in the United States. Subsequent actions by the cartel of oil-exporting nations to limit supplies and raise prices have prolonged the dilemma for the United States and all other importers of petroleum.

The spatial pattern of energy shortage in the United States has been of particular interest to the economic geographer. The first persons to be affected have been those at the far ends of the oil and gas pipelines and those at the ends of tank truck routes. This has represented a pulling back of service from those peripheral areas that are most costly to supply. Also damaged by the reduction in oil supplies have been the independent gasoline distributors and dealers, who have traditionally assumed an important economic function by taking surplus refinery runs of the major oil companies. This "unbranded" gasoline was then sold at reduced prices. Thus, it has been those persons in the lowest income groups who have been the first to be adversely affected by shortages: the rural poor remotely located at the end of distribution lines and the urban poor dependent upon cut-rate gasoline from independent dealers.

Why should the United States be afflicted with energy shortages? After all, the country's stocks of oil and natural gas from conventional domestic sources is considered sufficient for at least two more decades, and coal reserves are among the world's largest. One answer

to this is given by the fact that the United States is the world's largest user of energy and thus peculiarly vulnerable to supply problems. Heavy use of energy is a function of American affluence; but it also results from social attitudes conducive to high energy consumption— the special role of the motor car in family and community life, an ingrained dependence upon appliances and mechanical contrivances, and a fascination with gadgetry. These attitudes have been encouraged by unusually low energy prices. Government regulation of utility companies has kept gas and electric rates lower than in many other parts of the world, but equally important has been the intense competition among energy suppliers for the available consumer market. This has assumed the form of gasoline "wars" among service stations, rivalry between gas and electric companies, and lavish advertising to promote energy use. In addition, the oil industry has maintained a world pricing system that has favored exploitation of nondomestic deposits (see Chapter 4).

An unfortunate result of these influences has been a profligate use of energy in all its forms. Although, as we have seen, Americans use one-third of the world's energy, they have been spending only 4 percent of their GNP to get it. One consequence is that 25 percent of all mechanical energy in the country is used for transportation. Oversized motor cars consuming large quantities of gasoline are wastefully used for often trivial trip purposes, while much cheaper and more efficient mass transit is avoided in urban areas by most of those having cars and able to drive. Manufacturers, who consume another 35 percent of the country's energy, are also careless in its use, encouraged in this practice by the special low rates granted by power companies to customers buying large blocks of power. The rest of the country's power goes for household and business use, where at least one-quarter is lost through poor insulation. Other losses are caused by overheating, inefficient appliances, and excessive use of air-conditioning.

In addition to a rapidly rising demand for energy, the pressure on available supplies has been aggravated by a delayed and inadequate response to the emerging problem. Citing low gasoline prices and government restrictions on oil imports, the petroleum industry has failed to construct sufficient new refinery capacity. Low prices have also been given as the reason for inadequate domestic exploration for oil and gas. Meanwhile the government has been reluctant to institute politically unpopular measures that would discourage wasteful consumption and would permit more realistic pricing of utilities. Moreover, the government has not been committed to the massive research effort required to ensure future domestic supplies of energy, and it has been hesitant to import larger quantities of oil and gas for fear of excessive dependence upon the Arab Middle East and of draining the country's foreign exchange reserves (see Chapter 11).

National response to the energy shortage has also been delayed by serious environmental questions that are yet to be resolved. Although these will be considered in more detail in a later section, we should note here that there is a direct conflict between the demand for more energy and the need to protect the environment from pollution. For example, clean-air laws have generally forbidden the burning of high-sulfur coal and oil, which precludes use of a major part of the country's domestic fossil fuel supply. Government-required anti-pollution devices on motor vehicle exhausts have reduced efficiency of fuel consumption by at least ten percent.

Full use of the country's large reserves of coal is severely restricted by objections to the environmental impact of mining operations, particularly the devastating effects of strip mining, which is the cheapest and most effective way to get at the coal. Major oil reserves lie beneath the country's continental shelves, but recent disasters such as the oil leakage in the Santa Barbara Channel have delayed efforts to exploit these rich off-shore deposits. Tapping the vast oil reserves on Alaska's North Slope was delayed because of the controversy over the environmental impact of transporting oil from that remote Arctic location. On the one hand there are the potential hazards to the landscape and wildlife that might result from piping hot oil across the frozen tundra and on the other there is the fear of oil spills from tankers moving the commodity down the Pacific coast. The construction of nuclear power plants has also been much delayed by environmental considerations.

The energy-supply questions confronting the United States are repeated in several other technically advanced countries today. On the whole, they can be considered only short-run problems. In the longer run it seems likely that advancing technology will provide answers from among the alternatives suggested earlier, although these solutions will undoubtedly require much money and a great deal of time for research and development. Indeed, as we shall see later, it is possible that certain critical side effects of energy production and use may be the determining factor in the end. The situation is less promising over the long run, however, for maintaining an adequate supply of certain metallic ores that must be teamed with mechanical energy for a modern economic system to function.

the metals

The metals are a class of elements that are hard, heavy, and opaque, have a "metallic" luster, and are capable of being drawn into fine wire (ductility), hammered into thin plates (malleability), and melted by heat, and they are able to conduct both electricity and heat (conductivity). However, each metal possesses these qualities in different combinations and degrees and consequently has its own set of uses. Many of the metals are versatile, a quality enhanced by their capacity for alloying, that is, for combining with other metals in varying proportions. This multiplies the already extensive range of special purposes that these elements are able to serve.

There is an intimate relationship between metals and the consumption of mechanical energy. Indeed, they are indispensable to all sectors of the modern economy. This is obvious in the case of manufacturing and transportation, but it is equally true of the extractive industries, including modern agriculture. Not only do the metals contribute to high agricultural yields through their use in farm tools, machinery, and transport equipment but also in the production of agricultural chemicals. A great many metals are required by an increasingly complex modern technology, in which subtle differences in metallic qualities can be vital. Although a certain amount of substitution of materials is sometimes possible there are certain key metals for which no feasible substitutes have been discovered.

For these reasons, we require a continuing supply of metals. But how good is this supply? The answer is different for each metal, some of which are still plentiful and others nearing exhaustion. But all are nonrenewable. One of the first things we discover when examining the future of our metallic reserves is that some of the most "common" metals are not really common at all. Of the so-called common metals only iron and aluminum are among the first ten elements in the continental earth crust, and these ten represent 99 percent of the total crustal weight. Relatively speaking, therefore, the other commercially important metals exist in only small quantities. Considering the great mass of the earth's crust, however, the absolute amounts are in fact much greater than this would seem to indicate and a more realistic dividing line between the abundant and the scarce metals is sometimes set at the 0.01 percent level. On this basis the most plentiful metallic elements are iron, aluminum, manganese, magnesium, chromium, and titanium, while the least plentiful include such familiar metals as copper, lead, zinc, and nickel. In many cases, these scarce elements are being extracted in large volumes despite severely limited reserves.

Certain metals are much more widely distributed over the earth than others. In some instances this results from a generally greater crustal occurrence, but in others it reflects the essential character of the ores from which they are extracted. Certain ores—such as iron, aluminum, and copper—have a metallic content that varies continuously from very rich to the very lean. This variability is a boon to the mining industry, since the limits to practical exploitation are set simply on the basis of cost and available technology. Many other metals, however, are discontinuous in concentration; they either occur in a place or they do not. This is true of such important metals as lead, zinc, tin, nickel, tungsten, mercury, manganese, gold, and silver. Certain of these are concentrated in only a few places.

Still another problem of world mineral supply is the fact that the countries consuming the largest quantities are not necessarily the ones that are best endowed with resources. The United States is the outstanding consumer of metals, but it lacks many vital metallic resources. Similarly, most European industrial nations are conspicuously deficient in metallic ores. Some of the largest reserves are found in the less developed countries and in those technically advanced nations with large territories and small populations, especially Canada and Australia.

THE HIGH-VOLUME METALS. Among those metals required by world industry in very large quantities are iron and its close partner, manganese. A second class of high-volume metals is the nonferrous group.

Of the metals, iron is the overwhelming leader in total annual tonnage of output—constituting 95 percent of all the metals extracted—and this volume continues to rise each year. This can be attributed partly to iron's being plentiful and very cheap (only a few cents per pound); but this popularity also results from its great strength and its readiness to form alloys with numerous other metals. When added to iron in even minute quantities, these elements can cause it to assume a variety of desirable properties that contribute still further to the metal's versatility. Iron technology is relatively easy, too, since the metal can be removed from its oxides (the most common occurrence in nature) by means of chemically simple processes.

Since the first discovery of a technique for making iron, about 2000 B.C., this metal has become one of man's most important materials and it is used by virtually every society today. Nevertheless, there is a decided relationship between the per capita consumption of iron and level of development. This is shown by the S-shaped curve of Figure 3.20. Usage is exceedingly low in such underdeveloped countries as Indonesia (7 pounds per capita), Ecuador (44 pounds), and India (24 pounds), but it climbs steeply with rising per capita income. Note, for example, that moderately developed Spain uses 529 pounds per person, while more prosperous Italy uses 776 pounds. Ultimately, however, per capita usage seems to reach a saturation point, as shown by the similar rates of consumption by the United States, Sweden, West Germany, Japan, and other technologically ad-

Fig. 3.20 *World steel consumption and GNP per capita. Per capita steel consumption is a commonly used measure of relative levels of development.*

Source: Meadows et al., The Limits to Growth.

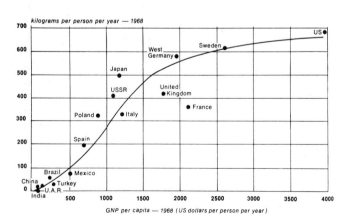

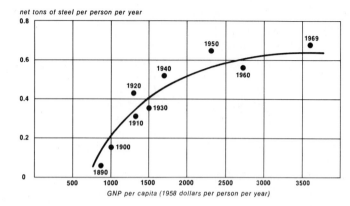

Fig. 3.21 *United States steel consumption per capita, 1890–1969. During the earlier stages of industrial growth in the United States, per capita steel consumption rose sharply and steadily. As the economy matured, steel use eventually leveled off at a fairly high point around which it has since fluctuated with the business cycle.*

Source: Meadows et al., The Limits to Growth.

vanced countries. This relationship is also seen in the changing rates of consumption by a particular advanced country. Note that the United States (Fig. 3.21) appears to have reached this point of saturation during the 1950s. (The lower figure for 1960 reflects the economic recession of that year.)

Rates of production of iron are likewise related to level of development. The leading producers of steel are the United States, the Soviet Union, Japan, West Germany, and other European countries; but production of steel is widespread even in the less developed countries, where the possession of steelmaking facilities is often an item of national prestige (see Fig. 3.22). Altogether some fifty countries manufacture steel, including Egypt, Colombia, and Peru, although the output of many is quite small.

As previously noted, some of the most important steel-making nations have little ore of their own. This is especially true of Japan and Italy and certain other European producers. Even the United States, which originally had large reserves, must now import much of its ore, as well as finished steel. The best Lake Superior deposits have long since been exhausted and lower grades of American ore are now being developed. Indeed, low-grade taconite deposits now contribute 40 percent of the iron mined in the United States. Today the largest reserves are found in the Soviet Union, India, Brazil, Venezuela, Chile, Peru, West Africa, Australia, and Canada. Note the prominence in this list of less developed countries as well as advanced nations having large areas and low population densities. All these countries are important exporters of ore, and the total volume of world trade in this commodity has become very great.

Because iron is the second most plentiful metal in the earth's crust, and since nearly all types of iron ore are now successfully treated by iron technology, total

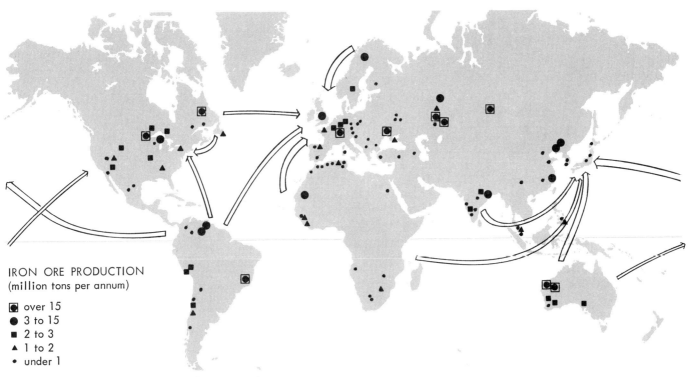

IRON ORE PRODUCTION
(million tons per annum)

- ◙ over 15
- ● 3 to 15
- ■ 2 to 3
- ▲ 1 to 2
- • under 1

Fig. 3.22 *Iron ore: world production and trade*

reserves of this element are enormous. One result of this is that iron is cheap for its bulk. Transport cost and accessibility to market are therefore important determinants in the selection of deposits for exploitation, more so than for any other metal. But the smelting of iron ore also requires great tonnages of other ingredients as well, especially coal for fuel and for driving off oxygen, and limestone to carry off other impurities. Therefore transport costs and accessibility of these other materials are likewise important locational considerations for the steel industry. For these reasons many large known deposits in remote areas remain ignored while ores of indifferent quality but close to market and to other ironmaking materials are actively pursued.

The projected life of world iron ore reserves is thus much greater than that of most mineral resources. The static index of this metal's reserve life is 240 years and the exponential index is 93 years (Table 3.2). However, vast resources of lower-grade iron ore are available. The main effect of iron ore usage for many years to come, therefore, will be rising costs as richer, more accessible reserves become exhausted. Since iron resources are in no immediate danger of depletion, the basic supply problem for iron becomes the adequacy of companion resources upon which its production and use depend, namely energy and alloying elements.

Manganese is a vital alloying metal for steel manufacture. It serves a dual function in the steel industry: (1) a process material acting as a "scavenger" to carry off sulfur and oxygen, an essential use for which there is no known substitute, and (2) an alloying element that imparts toughness to the metal. Although manganese has other industrial applications, they are minor. Be-

cause manganese is a relatively plentiful element in the earth's crust, its total world supply presents no immediate problem. Conventional reserves have an exponential index of reserve life of 46 years (Table 3.2), although lower grades are available at higher cost. So plentiful are current supplies, in fact, that the metal tends to be overused: 16 pounds are being used in the average ton of steel whereas only 4 pounds are needed for satisfactory results.

The main difficulty of manganese supply today is the spatial distribution of reserves: the best deposits are not always in the places where the metal is most needed (see Fig. 3.23). The United States, in particular, has virtually no domestic reserves of high-grade manganese ore and an inadequate supply of low-grade ore. Other big industrial nations also lack manganese, except for the Soviet Union, which has at least one-half of the known world supply. The remaining reserves are mainly in the less developed nations of Africa and Asia. Consequently, a major part of the world output of manganese travels between continents. Fortunately for the United States, there are very large deposits of manganese at the bottom of the ocean. Nodules of manganese have been found at depths of 500 to 3,000 feet off the southeastern coast of the United States and at depths of 5,000 to 14,000 feet in the eastern Pacific. Commercial extraction, using dredges and vacuum devices, is about to commence at present. Thus the supply problems of iron and its close companion, manganese, are not immediately pressing.

The prospect is less promising for a number of nonferrous metals essential to technologically advanced countries.

Manganese

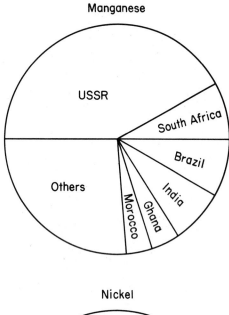

Nickel

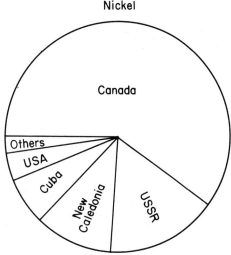

Fig. 3.23 *World production of manganese and nickel*

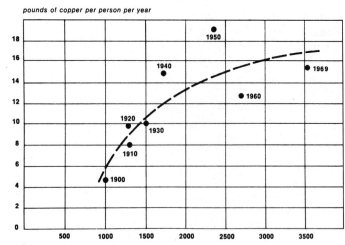

Fig. 3.24 *United States copper consumption per capita, 1890–1969.*

Source: *Meadows et al.,* The Limits to Growth.

Fig. 3.25 *World production of bauxite and lead*

Bauxite

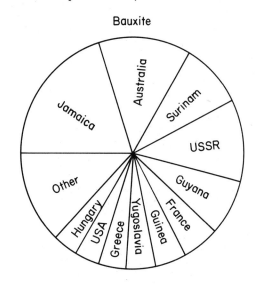

Lead

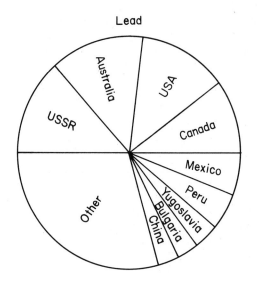

Metals in this group—aluminum, copper, lead, and zinc—are widely used and consumed in very large quantities, often with little relationship to the total reserve supply available. Moreover, the rate of consumption of each continues to rise, as shown by the case of copper in the United States (Fig. 3.24). All of the nonferrous metals normally occur in low-grade ore, except aluminum. These elements are also erratically distributed in the world, resulting in a large volume of world trade both in the metals and their ores. All four metals are more costly than iron, owing to the complexity of their ores, intricate technology of extraction, and expensive processing methods.

Aluminum is an exception in this group in several respects. First, it is the only nonferrous metal that appears abundantly in the earth's crust (8 percent of the total). Moreover, it is the only one of the four that occurs in high-grade ores, mostly over 32 percent metallic content (Fig. 3.25). Aluminum therefore has a static index of reserve life equal to 100 years. However, consumption of this metal has been growing very rapidly, its annual rate of increase averaging 6.4 percent. The exponential index for aluminum is therefore only 31 years. It is true that there are very large low-grade supplies of aluminum ore, but it is not commercially feasible to extract these with today's technology. The best hope is that the present rate of growth in consumption will level off in the future; indeed some evidence of a slowing trend is already appearing.

The other nonferrous metals are rare in crustal occurrence, copper being only 0.0058 percent, lead 0.0010, and zinc 0.0082. These three have become sufficiently concentrated for commercial extraction only through fortuitous acts of nature. Their world supply situation, already difficult, is to become much tighter in the near future. None has an exponential index of reserve life much in excess of two decades. Of the three, only copper occurs in continuously variable concentrations, which means that lower grades may be mined. Copper is already being extracted from incredibly lean ores: only 0.9 percent metallic content in the United States, 1 to 2 percent in Canada and Chile, 4 percent in Zambia, and 6 percent in the Congo. However, turning to even lower grades appears feasible, especially in view of the cheap open-pit mining that prevails in the copper industry. But this alternative does not apply to lead and zinc, which usually occur together. Their ores are generally much richer than those of copper, but their deposits are small and require costly underground mining. This cost tends to be partially offset by the valuable byproducts, such as copper, gold, and silver, which are frequently obtained in lead and zinc mining operations. The prospect for a continuing world supply of these elements is rather dismal.

In the case of the nonferrous metals, the technically advanced nations, especially with the inclusion of Canada and Australia, are able to provide a fairly high proportion of world output (Fig. 3.26). Even so, consumption rates in those lands are so great that the less developed countries must give important help. More than one-third of the known reserves of the chief aluminum ore, bauxite (aluminum hydroxide), are in Australia, and the technically advanced countries as a whole have about one-half of the total. Africa and the Caribbean have most of the rest, while South America and Asia possess somewhat lesser quantities. Nearly half of the world's copper reserves are in the developed countries, too, especially the Soviet Union and the United States. The rest is mainly in South America (principally Chile and Peru) and Africa's rich copper belt (Zambia and the Congo). Most of the world's larger deposits of zinc and lead are found in the United States, Canada, and the Soviet Union.

Although these metals cost more per pound than iron, they are surprisingly cheap, considering their relative scarcity. Nevertheless, their cost is rising as reserves decline in size and richness. The pressures on these supplies continue to grow as more and more vital uses for the nonferrous metals appear. Copper and aluminum are virtually indispensible in electrical applications because of their high conductivity. All four are used variously in the manufacture of important alloys such as bronze, brass, monel metal, solder, bearing metal, type metal, casting metal, and special alloys for aircraft applications. Aluminum, because of its lightness, is valuable as a structural metal. Copper and aluminum are much used for cooking utensils, owing to their heat-conducting properties. Copper, lead, and zinc each have their special applications because of their resistance to corrosion: sheathing, storage batteries, and galvanizing, for example. All four have essential uses in the production of chemicals.

The nonferrous metals thus have a multitude of vital applications, and they have become interwoven into modern production in a variety of ways. With the

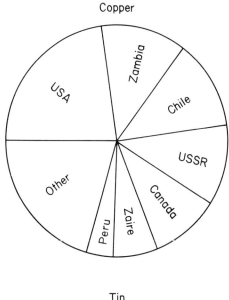

Copper

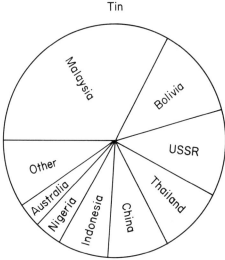

Tin

Fig. 3.26 *World production of copper and tin*

possible exception of aluminum, their supply situations are in jeopardy, however. Some substitution is possible, as, for example, the increasing use of aluminum in the place of more expensive copper in applications requiring conductivity; unfortunately, the substitution is not always feasible. It should be noted also that the production of nonferrous metals causes a serious drain on other resources. This is especially true of mechanical energy, which is used in great quantities in their extraction and processing. Much heat is required for zinc processing in particular; and large amounts of electricity are used in copper and aluminum refining, both of which are electrolytic processes.

THE LOW-VOLUME METALS.   Most of the metals produced and consumed in small volumes are also limited in crustal occurrence, but all of them are relatively expensive. Several are obtained as joint products of mining operations aimed at simultaneously obtaining other metals occurring in the same ores. Despite their low levels of use, these metals are essential to modern industry. Among the many elements fitting this description two categories are especially prominent: the alloying metals and the precious metals.

The alloying metals have a great many individual characteristics and a multitude of uses, but one kind of application they all share: their use in combination with other metals, especially in steel, to give special properties to the finished product. For most of them this is the principal way in which they are employed. Since this is a derived use, their demand structures and price levels are usually derived also. If the price of one of the alloying metals should fall, for example, it is unlikely that any more of it would be consumed, since the quantity required depends upon the current level of steel production. Pricing is further complicated for those alloying metals obtained as joint products. Because their output is tied to that of other metals with different demand conditions, changes in price have little effect on quantities produced. Although the alloying metals are often used in minute quantities, they have such an essential function that they are often referred to as *vitamin elements*. Some substitution among them is possible, but in many cases it is not.

Although a few of the alloying elements are plentiful in the earth's crust, others are rare. It is important here to distinguish between *rarity,* which is determined by an element's relative physical abundance in the earth's crust, and *scarcity,* an economic concept that refers to the costs of acquisition at a particular time and place. Three alloy metals appear to present no immediate problems of scarcity: chromium, titanium, and magnesium.

Because chromium helps steel to keep a sharp cutting edge even at high temperatures, it is employed in high-speed steels, a use for which chromium has no satisfactory substitute. Together with iron and nickel, it is also one of the principal constituents of stainless steels, a large and particularly important family of al-

loys. Chromium is fairly plentiful, having an exponential index of 95 years. Eighty percent of total output comes from South Africa, the USSR, Turkey, Rhodesia, and the Philippines, in that order. Another of the abundant alloying elements, titanium, comprises 0.86 percent of the earth's crust, with most of its current output coming from Canada, Japan, the United States, Australia, and Brazil. It is a lightweight, high-strength, corrosion-resistant metal used as an alloy of steel as well as in aero-space applications and in paint pigments. Magnesium is the lightest of all the metals, however, and it is also very strong. It is used to produce lightweight, corrosion-resistant alloys and in chemical production. It, too, is very widespread in occurrence. Magnesium is consumed only in small amounts and total output is not great. At present most of the world supply is obtained through electrolysis of sea water. There is no supply problem for magnesium at current levels of demand.

The supply situation is more critical for most of the other alloying elements, especially nickel, molybdenum, tin, and tungsten. Severe shortages of tin and tungsten appear imminent at this time. Occasionally these four elements occur separately; but these individual occurrences are in special metallogenic provinces —regions that have undergone a rare combination of geological events. More often they occur as byproducts or joint products with other elements, which means that a shift in demand and price may have little effect on the supply.

Most of the nickel that is mined is used in stainless steels and high-temperature and electrical alloys. Its crustal occurrence is small and it is found concentrated in only a few places: Canada (half of world output), the Soviet Union, New Caledonia, and Cuba (Fig. 3.23). Its exponential index is 53 years. Molybdenum imparts toughness and resilience to steel, and this is its chief use. Like nickel, its occurrence is highly erratic. Some of it is obtained as a byproduct of copper, but most comes from a metallogenic province that extends north and south through the Canadian and United States Rocky Mountains. Its exponential index is 34 years.

Tin, long valued for its corrosion-resistant properties, is used for plating iron and steel and as an alloy of copper in the production of bronze. Most of its output comes from two metallogenic provinces—one in Southeast Asia and the other in the high Andes of South America (Fig. 3.26). The tin supply from these sources is dwindling, however, and its exponential index is only 15 years. Tungsten often occurs together with tin in its main source region, which extends from Korea to Malaysia in East Asia. It makes exceedingly hard alloys with steel and is also used to manufacture tungsten carbide for cutting tools. Its exponential index is but 28 years.

The precious metals—silver, gold, and the platinum group—are another important class of elements whose supply is diminishing. Since ancient times silver and gold have been prized for their beauty and indestructibility. The precious metals have always been rare but they are becoming critically scarce today as their demand increases. Silver has a number of very useful properties and much more would be used if it were less costly. Its principal applications are in coinage, household silver, and jewelry, but industrial applications constitute its greatest market. Silver is the main ingredient of photographic film and it is also used in critical electrical applications because of its conductivity, which is even greater than that of copper.

Silver is naturally rare (only 0.000008 percent of the earth's crust by weight). The world's major source area is the Great Cordillera of the western Americas; smaller amounts are found in the Soviet Union and Australia. Today most of the newly mined silver is obtained as a byproduct of lead, zinc, and copper operations. Very little is mined for its own sake since the ore is rarely rich enough. Because of its growing scarcity, silver has doubled in price within the last decade; yet its output has increased but little in response, so inelastic is its supply. Although the exponential index of silver's reserve life is calculated at only 13 years, the byproduct nature of its output probably means that total annual demand will simply not be met and its projected life span will therefore be spread over a longer period of time.

Because it occurs in the native state and is easily worked, gold was used for coinage and shaped into jewelry by the earliest civilizations. The antiquity, beauty, and rarity (0.0000002 percent of the earth's crust) of gold have endowed it with a mystical aura. This esoteric quality of gold is apparent in the tenacity with which modern governments cling to it as a basis for their currencies in the face of a steadily dwindling natural store of the metal. One of its principal commercial uses continues to be in jewelry making, where it is prized for its lustrous appearance and great value. However, gold's inertness and resistance to corrosion account for many of its growing number of industrial applications. The exponential index of gold is a mere 9 years; but, like silver, it will probably continue to appear on the market in a diminishing flow. Although some gold is produced in 71 countries, 90 percent of the total output comes from South Africa (two-thirds), the USSR (one-eighth), Canada, the United States, and Australia.

In modern times, gold and silver have been joined by another group of precious metals, the platinoids. In addition to platinum, the main member of the group, these include five other closely related metals that invariably occur together in nature. They are not quite as rare as gold and the world supply seems fairly secure at present rates of consumption. The platinoids are acquiring a growing number of industrial applications, in addition to their use in jewelry, and current projections could prove excessively optimistic. The Soviet Union, South Africa, and Canada are the principal sources.

Another valuable element that does not fit into any of these categories is the industrial metal, mercury, which appears in the liquid state at ordinary temperatures. Although mercury is generally regarded as indispensable to any number of industrial applications its supply is now dwindling. The ancient Spanish mines still remain the leading source and their expected life is decidedly limited. The exponential index of mercury is only 13 years.

other nonrenewable resources

Two other classes of nonrenewable resources remain to be considered: (1) the mineral raw materials used for the manufacture of fertilizers and other chemical products, and (2) the nonmetallic-mineral building materials. Both of these are essential to the functioning of a modern economy, and they affect every member of society either directly or indirectly. Will there be an adequate supply of these to support a growing population?

MINERAL RAW MATERIALS FOR CHEMICALS AND FERTILIZERS. As we noted earlier, the best hope for feeding the expected additions to the world population is to increase the yield of land currently under the plow. Chemical fertilizers will be necessary to achieve this increase, along with improved seeds and more water. Although every plant type has its own particular combination of requirements, all crops must have nitrogen, phosphorus, potassium, calcium, and sulfur. These are the natural constituents of some soils but not all. Moreover, some plants make unusually heavy demands on certain elements and quickly deplete them from the soil. These nutrients must be replaced for subsequent plantings.

Farmers have traditionally restored plant food element to the soil either by fallowing—that is, resting the soil so that it can recuperate naturally—or by crop rotations that alternate soil-depleting crops with soil-restoring ones such as the legumes. But these practices are not always effective and they are too extensive in their use of land under conditions of increasing population pressures. One way of restoring nutrients to the soil is through the application of organic fertilizers, especially animal manures and, in the Orient, "night soil," or human wastes. Even this is inadequate for today's needs and manufactured fertilizers are required in rapidly increasing quantities.

The mineral raw materials for manufacturing fertilizers are also used to produce other chemical products and have other industrial applications. However, fertilizer manufacture is the largest single market for these materials and the demands are accelerating. The United States is currently the largest producer and consumer of chemical fertilizers, accounting for between one-third and one-half of the total volume of each type.

The original source of nitrogen for fertilizers was from naturally occurring compounds, the most important deposits being those in Chile's Atacama Desert. Today Chile supplies only three percent of world needs. Much of the remainder is extracted directly from the atmosphere, of which nitrogen is the largest constituent element. In addition to large quantities of electricity, the other major requirement for synthesizing nitrogenous fertilizers is hydrogen, with which the nitrogen is combined to produce a water-soluble ammonia compound that plants can readily assimilate. Ammonia is also obtained as a byproduct of coke oven operations, most of which are associated with the steel industry. The United States produces one-third of the world's supply of nitrogenous fertilizers.

Phosphorus is essential to plant growth, but it is easily exhausted by intensive cultivation. The chief commercial source of phosphorus is phosphate rock (apatite), which is treated with sulfuric acid to make it water-soluble and thus accessible to plants. The resulting superphosphate is very concentrated. Phosphorus is an abundant element, constituting 0.1 percent of the earth's crustal weight, but most phosphate rock is found

among the marine sediments of old sea beds. Despite the great world reserve of this mineral, deposits of commercial size and quality are found in only a few places (Fig. 3.27). The United States produces nearly half of the total world output, most of the rest coming from the Soviet Union and North Africa. One consequence of the unequal distribution of this vital material is the large quantity of it that moves in international trade.

Another abundant element that produces a particularly vital fertilizer is potassium, which comprises 1.68 percent of the earth's crust. Potassium is widely distributed throughout the world but not in a readily usable soluble form. Most of it is obtained commercially from salts resulting from the evaporation of sea water. Total reserves are very great, but the chief source areas are western Canada and the United States, Europe, and the Soviet Union (Fig. 3.27).

Calcium is important to certain crops, especially corn and other grains. It is a natural constituent of certain soils in sedimentary regions and it reaches high levels of concentration in subhumid lands, such as the plains and prairies of western United States and Canada and the steppes of Russia. These are all extremely productive soils. The calcium content of many other soils is inadequate, however, and easily exhausted by intensive cultivation in humid areas. Lime needed for replacement of this lost element is easily obtainable in many parts of the world wherever limestone is available. Calcium is one of the most plentiful elements and processing is simple.

The most basic chemical raw material is sulfur, which has an endless number of uses in chemical production and manufacturing in general. The largest single application, however, is in fertilizer production, which takes two-fifths of total output. Sulfur is used both in the manufacture of superphosphates and ammonia sulfates. In addition, much of the chemical industry's use of sulfur goes eventually into agricultural applications, including insecticides and herbicides. Sulfur is widespread and abundant, being united in nature with many other elements (Fig. 3.27). Relatively pure elemental sulfur is also available in limited quantities and in specific places. Volcanic cones in Japan, Sicily, and the Chilean Andes provide a certain amount, but the largest sources are coastal salt dome deposits along the margins of the Gulf of Mexico. Native sulfur reserves cannot be expected to last for long, however, and increasing output is coming from fossil fuels, where it is obtained in the purification of oil and gas and collected from coal smoke. It also constitutes a byproduct from the processing of sulphide metallic ores. These and other similar occurrences assure an ample supply of sulfur, though possibly at rising costs.

Total reserves of all the principal fertilizer raw materials are thus very large. No world shortage is apparent for the foreseeable future despite increasingly heavy demands for agricultural, chemical, and general industrial applications. The resource problem resulting from consumption of these minerals concerns the drain that their use imposes indirectly on other re-

Fig. 3.27 *World production of mineral fertilizers. Three of the four principal fertilizer raw materials are mineral products; most of the fourth, nitrogen, is extracted from the atmosphere and combined with hydrogen to form ammonium nitrate. Much of the world's sulfur comes from native sulfur deposits but increasing amounts are extracted from pyrites.*

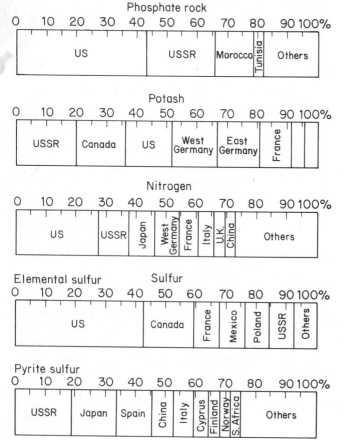

sources. Because the nations of the world are unequally endowed with fertilizer materials (except for atmospheric nitrogen), much long-range transporting of bulky commodities is required, thereby consuming much energy and other resources. Moreover, fertilizer production involves large inputs of capital and draws heavily upon fossil fuels, electric power, and other chemicals.

NONMETALLIC-MINERAL BUILDING MATERIALS. The rocks and earthen materials that are used for building purposes are so common that their true importance is often overlooked. In volume of output they lead all the minerals, and in value they are second only to the fossil fuels. Some of the building materials—such as sand and gravel, crushed stone, and dimension stone—are used directly with almost no further treatment after extraction. Others—including asbestos, clays, and the raw materials for glass and cement—receive considerable processing before final use.

Some of these commodities are among the most plentiful natural resources, and, with special exceptions, tend to be found in a great many places. As in the case of the fertilizer raw materials, therefore, the main long-run supply problem that the mineral building materials present is their effect on other resources. Their extraction is highly mechanized, using power machinery made of metals and burning fossil fuels. Most of the building materials are heavy and bulky, and their transportation makes further demands on the mechanical energy supply. Their processing, too, in some instances consumes large amounts of heat. Any projections of future use of these commodities must therefore take into account their substantial effects on the energy supply.

TECHNOLOGY AND THE NONRENEWABLE RESOURCES

Every mineral resource has its ultimate limit, yet the demand for minerals continues to grow relentlessly. In the past, the Americas, Africa, Asia, and Australia quickly yielded up fabulous finds of rich ores occurring in deposits at or near the surface. Today exploration must proceed more painstakingly in the search for hidden deposits. Final exhaustion of the nonrenewable resources would thus appear to be inevitable.

How, then, is the end likely to come? For a given mining operation the final day may appear very suddenly, but it is not likely that all mines will fail simultaneously. Rather, they will probably give out one by one and the total amount of the commodity appearing on the world market will gradually diminish. For this reason, noted earlier in the cases of silver and gold, it is probable that the indices of reserve life indicated in Table 3.2 will actually be exceeded as annual output falls and as the amount demanded is reduced by accelerating prices. Approaching exhaustion will be signaled well in advance as the growing shortage forces prices upward until they finally become prohibitive. We see this happening now in the case of mercury.

If eventual depletion of reserves is thus unavoidable, is there any way to postpone that final day? The optimists answer yes to this question and some confidently predict that technology may prevent that day from appearing at all. Those who place their trust in technology cite the impressive accomplishments of the past, when one spectacular breakthrough often followed close on the heels of another. Let us consider, therefore, some of the ways in which technology may come to our aid, either by stretching out the life of our resources or by conserving the existing supply.

techniques for maintaining reserve levels

Among the developments that are being depended upon to keep known reserves at satisfactory levels are new methods for discovering, mining, extracting, and refining minerals and for producing electricity. In the past this type of technological advance has had the effect of reducing costs (or at least preventing prices from rising unduly). It has also made feasible the exploitation of materials that had not previously been classified as resources because of their remoteness or poor quality.

energy supply

Advancing technology has improved the prospects for supplying more energy. Though fossil fuels should eventually become exhausted, there will probably be continuing supplies of energy from alternative sources, particularly breeder reactors and nuclear fusion. Indeed, we have been promised very large quantities of cheap electricity from these and other new sources. The prediction is being made that electricity may, in fact, become so plentiful that it will become feasible to use this to extract and process minerals from sources now considered unorthodox.

It is being suggested, for example, that with abundant electrical power it will be possible to process increasingly poorer ores until eventually useful minerals can be extracted directly from "country rock," the average rock of the earth's crust. Most geologists are not optimistic about this, however, because of the waste disposal problem this process would entail. In extracting one ton of metal from average granite it would be necessary to discard 2,000 tons of leftover rock.

The idea is also being advanced that vast quantities of metals could be extracted from sea water since oceans cover 71 percent of the earth's surface to an average depth of nearly 2.5 miles. This great volume of salt water contains much dissolved material—as much as 160 million tons of solids per cubic mile. Salt, magnesium, sulfur, calcium, and potassium constitute 99.5 percent of this. Other, more valuable, elements in a cubic mile of sea water include 47 tons of zinc, 14 tons of copper, 14 tons of tin, 1 ton of silver, and 40 pounds of gold. Sodium, chlorine, magnesium, and bromine are already being extracted electrolytically from the sea and the idea of removing some of the others is very tempting. Again, one of the problems that makes this a formidable undertaking is the disposal of enormous tonnages of waste materials. Even more serious is the fact that the valuable metals are contained in extremely dilute solutions and huge quantities of water would have to be treated. And the most serious problem of all is the amount of energy needed to do the job. Later we shall consider the environmental effects of such large-scale energy consumption.

better methods of discovering and treating ores

Fanciful as some of these ideas may appear, still other radical methods are being actively pursued with some success. One of these is the development of techniques for seeking out ores deep beneath the earth's surface; other methods are being devised for finding the most promising areas in which to concentrate exploration. On the other hand, many persons still insist that more resources are yet to be found both in areas that have already been explored and in some that have not yet been thoroughly surveyed. These individuals believe that better exploration techniques and an improved knowledge of regional geology will substantially expand reserves of many commodities.

techniques for conserving resources

Even the most optimistic of those experts putting their faith in technology, however, are coming to agree that we should take better care of the resources available now. There are a number of techniques that are being developed to accomplish this.

reduction of waste in extraction and processing

Surprisingly large quantities of valuable mineral materials are lost in the earlier stages of production. Underground mining is especially wasteful. Pillars left to support mine roofs are often rich in minerals but these have traditionally been left behind after the mine is abandoned. Many minerals are often overlooked, owing to ignorance of irregularities in the shape of the ore body; others are ignored because the ores are considered too lean for economical extraction. Although improved techniques may allow these residues to be of use later, reopening an abandoned flooded mine is usually difficult. Earlier methods of petroleum extraction invariably left a very large proportion of the oil underground. Today techniques are being developed for reducing this waste, and methods for reviving abandoned oilfields have proved especially effective.

Open-pit or strip-mining operations are ordinarily far more efficient in extracting most of the valuable mineral. The best example of this, perhaps, is the mining of porphyry copper ores, which results in virtually 100 percent recovery of the copper from ores averaging below 0.9 percent in the United States. In addition, valuable byproducts, such as gold and silver, are obtained.

more efficient use of metals

Several techniques can be applied to use resources more efficiently in manufacturing. The quantity of a metal that is required for a given application can often be reduced, for example, by producing the metal to closer tolerances or by adding alloys to increase its strength. Today a ton of steel gives about 43 percent more structural support than the same amount would have provided only ten years ago. Because of this, it is possible to make both structural members and sheets thinner than before. This is one reason why the United States produces relatively less tonnage of steel than does the Soviet Union, where steel products tend to be heavier than necessary in order to fulfill official quotas specified in terms of total weight.

Modern developments have also brought greater efficiencies in fuel use. Design improvements in internal combustion engines have made it possible for buses, trucks, locomotives, and ships to move greater ton-miles of payload per unit of fuel than a few years ago. Some of the greatest improvements have been in the efficiency with which coal is used to generate electricity. Much smaller quantities of coal are required to produce the same amount of electric energy and it is possible to burn cheaper grades.

In addition to these advances, there are others that are equally feasible but require a change in society's attitudes and goals. One way to husband large quantities of valuable resources would be to increase the durability of manufactured products. This is desirable not only for goods employing scarce materials but also those using abundant ones, since valuable energy resources are required for their manufacture in either case. Along with this might logically go a radical change in life style in ways that would deemphasize high per capita levels of resource use.

reclaiming and recycling discarded metals

The idea of reusing valuable metals and other materials has received much popular attention, some of it quite fervent; but the notion is by no means a new one. Today approximately 40 percent of the copper consumed each year has been reclaimed, as has a high proportion of the tin. An unusually large percentage of lead (44 percent in 1970) is also recycled, most of it coming from old automobile batteries. Far more reclamation of metals and other materials is desirable and possible, especially reusable materials from discarded automobiles and household wastes.

the use of substitutes

To an ever increasing extent the substitution of one material for another has been forced upon us by growing scarcities and rising costs of certain commodities.

More aluminum is replacing copper in electrical applications, and aluminum is beginning to substitute for tinplated steel in the container industries. Tinplated cans are also being replaced more and more by lacquered ones. Plastics are increasingly substituting for metals in a great many uses, from plumbing pipes to automobile fittings.

It must be accepted, of course, that these and other conservation techniques raise resource costs. Recycling of most materials is expensive, and so are improved product designs and more intensive mining methods. Often forgotten too is the fact that the recovery of metals is only partial after each cycle of use. Some metal is essentially lost altogether, and all of it is therefore due to be permanently consumed in the long run.

Although past achievements may seem to give grounds for continued faith in the ability of technology to bring salvation, previous experience is no longer a reliable guide to the future. With demand currently at the highest absolute levels in history, projected consumption rates are enormous. Consequently, many authorities now recognize that excessive optimism diverts attention from the real problem of ultimate exhaustion of our nonrenewable resources.

implications of resource exhaustion

What will the final depletion of our natural resources mean to us as individuals and citizens? Ultimately it will touch each one of us, but in the near term persons living in technically alvanced lands will be affected differently from citizens of less developed countries.

technically advanced countries

The real problem of resource use today arises from the high consumption rates in the developed countries. Per capita resource use in the less developed areas is generally very low. High levels of consumption affect advanced countries in several important ways. They show up first in the intensive exploitation of domestic reserves, such as the Lake Superior iron ores, followed in time by depletion, or the threat of it. Even prior to exhaustion, consumption may greatly exceed the resource endowment and the country will begin to rely more and more on imports. The United States used to be a net exporter of minerals, but since World War II it has been a net importer. By 1970 the country was importing five-sixths of her nickel, three-fourths of her bauxite, nearly half of her zinc, more than a third of her iron ore, and almost all of her tin and manganese. When current plans are implemented, moreover, American imports of oil and natural gas will rise sharply. As total world reserves of a particular resource diminish, however, those countries still possessing reserves may be unwilling to export to deficit countries. Many of the mineral-rich nations are in early phases of development and may prefer to retain their raw materials for use in domestic industries.

less developed countries

Known world reserves of even the most abundant mineral resources are grossly insufficient for global consumption patterns that reach the per capita rate now prevailing in the United States. Burdened by their huge populations, the less developed countries as a group can never expect to attain the current rate of United States consumption. It thus follows that the possibilities for industrialization of most underdeveloped nations are dim. Already some voices in the less developed world are expressing concern that the technologically advanced lands are using up their heritage, and they wonder what resources will be left when the time comes for them to need them.

Contrary to common belief, growth actually tends to reduce equality. The gap between the rich and the poor widens and high rates of population growth serve to exacerbate this difference. With increasing numbers and rising consumption, distribution may become less equitable; those who have anything of value hang onto it. Therefore, since dwindling resources affect everyone ultimately, the need for a careful appraisal of resource availability is gaining wider acceptance. Since we must all eventually revert to lower levels of resource use, now is the best time to begin the change.

ENVIRONMENTAL QUALITY

Up until now our attention has been directed toward the quantitative results of man's increasingly intensive exploitation of his physical environment. The most pressing question has been whether there will be sufficient resources to support larger numbers of people at ever higher levels of per capita consumption. Now we consider the qualitative aspects: How have rising levels of human activity affected the world as a place in which to live?

the physical environment

Pollution is a problem that has many facets. At the least, it concerns aesthetics; at the most, it concerns a threat to the ecosystem involving the survival of human life itself. Pollution entails wasting important resources, including contamination of air and water. Thus, the compounds of mercury and lead entering the atmosphere and water supplies are serious pollutants, but they also represent the loss of critically scarce metals. Moreover, just as resource use is growing even more rapidly than the population, so also is pollution rising at ever increasing rates. This is merely evidence of the degree to which pollution is related to levels of agricultural activity and industrialization.

The impact of pollution tends to be delayed so that there is grave danger of exceeding the limits of safety before we are aware of the problem. Many long-lived toxic substances travel great distances and accumulate in unforeseen places. Besides the problems of mercury and lead poisoning, chemicals such as DDT pose serious threats. DDT evaporates and is carried long distances in the air, precipitating out of the atmosphere, entering the food chain, and persisting in the tissues of living organisms. At least two decades may be required for it to lose its potency.

contamination of the atmosphere

Air pollution occurs when waste gases and solid particles enter the atmosphere and spread. In the form of smog (smoke plus fog) it hangs visibly over large industrial cities, so thick at times that it shuts out much of the sunlight. It assails the other senses too, irritating the eyes and lungs and issuing repulsive odors. Some other common forms of air pollution are corrosive of paint, steel, rubber, nylon stockings, and statuary.

To a major extent, air pollution is a product of the consumption of energy, especially the combustion of fossil fuels, as well as many industrial processes. Among the greatest offenders are the internal combustion engines that power passenger cars, buses, trucks, and aircraft, which emit vast quantities of noxious gases: carbon dioxide, carbon monoxide, sulfur oxides, nitrogen oxides, particulate matter (soot), and tetraethyl lead. The most serious industrial offenders are pulp and paper mills, iron and steel mills, petroleum refineries, smelters, and chemical plants, which contribute enormous tonnages of carbon monoxide, sulfur dioxide, nitrogen oxide, and fly ash to the atmosphere.

The cleanest form of energy, electricity, causes some of the worst pollution. Thermal generating plants contribute one-fifth of all the particulates and nitrogen oxides and half the sulfur oxides sent aloft from the United States annually. Nuclear power plants, which are to contribute half the world's power by the year 2000, avoid most of the pollution problems of conventional power plants but add new ones of their own.

One further source of atmospheric pollution is space heating. The use of fossil fuels to heat homes, offices, and factories adds much to the total load. The burning of trash by householders and also by municipalities, commercial junk dealers, and others is still another source.

Each of the principal contaminants of the atmosphere is capable of becoming extremely hazardous to human beings. These toxic substances in the atmosphere tend to be slow-acting with people of normal health, but they may affect the very old, very young, or those with respiratory ailments with tragic suddenness.

Evidence is also mounting that atmospheric pollutants may affect our weather and perhaps alter our climatic patterns. Since all energy is ultimately dissipated as heat, the cumulative effect of energy consumption on a large scale is to warm the atmosphere. It has been estimated that by the year 2000 the amount of heat released by human activities may be equal to 18 percent of incoming solar energy. This may eventually impose a limit to the amount of mechanical energy that can safely be used.

water problems

Probably the most valuable resource of all is water. The total amount on the earth's surface, below it, or above it, is vast; but 99.35 percent of this is in the oceans or locked in the polar ice caps and thus not directly accessible for human consumption. The remaining 0.65 percent is all that we have to use (except for navigation); this occurs as ground water or is in lakes or streams. When viewed on a global scale, water is a renewable resource; at the local level it can be a vanishing resource.

During its stay on earth, water is often used and reused many times for municipal purposes, industrial cooling, process water, or irrigation. Almost every time that water is used contaminants are added to it. Flowing water has natural recuperative powers, but these can easily be exceeded under intensive use. It must usually then be treated before reuse, but much of the water containing municipal and industrial wastes is incompletely treated, and some is dumped into streams with no treatment at all.

the cost of growth

The accelerating pace of modern living has thus brought with it a multitude of problems, whose dimensions we are only now beginning to comprehend. Increasing numbers of people and rising volumes of industrial production have resulted in contamination of the atmosphere, pollution of water, disfiguration of the landscape, and deterioration of human relationships is an environment that is being used with ever greater intensity. These are the complications that have accompanied our efforts to attain successively higher levels of material well-being in terms of more and better transportation, housing, appliances, clothing, recreation, medical care, and other specialized services of a proliferating variety—in other words, all that is contained in that familiar measure called the Gross National Product, or GNP. More formally defined, GNP represents a country's total annual output of goods and services.

Today some people are saying that the GNP has been misleading us, that it does not take into account hidden costs exacted by problems of the kinds just described. Such costs, it is said, actually reduce the total benefits gained from rising output. As a more realistic index of how well off a population may be, economists Nordhaus and Tobin have proposed a Measure of Economic Welfare, MEW. This is derived by adjusting the GNP to allow for the costs to a society resulting from environmental deterioration and the problems of contemporary urban life. More euphoniously, and perhaps more accurately, Samuelson has relabeled this measure Net Economic Welfare, or NEW.

Figure 3.28 illustrates the relationship between GNP and NEW as this has evolved during the past four decades. Note how steeply per capita GNP has climbed

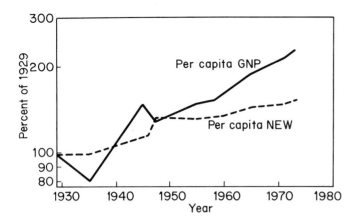

Fig. 3.28 *Differential growth of net economic welfare and gross national product. Note that as per capita GNP dropped during the Great Depression, net economic welfare (NEW) remained little changed. When war production brought a sharp rise in GNP during the 1940s, NEW lagged behind until the period of postwar readjustment. Since that time GNP has continued to rise more rapidly than NEW. (Drafted from trends suggested by Paul Samuelson.)*

since World War II. Meanwhile NEW has risen much more slowly, owing to the cumulative effects of modern urban problems. Because the two curves are rising at different rates, the gap between them is widening. If effective steps should be taken to solve the problems of growth, NEW would begin to rise more steeply; however, the costs of such remedial measures—for example, sewage treatment plants and devices for precipitating pollutants in factory stack gases—would reduce the slope of the GNP curve. In this way the gap between the two would begin to close and GNP would thereby gain increased reliability as a measure of a society's wellbeing.

PROJECTION FOR DISASTER?

Our assessment of the problems of supporting an increasing population at higher levels of material comfort, while attempting to minimize the distorting effects of growth, has further reinforced our impressions of a world system that is intricately interrelated. We have seen that an increase in population requires larger supplies of food, clothing, shelter, transport facilities, services, and an ever expanding array of other needs. Satisfying these enlarged demands in turn calls for heavier investments of capital. Greater allocations must be made for the production of fertilizer, farm machinery, and chemicals; for the construction of irrigation works and farm-to-market roads; for building textile and clothing factories; for constructing dwellings and so forth. But these uses of capital make rising demands upon nonrenewable resources: fertilizer and chemical raw materials and other metallic and nonmetallic minerals, as well as fuels.

Some of these resources, we have learned, are plentiful; but a great many others are not. Yet exploitation and use of even the abundant resources makes demands on other resources more limited in supply. Iron, for example, is plentiful, but steel production requires carbon and heat, provided by fossil fuels, together with a wide variety of scarce alloying metals. The raw materials of cement are abundant, but their manufacture consumes much heat. The ultimate solution to the energy problem appears to be electricity obtained from unconventional sources, but scarce nonferrous metals are needed to transmit and use this electricity.

Moreover, the consumption and final discarding of resources results in pollution, which adversely affects both population and production. Not only does pollution present severe health hazards but it imposes a mounting cost burden on the economic system. Its ultimate effects we cannot anticipate with accuracy because of the time lag in its impact. Yet it is most certainly a grave problem that cannot be avoided, because both the United States and world populations are now too large to survive without intensive and mechanized agriculture, industry, and an integrated transport system. It is no longer possible to retreat entirely to a simpler era. There are too many of us.

All projections thus point to continued growth in population, investment, resource use, and pollution, at least in the near term. Yet, considering the ultimate limits to the total supply of food and resources and to the amount of contamination the environment can absorb, where will these projections of growth take us? How long can the world system continue to expand without tempting disaster?

One attempt to find answers for these questions was presented in the Club of Rome report, *The Limits to Growth* (1972). In this study an elaborate mathematical model of economic growth was developed, employing a large number of variables representing capital investment, population numbers, population birth and death rates, per capita food production, per capita industrial output, nonrenewable resources, and pollution. As in Malthus's work, two kinds of curves resulted. Those representing population, industrial output, and pollution rose exponentially, that is, at an increasing rate, until they encountered those curves representing a fixed supply of nonrenewable resources and worsening pollution. The suggested solution for this problem was to halt population growth and economic growth, to recycle physical resources, and to emphasize food production.

Before we can reasonably assess the validity of the Club of Rome's diagnosis and prescribed solution, we must examine more closely a variety of important facets of the world economic system as it is structured and functions. These will be the subjects of the next several chapters, and the information presented there should enable us to think more analytically about the issues of growth and change when we return to them at the conclusion of the book.

RECOMMENDED READINGS

Ehrlich, Paul R., and Anne H., *Population, Resources, Environment: Issues in Human Ecology*. San Francisco: W. H. Freeman, 1970.

Meadows, Donella, Dennis L. Meadows, Jørgen Randers, and William W. Behrens III, *The Limits to Growth*. New York: Universe Books, 1972.

National Research Council of the National Academy of Sciences, *Resources and Man*. San Francisco: W. H. Freeman, 1969.

Netschert, Bruce C., and Hans H. Landsberg, *The Future Supply of the Major Metals*. Washington: Resources for the Future, 1961.

Skinner, Brian J., *Earth Resources*. Englewood Cliffs, N.J.: Prentice-Hall, 1969.

economic
fundamentals
two

The issue to which we turn first is in many ways the most fundamental raised in Chapter 3, that of the mechanisms by which limited supplies of resources and products are shared among the growing demands of an escalating world population. In smaller-scale pre-industrial societies, sharing was most often based upon social rules, traditional rights, and customary obligations. In more complex modern economies, regulation of exchange is achieved by means of prices.

In this chapter we look at both the traditional types of exchange in what some anthropologists have called the world's "little" or "folk" societies, and at the geography of prices in larger-scale, more highly specialized economies. It will be found that just as several different means of noneconomic exchange (householding, redistribution, and reciprocity) have been observed in simpler societies, the geography of price assumes different forms in the several types of modern political economy listed in Chapter 1.

We will therefore discuss not only how prices are determined and why they vary geographically in free-enterprise economies, but also what happens to pricing when free enterprise is absent.

HOUSEHOLDING, REDISTRIBUTION, AND RECIPROCITY IN SMALLER-SCALE SOCIETIES

Recall the discussion in Chapter 1, where it was pointed out that people have a variety of wants in any society—for food, clothing, shelter, prestige, and social standing. As producers they work to satisfy these wants. Economic systems develop out of the need for some form of organization to ensure that demands are met by production of the proper kinds and quantities of supplies.

a simple case

Consider Robinson Crusoe before his man Friday happened along. Responsible for satisfying all his own demands, he decided what he wanted, had to *extract* his raw materials and crops, *transport* them to his workshops, *process* them to create desired products, *store* the products at some convenient place until the need for them arose, and finally *distribute* them in proper proportions to the spots where they would finally be consumed. His *productive process* (comprising the stages of extraction, processing, and distribution, and the attendant operations of transportation and storage) thus led to final satisfaction of his needs in *consumption*.

Crusoe was a complete *economic system* unto himself, for he originated the *demands*, created the *supplies*, and so organized his work that his demands and supplies were maintained in overall equilibrium, consistent with his needs and capabilities and the resources available to him.

Both historically and presently—especially in the less "westernized" parts of the world today—examples may be found of small groups of people subsisting in communities with simple, self-sustaining "Crusoe-like"

price and other mechanisms for regulating exchange

4

economies in which the proper quantities and varieties of products are distributed among the members without the need for markets, money, or prices. In many of these communities, a primitive form of affluence also may be seen: many hunters and gatherers, for example, satisfy their needs with only a two- to four-hour workday. To the extent that there is production above subsistence levels, kinship structures and the institution of chieftancy organize the production, effort, output, and distribution of surplus goods.

Thus, in Crusoe's case, the decision as to how much to produce and how to distribute the output was *individual.* In Crusoe-like economies the decision is *social;* the rules, obligations, traditions, and group decisions of the community determine who shall produce what and how it will be distributed. Three such patterns of social control have been identified: householding, redistribution, and reciprocity.

householding

Householding is a literal translation of the Greek word *oeconomia,* the etymon for our word *economy.* A more appropriate rendering of the meaning is "production for one's own use," or, as the economic historian Karl Polanyi has expressed it in his book *The Great Transformation,*

Whether the different entities of the family or settlement or the manor form the self-sufficient unit, the principle is invariably the same: that of producing and storing for the satisfaction of the wants of the members of the group . . . Production for use as against production for gain is the essence of householding.

The householding unit is a self-sustaining entity. The medieval manor, the Roman *familia,* and the south Slav *zadruga* are all comparable examples of such householding economic systems. Large numbers of these independent economic units were the basis of feudal society in Europe.

In its pattern and organization, the householding unit is closest to the Robinson Crusoe example of a complete economic system. Instead of the single consumer, there are several members of several households; instead of the single producer there are several, with traditional division of labor based upon age, sex, social standing, and community traditions. Under most conditions, the householding unit obeyed what anthropologists call Chayanov's rule. This rule states that "the greater the relative working capacity of the household, the less its members work," and is intended to indicate that householding production it designed to meet the household's needs, and nothing more. Only to the extent that kinship or political organization demanded more than subsistence production was Chayanov's rule overridden.

Thus, the medieval manor comprised a series of families who worked cooperatively in cultivating their communal fields, woods, pastures, and ponds. Each family had an established right to the output from certain strips of land, to pasture a certain number of animals, or to use a certain amount of wood, but also had the responsibility to produce a surplus for the feudal lord. Equity was maintained by these rights. Local demands and supplies were kept in balance.

redistribution

There are certain societies in which equity is maintained through the institution of a strong central authority, whose function is redistributive. Goods are, upon production, delivered to this head man or chief, then parceled out by him to members of the social group in ways determined by custom. Many of the ancient empires, such as the New Kingdom of Egypt, were founded upon this principle of redistribution. It is also common among many of the cattle-raising tribes of East Africa. One interesting manifestation was found in the *potlatch* of the Kwakiutl of the Pacific Northwest, in which the chief assembled the wealth of the tribe and redistributed it by giving to others in elaborate ceremonies, with the ultimate objective of making the receiver the social debtor, and ultimately the retainer.

reciprocity

A third pattern of economic organization is reciprocity in the assurance of needed exchange. An example will illustrate. In the Trobriand Islands of western Melanesia, inland communities are paired with coastal villages in a pattern of exchange of inland breadfruits for coastal fish. The pairing extends to particular individuals being responsible for the direct exchange, in symmetrical arrangements of remarkable regularity and persistence. Many such exchanges are often disguised in the form of reciprocal gift-giving, but the principle is no less effective.

Karl Polanyi, whose impressive and massive work of synthesis is responsible for current understanding of the subordination of primitive economic life to social rules and traditions, did the pioneering work to increase our knowledge of these small-scale self-sustaining space-economies. He argued that all economic systems known up to end of feudalism in Western Europe were organized either on the principles of reciprocity, redistribution, or householding, or on some combination of the three. The orderly production and distribution of goods were secured through a great variety of individual motives disciplined by traditional principles of behavior. Gain was not prominent among these motives. Custom and law, magic and religion, cooperated in inducing the individual to comply with the rules of behavior which, eventually, ensured his functioning in the socioeconomic system. Furthermore, Polanyi argued, as long as social organization ran in ruts of tradition, no individual economic motives needed to come into play; no shirking of personal effort need to be feared; division of labor was automatically ensured; economic obligations were duly discharged; and material means for an excellent display of abundance at all public festivals were ensured. Such are the basic considerations guiding the simplest forms of exchange, not simply in feudal Europe, but in all societies in which the marketplace is absent.

BARTERING AND PRIMITIVE HIGGLING IN PEASANT SOCIETIES

The gradual emergence of both local and long-distance trade between social groups was responsible for the gradual transition of many self-sustaining groups into peasant societies, and in turn, the transformation of peasant societies into fully-fledged exchange economies. A *peasant society* is one in which the household or local social group remains relatively self-sustaining with respect to necessities such as food and shelter, but trades a surplus or a specialty product for outside manufactured goods or luxuries. A full *exchange economy* is one in which the principles of the division of labor apply to every producer, and very few producers, even farmers, consume even a small part of their own output.

Perhaps the earliest long-distance trade was exploration beyond the limits of the local area. Such exploration might involve warlike forays or irregular trading, often associated with the god-king, who maintained social controls, and the temple, the early focus of society. So long as the resulting exchange of goods was sporadic, market centers did not develop. Only when regular trade connections emerged was there justification for the establishment of permanent market places.

One regular form of long-distance exchange was between complementary production zones, for example, between plains dwellers and hill folk, each trading surpluses of their own specialty for those of the other. Market sites would often develop along the territorial boundary zone. At the appropriate season, often in conjunction with religious festivities, people from surrounding areas would converge upon the market sites to barter surpluses. Where relations between the different groups were strained, such an occasion would be a time of truce, and the market site would be neutral ground.

Local trade emerged on the basis of regular intercourse among peasants, local craftsmen and specialists, and town merchants and middlemen. Local surpluses would be traded for necessities, such as salt, iron, or durables, and merchants would have available some luxuries and trinkets obtained from the great fairs. To accommodate the cycle of agricultural labor, markets would be held periodically. Links connecting long-distance trade, the great fairs, and local periodic markets were provided by the town merchants, who transported the goods by traveling from one site to the other.

It was only with the emergence of local and long-distance trade that market sites and trading posts became widespread in peasant societies. For example, in Yorubaland in West Africa, the earliest markets were located along the contact zone between forest and savanna, along coastal lagoons and creeks, or at the boundaries between different peoples. The larger markets were along the chief trade routes, and changed in importance with these routes. One important origin of Yoruba markets was the resting place where local populations provided services to passing traders. If such resting places became popular, a market into which farmers brought their wares sprang up, and periodic market days developed. Extra large meetings would be held less frequently, when large numbers of traders converged.

Initially, *bartering* was the dominant means of exchange at these meeting places. But gradually, some form of *money* took over as the medium of exchange, and goods began to move at prices determined by *higgling*, face-to-face bargaining between buyer and seller with both trying to maximize their advantage, ultimately agreeing on payment. Under such conditions, prices are highly variable and flexible from time to time and place to place. The only general statement that can be made about price levels is that they ultimately lead to a balance or agreement between buyer and seller that transfers a commodity or a service from one to the other.

THE GEOGRAPHY OF PRICE IN FREE-ENTERPRISE SYSTEMS

Now consider the problem in a much larger-scale free-enterprise economy in which there are many buyers and sellers who cannot meet face-to-face to bargain, yet for whom some type of balance ultimately must be achieved. It is in this case that the classic economic theory of price applies.

According to this theory, price is the rate at which a good, service, resource, or factor of production can be exchanged for any other good, service, resource, or factor of production in a manner that clears the market and equates demands with supplies. Goods have prices because they are useful and scarce in relation to the uses people want to put them. When something has no use, it does not command a price; when it is useful but available to all in unlimited amounts, like air, it cannot command a price.

Whether or not a thing is useful is determined by the demands expressed by consumers; scarcity is determined by the capacities and willingness of producers to generate the supplies needed. Price, then, is determined by the demands and supplies of many consumers and producers jointly interacting in a market where goods and services are exchanged.

The most fundamental characteristic of such free enterprise markets is that the individual buyer or seller is a "price taker," because he has no control over the price he must pay or can receive. The prices are determined competitively in the market, and the actions of any particular individual cannot change them. Indeed, very elaborate legal safeguards have been developed in free enterprise societies to preserve this situation as the way of conducting business. Competitive markets work best in agriculture, the precious and nonferrous metals industries, the stock exchanges, and the markets for land, homes, and other kinds of property.

demand, supply, and price

Several elementary concepts should be remembered about the relations of demand, supply, and price in competitive markets. As the price of a product falls, more of it will be bought. This is because some people who could not buy at the higher price will begin to make purchases, and because all buyers can increase their purchases of the cheaper commodity at the expense of alternative goods that have become relatively more costly. Similarly, the theory of supply postulates that the higher the price, the more of a good will be offered for sale because sellers are eager to sell while conditions are good. If prices fall, supplies will be withheld in the hope that prices will rise again. These relationships can be diagrammed, as in Figure 4.1

A demand schedule shows the functional relationship between price and amount demanded. A supply schedule shows the relationship between price and amount offered. The two schedules cross at a point of *market equilibrium* at which buyers and sellers, by matching purchases and sales of the good in question at price *P,* are able to clear the market of the available

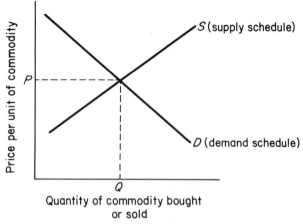

Fig. 4.1 *Demand, supply, and price relationships*

supply. In such a situation total demand equals total supply and is $P \times Q$, the price per unit multiplied by the number of units consumed.

Economists call this a *partial equilibrium market solution* to the problem of demand, supply, and price

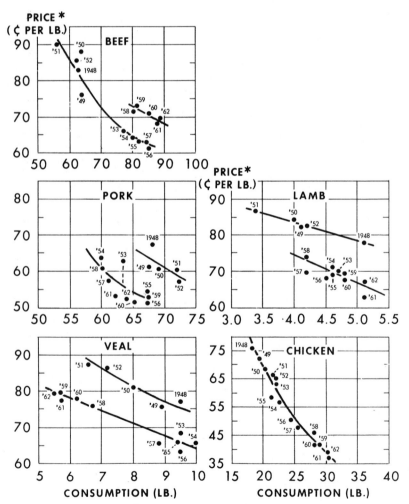

* DEFLATED BY CONSUMER PRICE INDEX.

Fig. 4.2 *Estimated demand curves relating per capita consumption and deflated retail prices for meats, 1948–1962*

The simplest case is that of chicken, where all the data for the entire period line up closely around a smooth line. Each dot is a yearly average price, found where a supply curve intersected the demand curve in that year. There was a fairly regular drop in price throughout the period and a corresponding regular increase in consumption. This involved yearly changes in supplies so that successive supply curves moved along a single demand curve. This demand curve is therefore approximated by the line fitted through the scatter of points. The individual yearly supply curves are not shown. In the other cases, two demand curves have been drawn. For example, the data for beef in the period 1948–1957 line up closely around one smooth line. The corresponding data for the period 1958–1962 line up closely around a higher line. This indicates that the demand curve for beef shifted upward in the latter part of the period. In the period 1958–1962, consumers paid higher deflated prices than they paid earlier for the same per capita quantities. Similar analyses indicate downward shifts in the demand for pork, lamb, and veal. These shifts came earlier than the shift in the demand for beef. Comparison of the different sections of the figure suggests that these shifts in demand for individual meats may have been due in part to shifts in supplies of competing meats. This is particularly true for beef and pork. The upward shift in demand for beef came several years after a 1953–1954 reduction in pork marketings. The drop in the demand for pork occurred simultaneously with the increase in per capita supplies of beef, as indicated by the great distance between the points for 1952 and 1953 in the beef graph. In other words, prices of the various meats were jointly determined.

Source: U. S. Department of Agriculture, Economic Research Service, Neg. ERS 2147-63(7).

because the market is only cleared for one particular commodity. General equilibrium analysis concerns the simultaneous relationships between demands, supplies, and prices of the many goods and services bought and sold within an economic system.

To illustrate this problem of simultaneity, Figure 4.2 shows the results of the U.S. Department of Agriculture's attempts to estimate demand relationships for a variety of meats in the United States, 1948–62. As the caption indicates, price shifts for beef, pork, lamb, and veal were interdependent because demand for any one of the meats responded to relative supply changes and price shifts for the others.

To make any discussion of demand, supply, and price meaningful in economic geography we cannot work with national average annual prices in the manner of Figure 4.2 however. It is first necessary to recognize that there are many kinds of prices, and that any of these prices may vary according to a variety of factors, most notably: (1) grade or quality of product; (2) season-

ality; and (3) location. We will illustrate the first two of these cases briefly, and devote the major part of this section to the principles determining geographic variations in agricultural prices.

seasonal movements of prices

Table 4.1 shows how the prices of Washington State red delicious apples varied seasonally in 1966–67 in several cities. Note how prices fell as supplies were released on the market during the Christmas season, and how they reached their highest levels in autumn just before the new harvest. Note also how the retail values increased with increasing distance from Seattle, and also the size of the price spreads or markups among the shipping point in Washington State, the wholesalers' or terminal market auction prices paid by retailers at the destinations, and the retail values received by consumers. The price variations and price spreads just referred to are defined explicitly in the notes accompanying Table

Table 4.1   Price per Carton, Washington Red Delicious Apples 1966–1967: Chicago, New York, Los Angeles, and Seattle

	Oct.	Nov.	Dec.	Jan.	Feb.	Mar.	Apr.
			(In dollars)				
Shipping point price, f.o.b.[1]	$ 5.00	$ 4.25	$ 4.25	$ 4.38	$ 4.35	$ 4.38	$ 4.60
Wholesale (W)[2] or auction (A)[3] prices							
Seattle (W)	6.45	5.50	5.50	5.00	5.15	6.00	5.50
Los Angeles (W)	6.25	5.25	5.38	5.75	5.38	5.63	5.65
Chicago (A)	6.34	5.74	5.15	5.98	5.17	5.11	4.85
New York (A)	6.89	6.60	7.40	6.70	8.33	7.53	6.68
Retail value[4]							
Seattle	8.79	7.90	7.86	7.90	8.23	8.59	9.07
Los Angeles	9.88	9.64	9.68	9.92	10.08	9.72	10.20
Chicago	9.96	9.07	8.87	9.72	9.00	9.44	9.75
New York	11.73	10.32	10.24	10.48	10.56	10.41	10.96

The prices reported in this table are defined by the USDA as follows:

[1] *Shipping point price (f.o.b.)* The simple average of the midpoint range of daily prices for a specified container of commodity of specified grade and size received by a broad sample of shippers in representative shipping districts during a specified week. The shipping point price is equivalent to the grower and packer return, the amount received by the grower and packer for a specified container of commodity of specified grade and size. F.o.b. means free-on-board, and signifies that the price excludes transport charges.

[2] *Wholesale price* The estimate of the average price received for a specified container of commodity of specified grade and size sold in less than carload lots by a broad sample of first wholesale handlers in a given market.

[3] *Auction price* An average price for a specified container of a commodity of specified grade and size sold through a terminal market auction.

[4] *Retail price* The estimate of the average price per pound paid for a commodity of specified grade and size by customers in a sample of retail stores in a given city.

Retail value The dollar value of a specified container of a commodity of specified grade and size sold at retail after allowing for waste and loss incurred in the marketing process. The retail value equals the retail price per pound times the net weight of the container less the allowance for waste and loss.

In addition, there are two important types of price-spreads or markups:

Shipping point–wholesale spread The wholesale or auction price of a specified container of a commodity less its shipping point price. This spread is the amount received by the transportation agency and the primary wholesaler or auction company.

Wholesale-retail spread The retail value of a specified container of a commodity less its wholesale or auction price. This spread is the amount received by those who perform the functions of retailing, intracity transportation, and secondary wholesaling.

Source: Prices and Spreads for Apples, Grapefruit, Grapes, Lemons, and Oranges Sold Fresh in Selected Markets, 1962/63–1966/67, USDA Economic Research Service, Marketing Research Report 888 (Washington, D.C.: USDA, 1968).

4.1 and will be of major concern after the question of price variability due to grade of product has been considered.

grading systems and qualitative price differences

Table 4.2 shows the current grading system for eggs in the United States, to illustrate how complex matters of grade are. Most trading in eggs is conducted on the basis of these uniform wholesale grade and size designations.

If consumers were indifferent to the quality and size of the eggs they purchased, prices for different grades and sizes would tend to be equal. Consumers, however, prefer high quality eggs and are willing to pay a price differential for quality. Storers also prefer high quality eggs because they keep fresh longer. Therefore, higher prices are received for better quality and larger eggs, but the price relationships among different classifications of eggs change throughout the course of a year due to seasonally varying supplies of the different qualities and sizes.

Seasonal variation in the production of high quality eggs arises because hot weather adversely affects the laying hens. In addition, hot weather contributes to a more rapid deterioration of egg quality while eggs are in marketing channels. The seasonal variation in egg size is associated with the age of a layer; pullets first coming into production lay smaller eggs than they do after they have laid several months. Consequently, greater quantities of large eggs are available in the spring, while greater quantities of medium and small eggs are available in the fall, and relative prices for the different grades move accordingly. Grade differences and seasonal changes are fundamental features of commodity pricing.

spatial variations in prices due to transport costs

Substantial shipping point-wholesale price spreads for apples were noted in Table 4.1. Table 4.3 shows the importance of transport costs in determining such spreads, using Idaho potatoes as an example. When variations in wholesale prices are so closely related to transport charges, distinctive spatial patterns result.

A dramatic example is that of the wholesale prices paid by fluid milk dealers in the United States. In 1958–59, the principal area of low milk prices was the dairy belt of the north-central region shown in Figure 4.3. There farmers received under $4.00 per 100 pounds of milk with 3.5 percent butterfat content, in contrast to prices on the Atlantic and Gulf coasts that exceeded $6.00 per 100 pounds, as Figure 4.4 reveals. The average relationship of price to distance was such that dealers' buying prices per 100 pounds of fluid milk increased at an average of 2.18 cents per 10 miles increase in distance from the center of gravity of American dairying,

located in Eau Claire, Wisconsin. This relationship of price to distance is graphed in Figure 4.5.

Many similar examples in which prices increase with distance from a principal source of supply can be found, and from what we have learned already, we should expect quantity demanded to drop in more distant areas as price increases. When this happens, a price "funnel" increasing with distance from the center of supply will be accompanied by a demand "cone" decreasing with distance, as shown in Figure 4.6. It is from knowledge of demand cones that it becomes possible to define and measure market and supply areas.

definition of supply areas and market areas

Let us assume that there is a market which receives output from a variety of producers in the surrounding territory, and then sells the output to surrounding consumers. What will be the supply and market areas of the market? The following definitions apply:

1. The *supply area* of any central market includes all potential suppliers for whom market price less transport cost will still be sufficiently high for them to be willing to sell some quantity in the central market.
   a. The *primary supply area* is that part of the total supply area in which the share of the market obtained by the central market is greater than the market penetration of any competing center.
2. The *market area* of any central point of exchange includes all potential customers for whom market price plus transport cost will still be sufficiently low for them to be willing to make purchases at that price in the center.
   a. The *primary market area* is that part of the total market area which purchases more from the central point in question than from any other center.

Maps of supply and market areas will appear later in this book, and so it is well to keep in mind their relationship to spatial variations in prices due to transport costs.

base-price quotation in central markets

Not all prices vary outward from shipping points located at the center of gravity of production at rates determined by transport costs. For many agricultural commodities and industrial raw materials, a base price is determined in one or more central markets, usually located in major cities. The agriculturalist receives the central market price *less* transport and other handling charges *to* the market. The purchaser pays the central market price *plus* transport costs and related charges *from* the central market. We just noted how distinctive supply and market areas result under such conditions.

This kind of central market determination of local price levels is a creation of the last two centuries. For

Table 4.2 U.S. Wholesale Grades and Weight Classes of Eggs

WHOLESALE GRADE DESIGNATION	MINIMUM PERCENTAGE OF EGGS OF SPECIFIC QUALITIES REQUIRED[1]				MAXIMUM TOLERANCE PERMITTED (LOT AVERAGE)				
	AA quality	A quality or better	B quality or better	C quality or better	B quality, C quality, dirties, and checks	C quality, dirties, and checks	Dirties and checks	Checks	Loss
					Percent	Percent	Percent	Percent	Percent
U.S. specials—percent AA quality[2]	20	Balance	None permitted except for tolerances	None permitted except for tolerances	7.5				2
U.S. extras—percent A quality[2]		20	Balance			11.7			3
U.S. standards—percent B quality[2]			20	Balance			11.7		4
U.S. trades—percent C quality[2]				83.3			11.7		5
U.S. dirties—percent								11.7	5
U.S. checks—percent									5

WEIGHT CLASS	PER 30 DOZEN EGGS		WEIGHTS FOR INDIVIDUAL EGGS AT RATE PER DOZEN	
	Average net weight on a lot basis[3] At least—	Minimum net weight individual case basis[4]	Minimum weight	Weight variation tolerance for not more than 10 percent, by count, of individual eggs
Extra large	50½ pounds	50 pounds	26 ounces	Under 26 but not under 24 ounces
Large	45 pounds	44 pounds	23 ounces	Under 23 but not under 21 ounces
Medium	39½ pounds	39 pounds	20 ounces	Under 20 but not under 18 ounces
Small	34 pounds	None	None	None

[1]Substitution of eggs possessing higher qualities for those possessing lower specified qualities is permitted.

[2]The actual total percentage must be stated in the grade name.

[3]Lot means any quantity of 30 dozen or more eggs.

[4]Case means standard 30 dozen egg case as used in commercial practice in the United States.

Source: U.S. Department of Agriculture, *The Demand, Supply and Price Structure for Eggs*. (Washington, D.C.: USDA, Agriculture Marketing Service, Technical Bulletin, No. 1204, 1959.)

Table 4.3 Shipping Point—Wholesale Spreads for Idaho Potatoes, Average 1933–1948, Related to Transportation Charges Per Cwt.

SEASON AVERAGE AND MARKET	SPREAD BETWEEN SHIPPING POINT & WHOLESALE PRICE	TRANSPORTATION CHARGE	DIFFERENTIAL
Average 1933–1941			
New York City	$1.20	$1.10	$ .10
Chicago	.80	.78	.02
Los Angeles	.50	.52	−.02*
Average 1942–1948			
New York	1.60	1.26	.34
Chicago	1.03	.89	.14
Los Angeles	.54	.53	.01

*Negative figure due to slight incomparability of date.

Source: *Effects of Increases in Freight Rates on Agricultural Products*, USDA Circular 847 (Washington, D.C.: USDA, 1950).

example, until the 1850s, agriculture in the United States was characterized by small production units. Transportation, communication, and marketing were largely local, and trading was usually a face-to-face matter between producer and consumer in a weekly market. In the last half of the century, however, many changes took place which led to the development of a nationwide commercial marketing system. Cities grew rapidly, western lands were brought into production, railroad mileage expanded quickly, and communications improved. These developments facilitated the long-distance flow of commodities to food-deficit areas.

Trading progressed to formal clubs organized to provide a common meeting place for traders. It was a logical next step for commodity exchanges to emerge and provide organized trading. Commodity exchanges are nonprofit associations of persons acting as principals or agents in the transfer of ownership of agricultural commodities. *Futures* markets are the major part of most exchange operations, involving speculative dealing in future demands, supplies, and prices. *Cash* or *spot* markets where available commodities are sold and delivered within a few hours are also part of the commodity exchange function.

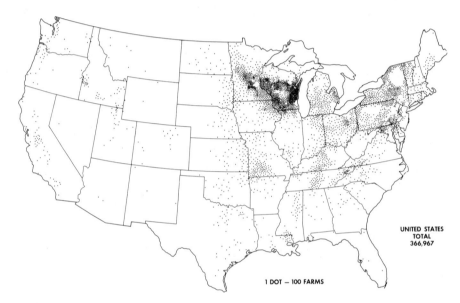

Fig. 4.3 *Dairy farms in 1964*

Source: U. S. Department of Commerce, Map No. 64A-M15.

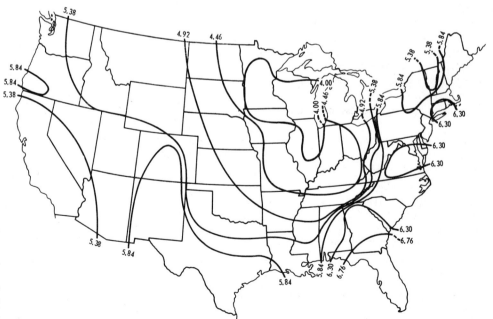

Fig. 4.4 *Spatial variations in milk prices, 1957–1958*
Dealers' buying prices per cwt., 3.5 percent butterfat for fluid use, based on prices in 185 markets.

Source: U. S. Department of Agriculture, Agricultural Marketing Service, Neg. 7215-59(6).

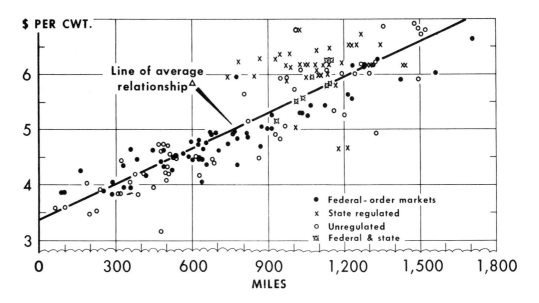

Fig. 4.5 *Fluid milk prices related to distance from Eau Claire, Wisconsin, 1957–1958. Dealers' buying prices per cwt., 3.5 percent milk for fluid use. Miles are the shortest highway distance from Eau Claire, Wisconsin. Regression line is* Y = 3.38 + .002175 X, *where* Y *is price and* X *is distance.*

Source: *U. S. Department of Agriculture, Agricultural Marketing Service, Neg. 7250-59(6).*

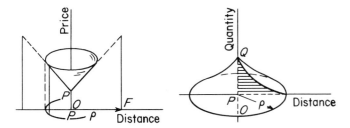

Fig. 4.6 *The price funnel and the demand cone*

What do such exchanges do? Cash markets in commodity exchanges provide continuous market trading for those who wish to buy or sell. Involving large numbers of buyers and sellers, they maintain quality standards, and permit a free flow of information so that competitive prices can be determined. In effect, they are the prime example of "the market" in classical free enterprise economies.

The actual process by which the base prices are determined can often be quite esoteric, however, as the example of egg prices illustrates. Quotations for selected grades and sizes of eggs are determined nationwide for the United States on each business day in New York, Chicago, Boston, and Los Angeles. The most widely used egg price quotations are those originating at New York and used throughout the middle Atlantic, northeastern and southern states. A private firm, the Urner-Barry Company, makes these quotations in the manner described in Appendix 4.1, "How Base Prices for Eggs are Determined in Terminal Markets." Different procedures lead to the terminal base-price quotations in Chicago, Boston and Los Angeles, as the example will show.

The Urner-Barry Company reports New York wholesale prices for many other agricultural commodi-

ties as well, and has been responsible for publishing daily price quotations and a weekly statistical market review, as well as other publications, since 1858. Market reporting services are sold via subscription to national publications and distributed through other communication facilities, such as telephone and wire services.

To repeat something we said earlier, the essence of *central markets* (also called market concourses) is that they bring together many buyers and sellers. Such markets exist today for many mostly agricultural products in the United States, including livestock, grains, fruits and vegetables, wool, cotton, naval stores, hides and tobacco. For example, U.S. corn prices are set by the price of no. 3 yellow corn on the Chicago Board of Trade, as are the prices of oats and soybeans. Barley prices are set by the quotations for no. 3 barley in Minneapolis. Sorghums are based on no. 2 yellow milo at Kansas City. American Cheese at factories in Wisconsin is priced at the Wisconsin Cheese Exchange. On the world scene, many metals are priced on the London Metals Exchange.

Chicago and London are examples of *terminal markets* where products from wide areas are concentrated, and it is for this reason that they developed their market concourses. Another example is that of Liverpool, which prior to 1940 was the major international market for wheat. Wheat prices registered on the Liverpool market were looked upon as the world base price. The United Kingdom was the largest single importer of wheat, and Liverpool was an ideal world market, as prices were little affected by special conditions in one or another of the world's producing areas, but reflected the general tendencies in all producing areas.

spatial patterns of prices when base prices are quoted

Let us return to the example of eggs. How does the map of egg prices (Fig. 4.7) relate to the map of egg production (Fig. 4.8) and to the fact that base prices for eggs are set in New York, Chicago, Boston, and Los Angeles?

The formula for explaining the spatial patterns, which applies in all cases where base prices are set in

terminal markets is as follows. Imagine that the supplier can sell his goods only at the central market. The price he receives is then the central market price minus transportation costs. The farther he is from the central market, the lower his price floor, as shown in Figure 4.9. Now suppose that other, smaller, local markets exist. The supplier will sell to these markets only if the local market price *exceeds* the central market price floor, as shown in the right-hand side of Figure 4.9. The central market price and transport costs thus set the producer's price floor, and provide him with an option to ship his output elsewhere if local demand is weak.

In the same way, central market prices set a ceiling which local consumers have to pay, as shown in Figure 4.10. Imagine that local production is inadequate to meet local demand. How high can the price of local production be bid before supplies are brought in from the central market? The local price could reach the price

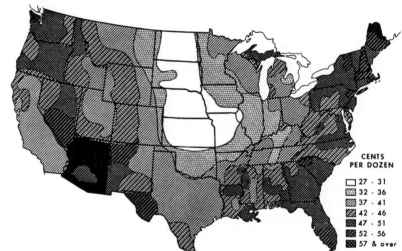

CENTS
PER DOZEN

☐ 27 - 31
▨ 32 - 36
▨ 37 - 41
▨ 42 - 46
▨ 47 - 51
▨ 52 - 56
■ 57 & over

Fig. 4.7 *Average prices received by farmers for eggs, 1953–1957*

Source: U. S. Department of Agriculture, Agricultural Marketing Service, Neg. 7066-59(2).

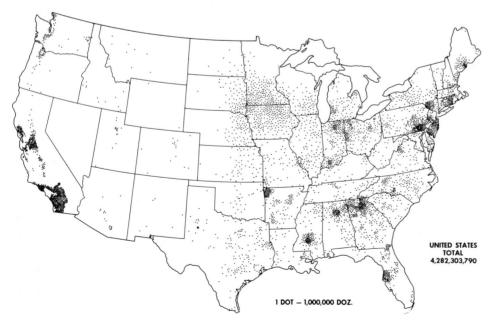

UNITED STATES
TOTAL
4,282,303,790

1 DOT — 1,000,000 DOZ.

Fig. 4.8 *Chicken eggs sold in 1964*

Source: U. S. Department of Commerce, Map No. 64A-M62.

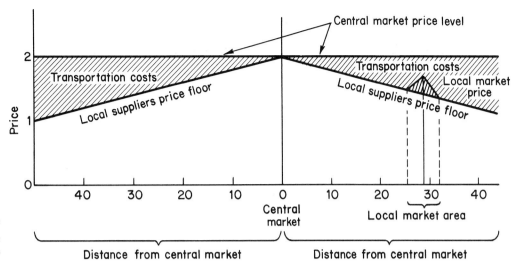

Fig. 4.9 *Determination of the local supplier's price floor*

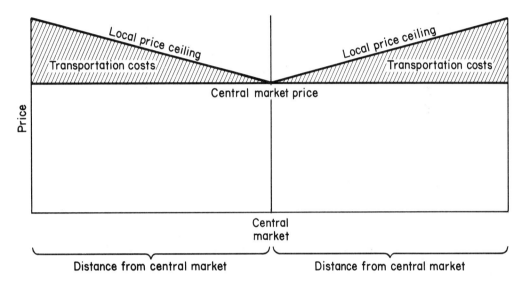

Fig. 4.10 *Determination of the ceiling price paid by local consumers*

at the central market plus transport costs from the central market, but no higher. This limit is the local price ceiling.

The result of the two price-distance gradients shown in Figures 4.9 and 4.10 is that differences between local price and central market price tend to increase systematically outward from the central market. Returning to Figure 4.8, local egg producers have the safety of a local price floor, knowing they can receive at least the base price, less transport costs to the central market, by shipping to the central market to sell. They will sell for a higher price locally if they can, but if local supplies so exceed local demands that local prices are likely to be driven down beneath the price obtainable in the central market, they will ship to the central market. In this way, the shipping point price in egg-surplus areas will always be the base price less transport charges. Conversely, in egg-deficit areas, the price ceiling applies, because whenever egg prices rise high enough, suppliers from the central market will ship in eggs, charging the base price plus transport charges. Finally, the central market price will be set to balance the receipts of eggs from producers

and the shipments required by deficit areas. In this way, the spatial variation in Figure 4.7 can be interpreted as follows. The lowest prices are received by surplus egg producers located in the north central region, with limited local demands, and far distant from terminal markets. The highest prices are paid in the large deficit urban markets of the northeast, southwest and southeast most distant from both surplus supplies and from the major terminal markets.

It is the market traders who make the whole process of balancing demands and supplies work. To illustrate, consider a trader who has been put in charge of a grain "desk" at the Continental Grain Company. A cable arrives from one of Continental's overseas offices—say, Paris. A buyer has bid for 10,000 tons of soybeans for July delivery in Rotterdam. Before accepting or countering with an offer, the trader considers future prices, world news, freight quotations, vessel bookings, the crop outlook, and the competition.

Then he makes a simple calculation. The basis for the final price is the futures quotation on the Chicago Board of Trade for July soybeans. The trader adds in the barge freight to New Orleans, the cost of handling at Continental's elevator there, and the ocean freight to Rotterdam. Then he cables the Paris office with a c.i.f. price offer—cost, insurance, and freight.

If the trader gets an "accept" from the other side, he begins the task of seeking out a profit. First, he "hedges" by buying July futures in Chicago. Since the futures price is the basis for his actual soybean sale, he can limit losses this way. Then he tries to find cheaper soybeans. If he does, he can sell his July futures, and his speculative profit will be the difference between the Rotterdam contract price and what he paid for the cheaper soybeans, less any cost of reselling the July futures.

The chartering department, meanwhile, will be speculating on shipping, trying to get the best deal possible for the July delivery in Rotterdam. It may take a section of a ship under charter by another company. Or it may charter a tanker for the 10,000-ton sale; 30,000 tons excess may be filled by another sale, or it may figure on selling the space later to a competitor at a profit.

All these facts, and more, determine what Continental's profit on the sale will be. At any rate, it will be months before the trader will know if the sale to Rotterdam was a success, but it is the possibility of making speculative gains that motivates the traders who keep the free-enterprise system of buying, selling, and price determination operational.

the geographic theory of prices

What we have described in the foregoing is a highly complex situation that may be understood by referring to Figures 4.11 to 4.16. Figure 4.11 has two parts; the left side relates the supplier's price floor and the consumer's price ceiling at different distances from the central market to a price-quantity relationship within the central market on the right side. The vertical axis plots price. M indicates the central market. To the right of the price-axis, in the price-quantity diagram,

CS is the supply curve in the central market formed by shipments from two surplus supply areas S_A and S_B. CD is the combined demand curve formed by two deficit areas D_A and D_B. P_M is the equilibrium central market price and Q_M the amount shipped from the two surplus suppliers via the central market to the deficit areas.

As a result, in the left hand side of the diagram, the line FGP_M is the price floor for the suppliers, whereas $P_M JH$ is the price ceiling for consumers. These two lines are determined by the equilibrium price P_M and by transport costs.

Exactly how is a combined supply curve of the kind shown in Figure 4.11 constructed? This is illustrated in Figures 4.12 to 4.16. Imagine that two producers, at A and B respectively in Figure 4.12, wish to supply goods to M (the central market). The local price at which A is willing to start production is AG and at B it is BC, so that although A is more distant from the market, it can supply M more cheaply (ME rather MC').

As price increases above ME and MC' each supplier will be willing to produce and ship more to the market. Assume that the supply curve for producer A is $EE'F$ in Figure 4.13 (this takes into account transport costs from A to M; at A, the supply curve would be lower because no transport costs need to be added in at the point of supply). As the price of M increases, a level will be reached at which B becomes willing to supply the market, in competition with A. That price is C'.

Once the price at M exceeds C', B begins to supply the market. B's supply curve is shown in Figure 4.14 by the upward sloping line $C'C''D'$. Since both A and B supply the market at prices above C', their *combined supply curve* in the market has to be derived. This is $EE'IJL$ in Figure 4.15, and it is formed by adding B's supply curve $C'C''D'$ to A's supply curve $EE'F$ horizontally, to show the total amount the two producers are willing to supply at each price level.

The foregoing materials are put together in Figure 4.16. $EE'IJL$ is the combined supply curve. The combined demand curve in the market is DD (note that DD

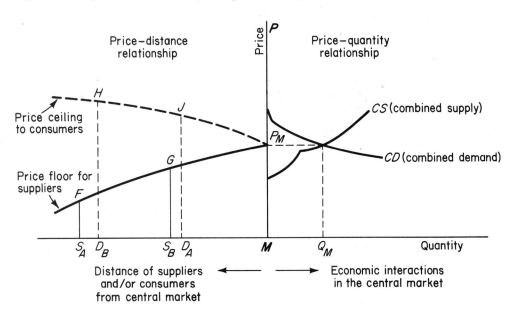

Fig. 4.11 *Central market equilibrium with resulting price gradients*

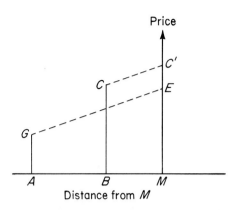

Fig. 4.12 *Initial prices at* A *and* B, *and in central market,* M

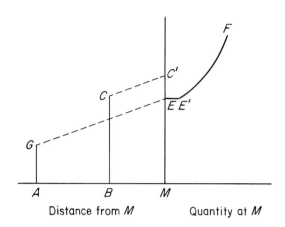

Fig. 4.13 *A's supply curve in the central market*

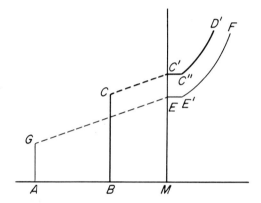

Fig. 4.14 *B's supply curve in the central market*

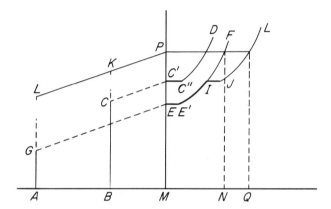

Fig. 4.15 *The combined supply curve. In this diagram, if* c″c″D′ *is added to* EE′IF, *the sum extends* EE′IF *to* EE′IJL. *The area* Pc′c″D′ *is therefore the same as the area* FIJL *added horizontally to the right of* IF.

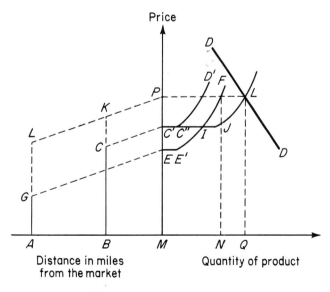

Fig. 4.16 *Derivation of the combined supply curve in a central market*

Adapted from: Hugh Nourse, Regional Economics *(New York: McGraw-Hill, 1968).*

can be derived in the same way as the foregoing). The point of equilibrium is L, the resulting market price is MP, and a total quantity MQ will be supplied. PKL is the local producer's price floor. At the price MP, A supplies the quantity MN (given by the intersection of A's supply curve and PL) and B supplies the balance, NQ.

MANAGED PRICES IN IMPERFECTLY COMPETITIVE SITUATIONS

Where there is a perfectly competitive free enterprise system, the actions of particular buyers and sellers do not affect prices; each individual is a "price taker" who is forced to accept the collectively determined price.

If the scale of economic organizations is such that their individual purchases or sales can materially affect prices, a situation of market imperfection exists. At the opposite extreme to perfect competition are market imperfections such as *monopoly*, in which a single seller dominates the market, or *monopsony*, in which there is a single buyer. In either case, price is determined by the dominant individual. Terms such as *oligopoly, oligopsony*, and *monopolistic competition* are used to describe organizational market-negotiated forms in which relatively few buyers or sellers are present who, either by following a price leader, or by engaging in collusive actions or various discriminatory practices can set the prices at which goods are bought and sold in the attempt to maximize their own returns or to achieve long-term organizational stability. We now turn to consider examples of these techniques in modern industrial states of the Western world.

oligopoly pricing and the basing-point system

A general class of such forms of discriminatory pricing arises under oligopolistic conditions, when a few large multiplant firms comprise an industry. These firms, while having discretionary power over price, tend to view pricing as an element in bargaining and negotiation. In following this view, firms ask themselves what the effects of their actions are likely to be on the price behavior of other firms. Smaller firms will follow the pricing policies of a dominant firm; to do otherwise would be to invite lethal retaliation, because large firms can combat local competition by cutting their prices in that area. When large firms confront each other, they quickly realize that their prices are closely interrelated, and that they must systematically restrain competition or be ruined by it.

Oligopolistic concerns desiring to restrain competition, invariably make their price leadership effective by the device of industrywide systems of identical delivered prices. Rival firms follow their leadership without making the effort to lower their prices that would promote greater competition. The most common delivered pricing scheme used is the *basing-point system* (*not*, it should be added, to be confused with basepoint pricing in

terminal markets). Although this system was used as early as 1880, it did not come into systematic use until after 1901 when it was applied to steel by the United States Steel Corporation.

The U.S. Steel scheme was known as "Pittsburgh plus." Under it, delivered prices for steel and steel products were quoted throughout the United States as the sum of a base price at Pittsburgh plus rail freight from Pittsburgh, regardless of the actual plant price or freight costs incurred from the actual producing point. Nearer or lower cost plants, which could actually deliver at lower cost than Pittsburgh plus, thus were able to earn extra profits. These profits were called "phantom freights." The overall effect was to raise prices, reduce demand, and protect U.S. Steel's Pittsburgh investments.

Soon after the adoption of the basing-point plan by the steel industry the practice was extended to the cement industry. Then, after 1912, the single basing-point practice spread rapidly to a variety of other industries—for example, cast-iron pipe, glucose, malt, maple flooring, welded chain, zinc, lead ("St. Louis plus") and copper ("Connecticut Valley plus"). The practice became worldwide. In Russia, for example, before the revolution, steel was priced according to a "Chelyabinsk plus" basing-point system.

In some industries multiple basing points were established. The principle is the same, except that two or more producing centers are quoted as bases, and market is divided among them according to base-price–plus-freight charges. Some of the industries adopting multiple basing points have been iron and steel (in 1924, following U.S. antitrust action), cement, hardwood lumber, gasoline, sugar, chemical fertilizers, milk and ice cream cans, asphalt roofing material, small arms ammunition, corn products, gypsum products, hard-surface floor coverings, linseed oil, rigid steel conduit, firebrick, lubricaitng oil, and plate glass.

competitive freight absorption

Where there are spatially distinct markets, another oligopolistic device that affects the geography of prices is that of freight absorption. In this scheme, local mill prices are quoted f.o.b., but potential customers may be quoted delivered prices less than "f.o.b. plus" to enable the firm to gain a foothold in the more distant market. In international trade, this practice is often called "dumping," as oligopolies controlling their domestic market try to gain access to foreign markets.

A reverse of this situation is found, for example, in the Frasch sulfur industry, in which higher prices are charged in export markets. This industry is a classical oligopoly that arose in the United States after the turn of the century when this unique technological innovation gave Frasch-processing producers a significant cost advantage over the Sicilian native sulfur industry. The industry has, since its inception, "administered" its prices in the interests of long-run stability, rather than letting them fluctuate with short-run variations in supply and demand. Domestic prices in the U. S. were quoted "f.o.b. mines" to satisfy governmental preferences for competition. In the early years of the industry, export prices determining the world pattern elsewhere were quoted c.i.f. New York City; in recent years this has shifted to f.o.b. Gulf port. Because of the level at which the export base price was set, the result was that net realized prices were consistently higher for exports than for domestic shipments.

PRICE REGULATION BY GOVERNMENTS IN WESTERN SOCIETIES

Explicit governmental regulations that affect or control prices are increasingly common in Western societies, whether they involve attempts to maintain free competition, regulation of prices charged by public utilities, regulations promulgated for public health and safety, or support of protective arrangements designed to maintain price stability despite wide seasonal or cyclical fluctuations.

In the transport utilities and in the postal service, for example, modifications of the price-distance relationship are permitted to simplify the charges that are levied, as in the postal service's zone-delivered pricing. In this scheme, uniform rates are allowed within broad distance zones so that instead of continuous price gradients with distance, price changes take on a "stair-step" form.

effects of health and safety regulations

Every governmental regulation affects pricing, production patterns, and market or supply areas in some way. Let us take as an example the effects of health and safety regulations on the U.S. dairy industry.

As the country industrialized, the growth of cities and the necessity of bringing milk from longer distances required improved practices to maintain the quality of milk from farm to consumer. This led to the requirements for pasteurization of milk and to a number of other public health measures applied to producers, haulers, and city handlers. The resulting city and state milk codes and the activities of public health officials have affected the production of milk in the following ways:

a. by increasing the size of investment required by farmers to produce milk for the fluid market and necessitating specialized types of farming practices for the production of high-quality milk

b. by determining which farms would be permitted to supply milk for use as whole milk or cream in the market.

The immediate effect of establishing higher standards for milk quality in any market is to raise production costs for many farmers. Some farmers have to invest in new equipment and change their methods of dairying, which results in higher costs per unit of output if their scale of operations remains unchanged. Some farmers are unwilling or unable to meet the new requirements,

and milk from new producers or additional output from old producers, or both, becomes necessary to meet the requirements of the market. The immediate result of all this is higher costs of production for the city's milk supply, requiring correspondingly higher prices to attract milk to the market.

Limiting the area within which farms may receive permits has taken various forms. In some cities, health authorities set a certain number of miles from the city as the maximum distance they will send farm inspectors. In other cities, the state line may represent the arbitrary boundary of part of the supply area. In the northeast, the Canadian border is the outer boundary or supply areas for New York and New England cities.

Several consequences follow from this restriction of the supply area. The shape of the more natural competitive supply area may be distorted. As part of the natural supply area is cut off, a depletion of supplies leads to somewhat higher prices. This induces producers in the remainder of the supply area to intensify their production and attracts new producers at parts of the outer boundary of the supply area where expansion is permissible. Beyond the boundary, supplies are completely immobilized no matter how attractive market prices may be.

price supports, output control, and direct payments to producers

Since the early 1930s, other activities of federal and state governments also have affected pricing, marketing, and consumption of many kinds of agricultural products. In the case of dairying, these activities may be grouped into three main categories. The first two affect prices directly, and the third indirectly.

1. The first group includes government activities in the marketing of fluid milk, such as the federal milk marketing order program. Although the main emphasis in the order program during the early 1930s was on raising prices, marketing orders basically are designed to maintain and improve stability of prices and bring about orderliness in the marketing process.

2. The second group includes price programs designed to raise prices of manufactured dairy products or prevent them from falling below a specified level. These programs also have affected prices of fluid milk indirectly. Purchases by the Federal Surplus Commodities Corporation prior to World War II were carried out to raise prices of butter and cheese when they were believed to be unduly low. Purchases of the Commodity Credit Corporation under the current price support program are carried out to prevent prices from falling below a predetermined level.

3. The third group of activities includes food distribution programs, such as the early low-cost milk programs and the school lunch and special milk programs. Some of these programs may have originated as a result of an attempt to give price assistance to farmers and to provide outlets for agricultural products acquired under price support programs, but their goal also is to improve national health and nutrition, and to expand the consumption of milk and dairy products.

Further governmental programs can be illustrated by taking the case of the U.S. wheat economy, in which important effects have resulted in prices, supplies and exports of wheat. These programs had their origins in the Great Depression, and have sought to provide a degree of stability to American agriculture despite the vicissitudes of a cyclical international economy. The continuation and improvement of these programs reflect the growing role of government in an increasingly organizational market-negotiated form of economy.

The first approach to stabilization of the depressed agricultural economy was the establishment of the Federal Farm Board—the first large-scale intervention by the government in the marketing of food products since colonial times—to purchase surplus wheat supplies in the attempt to raise prices.

Second came attempts—formulated in the International Wheat Agreement of 1949—to control international prices and trade (since, as we saw earlier, wheat prices are determined internationally). The 1949 agreement provided maximum and minimum prices for each of the four years that the agreement was to be in effect. The maximum price was the same for each year, but the minimum price was lowered each year. Each importing country could be required to purchase a specified "guaranteed quantity" at the minimum price for the particular year, and each exporting country could be required to sell this quantity to it at the maximum price. Total guaranteed purchases by importers and total guaranteed sales by exporters were equivalent to about half the current world trade in wheat. Flour could be substituted for wheat by agreement between buyers and sellers.

More recently, price supports have been maintained by the U.S. Department of Agriculture for a number of agricultural commodities. Support for six "basic commodities," including wheat, is mandatory. Prices are supported by loans, purchase agreements, and direct purchases. For wheat, the bulk of the price-support activities involve loans and purchase agreements.

Loans support prices in two major ways: (1) by providing farmers a cash return for the commodity at the support level during the period loans are available, and (2) by strengthening market prices of the commodity through the withdrawal of supplies from the market. *Purchase agreements* are agreements to purchase from a producer at the producer's option not more than a stipulated quantity of a commodity at the support price.

Beginning with the Agricultural Adjustment Act of 1933, acreage allotments and marketing quotas have been a condition for price support. The Agricultural Adjustment Act of 1938, as amended, stated:

The national acreage allotment for any crop of wheat shall be that acreage which the Secretary determines will, on the basis of the national average yield for wheat, produce an amount thereof adequate, together with the estimated carry-over at the beginning of the marketing year for such crops

and imports, to make available a supply for such marketing year equal to a normal year's domestic consumption and exports plus 30 per centum thereof.

In effect, the allotment and marketing quota provisions provide a mechanism for adjusting supply to demand, since the law now requires that acreage allotments and marketing quotas be put into effect when the supply of wheat exceeds a certain defined quantity. The attempts of the government are therefore directed towards maintaining agricultural prices and incomes at certain minimum levels by trying to curtail production by limiting the acreage allowances for growing particular crops. However, this continuing attempt to balance production with anticipated domestic use and export has missed its mark by a considerable margin. In the case of wheat, the chief reason was that average yields kept climbing: 25.9 bushels per acre in 1967; 28.4 in 1968; 30.6 in 1969; and 31.1 in 1970. The effect was that in spite of acreage restrictions, carryover as of July 1 was 425 million bushels in 1967; 539 million in 1968; 818 million in 1969; and 883 million in 1970.

ADMINISTERED PRICES IN THE SOCIALIST STATES

Pricing follows different rules and has different patterns in the "command economies" of the socialist states. Recall how those economies were described in Chapter 1: monolithic authoritarian governmental systems are dominated by a single party; the state owns the means of production, operating nonagricultural industries—and, in some countries, agriculture too; and there is centralized direction of the economy. In the classic socialist scheme, each industry is supposed to produce according to preset physical targets. Performance—at least until the late 1960s—was measured by output rather than sales, which meant that commodity movements were managed through rationing systems rather than through the interplay of demand and supply. Prices have played little, if any, role in economic management. Finally, socialist economies have been geared to ensuring rapid growth above all else.

the example of Czechoslovakia

For example, when the Communist regime came to power in Czechoslovakia, the economic system of that country was reshaped to conform to that of the USSR. Czechoslovakia adopted a program of expanding production along the entire spectrum of raw materials, metals and heavy equipment, often at the expense of the high-value precision machinery that had been the mainstay of prewar Czechoslovakia's foreign trade.

Enforcement of these investment decisions required a huge party-controlled bureaucracy. The bureaucrats devised economic plans, determined the allocation of resources, set production quotas, fixed prices on 1,500,000 different categories of goods, decreed their distribution, and conducted all foreign trade.

Ota Sik, who played a leading role in this design, and fled to the West after the abortive attempt to liberalize Czechoslovakia in 1968, has commented that all the economic problems that arose in the country can be traced to the removal of prices as the "thermostat" controlling the economy. The central role of market prices is too little appreciated, even in the U.S., among businessmen who thoroughly understand the central function of prices in the operation of their own enterprises.

The situation is beyond the control of the best managers, planners, and government departments [Sik says]. Involving, as it does, such a multitude of contradictory processes, no planning mechanism, even with the aid of the most sophisticated computers, can possibly function successfully. It has been demonstrated that, despite its deficiencies, the market mechanism is the sole medium capable of dealing with the complex interrelationships in a modern industrial economy.

Destruction of the market-price mechanism had a devastating effect on the Czech economy. Planners fixed prices on the basis of their notions of social utility, and in some cases this resulted in heavy losses for producers —or would have, if anyone had been keeping accurate accounts. And industrial managers, judged solely on their ability to meet production quotas, churned out great quantities of goods so shoddy that they could not be sold even at subsidized prices. In 1967, Sik says, Czech warehouses were bulging with many billions of dollars worth of unsalable goods.

Even worse over the long run, elimination of market prices left the planners without any sound way of determining where to invest the country's resources. Funds were poured into new factories—often in low-profit, low-technology industries—and huge construction projects. Little or nothing was devoted to modernization of existing plants.

Soviet pricing schemes

To repeat, in free-enterprise economies, prices limit demand for each product to available supplies. But in socialist countries, following the lead of the Soviet Union, prices have been set differently. In the USSR—apart from collective farm markets—foodstuffs and manufactured goods are made available to the consumers entirely through publicly owned or cooperatively owned retail shops. In these shops, the actual prices charged are determined directly by the all-union Council of Ministers, or executive agencies working on its behalf, usually as a fixed markup over wholesale prices, which are also dictated.

In general, these "official" or "administered" prices have not been set at clearing levels. Rather, for some commodities they have resulted in rapid buildups of unsold inventories, while for others they are so low that persistent shortages exist and many demands go unmet.

The reason for these divergences is that the Soviets have tended to relate prices ultimately to production costs and to some concept of social value rather than to the interplay of demand and supply. In the case of manufactured goods, for example, retail prices are ultimately related to the pricing of industrial materials, taking into account standard markups, and a turnover tax that varies between commodities to reflect social desirability. Industrial materials are, in turn, priced so that the return equals the average production cost plus a limited planned profit. Since, as we shall see later, average costs change with the scale of output, this pricing policy has the effect of ultimately relating all prices back to the nature, scale, location, and efficiency of production—all of which are set by the command structure of economic planning in the state. Demand plays no role whatsoever in price determination in this scheme.

Since the 1960s the Soviet economic planners have relied increasingly on methods of mathematical programming in order to provide ways of estimating more efficient relationships between planned targets, output levels, and commodity flows as a substitute for the free market's prices. These methods produce what the Soviet planners call "objectively determined values" for products. Similar values are called by Western scholars *shadow prices* that, if charged, would ensure that the economic relationships that are sought are achieved. Such shadow prices can be calculated in ways that reflect both scarcity and productivity, and they would avoid some of the problems of shortages and surpluses that now exist in the USSR. However, since consumption targets have to be preset by the planners before the mathematical methods may be used, the prices still reflect only production and supply considerations. The free play of consumer preferences and demands that characterize Western societies play no role in determining the mix of things produced.

how base prices for eggs are determined in terminal markets
appendix 4.1

NEW YORK

Before the opening of the market at the Mercantile Exchange in New York, the Urner-Barry Company representative reporting on eggs contacts a number of wholesalers in the Manhattan area. In these personal contacts, he learns how the dealers feel about the current market situation and whether eggs are moving rapidly or slowly into distributive channels in relation to the actual or expected receipts. Contacts are also made in the morning or the previous afternoon with major egg buyers in the New York area, but outside the Manhattan market. Calls and contacts are made with firms in the major production areas, particularly those supplying eggs to the New York metropolitan area. The Urner-Barry reporter is on the trading floor of the New York Mercantile Exchange during the fifteen-minute spot call each day. After observing trading activity; he announces his egg price quotations a few minutes after the close of trading. These are the new base egg quotations until the next spot call on the exchange. These quotations are announced by posting them on a blackboard on the trading floor of the exchange.

CHICAGO

The Chicago egg price quotations are issued Monday through Friday each week and are used by egg handlers in Chicago and adjacent areas of the Midwest. The Chicago base price quotations are established at the close of the Chicago Mercantile Exchange daily spot call. A private market reporter, who is usually not present at the time of the spot call, receives the phoned report of trading as recorded on the spot call board. This is his sole source of information. The reporter usually decides at once what the new quotations will be. These are posted on a blackboard above the trading floor where they are readily visible to all traders on the floor.

BOSTON

The quotations that are the basis for most sales in the New England area are compiled by a reporter for the Boston *Herald Traveler*. Normally from about 10:00 A.M. to 11:30 A.M., Monday through Friday, he receives reports of bids, offers, and sales of first receivers in wholesale lots in the Boston market area. The activities of the reporter are controlled by a consent decree of December 1949. This decree settled an antitrust case filed against the Boston Fruit and Produce Exchange and most of the major handlers who were members of the Exchange, charging them with collusion in fixing prices. The decree sets out in some detail the rules under which the reporter and the handlers are to operate. It is the responsibility of the traders to report sales, offers, and bids to the reporter. During the trading period, the reporter aids trading by directing traders desiring to buy to traders desiring to sell and vice versa. Toward the end of the morning period, trading usually stabilizes around price levels that will (1) clear the supply present in the New England area, or (2) will entice needed supplies from other areas outside New England by setting a price level which, less transport costs, induces producers elsewhere to ship to New England rather than selling locally. The resulting prices are then issued as the Boston quotations. They are published in the newspapers and released to wire services and private market reporters over a wide area. Quotations are issued for jumbo, extra large, large, medium, and pullet sizes for both brown and white eggs. The quotations for brown eggs are widely recognized as the primary quotations, since New England is the major brown egg preference area in the nation.

LOS ANGELES

A guiding factor in West Coast egg pricing is the price of eggs to dealers in the Los Angeles market area as re-ported by the United States Department of Agriculture (USDA) Market News Service. Historically, there have never been price quotations in Los Angeles or elsewhere on the West Coast of the type available in the New York, Chicago, and Boston areas. Since early 1966, a major factor in egg pricing in the Los Angeles area has been the weekly prices established by Southwestern Egg Producers, Inc. (SWEP), a cooperative. The Chicago and New York price quotations are closely watched by SWEP and may be considered in establishing weekly prices. The remainder of the West Coast is strongly influenced by prices in the Los Angeles area.

PREVENTION OF PRICE FIXING

Obviously, the arrangements described above could be abused. To ensure honesty, in the United States, the Commodity Exchange Authority, an agency of the United States Department of Agriculture, acting in the administration and enforcement of the Commodity Exchange Act, regulates commodity exchanges. It is a violation of that act to manipulate or attempt to manipulate prices on the spot markets, as well as in the futures markets. If violations are established, the Secretary of Agriculture may move against the individual violators administratively or may seek criminal action against them through the Department of Justice. In addition, if it is found that a contract market has not provided for the prevention of manipulation of prices, action may be taken under the act to revoke the exchange's designation as a futures contract market.

RECOMMENDED READINGS

Bressler, R. G., and R. A. King, *Markets, Prices and Interregional Trade.* New York: John Wiley, 1970.

Reynolds, L. G., *The Three Worlds of Economics.* New Haven: Yale University Press, 1971.

Wagner, P. L., *The Human Use of the Earth.* New York: Free Press, 1960.

Warntz, W., *Toward a Geography of Price.* Philadelphia: University of Pennsylvania Press, 1959.

Waugh, F. V., *Demand and Price Analysis.* Washington, D. C.: U.S. Department of Agriculture, Technical Bulletin 1316, 1964.

preference structures and spatial variations in demand

5

Demand and supply together determine price. Having examined some of the major characteristics of the geography of price, we shall now consider the geographies of demand in this chapter and supply in the following chapter.

CONSUMER PREFERENCES AND THE PRINCIPLES OF CHOICE

Ultimately, demands are based upon preferences—what people like and do not like—and preferences are based upon need. Consumers in cold climates for instance, must think about warm clothing and adequate shelter. Food consumption on the other hand, may be related to cultural factors. Jews and Moslems will not eat pork; most Hindus will not eat meat at all; until recently, natives in parts of New Guinea ate humans; and Aztecs were known to eat dogs. Food preferences also reflect income and social class in most parts of the world. In Southeast Asia, for example, corn is fed to the animals, and only the very poor will use it as table food if rice is too expensive. Food and clothing preferences also vary within social groups. In Japan, an increasing number of young people prefer Western food and dress, but their rural elders still choose the traditional ways. Finally, preferences within any culture depend on individual likes and dislikes.

In this discussion, we will consider preferences at the individual level. We will explore the relationships among preferences, the principles of choice, and the geography of demand. We will then apply these principles to the study of major spatial variations in demand.

tradeoffs among alternatives

Every consumer is faced with a basic problem—how to choose among alternative satisfactions, given his own set of preferences. He must choose some mixture of work and leisure. Given the limits of the income he derives from work, he must make choices among the alternative goods and services that are available to him. To buy one thing he must forego another, so to realize his preferences the consumer must allocate his available resources by choosing the goods he feels to be most desirable. Any such choice carries with it costs—the costs of alternative opportunities foregone.

To make choices, a consumer must build up a capacity to trade off alternatives. In choosing between work and leisure, for example, he must ask whether one more hour of work is worth more to him than using that time for leisure. Clearly, if it is, work is worth more, and he will work; if not, the time will be spent in leisurely pursuits. This process of trading off alternatives is called making choices *at the margin*.

Sometimes the consumer will be indifferent to which alternative to choose; he feels, at that point, that both choices are worth about the same. The identification of such points of indifference is of real importance, for, as we shall see in the next section, they enable the consumer's *indifference curves* and *preference map* to be charted. The curves and map tell us what his preferences and choices are likely to be and enable his demand schedule to be estimated.

construction of indifference curves

Consider the case of Farmer Jones, engaged in dairying in the state of Iowa. He wants to know what combination of grain and hay he should feed his cattle to maximize milk output and he wants to be able to determine how to crop his land to feed his cattle. He decides to ask Professor Smith at the Iowa State Agricultural Experiment Station for advice. Professor Smith suggests an experiment. Farmer Jones has a herd of larger-sized Holstein and Brown Swiss cows, each of which has an expected output capacity of 300 to 400 pounds of butterfat annually. The professor suggests that Farmer Jones feed the cattle different combinations of legume hay, corn silage, and grain, and chart the resulting variations in milk output.

This Farmer Jones does, and later on he brings the results to Professor Smith for analysis. The professor begins by plotting Farmer Jones's data in a graph, as in Figure 5.1. The two axes record amounts of grain and hay fed to the cows. Each dot represents one cow, with the milk output noted beside each dot. The next step is to interpolate contour lines showing combinations of feeds resulting in identical levels of output. For example, the 8500-pound contour traces out those combinations of grain and hay that yield 8500 pounds of milk per cow. From a production standpoint, the professor tells Farmer Jones that if he wants this level of output per cow he can feed each of his cows 6000 pounds of grain and 5000 of hay or 3000 pounds of grain and 9000 pounds of hay, or indeed any combination of feeds along the line between. What is important, the professor says, is that Farmer Jones is *indifferent* to these combinations from a milk-production standpoint along any particular indifference curve. Each combination on a given curve works equally well, yielding equal milk outputs. The contours can therefore be called *equal-product curves*. or *indifference curves*.

indifference curves and the preference map

In Figure 5.1, a second indifference curve has been drawn at a higher level of output (9,500 pounds). Clearly, many such curves could be interpolated in the graph, and one thing Professor Smith calculated was the mathematical equation describing the shape of the curves so that he could visualize them on the figure. This equation appears in the caption for Figure 5.1. A whole set of curves in a tradeoff graph, such as Figure 5.1, describes Farmer Jones's *preference map,* with higher levels of achievement moving upwards to the right. The curves are all convex to the origin because grain and hay are

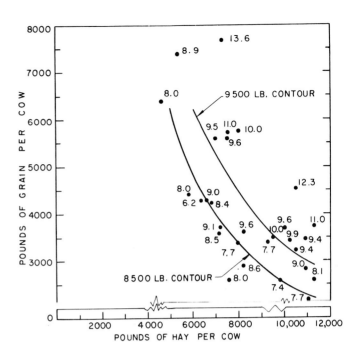

Fig. 5.1 *Equal product contours (feed combinations), at 8,500 and 9,500 lbs. of milk per cow. Contours interpolated using the production function,* $Y = 3.56X_1^{.5035}X_2^{.4}$ *where Y is the output of milk and* X_1 *and* X_2 *are hay and grain respectively. Thus, for 8,500 lbs. of milk, the input combinations yielding the 8,500 lb. contour are given by* $X_2 = (8500/2.56X_1^{.5035})^{2.5}.$

Source: Earl O. Heady and Russell O. Olson, Substitution Relationships, Resource Requirements and Income Variability in the Utilization of Forage Crops *(Ames, Iowa: Research Bulletin 390, Agricultural Experiment Station, Iowa State University, 1952).*

not perfect substitutes for each other in feeding the cattle. For example, if a cow is producing 8500 pounds of milk, and it is being fed 5000 pounds of hay and 6154 pounds of grain, 1 pound of hay can be substituted for 1.55 pounds of grain and the milk output will remain the same. At the other extreme, however (reading along the indifference curve), if 11,000 pounds of hay and 2281 pounds of grain are being used to produce 8500 pounds of milk, 1 pound of hay only does the same job as .26 pounds of grain. When a great deal of any one item is being used or consumed, its relative worth is much less than if a little of it is being used.

the production-opportunity line and the system of isoquants

The preference map is the first ingredient that Professor Smith needs to answer Farmer Jones's question about feed mixtures and cropping patterns. The second ingredient relates to what Farmer Jones can produce on his land. Let us suppose that he has 100 acres at his disposal to grow hay, grain, or some combination of the two. He might be able to produce, say, 200,000 pounds of grain (2000 pounds per acre) or 500,000 pounds of hay (5000 pounds per acre) by using the land entirely for one or the other, or some combination of the two.

What should he produce, he asks Professor Smith, to maximize milk yields if he restricts his herd to 8500-pound milk-yielders? And what size herd should he maintain? Professor Smith makes some rapid calculations. Ten times the figures that can be read off the 8500 pound contour in Figure 5.1 shows feed needed for ten cows; adding a zero to that obtains the input requirements for 100 cows.

The professor then draws another graph—Figure 5.2—with the results of these calculations in it. First, he plots Farmer Jones's *production-opportunity line,* which shows what feeds he can produce on his 100 acres: either 200,000 pounds of grain, or 500,000 pounds of hay, or some combination of the two, depending on how much land he uses for one or the other. Second, he plots contours for the results of his calculations showing total input requirements for different herd sizes. These contours are called *isoquants,* and were the ones produced by the calculations described above. Each isoquant records the input combinations that will produce an equal quantity of output. Thus, the lowest isoquant in Figure 5.2 charts the varying combinations of inputs required to support a 25-cow herd of 8500-pound–milk-yielders. The highest isoquant is for double that herd size, and the middle one is for 30 cows, which will together yield 255,000 pounds of milk.

The professor then shows Farmer Jones why it is impossible to feed a herd of 50 cows and expect 8500 pounds of milk per cow. The highest isoquant in the graph requires far more feed than can be produced on 100 acres of land. Similarly, although the farmer could crop his land in a way that would just feed a 25-cow herd of 8500-pound producers (point *A* in Fig. 5.2), he can do better than that. The production-opportunity line extends above the 25-cow isoquant in places, so that by producing somewhat more hay and less grain on his 100

acres he can still get 8500 pounds of milk per cow and support a herd of 30 cows (point *B* in Fig. 5.2). At this point, the highest isoquant reachable with the production-possibility line, some 270,000 pounds of hay and 90,000 pounds of grain are produced on the farm and result in a total output of 255,000 pounds of milk. This, Professor Smith tells Farmer Jones, is the way to maximize milk output in any *given* year.

the effect of complementary production relationships over time

But Professor Smith points out that Farmer Jones can do even better than this if he grows his crops in rotation, managing his farm properly over a *period* of years. In Figure 5.2 it was assumed that the crops were *competitive,* that is, that any increase in acreage of one resulted in a correspondingly proportional decrease in acreage—and therefore in output—of the other. But crops grown in rotation may be *complementary* in that growing one may increase the yields of the other in the following year. Grasses and legumes, for example, accumulate nitrogen and therefore increase yields of the subsequent year's crops. Professor Smith provides a simple example to Farmer Jones (Fig. 5.3). This was drawn from experimental data he had previously obtained from rotations grown on Marshall silt loam soil at the Page County Experimental Farm in Iowa. In the figure, the curve *CabcdR* indicates the output of grain and forage derived from 100 acres of land when the two crops are grown in rotation. The complementary production-opportunity line is not straight, but convex upwards, indicating that the farmer might be able to crop his land and support a herd of 35 8500-pound producers, giving a total output of 300,000 pounds of milk, if he practiced proper crop rotations. Farmer Jones, seeing

Fig. 5.2 *Determination of cropping pattern and herd size*

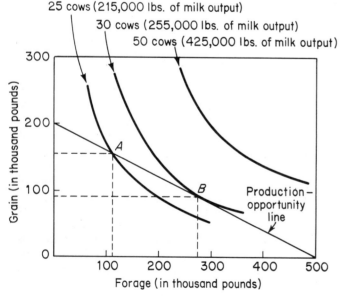

Fig. 5.3 *Substitution of forage for grain in crop production and milk production*

Source: Heady and Olson, Substitution Relationships.

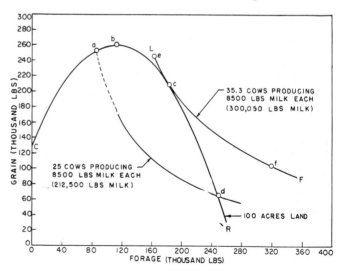

Table 5.1 Complementary and Competitive Relationships in Forage Production for Two Soil Types (Data for 100 Acres of Land)

ROTATION[1]	ACRES OF LAND OUT OF 100 IN		TOTAL PRODUCTION (LBS.)		POUNDS OF GRAIN SACRIFICED FOR EACH POUND OF HAY ADDED OVER PREVIOUS ROTATION
	GRAIN	HAY	GRAIN	HAY	
Wooster and Canfield silt loams, Wooster, Ohio, 1937–1943[2]					
C	100	0	217,840	—	
C–C–C–W–A	80	20	229,776	128,800	Complementary
C–W–A	67	33	215,480	203,200	.19
C–C–W–A–A	60	40	190,672	316,000	.22
C–W–A–A	50	50	165,928	363,000	.53
Clarion-Webster silt loam, Ames, Iowa, 1945–1948[3]					
C	100	0	180,320	—	
C–C–O–Cl	75	25	217,360	85,000	Complementary
C–O–Cl	67	33	182,333	132,660	.71

[1] C corn, O oats, W wheat, Cl clover, A alfalfa.
[2] See Yoder, R. E., "Results of Agronomic Research on the Use of Lime and Fertilizers in Ohio," Ohio Agr. Exp. Sta. Agron. 96 (Mimeo), 1945.
[3] From unpublished data, Dept. of Agronomy, Iowa Agr. Exp. Sta. Ames, Iowa, 1915–1948.

Source: Earl O. Heady and Russell O. Olson, *Substitution Relationships, Resource Requirements and Income Variability in the Utilization of Forage Crops* (Ames, Iowa: Research Bulletin 390, Agricultural Experiment Station, Iowa State University, 1952).

that point c is higher up in his preference map than, for example, points a and d, at either of which he could only support a herd of 25 cows, readily agrees that he should find the right crop rotation for his soils and climate.

What rotation scheme should then be used? Farmer Jones inquired next. The professor provides a series of examples of three-, four- and five-year rotations, compared with single-cropping corn (Table 5.1). From such data, he and the farmer quickly determine an appropriate cultivation plan. Farmer Jones has the information he needs to make the best choices among the alternatives available to him. The critical ingredients are his preferences and the limitations imposed upon him by the resources at his disposal.

ADJUSTMENTS TO PRICE CHANGES

price changes and the price consumption curve

If Farmer Jones operated a feed lot instead of cultivating the land and bought his forage and grain on the open market, his herd size and feed mix would be determined by the funds available to purchase feeds, rather than the cropping capability of his land. Herd size and feed mix would also be subject to fluctuations in grain and hay prices. The effects are illustrated in Figure 5.4.

The graph shows a succession of isoquants. For purposes of this example, it is assumed that the farmer spends a fixed sum on forage and grain. If all the money is spent on forage, OF can be purchased.

Now, let forage prices remain constant, but grain

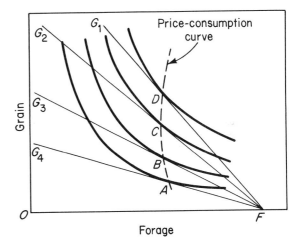

Fig. 5.4 *Effects of relative price changes*

prices change. When grain prices are high, only G_4 can be bought, and the farmers *price-possibility line* is G_4F. This line, in a manner analogous to the production-possibility line discussed earlier, describes what can be purchased with the funds (or resources) available. The optimal herd size and mix of input purchases is given by point A. If the grain price falls, however, purchases of grain can be increased to G_3, G_2, etc. The price-possibility line becomes steeper. The equilibrium moves from A to B, C and D on higher isoquants. Because grain prices are lower, more milk can be produced, and relatively larger shares of grain will appear in the feed mix. The line charted by the successive points A, B, C and D is a *price-consumption curve* (or "satisfaction path").

price effects, income effects, and substitution effects

Movement along the price-consumption curve as prices fall is called a *price effect*, which has two parts:

a. An *income effect;* i.e., as price falls, the farmer moves on to a higher isoquant, maintains a larger herd, produces more, and becomes better off.
b. A *substitution effect;* i.e., because the relative price of grain and forage changes with a move along the curve, the farmer tends to use more of the input that has become relatively cheaper, substituting it for the other in his input mix.

construction of demand curves

It is from the price-consumption curve that the farmer's *demand schedule* or *demand curve* can be constructed. For example, each of the points, *A, B, C,* and *D* in Figure 5.4 shows how much grain will be purchased at different grain prices. If this information is plotted in a price-quantity graph, the farmer's demand schedule for grain will be apparent.

CONSEQUENCES OF SPATIAL VARIATIONS IN PRICES

spatial demand cones

In Chapter 4, we saw how many prices increased with increasing distance from market centers due to the effect of transport costs. What are the consequences? Restricting ourselves for the moment to the agricultural example presented above, if forage prices vary less than grain prices because forage is produced locally, whereas grain is shipped in from some central market, the more distant farmers

a. use more forage, substituting the cheaper input for the more expensive one.
b. have smaller herds, and produce less on a given acreage, i.e., they are less intensive.
c. earn less.

Fig. 5.5 *The spatial demand cone*

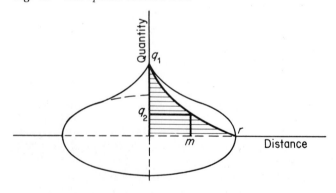

Because there are both income and substitution effects of price changes, as prices increase with distance, quantity consumed decreases, producing as a result, *spatial demand cones* of the kind charted in Figure 5.5.

regional variations in welfare

In general, then, the price effects of increasing distance include both income effects (people are less affluent) and substitution effects (activities are less intensive). The resulting regional variations appear and reappear in a variety of aspects of life throughout the world, where one of the most marked spatial differences is between affluent, growing activity in core regions where prices are determined, and lagging peripheries, less advanced, with greater poverty populations, and with far more extensive production patterns. These differences are the theme in the chapters that discuss the world's heartland and hinterland regions.

the pervasiveness of distance-decay

To illustrate, Figure 5.6 presents a series of graphs constructed as part of a study of regional development in the United States using data from the 1960 census. The horizontal axis in each of the twelve cases covers the 270 miles from Dallas to Houston-Galveston, Texas. The vertical axis of each shows how different characteristics vary from place to place along this 270-mile stretch. The first graph on the second row shows that income levels drop with increasing distance from Dallas, rise around Bryan, fall again, then rise towards Houston. This is the income effect described above. Similar patterns will be found in each of the other graphs. In each case the *distance-gradients* reflect spatial adjustments resulting from the income and substitution effects of price increases. For example, as the extent of commuting to jobs in the metropolitan centers declines with distance from the metropolises (top left-hand graph), population densities, the proportion of the population classified as urban, the value of land and buildings, income, amount of schooling, rate of population increase, and percent change in the population through migration all decline. The percentage of the population classified as *rural nonfarm* rises and then falls. Both the percentage of families with incomes less than $3,000 (the 1960 poverty line) and the unemployment rate increase with distance from the central city.

The rhythmic changes rise and fall like the tune of a well-known song. This rhythm symbolizes a *regional welfare syndrome* in which the lowest levels of welfare are to be found at the peripheries of major metropolitan regions, where prices are highest and economic opportunities are least.

That the population is responding to these systematic variations in welfare is also implied, for population is generally decreasing at the outer edges of the metropolitan regions, responding to differences in in-

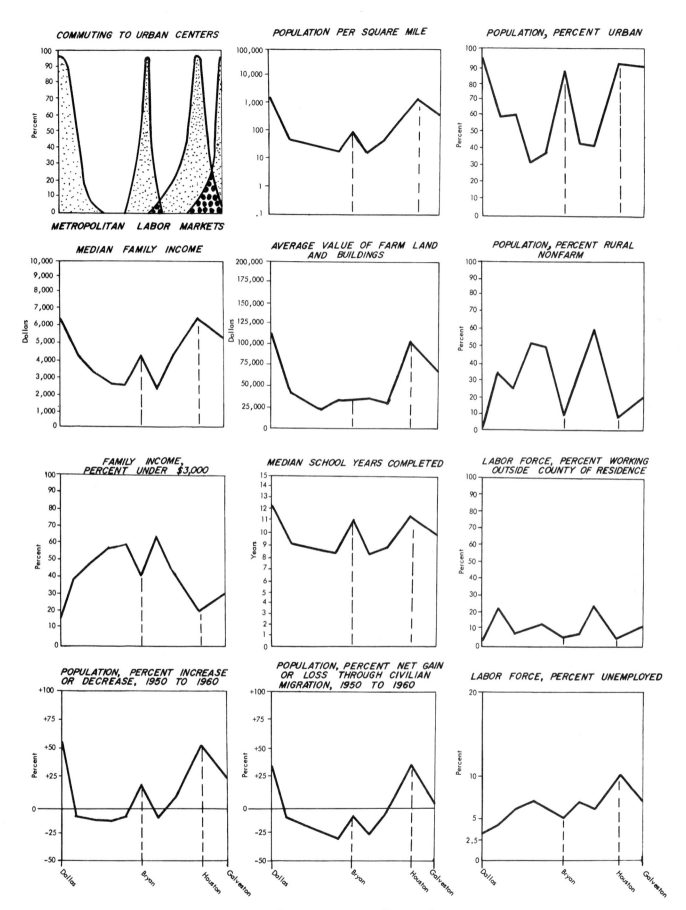

Fig. 5.6 *Socioeconomic gradients along a 270-mile traverse from Dallas to Galveston*
The graphs have been plotted using U.S. Census data from 1960. Each graph illustrates the same 270 miles from Dallas through Bryan, to Houston and Galveston. Locations of the towns are indicated at the bottom of each column. Note how incomes rise and fall in relation to the intensity of commuting to urban centers. Other characteristics rise and fall in the same manner.

comes and opportunities by migrating from areas of low opportunity to the metropolitan centers that are perceived to offer greater advantages.

MARKET POTENTIALS AND THE GEOGRAPHY OF DEMAND

It follows from the foregoing that more accessible areas are more likely to have a higher density of population and a higher per capita demand than less accessible areas, and that distance reduces demand and incomes. This idea has been used to develop measures of *market potentials,* designed to show spatial variations in the demands that can be served from different locations.

The computation of market potentials is relatively simple. Refer to Figure 5.5. Quantity demanded drops off with distance in any spatial demand cone. Total demand at any center can be calculated by finding the area under the spatial demand cone—that is, by adding up the quantity demanded at each point within the market area traced out by the demand cone.

Now imagine a map that plots the *results* of such summations for each of a series of possible business locations. In places with higher population densities and incomes, the market potential indicated will be higher; in the inaccessible peripheries it will be lower. The data can be contoured and a map of market potentials can be produced.

Because the exact quantity likely to be demanded by consumers at all locations is unlikely to be known for all locations, so various approximation methods are used to indicate likely variations in market potentials. One such approximation uses population numbers rather than quantities demanded; another uses total incomes. The approximation techniques thus result in maps of *population potentials* and *income potentials* as conveniently calculated substitutes for exact market potentials.

calculating population and income potentials

Population potentials measure the influence of population at a distance, as a surrogate for actual data on demands. They are calculated on the assumption that the strength of the *gravitational influence, V,* of a population P, at some other point c located r miles away, is

$$V_c = \frac{P}{r}$$

where
V_c = population potential, V, at point c
r = distance to some other point.

In other words, the attraction varies directly with population and inversely with distance. But there are many

Fig. 5.7 *Income potential of the world*
Source: Warntz, 1965.

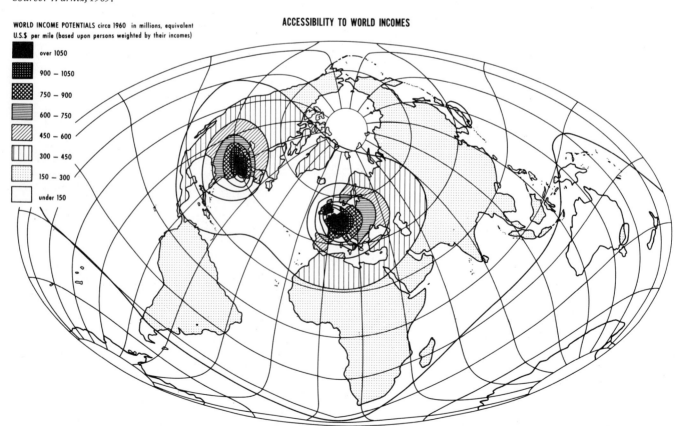

WORLD INCOME POTENTIALS circa 1960 in millions, equivalent U.S.$ per mile (based upon persons weighted by their incomes)

■	over 1050
▦	900 – 1050
▩	750 – 900
▤	600 – 750
▨	450 – 600
▥	300 – 450
░	150 – 300
□	under 150

ACCESSIBILITY TO WORLD INCOMES

other places for which an attraction exists. Therefore the expression becomes

$$V_c = \Sigma_i \frac{P_i}{r_{ic}}$$

where
V_c = population potential, V, at point c
P_i = population at point i
r_{ic} = distance from i to c

and Σ_i signifies that each "bit" of gravitational influence on c of all i points surrounding c is being added together. If I_i, the total income at point i is substituted for P_i in the last equation, one calculates income potentials in a directly analogous manner.

potentials in map form

Potentials are easily mapped. This is simply a matter of joining all points of the same potential on the map, just as contours on a physical relief map are made by joining all points of the same elevation above sea level.

An example is given in Figure 5.7, a map of income potential for the world. Two important peaks of potential appear. The first of these summits is the New York-Chicago axis, the North American industrial heartland, and the second is the Western European peak extending from southern Great Britain to West Germany and thence to northern Italy. Observe that the peaks are sharply delineated and are surrounded on all sides by steeply declining gradients. Both peaks are enclosed by a single $300 million isopotential line.

Two much smaller high points on the income potential map also appear. One of these is defined by the $300 million isopotential line encircling the main Japanese island of Honshu and the other is the small area of southeasternmost Australia enclosed by an isopotential line of $150 million. Note the absence of peaks corresponding to the East Asian and South Asian population clusters. Despite their enormous populations, China and India have per capita incomes so low that they are unable to generate concentrations of income potential. Only the world's modern urban-industrial core regions stand out. They are, of course, the centers of demand on a world scale, the world's "heartlands."

RECOMMENDED READINGS

Greenhut, M. L., *Microeconomics and the Space Economy*. Glenview, Ill.: Scott, Foresman, 1963.

Warntz, W., *Macrogeography and Income Fronts*. Philadelphia: Regional Science Research Institute, 1965.

costs and scale: basic supply relationships

6

From demand we should now turn to supply. To understand why supply curves have the form they do it is necessary to look at the economics of the production unit, for answers are to be found in the relationships of production costs to the scale of output. It is these relationships that will be explored in this chapter. We begin by exploring cost-scale relationships, and then show how supply curves are derived. Along the way, as in the previous chapter, the effects of spatial factors are discussed. The chapter concludes by exploring the effects that different output scales have upon the degree of concentration of production within industries, and, in turn, the effects of concentration on the competitive structure of these industries.

INCREASING AND DECREASING RETURNS TO SCALE

fixed and variable costs

Two kinds of costs are involved in all business operations, fixed costs and variable costs. Fixed costs must be paid even if the plant produces nothing at all. They include rents, interest, maintenance, and administration. At different levels of output, however, these fixed costs have different effects on costs per unit of output (unit costs). This is because fixed costs constitute a lump sum, whose effect on unit costs decreases as output increases, allowing the lump sum to be distributed over more units of output. Variable costs—those which change with level of output—include payments for wages, raw materials, fuel and power, and—as we shall see in a moment—transportation.

the U-shaped short-run cost curve

Because fixed costs decrease per unit of output with increasing output while variable costs tend to increase, total costs—the sum of the two—tend to decrease, then to increase. This results in a U-shaped unit cost curve, as illustrated in Figure 6.1. Both transportation costs and resources are important factors in producing the U-shape. Because greater output must be distributed to a wider market area, each increment to output involves a greater-than-proportional increment to average costs. If the business incurs substantial transportation charges, the U-shape of the cost curve will be relatively steep; where transportation charges are a smaller proportion of variable costs, the U has a shallower shape, as shown by Figure 6.1.

Similarly, the best resources are brought into production first and can be supplied at the lowest prices. Expanding the supply entails use of lower-grade or less accessible raw materials, cultivating less productive or more distant farmland, employing less-skilled labor, or the same labor at higher overtime pay scales, and less-efficient reserve equipment. For this reason, too, the cost curve is likely to be U-shaped.

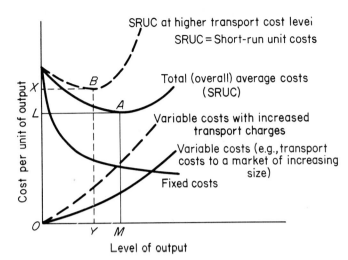

Fig. 6.1 *Fixed, variable, and overall average costs related*

an optimum scale of output

A U-shaped cost curve implies that there is some scale of output that is "optimum" in the sense of yielding least-cost output. For the lower transport cost level, this is at point *A* in Figure 6.1, at which cost per unit of output is *OL*, and *OM* units of output are produced. At the higher transport cost level, *B* is the optimum, but average costs rise to *OX* and the output level falls to *OY*. This implies that as transportation charges increase, unit costs will rise and the scale of output—and therefore the size of market areas—will fall, and vice versa. Transport improvements thus will increase the scale of production and the size of market areas.

returns to scale

This U-shaped pattern of average costs is a consequence of increasing and then decreasing *returns to scale,* a phenomenon first noted by Adam Smith in *The Wealth of Nations* and analyzed by the famous nineteenth-century economist Alfred Marshall. Marshall said the shape of the curve also can result from internal economies and diseconomies of the firm, those changes in production costs that can be created within the firm itself when the scale of output increases. Among the reasons usually given for internal economies are:

a. *labor economies*—the so-called advantages of the "division of labor," which arise because workers become more efficient through specialization
b. *technical economies*—these arise because many tools and machines are very expensive, so that their cost per unit declines as output increases
c. *marketing economies*—put simply, it may not be as hard or as costly per unit sold to sell 100 units of output as it is 10
d. *managerial economies*—a first-rate manager is expensive but can organize larger-scale output as well as smaller-scale

Internal economies arise because many of the factors of production (inputs) are indivisible and cannot be used as efficiently at small scales of output as at large. But equally, these indivisible factors can be overloaded, so that beyond some scale of output, costs will rise as managerial efficiency declines, space becomes too crowded, and it becomes too difficult to maintain good coordination of highly-specialized workers. The result, according to most economists, is that after some point businesses experience a *law of diminishing returns* (sometimes called the *law of variable factor proportions*) in the short-run. The combination of internal economies and diminishing returns produce the U-shaped unit cost curves.

Geography makes this relationship more pronounced, as we noted earlier. As output increases, not only are lower quality resources used, but products must be sold to wider market areas. Because the additional consumers are located at greater distances, transport costs per unit of output will increase at a rate depending upon transport rates and the mode of transportation. Accordingly average costs will climb.

SHORT-RUN AND LONG-RUN COST CURVES

Most of the previous discussion refers to the shape of *short-run* unit cost curves. *Long-run* average cost curves (also called *planning curves*) differ from these, because the assumption of a fixed investment in a given plant is dropped; all costs can be considered variable. In the short-run, it is assumed that one is dealing with cost variations from operating a given farm or factory at different levels of output. In the long run, the business can be modified or sold, or a new unit with a different amount and configuration of investment can be planned and built for a different scale of output.

One way of looking at the long-run average cost curve is by comparing average cost levels for a variety of different facilities, as in Figure 6.2. But each of the individual facilities representing different investment "packages" will have its own short-run cost curve, and the relationship between the two is more properly expressed by a relationship in which the long-run cost curve appears as an "envelope" embracing the many possible short-run curves, as in Figure 6.3.

the lazy-J long-run cost curve

An outstanding feature of Figure 6.3 is that it shows that the long-run returns to scale of investment may not be U-shaped, but instead that the envelope may take the shape of a reverse- or "lazy"-J. The graph shows the short-run cost curves for each of several types of dairy farm in Minnesota and the characteristics of the least-cost farm are described in each case. For example, the least-cost three-man dairy farm (farm *D* at the top of the illustration) is one with an investment of $325,000, working 623 acres of land with a 100-head herd, and produc-

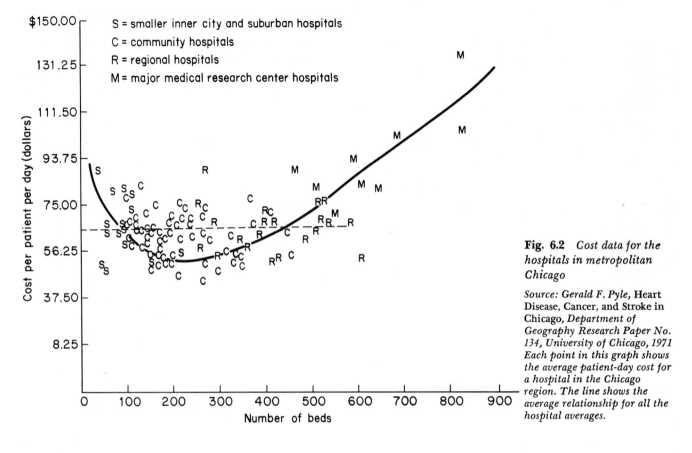

S = smaller inner city and suburban hospitals
C = community hospitals
R = regional hospitals
M = major medical research center hospitals

Fig. 6.2 *Cost data for the hospitals in metropolitan Chicago*

Source: Gerald F. Pyle, Heart Disease, Cancer, and Stroke in Chicago, *Department of Geography Research Paper No. 134, University of Chicago, 1971 Each point in this graph shows the average patient-day cost for a hospital in the Chicago region. The line shows the average relationship for all the hospital averages.*

Fig. 6.3 *Short- and long-run cost curves for Minnesota dairy farms*

Source: Buxton and Boyd, Minnesota Dairy Farming, *Fig. 4, p. 20.*

	Least-cost farms under differing assumptions				
	A	*B*	*C*	*D*	*E*
Net return	−$429	$4,633	$11,869	$16,925	$24,194
Milk cows	19	40	81	100	141
Land (acres)	109	234	467	623	817
Investment	$89,000	$149,000	$263,000	$325,000	$416,000

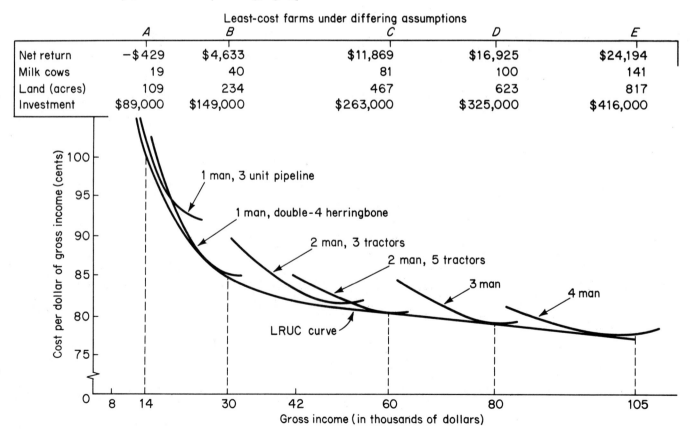

ing a net return of $16,925 per annum on a gross income of $80,000. The long-run curve traces out the best achievable cost per unit of output at each scale of production by forming an envelope embracing each of the short-run curves. Note how the long-run curve continues to slope downward to the right, indicating continuing cost advantages of increasing farm size.

Agriculture is pursuing these long-run cost advantages, resulting in rapid decline of smaller farms and a progressive increase in numbers of larger operations. Such results of cost advantages to larger-sized farms, accruing as they did throughout most of American agriculture, were responsible for the decline in the U. S. farm population from 15 million in 1960 to 10 million in 1970 as the small-scale farmers moved into urban occupations.

returns to scale and threshold size

Lazy-J long-run cost curves indicate a particular pattern of returns to investment. First, for the reasons cited in the case of short-run curves, there will be economies of scale, and the long-run unit cost curve will fall with increasing output. But only if there are long-run constraints will there be diseconomies of further increases in scale, producing a U-shaped LRUC curve. What occurs with the lazy-J is that the zone of increasing returns to scale terminates at a critical *size threshold,* but there is no onset of decreasing returns beyond this point because of the flexibility of different investment

configurations that may be designed and built. Instead, beyond the threshold, average costs per unit of output tend to be relatively stable, as for example, to the right of the $90,000 gross-income level for Illinois cash-grain farms (as indicated in Figure 6.4). Above the threshold point there is no apparent cost advantage of operating at either one scale or another. The critical factor that determines whether a firm can operate competitively is the factor of threshold size. The smallest and most inefficient producers beneath the threshold go out of business. Not only do competitive pressures force readjustments in the form of increasing scale, however; so do profits. With a reverse-J LRUC curve, total profits rise with increasing scale.

DERIVATION OF SUPPLY CURVES

What is the relationship of supply curves to the short-run and long-run cost curves discussed in the previous paragraphs? To establish the link, it is necessary first to define *total, average,* and *marginal* revenues and costs, and then to see what the short-run and the long-run responses of producers are to price changes.

total, average and marginal revenues and costs

Figure 6.5 provides a beginning point, graphing total revenues and costs against level of output for a hypothetical business firm. Total revenues equal total

Fig. 6.4 *Cost curves for Illinois cash grain farms*

Source: Van Arsdall and Elder, Illinois Cash-Grain and Hog Farms, *Fig. 7, p. 24.*

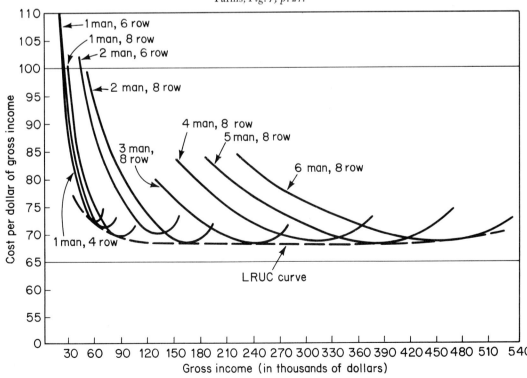

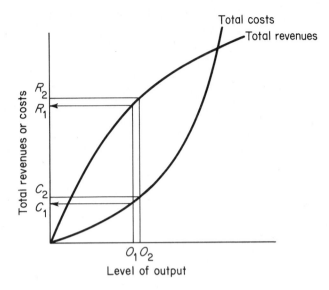

Fig. 6.5 *Total costs and revenues related to level of output*

costs at two production levels: *A*, with zero production, and *B*. At these two production levels the firm makes no profit. The greatest profit is achieved where the total revenues and total costs reach their maximum difference. In Figure 6.5 this production point is at output level O, where costs are C_1 and revenues are R_1. *Average revenues* and *average costs* for the output level yielding maximum profit can now be defined. Average revenues are R_1 divided by O_1 and average costs are C_1 divided by O_1. Profits are simply R_1 minus C_1.

Suppose the producer decides to turn out one more unit of output, producing at level O_2. Now $O_2 = O_1 + 1$ and the incremental unit of output is called the *marginal increment*. By the same token, *marginal revenue* is R_2 minus R_1 and *marginal cost* is C_2 minus C_1.

Several things need to be said about the relationships between marginal, average, and total revenues and costs. Consider first marginal revenue and cost. If profits are a maximum at O_1, then the difference between total revenues and total costs must be less at O_2 than they were at O_1; hence marginal costs at O_2 must exceed marginal revenue. Conversely, since profits are increasing to a maximum at O_1, marginal costs must be less than marginal revenues at production levels from *A* to O_1. It follows that the point of *maximum profit*, O_1, occurs where *marginal costs equal marginal revenue*. This point is also the production level at which *marginal cost* equals average revenue under conditions of perfect competition (for then, since the producer will be a price taker, average revenue equals price) and the producer can increase profits with expanding production only so long as each increment to production costs less than the revenue it brings.

What is the relationship between the marginal and average cost curves? This is shown in Figure 6.6. For the first unit of production they are the same. Beyond it,

the average curve lags behind the marginal curve, continuing to decline as long as the marginal curve is falling, but doing so more gently. When the marginal curve rises, the average curve eases off still more, turning upwards when marginal costs exceed average costs, but again, increasing more slowly. Note that the point of highest profits is not necessarily the point of lowest average production costs. The point of lowest average production costs occurs where marginal costs equal average costs.

the shape of the supply curve

Consider the model situation in Figure 6.6 in more detail. If the producer whose cost curves are depicted has many competitors, he can compete most effectively if he produces at output level *OA* and sells at price *OL*. Under conditions of perfect competition, *OL* will become the market price, and the industry will consist of many firms, each of size *OA*, and each a "price-taker." Because of the competitive conditions, the same price is received for each unit of output produced, so average revenues will equal marginal revenues.

If, for some reason, prices were to rise to the level *OR*, how should the producer respond to maximize his profits? As was noted earlier, he should increase his output to the level *OB*, to enable marginal revenues to equal marginal costs again at point *E*. But while his average revenues increase from *OL* to OR_1, his average costs only increase from *AD* to *BC*, so that the difference *CE* represents an increase in average profits.

The "production-expansion" path for the individual firm is described by the shift from *D* to *E* along the marginal cost curve; this, then, is that individual *firm's* short-run supply curve. If there are, say, 100 firms in the industry, total output at price *L* would be 100 × *OA* and at price R_1 it would rise to 100 × *OB*. A graph in which price is plotted against total output supplied,

Fig. 6.6 *The short-run unit cost curve and the marginal cost curve. The model shows two optimum levels of firm operation: one for cost minimization and one for profit maximization.*

Source: Van Arsdall and Elder, Illinois Cash-Grain and Hog Farms, *Fig. 1, p. 4.*

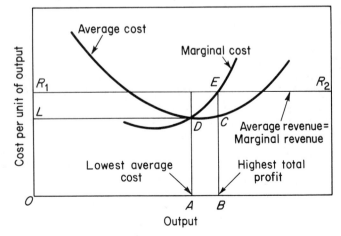

derived in the manner just described, yields the *industry's* supply curve.

the concept of elasticity

If a given price change elicits a substantial change in output, the supply curve will be relatively steep and *elastic*. On the other hand, if output levels are unresponsive to price changes, supply curves are relatively flat and are said to be *inelastic*. Returning to Figure 6.1, this suggests that, for example, the elasticity of supply will be more in the smaller-scale higher transport cost situation that is depicted than in the larger-scale lower transport cost situation. Other examples will occur to the reader.

THE RELATIONSHIP OF SCALE TO INDUSTRIAL CONCENTRATION

Variations in scale thresholds can be measured, and are closely related to the concentration of power and decisionmaking in small numbers of firms, the emergence of oligopolies, product differentiation and barriers to new competition, and pricing behavior within industries.

measurement of scale thresholds

One economist, J. S. Bain, has identified the size thresholds associated with lazy-J cost curves in a variety of industries in North America. By expressing the scale of individual manufacturing plants as a percentage of the total national capacity of an industry, costs were shown to decrease with increasing scale, and then to level off. This enabled threshold sizes to be measured in relation to the proportion of national industrial capacity contained in one plant of minimal efficient size by selecting as the threshold the point at which costs levelled off. It also enabled the capital requirements for a new plant to enter the industry at the efficient cost threshold to be calculated. The threshold conditions for entry in many of the industries that Bain studied were substantial.

economics of the multiplant firm

But Bain did not stop there. He argued that significant economies also may arise from the emergence of multiplant firms, and he tried to estimate them. The growth of such firms is responsible for the emergence of large-scale market negotiation in Western societies, because they prefer negotiation to competition. What are these economies of the multiplant firm? Bain distinguished three:

1. Economies of large-scale management
2. Economies of large-scale distribution
3. Economies of large-scale buying from suppliers

In some industries, economies from the centralized and coordinated management of several plants are claimed to be present. In some, operation of multiple plants may reduce costs of delivery if several branch plants are geographically scattered so as to be near different buying markets, and may also permit the building up of an efficient volume of sales through each geographically-separated distributive center. Existence of such distributive economies presupposes that the firm for some reason —perhaps for more effective sales promotion—finds it advantageous to distribute its output over a wide geographical area, such as the entire national market. Finally, the buying power of a multiplant firm that uses vast quantities of materials may permit it to bargain for lower buying prices than smaller firms can obtain.

horizontal and vertical integration

Bain's list of three considerations refers, of course, to the size of the firm relative to the size of the total industry. This dimension of size is often called *horizontal integration* ("across the market"). There is, however, another dimension of size and growth: extension via integration of preceding or succeeding productive processes. For example, a steel firm producing steel ingots by feeding pig iron into an open-hearth steel furnace may grow not only horizontally—by equipping to produce more ingots—but also vertically. This *vertical integration* may be *backward*, as the firm constructs new facilities or acquires them from others to produce its own pig iron, or it may be *forward* as the firm secures facilities for rolling or drawing its steel ingots into semifinished products, such as steel sheets or wire. Again, a firm engaged in petroleum refining may integrate backward to secure its own crude oil supply, or forward to acquire its own wholesale storage and distribution depots in various local markets for refined petroleum products.

The vertically integrated firm can perform a series of successive productive functions more efficiently than individual firms that each perform only one function. Economies of vertical integration are especially apparent where technologically complementary productive processes can be brought together in a single plant. For example, integrating in a single plant the processes of making pig iron, converting iron into steel, and shaping of steel into semifinished products permits considerable savings in the total fuel requirement for heating the iron and steel. If all functions are performed in a single plant, neither the pig iron nor the steel ingots have to get cold and then be reheated before passing to the next productive process. Some economies of vertical integration are also claimed where the firm's functions are not technologically complementary and are not able to be unified in a single plant: production of the components of a machine, assembly of the components into a finished machine, and distribution of the machine. In such cases, economies are usually attributed to improved coordination of the rates of output at the successive stages (through placing them under one management), consequent reduction of intermediate inventories, and elimination of the expense of purchase-sale transactions in moving goods from one stage to the next. Additional economies may result from forward or backward integration because the firm does not have to pay suppliers' or customers' profits, provided that this saving exceeds the interest payments a firm has to pay on the added investment required to integrate.

emergence of oligopolies and administered prices

There are several consequences of reverse-J long-run cost curves with high conditions of entry. Generally, high conditions of entry limit potential new competition and tend to create oligopolies in which the industry is controlled by a small number of multiplant firms. An example of a typical oligopoly in which a few firms have consistently controlled a large share of the market is that of the sulfur industry, in particular the Frasch sulfur industry, which produces sulfur from brimstone deposits found in the salt domes of the United States and Mexican Gulf coasts.

The Frasch sulfur industry is oligopolistic because of the high conditions of entry, and the LRUC is reverse-J. The difficulties faced by potential new competitors in gaining entry to the industry are threefold:

1. *Absolute cost barriers*—Established firms control existing Frasch sulfur deposits, and there is great competition for new deposits when discovered. A new sulfur firm enters this arena by having to raise capital for the cost of entry at the same time that it competes with existing producers owning less costly deposits. The effect is to raise the price that must be paid for the new deposits.
2. *Product differentiation barriers*—Firms who have an established reputation with their customers have a sales advantage over new competitors.
3. *The economy of scale threshold*—The minimal scale at which a new firm may achieve the lowest attainable cost is a significant fraction of the total capacity of the industry. The entry of an additional firm may induce established firms to lower their price to preserve their market share. In this case, the newcomer must compete against a price that is even lower than the prevailing price when the firm entered. This discouragement is often sufficient to turn away potential new entrants.

Relatively free from new competitors, Frasch sulfur producers let their prices be determined by administrative decisions rather than allowing them to fluctuate with market conditions. First, prices were determined by the industry in response to long-run criteria, rather than with respect to short-run economic changes. Second, the industry practiced price discrimination, charging one price in domestic markets and a second, higher basing-point price for foreign markets. The higher price was quoted f.o.b. vessels, Gulf port through the Sulfur Export Corporation, to which all Frasch producers belonged. The domestic price was established competitively by producers; the foreign price, however, was an arranged one producing a world pattern of Frasch sulfur prices rising with transport costs from U.S. Gulf ports.

product differentiation as a barrier to entry

In most such oligopolistic circumstances, product differentiation is as powerful a force in restricting entry as is the condition of entry itself. The most obvious sources of product differentiation are differences in quality of design among competing outputs. For example, one brand of shoes may have better materials and workmanship than another, or one make of clothes may be fashionable while another may not. In either case, different buyers may rank the competing products differently. One buyer may be fashion-conscious, looking for the latest styles. Another may be quality-conscious, willing to pay a considerable premium for quality shoes. Yet another may be price-conscious, accepting the lower quality if there is only a relatively small price concession.

A second source of product differentiation is the ignorance of buyers regarding the essential characteristics and qualities of the goods they are purchasing. This is likely to be an important consideration particularly with durable consumer goods, which are infrequently purchased and complex in design or composition. In this situation, the buyer is likely to rely on the "reputations" of the various products or their sellers—on popular lore concerning the product's performance and reliability, or on whether or not the seller has successfully remained in business for a long time.

Third, buyer preferences for certain products are developed or shaped by the persuasive sales-promotion activities of sellers, particularly by advertising of brand names, trademarks, or company names.

J. S. Bain has classified industries according to degree of product differentiation. He concludes that product differentiation is generally negligible in the producer good segments of the agricultural, forestry, fisheries, and mining industries. Because goods produced by these industries are likely to be standardized at various grades and qualities, the sellers' efforts to introduce product differentiation have generally been unsuccessful. Moreover, these industries comprise many small sellers, thus providing a close approximation to the theoretical "pure competition."

On the other hand, in manufacturing and processing industries—particularly those producing consumer goods—product differentiation becomes very important. The consumer-buyers tend to be poorly informed, especially when faced with choosing among goods with complex designs. Even when the goods are not complex, buyers are susceptible to persuasive advertising campaigns that emphasize the sometimes nominal differences among products. In addition, producers can purposely vary the designs or quality of their goods in ways whose significance is not easily understood by consumers.

In some consumer-good manufacturing industries, however, product differentiation is relatively unimportant. This seems to be especially true of basic necessities—food, clothing, and household supplies. Thus, in these industries the efforts of competing sellers to differentiate their products significantly have not been too successful. Thus, the establishment of brands and their support by advertising has not been automatically efficacious in creating strong product differentiation within a consumer-good industry.

In manufacturing industries making producer goods, product differentiation is most frequently slight or negligible, and for the usual reasons—expert buyers, and goods that may be produced to standards or specifications. Basic industrial chemicals, for example, clearly come under this heading. Buyers purchase to specification or rely on established grades, and generally do not prefer one seller's output to another sufficiently to induce them to pay any higher a price for it. The slight buyer preferences that do introduce some product differentiation generally depend on ancillary services that the seller performs for buyers, such as promptness in filling orders, or making deliveries. But with producer goods for which the provision of services by the manufacturer is an important element of the transaction (often when the producer-buyers represent rather small firms) and with large, complex producer goods (specialized machinery of various sorts), product differentiation may become as important as it is in consumer-goods categories. This would be true, for example, of farm machinery and business office machines of various sorts.

Other sectors of the economy may be characterized more briefly with respect to the incidence of product differentiation.

1. *Wholesale and retail trade* (groceries, clothing stores, drug stores, etc.). In retail distribution, product differentiation based on type and quality of service offered by the retailer and on the convenience of his location to the buyer is generally quite important. Product differentiation is evidently less important in wholesale markets in which retailers purchase from wholesale distributors.
2. *Service trades* (barber shops, dry cleaners, entertainment enterprises, etc.). Product differentiation is again important, for the same general reasons as those that apply to retailing.
3. *Contract construction*. On large-scale construction for industry or government where contracts are awarded after a process of bidding to specifications, product differentiation is a minimal factor. In residential construction, product differentiation based on design and location is generally quite important.
4. *Finance* (real estate firms, insurance companies, banks, etc.). Product differentiation is important in some cases and not in others.

5. *Public utilities and transportation*. In most utility industries, including suppliers of electricity, gas, and communications services, local monopoly by a single firm typically forestalls the emergence of product differentiation. In the transport field, product differentiation among the services of competing types of carriers and between competing carriers of the same type is present, but is evidently more important in passenger transportation than in freight transport.

conditions of entry and pricing behavior

The degree of difficulty that a new firm has in entering a field of industry determines how much the already established firms can raise their prices above the defined competitive level without attracting new competition. In effect, the established firms administer a geography of price, with their selling prices restrained according to the barriers of entry. In industries where the conditions of entry are not difficult, the established firms can exceed only slightly the competitive selling price before new competitors will enter; if entry conditions are difficult, the established firms can perhaps attain a monopolistic price—substantially higher than the competitive level—without attracting competitors; if entry conditions are moderately difficult, the established firms can only raise their prices moderately to keep out new competitors.

Thus, J. S. Bain found in his studies that:

1. When barriers to entry are either high or moderate, then
   a. among industries of high seller concentration, "limit pricing" to exclude entry is likely. This will result in higher prices and greater monopolistic output restriction according to the height of the barriers to entry.
   b. among industries of moderate to low seller concentration, the preceding tendency is likely to be modified or obscured because intra-industry competition will frequently keep price fairly close to the competitive level.

2. When barriers to entry are low, then:
   a. among industries of high seller concentration, periodic high prices and monopolistic output restriction are likely to emerge, followed by induced entry, and further followed by excess plant capacity. The ultimate result may be a significant decrease in seller concentration, an increase in intra-industry competition, and a lessening or elimination of monopolistic tendencies.
   b. among industries of moderate to low seller concentration, the pressure of entry plus the inherent tendencies toward strong intra-industry competition are likely to produce close approximations to competitive pricing and output.

Costs, prices, and the degree of concentration of production are thus closely interdependent.

RECOMMENDED READINGS

Bain, Joe S., *Barriers to New Competition.* Cambridge, Mass.: Harvard University Press, 1956.

Karaska, G. J., and D. F. Bramhall, *Locational Analysis for Manufacturing.* Cambridge, Mass.: M.I.T. Press, 1969.

Manners, G., *The Geography of Energy.* London: Hutchinson University Library, 1964.

Mund, V. A., and R. H. Wolf, *Industrial Organization and Public Policy.* Englewood Cliffs, N. J.: Prentice-Hall, 1971.

Wiles, P. J. D., *Price, Cost and Output.* New York: Praeger, 1961.

theories
of
location
three

The uses to which man puts the land resources available to him reflect, in part, differences in physical factors, such as soil fertility and climate in rural land use, and amenities, such as high elevation with imposing views in urban land use. Historical and cultural factors, too—including the timing of settlement and the cultural traditions of a population—affect land use. But even on a homogeneous plain, where the population is culturally homogeneous, the efforts of farmers or city residents and developers to maximize their returns and satisfactions produce systematic land-use patterns. The exciting discovery of these spatial patterns was first presented by Von Thünen in his study *The Isolated State* in 1826. The importance of Von Thünen's contribution should be emphasized. He provided the earliest theory of the spatial organization of land use. Although world economic geography has changed dramatically in the century and a half since Von Thünen made his seminal contribution, the basic principles that he stated still apply today to rural land use, and with some complications, to urban land use. Von Thünen's principles rely in turn on the ideas presented in the preceding section, particularly on the laws of returns. It is appropriate, therefore, to preface the discussion of Von Thünen's theory with a review of the laws of returns.

THE LAWS OF RETURNS

We should start by recalling the preference analysis introduced earlier. The manner in which a producer might blend inputs in order to achieve maximum output was presented in Chapter 5. The case where one input was strictly limited, as in the case of arable land available to a farmer, however, was not considered. We now turn to this case, beginning with a producer who has two different inputs, X and Y, as illustrated by the preference map in Figure 7.1. As usual, this preference map is drawn in the form of an ascending series of equal-product lines (isoquants), along any one of which inputs of X and Y produce the same volume of output. In addition, the diagram shows the producer's production-possibility lines, along which total input costs remain constant, and the scale line tracing out the optimum expansion path of the business at successively higher levels of output, i.e., that way of combining inputs to achieve maximum output at each successive level of expenditure upon inputs.

constant and variable input proportions

If the scale line is straight, increasing production is accompanied by constant factor proportions. For example, a doubling of output would require a doubling of both inputs. On the other hand, if the scale line is curved, increasing production involves substitution effects. Depending upon the curvature, increasing shares of either X or Y are required to achieve optimum output levels.

the spatial organization of land use

7

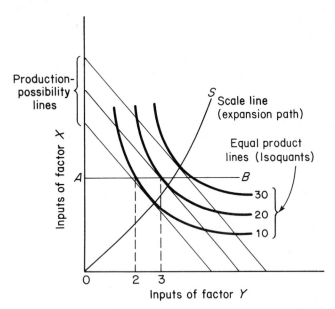

Fig. 7.1 *Production-possibility, equal-product, and scale lines*

marginal productivity and returns to scale

Now assume that there is a fixed supply of one input available (see *OA* in Fig. 7.1.). For example, let factor *X* be land, and assume that the farmer has a fixed number of acres under cultivation, *OA*. Output then will be changed solely as a result of increased inputs of factor *Y*, inputs of *X* necessarily being held constant

along the line *AB*. The *marginal physical productivity* of *Y* is the amount by which the *volume* of output changes following a unit increase of *Y*, with *X* constant (e.g., output moves from 10 to 20 when *Y* moves from 2 to 3, if inputs of *X* are limited to *OA*; the marginal physical productivity of *Y* is thus 10). The *marginal revenue productivity* of *Y* is the amount by which the *value* of output changes under the same circumstances. Such marginal productivity data enable us to understand the concept of returns to scale.

Figure 7.2 provides a numerical example. A fixed amount of land is in grain production. Variable inputs (*Y*) are measured as dollars of capital and labor spent on the land. As more capital and labor are applied, the grain yield in bushels per acre—and therefore the value of output—first increases (*increasing returns to scale*) and then decreases (*decreasing returns*).

The marginal revenue productivity curve describes the value of output received for each marginal increase in inputs of the variable factor *Y*. At what point should the farmer stop making incremental inputs of *Y*? In this case, the answer is provided by the data accompanying Figure 7.2. In Chapter 6 we saw that the general answer is where marginal revenue equals the marginal cost of the inputs, beyond which the inputs cost more than they return. For most producers, of course, the cost of an input is a given market price—say, for labor. Thus, the optimum level of any variable input (that which will maximize returns) occurs where marginal revenue equals marginal cost (or price) of the input. *The marginal revenue productivity curve is therefore the demand curve for the input.*

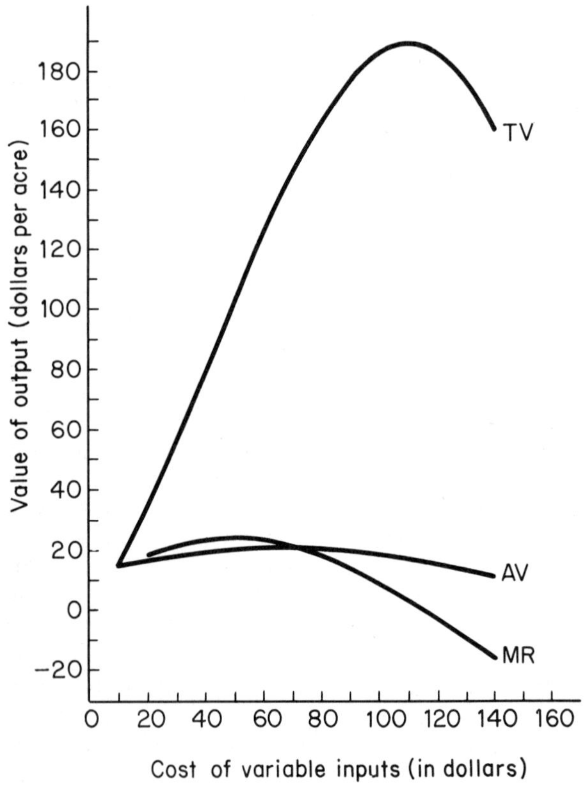

Fig. 7.2 *Total, average, and marginal value of output under conditions of increasing and decreasing returns. This figure compares the cost of variable inputs with total value of output, the average value of output at the scale of output reached, and the marginal value of the last $10.00 increase in outputs. The data from which the graph is plotted are shown below.*

Cumulative cost of inputs of variable factors (capital & labor)	Yield (bushels per acre)	Total value of output @ $1.50 per bushel	Average value of output per $10 input of variable factors	Value of additional output per $10 input (marginal value of product)
$ 10.0	10	$ 15.0	$ 15.00	$ 0
20.0	22	33.0	16.50	18.0
30.0	36	54.0	18.00	21.0
40.0	52	78.0	19.50	24.0
50.0	68	102.0	20.40	24.0
60.0	83.3	125.0	20.83	23.0
70.0	97.3	146.0	20.86	21.0
80.0	109	163.5	20.45	17.5
90.0	118	177.0	19.67	13.5
100.0	124	186.0	18.60	9.0
110.0	126	189.0	17.18	3.0
120.0	124	186.0	15.50	−3.0
130.0	117.3	176.0	13.54	−9.0
140.0	106.6	160.0	11.43	−16.0

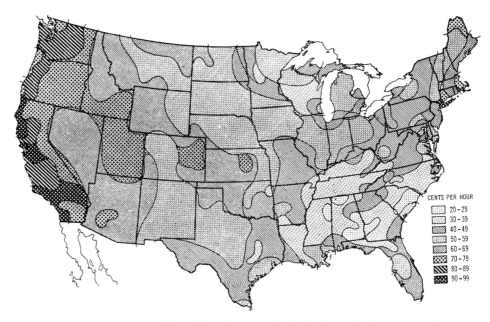

Fig. 7.3 *Farm wage belts in the United States, April, 1950. The values are delineated on the basis of composite hourly wage rates by state economic areas.*

Source: U.S. Department of Agriculture, Agricultural Marketing Service, Neg. 4131–57(4).

Consider what is implied. Figure 7.3 shows the variations in farm wages in the U.S. in 1950. If the above concept is valid, the variations in wages should reflect variations in the marginal revenue productivity of America farm labor, lowest in the South and highest in the specialized agricultural regions of the West Coast, a conclusion that is probably valid.

THE CONCEPT OF RENT

From the idea of the marginal revenue productivity of land as an input factor and its relationship to the price of the factor comes the concept of *land rent*. This concept is basic to the development of theories of agricultural and urban land use, because the core idea of land use theory is that land use is determined by land rent.

rent as a scarcity payment

Assume we are dealing with an island that contains a fixed amount of homogeneous land available for cultivation (*OS* in Fig. 7.4). The first farmer settles on the island, bringing with him a fixed amount of capital and labor. How much land will he use, and what rent will he pay?

Suppose he is a grain farmer selling wheat on the world market. Because of the nature of that market he must be a price-taker, accepting a fixed world price. Let his marginal revenue productivity curve for land then be *NM* in Figure 7.4, as he increases output by increas-

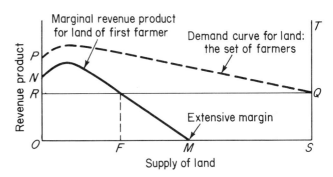

Fig. 7.4 *Marginal revenue product and the emergence of land rent*

ing inputs of land. The price paid by the farmer for the land (i.e., the land rent) and the quantity of land consumed will be determined by the intersection of the demand and supply curves for land. The demand curve is the marginal revenue productivity curve *NM*. The supply curve is the line *OST*. Thus, the farmer will use *OM* land. The rent will be zero. This is because there is land to spare. The farmer could always move if a landlord tried to charge him rent.

Rent is payment to a landowner for use of his factor of production, land, which arises solely because land is *scarce*. This can be seen in Figure 7.4, if we let additional farmers arrive on the island. The total demand curve increases as each individual's marginal revenue productivity curve is added to that of the others. For example, *PQ* might be the total demand curve for land of one group of farmers (the summation of the individual marginal revenue productivity curves). It intersects the supply curve *OST* at *Q*. Since there is only *OS* land available, farmers compete for the land, balancing demands and supplies at price *OR* (=*SQ*). The marginal cost curve for land is thus the price line *RQ*, and our first farmer, maximizing profits by equating marginal revenues and marginal costs, will cut his land consumption to *OF*. The other farmers will cultivate the rest of the island, *FS*.

differential rents due to productivity differences

Although the preceding example suggests that rents are uniform across the island, in reality rents do differ. Differential rents arise because

a. the productivity of different parcels of land varies, and
b. land is located at different distances from market.

Both types of variation are central to the theory of agricultural location, in which the basic idea is that each parcel of land is used for the activity that can pay the highest rent. If we can understand the reasons for the variations, we will have gone a long way towards understanding one of the basic problems of economic geography—that of explaining land use.

First, let us take the question of productivity differences. The idea of rent variations being attributable to productivity of the soil was first discussed by David Ricardo in his *Principles of Political Economy and Taxation* (1817). Ricardo said that high rents were due to the "niggardliness of nature" (i.e., to scarcity) and were related to the "original and indestructible power of the soil" (i.e., to productivity differences). Further, he said that the most fertile lands are put to use first, with production extending to less favorable lands only as demands increase.

Fig. 7.5 *Marginal revenue product differences for differing land qualities*

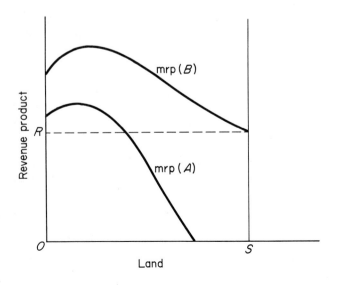

Why is this so? Productivity differences change the marginal revenue productivity curve for land because they change marginal physical productivity. For example, in Figure 7.5 the marginal revenue productivities of two grades of land, *A* and *B*, are shown. Assume situations in which both are in equal supply *OS*. The lower quality land will not command a rent, whereas that of higher quality will command rent *OR*. In agricultural terminology, the lower quality land is "marginal" because it does not pay any rent, and the rent charged for the superior quality land is entirely due to its greater productivity.

A generalization of Ricardo's idea has been provided recently by geographers H. H. McCarty and J. Lindberg in the form of an "optima and limits" scheme (see Figs. 7.6 and 7.7). In Figure 7.6 two variables—temperature and moisture—provide the basis for their

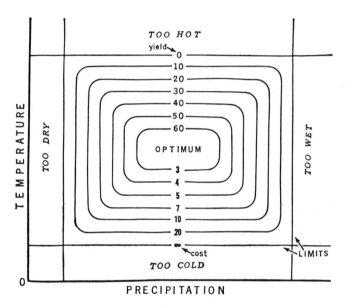

Fig. 7.6 *The optima and limits schema*

Source: H. H. McCarty and James B. Lindberg, A Preface to Economic Geography (Englewood Cliffs, New Jersey: Prentice-Hall Inc., 1966), pp. 61–62.

hypothesis. In some restricted area, those variables are presumed to combine ideally for producing a particular crop. That area is identified as having "optimum" conditions. Outward from it, conditions become less and less favorable until, finally, the physical limits are reached, beyond which production of that crop is impossible. In most cases, however, greater significance attaches to the "economic limits," which appear in Figure 7.7. When the productivity data of Figure 7.6 are translated into unit-costs of production and when those unit-costs are converted into rent (per unit of output), the areas of production that would appear in response to various price levels for that commodity can be estimated. Assume that a price of "7" will cover costs in the four inside zones of the model. No production will occur out-

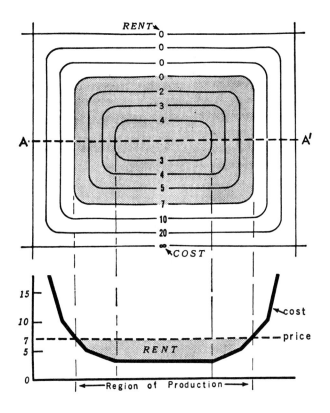

Fig. 7.7 *Rents in the productivity schema*

Source: *McCarty and Lindberg*, A Preface to Economic Geography

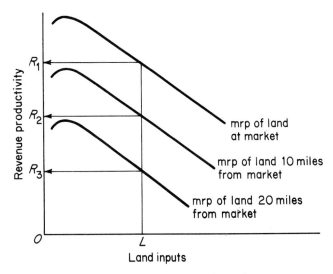

Fig. 7.8 *Marginal revenue productivities of land of identical quality at different distances from market*

side that zone (in the "no-rent" areas). Further, rent will increase towards the optimum.

What will happen if the price rises for the products of the land due to increasing demand? Marginal revenue productivity will rise, and the extensive margin of production will move into uncultivated lands. By the same token, the higher-rent land will also be used more intensively, because—recalling the earlier discussion of input substitution—if rents are higher for better quality land, and if other factors are constant, it will pay farmers to substitute inputs of the other (cheaper) factors for inputs of the more expensive land to achieve the same resulting output.

differential rents due to locational differences

The same relationship holds in the case of rent differences due to transport cost. Marginal revenue productivity is defined in terms of market prices. Yet the at-farm price involves market price less transport costs. Holding land quality constant, the effect of increasing transport costs therefore progressively reduces the more distant farmer's marginal revenue productivity curve (even though marginal physical productivity remains unchanged), and thus reduces the rent he pays for a given amount of land. See Figure 7.8, in which a farm of size OL pays OR_1 at the market, declining to OR_3 twenty miles away. The difference ($R_1 R_3$) is accounted

for by the reduction in revenues due to the cost of transporting output the twenty miles to the market.

In such a situation, rents display a pattern of distance-decay from the market center. Further, just as higher quality land will be used more intensively, so will more accessible land. We should expect to see both farm costs and returns decline with increasing distance from markets, and this is exactly the case in the agricultural example depicted in Table 7.1. Note that as rents fall with increasing distance, farm size increases because farmers substitute the cheapening factor of production (land) for others in their productive process.

Table 7.1 Some Variations in Agricultural Characteristics with Increasing Distance From Louisville, Kentucky (1918)

Distance from Louisville (miles)	Rent of land per acre	Value of land per acre	Percentage of receipts from		
			Truck and potato	dairy	other
8 or less	$11.85	$312	68%	10%	22%
9–11	5.59	110	35	12	53
12–14	5.37	106	34	20	46
15+	4.66	95	20	27	53

Distance from Louisville (miles)	Average area of improved land (acres)	Operating expense per acre	Gross receipts per acre	Land earnings per acre	Value of fertilizer used per acre
9	44	$73	$96	$23	$19.25
12	121	36	45	9	6.50
13	212	15	20	5	5.20
16	420	14	18	4	4.25

Source: J. H. Arnold and Frank Montgomery, *Influence of a City on Farming*, Bulletin 678 (Washington, D.C.: U.S. Department of Agriculture, 1918).

relationship of land rent to everyday "rents" and to land values

Is land rent the same thing as the rent paid to a landlord for an apartment? There is an important difference that must be clearly understood. What we call *rent* in an everyday sense is a payment to a landlord for a variety of things: land, building, furnishings and other services. Only a portion of this payment is the land rent. The rest is a "rental" for the capital, labor, and enterprise involved in constructing and maintaining the apartment occupied. The difference is clearly seen on local property tax bills, which separate assessments for the land and for the "improvements."

The assessor talks of land and building *values*, not rents, however. What is the difference? Land value is the price paid to purchase the land; land rent is the payment to an owner to use his land. There is a simple accounting relationship between the two: land rent capitalized at the current rate of interest equals land value, or the price of land is the present or capitalized value of the rent the land will earn during its useful life.

VON THÜNEN'S ISOLATED STATE: THE FIRST ECONOMIC MODEL OF SPATIAL ORGANIZATION

This simple idea that rents decline with distance was the basis of the first economic model of spatial organization, Johann Heinrich Von Thünen's 1826 classic *Der Isolierte Staat*. It is worth spending some time with Von Thünen's model, not simply out of historical curiosity, but because of the systematic way he linked the economic logic of rent theory to the spatial organization of land use.

Von Thünen had a university education in philosophy, biology, economics, and languages, and in 1810 when he was twenty-seven, he bought an 1,146-acre estate at Tellow, southeast of Rostock in Mecklenburg. As he operated and managed Tellow he kept meticulous records, and his early training led him to speculate about the best way of using his land.

nature of the abstraction from reality

He found it most helpful to develop the abstract ideas underlying the everyday operation of Tellow, pointing out to the readers of *Der Isolierte Staat* that "the reader who is willing to spend some time and attention" to his work should not "take exception to the imaginary assumptions . . . because they do not correspond to conditions in reality" since the reader will find that they allow him "to establish the operation of a certain factor, whose operation we see but dimly in reality, where it is in incessant conflict with others of its kind." This is to be said of all location theories, which are abstract because they seek to understand the basic processes at work shaping the complex reality of the everyday world, and it also explains why we spent so much time with rent theory at the beginning of this chapter.

Von Thünen was unremittingly logical. He stated his assumptions, posed his problem, deduced the consequences, and tested the deductions with empirical evidence that he collected on his estate over many years. As such, he was a model scientist.

the assumptions

The assumptions enabled him to focus on spatial differences, and in particular upon the effects of transport costs on land use:

Imagine a very large town, at the centre of a fertile plain which is crossed by no navigable river or canal. Throughout the plain the soil is capable of cultivation and of the same fertility. Far from the town, the plain turns into an uncultivated wilderness which cuts off all communication between this State and the outside world.

There are no other towns on the plain. The central town must therefore supply the rural areas with all manufactured products, and in return it will obtain all its provisions from the surrounding countryside.

The mines that provide the State with salt and metals are near the central town which, as it is the only one, we shall in future call simply "the Town".

These assumptions are severe: a plain with complete physical homogeneity; a single market, the "Town"; a single source of food supply, the plain; transportation costs related only to volume and distance shipped; and decisions made by economic man, relentlessly organizing space in an optimal way. But these assumptions are needed in order to establish the role of distance, whose operation in reality is in constant conflict with other factors affecting land use, including variations in climate, soil fertility, management, and the transportation network with its freight-rate structure.

the problem

Von Thünen then presented the problem that concerned him.

The problem we want to solve is this: what pattern of cultivation will take shape in these conditions?; and how will the farming system of the various districts be affected by their distance from the Town? We assume throughout that farming is conducted absolutely rationally.

It is on the whole obvious that near the Town will be grown those products which are heavy or bulky in relation to their value and which are consequently so expensive to transport that the remoter districts are unable to supply them. Here also we find the highly perishable products, which must be used very quickly. With increasing distance from the Town, the land will progressively be given up to products cheap to transport in relation to their value.

For this reason alone, fairly sharply differentiated concentric rings or belts will form around the Town, each with its own particular staple product.

From ring to ring the staple product, and with it the entire farming system, will change; and in the various rings we shall find completely different farming systems.

What Von Thünen is suggesting is that locational differences alone are sufficient to cause a complete system of spatial organization of land use, embodying concentric circles of crop production and farm types. But he did not stop there. Once the effect of distance had been observed, the assumptions were relaxed, and other variables introduced into the model to see how they modified the "ideal" pattern of rural land use that results from distance effects alone.

location rent for a single crop at a single intensity

Let us proceed stepwise through Von Thünen's model. He recognized that land inputs embody two different goods, *space* (physical area) and *location* (accessibility). The basic assumption in *Der Isolierte Staat* is that space is physically homogeneous, so that all variations in land quality involve the second quality, accessibility to the Town. The impact of diminishing accessibility on net income per unit land area is thus measurable as total income minus production and transportation costs. Since production costs for any single farm commodity were also assumed to be virtually invariant with distance from the Town, variations in net income could then be attributed to differences in accessibility alone. Income net of all costs Von Thünen called *location rent*. The question he then asked was how location rent differences were related to transport costs.

Von Thünen essentially calculated location rents as follows. Where:

R = location rent per unit of land
E = output per unit of land
p = price per unit of output
a = production expenses per unit of output
f = transportation costs per unit of output per mile
k = miles from market

Then:

$$R = E(p - a) - Efk$$

To illustrate the change in rent gradient with distance, let us assume production of a crop such that $E = 40$ bushels per acre; price (p) = $2.00 per bushel; expenses (a) = $1.00 per bushel; and the transportation rate (f) = 2 cents per bushel per mile. For farm *A*, directly at the market and with no transportation costs, $K = 0$, and the equation reduces to:

$$R = E(p - a)$$

Substituting gives:

$$R = 40(\$2 - \$1)$$
$$R = \$4 \text{ per acre}$$

For a second farm *B*, 25 miles from the market:

$$R = 40(\$2 - \$1) - 40(\$0.02 \times 25)$$
$$= \$20 \text{ per acre}$$

At 25 miles the rent has fallen to half. At what distance will it fall to zero? If:

$$R = E(p - a) - Efk = 0$$
$$k = \frac{(p - a)}{f}$$

Substituting our hypothetical values gives:

$$\frac{2 - 1}{0.02} = 50 \text{ miles}$$

A rent gradient, sloping downward with increasing distance from the Town, can be identified by applying the rent formula to different distances as in the above example. Figure 7.9 shows how the components of gross farm income will vary with distance from the

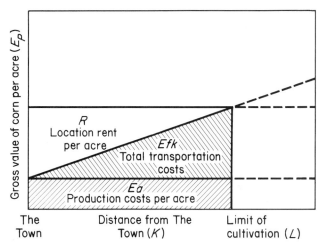

Fig. 7.9 *Components of gross farm income with increasing distance from the Town. Gross income per acre is invariant with distance from the Town. The residual amount,* R, *left after production costs,* a, *and transportation costs,* Efk, *are paid, diminishes with distance. This residual is termed location rent and is a measure of market accessibility.*

Town. Then, as in Figure 7.10, we plot only the spatial variations in rent with distance. Rotating the rent gradient around the Town, we find it becomes a rent cone, the base of which maps out the extensive margin of farm land, as demonstrated by Figure 7.10.

Who receives the location rent? Imagine that all the farms are rented out each year on a fully competitive basis at an auction. The farmers know that net return increases with accessibility and bid up the rents for farms closer to market. It pays to continue bidding until the bid rent equals the location rent; indeed, it is necessary for the farmer who wants to occupy the

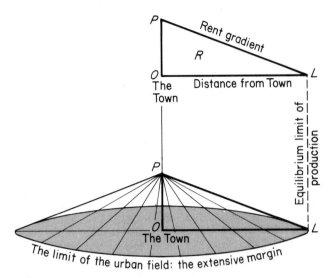

Fig. 7.10 *The rent cone and the extensive margin of production. The components of gross farm income in Figure 7.9 have been reversed to display the rent gradient. Economic rent at the Town is OP. At L, the equilibrium limit of production, O. The △ OPL is rotated to describe the rent cone and to map the extensive margin, where farm land gives way to wilderness.*

land to do so. At that price the farmer just recovers his production expenses (including what he expects to receive for his own labor) and transportation costs, and the landowner receives the location rent as a payment for his land. The competitive bidding eliminates the income differential to farmers that otherwise would be attributable to accessibility; and the bid rent, or contract rent, is the location rent. This bid rent produces a spatial equilibrium situation in which bid rent falls just enough from market to cover additional transportation costs so that the farmer is indifferent as to his distance from market. In essence, there is a tradeoff between transportation costs and accessibility rent.

location rent for a single crop at differing intensities

The higher location rent paid for land with greater accessibility is an incentive to increase output per unit of land by increasing inputs of capital and labor. Even in Von Thünen's day when technology was limited, distinct intensities of grain production existed involving different proportions of the three factors of production—capital, land, and labor. As noted earlier, however, factor substitution is imperfect. The incremental output for each additional unit of input of labor and capital is not uniform. At some point in the intensification of production extra units of labor, machinery or fertilizer add a smaller amount of product than the previous unit. Total physical product may continue to rise, but marginal physical product begins to fall.

This law of diminishing returns has important spatial ramifications. Consider the location rent formula again, $R = E(p - a) - Efk$. The difference between

market price (p) and production costs (a) diminishes per bushel as intensity increases, and the transportation cost per bushel (fk) increases with distance. The optimal level of intensity occurs where the marginal addition to yield by the final increment of capital and labor just pays for the transportation of that marginal yield to market. The lower the transportation costs are, the lower that marginal addition to yield need be to pay for itself. The closer the farm is to market, the further along the marginal physical product curve the farmer can proceed and the more intensive his farming system can be.

The spatial ramifications in the case where two intensity levels reflect two different types of farming organization (the *improved* and the feudal *three-field* systems) were explored in some detail by Von Thünen. The data came from the Tellow accounts for 1810–1819, but were standardized for an area of 100,000 rods, or 217 hectares, an area slightly smaller than Tellow, and for soils a little poorer.

The improved system yielded a gross product of 3144 bushels of grain with costs of 1976 bushels and 641 thalers. Location rent fell to zero at 28.6 miles, at which distance the 1168 bushels of grain for sale (3144 minus 1976 bushels) just fetched enough to pay the town-based costs (641 thalers).

Fig. 7.11 *Rent gradients for the improved and three-field systems. The improved field system yields a higher rent up to a distance of 25 miles, beyond which the three field system is more profitable. The improved system has a steeper rent gradient.*
Source: Data are derived from Peter Hall, ed., Von Thünen's Isolated State *(Oxford: Pergamon Press, 1966), p. xxvii.*

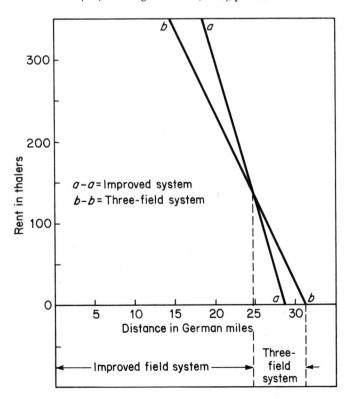

Table 7.2   Location Rent for Competing Crops

	MILK	POTATOES	WHEAT	WOOL
Annual yield, E	725 gal.	150 bu.	50 bu.	50 lbs.
Market price, P	$ 0.65 per gal.	$ 1.75 per bu.	$ 1.70 per bu.	$ 0.60 per lb.
Production cost, a	$ 0.05 per gal.	$ 0.25 per bu.	$ 0.20 per bu.	$ 0.10 per lb.
Transport rate per mile, f	$ 0.05 per gal.	$ 0.075 per bu.	$ 0.025 per bu.	$ 0.005 per lb.
Location rent at town	$435.00	$225.00	$75.00	$25.00
Rent at $0.00 at	12 miles	20 miles	60 miles	100 miles

Note: The data are hypothetical.

The three-field system produced a much smaller gross product—1720 compared with 3144 bushels—but both farm-based and town-based costs were smaller. A 45 percent reduction in yield contributed a 48 percent reduction in grain costs and a 49 percent reduction in town-based costs. The economic rent was lower, but it fell more slowly with increasing distance because the ratio of the 327 thalers of town-based costs to the 696 bushels for sale at the market in the three-field system was smaller than the corresponding ratio for the improved system. Plotting these data indicates that at 24.7 miles from market the three-field system provides the same location rent as the improved farming system (Fig. 7.11). The improved system is better up to 24.7 miles from the market, and the three field system from there to the extensive margin at 31.4 miles.

A spatial separation of the two farming systems occurs, with an inner circle of more intensive grain farming and an outer ring of less extensive farming. This separation illustrates the principle of highest and best use, which states that land is allocated to that use earning the highest location rent.

land use organization in the multicrop case

The most prominent contribution of Von Thünen's study was the determination of land use organization for the multicrop case. Activities are ordered according to the principle of the highest and best use as measured by their location rent at each distance from the market. Market price, transportation costs, and production expenses vary between crops so that the simple intensity law that applies to any single commodity is inappropriate. Instead the general rule becomes that land uses are sequenced outward from the market in the order of the price-spreads they achieve between market price and production plus transport costs. The site nearest the market will be appropriated by the product that can pay the highest location rent.

The details are complex but the basic operation of these principles may be illustrated by using hypothetical data for four commodities—milk, potatoes, wheat, and wool (Table 7.2). To graph the rent gradients, only the rent at the market and the limit of cultivation need be computed. Thus wheat commands a rent of $75 per acre at the market and can extend 60 miles from market.

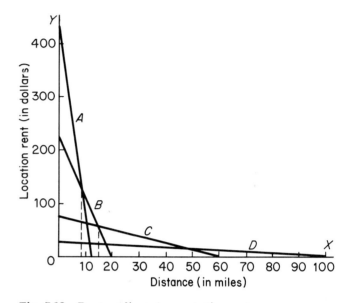

Fig. 7.12 *Rent gradients for competing crops*

The rent gradients for the four crops, based on their market rent and distance values shown in Table 7.2, are superimposed to construct the rent diagram, Figure 7.12. In accordance with the law of highest and best use, the land use with the largest location rent at any given distance from market, outbids the others. The four competing land uses are sequenced outward from the market to form concentric zones of milk, potato, wheat, and wool production.

Von Thünen's farming systems

Von Thünen described six farming systems in the *Isolated State*, ordered outwards as follows (Fig. 7.13):

1. *Free cash cropping* included horticulture and dairying for which perishability dictated a location as close as possible to market. Land use is intensive involving large labor inputs, multicropping, and heavy fertilizing; its outer limit of four miles is the maximum range of manure shipments from the city, where horses provided the principal motive power in Von Thünen's day. The land is too valuable for open grazing and the milk-cows are stall-fed.

2. *Forestry*. The location of forestry in the second zone comes as a surprise from the perspective of modern technology. It was logical at a time when forestry products

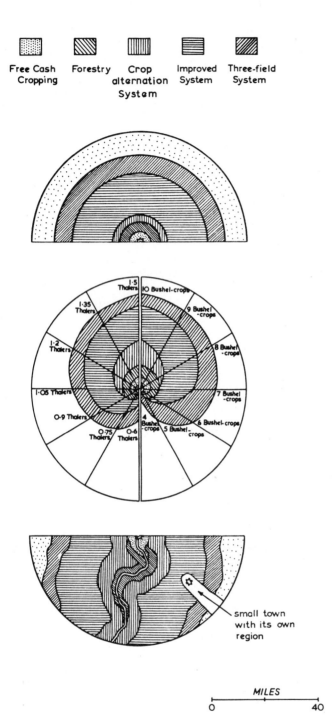

1·5
Thalers | 10 Bushel-crops

1·35
Thalers

9 Bushel
-crops

1·2
Thalers

8 Bushel
-crops

1·05 Thalers

7 Bushel
-crops

0·9 Thalers

6 Bushel-crops

0·75
Thalers

0·6
Thalers

4
Bushel
-crops

5 Bushel-
crops

small town
with its own
region

MILES

0   40

Fig. 7.13 *Agricultural regions in the isolated state, showing effects of changing prices or yields, and of a navigable river and a small second town*

Source: *Hall,* Von Thünen's Isolated State, *pp. 216–17.*

were in great demand for both building and fuel and when transportation costs, by the primitive means available, were high so that it achieved a substantial cost reduction by proximity to market.

3. *Crop Alternation Systém (Belgian System).* Rings 3, 4, and 5 represented decreasing intensities of crop and livestock farming modified by Von Thünen from contem-

porary agricultural practice. The crop alternation system involved a six-year crop rotation without fallow in which a given field was devoted for two years to rye, the staple grain crop, and for one year each to potatoes, barley, clover, and vetch (a legume fed to livestock). Rye and potatoes were cash crops, and the others used for livestock production, which also provided some cash income. Soil fertility was maintained under this intensive crop system by the rotation which included two soil-builders, clover and vetch, and by farm manure.

4. *The Improved System (Mecklenburg-Koppel System)* and

5. *The Three-Field System* were used to illustrate Von Thünen's crop intensity theory earlier. The improved system involved a seven-year rotation, six of crops and one year fallow. The crops were rye, barley, and oats for one year each and three years of pasture. The three-field system commonly entailed the division of the farm area into a permanent pasture and an arable area with a rotation of winter grain, spring grain, and fallow. Production costs and yield were about halved in this system compared with the Koppel system (ring 3). Cash income in both systems came from rye and livestock products, the same commodities as the crop alternation system, with the exception of potatoes.

6. *Grazing,* the farthest zone functionally linked to the town, extended outward to a **50** German mile radius (230 English miles). In Von Thünen's day this zone was too distant for economic shipment of most grain and other crops and beyond it the land was wilderness. The grazing zone was devoted primarily to permanent pasture, although surprisingly, it could successfully market some intensive cash crops such as oilseeds, hops, tobacco, and flax.

**modified patterns with
relaxed assumptions**

Von Thünen recognized that his assumptions needed to be relaxed to approximate actual conditions more closely, even in 1826. He wrote:

Actual countries differ from the Isolated State in the following ways:

1. Nowhere in reality do we find soil of the same physical quality and at the same level of fertility throughout an entire country.

2. There is no large town that does not lie on a navigable river or canal.

3. Every sizeable state has in addition to its capital many small towns scattered throughout the land.

What changes in spatial organization result from taking account of these factors? And what effects do increasing prices or yields have on the pattern? The central diagram in Figure 7.13 represents Von Thünen's description of the effects of increasing prices and yields on crop zonation. The effects maintain the concentric zones.

An irregular pattern of natural soil fertility, on the other hand, might completely disrupt the ordered pattern of concentric land-use zones. A pocket of fertile soil beyond the limit of cultivation for low-yield soil might support the intensive crop alternation system. Such variations in soil fertility distort the spatial pattern of interaction and the simple rent-gradients.

Finally, as shown in the bottom diagram of Figure 7.13 a substantial reorganization in the land-use pattern occurs with the introduction of a navigable river, for which Von Thünen assumes a transportation rate of only one-tenth the land rate. A farm 100 miles from the Town but located on this river has the same relative accessibility as a farm 10 miles from the Town by road. A farm 5 miles from that riverside farm has the same relative accessibility as one 15 miles by land from the Town. Von Thünen pictured the crop alternation system that results extending along the banks of the river to the limit of the cultivated plain with the land-use zones changing from a concentric to a sectoral pattern. One can imagine, of course, radiating highways of superior quality producing a "starfish" pattern.

Von Thünen also raised the question What determines the relative position of the towns in the *Isolated State* in respect of size and distance from each other? For example, towns of one size, distributed evenly throughout the country would support higher location rents and farm population density. But a number of disrupting factors are discussed by Von Thünen. Mineral deposits, notably ore, salt, and coal, are unevenly distributed resulting in an irregular distribution of mining towns and of the manufacturing towns processing raw materials of little value in relation to their bulk. The largest town, on the other hand, as the focal center of the country, would attract those industries enjoying large economics of scale, as will the functions and amenities, such as government administration, institutes of higher learning and art collections associated with the capital city of a state.

Von Thünen was satisfied, then, to leave the Isolated State with one primary center, introducing only one small town to illustrate the effect resource-oriented centers would have on land-use pattern, as in the bottom of Figure 7.13. The small town would compete with the large town for food supplies, and have a region skewed away from the big towns.

How might one determine the market area boundary between the large and small town? Figure 7.14 provides the answer. First, market price is lower in the small town because of lower population and, hence, demand. Rents fall with distance from each town, as in the top diagram of Figure 7.14. The spatial pattern of rents is shown in the middle figure, as is the market "indifference" line (i.e., that line along which rents from selling in the two centers are equal). The bottom diagram thus illustrates the subdivision of the plain into market territories, and the rent patterns that result.

VON THÜNEN'S PRINCIPLES, THEN AND NOW

Great changes have occurred in agricultural and transportation technology, and world population has grown considerably since the *Isolated State* was written. At

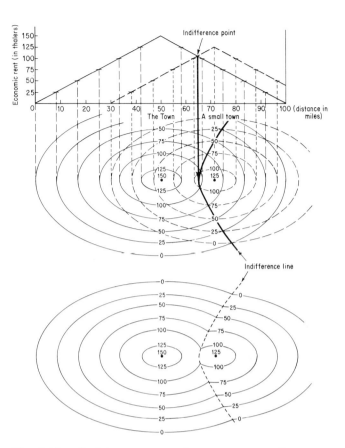

Fig. 7.14 *The impact of a second town on rent gradients and supply areas in the isolated state. The data are hypothetical and assume a single crop, single intensity land use with simple transportation cost-to-distance relationships.*

that time in many parts of the world, broad distance-related production zones could be distinguished not only in agriculture, but in other kinds of resource exploitation. W.R. Mead, for example, has described how exploitation of the forest resources of Scandinavia responded to "the discipline of distance" in the early nineteenth century (see Fig. 7.15). The sailing vessel, with complementary horse haulage or riverboat transport, gave rise to the distinctive regional zonings of farmland and woodland use. There was a sharp gradient in softwood timber values from coast and tributary waterway to the interior, with corresponding differences in their use. In general, accessible woodlands tended to provide the bulkier, less-refined materials, while less accessible woodlands produced the refined more transportable commodities. Norway, closer to western European demand, produced relatively more of the transport-sensitive forest products than Finland.

Similar examples have been reported in many other historical instances, and even today, in those parts of the world where people still walk or use animals for their principal motive power, distance-related adjustments of land use take place. One example explored by P.M. Blaikie involves villages in north India, where minute adjustments of land use to distance have come

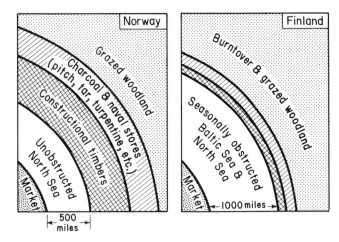

Fig. 7.15 *Zones of softwood exploitation in Scandinavia in the early nineteenth century*

Source: *W. R. Mead*, An Economic Geography of the Scandinavian States and Finland *(London: University of London Press, 1958), p. 95.*

Fig. 7.16 *Crop zoning in a North Indian village*

Source: *P. M. Blaikie, "Organization of Indian Villages,"* Transactions of the Institute of British Geographers, *No. 52, London (March 1971), p. 15.*

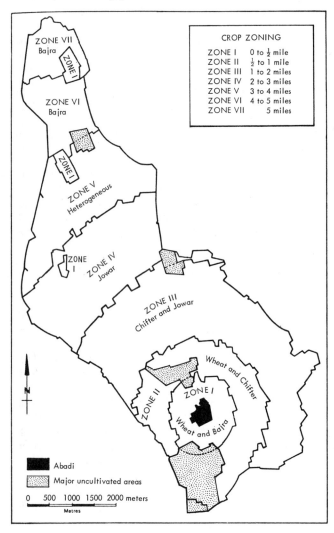

CROP ZONING	
ZONE I	0 to ½ mile
ZONE II	½ to 1 mile
ZONE III	1 to 2 miles
ZONE IV	2 to 3 miles
ZONE V	3 to 4 miles
ZONE VI	4 to 5 miles
ZONE VII	5 miles

about because self-sustaining farmers existing close to the basic survival level have to economize upon use of their own time travelling to and from their fields (Fig. 7.16).

Zonation also characterizes dairying industries throughout the world. For example, in the United States, a hundredweight of 4-percent milk can be converted approximately into (a) 10 pounds of 40 percent cream, and 8 pounds of skim milk powder, or (b) 10 pounds of American cheese, or (c) 5 pounds of butter and 8 pounds of skim milk powder. These differences in densities cause substantial differences in the costs of shipping milk in the different forms. In addition to density, weight and perishability cause transportation costs to vary directly with the value of the product. Thus the ratio of transportation costs of milk to an equivalent amount of cream is roughly 7 to 1, to skim milk powder 15 to 1, to American cheese 12 to 1, and to butter 25 to 1. Concentrated dairy products, whose values are high relative to their weight, can be shipped economically for longer distances than relatively bulky and perishable fluid milk. The result is a concentric zonation of milk specialization around central markets, as illustrated in Figure 7.17.

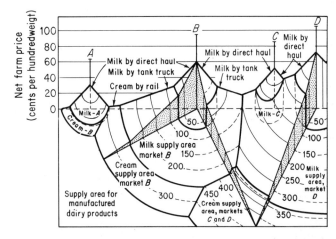

Fig. 7.17 *The net farm prices and supply areas for fluid milk, cream, and manufactured milk products, four-market model. Relative to base price for milk sold in manufacturing outlets.*

Source: *William Bredo and Anthony S. Rojko, "Prices and Milksheds of Northwestern Markets,"* University of Massachusetts Agricultural Experiment Station Bulletin *No. 470, Amherst, 1952.*

In Western Europe, the intensive cash cropping areas that extended only four German miles from the Town in 1826 have expanded far beyond Mecklenburg to encompass much of Europe, and some authors see a single Von Thünen pattern for this area (See Fig. 7.18). Moreover, the stock farming belt and the extensive grain production regions have migrated largely to the New World and the Southern Hemisphere. In a sense, then, the Isolated State has become the world, and the urban-industrial complexes of northwest Europe and

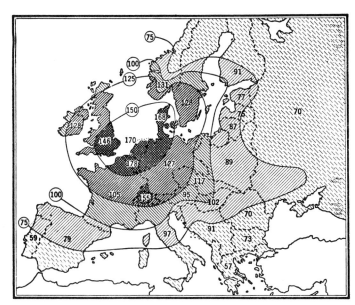

Fig. 7.18 *Intensity of agricultural production in Europe. The index of 100 is the average European yield per acre of eight main crops: wheat, rye, barley, oats, corn, potatoes, sugar beets, and hay. 1937 political boundaries.*

Source: Michael Chisholm, Rural Settlement and Land Use *(New York: John Wiley and Sons, Inc., 1967), p. 108, reproduced from S. van Valkenburg and C. C. Held,* Europe. *(New York: John Wiley and Sons, Inc., 1952).*

as the foundations of land-use theory. His conception of economic rent as a standardized measure of accessibility was, of course, his most important single contribution. Combined with the principle of highest and best use, the concept of economic rent identifies the three most fundamental components of the spatial organization of economic systems (to be discussed more fully in the next section):

1. *concentric-circle arrangements* around centers of activity defining points of greatest accessibility
2. *development axes* along major transportation routes
3. *multiple nuclei,* with the introduction of additional points of interaction.

THE ORGANIZATION OF URBAN SPACE

Von Thünen noted that rural land values increase toward a large town, but that this increase is only a prelude to a far greater rise in land values within urban areas. He went on to suggest that his principles govern this determination of land values and the allocation of land use in urban areas, just as they do in rural areas.

The first applications of the principles to urban land-use were not provided until the classic statements of R. M. Hurd in 1903 and of R. L. Haig in 1926; however, just a hundred years after *Der Isolirte Staat* was published. Hurd wrote:

As a city grows, more remote and hence inferior land must be utilized and the difference in desirability between the two grades produces economic rent in locations of the first grade, but not in those of the second. As land of a still more remote and inferior grade comes into use, ground rent is forced still higher in land of the first grade, rises in land of the second grade, but not in land of the third grade, and so on. Any utility may compete for any location within a city and all land goes to the highest bidder . . . Practically all land within a city earns some economic rent, though it may be small, the final contrast being with the city's rentless and hence, strictly speaking, valueless circumference. . . .

Since value depends on economic rent, and rent on location, and location on convenience, and convenience on nearness, we may eliminate the intermediate steps and say that value depends on nearness.

Haig's "principles," following on from Hurd, were:

1. Each activity seeks the location of maximum accessibility; *rent* is the charge which the owner of a relatively accessible site can impose because of the saving in transport costs which the use of his site makes possible.
2. The activity which can most successfully exploit the locational attributes of a given site will probably gain it through competitive bidding in the real estate market.
3. Land-use organization reflects the evaluation of the relative importance of accessibility to particular land-uses.
4. The efficiency of urban spatial organization is inversely proportional to the aggregate costs of friction in overcoming spatial separation of urban functions.

A land economist, Richard Ratcliffe, succinctly restated these principles as "the structure of the city is de-

northeast North America great "world Thünen-Towns," albeit affected by major world-scale differences in resources. Relaxing his initial assumptions did not lead Von Thünen to anticipate this ultimate scale in the hierarchy of spatial organization, or the growing importance of urban centers and of manufacturing activity that have accompanied it.

Von Thünen did probe urban matters—indeed he suggested that his model was applicable to urban land use—but it was not until some eighty years ago that his principles began to be applied to an understanding of urban land use and that significant extensions to location theory were made by formulation of a theory for the location of manufacturing activity by Alfred Weber. On the other hand it will be agreed that Von Thünen's propositions—or more generally, those of rent theory—attach to every kind of resource use. Every resource commands a price, determined by scarcity commensurate with its quality and accessibility. The higher quality and the more accessible resource will be used first. Each price level calls forth a particular intensity of use. In the case of human resources, the argument extends to wages and incomes; the better educated and more skilled the worker, the higher the prices; the less the accessibility to a center of demand, the lower the price. In the case of natural resources the argument is the same: as exhaustible supplies of higher quality and more accessible resources are used, scarcity pushes up the marginal revenue productivity of lower quality and less accessible items.

Although Von Thünen's study captured at best only a fleeting reality in its empirical details, his work presents principles of lasting value that today still serve termined by the dollar evaluation of the importance of convenience."

However, four sharp differences complicate the extension of Von Thünen's principles to the urban case:

1. The allocation of transport costs is different.
2. For urban residents, income is not earned at the place of residence.
3. Values may be affected by "externalities."
4. Urban development, once committed, has a long life, and age and obsolescence of a committed building stock affect values. Rapid changes of crops are, on the other hand, possible in the countryside.

transport costs and urban rent gradients

In the rural case, the farmer bears the transportation cost, whereas in the urban case the costs of travel may be paid by the worker, the customer, the shop, the businessman, or the factory. The response of each to travel cost differences is complex, and may vary according to such characteristics as trip purpose or distance from the central business district. Interaction tends to decline as distances increase, but with no simple or single association with travel cost. The location rent, or net revenue accruing to any location therefore is not necessarily related in any simple way to the savings in transportation costs offered by the location.

Two examples may serve to illustrate this point. Consider the shoeshine boy; his rent gradient is almost vertical. On the main street, where pedestrian traffic is heavy, he may be able to afford a high rent, whereas a short distance away on a quiet sidestreet, it may be impossible for him to afford any rent at all. The decrease in residential land values according to distance from a scenic attraction such as a river or lake similarly may be very steep. Residential land in north Chicago adjacent to Lake Michigan, for instance, tends to fetch twice as much per lakefront foot as land one hundred yards away. The criterion of highest and best use as measured by location rent is not brought into question by these examples; rather, the simple relationship of location rent to transportation costs is questioned.

residential land and consumer preferences

The farmer derives his income from the land and his total production is related to the total amount of land that he farms. Most urban families earn their income away from home and, generally, their income does not depend on the size of their residence or lot. Families who are looking for a house make two distinct decisions, lot-size and location.

Compare two families at different income levels who decide they can afford to buy lots of 10,000 and 2,500 square feet, respectively, and assume they both consider a suburban location where prices are 50¢ a square foot less, but the journey to work costs $500 a year more, than at an alternate location closer to work. The higher-income family stands to save $5,000 in land costs at the suburban location, compared with $1,250 for the lower-income family buying the smaller lot. Conversely, the additional transportation costs are the same for both families but they average out to 5¢ per square foot on the larger lot and 20¢ on the smaller.

The progressive substitution of transportation costs for location rent outwards from the point of greatest accessibility envisaged by Von Thünen for farmland does not apply in quite the same manner for residential land. For unlike the farmers of the Isolated State —all of whom Von Thünen assumed shared an equal standard of living—city residents have different income levels, and the higher-income families tend to use their superior purchasing power to buy larger quantities of less expensive land involving higher transportation costs, while lower-income families occupy more expensive land, but consume very little of it.

the problem of externalities

A third difference between urban and rural land use is the complexity of interaction patterns and externalities in the urban scene. The productivity of a farm, for instance, normally will not depend on what is being produced in adjacent fields, but the value of an urban lot may very much depend on adjacent land uses and on the area's character that they help to determine. The proximity of special services and functions may help to reduce a manufacturer's costs or enhance the prestige of a commercial or residential area. Conversely, nonconforming uses may create environmental blight that lowers the general economic status of an area.

An example of the first effect is the special set of communication-oriented industries in the New York metropolitan area that includes the garment center and related manufacturing, such as jewelry, trimmings, and fabrics, as well as printing and publishing. Typically, these are small plants operating under constant pressure from tight production schedules that vary with each job contract. The concentration of such industries in the central business district of Manhattan facilitates contact with customers, whether it is a city legal firm urgently wanting a brief printed, or a Midwest buyer selecting women's coats and suits. The concentration also facilitates subcontracting. The manufacturer of costume jewelry can respond rapidly to changes in his customers' demands by turning for supplies of such items as clasps, ear clips, hinges, blanks, joints and pin stems to subcontractors who can stabilize aggregate demand and increase mechanization of production by serving a cluster of jewelry plants. The industrial linkages so created enhance the value of proximity. The typical rental for manufacturing loft space in the garment center of New York has been about 50 percent higher than for similar space in other parts of the region. This premium paid for accessibility is not related in a simple way to reduced transportation costs.

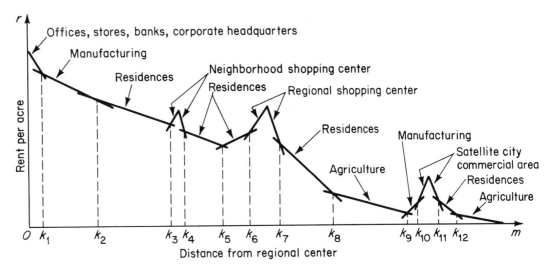

Fig. 7.19 *Hypothetical land rent profile in a multicentered urban area*

Source: William Goldner, A Model for the Spatial Allocation of Activities and Land Uses in a Metropolitan Region *(Berkeley: Bay Area Transportation Study Commission, Sept. 1968).*

At the other extreme are nuisance industries that cluster together in relative isolation to reduce protests against noxious odors, heavy smoke, or peril of explosion. Examples are meat-packing, soap, grease and tallow, paints and varnishes, and explosives plants. In the case of these nuisance industries, location is determined more by social costs than rent-earning capacity.

obsolescence and redevelopment

A fourth difference between urban and rural land use is the inflexibility of land use and the long effective life of building stock in an urban area, compared with the short seed-to-harvest periods for most agricultural crops. The urban problems of obsolescence and redevelopment that result from this inflexibility of land use may be illustrated by commercial activities, a highly competitive sector of the economy with fairly rapid turnover.

Commercial activities occupy only a very small proportion of urban land—about 4 percent compared with 32 percent for residential land in Chicago, for instance; they gain visual prominence by accessible location along major streets or in shopping centers. Changes in retailing technology and increasing consumer mobility create *functional blight* by undermining small owner-operated stores, such as the "ma and pa" groceries. The resulting blight constitutes one of the major land-use problems facing American cities. Functional blight is reducing the number of retail establishments in Chicago, for instance, by 5.87 percent average per year.

The reduction is greatest in areas of ghetto transition in which middle income white families are replaced by lower income black families. During the first phase of ghettoization, the speciality stores located in the shopping centers are forced to vacate, rapidly increasing vacancy rates there. As the neighborhood continues to change, land values and rents drop in the business centers. Businesses that serve the demands of lower income groups move from the adjacent ribbons into the shopping centers, shifting the vacancy problem from the centers to the ribbons. Vacancy rates in the ribbons may rise to one-fifth of the establishments, especially affecting the more deteriorated buildings. Unlikely to be reoccupied, such buildings accelerate the process of deterioration of the ribbons in a combined form of physical and economic blight.

Technological change and blight, however, are not only confined to urban areas; land abandonment is severe in many rural areas, and some farmers keep their farms in operation only by accepting a reduced living standard. Nevertheless, there is an important distinction between the urban and rural case. In general, rural land is abandoned because it fails to provide any location rent, whatever its land use. By contrast, the vacant store in the commercial ribbon occupies a site of potentially higher location rent than land being brought into urban use at the periphery. Urban renewal and redevelopment of the ribbon can bring such land back into active use—as a shopping center or as town housing, for example—but the problems of adjustment to change of the physical stock of a city are complex.

the concentric land use zones of E. W. Burgess (1923)

All these factors notwithstanding, there is considerable evidence to show that urban rents do decline outwards from a city center to produce rent gradients. These rent gradients are different for each different type of land use and so urban land uses become sorted concentrically around the city center to produce the kind of results illustrated in Figure 7.19. Note the land use progression: commercial; manufacturing; residential and agricultural. Indeed, apart from secondary rent peaks and land uses associated with neighborhood and regional shopping centers and at satellite cities, the pattern is little changed from the now classical formulation of E. W. Burgess, who first presented his hypothesis that urban land use is organized into concentric zones around the city center in 1923. He believed that these zones, illustrated in Figure 7.20, developed because (a) cities grow outwards from their original center, with the newest housing always found at the edge of the de-

veloped area, and (b) socially mobile individuals move outwards geographically as they move upwards in the socioeconomic system. Thus, higher-income families build new houses on the periphery of the city where open land is available and sell their old homes to lower-income families. The market provides housing for lower-income families not by building for them directly, but by a "filtering" process, letting higher-income families absorb depreciation costs before the house is handed on. This, in turn, produces very definite patterns of urban development and community change as the city grows

Fig. 7.20 *Burgess' spatial model*

Source: Robert E. Park and Ernest W. Burgess, The City *(Chicago: University of Chicago Press, 1925), pp. 41–53.*

The five zones E. W. Burgess said characterized the internal structure of the city were:

Zone I: The Central Business District. *At the center of the city as the focus of its commercial, social, and civic life is situated the Central Business District. The heart of this district is the downtown retail district with its department stores, its smart shops, its office buildings, its clubs, its banks, its hotels, its theatres, its museums, and its headquarters of economic, social, civic, and political life. Encircling this area of work and play is the less well-known Wholesale Business District with its "market," its warehouses, and storage buildings.*

Zone II: The Zone in Transition. *Surrounding the Central Business District are areas of residential deterioration caused by the encroaching of business and industry from Zone I. This may therefore be called a Zone in Transition, with a factory district for its inner belt and an outer ring of retrogressing neighborhoods, of first-settlement immigrant colonies, of roominghouse districts, of homeless-men areas, of resorts of gambling, bootlegging, sexual vice, and of breeding-places of crime. In this area of physical deterioration and social disorganization studies show the greatest concentration of cases of poverty, bad housing, juvenile delinquency, family disintegration, physical and mental disease. As families and individuals prosper, they escape from this area into Zone III beyond, leaving behind as marooned a residuum of the defeated, leaderless, and helpless.*

Zone III: The Zone of Independent Workingmen's Homes. *This third broad urban ring is largely constituted by neighborhoods of second immigrant settlement. Its residents are those who desire to live near but not too close to their work. It is a housing area neither of tenements, apartments, nor of single dwellings; its boundaries have been roughly determined by the plotting of the two-flat dwelling, generally of frame construction, with the owner living on the lower floor with a tenant on the other. While the father works in the factory, the son and daughter typically have jobs in the downtown area, attend dance halls, and motion pictures in the bright-light areas, and plan upon marriage to set up homes in Zone IV.*

Zone IV: The Zone of Better Residences. *Extending beyond the neighborhoods of second immigrant settlements, we come to the Zone of Better Residences in which the great middleclass of native-born Americans live, small business men, professional people, clerks, and salesmen. Once communities of single homes, they are becoming apartment-house and residential-hotel areas. Within these areas at strategic points are found local business centers of such growing importance that they have been called "satellite downtowns." The*

typical constellation of business and recreational units includes a bank, one or more United Cigar Stores, a drug store, a high-class restaurant, an automobile display row, and a so-called "wonder" motion picture theatre. With the addition of a dancing palace, a cabaret, and a smart hotel, the satellite Loop also becomes a "bright-light" area attracting a city-wide attendance. In this zone men are outnumbered by women, independence in voting is frequent, newspapers and books have wide circulation, and women are elected to the state legislature.

Zone V: The Commuter's Zone. *Out beyond the areas of better residence is a ring of encircling small cities, towns, and hamlets, which, taken together, constitute the Commuters' Zone. These are also, in the main, dormitory suburbs, because the majority of men residing there spend the day at work in the Central Business District, returning only for the night. Thus, the mother and the wife become the center of family life. If the Central Business District is predominantly a homeless-men's region; the rooming house district, the habitat of the emancipated family; the area of first-immigrant settlement, the natural soil of the patriarchal family transplanted from Europe; the Zone of Better Residences with its apartment houses and residential hotels, the favorable environment for the equalitarian family; then the Commuter's Zone is without question the domain of the matricentric family. The communities in this Commuter's Zone are probably the most highly segregated of any in the entire metropolitan region, including in their range the entire gamut from an incorporated village run in the interests of crime and vice, to exclusive villages with wealth, culture, and public spirit.*

Source: Ernest W. Burgess, "Urban Areas" in T. V. Smith and L. D. White, eds., Chicago: An Experiment in Social Science Research *(Chicago: University of Chicago Press, 1929), pp. 114–23.*

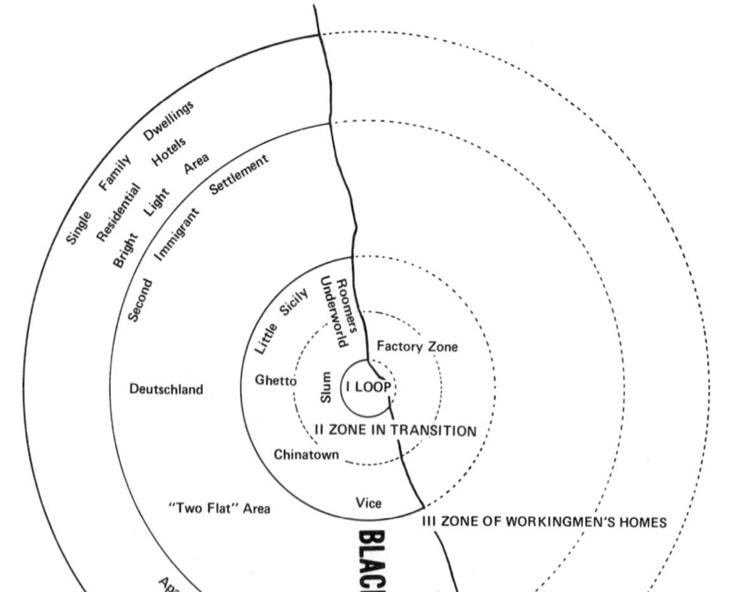

Single Family Dwellings
Residential Hotels
Bright Light Area
Second Immigrant Settlement
Little Sicily
Ghetto
Roomers
Underworld
Slum
Factory Zone
I LOOP
II ZONE IN TRANSITION
Deutschland
Chinatown
Vice
"Two Flat" Area
III ZONE OF WORKINGMEN'S HOMES
BLACK BELT
Apartment Houses
Residential Hotels
IV RESIDENTIAL ZONE
Bright Light Area
Restricted Residential District
V COMMUTERS ZONE
Bungalow Section

and as new immigrants on the lowest rungs of the socio-economic ladder find initial residences in "ports of entry" in the oldest neighborhoods closest to the city center. The growth of the city increases the space needs of residents of each zone causing an *invasion* by each zone into the next outer zone so that at any given distance from the city center there is a "succession" of land uses. Burgess called this the process of invasion and succession.

C. C. Colby's centrifugal and centripetal forces (1938)

Burgess's theory related residential land use to the social characteristics of city dwellers in a concentric scheme continually directed outwards. In 1938, Charles C. Colby offered a view of the city's function, form, and pattern as the resultant between two opposing forces, centripetal and centrifugal. The centripetal forces comprise the special assets of the central zone of the city. Colby classifies these into natural site attraction, accessibility and functional convenience, externalities that produce functional magnetism, the movement of acquired advantage producing functional prestige, and the human desire to be at the center of things. Opposing these centripetal forces are centrifugal forces comprising the uprooting conditions in the central zone and the attractions of the periphery. Ever-increasing land and property values and the accompanying higher tax rates add directly to costs of operating in the central business district (CBD). Downtown traffic congestion and space needs, perhaps with special site characteristics, are also strong centrifugal forces. The combination of these powerful centripetal and centrifugal forces produces a concentric ordering of urban land use around the CBD.

population density gradients: the Colin Clark model (1951)

Related to rent gradients are decreasing intensities of land use and of population density outwards from a city center. Colin Clark, the economist, has claimed that urban population densities are characterized by a particular type of distance-decay—the negative exponential decline from the city center. This gradient can be expressed by the formula:

$$d_x = d_o e^{-bx}$$

where:

d = population density
x = distance from city center
d_o = density at city center
e = natural logarithmic base
b = density gradient (a measure of city compactness)

or $ln d_x = ln d_o - bx$ when the natural logarithm (*ln*) of density is used.

Clark provides thirty-six examples of cities for which this equation provides a good fit of population density gradients. These examples range in time from 1801 to the contemporary period and from Los Angeles to Budapest. Subsequent research has added about a hundred more examples including all large U.S. cities in 1950, all Canadian metropolitan areas in 1971, Asian cities such as Colombo, Hyderab, Calcutta, Manila, Rangoon, Singapore, Djarkarta and Tokyo; as well as Sydney, Australia, and Kingston, Jamaica. Moreover, as transportation improvements have increased personal mobility, population density gradients have decreased. These decreases are illustrated for four Canadian metropolitan areas (Fig. 7.21).

Homer Hoyt's axial model (1939)

Burgess and Clark chose to stress a single geographic component—distance from city center—in their descriptions of urban land-use zones and population density gradients. As early as 1903, however, Richard Hurd had noted the importance of a second component—direction—with concentric growth around the city, and axial growth along the transportation lines combining to produce a star-shaped, rather than a circular city. The importance of axial growth in residential land use was documented in 1939 by Homer Hoyt who employed block data on rents for sixty-four medium to small American cities, provided by the Works Progress Administration of the United States federal government, supplemented by his own surveys of New York, Chicago, Detroit, Washington, and Philadelphia. Hoyt used rent as a measure of the economic status of residential areas and a historical model of urban land use, like Burgess, but he argued that the directional or sectoral component of land use is more important than the concentric.

Hoyt noted, like Burgess, that high-rent residential areas are typically found on the periphery of the American city as a result of the continued centrifugal movement of high-income population. But high-rent areas are small compared with low-rent areas, and they do not occupy the whole periphery. Instead, Hoyt argued that high-rent areas occupy only one or more sectors of the periphery. Status of residence declines from these peaks toward the center of city where low-status housing occurs and spreads out along some sectors to the periphery. Hence housing status describes a sectoral rather than a concentric pattern, and high-rent neighborhoods follow a definite path in one or more sectors of the city.

The high-grade residential area has its point of origin near the retail and office center where the higher income groups work and farthest from the industries and warehouses where the lower-income groups work. Expansion can be outward only, because other growth points having a different character also grow, thus preventing lateral expansion. Hoyt noted that higher-priced residential construction tends to expand along the fastest existing transportation lines and toward the homes of community leaders. It is also attracted toward high ground and to waterfronts and riversides free of industrial use. It tends to follow the same direction of

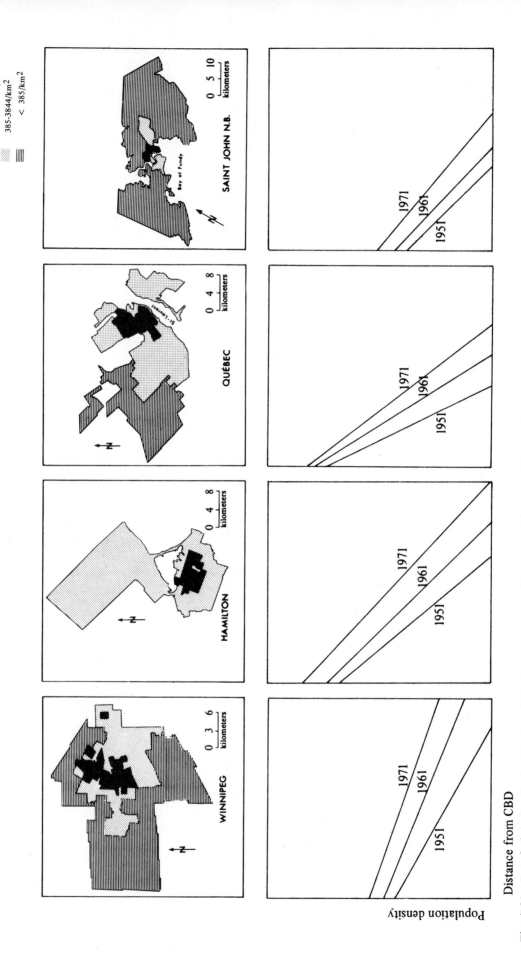

Fig. 7.21 *Population density profiles for selected census metropolitan areas. The maps illustrate how population density varies within a city. Population density gradients over time illustrate an increase in the size of the metropolitan areas and an increase in these average densities.*

Source: Data were tabulated by the Ministry of State for Urban Affairs and the Census Division of Statistics Canada.

growth for long periods but is influenced by the location of new office buildings, banks, and stores. Hoyt noted finally that the direction of the growth of better residential neighborhoods may be changed by estate developers.

Harris and Ullman on multiple nuclei (1943)

Neither concept of distance or direction separately or in combination are sufficient to explain all details of the spatial organization of urban activities, however. Thus, in 1943, Chauncy D. Harris and Edward L. Ullman suggested that models of urban land use must recognize the existence of more than one nucleus within a city around which growth occurs. The nuclei may date from the origin of the city as in London where "The City," the center of finance and commerce, and Westminster, the political focus, were at one time separated by open country. In addition, new centers may develop with city growth, as in Chicago where heavy industry, at first localized along the Chicago River in the heart of the city, migrated to the Calumet District, serving there as the nucleus for extensive new development.

The emergence of separate nuclei and differentiated districts are related by Harris and Ullman primarily to three centrifugal and one centripetal factors. The centrifugal factors are the rent gradient coupled with space requirements, the need for specialized facilities, and incompatibilities among different land uses. The centripetal factors that convert simple dispersion to multiple nuclei are the functional convenience, magnetism, and prestige that are not entirely restricted to the central nucleus.

The number of nuclei, Harris and Ullman said, may vary according to the historical development and localization forces involved. Typically, however, five distinct nuclei occur: the central business district, wholesaling and light-manufacturing, heavy industrial, specialized nuclei, and suburban and dormitory satel-

lites. The resulting internal structure of the city does not follow any simple or single pattern.

a hierarchy of commercial nuclei

One group of nuclei bringing some regularity to city structure is suggested by Figure 7.22, which describes the elements comprising the commercial structure of the large North American city, as summarized by B. J. L. Berry in 1963.

The elements are these:

(a) *Commercial Centers.* The hierarchy of commercial centers ranging from convenience and neighborhood centers to the metropolitan CBD is defined by the number and variety of functions offered, and by the trade area served. The hierarchy of centers is "nested," as suggested in Fig. 7.22, so that centers of each "order" offer, in general, all the functions performed by lower-order centers, and are distinguished from them by their performing additional functions, unavailable in smaller centers.

The hierarchy of commercial centers is thus created by a hierarchy of commercial functions. Moreover, the accessibility of business functions is related to their order in the hierarchy. Even within the centers, an inner core area of high land value is occupied by functions that rank the center above lower orders, and this core is surrounded on successively lower-valued land by functions typical of each lower order of the hierarchy.

Thus, central business districts may be divided into a "core" and "frame," as suggested in Fig. 7.23, on the basis of accessibility, land values, and intensity and type of land use. The frame has lower intensity uses such as manufacturing, wholesaling, and warehousing. In the core, clusters of associated activities form distinct districts or specialized areas. The retail district is centered on the street intersection of highest pedestrian densities, with surrounding districts devoted to finance, insurance, medical services, entertainment, hotels, and down-

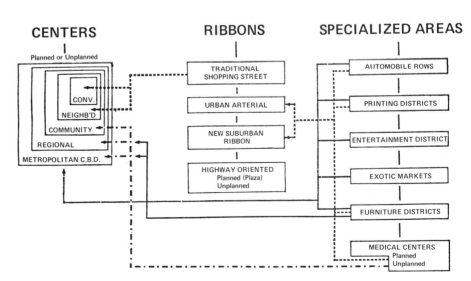

Fig. 7.22 *Typology of business areas in a large city*

Source: Brian J. L. Berry, Geography of Market Centers and Retail Distribution *(Englewood Cliffs, N.J.: Prentice-Hall, 1967), p. 46.*

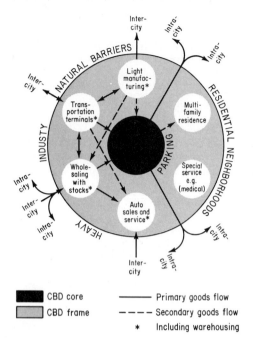

Fig. 7.23 *The core-frame concept of the central business district*

Source: E. M. Horwood and R. R. Boyce, Studies of the Central Business District and Urban Freeway Development (Seattle: Universiy of Washington Press, 1959), p. 21.

town apartments; scattered throughout are lower-order and complementary functions. Thus office buildings contain restaurants, beauty and barber shops, or newsands.

Many of these functions are eliminated in the regional shopping centers in which a typical zoning of activities, ordered by distance from the principal intersection may include (1) at the core: distinctive regional-level functions with branch department stores, women's clothing and accessories, candy, drugs, and jewelry followed by (2) a mixture of regional and community functions, such as household appliances, bakeries, movie theaters, restaurants, banks, optometrists' and insurance offices; and (3) in the periphery, personal service establishments at the neighborhood level, such as hardware, furniture, supermarkets, cleaners, liquor, real estate offices, laundromats, and barber and beauty shops. Similarly, in community centers, the regional level is in turn eliminated, to be succeeded by community-order functions in the core and neighborhood level functions in the periphery.

(b) *Ribbons.* A variety of sectoral or ribbon developments can be identified, including strings of establishments serving highway-oriented demands, such as service stations, motels and restaurants; arterial developments demanding too much space to be able to afford central locations, such as automobile dealers; and services independent of accessibility because servicemen travel to the consumer, such as plumbers and TV repairmen; or merchants whose customers are prepared to make a specific single-purpose trip, such as for furniture.

In much of the literature of urban geography, sociology, and economics, the concentric, axial and multinuclei schemes have been presented as competing alternatives. Within the past ten years, however, a great deal of research on the relations of urban land use, activity systems and socioeconomic structure has found that they are complementary arrangements relating to different facets of urban life.

The beginning of this work was in the field of *social area analysis,* introduced in the early 1950s by Eshref Shevky and Wendell Bell in their studies of Los Angeles. They postulated that three fundamentally distinct groups of characteristics differentiate residential land use, relating to economic status, family status, and ethnic status. *Economic status* measures educational attainment, income-level and occupation mix. *Family status* measures family type, including number and ages of children, and female participation rates in the labor force. *Ethnic status* measures segregation and the ethnic composition of the city. Shevky and Bell deduced these indexes from basic postulates concerning changes in urban life brought about by industrial society (Table 7.3). Economic status—or, in their terms, social rank—is related to changing occupation structure with the relative growth of clerical, supervisory, and management operations. Family status, or urbanization, is related to the changes in life style and the emergence of specialized family types as women enter the labor force, and to other changes associated with urbanization. Family status contrasts areas with large, young families, few women working outside the home, single-family dwellings, and high car and home ownership with areas with small families, more women in the labor force, a high proportion of multiple dwellings, and less car and home ownership. Ethnic status, or segregation, is related to the growing diversity and changing composition or urban population with migration.

A good deal of research has supported the validity of the Shevky-Bell propositions whose applicability to urban land use analyses has been generalized more recently by the development of new kinds of studies called *factorial ecologies.* The factorial ecologies have linked the Shevky-Bell indexes to the various spatial models of the city in an interesting way, finding that:

1. economic status tends to be distributed in a sectoral pattern
2. family status tends to vary concentrically
3. ethnic status tends to form separate districts, with their own community nuclei, superimposed upon the economic and family status patterns
4. over time, the economic status pattern tends to expand sectorally, the pattern of family status tends to move outward from the city center in a wavelike concentric fashion, and minority groups expand by spatial diffusion into the economic sectors of least social resistance

Table 7.3   Shevky's Model of Urbanization and Its Consequences

POSTULATES CONCERNING INDUSTRIAL SOCIETY (ASPECTS OF INCREASING SCALE) (1)	STATISTICS OF TRENDS (2)	CHANGES IN THE STRUCTURE OF A GIVEN SOCIAL SYSTEM (3)	CONSTRUCTS (4)	SAMPLE STATISTICS (RELATED TO THE CONSTRUCTS) (5)	DERIVED MEASURES (FROM COL. 5) (6)	
Change in the range and intensity of relations	Changing distribution of skills: Lessening importance of manual productive operations; growing importance of clerical, supervisory, management operations	Changes in the arrangement of occupations based on function	Social rank (economic status)	Years of schooling, Employment status, Class of worker, Major occupation group, Value of home, Rent by dwelling unit, Plumbing and repair, Persons per room, Heating and refrigeration	Occupation Schooling Rent	Index I
Differentiation of function	Changing structure of productive activity: Lessening importance of primary production; growing importance of relations centered in cities; lessening importance of the household as economic unit	Changes in the ways of living; movement of women into urban occupations; spread of alternative family patterns	Urbanization (family status)	Age and sex, Owner or tenant, House structure, Persons in household	Fertility, Women at work, Single-family dwelling units	Index II
Complexity of organization	Changing composition of population: Increasing movement; alterations in age and sex distribution; increasing diversity	Redistribution in space; changes in the proportion of supporting and dependent population; isolation and segregation of groups	Segregation (ethnic status)	Race and nativity, Country of birth, Citizenship	Racial and national groups in relative isolation	Index III

Source: Robert A. Murdie, *Factorial Ecology of Metropolitan Toronto, 1951–1961* (Chicago: Department of Geography Research Paper No. 116, University of Chicago, 1969, pp. 20-21)

The model thus shows the three spatial patterns—concentric-circle, sectoral, and multiple-nuclei—to be complementary, in that each refers to different subsets of phenomena. It follows that a combined model expressing the totality of socioeconomic characteristics of urban neighborhoods may be produced by superimposing the three spatial patterns, thus overlaying a spider's web on the physical space of the city (Fig. 7.24).

In many factorial ecologies of cities completed throughout the world, the same three major patterns of socioeconomic differentiation have emerged. Some spatial differences between North American cities and those of other culture areas have been discovered as a result. For example, large families of lower economic status occupy the periphery of the metropolis in relatively unindustrialized societies throughout the world, where members of the highest social rank preempt central locations. In many cities in cultures in which centrality remains important (in India, for example, or Latin America), social status thus is concentric, dropping from a peak in the city center. Ethnic factors are generally less prominent in European than in New World cities where immigration has made a relatively greater contribution to population growth.

Any understanding of the spatial organization of cities must delve beyond simple identification of these spatial patterns, of course. The decision makers, their decisions, the constraints, and the processes resulting from these decisions need to be considered. The matching of housing characteristics such as house value and type and neighborhood type with family characteristics such as family income, stage in life cycle, and life-style preferences varies regionally and locally with differences in culture and level of economic development. Furthermore, socioeconomic structure is not superimposed on space but evolves under continuous interaction with it.

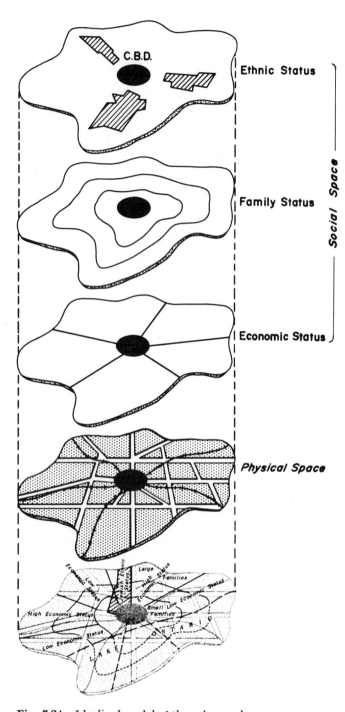

The social values invested in land and administrative factors, such as zoning ordinances, urban renewal projects, and transportation developments produce deviations from any single idealized pattern and modify the narrower economic logic of urban and rural land use.

RECOMMENDED READINGS

Beckmann, Martin, *Location Theory.* New York: Random House, 1968. See Chapter 4, "Allocation of Land."

Chisholm, Michael, *Rural Settlement and Land Use: An Essay in Location.* New York: John Wiley, 1962.

Gregor, Howard F., *Geography of Agriculture: Themes in Research.* Englewood Cliffs, N. J.: Prentice-Hall, 1970. See Chapter 4, "Spatial Organization."

Hall, Peter (ed.), *Von Thünen's Isolated State,* trans. Carla M. Wartenberg. Elmsford, N. Y.: Pergamon Press, 1966.

Hauser, Philip M., and Leo F. Schnore, *The Study of Urbanization.* New York: John Wiley, 1966. See particularly Chapter 10, "On the Spatial Structure of Cities in the Two Americas."

Hoover, Edgar M., *The Location of Economic Activity.* New York: McGraw-Hill, 1948. See Chapter 6, "Land Use Competition."

Mayer, Harold M., and Clyde F. Kohn (eds.), *Readings in Urban Geography.* Chicago: University of Chicago Press, 1959. See Section 10, "General Nature of City Structure."

Fig. 7.24 *Idealized model of the urban ecology*

Source: R. A. Murdie, Factorial Ecology of Metropolitan Toronto, 1951–1961 *(Chicago: University of Chicago, 1969), pp. 9, 169.*

From land use, let us now turn to industrial location. This chapter will review the basic elements entering into plant location decisions, and industrial location theory, which describes those circumstances determining successful locations under competitive market place conditions. Chapter 9 follows with several case studies, illustrating the complex dynamics of locational change in different kinds of industries in response to changing technology and shifting market conditions.

The questions we want to answer are: Why are plants in the manufacturing industries located where they are? What factors and decisions enter into the firm's initial choice of plant location? To what extent are the locational patterns of plants within any manufacturing industry determined by the initial location decisions of the firm? To what extent do such locational patterns represent successful survivors, after competition has weeded out those plants initially located with least concern for or awareness of market place conditions? We look at the firm's plant location decisions first and then turn to industrial location patterns and the factors apparently entering into successful performance in the market place.

Throughout the discussion, we will use the term *plant* to refer to the individual producing unit, *firm* to refer to the corporate management and decision-making unit, which may be single or multiplant, and *industry* to refer to a group of firms engaged in creating the same or similar types of product.

PLANT LOCATION DECISIONS

When manufacturers are asked why they located their plants where they did, the answers are quite surprising. For example, in a survey of Michigan manufacturers made by Eva Mueller and John Lansing in 1960 firms were asked why they located in Michigan, and then why they chose the particular site within Michigan. The dominant response was "personal reasons" or "chance" or "opportunity—found a good site."

This hardly speaks for careful prior analysis of locational alternatives, as one might expect from rational businessmen attempting to select the most profitable potential locations for their plants. One possible conclusion might be that because so many personal reasons enter into individual plant location decisions, generalizations or theories that assume rationality of choice cannot be proposed. Yet many students have observed that there is an apparent rationality or regularity to industrial location patterns. How can we reconcile what industrialists say they do with what researchers say they see? One answer comes from competitive economics, which says that we must distinguish between apparently rational industrial location patterns in fact created by the "guiding hand" of the market and the apparently haphazard initial decisions of the firm. Another type of answer is provided by study of actual management behavior of large-scale multiplant firms. Lansing and Mueller's surveys show that for larger firms "personal" accounts for a smaller percentage of the reasons for lo-

industrial decisions and location patterns

8

cation and selection of particular plant sites. Larger firms, do, in fact, engage in objective systems analysis.

adoptive and adaptive locational behavior

The difference between the two cases has been highlighted by Armen A. Alchian and Charles M. Tiebout, two American economists. They distinguished two circumstances leading to the apparently rational locational patterns about which people think they can theorize. These circumstances were termed *adoptive* and *adaptive* locational behavior.

The idea of adoptive economic behavior has its intellectual roots in the "survival of the fittest" philosophies of the nineteenth century. The behavior and locational choices of individual firms, it is acknowledged, may appear quite random when viewed case by case. But, it is argued, this random behavior takes place within a competitive economic environment. Thus, although many firms pursue their activities without investigating alternative locations and despite the fact that businessmen choose locations for many strange reasons, the conditions imposed by the economic environment do make locations matter to these individual firms in the long run, because some locations are by their nature more profitable than others. The initial or individual location decisions of the firms may turn out to be *irrelevant* to the emergence of spatial regularities, because locational differences affect the ability of firms to survive in a competitive environment. In the long run, if a plant's location is inconsistent with the calculus of economic advantage it will find itself threatened by more favorably located competitors. The competitors will grow and the unprofitable plant will finally shut down. Such differential industrial growth leads to apparently rational locational patterns of plants within the industry, made up of the successful survivors. The theory of industrial location with which we will be concerned later on in the chapter basically helps explain what happened and why the locational patterns emerged. As market place conditions change, it also explains why locational change takes place, and what the resulting patterns are likely to be.

The adaptive viewpoint is somewhat different, focusing on rational decision making and locational choice. From this point of view, large firms with substantial investment in market research and with systematic processes of internal decision making can so analyze the economic environment that they can find out how to locate themselves in the way that best achieves corporate goals. This automatically creates a "rational" economic geography consistent with predetermined goals: by design and analysis firms ensure that they will be successful as the competitive process operates.

Now clearly, this is a very different point of view from that of the survival of the fittest. Whereas the adoptive viewpoint says that there is irrationality in individual decision making and competition within the economic system determines who will be successful, the adaptive viewpoint says that optimal locations can be determined by analysis and that rational decisions can determine for the individual business the location that will result in the greatest economic advantage.

industrial location decisions

Let us look at an example of the locational decision process of a large corporation establishing a branch plant. Summarizing the results of several studies, John Rees, a British geographer, has developed a decision-making model. He argues that branch plant locations are determined in a specific decision-making environment that involves the short- and long-term goals of the firm, and he builds into the model perceptions of need, aspirations, and motivations of the decision makers, and the fruits of past experience.

The firm becomes concerned about possible branch plants either because potential demand is perceived in its various sales territories, or in untried territories, or because growth has produced difficulties in expanding on-site. A location problem is recognized that can be met by a short-term response of on-site increases in output, or by a long-term response of one of three kinds: relocation of the existing plant; acquisition of a plant from someone else; or construction of a new branch plant.

If the firm chooses to construct a new branch plant, it begins to seek location alternatives. There are three stages: (a) the selection of a potential sales *region* within which sufficient demand is thought to exist to warrant a branch plant; (b) the selection of a *community* within this region, using a comparative cost approach, to find the place most likely to satisfy the firm's profit goals; and (c) the selection of a *site* or sites for the plant within the community, often based on social, rather than economic, grounds (e.g., where it is thought the probable manager would prefer to live).

Then the decision is finally ratified, and the firm's resources are allocated to build the plant. Whatever is learned from the decision process, and from later evaluation of the plant's performance "feeds back" to the decision-making environment within which future decisions will be made.

Similar models have been developed by P. M. Townroe in his studies of locational decision making by British firms. He found it necessary to distinguish three kinds of firms: the private capitalist, the corporate capitalist, and the state. For all three profit, security, and growth are basic goals. In Britain, however, the state, on its own behalf and by restrictions placed upon others, also insists that social goals be served.

Two different profit motives also are present. In the short-run, firms may try to maximize their profits, but often in the long-run they seek the greater security of *satisficing*. A satisficer is one who seeks a more-likely-to-be-guaranteed rate of return on investment, rather than trying always to reach the maximum.

Townroe also points to the other elements in the complex decision environment: responsibility to shareholders, employees, and the public; the management structure of the firm; management and investment policy. All serve to illustrate the complex context of locational decision making. He also cautions that the search process and generation of alternatives was characterized in many of the cases he studied by lack of any systematic approach, by the ample opportunity for subjective assessment, and by the frequency with which, in retrospect, even the largest companies felt that important aspects of the new location had been overlooked before the choice had been made.

THE DEMAND FACTOR IN LOCATION

Both Rees and Townroe point out that the prime consideration in industrial location relates to demand (i.e., to whether there exists a potential market area of sufficient size to consume the output of a manufacturing plant). Such an assessment depends on the computation of *market potentials* for different locations, as was demonstrated in a classic study of the market as a factor in industrial location in the United States, completed by Chauncy D. Harris in 1954.

Harris first constructed a map of income potentials, such as that already discussed in Chapter 5. He then showed that manufacturing potentials, calculated in the same way, had the same spatial pattern in the United States. Finally, he demonstrated that manufacturing employment was increasing most rapidly where national market access, as measured by income potentials, was greatest. The exception was where the textile industries were expanding close to sources of cheap labor in the Piedmont of the Carolinas and Georgia. Later, Allan Pred confirmed Harris's results and emphasized that the demand factor was apparently most significant for high value-added manufacturing (i.e., for those activities, such as the engineering trades, that convert simple inexpensive raw materials into complex costly products using large inputs of capital and labor).

Why should this be so? One useful insight has been provided by another location economist, Martin Beckmann. Beckmann points out that the prices received by producers for their output can be either the same from place to place, or they may vary spatially. The same is true for the prices paid by the producers for their needed inputs.

If both input and output prices are uniform from place to place, the firm is *locationally indifferent*. If, however, output prices are uniform from place to place but input prices (costs) vary locationally, then the firm can optimize by *minimizing cost*.

If input prices are uniform from place to place but selling prices vary locationally, the obvious strategy for the businessman is to locate where he can *maximize revenues;* this implies getting into the position that is most sensitive to the variations in output prices. Finally, if both input and output prices vary locationally, the optimum location behavior—that which *maximizes profit*—is to find the location that maximizes the spread between revenues and costs.

Now recall what was said about the relationship of costs and prices to firm characteristics in Chapter 6. Where goods are highly complex, there is substantial product differentiation and selling price variability. But often such high value producers purchase simple semi-processed parts at input prices that vary little. In other words, the revenue maximizers in Beckmann's scheme will, in general, be the high value-added producers who, in turn, seek out demand-maximizing locations rather than cost-minimizing locations.

PRODUCTION COSTS AND PLANT LOCATION

On the other hand, many firms are still extremely sensitive to cost factors in location, whether they are "adaptive" producers seeking the best location, or competitors finding out who is being "adopted" by the conditions in the market. As a result, a considerable body of literature has emerged in which the relationships of production costs to plant location have been codified.

This literature begins by recognizing that any business must go through several stages in getting its product onto the market:

1. *procurement* of raw materials;
2. *processing* of raw materials into finished products;
3. *distribution* of products to the consumer.

The first and third of these stages involve transportation costs. The second involves the productive operations—capital inputs and scale, for example—plus labor costs.

A variety of situations has been studied in which plant location is affected by variations of procurement, processing, and distribution costs. For example, cases have been noted in which plants are all very much alike in their labor requirements and scale of operations wherever they are located, so that these costs do not vary much spatially, but which incur substantial transport costs that do vary considerably from one location to another. Under these conditions plants have to minimize transport costs to maximize their competitive advantage. Such plants have been called *transport oriented*. Two forms of transport orientation have been noted: (1) where procurement costs are large and variable, in which case the plant is *raw-material oriented,* and (2) where distribution costs are large and variable and the plant is *market oriented*. As we will see later, there are strong pressures for transport-oriented plants to be either raw material or market oriented rather than being located between raw materials and markets.

Industries in which plants are quite insensitive to transport cost variations also have been studied. Transport costs for these industries played a minor role in determining final cost and competitive position. Location analysts speak of plants in these industries as being *footloose*. For some footloose plants, however, processing costs often have been a large and variable part of total cost, leading to other kinds of locational patterns. One type arises from short-run differences in processing costs. Labor costs and taxes, for example, may vary locationally in the short run. Plants whose competitive advantage has depended upon minimization of labor costs are called *labor oriented*.

Other processing cost differentials persisting in the long run have been studied. Among these are economies of scale. When the threshold scale of plant alone determines cost levels, and the degree of concentration is substantial (as discussed in Chapter 6), plants are relatively insensitive to location. In such cases the advantages of an *early start* have often determined which firms achieve a superior ability to compete whatever their initial location.

Other long-run differences in processing cost have been attributed to *external economies* (the so-called economies of agglomeration) of which several kinds have been identified.

1. *Economies of localization,* which result from similar plants clustering together and achieving benefits from joint use of subsidiary facilities, such as a common pool of skilled labor or uniquely specialized financial institutions.
2. *Economies of urbanization,* which result from many businesses of many kinds serving a common market, drawing on a large pool of labor, and making joint use of public facilities (housing, transport, recreation).
3. *Industrial complex economies* in which closely related productive processes are linked together by materials and byproducts flows.

Some of these economies strengthen the snowballing effect that the biggest cities have upon otherwise relatively footloose kinds of industry, and together they produce *hierarchical organization* of industrial locations. Industrial complex economies, in particular, have also been shown to produce major industrial groupings in rural areas.

Let us now attempt to probe more deeply into the findings of actual locational analyses of each of the factors in turn.

THE FORMS OF TRANSPORT ORIENTATION

When transportation costs form a high proportion of total costs, research has confirmed that the plant tends to be transport oriented, minimizing transport costs so as to be able to put its products on the market at lowest cost. Transport-oriented firms survive in such circumstances while their competitors falter and sometimes fail altogether.

dispersion as a form of transport orientation

The earliest form of transport orientation emerged under circumstances in which consumers were widely scattered and raw materials were available everywhere as ubiquities. If products were, in addition, expensive to transport, a locational pattern comprising many small, widely diffused firms resulted. Each plant would

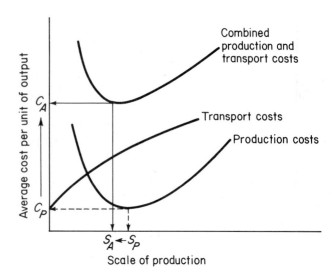

Fig. 8.1 *Effect of high transport costs on the scale of output*

have to be small, sacrificing economies of large-scale production to save transport costs and serving a small market area with a radius effectively limited by rapidly escalating transportation costs.

Figure 8.1 illustrates this situation, recalling the presentation in Chapter 6. The plant has a U-shaped cost curve. If transport costs were zero the optimal scale of production would be S_p, with average production costs C_p. But as scale of production increases, the size of market area and the average transport cost burden must also increase. Hence, the combined production and transport cost curve, although still generally U-shaped, lies much higher. The optimal scale of output is lower (S_A) and average costs are much higher (C_A), the amounts depending upon the steepness of the transport cost gradient.

This industrial pattern was common in Western Europe and North America prior to the development of cheap transport by canals and railroads during the nineteenth century. Transportability of goods was low and production was local, intended only to serve local needs. During the nineteenth century, however, several basic changes occurred as the Industrial Revolution ran its course. Market areas were widened by transportation improvements that slashed overland shipping costs; production was concentrated in larger plants that made use of newly-developed technologies and tended to cluster in areas with superior resource endowments; industrial areas with associated urban complexes developed, and industry was therefore also effective in creating major centers of consumption. In many kinds of industrial activity—for example, production of iron (to be discussed in Chapter 9)—small diffused plants failed as the new large-scale producers put superior products on the market at lower cost. A new industrial order and pattern was created.

Thus, in Figure 8.2 we see how the lowering of the production and transport schedules leads to expansion of the optimal scale of output to S_B, together with a lowering of cost to C_B. In consequence, plants and

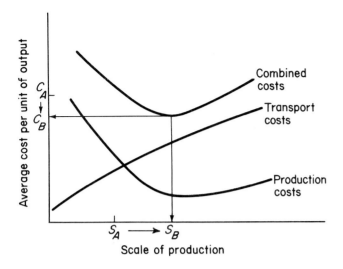

Fig. 8.2 *Consequences of improved production and transport technology for the scale of output*

market areas become larger and fewer. As scale increases, however, diffusion declines for other reasons. Larger and fewer modern firms have been shown to seek out and use superior sources of raw materials and serve national markets from points central to these markets. Because they seldom have been fortunate enough to find raw materials near the central locations, they have been impelled to one or the other location or to some intermediate point.

raw material orientation

Raw material orientation arises when:

1. there is a great deal of loss of weight or bulk of raw materials in manufacturing, so that if the plant is raw material oriented a lighter and more compact product can be shipped to market;

2. when raw materials are more perishable or fragile than the finished products.

Raw material oriented industries are characteristically the "heavy industries": iron and steel plants, chemical plants, and so on. They may be identified by the following features: costs of raw materials form a large percentage of the value of gross output; the value of products per ton is low; high weights of raw materials are used per operative; and the labor force is predominantly male. These are industries of low mobility, tied to sources of raw materials, which produce commodities which are heavy and bulky in relation to value and add substantially to the price of finished products if they are transported. Such were the industries that created the first large industrial towns during the Industrial Revolution.

market orientation

Manufacturing plants, on the other hand, are market oriented when:

1. there is a weight or bulk gain in production, so that products add more to price if transported than do the raw materials;

2. products are perishable or fragile;

3. frequent or rapid contact with consumers is required;

4. raw materials are simple and homogeneous and can be carried in bulk but there are several complex products that must be conveyed separately, as in the case of crude oil and separate refinery products;

5. there are differential transport rates such that more is charged to ship higher-value finished products than lower-value raw materials (called "charging what the load will bear").

This type of transport orientation has been of increasing importance during the twentieth century, even for such traditionally raw-material-oriented industries as iron and steel.

Also, more and more industries are of the assembling kind, procuring semiprocessed raw materials and converting them into bulky products. By their very nature, these industries are market oriented, and increasingly sensitive to demand rather than cost factors, as we saw earlier. Some examples are the American Can Corporation and Continental Can Corporation, both of which have experienced distinct economies from diffusing branch plants to many local markets. Because their products are bulky and expensive to ship, costs are minimized by minimizing the distances over which cans are shipped. Growth of the industry has occurred by establishing branch plants wherever the demand in a market area justifies it. A similar scatter of plants related to scatter of demands is found in the case of the Metal Box Company in England. Indeed, the entire branch plant movement in the United States, Canada, and Western Europe has been promoted by decentralization. Although decentralization forfeits some of the internal economies of scale, it produces great savings in transport costs and speedy servicing of customers. Another example is the British Oxygen Company, which produces oxygen and acetylene. Their gases are produced in one plant in the western suburbs of London, transported in liquid form to market areas and there passed under pressure into the cylinders in which they are sold to consumers. The advantage is to minimize costs of transporting the cylinders, which are eight times the weight of the gas which is put into them. Bottling centers are thus decentralized. The same is essentially true in the soft-drink industry, where flavors and essences are shipped in liquid, or syrup, form to many local bottlers who add a ubiquity (water) and bottle. The economy is in shipping the end product, which consists mainly of water and bottles.

intermediate transport orientations

Market orientation is increasing. But what of locations intermediate between raw materials and markets? Such orientations have been shown to be generally unfeasible, as illustrated by the combined cost curve in

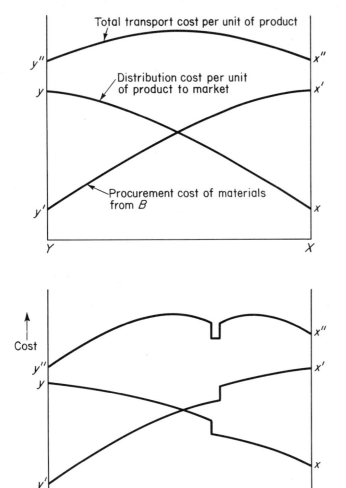

Fig. 8.3 *Endpoint and transshipment point locations.*
This figure illustrates a plant that uses a single material at X and sells its product at the market Y. The transfer–cost gradients xy and x'y' indicate, respectively, the cost of moving material away from X and the cost of distributing to the market at Y. The vertical distance X to x is the terminal or loading charge at the material source, and Yy' is the cost incurred in distributing if the factory is at the market. The curve x"y" is the total transfer cost (the sum of xy and x'y'), and shows the least–cost location at Y. With convex gradients, the total cost is bound to be more between Y and X than at these points, as indicated in the upper diagram. The effect of a transshipment point is illustrated by assuming a town, T, at which additional transfer costs are incurred through, perhaps, unloading from railroad to canal, as shown in the lower figure. Both curves xy and x'y' take a jump here. A location in this town avoids these transshipment charges and is in fact as advantageous as being at the source of material X.

the upper half of Figure 8.3. One exception is where "processing-in-transit" privileges are granted by the railroads, as in the example of the U.S. flour-milling industry concentrated at Buffalo or where there is a break-of-bulk in the course of transportation, a situation illustrated in the bottom part of Figure 8.3. Ports, for example, are favorable spots for processing of raw materials that have been shipped by water. In Western

Europe flour mills and sugar and oil refineries are concentrated at port locations. Most "colonial" raw materials brought in from the world's hinterland regions are processed at ports in Western Europe. Such transshipment centers are called *break-of-bulk* points. Other kinds of transshipment centers are *collection points*, where agricultural or other products are assembled prior to shipment, or *distribution points* central to diffused markets. In the United States much wheat is processed into flour at collection points. The flour is then made into bread at distribution points. Many other examples will occur to the reader.

LABOR ORIENTATION: TYPES AND CASES

A variety of studies also has shown that when transport costs are a low proportion of total costs, the ratio of labor to total cost is high, and labor costs vary a good deal from place to place, plants tend to be most competitive when they are located in areas in which labor cost is least. It is under such conditions that plants are described as being *labor oriented*. In the world today, there are major industrial shifts taking place in labor orientation as part of a global scramble for cheap labor. Accelerating wage inflation in established industrial areas is pushing manufacturers into new efforts to tap the vast pool of willing and cheap labor in poorer countries. Manufacturers are farming out production of component parts, subassemblies, and even finished products sometimes for export to other areas but often for use back home. In the process they are not only cutting their own costs but speeding the industrialization of underdeveloped countries, some of which are coming to relish the role of workshops for distant, richer lands.

tradeoffs between money wages and skills

What are the bases of this movement? Clearly, the prime reason is labor costs, but studies of labor costs show how important it is to recognize that labor costs involve not only money wages. There are many situations where money wages vary apparently without effect on industrial locations because the benefits of lower wages are offset by a lack of skill and lower productivity of the lower-wage labor force. In such cases, skills are far more important in determining the least labor cost location than money wages alone. However, the importance of labor orientation to skills may be offset by technological advances that make unskilled and semi-skilled workers as productive as the skilled workers who previously dominated the industry. For example, in 1970 it cost $2 million less on Taiwan to employ 1,000 women than in the United States, and they took one-third the time to train. In such cases, an orientation to low wage areas rather than to skills has arisen, and is apparently the source of the world trend noted above. Labor costs, therefore, vary first in terms of money wages, and second in terms of productivity and skills.

short- and long-run labor advantages

If the supply of labor is great relative to local demands for labor, wages will be low compared with areas where competition for labor is relatively greater. But research has shown that low wage conditions tend to be ephemeral: if industry comes to an area in search of the low wages, the very act of movement changes the local supply and demand schedules for labor and raises the price. Also, labor tends to migrate from areas of low opportunity to areas of higher opportunity, tending to equalize geographic differentials in wages for that reason, too. Thus labor cost variations due to money wages tend to be short-run differentials that can only persist in longer periods of time either because there is a substantial immobility of labor due to ignorance, poverty, or local social ties, or political barriers between countries that inhibit the free movement of labor. But even such immobilities will tend to be eroded in longer periods of time.

Persistent long-run money wage differentials have been studied in two types of conditions. First, are those cases in which money wage differences do not represent differences in real wages; for example, in areas where the cost of living is low. Second, there can emerge those dynamic conditions described by Gunnar Myrdal in *An American Dilemma* for the U.S. or in his work *Asian Drama* for conditions on an international scale. Myrdal argues that processes of "circular and cumulative causation" can be identified such that labor cost differentials, rather than being equalized in the long run, tend to increase over longer periods of time. The principal reasons that he cites are the differential nature of the migration flows from areas of low to areas of high economic opportunity. Put simply, the most able people move to find better jobs, leaving behind an older and less able population group. This migration decreases the economic viability of the home area, although it increases the quality of skills available in the reception area. These skills impart advantages for further growth, so that the reception areas gain more and more relative advantages.

regions with money-wage advantages

Money wages have been shown to be low in four kinds of areas, which therefore represent the most attractive zones for industry decentralizing in search of low labor costs.

1. *Where the supply of labor is increasing more rapidly than the demand for labor.* This is typical in rural and backward areas where net reproduction rates are substantially greater than elsewhere. Such a condition is typical of the rural parts of the United States in which particular minority groups live. Today, the net reproduction rate of the American Indians, for example, is much higher than that of any other group in the population. On an international scale, this is the characteristic of the Far Eastern countries. In each of these cases, migration rarely tends to offset the natural increase completely, so that a persistent labor surplus develops which keeps the price of labor at a minimum.

2. *Where economic opportunities are declining in relation to a sizable local labor force.* Such a condition is typical of any kind of economically depressed area. The coalfields, for example, were in this position during the peacetime between the world wars. For a long time the anthracite towns of eastern Pennsylvania have faced this situation, as have many other mining areas. This was the history of the cotton textile towns of New England when the cotton textile industry moved to the Piedmont area of the Carolinas and Georgia. Of course, where economic opportunities are declining in relation to the labor force, wage rates will drop.

3. *Where employment opportunities are available only for part of the population.* This has been a general characteristic of female labor in heavy industrial areas where the demand is traditional only for male labor—in the coalfields, in mining areas, in fishing towns, or in railroad towns. In these areas of heavy industry, female labor has traditionally been available at very low wage rates. Where the size of the local female labor pool is large, however, labor-intensive, low-wage industries have been attracted.

4. *Where the cost of living is low so that real wages are high relative to money wages.* For example, housing prices in the American South and Southwest are much lower than in the Northeast because homes in the Northeast must be protected against the very severe winters. Lower housing prices mean that people can maintain the same real level of living at lower money wage rates because they need to put less into the housing that they purchase. A similar situation is where superior residential amenities create a substantial "psychic income" that people are willing to take instead of the higher wage rates offered in areas with fewer residential advantages. It has often been said, for example, that during the 1950s and early 1960s the University of California in Berkeley was able to attract top flight faculty for $2,000 a year less than major universities in the Northeast because of the superior residential environment that the Bay Area offered. In such conditions, of course, money wages will tend not to reflect the real level of living, and the money-wage differential will act to the competitive advantage of labor oriented firms.

technological change and the ties of localized skills

We made the point earlier, however, that money wages are only significant locational factors where skills are relatively insignificant. We will turn later to instances in which the advantages of certain highly localized skills lead to the long-term ties of particular industries to particular locations, and we will discuss the reasons for the development of these localized skills. What is significant is the condition under which skill factors have been shown to exert a diminishing pull on industries. Localized skills are usually relevant to only one industry and are relatively immobile. They are thus very powerful causal factors in geographical inertia. Many operations can only break out of the bonds of localization in a skilled labor area by diminishing reliance upon the skill factor. Only when higher productivity is not related to skills will lower labor cost mean lower wages.

Industry has been shown to shift into areas of lower money wages most generally only under conditions of technological change, when increased mechanization, routinized operations and processes have tended to diminish the importance of skills. The introduction of line methods of production facilitates the use of relatively "green" labor, for example, so that operations can become routinized and can be performed efficiently with only a short period of training. Thus, when semiskilled labor force requirements become increasingly uniform, decentralization of routinized operations is facilitated in the direction of low wage areas, and a wider source of labor is available. But, of course, we have to repeat that this movement to low-wage areas is essentially a movement of routinized operations. Quality products have to stay in the traditional areas, for style cannot be routinized and the skills required for production of high style are localized. In the clothing industry, for example, ready-made clothing production has moved to cheap labor areas, but style lines remain in the world style centers—New York, London, Paris, etc.

In routinized operations, on the other hand, low wage areas may even have an advantage in productivity. First of all, a new plant coming into a previously non-industrialized area can "skim the cream" off the local labor force by offering higher wages than those offered by the alternative occupations of the previously non-industrialized area. This new labor force in general, having no previous experience in factory employment and no preconceived notions about the organization of the industry, or about workloads, is more plastic to requirements of a changed technology, and will be willing to operate with more pieces of machinery than the worker in the traditional industrial areas. Also, too, low wage areas tend to be those areas that have the least restrictive labor codes—we are all well aware of the substantial differences in legislation relating to employment and labor conditions among the States. The areas that have the most restrictive forms of legislation also tend to be the areas in which the trade union movement is strongest. In the United States this reflects, in general, the differences between North and South and between large city and small town. The relative abundance of labor in the South and in small-town locations means the inability of trade unions to establish themselves. Smaller towns, too, will tend to be dominated by one producer, who controls whatever he does not own locally. There, workloads are likely to be higher, employee benefits lower, and the employer much freer to adapt the productive process to his wishes.

SCALE AND AGGLOMERATION ECONOMIES

Processing-cost differentials also may arise from internal economies of scale (discussed in Chapter 6), and a variety of external economies representing different forms of agglomeration. These forms have been called the economies of *localization* and *urbanization,* although there can also be economies of *industrial complexes* in which the traditionally external localization and urbanization economies have been captured and "internalized" by a single firm that has integrated various formerly independent specialized operations. We will discuss these cases in turn.

localization economies

Localization economies have been shown to arise from the clustering of plants engaged in similar activity in a very restricted geographical area. The local scale of the industry that results benefits individual plants within the group and tends to perpetuate the localization of the industry. There are several kinds of economies that have been associated with this type of agglomerative factor:

1. *The reputation acquired by goods produced in a given locality.* This generally leads to substantial product differentiation, because goods produced in some localities, whether or not they meet the standards of that locality, do carry with them the aura of high standards of workmanship and quality. A typical case is that of the cutlery and steel produced in Sheffield, England; others would be Brussels lace and Irish linen.

2. *The consequences of the industrial atmosphere pervading the localized area,* arising out of the close association of manufacturers who meet frequently. Rivalries among these manufacturers breed innovation; at the same time there can be interchange of personnel and information. Knowledge under such circumstances is more rapidly diffused among firms located within the cluster. Firms in the same industry but outside the cluster operate at a disadvantage. This factor of geographic association was, of course, more important during the nineteenth century than the twentieth. It is of less importance today because of the growth of nationwide selling organizations and of a trade press that tends to diffuse ideas rapidly.

3. *The creation of a pool of skilled labor,* which tends thereby to strengthen localizing economies.

4. *Local utilities and services become adapted to the particular needs of the industry.* Banks, insurance agencies, and transportation companies supplying special facilities appropriate to the needs of the industry dominate the kinds of service provided in the locality.

5. *Most important, the local scale of industry permits the subdivision of operations between plants.* There arise auxiliary specialists meeting requirements of several firms who can provide particular items more cheaply than if the individual firms had to provide their own. With a localized industry, then, vertical disintegration proceeds further, arising from the close geographical association of firms, short hauls, speedy delivery, and the lessening of stock requirements. Thus interdependence facilitates those real economies of subdivision that are exhibited by the most localized activities, the most outstanding examples being in the cutlery trades and in the clothing industry (for example, in the garment industry of New York or at the East End of London). Another example is the metal trades of the West Midlands where three main types of

activity constitute the localization: (a) a large number of firms performing common metal processes, but not producing finished goods; e.g., the founders, rerollers, forgers, welders, galvanizers, (b) a large number of firms making common components, screws, bolts, nuts, tools, springs, and (c) service trades; e.g., small establishments making wooden patterns or machine tools, the scrap merchants, and so on. These three main types of activity support the highly localized metal goods manufacturers who engage in assembly and the further processing of the components made by the three main types of activity. Good examples are motor vehicles, bicycles and motorcycles, guns in Birmingham, locks at Wolverhampton, and so on.

P. Sargent Florence, in his book *Investment, Location, and Size of Plant,* has distinguished four main types of industrial linkages that characterize localizations. These are as follows:

1. *Vertical linkages.* In this arrangement, a series of processes linked to each other in succession contributes to the gradual transformation of raw materials into finished products. For example, in the iron and steel industry, there is preliminary processing of iron ore followed by a blast furnace stage, followed by a smelting stage, followed by the steel converter stage, followed by a variety of subsequent hot and cold metal rerollers, etc., as we have discussed earlier in this chapter. This characteristic can lead to vertical *disintegration* of an industry, such that each of the successive stages is carried on by different plants, or it can lead to *vertical integration* such that successive steps in the transformation of raw material into finished products are brought within the ownership of a particular company and with the confines of a particular plant.

2. *Diagonal linkages.* These are characterized by trades that serve a number of different industries and need contact with all of them to maintain viability. Here, good examples are the engraving, plating, and polishing activities in the jewelry quarter of the city for example, or in the machine tool industry.

3. *Lateral linkages.* These involve industries producing parts, accessories, or providing services that feed into an assembly-type industry at different stages of the assembly process, so that the industries converge upon the flow of the assembly line at different stages. A typical case is that of the automobile industry where a variety of services and products feeds into the assembly line.

4. *Common service linkages* of industries using the common processes and skills provided in a local area. For example, each of metal trades draws on the same skills and common processes; the nut and bolt industry, nuts, screws, buttons, chains, cables, locks and bolts, etc.

The economies of localization are therefore those of the *acquired* advantages an industry develops within particular areas, contrasting between the initial attractive advantages of that area and the acquired advantages that arise from the persistence and growth of some localized activity. Over the years the initial advantages may disappear and the persistence of an industry in an area is then ascribable to the accumulation of acquired advantages. Very often *industrial inertia* is tied up with acquired advantage, for subsequent survival may be based upon economies derived from growth, agglomeration, and persistence. Again, we must distinguish between two kinds of inertia. First, there are those forms sustained by cost advantages acquired through localization. Second, there are forms that are sustained by imperfect competition, in which progressive product differentiation insulates a firm from the fully competitive arena.

urbanization economies

Urbanization economies have been shown to derive from the close association of many different kinds of industry in large cities, although it is important to distinguish between urbanization economies and other factors that draw industries to cities, such as the availability of fuel and materials, the locational advantages of ports, and so on. The latter are merely examples of strongly-marked material or market orientations and represent neither the economies of localization nor those of urbanization. Urbanization economies arise because location in a large and diverse group of industrial plants within large population centers may have significant effects upon the costs of individual plants. The cost advantages derive from several sources:

1. *Transport costs.* A large city will have superior transport facilities offering significantly lower transport costs to regional and national markets. A city located in such a way, at a focal point on transport networks, is especially suited for easy assembly of raw materials and for ready distribution of products. There are thus market advantages for speedy and cheap distribution that may be accentuated by the advantages arising out of the size of the local consuming market. In the bigger cities, this local market will account for a very substantial share of service and residentiary activities and of the regionalized activities that need to minimize transport costs, since the local population may form a large part of the total national market. Greater London, for example, has one-fifth of the British consumer market and the New York metropolitan area has been called "one-tenth of a nation." In both cases, these markets account for a significantly larger proportion of the higher quality and fashion-oriented demands. Thus the large city, because of its dominance even on a national market scale, may be the ideal plant location: substantial demands are local and the rest of the plant's output is more easily distributed. If a plant locates in New York, for example, it has easy access to facilities, such as showrooms and warehouses, that it may have to provide for itself in a smaller city.

2. *Labor costs.* The large city labor market is diverse and dynamic, and the labor demands of single firms are only a small part of the total demands for labor. This available labor supply is especially important where firms have seasonally varying labor needs, for example. The big city labor market also offers a whole range of skills; consequently, the advantages of city over the small town are obvious even though its wage rates may be somewhat higher than those of the small town. Facilities for labor that are readily available in the large city may often also have to be provided in the small town, which raises the real labor costs to the firm.

3. *Advantages of scale.* The larger the city the higher the scale of services it can supply. Thus, services such as fire-fighting, police, gas, electricity, water, waste disposal, education, housing, and roads are generally better in the larger city than in the small town. Firms developed in otherwise unindustrialized areas generally have to spend much more capital on infrastructure and social facilities than those that have been developed in large cities. These kinds of scale advantages came into play particularly in the industrialization of the largest metropolitan areas in the period following World War I, although interrupted by World War II. Urbanization economies are those that, in particular, had a magnetic effect upon those industries in which coal was replaced as motive power by electricity, and in which rail and water transportation was replaced by trucking. This new industry is "light" industry concerned with the manufacturing of consumer goods. These goods are often branded and serve sheltered markets because of imperfect competition deliberately created by advertising. For these industries, transport costs are a low proportion of total costs because the materials used tend to be semiprocessed and because the products are compact and have high value in relation to weight. Because unskilled or semiskilled workers are needed, the firms therefore are more likely to be attracted by large cities, especially by the markets and the marketing facilities of these large cities. As light industry is attracted to large cities, the magnetic power of large cities for this kind of industry is increased, creating conditions favorable to further growth. This kind of an effect has been called "circular and cumulative causation."

However, in some respects the addition of industries to the larger cities has added to the costs of existing industries. Private firms may be hit by many disadvantages that accrue in the inner areas of large cities, such as transport congestion, parking problems, and difficulties of loading and unloading. There are also disadvantages in terms of labor: competition for labor and the higher cost of living in cities means that workers must earn higher wages, and this outlay on the part of the firm may not be offset by improved efficiency. And most significant are the effects of high land values in the hearts of the bigger cities, which result from the intense competition for space in and around the central business district, as we saw in Chapter 7.

central area industries

Industries remaining in, or close to, the central business district are those which find a great advantage in the accessibility of the CBD. As the point of convergence for all city and regional transport routes, the CBD offers unusual convenience for buyers as well as for workers. But industry in central business districts also faces severe competition for sites from many other functions seeking the same advantages of centrality. They compete through the prices they are willing to pay to occupy space. Hence, as we saw in Chapter 7, a hierarchy of land usage is found in the city. The "highest" uses are those that derive the greatest advantage from centrality and that can therefore pay most

by turning the advantage into profit and rents. Housing is generally low on the hierarchy, except for high income apartment houses. Most types of industry are also driven out of the core of the city because for them the advantages of centrality are relatively small whereas production costs are lower on the periphery of the city. Therefore, as the process of land use competition takes place, the higher uses occupy the central area and the only industries that remain localized within the boundaries of the central business districts are of the following kinds:

1. The *financial district* of banks, brokers, and the like, relying upon speedy personal contact within a closely intertwined set of activities and relationships
2. A variety of *specialized retail functions,* including department and specialty stores that require large population support at the point of convergence of population.
3. A variety of *social and professional functions,* including the *headquarters and main office function.*

These activities tend to squeeze out housing and industry from the most accessible points. The industry that survives in the city has very special features. It tends to be found on the edges of the central area in the back streets where land values are lower. For this kind of industry central location is imperative; there is no alternative. The industry must be in central areas because of its marketing needs in meeting demands. Marketing and manufacturing functions cannot be separated. A simple showroom in the central area will not do. Also, many of these industries have been long established in the inner areas because these areas support relatively immobile skilled labor forces and because the industry is part of the extreme subdivision of processes within the cluster of interdependent firms. The scale of operations of such firms is generally small. They use ground very intensively, their space requirements being very low in relation to their level of output. In this sense, they can adapt relatively obsolete multistory building space in a variety of ways. This kind of space is, of course, available at the lowest rents until it is cleared and rebuilt for some other more intensive higher-paying use. Industry in central areas thus tends to move from building to building, being displaced as those buildings are cleared for reuse. Two good examples of central area industries are printing and clothing.

For printing, the marketing factor is important. Generally it is involved with so-called job printing for rush jobs that must be completed in a very short time. Firms are generally located on the margins of the professional and financial districts. Newspapers also tend to be produced in central locations, usually in very large modern buildings near the zone of highest land values. Here, centrality is essential to speedy news-gathering. There has to be close contact among the reporters who gather the news, the editorial staff, printers, and the truckers for speedy delivery of the newspapers. On the other hand, periodicals, books, and standardized kinds of job printing are not found in cities but tend to decentralize into the suburban areas and rural and small town locations.

Central area clothing industries involve those branches where fashion and style are important; for example, ladies dresses, gowns, coats, and so on. More than 50 percent of the labor force in these activities in England in 1950 was concentrated in London. More than 60 percent of all such garments made in the U.S. are made in New York. In the New York garment center there are three types of employers:

1. *Manufacturer,* who has an "inside" shop—that is, besides buying the cloth and selling the final product he runs his own production plant, in which his workers cut and sew the material into apparel.

2. *Jobber,* who buys the raw materials, designs the garments, and later sells them, but does not actually manufacture them. (In knit outerwear such a man is called a "converter" rather than a jobber.) The jobber has a showroom and usually a cutting room, but sends the fabric to "outside" shops to be sewed into apparel.

3. *Contractor,* who runs the "outside" shop, where the fabric is sewn into garments. He hires the workers, and is, in effect, a labor contractor. He produces to specification, never takes title to the goods, and is in no way involved with the marketing of the product.

The jobbing-contracting relationship has become a solidly established method of operation because it conveys two strong advantages. First, it permits specialization; the jobber concentrates on the merchandising while the contractor is a production expert. Second, it adds flexibility to an industry where uncertainty reigns; it provides a means of keeping down the unused plant capacity of all concerned.

This second advantage offers a key to understanding the business organization in the women's and children's apparel industries. Although aggregate demand for these products is predictable, the style factor prevents any single firm from knowing what its volume of sales for the season will be; thus the use of contracting relieves each firm of the need to maintain factories large enough to fill maximum orders. The jobber can find additional contractors to produce for him when his orders rise, and the contractor, in turn, is not dependent upon orders from only one jobber, but may turn to others to keep his plant occupied. Contracting even helps the manufacturers who operate their own plants, because those plants need only be large enough to handle normal demand; peak demand can be contracted out.

Contracting is used most in women's outerwear and least in undergarments. Children's outerwear falls between the two. In only one industry, corsets and brassieres, as many as two-thirds of the establishments are those of manufacturers. This industry, producing more standardized products than the other types of women's and children's apparel, differs in many re-

spects from the rest of the garment industries. On the other hand, blouses and unit-priced dresses are subject to frequent style changes and in these two industries, only about one-quarter of the establishments are those of manufacturers.

The crucial consideration is *style,* which involves rapid changes in design. Large cities are the places from which new designs are disseminated. The style factor means that output for stock is impossible, large varieties and small quantities of output are essential, and small scale of activity is appropriate. There is no division of processes or line methods of production, and only a few persons work on a single garment. The work is highly skilled. Thus in central London there are more than 2,000 firms making women's clothing. Women's outerwear firms have small space requirements; they can use converted obsolescent buildings. The industry's demand for skilled labor, as well as its demand for capital, coincided in the 1880s with the influx of Jewish refugees from Eastern Europe into London and New York. The garment trade thus became highly localized with interdependence of specialized subcontractors that produced accessories, such as embroidery, belts, and buttons. Reliance on common specialists arises out of the fashion nature of the trade.

The crucial point binding the industry to central locations is marketing: the industry has to be localized where buyers can cluster and have the garments immediately displayed to them. Therefore, the women's outerwear firms are close to London's West End and to the style centers of Manhattan. On the other hand, branches of the clothing industry manufacturing standardized products by line methods where there is a subdivision of processes and no skilled labor force requirements have decentralized to small town locations.

the decentralizing effect of land values

During the last two decades the principal theme in urban industrial location in North America and Western Europe has been decentralization within metropolitan regions. The increased costs to industry from high land values, including the accompanying property taxes, provide the principal centrifugal force. Moreover, high land values in inner city areas result in cramped and restricted sites, parking difficulties, deficiency of light and air, and environmental pollution. Industries that seek space, light, and air go to the periphery of the big city, to smaller towns, or to nonurban areas; often a relocation is planned to bring the plant closer to the owners' or managers' preferred place of residence.

A moment's reflection will suggest that the central-city diseconomies described above do not necessarily repel industries from cities altogether, however; rather they cause a particular arrangement or *sorting* of industry *within* urban regions. There is a centrifugal push to the fringe of the urban regions where land is cheap and plentiful. The peripheral area avoids the diseconomies of centrality while retaining the advantages of proximity. There the best of both worlds may often be obtained.

This trend of the margins took place slowly in the industrial areas of the U.S. and Western Europe in the interwar period. Despite the initial development of road transport and of highway improvements—alleviating and reducing the pull of rail terminals and docks in central areas on industrial locations—a long period of depression prevented relocation or many new suburban plant locations. The great change came after World War II: in many countries highways were further improved, and new large-scale trucks came into operation, often in combination with rail transport ("piggyback"). Rapid decentralization of industry from the central cities began in force.

But decentralization does operate selectively. For some kinds of activities central locations may be so crucial that they outweigh the disadvantages of congestion.

The industries that move out and decentralize are those for which centrality is not so crucial; they may be larger-scale operations with more specialized space requirements.

INDUSTRIAL COMPLEXES

Industrial complexes arise from another kind of scale and agglomeration economy that is very much like that of localization: when a set of activities involving closely interlinked production processes are managed so that their production, marketing, or other operations are coordinated at a given location, economies of an industrial complex may be said to exist. In the extreme case, the set of activities may be so closely interdependent that they can be operated as a single plant.

types of linkages in industrial complexes

One type of industrial complex arises when successive stages in the manufacture of given end products may be linked at a single location, as in the case of a vertically integrated iron and steel mill (see Chapter 9). Another type of complex results when there is joint production of several products from a single class of raw materials, as when foodstuffs, fertilizers, and industrial products are made from cattle. Yet another type arises when raw materials are processed to yield intermediate products that may combine to form end products. An example is where acetylene and hydrogen cyanide can be produced from alternative sources of hydrocarbons (oil, natural gas, coal). These intermediates can be used to manufacture other intermediates—for example, acrylonitrile, which can be turned into final-stage intermediates such as orlon fiber, and ultimately into such final products as textile fabrics. Three industries are represented in these industrial linkages: petroleum refining, chemicals, and textiles. But what is important about the *complex* is that the particular production sequence is interdependent, demanding *joint* locational evaluation of each of the elements to derive the best location for the complex.

Kolossovsky's territorial production complexes

Walter Isard has pioneered joint locational analysis for industrial complexes in the United States. In 1947, a Moscow geographer, N. Kolossovsky provided a general classification of the circumstances in which industrial complexes might arise. In his article on the development of the "territorial production complexes," Kolossovsky based his classification upon the energy cycles involved in the production process.

Corresponding to each type of territorial production complex in the USSR, he also said that there were distinct types of *economic regions*. His classification of the USSR's production complexes was as follows:

1. *The pyrometallurgical cycle of ferrous metallurgy,* which includes coking coal and iron ore mining, enrichment of metals, coking of coals, blast-furnace processes, recasting of pig-iron into steel, rolling processes, heavy-machine building and, to some extent, machine and tool building. This cycle also includes the chemical industry's processes that use the products of coal coking. The electric power of the cycle is based mainly on thermal-electric stations using coal dust.

2. *The pyrometallurgical cycle of nonferrous metals,* which includes mining and enriching of ore of nonferrous metals, coal mining, nonferrous metallurgy, smelting and refining the main nonferrous metals, and extracting their rarest concomitant minerals, recovery of sulfurous byproducts, and the development of the chemical industry using these byproducts, the working of nonferrous metals, and machine-building consuming these metals in considerable amounts: production of cables, electric and technical appliances, etc. The electric power base of the cycle often consists of thermal-electric stations using local brown coals.

3. *The petrochemical cycle* of oil, power, and chemical production, including extraction and processing of natural deposits of oil, natural gas, common potassium and other salts. To this cycle belong the oil refining industry, and organic synthesis of alcohols, rubber, plastics, and other products of the chemical industry. The electric power base of the cycle is based mainly on thermal-electric stations using the final byproducts of the oil-refining industry and gases.

4. *The hydroelectric power industrial cycle,* based on the use of cheap power produced by hydroelectric power stations, and wide use of electric power in all the main and auxiliary processes of production. To this cycle belongs electrical metallurgy of ferrous and nonferrous metals, electrical chemistry, electricothermics and other branches of industry consuming large quantities of power. The most important link in this cycle is the hydroelectric power station.

5. *The consuming district cycles,* far from sources of raw materials, high quality fuel, and cheap hydroelectric

power. These cycles are based on transportable raw materials and semimanufactured materials brought from other parts of the country. Intensive development of manufacturing industry permits wide use of second-rate local fuel (peat, combustible slates, brown coals), but these cycles use a still greater amount of fuel brought from other regions. It is characteristic of such cycles that they create "secondary" branches of industry that make use of the byproducts of manufacturing industry—secondary ferrous metallurgy, secondary nonferrous metallurgy, etc. Productive cooperation of plants and factories is common, based on full use of local raw materials and their byproducts and on those brought from other regions. The electric power base of the cycle is the combination of thermal-electric stations working on local second-rate fuel, and local hydroelectric power stations of medium capacity with electric power stations working on fuel brought from other parts of the country. Shortage of electric power and fuel is filled in by transmission of electric power by wire, and of oil and natural gas by pipelines, from other industrial areas.

6. *The timber industry cycle,* including lumbering, saw mills, forest chemistry, and a number of other branches of industry using pulp. Byproducts of the timber industry create the power base of this cycle.

7. *Agricultural cycles,* including branches of industry treating products of agriculture-vegetable fiber and wool, corn, skins, vegetable oils, etc. Small and medium thermal-electric stations, often using fuel brought from other regions, usually constitute the power base of this cycle.

8. *The irrigation cycle,* including branches of industry processing products of irrigated farming, and also comparatively large irrigation works that include hydroelectric power stations producing cheap power.

It must be admitted that Kolossovsky's typology of industrial complexes was probably developed more for describing the economic regions of the USSR than for analyzing the interdependencies involved in the location of industrial complexes. However, his classification does provide a concise overview of the circumstances under which such complexes might arise, as seen through the eyes of a Soviet scholar concerned with the central planning of industrial locations. In each case, *joint* location of several closely related activities might produce a different, and superior, locational pattern.

INDUSTRIAL LOCATION AND THE URBAN HIERARCHY

hierarchical location differences

Large cities will have larger local markets and provide greater ease of access to regional markets than smaller cities. Likewise, smaller cities will offer labor at lower wage rates than larger cities will, because competition for labor is less. And the very idea of urbanization economies is one associated with city size. Because the cost factors in plant location vary systematically with city size, it is expected that plant location

should vary significantly w... the urban hierarchy, as fo... centrated in large metropo... markets. They derive their ... externalities (economies of ... tion), and from national ma... extreme, small town industry ... material-oriented processing i... ture, fishing, and forests and lo... weight-reduction before the p... ... national markets; and (2) activitie... ...ing their locational advantage in the low labor costs of small towns. In between, medium-sized cities appear to have concentrations of larger-scale agricultural processers, and a broad range of large- and medium-scale industries engaged in fabricating intermediates and producers' goods from metals.

costs, infrastructure, innovation, and filtering processes

What are some of the reasons for the differential importance of cost factors from larger to smaller cities? An urban economist, Wilbur Thompson, offers one set of reasons. He argues that the larger urban areas are places of creative entrepreneurship, continually inventing or adopting new activities and enjoying the rapid growth characteristic of the early stage of an industry's life cycle when a new market is exploited. Thompson says that the economic base of the large metropolis derives from the creativity of its universities and research parks, the sophistication of its engineering firms and financial institutions, the persuasiveness of its public relations and advertising agencies, the flexibility of its transportation networks and utility systems, and all the dimensions of infrastructure that facilitate the quick and orderly transfer from old dying economic bases to new growing ones. But when an industry matures, the rate of job formation in that industry slows, and the local rate of job formation in the large city may slow even more as the maturing industry begins to decentralize—a likely development, especially in non-unionized industries, because with maturity the production process becomes rationalized and often routine. The high wage rates of the innovating area, quite consonant with the high skills needed in the beginning stages of the learning process become excessive when the skill requirements decline and the industry, or parts of it, "filters down" to the smaller, less industrially sophisticated areas where the cheaper labor is now up to the lesser occupational demands.

A filter-down theory of industrial location would go far toward explaining the small towns' lament that they always get slow-growing industries feeding on lower wage rates. The smaller, less industrially-advanced area struggles to achieve an average rate of growth out of enlarging shares of slow-growth industries, originating as a by product of the area's low wage rate attraction.

The larger, more sophisticated urban economies

to earn high wage rates only by continu-
ming the more difficult work. Consequently,
ust always be prepared to pick up new work in
early stages of the learning curve, inventing, inno-
ating, rationalizing, and then spinning off the work
when it becomes routine. In its early stages an industry
also generates high local incomes by establishing an
early lead on competition, and thus smaller towns receiving "filtered-down" industries are, almost by definition, destined to have lower income levels than those
prevailing in metropolitan areas.

In support of his formulation, and to illustrate
the consequences for the welfare of the citizenry,
Thompson reports on a variety of analyses that show
that median family income in American cities is a
positive function of local educational levels, degree of
manufacturing specialization, city size, the male labor
force participation rate, and percentage of the population foreign-born. Thus, larger cities have higher educational levels, more diversified occupational skills, and
more culturally enriched environments. These qualities
combine with the higher-skill mix in manufacturing—
more capital per worker and greater productivity—kept
high at the margin by union control of the labor supply, and by the combined product and factor price
power of oligopolies and unions. Such a nexus of oligopoly, unions, and capital-intensive production, particularly in heavy industry, contributes to the higher
income levels of the metropolitan resident.

Economic growth benefits the smaller town only
through the downward "filtering" of industry in this
scheme. The mechanics of filtering are as follows: The
higher the capital-labor ratio in a region, the higher
the wage rate of the unskilled. The implication of this
is that, in any economic expansion, the high income
region experiences rising wage rates first. Some industries will be priced out of the high income labor market
and there will be a shift of that industry to low-income
regions, increasing their employment and incomes. If
the boom can be maintained, industries of higher labor
productivity will shift into the growing regions and
some industries will be driven even further into the
countryside. At any point in time, then, industries will
be differentially located in urban areas and labor markets of different sizes. And the shifts can be seen operating not only in the U.S., but throughout the world
today. While newer forms of market-oriented industries
tend to be centralizing towards major population centers, manufacturing—particularly such sectors as apparel and textiles and electrical machinery—is moving
interregionally and internationally from rich to poor
areas, and from larger to smaller urban centers.

the case of the apparel industry

In the apparel industry in the United States, to
consider one example, locational shifting has consisted
of a continual process of "peeling off" particular
branches of production from the body of the New York

metropolitan region's employment. The process began
in men's work clothing and women's housedresses. Both
industries employ relatively unskilled female labor, and
their products are highly standardized. Producing on a
large scale, and not governed by rapid style changes,
these firms do not require the external economies available in the New York metropolitan region. At the same
time, labor cost is a crucial factor for survival. As the
immigration laws cut off the influx of cheap labor, and
as improved transportation made it feasible to locate
in low-wage labor markets, these industries began to
leave the region. While New York firms declined, the
production of work clothing and housedresses expanded
in Pennsylvania, in the southeast, and in the low-wage
urban labor markets of St. Louis and Kansas City.

But the wage-oriented shifts in location were not
confined to these cheapest products. In the 1920s, New
York City emerged clearly as the highest wage area in
women's and children's garments. At the same time, it
appeared as the highest wage area in men's clothing,
except for Chicago, which specialized in quality production. As a consequence, producers in other lines of
garments—lines less standardized than housedresses or
work clothing—began to search for locations with lower
labor cost. In the two main branches of women's clothing—women's and misses' dresses, coats and suits—the
shifts were facilitated by two factors that gained in
importance during the late 1920s. One was the physical
separation of the actual production—the sewing of the
garments—from the merchandising and cutting operations. The other was the rise of "section work," which
required relatively unskilled labor. As a consequence
of these developments, contractors producing cheaper
types of dresses, coats, or suits could locate outside
New York City and still provide the jobbers with quick
truck delivery. In this way it was possible for firms to
retain many of the advantages of proximity to the
center of fashion and skilled labor in New York City
while enjoying lower labor costs in the sewing of the
garments.

The search for cheaper labor thus did not always
push the garment firms entirely out of the region.
Many firms moved to the region's suburban counties;
indeed, in women's coats and suits the bulk of the city's
loss has been made up by employment in those counties.
But the labor available in the mining communities of
Pennsylvania and the textile towns of New England
has been even cheaper than that available in the region's
outlying counties. Overnight by truck from New York
City, these communities could maintain close ties with
Manhattan's garment center. Under the "section work"
system, the producers could employ local women who
had had no previous experience in the needle trades.
As a consequence, dress contractors in the lower price
lines moved increasingly to these communities. The
relative decline of inexpensive dress production in the
metropolitan region has been accelerated by expansion
in still other areas in the South and Midwest.

Locational changes in other New York clothing

industries displayed many similar features. In the more standardized and cheaper branches of women's undergarments, children's outerwear, and men's clothing, the New Jersey counties of the region gained at the expense of New York City; but the search for lower labor costs again led eventually outside of the New York metropolitan region. In men's clothing, for instance, the first outside gainers were the competing urban centers of Philadelphia and Baltimore; but in the 1930s relative gains were registered by smaller communities in Pennsylvania, Maryland, and the Midwest. A more recent expansion of employment took place in the low-wage Southeast in the manufacture of children's outerwear and women's undergarments. Among other industries showing the beginnings of "filtering-down" as mass production operations are separated from activities demanding higher skills are, for example, book manufacturing, which is decentralizing while composition and printing remain highly concentrated in major metropolitan areas, consistent with the high skill component and the continuing need for specialized external services and close contacts with customers and supplies. The filtering industries moving into the smallest towns have been those traditionally displaying the least dependence upon urbanization economies, generally involving mass production of goods for final consumption. On the other hand, industrial complexes of highly interdependent activities producing intermediate products and capital and producers' goods are showing some tendency for increased concentration in moderate-size markets.

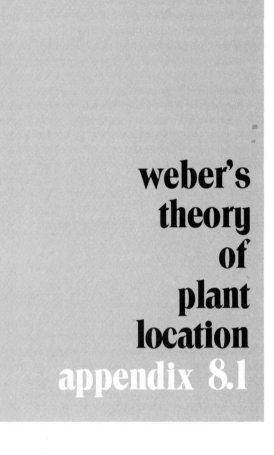

weber's theory of plant location
appendix 8.1

The original theory of plant location, on which all the research leading to the previous findings has been based, was formulated in 1909 by a German location economist, Alfred Weber, in a book entitled *Über den Standort der Industrien.* Although his theory has subsequently been enriched and enlarged upon by a variety of persons, most notably Tord Palander, Edgar Hoover, August Lösch, Melvin Greenhut, and Walter Isard, it is appropriate that we summarize the essential parts of Weber's theory here, to set aside Von Thünen's theory in Chapter 7.

Weber, like Von Thünen sought to develop both a "pure" theory of industrial location applicable to any political or economic system, and a "general" theory, applicable to all types of industry. In the manner of Von Thünen, Weber derived his theory using a method of successive elimination, singling out certain major elements for attention and eliminating all other complications by means of simplifying assumptions. This approach, he acknowledged, cannot be expected to explain actual locations but merely to clarify the underlying influences.

In order to understand Weber's analysis we need to familiarize ourselves with the assumptions upon which his argument is based and with the meaning of certain terms that he employed. The formal assumptions are as follows:

1. Weber postulates a uniform country like that of Von Thünen's uniform plain

2. He proposes to consider a single product at a time. Goods of different quality, though of similar type, are treated as different products

3. The position of sources of raw material is assumed to be known

4. The position of points of consumption is also assumed to be known

5. Labor is geographically fixed. Weber assumes that there exists a number of places where labor at definite, predetermined wages can be had in unlimited quantities

6. Transportation costs are a function of weight and distance. Differences in topography are allowed for by appropriate additions to distance and differences in transportability by additions to actual weight

Among the terms that Weber uses are the following:

1. *Ubiquities*—materials available practically everywhere, and presumably at the same price everywhere.
2. *Localized materials*—materials obtainable only in geographically well-defined localities.
3. *Pure materials*—localized materials that enter to the extent of their full weight into the finished product. Thread to be woven into cloth is perhaps an example of this category.
4. *Gross materials*—localized materials that impart only a portion of, or none of, their weight to the finished product. Fuel is the extreme type of gross material, for none of its weight enters into the product.
5. *Material index*—indicates the proportion that the weight of localized materials bears to the weight of the finished product. A productive process which uses pure material has an index of 1.
6. *Locational weight*—the total weight to be moved per unit of product. An article made out of ubiquities would have a locational weight of 1 because only the product itself would be moved; if it were made from pure material the locational weight would be 2 because for transportation of the product an equivalent weight of materials would be required.
7. *Isodapane*—the locus of points of equal transportation cost. The meaning of the term will become clear in the discussion.

Working with these assumptions, employing these terms, and seeking in the first instance to measure the effect of transportation upon location, Weber then imagined certain cases and developed conclusions about them. Let us look at these cases, reformulating Weber's initial arguments where modern theorists have improved upon them.

CASE 1: ONE MARKET AND ONE SOURCE OF RAW MATERIALS

The first case supposes a raw material to be produced at *A* and the finished product made out of the material to be consumed at *B*. The problem is to determine where the manufacture or processing is to take place. Weber states four possibilities:

1. If ubiquities only are used, the processing will occur at point of consumption *B*, because the selection of *B* will make transportation unnecessary.
2. If one pure material is used, processing may occur at *A,* at *B*, or at any point between *A* and *B*. This conclusion is based upon the fact that the weight to be transported and the distance to be covered is the same in all instances.
3. If pure material plus ubiquities is used, the processing will occur at the point of consumption *B*, because the pure material will be without influence, and the ubiquities will govern.
4. If one weight-losing material is used, processing will occur at point of production, because the weight that is lost will not have to be transported.

CASE 2: ONE MARKET AND TWO RAW MATERIAL SOURCES

Weber's second case assumes that raw materials are available at two places, *A* and *B*, at equal prices. The finished product is to be consumed at *C*, and the problem as before is to determine where manufacture or processing is to take place. Three possibilities are now considered:

1. If ubiquities alone are used, manufacture will occur at the point of consumption for the same reasons as when only two points were involved.
2. If several pure materials are employed, manufacture will also take place at point of consumption. On this supposition, the weight of materials exactly equals the weight of the product. All weights, whether in the form of materials or in the form of product, have to be moved from their deposits to the place of consumption. They should not deviate unnecessarily; therefore each material will proceed along the straight line that leads from the origin to the point of consumption. Unless the way of one should lead, by chance, through the deposit of another, all of these ways will meet for the first time in the place of consumption. Since the assembly of all materials at one spot is the necessary first condition of manufacture, the place of consumption is the location where manufacturing will be carried on; a productive enterprise, using several pure materials alone, will always locate at the place where its products are consumed.
3. The conclusion is different if several localized weight-losing materials are used. In analyzing this case Weber sets up what he calls a "locational figure." Let us suppose a process which uses two weight-losing materials produced at *A* and at *B*, and let us suppose that the product is to be consumed at *C*. Manufacture will not take place at *C* because it is undesirable to transport from *A* and *B* to *C* the material weight that does not enter into the weight of the finished product. It will not, according to Weber, occur at *A* or *B* unless the importance of one material happens to be so great as to overcome the influence of all other elements. Instead, it will usually be found somewhere *within* the triangle, at that location determined by the relative balance of the locational weights.

THE "FIRST DISTORTION": LABOR COSTS

Weber treated labor costs as "a first distortion" of the industrial locations determined by transport costs. The second step of his locational analysis, then, was to plot the spatial variations in transport cost away from the optimum transport-cost location in order to observe the background against which differences in labor cost operate. If, at some other place in the region, the cost of labor per unit of product is less than it is at the optimum transport location, perhaps because an established industry closed down or an unusually high rate of population growth occurred, or a pool of particularly skilled workers is available, and if the increment to transport costs at this alternative location is less than the labor savings, a "deviation" from the "optimum" least transport cost location will arise.

AGGLOMERATION AND DEGLOMERATION

Having combined the effects of transport and labor costs, Weber then turned to the problem of determining how that location may be deflected within the region by the tendency of firms to agglomerate. In Weber's view, there are two main ways in which a company can gain the benefits of agglomeration. First, it may increase the concentration of production by enlarging its factory, thus obtaining savings through a larger scale of operation. Second, it may benefit by selecting a location in close association with other plants. This "social" agglomeration yields benefits from sharing specialized equipment and services, greater division of labor, and large-scale purchasing and marketing.

Weber confined his attention specifically to what he calls "pure" or "technical" agglomeration, omitting from consideration all types of "accidental" agglomeration, that is, industrial concentrations formed for reasons other than to take advantage of agglomeration economies per se. On such grounds he eliminated those agglomerations that occur because of the common attraction of industrial establishments to large concentrations of people or to ports, highway and railway junctions, and other transport features. Deglomeration—the "weakening of agglomeration tendencies"—he attributed to the competition for land, which becomes increasingly scarce and more expensive in areas of industrial concentration until high rents begin to outweigh the original advantages of agglomeration.

As a "second altering force," agglomeration acts to divert manufacturing from either a least transport-cost location or a least labor-cost location, depending upon which was originally the dominant locating influence in a given instance. For an establishment that would normally be transportation-oriented, the savings from locating close to other firms may be sufficient to justify some sacrifice of transport cost. To determine whether or not such a diversion from the least transport-cost was feasible, Weber employed a similar logic to that previously used for weighing the counterattractions of transport and labor locations.

Because the attractions of agglomeration and labor-cost savings both represent deviations from the least transport-cost location, however, in Weber's view, these two influences may conflict. The decision will go to the one that provides the greater savings. Weber indicates that the winner is more likely to be the labor location because that is a place where "accidental" agglomeration may be expected to occur as a result of a concentration of population or the presence of special transport features. "Pure" agglomeration, he felt, can prevail only with industries having very low labor requirements, such as oil refining or chemical manufacture. The main effect of the conflict, then, is to increase the tendency of industry to collect at only a few locations.

RECOMMENDED READINGS

Estall, R. C., and R. O. Buchanan, *Industrial Activity and Economic Geography.* London: Hutchinson University Library, 1961.

Greenhut, M. L., *Plant Location in Theory and Practice.* Chapel Hill: University of North Carolina Press, 1956.

Hoover, E. M., *An Introduction to Regional Economics.* New York: Knopf, 1971.

Segal, M., *Wages in the Metropolis.* Cambridge, Mass.: Harvard University Press, 1960.

Smith, D. M., *Industrial Location.* New York: John Wiley, 1971.

Industrial locational patterns, whether produced by survival of the fittest in a competitive market place, by careful corporate locational research, or by governmental constraints on individual locational choice, are never static. Not only is there continual innovation and filtering down the urban hierarchy but populations and markets change, resources become depleted, and changing technology reduces distance, introduces new modes of production, and provides new products. To all such changes, the calculus of locational advantage must respond. Even if locations were rationally determined under one set of conditions, they cease to be when these conditions change. A situation of stress is created, and the locational pattern will adjust.

It is to examples of the adjustment process that we now turn. We look first at how changing production and transport costs affect the size and shape of market areas. Then, the role of technological changes in producing successive transport orientations of the iron and steel industry are explored. Third, the replacement of power-source orientation by labor costs as the dominant locational factor in the textile industries is analyzed. Finally, the rapid locational shifts in the modern electronics industry are described.

PALANDER'S MARKET AREA ANALYSIS

One interesting portrayal of the effects on locational patterns of transport cost and production cost differences was provided by the Swedish economist, Tord Palander, in *Beiträge zur Standortstheorie,* perhaps the next most important book on industrial location after Alfred Weber's. While Palander's method was to compare a series of cases, it does reveal how careful use of theory can cast light on likely spatial dynamics as transport and production costs change.

Palander first took the case of two identical producers, and asked where the boundary between their market areas would occur. This is illustrated in Figure 9.1a. *A* and *B* are two plants serving a market distributed along the horizontal axis of the diagram. The plant cost, or price charged for the product at source, is given by the vertical distance A^p for firm *A*, and B^p for firm *B*. Away from the plant, the price the consumer has to pay is raised by the cost of transportation, as shown by the lines rising in both directions, A^f and B^f. Thus, at any point, the price charged includes a fixed plant cost and a variable cost of transportation. The boundary between the market areas of the two firms will be at *X,* where the delivered price from both producers is equal and customers will be indifferent as to which firm they buy from.

Figures 9.1b through 9.1e illustrate variations on the theme, in which Palander changed the relative values of plant price (*p*) and freight charges (*f*). Figure 9.1b shows equal freight rates but lower plant price at one location (*B*), enabling it to control more of the area between the two firms than *A* can. *B* should then have a greater output level than *A*. In Figure 9.1c, firm *B*

industrial location dynamics: case studies

9

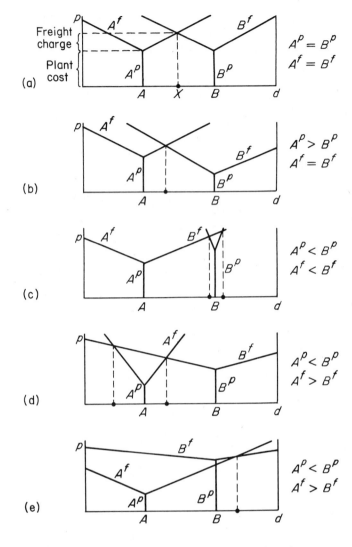

Fig. 9.1 *Market area boundaries in different situations*

has both a higher plant price and higher transport costs per unit of distance than *A* has, but it is still able to control a small market area by virtue of the higher delivered price from *A* near *B*. Figure 9.1d shows that where one firm (*A*) has a lower plant price but higher transport costs it is able to control a fairly extensive section of the market. To the left of *A*, however, there comes a point where *B* regains control by virtue of its lower freight cost. Finally, Figure 9.1e shows a more extreme version of the case at Figure 9.1d, in which firm *B* cannot serve the market immediately adjoining its factory because the price at the plant is so high; it is only at some distance to the right that the relatively low freight rate from *B* allows the firm to sell at a lower price than that of *A*.

Some excellent examples of the above cases can be drawn from Britain's Labor government's post–World War II White Papers on the sand and gravel, brick, and cement industries. These examples reveal increasing concentration of production as relative transport and production costs decline from one case to the other.

This indicates what happens to locational patterns as, through time, similar changes in transport and production costs occur: production becomes concentrated in the least-cost locations.

sand and gravel working

Sand and gravel are widely available in superficial deposits in Britain. They are usually worked together, because gravel aggregates are found surrounded by sand. The product has a very low value in relation to bulk: in 1948 the pit price was five shillings per ton, including all costs of excavation and dressing. Pit price does not vary much from one part of the country to another. Transport costs loom large in final delivered prices: transportation of only two miles increases selling prices by thirty percent (the markup being for the fixed costs of loading and the variable costs of carriage) and shipment of thirteen miles doubles the pit price. Since the consumer makes his purchases on the basis of final delivered price it is easy to see how small sand and gravel pits multiply, each serving small market areas limited by increasing transport costs. Few pits sell sand and gravel further then thirty miles from the pit in Britain; the few exceptions are where cheap water transportation is available.

The lesson is one that was introduced in Chapter 8: transport costs force an industry that sells a ubiquitous low-value product to assume a diffused locational pattern, in the manner of Figure 9.1a. Figure 9.2 is probably a more accurate graphical presentation of the transport gradient-production cost relationship, however. This figure was prepared by another location theorist, Edgar M. Hoover, in a 1937 book entitled *Location Theory and the Shoe and Leather Industries*. Hoover observed that in the extractive industries, average costs rise with increased production due to increasing transport costs as the market area gets bigger at an increasing rate, because the cost curve of the firm tends to be U-shaped. Thus, if a mineral is extracted at point *X*, *A*, *B*, and *C* indicate possible edges to its market area in one direction. If the area *XA* is supplied, production costs are represented by the distance *Xa* on the ordinate, and the line *aa'* shows how delivered price increases away from *X* as transport costs are added. If the market is extended to *B*, the cost of extraction rises to *b*, and a new transport gradient (*bb'*) is introduced. Extension to *C* has a similar effect. Joining together points *a'*, *b'*, and *c'* with the delivered price at all other possible edges of the market area produces what Hoover terms the *margin line*. The introduction of a margin line relating to a second source of the mineral (*Y*) reveals a point of intersection, which represents the boundary between the two market areas.

the brick industry

In 1950 there were almost 1500 brick-making plants in Great Britain. There are very few clays in the country that have not been worked for brick making.

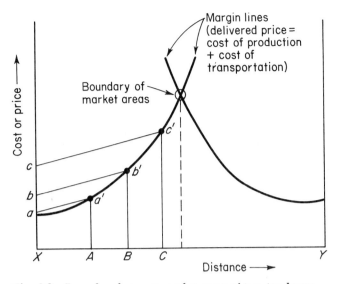

Fig. 9.2 *Boundary between market areas of two producers under conditions of diminishing returns to scale*

Transport costs are lower in relation to production costs than for sand and gravel. Prices increased 20 percent with shipment of 50 miles, and doubled if shipped 150 miles. Lower transport costs imply larger market areas, and more latitude in location of the brick-making plants, as suggested in Figure 9.1b. Thus, plants tend to concentrate on the best brick-making clays. One-third of the productive capacity of Great Britain was found at the time of the White Paper in 46 plants at Bedford, Bletchley, and Peterborough in the Midlands where the superior Oxford clays are used to make "Fletton bricks," the familiar red bricks that characterize the English landscape. This concentration is made possible because production costs on the Oxford clays are lower than elsewhere. Peculiar advantages are thick homogeneous beds that reduce excavation costs, the fact that 5 percent of the volume of the clay is carbonaceous, which reduces the amount of coal that has to be purchased to bake the bricks, and the plastic qualities of the clay, which eliminate pretreatment, such as pulverization, normally required before bricks can be moulded. The Fletton producers sell over longer distances by virtue of lower production costs. In England these longer distances are adequate for the Fletton producers to be able to dominate the entire market on the London-Birmingham axis.

the cement industry

A third case is illustrated by the British cement industry. There are two kinds of cement: (a) Portland cement, formed by burning clay and chalk together until they fuse in a clinker, which is crushed to make cement, and (b) blast-furnace cement, a byproduct of the steelmaking industry. The former is most common in England, and provides this third example of the joint role of transport and production costs in reducing the diffusion of industry.

Several raw materials are needed to produce Portland cement. To obtain 100 tons of cement requires 225 tons of chalk, 75 tons of clay, 60 tons of coal, and 5 tons of gypsum. Clay and chalk are usually found close together in England, and because chalk inputs are greatest, cement plants tend to be tied to sources of chalk. But since costs of transporting cement are high, cement plants tend to be small, located centrally to small scattered markets. Price increases with overland transport are such that the cement is not sold farther than 25 miles overland from the cement plant.

In spite of such obvious pressures for diffusion, however, 50 percent of Britain's Portland cement is produced in the Thames-Medway area, southeast of London. Why should there be this concentration? First, the Greater London market, accounting for 25 percent of Great Britain's consumption of cement, lies within a 25-mile radius of the Thames-Medway cement plants. Second, the chalk of lower Thamesside is pure, easily extracted and converted into cement so that production costs are lower than elsewhere. As in the use of Fletton bricks, this leads to increases in the market area of the cement plants. Third, the plants are located by the river Thames, and cheap water transport is available to cement markets around the coasts of England. Thamesside is able to dominate the coastwise cement trade for several hundred miles, in the manner suggested by Figure 9.1d. The lesson is that the size and shape of market areas, and amount produced in any area, may be modified by the size of local markets and by differentials in transportation rates.

CHANGING TRANSPORT ORIENTATION IN THE IRON AND STEEL INDUSTRY

The foregoing comparative cases suggest that as transportation and production conditions change, the preferred transport orientation of an industry may change through time. If we trace the effects of technological development on the changing locational patterns of the iron and steel industry, the complexity of the relationships involved can be illustrated. It will be useful to begin during the eighteenth century—even though, of course, the iron industry dates much further back—because at this time processes became clearly defined and certain regional patterns had emerged.

diffusion during the eighteenth century

During the eighteenth century, the industry produced pig iron. Furnaces tended to be found in wooded areas near the sources of iron ore. About 8 to 9 tons of pig iron could be produced using the charcoal obtainable from one acre of woodland. The largest furnaces could produce 20 to 30 tons of pig iron each week, consuming 150 to 200 acres of woodland each year. It was uneconomical to transport charcoal more than 15 miles. The amount of iron produced in any area was therefore limited by the available charcoal supplies: if the entire 15-mile radius were completely wooded and produced charcoal on a self-sustaining 50-year cycle, it could only support 40 furnaces making 60,000 tons of iron per year. Local concentrations of industry were out of the question, and in Europe and the settled parts of North America the industry had a highly diffused locational pattern. The industry could only grow by becoming more scattered. Perhaps the biggest iron producers of the time were Sweden and Russia.

Blast in the furnace was produced by direct water power, which had replaced foot bellows a century earlier, and most furnaces therefore tended to seek streamside sites. Since the amount of power available from a water wheel was necessarily limited, reliance on water power had the same effects on the industry as charcoal; it kept the scale of operations small and the industry scattered.

During the eighteenth century markets were also scattered, and the costs of transporting the finished products of the industry—castings, blooms, bars, and strips—were also very high, and these considerations reinforced diffusion trends.

transformation of techniques and locations during the industrial revolution

This early iron industry was transformed by a series of major innovations at the end of the eighteenth century. Abram Darby had used coal to smelt iron as early as 1709, but his invention had limited application, since the process he proposed resulted in a "cold short" pig iron, a very brittle product of little general value. The ultimate triumph of coal as a source of fuel awaited inventions that would permit it to be forged into a valuable and desirable commodity like wrought iron. Such an invention became available in 1789 when the patents on Henry Cort's "puddling" furnace lapsed. Puddling was a means of processing iron as it was being smelted to reduce the carbon content and transform the brittle pig iron into more malleable wrought iron. The impact of Cort's process was immediate and widespread. In England, for example, charcoal was replaced as a fuel by coal within one decade. Simultaneously, the industry was freed from ties to water sites, because of the harnessing of steam to provide the blast in the furnaces and to rotate the rollers in the puddling furnace. Between 1790 and 1800 the scattered charcoal-iron industry was replaced by a more competitive coal–wrought-iron–steam industry. These changes made possible substantial increases in iron production at the same time as demands for iron were increasing because of industrialization, construction of the railroads, and other developments reflecting the increasing momentum of the industrial and transportation revolutions.

The net effect of these changes was the development of a larger scale industry, concentrated on coal fields where both fuel and clayband iron ores were available. Wrought iron could be made at lowest cost on the coal fields because the assembly costs of the requisite raw materials (coal, iron ore, and refractory materials) were lowest. As concentrated iron-producing districts developed, so did some of the first industrial towns of Western Europe and the United States.

This pattern was not allowed to crystallize, however. A series of additional technological changes took place during the first decades of the nineteenth century and these also had marked effects upon the locational pattern of the industry. First, local iron ores on the coal fields were worked out rapidly and the industry had to reach further afield for iron ores. In England in particular this problem became critical: in 1850, 95 percent of the ore used was from coal measure sources; by 1880 this had declined to 30 percent, and by 1913 to 6 percent. Overseas sources of ore became increasingly important, first from northern Spain, and later from Sweden after a railroad was built from Kirunavaara to Narvik in 1894. Increasing ore imports gave importance to intermediate (port) locations at which ore had to be transshipped. Otherwise empty railroad cars coming back from carrying ore to the coal field iron mills could be used to carry coal on the return haul to the port. By keeping some of the imported ore, the ports could develop iron plants. This was especially apparent in the United States with the westward movement of the country, the development of the Lake Superior ores, and the subsequent growth of the various lakeside steel plants (for example, at Cleveland and Chicago).

A second change was a steady decline in coal consumption, coming about because of introduction of the hot blast, which allowed furnace temperatures to be increased and lowered inputs of coal. In 1829, 8 tons of coal were required to produce 1 ton of pig iron; by 1850 this had been reduced to between 2.5 and 2 tons, and the pull of coal fields on the iron industry was relaxed accordingly.

The third, and perhaps most basic change, was the introduction of large-scale methods of producing cheap steel, a product superior to wrought iron for most purposes. Until the 1850s steel was an expensive item produced in small batches by the Huntsman crucible process at places like Sheffield in England and Solingen in Germany, and wrought iron was used for most purposes. After 1880 the era of wrought iron had passed. The first steel converter was invented by Bessemer in 1856. This was followed by the invention of the open-hearth converter by Siemens and Martin in 1864.

At least two new elements were introduced into the locational calculus by the introduction of steel converters. In addition to the pulls of raw materials and markets, scrap could be used in the open hearth furnace, implying that cheap scrap locations could become feasible competitive locations for the industry. Further, invention of the basic Bessemer process by Gilchrist Thomas in 1879 enabled phosphoric ores to be used in steel production. This was of particular importance in Europe where vast iron ore deposits such as those of Lorraine in France are phosphoric. The discovery that lining the steel furnace with a limestone flux would

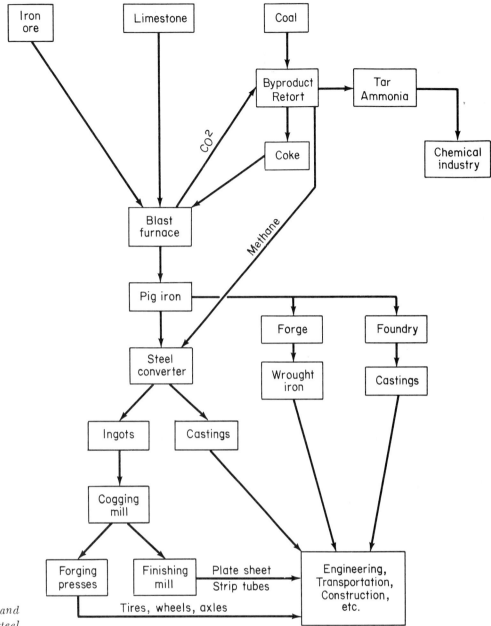

Fig. 9.3 *Production of iron and steel*

remove the phosphorus immediately made these ores available to the steel industry. Basic Bessemer converters were introduced rapidly in France, Belgium, Luxembourg, and Germany. Acceptance was less rapid in Britain, where acid (nonphosphoric) ores were produced locally in Cumberland or imported. However, during the twentieth century Britain has made increasing use of the low-grade phosphoric iron ores of Oxfordshire, Northamptonshire, Lincolnshire, and Yorkshire. Even today most of the steel produced in the United States is acid. Only at Birmingham, Alabama, is there a basic Bessemer plant. Thus a regional differentiation of steel-producing facilities emerged, based upon the types of ores used. The ability to use the new sources of ore led to new locational opportunities, particularly in Western Europe. In France today the greatest part of the iron and steel industry is ore-field oriented.

After this wave of technological change, concentrations of new steel mills were to be found in urbanized coal field locations, at intermediate port locations, and at low-grade phosphoric iron ore deposits. This pattern persists, although continued relocation has taken place as availability of raw materials has changed, and a new strong pull of markets is evident. The next sections examine the contemporary patterns in more detail, and evaluate trends.

the modern steel industry

Today there are three major stages in the steel making process between the time that raw materials are assembled and finished products are available for consumers. (Fig. 9.3). The first of these stages centers on the blast furnace, in which three basic raw materials are placed: iron ore, coke, and limestone. Coke provides heat, which releases carbon monoxide and carbon dioxide from the limestone. The carbon monoxide acts on the iron ore so that the iron is separated from the sands and clays and other impurities that are also present in the ore; the carbon dioxide can be led off to the coke oven to assist in converting coal to coke. Impurities combine to form a slag, which can be used for construction or, as in the United States, a raw material for the cement industry. The iron is led off into pigs—hence the name pig iron—and may be used by forges, which produce wrought iron, by foundries which make castings, or it may be transferred to the second stage of the steelmaking process, the steel converter, and transformed into steel.

Pig iron is a brittle product because of its high carbon content (3 to 4 percent), and is therefore relatively useless. Cort's puddling furnace provided a means to reduce the carbon content (to 2.5 percent), and the resulting wrought iron—a tougher and more malleable product—was of correspondingly higher value. The invention of the steel converter was revolutionary because it facilitated drastic reductions in carbon content (to 1.4 percent) and, accordingly, allowed a stronger, tougher product to be made.

Until the recent invention of the basic oxygen process, there were three types of steel converters in use in the world, all over a century old. The first was invented in 1856 by Henry Bessemer. This Bessemer converter requires an input of hot pig iron, through which air is blown to burn off carbon. It is a small batch process (converters average 20 tons), and it is quick (a batch can be "cooked" in 20 minutes). Although it has low capital and operating costs, it provides relatively poor quality control. If the converter is lined with dolomite, it is ideal for removing phosphorus from ores, and hence phosphoric ores are charged into Bessemer converters to produce so-called basic or Thomas steel (after the inventor of the phosphorus-removing process). The Open Hearth Converter was invented in 1864. Hot and cold pig and scrap iron can all be placed into this converter. It produces large batches (100 tons and over) and works slowly as air and methane are passed over the metal to provide heat (14 hours is an average). Exact quality control is possible. One advantage of the converter is the ability to charge cold scrap metal without prior heating, because in an average steel mill possibly 40 percent of the metal moving through is scrap that arises within the plant, so-called circulating scrap. A third, but special-purpose, steel converter is the Electric Arc. This converter is used mostly for producing special alloy steels. It uses large amounts of electric power, plus scrap, pig, and alloy metals such as chrome (for resistance to abrasion, stainless steel), vanadium (for flexibility), manganese (for hardness), tungsten (for "high-speed" steels), and molybdenum (for toughness).

From the converter, steel moves on to the cogging mill and forging press, where it is shaped into wheels, axles, etc., or it moves to the finishing mill where plates,

sheets, strip, tubes, rails, and so on are produced. These products then go to the automotive, construction, container, and engineering trades, which constitute the main consumers of the products of the steel industry.

Successful locations of blast furnaces, throughout the history of the industry, have depended upon cheap assembly of raw materials. Coal-to-iron ratios of 8:1 were powerful enough to pull the wrought iron industry to the coal fields in the early nineteenth century. Economies in coal consumption reduced this pull, however, by lessening the extent to which minimization of transport costs on coal determined the least-cost location of blast furnaces. Since the middle of the nineteenth century, coke rather than coal has provided the charge for the blast furnace. In the early days coke was produced near the pit head and shipped by rail to the blast furnaces. Approximately 2 tons of coal were needed to yield 1 ton of coke. "Beehive" coke ovens were used. These beehives needed special coals, which would swell into a coke strong enough to let iron filter down through it as it was separated from impurities in the iron ore. The coals also had to be phosphorus-free and sulphur-free, because the early steel industry had no means of eliminating these impurities. Such coals were only available in limited localities: Connellsville in Pennsylvania; Durham, South Wales and West Yorkshire in the United Kingdom; the Ruhr in Germany. Great concentrations of beehives therefore developed on these coal fields. In the beehive all volatile materials were wasted, and no byproducts were recovered.

To the developing chemical industries, however, byproducts proved too valuable to be wasted, and after the turn of the twentieth century a dramatic change took place in coke production. In 1900, 80 percent of British and 84 percent of American coke capacity was beehive; by 1953, 96 percent of British and 97 percent of the United States's coke was produced in byproduct retorts. These new retorts could use a wider variety of coals, freeing the industry from reliance on a few coal fields. Byproducts provided bases for chemical and, later, for artificial fiber industries. Also, instead of coke being shipped, it became common to ship coal to blast furnace locations, where the new coke ovens were constructed. Methane produced in the coke ovens provided heat for steel converters. Economies in byproduct ovens reduced the coal-to-coke ratio to 1.5:1.

Until Gilchrist Thomas invented the basic steel-making process in 1878 all ores used in steelmaking were of necessity acid, or phosphorus-free, for the industry had no means of removing phosphorus, which made steel brittle. After this invention large reserves of lower-quality phosphoric iron ores became available to the basic Bessemer steel industry—particularly the Lorraine ores of France. The Bessemer converter, rather than the open hearth, is used to produce basic steel because the dolomite lining placed in a converter to facilitate the basic process doubles the length of time needed to produce a batch of steel. Increases in the cost of heat required for this longer period of time are substantial in

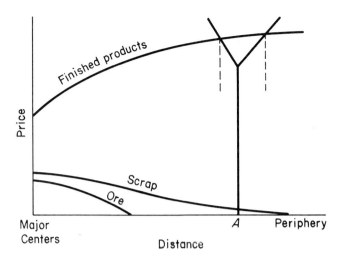

Fig. 9.4 *Success of a peripheral cold-metal shop at a great distance from major integrated producers*
Producer A is located at a great distance from major centers but is able to compete because: (a) scrap is cheaper on the periphery (price at major centers of demand less transport costs) and (b) cost of finished products is greater (price at centers plus transport costs). Therefore, in spite of smaller scale and higher production costs, A works against a greater pricespread and is able to control a small market area at the periphery, provided, of course, the demands in the small market area are large enough to absorb A's output.

the open hearth, but the Bessemer converter just requires air to be blown through hot metal for a longer period.

Today the three stages of steelmaking tend to be located together in *integrated* steel mills. Many benefits accrue in such industrial complexes. Intermediate transport and handling is eliminated. Hot metal may be transferred from one process to another, eliminating costs of reheating. Wastes may be transferred from one stage to another and become items of real value. Transfers of carbon dioxide from the blast furnace to the coke oven and methane from the coke oven to the open hearth are examples.

On the other hand, three forms of *disintegration* persist:

1. market-oriented forges and foundries
2. re-rollers producing tinplate, wire and nails, and similar products, which are also market-oriented because they use compact pig iron inputs, and convert them into bulky products without weight loss
3. cold metal shops.

Cold metal shops usually start out with an open hearth or electric arc furnace, charging scrap and only a little pig. They lose the economies of integration and their locations are not determined by the same considerations as for hot metal plants. Cold metal shops tend to be tied to cheap sources of market scrap, which does not compete with coal and iron ore as a location factor, and they are able to compete in outlying locations be-

cause scrap is sold at lower prices at greater distances from major industrial regions; moreover, in such places the spread between raw material costs and the price of finished products tends to be higher, as Figure 9.4 suggests. This figure is reminiscent of Figure 9.1c. The pattern is noticeable in the United States, where Pennsylvania steel mills charge 40 percent scrap ("circulating" or in-plant scrap) while plants in California charge 85 percent and in Texas charge 97 percent scrap.

Location of integrated steel mills is today governed by a least-cost balance between locating blast furnaces (involving raw material assembly costs) and location of finishing mills (involving least-cost distribution of products to markets). Costs of labor and taxes vary much less from place to place than procurement and distribution costs and, accordingly, are of lesser impact upon locations. Also, because steel mill costs are reversed-J shape, once a certain minimum scale of output has been reached, production costs within plants do not tend to vary much per unit of output.

Table 9.1 provides the best information to have become available in the United States on costs of assembling raw materials and distributing finished products. These data are for 1939, but they will facilitate the following discussion. Regretfully, more recent data of equivalent detail are simply unavailable.

An ideal location is where ore, coal, and markets are juxtaposed, and the markets are large enough to consume the output of a "threshold" plant. Seldom, however, do plants find this fortunate situation. Note in Table 9.1 how Birmingham, Alabama, benefits from very low assembly costs of juxtaposed sources of raw materials, but has extremely high costs of distributing finished products.

Today, steel mills must elect to locate at coal fields, ore mines, markets, or at some intermediate point, depending upon the particular balance of forces working. Note how Pittsburgh benefits from low coal costs but incurs relatively high ore costs, while Duluth has the reverse. Each location pulls the plant, in the sense of Weber's model discussed earlier, and the strongest pull is exerted by the factor contributing most to reduce the transport bill; by minimizing transport costs the greatest reduction in total costs is achieved.

Coal has traditionally exerted the strongest pull upon locations and led to the early concentration of industry in the Pittsburgh area of the United States, the Midlands of England, central Scotland and south Wales, the Ruhr region of Germany, the Nord-Sambre-Meuse region of France, Belgium and Luxembourg, and the Donbas region of the Ukraine in Russia. In the twentieth century the pull of coal lessened because of blast furnace economies and heat transfers in integrated steel mills. Whereas the coal-to-iron ratio of the early industry was 8:1, the coal-to-steel ratio of the modern industry is now 1.3:1.

Ore sources have been of increasing importance with the decline in the pull of coal, particularly in Western Europe. For ore, the strength of pull depends upon

Table 9.1 Costs of Steel Production in Alternative Locations

ASSEMBLY COSTS ON RAW MATERIALS PER TON OF FINISHED STEEL FOR SELECTED LOCATIONS IN 1939 (IN DOLLARS)

Location	Ore	Coal	Limestone	Total
Sparrows Point	$7.16	$ 5.65	$1.05	$13.86
Bethlehem	1.81	5.93	.51	8.25
Buffalo	3.57	4.78	.45	8.80
Pittsburgh	6.24	.50	.62	7.36
Youngstown	5.61	2.71	.34	8.66
Cleveland	3.57	4.11	.45	8.13
Detroit	4.12	5.15	.31	9.58
Chicago–Gary	4.12	5.79	.37	10.28
Duluth	1.77	5.54	.37	7.68
Birmingham	1.46	2.39	.15	4.00
Pueblo	4.47	3.06	.79	8.32
Provo	3.55	3.86	.26	7.67
San Bernadino	3.89	11.68	–	15.57

TRANSPORTATION CHARGES FOR SUPPLYING CERTAIN MARKETS WITH 1 TON OF FINISHED STEEL FROM SELECTED PRODUCING CENTERS, 1939

Producing center	Assembly cost	Freight charge on steel	Total
Chicago			
Chicago-Gary	$10.28	–	$10.28
Cleveland	8.13	$ 1.68	9.81
Pittsburgh	7.36	6.16	13.52
Birmingham	4.00	12.54	16.54
New York			
Bethlehem	8.25	3.81	12.06
Buffalo	8.80	3.64	12.44
Pittsburgh	7.36	8.06	15.42
Sparrows Point	13.86	1.68	15.54
Seattle			
Birmingham	4.00	15.46	19.46
Provo	7.67	16.24	23.91
San Bernadino	15.57	9.41	24.98
Sparrows Point	13.86	11.20	25.06

Source: *The Economics of Iron and Steel Transportation*, U.S. Senate Documents, No. 80, 79th Congress.

its quality, or percentage iron content; the higher this percentage, the more iron is carried per ton of ore and the more transportable it is. Discovery of the high-quality Lake Superior iron ores and the westwards movement of the center of gravity of the United States together enabled the steel industry to decentralize from Pittsburgh to Cleveland and Chicago-Gary: intermediate locations at break-of-bulk points between water and land transport where coal could be carried back to transshipment points in the same railroad cars that had carried iron ore inland to the coal fields. More recently, the Sparrows Point and Fairless steel mills have been built on the east coast at intermediate points that import coal by rail and coastal steamer from West Virginia and Tennessee, and high quality ores from Canada, Chile, and Venezuela by specialized ore-carrying ships.

Actually, the situation is now such that *combined* costs of coal and ore are much the same everywhere in the northeastern United States. This is because coal field centers have higher ore costs, and at intermediate points, the savings in ore costs are offset by increased transport bills on coal.

In Europe, steel mills were built during the late nineteenth and early twentieth century at intermediate point locations. But in England, France, and Germany, ore sources have exerted an ever-increasing pull upon the location of integrated steel mills. More and more low-quality phosphoric ores are being used (i.e., ores with less than 40 percent iron content), and assembly-cost advantages have therefore accrued from ore field locations. Examples are the Scunthorpe and Corby steelworks in eastern England, the Salzgitter mills in Germany, and the Lorraine mills in France. In England the coal-to-pig ratio is only 1.3:1 today, whereas the ore-to-pig ratio varies from 2 to 2.5:1 with foreign ores and 3:1 to 5:1 with domestic low-grade ores. These ratios indicate reason enough for the new ore field steel mills.

Markets have had an increasing pull on the location of integrated steel mills for several reasons. Modern low-cost mills have to enter production at a definite minimum size (approximately 800,000 tons of pig capacity) if they are to obtain economies of large scale production. Mills usually locate in an area if the market is large enough to consume this output. This minimum scale is the main barrier to development of an iron and steel industry in backward areas today, since such areas do not have large enough steel markets. Freight rates on finished steel tend to be at least twice as high as those on coal and iron, because transportation agencies tend to charge according to the value of the item carried rather than according to the cost of service. This means that for the same outlay of funds outputs can be shipped less than half the distance of inputs, a compelling motive for market orientation, incurring costs of shipping raw materials rather than of shipping finished products. Markets also tend to be sources of cheap scrap metal, which may be substituted for pig iron in the steel converter. Hence, orientation to scrap supplements the pull of markets. In the United States today steel mills tend first to satisfy conditions of market orientation by locating within the country's major market for steel products, which is the northeastern manufacturing belt. They then try to locate themselves within the belt to minimize assembly costs on raw materials, although as we have noted, combined assembly costs of coal and ore tend to be the same throughout this belt.

In the past, the iron and steel industry has been highly mobile as raw material sources, markets, and technical characterisics of the industry have changed. Some authorities argue, however, that today the industry displays considerable *inertia* persisting in old localities long after these localities have lost their initial cost advantages, and failing to grow in new locations where costs may be lower. Two cases may be distinguished: when the industry is competitive, and when competition is absent.

Inertia may exist in competitive steel industries because original advantages have been lost but new advantages have been acquired. For example, in Sheffield, England, advantages of low assembly costs have long passed, but the industry persists because it now uses market scrap, and has tied to it a large specialized local market for special grades of steel. The specialized steel industry in Sheffield therefore remains competitive. On the other hand, inertia may exist because of artificial restraints upon the competitive process that restrict new centers and maintain old ones. Steel mills are enormous capital investments. In the U. S. in 1950, $250 million were required to develop a mill with ingot capacity of 1 million tons. Such investments are not easily abandoned. Because of the scale of plants in the industry, there is a very limited number of firms. Ten companies account for well over 90 percent of U. S. steel output. Capital requirements are such that entry of new firms into the industry is not easy. In most industries entry of new firms in better locations pushes old firms to the margin, but in the iron and steel industry a limited number of firms control development, and they have a stake in old locations that they are unwilling to sacrifice. This means that existing concerns have in mind the effects of new developments on present capacity involving durable, specific, and immobile investment. A shift involves considerable financial loss that firms are understandably unwilling to bear. The industry has a desire for stability, because costs can only be minimized when the large plants are running to capacity and fixed costs are spread over large amounts of output. New developments will only be undertaken in these circumstances when demands are increasing rapidly and old capacity will not be affected adversely by new construction. Social and political pressures also promote inertia, for many steel plants dominate one-industry towns. The closing of a plant would have calamitous local effects, which are inadvisable both socially and politically.

Since most new developments are undertaken by existing firms, there are two consequences: plants in new areas are the property of major concerns in old, and their operations are designed to have least impact upon the affairs of the older plants; pricing systems reflect interests in stability. The old "Pittsburgh plus" pricing system that protected Pittsburgh against competition from lower cost producers in new locations (until it was finally declared illegal by the Supreme Court in 1948) was a good example of a pricing system developed in an industry for which stability was the major goal.

THE SEARCH FOR CHEAP POWER
BY THE ALUMINUM INDUSTRY

Transport orientation exists in many industries in addition to iron and steel. A modern case in point is the aluminum industry, in which transport orientation reflects the search for cheap power. This industry is a product of the twentieth century, producing a metal that does not exist as a free element in nature. A hundred years ago aluminum was semiprecious, selling at over $500 per pound. It could only be produced cheaply and at scale after 1886 when Hall in the United States and Heroult in France simultaneously invented a process whereby aluminum could be derived readily from aluminum salts, called alumina. The invention was adopted widely and quickly; by 1895 there were five large producing companies, and the price of the metal had fallen to 35¢ per pound.

stages of production

Today the industry is organized around four distinct stages of production. Each of these has a different transport orientation:

1. Bauxite mining, and initial reduction of the bauxite clay, which contains the aluminum salts, to a more transportable product by elimination of the most evident dross. This stage is oriented to sources of raw materials. Within the United States, Arkansas is the center, accounting for 90 percent of domestic bauxite production. The U.S. industry also imports large amounts of bauxite from such places as Jamaica and the Guianas via Gulf of Mexico ports such as Mobile, Corpus Christi, and Baton Rouge.

2. Chemical reduction of bauxite to alumina by a caustic soda process, which halves the weight of the raw material. In the U. S. this stage is found either raw material oriented in Arkansas, or at the Gulf of Mexico break-of-bulk points prior to rail shipment, resulting in obvious economies in transportation. One-hundred-thousand-pound boxcars of alumina then move from the alumina plant by rail, to aluminum plants elsewhere in the U.S.

3. Electrolytic transformation of alumina into aluminum, a process which again halves the weight of the material as it passes through the plant. This stage is oriented to least-cost power sites to minimize costs of transporting power. To illustrate, a one-mill difference in power cost, assuming 15,000 kilowatt hours per ton, affects ingot cost by $15 per ton. At 1.5 to 2 mills per ton-mile, this amount would be the cost of moving 2 tons of alumina 3,700 to 5,000 miles, or a ton of aluminum 3,000 miles, at 5 mills per ton-mile, both rates appropriate for long ocean hauls.

4. Processing of aluminum pig into finished products. This stage is market oriented, since a compact raw material (pig) is shipped and transformed into bulky finished items, which are then distributed to consumers.

In the United States four large companies control the bauxite-alumina-aluminum stages of the industry: Alcoa, Kaiser, Reynolds, and Anaconda. Olin Mathieson is the only other company with a large aluminum plant. Processing, however, is carried on by a myriad of 3,500 small market-oriented firms, few of which have any connection with the large producers who control earlier stages of the productive process.

Table 9.2 indicates what the relative costs of Alcoa, Kaiser, and Reynolds were in 1948. (Again, it is always a problem to obtain thorough data on locational costs for research in economic geography.)

Note the contrast in bauxite prices. This is because Reynolds controlled Arkansas bauxite production and transferred it immediately to alumina plants in

Table 9.2   Costs of Producing One Pound of Pig Aluminum, 1948 (in cents)

	RAW MATERIAL	TRANSPORTATION OF Bauxite	TRANSPORTATION OF Alumina	POWER	MANUFACTURING	TOTAL
Alcoa	2.28¢	1.08¢	0.64¢	1.78¢	4.73¢	10.51¢
Kaiser	3.18	1.16	0.84	1.81	4.64	11.63
Reynolds	3.03	.096	0.58	2.32	5.01	11.036

Note: 1948 market price was 15.5 cents per lb.

Source: Office of Defense Mobilization, *Materials Survey: Aluminum,* 1956.

Arkansas, whereas Alcoa and Kaiser obtained their bauxite from British Guiana, Surinam, and Jamaica, and incurred the costs of transporting it to Mobile (Alcoa) and Baton Rouge (Kaiser). Reynolds had also invested in Jamaican bauxite as a safeguard and had an alumina plant at Corpus Christi.

Alumina is transported to power-oriented aluminum plants, e.g., Reynolds in Arkansas, using TVA power, at Longview, Washington, using power from Bonneville, and in Louisiana, where natural gas is plentiful; Alcoa at Massena, New York, and at Point Comfort, Texas, again using water and gas power sources, respectively; Kaiser at Spokane, Washington, and at Baton Rouge, Louisiana. Power orientation is imperative, since producing 1 ton of pig aluminum requires 2 tons of alumina and 15,000 to 20,000 kilowatt hours of electricity, plus about a half ton of carbon for anodes, and a cryolite solvent.

In the past, great power requirements have affected not only locations, but the price and production policies of the industry as well. The earliest industry used thermal electricity, at Pittsburgh, but soon graduated to cheap hydroelectric power sites in Washington State (Columbia Valley Project), New York (Niagara Power), and Arkansas (Tennessee Valley Authority). Outside the United States, there is a similar hydroelectric power-oriented aluminum industry, for example, Alcan's Arvida and Beauharnois sites in Quebec and Kitimat in British Columbia, and British Aluminum's Scottish and Norwegian capacity. Similarly, capacity in the USSR, the world's third largest producer of aluminum after the United States and Canada, is found at hydroelectric sites.

changing industry economics

In recent years, however, the economics of aluminum production in the United States has tended to change. Demands have grown, but new cheap hydroelectric power sites have not become available. Costs of hauling bauxite and alumina have increased, yet costs of thermal electricity produced from coal or natural gas have fallen rapidly. Costs of transferring aluminum to customers have tended to rise steadily. The result has been (a) construction of plants in Texas and Louisiana, oriented to low-cost electricity produced from natural gas and eliminating long hauls of alumina by rail, and (b) more recent interest in the Ohio Valley, with plants

using cheap coal-produced electricity, reducing costs of hauling alumina vis-à-vis the west coast, and locating close to major markets in the U.S. manufacturing belt.

In the mid–1950s, combined costs of power and transportation were lower in the Ohio Valley than anywhere else in the country. However, the construction of new Ohio Valley plants was held back in the years 1957–1960 because of a recession in the U.S. economy that tended to reduce all capital starts. At that time, too, came increased international competition in the aluminum industry from the USSR. The Soviets apparently developed a large aluminum industry to supply conventional armed forces, and then after 1957 began to reduce conventional armaments and therefore demands for aluminum. Surplus aluminum was sold at 24 cents per pound in western European markets in 1958, while the world price was 26 cents. This competition had adverse effects upon Alcan, which had previously supplied Western European countries, and in late 1958 Alcan was forced to cut prices to meet competition. Alcan also supplies U.S. markets, and the cut in prices forced Alcoa, Kaiser, and Reynolds to follow suit. Severe domestic competition resulted, and less efficient domestic capacity was closed down for several months. Expansion plans in the Ohio Valley were shelved accordingly, illustrating the fact that any locational decision is intimately related to demand-supply-price relationships for an entire industry on an international scale and cannot be considered simply in terms of local circumstances. New capacity, even though more economical, will not be constructed when a surplus of capacity exists already, especially in industries that are controlled by a few large firms, because of the large capital requirements involved in setting up productive operations.

EMERGENCE OF LABOR COSTS AS A LOCATIONAL FACTOR IN THE TEXTILE INDUSTRIES

The textile industries provide an ideal example of the emergence of labor costs as a location factor in modern industry, as well as providing insights into the locational dynamics that accompanied the technological changes of the Industrial Revolution. Since most of the early changes took place in Britain, we will look at the experience of that country first. Therefore, the analogous American experiences will be described, and then current world dynamics will be analyzed.

the early British textile industry

As late as 1851, British textile industries employed far more workers than the iron and steel industries. In 1851, 1 in every 19 workers was engaged in textile production, although the growth of other industrial sectors in later stages of the Industrial Revolution reduced this figure to 1 in 37 by the end of the nineteenth century. As the textile industry grew, its distribution changed. Growth was accompanied by increased concentration in particular locations and then increasing shifts of one such concentrated location to another. For a beginning, however, as in the case of the iron and steel industries discussed earlier, we can go back to the eighteenth century. In the late eighteenth century, cotton could only be used in the textile industry when combined with other fibers, notably linen, to produce fustians. The early locations of the industry, as in the case of woolens and fine worsted production, were determined by the medieval organization of production.

In the Middle Ages, the textile industry was closely connected with farming. The peasant families cultivated and harvested their own foods; the spinning and weaving of animal fibers were done by hand. During the fifteenth and sixteenth centuries, settlements extended from the neighboring lowlands into the central mountainous spine of the British Isles, the Pennines, proceeding on a copyhold basis by a process of "intaking" of 15 to 25 acres per family. Because these holdings afforded inadequate support, farming families had to seek ancillary employment in the production of textiles. Indeed, the spread of new farms into the Pennines into previously manorial cattle-breeding areas was specifically governed by industrial opportunities. One act of Parliament, the so-called Halifax Act in the sixteenth century, for example, talks explicitly of settlement taking place on the basis of growing opportunities in the textile industry. Farming in such areas was essentially secondary to textile output. Agricultural produce was not sold but was consumed by the household, and the rent paid by the household for its land was paid in kind by the output from the loom.

With such a wide diffusion of textile production throughout the central mountains and moors of England, neighboring towns functioned as the marketing centers of large parishes from which they drew their trade. The towns were commercial, rather than manufacturing centers, and the characteristic pattern of urban settlement involved a large number of small towns, the most important building of which was the "piece hall" where the textile pieces were brought in for sale. Only Manchester grew larger because it had an urban cottage textile industry as well as a service function and also because it had finishing trades to which the produce of the countryside was brought for bleaching and dyeing. Only one branch of the textile industry—fulling, drawing the cloth from the local areas—was mechanized at this time.

New techniques in the first phase of the Industrial Revolution transformed this local medieval industrial pattern. The change came in spinning before it came in weaving. In 1785 the patent was withdrawn on Arkwright's water frame. Then, in 1813, Horrock's power loom was invented, although it was not widely used until after 1820. The result of the first of these changes was that hand spinning was replaced by machine spinning, thirty years before hand weaving was replaced by machines. The techniques were applied first in the cotton industry, in the woolen industry after 1820, and in very fine woolens and the worsted industry after 1810. Therefore there was a time lag between the emergence of mechanized spinning and weaving and in the pace of mechanization in the cotton, woolen, and worsted industries.

Initially, the only source of power was water. In the period from 1718 to 1825, the spinning industry was mechanized, and the new factories were located at water-power sites, surrounded by a cottage hand loom weaving industry associated with the scattered farmsteads on the hillsides. The cotton industry spread to take up most of the available water power sites, moving from the most accessible sites to more and more inaccessible spots, so that the manufacturing industry diffused quite widely throughout the British countryside. The limitation of the water power source meant that local scale of industry was impossible. Spinning was undertaken by a very large number of small dispersed factory units, and a much wider spread of the cottage hand loom weaving industry also took place, although without the ties to agricultural "intakes" that had characterized its earlier scatter.

After 1825, hand loom weaving was gradually replaced by power loom weaving, first in the cotton industry and then in the woolen industry. At the same time, water power was replaced by the use of steam. New towns grew around the new large-scale textile mills, generating the first phase of large-scale urbanization associated with the industrialization of the early nineteenth century. By 1840, the change from water to steam was relatively complete. In 1838, only 11 percent of the total horsepower was still drawn from water.

Because the pace of change was slower in the woolen and worsted industries than in the cotton textiles industries, it meant different rates of change obtained for each part of England where each type of textile industry was concentrated. The cotton textile industry, for example, was concentrated west of the Pennines in Lancashire from Blackburn south to Manchester, Stockport, and Oldham. Initially, this industry was not of pure cotton textiles, but of fustians, a mixture of cotton and linen. A subsidiary concentration of cotton textile production was in the Lanark area of Scotland; however, this area declined during the cotton famine of the American Civil War and its capital and labor shifted to iron production and shipbuilding.

Worsted had been produced in East Anglia and in the West Riding of Yorkshire during the eighteenth century. During the early nineteenth century mechanization and expansion of worsted, the agriculturally based industry of East Anglia declined and by 1851 over 90 percent of the labor force in this industry was in the West Riding of Yorkshire, especially in the Bradford-Halifax area. A good deal of the decline in East Anglia was attributable to the fact that the industry shifted from water power to steam. The West Riding of Yorkshire was located on the coal outcrops where coal was readily available, whereas East Anglia had to ship in coal at great cost. The increasing coal costs raised the cost of worsted output in East Anglia and the industry lost in the competitive process to the coal-oriented West Riding producers.

The woolen industry was much more scattered than either cotton or worsted production, although much wool was produced in the West Riding of Yorkshire, in Wales, and in the southwest of England. During the early nineteenth century, each of the outlying centers maintained their importance so that by 1851 only 45 percent of workers in the woolen industry were found in the West Riding of Yorkshire. However, the West Riding grew faster, and the Tweed Valley arose as another production center in the mid-nineteenth century. These changes were attributable to the shifts in locational patterns associated with replacement of water power by steam power. First, the costs of coal became dominant in the productive process. Prices of the final product rose quite steeply when coal had to be transported over any great distance. Therefore, the steam mills were located on the coal fields. The large scale of the coal field steam mills meant that they required a very large labor force. The workers' cottages clustered around the mills contributed to the growth of coal field towns in which not one but a variety of mills were located. These towns became the dominant centers attracting labor flowing out of the countryside where economic opportunities in the declining cottage industries were vanishing.

Ancillary advantages also induced the steam mills to concentrate increasingly in towns, particularly in the larger towns. The towns provided many public facilities, such as the local gas plant that supplied light and local schools (meeting the terms of the earlier factory legislation) that provided a work force with basic levels of education. In towns, manufacturers could easily share costs of facilities with others, while in the country they had to provide these services for themselves. Moreover, manufacturers could pass on many of the costs to the workers. For example, rather than having to build housing out in the countryside, they could rely upon developers to build the housing and to rent it to the workers. The textile towns as we know them thus emerged. Great specialization developed from one town to another. Some towns emphasized cotton, woolens, or worsted; some emphasized spinning or weaving; some made relatively coarse products, while others produced relatively fine material.

There is no satisfactory answer to explain why these very substantial differences in local specializations developed. In general, the initial spark was some historical accident. However, when specializations did develop, the whole town became adapted to the requirements of the specialty—the schools, the productive processes, the ancillary services, the merchants' associations, the forms of banking, the provision of capital. In this way, the phenomenon of industrial localization emerged, involving higher productivity based upon the particular skills founded in some local specialization.

the American textile industry

A similar history characterized the American cotton textile industry. There the initial concentration of the industry developed in New England. The start had a double origin—the 1793 invention of the cotton gin and the 1812 War blockade that prevented British imports from reaching North America and providing the impulse for new machinery to be imported from Europe.

The early start in New England was favored in several ways. Factories were established on the Merrimac, Connecticut, and Blackstone rivers at such towns as Concord, Lawrence, and Lowell. Each of these was a Fall Line site where an ample water supply was available. Capital was forthcoming for this stage of industrialization from the merchant classes and the shipping interests of Boston, and there was a substantial rural population available to supply the labor force. Furthermore, these locations were at the heart of U.S. markets and they also had easy access elsewhere by sea.

As in Britain, shifts in location came with the application of steam power. Fall River and New Bedford were the principal coal importers, and they became centers of the coal-steam textile industry, although the quality of the water power sites in North America led to a substantial lag behind similar changes in Britain. By 1870, 25 percent of the U.S. industry was steam powered, and only by 1900 did it become 67 percent. The coastal locations obviously were ideal for the coal-oriented textile industry because they had the lowest assembly costs of coal. In 1870 Lowell's coal costs were 15 percent greater than those at the coastal sites. New Bedford was especially favored because after the Civil War it experienced a substantial decline in its whaling and shipbuilding industries. The surplus labor force was absorbed by the growing textile industries. After 1840 as well, it recruited substantial new immigrant labor, and as late as the 1920s New Bedford was the center of the U.S. yarn spinning industry.

changing orientation to areas of lower labor cost

However, the twentieth century saw a fundamental shift in the location patterns of the textile industry. In the U.S., the regional shift was from New England to the Piedmont fall line sites of the Carolinas and Georgia. As in the case of the early industry, the first shift came in cotton followed by woolens and worsteds, and spinning moved ahead of weaving. First of all, there was a relative decline in the New England textile industry, followed by an absolute decline and even a physical shift of many plants southwards. In 1880 the Piedmont fall line had only 5 percent of the U.S. spinning capacity. By 1900 this had increased to 22 percent; in 1920 it was 42 percent, and in 1952 it was 81 percent. New England, on the other hand, had 95 percent of the capacity in 1880, 78 percent in 1900, 58 percent in 1920, and 19 percent in 1952. The change came because of the labor cost advantages of the South.

First of all, in the late nineteenth century the New England industry had to compete for labor with a variety of other industries, for example, the boot and shoe industry and a variety of commercial activities. As a result of this competition, wage rates rose. Also, the new immigrants tended not to stay in New England but to head West. Because of this westward expansion and because of the intensity of union activity in New England, labor became increasingly expensive. In 1881 through 1886, Fall River had 15 strikes. Consequently, the wage rate increased very rapidly, while productivity of labor was relatively low because of the very strict labor codes that also resulted. The South, on the other hand, had much cheaper labor that was more easily available and more productive.

Of course, the initial money wage advantage of the South has not persisted, because as industry moved South it raised southern wages. If we call the 1900 wage rate in New England 100, then in the South it was 50. In 1925 the ratio was 100 to 75, but by 1950 it had become 100 to 90. There was little initial competition for labor in the South. Mechanization encouraged the standardization of labor at a relatively low skill level, so that small town locations became feasible for the new decentralizing industry. And in these small towns the textile mills tended to be the only industry. Because the mills could pay a slightly higher wage than that of the agricultural activities of the hinterland, they could command the cream of the local labor force.

As operations in the textile industry became increasingly routinized, productivity of the skilled labor in New England and the unskilled in the South was first equalized, then gradually shifted in favor of the South. First, there was little unionization in the work force. This meant that, in the Piedmont weaving industry for example the average load per worker was 18 looms, whereas in New England it was less than 12. Moreover, the factory exerted its command over the local community to oppose the organization of unions and the enforcement (and even in some states, the enactment) of labor codes. Another very substantial contributing cause to the industry's shift to the South in the period 1919 to 1939 was a technical revolution in the textile industry: Northrop looms were introduced in the southeast whereas the New England weaving industry remained concentrated in the older technology. These new looms reduced production costs by 40 percent.

The advantages of the South tended to diminish from 1940 onward. First of all, the coming of new industry meant a gradual increase in economic opportunity in the South, and a tendency for equalization of labor costs. After spinning came weaving, after cotton came woolens, then worsted. Thereafter came the textile machinery industry and the plants producing synthetic fibers. More recently, a range of electronic industries and engineering have located in the South. An increasing tightness of the labor supply in the Piedmont areas of the South has resulted.

This has led to a continuing trend for the industry to migrate further afield: into the Deep South; to Puerto Rico; over the Mexican border; to locations in the U.S. where "by product" female labor persists, for example, in the anthracite towns of eastern Pennsylvania or in the mining and forest cities of the upper Great Lakes, where heavy industries employ mostly male workers. In addition of course, the U.S. is facing very substantial competition from textile production of the Far East. Initially this competition was from Japan, followed by that from Hong Kong, followed increasingly today by products moving out of Taiwan and Korea.

This trend has been even more profound in northern Britain, the traditional center of the mechanized textile industry. In 1882, 80 percent of the world's textile exports came from the United Kingdom, and these amounted to 60 percent of Britain exports by value. In that year 4 billion yards of fabrics entered world trade. By 1949 to 1951, 14 billion yards were produced, but only 18 percent of this was made in the United Kingdom. In that year, 35 percent of the world output in textiles came from Western Europe, over a quarter from Southeast Asia, and 20 percent was accounted for by Japan. Except for Japan, Southeast Asia remains the great growth area in the textile industry.

In both Europe and the U.S., the pattern that has emerged is that of the very specialized high skill products remaining concentrated in the old areas of production, whereas mass production for the textile markets of Western Europe, America, and indeed, for the world, is produced in the Far East. The reason for this is clear. It is to be found, first of all, in the replacement of coal as a locational factor by labor, once the coal-steam powered industry changed over to electric power during the early twentieth century. By 1953, the average cost of production of cotton textiles in the United Kingdom was 108.1 pence per pound. Of this, the average cost of raw cotton was 45.5 pence ± 3. Power costs were 4.8 pence per pound, with insignificant variability from place to place. Capital costs averaged 39.6 pence per pound and again varied insignificantly, while distribution costs averaged 3.5 pence and again varying insignificantly from place to place. However, labor costs, 16.7 pence per pound on the average, varied regionally from half to double that amount (8 pence to 32 pence per pound). Thus, with raw material costs not varying greatly with location, a product with high value per unit of weight, no weight loss, variable distribution costs, and electric power costs with little locational pull, capital costs perhaps offering some advantage to already developed areas because of lower interest rates, and labor costs varying greatly from location to location, labor became the factor conducive to low processing costs. Cheap labor became the critical location factor that determined success, particularly because mechanization had already eliminated the advantages of skill in the industry. Cotton textiles could then spread very rapidly, often becoming the springboard for further industrial growth. The relatively inexpensive machinery meant low capital thresholds, and very simple repetitive skills meant that a very poorly educated mass labor force could be employed. The growth of the industry in India, China, Japan, and Korea thus reflects the low labor costs and ease of entry in the industry.

The history of textiles chronicles an industry that shifted very rapidly from a very widely scattered eighteenth-century cottage handicraft industry to a nineteenth-century mechanized industry that concentrated on the coal fields of Western Europe after initial spread of factories seeking water power, to a twentieth-century industry transformed by electricity, in which labor costs became the dominant locational factor. During the last half century, there has been continuing decline of traditional areas and rapid growth of the industry in those parts of the world where labor supplies are abundant and cheapest. The industry remaining in the traditional areas (e.g., the linen industry in Belfast, the very fine worsted industry of Yorkshire, or the lace industry of Brussels) involves the highest skill lines and the prestige based upon historical localization. Elsewhere, as routinized textile operations based upon natural fibers continue to diffuse into low labor cost areas, the residual industry in Europe and the U.S. concentrates on lines of production using the artificial fibers, such as rayon, nylon, or dacron. The forces operating in these cases are the great capital requirements and substantial economies of scale involved in the production of artificial fibers.

ELECTRONICS: RAPID CHANGES IN A MODERN INDUSTRY

A twentieth-century example of an industry whose locational orientation has shifted radically towards increasing labor orientation is that of electronics. The electronic industries are those which, according to the definition of the Electronic Industries Association in the United States

are engaged in that branch of science and technology which deals with the study and application of techniques to direct and control the conduction of electricity in a gas, vacuum, liquid or solid state material. Electron tubes and semiconductors are combined with resistors, capacitors, transformers and similar components in equipments which detect, measure, record, compute and communicate information. The distinguishing feature of electronic products as opposed to purely electrical ones is that although electricity flows through the circuitry of both, electronic products also include tubes and semiconductors which can discharge, direct, control, or otherwise influence the flow of the electricity.

Because there are more than 30,000 types of electronic products manufactured—all extremely varied in function, value, and form—it would be helpful to distinguish four categories: consumer, industrial, government, and components.

Consumer products include some of the most familiar kinds of electronic equipment, such as televisions and radios, phonographs, high fidelity and stereophonic sound equipment, tape recorders, hearing aids, citizens' band transceivers, and home intercommunication systems.

Industrial and commercial electronic products include computers; testing and measuring instruments; industrial control and processing equipment; electronic instruments for nuclear work, such as reactors, sensing controls and radiation detection devices; television and radio broadcasting equipment; microwave devices; medical and therapeutic equipment, such as X-ray systems and diathermy units; and navigational instruments for civil and private aircraft and ships.

Government products are vital parts of missiles, spacecraft, aircraft, tanks, ships, and other items used in national defense and space programs. Representative examples of these products include guidance and checkout systems, telemetering, ground tracking and support equipment, radar, sonar, infrared and other detection systems and devices, gyroscopes and other navigational equipment, fire control devices, and high-speed communication equipment.

Components are usually classified in four broad groups:

1. Electronic tubes, including receiving, television picture, and various power and special purpose tube types.
2. Principal semiconductor devices, including transistors, diodes, and rectifiers.
3. Passive components, including such items as capacitors, resistors, transformers, relays, connectors, and switches.
4. Integral circuit packages, a more recent innovation providing a high degree of compactness and reliability, is a combination of two or more components, excluding electron tubes.

early history of the U.S. industry

Electronics is a twentieth-century industry. The first patent for wireless telegraph was granted to Marconi in 1896, just 13 years after Thomas Edison succeeded in inducing electrons to jump across the partial vacuum between a carbon filament and a metal plate in his light bulb. The wireless technique was put into use by the British to communicate with ships at sea and in 1901, Marconi successfully demonstrated the first transatlantic wireless communication. Other significant developments occurred at about the same time. The invention of the three-element vacuum tube by DeForest in 1906 made possible both the development of radio broadcasting and the practical application of television. Between 1910 and 1920 rapid progress was made in the theory, application, and construction of vacuum tubes and their circuits. During World War I the United States government realized the value of radio to the military forces. This concern led to the formation in 1919 of Radio Corporation of America as a method of pooling the patents of American corporations. The resulting chain of events was to set the stage for rapid expansion of radio broadcasting in the United States during the 1920s.

In 1920 the nation's first broadcasting station was established in Pittsburgh, Pennsylvania. Within two years, 99 stations were in operation in the United States. Such rapid expansion of radio broadcasting facilities was accompanied by a corresponding boom in the demand for radio receiving sets as radio became a means of mass communication. In 1922, it was estimated that there were approximately 60,000 radio sets in use, but by 1927 the number had reached 7,500,000. During the 1930s research continued toward the development of television. A few commercial sets were manufactured near the end of the decade, but full commercial development was delayed by World War II.

While commercial development in electronics came to a halt during World War II, research in the field was continued for purposes of national defense. In fact, the concentration of research and development carried on in the emergency of war yielded significant innovations that were to play a great role in the postwar growth of the electronics industry. Throughout the war, most of the nation's consumer electronic production capability was transferred to the production of radio communications equipment for the armed services. Although there was little production of television until after the war, work on related technologies continued because of potential wartime applications. Defense research efforts brought about improvements in radio communications and important new developments, including radar, sonar, fire control systems, and the proximity fuse.

Immediately following the end of World War II the nation's radio manufacturers turned to the production of television. Between 1947 and 1950, the production of televisions rose from 179,000 units with a shipment value of $50 million to $7.5 million units with a shipment value of $1.35 billion and electronics employment rose by nearly one-fifth.

The sudden spurt in consumer electronic products following the war was soon eclipsed by the need for military and space products stimulated by the Korean War. Sales of military and space products exceeded that of consumer products by 1952 and continued to rise until in 1964 factory sales of military and space products were over three times that of consumer items. Sales of industrial products also increased rapidly. In 1950 they were only about one-fifth that of consumer products, but by 1961 factory sales of industrial products exceeded that of consumer products. This growth resulted to a large extent from a steadily growing effort in research and development work by both government and private industry. The computer, transistor, and integrated circuit are prime examples of the many innovations accruing from research and development work.

locational shifts

In the early years of wireless communication, the United States electrical machinery industry was located in the East, close to the nation's trade, transportation, and major manufacturing complexes, as well as close to the laboratories of the inventors. Subsequent growth of parts of the industry occurred in the Midwest. The manufacture of telephone apparatus in Chicago was associated with that city's early development as a major transportation, communication, and manufacturing center. Of particular importance appears to have been the availability of low cost labor together with lower transportation costs derived partly from favorable transportation rates for rail shipment eastward to markets and favorable access to markets in midwestern population centers.

Major changes came during and after World War II, first as a result of governmental programs and expenditures, and thereafter as a result of the rapid growth of the consumer electronics industry. During World War II, growth of electronics manufacturing in the Boston area was based on the access to scientific talent attracted to major research programs associated with Harvard University and the Massachusetts Institute of Technology. Likewise, the stage was set for rapid growth of electronics in California as a consequence of wartime growth of aircraft production in that state.

After the War, two trends were evident in the electronics industry: (a) the dependence of industrial and governmental production upon federal contracts, and (b) the pursuit by the consumer products and components sectors of the industry for cheap labor. Thus, California, and later Texas, grew rapidly on the basis of prime contract awards by the government. Radio and television production, on the other hand, diffused rapidly into small towns throughout the Midwest, and moved into the gap left in the former textile towns of New England by the migration of the textile industries from that region.

By far the most rapid rise of electronics production in the consumer goods and components has been that of the Far Eastern producers, most notably Japan, Hong Kong, and Taiwan. Governmental incentives, combined with ample supplies of cheap yet highly productive labor have combined to transfer world leadership in much electronics production to these regions. Indeed, many final consumer products assembled in the United States are made of components manufactured in those countries.

growth of Taiwan's electronics industry

Let us examine the case of Taiwan, whose electronics industry is only a decade old. The first large-scale Chinese-owned factory specializing in transistor radio production was built in 1961, while the earliest electronics plant built using foreign capital was constructed in 1964. Although still in its infancy, the industry has surpassed the growth rate of electronics elsewhere. Since 1965, Taiwan has been the third largest Asian producer of electronics products (after Japan and Hong Kong). Many economic indicators provide a concrete manifestation of its momentum of growth. The number of electronics factories in Taiwan rose from 15 in 1966 to 150 in 1969. A decade ago production was limited to a few types of inferior and unattractive tube radios and phonographs. Practically all the parts needed by the assembly plants had to be imported. Now, the range of electronics products has increased to more than a hundred types, including components such as electronic tubes, magnetic parts, resistors, computer subassemblies to radios, TV sets, communication and observation equipment, and electronic computing machines.

The electronics boom in Taiwan has been a function of the availability of overseas investment which, in turn, has been a response to the congenial local conditions, especially cheap labor. Average wages for female workers in electronics factories are US$20 per month in contrast to US$300 per month in United States. This wage rate is approximately one-third that of Japan and one-half that of Hong Kong. At this rate, the Taiwan industrialists are proud to say, an American firm is able to effect a saving of US$2 million yearly if it shifts the work of 1,000 women from its U.S. plant to Taiwan. Furthermore, U.S. executives remark that on the average it takes Taiwanese women one-third less time to learn the same operation than their American counterparts, and strikes are relatively rare. Such a labor cost differential is an attractive bait to foreign investment.

The labor cost lure is bolstered by government programs. A number of tax incentives are included in the "Statute for Encouragement of Investment" and other relevant laws to work towards this goal. A brief inventory of these is presented below so that their magnitude and direction can be realized.

A. Customs Duties
   1. Imports of machinery and equipment
      (a) Import duties amounting to NT$100,000 (US$25,000) or more may be paid in installments.
      (b) Where one-time capital payment and capital expenditure exceed NT$90 million (US$2.25 million), no import tax may be imposed on machinery and equipment brought in for the investor's projected factory.
      (c) Factories planning to export 90 percent or more of their products and planning to re-export their machinery and equipment within five years may apply for deferred import duties payment for these imports. No payment will be necessary if the promises are fulfilled.

   2. Imports of raw material
      (a) Import duties on raw materials may be returned or otherwise compensated when products processed from these materials are exported.
      (b) Bonded warehouses may be utilized. Bonded factory treatment may also be accorded.

B. Income Tax
   1. Newly established factories are given a five-year income tax holiday beginning from the day products are first put on the market.
   2. When additional investment is effected for factory expansion, a similar tax holiday is accorded the portion of income resulting from the expansion.
   3. When undistributed profit is invested in factory expansion projects, no income tax shall be levied on the reinvested portion up to 25 percent of the year's total profit.

C. Business Tax
   None is imposed on electronics exports.

D. Stamp Tax
   Revenue stamps equivalent to only 0.1 percent of the amounts stated on invoices are required for export electronics products.

Tax incentives and other massive concessions, combined with the low wage rates have been responsible for the explosive growth of the electronics industry on Taiwan.

RECOMMENDED READINGS

Estall, R. C., *New England: A Study in Industrial Adjustment.* London: Bell, 1966.

Helfgott, R. B., W. E. Gustafson, and J. M. Hund, *Made in New York.* Cambridge, Mass.: Harvard University Press, 1959.

Lichtenberg, R. M., *One Tenth of a Nation.* Cambridge, Mass.: Harvard University Press, 1960.

Martin, J. E., *Greater London: An Industrial Geography.* London: Bell, 1966.

Robbins, S. M., and N. E. Terleckyj, *Money Metropolis.* Cambridge, Mass.: Harvard University Press, 1960.

Smith, W., *An Historical Introduction to the Economic Geography of Great Britain.* London: Bell, 1968.

exchange
and
interaction
four

The last three chapters dealt with the spatial organization of land use and the location of industrial production. For the resulting supplies to reach consumers, there must be spatial interaction. Only through trade can demands and supplies be balanced. Only by means of trade can the price mechanism play its role.

We thus turn to the theory of international trade and to the dynamics and contemporary patterns of world commodity flows in Chapters 10 and 11. This will enable us to consider in subsequent chapters the relationship between interregional and local trade and the development of urban hierarchies, the relationships of trade flows and transportation networks, and the creation of international regions and international systems by means of the two-way relationship between regional specialization and trade.

That trade is indeed intimately bound up with the question of the location of production and consumption was noted by Alfred Weber and later developed theoretically by Bertil Ohlin in his book *Interregional and International Trade* (1933). As Walter Isard stated later, "Location and trade are as the two sides of the same coin. The forces determining one simultaneously determine the other." It is clear that locational decisions, such as those faced in manufacturing and agriculture, often involve problems of securing raw materials from one set of places and distributing products to another. This interregional exchange of physical commodities is trade. In the broadest sense, trade can be taken to include not only movements of commodities but also of services, although it is usually convenient to concentrate more particularly upon physical flows.

We emphasize *international* trade in this chapter for a variety of reasons. Most important, it will enable us to discuss the role that sovereign governments play in determining or controlling trade flows, and therefore in influencing the location of production. While international and domestic trade take place for many of the same reasons, governments impose a number of obstacles that interfere with exchange between countries. Also, whereas economic conditions within the boundaries of a particular nation tend to be fairly uniform from one place to another, this is not usually true between countries. National political systems often differ from each other in their fiscal policies, in subsidies and taxes applied to their citizens, and in many other ways. Legal frameworks tend to vary in such important matters as the rights, liabilities, and obligations of firms and individuals. The existence of these complexities helps to explain the large amount of theoretical literature on the international aspects of trade.

HISTORY OF TRADE THEORY

The theory of international trade emerged as an independent body of thought at a very early date. From the outset it developed in response to specific practical needs of the times, although much of it has subsequently reached high levels of abstraction. In large measure the

theories of international trade

10

character of the trade theory we have inherited reflects the way in which it has evolved, particularly in its form and emphasis.

It is customary to separate the history of international trade theory into three or four periods. The first of these is the preclassical or *mercantilist* era, which followed the Middle Ages and reached its zenith within about a century prior to the 1750s. It is generally agreed that mercantilism did not actually attain the status of a true theory, however, and the beginnings of trade theory as we know it today are considered to have come with the *classical* period, which appeared coincidentally with the English Industrial Revolution in the middle of the eighteenth century and continued for another 150 years or so. Contemporary trade theory, or the *modern* period, has formed during this present century and has largely superseded the more simplistic notions of earlier eras, although some of the ideas of mercantilism and of the classical period persist in certain national policies even today.

mercantilism

Those who wrote on trade topics during the mercantilism era have been described as mainly political pamphleteers, since they were less concerned with producing a theory than with fostering a set of national policies of self-interest. This economic nationalism was a natural component of a period when strong central governments were forming. Since these writings fall within a number of distinct national groupings they cannot be generalized very satisfactorily, but several common features were shared by the various mercantilist policies.

First, it was considered essential that a country have merchandise exports in excess of imports, thereby acquiring a "favorable balance of trade," that is, one which would contribute a surplus of money or gold to the royal treasury. Second, there was an emphasis on foreign trade rather than domestic trade, on manufacturing rather than agriculture, and on plentiful cheap labor. Manufacturing was favored because it could support a denser population and because its output yielded exports of higher value. A large population of low-wage labor was regarded as a source of national strength. Finally, mercantilism promoted the use of various artificial measures by which countries could enforce these aims. Despite their antiquity, many of these notions sound surprisingly contemporary since even today some national policies are at least implicitly mercantilistic. Although modern trade theory emphatically rejects most mercantilistic ideas, it continues to stress the "normative": that which *ought* to be.

classical theory

The classical period was an era of great theorists such as Adam Smith and David Ricardo, men who reacted sharply to the errors and excesses of the mercantilist philosophy. The basic normative premise of classical theory was that free trade is beneficial to all trading partners. The questions asked by classical theory were these: Why is international trade mutually advantageous? What determines the goods to be exchanged? What decides the amounts of goods to be traded (and thus the international price level)? The emphasis, therefore, was on the gains from trade. Trade among countries, it was argued, results in increased international specialization in production, a division of labor like that which accompanies domestic trade. Classical theorists used the *labor theory of value* to measure the effects of trade. This was the notion that all costs can be reduced ultimately to units of labor, which in turn is directly related to the price that must be charged for the product.

Toward the latter part of the nineteenth century and during the early years of the twentieth, trade theorists added many refinements to classical theory and also introduced a number of new concepts and useful geometric techniques of analysis. This interval near the close of the classical era is sometimes called the *neoclassical* period.

modern theory

Modern theorists have discarded the rather simplistic approach of the classical period and have attempted to deal with the complexities of the real world of international trade. The labor theory of value has been abandoned by all except the followers of Karl Marx. In addition to this single factor of production, modern theorists admit other factors, namely, land, capital, and entrepreneurship. It has become more common to speak of differences in "factor endowments" or "units of productive power" as determining the nature of trade among countries. Thus the relative scarcity or abundance of capital or labor or products of the land are reflected in the kinds of goods that are produced and advantages that countries may have in trading. It is from this perspective that we examine some of the basic elements of trade theory and see how these operate in both international and interregional trade.

THE DETERMINANTS OF TRADE

The geographer's efforts to understand better the form and nature of trade flows raise issues that have long been central to trade theory, especially the question of why trade should occur at all. The most obvious answer, but one which is not as simple as it might appear, is that trade serves to reconcile limited productive capacities with widely ranging needs and wants. As we shall see, however, participants in trade gain a number of other benefits as well. In learning why trade takes place, we can also expect to find out what commodities will be traded and in what quantities, and who will do the trading. Thus as we look at the bases for trade we also observe its structure and its direction of movement.

Table 10.1   Production Possibilities and Domestic Exchange Ratios of Corn and Potatoes in Canada and the United States, Before Trade

| | PRODUCTION POSSIBILITIES | | | DOMESTIC EXCHANGE RATIOS | |
	Potatoes	(or)	Corn	Potatoes/Corn	Corn/Potatoes
Canada	75		50	1.50	0.67
United States	100		200	0.50	2.00

The forces affecting trade can be grouped into two broad classes. Under ideal conditions the principal trade determinants are those relating to supply and demand. In the real world, however, another group of influences often distort the ideal pattern and act as barriers or impediments to trade. These latter conditions can make trade more difficult, or even impossible, or merely alter the commodity mix and price structure. It is mainly this second group of influences that causes international trade to be more complicated than interregional trade.

conditions of production and consumption

To isolate the effects of supply and demand on trade, we begin with a set of simplifying assumptions that can later be relaxed to admit the many complexities of the real world. Let us assume at the outset that there are no artificial impediments to trade and that no cost is required for overcoming the friction of distance. With these complications removed, two principal concerns remain. First, what characteristics of a country's (or a region's) production affect its capacity to supply its own needs and perhaps to sell to some other area? Second, what conditions affect the mix of commodities consumed by a country and thus influence its purchases abroad? Admitting the realistic assumption that countries differ from one another in both of these respects, it is to be expected that certain complementarities will exist among them. The surpluses of some areas may match the deficiences of others. What then is the basis for reconciling these varying supplies and demands?

comparative advantage

The classical answer to this question is given by the principle of relative costs, or, as Ricardo termed it, the *law of comparative advantage.* Briefly stated, the law of comparative advantage is this: A country will benefit from exporting a commodity that it can produce at a lower relative cost, and it will benefit from importing a commodity for which its own production costs are relatively higher. The key word here is *relative,* as the following example illustrates.

Let us take two countries that are entirely isolated from the rest of the world and which, as we first find them, have no commercial relations with each other. Each produces and consumes the same two commodities, potatoes and corn. As Table 10.1 shows, the first of these countries, Canada, is capable of producing 75 units of potatoes per unit of production cost, or alternatively, it can turn these same resources to the production of 50 units of corn per unit of cost. This implies, of course, that Canadian resources are better suited to potatoes than to corn. So long as there is no trade with the United States, the two goods are traded within Canada at the rate of 1 unit of corn for 1½ units of potatoes, or conversely, 1 unit of potatoes equals ⅔ unit of corn. Thus corn has the higher price of the two commodities because it is more costly per unit to produce and thus scarcer. Since both commodities are demanded by Canadian consumers some of each must be grown, and Figure 10.1a shows all the possible combinations of corn and potatoes that the country is capable of producing. The Canadian production possibilities curve, *XY,* ranges from the extreme case where all resources are allocated to potatoes, *Y,* to the other extreme, *X,* where everything is put into corn, together with the various combinations of the two crops.

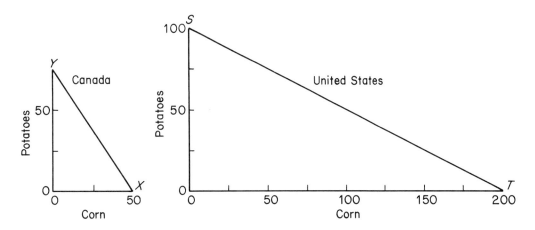

Fig. 10.1 *Production possibility curves, Canada and the United States, before trade*

| | PRODUCTION POSSIBILITIES | | | DOMESTIC EXCHANGE RATIO | DOMESTIC CONSUMPTION | | |
	Barley	(or)	Wheat	Barley/Wheat	Barley	Wheat	Total
United Kingdom	100		100	1.00	50	50	100
France	50		200	0.25	12.5	150	162.5

Meanwhile, we find that the second country, the United States, has the capabilities for growing 100 units of potatoes per unit of cost, or for producing 200 units of corn with the same resource allocation. Therefore, on the domestic market of the United States, 1 unit of corn can be exchanged for ½ unit of potatoes. The range of conceivable combinations of the two crops is shown by the production possibilities curve in Figure 10.1b.

Comparing the production costs of the two countries, we see that the United States has greater capabilities for both crops. It has an *absolute advantage* in potatoes, since it can turn out 1⅓ units for every one that Canada can grow; and similarly it can produce 4 units of corn for every unit of Canada's. However, we note also that the *margin of difference* between the countries is greater for corn than it is for potatoes. In domestic trade a Canadian farmer sacrifices 1½ units of corn for 1 unit of potatoes, while a farmer in the United States gives up only ½ unit of corn for 1 unit of potatoes. Therefore, the United States not only has an *absolute* advantage in corn but a *comparaitve* advantage as well. Still, a Canadian farmer needs to give up only ⅔ unit of potatoes for 1 unit of corn, while the United States potato farmer must sacrifice 2 units of potatoes for 1 unit of corn. Despite its *absolute disadvantage* in potatoes, therefore, Canada has a *comparative advantage* in that crop.

With the opening of trade between the countries, Canadians discover that they can receive up to 2 units of corn in the United States for every unit of potatoes they sell there instead of the ⅔ unit to which they have been accustomed at home. The Americans, on the other hand, learn that in Canada they can get up to 1½ units of potatoes for 1 unit of corn as opposed to merely ½ unit in their own country. The ensuing trade

benefits both countries as Canadian potatoes move southward into the United States and corn makes the return journey northward. So beneficial is this exchange, in fact, that Canadian farmers begin to specialize in potato production and transfer their resources out of corn, while United States farmers turn their emphasis to corn at the expense of potatoes. Obviously, the initial exchange ratios for potatoes and corn do not last long after trade begins and as specialization increases. Trade tends to close some of the gap in prices but not all of it. Differences between the two countries will continue so long as there are disparities in their productive possibilities and the exchange between them will remain mutually advantageous. This analysis has thus given us the *direction* of trade flows, but it has not given us the actual amounts traded or the final *equilibrium* price, that is, the exchange ratio that is settled upon after trade and specialization have developed to their optimal levels.

To discover how prices and quantities are determined, we take the example of two countries with economies assumed to be of similar size, the United Kingdom and France. Both grow the same two crops, barley and wheat; but in the United Kingdom barley is produced at the same cost as wheat, whereas in France wheat is grown more cheaply. The situation in each country in the absence of trade between them is given in Table 10.2 and is illustrated in Figure 10.2. Note here that, as in the Canadian-United States example, the production possibilities curves of the two countries (*PR* and *NT,* in Fig. 10.2) appear as straight lines. This indicates that the production costs in each country are assumed to be constant; that is, each unit of cost input yields the same increase in output as the previous unit. This characteristic becomes important in the argument that follows.

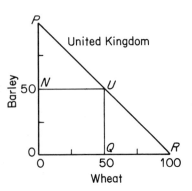

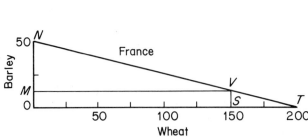

Fig. 10.2 *Production possibilities of the United Kingdom and France, before trade*

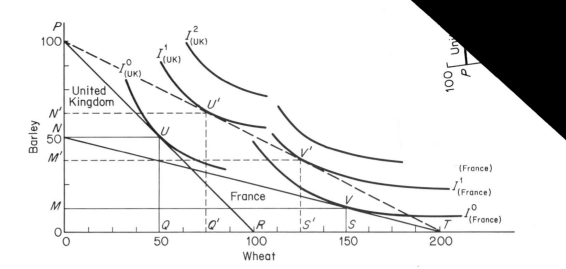

Fig. 10.3 *Gains from trade, two-country, two-commodity case*

From the information at hand it is clear that barley and wheat are exchanged on equal terms in the British domestic market. This is true even though Britons might wish a bit more wheat since it is more useful as a human food than barley, which serves mainly as feed for animals and for malting purposes in the production of beer and ale. Nevertheless, growing conditions do not permit greater emphasis upon wheat except at unduly high costs. In any event, 50 units of each of the two grains are produced and consumed within the country, which is shown in Figure 10.2a as ON of barley and OQ of wheat. Meanwhile, in France, where climatic conditions are especially favorable for wheat, that grain can be produced at a cost only one-fourth the cost of growing barley. The French therefore produce and consume 150 units of wheat (OS in Figure 10.2b) for every 12.5 units of barley (OM) despite a latent desire for larger quantities of the latter, more expensive (in France) grain. From the differences in the steepness of the slopes of the two production possibilities curves and from the domestic exchange ratios shown in the table, therefore, we find that the United Kingdom has a comparative advantage vis-à-vis France in barley production, while France has a comparative advantage in wheat.

As trade between the countries commences, there is a movement toward increasing production of barley in Britain and wheat in France until, under the conditions of constant costs assumed here, specialization becomes complete. Britain allocates all her resources to barley (OP in Figure 10.3) and supplies this commodity to consumers of both countries. France puts all her productive capacity into wheat (OT in the figure) and shares the output with Britain. From Figure 10.3 we are also able to determine the price at which the wheat-barley trade is to take place between the countries. The *international exchange ratio* is given by

$$\frac{OP}{OT} = \frac{100}{200}, \text{ or } 0.50$$

In other words, one unit of wheat is exchanged for 0.50 of barley. This ratio, often called the *international*

terms of trade, is indicated by the dashed line, PT, the *exchange possibilities curve.*

The quantities traded depend not only on *production* but also on the levels of *consumption* in both France and the United Kingdom. The demand patterns of the two countries are given in Figure 10.3 by the families of *indifference curves,* the British consumption by those curves labeled I_{UK} and those of France by I_F. The indifference curves indicate the various proportions in which the British and French consumers are willing to substitute wheat for barley or vice versa. Each curve corresponds to a given level of consumption of a country. Thus I^0 refers to one level, I^1 to the next higher level, and I^2 to a higher level yet. It is clear that a people will wish to reach the highest curve that they are capable of. The actual amount of a grain consumed prior to the opening of trade is indicated by the *point of tangency* of an indifference curve with the production possibilities curve of a particular country, U being the amount consumed by the United Kingdom and V by the French. After trade, the consumption point is taken as the point of tangency of an indifference curve with the exchange possibilities curve (PT). Therefore, with the advent of trade, British consumption moves from U to U' on the next higher indifference curve (from I^0_{UK} to I^1_{UK}). This means that trade makes it possible for the British to consume 62.5 units of barley instead of 50 (ON' instead of ON) and 75 units of wheat instead of 50 (OQ' rather than OQ).

French consumption likewise moves up from V to V' (from curve I^0_F to I^1_F). France is able to consume 37.5 units of barley instead of 12.5 (OM' rather than OM). Note, however, that in this example wheat consumption in France actually falls slightly, from 150 units to 125 (from OS to OS') as a result of trade. In this case the French are giving up a cheaper grain, wheat, for one which in France has previously been more expensive and for which latent demand is strong. For example, before trade, France would have had to sacrifice 150 units of wheat output to get the 37.5 units of barley now obtained from the United Kingdom for only 50 wheat units. Thus greater consumer satisfaction is attained by both countries as a result of trade.

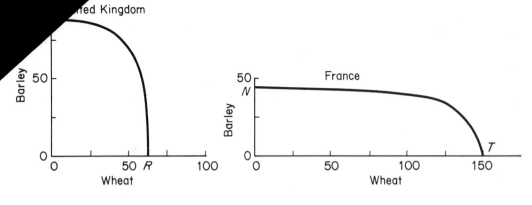

Fig. 10.4 *Production possibilities curves, increasing costs*

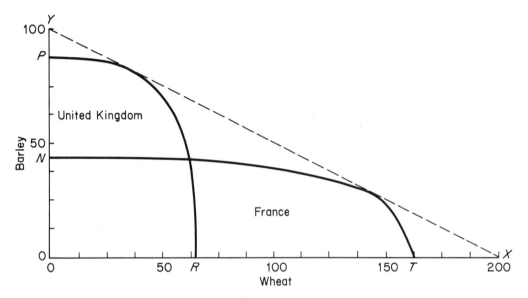

Fig. 10.5 *Exchange possibilities curve, increasing costs*

To summarize, then, trade has brought complete specialization of production by both countries, each supplying the other with part of its output. The United Kingdom now produces *OP* barley, exports *N'P* of it to France, and consumes the rest (*ON'*) while importing all her wheat needs (*N'U'*) from the French. At the same time, France produces *OT* of wheat and exports *S'T* of it to Britain. The remaining wheat output (*OS'*) she consumes herself, while importing *S'V'* of barley from the United Kingdom.

It should be noted at this point that complete specialization such as described here is uncommon in the real world, although as we shall see later, several less developed countries come very close to it. One important factor preventing specialization from reaching its extreme limits is the tendency for unit production costs to begin increasing after a certain level of inputs is reached. For this reason the previous assumption of constant costs and linear production possibilities curves is not realistic (see Figs. 10.1, 10.2, 10.3). Thus, under conditions of increasing costs, Figure 10.2 would look more like Figure 10.4. The curvature of lines *PR* and *NT*, production possibilities of the United Kingdom and France, results when limits of efficiency are reached by either type of production as additional resources are applied. This happens if, as is usually the case, not all of a country's resources are suited to a particular line

of production. As new resources are allocated to wheat, for example, a point is eventually attained where each additional new unit of input (machinery, fertilizer, manpower) no longer yields a proportionate gain in wheat production.

How this affects trade is seen in Figure 10.5. There the modified nonlinear production possibilities curves of the United Kingdom and France (see Fig. 10.4) have been superimposed and an exchange possibilities curve, *XY*, constructed as shown.

THE BENEFITS FROM TRADE

It has been shown above that several desirable results may follow the introduction of trade between countries with different production possibilities. The parties to trade benefit in two ways: (1) from the exchange of goods in and of itself, and (2) from the areal specialization that follows from this trade.

The gains from trade per se have been demonstrated in the preceding pages. As Figures 10.1 through 10.5 indicate, the introduction of trade permits the commodity mix of a country to be adjusted in such a way that the country can move as a whole to a higher level of consumption than was possible in isolation. In short, the production pattern no longer needs to coincide with the consumption pattern.

Over and above these benefits, however, there is still a second set of gains. The increased regional specialization of production that follows trade offers important opportunities for more efficient production, for a greater output from each unit of resources. If the people of a district, region, or country concentrate their efforts upon producing a limited number of goods, they are able to use effectively those existing skills and resources that are best adapted to the purpose. In addition, with experience and continued practice in these lines, many new skills of an even higher order accumulate. A fertile environment for invention and innovation is created, as research and development become focused along narrow channels and specialists in the field live and work in close association with one another.

Business enterprises gain in competitive strength from operating in such a climate. These benefits are both *internal* and *external* to the firm. Among the internal effects are economies of large scale production, such as more efficient use of machines and manpower, lower prices for raw materials purchased in bulk, reduced transport rates for assembling materials and distributing products in large quantities, and lower unit operating costs as a result of spreading output over longer model runs. External economies enjoyed by the firm located in an area of specialization include access to a large pool of labor with the requisite skills and experience as well as opportunities for sharing ideas and information with others engaged in the same type of production. Equally important is the availability of specialized facilities of many kinds. Among these are auxiliary or related industries with which there are direct ties, such as those linking steel mills with suppliers of fire bricks for lining furnaces or with firms using steel for fabricating bridge members. Often such areas acquire a variety of specialized service agencies. Associated with the cotton textile industry of Lancashire, England, for example, are cotton brokerage and exchange activities as well as banking and insurance firms having a particular knowledge of the peculiarities and problems of that trade.

In this way areal specialization further enhances the comparative advantage that a country or region may have possessed in the first place. Once it has gained sufficient momentum, the specialized area increases its competitive edge over other areas that might wish to enter the market. Indeed, even if no resource advantage had existed initially and the specialization had developed merely through historical accident, the area might well have acquired a comparative advantage by reason of economies of the kind described here. This factor helps to explain the existence of many industrial concentrations around the world whose original reason for locating may now have vanished. Examples are Britain's clay products industry at Stoke-on-Trent, France's textile manufacturing of Le Nord, and the optical instrument specialization at Rochester, New York.

In sum, if trade is truly free, it should be expected to result in an optimal use of the world's resources through greater efficiency and thus smaller resource use per unit of output. It should also bring higher standards of living from the same resource base. These benefits, at least in theory, should produce more goods for everyone concerned and perhaps more leisure as well. Let us next examine those characteristics of areas that cause them to differ from each other in their production and consumption.

EFFECTS OF SUPPLY CONDITIONS ON TRADE

We have previously seen how trade can be generated between areas that have comparative advantages arising from differences in production costs. At this point, we shall attempt to learn why costs vary spatially, paying particular attention to the parts played by the individual factors of production—*land, labor, entrepreneurship,* and *capital*. First, however, we shall examine the general nature of production factors. Two aspects are important here: (1) factor requirements of particular industries and (2) variations among regions and countries in the proportions in which they possess these factors.

factor proportions and intensity

To some degree all four factors are used in virtually every type of commercial production, whether it be farming, mining, manufacturing, or some other economic activity; but different activities tend to require these factors in varying proportions. Most primary activities, such as farming or forestry, make heavy demands on the factor of land and are thus said to be *land-intensive*. Some types of manufacturing, such as cotton textiles, need much labor; other industries, such as oil refining, need much capital and relatively little labor. Thus *factor intensity* differs widely from one type of production to another.

In many economic activities it is possible, within limits, to substitute one factor for another. In agriculture, labor and capital (in the form of equipment or fertilizer) can often be applied to a unit of land in varying proportions. Manufactured goods, in many cases, can be hand- or machine-fabricated, thus partially substituting capital for labor. Yet, sometimes the factors of production occur in forms that are so highly specialized in their applicability that they are difficult to shift out of one use into another. This is true of certain kinds of land, such as high-acid soils that are good for growing potatoes or blueberries but poor for wheat, which requires high-alkaline soil.

Ironically, labor is another factor that is sometimes difficult to transfer from one activity to another. One reason for this is that skill requirements vary so much, especially in lines of production for which a great deal of training and experience are needed. Quick shifts of labor are often difficult to effect because workers may be reluctant to learn new skills or unable to be retrained. A farm worker could not be employed immediately as a petroleum chemist, and a lathe operator could not be converted quickly into a crane operator or dairy farmer. Even some forms of capital can be highly specific: it would hardly be feasible to convert a refinery to the manufacture of textiles. What is important here is the time dimension; although certain factors cannot be shifted instantaneously to other uses they may be converted over longer periods. This is especially true of labor, which, given a sufficient number of years, can acquire new skills.

Scale of operations is another important consideration. Factors may be combined in different proportions at a low level of production than at a high level. This can be seen in two contrasting forms of European agriculture. Peasant farming, found in parts of France, Germany, Switzerland, and elsewhere, is characterized by very small holdings with scattered, fragmented fields. Because large farm machinery would be useless in most cases, peasant agriculture is particularly labor-intensive. On the other hand, commercial farms in Europe may produce the same crops as the peasant farms; but, with their large acreages and big fields, most have been able to mechanize their operations, thus becoming relatively capital-intensive. The same is true of manufacturing; a given line of production may be carried out in small, labor-intensive establishments during the infancy of the industry, but as the scale of operations grows, labor-saving machinery and mass-production methods become both feasible and necessary.

The factors of production are present in different countries in widely varying proportions. Australia and Canada have large land areas with sizable and varied natural resources, but they have comparatively small populations to go along with those resources. Consequently, both countries are short of labor and also lack adequate supplies of capital and entrepreneurship. At the other extreme are several small European countries, such as Belgium and Switzerland, that have well developed capital markets, large pools of highly skilled labor, and accumulated managerial skills of a high order, but have meager quantities of land or other physical resources to which these factors can be applied. Several less developed countries—India and Pakistan, for example—have large oversupplies of workers, most of whom are uneducated and untrained; yet these countries lack the capital and managerial requirements for putting their masses to productive activity.

the Heckscher-Ohlin theory

How does a country's particular combination of factors affect its foreign trade? One attempt at answering this question is the *Heckscher-Ohlin theory.* This theory begins with the premises that (1) countries differ in their proportions of factors; that is, their *factor endowments,* and (2) commodities differ in the combination of factors they require; that is, their *factor intensities.* If it is assumed that factor intensities of given commodities remain the same in different countries, the Heckscher-Ohlin theory holds that each country will export those goods whose production is relatively intensive in the country's abundant factor and import

those which are intensive in the factors that it lacks. This would seem to be confirmed by the exports of Hong Kong, Taiwan, and Singapore, all of which have large supplies of cheap labor and export labor-intensive goods such as cheap shoes, garments, toys, and novelties. The Swiss, with much capital and skilled labor but little land, produce and export watches and scientific instruments. With her vast land area, Canada exports primary products such as wood pulp, paper, potash, and wheat to a greater extent than most technically advanced nations. On the other hand, Hong Kong and Switzerland both import raw materials and foodstuffs, while Canada tends to import goods that are intensive in labor and capital. The Heckscher-Ohlin theory is much criticized as being too simplistic, yet there is evidence to suggest that it helps to explain a number of trade patterns. Before considering other influences on trade, let us first explore the effects of specific factors of production.

land as a factor

As a factor of production *land* occupies a central place in determining the size and nature of world trade flows. By land, we mean the territory of a country, region, district, or other areal unit, together with its quantities and particular qualities. The properties of land in which we are particularly interested are its physical resources that are useful to man. What is significant about these resources as they relate to trade is that they are distributed in a most uneven fashion throughout the world (see Chapter 3). For this reason the resources of most countries are "skewed," that is, there are large stores of some resources—perhaps more than can be used locally—and short supplies of many other needed resources.

This is especially true of *mineral resources.* Among the metallic minerals are a few, such as iron ore, that are abundant in the earth's crust and found in many places; usually, however, even these common minerals are concentrated in commercial quantities in a limited number of areas. The result of this resource skewness is a voluminous and rapidly growing interregional and international trade in minerals. Much of the world's ocean tonnage is devoted to transporting oil from Venezuela, North Africa, and the Middle East to Western Europe, Japan, and the United States.

Biotic resources are spread inequitably too, partly because of climatic and other physical reasons but also because of the destructiveness of man. Today the forested areas of the Pacific Northwest of Canada and the United States, together with northern Ontario and Quebec, send their wood products to the more populous parts of North America. Large flows of these commodities also converge upon central and western Europe from Scandinavia and the Soviet Union. At the same time, tropical hardwoods move from equatorial regions to industrialized areas of the temperate latitudes.

The widespread trade in agricultural commodities clearly reflects world variations in *climates, soils* and *relief.* The Mediterranean basin and similar areas in

California and elsewhere are able, by reason of their long growing season, to specialize in growing fruits and winter vegetables for populations in colder areas thousands of miles distant. Among the largest volumes of agricultural commodities entering international trade are the exchanges of temperate-land grains, particularly wheat, for the sugar and tropical fruits of warmer areas. An important characteristic of the very large trade in wheat is its unpredictability from one year to the next. This is attributable in large degree to the variability of harvests typical of the leading wheat growing areas, whose rainfall patterns are highly uncertain. Hence the Soviet Union, which leads the world in wheat output in most years, has been forced to import vast quantities of grain during years of crop failure.

Differences in soils can also contribute to world trade flows, and many crops such as grapes, tea, and sugar cane have fairly exacting requirements. Important quantities of vegetables are exported from regions having muck soils, such as southern Florida and the Holland Marsh area of Ontario. Finally, there is the influence of physical relief. Regions with great expanses of low-lying level terrain are often producers and exporters of foodstuffs to mountainous areas unable to grow sufficient quantities of food. The exchanges of the Netherlands and Denmark with the Alpine countries of Austria and Switzerland illustrate this element in the world food trade.

It should be noted that the patterns of commodity movements described here are by no means constant through time. One reason for this is the changing nature of resources; even the view of what constitutes a resource changes from one time to another (see Chapter 3). The state of the arts thus has much to do with the trade in products of the land, as does the level of development of countries and populations (see Chapter 11). Moreover, new resources are constantly being found, often with startling effects upon world trade patterns, as in the case of the North African oil discoveries. Resources can be exhausted, as, for example, some of the cotton lands of the southern United States and the high grade iron ores of the Lake Superior region. Each of these events has helped to reorient trade flows.

The trade between countries is affected in many ways by the *physical dimensions* of trading units. Obviously, the larger the country the more likely that it will have a wide range and abundant supply of resources, and this is reflected in a more diversified production. Being more nearly self-sufficient in their own output, the United States and the Soviet Union do not have to depend so heavily upon trade with other nations as some smaller countries do. Although in absolute terms the United States, with its great economy, is the largest single trading country, her exports have, in the past, seldom exceeded 4 to 5 percent of the nation's gross national product. By contrast, the Netherlands, which is about the size of Massachusetts plus Connecticut, exports from 35 to 40 percent of her total output. Moreover, a small country is unlikely to have a sufficiently large production to be able to influence the international terms of trade and will thus be forced to accept prices set for her in the larger world markets.

A second physical characteristic of countries that may affect their trade is their *shape*. This is especially true of agricultural production, where a greater north-south extent means a wider climatic variation and thus a much wider variety of farm products. Because Canada's agricultural lands are confined to a long narrow strip extending east-west just above the United States border, only a limited number of temperate-land crops are possible. Long borders between countries are conducive to trade. Thus, while Ontario relies mainly upon coal imported from the eastern coal fields of the United States, British Columbia in the far west supplies that same commodity to the adjacent Pacific states of the United States. One last physical attribute of countries, though not the least important, is relative location, to be discussed separately in the next section.

The complementarity of the factors of production has already been stressed, and this is no less true of land than the others. From an economic standpoint, land becomes useful to man only when capital, labor, and management are applied to it. This has been noted previously with regard to Canada and Australia, where land is by far the most abundant factor and its development has been retarded by the shortage of the other factors. Viewed in another way, each of these examples illustrates the fact that physical extent of a country is not an adequate measure of effective size unless it is coupled with an economy of equivalent dimensions. The net effect of such an imbalance of factors is to create trade, since both countries export large quantities of land-intensive commodities that larger economies could absorb domestically.

labor as a factor

Historically, the factor that has most interested theorists has been *labor*. Indeed, the law of comparative costs was originally posed in terms of the labor theory of value, according to which the values of all commodities can be measured by their labor inputs, such as mandays. The output of a unit of labor is considered constant everywhere and for all economic activities. In other words, laborers can be transferred from one industry into another without affecting total labor cost. The other factors are either ignored or they are treated as stored-up labor. The labor theory of value is no longer widely accepted, but labor is still acknowledged as an important influence on trade. Two aspects of labor are of special significance: (1) its relative abundance or scarcity and (2) its productivity.

Countries (and regions) vary considerably in the *size* of their labor forces; many have inadequate numbers of workers to man their farms and factories while others have more workers than they can employ economically. For labor-scarce economies—those having a low ratio of labor to land—the Heckscher-Ohlin theory predicts resource-intensive exports and labor-intensive imports. Thus Finland, Canada, and Australia export commodities having a large resource content, such as minerals, wood products, or animal products.

Contrary to the labor theory of value, labor inputs for the same goods do vary from one place to another, especially where there are differences in resource endowments. Both the United States and China produce wheat, cotton, and rice; but China uses labor-intensive methods while the United States employs methods that are at the same time land-intensive and capital-intensive.

In those countries where the labor-land ratio is very high, the expectation is for labor-intensive exports and land- or capital-intensive imports. A number of countries fall into this category, especially the island nations of Japan and the United Kingdom, both of which have traditionally imported large volumes of raw materials and foodstuffs and exported finished manufactured goods. A surplus of labor is usually accompanied by low labor costs, which prove very attractive to those industries using large numbers of unskilled or semiskilled laborers. Many manufacturing activities of this type might be described as mature industries; this is to say that they have passed through the innovative stages where highly skilled workers and engineers were needed and have now acquired mass-production techniques that may require large numbers of workers performing simple tasks on assembly lines. Examples of this are factories making cheaper grades of cotton textiles, standardized types of low-priced clothing, and even the better established forms of electronic production, such as the assembling of radios and television sets. Hong Kong and Taiwan have many such industries; Puerto Rico has likewise succeeded in attracting a rapidly growing community of mature industries.

Many less developed countries have labor surpluses that have hindered them in competing for new industries. One type of less developed country is both labor-rich and land-rich but lacks the capital and entrepreneurship necessary for industrialization. A majority of the Latin American countries fit this description. With their chronic unemployment and underemployment, they are able to attract only plantation agriculture, with all the problems that entails (see Chapters 11 and 20).

Much of the trade between countries can be attributed to differences in the quality of labor. This is expressed in terms of labor *productivity,* which measures the relative value of output of a unit of labor. Productivity of workers is affected by (1) their skill and work habits, (2) their wage levels, and (3) the availability of capital in the form of labor-saving machinery.

The effects of labor productivity on trade have been analyzed in a number of studies. One of these was designed to test the labor theory of value, based on the notion that differences between countries in labor productivity in the manufacture of a given commodity should be reflected in differences in production costs and thus in selling prices. Countries should be expected to export those goods in which their labor productivity is highest relative to other countries. In a comparison

of exports from the United Kingdom and the United States it was found that there was a direct linear relationship on a log-log scale between the productivity ratios of the two countries and their export ratios for a number of goods. British exports were relatively greater than American exports in those goods, such as textiles and clothing, where the productivity of British workers most closely approached that of American labor. Where the unit output of United States labor greatly exceeded that of the British, as in the case of machinery and motor cars, American exports were relatively greater.

There are many characteristics of labor that can affect its productivity. A number of countries export labor-intensive products that require special manufacturing skills acquired over long periods of time, as for example, Swiss watches, Belgian cut diamonds, women's garments from Paris, and cutlery from Sheffield, England.

Conversely, those countries lacking industrial traditions often find great difficulty in introducing new forms of export production. It may take many generations for a country to acquire a work force having the skills and work habits necessary to man a modern industrial enterprise. Members of a folk society usually have wholly different cultural attitudes, incentives, and value systems than those required for working on an assembly line or operating a power shovel.

enterprise as a factor

Although the trade literature has little to say concerning *entrepreneurship,* the quality of management is an essential element. In some less developed areas it is a central issue. The character of decision making by the business community has much to do with the rise and decline of trading nations and regions. Wise managers have the vision to assess the foreign market and then to develop those industries having the growth potential needed to give a competitive edge in that market. Thus British industrial leaders were able to anticipate, and in some cases to create, the world demand for textiles, iron and steel, and machinery at the time of the Industrial Revolution. On the other hand, lethargic and complacent British management clung tenaciously to declining industries and obsolete technology during the latter part of the nineteenth century and the early part of this one.

capital as a factor

The other factor of production, *capital,* is of two principal types. Money capital is the more intangible, fluid form available for investment in any undertaking; while a more tangible type is capital in the shape of equipment, buildings, or land. Capital is sometimes difficult to treat as a separate factor, since it becomes so readily tied up with the other factors, as, for example, in improving land, educating managers, or training workers. Nevertheless, capital very clearly serves as an important determinant of trade. Any country having an abundance of capital eventually acquires a comparative advantage in exporting capital-intensive merchandise.

The United States is often cited as a capital-rich country, evidenced by American foreign sales of chemicals. The chemical industry as a whole has a very high capital-labor ratio, since it involves heavy investment in complex plant and equipment and large outlays for research and development; but it employs relatively few unskilled workers. However, the United States also exports large quantities of primary goods such as wheat, corn, soybeans, and cottonseed products, which are not usually regarded as capital-intensive commodities. This paradox has received much attention in the trade literature. The answer appears to lie in the fact that capital is almost invariably a complement to other factors and in the United States agriculture is highly capital-intensive. So successful has been the heavy agricultural use of capital—in the form of machinery, pesticides, herbicides, and chemical fertilizers—that only 2.7 million American farmers are able to support a domestic population of more than 208 million people and at the same time maintain a comparative advantage in many farm products in the international market.

Capital substitution for other factors of production has been increasing in this manner throughout the developed world. European agriculture has been closely following the American lead in recent decades and even Japanese farmers have been mechanizing their relatively small acreages. The most striking example, however, has been in Japanese manufacturing industry, which during the postwar era has turned to the production of capital-intensive merchandise such as cameras, machinery, electronics, and motor cars (see Chapter 17).

Money capital is the most mobile of factors and an important trend in recent years has been the increasing substitution of flows of capital for trade flows. More and more companies are building factories in those foreign lands to which they formerly exported their products. This often results when trade barriers are erected in the customary foreign markets. Rather than lose this income, manufacturers transfer their production to the foreign countries whose markets have been closed to imports. This, of course, reduces the companies' dependence upon domestic labor, a fact of much concern to the labor movement.

A second major reason for sending capital abroad in the place of merchandise is to take advantage of complementary factors of production in the foreign areas. Investment in other countries may be undertaken by agricultural concerns in order to obtain the use of land having specific qualities, as in the case of plantation agriculture. Similarly, manufacturers of labor-intensive goods may take advantage of cheap labor in other countries by developing new factories in such locations. The rash of new radio and television assembly plants on the Mexican side of the United States-Mexican border is an example of this.

Although capital in this fluid form moves easily between countries, other types of capital can be highly immobile. When invested in steel mills, shipyards, or auto assembly plants, capital can be a strong inertial factor. This helps to explain the slowness with which some countries adjust the composition of their exports to changing world conditions.

This discussion of supply factors brings into question certain parts of the Heckscher-Ohlin theory, especially its basic assumption that particular goods have the same factor intensities everywhere. Thus we have noted substantial changes in the ratios between capital and labor, and capital and land. Most important of all, however, this theory places excessive emphasis upon production factors. Trade is determined only in part by supply conditions; demand considerations are also important.

EFFECTS OF DEMAND CONDITIONS ON TRADE

We have noted that trade permits a region or country to maintain a pattern of consumption that differs from its production pattern. Reflecting the wide differences in resource endowments from one area to the next, there are many spatial differences in production possibilities; yet, at the same time, there are considerable variations in consumption. The fact that the structure of demand rarely seems to coincide with production in any one place is a prime reason for the existence of trade.

However, spatial differences in production are not absolutely essential for trade to develop. Trade can be created between two regions with identical production possibilities if they have unlike structures of demand. Take the case of two countries, A and B, both of which are able to grow potatoes and corn in equal proportions. Most of the people in country A prefer potatoes to corn, however, and those in B tend to like corn better than potatoes. With the opening of trade between the two, each country can produce both crops and exchange its unwanted surplus with the other country for the preferred commodity.

income as a factor

What are some of the reasons for spatial variations in demand if it is true that fundamental human needs are essentially constant? Perhaps the most important determinant of all is income. Rising per capita incomes obviously produce an increase in purchasing power and hence a larger effective demand. This extra demand does not extend in equal degree to all commodities, however. One explanation for the fact that rising incomes create stronger demand for some goods than others is given by *Engel's law,* which states that poor families (or poor countries) spend a larger proportion of their incomes on food than do rich ones. A poverty-stricken population may be able to afford only the barest necessities, and some parts of the world today are hardly capable even of this. For such people a rise in income may at first actually bring increased expenditures for food and other necessities until some minimum level is reached; but thereafter, as incomes continue to go up, the additions to income are spent increasingly on other goods, including nonessentials and even luxury items. Because so many of these tend to be manufactured goods—for which demand is virtually unlimited —sellers of industrial commodities tend to gain a growing share of the increase. Nevertheless, even agricultural products are affected differently by rising purchasing power. Poor populations consume mainly starchy foods, but as their incomes rise they tend to substitute increasing amounts of meats, green vegetables, and dairy products for the starches (see Chapter 2). These variations in demand for different commodities at different income levels are referred to as the *income elasticity of demand*.

There have been several attempts to measure variations in elasticities of demand. One such study found that elasticities of particular categories of goods were roughly similar in different countries, but that they were not identical. Some of the greatest variations were for food, which proved to have a very low income elasticity of demand but ranged from an index of 0.3 to 0.7 in different countries. This low elasticity means that a unit rise in income would not increase the demand for food to a corresponding degree. Thus if food expenditures had been averaging $15 per week and per capita weekly incomes rose from $30 to $40, the amount allocated to food out of the additional $10 income would come to another $5 if the raise in pay were proportionally distributed; but if the elasticity of demand for food was only 0.3, the addition to the food budget would amount only to $1.50. Housing had an income elasticity of demand of nearly 1.0, which means that expenditures for housing would rise at a rate approximating the increase in income. Clothing and other expenditures would both increase more than proportionally to the rise in income. This study found that, although there were relatively small variations in the income elasticities of demand *between* countries, variations *within* countries were very slight.

Because commodities differ in their elasticities, a comparison of countries at different levels of per capita income will show great contrasts in consumption patterns. This is explained by the fact that, as countries have ascended in the income scale, their patterns of consumption have changed, with certain commodities increasing in demand much faster than others. Trade flows among nations mirror these income differences. Goods exchanged by North America and Western Europe are very different from the goods moving between Europe and West Africa or Southeast Asia. This difference can be attributed to differences in consumption patterns as well as to different production possibilities.

Among those countries at the upper levels of development the disparities in demand patterns tend to narrow with the passage of time. Since the Second World War, with growing prosperity in Western Europe and Japan, the populations of those areas have developed increasingly similar life styles. Meanwhile the gap between developed and less developed countries widens further (see Chapter 11). Hence an important part of the explanation for demand differences between countries is yet to be accounted for.

the role of cultural differences

Another reason for demand variations among countries is the influence of cultural differences. The trade effects of culture can be shown by the influence of religious beliefs among certain populations. Some predominantly Catholic populations, such as those of Portugal, Spain, and Italy, import large quantities of fish to add to their own sizable production of this food; prohibitions of Hinduism limit India's consumption and importation of beef, and Moslem and Jewish restrictions on the eating of pork adversely affect meat sales to the Middle East nations. Differing consumption habits also affect trade flows, as shown by the unusually high per capita tea shipments reaching Britain as compared with the large importations of coffee into the United States.

domestic consumption and exports

Still another aspect of demand that is often overlooked is the effect of a country's domestic consumption pattern upon its exports. Usually a country competes most successfully in foreign markets by trading products for which its own domestic market is great. One reason for this is that large domestic sales permit the industry to develop economies of scale and achieve lower unit production costs, thereby adding to the country's comparative advantage in that commodity abroad. Before World War II Japan had very large home consumption of mass-produced, low-cost textiles and was therefore able to sell these abroad at favorable prices. More recently, Japan has managed to accomplish the same results with automobile exports, now that her population has attained the per capita income necessary for mass automobile ownership (see Chapter 17).

Summarizing the effects of production and consumption, we can say that while each contributes to trade, it is their interaction that is most important. Perhaps if all trade occurred at a single spot rather than flowing between different places on the earth's surface and if supply and demand were permitted to act upon each other unhindered, then the story might end here. However, the real world of trade is much more complicated than this; there are other forces that interfere with trade in one way or another.

BARRIERS TO TRADE

Leaving behind the ideal conditions with which we have been dealing, we find two kinds of obstacles to trade: (1) the effect of distance and (2) governmental interference.

distance

The most noticeable way in which distance can act as a barrier to trade is simply through the cost of

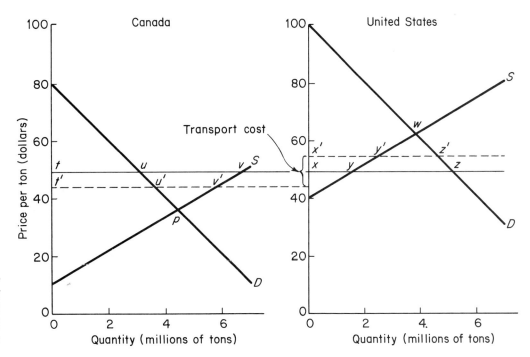

Fig. 10.6 *Price of paper in Canada and the United States, quantities traded and consumed with and without transport costs*

transporting goods. This cost does not correlate perfectly with the actual number of miles to be covered between origin and destination, since some routes are cheaper to travel than others. Mountainous terrain can add many miles to straight-line distances and steep grades can impose high fuel costs. Irregular coastlines prevent vessels from taking the shortest route between ports. For these and many other reasons transport routes are often more circuitous than might appear from a cursory glance at the map and therefore impose higher costs. Consequently, for purposes of analysis, it is often advisable to measure the intervals between places in terms of the actual costs entailed. This measure is often termed "economic distance."

It should also be noted that the expense of transporting goods is not restricted to just the cost of operating the motor vehicle, aircraft, or steamship. There are also bank collection charges, freight forwarders' and customs house brokers' fees, consular charges, and outlays for cartage. Adding these extra expenditures to the actual costs of moving the goods gives a total that is more accurately described by the collective term "transfer costs." Nevertheless, transport costs normally account for the major part of the total.

Introducing transport costs into the analysis complicates the problem considerably. First of all, these costs effectively prevent prices from actually becoming fully equalized by trade between regions or countries as implied earlier in Figure 10.3. Transport costs make goods more expensive to their importers and less valuable to their exporters, producing effects that can be seen with the aid of a simple example involving two countries and a single commodity.

Figure 10.6 shows hypothetical demand and supply curves for paper in both the United States and Canada. As usual, the demand curves, *D,* slope downward to the right, indicating that consumers in each country

Table 10.3 Effects of Transport Cost on Exports of Paper by Canada to the United States

| | WITHOUT TRANSPORT COST | | WITH TRANSPORT COST | |
	Canada	United States	Canada	United States
Price per ton (in dollars)	$49	$49	$44	$54
Quantity produced*	6.6	1.6	5.8	2.4
Quantity exported*	3.5	—	2.2	—
Quantity imported*	—	3.5	—	2.2
Quantity consumed*	3.1	5.1	3.6	4.6

*All quantities in millions of tons.

will take larger quantities of paper if the price drops. The supply curves, *S,* slope upward to the right since producers are able and willing to make more paper if the price goes up. The diagram shows that, in the absence of trade, the price of paper would be lower in Canada than in the United States. This is indicated by the points where the supply and demand curves cross—*p* for Canada and *w* for the United States.

The figure shows the results of trade, first in the absence of transport costs and then with the addition of transport costs. These effects are also summarized in Table 10.3. Without transport costs the price after trade in both countries—that is, the international terms of trade—becomes $49 per ton of paper, shown by the horizontal line extending from *t* to *z*. At this price Canada produces 6.6 million tons of paper (indicated by the distance *tv*), consumes 3.1 million tons of this (*tu*), and exports the remaining 3.5 million tons (*uv*) to the United States. Under these conditions the United States consumes 5.1 million tons (*xz*) of paper, of which 3.5 million tons (*xy*) are imported from Canada. United

States producers, then, are able to supply the other 1.6 million tons (yz) that the country needs.

On the other hand, if transport costs between the two countries amount to $10 per ton, the price of paper rises to $54 in the United States and falls to $44 in Canada. At the $54 price the United States is no longer willing to use as much paper and consumption then drops to only 4.5 million tons ($x'z'$). However, at this price domestic producers of paper are able to supply a larger quantity, 2.4 million tons ($x'y'$), and United States imports are thus reduced to only 2.2 million tons ($y'z'$). At the reduced Canadian price of $44 producers in that country will supply only 5.8 million tons ($t'v'$), but Canadian consumers will take a larger quantity, 3.6 million tons ($t'u'$). Still, the extra home consumption makes up for only a part of the lost exports to the United States, which are now reduced to only 2.2 million tons ($u'v'$).

It is important to note that in this example transport cost does indeed decrease specialization. The United States produces more of her own paper and buys less abroad, and total output falls in the supplying country even though more of the product is used at home. Observe also that the impact of transport costs falls with equal weight upon both importing and exporting countries. Of special significance, too, is the fact that if the transport cost should become so great as to exceed the production cost differential between the two countries, trade would not be feasible at all. Each country would produce all her own needs. Throughout the world innumerable types of localized production owe their existence to the sheltering effects of a prohibitively high transport cost barrier to trade with lower-cost regions elsewhere. Herein, then, lies one of the firm links between trade theory and location theory.

These general statements must be modified, however, to take into account the exceedingly wide variations in the costs of transporting different classes of merchandise. Most manufactured goods have a high degree of transportability owing to the low cost of shipment relative to their value, which has been estimated to average about 2 percent. Such products therefore tend to move freely over long distances throughout the world. The transportability of primary commodities varies widely, however, depending upon their relative value, bulk, weight, or perishability. Natural fibers such as cotton, hemp, sisal, and linen are valuable, light, and nonperishable and are therefore traded over very long distances. By contrast, many grains and ores are low in value per unit of weight and transport cost considerations have much to do with the resulting trade patterns of such goods.

Transport costs are not the only means through which distance affects trade, and in some instances they may not even be the main ones. Propinquity can contribute importantly to trade between countries or regions for other, more subtle reasons. Perhaps equally important are differences in population characteristics, which are likely to be much less in adjacent or nearby areas. Tastes, customs, languages, business methods, and laws all tend to become increasingly different with distance. For another thing, businessmen are likely to have a greater knowledge of sales opportunities in neighboring areas than in distant ones, perhaps through personal acquaintances, mass communication media, travel, or through other first-hand means.

Although in the past distance has been much neglected in studies of trade, increasing attention has been given to this variable in recent years. An example is Beckerman's study of the effects of distance upon Western European trade. Using transport cost as a substitute for actual mileage, Beckerman compared two separate rankings of the same countries: (1) ranked by the average amount of transport cost separating them, and (2) ranked by value of trade with each other (adjusted for size of country). The correlation between these two rankings proved very good, tending to confirm the importance of transport cost as an influence upon trade patterns in Western Europe.

Important as distance has proved to be, however, it is but one of several factors that determine trade, and later examples will show this relationship. Meanwhile, we should note that both transport cost and non-cost effects of distance are highly susceptible to technological change. As will be seen in Chapter 11, technology has contributed substantially to the long-term downward trend in transport costs and to vastly improved communications between areas, twin developments that tend to alter the role of distance.

governmental interference

With their police powers and authority for taxation, governments are capable of substantially distorting basic patterns of trade. At the national level this capacity is reinforced by physical as well as administrative control of border crossings. Although the trade effects are readily apparent in most countries, they are highly visible in the Communist lands.

In the case of Communistic governments, state control of the economy as a whole is an obvious ideological necessity and this dictates close supervision of commodity movements; but even in the capitalistic world there are strong incentives to interfere with trade whenever it is considered essential to the well-being of the economy. For this reason careful attention is given by every country to its *balance of trade,* which is the difference between the value of its merchandise exports and imports within a given time span (usually a year). The mercantilist view, which is still very much alive in political circles, is that an excess of exports over imports is to be desired and is thus termed a "favorable" balance of trade.

Yet exports and imports of goods rarely tell the whole story. Shipments of merchandise represent only the "visible" trade of a country; before a full assessment of economic impact can be made account must also be taken of "invisible" exports and imports. These include services rendered by the residents of one country to those of another, such as insurance, banking, transportation, and the care and feeding of tourists. To these must be added income from investments, royalties on patents and books, and gifts between nationals of different countries. For most countries the merchandise trade is the major part, but in certain cases the invisibles are especially crucial. This is true, for instance, of the United Kingdom, whose earnings from financial and transport services and tourism help to offset a sizable annual deficit in the balance of merchandise trade. Norway's very large ocean fleet performs a similar function for that country. An analogous economic relationship often exists between large urban centers and their hinterlands. Besides flows of goods and invisibles, there are also interregional and international movements of capital in the form of investments or loans. Finally there are exchanges of monetary gold between nations. All of these flows need to be taken into consideration in determining the economic relationships among countries. Hence each country maintains a detailed record of all its foreign economic transactions. This is commonly termed the *balance of payments.*

Political interference in trade is often quite deliberate, but there are also many occasions when governmental decisions have unforeseen trade effects. The measures taken by political bodies may have either positive or negative impacts upon trade, depending on whether they create, diminish, or rechannel trade. Positive measures of an intentional nature are most often taken for the purpose of increasing the exports of a region or nation. Examples of these are trade promotional devices such as fairs and exhibits or even financial aid to exporters in the form of subsidies, loan guarantees, or tax rebates. The countries of Western Europe, to whom trade is so vital, depend heavily upon methods of this type for increasing their international sales. Special trade ties are often formed with other countries to increase sales. Some countries maintain commercial attachés in their embassies for the purpose of assisting their exporters in doing business in those places. Indeed, it has been found that there is a direct relationship between the size of diplomatic staffs and the trade between countries.

On the other hand, restrictive measures are used to control the volume, composition, or direction of trade. Many of these techniques are relics of mercantilist days. Many governments are under almost incessant political pressures from special interest groups to make use of such devices. One technique favored since early times is the *tariff,* which is a tax or duty exacted against a particular category of merchandise entering or leaving a country. There are *export tariffs,* most common in raw-material-exporting lands, and *import tariffs,* which are applied nearly everywhere. Tariffs may be levied primarily to earn governmental revenue or to protect domestic producers from import competition. Examples of the former are Chile's tariffs on exports of copper and nitrates. Newly developing countries often rely heavily on the income from import tariffs; such tariffs represented the chief source of revenue to the government of the United States during its earlier years. Countries at all stages of development tend to use

import tariffs for protection against foreign producers. Such tariffs are often justified on the basis of the "infant industry" argument. Newly developing industries are given tariff protection from foreign producers during their early years when unit costs of operation are still higher than those prevailing abroad. It is implicit in this argument that tariffs will be removed when the new industries reach full competitive strength. Industries established under these conditions are sometimes referred to as "tariff factories." Canadian manufacture of chemicals and household appliances began with government assistance of this type, as did the fabricated metals trades of Mexico. Protective tariffs are also used to save declining industries that are losing their competitiveness in world markets. In recent years the United States garment trades, shoe manufacturers, and steel producers, and their respective labor unions have been agitating for such governmental help against lower-cost foreign competitors.

Tariffs have still other effects, as Figure 10.7 and Table 10.4 illustrate. Here a hypothetical tariff is imposed on United States imports of shoes from Italy (assuming that the two countries trade with each other in isolation from the rest of the world). It will be noted, first of all, that a tariff produces changes in supply and demand conditions similar to the effects of transport cost shown previously in Figure 10.6. In this present case we see that in the absence of trade the Italian price would have been $6.80 (shown by the intersection of Italy's supply and demand curves at *x*), while the American price would have been $13.30 (given by the intersection at *y*). With trade, however, the price in both countries settles at $10 (*Oj*). At this price the United States will consume 13 million pairs of shoes (*dh*), 5 million of which are imported from Italy (*eh*).

With the introduction of a tariff of $2 per pair (equal to *ia*), the Italian price drops to $9 (given by *or*) and the United States price rises to $11 (*oa*). This causes Italian production to drop by 1 million pairs to only 8 million and exports to the United States to fall to 3.4 million pairs. At the new higher price, consumers in the United States will buy only 12 million pairs, 8.6 million of which are now produced at home. On those shoes still imported from Italy the United States government receives tariff revenue amounting to $6.8 million ($2 times 3.4 million pairs, or *ia* times *bc*). This is equivalent to the combined areas *bcgf* and *lmsq* in the figure. Meanwhile domestic producers enjoy an additional $14.6 million (on sales of 8.6 million pairs at $11 instead of 8 million at the earlier price of $10). Note, however, that producers receive this benefit not only at the expense of foreign producers but also of domestic consumers, who now get only 12 million pairs of shoes for $132 million where they used to get 13 million pairs for $130 million. In balance, the United States profits by this arrangement, since both the domestic shoe mills and the government gain added income. Although there is some loss to United States purchasers of shoes, the principal losers are the Italians, who are able to sell fewer pairs to the United States and get a lower price for them. In

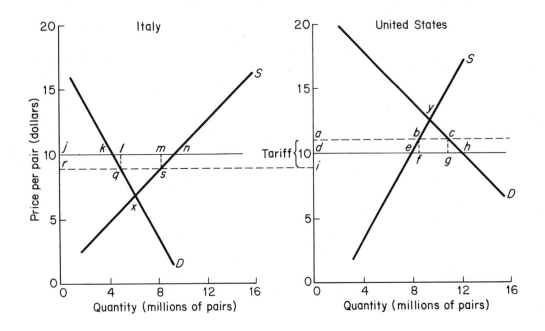

Fig. 10.7 *Effects of tariff on United States imports of shoes from Italy*

Table 10.4 Effects of United States Tariff on Shoes Imported from Italy

	BEFORE TARIFF		AFTER TARIFF	
	Italy	*United States*	*Italy*	*United States*
Price per pair (in dollars)	$10	$10	$9	$11
Quantity produced*	9.0	8.0	8.0	8.6
Quantity exported*	5.0	—	3.4	—
Quantity imported*	—	5.0	—	3.4
Quantity consumed*	4.0	13.0	4.6	12.0
Tariff revenue (in millions of dollars)	—	—	—	$6.8
Additional revenue to producers (in millions of dollars)	—	—	—	$14.6

*All quantities in millions of pairs.

other words, basically what we have in the tariff is a way of taxing the foreigner.

Still, there is always the risk of retaliation, since Italy is also a customer for American products. If, in retribution for the United States tariff on Italian shoes, Italy were to place a tariff on her imports of American corn, the results would be like those of Figure 10.7, only in reverse: Italy would buy less corn from the United States, the price of American corn would fall, less corn would be produced, and American corn farmers would be hurt. Thus, where retaliation is possible both countries are harmed by imposing tariffs; total trade is reduced and production and consumption are reduced. Some of the benefits of international specialization of production and exchange are thereby lost.

An even more drastic form of governmental intervention in trade is the *quota*. A quota is a specific limitation on the *quantity* of exports or (more usually) imports that a country will permit. This device is of more recent origin than the tariff, being largely a product of the world depression of the 1930s. Like tariffs, import quotas are used as a form of aid to domestic pro-

ducers. Quotas are especially favored as a means of protection from foreign competition for farmers and for producers of standardized manufactured goods such as textiles. Governments tend to prefer quotas where the foreign supply of a product is very great and available at particularly low prices. Under these conditions tariffs would likely be unsuccessful in stemming the flood of imports. Administrators favor quotas especially because of their sudden, drastic, and certain results and also because they are easy to impose, remove, or adjust. Allocations to importers under a quota system are usually made by means of import licensing arrangements, which have the further advantage of permitting assignment of specific shares of the market to favored nations.

Figure 10.8, which represents a hypothetical quota on Japanese rayon imported into the United States, illustrates the possible outcome of a recurrent issue in the United States, where textile manufacturers have long insisted that such protection is needed for their survival against foreign competition. Let us say that each year the United States has been consuming 70 million yards of rayon (*OD* in Figure 10.8) at a price of $2.50 per yard (*OE*). Of this amount, 50 million yards (*AD*) have been imported. If the government should yield to the demands of the domestic manufacturers and impose a quota limiting imports to 30 million yards (*BC*), this would, first of all, cause the price in the United States to rise to $3.00 (*OJ*) and total rayon consumption in the country to fall to 60 million yards. But out of this total American mills would be able to sell an increased quantity—30 million yards (*JK*) instead of the former 20 million yards (*EF*)—at the new higher price. The revenue increase to domestic producers would be $40 million (area *JKBO* instead of *EFAO*). Meanwhile, United States consumers would have to pay a total of $180 million (*JLCO*) for less cloth than they formerly got for only $175 million (*EIDO*). Thus the domestic mills gain at the expense of both domestic consumers and foreign suppliers. The effects are inflationary for the importing country and at the same time they are conducive to

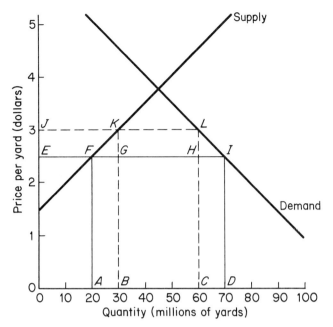

Fig. 10.8 *Effects of United States quota on imports of Japanese rayon*

monopoly control of production. Quotas of this type are highly arbitrary, since they freeze the volume and direction of trade into some predetermined pattern. Note also that, unlike tariffs, quotas yield no revenue to the government unless a high fee is assessed for import licenses.

Export quotas have also been used extensively in recent years to prop world prices of certain primary exports. Agricultural commodities and some minerals have chronically suffered from recurrent problems of oversupply and price instability. In such cases quotas may be imposed by exporting countries in an effort to reduce world supplies and thereby raise prices abroad. At various times Brazil has tried this means for limiting her exports of rubber and coffee, and the United States has attempted similar controls on cotton exports.

In the past, export restrictions of this type have not been very successful. Either substitutes would be found elsewhere for the country's products or new foreign sources of supply of the commodity would be developed. Thus nitrates have been synthesized to replace the artificially priced Chilean natural product; plantation rubber in the Far East has largely usurped the former markets for Brazilian rubber; Central American and Colombian growers have entered world coffee markets; and American price supports have encouraged cotton production in Africa. Producers in different countries have attempted to cooperate in controlling foreign sales of their products, but commodity agreements to this type uniformly failed, until the winter of 1973–1974, when members of the Organization of Petroleum Exporting Countries (OPEC) managed to agree on quantitative limits and prices for their oil exports.

A device rather similar to quotas involves the use

of *exchange controls,* by means of which a government buys all foreign moneys brought into the country through the earnings of its exporters and then distributes these currencies to importers in a carefully regulated manner. The allocation of foreign exchange is usually made through licensing schemes or auctions (as in Brazil). This is done in such a way as to control not only the volume of imports but also their composition, thereby conserving the country's money supply and assuring its most economical use. Such allotments are often made in such a way to discriminate against luxuries and favor necessities. Quota systems are sometimes accompanied by multiple exchange rates, in which case foreign currencies are sold to importers at higher prices for some purposes than others. Exchange controls were common in post–World War II Europe when shortages of foreign exchange were especially acute, and similar schemes continue in wide use throughout Latin America today.

In some parts of the world, governments go a step further and participate actively in buying and selling abroad, a practice that is termed *state trading.* This is the standard procedure in Communist countries, which operate through state agencies in making bulk purchases and sales in other countries. This device is less common among capitalistic countries, except for state monopolies in specific commodities such as salt, sugar, tobacco, and alcoholic beverages. During times of war, of course, bulk buying and selling by governments becomes necessary.

Intergovernmental relationships can alter trade patterns, as, for example, trade agreements granting special tariff concessions or generous quota allocations to favored trading partners. In general, their effects are to divert trade from the normal channels of a freely operating world market. Some of the more elaborate arrangements will be discussed later.

Nationalistic feelings, expressed through wars, hostile attitudes, or mere rivalries between populations can influence trade. Although there are natural complementarities between the Arab nations and Israel, their continued hostility discourages most Israeli-Arab trade. Trade between Eastern and Western Europe was highly developed before World War II but is much reduced now that the Eastern countries are controlled by Communists. Wars have often forced contending nations to industrialize, but on occasion they have had similar effects on noncombatants too. When cut off from European sources by World War I, Argentina began manufacturing a number of necessary items for herself. This process was accentuated still further when trade was again interrupted during World War II.

There is a wide range of minor governmental acts that sometimes interfere with foreign trade. Special labeling and packaging requirements may tend to exclude goods from some markets if the cost of changing the usual practices of producers in the exporting country is excessive. Sanitary and safety regulations can have the same effect. Some European countries maintain very specific requirements for the ingredients of prepared foods; Canada requires labels in both French and English; and the United States is specifying an increasingly costly array of safety and pollution-control devices on motor cars. Some of these measures are enacted without conscious thought of their effects on imported commodities, but others are used quite deliberately to exclude foreign competition that cannot readily comply with them. Even the mere existence of a border that must be crossed is sufficient to deter some trade movements. Small producers in particular are reluctant to spend the time and effort for the great amount of red tape usually required for entering goods through customs.

the extent of governmental interference and its cost: an example

Although it is theoretically advantageous for countries to specialize in their production and to trade with one another, each making the best of its comparative strengths in resource endowments, we have found that there are many obstacles to trade. In addition to the barrier of distance, there are innumerable artificial stimuli to domestic production. Since the Second World War there has been a trend toward liberalization of trade in manufactured goods, but the restraints on agricultural movements remain one of the most nagging trade problems of recent years. In looking at this problem two questions arise: (1) just how great is the extent of this interference, and (2) what does it cost the countries affected?

The United States Department of Agriculture has reported on recent attempts to answer these questions. The first problem is one of measuring the *degree of protection* that countries are giving their farmers. In view of the variety of protectionist devices, how do we determine their net effect? The best answer so far seems to be to derive a single measure, an *equivalent tariff*, which serves as a composite of all kinds of trade barriers. One way of doing this for a particular country is to take the difference between the price received by farmers for a given commodity, that is, the producer price (P), and the price at which that item is bought or sold abroad, in other words, the trade price (T). Combining these in the following manner

$$\left(\frac{P-T}{P}\right)100$$

gives the percent of change that the producers' price undergoes when the commodity is traded. This change can presumably be attributed mainly to governmental interference. If the producers' price is higher than the trade price, then the resulting percent of change, or equivalent tariff, is a positive number, and by its magnitude, indicates the amount of trade protection that good receives. If the trade price is higher than the producers' price, the equivalent tariff is a negative number, indicating the absence of protection.

The Department of Agriculture study covered trade in a number of grain, livestock, and dairy products for Canada and the United States, and for Denmark, France, the Netherlands, the United Kingdom, West Germany, and Italy. Of the goods analyzed, the most heavily protected was milk products, for which the degree of protection ranged from 31 percent of the producers' price up to 62 percent. For the other commodities, protection was generally greater for importing countries than exporting countries (note that some countries are both exporters and importers). Wheat is fairly typical of these, except that, in the case of Italy, an unusually high degree of protection is given to both imports and exports. For commodities as a whole, the greatest amount of import protection was that provided by France and the Netherlands, both of which are members of the European Economic Community.

The USDA study also measured changes in the degree of protection of imports and exports by the six European countries in this group. It was found that these countries had greatly increased their protection of milk products in recent years. For example, the Netherlands had increased her equivalent tariff from −6 percent in 1950 to 45 percent in 1961 and Denmark's protection had gone from −3 percent to 35 percent. Significantly, it was found that many countries had joined this move toward more protection, presumably for reasons of retaliation.

How much did the people of those countries pay for protection of their farm exports and imports? The Department of Agriculture's study estimated these costs for all eight countries, this time including Canada and the United States, and discovered that it ranged as high as $81 million. Canada's protection cost was the least, but the European countries' costs were all in the upper range. Highest of all were Italy and West Germany, the latter case illustrating the political influence of Bavaria's large farm population. These outlays naturally represent a redistribution of income to the farmers of these countries.

The implications of the USDA study are that expansion of world trade in agricultural goods is threatened by a swelling tide of protectionism. This is a matter of grave importance to at least four of the countries studied—Canada, United States, the Netherlands, and Denmark—all of which rely heavily upon their earnings from agricultural exports. However, this matter more directly concerns consumers of the importing countries who must pay higher prices for their food, and the taxpayers of the producing countries that subsidize their exports.

EFFECTS OF TRADE ON THE FACTORS OF PRODUCTION

We have seen that trade between regions and countries is affected by their relative endowments in the factors of production. Like other systems, however, the trade system has its feedback effects. Trade affects the factors of production in two ways: (1) the prices of these factors—capital, labor, and land—may rise or fall; and (2) their relative quantities may expand or contract. But capital and labor have a certain amount of mobility, and if any movement of these should take place, still other changes are possible.

factor prices and quantities

The introduction of trade may affect the prices of factors of production in both the exporting and importing regions or countries. As trade begins, Country A exports the good that is intensive in the factor that is relatively abundant in that country. If the abundant factor happens to be agricultural land, perhaps corn will be the land-intensive commodity and thus becomes the exported good. The first effect of trade will be that the domestic price of corn rises in the exporting country, reflecting the new international terms of trade. Resources are progressively taken out of other industries in Country A and put into producing more corn. But as more and more land is transferred to corn the additional land becomes available to corn production at ever higher prices. Thus land, the intensive factor in corn production, becomes more costly in relation to capital and labor. Further reducing the return to capital and labor in this case is the fact that these factors are not needed in such large amounts in corn production as for, say, cotton textile manufacture.

The opposite happens in the importing country, Country B. Before trade took place Country B grew her own corn, even though her land was not very good for corn production. When trade begins B's resources are taken out of corn and transferred into production of the good in which B has a comparative advantage, labor-intensive textiles. Paradoxically, trade has reduced the return to the scarce factor, labor in the case of Country A and land in Country B. This sort of effect has been seen in the depressing of wages that occurred when labor-intensive goods were imported into labor-short Australia and Canada.

Ultimately with free trade we theoretically should expect the return to factors of production to become completely equalized in the trading nations. In other words, in all countries trading with one another wages for labor should be the same, interest rates should become standardized, and land should obtain the same rent. All differences would have been erased by trade. In reality, however, perfect conditions rarely exist and factor prices stop short of complete equalization. Ordinarily it is physically impossible to shift all resources from one line of production to another. Furthermore there are the barriers to commodity movements noted earlier. The existence of transport costs, tariffs, and other impediments to trade helps to maintain factor price differentials from being eliminated altogether.

It will have been noted that not only are factor prices affected by trade but so are the relative scarcity and abundance of factors in the trading nations. We have seen that when trade causes the abundant factor of land, labor, or capital to rise in price, there follows an increase in the quantity of that factor. At the same time the scarce factor, being in less demand, falls in price and decreases in quantity. Thus trade has caused increasing specialization and at the same time has tended to exaggerate the differences in factor quantities.

factor mobility

Earlier we observed that the factors are not entirely confined to one place. Capital, labor, and entrepreneurship are more or less mobile between regions and, with some limitations, between countries. Some forms of these factors have more mobility than others, especially internationally. In a previous section we saw that money capital is highly mobile and can even act as a substitute for trade when the latter is restrained by tariffs or other artificial impediments.

Another effect of interregional and international movements of factors is to produce some equalization of their prices: interest rates, wages, and salaries. For example capital will tend to seek the market where it will receive the highest interest rates. But when the new market becomes saturated with capital, interest rates at that location will fall. Meanwhile, the drain of capital from the old area will cause its interest rates to recover somewhat. In this way the return to factors tends to become equalized. Yet, once again, there are limitations on the amount of equalization that can take place. Complete mobility of capital and labor is seldom attained, even between regions of the same country, because of the impediments noted earlier.

RECOMMENDED READINGS

Balassa, Bela, "Tariff Reductions and Trade in Manufactures Among the Industrial Countries," *American Economic Review*, 56, No. 3 (June, 1966), 466–473.

Corden, W. M., *Recent Developments in the Theory of International Trade*. Princeton, N. J.: Princeton University Press, 1965.

Heller, H. Robert, *International Trade: Theory and Empirical Evidence*. Englewood Cliffs, N. J.: Prentice-Hall, 1968.

Kenen, Peter B., *International Economics*. Englewood Cliffs, N. J.: Prentice-Hall, 1964.

Kindleberger, Charles P., *Foreign Trade and the National Economy*. New Haven, Conn.: Yale University Press, 1962.

Ohlin, Bertil, *Interregional and International Trade*, (rev. ed.). Cambridge, Mass.: Harvard University Press, 1967.

Thoman, R. S., and E. C. Conkling, *Geography of International Trade*. Englewood Cliffs, N. J.: Prentice-Hall, 1967.

world trade patterns and dynamics

11

The trading scene is constantly changing. Flows between areas increase or decrease in volume, shift direction, or change composition. One reason for this is that the resource endowments of regions and countries do not remain constant through time, and comparative advantages therefore undergo considerable change. An area may experience an increase in the size of its labor force or some other change in its demographic makeup. There may be an accumulation of capital through savings, the discovery or depletion of resources, or an advance in technology affecting productive capacity. Change does not come at the same time or in equal measure to all places, however, and areal variations in production and consumption resulting from unequal rates of change can have important effects on trade. Trade problems often arise as a result of these differences, causing the development of a variety of techniques for attacking them.

TRADE AND GROWTH

Precisely how trade affects economic growth is something that is much disputed. But there is general agreement that trade plays a central part in the growth process and that the relationship between trade and growth is a reciprocal one. This is to be expected in view of the close interplay between production and consumption on the one hand, and trade on the other. Two aspects of growth are apparent in this context. First, there is the kind of growth that takes place through an increase in the available factors of production—additions to the supply of capital, labor, and arable land, for instance. Then there is the kind of growth that results from technological advances.

In the growth of a region, trade may lead the way for the rest of the economy, as it so frequently did during the nineteenth century. This was clearly the case in Canada, whose rapid growth occurred as her staple export industries expanded in answer to strong demand in other countries. Among those countries currently in the earlier stages of expansion, however, growth of the economy seems more often to precede trade growth. In other instances trade and economic growth appear to have gone hand in hand, with trade serving to balance production and consumption. This has characterized Japan's recent history.

growth and the propensity to trade

There is evidence that countries participate in trade to a changing degree as their economies grow. At the outset, when it is particularly important to the region, trade expands very rapidly. Thereafter the amount of trade tends to increase at a slower rate than that of the economy as a whole. In the later stages of economic growth there may be a relative decline in a region's trade as comparatively less emphasis is placed on goods than on services, most of the latter being provided locally.

The world economy has expanded at an exceptionally rapid pace since 1750, bringing fast growth to those countries able to participate in international trade. When a country's exports make their first successful entry into the world market the domestic economy is spurred to a quick expansion. This is particularly true where individual families have previously tended to be self-sufficient. Production for export requires specialization of production and an increasingly fine division of labor. At the same time the domestic market expands as money begins to circulate and incomes rise.

At the outset there is often a single staple export, such as cotton fibers in the early United States or cotton textiles in Britain. The effects spread quickly to other related industries, which likewise expand, as do transport facilities. This growth creates new needs, both in volume and diversity, many of which cannot be supplied locally, particularly industrial raw materials and machinery. At the same time, rising incomes make it possible for the country's citizens to demand a growing number of foreign-produced goods. All imported commodities are not equally favored by this growth in incomes, however. In accordance with Engel's law, families allocate smaller and smaller proportions of their additional income to purchases of foodstuffs and spend increasing amounts on manufactured products and services. These changes, of course, show up in the structure of imports.

Meanwhile, as larger quantities of certain imported goods are consumed in the country, entrepreneurs begin to see the feasibility of manufacturing these items locally. The consequence of this "demonstration effect," therefore, is the appearance of a growing number of factories making goods that have previously been imported. Such "import substitution" naturally reduces dependence on foreign supplies. In the end both exports and imports thus grow more diverse but both tend to become a smaller proportion of total income. This relative decline of trade dependence with maturation of the economy is further exaggerated as the population allocates increasing amounts of income for services.

growth through technology

The kind of growth that results from improved technology yields an increased output from the same amount of resources. Thus a new device, such as the mechanical reaper, the cotton gin, or the self-doffing spindle, frees large numbers of workers for other purposes, while at the same time expanding the volume of exportable product. Technological change has occurred at an accelerating pace in recent times, and this has had important effects on trade. Presenting a new technology to the world involves two related processes, *invention* and *innovation*. The more fundamental process is invention, which describes the conception of a basic idea, such as the steam engine. Innovation, on the other hand, is the application of that idea to something directly useful to man, such as the steam-powered textile mill.

Invention and innovation are highly uneven in their occurrence and impact. There seem always to be certain regions where innovation takes place much more rapidly than elsewhere, although this leadership has tended to remain with a particular country for only a limited time.

the trade effects of technology

A new production technology can create exports for a country, it can make possible a substitution for imports, or it can give rise to a new demand for imports. If a new product is developed and the originating country is able to retain exclusive control of its manufacture, perhaps through secrecy or because that country is more advanced technically, and if there is a widespread demand for this product in those lands that cannot make it, then the effect is the creation of trade. The United Kingdom acquired much of its trading strength through the development of such exports as railway equipment, steam engines, and mechanical pumps. The United States has led in producing and exporting aircraft, farm machinery, construction machinery, chemicals, and machine tools. Sometimes the innovation is merely a new method for making a familiar product, such as Britain's machine-made textiles, ships, and steel.

Thus technology may yield a product that people all over the world want to import. But sometimes it is possible for an importing country to use its technology to develop substitutes for products formerly imported, thereby reducing trade. The United States has been active in this type of invention and innovation, as shown by the large variety of substitutes that have been synthesized as replacements for natural products formerly obtained from abroad. Synthetic rubber and nylon are familiar examples. The effects of developments such as these are compounded when the technology is then transmitted throughout the world, reducing world trade in rubber, natural fibers, and other replaced commodities. It seems probable, however, that in general technology acts to expand trade. Evidence for this is the enormous increase in high-technology goods entering world trade.

Technology affects trade not only through new production techniques but also through improvements in communication and transportation. Because communication is essential to trade, anything that makes the transmission of information quicker, easier, or cheaper tends to facilitate the flow. Such developments as the overseas cable, telephone, telegraph and radio, and more recently, satellite communication, have had important results for world trade.

In the long run, the transport rate curve has trended steadily downward, at least in relative terms. This has contributed substantially to the gradual spread of trade to remote parts of the world. Numerous transport innovations such as the screw propeller, steel hulls, refrigeration equipment, and jet aircraft, have helped to bring down the cost and time required for moving both goods and people.

trade growth and the diffusion of innovation

As we have seen, one export industry tends to give rise to others and the effects are spread throughout the regional economy. Thus, in the United Kingdom, this diffusion began with the textile industry, then extended into other industries, such as iron, metal products, and coal. The impact does not remain confined to one country, but diffuses internationally as well. British investment moved into France, followed by technical aid and skilled workers, enabling that country to join the United Kingdom as a supplier to the world market. These developments quickly spread thereafter to other Western European countries, particularly Germany, Austria, Switzerland, and Italy.

The diffusion of ideas occurs in a variety of ways. Some ideas have reached new areas through the theft of technical secrets, as in the transfer of textile technology from Lancashire to New England during the early nineteenth century, thereby creating a new center from which textiles could be exported to the world in competition with the original center. The same result is achieved in a more open and legal fashion through licensing arrangements, the publishing of technical articles, and foreign education for technicians, engineers, and scientists. In earlier times colonization was conducive to the spread of ideas through the world, and the trade links that France and Britain still maintain with their former colonies testify to the durability of that avenue of communication. In recent years one of the most effective means for the rapid transfer of business and technical information has been the multinational corporation. An innovation developed in centrally located company laboratories can spread rapidly to corporate outlets in other parts of the world.

Another avenue for diffusion of trade has been through the foreign procurement of industrial raw materials and foodstuffs. As nineteenth-century Britain reached farther and farther afield for ore, timber, grains, animal products, and other needs, trade and economic growth were transferred to such suppliers as Spain, Sweden, Denmark, the Netherlands, Canada, and the United States. Eventually such distant regions as Australia, New Zealand, South Africa, and Argentina were brought into the British commercial orbit, to be followed later by suppliers of rubber, vegetable oils, and other tropical goods.

In the outward movement of particular types of production from centers of innovation there tends to be a certain selectivity that has been explained in terms of the "product cycle" of industrial development. Manufacture of a new product usually requires proportionally large numbers of engineers and skilled workers in what is at first a highly experimental and low-volume operation. Eventually manufacture becomes sufficiently routine for the introduction of mass production techniques that yield economies of scale. With less demanding skill requirements the product can now, in this second phase, be made in areas other than the center of innovation.

When the industry becomes fully mature, still more of the production can be assigned to highly specialized machines that require only unskilled operators. At this point the industry becomes strongly attracted to areas having a surplus of cheap labor.

The electronics industry is an example of this cyclical type of development (see Chapter 9). Much of the initial development of new electronic equipment occurs in such centers of innovation as eastern Massachusetts, but once production becomes standardized it does not remain in that location for long. Thus some of the first television picture tubes were built in the Boston area, but the mass production of television sets quickly became established in the American Midwest. More recently much of the television output has been transferred to border areas of Mexico and to Japan and Taiwan as the industry has entered its mature phase. The result, of course, has been for the sources of television exports to diffuse outward from the original center of innovation. In the absence of further discoveries in the original source areas, the ultimate effect would be to reduce trade based on technology and to leave as the dominant cause of trade simple comparative advantage in the factors of production. This appears to be happening in the motor car industry, which is growing most rapidly in those countries with the relatively low-cost labor, abundance of capital, and large domestic market for consumer durables required by this fully matured industry.

Leadership in invention and innovation has tended to concentrate in one particular region or country at a given time. This has provided the leader with an important competitive edge in the exportation of high-technology goods. The principal center of innovation must work hard to preserve this comparative advantage and must try to remain one step ahead of its competitors. In the past, no country has succeeded in retaining the technological lead permanently. In the beginning it was Britain that assumed first place in technology, a position she managed to hold without challenge until about 1850. Western Europe and the United States subsequently gained ascendency, with much of the basic science originating in Europe and applied technology originating in the United States. By the time of World War II, however, the United States had attained a commanding place in both invention and innovation.

the United States as an exporter of technology-intensive goods

In the years following the War the "technology gap" between the United States and its nearest rivals widened substantially, as shown by the excess of technology-intensive exports over technology-intensive imports. Intensity of technology in a given industry is measured by several indexes, including proportionate use of scientific and engineering manpower, numbers of skilled workers, and expenditures on research and de-

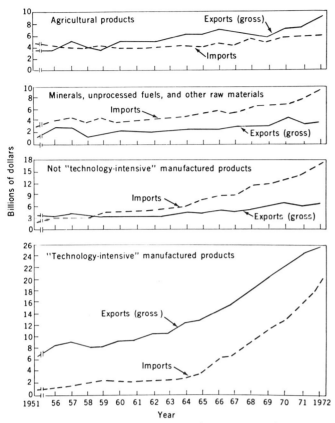

Fig. 11.1 *Changing structure of United States' trade. The United States has relied upon its trade surplus in high-technology manufactures to compensate for its trade deficit in low-technology manufactured goods; but, as this diagram shows, the nation may be losing this comparative advantage.*

Source: Deborah Shapley, "Technology and the Trade Crisis: Salvation through a New Policy?", Science, 179, No. 4076 (March 2, 1973), 881–83.

velopment. Some of the industries ranking high on this scale are chemicals, electrical machinery, electronics, nonelectrical machinery, transport equipment, scientific instruments, professional instruments, and controls.

Figure 11.1 demonstrates how importantly technology-intensive goods have contributed to the American balance of trade in recent times. The big surplus of exports over imports in this category has supported other major classes of trade that have done less well. For many years the country has had a deficit in its trade in raw materials (see Chapter 3), evidence of the insatiable appetite of American industry. Imports of low-technology manufactured products have likewise exceeded exports. A fourth category, agricultural commodities, has maintained a slight surplus, although this has varied from time to time, depending on world harvest conditions. Farm exports are vulnerable to protectionist policies of potential importing countries, particularly those of Western Europe, where tariffs, quotas, and high subsidies to farmers have raised difficult barriers for American agricultural exports to surmount.

Something else shown by Figure 11.1 is that the surplus of United States technology-intensive trade is narrowing. Does this mean that the country is losing its lead in technology? Although the excess of exports over imports in this vital class remained very substantial until 1965, high-technology imports have since been rising much faster than exports, especially in 1971 and 1972. The progressive shrinking of this cushion has contributed to a worsening American balance of trade (Fig. 11.2). Total exports of the United States exceeded imports by a comfortable $6 billion in 1965, but by 1971 this surplus had been converted into a deficit of $1.5 billion. According to preliminary trade figures for 1972, this deficit has since increased alarmingly to $5.9 billion, aggravating an overall gap of $8 billion in the country's balance of payments, which includes all of its transactions with the world at large.

Apparently the American lead in basic science is still fairly intact, but the nation's dominance in applied technology seems to be slipping away. In large measure

Fig. 11.2 *United States balance of trade, 1955–1971, with the world and with Japan. The growing deficit in United States world trade during the early 1970s can be attributed to a worsening balance of trade with Japan.*

Source: Statistical Abstract of the United States (Washington, D.C.: U.S. Government Printing Office).

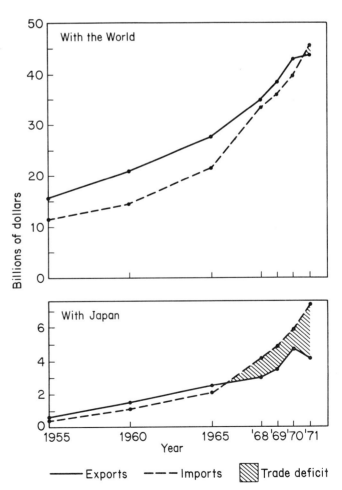

this can be attributed to a general modern tendency for a drastic decrease in the time required for diffusion of innovation. Nevertheless, there are several special reasons why the United States may be relinquishing this vital advantage in world commerce. One is a weakening of the country's competitive position because of failure to apply its technology adequately to cutting production costs as well as to developing new products. Lack of attention to production technology has permitted wage costs to soar as labor productivity declined. Inflation in the United States, while no greater than in most other industrial countries, has contributed to an overvaluation of the dollar in relation to Japanese and European currencies, whose exchange rates had been set during the abnormal period of their postwar reconstruction.

Meanwhile, the affluent American public has acquired increasingly expensive tastes for sporty imported motor cars, high-style European-made clothing, electronic appliances, and other foreign merchandise. Even as this excess of demand was building up in the United States, technology-intensive industries were expanding rapidly in Western Europe and Japan, especially the latter (see Chapter 17). The combined effects of these events are graphically apparent in America's rapidly widening trade deficit with Japan (Fig. 11.2).

Another factor contributing to this apparent deterioration in United States high-technology trade is the growing tendency for American firms to shift their output abroad, thereby accelerating the spread of innovation. As noted earlier, multinational corporations undertake locational decisions from a global perspective, and the outcome usually turns on objective considerations of comparative advantage rather than concern for any one country's balance-of-payments position. Partially compensating for this, of course, are the substantial returns on overseas investments. For the United States repatriated business profits amounted to $7 billion in 1969.

Finally, there is little leadership in scientific development emanating from Washington at this time. Unlike most of her principal competitors, especially Japan (Chapter 17), the United States allocates comparatively minor governmental assistance to research and development. Indeed, the federal budget for 1974 contained sharply reduced amounts for research, and at the same time the post of scientific advisor to the president was abolished.

The American position is decidedly weaker in some kinds of technology-intensive products than others, as Figure 11.3 illustrates. The poorest performance is in those industries in the maturer phases of the production cycle. One of these is motor vehicle manufacturing, a very large and important industry in the United States. According to Figure 11.3 the American trade deficit in automobiles has reached great proportions and is still increasing. Although United States manufacturers have been attempting to automate motor car production, others have been automating much faster, especially the Japanese. Several other lines of production have had

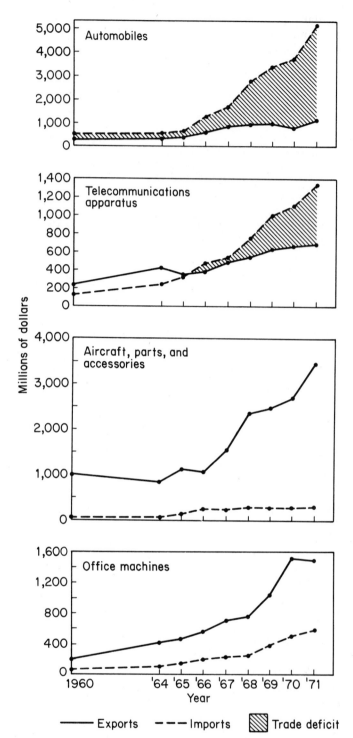

Fig. 11.3 *United States balance of trade in automobiles, telecommunications, aircraft, and office machines.*
These four trade categories are important constituents of the "technology-intensive" manufactured goods shown in Figure 11.1. Note the importance of export earnings from aircraft and office machines (including computers) and the growing trade deficit in automobiles and telecommunications (including radios and television sets).

Source: Statistical Abstract of the United States *(Washington, D.C.: U.S. Government Printing Office).*

similar experiences, including a major segment of the electronics industry (combined under the heading "telecommunications apparatus" in the figure). Here again it is the maturer phases of production within the industry that have moved to Japan and elsewhere.

The situation is more promising for the United States in the most sophisticated high-technology industries, such as computer manufacture. Although official import figures do not list computers separately, the trade performance of the general category "office machines" (Fig. 11.3) in large measure reflects the continued world dominance of American computer manufacturers. An even greater contribution is made by the aircraft industry, whose sales abroad have risen rapidly in recent years (Fig. 11.3). Some uneasiness for the future of this industry is being expressed, however, since the most advanced new designs are currently being developed in Europe.

Growing public concern over the perceived danger to the United States foreign trade position in technology-intensive goods has brought several proposed solutions, most of these calling for governmental action. For example, it has been suggested that a national office to foster advanced technology be established for the purpose of allocating scientific and technical manpower, currently being used most ineffectually, and making an inventory of United States technology, industry by industry. A further recommendation is to tighten patent laws to avoid premature loss of technology to competing nations. Tax incentives and low-interest loans and grants for business and university research are still other governmental initiatives proposed. Perhaps of equal importance, however, is the suggestion that manufacturers of technology-intensive goods be induced to design their products to conform more specifically with foreign demand and to give a more global emphasis to their marketing efforts, following the Japanese and German examples.

America's problems with sustaining a positive trade balance in technology-intensive goods illustrate not only the vital role of technology in world trade but also the fragile nature of trade based upon a lead in innovation. Preserving a technological lead is difficult, but doubtlessly even more trying is the problem of the lagging region or underdeveloped country that is striving to narrow the technology gap separating it from more advanced producers. Less developed countries generally lack the research and development funds, skilled technicians, professional, scientific, and engineering personnel required to invent and innovate. Instead, they are reduced to copying the techniques of the leaders. Often, by the time production in a new line can get underway, the more highly developed countries have already perfected a better way of making the product or have moved on to a superior replacement for it.

TRADE AND THE LAGGING REGION

There are many respects in which the trade experience of underdeveloped countries differs from that of advanced countries, and indeed it seems likely that the circumstances facing today's newer nations are unlike those that confronted the presently advanced countries when they were beginning their growth. The evidence seems to suggest that the benefits of trade, so obvious in the case of advanced countries, are not so automatic for underdeveloped ones. The important question is why that should be so. What is there about today's newly developing countries that is so different from yesterday's? If there is such a difference, can we apply the same theories of trade to both? The matter is complicated further by the fact that the kind of trade that takes place between developed and underdeveloped countries is not like that which occurs among the underdeveloped nations.

Before attempting to answer these questions, however, it should be noted that underdeveloped countries are not a homogeneous group. Development is a relative matter; the countries of the world can be arrayed along a scale of development that extends from the most advanced nations to the most backward, with the great majority scattered between. Those which are considered underdeveloped can be conveniently divided into two groups: the *developing* and the *backward* countries. Those classified as developing have all the usual traits of "underdevelopedness," such as low per capita incomes, high proportion of the labor force in agriculture, high birth rates, high population growth rates, low literacy rates, and so on. Despite this, however, they appear to have a real capability for the sustained growth required to become at some time advanced countries. The *backward* countries, on the other hand, are saddled with all the typical problems of underdevelopment, but in addition they seem to be confronted with so many serious obstacles for development that there is little immediate hope for advancement beyond their present subsistence economies.

trade problems of underdeveloped countries

We have seen how in the beginning trade served as a vehicle for growth for those countries now regarded as technically advanced. The lead having been assumed by a particular center, Britain, there was an outpouring of capital, labor, and entrepreneurship, as well as goods, from that center to such countries as Canada, the United States, and Australia, whose economic development rapidly followed. Today's less developed countries, however, have a different set of problems affecting their growth and the role of trade in that growth.

excessive dependence on a limited range of primary exports

One of the most difficult problems for the developing countries is their overspecialization in export production. Many such countries rely upon only one or two commodities, usually agricultural goods or minerals, for nine-tenths or more of their export earnings. Barbados, for example, obtains at least ninety-five percent of her foreign exchange from the sale of sugar and sugar products. Honduras and Costa Rica depend upon just two crops, coffee and bananas, for most of their overseas earnings. Theoretically such specialization should be beneficial to a country because of the high level of efficiency and the economies of large-scale production this makes possible. For exporters of primary goods, however, this is not usually the case. Excessive specialization in this instance risks heavy losses due to crop failures, uncertain demand abroad, and price fluctuations. Another problem of primary producers is the temptation to increase output even during those periods when the world market is saturated and prices are falling. Farmers, seeing their incomes decline as unit prices drop, are inclined to plant still larger acreages in the hope of making up their losses with increased volume. This response is directly opposite to that of factory managers when faced with surpluses and falling prices.

foreign ownership and control

Primary export industries of less developed countries are frequently owned by outsiders. Typical is plantation agriculture, which is prevalent in the sugar, banana, and rubber industries. Not only does capital come from abroad but so do the managers, while the unskilled labor that these highly modern enterprises require is obtained locally. Side by side with such enclaves of commercial agriculture is the traditional subsistence agriculture practiced by the majority of the indigenous population. This juxtaposition of the primitive and the modern is referred to as a "dual economy," examples of which are to be found throughout tropical America, Africa, and southern Asia (see Chapters 19, 20, and 22).

traditional social structure

In the organization of their societies most of today's less developed nations differ from those lands colonized by Europeans, especially the British. Unlike the transplanted Europeans of the early United States, the current populations of less developed regions lack an industrial tradition. Most have inherited social attitudes and value systems that are incompatible with the competitive, profit-oriented attitudes prevalent in advanced societies. Because of this it is difficult for such peoples to adjust to the changes required for modern production. The less developed countries of this present era are also confronted with grave demographic and employment problems. Among other problems, overpopulation, which is daily worsening due to high birth rates, creates a surplus of labor, resulting in severe unemployment and underemployment. None of these problems was encountered by the current group of technically advanced nations.

So different, then, are the less developed countries as a whole than nations at the other end of the develop-mental scale that we must ask whether the trade theory that is customarily applied to the developed nations has any relevance to the underdeveloped nations. According to this theory, free trade is invariably beneficial to all participants. Evidence that this may not necessarily be so is suggested by the almost universal use by less developed countries of a wide range of trade restrictions. Classical comparative cost theory would relegate the less developed countries to a permanent role as suppliers of primary goods to the advanced countries, would prevent their industrialization, and thus hamper their economic growth. This is a fate that few nations would willingly accept. Let us look more closely at the trading relations of less developed countries and see how theory has to be modified to cover their case.

trade between developing and developed countries

Of the enormous volume of merchandise now flowing in world trade only a fraction moves between underdeveloped and advanced countries; yet, relatively small though it be, this trade is exceedingly important to the poorer nations. For the underdeveloped countries the industrial nations are the only source for certain needs and the only important market for their traditional exports. These imports and exports are indispensable to the development process itself.

import needs of less developed nations

Among the imports required by underdeveloped countries are those consumer goods that such nations are not capable of providing for themselves through domestic production. Equally important, however, are those commodities required for economic growth, which include all sorts of machinery and other capital equipment needed to modernize agriculture and to build factories, supplies of spare parts and other items to keep the machinery running, and industrial raw materials not available domestically. Many of the industries thus established produce goods formerly imported and their output is therefore described as *import substitution*.

exports to advanced countries

To pay for these imports underdeveloped countries must sell their own goods in the world market. These are, of course, the primary commodities for which the poorer countries have both absolute and comparative advantages. The nature of these goods is dictated by the resources they may possess, such as soils and climatic conditions conducive to the raising of, say, bananas. It should be noted that the less developed countries are classified as primary producers because they export only primary products. The industrialized nations such as Canada, United States, Soviet Union, and France actually export greater amounts of primary commodities, mainly grains and other temperate agricultural commodities.

In exporting primary goods to the advanced countries, the underdeveloped regions operate under severe disadvantages. For one thing, manufacturers are becoming increasingly efficient in their use of raw materials today and are processing them more thoroughly, thus requiring relatively smaller amounts of these items, many of which come from underdeveloped areas. Moreover, there is greater use of synthetic raw materials that compete with the natural substances. The one exception is petroleum, the need for which is growing steadily and rapidly in the developed nations. Otherwise the share of less developed countries in world exports is shrinking relatively; it now stands at about one-fifth of the total and is declining.

Another tenacious problem is that the demand for agricultural commodities and certain other primary goods grows very slowly (owing to Engel's law) and responds only slightly to changes in prices. The world supply of these commodities continues to fluctuate widely, however, and prices therefore tend to remain unstable. At the same time, less developed countries are individually weak and disunited and thus unable to influence prices of their commodities in world markets. Instead such prices are set in the great commodity markets of London, New York, Chicago, and other industrial centers. A notable exception is petroleum, as we shall see in a subsequent section.

Underdeveloped countries as a group do export some manufactured goods and the volume of this trade is rising, but at a rate substantially below that of the world as a whole. Most of the manufactured goods exported by less developed countries are of a technically simple nature, usually the first-stage processing of metallic ores. Although some of these countries do make more sophisticated manufactured goods, there are several deterrents to their exporting these to advanced countries. First is the technological gap, which makes it difficult for less developed countries to compete on equal terms with the superior quality and lower prices of commodities produced elsewhere. Another problem is the lack of home market of sufficient size to provide the basis for economies of scale in production of these goods. Added to these difficulties is the natural inefficiency of newly started industries, including their initial high unit costs. Finally, there is a lack of familiarity among producers in less developed lands concerning the standards of quality, delivery schedules, and normal sales channels prevailing in major world markets.

the balance of payments

Most underdeveloped countries are troubled with chronic deficits in their foreign trade. Because of the problems just noted, exports are usually insufficient to pay for all the imports required both to sustain a country and to support its developmental needs. On this account there is much interference by governments in the trade of developing countries. Import restrictions of many kinds are used, especially licensing, exchange controls, and tariffs. These are needed to limit the total amount of expenditures and to reduce the importation of "inessentials" so as to husband scarce exchange needed for necessary items. Tariffs are used to improve the price ratio (terms of trade) with advanced countries, whenever this can be done without retaliation, and to protect infant industries. The protection of infant industries is especially important because a variety of industry is required to provide the kind of agglomeration advantages needed to attract still other industries and reach self-sustaining growth.

Among underdeveloped countries, those that can be classified as "developing" probably have the most pressing current import needs, but the "backward" countries possibly have the gravest trade problems. Trade with advanced countries can quickly extinguish any unprotected import-competing industry that might have served as a basis for development, as happened when cheap imports killed much of the cottage industry of India. In many backward countries the obstacles to development are so great that even a large export income fails to nudge the nation toward advancement. This problem is common among some of the oil-exporting countries of the Middle East.

trade among underdeveloped countries

Only a tiny fraction, from 5 to 7 percent, of world trade takes place among the less developed group. Nevertheless, the opportunities for such trade appear attractive. The nature of demand and supply are much alike in countries at similar levels of development; and having economies of similar size, they are able to trade and compete with each other on more nearly equal terms. Free trade is more feasible and a traditional trade theory becomes appropriate once more. One of the benefits cited for trade among underdeveloped countries is the opportunity this offers for them to increase their exports and thereby achieve economies of scale. Their industries can be made more efficient by the stimulus of this competition among equals. Moreover, it can reduce the needs for imports from advanced countries. That is to say, the developing countries can supply each other with those simpler commodities they are capable of producing and thus save the foreign exchange needed for unavoidable purchases from advanced countries.

The problem with this is that often underdeveloped countries are actually too similar to one another. This is especially true of neighboring countries, whose traditional primary exports are frequently so much alike that they do not need one another's wares. In some parts of Latin America, for example, every country exports sugar. What is needed, then, is to foster trade among developing countries in new types of production, especially manufactured goods, which vary much more widely. One solution for this problem is an arrangement called regional integration.

TRADE AND REGIONAL INTEGRATION

The idea of joining sovereign nations together to form a single economic region is not new; this was tried a number of times more than a century ago. But since World War II the technique has been eagerly revived as a means for overcoming the many problems of disintegration that had burdened Europe during the 1930s as well as a means of speeding recovery from the war. Integration has been called a form of "selective discrimination," since it combines some aspects of free trade with greater protection: free trade for its members and a common trade barrier to nonmembers. Regional economic integration comes in several types and degrees and it may or may not cover all activities in the countries of the union.

The aims of integration may go well beyond mere trade considerations. Among its main purposes, integration is intended to achieve economic growth through formation of an enlarged market, attain higher standards of living, solve problems of regional disparities, enhance the standing of member countries in world political councils, and gain a number of social and other noneconomic ends. The subject of integration is one of the more complex aspects of trade and we shall confine our attention here to examining the various degrees of integration, the factors that are expected to contribute to the success of union, some of the effects of integration on members and on the world at large, and the role of integration as a device for overcoming the problems of less developed countries.

organizational arrangements and characteristics

According to one classification scheme, five different levels or degrees of integration are possible. The first three are well represented in various parts of the world today, while elements of the other two are implied in the organizational arrangements of some existing unions or in their future plans.

types of integration

First and least restrictive of all is the *free trade area,* whose members agree to remove all tariffs and other barriers to trade within the group but continue to pursue their own independent trade policies with respect to nonmembers. The next higher degree of integration is referred to as the *customs union,* a much favored type of integration in the past. It calls for the free movement of goods among member countries but erects a common protective wall against outsiders. The third type is the *common market,* which, like the customs union, provides for free trade in merchandise among the group while maintaining uniform restraints against trade with nonmembers, but in addition permits unrestricted movement of capital and labor within the union. At a still higher level the *economic union* has all the char-

acteristics of the common market plus a provision for integrating matters of economic policy among member countries. The ultimate form is termed full *economic integration.* At this point all barriers to intrabloc movements of goods and the factors of production have been eliminated; there is complete unification of social as well as economic policies; and all members are subject to the binding decisions of a supranational authority, which includes executive, judicial, and legislative branches.

One of the earlier examples of a free trade area was the nineteenth-century attempt by Sweden and Norway, which was eventually dissolved. Some of the first customs unions, however, produced more lasting results. One of these was the German *Zollverein,* which joined together most of the many small kingdoms and grand duchies that eventually became modern Germany. Also still in existence are several "customs accessions." These are customs unions that unite a very small country with a larger one. Examples are Switzerland and Liechtenstein, France and Monaco, and Belgium and Luxembourg.

The modern movement toward integration began in 1944 with the formation of Benelux, a customs union that was intended later to become an economic union. Included were Belgium, the Netherlands, and Luxembourg. A short time later these three were joined by France, West Germany, and Italy to form the European Coal and Steel Community. The ECSC is a type of common market whose jurisdiction is restricted to two related sectors of the six national economies, namely their coal and steel industries. Interestingly, however, the ECSC has an organizational arrangement that includes executive, judicial, and legislative functions. Both Benelux and the ECSC were immediately successful and the same six countries agreed in 1957 to unification of all sectors of their economies. The result was the European Economic Community (EEC), basically a common market (and usually referred to as the European Common Market) but with a supranational authority and economic and social policy aims that foreshadow a much higher form of integration. Seven other countries—the United Kingdom, Norway, Sweden, Denmark, Austria, Switzerland, and Portugal (later joined by Finland, and more recently by Iceland)—thereupon formed a free trade area called the European Free Trade Association (EFTA). Finally, after a long period of intermittent negotiations with the six founding nations of the EEC, Britain, together with Denmark and Ireland, joined that organization on January 1, 1973. On that same date Denmark and the United Kingdom also withdrew from the EFTA, which is now left with seven members. Meanwhile the new nine-member EEC has signed a free trade agreement with those countries still remaining in the EFTA.

These postwar experiments in regional integration appear to have achieved many of the aims intended for them, especially the EEC. Because of this success, they have been much copied in other parts of the world, including Africa, the Middle East, and especially Latin America.

requirements for success from union

From a theoretical standpoint the best results can be expected from a union of countries whose economies are similar than countries whose economies are dissimilar. If member countries have the capability of producing the same goods in competition with each other they will be forced by union to become more efficient in their methods.

Greater benefits can also be expected from a union of countries which are not separated from one another by long distances. Propinquity reduces transport cost, increases the likelihood that the tastes of constituent populations will be similar, and is conducive to a greater knowledge of business opportunities. Ideally, member countries should be contiguous to one another and comprise a combined territory of compact shape in order to reduce total aggregate transfer costs. The total area of the union should be sufficiently large to permit diverse production and a division of labor. Each member is likely to experience relatively greater gains, however, if the countries are individually small, since this provides greater room for improvement with enlargement of the market. Probability of success is further increased if member countries prior to union (1) were one another's best customers and principal suppliers, (2) previously contributed in the aggregate a substantial proportion of the world's output and trade, and (3) were formerly prevented from trading freely with one another because of high tariff barriers.

Both the EEC and the EFTA have progressed markedly since integration; but the EEC has made the more impressive gains. At the time of its formation, the Common Market (EEC) was expected to do well because member countries had resources that complemented each other—France and Luxembourg with iron ore, Germany with coal, Italy with surplus labor, and Belgium and the Netherlands with their large output of intensively produced food crops. In actuality, however, the Common Market countries have proved to be highly competitive in most of their output. They have not relied importantly on one another's minerals, labor, or food supplies but instead have tended to exchange large quantities of finished and semifinished manufactured goods. All six countries make iron and steel, fabricate metal products, and produce an enormous variety of consumer goods.

Although individual EEC members are small or moderate in size, together they comprise a large part of Europe. They are mainly contiguous and are linked by well developed transport systems. The group includes some of the world's greatest trading nations, most of whom are one another's best customers. All nine have a high degree of dependence upon trade, especially the Benelux countries, where nearly two-fifths of total output is exported. This contrasts with pre–World War II days, when intra-European trade was much reduced by high tariffs and national policies of self-sufficient production.

The remaining EFTA countries are fairly complementary in the goods they produce and they also range more widely than the EEC in levels of economic development. Scandinavia exports forest products and minerals, as well as manufactured goods; Switzerland and Austria are principally manufacturing nations; while Portugal and Iceland are largely primary producers. Unlike the EEC, the EFTA countries tend to be widely separated, and the group as a whole occupies locations peripheral to the European continent. There are important trading nations in the group, although they are not the equals of most EEC members. Union has benefited the EFTA as a whole; but it is interesting to note that the greatest relative gains have gone to the Scandinavian members, which are contiguous, highly competitive with one another, and similar in many other respects. Significantly, the four Scandinavian countries have agreed to form a more highly integrated group (while still remaining within EFTA) called *Nordek,* or Nordic Economic Union.

effects of integration on trade and location

trade creation and diversion

One of the fundamental tests of integration is whether it has tended to create trade that did not exist before or has acted to divert trade out of its natural channels. This is a normative view of the problem, since the presumption is that trade creation is "good" while trade diversion is "bad." A union is said to have created trade if integration has resulted in shifting production from high-cost to low-cost sources. Trade diversion involves a shift from low-cost to higher-cost suppliers. Trade creation thus results in a more efficient allocation of world resources, while trade diversion has the opposite effect.

Any increase in trade among union members resulting from removal of internal trade barriers can be considered creation of new trade. This comes about in exactly the same way as the case illustrated previously in Figures 10.3 and 10.5, where the initiating of trade between countries permitted buyers to obtain savings and sellers to increase their incomes. Countries that do not belong to the union, however, tend to lose some of their former exports, for these are taken over by suppliers from countries within the group. To the extent that the old sources of supply were more efficient producers than the new ones in the bloc, trade diversion has taken place. In the long run, however, integration can result in trade gains even for nonmember countries if the union causes members to enjoy accelerated economic growth and thus demand more products from the rest of the world. Depending upon the way in which trade gains and trade losses balance each other, therefore, integration can result in either a net gain in total world trade or a net loss.

How these influences have operated in practice is shown by the experience of Western Europe. The total trade of the EEC countries has grown at an accelerated rate since union. The largest share of this new trade is with other EEC members, which of course, represents trade creation; but trade between the EEC and the rest of the world has risen sharply because EEC prosperity has increased the general level of demand in member countries. Yet when we look at the trade in specific commodities we can see that the EEC has caused some trade diversion. This is especially true of agricultural goods, which have been subjected to a uniformly high level of protection by EEC. Trade data show that Denmark, a traditional supplier of foodstuffs to neighboring West Germany, lost much of that trade after formation of the union and before her belated entry into the group. Presumably the Netherlands, a founding member that competes with Denmark in those same farm products, gained at least some of what Denmark lost in shipments to Germany. Sales of wheat by the United States to the EEC have also suffered because of the new tariffs, while French wheat producers have been able to pick up additional sales from their secure position inside the tariff wall. Many other farm products similarly have been affected, as have certain manufactured goods.

production and consumption effects

Removing the barriers to intrabloc trade should permit each member country to concentrate on producing those goods for which its comparative advantage is greatest. This specialization, together with increased competition and the economies of large-scale production for an enlarged market, could be expected to make producers more efficient. Reduced prices and higher incomes, together with a greater variety of merchandise on store shelves and more efficient distribution of goods, should raise levels of consumption.

The European experiments in integration tend to bear out these theoretical expectations, but not quite in the way anticipated. Studies of trade among members of the EEC and EFTA indicate that there has not been an increased specialization of one country in steel, another in grain, another in textiles, and so forth. Instead these industries have pretty well remained where they were before union, while there has been a marked change in the location of production in certain subcategories. This suggests that regional concentration has indeed occurred but that it has taken the form of *intraindustry* specialization. Thus, even though all Common Market countries make steel, one may emphasize sheet steel products and another, structural steel members.

locational effects

From the world perspective, a high common tariff wall would be expected to discourage some imports from former suppliers outside the union. One reaction to this is for the foreign supplier to build factories inside union territory in order to get under the tariff wall with his goods, thus substituting capital for trade. This has been confirmed by the enormous investment by United States companies in manufacturing facilities within the EEC and EFTA countries.

Because integration brings a free flow of goods among member countries, it is anticipated that a certain relocation of production may occur within the union itself. First there is likely to be an increased tendency for related industries to cluster together at a limited number of the most desirable locations, thereby eliminating production in less viable locations remaining from the pre-integration period when each country tended to make everything, however inefficiently. These areas of industrial agglomeration will then exert an increasingly strong attraction to newly established industries and thereby cause an even greater polarization of production. Studies of industrial location in the European Common Market countries since integration show this to have been the case; in fact, industrial concentration in certain favored locations has intensified. The net locational result therefore appears to be an increase in both intraindustry product specialization and regional specialization.

noneconomic effects

It was openly declared by many of the signatories to the Treaty of Rome, which authorized formation of the EEC, that the ultimate aim of the European Common Market should be a United States of Europe. Past experience lent credence to these expectations. The *Zollverein* or customs union of the eighteenth century German states had been quickly followed by political unification and the establishment of imperial Germany, and the customs union of South African colonies evolved into the modern Republic of South Africa.

Members of the tightly integrated EEC have cooperated in a number of social ventures, such as the establishment of schools and technical institutes as well as certain types of social legislation. The social effects of freer movement of peoples within the enlarged territory of the union have also been important, especially the migrations of Italian workers to West Germany and Belgium.

growth effects

One of the prime purposes of integration is to accelerate the growth of member countries, which is expected to result from greater efficiencies in resource use. This growth creates additional demand, which attracts both domestic and foreign investors. There should also be increased expenditures for research and development as domestic firms grow in size and capital strength; this of course, implies rising incomes. The lessons of these growth effects by the unions of technically advanced countries in Western Europe were not lost on the less developed countries or on the Communist countries of Eastern Europe.

trade, integration, and development

With active encouragement from the United Nations, less developed nations in several parts of the world have begun experiments in regional integration. The domestic markets in less developed countries, however, are severely limited by low per capita purchasing power and by the fact that often only a fraction of the population actually participate in the commercial economy. The subsistence part of a dual economy provides an insignificant market for most types of merchandise. Even in the commercial sector of the economy a high proportion of the labor force is usually engaged in agriculture. Because neighboring underdeveloped countries often export the same primary goods, they usually have little trade with one another prior to integration. Less than one-tenth of all Latin American trade, for example, is among the Latin American countries themselves.

In these circumstances integration is undertaken for somewhat different purposes by less developed countries than advanced ones. Although growth is an important goal of union in either case, among the less developed countries it is the main reason for integration. Integration offers developing countries an attractive means for simultaneously solving two trade problems. It provides an opportunity for engaging in free trade with other countries who are at similar levels of development and thus able to compete on equal terms and it serves as a technique for trading with advanced countries without suffering damage from their superior economic power.

the effects of union on the trade of developing countries

The gains from integration are similar for developing countries and advanced countries, with some important differences. First of all, less developed countries have possibilities for proportionately greater benefits if only because they have so much further to go. In addition to the opportunities to develop individual manufacturing specialties and trading these with other members, there are chances for improving the allocation of resources through union, especially manpower, which is usually employed wastefully or not used at all. Union offers producers the opportunity to operate their facilities at full capacity and to gain instant economies of scale from the enlarged market, while the intensified competition forces them to become more efficient.

With union, individual countries no longer have to think about developing a full range of economic activities, something that is difficult to manage. It becomes unnecessary for each country to acquire every major type of production, so long as all the members of the union can manage it together. The likelihood of this is increased by the fact that there are greater

probabilities that at least one member has the right combination of resources for efficient production of a given commodity.

The problem of trade creation and diversion is a critical one for experiments in integration among advanced countries, but it assumes a different complexion among less developed ones. For the latter, the all-important consideration is the effect of integration upon growth. Trade creation is still regarded as "good"; but trade diversion is no longer considered to be necessarily "bad." It is true that when less developed countries acquire import-competing activities, this represents a diversion of trade away from advanced countries; but these activities serve the much needed function of freeing foreign exchange for the purchase from those advanced countries of the high-technology machinery and other capital goods essential to growth—commodities that only the advanced countries offer.

Certain special problems complicate the integration attempts of less developed countries. For members to acquire individual manufacturing specialties as a basis for intrabloc trade, they must agree on the specific role of each country; but such agreement is difficult to achieve. Indeed, one of the principal obstacles to cooperation of any kind among developing countries is excessive nationalism, often reinforced by traditional rivalries between neighboring lands and by other considerations of national self-interest. The benefits of integration to developing nations, as well as its many problems, are illustrated by the experience of the Central American Common Market, to be described in Chapter 20.

other integration efforts

Many unions have been proposed or established throughout the world—in the Americas, Africa, Asia, Oceania, and Communist Europe. Some of these are as follows.

non—Communist groups

The Central American Common Market is only one part of the ambitious overall plan promoted by the United Nations Economic Commission for Latin America. The ultimate goal was a wider grouping that would integrate all the lands south of the Rio Grande into a single Latin American common market. In addition to the CACM, another regional bloc is the Latin American Free Trade Association (LAFTA), which includes the countries of South America plus Mexico.

Although its members need this kind of help for their many trade problems, LAFTA has had grave difficulties. Little trade has taken place among these countries, either before or since union, except for some modest exchanges in particular instances. In part, this lack of trade is attributable to the great distances separating the economically active parts of these countries, which are typically confined to the coastal margins of the continent. The LAFTA countries have generally been competitive with one another in their principal exports and have found it difficult to harmonize differing monetary policies, tariffs, and exchange controls. They have also been unable to agree on an assignment of manufacturing specialties among the membership.

While LAFTA has struggled with these problems, a regional organization has recently begun to form along the west coast of South America. This Andean Group, comprising Venezuela, Colombia, Ecuador, Peru, Bolivia, and Chile, operates within the broader framework of LAFTA. Another integration experiment in the Western Hemisphere is an association of island nations in the West Indies, which have attempted at various times to form a customs union.

Efforts elsewhere include two groups that have formed ties in the Middle East and North Africa, a federation of former British colonies in East Africa, and a free trade area initiated by Australia and New Zealand. For a variety of reasons little concrete progress has been made by these organizations.

Finally, there has been a fairly successful sectoral approach to integration in the case of the Canada–United States automobile agreement. This is essentially a free trade area limited to the components and products of a single giant industry. Free movement of these items between the countries is permitted only for the manufacturers themselves; customers cannot transport cars or parts across the border without paying duty. The arrangement has generally benefited the automobile industry, especially in Canada, where it is now possible to concentrate on long production runs of a limited number of models and thus gain important economies of scale that the small market in that country would not otherwise justify.

the Communist countries

The Communist Council for Mutual Economic Assistance (CMEA), or Comecon as it is usually called, is an association comprising the Soviet Union and most of the other Communist countries of Eastern Europe, with the addition of Outer Mongolia, a pastoral state lying partly between Siberia and China. Comecon is ostensibly a form of regional integration, but it necessarily differs from any of those described previously owing to the peculiar role of trade in Marxist countries. As with all economic matters, trade is subject to a number of ideological and political considerations. First, there is the Marxist labor theory of value, which tends to exaggerate the role of labor as a factor of production and to underrate the place of capital (even though the latter is essential to development). Second, because of a deep suspicion of the rest of the world, the Communist countries have strived for as close an approach to national self-sufficiency, or *autarky,* as possible. In the case of the Soviet Union this is very nearly attainable because of the unusually varied resources of that large country (see Chapter 18).

Despite this goal, however, trade with other countries is unavoidable, even for the USSR. For Communist nations the principal function of such trade is to solve problems of imbalance. It is frequently necessary to import raw materials and products that cannot be produced domestically or are in temporary short supply because of errors in planning, crop failures, or other unexpected events. There is also the need to import capital goods needed to commence manufacture of new products. At the same time, it is necessary to export surpluses to earn the exchange needed to pay for imports. Naturally this kind of trading is highly erratic. The ultimate purpose, from an ideological standpoint, is to permit the growth required to reach still higher levels of autarky.

When first established during the early post–World War II days, Comecon was not regarded as integration. It was designed originally to remake the Eastern European economies in the Stalinist mold, which meant striving for autarky for individual members. This scheme failed and in 1958 Comecon was reorganized by Khrushchev. The goal of autarky was dropped, mutual trade among the Soviet bloc was fostered, and some exchange with Western Europe was permitted.

Grave problems remain, however. There are wide disparities in level of development and size and much dissatisfaction with the individual roles assigned to members. As a consequence, intrabloc trade has not been greatly enhanced by the union. Ironically, trade with non–Communist countries has been rising rapidly, especially with Western Europe, with whom the eastern countries have many complementarities in resource endowments, a traditional basis for east-west exchanges in Europe since early times.

other types of trade groups

In the early postwar period countries tended to be arranged into trade groups according to the major currency used for international exchange among them, as for example, the Sterling Bloc and the Dollar Bloc, which have since largely disappeared. In the past there have also been strong trade ties among members of the British Commonwealth and within a similar grouping known as the French Community. In addition, a myriad of bilateral and multilateral trade agreements and commodity agreements have appeared around the world. Especially prominent today are two other organizations of wider scope: GATT and UNCTAD.

gatt

Most of the non–Communist trading countries belong to an association known as the General Agreement on Tariffs and Trade. GATT is the outgrowth of a postwar attempt to form an international trade organization intended (1) to untangle the snarl of special trade agreements and complex trade restrictions that had accumulated during the first half of the century and (2) to promote a closer approach to worldwide free trade. When this organization failed to receive ratification, the principal trading nations continued a series of negotiations, or "rounds," aimed at reducing trade barriers. Collectively the resulting treaties have been termed the General Agreement on Tariffs and Trade, administered from offices in Geneva, Switzerland. GATT has made a vital contribution to the enormous growth in world trade in recent decades.

unctad

For the newly developing countries, however, GATT has been of limited help. After all, GATT is designed to conform with neoclassical trade theory and its goal of universal free trade, which is not wholly appropriate for the trade problems of less developed regions. The United Nations Conference on Trade and Development has focused specifically on the difficulties that developing countries have in marketing their goods in advanced lands, sponsoring a series of conferences to find ways of reconciling the supply and demand of commodities sold by developing countries and with breaking down artificial restrictions imposed by advanced countries on these goods.

WORLD COMMODITY FLOWS

The emphasis up to this point has been upon the interplay of forces that serve to create trade, or to divert, inhibit, or otherwise distort it. In this final section we shall focus more specifically upon actual flows of merchandise and to look for meaningful patterns that may emerge from the conflicting influences described earlier. We shall first note the ways in which actual trade flows have been shaped by these influences, as measured by various world trade models. Then we shall examine these flows to see how they have evolved in modern times and how various countries of the world group themselves together in their trade connections.

world flow models

One recent study by Hans Linnemann, a Dutch economist, examined the movements of goods among eighty countries or colonies. Included were all of the major trading entities, except the Communist countries (for whom inadequate data were available); those countries whose trade consists mainly of goods in transit to and from other countries, rather than items actually produced or consumed domestically (this disqualified Singapore, Hong Kong, and the Netherlands Antilles, among others); and those for whom data were missing (this, unfortunately, excluded a number of less developed countries). The year selected was 1959 (actually an average of three years—1958, 1959, and 1960), since this was considered a "normal" period having fewer distorting international events of an economic or political nature. It was also regarded as fairly representative of modern conditions, since overall changes in trade patterns take place at a slow rate.

The basic data consisted of a total of 6,300 flows between pairs of countries. Other information incor-

porated into the model fell into three categories: demand, supply, and resistance to trade (distorting influences). The actual variables relating to each country were (1) gross national product, (2) population, (3) distance (shortest navigable distance between principal ports plus overland distance to main economic centers), (4) preferential trading relations, and (5) commodity composition of the flows. The preferential trade relations consisted of the connections between Portugal, Belgium, the United Kingdom, and France with their colonies and former colonies. The effects of commodity composition were measured by the degree to which the total structure of a country's exports resembled the total import structure of each of its customers.

All of these variables proved to be important determinants of trade. The greatest influence of all was exerted by gross national product (a measure of total demand) and distance (a measure of resistance to trade). Preferential trading relations also explained much of the pattern of flows among the eighty countries, especially between mother countries and their associated colonies, past or present. This influence was strongest of all in the case of France and her associates. France and other members of the French Community also showed the greatest complementarity in the commodities exchanged among them. The model gave poorest results when predicting the trade of the least developed countries among the eighty. In this connection it was discovered that flows below about one million dollars in size were particularly difficult to predict. This suggests that small flows, which are mainly to or from small economies, are erratic in occurrence. When an adjustment was made to allow for this effect, the explanatory powers of the model rose substantially.

the trade of Israel and Lebanon

This problem of small trade flows has been explicitly addressed in a study by James McConnell in which similar methods were used to analyze the trade connections of Israel and Lebanon. The two countries are below the mean level on most scales of development, they occupy adjacent locations at the eastern end of the Mediterranean, and both tend to trade very little with their immediate neighbors in the Middle East. Using 1967 data, the study examined individual trade flows between each country and all its trading partners. In the case of Israel this came to 51 countries; for Lebanon it was 53. The variables included in the two tests were (1) gross national product of the trading partners of Israel or Lebanon, (2) distance, (3) preferential trading arrangements (membership of trading partners in EEC, EFTA, the Communist bloc, or in the case of Lebanon, membership in the Arabian and North African blocs), and (4) a variable designating flows falling beneath the one-million-dollar level.

In the case of these two countries with below-average per capita GNP, the variable identifying individually small trade flows proved strongest of all. In other words, taking care of the erratic small flows greatly increased the explanatory capabilities of the model, which suggests that one million dollars is indeed a critical cutoff point in predicting trade flows. Gross national product and distance were also very important. In their trading connections, both Israel and Lebanon are strongly oriented to large economies such as those of the United States and the EEC countries. The trade preference variables showed that both EEC and EFTA memberships are positively related to Israeli trade, while membership in the Communist bloc is negatively related. For Lebanon, the Arabian group proved a strong connection. Nevertheless, such trade preferences exerted much less effect upon Israel and Lebanon than previously found to be true of more highly developed countries.

modern developments in world trade

The wide fluctuations in total world trade during modern times show how sensitive trade is to the vagaries of war and peace and of prosperity and hard times. Following World War I, which caused the first major disruption of trade in this century, world exports rapidly soared until, by 1929, they had doubled their level of ten years earlier. The total value of trade dropped precipitously as the Great Depression struck, falling by at least 60 percent in a remarkably short time. This was much greater even than the decline in total output, since countries quickly resorted to such protective devices as tariffs, quotas, and prohibitions to close their borders to foreign competition when domestic conditions became difficult. By 1938, however, trade had recovered to the 1929 level despite the persistence of artificial barriers that caused trade growth to lag behind the increasing world output.

At this point, world trade was again interrupted by war, followed by an extended period during which the customary flows were much distorted due to the wartime destruction of productive capacity in the leading economies of Europe and Japan. With the return to normal, world trade quickly gathered strength, and with the aid of GATT and other moves to free trade from its prewar encumberances, the flow of goods rose at an ever accelerating rate. Between 1948 and 1968 the total increased by more than fourfold (not allowing for currency inflation) and by 1969 it was rising at the unprecedented rate of 18 percent per annum.

current world trade

What is the nature of world trade in this period three-quarters of the way through the twentieth century? At present the non–Communist technically advanced countries supply over 70 percent of the world's exports, a proportion that has increased steadily for two decades (Table 11.1, pp. 214–15). In absolute terms the Communist countries have also increased their exports, but this rise has been at less than the world rate. In value terms, exports of the less developed countries have failed to keep pace with the growth of trade in the world at large. Their share in 1968, a little over 18 percent of the total, is decidedly less than it had been earlier in the decade. If it were not for the oil-exporting members of the group, the relative decline would be even greater.

Looking at particular areas, we find that the leading source region is the EEC, with 28 percent of the total. The United States is the largest single exporting country, followed by West Germany, Japan, France, and the United Kingdom. Not only has the trade of industrial countries grown at a rate well above that of the world as a whole, but the greater part of this increase has been in the trade of industrial countries with one another. Moreover, the fastest growth has occurred within continents rather than between continents. Thus much of the trade expansion is taking place among members of the EEC and other countries of Western Europe on the one hand and between Canada and the United States on the other. The pace of growth is set by the EEC, especially West Germany and Italy, and by Japan. The United States is lagging in its rate of trade growth, as is the United Kingdom, which was the leading trading country during an earlier era.

The commodity composition, or structure, of trade has undergone important changes in modern times. Most notable of all has been the fourfold increase during this century in the trade in manufactured goods as opposed to a mere 50 percent rise in the exchange of primary commodities. The relatively poor performance of primary exports has occurred in spite of a rising demand for industrial raw materials, particularly petroleum. This discrepancy is explained to some degree by the increasingly elaborate processing that takes place today, together with the rising proportion of finished goods entering trade. One fairly reliable measure of a country's level of development, in fact, is the quantity of its finished goods exports expressed as a percentage of its shipments of all manufactures. The increased exchange of manufactured goods provides further evidence of the growing interdependence among industrial countries.

Changes have also taken place in the composition of manufactured goods entering trade. There has been a steady decline in shipments of textiles and clothing, which were leading items of international commerce in an earlier time. At the same time, exports of metals and miscellaneous manufactured goods have remained fairly static. The categories that have grown most rapidly of all are machinery, transport equipment, and chemicals.

regionalization of trade

One way to gain a better insight into the nature of world commerce is to examine the trading characteristics of regional groupings of countries. Although continental areas have customarily served as a convenient basis for regional analyses of trade, they have not proved wholly satisfactory because countries do not always group themselves so neatly. A more objective approach to regionalization has been found in the use of special statistical techniques for grouping countries on the basis of their interdependence in trade. In two such studies by Bruce Russett, the degree of interdependence of pairs of countries was measured by expressing the trade passing between them as a ratio of their gross domestic products; those countries having similar linkages were then sorted into groups. This operation was performed on all the world's trading nations for which data were available, using information for 1963 and, for purposes of comparison, 1938 and 1954.

The outcome was a number of distinct multinational trade groups that tend to emphasize the degree to which world trade is becoming compartmentalized (Table 11.2, p. 216). Even so, most of the groups tend to overlap, with some countries appearing in more than one region. Certain of the major trading nations, especially Japan and the United Kingdom, participate actively in several regions. Other countries do not fit securely within one group or another (shown by their low numerical scores in the table) but tend to float on the fringes of two or more trade regions. The nature of the regionalization that has come from these studies confirms much that has been said previously concerning the ordering effects of distance. This influence is shown to be modified by access to cheap ocean navigation, however; and it is distorted considerably by strong political and cultural ties among nations, especially those relationships resulting from colonialism. The cohesive effects of particular levels of economic development are also clear.

Altogether, nine world trade regions appear in the 1963 data (Table 11.2). The first of these regions is referred to in the study as North and Central America, although it includes South American countries along the rim of the Caribbean. Principal members of the group are the United States, Canada, Mexico, the Central American republics, Venezuela, Trinidad, and Colombia. Ties to other continents also appear, particularly the four Scandinavian countries, West Germany, the United Kingdom, and Japan. The second region is labeled South America and includes most of the countries south of the Caribbean rim. Venezuela reappears again in this group, however, because of its role as a supplier of petroleum. Another major oil exporter, Saudi Arabia, has strong links with this region also, despite its remoteness from it. Likewise associated with the group are certain European countries, especially Spain (reflecting strong linguistic and cultural ties), Italy, and Switzerland. A third Western Hemisphere region emerging from the data is the British Caribbean, a group that combines the United Kingdom with several of her former colonies, principally in the Caribbean but also includes certain others as well. Among the latter are Canada, New Zealand, Ghana, and Nigeria. Saudi Arabia is once more present as a supplier to the region, as is Norway.

Four other clusters of countries are centered upon the European continent. One large group is called the Commonwealth, containing the United Kingdom and a considerable number of British Commonwealth members. All of the EFTA members are present, together with several other Western European countries, although the latter are weakly linked to the group. Japan likewise appears in this bloc. The French Community shows up as another large association of countries, including, besides France, many of France's former African colonies, together with some of her European neighbors. A third cluster, called Western Europe contains principally EEC countries plus the United Kingdom and the contiguous states of Denmark, Switzerland, and Austria. Israel is loosely associated with the group. The other trade region of the continent is Eastern Europe, which comprises nearly all the Comecon countries together with Cuba and Egypt. A few of the Western European nations have ties with this group, as do certain Asiatic countries. Among these are Japan and China, although the latter is weakly represented. Albania is notably absent.

Asia is the focus of two final groups. The "Arabs" include nine of the Arab League countries of the Middle East, together with nearby Italy and Cyprus. The other association is a large cluster called "Asia," which features Japan near the top of the list and contains several of the non–Communist Asiatic nations as well as New Zealand, the United Kingdom, and the United States.

The same procedure was also used with data for earlier years: 1938, the last normal prewar year, and 1954. A comparison of these older groupings with the more recent ones discloses a number of important changes attributable to ideological realignments of countries. The Soviet Union's present ties with Eastern Europe were absent in 1938; indeed that country did not appear importantly in any of the prewar groupings, clear evidence of Stalin's policy of economic self-sufficiency. The 1954 data first show these linkages among the Communist bloc and by 1963 the group has been joined by Cuba, which had previously been associated with the Caribbean group. The comparison also indicates very little decline of empires during the period of studies. Such weakening of colonial ties as occurred has largely been confined to the British group. France's cluster remains mostly intact.

The results confirm once again that a major part of the rapid postwar growth in trade has taken place within continents rather than between them. In both 1938 and 1954, Western Europe appeared as part of a much broader group, called the North Atlantic Community, that included the United States and Canada as well as Britain. North and South America were more closely linked in those earlier years, and the ties between Europe and Latin America were also generally stronger. Aside from these changes, there was an unusual amount of continuity in the associations of trading countries throughout this long period.

EXPORTS TO→ / EXPORTS FROM	WORLD	MARKET ECONOMIES Developed[1]	MARKET ECONOMIES Developing[2]	CENTRALLY PLANNED ECONOMIES[3]	UNITED STATES	CANADA	LATIN AMERICA	DEVELOPED MARKET ECONOMIES EUROPE TOTAL	EEC	EFTA Total	EFTA United Kingdom
World	272,710	191,240	52,260	27,790	35,320	12,420	13,290	123,500	72,320	38,910	17,560
Developed market economies[1]	193,190	147,900	37,460	7,140	25,880	11,330	10,210	97,600	57,330	30,850	12,280
Developing market economies[2]	49,780	36,400	10,270	2,600	9,240	1,000	2,060	20,050	12,320	6,130	4,410
Centrally planned economies[3]	29,750	6,940	4,530	18,060	200	93	1,020	5,900	2,680	1,920	870
United States	37,460	26,070	11,130	250	—	8,960	4,810	12,190	6,900	3,860	2,280
Canada	13,750	12,770	840	140	9,800	—	410	2,130	790	1,230	1,030
Latin America	13,510	9,920	2,810	780	4,100	460	1,600	4,530	2,770	1,250	750
Developed market economies, Europe	118,720	95,010	17,410	5,760	10,170	1,730	4,130	78,310	47,640	23,310	6,960
European Economic Community	75,690	62,100	10,180	3,050	5,960	710	2,440	53,370	36,460	12,750	3,370
European Free Trade Association	35,620	27,510	6,310	1,650	3,480	960	1,300	20,460	9,050	8,470	2,340
United Kingdom	16,890	12,060	4,030	670	2,080	720	580	7,240	3,370	2,250	—
Centrally planned economies, Europe and USSR[4]	27,500	6,220	3,480	17,580	200	68	940	5,490	2,430	1,780	790
USSR	11,660	2,580	2,260	6,810	61	12	650	2,150	860	660	425
South Africa	2,140	1,630	410	1	155	40	13	1,200	400	750	710
Developing market economies, Africa	11,470	9,340	1,160	740	700	75	69	7,880	5,430	2,010	1,440
Japan	15,990	8,400	6,820	760	5,020	480	800	2,070	970	720	350
Developing market economies, Asian Middle East[5]	9,380	7,120	1,920	205	400	81	145	4,530	2,680	1,400	1,060
Other, Asia	12,940	7,930	4,020	870	2,960	220	145	2,440	1,190	1,080	860
Centrally planned economies, Asia[6]	2,250	720	1,050	475	2	25	80	405	225	140	83
Developed market economies, Oceania[7]	5,110	4,030	850	225	740	120	57	1,700	630	990	940
Developing market economies, rest of the world[8]	2,490	2,090	360	1	1,090	160	105	680	250	400	285

[1]United States, Canada, developed market economies of Europe (including Turkey and Yugoslavia), Australia, New Zealand, South Africa, and Japan.

[2]Regions other than developed market economies and centrally planned economies.

[3]Centrally planned economies of Asia and Europe and USSR.

[4]USSR, Albania, Bulgaria, Czechoslovakia, German Democratic Republic, Hungary, Poland, and Romania. The transactions between Germany, Fed. Rep., and German Democratic Republic have been omitted.

[5]Including Cyprus and Iran.

[6]China (mainland), Democratic People's Republic of Korea, Mongolia, and Democratic Republic of Viet Nam. Estimates based partly on imports

EXPORTS TO → / EXPORTS FROM	CENTRALLY PLANNED ECONOMIES Europe and USSR[4]	USSR	SOUTH AFRICA	DEVELOPING MARKET ECONOMIES, AFRICA	JAPAN	DEVELOPING MARKET ECONOMIES ASIA Middle East[5]	Other Asia	CENTRALLY PLANNED ECONOMIES ASIA[6]	DEVELOPED MARKET ECONOMIES OCEANIA[7]	DEVELOPING MARKET ECONOMIES REST OF WORLD[8]
World	25,240	10,050	2,950	10,040	12,500	7,090	17,470	2,550	4,500	3,790
Developed market economies[1]	5,960	2,540	2,580	7,670	6,750	5,120	12,020	1,180	3,760	2,440
Developing market economies[2]	2,200	1,220	370	1,520	5,070	1,220	4,130	400	670	1,350
Centrally planned economies[3]	17,090	6,290	4	860	680	750	1,310	970	60	10
United States	250	105	510	860	3,460	1,250	3,470	—	950	750
Canada	28	9	74	42	580	39	220	115	190	135
Latin America	670	345	27	53	790	66	140	115	15	960
Developed market economies Europe	5,240	2,100	1,660	5,510	1,340	3,220	3,380	520	1,800	1,160
European Economic Community	2,700	1,060	780	3,560	740	1,720	1,820	350	540	640
European Free Trade Association	1,480	480	850	1,710	550	1,340	1,470	165	1,210	490
United Kingdom	540	230	690	1,030	295	960	1,030	125	1,040	425
Centrally planned economies, Europe and USSR[4]	16,620	6,060	4	730	435	670	560	970	23	5
USSR	6,200	—	—	415	355	335	280	610	3	—
South Africa	1	—	—	355	210	5	35	—	21	1
Developing market economies, Africa	660	370	130	660	530	145	225	79	26	57
Japan	340	270	280	860	—	550	4,450	425	560	170
Developing market economies, Asian Middle East[5]	190	87	165	385	1,730	660	650	19	215	71
Other, Asia	680	415	45	380	1,920	345	3,080	190	345	75
Centrally planned economies, Asia[6]	475	225	—	130	245	85	760	—	36	5
Developed market economies, Oceania[7]	99	60	60	41	1,160	59	465	125	250	230
European market economies, rest of the world[8]	1	—	2	28	89	2	38	—	72	185

data of trading partners. Where exports to China (Taiwan) could not be distinguished from exports to China (mainland) they are shown as exports to China (mainland). The intertrade of these countries is excluded.

[7] Australia and New Zealand.

[8] Consists mainly of islands in the Caribbean and Pacific areas.

Source: UN Yearbook of International Trade Statistics.

Table 11.2 International Trade Regions, 1963

NORTH AND CENTRAL AMERICA

Country	Value	Country	Value
El Salvador	2.42	Switzerland	1.45
Panama	2.41	Denmark	1.41
Costa Rica	2.25	West Germany	1.39
Nicaragua	2.24	Canada	1.30
Guatemala	2.10	Finland	1.28
Honduras	2.05	Spain	1.20
Venezuela	2.02	Mexico	1.19
Trinidad	2.01	United States	1.18
Netherlands	1.67	United Kingdom	1.13
Colombia	1.60	Austria	1.07
Belgium-Lux.	1.50	Japan	0.99
Sweden	1.49	Italy	0.92
Norway	1.46	France	0.82

SOUTH AMERICA

Country	Value	Country	Value
Peru	1.33	Spain	0.75
Uruguay	1.27	Saudi Arabia	0.67
Argentina	1.27	Venezuela	0.65
Paraguay	1.23	Switzerland	0.64
Chile	1.18	Italy	0.63
Brazil	1.09	Ecuador	0.61
Algeria	0.78	Sweden	0.59

BRITISH CARIBBEAN

Country	Value	Country	Value
British Guiana	1.31	New Zealand	0.75
Trinidad	1.25	Canada	0.75
Jamaica	1.22	Norway	0.63
Ghana	0.92	Nigeria	0.62
Saudi Arabia	0.77	United Kingdom	0.60

COMMONWEALTH

Country	Value	Country	Value
Kenya	1.95	Netherlands	1.04
Iran	1.77	India	0.93
Mauritius	1.74	West Germany	0.91
Uganda	1.68	Madagascar	0.90
Tanganyika	1.55	Israel	0.89
South Africa	1.44	Canada	0.87
Ceylon	1.43	Switzerland	0.86
Congo (L)	1.41	Finland	0.80
United Kingdom	1.37	Sweden	0.80
Belgium-Lux.	1.25	Italy	0.79
Pakistan	1.18	Japan	0.76
Ireland	1.16	Portugal	0.73
Australia	1.15	Greece	0.68
New Zealand	1.12	Austria	0.66
Iraq	1.12	France	0.65
Sudan	1.09	Norway	0.64
Malaysia	1.07	Spain	0.60
Burma	1.06		

FRENCH COMMUNITY

Country	Value	Country	Value
Ivory Coast	2.38	Netherlands	1.19
Senegal	2.27	Iraq	1.15
Congo (B)	1.91	Belgium-Lux.	1.12
Cameroun	1.84	Portugal	1.10
Dahomey	1.80	Ghana	1.08
Niger	1.67	Italy	0.92
France	1.65	West Germany	0.89
Upper Volta	1.63	Spain	0.89
Togo	1.62	Venezuela	0.86
Morocco	1.60	Switzerland	0.84
Mali	1.45	Norway	0.82
Algeria	1.42	Denmark	0.77
Cambodia	1.39	Sweden	0.76
Madagascar	1.34	United Kingdom	0.74
Nigeria	1.33	South Africa	0.69
Tunisia	1.29		

WESTERN EUROPE

Country	Value	Country	Value
Netherlands	1.36	Switzerland	0.83
United Kingdom	1.23	Italy	0.76
Belgium-Lux.	1.18	France	0.70
Denmark	1.13	Austria	0.64
West Germany	1.00	Israel	0.63

EASTERN EUROPE

Country	Value	Country	Value
Romania	2.66	Sweden	1.71
Czechoslovakia	2.37	Italy	1.66
Cuba	2.30	West Germany	1.63
Egypt	2.21	USSR	1.59
Finland	2.13	United Kingdom	1.55
Hungary	2.10	Burma	1.41
Poland	2.09	India	1.23
Austria	2.07	France	1.23
Yugoslavia	2.04	Indonesia	1.10
Bulgaria	1.91	Pakistan	0.93
East Germany	1.77	China	0.81
Switzerland	1.73	Japan	0.79
Netherlands	1.72		

ARAB

Country	Value	Country	Value
Lebanon	1.81	Sudan	0.99
Saudi Arabia	1.53	Egypt	0.87
Syria	1.47	Libya	0.84
Jordan	1.46	Italy	0.68
Kuwait	1.27	Cyprus	0.68
Iraq	1.23	Netherlands	0.61

ASIA

Country	Value	Country	Value
Malaysia	1.99	United States	0.88
Thailand	1.84	Netherlands	0.87
Taiwan	1.82	Pakistan	0.85
South Vietnam	1.72	United Kingdom	0.84
Philippines	1.69	Belgium-Lux.	0.80
Japan	1.63	Switzerland	0.80
Indonesia	1.49	Denmark	0.79
Australia	1.45	Canada	0.78
Burma	1.42	Saudi Arabia	0.77
Laos	1.41	India	0.75
Kuwait	1.41	Italy	0.70
South Korea	1.35	Norway	0.69
Saudi Arabia	1.33	Austria	0.68
Iran	1.16	Sweden	0.67
Ceylon	1.15	Mexico	0.64
Iraq	1.14	Yugoslavia	0.64
New Zealand	0.99	France	0.62
West Germany	0.89	Brazil	0.61

NOT LISTED IN ANY GROUP

Afghanistan	Haiti
Albania	Iceland
Bolivia	Liberia
Central African Republic	Mauritania
Chad	Nepal
Dominican Republic	Sierra Leone
Ethiopia	Somalia
Gabon	Turkey
Guinea	Yemen

Source: Bruce Russett, *International Regions and the International System*, pp. 134–38.

trade flows of major regions

The groupings of countries described above will serve as a partial guide for a brief general survey of world trade, giving particular emphasis to major trade blocs.

the Western Hemisphere

The United States is the central focus of North and Central America. Although lagging behind much of the industrial world in the rate of her trade growth, the United States is still the largest single exporter and importer, accounting for nearly one-seventh of all international commerce. This is in spite of the fact that only 4 to 5 percent of her gross domestic product enters foreign trade. This combination of large absolute trade and low trade-GDP ratio is made possible by the vast size of the United States economy, which has a total output of goods and services approaching the trillion-dollar mark. Exports are highly diverse and include a great variety of agricultural and other primary commodities, as well as processed goods of all types. The United States has an important comparative advantage in many farm products owing in part to the exceptional productivity of labor on her highly mechanized farms. As mentioned earlier, the country has also relied upon a comparative advantage in high-technology goods, although this margin is now beginning to diminish. The American economy has an insatiable appetite for a wide range of industrial raw materials that can no longer be supplied entirely from domestic sources, and imports of such goods are therefore indispensable for maintaining current levels of production. For this and other reasons trade is far more important for the United States than most of her citizens realize. Moreover, because of the growing need to import fuels and raw materials and the rising foreign demand for American industrial and farm products more cheaply obtainable now that the dollar has been devalued, it is likely that the country's trade-GDP ratio will increase in the future. The high per capita income makes the country as exceedingly attractive market for foreign suppliers, and her nearest neighbors have become quite dependent upon trade with the United States.

Canada is the chief trading partner of the United States. The Canadian economy has been described previously as being land-plentiful and labor-short, and the exports and imports of the country reflect these characteristics. Land-intensive commodities are prominent in Canadian exports—such items as grains, mineral ores and fuels, and wood products. A high proportion of these commodities have received at least some initial processing before shipment, however, since manufacturing is well developed in the country. Indeed, industrial products figure importantly in Canada's foreign sales, especially transportation equipment. Much of the manufacturing development of Canada has occurred with the aid of foreign investment, induced in large part by high Canadian tariffs on finished goods.

Despite the small size of her population, which is only slightly greater than that of California, Canada ranks sixth among the world's trading nations. More than one-fifth of Canadian production enters foreign trade and per capita exports are very high. Canada trades with a large variety of countries, including the United Kingdom and other Commonwealth countries, Japan (an important customer for coal and agricultural and forest products), the EEC countries, and Venezuela (principal source of petroleum for Canada's eastern provinces). Nevertheless, Canada is particularly dependent upon trade with the United States, which is the customer for more than one-half of the country's exports and supplier of two-thirds of her imports.

A prime reason for the high level of exchange between the two countries is contiguity. The next most important trading partners of each country are in the Eastern Hemisphere. The long border between them is itself a factor in the trade between Canada and the United States, as noted earlier. The two countries have similar demand structures, similar standards of living, similar customs, and (with the exception of French Canada) the same language. There are a number of important complementarities in production, too. This does not result in merely an exchange of Canadian primary goods for United States manufactures. The United States is a supplier of primary commodities as well, reflecting climatic differences (winter vegetables from California, Texas, and Florida), and differences in mineral resource endowments. The two also exchange both semifinished and finished manufactured goods in large quantities, owing in some measure to intra-industry specialization of production. Trade in manufactured goods is also enhanced by close linkages within major industries, including much United States ownership of Canadian industry and a great deal of Canadian investment in the United States.

Close trade ties also exist among the countries ringing the Caribbean. The Central American countries, Venezuela, Colombia, and Mexico have linkages with one another and with the United States. As in its relations with Canada, the United States has natural complementarities with these nations of Middle America—in climates, soils, biotic and mineral resources, labor supply characteristics, and other bases for comparative advantage. The trading relationships of the Caribbean rim countries are typical of countries at opposite ends of the developmental scale, with the United States serving as a market for tropical foodstuffs, minerals, and other primary goods and as a supplier of manufactured goods to other members of the group.

Proximity to the United States and the great distance separating her from other members of LAFTA have made it difficult for Mexico to reduce her dependence upon trade with the United States. However, Mexico has been industrializing rapidly in recent years, much of this taking the form of "tariff factories" built by investors from the United States, Japan, and Western Europe to get under the Mexican tariff wall. Mexico's circumstances in this case are quite similar to those of Canada, except that the Mexican government has insisted upon majority control of manufacturing and mining concerns by Mexican nationals. Per capita incomes are rising in the country despite a high birth rate. Because of population pressures, Mexican outputs tends to be labor-intensive. For this same reason Mexico is also a large exporter of labor to the United States.

As shown by Russett's studies, the islands of the West Indies retain close trade links with their respective mother countries, even though most of the British islands have now formally shed their colonial status. There are few ties to mainland Latin America and little trade among the islands themselves, which are separated from each other by long distances and tend to compete with each other in the sale of tropical foodstuffs. One of the major clusters in this area comprises the former British colonies. The French islands of the Caribbean all belong to the French Community cluster, and their trade is clearly oriented to France. The Netherlands Antilles, on the other hand, with their output of oil refinery products, have wider trade connections. The United States maintains strong trade links with Puerto Rico and the Virgin Islands, reflecting political connections, and with Trinidad and Jamaica, both suppliers of minerals to the United States. In addition, American influence is felt throughout the Caribbean in the form of tourism, which is assuming an increasing importance to local economies.

South America has not been able to achieve much unity in its trading relationships. Aside from the physical isolation and the competitive nature of their exports, members of the group are also at different levels of development, Argentina, Chile, Uruguay, and Brazil being more industrialized than their other partners. Although trade ties to North America and Western Europe have weakened in recent decades, South America remains an important source of metallic minerals, foodstuffs, and petroleum.

Europe

In 1969, 44 percent of all the world's trade originated or terminated in Western Europe and 41 percent of this was accounted for by EEC and EFTA alone. Western Europe constitutes a very large market, with its dense population and high per capita purchasing power. The European countries have some of the highest trade-GNP ratios in the world; indeed, the Benelux countries annually export from 35 to 40 percent of all their output.

Trade of Western Europe has been growing increasingly cohesive in recent decades and in 1969 two-thirds of all the trade of these countries took place within the region. Trade is facilitated by the world's densest transport networks and by a considerable degree of complementarity of production. Extending from the subtropical Mediterranean to the arctic tundra of northern Scandinavia, Europe has a great diversity in output of agricultural and forest products. The continent is becoming increasingly self-sufficient in many lines of production, including agriculture, which is undergoing substantial modernization. Europe is also endowed with a great variety of mineral resources, although it is very dependent upon the Middle East for petroleum. Above all, however, the Western European economies are competitive in their manufacturing output. Despite this, these countries have a particularly active exchange of manufactured goods, which are exceedingly diverse and have a high degree of intra-industrial specialization. Like the United States, Europe tends to emphasize high-technology exports.

The countries of EEC alone contributed nearly two-thirds of Europe's trade, even before Britain's entry in 1973, and this bloc constitutes the nucleus of an expanding group of trading nations. The EEC members are all industrialized, and their rate of trade growth is rising steadily. For example, while the trade of EEC with nonmember countries was rising by 18 percent in 1969, intrabloc shipments were growing by 26 percent.

All the members of EFTA are highly trade-dependent, but even before Britain's departure EFTA generated less than half as much trade as EEC. The United Kingdom's trade has been stagnating for some time. The long-term downward trend in Britain's foreign commerce stems partly from the fact that she has traditionally sold her goods in markets that are now growing at a slow rate and partly from a declining competitiveness of British industry in the world economy.

The addition of Britain and Denmark to EEC concentrates a major part of Western Europe's trade within a single tightly-knit unit of active trading units. It must be remembered, however, that Europe is a politically fragmented continent of many individual small countries. If political unification were to accompany economic integration, intra-European trade would then be counted as domestic commerce. After subtracting this from the total, trade between this new political entity and the rest of the world would then constitute only 15 percent of total world trade, only slightly more than the trade of the United States alone.

Trade ties between Western Europe and politically associated countries and colonies outside the continent continue to persist strongly despite the growth of nationalism among the newly independent states. The EEC serves as a special incentive to the former colonies of the European powers to keep their old links intact and does much to explain the tenacity of the French Community. Although the British Commonwealth is less cohesive, it remains a strong force nevertheless, especially for remotely located Australia and New Zealand.

The countries of Eastern Europe, including the Soviet Union, are tightly bound within an ideological grouping that has tended to isolate them from the world. During the Stalinist era the eastern lands traded very little, even with one another. Today their trade is rising and, counting the USSR, they contribute one-tenth of the world total. Three-fifths of this is still intrabloc trade, but commerce with the non–Communist world is rising.

the Middle East

The Arab nations are joined together by fervent political ties and their trade shows this. These countries occupy a particularly strategic location at a world crossroads, including the Suez canal and the junction of major air routes. Members of this bloc appear in several of the trade groupings cited earlier, owing to their important function as suppliers of petroleum throughout the world. The most important suppliers to the Middle East are the industrial countries of Western Europe, the United States, and Japan. Because of her political isolation from the other Middle Eastern countries, Israel trades mainly with Western Europe and the United States.

Asia

After the United States and the Soviet Union, Japan is the world's third largest economy; and, following the United States and West Germany, she is also the third most important trading nation. For a number of reasons developed at length in Chapter 17, Japanese products compete on favorable terms throughout the world despite the severe transport-cost disadvantage of a peripheral location with respect to the main centers of world trade in Western Europe and North America.

The other non-Communist countries of Asia are all at a lower level of development. Although the aggregate of the trade of this fairly large group of countries is substantial, trade per capita is quite low for all but a few. Most of the exports from this bloc consist of primary goods that are either unprocessed or only semi-processed. The most notable exceptions are the small island nations of Hong Kong, Taiwan, and Singapore, each of which has succeeded in attracting large numbers of labor-intensive industrial concerns producing for export. India has also become an exporter of textiles and other mass-produced consumer goods. About two-thirds of the exports of non–Communist Asian countries (other than Japan) go to the industrial nations, but most of the remainder is traded among the Asian nations themselves.

This leaves the Communist countries of Asia—China, North Korea, North Vietnam, and Outer Mongolia. Despite the huge population within this group, especially China with her 800 million, the level of trade generated is still very small. More than half of this exchange takes place with other less developed countries. Nevertheless, the world's principal trading nations are intensely interested in the prospects for expanding trade with Communist China, since aggregate demand in that country promises to be enormous. At present, however, trade with China is slow to develop because that country has very little surplus output as yet to exchange with the rest of the world (see Chapter 23).

CURRENTS OF CHANGE

The world's trade is an intricate system that operates in a state of delicate balance. Over the long run it has experienced growth and change, sometimes orderly, sometimes disorderly. What are the current trends in trade, what kinds of problems are appearing, and what are their implications?

trends

The history of trade has shown rapid growth whenever conditions have permitted. The exchange of goods among people from different areas is a form of spatial interaction that has persisted since earliest times. Today modern technology and economic trends are reinforcing this impulse to trade, and there is the promise of much potential trade growth ahead as barriers to the movement of goods continue to fall. There is also a changing commodity emphasis as the variety of world output continues to increase, as the location of production shifts to new areas, and as populations develop more diverse needs and wants.

unequal growth

These developments have favored some parts of the world above others. Unequal growth has taken place among the technically advanced nations as well as the less developed ones. The rapid upsurge of trade by Japan and the more aggressive Western European nations contrasts with the lagging growth of such older leaders as the United Kingdom and the United States. Meanwhile, as the trade of advanced countries has risen at accelerating rates, that of most less developed countries has stagnated.

compartmentalization of trade

Trading nations have always tended to show favoritism in their choice of markets and sources of supply, as shown by the persistence of old groupings of countries. Indeed, the traditional patterns have been further reinforced by the higher rates of intrabloc trade growth than in the world at large. Although groupings of countries according to currency blocs as such are disappearing, there is a remarkable tenacity among the political empires with which such monetary blocs were associated. The French Community has been the best example of this. Among the most revolutionary changes in modern trading relationships have been (1) the ideological division of Europe into eastern and western blocs and (2) the renewed popularity of regional integration schemes.

substituting capital for trade

Another important contemporary trend is the replacement of exports by foreign investment, in part a reaction to the increasing compartmentalization of trade noted above. The exportation of capital has provided an attractive means for surmounting the artificial trade barriers presented by trade blocs. It is also a natural accompaniment to the emergence of large multinational corporations that pay exclusive allegiance to no single nation.

current issues

A number of new developments have subjected the international trading system to severe strains. These pose difficult problems of adjustment for many of the world's nations and are the subject of much contemporary debate.

integration and trade diversion

One argument concerns the appropriate reaction of countries cut off from their traditional markets by the trade-diverting effects of integration, a problem of both Danish and American exporters of agricultural commodities to the EEC. The question in this case is whether to reach some accommodation with the Common Market countries or to withdraw behind one's own trade barriers. Having a relatively small economy, Denmark is following the former course with her decision to join the EEC; having less trade dependence, the United States seems to be tending toward the latter alternative.

foreign investment and the multinational firm

The barriers to trade resulting from integration have moved entrepreneurs to protect their threatened foreign markets by establishing overseas affiliates to produce the goods and services previously exported by the parent firm. This international flow of capital, augmenting an already growing stream of foreign investment into many parts of the world, has aroused criticism, and sometimes active resistance in both sending and receiving countries. In the capital-exporting nation, labor unions and others complain that jobs are being exported from the country; in the capital-importing nation, many persons object to increasing foreign control of the economy. Concern over this issue has mounted steadily in Canada, Western Europe, Latin America, and, more recently, in the United States. At the center of the controversy is the *multinational corporation.*

Also referred to as an *international, transnational,* or *supranational* corporation, the multinational firm is a company that operates in several national jurisdictions but (with a few important exceptions) is incorporated in only one country. A multinational firm conducts its foreign operations through partially or wholly owned subsidiaries, as well as through sales offices and overseas affiliates. One reason for the growing alarm multinationals are encountering in foreign lands is that so many of them are corporate giants; in 1971 there were 211 such firms with annual sales of $1 billion or more.

General Motors, for example, had yearly sales of $25 billion in 1971, an amount that dwarfs the gross national products of all but a dozen sovereign countries. Other United States-based multinational firms of great size are International Business Machines and International Telephone and Telegraph, the latter being the world's largest conglomerate—a firm engaged in a variety of different and sometimes unrelated activities. Switzerland is the home base for other mammoth multinational concerns engaged in banking, foods (Nestlés), and chemicals. Firms headquartered in the Netherlands and the United Kingdom are also among the world's largest, especially Unilever (soaps and detergents) and Royal Dutch Shell (petroleum), each of which is incorporated in both countries and therefore is an exception to the general rule that only one country serves as home base. So large are these and other similar multinationals that they play dominant roles in their home countries as well as in foreign lands.

Multinational concerns have also met adverse reactions because of their rapid growth since World War II. The real value of multinational sales has increased at a rate of 10 percent per annum for almost a quarter of a century, and the sales of United States-based concerns have grown tenfold within the past two decades. Depending on how it is reckoned, the current output of goods and services each year by all multinationals is approximately $300 billion; sales by United States-owned foreign subsidiaries alone are now five times the size of American exports.

The multinational corporation in its modern form was pioneered by Americans, whose first ventures of this sort actually predate the War by a number of years. Producers of petroleum, copper, aluminum, and other basic commodities were among the earlier multinational concerns, all of whom began their overseas operations as exporters but later turned to foreign sources for their raw materials and eventually to foreign markets for disposal of their expanded output. Subsequently, a group of United States firms principally engaged in manufacturing, most notably the Singer Sewing Machine Company, began to introduce labor-saving machines into other countries.

The accelerated growth of American-based multinationals during the postwar era resulted first of all from the effects of foreign restrictions on United States exports during the 1950s, especially those by the members of the EEC. Rather than lose their foreign markets, these firms began producing abroad. During the 1960s, foreign expansion by United States companies received its chief stimulus from rising production costs at home, particularly wages, at a time when European firms were finding it possible to cut costs through the economies of scale provided by the EEC. At that time many foreign currencies were so undervalued that overseas investments could be made very cheaply in U.S. dollars; moreover, foreign governments were beginning to insist upon local manufacture of certain key products regardless of their cost.

Of the three main types of multinational corporations, the raw-material producers—those exploiting the natural resource endowments of their host countries—are least successful today and are confronted with the most difficult problems. The large banks, insurance companies, and other financial institutions operating in more than one country are also experiencing difficulties. Most successful of all are the concerns that exploit the labor skills of host countries more capably than do the native entrepreneurs of those countries. These are the manufacturers of such commodities as motor cars, chemicals, drugs, electrical machinery and equipment, electronics, and fabricated metal products of all kinds.

At present the multinationals are highly concentrated in technologically advanced countries. Eight of the world's ten largest firms are based in the United States, and American-owned firms as a whole account for one-third of the total number of foreign affiliates and more than one-half of the total value of foreign investment. Together, the United States, the United Kingdom, West Germany, and France are the home bases for more than three-quarters of the multinational firms and more than four-fifths of the total foreign investment. Dutch, Swiss, and Japanese firms are also very important and are becoming increasingly so. Although multinational companies place a major part of their investments in developed countries, they are also investing in underdeveloped lands, where their impact is great.

One of the most frequent charges that their critics lodge against multinationals is that they are answerable to no sovereign authority. Although in fact these firms are not entirely without restraints, they nevertheless have considerable latitude because their operations take place in more than one country. In deciding where to locate their production facilities, for example, they are in the enviable position of being able to capitalize on the comparative advantages of many countries in their efforts to minimize outlays for raw materials, labor, and other production costs. The world's nations are at their disposal, and many countries are ardently wooing corporate investors with such special offers as tax concessions.

Multinational firms have unique opportunities to maximize their returns because of the variety of choices they have in making intracompany transfers. At will they can shift materials, products, technology, and capital among affiliates and parent, labeling these transfers however they wish and pricing them in the most advantageous manner. One of the most important uses for this capacity is to minimize taxes. Because multinationals operate in several tax jurisdictions, they can minimize overall tax bills by setting prices for intracompany transfers to show the highest profits in low-tax countries and the lowest profits in high-tax countries. When repatriating profits from an affiliate to the parent, the firm can sometimes conceal these by relabeling intracompany money transfers, calling them fees for consulting, licenses, or other services rendered the affiliate. In addition to "tax games," multinationals may engage in

"exchange-rate games." When there is a likelihood that major world currencies are about to be revalued, these companies can shift spare financial reserves from one country to another to make a profit on the change. Because of the prevalence of these practices, the multinational firm is often described as a company that makes its product in the country where production costs are least and channels its profits to the country where taxes are least.

Anything involving many billions of dollars inevitably has a deep impact on the economies and politics of nations and the world. Because multinational firms have the capability for investing vast sums of money, they are in a position to contribute substantially to the growth of national economies, as the Republic of Ireland has discovered since joining the EEC. At the same time, these companies can help reduce the technology gap among nations with their rapid transfers of information to foreign affiliates.

The potential impact of multinational investment decisions is greatest for underdeveloped countries. Among the bases for selecting such a nation for foreign investment, some of the most important are political stability, wage levels, and labor force characteristics. Indeed, there is a growing trend among multinationals to seize on the comparative advantages of underdeveloped nations, particularly the availability of much cheap labor. Companies are gearing their technology to the production capabilities of underdeveloped countries by breaking down complex assembly operations into a series of simple tasks that can be performed by unskilled workers. Although textile firms have traditionally been the first industries to spring up in a newly developing land, today the first may be electronics firms. Companies of this latter type are developing mobile production systems that can be farmed out quickly to foreign affiliates before the parent operation can become unionized and the transfer blocked. As a result there appears to be a new trend toward establishing *exporting* industries in underdeveloped lands rather than *import-competing* industries as in the past.

The benefits of this change in emphasis are shown by the rapidly rising prosperity of a select group of Asian countries offering political stability and large, industrious labor forces. Multinational firms manufacturing a wide variety of products chose first to enter Taiwan and Hong Kong; but now that wages have risen in those lands, foreign investors have begun to favor Singapore, South Korea, and, more recently, Malaysia and Indonesia (see Chapter 22).

One problem that this trend presents is the vulnerability of underdeveloped nations to exploitation by multinational concerns, as implied by the investment figures at hand. Although underdeveloped nations have received only 17.1 percent of the world's total foreign investment capital, they are contributing 46.5 percent of all foreign investment income. Thus foreign assets in underdeveloped lands are yielding a 14 percent return while those in advanced countries are providing a 7.5

percent return. This suggests that multinationals are extracting excessive payments from their affiliates and licensees in underdeveloped areas.

The impact of multinational firms on the foreign lands in which they operate is at least matched by their influence upon the economies of their home countries. Multinationals are usually the largest firms in their fields: they contribute a major part of domestic output, do most of the research and development, and employ the largest numbers of workers. General Motors, for example, regularly accounts for more than one-half of the motor vehicles sold annually in the United States. Contrary to the public stance of many American unions, multinational corporations, as a group, have better employment records than other companies. In balance, their foreign activities do not appear to have proved harmful to domestic labor.

Although multinationals are responsible for large outflows of capital from their native lands, these capital exports occur mainly during the first stages of foreign investment. Repatriated profits rise steadily thereafter and the net effect on the balance of payments is ultimately positive. This latter point has now been reached in the United States; indeed, by 1980 the net return from foreign operations by United States corporations is expected to reach $20 billion. Although there is an obvious substitution of capital outflows for exports at first, the overseas operations of these concerns eventually generate much exporting of raw materials and components to foreign affiliates. American-based multinationals currently export more goods than they import.

The political influence of multinational corporations is gaining much world attention at this time. Business operations of such size do tend to gain places close to the seats of power, both in their home countries and abroad; indeed, they may even bypass their own governments in dealing with foreign powers. This is suggested by the allegations against the powerful multinational conglomerate, ITT, which was at the same time accused of attempting to influence unduly the decisions of the United States government and of trying to prevent the installation of a socialist president in Chile. Other examples are provided by the public positions taken by United States-based oil companies toward the Israeli-Arab question in the Middle East.

Many observers have accused multinational corporations of assuming too important a role in the world currency crises of recent years. Supposedly, multinationals contributed some of the "hot money" that flowed from one country to another during the period and provided the pressures against the dollar and the pound that eventually led to their devaluation. Although these large corporations undoubtedly engaged in a number of defensive moves, sending excess funds to what appeared to be the most secure place at the time for example, there is no clear evidence that as a group they engaged in any concerted action for financial gain per se. Financial manipulation is incidental to the operations of such firms, most of which were established to produce and market goods and therefore have available at any one time only limited sums after providing for their other needs.

As the public becomes increasingly aware of the many facets of multinational operations, there are many calls for the regulation of these firms. Supranational controls on world business have been proposed, leading to a study of the problem by the United Nations, which in 1973 sponsored an international conference on this subject. Meanwhile the EEC has become concerned by the swelling role of multinational corporations within its jurisdiction, especially those based in the United States, and the organization is currently attempting to limit the freedom of multinational operations. In the United States the AFL-CIO is waging a campaign against what it conceives as the exporting of jobs by multinationals, and Congress is entertaining motions for curbing foreign investment. In Canada, investment and economic control by foreign interests has been an emotional issue for several years and feelings are now reaching new levels of intensity. In Latin America several governments have begun to expropriate foreign enterprises.

With all the public agitation against multinationals, controlling them, short of nationalization, is not a simple matter. First, it is administratively difficult for countries to obtain accurate information on multinational operations within their jurisdictions and to share this with other countries where those concerns may be represented. Moreover, such concerns have been adroit at evading controls: when the United States placed limitations on capital outflows during the late 1960s, the multinational companies merely financed their overseas expansion by foreign borrowing and by using retained profits abroad. Indeed, during the 1966–1970 period the parent companies of American-based multinationals supplied only 15 percent of their affiliates' funds. Most of the rest was generated internally by the affiliates or borrowed overseas.

Although the financial needs of multinational corporations necessarily differ from those of governments, open conflict between these businesses and the nations in which they operate is rare today. The legal authority of governments ultimately forces the companies to accept any conditions imposed upon them; multinationals often go to great lengths to accommodate when they have to. Moreover, it is the largest of the multinational concerns that are the most vulnerable. Because of their size and visibility, they are most subject to labor-union pressures and hence are more highly unionized in their home countries. For the same reason, political pressures are exerted more intensively against large firms than small ones.

The evidence seems to indicate that United States-based multinational corporations are entering a period of consolidation and that during the next several years they will grow more slowly than in the past, perhaps at annual growth rates of 5 to 7 percent rather than the 10 percent rate to which they have become accustomed. One reason to expect slower growth is that tariffs in the world at large have fallen substantially since the 1950s, and other barriers are under assault at the current round of GATT negotiations. Another reason is that overseas production is no longer as cheap as it was in the past. European wage levels are reaching those of the United States, Japanese labor costs are rising rapidly, and pay rates are going up in some underdeveloped countries. Currency revaluations are partly responsible for closing the wage gap, and they are causing American products to become more competitive in the international economy. Meanwhile, some of the United States-based multinationals have become so large that they are beginning to exceed their entrepreneural capacities, and management problems are hampering their growth. For these reasons production by American firms is beginning to return home.

Some of these same events are creating opposite conditions for multinational concerns based in other countries. Two successive devaluations of the dollar have suddenly made investment in the United States more attractive to European- and Japanese-based multinationals. The latter now find that they must establish factories in the United States if they are to preserve the shares of the American market they have gained for their products. Thus the Japanese electronics firm, Sony, and the Swedish motor car manufacturer, Volvo, among many others, are sending capital to the United States in substitution for their exports.

At the same time, there appears to be a growing role in world business for smaller multinational concerns. Because they are less visible they are not so vulnerable to public or political hostility; because they are small they can maintain tighter and more efficient managerial control; and because they are more mobile they can adjust more quickly to changing conditions at home and overseas.

As the complex issue of multinational corporations comes under closer scrutiny from many directions, the nature and role of these firms are changing. Although some form of international control over their operations appears inevitable, it is easy to see that multinationals will continue to play a central part in a world economic system that is becoming more and more interconnected.

nationalism: the new mercantilism

Accompanying and often exacerbating these problems is the resurgence of a new nationalism in much of the world. The old argument of protectionism versus free trade has been renewed as countries react to the strains in the trade system caused by integration, foreign investment, and the growing problems of an obsolete international monetary structure that is no longer capable of sustaining that system. Basic to this problem is the varying ability of individual nations to adjust to change.

Trade inevitably benefits certain industries in a country more than others. Those industries producing commodities for which the country has a comparative advantage are better off as a result of trade, while those making goods in which there is a comparative disadvantage are worse off. As we have seen earlier, the anticipated result of trade in such a case is a net gain for the country as a whole. This gain should be sufficient to enable the gaining industries to be taxed by an amount needed to compensate the losers and leave the gainers and the country as a whole still ahead.

The difficulty with this solution is that industries often form special-interest groups having sufficient political power to enforce their wills upon the country. Often overlooked is the fact that adjustments of the type called for in the international situation occur naturally between regions within countries. This was the case, for example, in the competition between New England and the Piedmont districts for the cotton textile industry earlier in this century. Although the Piedmont won that contest, little if anything was done to ease the situation of the New England region in return. Where two countries are involved, it frequently happens that the disadvantaged industry is able to prod political leaders to provide tariff or quota protection against the outside competition. This occurred recently as the U.S. established rigid quotas against textile imports from several Oriental countries in fulfillment of political campaign promises to domestic textile interests. The ultimate effect, of course, is to encourage inefficient producers and to reduce a country's ability to compete in international markets.

world trade and the energy crisis

In addition to these more or less chronic trade problems, world commerce is now beginning to feel the first effects of the growing energy crisis. In Chapter 3 we noted that the accelerating demand for mechanical energy is straining the world's fossil fuel reserves. Petroleum consumption is rising especially fast because petroleum is so versatile and easy to transport and store. We saw, however, that major petroleum reserves are concentrated in only a few places, notably in North Africa and the Middle East, where two-thirds of the world's supply is controlled by a small group of underdeveloped nations.

On the other hand, most of the technically advanced countries, which consume the major part of the world's oil output, are severely short of domestic supplies. European reserves are inadequate to its growing need, United States domestic supplies are dwindling steadily after a century and a quarter of intensive exploitation, and Japan's home supplies are exceedingly meager. The natural consequence of this world imbalance in the location of supply and demand is a rapid growth in the global oil trade. The stream of oil flowing by supertanker from the Middle East to deficit countries increases in size day by day (see Fig. 3.16).

This situation has ominous overtones for those petroleum-short countries dependent upon Middle Eastern supplies, as shown by the dilemma now confronting

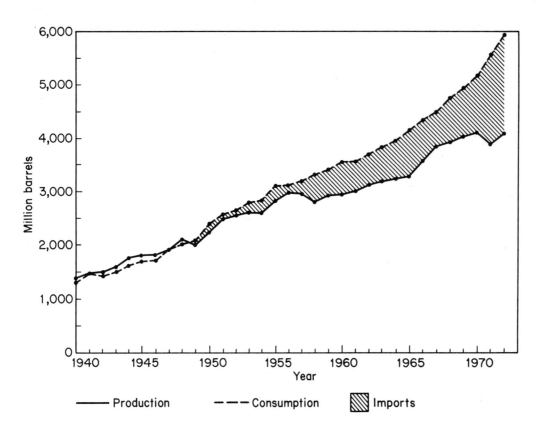

Fig. 11.4 *United States consumption, domestic production, and imports of all oils including natural-gas liquids, 1940–1972. The oil crisis of the 1970s had actually been building up for several years.*

Source: U.S. Bureau of Mines, Mineral Yearbook *(Washington, D.C.: U.S. Government Printing Office).*

the United States, which currently consumes one-third of the world's energy. The dimensions of the United States's growing petroleum pinch are graphically defined in Figure 11.4. There we see that demand for oil began to outrun domestic supplies soon after the Second World War, and the ever-widening gap has since had to be filled in by imports. By 1950 the annual deficit was about 400 million barrels; by 1960 it had risen to a billion barrels; and by 1972 it had reached 2.4 billion barrels. Even this quantity of imports has proved inadequate and severe shortages are appearing (see Chapter 3). Moreover, it is unlikely that Canada and Venezuela will be able to continue satisfying the United States's ever-growing requirements. Until the renewed fighting in 1973 between Israel and the Arab countries, oil from the Middle East had been regarded as the only feasible short-run alternative.

The financial threat this supply problem presents to the United States is a typical one for major petroleum-importing nations. The cost of American oil imports in 1973 reached $8 billion, equivalent to the entire balance-of-payments deficit of the preceding year. If current trends should continue, however, the bill for imported oil will reach $17 billion by 1980. This presumes that oil prices will not change in the meantime, a condition that is certain not to hold. The oil-exporting nations, who are probably the first underdeveloped producers of a primary good to succeed in joining together to control the world price, raised that price by 72 percent during the three years from 1970 to 1973 and were assured a further 10 percent increase in 1974 and again in 1975. Subsequent to these agreements, however, the oil-producing nations unilaterally announced substantially greater price increases.

As they continue to ship larger quantities at ever-rising prices, the oil-exporting countries are accumulating truly fabulous sums of money. It is estimated that the Middle Eastern countries alone will have amassed a quarter of a trillion dollars by 1980. At their present state of development they cannot spend it as fast as it reaches them and they are considered partly responsible for the currency speculations that have recently disrupted world financial markets.

No less worrisome to the larger oil-using countries is the political threat inherent in this situation. Aid to Israel has been forbidden by Arab governments as a price for continuing their supply of oil. During the 1973 Arab-Israeli war, countries failing to heed this warning, notably the United States, were summarily deprived of all Arabian oil, and the rest of the world was put on short rations to prevent transshipment to the "offending" nations. This crisis thereupon produced rancorous disputes between the United States and several European nations. The incident graphically demonstrated the strategic danger posed by dependence upon potentially hostile governments for this vital commodity, as well as the excessively lengthy and vulnerable supply lines this source of oil entails.

Some of the proposed responses to this difficult set of problems were outlined in Chapter 3. As a short-run solution to the present emergency, the United States government dropped its 14-year-old system of oil-import quotas. New deep-water ports are to be constructed for receiving imported oil, and major oil companies have announced large-scale plans for new refinery construction at coastal sites. To counter the threat of higher oil prices it has been suggested that the national government assume the responsibility for bargaining with oil-supplying nations. Meanwhile, in response to the 1973 Arab embargo on oil shipments, the United States government initiated energy-conservation measures to ease the immediate shortage and began a program to accelerate some of the longer-range plans for developing alternative sources of energy described in Chapter 3.

the future of the world trade system

Satisfactory solutions to these many old and new problems of international trade are required if current rates of world trade growth are to be maintained. First, it will be necessary to overhaul the present international monetary system, which is in disarray, largely because several countries are unable to adjust to changing conditions. Means also need to be found for reducing disparities among nations and especially for eliminating the trade disadvantages of less developed lands. Furthermore, solutions to global energy-supply problems will have to be devised. Finally, it is essential that countries avoid entering into a trade war that forces each nation into a stultifying economic self-sufficiency.

Two alternatives seem to present themselves. One is to perfect the world trade system, with the purpose of promoting general growth in trade and higher standards of living. The other is to permit the system to fall into disuse, which would mean retrenchment, economic isolation, stagnation, and a general return to the distressing conditions of the 1930s.

RECOMMENDED READINGS

Balassa, Bela, *The Theory of Economic Integration*. Homewood, Ill.: Richard D. Irwin, 1961.

Hanson, Roger D., *Central America: Regional Integration and Economic Development*. Washington: National Planning Association Studies in Development Progress, No. 1, 1967.

Kaser, Michael, *Comecon: Integration Problems of the Planned Economies*. London: Oxford University Press, 1965.

Linder, Staffan Burenstam, *Trade and Trade Policy for Development*. New York: Praeger, 1967.

Linnemann, Hans, *An Econometric Study of International Trade Flows*. Amsterdam: North-Holland Publishing, 1966.

Maizels, Alfred, *Exports and Economic Growth of Developing Countries*. Cambridge: Cambridge University Press, 1968.

Manser, W. A. P., *The Financial Role of Multinational Enterprises*. New York: John Wiley, 1973.

Russett, Bruce M., *International Regions and the International System: A Study in Political Ecology*. Skokie, Ill.: Rand McNally, 1967.

Viner, Jacob, *The Customs Union Issue*. New York: Carnegie Endowment for International Peace, 1950.

local trade and urban hierarchies

12

$\mathbf{T}$rade and growth are also related within nations and at the local level. The relationships may be understood by developing the concept of an urban hierarchy.

THE IDEA OF AN URBAN HIERARCHY: MUQADDASI'S SCHEME

The idea that urban centers are arranged in echelons according to their size, the functions they perform for the surrounding regions, and the nature of local trading relationships, is not new. For example, a description of the Moslem lands written over 1,000 years ago was phrased entirely in hierarchical terms. The description, shown in Figure 12.1, comes directly from the work of Al-Muqaddasi (or al-Maqdīsī), so-called because he was born in Jerusalem (Bayt al-Maqdis). Al-Muqaddasi was a geographer who visited all the Moslem lands except Spain, Sijistan, and India, and who, in A.D. 985–986, embodied an account of his twenty years of travel in *Ahsan al-Taqāsīm fi Ma'rifat al-Aqālīm* [*The Best Classification for the Knowledge of Regions*].

Muqaddasi was one of several medieval Arab geographers who divided the Islamic world into regions, based on the historical and sociopolitical identity of each region, as well as on the relationships between cities and regions. Within each region, or *iqlīm*, he classified the settlements according to a hierarchical grading system. As he noted: "In my grading system of settlements, the *amsār* (singular *misr*) are comparable to kings; the *qasabat* (singular *qasabah*) are comparable to ministers; the *mudun* (singular *madīnah*) are comparable to cavalry men; and the *qurā* (singular *qaryah*) are comparable to soldiers . . ." A definitive hierarchy of dominance and subdominance was implied. Further, relating the successively smaller settlements to an analogous hierarchy of subregions, he noted: "every *iqlīm* must have *kuwar* (singular *kūrah*); every *kūrah* must have *qasabah;* every *qasabah* must have (or attract) *mudun* (singular *madīnah*) . . ." To Muqaddasi, the Arab world of A.D. 985 was layered spatially into an urban-regional hierarchy comprising four distinct echelons.

SPATIAL HIERARCHIES AND THE LOCATION OF CITIES

Throughout the world, urban centers and the regions they serve are organized into such spatial hierarchies. As we saw in Chapter 8, industrial activities have distinct locational preferences for one or another rank of the urban hierarchy, based upon the differences in market opportunities, urbanization economies, and types of labor force that cities of different sizes provide. In this chapter, we will show similar relationships for retail and service businesses, the local and regional trade flows that support these businesses, and the service areas and marketing patterns resulting from the trade relationships. Regularities of the same kind also characterize the provision of administrative services in political systems.

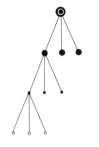

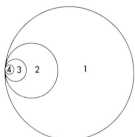

a. Theoretical hierarchy of
   settlements
   1. *Amsār (sing. misr), metropolis*
   2. *Qasabat (sing. quasabah),
      fortified provincial capitals*
   3. *Mudun (sing. madinah),
      provincial towns, a main town
      of a district, or a market town*
   4. *Qurā (sing. qaryah), villages*

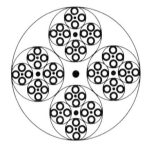
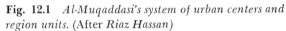

b. Theoretical hierarchy of regional
   units
   1. *Aqālīm (sing. iqlīm), regions*
   2. *Kuwar (sing. kūrah), provinces*
   3. *Nawāhy (sing. nahiyah),
      districts*
   4. *Rustaqāt (sing. rustāq),
      agricultural units*

c. Theoretical spatial distribution of
   settlements

Fig. 12.1 *Al-Muqaddasi's system of urban centers and
region units. (After Riaz Hassan)*

Source: Riaz Hassan, "Islam and Urbanization in the Medieval
Middle East," Ekistics, 33, (February 1972), 108.

the questions addressed by
central-place theory

The basic theory we are concerned with is called
central-place theory, and it attempts to answer such
questions as Why do urban hierarchies exist? What
determines the size and spacing of cities and the configuration of their market areas in such hierarchies?
There are, of course, many reasons for cities and their
locational patterns, often working in concert, as Figure
12.2 illustrates. For example, *transportation centers*
perform break-of-bulk and allied services along transportation routes and tend to be arranged in linear patterns with respect to railroads, highways, coastlines, and
rivers. *Specialized-function cities* perform services such
as mining, manufacturing, or recreation. Since the principal localizing factor is often a particular resource
such as a coal field, or a sandy beach and a warm sunny
climate, such cities occur singly or in clusters. Central-
place theory abstracts certain economic functions, the
tertiary activities of retail and service business, and
shows how their locational patterns lead to the broad
dispersion of market towns or central places of differing
sizes across the economic landscape, in hierarchies that
are precisely meshed with their market areas.

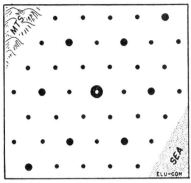

Theoretical distribution
of central places. In a
homogeneous land,
settlements are evenly
spaced; largest city in
center surrounded by 6
medium-sized centers that
in turn are surrounded
by 6 small centers.
Tributary areas are
hexagons, the closest
geometrical shapes to
circles that completely
fill area with no unserved
spaces.

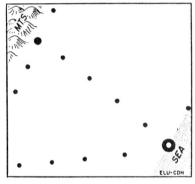

Transport centers,
aligned along railroads or
at coast. Large center is
port; next largest is
railroad junction and
engine-changing point
where mountain and
plain meet. Small centers
perform break-of-bulk
principally between rail
and roads.

Specialized-function
settlements. Large city is
manufacturing and
mining center surrounded
by a cluster of smaller
settlements located on a
mineral deposit. Small
centers on ocean and at
edge of mountains are
resorts.

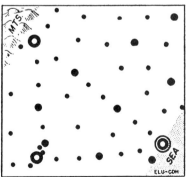

Theoretical composite
grouping. Port becomes
the metropolis and,
although off center, serves
as central place for whole
area. Manufacturing-
mining and junction
centers are next largest.
Railroad route in upper
left has been diverted to
pass through
manufacturing and
mining cluster.
Distribution of
settlements in upper
right follows central-place
arrangement.

Fig. 12.2 *Differing patterns of urban location*

Source: Chauncy D. Harris and Edward L. Ullman, "The Nature
of Cities," reprinted from Annals of the American Academy of
Political and Social Science, CCXLII (November 1945), 7–17 in
Harold M. Mayer and Clyde F. Kohn, eds., Readings in Urban
Geography (Chicago: University of Chicago Press, 1959), pp. 278–79.

It is to the central-place abstraction that we now turn, concerning ourselves therefore with the geography of retail and service business, and with the hierarchy of urban centers *insofar as they are market towns.* Because the leading central places in any region are also centers of wholesale trade which have their locational patterns determined by larger interregional trade flow relationships, the discussion of central places is followed by the elaboration of a "mercantile model" of wholesale trade. Finally, the chapter deals with local trade and periodic markets in peasant societies.

CITIES AND THE ORGANIZATION OF LOCAL TRADE

Throughout the chapter it will be well to remember why we are concerned with the urban hierarchy in studying the geography of economic systems: the basic reason is that of the interdependence of urbanization and trade. As metropolitan wholesaling centers, cities are the instruments whereby the specialized regions of a national economy are tied together. They are the centers of activity and of innovation, focal points of the transport network, locations of superior accessibility at which firms can most easily obtain the advantages of economies of scale and economies of localization and urbanization. Agricultural enterprise is more efficient in the vicinity of cities. The more prosperous commercialized agricultures encircle the major cities, whereas the inaccessible peripheries are characterized by backward, subsistence economic systems.

The sub-regional organization of the larger metropolitan-centered regions is provided by the system of central places, which involves:

a. a system of cities, arranged in a hierarchy according to the functions performed by each

b. corresponding areas of urban influence or urban fields surrounding each city in the system

The size and functions of a city and the extent of its urban field are proportional. Each region within the national economy focuses upon a center of metropolitan rank. A network of intermetropolitan connections and interregional trade-flows links the regions into a national whole. The spatial incidence of economic growth with these regions is a function of distance from the metropolis. Troughs of economic backwardness lie in the most inaccessible areas along the intermetropolitan peripheries. Each major region is, in turn, sub-regionalized by successively smaller centers at progressively lower levels of the hierarchy—smaller cities, towns, or villages that function as market centers for the distribution of goods and services to the region's consumers.

CHANGE IN THE URBAN SYSTEMS FRAMEWORK

Impulses of economic and social change in such a system are transmitted simultaneously along three planes:

a. outward from "heartland" metropolises to those of the regional hinterlands

b. from centers of higher to centers of lower level in the hierarchy, in a pattern of "hierarchical diffusion"

c. outward from urban centers into their surrounding urban fields, producing "spread effects"

Hence, the urban hierarchy serves not only to service the consumption needs of the various regions within a national economy, it also serves to pattern how and when change takes place. One result (which we discuss in Chapters 13 and 14) is that incomes fall as city size decreases and as distance from urban centers increases, in a distinctive hierarchically structured pattern of economic welfare.

WALTER CHRISTALLER'S CENTRAL-PLACE THEORY

Although many antecedents can be cited, going back to Al-Muqaddasi and before, the first explicit statement of central-place theory was made by the German geographer Walter Christaller in 1933 in a book entitled *Die Zentralen Orte in Süddeutschland* [*The Central Places of Southern Germany*]. The essential features of Christaller's argument may be summarized in six points.

1. The main function of a market town is to provide goods and services for a surrounding market area. Such towns are located centrally within their market areas, and hence they can be called "central places."

2. The greater the number of goods and services provided, the higher is the order of the central place.

3. Low-order places offer convenience goods that are purchased frequently within small market areas (Fig. 12.3) and hence the *range* of low order convenience goods (i.e., the maximum distance consumers are willing to travel) is small (Fig. 12.4).

4. Higher-order places are fewer in number and are more widely spaced than lower-order places providing goods with greater ranges (Figs. 12.5 and 12.6). Generally, the greater the range, the greater is the threshold (i.e., the minimum sales level necessary for the seller to make a profit).

5. A hierarchy of central places exists, to make as efficient as possible the arrangement of convenience and shopping goods opportunities for consumers, who have a basic desire to travel as little as possible to obtain the goods and services they need to maintain their households and persons, and for producers, who must earn at least a minimum "threshold" to survive.

6. Hierarchies have three spatial forms, organized according to

   (a) a marketing principle,

   (b) a transportation principle, and

   (c) an administrative principle.

Christaller proceeded, in the manner of Von Thünen and Weber, to a case in which extraneous variables were controlled by simplifying assumptions. As-

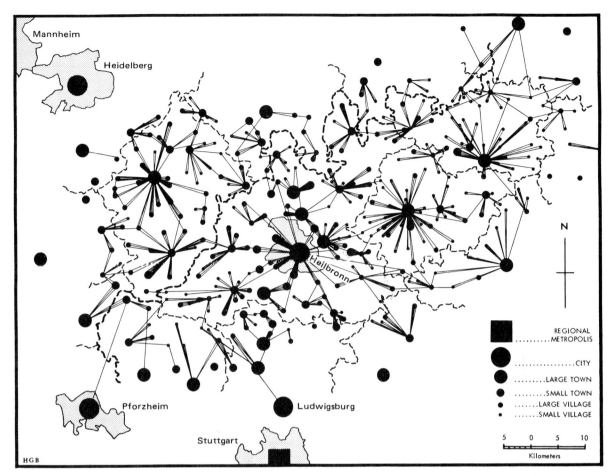

Fig. 12.3 *Travel to obtain pharmaceutical service in a portion of southern Germany*

Source: H. Gardiner Barnum, Market Centers and Hinterlands in Baden-Würtemberg *(Chicago: Department of Geography, Research paper no. 103, University of Chicago, 1966), p. 60.*

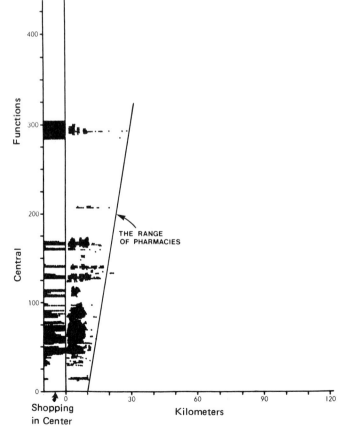

Fig. 12.4 *Relationship between distance traveled by consumers and size of center in Figure 12.3. The left hand column shows cases where consumers shop in the central place in which they live.*

Source: Barnum, Market Centers.

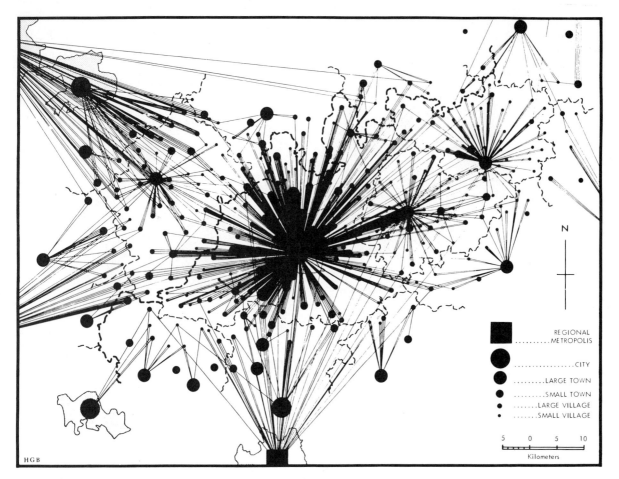

Fig. 12.5 *Travel to purchase clothing in a portion of southern Germany*

Source: Barnum, Market Centers.

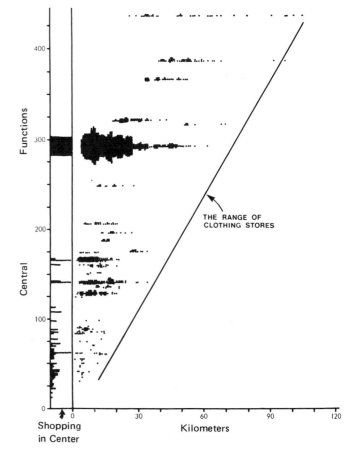

THE RANGE OF
CLOTHING
STORES

Fig. 12.6 *Distance relationships in Figure 12.5*

Source: Barnum, Market Centers.

sume, he said, identical consumers distributed at uniform densities over an unbounded plain on which access is equally easy in any direction. Under such circumstances the range of any good has a constant radius. How can centers be located so as to provide for the most efficient marketing of the goods? Given the homogeneity of the plain, Christaller concluded that each good should be supplied by a uniform net of equidistant central places, close enough together so that no part of the plain is left unsupplied.

The resulting distribution is one in which the central places are located at the apexes of a network of equilateral triangles, with each set of six centers forming a hexagon. This organization permits the maximum packing of central places into the plain.

the hierarchical principles

After developing his basic model, Christaller suggested three spatial alternatives, organized according to marketing, transportation, and administrative principles.

the marketing principle

The marketing principle assumes that the location of a central place of any order is at the midpoint of each set of three neighboring places of the next higher order (Fig. 12.7). These midpoints are the corners of the hexagonal market areas of the higher-order centers, and every higher-order center is surrounded by a ring of six centers of next lower-order located at the corners of its hexagons. The boundaries of the lower-order complementary regions are the perpendicular bisectors of the higher-order complementary regions.

The progression of centers and market area sizes derived by Christaller can be observed in Figure 12.7. Each higher-order market area contains the equivalent of three market areas of the next lower order—its own, plus one-third of each of the surrounding six, and the

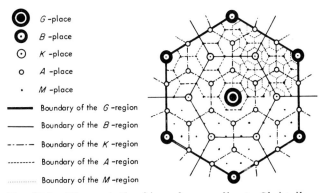

Fig. 12.7 *The marketing hierarchy according to Christaller*

Source: Walter Christaller, Central Places in Southern Germany, *trans. Carlisle Baskin (Englewood Cliffs, N.J.: Prentice–Hall, 1966), p. 61.*

equivalent of two central places of the next lower order —each ring of the six surrounding centers lies within the hexagons of three centers of higher order. The progression of market areas is $1(3^0)$, $3(3^1)$, $9(3^2)$, $27(3^3)$, $81(3^4)$, and of centers $1(3^0 - 0)$, $2(3^1 - 3^0)$, $6(3^2 - 3^1)$, $18(3^3 - 3^2)$ and $54(3^4 - 3^3)$. The progressive increase by a rule of threes leads to a description of this marketing-principle arrangement as a $k = 3$ network.

Christaller elaborated the marketing principle for the *landstadts* of southern Germany, namely Munich, Frankfurt, Stuttgart, and Nuremberg-Furth (see Table 12.1 and Fig. 12.8). Christaller's map also includes Strasbourg and Nancy in France and Zurich in Switzerland, which also rank as landstadts. The table presents a relationship among size, spacing, number of functions, and hierarchical interdependence that is surprising in its closeness to the theory. The strict regularity has been disturbed by a variety of historic, economic, and geographic circumstances. Among the economic factors causing local deviations that were noted by Christaller are population density and income, the economic base of the region, and interregional competition.

Table 12.1   Characteristics of Central Places in Southern Germany, 1933

TYPE	NUMBER OF PLACES	NUMBER OF COMPLEMENTARY REGIONS	RANGE OF REGION (KM.)	AREA OF REGION (SQ.KM.)	NUMBER OF TYPES OF GOODS OFFERED	TYPICAL POPULATION OF PLACES (IN THOUSANDS)	TYPICAL POPULATION OF REGION (IN THOUSANDS)
M	486	729	4.0	44	40	1	3.5
A	162	243	6.9	133	90	2	11
K	54	81	12.0	400	180	4	35
B	18	27	20.7	1,200	330	10	100
G	6	9	36.0	3,600	600	30	350
P	2	3	62.1	10,800	1,000	100	1,000
L	1	1	108.0	32,400	2,000	500	3,500
Total	729						

Note: The levels of the hierarchy described by Christaller are: I. Marktort M; II. Amtsort A; III. Kreisstadt K; IV. Bezirkstadt B; V. Gaustadt G; VI. Provinzstadt P; VII, Landstadt L.

Source: Walter Christaller, *Central Places in Southern Germany;* trans. Carlisle W. Baskin (Englewood Cliffs, N.J.: Prentice-Hall, 1966, p. 67)

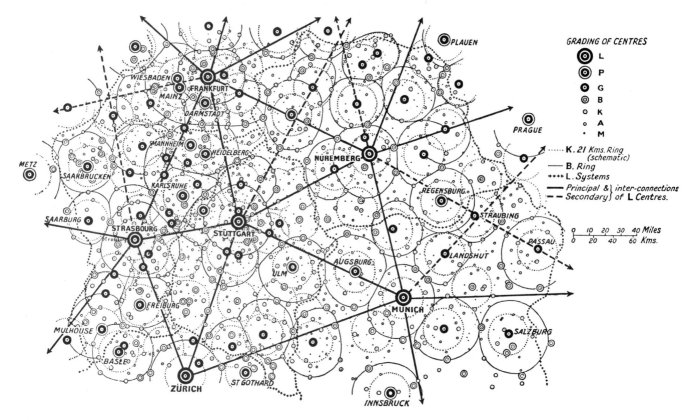

Fig. 12.8 *The central place system of southern Germany*

Source: Christaller, Central Places in Southern Germany, *pp. 224–25.*

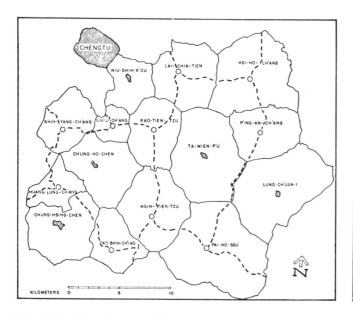

Fig. 12.9 *A portion of Szechwan near Chengtu. (After G. William Skinner)*

Source: Brian J. L. Berry, Geography of Market Centers and Retail Distribution *(Englewood Cliffs, N.J.: Prentice–Hall, 1967), p. 67.*

G. William Skinner, an American anthropologist, has provided an outstanding example of the relationship between actual central-place patterns and Christal-

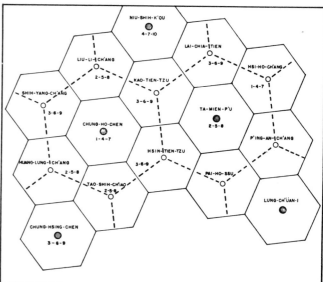

Fig. 12.10 *The K-3 network*

Source: Berry, Geography of Market Centers.

ler's abstract $k = 3$ network in a study of rural marketing in pre-Communist China, illustrated by Figures 12.9 and 12.10. In Figure 12.9 is the actual urban pattern which is easily transformed into the $k = 3$ network of Figure 12.10.

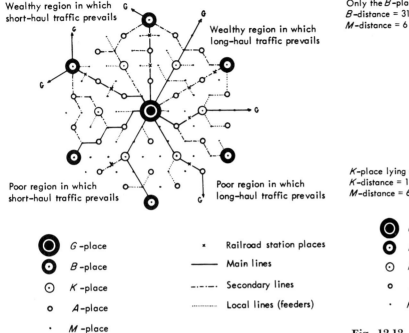

Wealthy region in which short-haul traffic prevails

Wealthy region in which long-haul traffic prevails

Poor region in which short-haul traffic prevails

Poor region in which long-haul traffic prevails

◉ *G*-place
◉ *B*-place
⊙ *K*-place
○ *A*-place
· *M*-place

× Railroad station places
——— Main lines
–·–·– Secondary lines
·········· Local lines (feeders)

Fig. 12.11 *Traffic routes in the marketing network*

Source: Christaller, Central Places in Southern Germany.

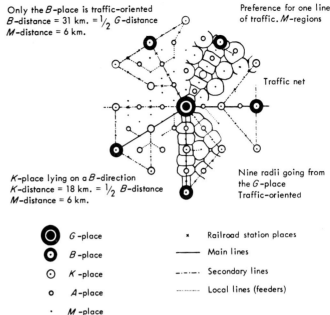

Only the *B*-place is traffic-oriented
B-distance = 31 km. = ½ *G*-distance
M-distance = 6 km.

Preference for one line of traffic. *M*-regions

Traffic net

K-place lying on a *B*-direction
K-distance = 18 km. = ½ *B*-distance
M-distance = 6 km.

Nine radii going from the *G*-place
Traffic-oriented

◉ *G*-place
◉ *B*-place
⊙ *K*-place
○ *A*-place
· *M*-place

× Railroad station places
——— Main lines
–·–·– Secondary lines
·········· Local lines (feeders)

Fig. 12.12 *Modification of market areas in the transportation solution to creation of a hierarchy, according to Christaller*

Source: Christaller, Central Places in Southern Germany.

Fig. 12.13 *The revised hierarchy solution to permit centers to align on major transport arteries: (a) the routes; (b) locations of centers; (c) regional hierarchies*

Source: Walter Christaller, Das Grundgerüst der räumlichen Ordnung in Europa *(Frankfurt am Main: W. Kramer and Co., 1950), p. 10.*

the transportation principle

Spatial organization according to the marketing principle makes it difficult to establish a satisfactory transportation system. The location of centers on the corners of hexagons means that no straight route can link centers at three consecutive orders on the hierarchy. A long-distance route linking "metropolitan" centers (*G*-places) can pass through the towns (*K*-places) but misses the cities (*B*-places) for which special routes are required. Christaller suggested a number of possible traffic route systems (Fig. 12.11). However, these alternatives are not as satisfactory as the reorganization of complementary regions according to a transportation principle.

The transportation principle states that the distribution of central places is most favorable when as many important places as possible lie on one traffic route between two important towns, the route being established as straight and as cheaply as possible. Christaller suggested that complementary regions would be distorted from the hexagonal form (Fig. 12.12) if one attempted to maintain the marketing hierarchy. He realized that a regular hexagonal form can be retained, however, by locating successive lower orders of centers at the *midpoints* of the transport routes running directly between the metropolitan centers (Fig. 12.13). Thus a hierarchy is produced maximizing the number of centers located on major transport routes. Because centers locate at midpoints, they bisect the sides of hexagons rather than locating at their apexes. The result is a "nesting" of hexagons inside one another according to

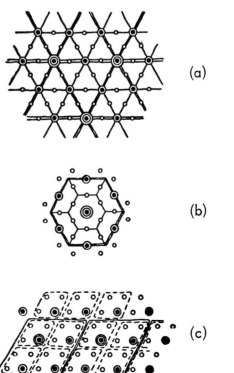

(a)

(b)

(c)

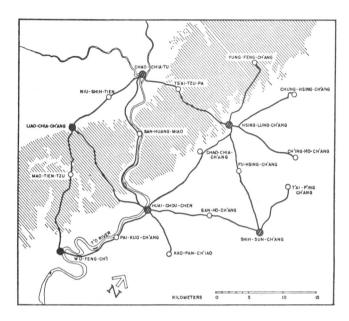

Fig. 12.14 *A second portion of Szechwan northeast of Chengtu. (After G. W. Skinner)*

Source: Berry, Geography of Market Centers.

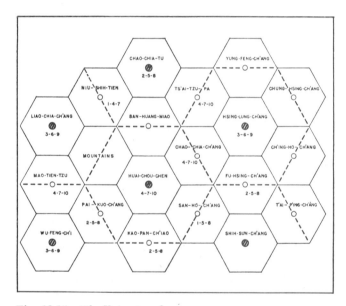

Fig. 12.15 *The K-4 network*

Source: Berry, Geography of Market Centers.

a rule of fours. For every center of a given order there will be, on the average, four market areas of the next lower order (its own, plus one half of each of the six surrounding) and three places of next lower order (each of the ring of six surrounding centers lies on the hexagon of two centers of higher order). The progression of market areas is $1(4^0)$, $4(4^1)$, $16(4^2)$, $64(4^3)$, $256(4^4)$ and of centers is 1, $3(4^1 - 4^0)$, $12(4^2 - 4^1)$, $48(4^3 - 4^2)$, 192 $(4^4 - 4^3)$. It therefore takes 192 village centers to support one metropolis by the traffic organization compared with only 54 by the marketing principle. Thus a traffic-

organized area too small to support 192 village regions could not support a metropolitan center. The traffic hierarchy is generally coarser with fewer levels than the marketing hierarchy for given-sized areas. The allocation of goods and services, therefore, involves broader groupings of goods at each level. Customers must travel farther, on average, to reach a center at a given level of the hierarchy, offsetting the advantage of a more efficient transportation system.

In another part of pre-Communist China, G. William Skinner has provided an example of a $k = 4$ hierarchy as startling as that shown in Figures 12.9 to 12.10. The relevant illustrations in this case are Figure 12.14, the actual pattern of central places, and Figure 12.15, the $k = 4$ hierarchy. In spite of the existence of mountains that have the effect of eliminating a center from one of the hexagonal cells, Figure 12.15 is only locally distorted.

the administrative principle

The transportation principle, like the marketing principle, presents a problem, however: the division of complementary regions at successive levels of the hier-

Fig. 12.16 *Hierarchical relationships and traffic routes in Christaller's administrative scheme*

Source: Christaller, Das Grundgerüst der räumlichen Ordnung in Europa.

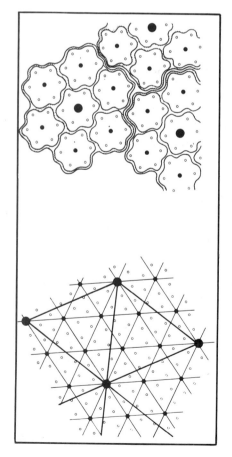

archy. The overlapping of smaller regions across the boundaries of higher-order complementary regions is inconsistent with administrative organization. Administrative principles involve the grouping of complementary regions of lower order, such as counties, *within* those of higher order, such as states, in their entirety. This is essential for unambiguous administrative control. The ideal organization, said Christaller, should have as the nucleus the capital, with a ring of lower-order administrative centers around it, and a thinning of population density toward the edge of the region. In this scheme, a central place of higher-order administers to the total area of the six surrounding lower-order complementary regions, thus following a rule of sevens (Fig. 12.16). The hierarchy is coarser, the transportation system less efficient and consumers must travel further than in either the market or traffic organization.

AUGUST LÖSCH'S ECONOMIC LANDSCAPES

A number of difficulties present themselves when all three principles are operating simultaneously in the organization of space. How do they relate to create some of the complex hierarchies observable in reality in modern urban-industrial societies? Christaller was unable to resolve these difficulties, but soon after he had written his book another German, location economist August Lösch, provided an answer in his book *Die Raümliche Ordnung der Wirtschaft* [*The Spatial Organization of the Economy*].

Lösch began, like all location theorists, with a wide plain, homogeneous in every respect and containing only self-sufficient farms that are regularly distributed in a triangular-hexagonal pattern. He then showed how an economic landscape could be built from the lowest-order centers upwards.

a progression of market area hexagons

His first step was to derive a spatial demand cone, and to prove why Christaller's triangular-hexagonal spatial patterns were the most efficient. He then found that Christaller's $k = 3$, $k = 4$, and $k - 7$ networks were the first three cases in an entire progression of market area sequences in which the spacing of centers or order could be calculated by the equation of

$$d_n = d_{n-1} \sqrt{k}$$

where k is the hierarchy ratio and d_{n-1} is the spacing of the next lower order of centers.

The nine smallest market area patterns found by Lösch are illustrated in Figure 12.17. These have k values of 3, 4, 7, 9, 12, 13, 16, 19, and 21. Centers are located with respect to the hexagons in three possible ways: at an apex, as where $k = 3$ and 12; at the midpoint of a side as when $k = 4$, 9, 16 and 25, and within the hexagon as when $k = 7$, 13, 19 and 21.

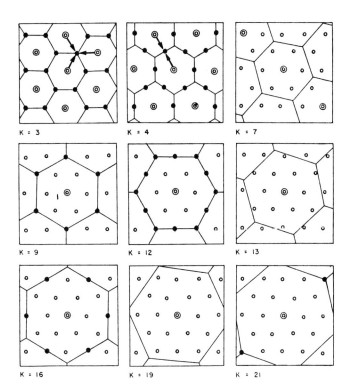

Fig. 12.17 *The nine smallest market areas in Lösch's analysis*

Source: Peter Haggett, Locational Analysis in Human Geography *(London: Edward Arnold Ltd., 1965), p. 119.*

city-rich and city-poor sectors around the metropolis

Lösch thought it desirable to devise a compound hierarchy incorporating all these possible arrangements of hexagons. Only such a combination, he felt, would adequately reflect the complexities of the real world. He thus built an "economic landscape" around a single metropolitan center using the ten smallest hexagonal configurations of market areas. Assume, Lösch said, that each network has one place in common, the metropolis. Then rotate the separate patterns around the metropolis until there is a maximum coincidence of central places in the different schemes—a solution that minimizes the number of centers. The result is a division of the region into six city-poor and six city-rich sectors (Fig. 12.18). Lösch provided sketch-maps of Indianapolis and Toledo as examples (Figs. 12.19 and 12.20).

The hierarchy is not "nested" in the Löschian landscape as it is in the Christallerian, so that apart from the metropolis, no center offers all the goods and services. On the contrary, each symmetric sixty-degree sector of the economic landscape displays considerable functional specialization. The twelve radii delimiting these city-rich and city-poor sectors are the busiest transportation routes, with cross-connections well developed in only the city-rich sector.

The city-rich sectors of adjacent metropolitan centers may be linked to portray the complete economic

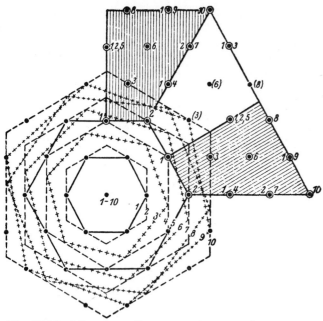

Fig. 12.18 *The ten smallest economic areas. The sectors containing many towns are hatched. Alternative regional centers are in parentheses. Simple points represent original settlements. Those enclosed in circles are centers of market areas of sizes indicated by the figures.*

Source: *August Lösch,* The Economics of Location, *Trans. William H. Woglom and Wolfgang F. Stolper (New Haven: Yale University Press, 1954), p. 118.*

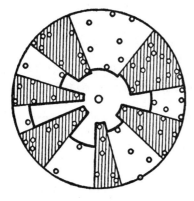

Fig. 12.19 *Indianapolis and environs within a radius of 60 miles.* (After *Andree's* Handatlas)

Source: *Lösch,* The Economics of Location.

Fig. 12.20 *Toledo and environs within a radius of 60 miles* (After *Andree's* Handatlas)

Source: *Lösch,* The Economics of Location.

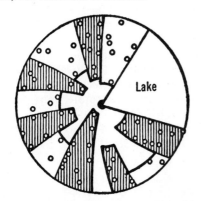

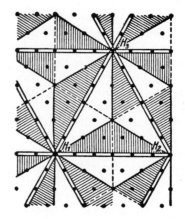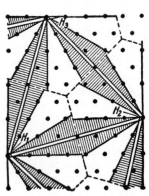

Fig. 12.21 *Alternate groupings of city-rich and city-poor sectors of adjacent metropolitan centers. Double lines connect routes between large cities; broken lines are landscape boundaries; hatched are sectors with many towns.*

Source: *Lösch,* The Economics of Location.

landscape in different ways (Fig. 12.21). The trunk lines of communication can be arranged to pass through the largest number of towns or a bypass pattern may be employed in which towns not directly on the main route lie within a relatively short distance on either side of them.

FUNDAMENTAL CONCEPTS OF CENTRAL-PLACE THEORY

Both Christaller and Lösch agree that the triangular arrangement of production sites or retail stores and hexagonal market areas represent the optimal spatial organization for a single good, under the assumption of uniform densities on an unbounded plain with equal access in all directions. Lösch provides explicit proof that this pattern of location of individual firms is as advantageous as possible. Although the two authors then disagree on how one builds spatial patterns of centers and market areas, they do agree on the three fundamental concepts of central-place theory, range, threshold, and hierarchy. These concepts have broad applicability in studying spatial organization and permit the statement of central-place theory without the restricting assumption of uniformity of purchasing power and the necessary consequence of hexagonal market areas. Indeed, Richard L. Morrill asserts that the crucial test of the usefulness of central-place theory does not involve the presence of the strict geometric (hexagonal) forms, but whether or not the following questions are valid:

1. Does the spatial organization of tertiary activity reflect the level and distribution of purchasing power?
2. Do tertiary services tend to be regularly spaced in areas with similar physical, cultural, and economic characteristics?
3. Do individuals tend to minimize the aggregate distance travelled to purchase goods and services?
4. Do individuals shop at a hierarchy of centers?

These questions apply to tertiary activity within individual cities as well as to systems of cities and, at both scales, permit investigation of the impact of physical, cultural, and economic heterogeneity on central-place activity.

WHOLESALE TRADE PATTERNS

Central-place theory deals with the relationships between retailers and consumers *within* given regions, as mediated by the urban hierarchy. The goods that are distributed by the retailers are brought into the region from other regions by wholesalers. The wholesale trade relationships that link regions are conducted in large measure *between* the metropolitan centers of the regions, and in consequence the locational patterns of the metropolises are determined by the *external* trade linkages. Hence, if as Christaller and Lösch maintain, local urban hierarchies are patterned around the metropolis they, too, must reflect some effect of the need for interregional trade.

the mercantile model

Such is the essence of James Vance's "mercantile model" of wholesale trade. Vance began by exploring the functions of wholesalers. Wholesaling, he said, connects, in trade, numerous specialized producers of commodities in many diverse regions with an even greater array of consumers, who within each region tend to demand the same array of goods and services. Direct access to the customer by the producer is impossible because of the great numbers involved and because of the considerable geographical distance that often separates the groups. Nonetheless, there must be ties between the two groups that will (1) provide the producer with both a market and some idea of its scale of demands, and (2) assure the consumer access to products of a determined type at a specific time.

Several different types of wholesalers were distinguished, based upon the manner in which the merchant conducts his business and the relation he bears to sources of his supply and locations and organization of his purchaser:

a. *The merchant wholesaler.* The first wholesalers almost certainly were merchants, in the original sense of that word—men who negotiated, or trafficked in, goods on a large scale, particularly in foreign trade. First as individuals and later as corporations these traders formed the fundamental body of wholesalers. They include distributors, jobbers, foreign trade merchants, or limited-function wholesalers—distributors primarily engaged in buying, taking title to, and where customary, physically storing and handling goods made by others, and selling the goods at wholesale principally to retailers or to industrial, institutional, and commercial users. Over the years the merchant wholesalers have been the largest component in the trade, and it is this type of establishment that matches most the standard conception of wholesaling. In the most recent census of wholesale firms and establishments, just over two out of three were classed as merchant wholesalers.

b. *The manufacturers' agent.* In contrast with merchant wholesalers are manufacturers' sales branches and offices. These establishments differ from merchant wholesalers in that they are owned by manufacturers or mining companies and maintained apart from manufacturing plants, primarily for selling or marketing their products at wholesale. There are two varieties: establishments that receive, store, and distribute the goods in which they trade, and those limited to the securing and remitting of orders for goods.

c. *The broker.* These sales agencies also are extensions of the manufacturing corporation; the distinction between the broker and the manufacturers' agent is that the broker serves many manufacturers, not one.

d. *Export-import agents.* Export and import agents fall into the general class of agents and brokers. These men provide a linkage between producers and consumers. Their knowledge of market conditions and sources of supply is for hire, and it earns their income. In some cases they may undertake certain financing functions, but in general the importer or exporter is a trader more than he is a banker. Often he may not take physical possession of goods, but it is his orders that start the flow of goods and determine their origin.

Vance argued that in the locational problem of the merchant wholesaler is found the quintessence of location theory for the trade. For such wholesalers, trade does not appear to be governed by competition among trading centers as much as by competition among wholesale establishments, possibly all in the same trading center. It is thus the quality of service, not its proximity, that is the key. Tributary areas must be as *small* as is consonant with the highest quality of service. As the tributary area population increases, the wholesaler must increase his product specialization, and thereby improve his service, in order to retain the same area of trade. If he does not increase his product specialization, then his tributary area will be forced to contract through the loss of integral parts to competitors who can prosper on no more than a part of an expanded market population. In these reduced tributary areas the frequency of trade would be increased at the expense of product specialization, which is a form of higher service.

In this scheme, the wholesale center is seen as the "unraveling point" in the geography of trade, linking specialized production areas, mediating trade flows, and determining the metropolitan centers from which central-place relationships can develop to meet the consumption needs of local areas.

The sequence of development linking the Old and New Worlds, and leading to the subsequent emergence of an urban hierarchy in the New World, Vance saw to be as follows (see Fig. 12.22):

1. Before settlement was attempted, the economic potential of the area was tested on the basis of information collected and the pattern of trade that might be anticipated.

2. Once the potential was determined, initial settlement took place in terms of a mercantile model. The dynamics were exogenic, the extent of the system was given by long-distance trading, and growth depended as much on the

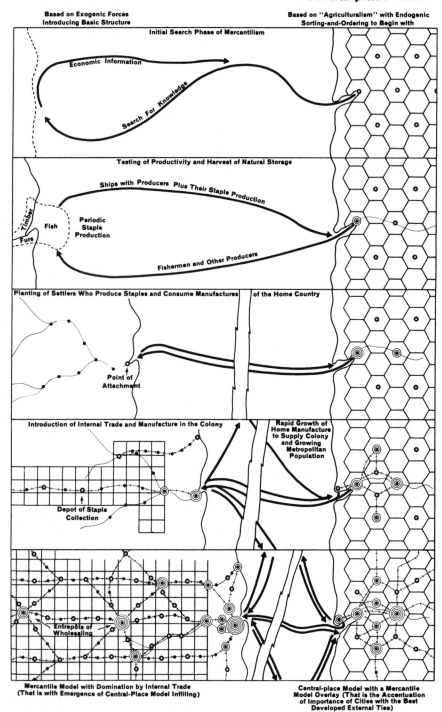

The Mercantile Model

Based on Exogenic Forces Introducing Basic Structure

Initial Search Phase of Mercantilism

Economic Information

Search For Knowledge

Testing of Productivity and Harvest of Natural Storage

Ships with Producers Plus Their Staple Production

Timber / Fish / Furs

Periodic Staple Production

Fishermen and Other Producers

Planting of Settlers Who Produce Staples and Consume Manufactures

Point of Attachment

Introduction of Internal Trade and Manufacture in the Colony

Depot of Staple Collection

Entrepôts of Wholesaling

Mercantile Model with Domination by Internal Trade (That is with Emergence of Central-Place Model Infilling)

The Central-place Model

Based on "Agriculturalism" with Endogenic Sorting-and-Ordering to Begin with

of the Home Country

Rapid Growth of Home Manufacture to Supply Colony and Growing Metropolitan Population

Central-place Model with a Mercantile Model Overlay (That is the Accentuation of Importance of Cities with the Best Developed External Ties)

Fig. 12.22 *Vance's contrasts between urban evolution in the mercantile model and central-place theory contexts*

Source: James E. Vance, Jr., The Merchant's World: The Geography of Wholesaling. *(Englewood Cliffs, N.J.: Prentice-Hall, 1970), p. 151.*

ability of the external world to consume as upon the parochial area to produce.

3. As the scale of the trading system enlarged, mercantile towns grew as "points of attachment" which, in turn, increased the demand for hinterland provision for those towns and for the collection of staples in greater quantity.

4. Only at this stage in the externally based system did the central-place model begin to characterize settlement. That characterization was limited (a) to the latter additions to the settlement pattern, and (b) to those areas characterized by areally based staple production.

5. Subsequently, there was parallel growth of settlement in accordance with both models. As new regions were opened up, metropolitan entrepôts were created on the basis of the external linkages needed to ship out exports. As local demands grew with the development of settlement, the metropolises also became importing centers, and in general, "unraveling points" in regional and interregional trading relationships.

Whereas the central-place pattern of the Old World gradually developed in triangular-hexagonal forms, that of the New World was laid down in rectangular patterns by the importation of both transport routes and the rectangular land survey system. The priority of mercantile towns in this process meant that they provided the basic points of focus—and ultimately the major metropolises—for the central-place systems responsible for the internal organization of retail trade.

PERIODIC MARKETS AND THE SPATIAL ORGANIZATION OF PEASANT SOCIETIES

So far we have talked about wholesale trade and central places in relatively specialized economies. What of the situation in those economic systems where specialization is relatively less advanced?

In most peasant societies, markets are periodic rather than permanent and continuous. The market is open only once every few days on a regularly scheduled basis, because the per capita demand for goods sold in the market is small, the market area is limited by primitive transport technology, and the aggregate demand is therefore insufficient to support permanent shops. Businessmen adjust by visiting several markets on a regular basis and accumulating the trade of several market areas.

Skinner's description of the periodic marketing system of traditional rural China may be used as an example, although details vary from one part of the world to another. Periodicity of the markets is related to the mobility of individual businessmen. The peddler toting his wares on a pole from one market to the next is the archetype of the mobile firm in China. Equally characteristic is the wandering artisan or repairman, itinerants purveying services from letter-writing to fortune-telling. From their point of view, periodic markets have the virtue of concentrating demand in specific places on specific days. When the firm is both producer and trader there are additional advantages, permitting sales and production to be undertaken on different days.

From the consumers' point of view, the periodicity of markets reduces the distance that must be traveled to obtain needed goods and services to a single day's excursion. Furthermore, the subsistence production activities of the household can be combined with needed trips to the market.

The periodicities of individual markets are synchronized; Figure 12.23 depicts one such system recorded by Skinner. There are three levels of centers: standard markets, intermediate markets, and central markets, which are the highest order and are located at strategic points on the transport network, providing important wholesaling functions. The central market receives imported items and distributes them to its market area via the lower-order centers, and it collects local products and exports them to other central markets and higher-order centers. The standard market is the lowest-level central place, with the exception of minor "green vegetable markets," and meets periodi-

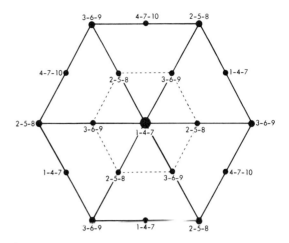

Fig. 12.23 *Periodicity of markets in a traditional Chinese 3-per-hsün cycle*

Source: Berry, Geography of Market Centers.

cally. The higher-level centers have permanent shops in addition to their periodic markets, and the central markets have smaller business centers at each of the four gates of the city, where the periodicity may even be on a twice-daily basis.

The periodic marketing system of Figure 12.23 is one in which a merchant can move between the central market and a pair of standard markets in a ten-day cycle divided into units of three: the central market (day 1), first standard (day 2), second standard (day 3), central (day 4), first standard (day 5), second standard (day 6), central (day 7), first standard (day 8), second standard (day 9), and central (day 10), when no business is transacted. The interlocking periodicities of a large number of market centers of different levels can be seen in the figure.

Such cycles are determined either by "natural" means, using the motions of the heavenly bodies, or they are "artificial," without reference to any natural cycles. Ten-day marketing weeks, for example, were tied to the lunar month, whereas the seven-day marketing week of the Christian calendar is entirely artificial.

In China, the two fundamental cycles were the lunar decade (*hsün*), beginning on the first, eleventh, and twenty-first of each lunar month, and the 12-day duodenary cycle. Skinner argues that a one per-*hsün* cycle was originally adopted by the Chinese ancients in the valley of the Huang Ho, whereas a one-per-duodenum cycle was adopted in the southwest. As market systems developed, first the higher-level and finally the standard markets doubled their schedules, and later the highest-level centers doubled their schedules again.

One factor influencing the periodicity of markets is population density. Generally, the more people in the area, the greater the aggregate demand and the greater the frequency with which any market can meet, until, at the most frequent, it meets every day. A similar statement can be made about per capita demands as incomes rise or the peasant household begins to

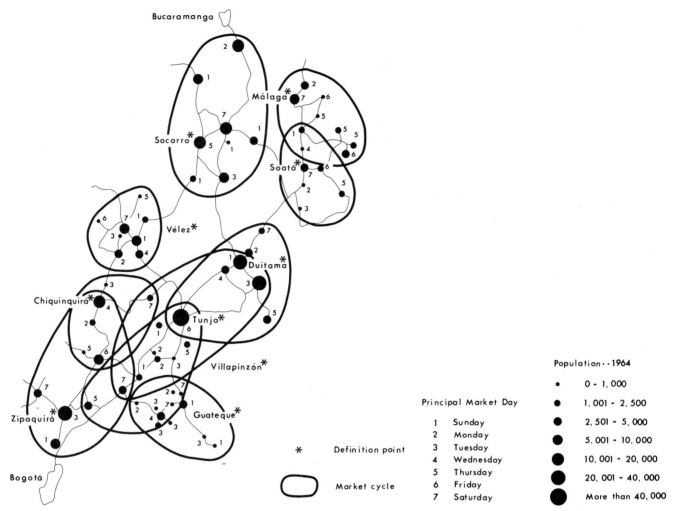

Fig. 12.24 *Market cycles in Andean Colombia*

Source: Richard Symanski, *Periodic Markets of Andean Colombia*
(Ph.D. dissertation, Syracuse University, 1971).

specialize more in production for sale: the more demands per capita increase, the greater the aggregate demand and periodicity, until permanency is achieved.

Across southern China, the periodicity of the duodenary cycle gradually increases from west to east, with the six-day week being very common (1–7, 2–8, 3–9, 4–10, 5–11, and 6–12) and in the densest areas further doubling resulting in 1–4–7–10, 2–5–8–11, and 3–6–9–12. Across northern China, one-per-*hsün* cycles are found only in remote peripheral areas. Two-per-*hsün* cycles are the most common in standard markets, and four-per-*hsün* in central markets. The three-per-*hsün* schedules are common for standard markets in the regions of higher population densities at the heart of the Szechwan basin and the plains of southeastern China, and where densities are higher owing to specialization in food production for urban markets closer to big cities. Figures 12.10, 12.15 and 12.23 depict such three-per-*hsün* cycles.

Elsewhere in the world other cycles are found: two-per-*hsün* cycles are most common in Korea, whereas a one-per-*hsün* cycle was found in Japan prior to modernization. Both are presumably related to diffusion of Chinese culture in the north. In Rome, markets were

held every ninth day. After the adoption of Christianity, the nine-day week was changed to a seven-day week and markets were held every Sunday. In time, clerical authorities became concerned with the worldliness of markets held about churches. In A.D. 906, for example, Sunday markets were prohibited in England. The weekday market that had sprung up, particularly in the trade of salt, iron, and local produce, took over the Sunday market functions. "Sunday towns" remain a common feature of life in Latin America even today, however, whereas "blue laws" and Sunday closing remain where Puritanical traditions are still strong. Figure 12.24 shows the seven-day periodic market cycles in a section of Andean Colombia.

Staggering market days to accommodate both buyer and seller seems to be a nearly universal pattern. In Africa, the market week varies from a three-day to a seven-day week. The three-day, four-day, five-day, and six-day weeks stem from ancient tribal differences, while the seven-day week resulted from calendar changes introduced by Islam into Africa. In Kusai, the economy is oriented to a three-day market cycle, and people think of three markets as being linked together. Each of these three markets is held on a consecutive day. Each, in turn, may be linked to another market cycle so that all of Kusai is covered by a connected net of market cycles. In Yorubaland the markets operate on a ring system. Each ring is composed of a four-day cycle or multiples of four days. This timing is related to the former four-day week in West Africa. Similar periodicities have been noted in India, and in Central and South America.

The standard marketing systems of China are shown by Skinner to be not simply exchange mechanisms, but the basic building blocks of that society. Other authors imply the same for other societies. Each standard market and its surrounding tributary area functions as an economic and social community, incorporating, on the average, eighteen villages.

Typically, one out of five adults living in the villages went to a market on a market day in traditional China to shop in the standard market in a multitude of petty market places, one for each product. This specialization is true elsewhere, and Figure 12.25 reproduces Fogg's diagram of the structure of a large *suq* in Morocco. The market serves as a place for the peasant to sell what he produces and purchase what he needs. For both buyer and seller, a profit motive dominates; bargaining and higgling may be intense, even though monetary standards of exchange exist. Local credit societies exist for villages within the system; landlords collect their rents and transport coolies can be hired there. In turn, each standard market links into higher-level market systems. The local elite patronize the intermediate and central markets, purchasing luxuries unavailable to the peasantry in standards markets.

Fig. 12.25 *Plan of a large suq* (After *Walter Fogg*)

Source: Berry, Geography of Market Centers.

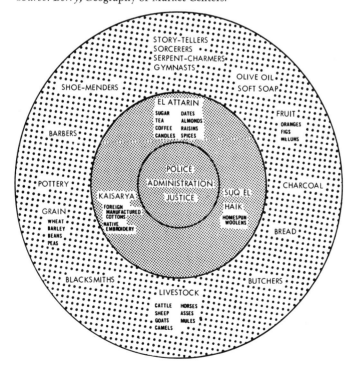

Furthermore, traders return to their bases to replenish stocks or dispose of purchases. Even at the higher levels, peddlers selling less frequently demanded goods can be found in the central markets.

The whole is thus an interdependent system, with exotic goods sold in the central market and itinerants circulating in lower-level markets. Merchandise produced in the central towns is distributed downwards by the itinerants. Both central and intermediate towns have a variety of producer-distributor and wholesale-retail relationships in addition to their retailing functions. The intermediate towns generally include only distributors, whereas the central markets have wholesalers with warehouses. Merchandise consumed by the peasantry or required by petty craftsmen flows down to every market, consumer goods for the local elite move no further than the intermediate markets, and consumer goods for the bureaucratic elite, and industrial supplies, never leave the central markets.

The upward flow of goods begins with the peasant selling his produce to local consumers or to dealers who process or bulk the product. These dealers pass the goods on to buyers, who carry them to intermediate or central markets, and perhaps up through successively higher levels of centers.

In what ways are the standard market communities social systems? They are endogamous for the peasantry; marriage brokers arrange marriages between villages within them. Leading shopkeepers and the local elite form committees responsible for the local religious festival. Voluntary and formal organizations use the standard marketing community as their unit of organization (for example, the composite lineage, the secret-society lodge, the committee arranging the local fair, the religious service society). Local variants of these elements of social integration repeat themselves elsewhere throughout the world. If a world map differentiating countries by level of economic development is examined, those parts of the world considered "underdeveloped" or with "isolated tribal economies" will generally be found to have periodic marketing systems in which basic economic units and basic social units are identical.

If the details of periodicity, commodities traded, and forms of social integration vary culturally, so do the locations of periodic markets. All locate to serve both buyers and sellers efficiently, but sites selected may differ among cultures. Most commonly, markets located at crossroads space themselves in a manner determined by the maximum distances consumers are willing to walk. The spacing is affected but little after an early period of development by differences in population density; instead, the periodicity of the markets adjusts as densities change, to serve increased demands by increased meetings. In Morocco, siting is determined by locations of springs and wells, to provide a reliable water supply, preferably close to a religious sanctuary or shrine, to guarantee protection. Larger *suqs* locate on the boundaries between production zones. In many places—for example, in Yorubaland and in North Africa—the rural population lives away from the market sites, and the hierarchy of rural settlements is not related to the hierarchy of periodic markets. This phenomenon also persists in Eastern Europe. Elsewhere, however, rural settlements and periodic markets coincide. An understanding of such local variability must be embedded in an understanding of local culture.

RECOMMENDED READINGS

Barnum, H. G., *Market Centers and Hinterlands in Baden-Württenberg*. Chicago: University of Chicago, Department of Geography Research Paper 103, 1966.

Berry, Brian J. L. *Geography of Market Centers and Retail Distribution*. Englewood Cliffs, N. J.: Prentice-Hall, 1967.

Brush, John E., and Howard L. Gauthier, *Service Centers and Consumer Trips: Studies on the Philadelphia Metropolitan Fringe*. Chicago: University of Chicago, Department of Geography Research Paper 113, 1968.

Christaller, Walter, *Central Places in Southern Germany*, trans. C. W. Baskin. Englewood Cliffs, N. J.: Prentice-Hall, 1966.

Dickinson, R. E., *City and Region*. New York: Humanities Press, 1964.

Garner, B. J., "Models of Urban Geography and Settlement Location," in *Models in Geography*, eds. Richard J. Chorley and Peter Haggett. London: Methuen, 1967.

Horvath, R. J., "Von Thünen's Isolated State and the Area Around Addis Ababa, Ethiopia," *Annals of the Association of American Geographers*, 59 (1969), 308–23.

Lösch, August, *The Economics of Location*, trans. William H. Woglom and Wolfgang F. Stolper. New Haven, Conn.: Yale University Press, 1954. See Chapters 9–12.

Sinclair, R., "Von Thünen and Urban Sprawl," *Annals of the Association of American Geographers*, 57 (1967), 72–87.

Skinner, G. W., "Marketing and Social Structure in Rural China," *Journal of Asian Studies*, 24 (1964), 3–43.

Stine, J. H., "Temporal Aspects of Tertiary Production Elements in Korea," in *Urban Systems and Economic Development*, ed. F. R. Pitts. Eugene: University of Oregon School of Business Administration, 1962.

Vance, James E., Jr., *The Merchant's World: The Geography of Wholesaling*. Englewood Cliffs, N. J.: Prentice-Hall, 1970.

regional economic structure

five

We began Chapter 12 with the Arab geographer Al-Muqaddasi's functional analysis of the Moslem lands in A.D. 985. Al-Muqaddasi realized that spatial organization is most easily understood in terms of the hierarchical division of space into *regions* arranged with respect to centers of political control or economic activity. Today, geographers are in fundamental agreement that regional study is an essential part of their discipline. Thus, in dealing with the geography of economic systems, they are concerned not only with the spatial behavior of economic forces (discussed in the preceding chapters) but also with regional economic structure and with the regional development problems that result. The next three parts of this book will turn to issues at the regional level.

The term *region* has several different meanings, however, and these need to be clarified in order to specify the relationships between regional structure and economic systems. These relationships take place at a variety of scales, from a worldwide scale to that of the smallest locality; the nature of these scales and the links between them must also be clarified. It is to these questions that we turn in this chapter. First, the various approaches to regional study are examined. Next, these approaches are applied to world-scale data to provide an overview of international regions. Then, in Chapter 14 the heartland-hinterland concept, an explanation of the system of international regions, is discussed. This concept provides the background for Parts VI and VII, which explore the world's heartland and hinterland regions in more detail.

APPROACHES TO REGIONAL STUDY

Traditionally, geographers have distinguished three kinds of regions: *functional regions* (also called *nodal* or *organizational* regions), *formal regions* (also called *homogeneous* or *uniform* regions), and *administrative regions* (politically bounded areas for the development or application of regional plans and policies).

functional regions and spatial interaction

Derwent Whittlesey, who was a strong advocate of the regional approach and regional methods in geography, stated that the "internal structure or organization [of nodal regions] . . . includes a focus, or foci, and a surrounding area tied to the focus by lines of circulation." A functional region is thus an area in which one or more selected phenomena of movement connect the localities within it into a functionally organized whole. For this reason functional regions may better be understood by considering the nature of the spatial interactions of which they are composed.

Spatial interaction, viewed most generally, involves the movement of people or goods, or the communication of ideas and information. It involves all behavior that helps to create socioeconomic systems, or that is required

the regional concept and the international system

13

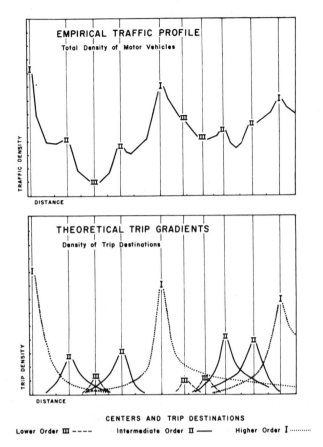

Fig. 13.1 *Travel gradients around a hierarchy of rural service centers*

Source: John E. Brush and H. L. Gauthier, Jr., Service Centers and Consumer Trips (University of Chicago, Department of Geography Research Paper no. 113, 1968), p. 9.

to maintain their spatial organization, or which stimulates system growth. Indeed, the spatial organization of a society is the spatial structure of its interactions; spatial organization would disintegrate without the sustaining flow of interaction.

Spatial interaction may be classified as *innovative* or *non-innovative* according to whether it helps a system to grow and develop or serves only to maintain it. Innovative interaction involves the diffusion of technology, ideas, and even fashions. It produces two contrasting and contradictory changes in spatial organization: *diminishing* regional differences in the geography of consumption (greater homogeneity) and *increasing* regional differences in the geography of production (greater specialization). Non-innovative interaction— that is, routine daily activities such as commuting, shopping, and so on—tends to increase proportionately within all systems according to the number of people involved, and to decrease within systems as distances increase and as intervening opportunities, boundaries, and barriers are met.

The most fundamental property to be seen in spatial interaction is that of *distance-decay;* this may be attributed to the cost, effort, or time required to overcome the friction that distance imposes on interaction. Money, energy, and time are limited resources. When more of these resources are allocated to interaction, fewer are available for other activities. The tradeoff between these other activities and spatial interaction is reflected in distance-decay, which is a measure of the spatial elasticity of demand. (See section entitled "Spatial variations in prices due to transport costs" in Chapter 4.)

In most cases, the focus of interaction is an urban center and the functional region is the trade or market area of the center. Figures 12.3 and 12.5 showed a whole series of such nodal regions. These regions display distance-decay gradients, and as interactions fall off with distance from a succession of centers, the separate distance-decay gradients produce distinctive traffic profiles along transportation arteries (Fig. 13.1).

Because most types of human interaction are similarly organized with respect to cities, the British urban geographer Arthur E. Smailes has suggested the term *urban field* for the functional regions defined using a comprehensive set of urban-centered interactions. If there is a hierarchy of urban fields, as would be the case in a central-place system, the highest order region that encompasses all the others Smailes calls a *holon*. The American planners John Friedmann and John Miller have increased the currency of the term urban field among planners, and Friedmann has postulated a series of stages through which urban fields and holons emerge as the level of development of countries changes.

More recently still, the Greek planner C. A. Doxiadis and Brian J. L. Berry have suggested the use of the term *daily urban system* because of the complex interdependency of everyday interactions relating to home, work, shopping, recreation, and education within modern metropolitan regions. In doing so, they were affirming a basic premise of Ludwig von Bertalanffy, the father of modern general system theory, that spatial interactions provide an opportunity to study the spatial organization of an economic system as an entity.

formal regions and the characteristics of places

Formal regions are areas within which the variations and covariations of one or more selected characteristics fall within some specific range. They may be *single criterion* regions, as in the definition of a manufacturing belt by the percentage of total employment in manufacturing or manufacturing production measured by value added, or they may be *multi-criteria* as in the definitions of agricultural regions that incorporate product mix and physical factors as well as the production and marketing system. Such agricultural regions are usually named by their predominant farming system, for example, the cotton belt, winter wheat belt, or corn belt.

The variety of homogeneous regions that can be

defined is as unlimited as the characteristics studied, and they may describe aspects of the population, regional production and consumption, physical environment, or resource base. But because the characteristics may be interrelated, many single-criterion homogeneous regions will be the same. To avoid the inevitable redundancy, mathematical techniques therefore are often used today to simplify the task of regionalization. Two ideas lie beneath the mathematics: (1) that the characteristics can be grouped into sets, with each set summarized by a "dimension" of variation, because the characteristics are interrelated; and (2) that formal regions can be defined by grouping together areas that have similar index values on each summary dimension identified, areas that would fall into identical regions with respect to the original characteristics.

Consider as an example the wide range of census characteristics available in most countries today. Censuses provide a mine of information on regions that have not yet been fully analyzed. In Canada, for example, the census population and household characteristics include age, sex, marital status, population that is urban, rural farm, and rural nonfarm; ethnic origin, mother tongue, place of birth, and period of immigration of the population; and education, income levels, and occupation structure. Housing characteristics include tenure and type of dwelling, number of dwellings in building and rooms in dwelling, the median value of owner-occupied housing and average rents paid, number of dwelling units built in each period, and details on the type and condition of the exterior, method of heating, plumbing facilities and other measures of the quality of the housing stock. In addition there are censuses of manufactures and agriculture. Similar characteristics are available for most countries, but differences in definition severely restrict data comparability between countries, and often between censuses in the same country. National atlases have been prepared in Canada mapping selected census characteristics following each census. Mathematical analysis reveals, however, that many of these characteristics have very similar distribution patterns. Indeed, it emerged that there were but three basic dimensions according to which Canadian regions might be defined:

1. *cultural*—the main differences being among French Canada, the English heartland of Canada in Ontario, and the Canadian West
2. *economic*—the contrasts between Canada's industrial heartland and its primary-producing hinterlands
3. *urban*—the important differences between urban and rural Canada on the one hand, and the special characteristics of Canada's metropolitan centers on the other

Because the census variables reflect only this smaller number of underlying dimensions of variation, the task of defining Canada's homogeneous regions is greatly simplified; far fewer than a full atlas of census maps need be used to depict Canada's regional differences.

interrelationships between functional and formal regions

Are formal and functional regions related? Yes, according to hypotheses advanced by the late Robert S. Platt and his student, A. K. Philbrick. Platt developed the first modern statement of the idea that *spatial organization at its most fundamental consists of points of focus, lines and channels of movement, and areas of organization. The areas of organization comprise, in turn, a successive hierarchy of formal and functional regions of increasing scale, the whole constituting a pattern of areal functional organization of spatial systems.* Philbrick provided an example of these ideas beginning with Boswell, Indiana, proceeding on up to the whole eastern United States and thence to the world. The hierarchy, he said, was based on two principles. First, any areal unit—for example, a farm field, a business district or a city—can be allocated to either formal or functional regions. Second, a hierarchy of alternating formal and functional regions can be identified with scale progression.

Consider a farm with its farm buildings and fields devoted to various land uses. Philbrick mapped a hypothetical farm in the United States Midwest with 160 acres, half in corn, and almost a quarter each in soybean and rotating pasture. The buildings and a few acres of permanent pasture make up the balance of the acreage. The fields are formal regions.

However small, such a farm unit constitutes a functional or organizational region. The distribution of land uses on the farm can be examined within the framework of land-use theory and relationships may appear between the intensity of interaction, measured as farm-labor input, and the distribution of land uses with distance from the farm buildings.

The hypothetical farm may also be classified as part of a larger homogeneous area (an agricultural region) composed of a number of similar farm units, with similar land-use patterns and probably with similar soil and climatic characteristics. Furthermore, these farm units are interconnected by a transportation and communication network connected by the same road and telephone system and are served by the same radio and television stations, the same schools and business organizations, and the same central places.

Closely following the urban hierarchy, Philbrick proceeded upwards until he reached a series of "fifth order" urban centers and their functional regions, such as Detroit, Toledo, Columbus, Buffalo, Cincinnati, and Cleveland. By virtue of their manufacturing specializations, these could be grouped into the "homogeneous" United States manufacturing belt, dominated by one sixth-order center (Chicago) and the only seventh-order center in the United States, New York. Philbrick noted that the hierarchy of alternating formal and functional regions could also be extended to the whole world. The final functional region then becomes a world manufacturing belt, the world "heartland" extending from the manufacturing belt of North America, across the manufacturing belt of northwest Europe, eastwards to include that of the Soviet Union, operating in the setting of "hinterlands" occupying the rest of the world.

spatial field theory

A complementary concept is spatial field theory, proposed by Brian J. L. Berry to focus on the forces producing areal functional organization. Berry began with the observation that a grouping of places with similar attributes would produce a homogeneous regionalization and that analysis of the information about the interactions between places reveals functional regions. But what are the relationships between attributes and interactions? After much study, Berry outlined three major conclusions:

1. *The characteristics or attributes of any place are directly dependent upon the volume and nature of its interrelationships with other places.*

   Discussion: This dependence of homogeneous regions on interaction patterns is most forcefully drawn in the location theories presented in Chapter 7. The rural land use zones and land values in Von Thünen's isolated state are dependent on interaction with the city, not inherent productivity differences of the land. Within the city, the highest land value is at the peak-traffic intersection. The density of housing and the variety and type of retail activity are also related to interactions with peak-traffic intersection.

2. *The characteristics of places directly affect their interactions with other places.*

   Discussion: That place-to-place differences in the variety and quality of the primary resource base influence the nature of interaction is seen clearly in Chapter 10, which discusses the role of factor endowments in determining comparative advantage, and therefore regional and international trade. This argument can be extended to many other arenas; for example, the role of cultural differences in reducing interactions across cultural boundaries.

3. *Because of 1 and 2, there is no simple, one-way causality between attributes and interactions or between formal and functional regions. Rather, they are interdependent, maintaining a relationship of mutual causality.*

   Discussion: This third conclusion implies that formal and functional regions arise simultaneously and are maintained in a state of mutual equilibrium, as in the joint operation of productivity differences and accessibility in the determination of land rents.

administrative regions and the spatial subdivision of power

A third way in which regions are defined is with respect to a politically bounded unit, such as a multinational union, a nation, a province, a county, or municipality, following the geographic separation of power. Of these, the most significant remains the nation state. Existing political boundaries may determine the areas for which regional plans are developed, or the

geographic units to which national economic and social policies apply. Frequently, too, special regions are defined for planning purposes and provided with their own planning staffs, as in the case of Appalachia or the Tennessee Valley. Seldom do the regional units used for the planning and administration of the several functions of government such as highways, education, health and welfare, and industrial incentive grants coincide, however. One reason is that boundary changes for such administrative areas generally do not keep pace with the changing geography of economic systems. Another reason is that major governmental agencies tend to be jealous of their functions and reluctant to collaborate with others. But many countries, notably Sweden and Britain, are trying to improve their local governmental organization today along functional lines.

Few attempts exist in the theoretical literature to define ideal administrative regions, although Walter Christaller developed a hierarchy of functional regions according to the administrative principle (Chapter 12). As will be seen in Chapter 18, the Soviets have made many attempts to improve their economic planning regions by experimenting with different hierarchies of functional regions, too. But in most instances, student and policy maker alike take the existing political-administrative structure as a given.

interrelationships between administrative, formal, and functional regions

The conclusions of spatial field theory also apply to the interrelationships between administrative regions and formal and functional regions. Both the attributes of places and of place-to-place interaction are influenced by administrative action, and vice versa. Interaction across international boundaries is affected by tariffs and trade quotas, product quality regulations and currency exchange, and language and consumer taste differences, as was seen in Chapters 10 and 11. Even at a subnational scale, barriers to interaction may exist because of licensing requirements, as in the case of heavy transport vehicles that must be licensed separately in North America for each province or state in which they operate, or changes in quality or type of transportation as in the former differences in railway gauge among states in Australia. Local laws on sale of alcoholic beverages, opening hours for retail stores, zoning, and prevailing levels of property taxes—all of which may vary from one municipality to the next—can affect land use, and thus, in turn, interaction.

Conversely, administrative regions are often defined in relationship to the attributes of places, whatever the size of the administrative region. The relationship is most obvious in the case of small regions designated to undertake a specific task, perhaps the comprehensive development of a river basin or the provision of public housing in a metropolitan area. Moreover, there are many examples throughout history of nations that have been called into existence to defend and administer a people with common kinship ties and cultural traditions.

It follows, again, that there are no simple, one-way relationships among the geographies of distribution, interaction, and administration; formal, functional, and administrative regions are interdependent. The exploration of these interdependencies recently has been attempted at the global scale by a number of social scientists. One of these efforts, by political scientist Bruce M. Russett, is reviewed in the next section to serve as an introduction to Chapter 14, and to provide a conceptual basis for Parts VI and VII, and for the final chapter on system growth and spatial dynamics.

DIMENSIONS OF INTERNATIONAL REGIONALISM

Russett's study, *International Regions and the International System,* delineated several sets of regions, the relationships between them, and, in several cases, changes in the regions during the post–World War II period. We will look at three of these sets:

1. International regions of *social and cultural homogeneity,* defined by grouping countries with similar attributes (formal international regions).
2. Regions composed of countries linked together by networks of supranational or intergovernmental *political institutions* (political-administrative international regions).
3. Regions defined on the basis of *trade* (functional international regions).

Russett's objectives in defining these regions were to explore the economic and social determinants of politics, and in turn, the influence of political variables on social and economic life. More specifically, he wanted to identify those areas of the world that have the greatest potential for further economic and political integration, and those areas where the necessary conditions seem weak or absent.

formal international regions

Russett's first regionalization, a grouping of countries into formal regions, was based on 54 economic and cultural variables for 82 countries. Many of these variables displayed similar spatial patterns, so they could be grouped by mathematical procedures (factor analysis) into dimensions of regionalism. Russett found that five dimensions accounted for 60 percent of the variation exhibited by the 54 variables. He named these dimensions economic development, intensive agriculture, communism, size, and Catholic culture.

economic development

The first dimension grouped such variables as gross national product per capita, newspapers and radios per capita; life expectancy; percentage of labor force in industry; pupils in primary and secondary schools;

literacy; hospital beds and physicians per capita; urbanization; and the infant mortality rate. Inversely related were the percentage of GNP derived from agriculture and the percentage labor force in agriculture and the birth rate. In other words, the higher a country's GNP, the lower the percentage of GNP from agriculture, the lower the percentage of the labor force in agriculture, the more hospital beds and physicians per capita, and the lower the birth rate, all clear indicators of development differences.

Similar results have been obtained by other scholars using different data, and they point to a pervasive dimension of differences among world regions involving accessibility, transportation, trade, external relations, technology, industrialization, urbanization, and gross national product—i.e., modernization, the social process of which development is the economic component.

Compare maps of six of them, which show similarities among the characteristics associated with the economic development dimension (Figs. 13.2 to 13.7, pp. 250–52). Gross domestic product per capita (Fig. 13.2) is the total market value of goods and services produced within a country, excluding any deductions or allowances for depreciation, divided by that nation's total population. GDP differs slightly from GNP, which includes production and income accruing to individuals and institutions normally resident in a country even if the income received is not earned in that country. Despite its acknowledged deficiencies, GDP is widely accepted as one of the best single measures of economic development. The map of GDP (Fig. 13.2) is based primarily on data for 1970. The countries in the three highest categories are the United States, Canada, the Western European nations, Australia, and New Zealand with values ranging from $4,734 for the United States to $1,726 for Italy and $1,315 for Ireland.

Values tend to be understated for lesser developed countries, but for many of the countries in Asia, the Middle East, Africa, and for some in Latin America, GNP per capita was well below the world median value of $362 per capita, with a low of $52 for Rwandi. Except for Bolivia ($205) and Paraguay ($249) South America achieves a generally higher GDP per capita than Asia or Africa. In some cases, such as those of Argentina, Uruguay, and Colombia, higher incomes reflect the widespread development of a commercial economy, but in others, notably Venezuela, the pattern is one of economic "dualism" with pockets of intense economic activity developed to serve foreign markets in what is otherwise a low-income, subsistence economy.

The map of percent of population in cities of 100,-000 or more presents a broad overall resemblance to the world map of GNP per capita with the percentage values extending over virtually the full range from 100 percent for Singapore to 1 percent for Cambodia (Fig. 13.3). The United States, Canada, the Western European countries, Australia, and New Zealand are again among the most urban although Canada has dropped from fourth rank

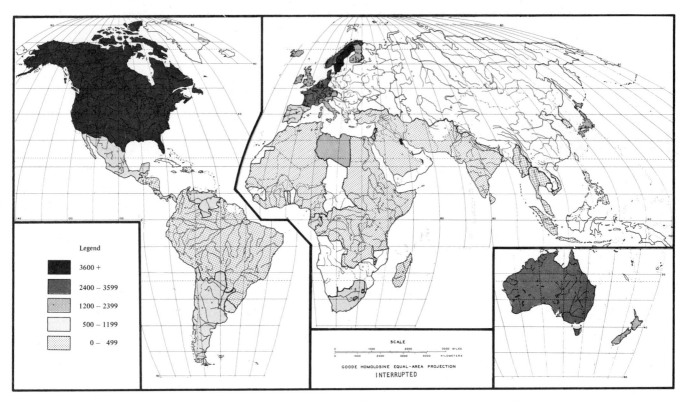

Fig. 13.2 *Gross domestic product, 1970*

Legend

3600 +

2400 − 3599

1200 − 2399

500 − 1199

0 − 499

SCALE

GOODE HOMOLOSINE EQUAL-AREA PROJECTION
INTERRUPTED

Fig. 13.3 *Percent population in centers of 100,000 or more, 1970*

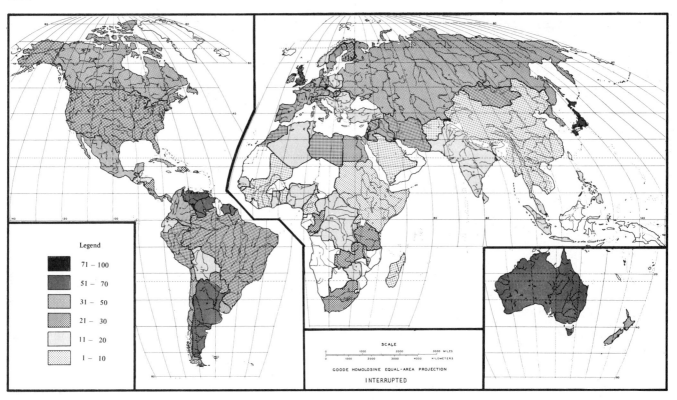

Legend

71 − 100

51 − 70

31 − 50

21 − 30

11 − 20

1 − 10

SCALE

GOODE HOMOLOSINE EQUAL-AREA PROJECTION
INTERRUPTED

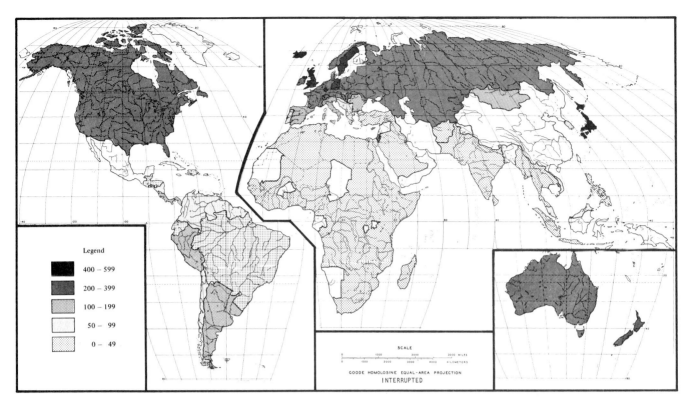

Fig. 13.4 *Daily newspaper circulation per 1,000 population, 1970*

Fig. 13.5 *Percent of economically active population in agriculture, 1970*

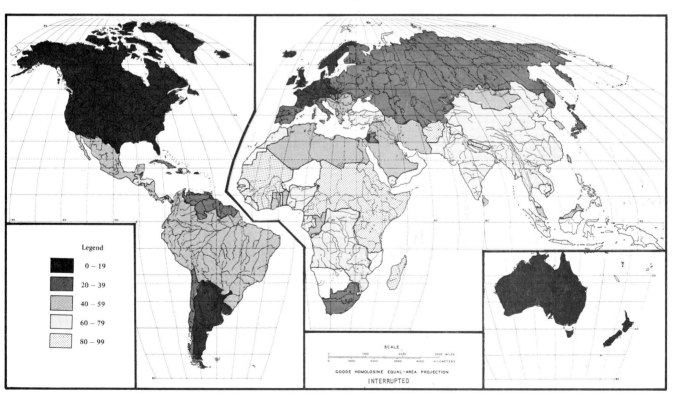

251

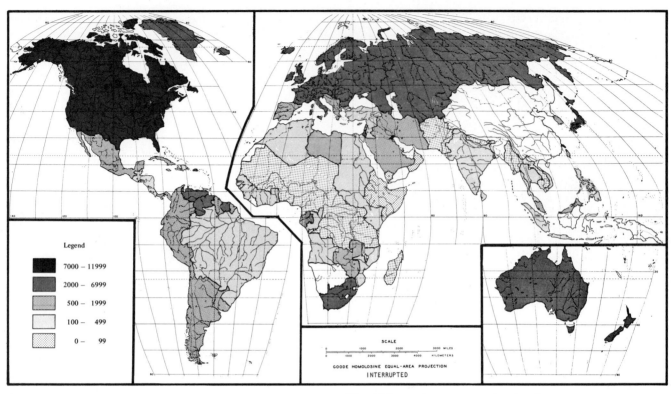

Fig. 13.6 *Energy consumption in kilograms, (coal equivalent), 1970*

Fig. 13.7 *Million freight ton-kilometers per railway kilometer, 1970*

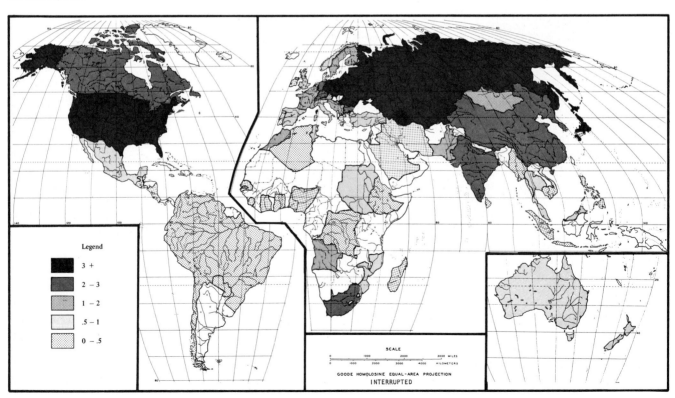

on GDP per capita to twelfth. On the other hand, some countries with relatively low GDPs per capita make considerable gains to join the ranks of the highly urban, including Singapore which moves from twenty-ninth to first place, Chile which ranks seventeenth on urbanization compared with thirty-ninth on GNP per capita, and Japan which ranks third on urbanization compared with twentieth on the income measure. In general, the countries that rank low on GDP per capita also rank low on urbanization, again forming a belt stretching from Asia across the Middle East and Africa to Latin America. Here again there are major exceptions with Egypt changing from seventy-eighth place on income to seventeenth on urbanization and Syria changing from sixty-eighth to thirty-sixth. However, these countries may offer examples of excessive urbanization, representing a severe lack of rural economic opportunities rather than vigorous economic growth in the urban areas.

Similarly, the maps of daily newspaper circulation (Fig. 13.4), percent of economically active population in agriculture (Fig. 13.5), and energy consumption (Fig. 13.6) all bear a striking resemblance to GNP per capita. Indeed, the difference among the maps of the economic development characteristics may represent in part data problems. International data series tend to have gaps and deficiencies, particularly for less-developed countries, which must be filled from alternative sources or by estimating procedures unless the data set is to be severely restricted both in terms of number of characteristics and countries. Definitions may vary among countries, perhaps reflecting conceptual difficulties in setting consistent criteria in different societies; and these data deficiencies are increased where the data values must be based on replies from individuals to questions involving their interpretation of complex census definitions. Agriculture, labor force, ethnicity, and literacy data provide numerous other examples of data gaps and deficiencies.

communism

Communism, with very extensive government ownership of means of production and tight control over the electoral process, Russett found to be identified by a separate grouping of six variables: Communist votes, central government expenditure and revenue as a percent of GNP, annual increase in GNP, and voting turnout, and, inversely, non-Communist voting and increase in hospital beds per capita. A weak association with the Communist factor was also displayed by such attributes as proportion of females in the labor force, slower population growth and low foreign trade relative to GNP. One economic variable not included by Russett, which has been closely associated with communism particularly in the early post–World War II years is intensity of freight railway traffic (Fig. 13.7). Railways in all Communist countries are heavily used. The USSR, which ranks first on this index, had a value of 8.03 million ton-kilometers of freight per railway kilometer in the mid 1950s, almost four times the world average of 2.04,

and more than three times the intensity for the United States (2.57). The only other countries that had values above world average were North Korea (3.78), China (3.64), East Germany (3.10), and Czechoslovakia (2.39). By 1970 the USSR's value had more than doubled to 18.60 million ton-kilometers of freight per railway kilometer, compared to the United States's value of 3.34 which was exceeded by those of Czechoslovakia (4.59), Romania (4.36), and Poland (3.67). Contributing to such high values among the Communist countries are long overland hauls of raw materials for heavy industry and agriculture, the comparatively small role of highway transportation, and in the USSR in particular, the physical limitations on movement of freight by inland and coastal waters. Political influences are important, too, including attitudes to regional development and "Western" least-cost location theory.

intensive agriculture

Russett's third dimension differentiated smaller countries with high population densities per unit of total area and of agricultural area in which farmland is fairly evenly distributed and in which the percent of the labor force in agriculture is declining more slowly than in the world as a whole. Population distribution and density are prime variables and have been discussed in Chapter 2. Population density is clearly independent of economic development and communism; there are, for instance, both poor and wealthy countries with dense populations as exemplified by many Asian and European countries, and poor and wealthy countries with sparse populations as exemplified by many New World and African countries.

Catholic culture and size

The last two dimensions identified by Russett were *size* and *Catholic culture*. Large countries tend to have a smaller amount of foreign trade as a percent of GNP, less foreign mail per capita and to have higher military expenditures.

Nations that comprise the fifth factor, Catholic culture, have the following distinguishing features: inequality of land distribution, a small share of the votes going to the Socialist parties, large numbers of deaths from political violence, and high proportions of military personnel as a percent of the working age population and of private consumption as a percent of GNP.

the formal regions

Using the dimensions of economic development, communism, intensive agriculture, and Catholic culture, Russett proceeded to group similar countries into homogeneous international regions. A group of twenty *Afro-Asian* countries, the first region identified, was characterized by underdevelopment. Next, twenty-six *Western community* nations were grouped, including the world heartland countries of North America, Western Europe, and Japan, together with Australia, New Zealand, and Israel. The group was characterized by high levels of economic development in particular. The Latin countries were divided into two regions by the mathematical analysis, one *Traditional Latin* group, clearly identified by intensive agriculture, and the other, the *semideveloped Latins*. The final group is that of the nine Communist countries, which form an *Eastern Europe* region with a mean score on the economic development factor a fraction below the semideveloped Latins.

political-administrative international regions

international organizations

Just as it is possible to group countries into international regions of sociocultural homogeneity, so it is possible to identify a corresponding international set of administrative regions, based on countries' memberships in the network of international organizations. Russett notes that international organizations, which forge formal links between nations, can originate for many reasons: to stabilize commodity prices and markets among major world producers; to foster trade among, and development within, member states; to facilitate international communications; to promote technical cooperation; to improve health conditions; to undertake joint military defense or to achieve ultimate political integration.

The number of international organizations has been growing rapidly—by Russett's count from 107 in 1951 to 163 in 1962, an increase of 52 percent, although this is not appreciably faster than the emergence of new nations over the same period, which increased by 48 percent from 77 to 114. The growth has been particularly rapid among regional organizations that are limited to clearly identifiable and virtually contiguous geographic regions, with the European Economic Community as the most striking example. In 1951, before the European Common Market (EEC) was established, France and Britain had 42 common memberships, the world's largest. In 1962, the world's largest number of common memberships, 76, was held by two EEC members, France and the Netherlands. Important regional associations have also sprung up in Latin America, Africa and Eastern Europe, generally linked with the trade associations such as CACM, LAFTA and COMECON (Chapter 11).

The simplest way of identifying the politically interdependent regions on the basis of membership in international organizations, Russett found, was to count the number of common memberships that every pair of countries has and to enter this figure into a table, with both a row and a column for every country. The actual counts were then scaled from 0 to 1 by dividing by the largest observed value. By analyzing the table, countries were grouped into regions directly.

the political regions

Seven regions emerged, with a few countries appearing in more than one region, reflecting global involvement with substantial numbers of comemberships in various parts of the world. The United States and United Kingdom fall in this category, but most of the countries belonging to two or more regions are middle powers, such as Japan, Australia, and Poland.

The regions and their member countries show a fairly close correspondence with the regions of sociocultural homogeneity previously identified. The Western Europe region is the largest with 27 member countries. The countries belonging to the Organization of American States together with Cuba, which has been expelled from that organization, form the second grouping. This region thus combines the Latin America and semideveloped Latins regions of the formal regionalization. The remaining five groups, although clearly identifiable, have fewer countries and fewer common memberships. The former British Africa region comprises nine countries; Kenya, Uganda, and Tanzanyika, the most closely linked members, have only twenty or so common memberships. Three of the remaining five regions, Eastern Europe, Asia, and the Arab states, relate directly back to the regions of sociocultural homogeneity. Eastern Europe is the same on the organizational as on the formal grouping with one exception: Yugoslavia, which groups with Western Europe. The Afro-Asia formal region divides into the Arab states and Asia.

The Asian administrative region comprises the non-Communist states of south and east Asia. The countries comprising the sub-Saharan African region, former French and former British Africa, were excluded from Russett's homogeneous regionalization because too few reliable data were available. The former French region includes all the former French African territories, except Guinea, which declared independence several years before the others, and included the former Belgium Congo drawn into many common organizations by its French elite. Similarly, the former British Africa group comprises Britain's former colonies: Uganda, Kenya, Tanganyika, Ghana, Sierra Leone, and Nigeria. It is possible that these two regions would have formed separate homogeneous regions if their member countries had been included in the formal regionalization. Considering only the countries included in both regionalizations, the two sets of regionalizations —the formal and the administrative—are remarkably similar.

functional international regions

In defining functional international regions, Russett limited himself to trade data, using aggregate trade between pairs of countries. This was because foreign investment, foreign aid, receipts from shipping, tourism, and other "invisibles" are not available on a complete country-to-country basis, and migration, tourism, and student exchange data have turned out to be rather unsatisfactory. World trade patterns and dynamics formed the subject of Chapters 10 and 11, and so we confine discussion here to Russett's results.

Nine functional regions emerged from Russett's analysis, but delimiting them proved more difficult than for the homogeneous and administrative regions. The functional regions are not mutually exclusive and some countries are listed in half or more of the trade groups. Consequently, the member countries invariably exceed the usual geographical boundaries associated with the regional names allocated, making the names less satisfactory than those for the other regionalizations and the regions difficult to map. Russett calls the regions North and Central America, British Caribbean, South America, Commonwealth, French Community, Western Europe, Eastern Europe, the Arab States, and Asia. The North and Central American region is led by the six Central American states, followed by Venezuela, Trinidad, and Colombia. But fifteen of the states listed are grouped with the twenty-six-country Western Community in the homogeneous regionalization. The Western Community countries are also fully represented in the Commonwealth and Asian trade regions, and well represented in the French Community and East European regions. By contrast, the South America, Western Europe, and Arab regions are smaller than in the previous regionalizations.

The Western Europe trade region, for example, comprises only the six Common Market countries, four of the European Free Trade Association countries, and Israel. The British Caribbean, a new region not distinctly defined in the previous regionalizations, is also small, and includes only ten nations, half of which are Commonwealth countries outside the Caribbean, namely Ghana, New Zealand, Nigeria, Canada and the United Kingdom, and Saudi Arabia.

interrelationships among the world regions

The interrelationships among the three types of regions —homogeneous, administrative, and functional—are statistically significant: the different regionalizations presented have closer matches than can be explained reasonably by mere chance. But Russett's analysis did not provide an adequate explanation of the *processes* by which the international system produces relationships among the characteristics of a country, its trade relationships with other countries, and its memberships in international organizations. Nor have we yet accounted for the greater apparent complexity of the functional regionalization than of the two other kinds. The reasons are to be found in the heartland-hinterland patterns that dominate the world economy. It is to these that we turn in Chapter 14.

RECOMMENDED READINGS

Berry, Brian J. L., "An Inductive Approach to the Regionalization of Economic Development" in *Essays on Geography and Economic Development*, ed. Norton Ginsburg. Chicago: University of Chicago, Department of Geography Research Paper 62, 1960.

Haggett, Peter, *Locational Analysis in Human Geography*. London: Edward Arnold, 1965. See Chapter 9, "Region-Building."

Olsson, Gunnar, *Distance and Human Interaction: A Review and Bibliography*. Philadelphia: Regional Science Association Bibliography Series, No. 2, 1965.

Philbrick, A. K., "Principles of Areal Functional Organization in Regional Human Geography," *Economic Geography* 33 (1957), 299–336.

Russett, Bruce M., *International Regions and the International System*. Chicago: Rand McNally, 1967.

Whittlesey, Derwent, "The Regional Concept and the Regional Method" in *American Geography: Inventory and Prospect*, eds. Preston E. James and Clarence F. Jones. Syracuse: Syracuse University Press, 1954.

the heartland–hinterland paradigm

14

The basic idea of the patterning of the international system by heartland-hinterland processes has been suggested many times. It was expressed, for example, by V. I. Lenin when he presented his "colonial model" of world spatial organization in which he argued that since the early nineteenth century the economic geography of the world has been strongly organized by and for the benefit of the industrial countries. The German location economist, Andreas Predöhl, gave the notion more substance when he described how, during the early nineteenth century, Britain became the focus of a unicentric world economy which, with the growth of new industrial core regions, has now become multicentric, with the rest of the world organized to produce raw materials for and to consume the products of the industrial heartlands. Europe was divided into an industrial heartland and agricultural hinterland by F. Delaisi in 1929 in a book with the graphic title *Les Deux Europes: Europe industrielle et Europe agricole*. Subsequent researchers have identified a regular pattern of distance-decay in agricultural productivity and per capita income from the European heartland, as was noted in Chapter 7, so that agricultural productivity is actually higher in "industrial" Europe than in "agricultural" Europe.

H. Perloff, an American planner, together with several associates, has described the emergence of the manufacturing belt as the economic heartland of the United States and the organization of the American space-economy along heartland-hinterland lines in the most graphic terms. He pointed out that North America's oldest cities were mercantile outposts of a hinterland resource area whose exploitation was organized by the developing metropolitan system of Western Europe. The initial impulses for independent urban growth came at the end of the eighteenth century when towns were becoming the outlets for capital accumulated in commercial agriculture and the centers of colonial development of the continental interior. Regional economies developed a certain archetype: a good deepwater port as the nucleus of an agricultural hinterland well adapted for the production of a staple commodity in demand on the world market. New resources became important from 1840–1850 onward, and new locational forces came into play. Foremost was a growing demand for iron, and later steel, and along with it rapid elaboration of productive technologies. Juxtaposition of coal, iron ore, and markets afforded the impetus for manufacturing growth in the northeastern United States, localized both by factors in the physical environment (minerals) and by locational forces created by prior growth of the urban system along the east coast (linkages to succeeding stages of production, in turn located closer to markets). The heartland of the North American manufacturing belt therefore developed westward from New York in the area bounded by Lake Superior iron ores, the Pennsylvanian coal fields, and the capital, entrepreneurial experience and engineering trades of the northeast. This heartland became not only the heavy industrial center of the country, but has remained the center of national demand, determining patterns of market accessibility ever since. The heartland had initial advantages of both excellent agricultural resources and a key location in the minerals economy. With development, it grew into the urbanized center of the national market, setting the basic conditions for successive development of newer peripheral regions by reaching out to them as its input requirements expanded, and it thereby fostered specialization of regional roles in the national economy. The heartland experienced cumulative urban-industrial specialization, while each of the hinterlands found its comparative advantage based on narrow and intensive specialization in a few resource subsectors, only diversifying when the extent of specialization enabled the hinterland region to pass through that threshold scale of market necessary to support profitable local enterprise. Flows of raw materials inward, and of finished products outward, articulated the whole.

It is little wonder that Perloff concluded that the American economy of the mid-twentieth century could be divided into

. . . a great heartland nucleation of industry and the national market, the focus of large-scale national-serving industry, the seedbed of new industry responding to the dynamic structure of national final demand and the center of high levels of per capita income . . .

and, standing in a dependent relationship to the heartland,

. . . radiating out across the national landscape . . . resource-dominant regional hinterlands specializing in the production of resource and intermediate outputs for which the heartland reaches out to satisfy the input requirements of its great manufacturing plants . . . in the hinterlands, resource-endowment is a critical determinant of the particular cumulative advantage of the region and hence its growth potential.

More recently, international heartland-hinterland contrasts have been identified by Raul Prebisch, who divides the world into an industrial center and a primary-producing periphery, and who blames much of the economic difficulties of the periphery on what he considers to be a long-term deterioration of the periphery's terms of trade. John Friedmann has elaborated the heartland-hinterland model as a "general theory of polarized growth" applying at all geographic scales. Friedmann perceives development as an innovative process that transforms the socioeconomic structure of spatial systems. Friedmann's organizing framework or paradigm thus explicitly identifies regions as a resultant of process with the main focus on the processes themselves. It thus complements Russett's approach, which identifies regions directly as a primary objective, by providing the needed understanding of underlying process.

FRIEDMANN'S GENERAL THEORY OF POLARIZED GROWTH

Friedmann's paradigm was presented as a framework for the study at all geographic s comprehensive set of processes—economic, se cultural, and political—that act to create hea hinterland contrasts. *Heartlands* are defined by F mann as territorially organized subsystems of socie possessing a high capacity for generating innovative change. *Hinterlands* are all the regions beyond the heartlands whose growth and change is determined by their dependency relationships to the heartlands. Heartlands share in common a heavy concentration of their labor force in manufacturing (secondary) activity and specialized (quaternary) services, representing a shift from development based on natural resources to development based on human resources. And both service and industrial activities are becoming less concerned with the processing and marketing of primary resources. As they become more sophisticated and scientifically oriented, the distinction between manufacturing-related and service-related activity becomes increasingly blurred. It is this new nexus of specialized activity that has become the modern engine of growth, making the term *heartland* almost completely synonymous with high per capita income and income potentials.

At both national and global scales, heartlands set the developmental path for the hinterlands, stimulating economic growth in the peripheries differentially according to the resource needs of heartland industries and consumers. Complementarities in the availability of factors of production between heartland and hinterland lay the foundations for interaction. Improvements in transportation and the organization of trade increase the transferability of staples from hinterland to heartland. Intervening opportunities impose spatial regularities in the timing of hinterland development and sequence the order in which unsettled areas and areas with a subsistence economy are drawn into the heartland's sphere of influence.

Friedmann also saw the diffusion of innovations from the core as controlling system growth and the form of the heartland-hinterland relationship, affecting economic activity and settlement patterns, sociocultural traditions and values, and the organization of power not only in the core, but also in the periphery. The periphery is thus dependent on the core in all respects. He summarizes as follows:

The volume of controlling decisions that emanates from the core is greater than the reciprocal volume of controls from periphery to core. This causes a net-flow of capital from the periphery which, in turn, gives rise to a net-flow of migrants into the core area. At the same time a continuous stream of innovations diffuses from the core to the periphery where it ultimately helps to create conditions that lead to demands for at least a partial restructuring of the fundamental dependency ratio . . . (John Friedmann, *Urbanization, Planning, and* s, Calif.: Sage, 1972, p.

pher, has noted the
e regional scale in his
ce of the Canadian

as corporations and
congregate in the
d and from which
y smaller cities to all
materials and people
hinterland to regional cities and on to the
metropolis. (Donald P. Kerr, "Metropolitan Dominance in
Canada," in *Canada: A Geographic Interpretation,* ed. John
Warkentin. Toronto: Methuen, 1968, pp. 531–55).

Even in the United States, where heartland-hinterland economic disparities have been narrowing since
1950, and where the sophisticated organization of financial institutions might have been expected to achieve an
interregional balance in the supply and demand for
capital, interregional disparities in interest rates persist
at the national scale. The Federal Reserve Bank of New
York attributes these interest disparities to a variety of
reasons, including legal, institutional, and investor attitudes toward the risk of investment in distant areas.

In essence, then, the heartland-hinterland paradigm identifies regional structure as the product of
"centripetal" and "centrifugal" forces operating at a
hierarchy of geographical scales. Centripetal forces are
set in motion when an emerging heartland attains the
necessary size for continued and self-sustaining growth
of a wide range of economic activities, enabling it to
achieve leadership in finance, education, research, and
planning, as Japan has done in recent years. Secondary
manufacturing and service activity tends to gravitate to
the heartland, leaving the hinterland increasingly
reliant on primary industries, which tend to play a
diminishing role in national economies. Heartland-
hinterland contrasts are strengthened by the concentration of corporation head offices, and the lower interest
rates at the center. Decisions regarding production, sales,
and research may be strongly influenced by where key
decision-makers live and work. The concentration of
corporate offices at the center of a national territory incurs a flow of corporate profits from the hinterland to
the heartland too, and creates a persistent shortage of
capital in the hinterland.

Centrifugal forces that reduce heartland-hinterland contrasts include the spread effects of growing markets and improving technology at the center, including
improved transportation and communications, which
can benefit industry in the hinterland; the protection
afforded hinterland industry by distance from the heartland; increasing congestion and environmental pollution of the heartland, combined with special amenities
that parts of the hinterland have to offer, and, increasingly (as will be seen in Parts VI and VII), the

attempts of governments to break apart the heartland-
hinterland form of spatial organization today on
grounds of regional and social equity.

Such a restructuring of a major regional economic
order will be exceedingly difficult, however. The development of the hinterland, according to the heartland-
hinterland paradigm, depends at first on supplying
staples to the heartland, then on the linkage effects of
the staples with other sectors on the hinterland economy,
and finally on restructuring the hinterland economy on
a human-resource base, like that of the heartland. Economic growth in a hinterland region may be sustained
for a time by increasing productivity in existing staple
production, or by the chance discovery of new staples
to replace depleted resources or those made obsolete
by technological change or by new discoveries and developments elsewhere. Economic growth in the hinterland can be augmented by linkage effects, which depend
essentially, on how the capital, generated by the exports, is invested. Such domestic investment can be
divided into three categories, according to whether it
generates "backward," "forward," or "final demand"
linkages. *Backward linkage* contributes supplies, equipment, and facilities needed to produce and ship staple
exports. The backward linkage with the greatest spread
effects is often the building of a transportation system
for export of the staple. *Forward linkage* involves further domestic processing of the staple before export
increasing the value added in the export staple. Forward
linkage includes such things as building pulp and paper
mills and petroleum refineries. *Final demand linkage*
includes the domestic production of consumer goods
for workers in the export industries. The strength of
final demand linkages depends on the level and distribution of income from the export industries, and
the proportion that is remitted abroad to foreign investors, or to families of foreign-born workers. More
generally, linkages can develop for the domestic as
well as the export sector of the economy, diversifying
production and stimulating industrialization. In all
cases, the development of these linkages depends both
on the ability of entrepreneurs, particularly domestic
entrepreneurs, to perceive market opportunities, and
on the appropriate economic, technical, social, and political framework to place these opportunities within
their grasp.

In light of the above, Friedmann sees four possible categories of hinterlands, according to their growth
potential and development history: upward transitional,
downward transitional, resource frontiers, and special
problem areas. *Upward transitional* hinterlands are
settled areas with growth potential and inflows of
capital and migrants. *Downward transitional areas* are
areas with declining economies, characterized by emigration. *Resource frontiers* are zones of new settlement
with lower population density and potentials for new
growth based upon staple exports. These are diagrammed in Figure 14.1. *Special problem areas* are
exactly what the name suggests.

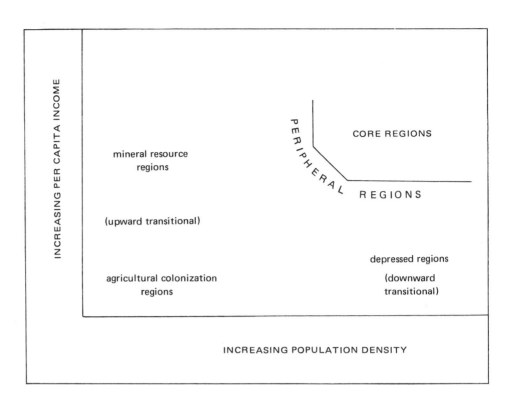

Fig. 14.1 *The income and population density relationship of peripheral regions and the core. (After Walter B. Stohr and John Friedmann, 1972).*

What this classification highlights is the fact that the socioeconomic characteristics of hinterland regions are so varied that it is unlikely that structural transformation of the hinterland economy can follow any single sequence of stages of growth or any one path of modernization. Indeed, the dimensions of international development are as complex and as varied as the international system itself (Chapter 25). Furthermore, the nations of the world periphery present a different socioeconomic situation than that of the heartland countries on the eve of their modernization. The hinterlands, therefore, embark on their economic development from a very different starting point than did the nations of the present world heartland.

We therefore turn in Parts VI and VII of this book to a detailed examination of the world's heartlands and hinterlands, for the systematic analysis of the earlier chapters must be complemented by an understanding of the ways in which the various economic factors come together to form total economic systems and subsystems. In pursuing this new direction we examine several examples of one of the most familiar, and at the same time most intricate, spatial systems of all—the national economy. These examples should serve to illustrate how many of the basic concepts of the geography of economic systems presented more abstractly earlier work in complex real world situations. They will, for instance, provide examples of the role of human and natural resources in the evolution of the state and its place in the world economic system. Similarly, they will show the effects of relative size—whether measured in terms of area, population, or output of goods and services—in assigning a country to its appropriate part in the global scene, as well as the

effects of relative location, both at the world level and within national territories. In each case the dichotomy between heartland and hinterland will be apparent; the locational strength of growth points will contrast starkly with the economic weakness of marginal regions and nations. The kinds of goods produced and traded, as well as the volume and direction of commodity flow, will demonstrate the effects of distance-decay.

Viewing these cases temporally, we can observe the effects of growth and decline, the dynamic elements of demography and the technology of production and transport. We shall also note the profound effects resulting from changes in effective attitudes, whether based on ideological considerations or national ethic and goals. Shifts in administrative control and its effects on the evolution of external commerce will be significant in some instances. In addition, there will be opportunities to examine deterrents to the growth and development of particular countries and regions within countries and to study the various planning measures that have been taken to combat their special locational problems.

As we view each country in turn, we shall make comparisons and contrasts with other countries wherever appropriate and note differences associated with relative location, level of development, and ideology. Certain essential characteristics of countries will be emphasized. One of these is the role each nation assumes within the world economic system, currently and in the past. In each instance we shall focus upon some characteristic activity or group of activities having a special significance for the country's growth or its failure to grow. National goals will be examined and locational problems will be analyzed.

EXAMPLES OF HEARTLAND ECONOMIES

The four heartland countries discussed—Canada, Britain, Japan, and the USSR—were chosen in part because of the range of political and economic systems they represent. At one extreme, Canada and Japan exemplify *organizational market-negotiated systems,* outgrowths of the *free-enterprise systems* of an earlier period (see Chapter 1). In each country major developmental decisions tend to be made by negotiation among large-scale autonomous organizations, while within the framework set by these decisions, substantial freedom in individual choice remains. The direct influence of government tends to be less in Canada than in Japan, where business, labor, and government have developed a uniquely close partnership in economic decision making called "Japan Incorporated." The United Kingdom is a *redistributive welfare state* typical of contemporary northwestern Europe. In Britain, the free-enterprise system has been modified by governmental action to the extent that publicly owned and operated productive and service enterprises exist side by side with a firmly regulated private sector. Together with taxation and social programs, this arrangement is intended to reduce social and spatial inequities and to guarantee every citizen a minimum degree of material welfare. At the other extreme of the political and economic continuum is the Soviet Union, the archetypal *socialist economy* with its monolithic governmental system dominated by a single party and with production, distribution, and consumption centrally planned and directed by the state.

The four nations further provide opportunities to look at a variety of industrial types, and in each case, to explore a particular theme relating to national problems of growth and development. For Canada the basic theme is that country's transformation from a resource-based rural economy to an urban-industrial one and the disparities that have arisen between the center and periphery during the course of this evolution. The theme for the United Kingdom is the early and continuing role of energy in national growth and development, the country's shifting horizons accompanying the changing nature of that development, particularly the recent shrinkage to "mini-Britain" and the effects these shifts have had on the perception of national problems and on the spatial economic system. The discussion of Japan will stress the rapid emergence to world economic leadership of a country lacking in physical resources but capable of adroitly mobilizing human resources by means of a unique set of political-economic-cultural arrangements. In the case of the Soviet Union, attention will focus upon the use of central direction to arouse a dormant giant to a position of economic strength, the particular emphases such an administered economy acquires, and spatial-organizational problems resulting from this approach to economic growth. In summary, we might say that Canada illustrates the operation of the forces of conflict and competition; the United Kingdom, competition tempered by government

regulation within the welfare state; Japan, consensus and cooperation in the relationships among government, capital, and labor; and the Soviet Union, absolute control and direction by the state. From this it is apparent that each of the four countries represents a different kind of response to the problem of growth.

Despite these differences, the four cases share with other heartland nations a number of common traits, especially demographic traits (see Chapter 2). All have population growth rates that are distinctly lower than those of the nations of the hinterland. The United Kingdom's population is growing at a rate of only 0.5 percent per year, which is typical of mature European populations. Canada's rate of 1.7 percent is on the high side of Type 5 countries in the United Nations classification system. Population growth rates for Japan and the USSR lie between these extremes.

All four countries are highly urbanized, the Soviet Union being somewhat less so than the others. The only demographic characteristic that differs markedly among them is their population densities. The island nations of Japan and Britain have attained very high densities. These populations are supported at relatively high standards by means of well developed urban-industrial systems. Recently settled Canada, on the other hand, has a low density. Both Canada and the USSR have much uninhabited and, by present standards, uninhabitable territory.

There are also similarities in production, consumption, and labor structure. In each case the proportion of the work force engaged in agriculture is low, especially in the United Kingdom. The percentage employed in manufacturing, however, is high, particularly in the Soviet Union and Britain. Tertiary activities also account for much employment, the most extreme case being Canada. As a widely accepted measure of development, per capita income is high in all instances. Likewise production of electricity per person is high. An even closer correspondence to level of development, however, is shown by the total energy consumed per capita. Among the heartland countries to be examined Canada is highest in this regard, although the United States is even higher. All the heartland nations have high per capita production and consumption of steel. The figure is especially high for Japan, being almost identical to that of the United States.

On the other hand, there are contrasts in the amount and type of transportation available. This is especially true of automobiles, which W. W. Rostow appropriately chose as his symbol of the "Age of High Mass Consumption." Soviet planners have chosen not to supply their citizenry wtih private transportation on a scale comparable to that of Canada, the United Kingdom, or Japan. Instead, the Soviet emphasis has been upon rail transportation. Per capita trade is likewise much greater for the non–Communist countries shown here than for the Marxist ones, although reasons other than Stalinist autarky help to account for the difference (see Chapter 11).

EXAMPLES OF HINTERLAND ECONOMIES

Four hinterland economies also are discussed—the countries of the Central American Common Market (CACM) considered as a unit, New Zealand, Indonesia, and China. These countries, despite their widely varying histories, cultures, ideologies, resource endowments, and levels of development provide a number of opportunities to develop certain central themes and to suggest a number of important parallels to the heartland countries. For instance, the CACM permits us to view a set of exploitive economies that rely upon a physical resource base, as does Canada. A further parallel to Canada is to be seen in the conflicts of cultures resulting from the confrontation between the indigenous Amerindian culture and the intruding Spanish culture. We shall also examine the problems of production and trade encountered by these small and economically weak nations: the difficulties of overspecialization in primary exports; problems of providing sufficient economies of large-scale production to attract modern industries; the harmful effects of dualism created initially by the Spanish invasion and subsequently replaced by neocolonialism from the United States, together with growing center-periphery contrasts within countries; and the difficulty of achieving faster economic growth. Finally, we shall examine the strategies for growth and development, including some Central American approaches to problems of internal disparities and the cooperative experiment in attacking problems of national growth and international trade.

The next case will be that of New Zealand, an island nation like Britain and Japan, but formed through the process of settlement by a European people. In this example the transplanted alien population and culture virtually displaced the indigenous population. The nation that subsequently evolved is patterned as closely after the mother country as circumstances have permitted. New Zealanders have adopted the British outlook and ways, sometimes in exaggerated forms, and usually belatedly, even to their British-type welfare-statism. Close cultural and economic ties to the mother country have persisted despite a relatively long period of independence. Although New Zealand has a resource-based economy like other hinterland nations, the country has attained a higher degree of prosperity than most peripheral regions. Nevertheless, New Zealand has a number of severe problems, and it has developed its own planning approach to solve these.

Still another island nation, Indonesia, serves as the third case study and represents a polar case to that of Japan. Unlike Japan it is a country of great diversity and considerable areal extent. Whereas the entire Japanese economy has absorbed its own peculiar adaptation of the Western system, Indonesia developed a dualistic structure as a result of Dutch colonial policies. Although there are center-periphery differences within each country, Indonesia's interregional contrasts are much greater, especially between the primate city, the areas of export economy, the large expanse of territory that retains its traditional subsistence base, and the undeveloped rich resources of its outer islands.

China, the final example, parallels the Soviet Union in several respects. Like the USSR it has a very large territory and a multitude of physical resources. China has also pursued a strategy for growth and development closely resembling that of the Soviet Union, a "bootstrap" operation based on central planning and control, separated from the world economy by the Bamboo Curtain. China's difficulties are numerous and of great magnitude, especially her problems of demography, organization, and control. In recent years, Chinese planning and development policies have begun to diverge from those of the Soviet Union, particularly in their unique approach to solving problems of regional inequality and of urban-rural differences.

the colonial imprint

Despite the many important contrasts between these four cases, a number of common refrains will also be explored stemming from the colonial imprint, for rather than seeing the benefits of polarized growth described by Friedmann, people in the hinterlands see their continuing dependency upon the heartland as an undesirable consequence of colonialism. Nearly all the hinterland countries share in some degree a past experience of European penetration. The form, depth, extent, and effects of European colonialism have varied considerably between the Americas, Asia, Africa, and the antipodes. Even within regions there have been considerable differences, certainly between North and Latin America, southern as opposed to eastern Asia, and from one part of Africa to another.

European penetration of the periphery occurred for many reasons—missionary zeal, easy riches, penal servitude, or escape from poverty and persecution—but most of all it was a reaching out for exotic commodities, raw materials, and foodstuffs. At first, Europeans directed their main effort toward acquiring exotic goods of the East: spices, silk, sugar, and other luxury items; after the Industrial Revolution they sought greater supplies of staple foodstuffs for their expanding urban populations and raw materials for their factories. Thus a flow of commodities into the center developed and has continued to swell.

To a considerable degree, the effects that colonialism has had upon hinterland countries depend upon whether this penetration resulted in permanent settlement or was mere exploitation. All the European imperial powers, particularly the British, established settlements that were needed to relieve temporary population surpluses and as safety valves for social, political, and religious unrest at home. The regions most attractive to permanent European settlers were those that were most familiar, having moderate climates and productive soils: eastern North America, New Zealand, eastern Australia, the Kenya highlands, the mountain basins of Central America and the Andes, and the temperate plains and valleys of southern South America. Immigrants came in large numbers to these lands (see Chapter 2) and succeeded in seizing territory from the Maoris, Cherokees, Caribs, Mayas, Patagonians, and other indigenous peoples. Even where the original motive was escape from difficult conditions in the homeland, some of these settlements eventually proved to be of great economic benefit to their mother countries because of the large quantities of grains and minerals the settlements shipped to European markets.

Other hinterland regions failed to attract European settlement, either because they had strong indigenous political organization and were already heavily populated, as in much of southern and eastern Asia, or because of extreme climates such as that of tropical Africa. Here the European impact took the form of political and commercial control for limited economic exploitation. Their purpose was to procure specific resources required by the metropolitan economy. This resulted in establishing enclaves of modern production and trade within a territory still devoted to indigenous activities of a mainly traditional and subsistence nature.

The metropolitan powers maintained tight political and economic control over their hinterland territories until changing conditions forced them to relinquish their empires. Political independence came to the American colonies of Spain and Portugal in the early 1800s. Having been granted internal self-government late in the nineteenth century, the British dominions were accorded full independence by the Parliamentary Statute of Westminster (1931). At the end of World War II the remaining British and Dutch possessions in southern Asia gained their freedom, as did the British, French, and Belgian colonies in Africa. And finally, during the 1970s Portugal has relinquished its control over major parts of the African continent.

Political independence has not always brought economic freedom to these lands, however. The metropolitan powers, especially the French, Belgians, and Portuguese, have been slow to relax commercial control over their former colonies. This is seen in the persistence of bipolar trade between these countries and their old territories (see Chapter 11). In its content, this trade reflects the complementarities of resource endowment between the two areas, which assign to the hinterland countries a permanent role as producers and exporters of primary commodities, thereby further reinforcing their condition of dependency. Multinational corporations headquartered in heartland countries help to maintain this hegemony, aided by formal and informal intergovernmental agreements. Thus the colonialism of an earlier time has been replaced by a "neocolonialism." Only those larger and more prosperous former colonies have managed to escape from this pattern and assume a place for themselves within the world heartland.

Because the hinterland countries remain economically dependent upon the heartland, their economic growth is conditioned by the resource needs of the metropolitan center and by the willingness of the metro-

politan powers to provide foreign aid and technical assistance. Growth and development are also affected by the degree of cultural affinity between countries, as we shall show by the differing experiences of Indonesia and New Zealand.

spatial organization

The internal organization of hinterland space that evolved also reflected the explicit requirements of colonial masters for political and economic control, access to sites of production for export, and links to points of embarkation. These needs are expressed in the locational pattern of urban places and their hierarchical arrangement, the nature of linkages between cities and their tributary areas in all hinterland regions, and the internal spatial structures of the cities themselves in the hinterland areas with substantial indigenous populations.

the regional structure of hinterland countries

One result of European penetration is that, although the great majority of hinterland people still are engaged in traditional rural activities, the city has assumed a dominant place in organizing the internal space of their countries. Because of the city's role in the exercise of administrative and commercial control, there has been a close interdependence between urban growth and regional development. Although urbanization has not proceeded as far in the hinterland countries as in the heartland, it is nevertheless occurring at an accelerating rate. As the hinterland city has grown in size and importance it has asserted increasing control over its tributary area through extension of the transport-communications network.

THE URBAN HIERARCHY. A distinctive feature of the hinterland country is the degree to which a single large city dominates the national system. Typically this *primate city* is at least five times the size of its nearest rival and has 70 percent or more of the urban population of the entire country. This describes San Salvador, Montevideo, Mexico City, Nairobi, Addis Ababa, Manila, Saigon, and many others. Virtually all such primate cities were established by the colonizing powers to serve as essential links between the mother countries and their sources of raw materials. Many years after independence, most of these cities continue to function in this relationship to the industrial nations today. The primate city is the focus of all modern functions and serves not only as the commercial capital but also as the capital for political and administrative control, the seat of an urban-based government and an urban-based power elite, and city-centered nationalism. As the center of intellectual activity, it contains the national university, and in many instances it is the seat of ecclesiastical control. Finally, the primate city is the center of innovation, the focus of change, and the principal point for the dissemination of new political, social, and economic ideas.

Given this set of functions, the principal city of a hinterland country is usually a port city as well, located in such a way to provide direct steamer access to the mother country and the world market. The principal exceptions to this are the primate cities of those tropical lands where the population and most commercial activities are concentrated in the healthfully temperate highland basins and plateaus. In such cases the primate city remains the main focus of modern production and trade but ships its exports through an outport, typically a much smaller, specialized place. Thus Mexico City has its outport of Veracruz, Guatemala City has Puerto Barrios, and Nairobi has Mombasa.

THE TRANSPORT-COMMUNICATIONS NETWORK. The primate city is also located to have superior access to those areas of export production that comprise its hinterland, reflecting its function as the main point for collecting, processing, and transshipping the primary commodities required by the mother country. Other urban centers in the country are decidedly smaller, less important, and perform fewer commercial functions, being, rather, provincial headquarters and local service centers. Thus the primate city is the supreme transport node in the domestic space-economy. By means of the transport connections that converge upon it, the primate city manages to integrate the commercial economy of the land. The network is designed in such a way to provide all the essential connections for asserting administrative control over the interior and reaching areas of agricultural and mineral production for the foreign market. Most places not engaged in such production are bypassed by the major routes, have poor connectivity to the transport system as a whole, and languish.

The transport and communications networks assume the shape of a fan, growing outward from the primate city in a tree-like, branching (dendritic) pattern. Figure 14.2 indicates the way the Indian railway network expanded outward from the main ports—Bombay, Calcutta, and Madras—during the second half of the nineteenth century. Note that, because of its great size, diversity of traditional princely states, and peculiar colonial history, the Indian subcontinent was penetrated simultaneously from more than one direction.

The case of contemporary India also illustrates the nature of the spatial organization that this type of development produces. Figure 14.3 shows the regional pattern of four main classes of economic organization. Comparing this with the map of urban population potentials (Fig. 14.4), we note a close coincidence between the more advanced types of activities and the country's urban population potentials centering upon the ports of Bombay, Calcutta, and Madras, and the administrative capital of Delhi. Finally, Figure 14.5 shows the functional regions of India as indicated by

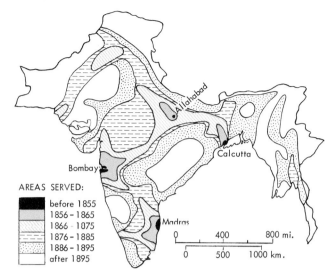

Fig. 14.2 *Diffusion of Indian railway network from Bombay, Calcutta, and Madras, second half of the nineteenth century*

Source: R. P. Misra, Diffusion of Agricultural Innovations *(Mysore: Prasaranga Manasa Gangotri, 1968), p. 15.*

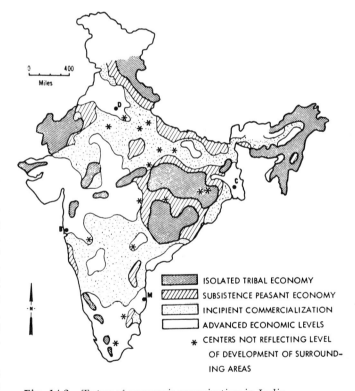

Fig. 14.3 *Types of economic organization in India*

Source: Brian J. L. Berry, "Interdependency of Spatial Structure and Spatial Behavior: A General Field Theory Formulation," Papers of the Regional Science Association, *21 (1968), 211.*

the flows of 63 commodities shipped interregionally. Each set of flows focuses upon one of the four major cities, and, in addition, the inland capital of Delhi is tied to the port of Bombay.

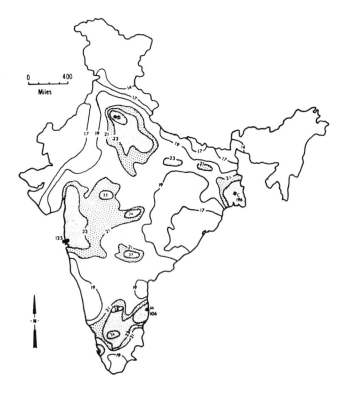

Fig. 14.4 *Urban population potentials in India*

Source: Berry, "Interdependency of Spatial Structure and Spatial Behavior."

Fig. 14.5 *Functional regions in India, based on commodity flows*

Source: Ibid.

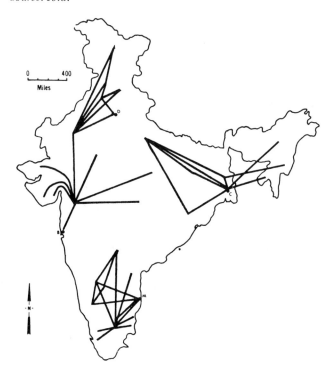

THE INTERNAL STRUCTURE OF THE HINTERLAND CITY.
The particular set of functions performed by the large hinterland city is reflected in the distinctive use of its internal space. As in the case of the large cities of North America and Europe, the non–Western city grows at a rapid rate and must therefore continually reach out for more territory along its margins. Unlike the usual heartland city, however, this centrifugal expansion does not occur in response to transport innovations, such as the construction of rapid transit and expressway systems. Instead, it results from the fact that the fast-growing primate cities of Asia, Latin America, and Africa cannot readily absorb all the rural immigrants converging upon them. Unlike the usual Western city, the hinterland city cannot provide sufficient housing in its already crowded center, and newcomers are forced to settle along the city fringes. There they form communities much like the rural villages from which they came, attempting to preserve the traditional rural social organization of their home areas. Whereas the population densities of inner cities in North America are falling (see Chapter 2), central densities of hinterland cities remain high.

The land use pattern within the non–Western city is likewise different from that of the heartland city. Among the reasons for this difference is the large proportion of the population engaged in the service sector in the hinterland city, most of the work force being clerks, administrators, transport workers, retail merchants, and street-corner vendors of trinkets and foods. Also complicating the pattern is the plurality of racial, ethnic, and cultural groups in the urban population. Finally, there is the mixed economy, which characterizes the hinterland city—the combination of Western capitalism, semicapitalism, and pre-industrial forms.

The most prominent feature of the city is the port, which was the center of economic activity during the colonial era and retains its supremacy in the post-independence period. Associated with it are many related activities: wharves, warehouses, and the kinds of manufacturing usually found at major ports. There are usually two main concentrations of retailing and other commercial services. One of these is the Western-style central business district, where products imported from the United States, Europe, and Japan are sold in modern, air-conditioned department stores and shops. Nearby, and contrasting in appearance, atmosphere, and hours and methods of doing business is the commercial alien center—the Chinatown or Indiantown, with its immense population densities. Although the alien merchants overwhelmingly dominated the commercial scene in the past, many of these groups have been expelled recently because of growing nationalism among the original population. In addition there are numerous markets that purvey a multitude of food-stuffs and other daily necessities, occupying large barn-like structures scattered throughout the city and operated by and for the indigenous population. These markets, in turn, are surrounded by innumerable street-sellers and hawkers.

Manufacturing in the hinterland city likewise assumes distinctive forms. The Western (or modern) types of production occur in specific zones, one of which is the area immediately adjacent to the port. As in the colonial era, these industries engage principally in the processing of foodstuffs: sugar, rice, tropical fruits, sago, tobacco, and other staple agricultural commodities for export. Often the port area provides sites for shipbuilding and repair, maintenance of railway equipment, and other transport-related activities. A second area of modern industry is located in recently constructed industrial estates (parks) along the margins of the city.

Unlike the usual European or North American city, many hinterland cities have not one but several peaks of population density, one for each of the major cultural groups in the area. The residential pattern established during the colonial period often persists, with the elite living close to the urban core or in the separate former colonial quarters, and the poor spreading outward toward the periphery. Although there are innumerable ethnic quarters throughout the city, the squatter settlements of newly arrived villagers are on the fringes of the builtup area. Western-style suburbs have also begun to appear on the outskirts of some hinterland cities as the growing middle class with their private motor cars seek escape from the crowded urban center. This intermingling of rich and poor is in addition to the traditional spatial associations of classes because of the custom of laboring families occupying living quarters on the premises of their employers.

The market-gardening zone, where intensive crops of fruits and vegetables that will be sold in the city are grown, is outside the city and adjacent to the builtup areas.

development and underdevelopment in the hinterland

In the world hinterland, the question of how to escape from endemic poverty is a dominant consideration. The great majority of hinterland countries are very poor by heartland standards, even though there is considerable variation in their levels of development. But what is it that we really mean by *development*? There is probably less agreement today than ever before on the definition of this term, which is commonly used in a normative sense—as a condition toward which every people unquestioningly aspire. It is customary for persons in the West to define development in terms of degrees of urbanization, commercialization, industrialization, modernization, and per capita production and consumption. This point of view is widely accepted in many of the hinterland countries themselves, which expect to experience the same sequence of events as those encountered by the West a century earlier.

Yet other paths have been taken. Although Japan ostensibly adopted the Western model, in actuality she did not so much *adopt* that model as *adapt* it successfully to her own peculiar indigenous attitudes and forms. The USSR has also adapted modern industrial technology to her particular ideological system. The problem for many of the hinterland countries in seeking to chart a similar independent path is that their current economies involve a problematic combination of Western and non–Western forms termed the *dual economy*.

the dual economy

When two social and economic systems that are clearly distinct from each other exist simultaneously within the same territory, each dominating a part of the society, that area has a dual economy. One of these systems, always the more technologically advanced of the two, has been imported from abroad; the other is the system indigenous to the area. Dualism usually occurs where an imported Western capitalism (or even socialism or communism) has penetrated a precapitalistic agrarian community and where the original system has managed to survive intact.

Precapitalism has a number of characteristics that contrast with those of modern capitalism. Typically it involves a communal way of life; tight all-embracing social bonds; and traditional class distinctions. The individual has limited, modest needs (unless he is one of the favored few belonging to the elite), and he engages in little or no exchange, except for luxuries when the periodic market or fair meets. He produces in and for the household to which he belongs, making finished goods rather than semicompleted commodities, and he seldom patronizes professional traders. The basic economic unit, both for production and consumption, is the family (or joint-family).

Wherever this kind of traditional subsistence production and consumption is carried out alongside a modern, efficient, highly capitalized structure tied to the world heartland, it can be said that a *dual economy* exists. The physical expression of dualism is the foreign capitalistic enclave with a life of its own: the trading city, commercial agricultural estate, the mining center, and all the modern transport and communication links that go with these. It is also manifested in the contrasting ways of life within the primate city: the Western-style CBD as opposed to the bazaar economy, scattered native markets, and streetsellers; the modern manufacturing establishments in the port area and suburban industrial estates as compared with the cottage industry scattered throughout the native residential sector.

Dualism is absent in a number of hinterland countries where the invading group exterminated the indigenous population, as in Argentina, or where the Europeans herded the native peoples into reservations. This latter practice was introduced by the early American republic, subsequently by Canada, New Zealand, and Australia and is being imposed upon the Bantu and Zulu in South Africa even today. In each of these cases except in the reservations, a Western type of homogeneous capitalistic nation has evolved as a replacement for the subsistence economy that preceded it.

The dualism described here must not be confused with the very special kind of *industrial dualism* prevalent in contemporary Japan. In Japan the term is used to describe the contrasts between the large, modern conglomerate firms known as *zaibatsu* and the small workshop enterprises remaining from an earlier era. Both types are wholly capitalistic even though one is more advanced than the other. The kind of dualism found in underdeveloped nations is of a very different sort, and it presents those countries with a particularly difficult set of problems.

DEVELOPMENTAL PROBLEMS AND DUALISM.   The regional structure of the world economic system, according to the heartland-hinterland paradigm, is the product of a set of centrifugal and centripetal forces. The centrifugal forces have had the effect of reducing contrasts between heartland and hinterland. Taking advantage of various spread effects from the heartland, certain hinterland nations have in the past managed to benefit from the growing markets at the center and to appropriate to their own use the technological improvements developed there, including the innovations in transportation and communication linking them to the center. The insulating effects of distance protected their infant industries from competing producers in the metropolitan center at the same time that worsening problems of overcrowding and congestion were raising rents and labor costs in the center. One growth became solidly established, these countries were able to generate the linkages, both forward and backward, that are required for a mature modern economy. Japan rose to economic power by following this track as did the United States and Canada during that earlier time when North America was on the periphery of the world economic system.

The majority of today's hinterland countries have not been able to make this transition, however. They have remained special problem areas because of the combination of *centripetal* forces that favor growth of the heartland at the expense of the hinterland. These less fortunate nations have therefore been consigned to what would appear to be a permanent role as primary producers, economically dependent upon the center, and beset by dualism. Such growth impulses as do reach them from the heartland remain confined to the enclaves of modernity, which are then inundated by migrants from a depressed countryside who came to the city and find only unemployment. Their disparities in material well-being have tended to grow instead of diminish, following the vicious circle of poverty, inadequate food supply, unemployment, and adverse demographic conditions described in Chapter 2. It has been estimated, for example, that the per capita incomes of today's underdeveloped nations are only one-sixth to one-third that of the present developed countries a century ago. Meanwhile, the underdeveloped lands as

a group are contributing a declining proportion of total world income. During their period of colonialism, the hinterland economies acquired a degree of dependency so great as to leave them excessively vulnerable to world trade fluctuations, a condition that has since continued as a result of neocolonialism. Drained by the heartland of their physical and human resources, they lack an effective voice in international economic affairs, which are decided by the advanced nations.

Problems of trade underlie many of their difficulties (see Chapter 11). Their unfavorable terms of trade, which appear to be worsening, represent one of the most intractable dilemmas confronting them. They must import increasingly expensive machinery and other capital goods in order to develop, but they have to continue exporting primary commodities for which there is a relatively static demand on a world market whose prices are set in metropolitan countries' commodity exchanges. Their excessive dependence upon a limited number of such primary exports is one of their heritages from colonialism. Their trade is often hampered by problems of remoteness. Either being too distant from the heartland or having inadequate transport connections to it burdens the hinterland nations with excessive transport costs for both their exports and imports.

Underdeveloped countries are troubled not only by the gap that separates them from the heartland but also by inequalities between regions within hinterland nations. The disparities of regional incomes in underdeveloped lands are usually greater than those in advanced countries, and they appear to be growing with time, even as regional disparities in the heartlands are diminishing. In much the same way that heartland countries tend to prosper at the expense of the hinterland nations, the primate cities of underdeveloped countries grow at the expense of the rural areas tributary to them. Transport innovation appears to intensify these regional inequalities; extending modern transportation into rural districts seems to intensify backwash effects.

Thus have arisen major sources of hinterland transformation: it has been in the disadvantaged peripheries that revolutions have been fought and won and old social orders replaced by new ones seeking alternative paths to national betterment, as in Castro's Cuba or Nyerere's Tanzania, where rural development takes priority over the primate city.

Similarly, as international access to depleting world resources becomes critical, the potentiality for creating resource-supplier cartels in the hinterlands grows and offers prospects for significantly transforming the balance of heartland-hinterland power. And so, after discussing the variety of examples of heartland and hinterland economies in Parts VI and VII, we return in Chapter 24 to the question of the changing balance of global economic power signified by OPEC, the Arab oil-producers' cartel, and in Chapter 25 to the issue of the limits to growth.

RECOMMENDED READINGS

Friedmann, John, *Urbanization, Planning, and National Development.* Beverly Hills, Calif.: Sage, 1972.

Kuklinski, Antoni, *Growth Poles and Growth Centres in Regional Planning.* Paris: Mouton, 1972.

McGee, T. G., *The Southeast Asian City.* New York: Praeger, 1967.

Meier, Gerald M., and Robert Baldwin, *Economic Development: Theory, History and Policy.* New York: John Wiley, 1957. See Part 2, "Historical Outlines of Economic Development."

the world's industrial heartland economies

six

A fundamental theme underlying much of what has taken place in the Dominion of Canada since confederation in 1867 under the British North America Act, and pervading much of what is written about future national prospects and problems, is the challenge of growth and change. Canada has grown very rapidly in land area, population, and productivity per capita. At the time of confederation, Canada comprised four small provinces extending along the Great Lakes—St. Lawrence lowlands and parts of the Atlantic maritime region. By the time Newfoundland joined Canada in 1949, Canada comprised ten provinces and two northern territories and covered half a continent, making it a little larger than Brazil, China, or the USA, and exceeded in land area only by the USSR. Toronto and Montreal, the two largest metropolitan centers in Canada, are two thousand miles from the third largest center, Vancouver, on the west coast and a thousand miles from St. John's, Newfoundland, to the east. Moreover, physiography and climate combine with sheer distance to make Canada's economic development an experiment in transportation, for transportation has always played a key role in the federal government's development policy.

Since confederation, Canada has sustained one of the world's fastest growth rates of population and of both GNP and GNP per capita and has changed from a largely rural to a predominantly urban nation (Tables 15.1 and 15.2). Population increased from a little over 3 million at confederation to 22 million by early 1973. Immigration has contributed a surprisingly small proportion of the population increase because of heavy emigration. The number of emigrants from Canada, 1851 to 1961, was about three-quarters the number of immigrants, and the total number of immigrants was less than half the number of births in Canada during the same period. But immigration has produced a cultural heterogeneity that increases progressively east to west across the country and that has significant occupational and social class attributes. Half the labor force in 1867 was employed in agriculture, lumbering, and fishing, and Montreal, the largest city, had a population of only 100,000. Currently only 8 percent of the labor force is in primary activities, all provinces are predominantly urban, and almost half the population live in metropolitan centers with populations over 100,000 (Tables 15.3; 15.4; and 15.5).

The course of regional economic development and population growth in Canada, in the past, has largely depended upon the exploitation of Canada's physical resource base in a laissez-faire, free-enterprise political climate, and Canadian economic historians have described it within the framework of a "staple" theory of economic development. The challenge of growth and change cannot be understood properly without reference to the role of export staples in the country's growth and to the resulting legacy of regional differences in the timing and nature of settlement and of economy across the country. But future economic growth

canada: the challenge of growth and change

15

Table 15.1   Rates of Population Growth in Major World Regions at Selected Periods, 1650–1971
(Average annual percentage changes)

	1650–1800	1800–1850	1850–1900	1900–1930	1930–1940	1940–1950	1950–1960	1960–1963	1963–1971
World	**0.3%**	**0.5%**	**0.6%**	**0.8%**	**1.0%**	**0.9%**	**1.7%**	**1.9%**	**2.0%**
Canada and United States	1.2	3.1	2.3	1.7	0.7	1.4	1.8	1.5	1.3
Latin America	0.3	1.1	1.3	1.8	1.9	2.3	2.7	2.9	2.9
Asia	0.4	0.4	0.4	0.6	1.1	1.1	1.8	1.9	2.3
Africa	(*)	0.1	0.5	1.1	1.5	1.5	2.1	2.5	2.6
Europe (including USSR)	0.4	0.7	0.9	0.8	0.7	−0.1	1.1	1.2	0.9
Oceania	(†)	(†)	2.2	1.7	1.0	1.4	2.1	2.3	2.1

*Slight change
†No significant change

Source: Economic Council of Canada, *Third Annual Review: Prices, Productivity, and Employment* (Ottawa, Nov. 1966), p. 9; and United Nations, *Demographic Yearbook, 1971* (New York, 1972) p. 111.

Table 15.2   National and Regional Population Totals at Selected Census Years, 1851–1971 (in thousands)

CENSUS YEAR	CANADA*	BRITISH COLUMBIA	PRAIRIES	ONTARIO	QUEBEC	ATLANTIC
1851	2,431	55	‡	952	889	533†
1891	4,734	98	152[a]	2,114	1,489	881
1931	10,363	694	2,354	3,454	2,875	1,009
1971	21,568	2,185	3,542	7,703	6,028	2,057
June, 1972 (est.)	21,830	2,247	3,563	7,825	6,059	2,081

Notes: *Canada total population excludes Newfoundland, Yukon Territory, and Northwest Territories. Regional figures may not equal Canada total due to rounding.

†Prince Edward Island population is for 1848.

‡Figures for Manitoba unavailable; Saskatchewan and Alberta not yet created.

[a]Manitoba only; Saskatchewan and Alberta not yet created. At the 1901 census, the population of the three Prairie provinces was 420,000 and Canada, 5,324,000.

Source: Leroy O. Stone, *Urban Development in Canada* (Ottawa: Dominion Bureau of Statistics, 1967); *1971 Census of Canada* (Ottawa: Statistics Canada, 1972); and *Estimated Population of Canada* (Ottawa: Statistics Canada, 1972), cat. no. 91201.

Table 15.3   Occupation Structure of National Labor: Canada 1881-1971

	CANADA	BRITISH COLUMBIA	PRAIRIES	ONTARIO	QUEBEC	ATLANTIC
Percentage distribution: 1881						
Primary	51	44	65	49	50	57
Manufacturing	24	28	16	27	25	18
Construction	5	6	5	5	4	4
Transportation	3	6	1	2	3	5
Trade	5	6	4	5	5	6
Service	12	11	8	12	13	9
Total	100	100	100	100	100	100
Percentage distribution: 1921						
Primary	37	29	55	28	31	43
Manufacturing	21	19	7	26	27	17
Construction	6	8	3	7	7	5
Transportation	8	11	7	8	7	8
Trade	9	11	8	11	10	8
Services	19	21	19	20	18	17
Total	100	100	100	100	100	100
Percentage distribution: 1951						
Primary	20	14	37	13	17	27
Manufacturing	25	24	14	30	29	20
Construction	6	7	5	6	7	6
Transportation	10	12	9	9	9	11
Trade	10	12	10	11	9	9
Services	28	32	25	31	28	26
Total	100	100	100	100	100	100
Percentage distribution: 1971						
Primary	8	7	20	5	5	8
Manufacturing	22	18	10	27	26	15
Construction	6	7	6	6	5	8
Transportation	9	11	10	8	9	10
Trade	17	19	17	16	16	20
Services	38	38	37	37	38	39
Total	100	100	100	100	100	100

Note: Columns may not total 100 because of rounding errors. See sources for definitions.

Source: D. Michael Ray, *The Urban Challenge of Growth and Change.* (Ottawa: Ministry of State for Urban Affairs, 1974), Discussion paper B.74.3. Tables are calculated from Dominion Bureau of Statistics, *Census of Canada: 1880-1881,* Vol. II, Table XIV (Ottawa, 1884); *Sixth Census of Canada, 1921,* Vol. 4, Table 2 (Ottawa, 1919); *Census of Canada, 1951,* Vol. 4, Table 2 (Ottawa, 1953); and *The Labour Force.* Cat. no. 71-001 (Ottawa, 1973.)

Table 15.4   Percent of Urban Population in Canada and in Major Regions at Selected Census Years, 1851–1971

CENSUS YEAR	CANADA*	BRITISH COLUMBIA	PRAIRIES	ONTARIO	QUEBEC	ATLANTIC
1851	13.1	–	–	14.4	14.9	9.0
1891	29.8	42.6	23.3†	35.0	28.6	18.8
1931	52.5	62.3	31.3	63.1	59.5	39.7
1971	76.1	75.7	66.9	82.3	80.6	55.6

Notes: *Excluding Newfoundland for all years except 1971.
　　†Manitoba only.
The 1851 and 1901 percent urban population figures refer to incorporated cities, towns, and villages of 1,000 and over. The 1931 and 1971 figures are based on the 1961 census definition of *urban* and include incorporated places of 1,000 and over and unincorporated towns and villages of 1,000 and over. Also included were unincorporated suburbs regardless of population size that were adjacent to cities, towns, and villages that had both a population of 5,000 and over and a density of at least 1,000 persons per square mile.

Source: Stone, *Urban Development in Canada*, p. 29; and *Canada 1973* (Ottawa: Statistics Canada, 1972), p. 114.

Table 15.5   Population for the Principal Regions of Metropolitan Development in Canada: 1901, 1941, and 1971 (in thousands)

PRINCIPAL REGIONS OF METROPOLITAN DEVELOPMENT	1901	1941	1971
Halifax	51	99	223
Montreal	415	1216	2743
Quebec	117	241	481
Hamilton	79	207	499
London	52	97	286
Ottawa	103	236	529
Toronto	303	1002	2628
Windsor	22	129	259
Winnipeg	48	302	540
Calgary	8	112	403
Edmonton	15	136	496
Vancouver	–	394	1082
Canada	**5324**	**11490**	**21568**

Note: Population figures for 1901 were calculated using an expanded definition of metropolitan area (see source, p. 132). Population figures for 1971 are CMA populations.

Source: Stone, *Urban Development in Canada; 1971 Census of Canada* (Ottawa: Statistics Canada, 1972).

will increasingly focus on the metropolitan centers with their skilled labor pools and their management and financial resources, creating a post-industrial society with distinctive value systems and life styles, and prompting increasing national concern to preserve primary resources for anticipated domestic requirements. And it is likely that government will play a widening role in the future course of development, attempting to direct it toward national objectives at the cost of reducing the free play of market forces.

Growth has been widely vaunted as an end in itself and has been actively encouraged by all levels of government. But many problems of pervasive concern to Canadians, such as urban congestion and environmental decay, are directly associated with rapid urban growth; and many other problems, including a steadily increasing population concentration in just a few metropolitan areas and persistent disparities in regional incomes and economic opportunities, are related to regional and sectoral disparities in growth rates (Fig.

15.1). As a result, the consequences of growth are beginning to receive more careful appraisal. The Economic Council of Canada in its 1969 Annual Review wrote, "Rapid growth will not be achieved easily or automatically. Nor, if achieved, will it solve all of our problems. In fact, it will create new problems, new wants and perhaps accentuated competition for resources."

The problems of accommodating growth and alleviating disparities in relative growth are pervasive. They occur at all geographic scales: local (such as "road improvement" to carry heavier traffic densities); metropolitan (with the contrast between suburban sprawl and inner city decay); national (regional income disparities) and even international (the regional impact of foreign investment and of trade and tariff policy). And they involve physical, demographic, social, economic, and political aspects at each of these geographic scales. An elaboration of all these problems would therefore involve a comprehensive statement on the form and growth of the Canadian space-economy. But of all the problems of pervasive concern to Canadians, three economic problems are especially prominent. These are the problems associated with regional economic disparities, rapid urban growth, and increasing foreign ownership, all of which are independent but which do interact. An attempt is made in what follows to outline the nature of these problems, the underlying processes responsible, and the sensitivity of these processes to public policy.

REGIONAL DISPARITIES

the problem

Regional disparities, measured by personal income differences at the interprovincial scale, are substantial and persistent (Table 15.6). The per capita incomes of the highest-income provinces, Ontario and British Columbia, have generally been twice as high as those of the Atlantic provinces, Newfoundland, Prince Edward Island, Nova Scotia, and New Brunswick. The 1971–1972 earned income per capita, as a percentage of the Canadian average is 66 percent for the Atlantic provinces, 89 for Quebec, 119 for Ontario, 92 for the Prairie provinces and 108 for British Columbia. Furthermore,

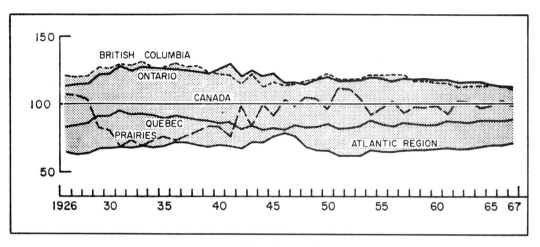

Fig. 15.1 *Regional personal income per capita as percentage of Canada average, 1926–1967*

Source: Economic Council of Canada, The Sixth Annual Review: Perspective 1975 *(Ottawa: Information Canada, September 1969),* p. 152.

Table 15.6   Regional Participation Income per Capita by Major Regions Relative to the National Average: 1910–1911, 1940–1941; and 1970–1971 *(Canada = 100).*

PERIOD	CANADA	BRITISH COLUMBIA	PRAIRIES	ONTARIO	QUEBEC	ATLANTIC
1910–1911	100	186	127	105	77	64
1940–1942	100	127	87	122	88	69
1970–1971	100	108	92	119	89	66

Note: Participation or employment income is income from wages and salaries and the net incomes of farm and non-farm unincorporated business. It differs from personal income by the exclusion of investment income and government transfer payments.

Source. Leroy O. Stone, *Migration in Canada* (Ottawa: Dominion Bureau of Statistics, 1969), p. 146, after R. Marvin McInnis, "The Trend of Regional Income Differentials in Canada," *Canadian Journal of Economics, I,* 1968; and *National Accounts* (Ottawa: Statistics Canada, 1972).

Table 15.7   Regional Disparities in Labor Force Participation, Age Structure, and Unemployment Levels: 1971

	CANADA	BRITISH COLUMBIA	PRAIRIES	ONTARIO	QUEBEC	ATLANTIC
Total population*	21,568	21,185	3,542	7,703	6,028	2,057
Percent population 15– 64† years	62.0	66.5	60.6	62.6	63.5	55.4
Labor force as percent of working ages‡	64.2	66.5	65.9	67.3	62.5	55.7
Unemployment rate §	6.4	7.0	4.5	5.2	8.2	8.6

Sources: *Canada, 1973* (Ottawa: Statistics Canada, 1972), p. 114.
†*1971 Census of Canada; Population by Age Groups* (Ottawa: Statistics Canada, 1972), cat. no. 92-7150.
‡*The Labour Force* (Ottawa: Statistics Canada, March 1973), cat. no. 71-001.
§*1971 Seasonally Adjusted Labour Force Statistics* (Ottawa: Statistics Canada, 1972), cat. no. 71-201. Note that the 1971 unemployment rates were the highest since 1961. In 1966 the Canada rate was 3.6, but regional differences were comparatively greater; unemployment in the Atlantic Provinces was 6.4 percent compared with Ontario's 2.5.

there has been little change in interprovincial disparities from 1926, the first year for which regular national accounts data are available. This persistence in interprovincial income disparities is in sharp contrast to the United States experience of a steady and significant convergence in the interregional spread of incomes since the early 1930s as personal incomes in the lower income regions, particularly the South, have grown more rapidly than in the United States as a whole.

The economic disparities are associated with interprovincial disparities in human resources and levels of productivity. The Atlantic provinces have, relative to the national averages, a low proportion of their population in the working-age group; a low labor-force participation rate; high seasonal fluctuations in work available and higher unemployment rates (Table 15.7). Lower productivity levels are associated with a relatively low educational level of the labor force, poorer physical resource and capital base, unfavorable industry structure and a smaller provision of public services.

Provincial data do not reveal the substantial intraprovincial differences that occur in settlement and economy. Canada's *ecumene* comprises a long belt that rarely stretches more than one or two hundred miles north of the United States border, and that is reduced in parts of the Western Cordillera, the Canadian Shield and the Appalachian mountains to a narrow corridor. The national pattern appears fragmented even when mapped in the form of potentials of population, income, and market—measures that convert the discrete locations of people, income, and retail sales into continuous statistical surfaces of accessibility.

The highest population and market potential values are at Toronto and Montreal, with very high values also at Ottawa, Winnipeg, and Vancouver. There is an Ontario-Quebec plateau of high values from Windsor eastwards to Quebec City, defining Canada's national heartland and manufacturing belt. The Atlantic region, consisting of a highly fragmented ecumene and mainly oriented toward the ocean, is isolated from the heartland by the northeastern extension of the Appalachian system. The Prairie ecumene, although somewhat larger than the heartland in area, has lower potential values than the heartland and is almost severed from it by the Canadian Shield. The Vancouver peak is isolated from the Prairie ecumene by the Western Cordillera where narrow corridors of higher potential follow the communications and settlement network.

Income potential is a weighted measure of *aggregate* income. An index of income disparity, in terms of income per capita, may be defined by subtracting the income potential value of each place from the population potential at that place and dividing the remainder by the average of the two potentials. The higher the index the greater is the disparity between population potential and income potential. Toronto, which has the highest income potential, has the lowest income disparity; in general, the heartland area of high income potential between Windsor and Toronto rates as comparatively prosperous. There is a gradual increase in the income disparity index northeastward along the St. Lawrence Valley and westward across the Prairies.

the heartland-hinterland process

How is the persistence of severe regional poverty to be explained in a country such as Canada, which has achieved a fivefold increase in the level of real per capita GNP in the hundred years since confederation, and has become one of the highest income countries in the world? The sheer size of the country and the concomitant contrasts in regional resources are important contributing factors. To these must be added differences in the timing of settlement, which appear to have operated within a heartland-hinterland system of development at a number of geographic scales. At the international scale, this process involved hinterland Canada supplying heartland Europe with staple exports according to Europe's needs and Canada's resource endowment and market accessibility. Commenting on this aspect of Canadian economic development, H. A. Innis, the leading innovator of the staple theory wrote:

The economic history of Canada has been dominated by the disparity between the center and the margin of western civilization. (H. A. Innis, "The Importance of Staple Products," in *Approaches to Canadian History,* eds. W. T. Easterbrook and E. Watkins. Toronto: McClelland and Stewart, 1967, p. 18).

Another prominent historian adds:

The St. Lawrence system that funnelled traffic from the continental interior out to the sea was closely connected with British finance and markets across the waters in an east-west trading network that thus reached halfway around the world. (J. M. S. Careless, "Frontierism, Metropolitanism, and Canadian History," *Canadian Historial Review,* 35, 1954, 1–21).

Canada's first staples were Atlantic salt codfish and St. Lawrence Valley furs, which were exported as early as the sixteenth century. Lumber, potash, pork, beef, and wheat from across eastern Canada were the major staple exports by the mid-nineteenth century, and wheat from the Prairies was added by the turn of the century. The east-to-west progression of staple production typically occurred with the growing demand for staples in Europe, the exhaustion of staples in the most accessible regions of Canada, the development of continental transportation facilities, and the introduction of new staple products.

Thus the heartland-hinterland process of regional development, operating at the intercontinental scale had already created, by the time of confederation, important east-to-west differences that remain as a basic dimension of Canadian regionalism. Immigrants as a percent of total population, particularly those landed before World War II, and cultural heterogeneity, average family size, dependency ratio, education levels, family income levels, and the percent of the male labor force in agriculture all tend to increase progressively east to west across Canada. And regional investment per head of population still displays a prominent east-west gradient (Fig. 15.2). Thus the low incomes and the lagging population and economic growth of the Atlantic region compared with the Prairies and British Columbia in part can be understood in terms of the Atlantic region's difficulty in coping with declining staples in contrast to the resource boom in western Canada.

Staple exports stimulate the domestic economy through economic spread effects to promote the growth of secondary and tertiary activity. These economic linkages are threefold: backward linkages to increase production in the export sector; forward linkages, involv-

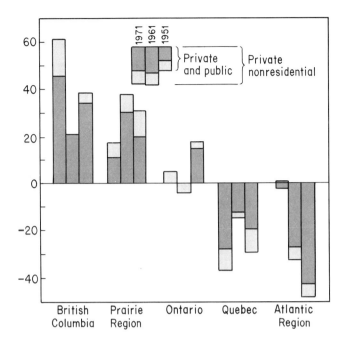

Fig. 15.2 *Regional investment per head of population:
1951, 1961, and 1971*

Source: After Regional investment per head of population:
Deviations from national averages in percent, *OECD Canada
(Paris: OECD, 1972), p. 77.*

ing domestic processing of staple exports; and final demand linkages, with consumer goods produced for domestic consumption by workers in staple export industries. Final demand linkages particularly favored the development of Ontario and Quebec and helped to establish a second heartland-hinterland process that operated at a national scale to make the spatial pattern of economic development in Canada more complex than the simple east-to-west pattern based on staple exports.

National heartland-hinterland differences, like east-west differences, have become a pervasive element of Canadian geography. Thus many socioeconomic characteristics have a significant correlation with distance from Toronto: average family-income levels tend to decline with increasing distance from Toronto; so does percent of male labor force employed in manufacturing industry and post–World War II immigration. Economic disparity increases significantly with distance from Toronto. And there is evidence that some heartland-hinterland contrasts are increasing. Population potential has decreased significantly with distance from Montreal (Fig. 15.3), the point of highest population potential since Confederation, but the gradient with which it declines has increased progressively since the turn of the century, indicating that population concen-

Fig. 15.3 *Population potential, 1971*

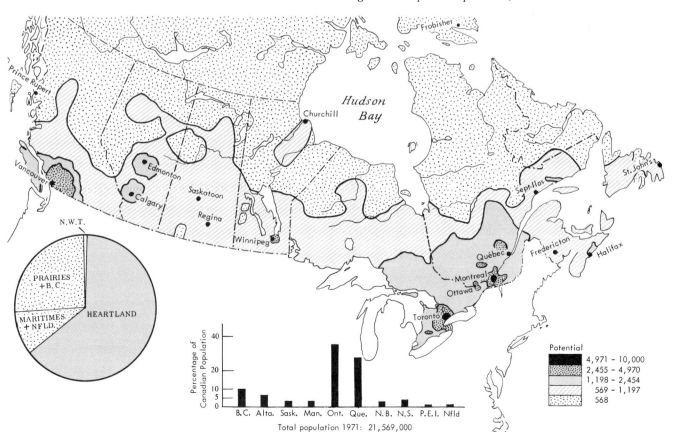

tration in the heartland is increasing. Comparison of 1961 census county data on incomes and economic disparity with the corresponding data for 1931, the first census year for which retail sales and income data are available, suggests some narrowing of heartland-hinterland economic disparities—in contrast, however, to the trend suggested by the provincial averages.

Assessing the impact of the national heartland-hinterland process on regional disparities and evaluating the persistence of regional poverty is complicated because urbanization itself reveals heartland-hinterland contrasts. Half the Canadian cities over 10,000 are located within four hundred miles of Toronto. Metropolitan growth, which reveals both west-east and heartland-hinterland gradients, has particularly lagged in the Atlantic provinces. Only 14 percent of the population in the Atlantic provinces lives in cities over 100,000 compared with 52 percent in Quebec, 55 percent in Ontario and 43 percent in the Prairie provinces.

Given the relationship between levels and rates of urbanization and regional disparities

the question must be asked if the persistence of generally lower levels of income in the Atlantic Region is not directly related to the continued dispersal of population and to the relative lag of concentration of economic activity in stronger urban growth centers. (Economic Council of Canada, *Fourth Annual Review: The Canadian Economy from the 1960's to the 1970's*. Ottawa: Queen's Printer, September 1967, p. 187).

Average income data provided by the Department of National Revenue indicate a strong relationship between income and city size and suggest that regional income disparities are primarily a reflection of disparities in regional city size (Table 15.8). Factor analysis also provides substantial support for this suggestion, indicating that heartland-hinterland differences can be grouped into two distinct sets. The first group includes characteristics that are primarily urban-rural, including a number of education, occupation, income, and housing characteristics. The second group identifies the relative emphasis on a lumbering-mining-fishing econ-

omy at the periphery, and associated with it, a higher male-to-female ratio of the labor force, higher unemployment rates and greater economic disparity.

The heartland-hinterland contrast in occupational structure is particularly well marked. After World War II the national proportion of total employment in agriculture, fishing, forestry, and mining was about 30 percent; by the early 1970s it was about 10 percent. But in the Atlantic provinces primary industries remain dominant; thus mining is the dominant industry in Newfoundland; forestry and agriculture in New Brunswick, agriculture in Prince Edward Island and agriculture, fishing, and mining in Nova Scotia.

Regional disparities in Canada can therefore be regarded as the product of the heartland-hinterland process operating at a hierarchy of scales: on an international scale to tie Canada to the export markets for its staple products; on a national scale to tie the Prairie and Atlantic hinterlands to the Ontario-Quebec heartland; and at successive subnational, or regional scales, to tie urban hinterlands to urban centers in systems of central places.

policy implications

Two Canadian economists, Helen Buckley and Eva Tihanyi, noted in a review of Canadian rural adjustment policies, "Geographical distribution has important implications for policy." (*Canadian Policies for Rural Adjustment*. Ottawa: Economic Council of Canada, 1967, p. 35). They illustrate the point: "If the rural poor are concentrated in specific regions or subregions, the programmes can be concentrated in certain areas. However, if rural poverty is widely dispersed among all regions, a real concentration will leave the majority of these people untouched."

But, the heartland-hinterland process, like other spatial processes of economic development, does not operate at a single geographic scale to concentrate poverty and economic disparity in a few regions. Indeed, there is ample empirical evidence to demonstrate the

Table 15.8   Average Income by Region and City Size Class: 1971 (National average for each size class = 100)

SIZE CLASS	ATLANTIC	QUEBEC	ONTARIO	WESTERN	NATIONAL AVERAGE
0–24,999	91.6	108.1	98.8	99.7	100
25,000–49,999	98.1	92.5	102.9	103.3	100
50,000–99,999	87.6	92.5	105.7	88.4	100
100,000–199,999	89.2	89.8	109.6	92.7	100
200,000–999,999	94.5	95.1	104.2	96.2	100
1,000,000+	n.a.	96.4	102.5	100.7	100
Average urban income for region	87.3	96.2	105.2	97.8	100

Note: 96 selected cities as given in *Taxation Statistics, 1973*.

Source: Calculated from *Taxation Statistics, 1973* (Ottawa: Department of National Revenue, 1972), pp. 10, 11, 17; and *1971 Census of Canada* (Ottawa: Statistics Canada, June 1973), Special Bulletin, cat. no. 98-701.

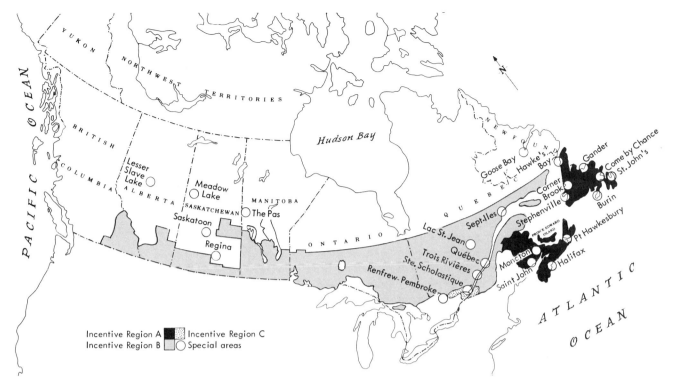

Fig. 15.4 *Areas designated for industrial incentive grants*

Source: Dept. of Regional Economic Expansion. Ottawa, Information Canada.

complex spatial structure and the widespread geographic distribution of economic disparity in Canada. Government programs to deal with these problems have therefore tended to designate large areas for special assistance (Fig. 15.4). But it follows that if large areas of the country are designated for development assistance without adjusting the level of incentives to compensate for heartland-hinterland gradients, such programs are likely to benefit the few designated regions with the greatest potential for development, thereby doing little to help less-favored regions that are more in need of assistance. The problem of how much of Canada should be designated under various government development programs remains a contentious issue and various approaches have been attempted. But the understanding of regional processes of economic development has not yet reached the point where supported recommendations can be made for the graduation of incentive grants to compensate for center-periphery gradients.

Second, the persistence of regional disparities at the provincial scale over the past fifty years for which data are available is remarkable in view of the rapid national economic growth over this period, a period that included a major depression and a world war, and the widening role of government and its increasing concern with regional disparities. At the time of Confederation, expenditures by all levels of government in Canada equalled less than 10 percent of GNP. By the late 1930s they reached a quarter of GNP and are now approximately a third of GNP.

Three historical phases in federal government policy on regional disparities have been distinguished. The first phase began in the 1930s with the depression when the federal government first introduced the policy of fiscal support to the poorer provinces. The second phase began with the recession of the late 1950s and the growing recognition of the persistence of regional disparities. The programs introduced in the 1950s were reorganized into a comprehensive approach in the newly-created Department of Regional Economic Expansion in the late 1960s. But fiscal and monetary policies, and policies affecting the longer-run development of the country, including growth-related budgetary expenditures, tariffs, transportation, and manufacturing training and mobility also have important regional implications. And in assessing the regional impact of these federal policies as well as the regional programs, the Economic Council of Canada concluded,

The unavoidable impression that emerges from a review of federal economic policies is that they have exerted a pervasive but inconsistent impact upon the various regional economies. (Economic Council of Canada, *Fifth Annual Review*, 1968, p. 177).

It is clear that regional disparities need to be given prominent and consistent attention in all aspects of federal policy if they are to be reduced. Much more attention will also have to be given to disaggregating regional totals and averages to identify the extent to

Table 15.9 Intercensal Percentage Change in Total, Urban, and Rural Population: 1851–1861 to 1961–1971

INTERCENSAL PERIOD	TOTAL POPULATION	URBAN POPULATION	RURAL POPULATION
1851–1861	33	62	28
1861–1871	13	31	10
1871–1881	17	50	10
1881–1891	11	42	2
1891–1901	12	32	4
1901–1911	35	62	21
1911–1921	22	34	13
1921–1931	18	31	7
1931–1941	11	18	3
1941–1951	19	34	–1
1951–1961	30	45	5
1961–1971	18	29	–6

Note: Newfoundland, Yukon, and the Northwest Territories are excluded. Data for Newfoundland are available only since 1951. The Yukon and Northwest Territories had only 14,000 persons residing in incorporated cities, towns, and villages of 1,000 and over in 1961.

Source: Stone, *Urban Development in Canada,* p. 28; and *1971 Census of Canada* (Ottawa: Statistics Canada, 1972), Preliminary Bulletin — Population Counts.

which "regional" disparities in Canada are actually disparities in the level of urban and metropolitan growth.

URBAN CANADA

urbanization and population concentration

Accompanying the persistence of regional disparities, there has been a sharp urban-rural disparity in Canadian population growth since before Confederation, and every decade has witnessed an advance in the proportion of the population that is urban (Table 15.9). The level of urbanization in Canada is comparable with that in the United States, and although Canada is far from being the most urbanized country in the world it may well be one of the most rapidly urbanizing.

Between 1970 and 2000, the Canadian urban population could more than double, and in the next three decades, Canadians will develop more urban area than they have since the beginning of European occupance. And more new housing units will have to be built over the next thirty years than the total in the existing stock.

Urban growth in Canada has been greatest in three provinces: Ontario, Quebec, and British Columbia. Thus interprovincial differences in urbanization parallel those in earned income per capita. Within these three provinces, most of the urban growth has occurred in the three largest centers: Toronto, Montreal, and Vancouver. If past trends continue, these three metropolises will account for almost a third of the total Canadian population by 1980 and more than a third by the year 2000 (Table 15.10).

Already three-quarters of the population are concentrated on less than 1 percent of the land area and urbanization is further increasing this level of concentration. In spite of Canada's vast size and empty spaces, the World's Fair at Montreal in 1966–1967 was located on new land artificially added to St. Helene's Island in the St. Lawrence River, and preparations for the 1976 Olympic Games in Montreal are causing serious concern because the facilities are to be built on city park land even though park land per capita in Montreal is already among the lowest in North America. Such problems are constant reminders that the impact of urban growth is in constant conflict with the quality of life and they create deep-rooted concerns about future urban growth.

Humphrey Carver has expressed this concern from the perspective of past performance:

We have to admit that though our motives are not regretted and our opportunities have been privileged, the results are only middling fair—and sometimes terrible. We have a sense of guilt because we have had the opportunity to build great cities in a way of our own choosing but we have settled for compromises and not really cared enough. . . . We are alarmed at what lies ahead. And we are frustrated because we possess no clear image of what we should be striving to accom-

Table 15.10 Population Projections to the Year 2000 for Canada and the Largest Metropolitan Regions (in thousands)

	1971	1981	2000
CANADA	**21,568**	**25,362**	**33,801**
Atlantic region	**2,058**	**2,086**	**2,061**
Halifax	223	239	294
Saint John	107	117	140
St. John's	132	133	182
Quebec	**6,028**	**7,261**	**9,112**
Montreal	2,743	3,528	5,091
Quebec	409	602	868
Ontario	**7,703**	**9,333**	**13,420**
Hamilton	499	628	894
London	286	290	425
Ottawa	602	711	1,031
Toronto	2,628	3,354	5,185
Windsor	259	266	344
Prairie region	**3,542**	**3,869**	**4,431**
Calgary	403	511	807
Edmonton	496	603	1,001
Regina	141	195	298
Saskatoon	126	194	321
Winnipeg	540	599	719
British Columbia	**2,185**	**2,831**	**4,777**
Vancouver	1,082	1,250	1,770
Victoria	196	239	330

Source: Canada 1973 (Ottawa: Statistics Canada, 1972), p. 113; and Systems Research Group, *Canada: Population Projections to the Year 2000* (Toronto, 1970), p. 16, 18.

plish. (Humphrey Carver, quoted in John N. Jackson, *The Canadian City: Space, Form, Quality.* Toronto: McGraw-Hill Ryerson, 1973, p. 7.)

Canada is just awakening to the extent of its urban problems: urban poverty, housing costs, transportation congestion, environmental decay, social unrest and fiscal squeeze. Urban poverty is different in socioeconomic character than rural poverty and so poses the need for additional policy thrusts in addition to those needed to cope with regional disparities. The problem of urban and rural poverty is selected, therefore, for more detailed comment.

urbanization and the socioeconomic structure of poverty

In essence, the socioeconomic structure of poverty in urban and rural areas results from the difficulty in making the economic, social, and political adjustments from a rural to an urban-industrial economy and the differential distribution of the benefits resulting from urbanization among socioeconomic groups and across space. Labor requirements change with urbanization from autonomous, unskilled, and irregular to functionally interdependent, increasingly skilled, and technologically regulated. Youthful, skilled, mobile workers are at a premium. The elderly bear the brunt of technological change in an urban setting; farmers unable to supplement their incomes with off-farm work bear the brunt of technological progress and changing terms of trade in a rural setting. The incidence and structure of poverty and the solutions that must be sought are different in urban and rural areas even though the process is the same in both cases.

The urban poor exceed the rural poor in absolute number, but the relative incidence of urban poverty is much lower. At the time of the 1961 census, 17 percent of the metropolitan and 26 percent of other urban families could be classified as poor compared with 46 percent of rural nonfarm families. The incomes of farm households were excluded from the 1961 census and the census of agriculture provides no equivalent indicator of farm incomes. However, a 1958 sample survey of farm family incomes suggests that farm incomes were lower again than rural nonfarm family incomes, equaling 63 percent of urban family incomes compared with a figure of 69 percent for rural nonfarm families.

Deficiencies in the cross tabulations of incomes with other census characteristics make it difficult to elaborate in detail on the differences between the structure of poverty in urban and rural areas. Major differences do emerge, however, in size of family, recency of immigration, and education. Almost half the urban poor are unattached individuals, compared with the rural situation where three-quarters of the poor are in family units. Furthermore, family poverty in urban areas is associated with female heads of the family and older families. In rural areas poverty is more general among families of all age groups and in families with male and female heads. Some 40 percent of the poor in the largest urban centers are foreign-born compared with 15 percent in rural areas. However, in both rural and urban areas, and regardless of size of urban place, pre-World War II immigrants are much more prone to poverty than Canadian-born. By contrast, postwar immigrants are much less prone to poverty. The very high incidence of poverty among prewar immigrants reflects, in part, the age of this group and the fact that many have now retired from the labor force. The lower incidence of poverty among postwar immigrants reflects their greater mobility, and higher education and skill levels. The urban poor are also better educated than the rural poor; one in six had completed high school and had some university training compared with one in fourteen of the rural poor.

The structure of the rural poor is complex and three independent dimensions can be distinguished: rural farm poverty, rural nonfarm poverty, and a third, smaller group, the socially-disadvantaged indigenous population and ethnic minority groups in rural areas. Rural nonfarm poverty increases in incidence with increasing distance from large urban centers and is more prevalent in areas of lagging urban growth such as eastern Ontario. Farm poverty is related to physiographic and climatic conditions, farm size, and the availability of off-farm work. One study of farm income in eastern Ontario found that, taking soil productivity into account, up to one-third of the farms were too small to survive; another study of farming in eastern Canada concluded that approximately half the farmers were redundant, in the sense that they could leave agriculture to the benefit of themselves as well as the remaining farm community and the national economy.

policy implications

The socioeconomic structure of poverty in Canada suggests then that urban and rural poverty are different problems requiring different policies. Urban poverty is specific to certain groups, particularly the old and unemployable, and constitutes an income-distribution problem. Rural poverty is more general and more complex and requires programs to increase employment opportunities for all the poor, whether farm or nonfarm, and whatever their ethnic origin. One objective of such programs will have to be to match more closely the distributions of population and employment. Thus more attention will have to be given to the spatial dimensions of population, poverty, and employment as well as to the socioeconomic structure of poverty.

But any attempts to tackle the poverty problem or any of the problems associated with rapid urbanization in Canada are faced with a number of acute difficulties. One of the most obvious is data deficiencies, which makes it difficult to probe and to document the extent and character of the problems. It is difficult to document the problems of Canada's rapid urbanization because of changes in definitions of metropolitan census tracts, census counties, and census characteristics; confidentiality rules that prohibit disclosure of manufacturing and other data; and enumeration errors. Often the data needed have never been systematically tabulated and are simply unavailable. No uniform financial data have yet been established in Canada to permit nationwide comparisons and analysis of the operations of even the largest cities.

There are sometimes difficulties, too, in identifying the spatial scale of the development processes responsible for problems and hence the scale at which policy solutions must be sought. Urban problems, particularly in the hinterlands, reflect changes in international trade, as when Elliot Lake's growth was temporarily eclipsed by the loss of uranium markets or when gold-mining communities suffered from a fixed price of gold. Regional problems associated with lagging urban growth may also reflect local problems, as when iron ore production was suspended at Bell Island, Newfoundland.

Furthermore, urban problems are highly interdependent. Thus, housing is related to transportation and land use; these affect the urban poor, the quality of the environment, and the fiscal resources of local governments; and these in turn have severe consequences for housing. Increasing recognition is being given to the interdependencies of transportation and land use planning. Location of diverse yet complementary activities, expressed in the land use patterns, dictate in large measure the density and direction of traffic flows, while at the same time, the transportation system has an impact on the structure of land use. Lack of attention by planners to these interdependencies frequently contributes to the failure of programs and may even create problems greater than those being corrected.

One dramatic example of the failure to take account of the interaction between transportation and land use developments is provided by the construction of the Queen Elizabeth Way through the rich agricultural fruitlands of the Niagara Region of southwest Ontario. The highway was built as a Depression relief project in the 1930s and widened and upgraded by the provision of service roads and overpasses between 1969 and 1972. These developments occurred in the absence of any regional development plan to direct and control urban development. The result is an emerging belt of continuous urban and industrial development from Niagara to Hamilton and Toronto along the so-called Golden Horseshoe. Urban form is thus created by public investments in transportation despite an Ontario government policy statement that

There has been increasing public concern about the encroachment of urban land uses upon the fruit lands of the peninsula.

. . . While it is too late to preserve many acres of farmland, drastic action should be taken to ensure the survival of those areas which are still economically viable.

FOREIGN OWNERSHIP

regional concentration of foreign ownership

The dominant economic function of most Canadian cities, particularly those in the heartland provinces of Ontario and Quebec, is manufacturing, and employment is related to the number of manufacturing functions performed. The location of manufacturing activity can be expected to have an important impact on urban and regional growth. But more of Canada's manufacturing industry is owned by residents of foreign countries than is owned by Canadians and there is evidence that the location of manufacturing plants by foreign companies is related to the location of their head offices. In particular, almost half of Canada's manufacturing industry is owned and controlled in the United States, and the spatial concentration of United States subsidiaries in southwestern Ontario appears to increase the level of interregional disparities.

The United States has more capital invested in Canada than in any other foreign country. By 1963, 46 percent of manufacturing industry in Canada was controlled by residents of the United States compared with 40 percent by Canadian residents. The remaining 14 percent was controlled by residents of other countries, principally the United Kingdom. These figures represent a substantial increase in foreign control since 1926, the first year for which official data are available, when 65 percent of manufacturing industry was controlled by Canadian residents. Furthermore, increasing foreign ownership has been associated with a trend from United Kingdom portfolio investment to U.S. direct investment (Fig. 15.5).

About 60 percent of foreign long-term investment in Canada is direct investment which constitutes a "package" of product, technology, management, and market access as well as capital. The vehicle for direct investment is the establishment of foreign subsidiaries by multinational corporations (the MNCs). It is estimated that in the next 20 years MNCs could easily account for half the goods and services produced in the Western world compared with the current 15 percent. Such multinational corporations are the most powerful agencies for regional and global economic unity that the twentieth century has produced, as was noted in Chapter 11.

The multinational subsidiary attempting to implement decisions must deal with the management of the parent company instead of with a multitude of relatively powerless shareholders; moreover, there may be less awareness of, and response to, regional cultural differences by multinational firms than by small, local, or even national firms. If the parent company insists

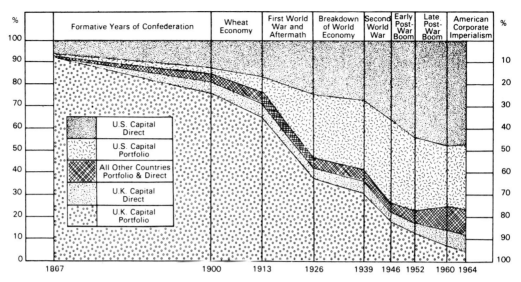

Fig. 15.5 *Composition of foreign investment in Canada: Confederation to Centennial*

Source: After *Kari Levitt,* Silent Surrender: the Multinational Corporation in Canada *(Toronto: Macmillan, 1970).*

that the subsidiary operate according to the methods and even the laws of the parent's home country, the political institutions and legal foundations of the subsidiary's host state are weakened. The most frequent problems of this "extraterritoriality" in Canada have concerned the United States' *Trading with the Enemy Act,* which restricts exports of U.S. subsidiaries. Other controls are exerted through antitrust laws and balance-of-payments policy.

Other problems of foreign direct investment include its impact on the Canadian capital market, on the size structure of industrial corporations, and on the Canadian balance of payments. Much less attention has been paid to the impact of foreign investment on industrial location, regional development, regional disparities, and social change.

United States-controlled establishments and employment contribute much more to those districts of the Canadian manufacturing belt that are contiguous to the United States, such as the Windsor district and the Golden Horseshoe extending from Niagara to Toronto, than to other parts of the manufacturing belt or other regions of Canada. Of the 1,618 United States-controlled subsidiaries listed in Canada in 1961, 1,132 are in the Toronto-southwestern Ontario region. The only cities outside these two contiguous manufacturing districts with large concentrations of United States-controlled subsidiaries are Montreal with 187, Vancouver with 50, and Winnipeg with 25.

Manufacturing employment in United States-controlled establishments shows a corresponding concentration in the two contiguous manufacturing districts. This concentration contributes to the disparity in manufacturing activity between the manufacturing heartland and the Western and Atlantic provinces. In 1961, 83 percent of the American-controlled employ-

ment was located within 400 miles of Toronto compared with 70 percent of the Canadian (Fig. 15.6).

source of capital and industry location

Differences in the location of manufacturing classified by country of control may reflect, in part, differences in the type of industry in which Canadian, United States, and United Kingdom capital are invested. United States investment is concentrated in fast-growth industries including the manufacture of rubber products, transportation equipment, and electrical products; it is very low in the slower-growth industries such as leather and knitted goods, clothing, wood, furniture, and printing industries. However, an analysis of county data, disaggregated both by industry type, country of plant control, and capital size-class of corporation revealed distinct spatial groupings of industry according to country of control rather than according to industry type or capital size-class. This suggests that country of ownership exercises a significant influence on branch-plant location.

This influence can be described by a spatial interaction (interactance) model: the number of subsidiaries in a Canadian city that is controlled by corporations within a United States metropolitan area is directly proportional to the number of manufacturing establishments in that metropolitan area and inversely proportional to distance from that metropolitan area. New York controls 307 Canadian subsidiaries, whereas Boston, much smaller but a little closer to Canada, has 48. Chicago and Los Angeles each have about the same number of manufacturing establishments, yet Chicago controls 197 Canadian subsidiaries compared with the more distant Los Angeles, which controls only 45.

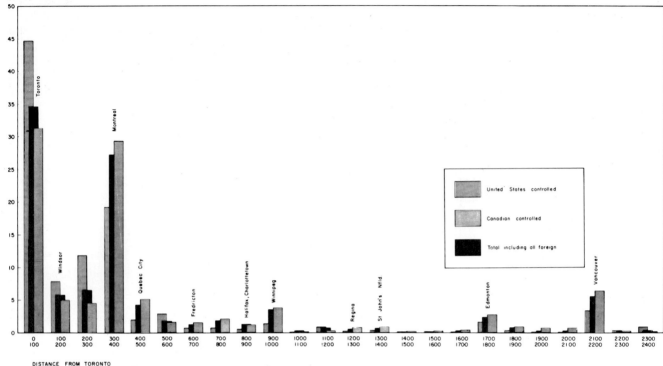

PER CENT

DISTANCE FROM TORONTO

Fig. 15.6 *The percentage of Canadian and United States controlled manufacturing employment within hundred mile distance bands from Toronto*

Because of the contribution of United States subsidiaries to the manufacturing industry in Canada, there are two important corollaries to the interactance model: (1) regional economic development and urban growth in Canada will tend to reflect the economic health of adjacent regions of the United States, and (2) the Canadian regions most likely to attract a large number of United States subsidiaries are those, such as southwestern Ontario, that are closest to the American manufacturing belt.

Two additional elements in the location of United States subsidiaries occur. The stronger of these is directional orientation: the tendency of subsidiaries to locate in the geographic sector that links the parent company with Toronto, the point of highest market potential. Toronto provides the optimal market location for American subsidiaries and few parent companies locate subsidiaries beyond it. Industrial interactance between a Canadian city and a United States city is severely restricted wherever Toronto becomes an intervening opportunity.

Furthermore, the distance that a parent company penetrates into Canada to locate a branch plant is directly proportional to the distance of the parent company from Canada. The Detroit manufacturer, for instance, can evade the Canadian tariff barrier and the prejudice against foreign products by locating a branch plant across the Detroit River. The marginal benefits of locating closer to the center of the Canadian market may not compensate for losing the convenience of operating the subsidiary close to the parent company.

Consequently, 34 of Detroit's 87 Canadian subsidiaries are located in Windsor where they comprise more than half the total of United States subsidiaries. Eight of Seattle's 11 Canadian subsidiaries are in Vancouver. Detroit controls only 20 subsidiaries in Toronto, and Seattle, none. By contrast, Los Angeles has half of its subsidiaries in Toronto, but none in Windsor. Urban growth concentrates along these development axes. One geographer, C. F. J. Whebell, has called them "urban corridors" and describes them as the "main streets" for the Ontario megalopolis of the twenty-first century.

Canada has been slow to examine the problems of foreign ownership and hesitant to take any action. There is little doubt that restricting foreign investment without taking strong compensatory action would drastically increase employment. But some policies have been put into effect, including the creation of a Canada Development Corporation and a federal government screening agency to evaluate foreign takeover bids in an attempt to improve the general efficiency of the Canadian economy within the framework of a national economic strategy.

CONCLUSIONS

The challenge of growth and change in Canada are therefore to accommodate the physical growth of urban centers to control the costs of congestion and the taxing of urban facilities; to share the benefits of urbanization among regions and social groups so as to reduce regional and social disparities in income and quality of life; and to accommodate foreign investment without increasing regional disparities.

Attitudes to urban growth and to the Industrial Revolution that has made such a fundamental contribution to urban growth, have long been mixed. Lewis Mumford, for instance, fears that the stage of the "manageable city" has been passed and that there is a serious danger of the metropolis decaying to become the *necropolis,* or the city of the dead. Ecologists, too, are warning of irreversible damage to the physical environment that is in part associated with increasing urbanization. The reality of these dangers is unquestionable.

Kenneth Boulding argues that human society in this century is passing through one of its great transitions: it faces the danger of collapse through an energy crisis by its extravagant use of physical resources. Such use may constitute an "entropy" trap, catastrophically halting the transition through the exhaustion or pollution of our resources before a more lasting man-land relationship can be established.

(The material in this chapter was drawn from D. Michael Ray's *Canada: The Urban Challenge of Growth and Change,* published by the Ministry of State, Urban Affairs, Ottawa, April 1974.)

RECOMMENDED READINGS

Brewis, T. N., *Regional Economic Policies in Canada.* Toronto: Macmillan of Canada, 1969.

Gentilcore, R. L., ed., *Geographical Approaches to Canadian Problems.* Toronto: Prentice-Hall of Canada, 1971.

Irving, Robert M., ed., *Readings in Canadian Geography.* Toronto: Holt, Rinehart and Winston of Canada, 1972.

Trotier, Louis, ed., *Studies in Canadian Geography.* Toronto: University of Toronto Press, 1972.

Warkentin, John, ed., *Canada: A Geographic Interpretation.* Toronto: Methuen, 1968.

the united kingdom: an imperial power turns inward

16

The United Kingdom contrasts markedly with Canada in a number of respects. Canada has about 40 times as much territory as Britain. The entire United Kingdom would fit in less than one-quarter of the space occupied by Ontario alone; indeed, Britain's area is about the same as that of Toronto's urban field. On the other hand, the United Kingdom has about 2½ times as many people as Canada, giving a density of 228 persons per square kilometer compared with Canada's two persons. Canada's population is growing at a somewhat faster rate, however. Urbanization has proceeded about as far in Canada as in Britain; in both countries, more than three-fourths of the population live in cities and towns.

The two nations are among the most technically-advanced countries, but most figures indicate that the United Kingdom is currently lagging in its economic growth. While Canada has attained a per capita GDP of $3,676, Britain's is only $2,128 (compared with $4,734 for the United States). By this measure, therefore, the United Kingdom's development is now less than two-thirds that of Canada; meanwhile Canada's GDP is growing at an average annual rate of 2.6 percent while Britain's increase is only 1.9 percent annually. Today Canada consumes nearly twice as much mechanical energy per capita as does the United Kingdom. Moreover, there is one automobile for every three people in Canada as against only one for every five people in Britain (the United States has one car for every nine-tenths person).

Both the Canadian and British economies depend heavily upon international trade—between one-fifth and one-fourth of their total output enters the world market each year (compared with only 4 or 5 percent for the United States). British workers are more dependent on manufacturing employment—36 percent as opposed to only 20.7 percent in Canada. This is changing, however; a decade ago at least half of Britain's work force was engaged in manufacturing. As noted earlier, very few British workers are in agriculture (about 3 percent), owing partly to the small amount of arable land (⅓ hectare per person compared with Canada's 3 hectares) and partly to the high productivity of British farm labor.

But most important, as an island nation the United Kingdom can draw upon only a limited domestic supply of physical resources today, except for a good (though finite) stock of fossil fuels. Unavoidably, therefore, Britain must trade actively with the rest of the world to redress the balance. Perhaps the country's most important indigenous resources today are nonphysical. The British people constitute a large stock of labor and entrepreneurship with skills accumulated over an exceedingly long period. Another accumulated resource is capital: money supply, capital equipment, and social overhead (such as transport and communications). But Britain's nonrenewable resources are being used up and her human and other nonphysical resources appear to be losing their competitiveness in the world economy. Britain, the first core of worldwide spatial organization, faces not the problems of growth, but those of retrenchment as the formerly imperial power that maintained the Pax Britannica adjusts to her new status as mini-Britain on the periphery of United Europe.

The successes of an expansionary past weigh heavily upon the British nation. We shall examine certain selected facets of that past, especially the country's emergence into the world economic system. Space does not permit a complete review of this subject; instead, the emphasis will be upon the role of energy in Britain's development. After looking at the country's traditional energy sources, we shall examine certain of the more recent forms of energy and attempt to assess their future possibilities. Finally, we shall view Britain's changing place in the world economy, the loosening of old ties to her former empire, the establishing of new links to her European neighbors, and her growing preoccupation with internal economic disparities.

ENERGY IN BRITAIN'S PAST AND FUTURE

From the Middle Ages onward the British people have relied upon a sequence of energy forms. At its first appearance each new type of energy has tended merely to supplement older forms, but in the end one after another of these has gained dominance, and with that dominance the locational structure of the economy has changed. In order of their exploitation by Britons, these energy types are human and animal power, wood used for fuel, water and wind power, coal, petroleum (both oil and gas), and nuclear energy. Two main sets of factors have influenced these changes in energy use. One is the evolution of energy technology: learning to harness and produce energy from new sources, developing new manufacturing techniques for using energy, and acquiring improved techniques in transportation. The other is the discovery and depletion of domestic energy reserves.

The many shifts in energy use have profoundly affected the British space economy. At first there was a strong orientation of production to sources of energy supply, influenced by the weight-losing character of early energy forms, the inefficiency of their use, and the primitive and costly nature of transportation. In nearly every instance the shift to a new source of energy led to a migration of manufacturing (refer to Chapters 8 and 9). Recently, however, many forms of production have been emancipated from locational dependence upon energy by growing efficiencies of energy use and transportation and changes in product emphasis.

New types of energy, together with innovations in manufacturing and transportation, have also influenced the character and orientation of British trade. Local and regional self-sufficiency were the rule in Medieval Britain. The only commodity to move far was raw wool, some of which was exported first to Italy and later to Flanders. When mechanical energy came to be applied to production and transportation, the volume of manufacturing output increased, unit production costs fell, and transport rates declined. Simultaneously, the areal range of manufactured exports expanded until it eventually encompassed the nation and the world. Let us trace this sequence of events.

early sources of energy

Before the Industrial Revolution the most important industry was the spinning and weaving of woolen and worsted cloth. The only other notable forms of secondary production at that time were leatherworking, ironmaking, nonferrous smelting, and metal crafts. Domestic transportation was mainly by horse, by foot or by boat. Fuels were used only for heating; power was supplied by human beings and animals and, to a minor extent, by water and wind. The location of production was partially related to the state of the arts in the use of energy.

human and animal power

Spinning was a part-time cottage industry, relying upon spinning wheels operated by women and children. Weaving was conducted by craftsmen using hand looms. Leather-making was likewise a handicraft. Smelters of metals and metalcraftsmen (goldsmiths, silversmiths, bellfounders, and cannon-makers) relied upon hand labor for molding, hammering, and shaping. Foot-bellows were used for raising furnace temperatures.

Human power remained important in British industry even during the early years of the Industrial Revolution, when it was used for operation of some of the first machines. Certain of these machines also relied on animal power. Hand looms persisted into the first half of the nineteenth century, and hand labor prevailed in British shoe and woolen manufacturing until 1850 and in coal mining until at least 1913. The locational effect of human labor is seen in the case of spinning, which was largely oriented to the rural population, as we saw in Chapter 9, and in clothing manufacturing, and other crafts, which took place mainly in the towns.

water power

Bellows operated by direct water power first appeared in the metal trades about the fifteenth century. By the sixteenth and seventeenth centuries water wheels became common for operating forge hammers, cutlery grindstones, mine pumps, spinning frames, fulling mills for the worsted trade, and grain mills. The early machine cotton industry passed through a water-powered phase from 1771 to 1786. The locational effect of water power was to further disperse rural industry, as was seen in Chapter 9, since running streams of any size are few and scattered in Britain.

charcoal

Charcoal was the most important fuel for British industry, especially for smelting metallic ores and metal finishing; some charcoal furnaces remained in operation well into the nineteenth century. By the sixteenth century, charcoal supply became a critical problem. Wood grew scarce as forests were cut down by a growing population that depended upon charcoal for heating its homes, by the smelting and woodworking industries, and by the shipbuilding industries. During the Elizabethan era, iron smelting was forced out of a number of districts because of competition from other wood-using activities, and much of the smelting industry retreated to remoter wooded areas such as the Forest of Dean, the Weald of Kent, and South Wales.

coal

first use

The first use of coal as a fuel dates back to the thirteenth century when it was introduced on a minor scale in the metal finishing trades and in tin smelting. During the sixteenth and seventeenth centuries, coal was adopted for domestic heating purposes, as the shortage of timber for charcoal grew and wood prices climbed. Tudor houses sprouted clusters of chimneys, and the coal fireplace assumed the role in Britain's hearth-oriented society they have held ever since. Slowly, fabrication of iron goods gravitated to coal field sites (Fig. 16.1), especially those of the West Midlands, which remains a leading area today, based on the acquired advantages created by this early concentration of the crafts (Chapter 8). Other coal-using industries followed, including the manufacture of glass, salt, soap, alum, copper, and bricks. As a consequence, a reorientation of British manufacturing was set in motion. The high cost of haulage restricted coal-using industries to coal field sites and those parts of the country readily accessible to them by coastal shipping or navigable streams. Because of the primitive state of mining technology the number of places where coal could be extracted was severely limited. Essentially a quarrying operation at that time, coal exploitation took place at outcroppings along coasts or streams. The result was that a limited number of coal-oriented industrial concentrations had already emerged by the eve of the Industrial Revolution.

coal and the Industrial Revolution

Mechanical energy was vital to the Industrial Revolution in Britain, based as it was on a power-driven machine industry capable of achieving economies of scale. Although coal ultimately became the principal motive power, its supremacy came only by degrees. Coal output rose steadily from 1711 onward, when the development of techniques for drainage and ventilation made deep-pit mining possible. Indeed, the first steam engines

Fig. 16.1   *The coalfields of Britain. Note that the coal seams extend under the sea in some of the coastally situated coalfields.*

were used to pump water from the mines. In the beginning (1750 to 1780) steam-powered pumps also supplied water for operating mill water wheels, but it was soon learned that steam could be applied as a direct power for machinery. Steam thereafter became the main energy source for textile mills (especially cotton), glass works, metals and metalworking, grinding, and grain milling. It was also during this eighteenth century period that coke-fired blast furnaces and refineries were introduced into the iron trades.

As coal rapidly gained ascendancy over other energy forms, its influence on the location of production grew. The attraction of coal fields was the more compelling because well into the nineteenth century coal remained expensive to ship. Furthermore, huge quantities of coal were needed because the primitive steam engines used it so inefficiently, as did the iron industry. Cold-blast furnaces, for example, required eight tons of coal for each ton of finished iron. The locational effect on cotton textile production was profound, and by 1831 virtually all the power-spinning operations had been lured to the West Yorkshire coal field towns. By the end of the eighteenth century ironmaking had finally been emancipated from forested areas and had instead become dependent upon coal field sites, especially those having a long metalworking tradition. These were the West Midlands, South Wales, and Scotland. The northeast coast was late to develop its metal trades because it did not have the acid nonphosphoric iron ores of the type required at the time (recall that the basic Bessemer process came much later). Manufacturing rapidly became urbanized during this period as labor was drawn to the factories, and towns sprang up on the coal fields.

In time this powerful attraction of coal was gradually alleviated. Transport costs for the fuel declined steadily after the canal-building era arrived and the railways appeared. Coal use also became increasingly efficient through such innovations as the Nielson hot blast, which by 1833 had reduced the coal-iron ratio to 2⅔ to 1. Both transport and industrial innovations came too late, however, to halt the self-sustaining momentum of new urban development on the coal fields.

the British coal industry today

The British coal industry reached its peak in 1913. In that year 287 million tons were produced, a third of which was exported, and more than a million workers were employed in the mines. By 1969 coal output had declined to 164 million tons, and no more than 300,000 workers are currently employed. Within the next decade annual production was expected to fall to 120 million tons or less. Meanwhile, British coal exports have disappeared altogether.

What caused this precipitous decline? It did not result from resource depletion, since total reserves are still large. The more accessible deposits have been exhausted, however, and those that remain are deep and costly to mine. The industry is burdened by the inefficient way mining was conducted in the past when operations were at too small a scale, causing deposits to become excessively fragmented. The heritage from that earlier period is a multitude of old, uneconomical pits and much inaccessible coal still remaining underground. During this century the coal industry has been plagued by labor problems, including low productivity, recruiting difficulties, and rising wage levels. Coal mining in Britain is a labor-intensive activity and is therefore particularly inflation-prone.

Meanwhile British coal has lost many of its principal markets at home and abroad. Exports have been curtailed by competition from Poland, the United States, West Germany, and the Soviet Union, among others—all lower-cost producers. Domestically, the coal industry has encountered competition from other fuels, especially oil and gas. Transport costs within the British Isles are decidedly higher for coal than for other fuels and it therefore has a greater spatial variation in delivered price. Furthermore, at the retail level coal sales are burdened with an inefficient distribution system.

Recognizing the vital place of energy in the national economy, the British government has made strenuous efforts to solve the coal problem. These began with nationalization of the industry in 1947, when it was placed under the control of the National Coal Board. The NCB has undertaken a program of rationalization with the closing of hundreds of small, uneconomical pits. By 1970 the total number of operating mines in Britain was down to 300, as opposed to 700 in 1960. Most of these mines are concentrated along the eastern flanks of the central Pennine upland, where efficiency is most easily attained. Modernization of mining operations has been sought by combining small

units into more efficient large ones, sinking new mines, using new mining techniques, and introducing mechanization. The handling and transporting of coal have also been aided by such innovations as unit trains. Nevertheless, many basic problems remain unsolved and it would actually be cheaper to import coal than to supply it from British mines—if coal imports were not prohibited owing to balance-of-payments considerations.

In recent years the home market for British coal has been changing. Dieselization of British railways has removed that major customer, and the largest user still remaining is the electric power industry, which takes nearly half the nation's coal output. Another third goes to coke ovens, gas works, and other industrial users, while household use has declined to about one-eighth of total production. All these markets are declining except coking for the steel industry. The total British market for coal is rapidly shrinking, both absolutely and relatively, and the decline would be even faster except for the inertia of long-time users. Coal supplied three-fifths of the United Kingdom's energy market in 1966; but three years later coal's share had fallen to less than one-half of the total; by the late 1970s it was expected to account for only one-third.

petroleum (oil and gas)

Despite the decline of coal, the United Kingdom's energy requirements, like those of other technically advanced nations, are soaring today. More and more energy is needed to sustain economic growth and to accommodate increased demand for consumer durables, especially automobiles and household appliances. With Britain's traditional energy source, coal, now proving inadequate to the expanding need, and with no real solution to the coal problem in view, the country is having to turn to other forms of energy. Although coal will surely remain a basic part of the total energy supply for some time to come, increasingly it is being supplemented or displaced by other energy types. These shifts are dictated by the compelling need to ensure a continuing adequate and dependable energy supply and by the rising cost of coal. The substitution cannot be avoided despite public concern for dislocations it may cause in local economies dependent on coal mining. The main beneficiary of this change in energy use is the petroleum industry—producers of both oil and gas.

oil

The consumption of oil products has risen steeply and uninterruptedly in recent decades. Much of the increased demand has come from industry, where the technical advantages of oil over coal have been eagerly seized upon (see Chapter 3). Steel mills have installed oil-fired furnaces, electric power stations have turned to oil-fired or dual coal-oil generators (as insurance against interruptions in supply), and chemical produc-

Fig. 16.2 *Location of British oil refineries*

ers have been replacing coal chemicals with petro-chemicals.

In the transport sector the changeover to oil has been very nearly complete. The navy, merchant fleet, and railways have become almost entirely dieselized, as has much of the truck fleet. Aviation is using ever greater amounts of jet fuel, and the growing number of private automobiles is increasing the demand for gasoline. More oil is also being consumed for central heating of homes, offices, public buildings, and factories. It should be noted that certain of these uses represent captive markets for oil, especially aircraft and automobile fuel. For all these reasons, therefore, oil consumption has accelerated since 1945, and in 1970 it passed coal as the leading energy source of the country.

A supply problem has resulted from this burgeoning demand for oil. Like most Western European countries, the United Kingdom's petroleum production from domestic wells has been negligible, and its oil imports have risen sharply. Within the fifteen-year period following 1950 British crude oil purchases from abroad increased tenfold. For Britain, as for other European countries, the character of these oil imports has changed since World War II. Before the war most of the oil entered the country in the form of refined products supplied from field refineries in the Middle East, especially Iran's Abadan refinery. In recent years, however, the United Kingdom has imported larger amounts of crude oil, which is domestically refined.

To supply this rising demand there has been a great increase in the size and number of British refineries, which have assumed a distinct locational pattern (Fig. 16.2). Refiners have managed to gain economies of scale in transportation by selecting coastal sites on deep-water anchorages capable of accommodating

modern 250,000-ton tankers drawing 66 feet of water (equivalent to a six-story building). The largest refineries (between 10 and 16 million metric tons capacity per year) are located within easy access of the main population concentrations of the country. Major refineries on Southampton Water and the Lower Thames serve London and the Southeast, and a second cluster along the Mersey supplies the Liverpool-Manchester urban-industrial complex. Other, smaller refineries geared to regional markets are at Milford Haven and Swansea (for the South Wales and Bristol Channel areas), on the Humber and Tees estuaries (for the Northeast Coast connurbation), and at Grangemouth (for the Scottish Midlands). It should be noted that wherever possible the emphasis has been on achieving economies of scale in refining by means of very large installations.

With the industry thus organized to accommodate large volumes of imported crude oil, Britain has been confronted with serious strategic and economic difficulties by this increasing dependence on foreign suppliers. British nervousness concerning the long and vulnerable supply line from the politically volatile Middle East was demonstrated by the country's involvement in the 1956 Suez crisis, and these fears were confirmed by the reduction of Arabian shipments during the Arab-Israeli conflict of 1973. Moreover, although oil has been cheap and convenient to use, the quantities now being imported place a severe drain on Britain's foreign exchange reserves at a time when the country's balance-of-payments problems have weakened the pound. The situation has become even more critical with the sharp rises in oil prices exacted by the recently-formed cartel of petroleum-producing countries. For all these reasons the United Kingdom has been making a concerted search for alternative sources of supply.

Just in time, important offshore oil discoveries have been made in the British sector of the North Sea. The seriousness of Britain's need for this oil, as well as the changing world price structure, is demonstrated by the willingness to confront the difficult problems of oil exploration and production in that locale. The waters are much deeper than those in the Gulf of Mexico offshore fields, and some drilling takes place at depths of 500 feet or more. Some of the world's most vicious storms strike this area, with hundred-mile-per-hour gales and hundred-foot waves. Operating in such waters is costly, since it requires special drilling rigs as tall as 60-story buildings as well as expensively constructed pumping and pipeline facilities. Off-shore oil production normally costs five times more than onshore, but North Sea costs are at least ten times those of the Middle East.

The first British North Sea oil discovery came in 1971, soon after Norway's important Ekofisk field came in. These finds were made in the northern part of the British sector opposite Scotland and the Shetland Islands (Fig. 16.3). The richness of these fields has exceeded expectations, and estimates of total reserves, already very high, are rising rapidly with each new discovery. The Argyll field was scheduled to provide the first crude oil from the British sector of the North Sea during the summer of 1974, and the giant "Forties" field was to follow in 1975.

Although the timing of these discoveries is fortunate, the United Kingdom is likely to remain partially dependent upon oil from the Middle East and North Africa until 1980, when the North Sea deposits can be brought into full production. Nevertheless, Britain's domestic output of oil should progressively reduce the drain on her balance of payments caused by fuel imports, a desirable turn of events just as Britain joins the EEC. Important locational effects are also expected, and indeed have already appeared along the east coast of Scotland. Aberdeen and Dundee, as bases for the exploration work, have become boom towns. Steel fabricating facilities for oil field equipment are under construction at Methil, Fife, and the demand for seagoing drilling and pumping rigs has revived the dormant shipbuilding industry of Glasgow. Another impact from the North Sea discoveries will be an increase in oil consumption by British industries and an accelerated decline in local coal field economies.

Fig. 16.3 *Oil and gas fields in the British sector of the North Sea*

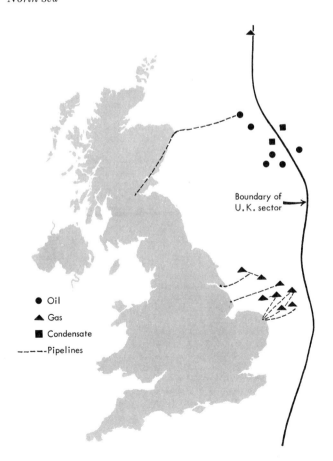

- ● Oil
- ▲ Gas
- ■ Condensate
- ---- Pipelines

Boundary of U.K. sector

gas

Manufactured gas ("town gas") has long been used as a secondary fuel by British industry and households. Having a lower BTU content than natural gas, it has traditionally been made from coal and distributed to local markets by Area Gas Boards. This "coal gas" yields valuable byproducts, including coke and raw materials for coal chemicals. Some of the gas is itself obtained as a byproduct of coke ovens in the steel industry. Postwar nationalization of the coal gas industry resulted in consolidation and technical improvements in production and distribution, including the construction of regional gas grids to interconnect the various gasworks to provide a dependable supply and meet peak demand. Coal gas was inadequate to the need, however, and new primary fuels for the manufacture of gas were introduced. First the industry turned to lower grades of coal, using new technology, then to the use of heavy fuel oil and finally to light petroleum distillate. Each new fuel successively reduced production costs.

At the same time, techniques were being perfected for transporting natural gas (methane) by seagoing vessels (see Chapter 3). The first regular shipment of liquified natural gas (LNG) arrived from Algeria in 1965 and entered a newly constructed British methane grid at Canvey Island, on the Thames estuary. This grid connects London and the southeast with Leeds and Manchester in the north. Although a technical success, the importation of LNG had the same disadvantages as oil imports: excessive dependence on politically unstable suppliers and a severe drain on foreign exchange holdings.

Meanwhile, in that same year, companies prospecting for oil (see above) struck natural gas deposits in Britain's southern sector of the North Sea. Production from this new source began in 1967 and at least nine major fields have been proved. The gas reaches Britain's east coast at three points, where it enters the newly expanding national methane grid. Significant onshore deposits of natural gas were also found in 1966 at Lockton.

As in the case of oil, Britain's natural gas discoveries have had a great impact. The United Kingdom was expected to achieve self-sufficiency in natural gas by 1975, effecting a saving of $250 million in foreign exchange. Providing low-cost competition for oil, and particularly for coal, in the industrial and home-heating markets, gas was supplying 15 percent of all Britain's energy needs by 1975. At present natural gas from the North Sea favors the country's east coast regions; but completion of the national grid will bring cheap gas to the entire island, yielding important benefits to areas now lacking indigenous energy supplies but further undermining local coal field economies.

electricity

The generating and distributing of electricity has been a nationalized industry in the United Kingdom since the late 1940s, its management being in the hands of a Central Electric Generating Board. The various parts of the country have been linked together by means of a supergrid, which has recently been converted to 400 kilovolts for more efficient transmission over long distances, to make possible more efficient continuous consumption by balancing demands across the country. The grid also makes possible important economies of scale from the use of larger generators. Although electricity is by nature a secondary form of energy, it is rapidly growing in importance in Britain as elsewhere. The primary energy types used for generating British electricity include both thermal and hydro sources. The thermal fuels include coal, oil, gas, and nuclear energy, each of which has assumed a particular place in the total scheme. Hydroelectricity is mainly of local significance.

conventional sources of British electricity

The character of electric power generation has changed markedly in the United Kingdom since World War II. The traditional primary generating source, coal, is no longer the cheapest even though it still accounts for three-fourths of the total power produced. Immediately following the War officials assumed that the country

Fig. 16.4 *Major thermal generating stations, early 1970s. Note the central concentration of large coal-fired generating stations in the valleys of the Trent and Calder rivers. Oil-fired stations are all coastally situated for receiving imported fuel, while most nuclear stations are located at a distance from major population centers.*

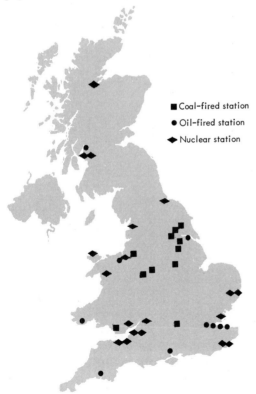

■ Coal-fired station
● Oil-fired station
◆ Nuclear station

would remain indefinitely dependent upon coal-fired generators. With respect to the supergrid, major new plants were to be centrally located along navigable waterways serving the coal fields, especially the Rivers Aire, Calder, and Trent (Fig. 16.4). Other stations were placed at coastal and coal field points to serve local demand. Technical advances in coal-fired generation tended to reinforce this initial decision. It was soon discovered, however, that coal supplies would remain neither adequate nor dependable and the CEGB turned increasingly to oil-fired generators to avert looming power shortages.

Oil has since proved decidedly cheaper than coal for power generation, especially in southern England. The resulting trend toward oil-fired stations was temporarily halted, however, when the Suez crisis of 1956 introduced uncertainties with respect to oil supplies. Some oil-fired generators were reconverted to coal and others were provided with standby coal-burning units. Above all, the Suez crisis stimulated development of nuclear energy for power generation. The appearance of alternative suppliers and lower prices for oil brought a return to that primary source in the 1960s, and by 1969, 15 percent of the total was from oil-fired units. Note that the major oil-burning generators are located adjacent to large refineries on the Thames estuary, Southampton Water, Milford Haven, Merseyside, and the Scottish Midlands (Fig. 16.4). Now, in the 1970s, the North Sea oil and gas discoveries have reinforced the trend away from coal-fired generators, and promise to become increasingly significant in future planning.

Another locally significant source of primary energy for electricity generation is falling water. The water power potential of Britain as a whole is low, but the mountainous areas of north and mid Wales and Scotland provide attractive opportunities to use this form of energy. Although these regions have scattered populations, water power has been used as a means of attracting electricity-using industries to bolster lagging local economies.

nuclear energy

The United Kingdom is currently the leading nation in the use of nuclear power for generating electricity (43.7 percent of the world in 1972). This emphasis has been official policy since 1955, at which time the likelihood of a long-run shortage of coal was being recognized, together with the apparent lack of other alternatives. Nuclear power development has also been stimulated by Britain's reluctance to become dependent upon foreign energy, for reasons cited earlier. The first British reactor was completed at Calder Hall in 1956, just as the Suez affair was adding gravity to the energy problem. Although easing of the oil supply situation in the 1960s subsequently reduced the sense of urgency surrounding the atomic energy program, the plan was not abandoned but continued to be viewed as a long-term answer to the energy question. Moreover, when the Arabian oil producers restricted shipments during the fall and winter of 1973, Britain's nuclear program again claimed national attention.

Clearly the country has paid a price for pioneering in nuclear power development, in the form of now obsolescent, high-cost installations. Nevertheless, atomic energy offers significant advantages for the British. Although initial capital investment is substantial, operating costs are low and tend to fall with advances in technology. In addition, nuclear power provides important savings in foreign exchange.

British nuclear stations are located according to a number of criteria. Because nuclear fuel has very little bulk, the generators can be placed in districts lacking other types of energy, especially coal-deficit areas. Cooling-water requirements are great, hence the British stress upon coastal or estuarine sites. Because of the popular fear of nuclear installations, they are kept at a distance from built-up areas. Moreover, they have been sited in such a way as to minimize damage to the environment. Current installations are thus mainly in remoter coastal locations outside the coal field areas. The principal sites are in the southwest of England, North Wales, Scotland, East Anglia, and southeastern England (Fig. 16.4).

Thus conceived as the long-term answer to Britain's energy needs, the atomic energy program now stresses perfecting of the fast-breeder reactor (see Chapter 3), which is expected to be in operation by the 1980s. It is believed that in the long run nuclear energy may reduce total costs by 15 to 20 percent. In any event, it remains as a resource for that inevitable time when fossil fuels approach final extinction.

British energy in summary

One of the central themes in British industrial history has been the availability of a dependable supply of cheap energy. The energy content of its exports provided Britain with an important comparative advantage that helped determine her unique place in the world economic system. Further, Britain has shown continuing capacity to shift from one indigenous energy source to another, and to rearrange its internal spatial order in response to these shifts.

At the dawn of the industrial era, wood, falling water, and coal each in turn exerted a locational attraction to certain key industries, especially coal, whose inertial influence remains even today. Nevertheless, the locational pull of energy has steadily weakened. Industry has been using energy more efficiently, better and cheaper means for transporting it have evolved, and the modern manufacturing has become increasingly drawn to the market. This market attraction relates partly to the changing structure of freight rates (see Chapter 8), but it can also be attributed to the greater amount of processing that manufactured goods receive

today. This has tended to emphasize the later stages of the manufacturing sequence, especially those aimed at the proliferating market for consumer goods. In addition, external economies have continued to gain in their importance to manufacturing. Finally, and not least, a greater variety of energy sources is available today in Britain, as elsewhere. Some, such as oil, natural gas, and electricity, are now distributed so efficiently that there is little spatial variation in their costs and they have essentially become ubiquities in the Weberian sense. As Weber observed, ubiquitous materials entering into a product add to the pull of the market (see Chapter 8).

For Britain, however, there is the question of which market should be stressed, the domestic or the foreign. The locational requirements for export production are not the same as for domestic industries. Although no one doubts that both markets must be served, emphasis upon one or the other of these has tended to shift in response to the impact of world events and changing British attitudes on the economy of the country. These changes in emphasis have affected the various regions of Britain in different ways, and therein lie the roots of a modern British dilemma.

BRITAIN'S CHANGING ROLE AND OUTLOOK

For more than a century, Britain dominated the world economically and politically, but in recent times that dominance has gradually dissipated. This decline in world power has brought a change of national focus and direction, causing international ties to weaken and domestic matters to receive more attention. Out of this situation a number of conflicting national goals and unresolved issues have emerged.

economic ascendency and decline

The first hundred years following the Industrial Revolution brought Britain to the pinnacle of world power. During this period the country turned from the ancient quest for continental territory to the acquisition of non-European possessions, colonizing those in the temperate lands and holding others in the tropics for commercial exploitation. Britain's role in this spatial order was to supply manufactured goods for which the principal markets were her expanding overseas empire. From the latter she received the primary commodities required by the British economy. Military power and political dominance ensured the development and maintenance of this colonial heartland-hinterland scheme. The global exchange was made possible by cheap ocean transportation with its long-haul advantage. It was a trade based on comparative advantage, both natural and acquired. At her zenith in the 1870s Britain was producing one-third of the world's manufactured goods, operating one-half of the world's merchant shipping, and maintaining direct or indirect control over a major part of the world's population. The next hundred years saw this lead slip away as other countries gained in industrial strength. Although in 1913 Britain was still first in manufacturing output, her proportion of the total was down to one-seventh. This relative decline has continued uninterruptedly since.

between the wars: the British commonwealth

The First World War cost Britain many of her overseas investments, including banking, insurance, and other commercial interests abroad, which were sold to finance the war. Much of the merchant fleet was destroyed by enemy action and former customers were lost to competitors or supplied more of their own needs. Internal self-government had previously been introduced to most British overseas possessions, and in 1931 parliament granted full sovereignty to the dominions (Canada, Australia, New Zealand, and South Africa). These newly independent countries nevertheless retained their close ties with the mother country through informal association, together with the remaining colonies. Thus empire was replaced by a "British Commonwealth of Nations."

After 1913 British trade likewise changed in structure. In that year exports still consisted of manufactured items and coal, while imports included little beyond the traditional foods and industrial raw materials. By 1937 exports were confined almost entirely to manufactured goods, British coal having virtually disappeared from world markets; however, imports now included manufactures as well as unprocessed commodities. Many of these new imports came from old customers, especially the United States and Canada. The British balance of trade had begun to slip.

At the same time Britain's commerce was assuming a different spatial pattern. During its nineteenth century global expansion, British trade with the industrializing countries of Western Europe had declined relatively. Between 1913 and 1937, however, her trade with Western Europe declined absolutely as well, a result of European efforts to achieve autarky during the depression and to prepare for the approaching Second World War. Only Britain's trade with the non-industrialized members of the Commonwealth grew.

Britain's reliance on world trade continued to deteriorate until by 1937 it represented only ten percent of national income. British investment and production were directed toward the domestic market during that era of world financial retrenchment, a move that was reinforced by the high tariffs on manufactured goods prevalent at the time. Because Britain's physical resources do not permit total self-sufficiency, the closest that Britain could approach to autarky was in consumer manufactures. British industry therefore turned more and more to the supply of these goods for the home market to replace lost foreign sales of the traditional export staples.

post–World War II: continued decline from world power

At the conclusion of the Second World War, Britain's Asian, African, and Middle Eastern territories gained full independence, and the country underwent a military retrenchment with the loss of naval bases in the Indian Ocean, the Red Sea, and the Mediterranean. The United Kingdom's industrial growth has also slowed since World War II and currently lags behind that of most other technically advanced nations. This economic weakness can be attributed to a number of causes in addition to the loss of Britain's vast overseas empire with its captive market and diverse resource base. One such problem is the increasing inadequacy of the domestic market to support the high levels of operation required to gain the economies of scale demanded by many modern industries. Another is the deterioration of domestic resources.

In addition to a shortage of physical resources, there has been a decline in nonphysical resources. For example, British entrepreneurship is not as innovative as in the past, tends to be poorly trained, and does not sponsor sufficient research to maintain a position of technological leadership. The brain drain of recent years appears to have caused the loss of many of the best trained and venturesome individuals among the managerial and scientific resource pool. The labor force has been restive, prone to frequent wildcat strikes, and hostile to automation; the country's labor unions have been loath to change goals developed in earlier eras when conditions were different. Worker productivity is therefore well below that of most contemporary industrial countries. British capital resources have been drained by wars and depressions, by the economy's declining competitiveness in the world market, and by heavy taxation to pay for social programs and income redistribution. Industrial plants and equipment are aging as a result of investment rates lower than those of Japan and Western Europe. The country's infrastructure is likewise growing obsolete, especially transport facilities. Because the canals, railways, and highways are all excessively narrow and low in carrying capacity by modern standards, they have become uneconomical in operation, a price of the country's pioneering in transport innovation.

British trade continues the trends of the 1930s, although GATT and other forms of international cooperation (see Chapter 11) have tended to reduce some of the artificial prewar barriers to commodity flows. The traditional export staples, especially textiles, have declined further, but they have been replaced by increasing exports of aircraft and motor vehicles, electrical goods, and chemicals, all high-technology items. Nevertheless, the country's balance-of-payments problems have continued to worsen, forcing a series of currency devaluations. In large measure, this can be attributed to the high unit costs of the export industries with their higher wages and lower labor productivity than those of competing nations, especially Japan. These difficulties are reinforced by a rising inflation rate.

"joining Europe"

Since Britian must continue trading for her survival, she has been forced to reorient her domestic economy and foreign commerce in recognition of changing realities in the world at large. As noted in Chapter 11, the United Kingdom's first attempt to join the EEC was rejected in 1963; however, her most recent application has been accepted and Britain officially entered the Common Market on January 1, 1973, along with Denmark and Ireland. The new nine-nation EEC provides Britain with a market of more than one-quarter billion people, having more than a fourth of the world's trade, and with an overall GNP second only to that of the United States. EEC membership represented a radical departure in British policy. Britain was required to relax her longstanding reliance upon Commonwealth and New World commercial ties and to abandon her customary aloofness to direct involvement in European economic affairs. It represented an admission that the old world economic order has passed.

domestic impact of Britain's changing place in the world

Another important result of the United Kingdom's altered international role has been the introduction of a new set of conditions affecting location of production within the country. The best locations for industry can be very different for a dominant international power with widespread commercial interests than for a small island nation thrown upon its own resources in a world of fiercely competing giants. The changing political and economic fortunes of the nation as a whole have therefore had considerable impact upon the economic welfare of the various regions of Britain.

location of British manufacturing during the imperial era

Throughout the long interval of British world dominance, the country's manufacturing reflected the prevailing international outlook. This included the location of manufacturing, with its focus on the export market. There were large concentrations of export industries along the coastal margins, especially the old coal field areas with access to facilities for the import of raw materials and shipment of the output. Many of these concentrations were situated peripherally to the country as a whole, as, for example, the Scottish Midlands, with its emphasis upon basic metals directed particularly to the shipbuilding at Clydeside (Glasgow). Another area where export manufacturing was concentrated was the Northeast Coast, centering on Middlesbrough, an area devoted mainly to iron and steel, shipbuilding, and

heavy fabricated items such as structural elements, bridge members, and locomotives. The Lancashire industrial complex, focused upon Manchester and Liverpool, was the great cotton textile region. Finally, there was South Wales with its long tradition of making iron and steel, nonferrous metals, tinplate and other flat-rolled metal products, and railway rails, as well as the mining of steam coal for export.

These were highly specialized regions, typical in this respect of much British production. As long as the foreign market for these goods held, the export regions enjoyed all of the many efficiencies of specialization: economies of scale, concentrations of technical skills, agglomerations of closely linked production units, and supporting services geared to the peculiar needs of local industries. This intense specialization had its disadvantages from the outset, however. The kinds of production upon which these regions depended were exceedingly vulnerable to wide swings of the business cycle and to the vagaries of international political and economic events. For a century and a half these export-producing regions rode the crest of a wave of long-term upward trends for their products, and on the whole, prospered along with the rest of the country; but when Britain's international fortunes turned, so did those of the export-based industries and the regions where they were located.

depressed areas in twentieth-century Britain

The deterioration of Britain's place in the world economy had a profound impact on the location of her industry. The loss of foreign markets struck hard at those regions having an export outlook. Declining foreign sales of ships, heavy steel products, textiles, and coal were a severe blow to the regions engaged in producing these goods. As the domestic market assumed greater relative importance the emphasis turned to consumer goods, both durables and non-durables. These activities have very different locational needs that tend to favor another set of producing regions. Benefiting most of all was London and the Southeast, the country's largest market, main focal point for the national transport network, and the center of government and commercial control, with all of the many related services and amenities of a capital city and world metropolis. This region is suited above all others for the manufacture of market-oriented consumer softwares, highly engineered products such as scientific instruments, and all the one-of-a-kind items required by a modern economy.

The other area to gain from the country's changed outlook has been the English Midlands, a region adjacent to the London area and likewise central to the national market. This old coal field district has the advantage of a local energy supply and a long industrial tradition based upon highly engineered goods. These include transport equipment, particularly automobiles, together with a wide range of other consumer durables enjoying a rising demand both at home and in the world at large. The London and Southeast and the Midlands regions have therefore benefited from maximum accessibility to the domestic market and both have a diversified output that tends to insulate them from the worst effects of cyclical variations in the economy. In these respects they contrast greatly with the less advantageous domestic locations and the extreme specialization of the old export regions on the country's margins.

Even before the world depression of the 1930s these peripheral areas were adversely affected by the United Kingdom's deteriorating international position, but the greatest economic depths were reached in 1933 and 1934. At that time Scotland and the North of England had unemployment rates of 22 percent, while those of South Wales ranged around 30 percent. Certain pockets of unemployment suffered rates as high as 40 to 80 percent. These figures reflect the devastated conditions nationally in the industries upon which these areas depended. Unemployment in shipbuilding reached 61 percent, metal manufacturing 35 percent, coal mining 26 percent, and textile production 24 percent. These rates contrast with those of London and the Southeast and the English Midlands, where unemployment rose no higher than 10 to 11 percent during the worst of the Depression. Despite these wide regional variations, little interregional migration of labor occurred during the Depression. In part, this can be attributed to the British tendency toward low mobility of labor, which maintains strong attachments to home communities; in large measure, however, it merely reflected the lack of vacancies anywhere in the country during that difficult period.

government measures to aid the distressed areas

Britain was perhaps the first country to address the problems of regional disparities. As early as 1928 an Industrial Transference Board established training centers and provided assistance for those wishing to migrate from the most seriously affected areas. For reasons given earlier, this approach availed little and the situation merely worsened. Finally, as the Depression reached its severest point, the Special Areas (Development and Improvement) Act of 1934 was passed. This designated four depressed regions to receive special governmental attention. These "special areas" were South Wales, Northeast England, West Cumberland, and Central Scotland. The act was subsequently amended to provide social overhead in the distressed areas, including sewerage and water systems, streets, utilities, and other facilities that might help to attract industry. Loans, tax incentives, and other subsidies were offered to small businesses locating in the areas. Industrial estates (parks) were to be established and furnished with ready-made, low-cost buildings for industrial occupancy. Little improvement took place in the depressed areas until

1938 and 1939, a time when the economy as a whole was showing renewed vigor owing to preparations for the impending Second World War.

New insights into the nature of regional problems were supplied by a government study issued in 1939, the Barlow Report. The Barlow Commission termed generally harmful the growing tendency for economic activities to concentrate in large conurbations such as London, and it argued for government control over industrial location with the purpose of directing it into the depressed areas. More specifically, it recommended decentralization of the industrial population from the congested metropolises, especially London, and a policy of industrial diversification in the peripheral distressed areas. The traditional industries of the special areas were too susceptible to economic fluctuations, the report declared, and the cure for this was to promote in those regions a greater variety of economic activities having a steadier demand for their products, especially consumer goods industries.

Responding to this influential study, Parliament approved a Distribution of Industry Act (1945), which established "development areas." These were the old special areas with the addition of the previously excluded nearby cities, which, it was now thought, might serve as growth points for regional development. Among other things, the act provided for the licensing of factory construction, which proved to be a powerful locational tool. Supplementing this measure, the 1947 Town and Country Planning Acts tightened the licensing provisions by requiring that construction of any industrial building over 5,000 square feet be covered by an Industrial Development Certificate (IDC) from the Board of Trade (the United Kingdom's equivalent to the U.S. Department of Commerce). This limitation affected all but the smallest workshops. The act also restrained urban growth so as to bring about a planned decentralization. To reinforce this aim, financial incentives and low-rent, government-built factories were provided for firms locating in the development areas.

Immediately after the Second World War there was an influx of new industries into the development areas, partly in response to government pressures and assistance but also because of other factors. One of these was the considerable number of World War II munitions factories now cheaply available for conversion to peacetime manufacturing purposes. Some of these formed nuclei for additional industrial estates. Of similar effect was the government rationing of building materials, which continued in short supply for some time following the war. In this manner, the development areas managed to acquire at least half of the new postwar industries. Unfortunately the British balance-of-payments crisis of 1947 forced curtailment of these development programs and produced an abrupt shift of emphasis to export industries and to those engaged in import-substituting types of manufacture. Devaluation of the British pound subsequently relieved the payments problem and a Second Distribution of Industry Act (1950) was implemented in an attempt to revive the now sagging fortunes of the development areas.

The following year the British Conservative party was returned to national political power on a "freedom from planning" platform, and aid to the development areas was thereupon sharply reduced. Only a brief boom in their traditional export industries sustained the distressed regions, but the economic decline that followed caused them serious problems. The development areas suffered through these stop-and-go government policies related to changing national politics.

These regions were given renewed attention with passage of the Distribution of Industry (Industrial Finance) Act of 1958, which added still other districts to the original list of those eligible for special consideration. In 1960, however, a Local Employment Act replaced the development areas with development districts, collections of employment exchange areas. These were scheduled for aid solely on the basis of their current unemployment rates. The constant scheduling and descheduling of districts in response to rising and falling unemployment rates introduced a new uncertainty that hampered efforts to attract new industries. In 1963 a National Economic Development Council (NEDC) was established for the purpose of identifying "growth areas" to receive preferential treatment. This was followed by the 1964 Industrial Training Act to aid unemployed workers in gaining new skills, and by still another act in 1965 that added sixteen new areas to the development districts so as to make continuous areas out of hitherto scattered ones.

When it became clear that this series of arrangements was producing few results, the Industrial Development Act of 1966 sought to bring a return to the broader, more regional concept of development areas. Other criteria in addition to unemployment rates were used to define these new, larger areas. Later, as a result of a Hunt Committee Report, a number of "grey areas" were also delimited. These "intermediate areas" had less severe economic problems than those of the development areas, and they received a less drastic form of special aid. Finally, in 1969 "special development areas" were designated and granted an extra measure of government help. These were particularly hard-pressed communities inside the boundaries of existing development areas. Virtually all were coal-mining districts stranded by the decline of their staple industry.

At the beginning of the 1970s, therefore, four types of areas were marked for special attention from government agencies within the framework of economic planning regions (see Figs. 16.5 and 16.6):

1. Development areas—large regions with many varied incentives for new industries and other forms of help

2. Special development areas—small communities within the development areas eligible for additional forms of assistance

3. Intermediate areas—"grey areas" marked for aid on a somewhat reduced scale

4. The remainder of the nation, for which no special developmental help was indicated.

To summarize this chronology of British regional development efforts since 1934, we may note that official policy has taken different directions within the thriving West Midlands and the South of England on the one hand and in the lagging regions of the North and West on the other. For the former, the problems have been those of preserving agreeable urban living conditions and providing adequate mobility for passengers and goods at a time when business firms and people have crowded into the regions to participate in their relative prosperity. The official response in these localities has been to promote urban renewal of inner-city areas and improved intraregional transportation, but at the same time to restrain economic growth and urban-industrial development to a feasible extent. Specific measures have been adopted to produce a decentralization of people and jobs to new towns within the

Fig. 16.5 *Economic planning regions of the United Kingdom*

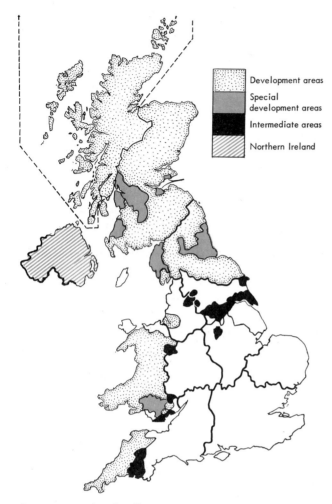

Legend:

- ⬚ Development areas
- ▨ Special development areas
- ■ Intermediate areas
- ▨ Northern Ireland

Fig. 16.6 *Regional policy areas*

London and West Midlands regions and to shift some of their economic growth to stagnating regions on the margins of the country.

In the latter areas the problems have been excessive unemployment, low levels of economic activity, and net out-migration of people. Through much experimentation, the government has developed a set of policies designed to ease the decline of staple industries such as coal, steel, shipbuilding, and textiles and at the same time to attract new forms of employment in order to diversify local economies. Positive measures have included building industrial estates, constructing standard factories in advance of demand, subsidizing factory rents and labor costs, extending investment grants and tax concessions to manufacturers, aiding the development of roads and other forms of infrastructure, promoting local amenities and improving the environment, retraining workers, and exerting locational pressures on such growth industries as motor car manufacturing.

We have also seen that the spatial pattern of developmental aid has shifted considerably as experience has accumulated throughout this period. Thus, when it was found that exclusion of major urban centers from the four special areas of 1934 was unrealistic,

development areas were subsequently formed to include both the regional capitals and to incorporate more territory. Again, during the early 1960s, the experiment with development districts was quickly abandoned when it was found to be too local in its impact, forcing industry into uneconomic locations and thus creating new problems. The emphasis then shifted to the fostering of growth points, and a return was made to even broader development areas, including "special" development areas that require an extra measure of help. Finally came the realization that certain localities adjacent to the development areas also need special consideration, although to a lesser degree.

With the advent of a new Conservative government in June of 1970, regional development was again deemphasized and investment grants were replaced with tax allowances. That year also brought a further deterioration of the national economy, which caused a sharp rise in unemployment in all of the peripheral areas. No doubt the Labour party, which subsequently regained control, will introduce further changes in regional development practices. Therefore, although nearly a half century of British experience with regional planning has brought general acceptance of such policies, little political agreement exists as to the exact form they should take.

The lagging regions have been receiving an average total of $730 million annually—a great amount of money for an economy the size of Britain's. Largely as a consequence of these expenditures, the cruel regional disparities of the 1930s are much diminished today. Nevertheless, a gap between the center and the periphery still persists, despite the many years of more or less intensive effort to close it. The Southeast and the Midlands continue to be generally favored with prosperity, and those areas immediately adjacent to them appear to benefit from the spread effects of growth at the center. It is here that Britain's greatest metropolitan development has occurred. These two concentrations of population and employment have merged to form a great megalopolis that contains 70 percent of the people of England and Wales living on only 24 percent of the land area. The functional interrelationships among the many parts of this metropolitan region are very close, as shown by the fact that it accounts for more than two-thirds of the flows of freight, mail, and railway passengers south of the Scottish border.

By contrast with the prospering metropolitan center, the peripheral areas continue to lag. They still suffer from comparative disadvantages in labor and entrepreneurial skills, external economies, amenities, and location with respect to the national market. Unemployment rates are therefore higher, per capita incomes are lower, and net out-migration continues. Even though much abated, disparities still remain.

Concurrently, Britain has pursued a program to redistribute national income, thereby narrowing the gap between the very rich and the very poor. This program includes high taxation of upper-income persons, through steeply graduated income taxes and high death duties (inheritance taxes) and an elaborate system of social services, such as old-age pensions, nationalized medicine, and unemployment insurance.

conflicting national goals

Contemporary Britain is a country with seemingly antagonistic national policies. These contradictions have produced lengthy public debate and contributed to the vacillations on domestic and foreign issues illustrated in the preceding sections. Thus the domestic policy of promoting industrial growth and diversification of employment in the lagging regions would seem to run counter to the persistent national economic need to export for survival in a competitive world.

Diversification almost invariably means increasing production of consumer goods mainly for domestic consumption and for reducing the emphasis upon manufactures intended for export. Yet, at a time when the balance of payments is dangerously unsettled and the pound is in continual danger, more exports are badly needed. Moreover, there is the drain on the national treasury caused by subsidizing the development areas. Then, too, the peripheral regions are not usually the most efficient points from which domestic markets can be served. Transport and communication links are indirect, and many agglomeration advantages for industry are lacking. Any such loss of efficiency burdens the national economy as a whole.

Another question now arising is whether or not these remoter parts of Britain are too far from the center of gravity of the new nine-nation EEC. Southeastern England, the location preferred by those serving the domestic market, would likewise appear to be a better place from which to reach continental markets, situated as it is opposite the Rhine delta and pointed directly at the economic heart of Europe. As measured by per capita incomes, the only British region that approaches the average level of prosperity of the EEC as a whole is the Southeast, followed by the West Midlands. Other regions of the country now lag well behind the Common Market standard. Yet, the United Kingdom's regional development efforts may run counter to her best opportunities for successful competition in the wider European economy. Finally, there is the question as to whether Britain's income redistribution policy does not weaken her capacity to generate capital needed for participation on equal terms in the Common Market.

These basic conflicts confronting British policy makers are reflected in the seemingly schizoid government approach toward national goals. While one agency may be working to promote industries making domestic consumer goods in order to achieve stability and raise employment, a second agency may be trying to stimulate export industries to reduce the foreign exchange deficit. Thus we have the contemporary British dilemma.

Deprived of the comfortable independence once afforded by her widespread colonial empire, the United Kingdom has only the natural and human resources of her home islands to draw upon as she enters into a union with strong competitors. But to use those resources with the necessary efficiency, she may have to sacrifice domestic programs that Britons have come to consider essential to their way of life.

RECOMMENDED READINGS

Chisholm, Michael, Gerald Manners, eds., *Spatial Policy Problems of the British Economy.* Cambridge: Cambridge University Press, 1971.

Manners, Gerald, *The Geography of Energy.* London: Hutchinson University Library, 1964.

———, "Some Economic and Spatial Characteristics of the British Energy Market," in Michael Chisholm and Gerald Manners (eds.), *Spatial Policy Problems of the British Economy.* Cambridge: Cambridge University Press, 1971, Chapter 6.

Manners, G., D. Keeble, B. Rodgers, and K. Warren, *Regional Development in Britain.* New York: John Wiley, 1972.

McCrone, Gavin, *Regional Policy in Britain.* University of Glasgow Social and Economic Studies, No. 15. London: George Allen & Unwin, 1969.

Smith, Wilfred, *An Economic Geography of Great Britain.* New York: Dutton, 1948.

Stamp, L. Dudley, and Stanley H. Beaver, *The British Isles.* London: Longmans, Green, 1958.

japan:
growth
pole
of
the
orient

17

As we enter the final quarter of the twentieth century, another island nation, also the former center of a large empire, has joined the select group of modern economic giants. Japan's advance has been so rapid that the world has been quite surprised by the profound change. Accustomed to a Japan exporting cheap, low-quality, labor-intensive textiles and novelties, American and European manufacturers were ill-prepared for the sudden appearance of highly engineered Japanese cameras, television sets, motor vehicles, and ships. Inevitably the Japanese people have been much affected by the swiftness of these changes. Economic growth has become a national preoccupation in Japan even as Britons have turned to the problem of redressing economic disparities among their people. While the United Kingdom strives to avoid being swept under by the tide of change, Japan rides its crest.

Despite the differences in their current fortunes, however, Britain and Japan are so similar in other respects that comparing the two has become a popular exercise. Both island groups, for example, lie offshore of the great Eurasian land mass. They also resemble each other in size, nature of production, and relationship to the world economy. Moreover, economic activity in both countries tends to concentrate in the southeastern part of the main island, producing congestion in the core area and economic distress in remoter regions.

Interesting as these comparisons may be, a perhaps more compelling reason for examining Japan's space-economy is its dominating influence in the world economic system. As Japan's material wealth increases, her citizens are attaining European levels of prosperity, and indeed may well become the most affluent people in the world before the end of the century. Meanwhile, her trade with the rest of the world has reached such proportions as to cause major realignments of the world's currency system. Japan's accomplishments are even more significant in contrast to her Asian neighbors, all of whom are in the early stages of development. The Japanese economy towers over the rest of Asia not only in level of technology but also in total volume of output and size of personal income.

Looking more specifically at Japan's characteristics we find that her national income of $207 billion (1971) is nearly twice that of the United Kingdom and substantially larger than West Germany's. Indeed, it is more than half again as large as that of all the rest of Asia combined. Yet, physically, Japan is a small country, her 143,000 square miles being less than the area of California, although somewhat more than the area of the British Isles. The Japanese archipelago, which stretches 1,400 miles from northeast to southwest (Fig. 17.1), includes four main islands and hundreds of small ones. Honshu, the largest, has two-thirds of the total land area and three-fourths of the Japanese population, and the greater part of the country's commerce and industry. The next largest island, Hokkaido, is the northernmost of the major group. It was the

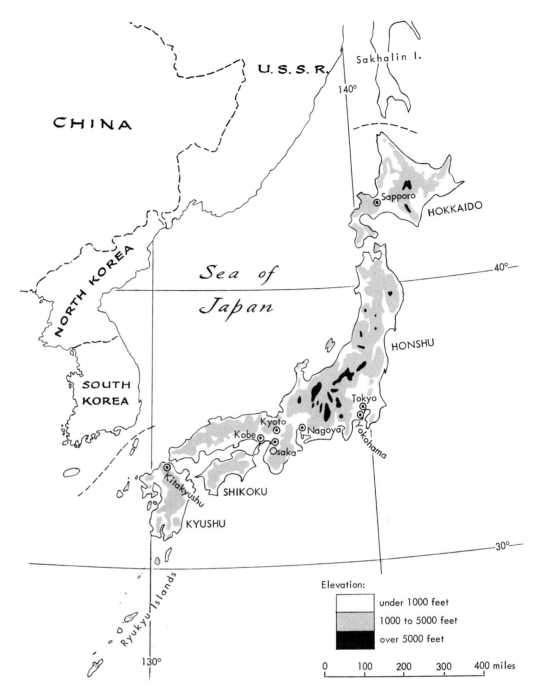

Fig. 17.1 *Japan: physical relief and largest cities*

latest to be occupied and has only five percent of the population. Kyushu and Shikoku in the south are much smaller.

In 1972 there were 106 million Japanese within this small territory, giving a population density of 739 persons per square mile (350 per square kilometer). This density is considerably higher than that of the United Kingdom, but it is less than that of Belgium and the Netherlands. Yet, when it is considered that 75 percent of Japan's surface is occupied by rugged mountains, some reaching 12,000 feet or more, the country's population is indeed crowded for living space. Most Japanese are found along the coastal lowlands in

the southern half of the nation. Until recently, Japan had a high population growth rate, and overcrowding was one of the reasons given for Japanese belligerence during the 1930s and 1940s. After a strenuous and typically well-organized effort, the population has now become stabilized, with an annual growth rate that is 1.1 percent and falling. Under the United Nations classification system (Chapter 2) therefore, it has become a Type 5 country. The current birth rate is very low, and the death and infant mortality rates are among the lowest in the world. Today's Japanese have an unusually long life expectancy. The per capita national income of $1975 (1971) is close to the average for

Western Europe; and the Japanese people have become visibly prosperous, as shown by the rapidly rising number of automobiles. Although per capita energy consumption is still somewhat below that of the United Kingdom, this too is growing very fast. Japan's literacy rate is one of the world's highest. At 98 percent, it is far above that of other Asian nations, most of whom have well under 50 percent literacy.

In a country with such a high standard of living it is surprising to discover that 19 percent of the labor force is still in agriculture, as compared with Britain's 3 percent. This proportion is falling rapidly, however. In 1963, 29 percent of the workers were farmers, and as recently as 1930 the figure was 51 percent. On the other hand, only one-fourth of the labor force is in manufacturing, a fact that belies the customary view of a labor-intensive industrial nation. Like other technically advanced nations of today, Japan's tertiary labor force is growing much faster than that of the other sectors.

From what has been said so far, it is apparent that the Japanese space-economy has unique characteristics. As we examine her resource endowment, output and trade, and incredibly rapid rate of growth, we shall see that Japan has assigned a special place to high-technology industries. Despite her successes, however, Japan has difficult spatial problems, both internal and international.

THE DISTINCTIVE JAPANESE SPACE-ECONOMY

resource base

Japan is severely short of the basic physical requirements for feeding her large population and supplying an increasingly ravenous industry. Her 16 million acres of arable land are hardly more than one-third of Britain's supply, since three-fourths of the territory is in steep slopes. This means only 0.15 acres per person, far less than is available to the average Briton; and it is a proportion that continues to shrink with population growth and urban encroachment upon some of the best cropland. Japan's agricultural land is scattered along the coastal plains, the narrow river valleys, and a number of small mountain basins in the interior.

Most of the country's domestic reserves of industrial raw materials, like those of Britain, are grossly inadequate, making necessary massive imports. By far the majority of these are procured from distant locations, imposing a special cost on Japanese industry. This burden of having to draw upon a global supply area is being eased for the Japanese, however, by transport innovations yielding ever greater economies of scale: gigantic bulk ocean carriers and modern port facilities with deep water channels and anchorages.

Wood is one of the few natural resources that has not been particularly scarce. Three-fifths of the

country is in forest, and much wood is used for housing, heating, synthetic fiber manufacture and many other purposes. Yet even this supply is proving inadequate for today's pace of resource use, and the Japanese must import increasingly large quantities of wood from Canada and the United States.

The energy problem is particularly severe for Japan. Demand for fuel is rising at least 10 percent each year and it is undergoing the same structural changes as in the United Kingdom. Oil is replacing coal, and electricity is becoming more and more important to the economy. Never self-sufficient in primary energy supplies, Japan is having to rely increasingly upon foreign sources. Although her domestic reserves are of fair size, Japan's coal is expensive to mine and is of poor quality. Very little of it is of coking grade, and large quantities must be purchased abroad to supply the rapidly expanding steel industry. Although the United States has been a principal source, the Japanese have been investing heavily in Canada's Rocky Mountain deposits and in newly opened mines in Australia.

Only tiny amounts of petroleum are produced domestically, and Japan has therefore become one of the world's principal oil importing nations. Most of the supply comes from the Middle East, where Japanese investment has been growing. This dependence upon the politically uncertain Arab nations has been a matter of much concern to Japan, however, especially since the Middle Eastern oil crisis of 1973, and Japanese companies have been undertaking extensive oil exploration in Asia, including recent developments offshore in southwest China. Most of the oil obtained by Japan is refined domestically at refineries sited along the industrialized coastal belt of southeastern Honshu.

Mountainous Japan has much falling water, and this has been the principal source of electric power in the past, along with coal-fired generators. Today these primary energy sources are proving inadequate for the expanding need and both sources of power are becoming increasingly costly. The Japanese have therefore begun to develop nuclear power, but this remains chiefly a resource for the future. At present the chief emphasis is upon oil-fired generators.

Domestic supplies of metallic ores are especially poor, consisting mainly of small amounts of iron, zinc, and copper. As a consequence, Japan must obtain very large quantities of these raw materials from abroad, especially iron ore, which is procured from all over the world in giant ore carriers. India, the Philippines, and Malaysia are important suppliers, and some of the rich iron deposits recently discovered in western Australia are being developed with Japanese capital.

Japan's poverty in natural resources has always been a cause for acute anxiety, having served in the past as a justification for Japanese belligerence and expansionist tendencies. The country's chief assets and the true basis for her prospering and growing economy are therefore her human resources.

nature of output

agriculture

Various characteristics of Japan's production resemble those of the British economy, yet it has some uniquely Japanese qualities. For example, although Japan is a net importer of food, the proportion supplied domestically is surprisingly great, considering the minute endowment in cropland. At least four-fifths of the nation's food needs are provided by Japanese agriculture, and the country is self-sufficient in rice, the staple crop. How has this been achieved? For one thing, although land is in short supply, the climate is particularly favorable for high yields per acre. The islands are well-watered and have a wide latitudinal range, extending from 30° to 45° north. The variety of climatic types is therefore comparable to that found in the United States between Florida and Maine. The two extremes are Kyushu, with subtropical conditions and a very nearly year-round growing season, and Hokkaido, whose long, cold winters leave only 150 growing days during the brief, mild summer.

Although Japanese farms still supply the country with rice and other small grains, more of them are turning to vegetables, dairy products, meat animals, citrus and temperate fruits, and other commodities demanded by a population whose rising prosperity permits them to enjoy improved diets. Despite the great variation in physical conditions and the fragmented nature of arable land areas, Japanese agriculture gives evidence of a classical Thünen-like locational pattern. It has been found, for example, that 80 percent of Tokyo's fresh vegetables, fluid milk, and eggs are supplied from an area within a thirty-mile radius of the city; remote Hokkaido, on the other hand, produces livestock, butter and cheese, and such relatively nonperishable vegetables as cabbages for shipment to the metropolis. Cereals also are grown farther from major urban centers, and there is a transition of grain types with increasing distance.

As measured by crop yields and farm size, the intensity of Japanese agricultural production likewise diminishes as one moves away from the urbanized areas. Nevertheless, if intensity is defined as the proportion of variable factors (labor and capital) to the fixed factor (land), then all Japanese agriculture tends to be more intensive than in most other parts of the world. Farms average only $2\frac{1}{2}$ acres in size, somewhat smaller in the south and larger in the north. In the southern half of the country, where the growing season is sufficiently long, there is much double-cropping and intercropping. It has been traditional to apply heavy inputs of labor to these small patches of land. As noted earlier, the proportionate size of the agricultural labor force, although unusually high for a technically advanced nation, is dropping steadily. A major exodus from the farms is now underway, this being both a cause and effect of the increased substitution of capital for labor in Japanese agriculture.

The growing capital-intensity of Japan's farms takes several forms, one of which is mechanization. Following World War II Japanese farmers rapidly adopted an ingenious type of hand tractor peculiarly suited to their specific needs. Today this multipurpose implement is used not only for plowing and cultivating but also as a versatile source of mechanical power for every sort of farm need. It is made to operate threshing machines, rice hullers, water pumps, power sprayers, and many other pieces of farm equipment. Its widespread acceptance has speeded up farm work manyfold, but it has also released for productive purposes much land that was previously needed to grow feed for draft animals. Another form of capital introduced by most Japanese farmers is the use of agricultural chemicals, such as pesticides and herbicides, and the application of both organic and mineral fertilizers. Capital-intensity is also evidenced by the unusual amount of irrigation, found on fully half of Japan's farm area.

The quality of agricultural entrepreneurship is especially high in Japan where farmers' incentives were further enhanced by the land reform program undertaken during the American postwar occupation. Because of this combination of conditions, the per-acre output of Japanese farms is currently very great. Already many times those of other Asian countries, Japan's agricultural yields have continued to rise steadily throughout recent history. Nevertheless, this type of agriculture is necessarily high-cost, and Japan could actually import many foodstuffs more cheaply than she can grow them herself if she chose to relax her high barriers to foreign agricultural commodities.

In the past most of the protein in Japanese diets came from fish, although today this is supplemented more and more with other animal foods. To supply this need Japan operates a large fishing fleet which currently leads the world in total catch of food fish. The country has an ideal natural location for a fishing industry, being surrounded by productive waters. These are becoming badly overfished, however, as well as heavily polluted by industrial effluents, and the fleet must now range throughout the world's oceans in order to maintain a continued supply of fish.

manufacturing

Following Britain's lead, Japan has been a manufacturing nation for many years, but full industrial maturity has been attained only within the past two decades. Today the country has a full range of industrial types, including basic metals and chemicals and a particularly wide selection of other producer and consumer goods.

Japanese industry enjoys several special advantages. One of these is low labor costs; another, perhaps of even greater importance, is the remarkable efficiency with which labor is used. Manufacturing workers comprise only 26 percent of the country's labor force, far less than in Britain, and their output is greater individually and in total. Efficiency also characterizes the country's transportation. High-speed railways represent the principal means for moving passengers and goods internally, while an ultra-modern merchant fleet and an effective airline system supply the overseas connections vital to a country so distant from foreign suppliers and customers.

Finally, there are the marketing skills of Japanese managers, who are keenly alert to changing conditions in both foreign and domestic markets. This is substantially aided by a government peculiarly sensitive to the needs of business. Japan's economic decision makers have always emphasized foreign sales, evidencing an unusual degree of "export-mindedness." Nevertheless, rising Japanese incomes have made the home market a valuable base for gaining the necessary economies of scale for successful competition in the world at large (see Chapter 11). Indeed, the Japanese domestic market is itself far more important than generally realized by foreigners or even by the Japanese themselves. Only 10 percent of the country's GNP is actually exported, a proportion half that of Britain and less than one-third that of the Benelux countries.

foreign trade

Nevertheless, Japan has become the third largest exporter, after the United States and West Germany, and her trade is growing faster than that of either of the leaders. In 1972, for example, Japanese exports grew by 20 percent over the preceding year to reach a total of $30.2 billion. Meanwhile, her imports were only $23.7 billion, giving a high surplus of $6.5 billion. Japan's trading role is dictated, as is Britain's, by a large population contained within a small area having an inadequate natural resource endowment. The structure of Japanese trade closely resembles that of Britain, too. Japan imports foods and industrial raw materials and exports finished manufactured goods.

This is true even of commercial relations with Japan's chief trading partner, the United States. It seems paradoxical that the exports to Japan of the world's largest industrialized nation should contain such a high proportion (about one-fourth) of agricultural commodities, especially soybeans, cotton, and grains, along with other primary goods such as lumber and coal. In return the United States imports Japanese manufactured products with a high technology content. America's trade with Japan thus has all the characteristics and problems of an *underdeveloped* country trading with a technically advanced country—including increasingly unfavorable terms of trade! This helps to account for the more than $4 billion trade deficit that the United States had with Japan in 1972 (see Chapter 11).

In addition to its function of providing Japan with the food and materials she lacks at home, trade has a second function for the country: it compensates for cyclical fluctuations in the growth of domestic markets. Whenever home demand slackens temporarily, Japanese manufacturers immediately look to alternative markets abroad where they can dispose of their surplus output.

JAPAN'S GROWTH AND DEVELOPMENT

Of all the characteristics that distinguish the contemporary space-economy of Japan, the most pervasive is growth—rapid and uninterrupted growth. As Japan has surpassed one after another of the major national economies, this remarkable achievement has not only captured the imagination and aroused the uneasiness of the world but has become an obsession with the Japanese themselves. And yet, growth is not a new phenomenon to Japan; it has characterized Japanese economic affairs ever since Commodore Perry's visit ended that country's centuries-old feudal isolation. The capable, well organized Meiji rulers who gained control from the feudal Tokugawa shoguns in 1868 immediately began to modernize and industrialize Japan after the Western model. They quickly mobilized a low-cost labor force that had already acquired a tradition of hard work and a respectful attitude toward authority.

At the same time Japan's leaders began their long drive to build a colonial empire to provide raw materials the home islands lacked. First, the Japanese acquired neighboring island chains and then the larger island of Formosa (now Taiwan), after which they occupied the neighboring mainland peninsula of Korea. In the 1930s they extended this continental toehold by taking over important parts of China, and during the Second World War they temporarily gained control over most of eastern and southern Asia. All these territories were lost in the final Japanese defeat.

Although the disorientation that followed was intense, it was also surprisingly brief. With the onset of the Cold War in 1947 and 1948, the American occupation shifted from a punitive policy to one of rebuilding Japan as an American-style democracy, as a buffer against Communist China. By 1951 the Japanese economy had recovered to its prewar levels of output, aided by United States defense procurement in Japan during the Korean War. Japan's subsequent economic growth and development have been uninterrupted.

dimensions of Japan's growth

Two decades of unprecedented growth have produced truly revolutionary effects upon Japan and the Japanese people and on their relations with the rest of the world. During the most recent fifteen years Japan's total output has increased 4.4 times. Between 1955 and 1960 the annual rate of growth was 9.2 percent, from 1960 to 1965 it rose to 9.7 percent, and during the 1965–70 period it reached an astounding 12.1 percent. This compares with recent annual growth rates of 2.3 percent for the United States and only 1.9 percent for the United Kingdom. Thus Japan's output has actually been growing at an accelerating rate. As a result Japan has now become the world's leading shipbuilder, has acquired one of the largest, and certainly the most modern, of merchant marines, has taken second place after the United States in the production of consumer durables, and is assuming first place as an exporter of motor vehicles.

All this has brought new prosperity to the Japanese people. With the population now stabilizing, per capita national income has risen from only $227 in 1955 to $395 in 1960, to $735 by 1965, and $1975 in 1971. Although Japanese per capita income is now about half that of the United States, the present rate of increase should make it possible for the Japanese to equal or surpass the American living standard before the end of the century, especially when the recent readjustments of world currency exchange rates are considered. The Age of High Mass Consumption has clearly arrived in Japan, and durable consumer goods are well within the reach of the average citizen. Color television, air conditioners, private cars, private home ownership, and central heating have become an accepted part of the Japanese way of life.

These developments have also promoted the growth and spread of Japanese economic influence internationally. Japan has been achieving closer economic relations with many nations, especially in Asia and Oceania, through direct investment as well as trade. Japan is now giving direct financial aid to less developed countries, and equally important, is providing technical assistance. Japan is in a good position to help Asian agricultural development, based on her own remarkable agricultural revolution during the past generation. The Japanese have also gained a central role in world monetary affairs owing to the strength of the yen and the accumulation of an almost embarrassingly large foreign exchange reserve.

factors contributing to growth

The most frequently asked question is How do the Japanese do it? Actually, as we have already seen, rapid growth has been an integral part of Japanese life for the past century, interrupted only briefly by World War II. It is only because Japan is now moving into world leadership that her amazing achievements have gained international attention. Some of the reasons for this extraordinary growth are of a short-run nature, while others are more lasting.

imported capital and technology

A stereotype that is widely accepted by most of the world and even by the Japanese themselves is that Japan merely copies other nations' innovations. At the outset of Japan's drive to industrialize this was largely true, as it is of any country at that stage of its development. It was certainly characteristic of the United States economy during the nineteenth century. The Japanese profited handsomely from their importations of foreign technology. For example, between 1950 and 1969 Japan was able to acquire, with a total outlay of merely $1.5 billion in royalties and licenses, a body of thoroughly tested American industrial technology that had cost the United States $20 billion per year in research and development. Today, however, the Japanese are themselves beginning to innovate at an increasing rate. This is especially apparent in the transport developments that have permitted the country to overcome her old handicap of distance to markets and sources of raw materials, but it has also been true of Japan's distinctive advances in production technology and product design. Currently the Japanese investment in research and development is reaching levels approximating those of Western Europe and exceeding those of the United Kingdom. Even larger allocations are budgeted for the future.

It is also frequently noted that Japan benefited greatly from developmental aid supplied by the United States. This was undoubtedly an important factor in Japan's quick rebound from the wartime destruction of her economy. Not only did the United States provide financial help, but she also spurred the Japanese to democratize the political institutions and to institute sweeping land reforms. The United States has also provided Japan with a military umbrella that has spared that country from the heavy defense expenditures that burden most countries. Nevertheless, Western Europe has had similar help and, although Europe's recovery was likewise quick and was followed by a period of strong economic growth, none of this occurred at the unusual rates achieved by Japan. In any event, the importation of capital and technology has provided only a short-run and temporary advantage. Foreign technology has now been exhausted; Japanese industry is at a level comparable to that of the most advanced countries, and factors other than borrowed technology will likely be more important in the long run.

nature of the labor force

Of all Japan's assets in world economic competition, perhaps the one most frequently cited is that of a "plentiful supply of cheap labor." There is no doubt that hourly wage rates in Japan are lower than those in the West, but they are by no means the lowest in Asia and they are rising steadily. Workers in Korea, Taiwan, and other newly industrializing nations of the Orient receive much less pay than in Japan, and the Japanese are losing their competitive edge in the world market for cheap, labor-intensive goods. Moreover, there is evidence that direct labor costs in the more sophisticated lines of Japanese production are now fairly comparable to those in Europe and North America, especially since revaluation of the yen. Then, too, labor is no longer plentiful in Japan; in recent years the country has been confronted with a worsening labor shortage.

As noted previously, however, Japan's work force is very productive. Japanese workers are well educated, thoroughly skilled, highly motivated, and hard-working. In large measure this can be attributed to the unique structure of Japanese society, the kinds of communal interests and loyalties that hold this people together. Western society tends to be organized horizontally, with membership based on common interests, income, status, or social class; but Japanese society is structured vertically, the group being created out of the fact of living in the same place, or more particularly, working for the same company. The Japanese are linked to each other by complementary roles in pursuit of a common end. This grows out of the Japanese concept of the "family" or "household," upon which the whole society is founded. Indeed, individuals often speak of their place of work in the language of the family. In essence, then, a person belongs to two families—the one into which he was born and the one that provides his livelihood.

In either case the result is strong loyalty to a vertically organized group. It also produces a feeling for authority and accords great prestige to that person at the top of the pyramid. On the other hand, the individual who occupies the leadership post likewise feels an intense loyalty to the group. He consults as many members as possible before coming to a decision on behalf of the household or firm, thus making certain that a consensus has been reached prior to any action. This arrangement forms closer ties between the executive and the worker in a particular firm than between persons of equivalent positions in different firms. An important feature of this is the system of "lifetime engagement." The individual joins a company upon completing his education and remains with it until retirement. Rarely does anyone change jobs and seldom is anyone fired. Income is based more on education and seniority than on the type of work performed. Out of this system emerges an energetically enthusiastic devotion to the firm, reinforced by such institutions as the opening exercises that begin the work day, complete with a recitation of the company creed and singing of the company song. The steadily rising standard of living has also helped keep labor contented.

All this provides managers with unusual flexibility in their use of labor. Since status and salary are not based on any particular task, workers can be shifted from job to job as needed. This system allows for no labor "featherbedding" nor does it include the rigid work rules that so afflict Britain today. This, as much as anything else, has contributed to the ease with which Japanese firms have adopted important innovations. Although this arrangement makes for unusual stability, it has its own rigidities too. Since labor costs cannot be quickly and easily reduced, Japanese companies have a particularly strong inducement to maintain full operating capacity at all times, thus tempting them to "dump" their surplus output in foreign markets (see Chapter 11) in order to keep production at optimal levels. Altogether, then, it is not so much a wage advantage that has contributed to Japanese industrial growth as the quality of the labor force and the efficiency with which it is used.

nature of business organization

Another consideration that is seldom noted but may be one of the most important of all is the quality of Japanese entrepreneurship, with its unusual capacity to mobilize the factors of production to implement innovations and to market the products. A prominent feature of the Japanese economy is the role of very large firms, which, although outnumbered by small concerns, nevertheless account for an overwhelming proportion of total national output. These are the giant combines called *zaibatsu,* whose closest Western equivalent are the "conglomerates" of the United States. The *zaibatsu* are characteristically composed of a closely-knit group of banking, manufacturing, and trading companies, whose operations are so diversified that they are almost invulnerable to the vagaries of the business cycle and whose resources are so vast as to permit them to seize new opportunities with unusual ease and alacrity. Significantly, many of the *zaibatsu* originated as family-held firms.

A further unique Japanese arrangement is the partnership between Japanese labor, business, and government, often referred to as *Japan Incorporated.* This heritage of the Meiji period has no parallel in the West and it is uncommonly favorable to high growth. It represents an active collaboration among business leaders and government ministries in economic planning, permitting an anticipation of new trends, efficiently allocating resources, and developing needed institutional arrangements. What this amounts to is a further extension of the Japanese concept of "household" or "family," the common goal in this case being the maximization of national income. Just as in the individual home or company, extended consultations take place among the interested parties in order to reach a consensus before taking action. It is interesting to note that such explicit ties between government and business are expressly forbidden by law in the United States and Canada.

One essential feature of this partnership at the national level is the provision for business loans guaranteed by the government. A steady flow of investment capital is provided by the extremely high rate of household savings in Japan, resulting in a ready pool of funds for channeling into increased industrial capacity. As a consequence there is an exceptionally high volume of business borrowing in Japan, at little or no risk to the firms themselves. At the same time, there is minimal risk in this for government, since the widely diversified *zaibatsu* are reliable borrowers and smaller businesses do not participate as freely in this arrangement. As a consequence, according to some estimates an incredible one-third of the country's gross national product is reinvested. Japan is thus a country that runs on credit but does so in relative safety.

Despite this unique service, the Japanese government appears to have relatively little direct participation in business operations, except in the areas of transport, communication, and steel production. The government is mainly an active collaborator that guides and assists but does not command. This is a consensual arrangement typical of Japanese affairs generally. The system is very flexible, being conducive to quick response to changing conditions and rapid growth, much more so than either Western capitalism or Marxism.

favorable trading conditions

Finally, there is the important contribution to Japan's economic growth made by the unusually favorable conditions under which she has traded with the rest of the world. This has been a central element in the total growth pattern despite the fact that only one-tenth of national output goes to foreign markets. One advantageous aspect of that trade has been the nature of Japan's price structure. Japanese exports were able to undercut the products of other advanced countries in their own markets at least in part because Japan's wholesale prices tended to remain stable or to decline even as those of the United States and Europe were rising. This was possible because of the gains in productivity noted above. Until recently, Japan was also able to keep marketing costs for producer goods particularly low.

Meanwhile, Japan maintained a built-in resistance to imports of manufactured goods. Import-competing industries were able to resist the general trend toward higher wages in the high-growth exporting industries because of the stable, exceedingly loyal labor force we described earlier. Prices of domestically made consumer goods thus did not rise as fast as those of imports. Imported products encounter the formidable barrier provided by Japan's archaic and very complex multilayered system for distributing goods to the consuming public. If this were not enough, the Japanese government has maintained one of the world's most effective systems of official import barriers. These include both tariff and nontariff measures for controlling entry of foreign goods.

Hence Japan has enjoyed a superior competitive position for her exports in world markets even while raising an effective resistance to imports. In this way trade has provided an ever-expanding outlet for Japanese-made goods.

the changing character of Japanese output and trade

Japan's production and exchange have undergone important shifts in emphasis in response to changing factor endowments and the evolving structure of demand.

the "old" industries of prewar Japan

The accepted picture of Japan as a country whose principal comparative advantage is abundant cheap labor and whose comparative disadvantages are land and capital was indeed true of prewar Japan. During that era Japanese industry stressed mass production of low-grade, standardized, simple consumer software, especially cotton and rayon textiles and the garments made from them. Chapter 9 has traced the evolution of the machine textile industry, its beginnings in Lancashire and New England, its eventual decline in those areas as the industry matured and became labor-intensive and diffused into low-wage areas such as prewar Japan. Moreover, such goods found a large domestic market among Japan's low-income population of that period, for whom they represented necessities. The resulting high volume of output and economies of scale permitted the surplus to be exported at prices below the general world level (see Chapter 11).

Japan's comparative advantage during that era also favored the manufacture of cheap novelty items, "bazaar goods" requiring much hand labor and produced in a myriad of small workshops. Hence "Made in Japan" came to be synonymous with cheapness and even shoddiness. This low quality of goods, however, was not a matter of insufficient skill but rather a response to a particular kind of demand that Japan was able to fill at home and in foreign markets at that time. Japan's high order of skills was demonstrated by the country's capacity for supplying a modern and efficient war machine, to the considerable surprise of her adversaries.

postwar developments: the "new" industries

Following the brief period of recovery from war, Japan's production and trade took some sharp turns. First, there was the loss of the comparative advantage of having the world's cheapest industrial labor force. One after another—Hong Kong, Taiwan, Singapore, India, and South Korea—began making cheap textiles, clothing, novelties, and other inexpensive goods, trading on their abundance of even cheaper labor. The reaction of Japanese textile manufacturers has been typical of the older areas described in Chapter 9, that is, to specialize in goods of higher quality, relying on accumulated skills not available to newer producers. At the same time, there was a rapid accumulation of capital in Japan, by means described earlier, together with the rise in per capita purchasing power by the Japanese public.

Decision makers in government and business were quick to recognize this shifting combination of production possibilities and demand. Adopting the most advanced Western techniques, they moved into the production of goods of higher quality and greater variety. The emphasis became twofold. First, there was a stress upon consumer goods of the types now demanded domestically: household appliances, sporting goods, cameras and other optical equipment, and more recently, motor vehicles. Second, came the development of producer-goods manufacture, especially transport equipment (ships, locomotives, trucks, and buses), machinery (machine tools, textile machinery, construction machinery, and instruments), chemicals and basic metals. In all this, close attention has been given to quality control, mainly to erase the stigma of shoddiness. Careful workmanship and inspection have been stressed in the effort to establish a new reputation for durability.

The production emphasis has thus been on high-technology goods demanding much greater engineering and labor skills than the old industries required. The goods involve greater capital inputs as well, something that the *zaibatsu* have in ample supply. Particularly strenuous efforts have been made to achieve higher levels of efficiency in order to obtain the greatest possible output from the factors of production. Ultra-modern facilities have been installed to gain the utmost productivity from capital and labor through the use of labor-saving machines and manufacturing techniques. Above all, there has been an attempt to achieve all possible benefits from large-scale production, permitting major reductions in unit costs.

stages in Japan's postwar development

What was the actual sequence of events that produced this transition? Altogether, three surges of industrial growth can be distinguished in Japan between 1955 and the present. Each of these appears to have been powered by a new industrial emphasis, a new set of "trigger industries." The first was associated with important advances in electric power generation. The traditional sources of electricity, coal and falling water, had provided an adequate supply until 1955, when power shortages began to occur. Industries dependent upon electricity were adversely affected. At the same time the output of pig iron proved insufficient and the capacity of the national railway was exceeded. Although several remedies were applied to these problems, perhaps the most significant was the development of increased efficiency and enlarged volume of output of the country's electric generating stations. Very large oil-fired generators were designed and installed, raising unit capacities of the largest stations from 75,000 kilowatts in 1953 to 1 million kilowatts by 1972. Aside from this enlarged output, fuel oil consumption per unit output was reduced by 30 percent while thermal efficiency rose from 23 percent to 39 percent, the latter being a particularly high figure. This meant equivalent reductions in per unit generating costs and an abundant supply of this cheap electricity for powering a modernized, electrified railway system and for the electricity-consuming industries. Especially benefited were the producer-goods industries, those making materials for use by other manufacturers. At the same time, other essential technological advances were contributing im-

portantly, advances such as automated controls and other mass production equipment.

These advances made possible the next surge of industrial growth, this time based upon developments in petroleum refining, petrochemical manufacture, and iron and steel making, all materials-producing industries. Petroleum refining in particular had important multiplier effects on the Japanese economy. To supply the demand for fuel oil from the large, new electric generating stations, refiners had to expand their output by a substantial amount. This they accomplished by drastically increasing the size of refinery operating units, which rose from an average of 10,000 to 38,000 barrels per day in 1955 to the present 200,000 barrels per day. To provide these great refineries with sufficient raw material the oil companies in turn introduced supertankers, which gave additional economies of scale in material procurement. Important reductions in the unit costs of fuel oil because of these twin developments were passed along to the generating stations. Meanwhile, these modern refineries were yielding a number of important byproducts, including petrochemicals, which in turn provided the raw materials for plastic manufacturing and a host of other industries.

At the same time, the Japanese steel industry was experiencing a great rise in capacity with the installation of some of the world's most modern and largest plants. Plant capacities reached the unheard-of level of 12 to 15 million metric tons per annum. This was accomplished by increasing the capacity of steel-making equipment (e.g., a tenfold rise in the daily output of blast furnaces) and by calling upon the services of gigantic ore carriers. The resulting economies of scale gave the cheapest per unit product costs in the world. This, together with greater quality control, was a great advantage to large Japanese steel users, especially the shipbuilders, who benefited doubly, first from the demand for ore carriers and supertankers and second from the availability of good, cheap steel for their construction.

By this date, the rising tempo of Japanese industry and the growing prosperity of the people had increased the demand for consumer durables described earlier. The more than sevenfold growth in personal incomes since 1955 proved to be an important stimulus to the manufacture of household appliances and other consumer items, and their efficient mass production carried the Japanese economy to its present high level.

Altogether, these three surges of growth and development have resulted in an industrial sector that is fully matured, with a full range of modern output of both producer and consumer goods, operating at exceptionally high levels, and enjoying unusually low unit costs. At this point, however, observers are detecting signs of potentially stubborn obstacles to continued growth at current high levels. Before examining this problem, let us first examine more closely some of the new industries that have helped give Japan a competitive edge in today's world market.

INDUSTRIAL EXAMPLES: HIGH-TECHNOLOGY PRODUCTION

The shift of Japanese resources into the production of modern high-technology, high-quality, capital-intensive, high-value-added goods is well illustrated by the evolution of the engineering industries, which are so characteristic of modern Japan. The basis for this type of manufacturing was established during the 1930s with the beginnings of bicycle manufacture and the production of light electrical equipment, textile machinery, and finally, during the Sino-Japanese and Pacific wars, shipbuilding, aircraft, and machine tools. After the postwar period of recovery, engineering output again rose sharply, exceeding prewar output by the early 1950s. Output doubled between 1955 and 1957 and doubled again by 1961. By 1963 the volume was five times that of 1955 and it has continued to double and redouble since. During this time engineering production has become extremely diverse, as manufacturers have ventured in any number of wholly new lines in their attempt to supply the growing domestic and foreign demand. Today the engineering industries are the largest segment of Japanese production and sales abroad.

machinery

One branch of engineering that got off to an early start in Japan is machinery production. Precision machinery manufacture in particular has served as a bridge between the old and new industries. As in the case of the old industries, precision machinery manufacture requires manual skills and efficient organization, but it also demands a high order of scientific and technical knowledge, the ability to work to fine tolerances, and much capital. Products successfully developed by manufacturers of precision machinery include cameras, binoculars and other optical goods, watches, clocks, and scientific instruments.

The camera industry was poorly developed until the late 1930s. Wartime requirements produced a new demand by the military for quantity output and for greatly improved lens quality. After the war these newly developed skills were converted to serve the consumer market, the emphasis this time being on high-quality cameras, especially the increasingly popular single-lens reflex. This kind of manufacture requires standardization and precision tooling; as it is not successfully automated, much skilled labor is necessary, especially for the grinding of lenses.

Today there are many firms in the industry, but only five make the completely finished units; the rest are subcontractors—a typical Japanese arrangement. After several years of successful operation the Japanese camera industry is still expanding, and cameras (together with other optical goods) represent one of the country's most important earners of foreign exchange. More than half the output enters the world market and the value of these exports is rising even faster than the number of units sold, an indication of the growing market for expensive cameras. Japan now dominates the world market for fine cameras, once an exclusive German province. The United States takes 30 percent of Japan's camera exports, but the European countries are becoming important customers as well.

Watches and clocks represent another booming Japanese industry with a history and a set of production requirements similar to those of optical instruments. Two large firms control Japan's manufacture of these items. The total value of watch and clock output is equivalent to that of cameras; however, a smaller proportion is exported and this consists mainly of the less valuable types. There is a different overseas market for these, too. Unlike the cameras, which are destined mainly for technically advanced Western countries, watches and clocks are exported mainly to southeast Asia. The volume supplied to other markets is rising, however, and the Japanese are investing in the manufacture of time pieces in such places as Brazil and Mexico. The more valuable Japanese-made watches are sold domestically.

Japan has gained a special place in the manufacture of electrical machinery and equipment, items such as generators, transformers, motors, and cables. Established on the eve of the Second World War, this industry had a complete line of production from the smallest household motors to heavy-duty industrial equipment. The chief manufacturers are subsidiaries of the *zaibatsu*, who developed the industry in connection with their shipbuilding operations. Close links were formed at the outset with General Electric and Westinghouse as well as with certain German firms. The attempted breakup of the *zaibatsu*, following the Allied victory, disrupted production for a time, but a vigorous resurgence occurred subsequently.

The manufacture of electrical machinery has benefited from Japan's rapid growth in electric power generating capacity and expanded use of electric power, from the increased diversification of electrical production, and an increase in the level of technological input. The electrical machinery industry has been growing at a rate three times that of Japanese industry as a whole. In the beginning most of the output of heavy electrical machinery and equipment was sold domestically and only the lighter items were sent abroad. Today, however, Japan has become a very important exporter of heavy electrical goods, especially to Southeast Asia. The Japanese have contributed numerous significant innovations to the industry, including giant turbines and motors and high-voltage transmission cables and transformers. Japan is second only to the United States in the manufacture of electrical machinery.

A similarly rapid expansion and diversification has occurred in other forms of industrial machinery production, including machine tools, textile machinery, and construction machinery, among many others. Machine tools—lathes, cutting tools, automatic screw machines, and others—have assumed an essential place in Japan's overall industrial growth. As in the United States, machine tool production is highly sensitive to fluctuations of the business cycle, but the industry has enjoyed great prosperity recently owing to Japan's acute labor shortage and the resulting demand for automated equipment. Machine tool production is another industry in which Japan has leaped into second place after the United States, ahead of the Soviet Union and far above West Germany, both traditionally important producers. Yet so great is Japanese industry's need for these items that Japan is a big importer as well as exporter of machine tools, although most of the imports are of special types.

electronics

One of the most rapidly advancing of all Japanese industries is the manufacture of electronic products. Indeed, its output exceeds that of the motor vehicle producers. The electronics industry has both its innovative and mature phases and Japan is well suited to both. Japan has large numbers of thoroughly trained engineers and technicians for the innovative aspects, and numerous important technological advances have recently been made by Japanese electronic research. A second asset is the country's large labor force, composed as it is of skilled and semiskilled workers, both of which are important in this industry requiring manual dexterity. The industry's early growth in Japan was aided also by the generally low capital requirements of electronics manufacture. For an island nation with few natural resources, the low raw material requirements of electronics production is an added attraction. The industry has benefited, too, from heavy government backing.

Innumerable types of electronics goods are represented in Japan. Consumer products have made very substantial gains in Japan's electronics industry, especially items such as television and radio sets, tape recorders, phonographs. At present color television accounts for 50 percent of the country's total output of consumer electronics goods. Exports of these are particularly brisk, especially to the United States, but an increasing volume is moving to Latin America and Western Europe. The domestic demand for these products is growing fastest of all, especially for color television.

The Japanese also make electronic computers, and the government is promoting the growth of this high-technology industry with special vigor. An increasing share of the computers in use in Japan is produced domestically, although it is still necessary to import the larger models as the Japanese market does not provide the necessary threshold for these. Also of considerable significance is the manufacture of electronic components and parts for export to the United States and Western Europe, especially integrated circuits, television tuners, resistors, and semiconductors.

transport equipment

Still another high-growth sector of Japanese industry is the manufacture of ships, railway equipment, aircraft, and motor vehicles. None of these is entirely new to Japan; all made essential contributions to the country's war effort. What is new, however, is Japan's mounting world prominence in their manufacture and sale. The country has acquired a commanding lead in shipbuilding and is an increasingly close second to the United States in motor vehicles. Sales on the world market are particularly vigorous, but the domestic need for these products is the essential foundation for the growth of this industry.

shipbuilding

One of the first industries to be sponsored by the Meiji during the 1870s was shipbuilding, but Japan's current world role is strictly a modern phenomenon. By 1972 Japan was building 50 percent of the world's new shipping, as opposed to only 8 percent for second-place Sweden. As an earner of foreign exchange for Japan, shipbuilding is outranked only by the steel industry.

Government policy was responsible for the industry's rapid expansion during the 1930s. Under a subsidy program called "scrap-and-build" the country acquired a large merchant marine; meanwhile the imperial navy was expanding quickly in preparation for the Second World War. Shipbuilding accelerated still more during the course of the war, but it suffered severely from Japan's defeat. With the onset of the Cold War, world demand for ships suddenly burgeoned. Because European and American shipyards were strained beyond their capacities, Japan's facilities were pressed into service. The Japanese shipbuilding boom of that period was considered temporary then, since Japanese steel was still inferior in quality and construction costs were high in the Japanese yards.

It is typical of the Japanese that they used this opportunity well. By 1956 Japan had become the world's leading shipbuilder and she has continued to increase that lead since. How this was accomplished tells much about the Japanese economic system. First, Japanese shipbuilders immediately invested heavily in new shipbuilding equipment, quickly acquiring the best outfitted yards in the world. Second, they introduced a number of important innovations. Whereas ships have traditionally been custom-built, the Japanese developed methods for mass-producing them. New construction techniques substantially reduced completion time and greatly increased labor productivity. Usually a major item in shipbuilding, labor costs in the Japanese yards were thus reduced to uncommonly low levels. Important advances in marine engineering were also made, yielding a product with high performance characteristics. As important as any of these, however, was the development of giant bulk carriers—tankers and ore carriers—well in anticipation of a world demand for economies in scale in transporting raw materials, a demand that is still growing. Finally, Japanese shipbuilders have acquired an important raw material advantage as steelmakers improved the quality, increased the quantity, and reduced the price of their commodity. Japan has thus become the lowest-cost producer of ships in the world.

The demand for Japanese-built ships has not abated. Domestically there is a continuing need for ships in the rapidly expanding merchant fleet, particularly the efficient supercargo carriers needed for procuring Japan's industrial raw materials and other primary commodities from distant sources. The export demand for great bulk carriers has risen steadily ever since the closing of the Suez Canal, accentuated still further by the rising oil needs of Western Europe and the United States. Japanese shipyards also do a lively business in ship repair and remodelling. Despite their uninterrupted prosperity, Japanese shipbuilders have actively diversified by venturing into other industries. This has especially been true of electric machinery production, begun originally to provide a dependable supply of these items for their marine engineering products.

motor vehicles

Japan's third largest export industry today, after steel and shipbuilding, is the manufacture of automobiles, trucks, and buses. Exports of motor vehicles reached the incredible figure of 2 million units in 1972, 40 percent of these going to the United States. In that year another 5 percent were sold in Europe, but this proportion has been rising so rapidly that Europeans have begun raising barriers to Japanese imports. Japan's motor car exports to Australia have encountered a similar reception. Meanwhile, Japanese motor vehicle sales have penetrated deeply into the markets in less developed countries, especially South Asia, now the second largest customer after the United States. Japanese car exporters have become formidable rivals to European manufacturers because of their adaptability to market needs and the low price and high quality of their product.

Even so, Japan is the largest single market for her own motor vehicle output, a result of the country's new-found prosperity. The Japanese production of trucks and buses represents a higher proportion of total motor vehicle volume than is true of other major producers. Nevertheless, the Japanese are buying ever larger numbers of passenger cars despite poor roads (only 15 percent are paved) and urban congestion. Altogether, therefore, Japan has assumed a place as the second largest producer of motor vehicles, rising from insignificance within less than a decade.

Again we may ask how Japan managed this achievement. Until the late 1930s the country depended mainly upon vehicles assembled in Japan from parts imported from the United States, the effective demand for this high-threshold good still being too meager at that period. In 1936 the Japanese government financed the purchase of American manufacturing equipment and hired United States consultants. By the time of the Second World War the country was self-sufficient in trucks. Two *zaibatsu* vehicles manufacturing firms of that period remain the leading producers even today.

The Korean War brought purchases of Japanese-made trucks by the United States military even as a growing domestic market was beginning to form. The subsequent rapid rise in vehicle output received still another important form of aid: a high import tariff (40 percent ad valorem) fortified by strict quotas and exchange restrictions. Unit prices remained high and the quality poor, however, until 1956, when the industry thoroughly reequipped its plants. Today Japan's motor vehicle manufacture is the most automated in the world, including such features as automatic welding machines. The current question being asked in Japan is whether or not this growth can be sustained. Clouds are appearing on both the domestic and international horizons that may affect this and other Japanese industries and perhaps her economic growth in general.

JAPAN'S CURRENT PROBLEMS

At this time it seems possible that certain potentially serious obstacles may interfere with the continuation of Japan's phenomenal rate of economic expansion. Some of these may be beyond Japanese power to control. In addition to external conditions, the country is encountering a number of internal problems. Disparities among industries, people, and regions within Japan have long been neglected, but they can no longer be safely ignored. A Japanese government white paper on science and technology has acknowledged these difficulties and has proposed steps for solving them. Possible new directions of industrial development are being explored, and the government has adopted bold measures for addressing regional disparities and other internal problems.

obstacles to continued growth

PROBLEMS OF INDUSTRY AND TRADE. There are signs that Japan is entering a "grey area" of diminished growth. To a certain extent this is to be expected as Japanese industry begins to experience diminishing returns from the scale economies that raised production efficiency to its current levels. The country is also reaching the limits to growth based on borrowed technology. Additional commitments to research and development are being made; together the Japanese government and business community allocated $5.9 billion to this purpose in 1972, an increase of 17 percent over the previous year. Since Japan does not have a large military and space research program, however, the nation will have to do a great deal more to avoid a technology gap.

Today Japan is beginning also to encounter industrial inefficiencies resulting from a longstanding neglect of essential social overhead. Roads and many other public facilities are so poor that they impose extra costs on producers. Moreover, Japan's intensive use of the land for urban and industrial purposes is causing a severe deterioration in the environment, especially in the form of polluted water and air. Public services have not kept up with the growing need; it is estimated, for example, that only 15 percent of the nation's homes are connected to sewers. Moreover, whole communities have been affected by such calamities from industrial wastes as mercury poisoning, named Miyamoto disease, after the heavily polluted bay whose fish poisoned many people in the 1960s. Problems of this sort can be attributed to the emphasis upon sustained growth of raw-material and energy-consuming industries confined within a severely restricted space; indeed, a postwar Japanese goal has been to encourage the growth of Tokyo into a megalopolis. Inadequate space is also a factor in the growing problems of congestion: traffic jams, high accident rates, housing shortages, meager park and recreational facilities, and the breakdown of public services from excessive use. Another area of public well-being in which Japan lags badly behind other technically advanced countries is in social-security coverage, which is wholly inadequate at present.

An unavoidable dependence upon foreign trade makes the Japanese sensitive to threats of trade restrictions and causes them to fear economic isolation. There is much justification for these fears, since Japan's rising economic role is arousing widespread resentment around the world. As we saw previously, her growth was not noticed until the competitive threat reached serious proportions. As Japanese dominance increases in many areas of the world economy, barriers to Japanese encroachment are being erected in Europe, Australia, the United States, and in many less developed nations.

An example of the kinds of trade problems Japan is now encountering is provided by the recent decline in her motor vehicle exports, heretofore one of the most dynamic elements in the Japanese trading scene. The rate of increase in foreign sales of vehicles, which averaged 25 percent per annum through 1971, fell to 10.5 percent in 1972; since then, exports of vehicles have declined absolutely. One major reason for this is found in the monetary changes implemented as a result of the Smithsonian Agreement of December 1971, which raised the yen 16 percent against the dollar. The second readjustment of February 1973, raised the yen still another 16 percent against the dollar, and the Japanese monetary unit has since been permitted to "float," that is, to seek its own level in world competition. As a consequence there has in all been a 40 percent deterioration in the price edge formerly enjoyed by Japanese-made cars. The rising prices of Japanese

vehicles in the American market has severely damaged exports to the United States.

Exports of motor vehicles to the rest of the world also show signs of declining at present because of growing resistance by other countries to Japanese incursions in their home markets. The United Kingdom, Italy, and other European nations are setting rigid quotas in an effort to hold Japanese sales in their markets to 5 percent of the total. Brazil has one of the most rapidly expanding markets for motor vehicles today, but that country is insisting upon a 95 percent domestic content in cars sold there. Australia has recently decreed a minimum of 85 percent local manufacturing content. Extension of the Japanese economic invasion of Europe to other lines—radios, television sets, tape recorders, and cameras—is likewise widely resented, causing barriers to be imposed. Japan's sales to Europe in 1972 were $3 billion, a rise of 22 percent from 1971. This growth was aided by the fact that European currencies underwent little change with respect to the yen.

Meanwhile, even domestic sales of cars may diminish. At present, 70 percent of total output is sold in Japan, and domestic sales may help to take up the slack in exports. However, 23 million automobiles are already on Japan's roads and a local reaction against cars is building up. Moreover, labor costs in Japan's auto industry are rising. At the same time, the domestic market appears to be reaching saturation for products of the other leading industries too. No opportunities for dramatic expansion seems to lie in that direction.

Japan's industrialists have already begun their response to retarded manufacturing growth. One solution is internationalization of production, exporting technology and capital as the United States has long been doing. Japan is now investing heavily in production facilities abroad: steel manufacturing in Brazil, and transistor and manganese dioxide production in Ireland. Auto assembly by Japanese companies has begun in Spain and Australia. In all, Nissan (which makes Datsuns) manufactures or assembles cars in 22 countries, and Toyota produces in 19. Corrugated plastic sheeting is being made by Mitsubishi in Belgium, Sony radios and television sets are now manufactured in California and in Wales. Japanese steel, chemicals, textiles, and ships are currently being made in Greece. Major Japanese investments are planned for the American southeast. In all, there was a net outflow of Japanese long-term capital of $6 billion during the 1972–1973 fiscal year, causing an unusually large balance-of-payments deficit for that country. By the end of 1973, Japan's overseas investments totaled $10 billion, an amount equal to West Germany's foreign holdings.

Other changes in direction can likewise be anticipated. There will surely be a reallocation of resources to social overhead, and a new generation of "trigger industries" may well appear. On the list of candidates for the next set of trigger industries are housing construction and transport improvements. The past fifteen years have seen a net increase of 7.63 million persons in the three metropolitan regions (Tokyo-Yokohama, Osaka-Kobe-Kyoto, and Nagoya), but those areas have severe housing shortages resulting from the high cost of land and a shortage of mortgage money. Part of the problem may be relieved by suburbanization to publicly developed new towns such as Tama outside Tokyo, with the aid of high-speed transport links. The government white paper also emphasizes the need for increased environmental protection, which should give rise to the introduction of antipollution equipment and changes in production technology.

THE ENERGY CRISIS. By 1973 Japan was confidently meeting these challenges to her economic growth. Although for the first time in many years a large balance-of-payments deficit was accumulating, this caused little concern because the nation's foreign exchange reserves were already so great. Indeed, the government had deliberately acted to reduce the large export surpluses of previous years by relaxing import controls and encouraging the *zaibatsu* to enter into the importing business. At the same time the country was making a strong recovery from a minor economic slump. In October 1973, however, all was changed by the abrupt actions of the Arabian oil producers, who were at war with Israel.

No country was more affected by the oil crisis than Japan, whose economy runs on oil, of which more than 99 percent is imported. These were alarming developments for a nation long concerned with maintaining a secure supply of nonrenewable raw materials. When the Arabs created a world shortage by cutting back production and then doubling their prices, Japan's oil import bill rose by an estimated $10 billion. This development was all the more grave because it was superimposed upon an accelerating price inflation caused in part by rising world prices of industrial raw materials and foods. By mid–1973 Japanese prices were already 13 percent higher than they had been the previous year.

The oil crisis was a severe shock to the domestic economy, prompting widespread predictions that Japan's "economic miracle" had ended and that the nation might actually decline. Reacting swiftly to the emergency, the government imposed dim-outs to conserve electric energy, began an intensive search for new sources of oil, and undertook a diplomatic offensive to gain Arab favor. In return for offers of developmental assistance, Japan was able to secure guarantees of future supplies of Arabian oil and thus to avert actual shortages. She could not escape a steep increase in oil prices, however.

Even as it dealt with the emergency, the Japanese government was developing a new long-term oil strategy. The first need was to find ways to pay for the more costly oil. To accomplish this, Japan opened an export offensive to gain the needed increase in foreign exchange earnings, meanwhile relying upon her still large

reserves as a cushion. At the same time she began a drive to diversify her foreign sources of oil, 43 percent of which had been coming from Arab lands. While continuing to rely upon such existing suppliers as Iran, Indonesia, and Nigeria, she began promoting joint oil exploration and developmental projects with the Soviet Union, China, and other Asiatic neighbors, as well as investing in Canada's Athabaska tar sands and in many other new petroleum ventures. The oil crisis had the further effect of renewing Japan's old concern for maintaining an uninterrupted flow of other raw materials. With a view to making long-term commitments for these commodities, the nation sought closer diplomatic and economic relations with a number of resource-rich countries.

Largely as a result of the emergency, Japan's economic performance suffered during the first half of 1974. The government's resolute actions, however, led to a general recovery during the latter part of the year, permitting an anticipated overall increase of 3 to 4 percent in GNP for the year as a whole and promising more rapid growth thereafter. Although consumer prices in 1974 were 25 percent above those for 1973 and workers gained a general wage increase of 30 percent during the spring, the volume of exports had risen by 20 percent (by 60 percent in terms of value). At the same time, the government had reimposed controls on outflows of capital from the country. As a consequence of these two developments, the balance of payments was returning to a state of equilibrium. Despite the nation's economic difficulties, Japanese workers escaped its worst effects because of their job security under the custom of lifetime engagement.

Although Japan was seriously affected by the oil crisis, she was one of the first nations to find successful answers to the problem. This represents another tribute to Japan's adaptive efficiency and to the resilience of her people.

disparities in the Japanese space-economy

Japan's preoccupation with fast industrial growth has exacerbated old inequalities in the economy and society and it has created new ones as well. One of these problems is the widening disparity between the old and new economic activities, which have given rise to what is termed a "dual economy." Another is associated with the unusual concentration of people and industry in the Japanese megalopolis in southeastern Honshu.

the dual economy

There is a sharp dichotomy between the giant conglomerates (*zaibatsu*), with their diversified manufacturing-commercial-financial operations, high degree of capitalization, and modern output and methods on the one hand and the small and medium-sized workshops with their specialization and their reliance upon manual skills on the other. The small firms serve both domestic and export markets. Some produce traditional Japanese goods, such as clothing, footwear, and textiles, while others engage in more modern types of manufacture for export. Many small firms function mainly as subcontractors to large companies, and each of the industrial giants tends to be surrounded by such satellites. More than half of Japan's industrial workers are employed by small firms, but the output of these establishments is a far smaller proportion of total output. The small companies are vulnerable to labor shortages, have high bankruptcy rates, and survive only with difficulty. Their problems are not particularly helped by the government, whose policies have consistently favored the larger firms with their many efficiencies.

center-periphery contrasts

A second dichotomy is that of the Japanese urban-industrial heartland and the remainder of the country, just as in the British case. The spatial arrangement of these contrasting regions in Japan also resembles that of Britain. The Japanese heartland, with its extensive megalopolitan development and its concentration of manufacturing, is confined to a limited portion of the coastal plain of southeastern Honshu. It extends from the Tokyo-Yokohama capital region to Nagoya in the Chubu region and the Osaka-Kobe-Kyoto complex in the Kinki region. The hinterland comprises the rest: northern Honshu and all Hokkaido, Kyushu, and Shikoku (see Fig. 17.2). The two regions differ markedly from each other in population densities, migration and growth rates, and the intensity of agriculture, manufacturing, and commerce, and each area has different problems. Figure 17.2 illustrates the contrasts in population and income between the heartland and hinterland.

Japan is fundamentally an urban-industrial nation and the Kanto plain is at the heart of it all. Three districts—Southern Kanto, Tokai, and Kinki—contain the capital city of Tokyo, itself one-tenth of the nation's population, and five other major cities (Fig. 17.2). Altogether, 48 percent of Japan's people live and work here, but they receive 58 percent of the income. Not only are these Japan's most prosperous citizens, but their incomes are rising at a faster rate than elsewhere. For this reason, if for no other, the heartland has become the natural focus for the rural-urban migration noted earlier.

If the entire coastal industrial belt from Tokyo to northern Kyushu is included, as in Figure 17.2, the heartland accounts for three-fourths of Japanese manufacturing and provides the great majority of deep-water ports capable of handling the largest vessels. The core region has other important functions as well, especially those centered in Tokyo, which is the principal corporate headquarters, the political capital, the site of major universities, and the focus of the country's most attractive urban amenities. Like London and the South

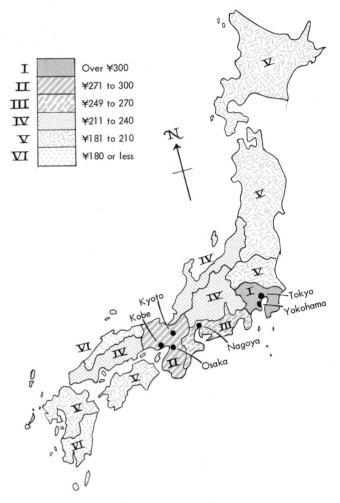

I		Over ¥300
II		¥271 to 300
III		¥249 to 270
IV		¥211 to 240
V		¥181 to 210
VI		¥180 or less

Fig. 17.2 *Regional contrasts in per capita income. Japanese incomes are highest in the national center, especially in the Capital region (Tokyo and Yokahama) and, to a lesser extent, in the Kinki region (Osaka, Kobe, and Kyoto) and the Chubu region (Nagoya). Incomes decline steadily away from the center, reaching their lowest levels in remoter parts of the country.*

Source: Data from Japan Economic Yearbook 1970.

of England, however, Japan's core area also has a growing list of problems. This region is particularly troubled with the excessive crowding, housing shortages, traffic congestion, and severe deterioration of the environment.

The hinterland is different in nearly every respect. Hokkaido and northern Honshu lag badly in their development, being the last areas settled and having a climate that most Japanese find severe. Western Honshu, all of Shikoku, and most of Kyushu are similarly peripheral. All are losing population; the young, in particular, wish to settle in more centrally located areas. Other troubles of the marginal areas are low incomes, limited economic opportunities, and a feeling of isolation. Thus Japan's center-periphery difficulties are very like those of the United Kingdom, except that Japan's marginal regions have not undergone the prior development and earlier prosperity experienced by Britain's distressed areas.

Unlike the United Kingdom, which has been concerned for half a century with the predicament of her lagging regions, Japan is only now addressing the question. In 1969, the Economic Planning Agency drew up a New Comprehensive National Development Plan that was adopted by the cabinet, including master plans for transportation. Then in 1972, the government of Prime Minister Tanaka assumed power with a program for solving this and other urgent domestic problems that had been neglected during the exhilarating national drive for economic ascendency.

the Tanaka plan for remodeling Japan

The rationale for the Tanaka plan stems from the realization that the price of economic success has been a poor and deteriorating quality of life. The Japanese have come to understand at last that, in selling the products of their hard labor at cut-rate prices, they have in effect been subsidizing their customers in other lands, a view that is entirely consistent with trade theory (Chapter 10). It is therefore logical to conclude that more of the nation's GNP should be allocated to domestic needs, even if this reduces Japan's competitiveness in world markets. The new national goal, then, is to catch up with other technically advanced countries

Fig. 17.3 *The Tanaka plan. This scheme calls for encouraging migration away from congested urban areas into the rural countryside and planned new towns while discouraging migration into large cities and suburbs. The plan also proposes an elaborate system of new expressways and rail lines to tie this dispersed population together.*

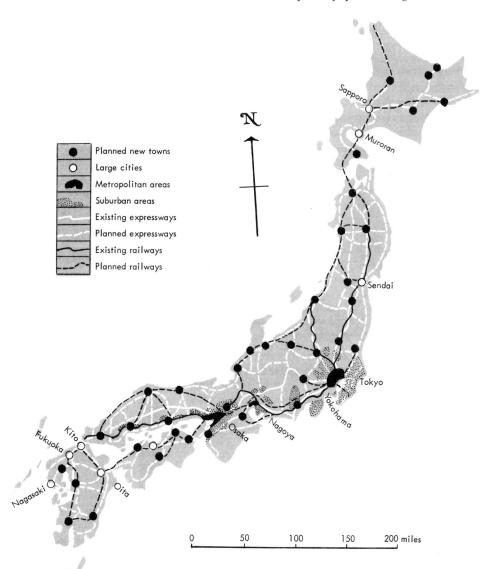

in a number of social objectives and perhaps even to surpass them.

The Tanaka plan itself is elaborate. Described as the largest peacetime project in human history, it aims at no less than restructuring the entire internal space-economy of Japan by a target date of 1985. This claim seems verified by the projected cost: $1 trillion in public and private funds, a figure that is four times the country's current total annual GNP. The plan has these main features:

1. to disperse the population and industry throughout the country
2. to connect these scattered locations with an efficient transportation and communication system
3. to effect a general improvement in the quality of Japanese life.

To accomplish the decentralization of manufacturing, an official agency, the Corporation for Relocation of Industry, has been provided with both positive inducements and penalties to use in its negotiations with industrial concerns. It is empowered, first of all, to offer financial incentives to relocating firms and to the communities that receive them. These subsidies have been expected to total $7 billion to $10 billion by 1985. The companies are to receive loans to cover their moving costs, and they are to be allowed an accelerated depreciation on buildings and equipment vacated at their previous premises in more congested parts of the country. The communities are to be given grants for building parks and for acquiring pollution-monitoring facilities. Second, as a penalty for uncooperative concerns, the agency will be able to impose a "factory-expulsion tax," that is, a surtax on firms that insist on remaining in their old crowded locations. Once the industrial slums of Japan's megalopolis of Tokyo, Nagoya, and Osaka have been emptied, the plan calls for razing the derelict factory buildings and converting the space into parks and housing.

The redistribution of Japan's population entails the addition of more than seventy new towns. Each new town of 250,000 people (see Fig. 17.3) is expected to cost $1.8 billion. Factories are to be sited within carefully landscaped industrial parks, and strict controls are to guard against pollution of the environment. High-speed rail and expressway systems are to connect all parts of the country so that no more than a one-hour journey separates any pair of major cities.

Social improvements are an integral part of the plan. It calls for increasing the number of parks and recreation facilities and for active measures to clean up the environment. Social security benefits are scheduled to be raised substantially, and the present six-day work week will be cut to a five-day work week. The country's progress in improving the quality of living will be gauged by a measure called "Net National Welfare" or NNW, which is analogous to the concept of Net Economic Welfare described in Chapter 3. To compute NNW, a deduction will be made from total GNP for all the undesirable side effects of growth (such as pollution, crowding, and traffic congestion) and an addition will be made for any new positive elements (such as increased leisure or new recreational facilities).

Since the business community of Japan appears to have reached a consensus on the need for such a program, unified national action can reasonably be expected. Ironically, the principal opposition comes from Japan's socialists, largely because it is a business-associated plan and in direct contrast with socialist regional planning elsewhere in the world! The effort will mean a sharply increased tax burden for business, which is lightly taxed at present. Japanese exporters will therefore find it more difficult to continue underpricing other producers in international markets. This does not necessarily indicate that the volume of Japanese exports will be reduced below levels they might otherwise attain, however, since a "soft-sell" approach may in fact be the only way that Japanese firms can overcome the mounting resistance they are encountering to their present sales methods. Thus the prime minister confidently forecast that Japan's GNP would reach $1 trillion by 1985 despite the costly remodeling scheme. Another anticipated effect of the plan is an accelerated popular interest in recreational activities. This shift is already becoming evident as the Japanese people develop more and more enthusiasm for baseball and bowling, European and American music and theater, and foreign travel.

It is not yet certain just how the Tanaka plan will be affected by the nation's financial problems, especially those relating to inflation and the energy crisis. There are some indications, however, that these difficulties may force a delay in implementation of the plan. Tanaka's fall from power in November 1974 may also result in some modification of Japan's approach to her center-periphery problems.

RECOMMENDED READINGS

Abegglen, James C., "The Economic Growth of Japan," *Scientific American*, 222, No. 3 (March, 1970), 31–37.

Allen, G. C., *Japan's Economic Expansion.* London: Oxford University Press, 1965.

Broadbridge, Seymour, *Industrial Dualism in Japan: A Problem of Economic Growth and Structural Change.* London: Frank Cass, 1966.

Hall, Robert B., *Japan: Industrial Power of Asia.* Princeton, N. J.: Van Nostrand Reinhold, 1963.

Still another strategy for stimulating national economic growth has been pursued by the Soviet Union. The USSR's leaders are guided by a comprehensive plan for the entire economy, shaped according to Marxist principles and prepared by a central agency. Implementation of the plan is the responsibility of a bureaucratic hierarchy of officials answerable only to those who control the Communist party machinery. This approach to growth ignores marketplace economics and attempts to create its own conditions of supply and demand. Although Marxists usually profess contempt for classical least-cost location theory, they often practice it in a purer fashion than elsewhere. In a more recent development, too, the Soviets plan to use general system theory as a basis for computerized management of their economy.

In addition to our interest in this different path to growth and development, we must recognize the importance of the USSR to the world economic system as a whole. Its immense physical size, large and varied population, and great economic, political, and military strength inevitably earn for it a central position in that system. The Soviet Union also provides many useful bases for comparison with the heartland nations discussed previously. It is a country with distinctive physical and human characteristics, and novel methods have been used for mobilizing these for national growth. The spatial effects of this Soviet strategy, the peculiar biases it introduces into the structure of the economy, and the complex problems of Soviet growth are of particular interest to the economic geographer.

NATURAL AND HUMAN ENDOWMENTS OF THE USSR

The vast physical resources of the Soviet Union contrast greatly with the meager endowments of the United Kingdom and Japan. The USSR is more like Canada in this respect, except that it has a larger and more diverse population. The Soviet Union resembles Canada in a number of other ways, too, such as territorial extent, northerly location with many great empty spaces, and a history of reliance on extensive land-consuming production. In their approach to the use of human and natural resources, however, the two countries have diverged substantially.

a large and isolated land

The Soviet Union is the world's largest nation. Standing astride two continents (Fig. 18.1), it occupies 8.6 million square miles (22.3 square kilometers), approximately one-sixth of the earth's land area. This is eight and one-half times the size of the United Kingdom, nearly six times that of Japan, more than twice Canada, and almost two-and-one-half the United States. So great is this territorial expanse that the USSR's population of 245 million, the world's third largest, produces a density of only 28.5 persons per square mile. This com-

the soviet union: growth through central planning

18

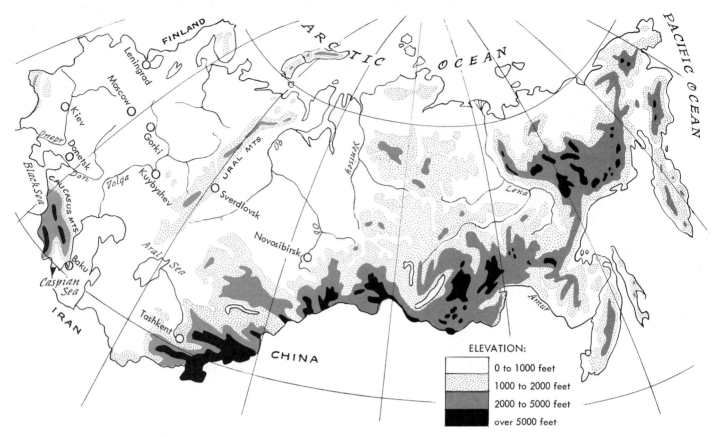

Fig. 18.1 *The Soviet Union*

ELEVATION:
0 to 1000 feet
1000 to 2000 feet
2000 to 5000 feet
over 5000 feet

pares with densities of 587.5 for the United Kingdom and 738.8 for Japan.

On another common measure, gross national product, the Soviet Union also ranks among the world's leaders, second behind the United States. Although dissimilar accounting systems in the two countries prevent precise comparisons, most current estimates indicate that the USSR's total output of all goods and services is now about three-fifths that of the United States. Because of her large population, however, the Soviet Union's per capita GNP is still less than half that of the United States.

Many of the USSR's unique characteristics derive from her position on the globe. First of all, the Soviet Union is a northerly country, with the southernmost point (in Soviet Central Asia) being at about the same latitude as Nashville, Tennessee, and the northernmost point (in the Soviet Arctic islands) being as close to the North Pole as the upper tip of Greenland. The economic heart of the country, and the focal center of population, Moscow, is at 55°45′ north, about the same as Sitka, Alaska; the second city, Leningrad, is very nearly at 60° north, equivalent to the northern tip of Labrador or to Skagway, Alaska. The Soviet Union is also a continental country. The nation's central area of maximum activity is deep in the interior of the Eurasian land mass, and its only ocean frontages are on cold seas, frozen much of the year. This continentality produces extremes of temperature, and it deprives much of the country of adequate rainfall.

physical endowment

As a natural consequence of its great size, the Soviet Union has a wide variety of physical conditions. Much of the land area consists of low plains. The north European plain penetrates deep into the western, or "European" part of the country; and the Ural Mountains (generally below 6,000 feet) hardly present a barrier to the movement of people, goods, or climatic conditions. Beyond the Urals much of western Siberia is similarly low-lying country. Farther east, however, the country becomes increasingly mountainous, while the southern borders are rimmed by the world's loftiest mountain system. Within this sprawling landscape are found a wide range and vast quantity of valuable natural resources, which have until very recently helped the country maintain an important degree of self-sufficiency.

food resources

Not only does the Soviet Union possess the largest land area of all the nations, she also has the greatest amount of arable land—607 million hectares (1,656 million acres). This is almost 100 times as much land as Japan has, nearly 10 times that of Canada, 35 times that of the United Kingdom, and 40 percent more than that of the United States. With the Soviet Union's large population, this works out to 6.2 acres of arable land per person, only slightly more than the United States's figure of 5.4 acres per person. Even so, the total output of Soviet farms is only three-quarters that of the United States, and the amount per person is even lower.

Some reasons for the poor productivity of Soviet agriculture are the abbreviated growing season, the unproductive, acidic nature of the forest soils in the northern parts of the country, and the inadequate, uncertain moisture conditions of the more southerly areas, despite the inherent richness of their grassland soils. On the average, therefore, per acre yields of Soviet farmlands are low. The productivity of Soviet farm labor is also low, far lower than that of the other technically advanced nations reviewed here. This problem can be attributed partly to low levels of investment in agriculture and partly to poor organization.

Nevertheless, the USSR's agriculture produces a varied output of grains, livestock, vegetables, root crops, sugar, oil seeds, fibers, and even subtropical fruits and beverage crops (Fig. 18.2). Moreover, the total production of certain key commodities is substantial during an average year. The Soviet Union leads the world in output of potatoes (29 percent of the world), wheat (24 percent), sugar beets (13 percent), sunflower seeds (69 percent), and flax (59 percent). The country is second only to the United States in cotton production. Significantly, however, the USSR ranks a poor seventh in production of livestock. On the whole, the greatest concern of Soviet farm planners is not so much with the total quantity produced over an average period but the uncertainty of output year by year. Massive crop failures are frequent and disastrous.

In an effort to ease her food supply problems and to remedy a shortage of animal protein, the USSR has developed a large fishing industry. Only Peru and Japan exceed the Soviet Union's total catch, more than a third of which comes from her own rivers, lakes, and adjacent seas. A wide-ranging, exceedingly modern ocean fishing fleet provides the remainder, which, however, falls far short of the amount needed to compensate for the inadequate Soviet farm output.

industrial raw materials

The Soviet Union depends to a surprising degree upon agriculture for industrial raw materials, especially in view of persisting food shortages. In addition to large

Fig. 18.2 *Agricultural regions of the Soviet Union*

Source: Paul E. Lydolph, Geography of the USSR *(New York: John Wiley, 1965), p. 18.*

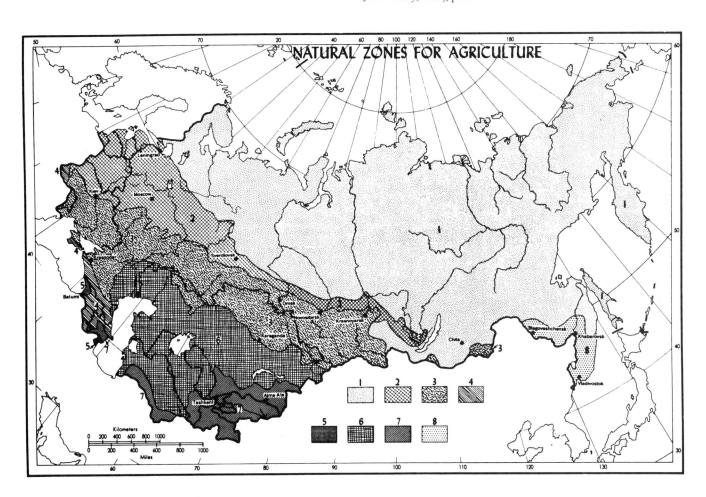

acreages devoted to plant fibers, such as flax, hemp, and cotton, agricultural commodities are much used as raw materials for chemistry. Immense tonnages of potatoes, grain, and molasses, for example, are used to produce ethyl alcohol, a principal ingredient of plastics, synthetic rubber, and other chemical materials.

The USSR is not dependent on foreign suppliers of mineral raw materials as are British and Japanese industry. Because of her vast territory and varied geology, the Soviet Union possesses the world's largest and most diverse supply of minerals. The USSR leads the world in output of iron ore, copper, chrome, manganese, nickel, and platinum, and is probably first in coal and natural gas reserves. The nation is second or third in mine production of crude oil, lead, zinc, bauxite, gold, mercury, asbestos, and tungsten, and ranks very high in output of silver, diamonds, and tin. Having the world's largest forest reserves, the Soviet Union produces 25 percent more timber than second-place United States.

The main problem of the Soviet Union's industrial raw material supply is that much of it is in the most remote parts of the country. As a result there are incredibly long rail hauls of minerals, mostly westbound, and wood, principally southbound. Thus Soviet industry bears a heavy transport burden for her raw material. To compensate for this, the Soviets have given much of their industry a raw-material orientation, thereby forcing finished products to move unusually long distances to their markets. Important exceptions are iron, coal, and alloying metals, which are generally well located for exploitation.

human resources

The Soviet Union's population—the largest of any country we have examined thus far (almost a quarter of a billion people)—is distributed very unevenly within the national territory and is exceedingly varied ethnically, linguistically, and in levels of education, skills, and development. Unlike Japan, the Soviet Union has not effectively mobilized her labor force. Despite a very large aggregate output of goods, the country is confronted with severe problems of supplying the needs of its consumers.

demography

Until recently the Soviet Union had a population growth rate of 1.7 percent and had been regarded as a Type 4 country in the United Nations classification system (Chapter 2); that is, she had a low death rate and a fairly high but falling birth rate. The growth rate has now been stabilized at 1.1 percent, very similar to that of the United States. The total population of the country would be much larger than it is today, perhaps as much as 70 or 80 million greater, had it not been for a series of calamities that have decimated the population. During the early Soviet period widespread famines cost millions of lives, and civil disorders and wars have been even more destructive, especially World War II.

the changing population distribution

Most of the population is concentrated in the central European part of the country. The highest peak of population density occurs at the capital city of Moscow, the largest urban center in the country and the focus of the Central Industrial Region. A secondary peak of population appears farther south in the Donets Basin of the eastern Ukraine. This is another old industrial area and is also central to the USSR's greatest densities of rural population. A smaller peak is in the far southeast at Tashkent, principal urban center of Soviet Central Asia and a focus of industrialization and irrigated agriculture.

For the Soviet Union as a whole, densities decrease outward from Moscow, declining steeply northward toward the Arctic parts of the country and more gradually westward into the long-settled parts of Old Russia and the Baltic States. Eastward densities fall gently, forming a wedge-shaped ridge extending from the central industrial region of Moscow to the Volga oil fields and industries and beyond to the industrial districts of the southern Urals and into the industrial-agricultural areas of the southern parts of western Siberia and northern Kazakhstan. Local areas of high density are found in the basins and valleys of the high Caucasus. Very low densities characterize most of the rest of the country, particularly the vast reaches of Siberia and the Soviet Far East.

The USSR is a country of large cities. There are at least 200 places with populations of more than 100,-000—as many large cities as the United States has—despite the fact that only 55 percent of the country's total population live in urban places. This figure is low for a technically advanced nation—much lower, for example, than the United Kingdom (79 percent), Canada (74 percent), or Japan (68 percent). Today eight centers have well over one million people each. Moscow, the present capital and principal center of economic control, leads with nearly seven million people. Leningrad, old capital of the tsars and once the principal city, now has only half as many people as Moscow but still remains in second place. Numerous other cities are rapidly approaching a million people each.

Modern Soviet history has seen important population shifts within the country. One component of this has been interregional, most notably the eastward movement. For many years the official policy to occupy the sparsely settled periphery was not particularly successful, mainly because of a long-settled population's reluctance to leave its home districts. Eventually, however, the eastward push was impelled by external events, most importantly World War II. Millions of people moved ahead of the German invasion of the populous western regions into the Urals and central and southwestern Siberia. As a result, the country's greatest increases have been outside the older regions; these experienced little population growth except in their principal cities. Other interregional population transfers took place with the resettlement of populations following the westward shift of the Soviet Union's borders at the end of the war.

The second major component of the USSR's modern population change has been the rural-urban movement. Although this is a universal phenomenon (see Chapter 2), only Japan among the leading nations has seen urbanization proceding at a rate as rapid as that of the Soviet Union. Soviet cities everywhere have grown faster than the rural population. A mere 18 percent of the population lived in cities in 1926, but the percentage has been going up steadily ever since. Between 1927 and 1959, 43 million Soviet citizens moved from the farm to the city, swelling the populations of existing places and occupying wholly new towns and cities.

To a great extent urbanization in the Soviet Union is a product of government policy and planning. The strong emphasis on natural resource development has produced a large number of new, planned cities in previously unexploited and little-inhabited areas, a program that required active labor-recruitment campaigns in the older parts of the country. Second, there has been an explicit policy favoring industrialization, generally at the expense of rural pursuits. This has entailed a reallocation of the labor force in a way that is consonant with Marxist theory, as we shall see later.

City growth in the Soviet era has produced profound spatial effects. During the 1926–1939 period there was an unusually high rate of growth among the cities of the Donets Basin of the Ukraine, the Kuznets Basin of southwestern Siberia, and the newly industrializing areas of the Urals (Fig. 18.1). Mostly these centers of high growth benefited from Stalin's emphasis upon coal as a basis for industrialization, but some also assumed importance as new centers of political and administrative control. The period from 1939 to 1959 included the war years, when retreat from the Germans and strategic considerations promoted rapid growth of cities deep in the country's interior, from the Volga to Lake Baykal in eastern Siberia. During the postwar part of this period it was the coal fields, oil fields, and cities of the virgin agricultural lands west of the Volga that benefited. Since 1959 urban growth has become more widespread, extending all the way from the European borders on the west to Baykal in the east, but above-average increases took place in Kazakhstan and southern central Asia and in the new chemical cities in Belorussia on the far west. A number of cities have stagnated in recent times, especially in the black-earth agricultural region west of the Volga.

population characteristics

A country spanning two continents and filling a space larger than all South America can be expected to have a great many different kinds of people. Beyond the matter of size, however, is the fact that the USSR contains the original homelands of many of the world's distinctive racial, ethnic, and linguistic groups. For millennia its territory was penetrated and repeatedly crossed by waves of migrants and hordes of invaders from the far reaches of Eurasia. As a meeting ground of oriental and occidental, its immense plains and low interior mountains offer few physical obstacles to the movements of peoples and cultures. In more recent times the characteristics of its present inhabitants have been shaped— and in some instances distorted—by events of history and the force of ideology.

One modern consequence of this rich past is that there are 108 distinct nationality groups within the Soviet Union as defined by the official census. Chief among these are the Slavs who comprise three-fourths of the country's total population and are mainly concentrated in the west. The Turkic peoples apparently originated in what is now Soviet Central Asia and that is still their chief location, plus sections of the southern Caucasus. There are many Turkic groups in the country, the most numerous being the Uzbeks (4 percent of the Soviet total) and the Tatars (3 percent). Other Turkic folk include the Kazakhs, Kirghiz, and still others in fewer numbers. In addition to these main ethnic types are smaller groups of Caucasians (Georgians, Armenians, and others), Finno-Ugrians (Estonians and Karelians), Baltics (Latvians and Lithuanians), as well as colonies of Jews, Germans, and other Middle Eastern and European peoples. Ethnicity has played an important role in the Soviet Union, having been a leading basis for defining territorial administrative units.

The country has a large labor force, which includes more than nine-tenths of the able-bodied adult population, as opposed to only three-fourths in the United States. One reason for this high participation rate is that entry into the work force customarily takes place at the age of 16. There is also a high female participation rate. More than half the USSR's work force is composed of women, whereas in the United States the figure is approximately 38 percent. Soviet women perform heavy laboring jobs in construction, maintenance, and industry; and they are well-represented in the professions, especially medicine.

For a technically advanced nation, the Soviet Union has a surprisingly large labor force in agriculture. Whereas in the United Kingdom the proportion is only 3.1 percent and in the United States but 4.2 percent, the USSR's farm workers represent 35 percent of the total. The proportion engaged in secondary occupations is about one-third, fairly comparable to other advanced countries. The tertiary work force is unusually small, however, constituting only about 28 percent. Canada and the United States have percentages at least twice that high.

A smaller percentage of the Soviet population receives a secondary education than in most advanced countries. The Soviet figure is less than half that of the United States, Canada, France, or Japan. This stems largely from the Soviet emphasis on vocational and technical training for her workers.

Considering its present fairly high per capita GNP, the Soviet Union's population does not enjoy a very satisfactory standard of living. Although the large number of medical doctors assures good health care and has indeed greatly reduced the death rate, diets remain poor by western standards. With the chronic food shortages of earlier years behind them, the Soviet people receive an adequate quantity of food; but they have a diet heavy on starches and deficient in proteins, fresh fruits, and vegetables, despite strenuous efforts to increase the output from the farms and fishing fleet.

Indeed, consumption levels are generally lower than in other advanced countries. Although the country's total national output of goods and services is now about three-fifths that of the United States, per capita consumption is much lower than that figure implies. Most estimates indicate that the average Soviet citizen consumes hardly more than one-third as much as an American. One of the main reasons for the disparity is the Soviet's high level of reinvestment of national income to accelerate national growth; this depresses personal consumption and makes consumer goods scarce. Thus, although housing is subsidized and very cheap, it is in exceedingly short supply. Moreover, the range of consumer goods is severely limited and most are of inferior quality.

THE SOVIET SPACE-ECONOMY

How is this great store of diverse human and natural endowments organized spatially? What is the Soviet approach to management and direction of its complex space-economy and how has this strategy influenced national economic growth? How has the Soviet system affected the nature and location of production? These are the questions to which we now turn.

administrative regions

A hierarchy of territorial units is employed in the political administration of this federated state. Below the top echelon of government, centered in Moscow, is a second level comprising· the Soviet Socialist Republics (SSR). Altogether there are fifteen republics, each ostensibly defined according to the area occupied by a major nationality group. The Russian Soviet Federated Socialist Republic is much the largest, in terms both of area and population. It takes in the northern part of the country from Finland to the Pacific, including all of Siberia. Other larger republics

are the Belorussian SSR, the Ukrainian SSR, and the Kazakh SSR. Each of the three Baltic states (Estonia, Latvia, and Lithuania) has also been designated a republic. Theoretically, the SSRs are accorded a considerable amount of sovereignty; in practice, administration of the country is highly centralized.

A third level in the hierarchy consists of subdivisions of the larger SSRs: oblasts, krays, and ASSRs. *Oblasts* are strictly administrative units, *ASSRs* (autonomous Soviet Socialist Republics) are assigned to smaller nationality groups, while *krays* combine small ethnic groups. There is also a further subdivision into fourth and fifth levels of administrative areas. Superimposed upon this political structure is a set of economic regions, whose size and functions have changed from time to time with shifts in national policy. The economic regions are used for planning and control of production and distribution.

The Soviet urban hierarchy is directly related to the administrative regionalization, since the primary functions of urban centers in the USSR relate to the planning, management, and administration of the centralized state. The highest order of the central place system consists of one city, Moscow, the top control center, while the second order contains 18 cities, corresponding to the major economic regions of the country and answering to Moscow. A third order, subject to cities of the second level, contains 50 headquarters cities of the USSR's industrial management regions. In the fourth order are 146 cities, centers of *oblasts* or their equivalent. It is through this system that the administered economy attempts to move toward the goals of the state.

administrative control: planning and direction

the command economy

The essence of the Soviet system is centralized planning and detailed control of all economic life. Such a command economy, or administered economy, is a mammoth undertaking; certainly it did not spring full-blown into being with the 1917 Revolution. Indeed, Lenin's administrative arrangements at the outset were pragmatic, and a mixed economy prevailed during the early years of Communist control. Yet the eventual pattern was foreshadowed with the establishment in 1921 of Gosplan, the State Planning Commission. At first Gosplan was attached to the council of labor and defense and charged with

1. working out a single general state economic plan, together with the methods and means for implementing it
2. preparing a state budget
3. considering questions of currency, credit, and banking
4. making industrial location decisions.

Although it had an essentially coordinating role, its decrees carried legal force. At first, however, its control was restricted to only a few economic activities.

During the late 1920s Gosplan gained prominence and power as it gradually assumed its eventual form. Today it is directly under the supreme executive, the Council of Ministers, and it controls the economy through preparation and execution of five-year plans, the first of which was begun in 1929. Gosplan has more than 30 departments, one for each main branch of industry, and one each for internal trade and foreign commerce. The departments are required to match production with needs (demand) and to control investments. Gosplan has specialized divisions for labor, transport, and communications, and it maintains a central statistical administration. It is a hierarchical organization with several operational levels.

Among Soviet decision makers there has been a long-standing conflict between proponents of vertical and horizontal principles of administrative organization. The Gosplan operation, with its essentially autonomous ministerial departments and their independent industrial empires, is a vertical arrangement. This approach was the rule until 1957. In a notable but largely unsuccessful experiment in decentralization carried out between 1957 and 1965, a horizontal regional system was tried. Administration subsequently reverted to the vertical plan, but with modifications still in progress today.

the Stalin planning model

A true command economy for the Soviet Union finally took shape during the 1930s. With its vertical organization, it provided for firm central control and accountability to party leaders at each level. Under the aegis of Gosplan, which set general policy and allocated resources, all state enterprises were directed by People's Commissariates (later Ministries). This included agriculture, which was organized into large undertakings, either collectives or state farms. Plans of binding force, described as the "will of the party," were handed down through the hierarchy. These plans governed quantity and variety of output and specified procurement arrangements, operating details, prices, and distribution of the final product. Priorities among the various enterprises were based on political considerations rather than on making a profit, and prices bore little relationship to actual costs. Operational plans were made annually within the context of the five-year plans. Allocation of materials and distribution of outputs among enterprises was planned in detail.

Following World War II several changes in the system were made. There was some subdivision of the ministries regionally, and a proliferation of new ministries occurred through subdividing the old. Specialists began to be appointed as ministers as replacements for the politicians who had previously held such posts. Gosplan was relabeled a committee and its functions were limited to planning.

This strategy produced impressive gains in quantitative terms, but it resulted in a sacrifice of quality and technical progress. It rewarded managers for fulfilling plans, placing the emphasis upon making everything in as large a quantity as possible. This could best be accomplished by continuing to use the same designs year after year. As a consequence the system acquired a deep conservatism, with few structural changes and little response to changing technologies and needs. The most flagrant example of this was the continued emphasis upon coal long after oil and gas proved plentiful, as well as cheaper and easier to use. This conservatism became even more exaggerated when Stalin insisted on "purging" some of his ablest administrators. From the outset the system emphasized heavy industry and the making of producer goods; at the same time it neglected agriculture, except as a source of capital for investment in industry. Consumer goods were given a very low priority, as was foreign trade (see Chapter 11).

the Khrushchev approach

Stalin's successors were quick to point out the defects built into the Stalin model: the competition among ministries for resources, the personal empire-building within the ministries, the lack of coordination among sectors, the duplication of supply arrangements, especially of intermediate products, of which many were being cross-hauled over incredible distances. Premier Khrushchev's solution, beginning in 1957, was to establish 105 regional economic councils (*sovnarkhozy*). Each republic was to have its own Gosplan, while the all-Union (or national) Gosplan was to perform only general planning and to coordinate plans of the republics. It was also to continue allocating essential commodities between republics. Foreign trade was reorganized, and Comecon was revived and given a new form and new functions (see Chapter 11). Khrushchev also determined to spur development of the chemical industry, which had remained backward under Stalin; to modernize agriculture and expand its output; to change the energy balance, ending the excessive emphasis on coal; and to increase the supply of consumer durables.

As logical and well-meaning as these reforms were, they were introduced precipitously and capriciously. The regional decentralization of control and production was unsuccessful because it fostered excessive localism, regional administrators lacked sufficient information, and resources were misallocated, all of which created general confusion. The patchwork administrative changes introduced by Khrushchev further added to the chaos. Economic growth, which at first proceeded rapidly, slipped sharply after 1958 and farm output actually fell.

Brezhnev and Kosygin

The party leaders who deposed Khrushchev quickly disassembled his reforms. They largely discontinued the regional planning system in 1965, although preserving some of its more workable features. They restored the ministerial system of planning and control, with Gosplan again in charge. Nevertheless, they did institute needed reforms and in particular they gave more latitude to decision makers at lower levels in the hierarchy. Serious planning and management problems continue to persist, however, and the Soviet Union is now undertaking further innovative steps, as we shall note later.

economic growth and development

In the world at large, the growth rates of the USSR's economy have been cause for much awe, admiration, alarm, skepticism, controversy, speculation, and analysis—depending upon the period during which this growth was being observed and the ideology of the observer. The nation's progress has been closely watched, especially by development planners in other Communist countries and in some of the less developed lands. The Soviet approach has been emulated rigidly by the former, and parts of it have been copied by the latter. Nevertheless, the Communist theory of growth and the Soviet Union's experience have not coincided in actual practice. Furthermore, when assessing the results achieved by the USSR and attempting to apply these ideas elsewhere it is essential that account be taken of the inherent advantages that the Soviet Union has had for growth and development as well as some of the serious obstacles it has had to confront. So far the results have been mixed.

the Communist strategy for growth

At least until recently, the only acceptable Communist strategy, as developed by Marx, Lenin, and Stalin, has been based upon the assumption that only industrialization can give rapid growth and development. Moreover, one of the basic Communist principles of industrialization is that growth must occur through the process of import substitution (see Chapter 11). In other words, the country must strive to produce domestically as many as possible of those items previously imported rather than to rely on increasing national income through expanding exports. Autarky (self-sufficiency) in raw material supply and in other basic goods was to be sought. The ultimate outcome would be a closed economic system.

A second principle is the maintenance of a high rate of savings and of productive investment. Stalin insisted that a country must develop as fast as it possibly could, while Marx had stated that the larger the proportion of GNP reinvested the more rapidly national income would grow. A third Communist principle of industrialization is that producer goods should be emphasized, since rapid growth supposedly requires a high ratio of producer to consumer goods.

To accomplish these aims, planners first allocated as much capital as possible to productive investments, that is, those capable of directly increasing the output of commodities. "Nonproductive" investment was limited to essentials only, such as education and training and scientific research. Planners made certain that industrial growth proceeded at a faster rate than other sectors of the economy. Third, they saw that output of industrial *producer* goods exceeded that of industrial *consumer* goods. For Stalin the former group was essentially confined to coal mining, iron and steel making, and machine production. This follows Lenin's "principle of decisive links of the chain," by which the administrator selects a prospective leading sector and then pours all resources in this, trusting all others to follow in time. Implementation of these principles requires strong centralization of planning and administration, suppressing market forces and setting high planning targets.

Soviet growth in practice

To what extent have the results in the USSR coincided with the prescriptions of Communist growth theory? Before attempting an answer, we should caution that Soviet data must be used with special care. Some of the data problems are unique to the command economy. Reported figures are suspect firstly because they come from a single source, the state. There are no independent sources of data to serve as a check or restraint on official exaggeration or distortion. Official agencies try to make themselves look good, because they are judged on the basis of the figures they are able to release. Second, there has always been an incentive to crusade for communism, which makes objectivity difficult to sustain.

These peculiarities of the system introduce a selectivity into data reporting. Poor performances are hidden or disguised whenever possible, good results are trumpeted, and military production is not reported. Reliability is also questionable because of a tendency to exaggerate absolute output and to overstate contrasts with the pre-Revolutionary period. Other data problems stem from the Soviet method of pricing, which, as we saw in Chapter 4, does not accurately reflect costs, and suffers from an ideological bias in accounting methods. For example, capital inputs tend to be understated and labor tends to be overvalued. Still another problem results from the planning emphasis on sectors where quick growth is easiest and quickest. Despite these deficiencies, Soviet data have steadily improved as the country's leaders have gained in self-confidence and maturity. Moreover, foreign students of the Soviet Union have gained skill in interpreting and weighing the figures reported by official agencies.

With this caveat we may examine the record of Soviet growth as reconstructed by analysts. Following the 1917 Revolution and continuing until 1920, the Communist leadership was forced to fight a civil war against opposing forces. This chaotic period caused a sharp decline of output from tsarist levels, manufacturing output falling by 80 percent and agriculture by 50 percent. The fighting and the famine and disease accompanying it reduced the country's population by 5 million people. The Communists managed to defeat their opponents in 1920, and from then until 1928 they passed through a period of pragmatic compromise between socialistic and capitalistic forms. This mixed economy resulted in further disorganization of production and distribution, but prewar levels of output were regained by 1928, if only because of the end of armed conflict.

The Soviet leadership made an abrupt change in direction in 1928 by introducing a true centrally planned economy aimed at promoting faster economic growth. Under the first five-year plan (1928–1932) agriculture was collectivized, with private land holdings combined into large jointly operated production units. The initial effect was a severe reduction in farm output and widespread famine. Manufacturing production, however, rose by 50 percent under government control, aided by heavy investment and a 60 percent increase in industrial employment. During the second five-year plan (1933–1937) manufacturing output rose even faster, by 85 percent; but the third five-year plan, interrupted in 1940 by the Second World War and hobbled by Stalin's purges, brought little change in total production. In addition, the German invasion caused enormous losses of population and much material damage. By 1946 Soviet output was only 60 percent of the prewar level.

Under the fourth five-year plan (1946–1950) the country experienced rapid recovery and managed to reach prewar levels by 1948 or 1949. In spite of interruptions caused by the Korean War and the struggle for power following Stalin's death, the fifth five-year plan (1951–1955) continued the rapid rise, adding another 60 percent to the total produced. The sixth plan, delayed by Khrushchev and revised to extend for seven years (1959–1965), introduced the new regionalization scheme, reorganized Comecon, shifted emphasis to oil and chemicals, and produced the spectacular sputnik venture into space-exploration. As suggested previously, it also brought much disorganization and mismanagement, and growth rates began to decline. Since 1965 growth has continued to slip.

Looking at the full record, we find that the Soviet economy has multiplied six or seven times since the Revolution. It has been an irregular growth, however, characterized by sudden spurts of growth interrupted by serious disturbances. The best years were from 1928 to 1940 and from 1948 to the mid-1960s. It has been estimated that Soviet output grew at an annual rate of only 0.1 percent between 1913 and 1928 but that the rate rose to 9.9 percent between 1928 and 1940 and again reached a level of 9.6 percent between 1950 and 1955. By 1963, however, it had declined to only 4.2 percent. In 1971 it fell to 3.5 percent and in 1972 it was

only 1.5 percent. Comparisons of the country's post-Revolutionary growth with earlier times have indicated that the Russian economy had probably grown at an average annual rate of 5.3 percent during the last 50 years of the tsars' reign but at an average rate of but 4.4 percent between 1917 and 1955.

There is also evidence of wide differences in the growth rates of different industries after 1913. For example, it is estimated that output of machinery and equipment had multiplied 58 times by 1955, but that manufacture of intermediate industrial products had increased only nine times and consumer goods but three times. This, of course, reflects the official policy under which nine-tenths of all Soviet industrial investment has gone into industrial producer goods.

elements affecting Soviet growth rates

The USSR has thus experienced periods of very rapid growth during the past fifty years, but the modern tendency is for the economy to grow at decreasing rates.

Soviet growth rates have benefited from strict application of the Communist principle of complete administrative control of production and distribution. This has permitted close allocation of investment capital, control over labor assignment and limitations on its mobility, and control over wages and prices so as to influence the level and nature of consumption. In short, it has made possible the selective mobilization of all resources, with great unity of purpose.

Growth has been further stimulated by the high rates of savings and investment, another practice that is basic to Communist theory. "Profits" are reinvested directly through the state budget or used by the government itself. The Soviet Union reinvests nearly one-third of its GNP, a rate comparable to that of Japan and twice that of the United States. The funds for this purpose are extracted from the population in the form of forced savings. In earlier times much came as forced deliveries from agriculture, which was in effect being required to pay for industrialization.

The Communist principle of stressing industry, and producer goods in particular, temporarily aided the USSR in achieving rapid growth. This meant shifting labor from a less productive branch of the economy into a more productive one. The Soviet Union was able to get much more output from a worker employed in this type of manufacturing than it could from his services in the inefficient Soviet-style agriculture. Moreover, the emphasis on producer goods was doubtless a necessity for the USSR in its earlier years, considering the lack of effective demand for manufactured consumer goods from the mainly subsistence farmers of that period. Under those conditions the producer-goods industries became virtually autonomous since they had assured markets for their wares. Thus one set of producer goods (coal and iron ore) could be used to make other producer goods (steel) to make still other producer goods (machinery to mine coal and iron ore and steel mill equipment). It was thus a circular process kept going by regular infusions of capital and labor extracted from other facets of the economy, especially agriculture.

For those looking to the Soviet model for possible application elsewhere, it is important also to note those special advantages enjoyed by the USSR but not necessarily shared by other developing nations, Communist or non-Communist. Foremost has been the advantage of size, which contributed importantly to the Soviets' attempts to achieve autarky. Few, if any, other nations can call upon the rich store of natural resources possessed by the USSR, which not only materially assisted the policy of self-sufficiency but also made possible the emphasis on producer goods. Indeed, it is often observed that the USSR is actually a case of development based upon *regional* specialization and interregional trade on a scale so vast that it differs little from trade among sovereign nations of the more usual size. In other words, the USSR is like a huge common market protected from external competition and enjoying the highly varied factor endowments of its different regions. The size of the Soviet Union's domestic market also assures the great economies of scale and resulting low unit costs of operation required for the manufacture of producer goods. For these reasons the Soviet Union does not make a satisfactory example for the small Communist countries of Eastern Europe or for most underdeveloped nations.

Another special advantage that was enjoyed by the Soviets at the outset was their legacy from imperial Russia. Most students of growth and development agree that Russia was already at the takeoff stage on the eve of the 1917 Revolution. The new rulers also inherited a large quantity of unused productive capacity, and they found already in existence a considerable amount of infrastructure, such as railways and communications, and institutions such as banking.

A number of unique circumstances were also at work during each of the Soviet Union's periods of rapid growth, namely from 1928 to 1940 and from 1948 to 1958. Some of these are unlikely to recur. After the Revolution, for example, a number of population and labor force characteristics favored growth. Between 1917 and 1940 the population increased sharply in size, augmenting the labor force and the market. During that same period the Soviet Union was successfully eliminating illiteracy. Even without the population increase there were large numbers of idle workers available in the beginning. Moreover, there was (and still is) the substantial amount of concealed unemployment in agriculture, a large pool of underutilized labor for manufacturing. Another valuable source of labor has been the unusually high female participation rate. Then too, at the beginning of the first five-year plan and again after World War II there was a favorable attitude among the work force, who were prepared by what they had already endured to work hard to make up for the time lost. Such attitudes cannot easily be sustained in normal times. Labor productivity rose in both periods of high growth, although it is still lower than in Western Europe or North America. Substantial output was apparently achieved also by the use of forced labor, gangs of political prisoners during the earlier growth period and a great number of German prisoners of war in the latter period.

Soviet growth in the postwar era was further augmented by the annexation of new territories having a combined area larger than that of France and containing 20 million people. This has been calculated to have added 11 percent to the country's gross output and another 0.3 percent to the annual growth rate. Moreover, the tight control exercised by Stalin over the Eastern European satellites was in some respects like an addition of territory.

During both high-growth periods the Soviet Union benefited from large amounts of borrowed technology. In 1928 the country could draw upon a great body of as yet unutilized Western technology available to it at a low cost through the use of consultants and in numerous other ways. During and following World War II the USSR experienced a second infusion of Western technology. In addition, as in the case of Japan, there was a large amount of foreign aid from the United States at that time, as well as reparations from the defeated enemy. The replacement of war-damaged factories with wholly new industrial plants and equipment incorporating the latest ideas provided important new efficiencies. Against these gains from postwar recovery must, of course, be placed the severe war losses in both men and material.

Although the exact rates of annual growth experienced by the Soviet Union have been much argued, there is general agreement that this rate of growth has declined over the long run and is still slipping. This trend, confirmed by official figures, is particularly disturbing to Communist theorists; it was not supposed to happen. Several explanations offer themselves for this turn of affairs. One is that early growth figures were illusory; the quick spurts of output in each case accompanied the resumption of production following a period of disruption. Mobilizing idle labor force and physical facilities for productive use can give quick results. The country now appears to be reaching the limits of effective demand for the products upon which it has been concentrating and is not yet making those things for which widespread demand still exists. The effects of conservatism in planning and management seem also to be felt. Planners have set high goals but they have been reluctant to try new methods or change the product mix in ways that are clearly needed. Moreover, the easiest, quickest approaches to growth have been exhausted. Growth is requiring increasingly large inputs of capital but this is not being reflected in high labor productivity.

We should note that the country's growth to this point has taken place at a cost that has been high in both material and human terms. It has required great expenditures of physical resources: fuels and metallic ores have been used lavishly, and rich, conveniently located deposits are nearing depletion. Forced growth has also exacted much human suffering and deprivation. It has taken place at a sacrifice of efficiency in the use of natural and human resources.

the nature and location of Soviet production

Soviet planning for industrial growth and development has had an impact on the location and structure of production over and above the effects of such customary influences as the physical character of the country, the locations of raw materials and markets, and the historic development of the economy.

the location of production

As we observed earlier, the Soviet Union has had to contend with an unusually uneven spatial distribution of human and natural resources. At the grossest levels, this problem is illustrated by the disparities between the Soviet west (including the areas of the Urals and the Caucasus) and the east (the Asiatic lands beyond the Urals). The Asiatic portion has 80 percent of the land area and 88 percent of the power resources but has a population density of only 2.6 persons per square mile. Investment costs are much greater in the east than for similar projects in the west. The east also has a severe shortage of labor and inadequate food supplies, since local farm output is meager and the country's main agricultural lands are hundreds or even thousands of miles to the west.

The country thus has had to overcome vast distances; and transportation has assumed a critical role in moving the raw materials of the east to manufacturing centers in the west and conveying food, labor, machinery, and equipment to the east. Transportation has therefore been a necessary condition for development, but its cost is high when such great distances are involved. For instance, it has been estimated that transport costs for moving coal and other minerals over distances of 900 to 1200 miles are three to three-and-a-half times the cost of mining. Transportation is a big consumer of the factors of production, requiring one-quarter of all the fuel output and one-tenth of the manpower. Aside from the matter of cost, the railways are overburdened with hauling primary materials.

The planning response to this problem suggests some disparity between Communist location theory and Soviet practice. The official line is to speak derisively of traditional location theory as "capitalistic" and useless for Communist planning, but in fact Soviet planners have been forced to apply Weberian principles more actively than most. They have had to take a cost-minimization approach to location because of the distance problem. Locational distortions have occurred because of political and military needs, but these have

been less than might have been supposed and they are diminishing at present. To only a limited extent have Soviet planners heeded the Communist doctrine of distributing industry as evenly as possible, developing backward areas and peoples, and encouraging regional specialties.

The spatial pattern of manufacturing illustrates these several influences. The temptations of the east were felt strongly by Stalin, who made strenuous efforts to develop industry beyond the Urals. In this he was motivated by his bias toward heavy industry and by the bountiful supply of raw materials for this kind of production in the east. To some extent he was influenced by military considerations in attempting to disperse production as security against invasion from the west and in occupying and strengthening lands adjacent to the Chinese border. Since Stalin's passing there has been a disillusionment with the east because of the exceptionally high development and transport costs industry must bear in those locations, together with a growing appreciation of the agglomeration advantages of the established industrial districts of the west.

Soviet planning, especially under Stalin, had a persistent bias toward coal field locations. Many of the coal fields are easy to reach, their locations were well known at an early date, and meanwhile oil and gas exploitation lagged. Even after petroleum development had begun to catch up, planners were slow to adjust to the change in resource availability. Coal fields have also acquired industries because of the policy of regional self-sufficiency in fuels, which has caused even low grade peat and brown coals to be used. The coal field bias was also perpetuated by the influence of intrenched special-interests groups in the national ministries.

The combined effects are apparent in Figure 18.3. The European portion of the country (including the Urals and Caucasus) still has 82 percent of Soviet manufacturing. Three-fourths of the total is found in the Soviet "manufacturing belt," where coal field orientation is particularly apparent. Within this belt the central industrial district leads as in the past, relying in part on local brown coal and peat augmented by imports of fuels from other regions. The eastern Ukraine and Urals, with their coal fields, follow, while the oil-rich Volga regions are close behind. Leningrad's industry lags behind other parts of the manufacturing belt.

Industrial output is increasing most rapidly in the European areas at present, despite the raw-material advantages of the east. This reflects an awareness of locational realities and of the problems of the east. Recent shifts to oil and gas and the growing pipeline capacity have had their effects, especially in the rapid industrial expansion of the Urals-Volga regions. The city of Kuybyshev, at the great bend of the Volga, is the focal point of this part of the country. In addition to its energy supply, Kuybyshev is a transport hub and

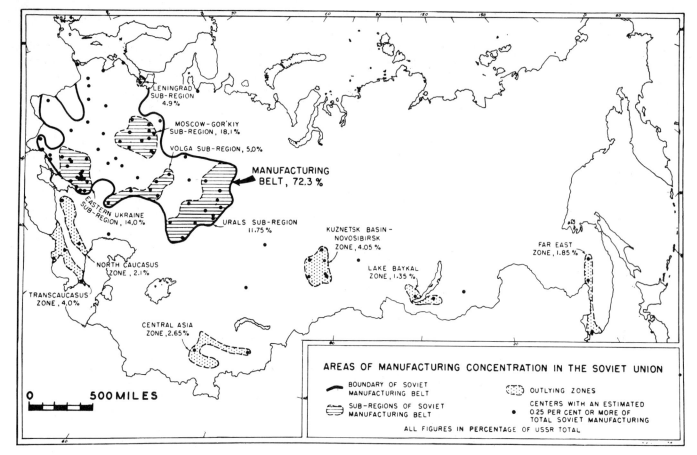

Fig. 18.3 *Soviet manufacturing regions*

Source: Richard E. Lonsdale and John H. Thompson, "A Map of the USSR's Manufacturing," Economic Geography, *36 (January, 1960), 42.*

it is surrounded by other important industrial concentrations: the Urals, the central industrial district, and the eastern Ukrainian district. The lone industrial growth point of consequence in the east is Novosibirsk Oblast, a rapidly developing metallurgical region in western Siberia. The center of gravity of Soviet industry is tending to shift eastward but still lies within the main orbit of European Russia.

How has the location of agriculture been affected by Soviet policy and planning? We have noted earlier that Soviet agriculture is subject to severe physical limitations. The greater part of the USSR is too cold, too dry, or too wet for agriculture, leaving only one-tenth of the entire territory suitable for farming. The specific aims of the Agricultural Ministry are to expand cultivated area, to increase yields, and to choose the appropriate land use for each production area.

One of the more successful tactics has been to irrigate the more suitable arid lands of Central Asia, permitting the replacement of extensively farmed grains with high quality cotton. Some of the marshlands of southwestern European Russia have also been reclaimed through drainage.

A third approach has been to extend commercial grain-farming into some of the subhumid grasslands that had previously been considered unsuited for agri-

culture. The most spectacular of such experiments was Premier Khrushchev's pet project, "the virgin lands scheme," initiated in 1954. In an undertaking unparalleled in world agricultural history, commercial grain-farming was pushed into the dry grazing lands of Trans-Volga and adjacent southern Siberia and northern Kazakhstan. Ultimately the area sown to grains reached a total of 40 million hectares, a territory equivalent to Illinois, Indiana, Ohio, and West Virginia. The project attracted 330,000 migrants, mainly from European USSR, who endured pioneering conditions on the newly established state farms.

Only single-crop agriculture is practiced in this area, the crop being spring wheat. Because of inadequate moisture, yields are low; but the huge acreage allocated to wheat was intended to compensate for this disadvantage, as on the plains and prairies of North America. One purpose for the undertaking was to relieve the Ukraine of some of its responsibilities for wheat production, freeing that more humid area for corn and other feed grains to support increased animal production. The "virgin lands" have had some good years; but they are subject to cycles of prolonged drought, and monumental crop failures have been frequent. The new corn areas in the Ukraine have not done well either, since this is not the ideal environment for dependably good corn yields. The Soviet grain supply has thus fluctuated wildly, and the USSR has had to import massive quantities of North American grains in bad years.

Some of the most significant contributions to increased Soviet farm output have resulted from higher yields. Fertilizer supplies have risen in recent years, supplying nutrients much needed by the poorer soils. Improved farming techniques and better equipment have contributed to yield increases. Land formerly used to grow feed for draft animals has been freed for more productive uses by the introduction of tractors, thereby adding to output per farming unit. Despite these measures, however, the USSR still lags far behind Western Europe and North America in average yield per acre.

To summarize, the expansion of arable lands has been most successful where special physical advantages have made this possible, as in the irrigation of specialty crops. Aside from this, the main locational effects of Soviet policy have been:

1. to replace grains with more valuable industrial crops where favorable conditions exist
2. to substitute high-yielding feed grains for low-yielding food grains, and
3. to intensify production.

In pursuing their policy of autarky, however, planners have often insisted on the production of crops not well suited to the Soviet Union's physical environment. On the whole, therefore, genuine success has tended to elude the USSR's agricultural planners, despite a few advances.

Transport policy is another area in which the USSR has taken a growth path different from many other technically advanced countries. Despite the magnitude of the problem of overcoming distances, transportation has been a lagging sector in the Soviet Union. Investment in transportation has been kept to a minimum; improvements and new facilities have been added to the system only after the need has become demonstrably pressing.

Transport policy has also emphasized railways at the expense of highways. In part this results from the special place assigned to heavy industry, which is more likely to require this type of transportation. Moreover, the physical character of the Soviet landscape is generally suitable for railways, a fairly extensive rail system having been inherited from the tsars. Soviet transport policy requires intensive use of existing facilities, which helps to explain the remarkable traffic densities on the railways. Finally there is a stress on regional self-sufficiency in raw materials and agricultural output so as to minimize haulage. Even so, goods are transported over surprisingly long distances.

More recently transport planners have given greater attention to the development of air transport for passenger travel. This is a ready solution for the problems of long-distance travel within the country and for accommodating the increasing number of international travelers. A second new development is the decision to increase substantially the nation's output of motor vehicles, a momentous policy reversal with many implications.

planning and the structure of production

Planning in the Soviet Union has possibly had an even greater effect on the kinds of commodities produced than it has had on their location. Some hard choices have had to be made in the allocation of resources. As we have seen, agriculture was until recently given only the most grudging support; it has been starved for investment funds and milked for development capital, which was used elsewhere. Tertiary activities were supported only to the extent necessary to support the growth of industry. Although the manufacturing sector was the beneficiary of this allocation scheme, only certain kinds of industry gained from it. Let us look more closely at one of those favored branches of manufacturing, metallurgy, and in particular, the iron and steel industry, an activity representative of Stalin's bias.

metallurgy: a top priority industry

In 1971 the Soviet Union at last achieved a goal that had been strenuously pursued almost from the beginning: it passed the United States to attain world leadership in steel production. At present the USSR is making one-third again as much crude steel as third-place Japan, although Japanese output is now rising at a faster rate. Soviet output is three times that of West Germany and five times that of the United Kingdom.

To achieve this goal, Soviet steel output has doubled and redoubled many times since the early 1920s (see Fig. 18.4), even though its rapid growth was at times severely interrupted by cataclysmic events, such as the Nazi occupation of the principal steel-making districts. Nearly everything has favored this rapid growth. None of the physical requirements is lacking; iron ore, fuels, alloying metals, and fluxing materials are abundantly available. The country is well endowed with iron-bearing ores at Krivoy Rog and other locations in the southern region, in the so-called Kursk magnetic anomaly south of Moscow, and in the Urals. Although the largest reserves of high-grade coking coals are in the east, the west has a good supply, especially in the Donets Basin of the eastern Ukraine. Today coke is being supplemented as a fuel by natural gas, also available in large quantities. Pipelines converge upon the eastern Soviet Union from major fields in the Volga-Urals, Caspian, South Central Asian, and Arctic areas. Finally, alloying metals are available in great variety, and manganese is so plentiful that it is used lavishly by Soviet steel makers.

Equally favorable to the rapid growth and de-

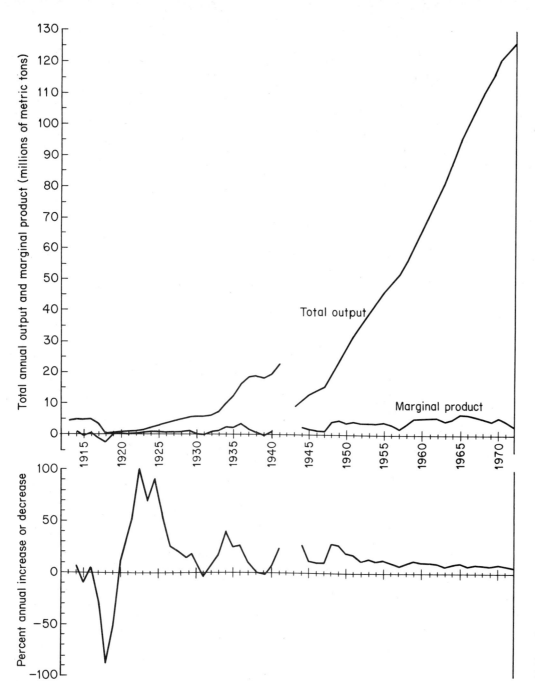

Fig. 18.4 *Soviet output of crude steel, marginal product, and percent change, 1913–1972.*

Sources: 1913–1954 data from **M. Gardner Clark,** The Economics of Soviet Steel *(Cambridge: Harvard University Press, 1956);* 1955–1972 data from Encyclopaedia Britannica Book of the Year.

velopment of Soviet steel has been Marxist ideology. Under the very first five-year plan the steel industry underwent a forced development, including special allocations of resources and especially capital. Heavy subsidization of steel production continued thereafter. A policy of low prices to steel-consuming industries spurred the unusually heavy use of steel characteristic of Soviet fabricators. Large government grants were required to make up the resulting deficits.

This illustrates the "perpetual-motion" machine of producer-goods manufacture in the Soviet Union. The steel industry had a guaranteed market for its products among the manufacturers of other producer goods: machinery for steel making and for mining and other heavy industry applications; transport equipment

for moving raw materials and distributing products; structural steel and other items used in construction. One of the principal markets for Soviet steel—and another reason for the Stalinist emphasis upon heavy industry—is the military. Munitions production reached high levels at an early date but investment in war industries accelerated rapidly from 1937 onward. The eastern European satellites have come to depend upon the USSR for iron ore and also for steel and machinery to supplement their own inadequate output. A further short-term advantage enjoyed by the Soviet steel industry came from the war reparations received from nations conquered in World War II. Soviet-occupied areas were stripped of equipment of all kinds and sent back to the USSR to help speed its recovery.

location: policy and practice

What kind of locational pattern has the Soviet steel industry assumed? Is there any basis in fact for the claim of Soviet writers that their industry has been able to remain independent of bourgeois locational principles? The tsarist spatial pattern showed a decided coal field orientation. Three-fourths of the production was in the Ukraine and most of the rest in the Urals. Soviet control of the industry at first reinforced the coal field emphasis, broadening it to include production on still other coal fields in the east. Subsequently other locational considerations were introduced. Although the pattern has undergone some recent changes, the old arrangement is surprisingly persistent.

Four main centers of integrated iron and steel manufacture predominate at the present time: the Ukraine, the Urals, European Russia, and Asian USSR (Fig. 18.5). In addition, there are scattered plants making ingot steel using pig iron and scrap metal as raw materials. The Ukraine currently makes more than 40 percent of the Soviet Union's pig iron. The "Ukrainian metallurgical base," as Soviet planners term it, provides a remarkable juxtaposition of raw materials and fuels. Coal comes from the Donets coal basin (the "Donbas") in the eastern Ukraine, which has been a major producing field since the early nineteenth century. High quality coking-grade bituminous coal occurs there in thin, tilted seams, some very deep underground and

costly to mine. Nevertheless, the Donbas still exceeds other richer and larger fields in the total amount of coal raised, because of its favorable location within one of the chief industrial complexes of the nation.

Some of the largest proved reserves of iron ore in the USSR occur in this region. Krivoy Rog's high-grade direct-shipping ores have been exploited since the latter part of the nineteenth century and are now nearing depletion. The industry is having to turn to plentiful low-grade ores, which must be beneficiated (that is, removing the non-iron-bearing materials); a new nine-million-ton concentrator has been installed for this purpose at Krivoy Rog. To the south are other ore deposits on the Kerch peninsula of Crimea. Near Krivoy Rog at Nikopol is the world's largest known deposit of manganese. Limestone for fluxing and a variety of other minerals are also at hand.

The integrated steel mills have three kinds of orientation in the Ukraine. Those at Donetsk and elsewhere in the Donbas are coal-oriented, while the mills at Krivoy Rog and Kerch are oriented to ore. In addition there are intermediate steel mill locations at break-of-bulk and other transport locations. Examples are Dnepropotrovsk and Zaporozh'ye, situated where the Donetsk-Krivoy Rog railway crosses the River Dnieper, and Zhdanov and Taganrog on the north shore of the Sea of Azov lying between the Donbas and Kerch. In the Ukraine, coal flows generally westward and south-

Fig. 18.5 *The Soviet iron and steel industry*

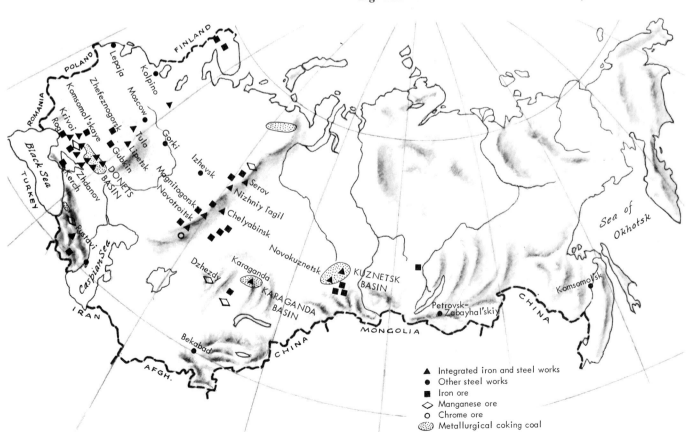

ward, ore moves eastward and northward, and back hauls are utilized wherever possible.

The second most important steel-making region is the Urals, which produces from 25 to 28 percent of the USSR's pig iron. The low Ural Mountains are highly mineralized, with an incredible variety of ferrous, nonferrous, and precious metals, as well as fossil fuels and other minerals. Although local iron deposits are nearing exhaustion, supplementary supplies are nearby in north Kazakhstan and western Siberia. Coal is less well represented in the Urals and must be supplemented by long-distance shipments from the large reserves of the Kuznetsk Basin (the Kuzbas), 1,400 miles to the east in Siberia, and Karaganda, 600 miles to the southeast in Kazakhstan. The Urals offer a wide range of alloy metals, including manganese, nickel, tungsten, and chrome.

The main surge of industrialization in this region took place before and during the Second World War, when it proved to be a secure location. The Urals steel industry performed a crucial service during Nazi occupation of the Ukraine and Central European USSR. Many fabricating plants moved to the Urals ahead of the advancing Germans, and they have remained there since to provide large local markets for steel. The Urals also have good access to the large markets in the West.

In addition to these major areas of steel production, there are two other smaller centers. Producers in European Russia pour a little more than one-tenth of the country's pig iron. This is a market-oriented location. Raw materials must be hauled long distances, the coal coming from Pechora in the Arctic and from the Donbas, and the iron ore from the Kola Peninsula or Kursk.

Less than 10 percent of Soviet pig iron is produced in the eastern USSR. Steel-making facilities were developed in the Kuznetsk Basin during the 1930s to use the exceedingly rich Kuzbas coking coal. At the outset the Kuzbas shipped coal 1500 miles to steel mills in the Urals, and iron ore was returned in the backhaul for smelting in the Kuznetsk furnaces. The arrangement was later terminated and the two steel districts now use materials nearer at hand. Another coal field location outside European USSR is at Karaganda, which draws upon the country's third most important coal basin. Iron ore is also found nearby. The main markets for the Asian output are far to the west in the European part of the nation, necessitating very long hauls of the finished steel.

The four major steel-producing districts illustrate the basic nature of steel mill location in the Soviet Union. Coking coal played a decisive part in locating the mills of Imperial Russia and it has continued important to several modern operations, especially those in the Donbas, the Kuzbas, and Karaganda. Yet the increasingly efficient use of coal has weakened its locational influence in the Soviet Union as in the United Kingdom and elsewhere.

This change in the coal-ore ratio has simultane-ously increased the influence of ore on steel mill location. The steadily falling iron content of the country's ores has further strengthened the pull of ore deposits. As in the United States, the deposits that have been worked for many years are now yielding poorer ores, necessitating beneficiation and agglomeration. In several places new deposits of lean ores are being exploited in order to reduce rail haulages. All of this has caused iron ore deposits to acquire greater locational influence.

Scrap iron and steel are generated mainly in districts where metal fabrication takes place. The locational effect of scrap supplies is therefore to increase the attraction of markets. However, Soviet planners have tended to underestimate the importance of locating close to markets. During the earlier years, the steel industry moved progressively farther from its markets even as steel was becoming increasingly market-oriented in the United States and Western Europe. A belated awareness of this problem has produced some reversal of the earlier trend. One solution has been to establish small consumer-oriented steel-ingot plants within or close to market areas. In addition, there has been a tendency to move some of the market for steel into the remoter producing areas by establishing steel-fabricating facilities at such locations.

Another flaw in earlier Soviet planning was the inclination to give too little attention to transport cost and to become preoccupied with production costs differentials, as illustrated by the Urals-Kuzbas combination cited earlier. The 1500 mile rail haul each way was made possible only by extracting an unrealistically low freight rate from the state-operated railway system. Since then the problem has been eased by increasing the self-sufficiency of each of the two steel districts. A second part of the solution has been to halt expansion of steel production in the east; no new furnaces have been added in Kuznetsk since 1934. Third, there has been an expansion of the Siberian rail net by developing a supplementary southern route to the east. Soviet decision makers thus appear to be accepting belatedly some of the fundamental principles of location previously rejected as inappropriate to the Communist system.

current trends

Aside from the locational changes taking place in the Soviet steel industry, a second important development has been the growing competence of the USSR's metallurgical engineers, whose technological advances have gained world attention. Despite the current preeminent position of the Soviet Union's steel industry, however, its rate of growth has fallen below the world rate and much below that of Japan. One of the problems of the Soviet steel industry is that it seems to be experiencing diminishing returns. Soviet steel producers find that their marginal costs are rising sharply; it is becoming much more expensive to add new capacity than it was in the past.

One of the major reasons why the country's steel industry is likely to grow at a slower rate in the future, however, is that planners are beginning to realize that they have been overproducing and overusing steel. It is now freely admitted that steel has been used wastefully in the past by making excessively heavy gauges and inappropriate applications. Competition is now being permitted from other materials, such as aluminum and plastics. Finally, Soviet decision makers would like to reduce the heavy burden of supporting a large munitions industry, by far the principal customer for steel. As this suggests, a number of major policy shifts appear to be under way in the Soviet Union at this time, as the nation's leaders take a new look at their country and its problems.

CONTEMPORARY PROBLEMS OF GROWTH IN THE USSR

The current reassessment of the Soviet Union's growth problems has at least two dimensions. The first of these had to do with imbalanced growth. Certain sectors of the economy and sections of the country are lagging badly behind the rest, violating basic doctrines of Marx and Lenin, and the nation's leaders therefore are feeling pressures to correct these disparities. Perhaps even more worrisome is the dwindling rate of growth being experienced by the economy as a whole. This is raising the suspicion that something may be wrong with the Soviet Union's basic strategy of development. As a result of this reassessment some radical changes seem to be imminent. These promise to reorder the Soviet Union's domestic system and to create a new role for the USSR within the world economic system from which the nation has remained aloof for so long.

unbalanced growth

The Soviet Union has provided the world with its longest and most thorough test of the Communist growth strategy. By forcing the growth of certain selected activities, it was thought that the rest of the national economy should follow along. The returns from this fifty-year experiment are now in and they indicate that the Soviet economy has not achieved well-rounded growth; important sectors have remained poorly developed and these are proving a drag on the entire system. Furthermore, large parts of the country and a substantial segment of the population are still in a relatively underdeveloped state. This was not supposed to happen.

structural problems

As the preceding pages have shown, several economic sectors have been neglected, especially infrastructure. Supporting facilities of all types have been provided in the most niggardly fashion, so great has been the reluctance of Soviet planners to divert investment funds from manufacturing. The most obvious example is transportation. Road and highway construction have lagged badly; there are few intercity routes of modern quality. The country has an uncommonly small number of motor cars in relation to its general level of technical advancement. Trucks are more numerous, but because of the poor roads they are ordinarily used only for local hauls. Intercity commodity movements are nearly all by rail, but even the railways are starved for investment funds and expansion is permitted only when facilities have become strained beyond their capacities. Housing is severely limited because the construction industry has had to focus mainly on building factories. Basic services of all kinds are kept to the barest minimum required to keep the economy running and to hold the society together. Secondary and higher education are only for the very few.

We have also seen that the farm population was treated with special brutality by Stalin, although conditions have improved under his successors. Independent holdings were consolidated into collectives or state farms, with a view to converting agriculture into an industry like manufacturing and to make farmers into an industrial labor force. Among other things, this approach has had the aim of (1) increasing total farm production, (2) channeling a larger proportion of that output into the national economy by completing the commercialization of agriculture, and (3) milking agriculture for capital to feed the expanding industrial sector. In return, only a minimum of investment was made in agriculture until Khrushchev assumed control. As a result of mismanagement, neglect, and the uncertainties of a harsh climate, the Soviet Union's agriculture has performed disappointingly.

On the whole industry has done much better, although, as we have noted, certain branches have been neglected. Consumer manufactures as a class have been kept at a minimum. More surprising was Stalin's myopia concerning certain producer goods, notably chemicals. The chemical industry was comparatively well developed under the tsars, mainly with foreign ownership, and it made a quick recovery from the First World War, the Revolution, and the ensuing Civil War. Under Stalin, however, it lagged badly. Chemicals had represented 6.4 percent of total industrial output in 1924, but by the early 1950s the proportion had fallen below 3 percent. Moreover, only the heavy chemicals branch of the industry received any significant investment. Basic chemicals therefore experienced most of the industry's total growth, and the Soviet Union actually led most of the European nations in this limited group of products. Other important branches of the chemical industry suffered badly, however; production of synthetic materials (with the exception of synthetic rubber) was negligible, and even fertilizer output remained inadequate. Only the most rudimentary organic chemicals were made, and these principally from food sources. Oddly for a country short of food, huge amounts of potatoes were used to make industrial alcohol.

Following Stalin's death feverish efforts have been made to catch up, and massive investments have been allocated to the chemical industry. It has recently experienced a rapid growth mainly based on petrochemicals. The chemical industry is much too complex for forced development, however, and the Soviet Union still lags far behind the rest of the technically advanced world in this respect. Indeed, most types of chemical output are growing much faster in Western Europe, the United States, and Japan than in the USSR, although the latter is now doing very well with synthetic fibers and chemical fertilizers. Thus, even with a single industry such as chemicals there is still much unevenness of development.

In addition to distortions such as these, the economy is being held back by gross misallocations of labor. Considering the way in which investment capital has been allotted, it seems paradoxical for industry to be experiencing a growing shortage of labor while agriculture remains greatly overstaffed. Even more surprising is the fact that, after more than half a century of deprivation, Soviet agriculture provides a total output that compares much more favorably with that of the United States than does the output of Soviet industry. Recent estimates indicate that total farm production in the USSR is about three-fourths that of the United States, while total nonfarm production is only half U.S. output.

regional disparities

Another unexpected form of economic imbalance, considering Communist views on the subject, is the problem of depressed areas in the Soviet Union. Even though this is regarded as a capitalistic problem not to be tolerated in a Communistic state, some parts of the USSR are lagging badly and some are decidedly backward. The problem is found in both the European and Asiatic parts of the country. Examples of the former are Belorussia, Lithuania, eastern Latvia, and the western Ukraine. These regions all have large, mainly rural populations, and each experienced retarded growth under Stalin. Similarly, much of Soviet Central Asia and the southern portion of Kazakhstan have had rapid population growth but have fallen behind the rest of the country in their development. Among their many problems are isolation from the center of national activity, the lack of agglomeration advantages for many forms of industry, and a number of cultural disadvantages of the labor force.

In addition to these areas, there are vast and remote reaches of the Soviet Union where negative environment and extreme isolation have thus far prevented modernization. On the deserts, steppes, high mountains, and endless expanses of northern coniferous forest and Arctic tundra are tribal folk still striving for a meager subsistence from nomadic herding, hunting and gathering, and primitive agriculture.

trade problems

Before World War II and until Stalin's death, the Soviet Union had virtually achieved its goal of autarky. However, some trade developed with the client states in Eastern Europe and, for a time, with China. These exchanges were intended to help solidify and develop the Communist economies of those countries and thus tighten political control. A certain amount of trade has taken place with underdeveloped nations, often with the aim of propagating the Communist ideology. Trade with non-Communist technically advanced nations served as an outlet for planning overruns and a means for relieving unexpected shortfalls. The Soviet Union has also imported machinery and other needed producer goods from these latter countries.

From the standpoint of orthodox trade theory (Chapter 10), the Soviet policy of autarky has exacted a high cost from the national economy. It has prevented the nation from obtaining goods in each case from the cheapest producer. It has also fostered inefficient domestic production of many goods that could have been imported more cheaply.

the problem of sustaining momentum

Of all the questions confronting the Soviet Union's leaders today, perhaps the most compelling is the problem of declining growth in the gross national product. The high rates of increase following World War II, particularly during the 1950s when for a time growth very nearly reached 10 percent per year, caused great satisfaction in the Soviet Union and much uneasiness among her rivals. The rate has been slipping since, however, falling to 4 percent in the 1960s, to 3.5 percent in 1971, and to only 1.5 percent in 1972.

This growth rate is lower than that of most other advanced countries and far below Japan's rate of growth. The Soviet leadership is understandably distressed since it casts doubt on the Marxist growth formula. Moreover, the low growth rate leaves the USSR at a stage of development that is now reckoned to be about on a par with that of Italy. The two countries have had similar per capita outputs for the past decade.

roots of the problem

Part of the growth problem has to do with the Soviet Union's current labor situation. The developing shortage of industrial labor is a serious matter, since the country's economic growth has been based heavily upon an ever-increasing labor supply. Between 1950 and 1970 the labor force increased by almost 28 percent: from 97 million workers to 124 million. Three-fifths of this additional 27 million consisted of women, many former housewives. With 92 percent of the eligible population either working or going to school full time, the labor participation rate is already exceptionally high (the present United States participation rate is only slightly more than three-fourths, and a far higher proportion of that number is in school). Consequently little room remains for further increases in the number of workers.

An alternative way of approaching the problem is to increase output per worker, but the Soviet Union's recent experience with labor productivity has been disappointing. Although productivity rose quickly during the early 1950s, it began to slacken later in that decade and during the 1960s it slipped further. This failure to increase labor productivity has occurred despite heavy investments in machinery. Even so, Soviet mechanization is still well below that of the United States, especially in the use of computer controls. Indeed, analyses of this problem indicate that for some reason the USSR has a very low elasticity of substitution of capital for labor in comparison with the United States. In other words, each additional ruble spent on new machinery contributes less than it should to reducing man-hour requirements.

The Soviet Union uses its labor inefficiently in both industry and agriculture. Factories assign large numbers of their workers to nonproductive supporting roles. There are many instances where employees are put to work at jobs other than those for which they have received extensive training. The problem is at its worst in agriculture, which employs more than one-third of the total work force despite the fact that the Soviet Union manufactures more tractors than the United States.

Although a major part of the country's industrial capacity has been reserved for making producer goods and munitions, it seems likely that the point has now been reached where growth based on capital goods will experience diminishing returns. The goal of military parity with the United States having been reached, further growth based on munitions appears improbable. Yet the private consumer is still deprived of many of his needs and wants.

defective planning and administration

These problems partly stem from inept planning and management. Although the Communist theory of growth has its builtin distortions, the Soviet bureaucracy has not done very well in applying this philosophy. Much of this can be blamed on Stalin, who kept important decisions to himself and punished or purged innovative planners and managers. This stultified initiative and turned the surviving planners and managers into mere yes-men. The rigidity and conservatism of its administrative hierarchy has cost the Soviet Union many opportunities for improving the system.

Aside from the qualities of the managerial group, there is much evidence that the Soviet Union is confronted with problems of entrepreneural capacity similar to those sometimes experienced by very large corporations in the capitalistic world. Centralized decision making tends to reach the limits of human capacity for comprehension when the system grows increasingly complex. The Soviet economy has evolved into a huge and very ponderous machine, requiring decisions that have become incredibly numerous, varied, and complex. An undertaking of such magnitude would cause such problems under any circumstances, but the Soviet system provides no realistic pricing mechanism to serve as an automatic check and guide. As a result, production norms must be expressed by planners in the form of gross indices, and plan-fulfillment has become an exercise in routinely trying to match targets. Added to this are horrendous planning mistakes, such as building huge industrial establishments to supply markets that do not exist and making vast investments in uneconomical locations.

the Soviet response

The slow growth rate, shortages (especially in agriculture), and consumer complaints have aroused concern among the country's leaders. They have responded by launching a number of initiatives affecting both the internal economy and the country's relations with the world at large.

domestic changes

From some of the new directions that are being prescribed for the Soviet economy, it would seem that the country's decision makers have been rethinking the Communist theory of growth. Orthodox notions concerning the apportioning of investments to producer and consumer goods are being reexamined, and technological progress is receiving more attention. Planners are starting to favor the "progressive" branches of manufacturing, regardless of sector. Such industries as aluminum, plastics, synthetics, and electronics are for the first time receiving priority treatment as the planning emphasis turns to relative potentials for growth.

New approaches to the processes of planning and administration are taking form. Former Premier Nikita Khrushchev had attempted to reform the system in 1957 but his impetuous schemes did not work. Since assuming control in 1965, his successors have subjected the problem to intensive study by thousands of experts, using a variety of econometric models to test alternative schemes. The results have begun to appear in a series of announcements by Soviet Party Leader Leonid I. Brezhnev and the official press. These were foreshadowed in 1971, but the details were not released until December 1972, and the following April. The announcements described a reorganization of the decision-making apparatus, economic structure, regionalization, and locational planning.

Particularly significant in this list of changes is the decentralization of control. Khrushchev had attempted to overcome the problems of excessive centralization by dismantling the central ministries, but he did not replace them with a workable substitute. The present leaders have announced the formation of large government corporations, or "industrial associations," which are to assume control gradually over a period ending in 1976. The associations represent a new intermediate administrative level between the central ministries and individual factory managements. The 33 Soviet ministries are to set overall policy and to provide guidance and supervision, but they are to relinquish most of the direct operational decision making. The USSR's 50,000 factories are to be combined into approximately 1,000 associations, which will assume responsibility for many of the decisions that had been delegated to individual factory directors in 1965. The latter are to be represented on the boards of their associations, however. This arrangement represents a compromise between centralized and decentralized control, a subject of much disagreement for years.

Each association is to be composed of related forms of production, and some are even to have their own research laboratories (state subsidized) and retail outlets. Most associations are to be regionally organized, with the headquarters located as close as possible to the centers of production. Some associations are to be nationwide, where, as in the case of petroleum refining, only a few large plants are involved. The associations are to have economic accountability, that is, they are to be financially self-supporting, turn a profit, pay taxes, and reinvest some of their proceeds. They are to draw up their own production plans, following ministry guidelines; but only the ministries are to assign suppliers and customers and make investment decisions. The associations are charged with controlling and improving product quality, developing new technology, and designing new export products. As this suggests, they are to have some ability to initiate foreign trade, although the Foreign Trade Ministry is still in charge. In preparation for this new arrangement the Soviet Union has for some time been conducting intensive training in management.

Complementing these changes is a massive experiment conducted to test the applicability of cybernetics to total social system transition in the USSR.

Effort has been addressed to automation, based upon the belief that such automation is required to achieve the organizational complexity necessary for social progress. The intent of the effort is to serve the perceived need for highly perfected systems of automatic control, and to this end cybernetics has been tied to the goal-seeking activity of the centrally directed state, linked as a science and technology to the concept of controlled social progress. Figure 18.6 depicts (in a very abbreviated form) the essential elements in the Soviet cybernetics program. The real world is made up of people, nations, factories, transportation systems, mines, and so on. Sensors are being developed to detect changes in each system in the real world. Comparators receive processed information and compare it with the kind

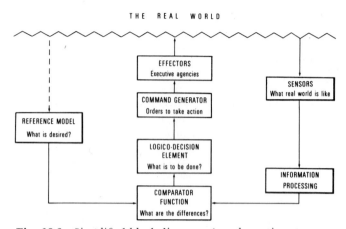

Fig. 18.6 *Simplified block diagram of a cybernetic system*

Source: Adapted from John J. Ford, "Soviet Cybernetics and International Development," in John Diebold, ed. The Social Impact of Cybernetics *(Lafayette, Ind.: Purdue University Press, 1966).*

of behavior called for by a reference model, which describes the devised goals. The results of the comparison are transmitted to the command element, which then decides whether to leave the real world as it is or whether commands should be transmitted to the effectors to change the behavior of the real world. If the latter course is elected, information about the ensuing change is sensed, processed, compared with the reference model and so on around the feedback loop.

The system will be made operational in the Unified Information Network of the USSR, scheduled for completion in 1970–1975. This is to be a "nervous system" tying together the systems' "sensors" of internal and external environments at all organizational levels with the highest decision centers. These can then determine optimal courses of action and transmit information to the effector organs of the social system-ministries, production complexes, schools, defense installations, and so on. The new behavior of the system is then transmitted to the decision makers, and new actions are undertaken in a continuous process analogous to that by which a helmsman steers a ship toward its destination.

Party Leader Brezhnev announced still another innovation, namely regrouping the nation's fifteen republics into seven large planning regions. The announced purposes of the change are (1) to coordinate planning and administration more efficiently, especially in implementing overall policies of national development extending to the year 1990; and (2) to shift emphasis from the narrow ethnic interests of the present republics to the national welfare, to generate a "Soviet" nationalism and pride that would replace ethnic loyalties.

A third initiative has been labeled *Genshema,* a general scheme for industrial location to the year 1980. Apparently Genshema is to base industrial location primarily on energy resources. This is reminiscent of the long-time orientation to coal, except in this case it is expected that by 1975 oil and gas will be contributing 76 percent of the energy supply. Nuclear energy is expected to have an important place also, seven large new nuclear power stations being specified in the general plan. Genshema is also stressing development of the northern regions of the Soviet Union closest to the United States manufacturing belt.

In the light of Communist growth theory the most radical set of changes has to do with recasting the structure of the Soviet economy. The ninth five-year plan explicitly emphasizes the needs of consumers. A major thrust of this plan is to provide more and better food and to make available a larger and more varied supply of consumer durables. It allocates larger sums for investment in agriculture, especially for feed grains and meat animals, with a view to increasing the level of animal protein in the Soviet diet. The food industry is to be expanded by the building of new processing plants. The Soviet Union's large imports of food and feed grains during recent years of crop failure is an indication of the leadership's resolve to maintain the country's food supply regardless of natural calamities.

The current five-year plan specifies substantially increased output of a number of consumer durable goods. Among these are common household appliances that had not previously been made and sold in the Soviet Union. The most vigorous efforts have gone into increasing the production of passenger cars. A new factory at Togliatti on the Volga River has been built under an agreement with Fiat of Italy, and overtures were made to the Ford Motor Company to secure assistance in expanding truck output. Attention is also going to consumer services, which have been notoriously slow and of poor quality. Planning officials authorized self-service stores in 1972 and have promised to add other services. The country will have to make major commitments to the service sector if only to prepare for the widespread ownership of private cars, since maintenance and repair services, spare parts distribution, and suitable highways are virtually lacking at this time.

The new five-year plan also attacks the center-periphery problem. It favors the poorer regions in the location of growth industries, especially chemicals, which are currently being introduced in backward sections of Belorussia, the Baltic Republics, and the western Ukraine. In this respect the Soviet Union is closely following the lead of Britain's development area policy. Finally, the USSR has joined the growing campaign among technically advanced countries to improve the quality of the environment. An example of this is the placing of pollution controls on industries that had been dumping refuse in Lake Baykal.

shifts in foreign economic relations

To make the radical transformation required for the Soviet economy to shift from producer to consumer goods would be a difficult and slow process under most conditions. It is especially so in a centrally planned system lacking the direct interplay of demand and supply. These difficulties seem to have been recognized by the Soviet leaders, who have found a quick solution at hand. Abandoning their autarky policy of more than half a century, they have turned to trade with other industrialized countries. Trade offers the opportunity to achieve a new structure of consumption more quickly and cheaply than by tooling up for domestic production.

This appears to underly the Soviet economic rapprochement with the United States, Western Europe, and Japan, which took place in a series of dramatic diplomatic and economic developments commencing in 1971 and 1972. One of the first results of this Soviet opening to the West was the USSR's agreement to purchase $750 million worth of grains from the United States. Other large purchases followed and a comprehensive trade agreement between the two countries was concluded in October 1972, to be followed the next year by further agreements.

The USSR's import needs are very great and exceedingly diverse. It is expected that the country will be importing new agricultural technology, specialized types of farm machinery, farm storage equipment, and food-processing equipment and technology. The recent agreement to permit production of Pepsi-Cola in the Soviet Union is a sample of the arrangements that can be anticipated. Other forms of production technology for consumer goods are to be imported, and several agreements are being negotiated with American, European, and Japanese concerns.

To pay for this great flow of imports the Soviet Union needs to develop new exports. Until recently the country has had a negative trade balance with the West. Several likely prospects suggest themselves. The Soviet Union has become a low-cost producer of certain types of machinery, which would seem to find ready sales abroad. Unfortunately Soviet machines do not meet the quality standards prevailing in the West; indeed most of the USSR's manufactured goods suffer from this disadvantage in competing with Western products. As the country participates more widely in the international economy this problem may be solved in time. Meanwhile the best hope for the present seems to lie in exports of fossil fuels, especially oil and gas, nonferrous and alloy metals, pig iron, steel ingots, and sheet and structural steels. Shipments of some of these are already finding their way into Western markets. The Soviet Union has set up a special fund to develop new export products to be added to this list. Meanwhile, rising prices for the nation's mineral products, including gold, have at least temporarily brought the USSR's foreign trading account into better balance.

The reorganization of planning and administration in the USSR apparently leaves the central Ministry of Trade in basic control of foreign commerce. It provides, however, a limited foreign trade role for the new industrial associations. Border regions are already permitted a certain amount of independent barter trade with their near neighbors. The Baltic republics and Leningrad trade with Finland under such an arrangement, and the maritime territory of the Soviet Far East has formed similar ties with Japan.

a perspective on Soviet growth

Despite uniquely varied resource endowments and centralized control of the economy, the Soviet Union has not been able to escape the problems of lagging growth and spatial inequality confronting countries with fewer resources and different political systems. The USSR's difficulty in maintaining forward economic momentum is a problem encountered earlier by the United Kingdom and more recently by Canada and Japan; the Soviet Union's regional disparities are also much like those of the other three. Moreover, the Communist strategy of unbalanced growth has produced a number of structural problems not duplicated in non–Marxist countries.

For the first time in the nation's history, however, the Soviet leadership seems to be attacking all these problems in a direct and comparatively realistic fashion. Without abandoning the basic features of the command economy, the nation's pragmatic rulers have not hesitated to relax some of the more rigid tenets of pure Marxist doctrine or to borrow from the experience of the non-Communist West.

RECOMMENDED READINGS

Clark, M. Gardner, *The Economics of Soviet Steel*. Cambridge, Mass.: Harvard University Press, 1956.

Harris, Chauncy D., *Cities of the Soviet Union*. AAG Monograph Series No. 5. Washington: Association of American Geographers, 1972.

Lydolph, Paul E., *Geography of the USSR*. New York: John Wiley, 1965.

Nove, Alec, *An Economic History of the USSR*. London: Penguin, 1969.

Nutter, G. Warren, *Growth of Industrial Production in the Soviet Union*. National Bureau of Economic Research. Princeton, N.J.: Princeton University Press, 1962.

Shabad, Theodore, *Basic Industrial Resources of the USSR*. New York: Columbia University Press, 1969.

If one theme has emerged more clearly than any other in the preceding case studies, it is one of growth. The post–World War II period, with its closer international economic cooperation and freer international trade, has been one of strong and relatively steady growth for the world's heartland countries. Most have sustained faster growth rates than their long-term averages, whether measured as a national aggregate or weighted per capita. Differences between growth rates also have been very large. Japan, for instance, averaged annual rates of real gross national product of 9.6 for the period 1955–1965 compared with the United Kingdom's 3.1 (Fig. 19.1). Compounded over a number of years, such differences become a serious concern to both heartland and hinterland countries whose growth rates, however rapid, have lagged behind the leaders. What has caused the differences? To answer this, let us now formalize and quantify the regional comparisons.

THE DENISON MODEL

One of the most notable approaches to evaluating the determinants of growth is that of the American economist, Edward F. Denison. His 1962 study, *The Sources of Economic Growth in the United States and the Alternatives Before Us,* has been recognized as a landmark in the quantitative analysis of economic growth. Deni-

Fig. 19.1 *Growth rates of national income, 1950–1962. Japanese data are real GNP for 1955–1965, other countries are real national income for 1950–1962.*

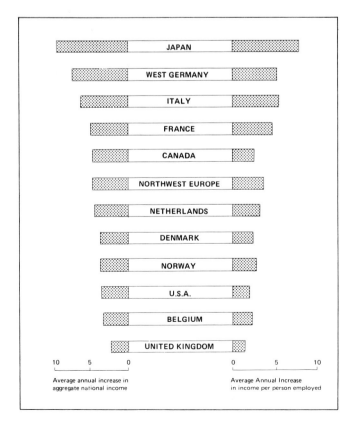

JAPAN

WEST GERMANY

ITALY

FRANCE

CANADA

NORTHWEST EUROPE

NETHERLANDS

DENMARK

NORWAY

U.S.A.

BELGIUM

UNITED KINGDOM

10   5   0   0   5   10

Average annual increase in aggregate national income

Average Annual Increase in income per person employed

determinants of growth in the heartland economies: the denison model

19

Table 19.1   Indexes of Real National Income, International Comparison: 1960 (United States = 100)

| | INDEXES BASED ON U.S. PRICE WEIGHTS | | | | INDEXES BASED ON NATIONAL EUROPEAN PRICE WEIGHTS | | | |
	Total	Per capita	Per person in the labor force	Per person employed	Total	Per capita	Per person in the labor force	Per person employed
United States	100.0	100	100	100	100.0	100	100	100
Northwest Europe	70.1	69	62	59	54.6	54	48	46
Belgium	3.1	61	63	61	2.7	53	54	53
Denmark	1.8	71	60	58	1.4	55	47	45
France	16.7	66	62	59	13.0	51	48	46
Germany	22.3	73	62	59	17.2	56	47	45
Netherlands	3.9	61	67	65	2.9	45	50	48
Norway	1.3	64	62	59	1.0	48	47	45
United Kingdom	21.0	72	61	59	16.5	57	48	46
Italy	11.9	43	41	40	7.1	26	25	24

Source: Edward F. Denison, assisted by Jean-Pierre Poullier, *Why Growth Rates Differ—Post-War Experience in Nine Western Countries* (Washington: Brookings Institution, 1967), p. 22; reprinted in D.J. Daly, "Why Growth Rates Differ—a Summary and Appraisal," *Review of Income and Wealth* Series 14, No. 1 (March 1968), 75-93.

son also applied his methodology to eight Western European countries in *Why Growth Rates Differ*. Dorothy Walters subsequently applied it to Canada, and Hisao Kanamori to Japan. It is currently being applied to other countries, including the USSR, but results in these other cases are not yet available.

facts on income levels and growth rates

Denison's analysis began with the measurement of real income per capita, using data on net national income totals adjusted to improve international comparability and on population, labor force and employment, and the relative purchasing power in the different countries. These last data are the weakest especially because of marked differences in relative prices of similar products in the different countries. Thus, automobile prices are relatively higher in Europe than other consumer prices compared with the United States and Canada, and the quantities purchased represent a smaller share of total consumer expenditure. By contrast, food expenditures are a much larger part of total expenditures in Europe than in the United States. These cases are typical of the contrast between the relative prices of manufactured goods and mechanized services as opposed to unprocessed foods and personal services between Europe and the United States. Thus, European price weights applied to the United States widen real income differences; United States price weights applied to Europe narrow them (Table 19.1). But the differences are large, whichever set is used. National income per person employed in northwest Europe was 41 percent lower than in the United States in 1960 using U.S. price weights. However, the difference has been narrowing in the postwar years, because United States growth rates are below those in northwest Europe, Italy, and Canada (Fig. 19.1). Denison asked why differences in income levels and economic growth

rates had occurred, and whether the United States could have been expected to do better. The first step in answering these questions was a sound classification of the determinants of growth.

quantity of factor inputs versus efficiency of factor use

Denison's model was based on meticulous examination and classification of the sources of growth.

The most fundamental distinction was provided by grouping all individual determinants of growth into two sets: growth due to increases in the *absolute levels* of the factors of production; and growth due to the *increasing efficiency* with which these resources are used and combined. Denison found that a country's production may grow mainly because the labor force and capital inputs increase, as in Canada, or because of increasing efficiency with which these factors are used, as in the countries of northwest Europe (Fig. 19.2). In northwest Europe, 3.1 percentage points, or two-thirds of the total growth rate of 4.8 percent arose from gains in the efficiency of resource use, the highest figure of 4.5 being for Germany and the lowest figure of 1.2 for the United Kingdom (Table 19.2). In Canada, only 2.1 percentage points arose from this source, and in the U.S. only 1.4. Conversely, 2.7 percentage points of the Canadian growth rate arose from increased inputs of labor and capital, compared with 1.9 in the United States and 1.7 in northwest Europe. Put another way, 60 percent of the economic growth in North America was produced by using more inputs and 40 percent by using inputs more efficiently. In Europe, on the other hand, the relative importance of quantity and efficiency was reversed. Only 40 percent of the growth was due to additional inputs of labor and capital and 60 percent to more efficient use of labor and capital inputs.

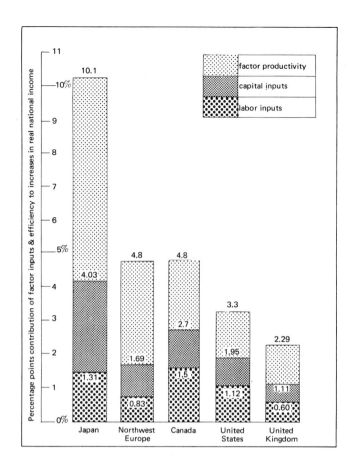

Fig. 19.2 *The contribution of labor inputs, capital inputs, and factor productivity to growth of real national income, 1950–1962. Data for Japan's real national income are from 1955–1968.*

Table 19.2 Contributions of Factor Inputs and Factor Productivity to Growth of National Income: 1950–1962

	CANADA	UNITED STATES	NORTHWEST EUROPE	UNITED KINGDOM	JAPAN
Average annual percentage increase in real national income	4.8	3.3	4.8	2.3	10.1
Contribution of:		*Percentage points*			
Total factor inputs	2.7	1.9	1.7	1.1	4.0
Labor	1.5	1.1	.8	.6	1.3
Employment	1.5	.9	.7	.5	1.0
Education	.3	.5	.2	.3	0.1
Age-sex composition	−.1	−.1	−	−	0.2
Hours of work	−.2	−.2	−.1	−.2	−0.1
Capital and land	1.2	.8	.9	.5	2.7
Enterprise capital	.9	.6	.8	.5	2.6
Residential capital	.3	.2	.1	−	0.1
Factor productivity	2.1	1.4	3.1	1.2	6.1
Resource shifts	.7	.3	.7	.1	n.a.
Economies of scale	.6	.4	.9	.4	n.a.
Other	.8	.7	1.5	.7	n.a.

Notes: Percentage points are the actual percentage increase in real national income contributed by each determinant. They are not to be confused with the percentage of the total increase contributed by the determinant. Thus total factor inputs in Canada contributed $\frac{2.7}{4.8} \times 100$ or 56 percent of the total increase in real national income.

Percentage points may not total national average percentage increases in real national income because of rounding.

Sources: Denison, *Growth Rates,* Tables 21-1 to 21-19, pp. 298–316; Walters, *Canadian Growth Rates,* p. 37; and Hisao Kanamori, "What Accounts for Japan's High Rate of Growth," *Review of Income and Wealth,* Series 18, No. 2 (June 1972), 157.

Table 19.3 Percentage Contribution of Factors of Production to National Income: 1950–1962

Net national income	CANADA 100.0%	UNITED STATES 100.0%	NORTHWEST EUROPE 100.0%	NORWAY 100.0%	UNITED KINGDOM 100.0%
Labor income	75.3	78.6	75.8	74.1	77.8
Income from housing	3.9	3.5	1.7	1.0	2.2
Income on foreign investments	−1.8	0.6	0.6	−0.8	1.8
Other property income	22.7	17.3	21.9	25.7	18.2
Nonresidential land	3.7	2.9	3.9	4.6	2.9
Nonresidential structures and equipment	14.3	11.2	14.0	16.4	11.9
Inventories	4.7	3.2	4.0	4.7	3.4

Note: The factors of production contribute a larger share to net national income than they do to the *increase* in net national income. Thus, increasing factor inputs in Canada, which earn 100 percent of net national income, contributed 56 percent of the increase in net national income, 1950–1962. The remaining 44 percent was contributed by increasing efficiency in the use of factor inputs.

Source: Dorothy Walters, *Canadian Income Levels and Growth: An International Perspective* (Ottawa: Economic Council of Canada Staff Study No. 23, 1968), p. 29.

These disparities between northwest Europe and North America have frequently given rise to the notion that North American growth can be accelerated by emulating northwest Europe. The truth is much more complex, however. Growth performance involves many components that vary among countries over time. More detailed classification and analysis of the determinants of growth suggested that northwest Europe began the 1950s with much lower outputs per employed person and that the greater contribution of efficiency to growth represented in part a narrowing of the gap between North America and northwest Europe, as we shall now see.

THE CLASSIFICATION AND CONTRIBUTION OF INDIVIDUAL GROWTH DETERMINANTS

classification of labor inputs

The sheer size of the labor force was the prime variable explaining levels of output in all countries, Denison found. In the countries analyzed, labor earned 70 to 80 percent of the national income (Table 19.3). Considerable variations in the composition of the labor force are evident, however, among heartland countries. For example, the proportion of the labor force employed on a part-time basis and the hours worked by full-time and part-time employees help govern the effective size of the labor force. More important, however, these factors affect the quality of work performed. The age and sex composition, the proportion of the labor force in the armed services, the education level, and many other characteristics also affect the quality of the labor force and, hence, productivity. Denison's study involved a very careful evaluation of all these aspects of the labor force, omitting only those characteristics that do not vary appreciably among the heartland countries; or over time within them; those that affect individuals or groups within countries rather than differences in labor productivity among countries; and those that

could not be quantified, however plausible they might be. Of all the aspects examined, two were particularly important: size of the labor force and education levels.

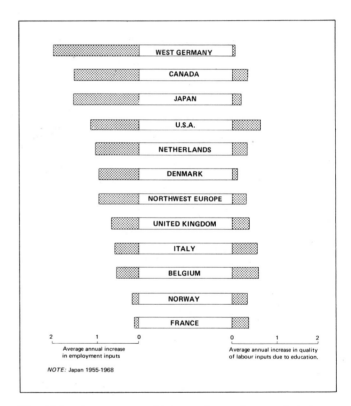

Fig. 19.3 *Average annual increase in employment inputs and in educational level of labor force, 1950–1962*

the size of the labor force

The labor force of the seven northwest European countries substantially exceeded that of the United States in the postwar years partly because of a larger population and partly because a much higher proportion of the population was gainfully employed. In 1960 the percent of population employed was 44.8 in northwest Europe compared with 38.3 percent in the United States. The difference was made up of a higher labor force participation rate (4.9 percentage points) and lower unemployment rates in northwest Europe (1.6 points). The higher labor force participation rates in turn result from the larger proportion of the population in the working age category and higher female participation in northwest Europe. The total labor force has been increasing more rapidly in both the United States and Canada than in northwest Europe, however (Fig. 19.3). Much of the United States increase is accounted for by growth in the numbers of female and part-time workers, in contrast to northwest Europe, where female participation was already at a high level and part-time work is less common.

quality of the labor force

The larger absolute size of the labor force of northwest Europe is offset by the higher quality of American labor, especially in education. Improvements in education are associated not only with shifts in the occupational structure of the labor force toward higher-grade occupations but, more importantly, with improving the quality of the work performed within any given occupation. Furthermore, a better-educated labor force is more likely to be geographically mobile—again increasing productivity—and may also improve the technical and managerial practices in a country. Advances in technology and management, however, constitute an independent and actually more important determinant of growth than advances in the education level of the labor force.

There are major contrasts in the educational profiles of the United States and northwest Europe (Table 19.4). In all European countries, a comparatively large proportion of the new additions to the labor force consists of young persons near the minimum legal working age. In North America, new additions to the

labor force are more evenly distributed among the age groups, since relatively more people, especially in the United States, complete secondary school and university before seeking employment. The contribution of education to improvements in the quality of the labor force and differences in this quality among different countries involves a number of difficult questions. How is each educational level of the labor force distributed among the different labor force categories—civilian and military, male and female, and agricultural and nonagricultural? How are years of education to be weighted to provide a single index applicable to all countries? Denison finally produced two different indexes, one based on number of school years completed and, because there are international differences in school starting age, another based on age of school-leaving. Either way, the educational level of the labor force in the northwest European countries and in Italy indexed much lower than that in the United States. Thus the labor force in Italy had an education quality index of 79.7 and northwest Europe 93.3 in 1960, based on years of school completed and a United States index value of 100. These differences have important consequences for productivity. For instance, if the only difference between Italy and the United States were the educational level of the labor force, real national product would be 15 percent lower in Italy than in the United States.

Denison also concluded that between 1950 and 1962 the amount of full-time education received by the labor force increased in all the countries examined but that the amount of increase was greater in the United States than in northwest Europe, increasing the disparity in labor quality (Fig. 19.3). Furthermore, improvements in the educational level of the labor force contributed more aggregate economic growth to the United States than to northwest Europe, even though any given improvement in education in the United States evidently contributed less growth than the same improvement in northwest Europe (Table 19.2).

Summary measures of the labor input were computed by Denison taking into account employment, hours worked, the composition of the labor force and education levels (Table 19.5). The higher proportion of Europe's population employed was found to be sufficient to compensate for lower inputs per person employed and thus yielded higher labor input per capita than in the United States. But labor inputs in 1950–1962 increased more in the United States and Canada than in northwest Europe (Fig. 19.3).

land and capital

The remaining two factors of production, land and capital, earned a surprisingly small proportion of total national income, less than 25 percent in both the United States and northwest Europe, Denison found. Land's share was particularly small because only rents and similar payments count as returns on land itself as a factor of production, as we saw in Chapter 7.

| Table 19.4 | Percentage Distributions of the Male Labor Force by Years of School Completed (Five Countries at Selected Dates) |

YEARS OF SCHOOL COMPLETED	UNITED STATES (1957)	CANADA (1961)	FRANCE (1954)	UNITED KINGDOM (1951)	ITALY (1961)
0	1.4 ⎫ 7.5		.3	.2	13.7
1-4	5.7 ⎭		2.4	.2	26.1
5-6	6.3 ⎫ 20.8		19.2	.8	38.0
7	5.8 ⎭		21.1	4.0	4.2
8	17.2	17.6	27.8	27.2	8.1
9	6.3	11.1	4.6	45.1	.7
10	7.3	12.0	4.1	8.4	.7
11	6.0	6.6	6.5	7.3	.6
12	26.2	14.9	5.4	2.5	1.8
13-15	8.3	3.9	5.4	2.2	3.0
16 or more	9.5	5.6	3.2	2.1	3.1

Sources: Denison, *Growth Rates*, p. 80; and Walters, *Canadian Income Levels*, p. 55.

Table 19.5 Indexes of Labor Input, International Comparison: 1960 (United States=100)

AREA	TOTAL LABOR INPUT	LABOR INPUT PER PERSON EMPLOYED	LABOR INPUT PER CAPITA
United States	100.0	100.0	100.0
Canada	8.8	100.0	n.a.
Northwest Europe	115.3	97.7	114.2
Belgium	4.9	97.9	97.6
Denmark	2.9	94.2	115.4
France	27.6	97.9	109.1
Germany	36.0	94.8	117.2
Netherlands	6.6	110.0	103.6
Norway	2.1	100.6	108.1
United Kingdom	35.2	98.6	121.0
Italy	26.2	89.1	95.5

Sources: Denison, *Growth Rates,* p. 115; and Walters, *Canadian Income Levels,* p. 67.

Rental income on nonresidential land and natural resources (i.e., returns to land as a factor of production) varied from 3 percent of national income in the United States to 4.6 percent in Norway (Table 19.3). There was little change in the amount of agricultural land in use from 1950 to 1962, with the biggest change in the United States, where agricultural land decreased 3.3 percent from 1950 to 1959. But the contrasts among land area and mineral production per person employed in Canada, the United States, and northwest Europe are very marked (Table 19.6). The weighting used by Denison in computing relative contribution of land to net national income was 73 for business-site land, 17 for farmland, and 10 for mineral land. Large disparities in land resources are translated into rather small contributions to the gaps in net national income per person employed. Land narrowed the Canada–United States income gap by 0.6 percentage points. It

increased the gap by 0.5 percentage points for northwest Europe, a very small figure considering the 41-point percentage gap in income per person employed.

Even the new oil and natural gas discoveries in Europe during the period analyzed did not have a large impact on growth rates. Their precise impact is the difference between production and import costs weighted by the value of fuel measured as a proportion of national income. Increased production of crude petroleum and natural gas equaled 16 percent of apparent 1962 energy consumption in Italy. If this increase were entirely due to new discoveries, if fuel costs equaled 4 percent of national income and the savings in the fuel costs were 50 percent, the contribution to growth would be 0.05 percentage points a year in Italy. The figure for Holland and France would be only half that for Italy.

In contrast to the small proportion of growth attributed to land, capital contributed 25 percent of the growth in the United States between 1950 and 1960, 27 percent in Canada, and 18 percent in Europe. In a number of countries in northwest Europe though, capital contributed more to economic growth than did labor—0.9 percentage points compared with 0.8 (Table 19.2).

The growth generated by investment was not exactly proportional to the rate of investment, however, although a general correspondence is evident (Fig. 19.4). Part of the difference among countries was due to the nature of the capital investments made. It is unlikely that investment in construction influences productivity the same way as does investment in equipment. In the case of Canada, for example, which has a particularly heavy proportion of its investment in construction, a higher rate of capital investment reflects in part the higher costs of doing business in a huge country with a low population density, a long severe winter, and a heavy emphasis on construction-intensive industries such as electric power and mining (Fig. 19.5).

Table 19.6 Land Area and Mineral Production Per Person Employed: 1960* (United States=100)

	LAND AREA PER PERSON EMPLOYED			VALUE IN $U.S. OF MINERAL PRODUCTION PER PERSON EMPLOYED	
	All land	*Arable land*	*Arable land adjusted†*	*Denison list*	*Expanded list*
Canada	1,213	226	199	134	171
United States	100	100	100	100	100
Northwest Europe	13	20	16	26	26
United Kingdom	7	11	9	26	26

*Land area data are from 1961 for Canada and 1958 for the United States.
†Includes one-third of permanent meadows and pastures.

Note: Dorothy Walters expanded the list of minerals considered by Denison to include minerals important in Canada but not in the Denison countries.

Source: Walters, *Canadian Income Levels,* p. 97.

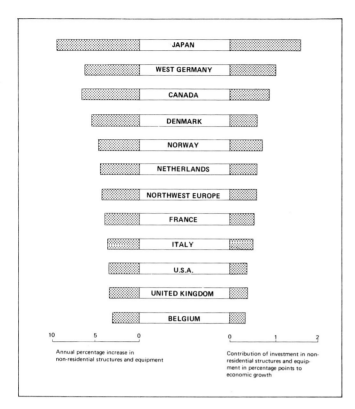

Fig. 19.4 *Increase in nonresidential structures and equipment and the contribution made to growth of a real national income, 1950–1962. Data for Japan are from 1955–1968.*

Fig. 19.5 *The percentage composition of total nonresidential investment*

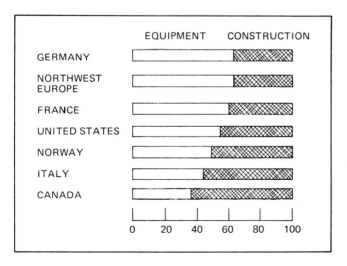

increasing efficiency in the use of factors of production

The second major group of growth determinants isolated by Denison made its contribution by increasing outputs per unit of input. Indeed, output per unit of input has contributed more to growth in all the individual European countries analyzed than have increases in factor inputs. Gains in efficiency have been lower in the United States, and lowest in the United Kingdom (Table 19.2). But even in the United States and Canada increasing efficiency has made substantial contributions to national economic growth.

The determinants of increasing efficiency are listed together with their actual contributions to growth in selected countries and regions in Table 19.7. They include the most important growth determinants of all: advances in knowledge related to technology, management, and organization; and lags in applying best knowledge. They also include two growth determinants, which, though smaller, go far toward explaining differences in postwar growth among heartland countries: improved allocation of resources and economies of scale.

Advances in knowledge and lags in applying it emerged in the Denison analysis as a single residual term because of the nature of national income measures. The output of service activity cannot be measured by any direct, concrete measure of production and so must be equated with input. An important contribution of new knowledge is the development of new products, but this contribution is impossible to isolate and measure because only those advances of knowledge that reduce the unit costs of products already in existence contribute to measured growth; and finally, in some countries the measured national income does not take into explicit account the development of new forms of business organization and their contribution to economic growth.

Knowledge and the level of best-practice technology, management, and organization differ even among the heartland countries because of the time taken for advances made in one country to diffuse to others, and because such advances are often more applicable in the country of origin than abroad.

The level of knowledge should probably be the same in all plants producing any given product within a country; but, in fact, there is a lag between best-practice and average-practice technology within countries, which has implications for national economic growth as well as for regional disparities. Adoption of new knowledge and techniques is often delayed to secure returns on existing durable capital equipment. In such circumstances, the flow of new techniques outstrips the flexibility of the system. For example, it took a decade and a half for the best-practice techniques in blast furnaces in the United States developed by the beginning of the century to be adopted throughout the country. If all plants had adopted best-practice technology immediately, labor productivity would have doubled.

Table 19.7   Sources of Increasing Output Per Unit of Input in the U.S.A., Canada, Northwest Europe, United Kingdom, and Italy: 1950–1962

SOURCES OF INCREASING OUTPUT PER UNIT OF OUTPUT	U.S.A.	CANADA	NORTHWEST EUROPE*	UNITED KINGDOM	ITALY
Total	**1.37%**	**2.1%**	**3.07%**	**1.18%**	**4.30%**
Advances of knowledge	.76	.6	.76	.76	.76
Changes in the lag in the application of knowledge, general efficiency, & errors & omissions					
Reduction in age of capital	–	–	.02	.00	.00
Other	–	–	.54	.03	.89
Improved allocation of resources					
Contraction of agricultural inputs	.25	.6	.46	.06	1.04
Contraction of nonagricultural self-employment	.04	.1	.14	.04	.22
Reduction of international trade barriers	.00	–	.08	.02	.16
Balancing of the capital stock	–	.3†	.08	–	–
Deflation procedures	–	–	.07	–	–
Economies of scale					
Growth of national market measured in U.S. prices	.30	.5	.41	.22	.55
Income elasticities	–	–	.46	.09	.60
Independent growth of the local markets	.06	.1	.06	.05	.07
Irregularities in pressure of demand	–.04	.1	–.01	–.09	–
Irregularities in agricultural output	–	–	.00	–	.01

*The Denison countries included in Northwest Europe are listed in Table 19.1.

†This is a statistical adjustment to include the amount by which the Canadian growth rate was increased by the use of productivity and profit-adjusted construction deflators. See Walters, *Canadian Growth Rates*, p. 37.

Note: Where a main growth determinant (shown in italics) is subdivided into its component parts, the contribution of the component parts *only* is given. The columns thus add up to the total, ± rounding error. This procedure explains the blanks for *Changes in lag* and *Improved allocation*.

Sources: Denison, *Growth Rates*, Tables 21–1 to 21–19, pp. 298–316 and Dorothy Walters, *Canadian Growth Levels Revisited, 1950–1967* (Ottawa: Economic Council of Canada, Staff Study No. 28, 1967) p. 37.

There is no doubt that the lag between best-practice and average-practice technology is much greater in northwest Europe than in the United States. Denison's analysis suggested that the lag has failed to narrow, except in France and perhaps Italy.

Improved allocation of resources, particularly labor shifts out of agriculture and self-employment, have varied considerably in their contribution to growth, the smallest contributions being in the United Kingdom, and by far the largest in Italy (Fig. 19.6). Agricultural employment was still considerable in many heartland countries in 1950, and there would have been little loss in agricultural output even if many farmers had left agriculture. Overallocation to agriculture and self-employment still explain most of the difference between Italy and northwest Europe in output per unit of total input, and large differences still exist in farm employment as a percentage of total employment (Fig. 19.7).

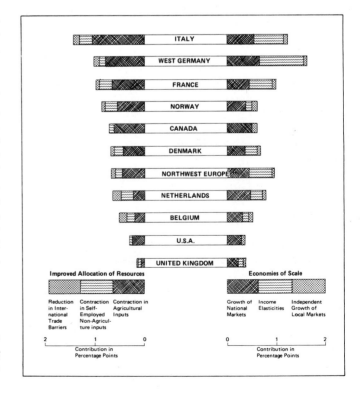

Fig. 19.6 *The contribution of improved allocation of resources and of economies of scale to growth of real national income, 1950–1962*

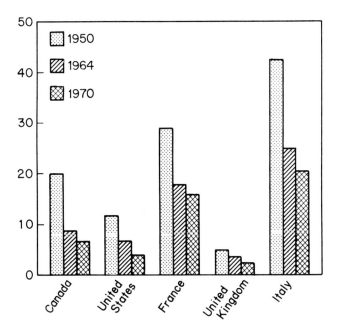

Fig. 19.7 *Farm employment as a percentage of total employment*

Another determinant that has contributed substantially to disparities in the postwar growth performance of heartland countries is economies of scale. Economies of scale are hard to measure and comprise several components that Denison groups into growth of national market, income elasticities, and independent growth of local markets.

The fast-growth European countries were in an unusually favorable position to benefit from economies of scale in the 1950s and 1960s. Their production levels of automobiles and other income-elastic consumer products was low in the early 1950s and rose more than proportionately with rising incomes. It is precisely in the early stages of production increase from low-volume to high-volume that economies of scale are largest and make their greatest contribution to economic growth. Furthermore the necessary technology did not have to be developed but could be borrowed from the United States or was introduced directly by American firms themselves.

Rapid urbanization and changes in shopping behavior associated with increasing automobile ownership have made an independent contribution to economies of scale. It appears that the contribution to growth made by this factor 1950 to 1962 has been the same in Europe as in the United States and much smaller than the contribution made by market growth (Table 19.7). But added together, the contributions made by all components of economies of scale are impressive. For example, they contributed .93 percentage points (.41 + .46 + .06, Table 19.7) to northwest Europe's growth which, without this contribution, would have been 3.85 percent instead of 4.78 percent. The contribution to growth in the United States was only half as great, and not much greater in Canada.

INTERREGIONAL CONTRASTS IN POSTWAR GROWTH PERFORMANCE

The main findings of the Denison model can best be summarized by interregional comparisons of postwar growth performance. Denison was particularly concerned with a comparison of the European and United States experience. Other researchers have used his model to assess the performance of Canada and Japan.

United States net national income grew more slowly than northwest Europe's between 1950 and 1962, averaging 3.32 per year compared to 4.78. But there was a 5-percentage point spread within northwest Europe, with Germany achieving a growth rate of 7.26 percent and the United Kingdom only 2.29. These measures say nothing, however, about the contribution made by the individual growth determinants or how well national economies performed when allowance is made for their different circumstances.

Ranking the determinants in order of importance shows the typical sequence in contributing to growth per person employed:

1. advances in knowledge;
2. capital investment in nonresidential structures and equipment;
3. contraction in agricultural inputs;
4. economies of scale: growth in national markets.

For aggregate national income the sequence is mixed, with advances in knowledge and employment growth vying for first place, nonresidential structures and reduced agricultural inputs vying for third place. But the rank-order contribution to growth of these determinants for northwest Europe and the United States is quite different except for the predominant contribution of advances in knowledge.

Three determinants, all involving increase in factor inputs, contributed substantially more to total economic growth in the United States than in northwest Europe: employment, education, and housing (Table 19.2). Northwest Europe's faster growth rate was primarily due to increasing efficiency in use of factors, including a better allocation of resources, particularly the contraction of agricultural inputs and nonagricultural self-employment, and economies of scale, particularly the growth of national markets. But northwest Europe also achieved more growth from capital inputs into nonresidential structures and equipment. But it was a case of Europe catching up rather than the United States falling behind. Denison ended his very detailed summary with an epilogue for American readers in which he says that Europe should continue to narrow the income gap between the two regions in the years ahead:

The conclusion, I believe, is clear. Although most of the European countries have achieved higher growth rates than the United States, this was not because they were doing more to obtain growth. They were able to secure higher growth rates only because they were operating in a different environment. Conditions were very different with respect to factor proportions; to misallocation of resources; to the existing level of technology, management, and general efficiency in the use of resources; and to economies of scale. Some have supposed that the United States could have matched the growth rates of European countries if only Americans had done as the Europeans did. I conclude that this is simply not so.

Comparisons with the postwar growth rates of European countries, therefore, do not provide grounds for dissatisfaction with the American growth record. The point needs stressing because the conditions that enabled Europe to obtain higher growth rates are not exhausted. Aside from short-term aberrations Europe should be able to report higher growth rates, at least in national income per person employed, for a long time. Americans should expect this and not be disturbed by it. Nothing in this analysis suggests that the conditions making for higher European growth would continue to operate if the European countries were to reach American levels of national income per person employed. (Edward F. Denison, assisted by Jean-Pierre Poullier, *Why Growth Rates Differ— Postwar Experience in Nine Western Countries*. Washington: Brookings Institution, 1967, p. 344.)

United Kingdom compared with northwest Europe

Similar considerations apply in comparing the United Kingdom's growth performance with that of northwest Europe. From the Denison model the United Kingdom appears to have had the worst of both worlds: on those determinants where Europe lagged behind the United States, the United Kingdom tended to match the European performance; on those determinants where Europe did better than the United States, the United Kingdom tended to match U.S. performance. This is true in the case of both factor inputs and increasing efficiency although it was the latter determinants that contributed most of the U.K.-Northwest Europe growth differential (Tables 19.2 and 19.7).

Consider the two factor inputs that differed most between Europe and the United States: employment growth and capital investments in nonresidential structures and equipment. These two contributed the bulk of the factor input differences in growth between the U.K. and northwestern Europe. Thus employment growth, which contributed less to growth in Europe than in the United States, contributed even less to that of the United Kingdom, and capital investment, which contributed more to Europe's growth than to the United States', contributed much less to the United Kingdom's.

Most of the growth differential between the United Kingdom and Europe was due to the very small increase in efficiency of factor use in the U.K., including contraction in agricultural inputs, contraction of non-agricultural self-employment, and growth of national markets. On these three determinants which contributed so much to the northwest Europe-United States growth differential, U.K. performance is below or equal to that of the United States.

But it could be argued that the United Kingdom was the victim of circumstances and that the other northwest European countries had easier opportunities to grow. For instance, the United Kingdom had the smallest decline in farm employment of any of the countries analyzed, from only 5.4 percent to 3.9 percent 1950 to 1962. But the economic growth achieved in different countries by reducing the agricultural labor force in agriculture reflected the degree of initial over-allocation of labor to agriculture rather than the degree of success in curtailing it. Reallocation of agricultural inputs in the United Kingdom had virtually reached the limit and the agricultural percentage of the labor force was by far the lowest of any of the countries. And again, self-employed and family workers constituted the smallest fraction of nonfarm employment in the United Kingdom of any country analyzed and it gained the least from reallocation of labor out of these groups because it had the least misallocation to eliminate. A failure to benefit from economies of scale also afflicted the United Kingdom. Slow growth inhibits gains from economies of scale. Furthermore, Britain was faced with economic retrenchment from the wider Commonwealth system to the new "mini-Britain."

The story is the same for factor inputs. West Germany's employment growth was remarkable due to the flight of refugees from East Germany, immigration from other countries, and sharply falling unemployment. But Germany's labor force participation rates were not appreciably greater than the United Kingdom's in 1960, and if the United Kingdom's labor force grew more slowly than did that of Western Europe, it was because it started at a higher level.

Denison's conclusions on the difficult subject of nonresidential structures and equipment are less certain, but Britain did invest a lower average annual percentage of GNP to this sector than any country, 11.7 percent compared with Germany's 16.8 and Norway's 24.1. And the gap in net stock of enterprise structures and equipment between the United Kingdom and the other European countries widened. In comparing the United States and Western Europe Denison noted that investment in nonresidential structures and equipment was the one important area where the United States had done less to stimulate growth than did northwest Europe. The same may well be true of the United Kingdom and it also seems likely that unless its entry into the European Common Market creates new avenues for growth, it can expect its growth rate to continue to lag behind that of Western Europe.

Canada and the United States

The application of the Denison model to Canada's postwar growth was initiated by the economist Donald J. Daly. The results were presented by Dorothy Walters in an Economic Council of Canada Staff Study, *Canadian Income Levels and Growth,* in 1968, and the results were summarized the same year in the Fifth Annual Review of the Economic Council entitled *The*

Challenge of Growth and Change. The Economic Council noted the slow growth in the efficiency with which factor inputs were used 1950 to 1962 and once again emphasized the imperative requirement for strong and sustained increases in productivity, since a high rate of productivity growth is essential in the long run for increasing the standard of living of Canadians, and for achieving the country's economic and social goals.

Shortly after this study was completed, a revision of the national accounts and expenditures was published to bring the Canadian system closer to the revised international system established by the United Nations, while maintaining and extending that part of the framework that reflects the particular structural and institutional features of the Canadian economy. The new accounts indicated an upward revision of the growth of real GNP from 4.1 percent to 4.8 for 1950 to 1962, and of net national income from 3.8 to 4.8. Rerunning the Denison model indicated no change in the contribution of factor inputs; they remained at 2.7 percentage points. But the contribution of output per unit of factor input doubled from 1.1 to 2.1 percentage points as a result of the national account revisions. These results, presented by Dorothy Walters in a second Economic Council Staff Study, *Canadian Growth Revisited: 1950–1967,* were published in 1970.

The revised national accounts raised Canada's growth rate to the same level as that of northwest Europe, and in fact, careful comparison of the contribution to growth made by the various determinants suggests that Canada did about as well or better than northwest Europe on every determinant except "residual sources" of growth. Deleting this determinant would reduce northwest Europe's growth to 3.5 percent but Canada's to only 4.2. And it would reduce the contribution of output per unit of input in northwest Europe 1.8, only a little above Canada's 1.5. What are these residual determinants of growth? Denison included advances in knowledge, reduction in the age of capital, changes in the lag in the application of knowledge, general efficiency, and errors and omissions. With this one important exception, Canada, in complete contrast to the U.K., seems to have come close to enjoying the best of both worlds, matching or exceeding the United States on the contributions made by factor inputs, excepting the contributions made by improved education of the labor force, and doing as well as northwest Europe on output per unit of input, with the exception of economies of scale due to income elasticities in consumption and the residual sources already noted.

By far the most important determinant of Canada's postwar growth was the increase in employment associated with the postwar baby boom and very high immigration rates. From 1950 to 1967 the Canadian population grew by almost 50 percent, compared with 30 percent in the United States and 9 percent in the United Kingdom. The labor force grew at an even faster rate because of increasing labor force participation rates, particularly by women. The rate is still below that of most industrialized countries (Table

COUNTRY	RATE
Canada	39
U.S.A.	47
Northwest Europe	
Belgium	39*
Denmark	52*
Germany	47
Norway	40
United Kingdom	51
Italy	29

Table 19.8   Female Participation Rates in Canada, U.S.A., Five Northwest European Countries, and Italy: 1967

*The rates for Belgium and Denmark are for 1966.

Note: Rates are calculated as women in the labor force as a percent of the female population aged 15 to 64.

Source: Walters, *Canadian Growth Rates,* p. 13.

19.8), but coupled with the increasing tendency for young males to stay in school (reducing the labor force participation rate for males aged 14 to 19, from 45 to 35 percent between 1950 and 1967) the result was that half of the increase in the labor force between 1950 and 1967 was accounted for by women.

The labor force improved in quality as well as quantity. New entrants to the labor force had a higher level of education than retiring workers. For instance, the 1965 median level of education was 11.0 years for the 20 to 24 age group in the labor force, compared with 7.9 years for the 40 to 64 age group in the labor force. The very rapid growth of the labor force in Canada thus has been associated with an increasing level of education. It is estimated that the contribution of education to annual growth has been about a quarter of a percentage point in the 1950s and a half of a percentage point during the 1960s. These figures sound very small unless placed in their proper context of a *total* annual growth of 4.8 in net national income, 1950 to 1962, and 6.0 from 1962 to 1967.

The faster rate of postwar growth in Canada than in the United States has reduced the income disparity between the two countries, unlike United States–United Kingdom differentials, which remained unchanged. But the lower level of output in relation to inputs has persisted in Canada for several generations and remains a serious concern. The disparity varies greatly between different economic sectors. Output per worker in manufacturing industry is estimated to have been 31.5 percent lower (using United States price weights) or 35.6 percent lower (using Canadian price weights) than in the United States in the early 1960s. This resulted in higher prices for manufactured items in Canada even though average hourly earnings in Canadian manufacturing were between 20 and 25 percent lower than in the United States.

A variety of reasons have been offered to explain these productivity differences, including the "miniature economy" explanation, which argues that economies of scale are reduced by producing the same variety of manufactured items as the United States in a country with only one-tenth of the population. But a number of commentators have stressed the relative scarcity of highly educated workers in Canada. The Economic Council's *Fifth Annual Review,* which summarized the first set of results of the Denison model, pointed out that universities in the United States produce four times as many business administration and commerce students per capita as Canada, and seven times as many Master of Business Administration graduates. At the doctoral level the disparity is even more startling, with a total of only two doctorates in business administration granted by Canadian universities up until the fall of 1968 compared with an annual total averaging more than 350 in the United States. Even when allowance is made for the flow of Canadian students to the United States for graduate education, the number of Canadians obtaining advanced training in business is appreciably lower than in the United States and may help to explain the disparity in residual sources of growth, which include advances in knowledge and changes in lag between best and average practice. Certainly such factors loom large in the conclusion of Dorothy Walters on Canadian growth. She ends her 1970 study with the following statement:

An improved productivity performance in Canada would require some combination of growth-oriented stimuli which would raise the residual sources of growth. These could include increased efficiency in the organization of factors of production; other gains from higher levels of management skill and efficiency; larger economies of scale and specialization, promoted perhaps by commercial policy; gains in efficiency via a reduction in factors constraining competition; and all those factors which create a mobile, flexible, responsive and efficient economy.

Japan

Japan's growth rate has been about double that of northwest Europe and Canada and three times that of the United States in the postwar period. Hisao Kanamori has attempted to account for these differences by applying the Denison model to Japan.

The average annual rate of increase of factor inputs in Japan exceeded that of all other heartland countries, both in total and in the separate inputs of labor and capital and in the output per unit of input. Growth of total labor inputs were only just above those of Germany, however, and the employment input of 1.5 was actually less than Germany's 2.0 (Table 19.9). And, surprisingly perhaps, the contribution of labor to economic growth (1.31) was a little below the labor contribution in Germany (1.37) and Canada (1.5), although ahead of the United States and northwest Europe (Table 19.2). The largest contributors to growth in Japan, in fact, were capital inputs and increasing efficiency, and it has been these same two sets of growth determinants that have contributed most to the growth

Table 19.9   Annual Percentage Increase of Factor Inputs in Japan, U.S.A., Northwest Europe, and the United Kingdom

	JAPAN	U.S.A.	NORTHWEST EUROPE	UNITED KINGDOM
Total factor input	**4.2**	**1.71**	**1.67**	**1.16**
Labor	1.9	1.42	1.08	0.77
Employment	1.5	1.14	0.93	0.65
Hours of work	−0.1	−0.21	−0.18	−0.19
Age, sex composition	0.3	−0.13	0.04	−0.05
Education	0.2	0.62	0.30	0.37
Capital	10.5	3.58	4.53	3.35
Nonresidential structures and equipment	9.6	3.74	4.55	3.58
Inventories	12.4	3.00	4.47	2.56
Land	0.0	0.00	0.00	0.00
Output per unit of input	5.5	1.36	3.04	1.18

Note: The Japan rates are based on the period from 1955 to 1968; the USA, Northwest Europe, and United Kingdom from 1950 to 1962. Northwest Europe includes the seven Denison countries: Belgium, Denmark, France, West Germany, Netherlands, Norway, and United Kingdom.

Source: Kanamori, "Japan's High Rate of Growth," p. 157.

differential between Japan and the other heartland countries (Table 19.10).

Thus capital increases contributed 2.2 percentage points more than the United Kingdom to Japan's annual percentage increase in national income and productivity increases 4.9 percentage points more than the United Kingdom. Compare these figures with the U.K.'s increase of national income of 2.3 percent: in one case the *differences* between the U.K. and Japan are almost the same, in the other case almost double the contribution of *all* growth determinants in the U.K. The rate of increase of efficiency in factor use in Japan has indeed been remarkably high, and by itself, would have been enough to place Japan first among nations in rate of growth.

As noted in the earlier discussion on Japan, this high postwar growth rate in productivity reflects the rapid shifts in the allocation of labor from agriculture to manufacturing industry, the swift introduction of foreign technology, and rapid increase in economies of scale. It is not clear whether the rapid-growth opportunities offered by these determinants are approaching exhaustion. The evidence from application of the Denison model separately to the periods 1955 to 1960, 1960 to 1965, and 1965 to 1968 is that the contribution to growth by increasing efficiency in use of factor inputs is actually increasing (Table 19.11); increasing productivity contributed 4.7 percentage points to Japan's growth from 1955 to 1960 and 5.9 percentage points from 1960 to 1965. The corresponding figures show a decline both for northwest Europe (from 3.9 to 2.5 percentage points) and for the United States (from 1.9 to 1.0). Thus increasing efficiency contributed 0.8 per-

Table 19.10 Differences in the Contribution of the Determinants of Growth Between Japan and the USA, Canada, Northwest Europe, and the United Kingdom

	U.S.A.	CANADA	NORTHWEST EUROPE	UNITED KINGDOM
National income	−6.8	−5.3	−5.3	−7.8
Gross input	−2.1	−1.3	−2.3	−2.9
Labor	−0.2	−0.2	−0.5	−0.7
Employment	−0.1	−0.5	−0.3	−0.5
Work hours	−0.1	−0.1	−0.1	−0.1
Age, sex composition	−0.3	−0.3	−0.2	−0.2
Education	−0.4	−0.2	−0.1	−0.2
Capital	−1.9	−1.5	−1.9	−2.2
Dwelling	−0.1	−0.2	−0.1	−0.1
International assets	−0.1	−0.1	−	−0.1
Nonresidential structures and equipment	−1.2	−0.7	−1.0	−1.2
Inventories	−0.9	−0.9	−0.8	−0.9
Productivity	−4.7	−4.0	−3.0	−4.9

Note: Figures are in percentage points. A *minus* sign indicates that the determinant contributed *less* than in Japan. Thus productivity contributed 4.7 percentage points less to growth in the USA than in Japan. If the productivity difference between Japan and the USA had been 0.0, USA national income would have risen by another 4.7 percent a year.

Source: Kanamori, "Japan's High Rate of Growth," p. 160; and Walters, *Canadian Growth Rates,* p. 37.

Table 19.11 Contribution of Determinants to Growth of Real GNP in Japan: 1955–1960, 1960–1965, 1965–1968, and 1955–1968

	1955–1960	1960–1965	1965–1968	1955–1968
Real GNP	8.9	10.0	12.3	10.1
Total input	4.23	4.13	3.89	4.03
Labor	2.10	0.87	0.97	1.31
Employment	1.12	0.87	1.18	1.03
Work hours	0.56	−0.40	−0.49	−0.07
Age, sex	0.35	0.20	0.07	0.21
Education	0.07	0.20	0.21	0.14
Capital	2.13	3.26	2.92	2.72
Dwellings	0.11	0.16	0.16	0.14
International assets	−	−	−	−
Equipment	1.16	2.09	1.73	1.62
Inventory	0.86	1.01	1.03	0.96
Land	−	−	−	−
Production per input volume	4.7	5.9	8.4	6.1

Note: All figures are in percentage points.

Source: Kanamori, "Japan's High Rate of Growth," p. 167.

centage points more in Japan than in northwest Europe during the first period, but 3.4 percentage points more in the second. And it contributed 2.8 percentage points more in Japan than in the United States in the first period, but 4.9 percentage points more in the second. The spiraling economic growth indicated by these fig-ures has, of course, suffered a setback because of the energy crisis and escalating raw-material costs, as we have seen in Chapter 17. The growth, though somewhat dampened, should continue to consolidate Japan's position as a new, major heartland giant.

RECOMMENDED READINGS

Daly, Don J., "Why Growth Rates Differ—A Summary and Appraisal," *Review of Income and Wealth,* Series 14, No. 1 (March 1968), 75–93.

Denison, Edward F., assisted by Jean-Pierre Poullier, *Why Growth Rates Differ—Postwar Experience in Nine Western Countries.* Washington: Brookings Institution, 1967.

Kanamori, Hisao, "What Accounts for Japan's High Rate of Growth," *Review of Income and Wealth,* Series 18, No. 2 (June 1972), 155–71.

Walters, Dorothy, *Canadian Growth Revisited, 1950–1967.* Ottawa: Economic Council of Canada, Staff Study No. 28 (1970).

the world's hinterland economies

Central America is a region of little countries with big problems. As we observed in Chapter 11, five of the seven nations occupying the narrow strip of land between southern Mexico and the South American continent have joined together in an organized effort to attack these problems. The countries of the Central American Common Market—Guatemala, El Salvador, Honduras, Nicaragua, and Costa Rica—illustrate a number of the common characteristics of the world hinterland. Each of the five is an example of the exploitive economy at lower levels of development, in contrast to the more advanced resource-based economy of Canada. Like most other underdeveloped nations, the CACM countries must combat problems of dependency that result from economic and political weakness, and they must try to overcome the disadvantages of small size in a world economy that rewards bigness. In their economic relations with the rest of the world they have to contend with the difficulties of excessively specialized export trade while burdened at home with some of the world's highest rates of population growth. All the center-periphery contrasts described in the preceding pages are present here: disparities between the world heartland and the CACM, inequalities among CACM member-countries, and differences between regions within individual countries.

The Central American nations are also representative of tropical Hispanic America. Although in some respects the colonial heritage of Spain's former overseas possessions resembles the legacy of the newly independent lands of Asia and Africa, it also has a number of distinctive traits. The cultural conflicts of Spanish and Catholic institutions with the traditional forms of the indigenous Indian societies, especially those of the relatively advanced Mayas, have reached merely an uneasy accommodation. The dualism that has grown out of this relationship bears a peculiarly Iberian stamp, upon which has been superimposed the neocolonialism introduced by United States' interests following each Central American country's independence from Spain. Much of what we shall say here has to do with Central America's second struggle for independence, the effort to gain emancipation from economic imperialism and its related poverty trap. This effort has produced unique strategies for growth and development, employed at three levels. First, there is the attempt to integrate the five economies into a common unit that is able to confront the world more effectively. Second, this in turn has required a new set of techniques for reaching a harmonious accommodation among the national economies of individual members. Third, each Central American country has initiated a program to overcome regional disparities within its own borders. These approaches have already measurably affected the nature of Central America's domestic and foreign trade, the structure and location of production, and the size of national incomes.

the cacm countries: development through cooperation

20

THE CENTRAL AMERICAN REALM

The rugged isthmus that curves southeastward from Mexico is politically fragmented despite its limited areal extent. The five CACM countries, which, taken together, cover an area a little larger than Japan (or California), are individually tiny. The smallest is El Salvador, about the size of Massachusetts, and the largest, Nicaragua, is the equivalent of North Carolina. The total population of the CACM in the early 1970s was about 15 million people, or approximately that of Ohio plus Indiana. Individually they range from 1.7 million (Costa Rica) to 5.1 million (Guatemala). Although little El Salvador is densely populated, the others have a considerable amount of space per person. Further reducing the effective size of these small economies is the fact that only a third of their people are economically active, that is, contributing to the national money economy.

The level of development in Central America is well above that of most of Africa and southeastern Asia, but it is not very high by Latin American standards. Although the average per capita GNP of 18 Latin American countries was $537 in 1971, the average for the CACM countries was only $355. There is a fair range within the Common Market, however, between the poorest country, Honduras, with a per capita GNP of $255, and relatively prosperous Costa Rica, whose

per capita GNP was $539. The differences in material well-being among the CACM nations are also apparent from other measures of their physical and human resources.

physical resource endowments

For economies so directly dependent upon primary production, the physical characteristics of their land—climates, soils, physical relief, and mineral deposits—assume a special importance. These attributes provide the bases for their comparative advantages in world trade, establish limits on the nature and scale of output, and help shape settlement patterns. The variety of physical conditions within the Common Market's combined territory is surprising, considering its limited size.

the land

Not only is Central America a mountainous land, but its surface features are exceedingly complex (Fig. 20.1). The central mountain core that runs the length of the isthmus is composed of folded and faulted ranges generally 2,000 to 7,000 feet in elevation, surmounted in many places by volcanic peaks reaching as high as 12,000 feet. This mountainous spine is not continuous, however; it is separated into two parts by a lowland

Fig. 20.1 *The CACM: physiography and principal cities*

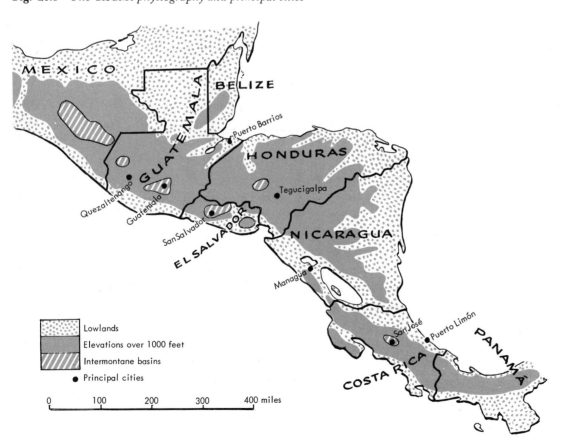

that crosses the isthmus diagonally through southern Nicaragua. One of the few large expanses of level land is the plain of northeastern Guatemala; other level areas are the coastal plains, mostly narrow but widening in a few places, together with numerous river valleys and basins within the highlands. The isthmus is divided politically in such a way that four of the CACM countries have land in the highlands and on both coasts; El Salvador is confined to the Pacific side.

Despite the tropical location (8°N to 18°N), Central America has extremely varied climates, soils, and vegetation, depending upon wind direction, slope, and elevation. Moisture-laden winds that have passed over the warm waters of the Caribbean supply the east coast with heavy rainfall throughout the year, supporting a luxuriant tropical rain forest. Because moist winds blow onshore from the Pacific only during the seven months of the high-sun period, that coast experiences a long period of drought and has a natural vegetation of savanna grasses and scrub growth. The windward slopes of the mountains are wet and heavily forested, but the leeward slopes are often very dry, with a desertic type of vegetation. Monthly average temperatures rarely fall below 70°F at sea level, but cool temperatures prevail on the upper slopes. Most intermontane basins have mild temperatures, producing delightfully springlike conditions throughout the year. Many areas have soils of volcanic origin, which are especially productive, though vulnerable to erosion on steeper slopes.

economic uses of the land

In addition to being small, the Central American countries are able to make productive use of only a fraction of their total land area. In the entire CACM, arable and pasture lands together comprise only 28 percent of the total, although this proportion reaches nearly 60 percent in crowded El Salvador. Forests occupy another 40 percent of the CACM territory, but only a part of this forestland is commercially useful and an even smaller percentage is actively exploited. The remainder of the CACM lands go unused because of excessively steep slopes, lack of moisture, or poor drainage.

Less than 12 percent of the CACM territory is classed as arable, a tiny amount for countries so dependent on the soil. This quantity of farmland, equivalent to the total areas of Vermont and New Hampshire, gives an average of only 0.8 acres per person, although the proportion varies among countries. Honduras and Nicaragua have only 7 percent of their land in crops, but overpopulated El Salvador has 30 percent under the plow. Limited as the arable lands of the CACM are, a surprising range of agricultural production takes place, including a wide array of grains, vegetables, and fruits for local consumption, and commercial crops.

Commercial production at lower elevations concentrates on the cultivation of bananas, cacao, sugar cane, pineapples and other tropical fruits, rice, cotton, oil palms, and rubber. These products grow under natural conditions along the rainy Caribbean coast; but they require irrigation on the Pacific side, where many mountain streams provide an ample supply of water.

The premier crop of the lowlands is bananas, which were first grown commercially in Central America. Following the first shipments to New Orleans in 1878, banana culture spread rapidly along the Caribbean coast, which, with its high temperatures and heavy rainfall, ample sunshine, excellent volcanic soils, and good drainage, provided perfect conditions for large-scale banana production. After a disastrous onslaught of plant diseases, however, much of the banana industry later shifted to the Pacific Coast, especially to the Golfito area of southeastern Costa Rica.

Another set of commercial crops occupies the intermediate elevations (2,000 to 5,000 feet) found on the lower slopes and in the intermontane basins. Coffee is the primary commercial export crop at these elevations and occupies as much as one-third of the total arable land in some Central American countries.

Physical conditions for growing coffee are excellent in the upland basins and on the plateaus and mountain slopes below 4,500 feet. These areas have volcanic soils, temperatures between 60°F and 75°F, well distributed rainfall, and a good labor supply. Secondary commercial crops at intermediate elevations include sugar, rice, and, especially since the Castro revolution in Cuba, increasing amounts of excellent tobacco. Corn, beans, vegetables, and subtropical fruits, for domestic sale in nearby urban centers, are also grown here.

At higher elevations, above 5,000 feet, temperatures are too low for most of the crops previously listed. Maize, or corn, is the major crop up to 9,500 feet, although wheat is produced at these elevations in some parts of Guatemala for domestic sale in the cities. Potatoes are dominant at the highest elevations (up to 10,500 feet) and are an important crop in Costa Rica, especially on the upper slopes of Irazú, an active volcano overlooking the capital city of San José. Temperate zone fruits are also common above 5,000 feet.

A large proportion of the cropped land in Central America is occupied by subsistence agriculture, especially the steeper, poorer slopes in the highlands and parts of the rain forest. The principal subsistence crops are maize, beans, rice, potatoes, and cassava. Maize is by far the main food crop of Central America; it occupies the largest acreage in every country. It is the staple of diet and the one major crop of the Indian areas of Guatemala, where it can be found in almost every field. It is grown on 37 percent of all cultivated lands in Honduras and on 54 percent of Nicaragua's crop land; it occupies the largest acreage of any crop in Costa Rica.

Grazing takes place on one-sixth of the total land area, which is more than all the land devoted to crops. It occurs at all climatic zones and elevations throughout the isthmus, but it occupies a particularly large percentage of the land in Honduras and El Salvador, nearly one-third of the total area, and it is the dominant land use along most of the Pacific coast. It is the only land use on the highest slopes, which are devoted to sheep pasturing. A large and rapidly increasing acreage along the Caribbean coast is now being converted to beef production, employing the latest breeds specially developed for tropical conditions.

Central America as a whole is 40 percent forested. The exception is El Salvador, where intensive use of the land has nearly denuded it of its former forest cover. In the hot Caribbean coastal lowlands, with their heavy year-round rainfall, dense tropical rain forests prevail. The Guatemalan *departamento* (county) of Petén, in the far northeast, has a luxuriant growth of tropical broadleaf trees. The rain forest belt extends southeastward along much of the Caribbean coastal plain, with pines appearing in the upper parts of the tropical zone, especially in eastern Nicaragua. The uplands are likewise forested in many places, where a wide variety of trees appear in a horizontally zonated pattern according to elevation. Semideciduous trees grow on the lower slopes, and oak, cypress, and pine occur higher.

In areas accessible to world and domestic markets, lumbering is an important activity. Mahogany and cedar are favored in the rain forest regions, particularly in Petén, which exports its lumber output through Puerto Barrios on the Caribbean. In a number of places there is active logging of pine and other valuable species. Forest-gathering takes place in the rain forests also; chicle gathering is the chief activity of this type.

The Spaniards were generally disappointed in their search for precious metals in Central America. Mining is currently important in only two countries, Honduras and Nicaragua. Honduras produces opals, antimony, gold, silver, and platinum. (The capital city of Tegucigalpa was settled originally as a silver-mining community.) Silver from the local San Jacinto mine is still an important Honduran export. Nicaragua has sizable gold-mining operations in the La Luz mines, whose vein deposits were discovered in the 1890s after having been overlooked earlier by the Spaniards in their intensive search for precious metals. Minor mineral production also occurs in El Salvador. Bauxite is now being mined in the San Isidro de General district of Costa Rica, and an alumina plant has been built by Alcoa to process the ore. Nickel deposits of substantial promise have recently been found in the Sierra de las Minas of eastern Guatemala and are awaiting development by the International Nickel Company.

For a food-short land there is much promise from the offshore fisheries, which are producing increasing amounts of shrimp, crawfish, tuna, and other varieties. Traditionally, there has been considerable inshore fishing in bracking waters, especially the fishing by Indians of large, tasty snook in the waters of Lago Izabal in eastern Guatemala.

human resources

Some of the severest dilemmas confronting Central America today are human problems, including the nature of settlement, population shifts, racial and cultural mixtures, and rigidities of a traditional social structure. The problems of population growth and of feeding, housing, educating, and employing these new additions to the population are equally severe. The character of the labor force is another basic problem.

settlement

Not only are the Central American countries small, but their populations are extremely concentrated in particular kinds of places. The typical pattern is one in which large numbers of people cluster around the capital city. Separating the population cluster of one country from the main population concentration of each neighboring country is a strip of land that is less densely settled. This arrangement is one that derives from the history of settlement, the physical character of the land, and subsequent development of the space-economy.

In Guatemala, El Salvador, Honduras, and Costa Rica, 70 to 90 percent of the population lives in the highlands, where the capitals and major cities are (Fig. 20.2). Relatively dense populations fill the upland basins, some of the wider valleys, and broader upland areas at elevations from 2,000 to 7,000 feet, especially in the western portions of the mountainous zones. In most cases these upland areas enjoy physical conditions superior to other parts of the country: ample rainfall, productive soils, moderate relief, and milder, pleasanter, and more healthful climatic conditions. It was in these places also that the invading Spaniards found dense sedentary Indian populations that were easy to enslave.

The main concentrations of population in Nicaragua are arranged differently. Only a third of the population lives in the highlands; the main centers are on the lowlands adjacent to Lake Managua and Lake Nicaragua (Fig. 20.2). As in other parts of Spanish America, it was the preconquest pattern of Indian settlement that anticipated the modern arrangement.

Outside these areas of concentration, the CACM countries are sparsely settled, except, of course, for overpopulated El Salvador. Areas avoided by Central Americans include inhospitable portions of the highlands—the extreme heights with their cold, rugged slopes—and those arid districts lying within the rain shadows of the high mountains. The coastal lowlands are also lightly populated; most of the people are in the port areas or in and around the plantations and estancias. The departamento of Petén in Guatemala, for example, occupies one-third of the national territory but has less than 1 percent of the population.

The five capitals of the CACM countries are truly primate cities. Guatemala City, with its 573,000 people, is ten times larger than its nearest competitor, Quezal-

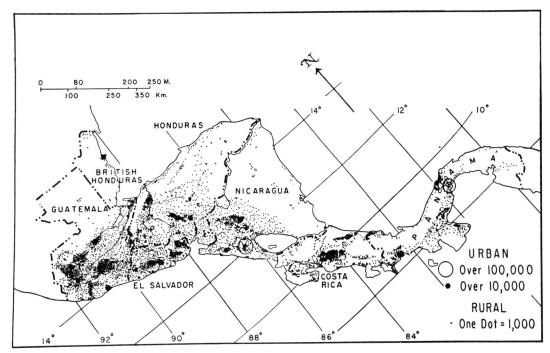

Fig. 20.2 *The CACM and Panama: population pattern*

Source: Preston E. James, Latin America *(New York: Odyssey Press, 1969).*

tenango, the ancient highland capital of the Mayas. Costa Rica's capital of San José (196,720 people) is seven times the size of second-place Alajuela (27,882), but the old colonial capital, Cartago, has a population of only 21,432. Managua, capital of Nicaragua, is the only one of the five that is not situated in an inter-montane basin.

Considering their vital function in the foreign trade of these countries, the port cities are surprisingly small. Except for El Salvador, every country has at least one port on each coast, linked by rail (except Tegucigalpa) and highway to the primate city (Fig. 20.3). The typical Central American port is almost wholly concerned with the transfer function and has little industry except possibly for a small oil refinery employing only a handful of men. Guatemala's twin ports of Santo Tomás and Puerto Barrios on the Caribbean serve much of the CACM territory and make use of the old banana railway to Guatemala City and San Salvador and, more recently, Highway CA-9, which ascends the highlands to connect with the Pan American Highway system.

Urban populations are rising rapidly, even faster than populations as a whole, as in-migration from the countryside accelerates. This movement is largely a search for employment opportunities lacking in the rural hinterland. The populations of Costa Rica, Guatemala, and Honduras are now one-third urban, and the urban populations of El Salvador and Nicaragua have reached 40 percent. By 1980 the urban proportion may be as high as 50 percent in most of Central America.

It should be noted, however, that some of this urbanization is deceptive, since many town-dwellers work on nearby farms. For example, most of the Costa Rican potato farmers on the upper slopes of Irazu, actually reside in Cartago at the base of the mountain.

population growth

This urban expansion is only one manifestation of overall rates of population growth that are among the world's highest. The average annual rates of growth between 1963 and 1970 were 3.2 percent for Costa Rica, 3.8 percent for El Salvador, 3.1 percent for Guatemala, 3.4 percent for Honduras, and 3.7 percent for Nicaragua. These high growth rates are the predictable results of rapidly declining death rates because of greatly improved control over communicable diseases and substantial reductions in infant mortality rates while birth rates remain at high levels of 45 to 49 per 1000. With this pattern, the CACM countries easily qualify as UN Type 3 countries in the midst of the most explosive period of population growth, with doubling times of 20 years or less (see Chapter 2). Only Costa Rica, which entered this cycle much earlier than the rest and has attained a higher level of material prosperity, shows some signs of reducing its growth rate. The very large family is a cherished institution in Central America, for it is a customary means of achieving social security in an uncertain environment, and a product of firm religious strictures against birth control.

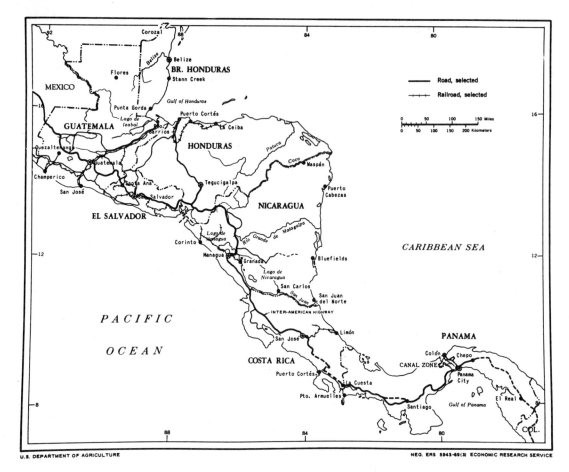

Fig. 20.3 *The CACM and Panama: highways and railways*

Source: Battelle Memorial Institute, Projections of Supply and Demand for Selected Agricultural Products in Central America through 1980 *(Washington: U. S. Department of Agriculture, Economic Research Service, 1969, frontispiece).*

As it is for most underdeveloped nations, rapid population growth is a matter of grave concern in Central America. It has encumbered these countries with large and growing numbers of persons in the dependent ages. More than half the Honduran population is under 15 years of age, and the other CACM countries have proportions almost as high. Not only does this population structure reduce the numbers who contribute actively to the economy but it also magnifies the problem of educating the young. Moreover, it produces a severe drain on family and national resources, especially the food supply.

Expanding food output rapidly enough to support this growing population has proved a difficult challenge for Central America, even though the overall man-land ratio is still relatively low by the usual standards of underdeveloped nations. The number of persons per square mile is only 88 in Costa Rica, 125 in Guatemala, 60 in Honduras, and 39 in Nicaragua. On the other hand, El Salvador has 429 people per square mile, a very high figure for a farming population in a mountainous land; it is the only country of the five that fully occupies its national territory. As yet only El Salvador is severely overcrowded; but the other four nations, with their 20-year doubling times, are also due for serious population problems before the century ends.

Aside from the matter of adequate food supply, there is growing concern about the quality of diets, which has traditionally been poor and is deteriorating among some segments of the population. The staples of the Central American's diet are maize, beans, and rice; maize alone represents 75 percent of the total diet. In more favored areas these may be supplemented by other vegetables and fruits. Wheat (grown in significant quantities only in the Guatemalan highlands) and animal products are eaten only by wealthier urban dwellers.

Population pressures are depressing living conditions in varying degrees in all five countries. Because of low family incomes and a general shortage of capital, housing cannot be built fast enough, either in rural areas or in the squalid settlements ringing the primate cities. It has been estimated that 40 to 50 percent of all houses are constructed of waste materials, have thatched roofs and dirt floors, and are too small. Half the homes of Central America lack potable water, toilets, sewerage systems, or plumbing of any sort. As in most things, Costa Rica is much better off than the others in these respects.

the labor force

Another consequence of rapid population growth, and a contributing factor to many of the problems cited earlier, is the difficulty of generating employment fast enough. The expanding farm population has resulted in rural underemployment, and the rural spillover into the cities has created rising urban employment. The rate of job formation in industry has not been nearly fast enough, swelling the numbers of street hawkers and other marginal service workers and leaving many persons with no source of income at all.

Central Americans are hard workers and eager to learn, but they are severely hampered by illiteracy and inadequate skills. The great majority are classified either as unskilled or semiskilled, 43 percent of the adult population of the CACM are totally illiterate, and many of the rest have low proficiencies in reading and writing. Once again the exception is Costa Rica, which is the only Central American country with both compulsory and effective school attendance. Only 15 percent of Costa Ricans over 15 years of age are illiterate, in contrast with Guatemala, whose illiteracy rate is 65 percent. This is one of the reasons that Central America has a general shortage of qualified teachers, skilled labor, qualified managers, and experienced entrepreneurs.

Within the CACM countries, between one-half and two-thirds of all employed workers are engaged in primary activities, mainly agriculture. The proportion working in factories ranges between one-tenth and one-fifth of the total. Honduras has the largest percentage employed in agriculture and the smallest proportion in secondary activities.

ethnic composition of the population

Nearly four centuries of intermarriage have produced a people of mixed ethnic backgrounds. Superimposed upon an already diverse indigenous Indian population were subsequent additions of Iberians, Negroes, and fewer numbers of other peoples. The ethnic makeup of the population varies considerably from one country to another, depending upon the history of settlement and the relative number of persons of each group present, but the most common in the CACM countries as a whole is the combination of Spanish and Indian, referred to as *mestizos*.

Guatemala is largely an Indian country; 60 percent of its people are of unmixed Mayan ancestry. Thirty-five percent are Indian-Spanish (with a higher proportion of Indian ancestry), and 5 percent are of European descent, mostly Spanish. Very small numbers of Negroes, who came originally from the West Indies, live in and near the Caribbean port of Livingston. Three of the other countries are populated mostly by mestizos: in El Salvador 11 percent of the people are Indian, 78 percent mestizo, and 11 percent Spanish; in Honduras 10 percent are Indian, 86 percent mestizo, 2 percent Spanish, and 2 percent Negro; in Nicaragua 5 percent are Indian, 60 percent mestizo, 17 percent Spanish, and 9 percent Negro. In Costa Rica 80 percent of the total population is Spanish, 17 percent is mestizo, 2 percent Negro, and less than 1 percent Indian.

THE COLONIAL LEGACY

The unique characteristics of Central America's people and their society—as well as their problems—are rooted in three and a half centuries of colonialism. What kind of spatial organization has evolved in this milieu? First, alien penetration, initially from Europe and subsequently from North America, has created a dualistic economic and social structure. Second, it has brought about a dependency upon the world heartland that these countries have not been able to shake off. An examination of the circumstances in which the five nations found themselves by the end of the 1950s will provide a clearer understanding of the problems that led at that time to the formation of the CACM and the various national planning councils.

alien penetration

The burden of its history weighs heavily on Latin America. To understand the contemporary Central American people and their culture, economy, and problems, we must know something of what went before. Many Central Americans still live in their past, especially those unassimilated Indians who exist as they always have, cut off from national life. Many people of European extraction preserve their old ways, too, clinging to customs, practices, and attitudes of an earlier time. Each group has its traditional religious practices, systems of land tenure, costumes, architectural styles, and foods. In some instances the traditions of the two cultures have become intermingled.

The clash of cultures occurred during two main periods of colonialism, and each period left its distinctive imprint. First came the Spanish conquest, followed by European settlement, the imposition of colonial administration, and the introduction of an agrarian economy based on a series of export staples. Later another alien invasion took place and partially supplanted the old Spanish colonial system with a neocolonialism of North American origin.

the Spanish conquest and rule

The first of these foreign intrusions arrived suddenly and violently, opposing a disciplined and relatively advanced band of invaders and a poorly organized and less materially developed indigenous population. It was a meeting of contrasting cultures and economies. Yet the indigenous peoples were by no means homogeneous: some had complex cultures, and others were exceedingly primitive; some were easily subjugated, others resisted strenuously; some were quickly and completely assimilated by the intruding culture, many were never assimi-

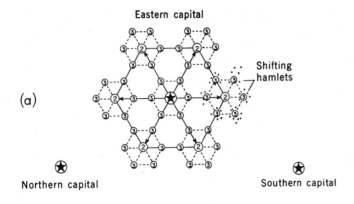

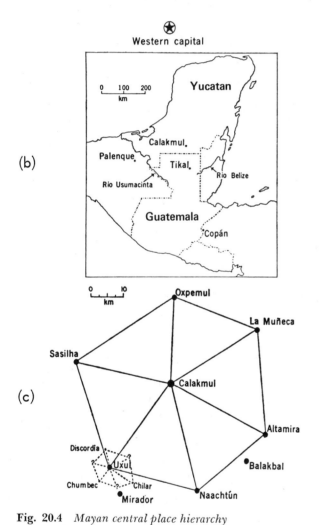

Fig. 20.4 *Mayan central place hierarchy*

Source: Joyce Marcus, "Territorial Organization of the Lowland Classic Maya," Science, 180 (1973), 911–16.

lated at all. Those differences among peoples have influenced the character of the nation that subsequently evolved in each area. The densities of aboriginal populations also varied greatly from one place to another, with lasting effects on the Central American settlement pattern.

Of all the pre–Columbian peoples, the most enduring legacy was left by the Mayas, whose culture was probably superior to that of any other indigenous group in the Americas. The Mayas occupied all modern Guatemala and adjacent parts of Honduras and Mexico; their descendents still live in these areas, speaking the many Mayan dialects and preserving the old customs and dress.

The peak of the Mayan period was reached before the arrival of Spaniards, by which time this ancient civilization had already begun to decline. At their zenith the Mayas built cities of 30,000 to 40,000 inhabitants. Each city was supported by the primitive agriculture in its hinterland. The Mayas constructed elaborate, tall structures without the aid of the arch, developed an accurate calendar, and acquired an impressive knowledge of mathematics and astronomy. Yet they did not have the wheel or use beasts of burden. Their sedentary but primitive agriculture was based upon maize, beans, squash, yams, peppers, and cacao.

The settlement pattern of the lowland Mayas is interesting to modern urban geographers because of the regularity of its form, which, to a remarkable degree, evidences certain features of central place theory. Deciphering the hieroglyphic inscriptions on *stelae* (freestanding stone monuments) found among the ruins of this civilization, archaeologists have confirmed that the Mayas had three levels of central places, forming a nested hierarchy. At each level in this hierarchy the centers were spaced equidistant from one another and each higher-order center was surrounded by centers of lower order arranged in a uniformly hexagonal lattice. Figure 20.4a illustrates this arrangement in an idealized manner.

The hierarchy accorded first rank to four regional capitals, one on the east of the national territory, another in the north, and others on the west and south, reflecting the Mayan cosmology, which conceived of a quadripartite division of heaven and a corresponding arrangement on earth. Ruled by an important dynasty, each capital was a ceremonial, administrative, and commercial center dominating the territory within its quadrant of Mayan earth-space. Around each regional center were six secondary centers forming a hexagonal lattice and located equidistant from one another. Although there was some variation from one region to the next, depending upon the agricultural carrying capacity of the land, there was remarkable consistency in the spacing of these centers within a given region. In one case, actual measurements have indicated a mean distance of 10.33 kilometers separating one secondary center from the next, with a standard deviation of only 1.9 kilometers. Apparently junior members of the regional dynasty ruled these secondary centers, thus giving a firm political cohesion to the system. Finally, nested within this spatial lattice, were the tertiary places, six for each secondary center (Fig. 20.4a). These were the villages, probably mere clusters of thatched huts inhabited by farmers.

Mayan records do not explicitly describe this neat geometrical arrangement; in all likelihood it simply grew out of the basic service functions of their urban places and the practicalities of travel and transportation. Fundamental to the system were the farmers living in their nucleated hamlets, each farm worker having an estimated capacity to provide food and fiber for twelve persons. That such an arrangement actually existed in the year A.D. 730 is shown by Figures 20.4b and 20.4c. The hieroglyphs on one stela identify the four regional capitals of that period as Tikal (eastern), Calakmul (northern), Palenque (western), and Copán (southern). Extensive ruins of great stone pyramids, innumerable stone monuments, and other remnants mark these four sites today. Figure 20.4c illustrates the pattern of secondary centers surrounding the northern capital, Calakmul, and supplies an example of the tertiary places focusing upon one such center, Uxul.

The Old Empire of the Mayas, centered in northern and eastern Guatemala and nearby Honduras, was replaced by the New Empire in the Yucatan peninsula, which in turn collapsed in the fifteenth century. When the Spaniards arrived, the Mayas were spread over a wide area; the majority were densely clustered in the western highlands and basins of Guatemala, especially Quezaltenango and such lesser centers as Chichicastenango. The Mayas still hold to these districts and to their ancient lands around Copán in northwestern Honduras.

Most of pre-Columbian Honduras was inhabited, however, by the Lencas, a much simpler folk. Unlike the Mayas, the Lencas were shifting cultivators and subsistence hunters and fishers, who sparsely occupied their lands. They also differed from the Mayas in that they were readily assimilated into the Spanish culture, giving up their Indian dress, language, and customs. The Pipils, a peaceful group of shifting cultivators in El Salvador, were also assimilated quickly.

The native population of Nicaragua, a docile group living around the shores of Lake Nicaragua, was made up of primitive subsistence farmers, fishermen, and hunters. On the Caribbean coast of that country were the Miskitos, who still live in primitive fashion in that isolated region. Costa Rica's exceedingly small Indian population was quickly extinguished by diseases brought by the conquerors.

This world into which the Spaniards suddenly appeared was the most populous part of pre–Columbian America and contained at that period more than one-third of all the Western Hemisphere's people. By contrast, the Spanish armies were small, but they were well armed and disciplined, mounted and highly mobile. The Spanish immigrants who followed were likewise limited in numbers; in all, only 300,000 heads of families left Spain permanently for this part of the Americas.

A combination of motives drove these outnumbered but audacious intruders: an obsession for precious metals, the prestigious life-style represented by a large cattle ranch (estancia), or a compulsion to spread Christianity among the "heathen." From their base in Mexico City, the Spaniards began the conquest of Central America with an invasion of the Guatemalan highlands in 1523, followed by an expedition along the Caribbean coast into Honduras. The remainder of Central America quickly fell to the conquerors, who placed all except Panama under the Captaincy-General of Guatemala.

Except in Costa Rica, Spanish settlement focused upon areas already occupied by large numbers of Indians. In Guatemala and El Salvador the colonists established estancias in highland basins below 5,000 feet, leaving the heights to the Mayas. Settlement of Honduras occurred in the isolated mining district around Tegucigalpa and in the agricultural lands of the north coast. Only in Nicaragua did the settlers occupy the lowlands first, selecting the area around Lake Nicaragua where the Indians were concentrated.

Costa Rica's initial settlement took place in the volcano-rimmed highland basin known as the Meseta Central. Unlike those who occupied the other Central American countries, the colonizers of Costa Rica were independent small farmers, who developed no aristocracy, sought no special prestige in landed wealth, engaged in no mining, and enslaved no Indians. From this humble pioneering stock came the most prosperous people of modern Central America. Although elsewhere the Spanish settlers freely intermarried with the indigenous peoples, the colonists of Costa Rica did not. Even today the Meseta Central is inhabited by a people of virtually unmixed Spanish ancestry.

Although the goal of most Spanish settlers was to grow wealthy from the land, their grand estancias could not fulfill this ambition solely from the sale of beef products, which had to be marketed locally at a low profit. Therefore, like the early settlers of Canada, the Spanish colonists developed export staples that could bring a large return on the world market despite high transport costs from their remote location. Experimenting with a number of high-value commodities that could be grown on the more fertile agricultural lands on their estates, they produced sugar cane at lower elevations and wheat in the uplands, and they adopted for commercial production and export a number of valuable indigenous products, particularly cacao, indigo, and cochineal. Throughout the colonial era the small farmers of Costa Rica remained largely subsistence producers, making a poor living from maize, beans, and other native crops.

independence and neocolonialism

Independence came much earlier to Spanish America than to other underdeveloped areas in Asia or Africa. Mexico became independent in 1821 and established a monarchy over the entire Vice-Royalty of New Spain, stretching from western Canada to the Costa Rican border with Panama. In 1823 the five Central American provinces, the Captaincy-General of Guatemala, separated from Mexico and formed a federal republic. Because of local ambitions and jealousies and the isolation of each population cluster from the others, the federation managed to hold together only until 1838, when it collapsed, leaving each province free to form a separate nation.

Soon thereafter the new states acquired a new staple export—coffee. Commercial production began first in Costa Rica, where the government actively promoted this crop by granting free land for coffee growers and constructing roads to the ports. Coffee proved to be an ideal export crop for Central America. The highland climates and rich volcanic soils provided perfect physical conditions, and the compact, valuable product could bear the transport costs from isolated locations. Thus coffee's role as an export staple paralleled that of wheat in Canada.

Also like Canada, Central America's laissez-faire attitude and tradition of private property made these countries vulnerable to foreign commercial encroachment. The first intruders from abroad were the German coffee planters, who emigrated to Guatemala in the 1860s. While retaining their German citizenship, they eventually controlled nearly one-third of the country's cropland.

Of far greater impact, however, was the appearance of the North American fruit companies, which profoundly affected Central American agriculture, trade, settlement, racial composition, infrastructure, and politics. The new export staple they introduced was bananas, first planted in Costa Rica by a North American railway contractor. So successful was this venture that it led in 1899 to formation of the United Fruit Company, which subsequently spread its operations throughout Central America, occupying coastal plains and broad valleys that were largely devoid of people before the company's arrival.

Although the United Fruit Company is the principal operator, other firms have followed. The industry is highly capitalized and has easily and quickly attracted North American investors. Its operations have been vertically integrated to an unusual degree and encompass production, transporting, marketing, and a number of other related functions. The company clears and plants the fields; cultivates, fertilizes, and harvests the crop; builds dams for flood control and irrigation; and constructs elaborate irrigation and spraying apparatus. It provides company towns for managers and workers, self-contained communities often in the midst of primitive surroundings. Bananera, the United Fruit Company operation in the Motagua valley of Guatemala, for example, not only supplies housing, utilities, and streets but also hospitals, stores, and recreation facilities for its employees. The company usually has to provide its own transport facilities for procuring supplies and marketing the product. It has constructed and operated rail lines linking its plantations with ports, where bananas are loaded on company owned refrigerator ships.

The management, staff, and technology are all alien to Central America. In the past, the company could not even obtain an adequate supply of labor from the indigenous population but had to import large numbers of Jamaican Negroes, whose descendents comprise a major part of the Caribbean lowland populations of Honduras and Costa Rica today.

Bananas came to dominate the exports of the Central American countries, and they still lead in Costa Rica and Honduras. As a consequence, the banana industry also dominated national economies and became a powerful political influence. Because the companies often dictated government policy, the term *banana republic* has been coined to describe the small tropical land that has become a puppet to outside commercial interests. This political influence subsequently became increasingly unpopular and is now much reduced. The United Fruit Company has been diversifying its land use in Central America, has relinquished ownership of its railways, and has begun purchasing part of its bananas from local growers.

dualism

Throughout the long era of Spanish colonialism and the period of North American-based neocolonialism that followed it, each new wave of intruders added another layer to the dualistic society and economy that evolved in Central America. This dualism appears in several forms. One is the *cultural dualism* that is apparent in the contrasts between the Iberian and indigenous ways of life. *Economic dualism* is expressed in the dichotomies between urban and rural, between central and peripheral regions, and between modern commercial production and traditional subsistence activities.

cultural dualism

One of the most persistent conditions surviving from the Spanish period is that peculiarly Latin American type of cultural dualism that distinguishes people on the basis of ancestry and family ties. Its visible manifestations are the accumulated wealth, prestige, privilege, and power accruing to one segment of society and the impoverished and subordinate role accorded the other. It is rooted in the collision of a pre-industrial European culture and a native Central American culture, each with its own attitudes and values.

As we have noted, there was much variation in the levels of advancement of the indigenous peoples of this region. Least advanced of all were the migratory, primitive subsistence hunters, fishers, gatherers, and farmers. Because their societies were also the least cohesive, they were largely assimilated and their cultures absorbed in the invading wave, leaving only their physical traits in the general mass of population. The most advanced native peoples were sedentary farmers with complex societies that still resist any external effort to submerge their unique cultural identities.

The Mayas, a particularly cohesive group have held to their traditional ways and ancestral lands. Today, in the western highlands of Guatemala and in the border areas of Honduras, they continue their communal existence in groups of up to 50,000 persons. The community owns the land that each farmer tills; although he has lifetime use of his assigned plot, he cannot bequeath it. The plot is returned to the community and is reassigned. Some live in separate farmsteads on the small plots they farm, but many live in nucleated agricultural villages and towns and go daily to the surrounding fields to work.

Each Mayan community is isolated physically and culturally from the other. Each has its own distinctive and colorful costume, its own traditions, and often its own Mayan dialect. Although nominally Catholic, they have not relinquished their Mayan religion. They may baptize their children, attend mass, and observe other Catholic rituals; but they continue to practice their traditional Mayan rites, too, making animal sacrifices and burnt offerings of herbs and incense to the Mayan gods.

Superimposed on this native culture are the distinctly European outlook and norms brought by the Spaniards, who also introduced their own administrative system and political organization and their laissez-faire, capitalistic economic system. To their adopted country they contributed the Spanish language, literature, and art, the Catholic church, and education and printing. This pre-industrial society of the Spanish colonials not only survived its transplanting in American soil but has persisted with little change through the centuries that followed the conquest. Many of its forms carry over even into the modern cities of Central America, since the same families who comprise the landed gentry often control the commerce, professions, and politics in the urban center.

These two contrasting societies, the Spanish agrarian and the pre–Columbian survivals, are often found adjacent to each other in the same rural and urban space. The striking dissimilarities between the two groups are reinforced by the rigid class and caste organization of the Latin American world. Moreover, when they are thrown together, the indigenous culture is no match for the European in any power contest. The descendents of the Spanish rulers retain unchallenged dominance economically and politically over the Indians and those of mixed ancestry.

The great mass of Indians, mestizos, and other subordinate groups live in a penurious state and endure all the wretched living conditions described earlier. In the midst are the landed aristocracy, a tightly knit group of old families who are greatly outnumbered by the poorer classes they dominate. The disparities are most extreme in El Salvador, where a small group of leading families maintain a firm grip on politics and on the rural and urban economy. To a varying and somewhat lesser degree this is also the case in Guatemala, Honduras, and Nicaragua.

The contrast between rich and poor is least in Costa Rica, especially in the Meseta Central, populated by the ethnically homogeneous descendents of the small farmers who originally settled the country. Costa Rica has provided the model for a democratic Latin America undominated by a land-owning aristocracy, unburdened by a standing army, and untroubled by massive rural poverty. The independent spirit of its ordinary citizens reflects their higher incomes (which would be greater yet except for the encumbering effects of a very high birth rate) and it is also an expression of their high degree of literacy. It has been no little accomplishment for this tiny country to educate and employ the large yearly additions to its population and work force.

the city and its region

The dichotomy between urban and rural in Central America and the carryover into the internal spatial structure and organization of the primate city is typical of most newly developing countries. The primate cities of Latin America differ from those of Asia and Africa only in the absence of a large alien Chinese or Indian merchant class. Here the most striking feature of the commercial sector is the contrast between the modern central business district with its array of expensive merchandise, much of it imported, and the nearby central market, the *mercado central*, housing innumerable crowded stalls offering agricultural produce and locally made handicrafts and inexpensive clothing.

In the residential sections there are also the contrasts between the stately homes of the wealthy inside the city and the squatters' shacks ringing the periphery. In the Central American city the meeting of two worlds is underscored by such common sights as barefoot Mayan women in bright native dress carrying burdens on their heads as they pass government employees in business dress in the central park or the sleek aircraft taxiing to an ultramodern terminal building while an oxcart loaded with bags of maize creeps down a nearby road.

The contrasts between city and countryside are especially acute in Central America, where politics is decidedly urban-centered; not only is the primate city the seat of government but it is the place where most of the nation's politically active citizens live. Except in Costa Rica, many of the rural folk are unaware of the struggles for power taking place in their land.

The primate city is the national center for domestic trade and all other kinds of commerce except, possibly, for that involving certain export staples such as bananas. Moreover, outside the main urban center, goods are exchanged in a very different manner, particularly in the traditional system of periodic markets. Each village in the countryside has its regular market day, a colorful event when farmers bring their surplus produce to town for sale or barter. Itinerant merchants follow a regular circuit as they travel from one village's market to the next, vending their wares or exchanging them for local merchandise.

In Central America almost all manufacturing of consequence is confined to the capital city, which is the only center providing the necessary agglomeration economies. Lesser urban places are merely rural service centers and the foci of regional and local political administration. Scattered through the countryside, however, are such native crafts as weaving and pottery making, and small-scale cottage industry.

agricultural dualism

Perhaps the sharpest distinctions of all are found within regions and even within communities, where the close intermingling of commercial and subsistence farming dramatizes their differences. The sequence of agricultural innovations in Central America has created a duality that is not surpassed anywhere else in the world. For centuries, the traditional agriculture of these countries has been the small-scale production of maize, cassava, beans, rice, sorghum, tomatoes, and squash. Commercial agriculture is of two main types: the growing of export staples and the production of crops for sale on the domestic market, and is divided between domestic and foreign ownership and management. The coffee estates and many of the cotton and sugar operations are under Central American control and most of the banana production is under North American management. Commercial crops for domestic consumption (especially maize, vegetables, and fruits) are produced mainly by Central American landowners. Meat production has been a favorite pursuit of the local landed aristocracy for centuries, but now that the Central American meats are entering the United States market in growing quantities, North American capital and management are increasingly important.

A summary of the differences between traditional (or subsistence) agriculture and the two types of commercial production in Central America follows:

1. Commercial farmers sell their products rather than keeping them for consumption, and they purchase almost all consumption needs. Subsistence farmers grow and consume virtually all their own food; make their own clothing, sandals, and many other consumer items; and barter for the rest at nearby periodic markets, which they travel to on foot.

2. Commercial agriculture is capital-intensive, although certain types (truck farming, for example) also have high labor inputs. Subsistence agriculture is labor-intensive and employs more than half of the workers in most regions and as many as 80 percent in some of the highlands.

3. Commercial operations have high levels of productivity; they account for half of Central America's total agricultural output. Traditional agriculture has very low productivity despite the large labor force involved. Output per worker on subsistence farms averages only one-fifth of that on commercial farms.

4. Commercial farming is highly capitalized; it requires heavy initial investment and entails much reinvestment of profits. Subsistence farming receives minimal investment and yields little if any savings. Credit is easily obtained for commercial production but is rarely made available to subsistence farmers.

5. Large production units are characteristic of commercial farming in Central America, where the grand estates (*latifundia*) of colonial times have been joined by the vast plantations during the modern era. In Latin America as a whole, only 1.5 percent of all farms exceeds 2,500 acres, but these give two-thirds of the output even though much good land on these farms actually goes unused. The subsistence farmers till minute plots of land (*minifundia*). Three-fourths of all Latin American farms are under 50 acres, and these contribute only 4 percent of the output. Operations of this size are too small to employ the methods and equipment necessary to give the scale economies enjoyed by commercial farms.

6. The ownership of commercial lands is concentrated. Some of it is in foreign hands, and the remainder is controlled by a small number of families among the local aristocracy. In some areas, subsistence farmers own the plots they till, individually or communally, but in other places tenancy prevails. Many hired laborers on large estates also practice subsistence farming during their off hours, working small pieces of ground provided by the estate owners.

7. Commercial agriculture virtually monopolizes the prime land—the richest soils, gentlest slopes, and best climatic conditions—most of which is scientifically managed. Subsistence farmers work the marginal land—the poor soils on steep slopes and high elevations—which has become exhausted and badly eroded from long continuous use.

8. The commercial operations employ elaborate equipment and tools and practice scientific production techniques. Traditional agriculture uses archaic methods, poor seeds, and primitive, inefficient tools—hoes, machetes, and, in the more fortunate instances, crude plows pulled by yokes of oxen.

9. The plantations and estates have access to market by modern highways or, in the case of the fruit companies, railways. Most subsistence farms are quite isolated, so any small surplus must be transported to market by primitive means—human porter or pack donkey.

domestic transportation and communications

One basic distinction between commercial and subsistence production that we have stressed is their relative accessibility. This underscores the general inadequacy of transportation in Central America, a region that owes much of its political and economic fragmentation to this weakness. Traditionally, each of these countries has been a self-contained unit, open to commercial exchanges with the world heartland but isolated from its immediate neighbors. Direct transport linkages between the Central American countries were severely limited in the past, and they are still inadequate.

The national transport system in each of these countries has two foci: capital cities and ports (see Fig. 20.3). Only one of Central America's railways crosses an international border: the narrow-gauge line connecting Guatemala and El Salvador. Major all-weather highways also converge upon the principal city, linking it to all or most of the principal regional administrative centers. The important districts of commercial primary production—the banana plantations and mining operations—are also provided with direct transport connections either to the ports or to the capital city; indeed, the fruit company constructed most of the early railways and the port works.

Connections between other regions are generally poor or nonexistent. For example, coffee produced in the Cobán district must first go to Guatemala City and then to Puerto Barrios, even though Cobán is fairly close to the port in terms of straight-line distance. A general lack of farm-to-market roads seriously affects subsistence farmers and tends to perpetuate their non-participation in political life.

Only with the establishing of national airlines were some regions finally given access to one another and to the outside world. But even the airlines focus upon the national capital. Although helicopters are used to transport high government officials to some remote districts, they are of no help in transporting low-value, bulky agricultural produce.

the consequences of dualism

The kinds of dualism that persist in Central America present many obstacles to growth and development. First, resources are concentrated in the commercial sector, which leaves very little for the subsistence sector despite the rapid increase in demand for daily necessities from the burgeoning population. This results in low and stagnating productivity in the traditional sector and to its continued isolation from potential markets for its commodities. The productivity of subsistence farmers is further reduced by their high rates of population growth, which cause further fragmentation of holdings that are already uneconomically small. At the same time that farm consolidation is reducing the number of production units in North America and Europe, Central American farms are multiplying and their tenancy rates are rising. This in turn reduces agricultural efficiency and depresses per capita farm incomes.

All this further aggravates the region's many grave social problems: poverty, hunger, malnutrition, illiteracy, poor housing, unemployment and underemployment, and political unrest. It also exaggerates the export dependence of Central America's commercial sector, leading to still another cluster of problems.

foreign trade problems before integration

Central America provides a dramatic example of the difficulties that underdeveloped countries experience with their foreign trade (see Chapter 11). Under conditions of free trade, the Central American countries were relegated to a subordinate and disadvantageous role in the world economic system.

trade with the heartland

Central America's comparative advantage has been the production of export staples—sugar, cacao, coffee, bananas, and fibers—whose land-intensive production is based on a special set of physical conditions. The selection of these exports was decided by alien entrepreneurs, who concentrated investment and resources almost to the exclusion of all else.

The imports required under these conditions include both manufactured and agricultural commodities. The former consists of the capital goods required to support the commercial sector: farm machinery and equipment, construction machinery, transport equipment, and so forth, together with many durable and nondurable consumer products. The agricultural imports are such foodstuffs as temperate-land grains.

A number of trade effects resulted. First, a large proportion of domestic output was exported; exports of the five countries represented nearly 18 percent of their combined GDP in 1960. Second, there was extreme specialization of exports, restricted to a narrow range of tropical agricultural commodities. Imports, on the other hand, were relatively diverse, reflecting the wide variety of needs, even in economies as simple as these. From the standpoint of conventional trade theory (Ricardo's law of comparative advantage, see Chapter 10), this was an ideal outcome. Central America could be expected to maximize its GNP by focusing on producing and exporting only those commodities that it could turn out most efficiently and importing those goods that could be produced more cheaply elsewhere.

Conventional theory, however, overlooks the peculiar trade problems that underdeveloped primary producers encounter: the result of extreme specialization and the characteristics of the commodities exported. Before union, the five countries were among the most highly specialized exporters in the world, with only four commodities (coffee, bananas, cotton, and cacao) accounting for nine-tenths of their combined exports by value. The most extreme case was that of Guatemala, who gained more than 99 percent of her export earnings from coffee and bananas alone. Costa Rica's position was almost as bad, since coffee, bananas, and cacao made up almost all her foreign sales. Honduras sold little more than bananas, coffee, silver, and lumber, while Nicaragua depended almost entirely upon cotton, coffee, gold, and lumber.

This excessive dependence upon primary exports produced adverse results: severe monetary instability due to fluctuations in world prices for the export staples; and increasingly unfavorable terms of trade (Chapter 11). Export prices for Central America's staples have risen slowly over a period of years. Meanwhile, prices of the region's manufactured imports have risen rapidly.

A further problem was the excessive dependence upon a small number of trading partners. A majority of the region's exports went to the United States and an even larger proportion of imports came from that country. Most of the rest of the trade was with Western Europe, with Japan becoming an increasing important supplier as well. Despite their proximity, the Central American nations sent only 7 percent of their exports to other CACM members in 1960. Indeed, there were few opportunities for such exchange because all of them produced the same export staples. Their import needs were supplied largely from advanced nations because the output of their own factories was inadequate in volume and variety.

the traditional industry of
Central America

The manufacturing output of the five nations contributed only 13.2 percent of their combined GNPs in 1960. At that time the region's industries were mainly engaged in the simple processing of domestic raw materials and foodstuffs for local consumption. The largest group were the food, beverage, and tobacco industries, which contributed 55.3 percent of the gross value of industrial output. Textiles and clothing provided another 16.1 percent and wood products and furniture supplied 5.8 percent. Together, then, these three major classes of production comprised 77.2 percent of the total. The remaining manufacturers consisted principally of paper and printing, cement and clay products, and a small number of lesser categories.

Small as the pre-integration industrial sector was, it assumed a particularly concentrated spatial pattern. A major part of the production took place in Guatemala, which, in 1960, accounted for 35 percent of the total value added by manufacturing within the five-nation group, and in El Salvador, which supplied another 25 percent. At the other end of the isthmus, Costa Rica provided 18 percent of the total. On a per capita basis, Costa Rica's share was substantially greater than the others, because that country was favored by foreign investors attracted by the higher level of development and greater political stability. There was very little industry in the territory between: Honduras' contribution of 10 percent was much less than its per capita share of the group's industrial output, and Nicaragua supplied less than 13 percent of the total. In general, however, the manufacturing output of the five nations was fairly proportional to their population sizes. This illustrates the market-oriented character of the industry at that time, which becomes even more apparent when we note that virtually all manufacturing took place in the capital cities then as it does now.

RECENT DEVELOPMENTAL POLICY INITIATIVES

By the late 1950s Central America was struggling with problems of sluggish growth of national output and generally stagnating economies at a time when population growth was accelerating. With populations increasing faster than output, the Malthusian trap appeared to be closing. These problems were duplicated throughout Latin America and elsewhere in the underdeveloped world. What has distinguished Central America has been the vigorous and well organized efforts that Central Americans have made to find solutions for these problems. The twofold approach adopted here has involved close cooperation among the Central American countries and detailed regional planning by the individual national governments.

Despite the many quarrels that have marred relations among the Central American countries, they have shown an inclination to turn to each other when a common trouble threatened. There is a tradition of unity dating to the colonial administration of the Captaincy-General of Guatemala and the federation that succeeded it during the early years of independence. The five countries have made more than a score of attempts to reunite since the collapse of federation. At last, in the 1950s the doctrine of regional economic integration in Latin America was developed and actively promoted by the United Nations' Economic Commission for Latin America (ECLA). Here was a solution that was made the more attractive because it originated with Latin American theorists; the idea of self-help appealed strongly to a proud people who had endured a subordinate role in world affairs for centuries. After a period of intensive discussion, the five nations formed the Central American Common Market in 1961.

Meanwhile, the member countries continued their own individual planning programs, which intensified further because of the need to solve problems appearing at the national and local levels. Thus at the same time that it was necessary to stimulate national growth, it was essential to relieve some of the adverse effects of growth. Foremost among the latter were the worsening problems of internal disparaties between people and regions.

the Central American Common Market

The framers of the CACM intended to accomplish a variety of aims, and because of the ambitious nature of their undertaking, they agreed upon a strong type of integration. Many important effects have followed those decisions and the vigorous organization they created to implement them. The CACM has contributed to a rapid acceleration of economic growth; has very substantially altered the volume, composition, and direction of trade; and has changed the structure and location of production.

objectives and obstacles

The general purpose of the CACM was to spur the Central American economies to a rate of growth exceeding the rate of population increase by:

1. reducing the excessive dependence upon the production and export of a limited number of agricultural specialties;
2. developing a new class of secondary exports and changing the structure of imports; and

3. establishing import-competing industries—firms producing for the enlarged domestic market goods that were formerly imported—including not only producers of the usual nondurable consumer goods (often termed easy import-substitution) but also manufactures of intermediates, such as basic metals and chemicals, and even producer goods (machinery and equipment) and durable consumer products (automobiles and appliances). These industrial specialties were to be allocated among the various member countries in an equitable but locationally sound manner to produce a diversified regional economy in Central America.

Serious obstacles stood in the way of achieving all these aims. One of the most serious was that of market size. The combined population of CACM is 15 million, but a majority is outside the market system. (Only 15 percent of Guatemala's population represents a market for manufactured goods at this time.) A second problem was the risk of encouraging inefficient production. Third, there was the danger of disguising normal imports and draining foreign exchange reserves by indiscriminately accepting new industries that merely do the final assembling or packaging of imported goods. Fourth, a number of political problems continue to threaten the CACM. One example is the insistence by poorer members upon special consideration in the location of new industries. More serious are the traditional rivalries, especially those in Honduras and El Salvador that have, in the past, erupted into open war. Finally, there is the instability of governments in a region where revolution has been endemic.

CACM organization and initiatives

To achieve the ambitious aims of the CACM against such obstacles called for closer integration and more elaborate machinery than most such unions have managed to achieve; indeed, the CACM is the most comprehensive integration that has been attempted by underdeveloped countries. Despite its title, the CACM is not a true common market according to Balassa's definition (see Chapter 11), because there is no provision for free movement of the factors of production. Now it is more of a customs union, although many of its organizational arrangements suggest one of the higher forms of integration.

The basic organization was created by the General Treaty on Central American Integration and ratified in 1960 by all except Costa Rica, whose signature was added in 1963. The treaty called for free trade among member countries on all goods not explicitly excepted. These exceptions, which were eventually reduced to only 5 percent of the total, included the staple export crops for the world market and certain special items (especially rum, alcohol, and refined oil products) that member countries depended upon for tax revenue.

The General Treaty also established a CACM executive branch. The ultimate authority in CACM affairs is the Economic Council, composed of the Central American ministers of economy, whose unanimous assent is required in all major decisions. Most of the preparatory work for the ministers, however, is done by an executive council of vice-ministers, who meet more frequently. The day-to-day operations of the CACM are conducted by a permanent secretariate (SIECA), which also makes studies of serious issues, produces reports, and compiles statistics. Its headquarters are in Guatemala City. More detailed technical studies and direct consultations with business enterprises are conducted by the Central American Institute for Industrial Research and Technology (ICAITI).

Another treaty, the Central American Convention on the Equalization of Import Tariffs (1959), specified uniform external tariffs to nonmember countries and created a Central American Clearing House to settle intra-CACM trade balances.

The CACM has also established a number of special instruments to spur growth and development. The most important of these is the Central American Bank for Economic Integration (CABEI), located in Tegucigalpa. The bank's lending policies emphasize economically sound projects expected to have a favorable impact on the whole region—manufacturing and agriculture as well as transportation, communications, and power. Lending decisions take into account the need for equalizing the economic gains of the five members.

One special CACM program is designed to attract "integration industries," technologically advanced types of manufacturing that can gain their required economies of scale by producing for the full CACM market. To supplement this program, the CACM has established the Special System for the Promotion of Production, which gives tariff protection to infant industries, and the Agreement on Fiscal Incentives to Industrial Development, designed to restrict competition among members for new industries.

the growth effects of union

The 1960s were a boom period in Central America. Domestic and foreign investment and the level of international assistance rose sharply. There were structural changes in production and more efficient use of Central American resources through reallocation and trade creation. Manufacturing output expanded, intra-CACM trade rose, and the traditional export staples enjoyed favorable conditions. Altogether the CACM countries experienced unprecedented growth, at least until 1966.

Total output of the five nations increased (at constant prices) by 84 percent between 1960 and 1971. Annual growth rates jumped after formation of the CACM: GNP had grown by only 2.8 percent per annum between 1957 and 1960 as population was rising at a rate of 3.1 percent, but during the first five years of union the GNP rose 6.3 percent per annum against a population growth rate of 3.3 percent. As a consequence, per capita

GNP, which had actually been falling before union, rose at an annual rate of 3.0 percent thereafter. This was an impressive achievement for a group of underdeveloped nations who were experiencing a frightening population expansion at the same time.

The five countries did not share equally in this growth, however. Although all experienced an immediate surge in growth at the outset, El Salvador and Nicaragua led the group and Costa Rica and Honduras lagged behind. By 1971 it was Nicaragua that had gained the most during the first eleven years, with Costa Rica close behind. Honduras and El Salvador had suffered setbacks due largely to their brief war.

Suddenly with the formation of their union, the Central American nations found themselves newly attractive to investors. In the past their citizens had avoided investing at home because of political and economic instability and a shortage of profitable investment opportunities. Formation of the CACM instilled confidence in the region's potential for growth and produced new avenues for investment in an enlarged market protected by high tariffs.

As a result, investment rates have risen substantially throughout the CACM. In 1960 the Central American countries reinvested only 14 percent of their GDP, but by 1971 they were reinvesting 18 percent, a figure that is much higher than the average for underdeveloped countries. The investment-GDP ratio in Costa Rica is especially high and reflects political and economic stability, higher literacy, and a greater variety of human skills than is common in such countries. By 1970 Costa Rica's ratio had risen to 30 percent, almost equal to the remarkable levels attained in Japan and the USSR (see Chapter 14). The ratio also rose in the other CACM countries, except for El Salvador.

The CACM experience is unusual in that three-fourths of this capital has been from private sources, both domestic and foreign. The traditional Central American source of capital accumulation—savings from sales of staple export crops—has provided a high percentage of these funds, which are now channeled into productive domestic investments, especially manufacturing. Private investment from abroad has multiplied many times. A major part of this money has come from the United States, but some of it has also originated in Japan, Mexico, West Germany, and other European countries. CACM members have gained a number of special benefits from these private foreign investments: the increased foreign exchange holdings they generate and the new technology and managment practices they introduce, which have even revitalized the traditional types of manufacturing.

Public sources have supplied the remaining one-quarter of this investment. Central American government funds have represented some of this, although much of it has been provided by loans and grants from abroad, mostly channeled through CABEI, the CACM's central bank.

production and location

Integration has had a substantial impact on Central American production. Manufacturing has been most affected, holding the attention of CACM officials for several reasons. Foremost among these is the influence of the development theory promulgated by the United Nation's advisory group, ECLA, which calls for Latin American countries to reduce their dependence upon agricultural production and export and to minimize their reliance upon manufactured imports, thereby improving their terms of trade with the heartland. In addition, with their populations growing at such enormous rates, the Central American countries can no longer expect agriculture to accommodate the flood of new workers; manufacturing might accomplish this, however. As a consequence, the CACM has increased the quantity of its manufacturing output and influenced factory location.

As the beneficiary of this favorable treatment, manufacturing grew much more rapidly between 1960 and 1971 than did the GDP; industrial output rose at an average annual rate of 8.3 percent while gross output was increasing by 5.7 percent per annum. The manufacturing sector of Central America was therefore producing 2.4 times as much in 1971 as it did in 1960. Whereas value added by manufacturing contributed only 13 percent to the region's GDP in 1960, it had increased to 18 percent by 1971.

In view of ECLA's theoretical emphasis on new kinds of industries, we might expect that the structure of manufacturing would have changed radically during this period of rapid growth in industrial output. This was not the case. New industries did make important quantitative gains, and so did the traditional industries. The market-oriented consumer-goods industries, which had always characterized Central America's manufacturing in the past, responded quickly and positively to the formation of the CACM. Increased demand, resulting from an enlarged market and rising incomes, spurred the pre-existing industries to put idle capacity to work, expand output, and build large new plants; the increased competition from other CACM producers forced them to adopt more efficient techniques. These measures resulted in greater economies of scale and reduced unit costs and prices for manufacturers of textiles, clothing, and other traditional goods. Most foreign investment went into concerns processing vegetables, fruits, tobacco, fish, and grain products for both CACM and overseas markets.

The CACM's drive to increase output of intermediates succeeded in attracting firms making wires and cables, reinforcing rods, steel shapes, electrical machinery and appliances, and oil refinery byproducts. The CACM now produces basic chemicals and chemical intermediates as well as finished chemical products. It also manufactures pulp and paper and paper products, rubber and rubber products, and nonmetallic mineral products.

Note that most of these old and new industries are of the mature type; that is, they are in the last phase of the industrial life cycle. They are well-established forms of manufacturing that use standardized machinery and employ mainly unskilled or semiskilled labor (see Chapters 8 and 9). Although Central American production is still predominantly market-oriented, the CACM has had some success in achieving backward and forward linkages. Common Market farmers, for example, now obtain their agricultural chemicals from local manufacturers and sell their farm commodities to CACM producers of frozen banana purée, meats, leather goods, cotton textiles, and clothing. This diversity provides security against fluctuating world prices for the CACM's staple exports.

Theoretically, we should expect that integration would have greatly altered the locational pattern of manufacturing in Central America. Freed from their former dependence upon individual national markets, industries should have been able to seek the optimal locations in the expanded five-nation area. The greatest growth should therefore have taken place in the larger existing centers providing ready-made agglomeration advantages and maximum access to market. In theory, we should expect an increased polarity of industrial growth within the combined territory of the union, focusing upon a limited number of growth centers, each with its own interregional specializations. Running counter to this is the CACM commitment to balanced growth, enforceable through the union's special instruments.

As a consequence, the actual locational pattern that has evolved represents a compromise. On the one hand, polarity of industrial production has tended to persist as certain growth centers have clung to their dominance. At the time of union there were already two principal areas of incipient industrialization: In the West, Guatemala City and nearby San Salvador acted as foci for manufacturing location, and in the East San José, Costa Rica, filled a similar role. Thus in 1960 Guatemala and El Salvador contributed 58 percent of the CACM's value added by manufacture, and Costa Rica provided another 18 percent. Honduras and Nicaragua together supplied merely 23 percent of the total, about equally divided between them.

By 1971 Guatemala and El Salvador still led the group, maintaining an undiminished share of a substantially larger total CACM output. Costa Rica and Nicaragua had meanwhile recorded ever greater gains, while Honduras slipped still farther behind. Thus, although both Nicaragua and Honduras had been favored for investment under CACM's balanced growth doctrine, the policy had succeeded in the one case and failed in the other. This underscores Honduras' difficulties in attracting private investment, and it shows how stubbornly the Common Market's bipolar pattern of development persists.

Another expected result of integration, in theory, is increased regional specialization. It is anticipated that each region within the union would specialize in certain commodities intended for the whole market area. Within the EEC and among the Scandinavian members of EFTA, this has assumed the form of intraindustry specialization. Evidence of a similar trend in Central America is provided by the pharmaceutical industry, which specializes in a different group of products in each of the five nations. The CACM explicitly locates its "integration industries" according to this principle.

infrastructure development

One facet of the Central American space-economy that has received indisputable benefits from integration is the region's infrastructure, which had traditionally been one of its basic weaknesses. At the inception of CACM, the Central American nations were still five wholly separate national systems, cut off from each other by a serious transport barrier. Not only was overland transportation poor between countries but it was inadequate even within countries. Many parts of Central America thus isolated from the outside world also lacked modern communications and electric power.

The CACM has therefore stressed transport development almost as much as it has stressed manufacturing. There has been a tendency to follow the Canadian example of making transportation a leading sector in regional growth. The CACM has received substantial assistance from foreign sources in this program. These include United States' contributions to the integration fund administered by CABEI, and the lending activities of the International Bank for Reconstruction and Development and the Inter–American Development Bank.

Efforts to develop the region's infrastructure have concentrated particularly on highway construction, because roads are quicker and cheaper to build than railways. Because a highway network also has a finer mesh, it can give improved access to more areas, especially in mountainous terrain that complicates railway construction and operation. In order to reduce transport barriers to intrabloc trade, the Central American regional highway program, instituted in 1961, has given priority to roads that are important to the entire CACM rather than to those roads that mainly serve national needs. This program has been well financed and has progressed rapidly.

Another infrastructive development goal of the CACM has been the coordination of electric energy supply systems. Although total output of electricity has tripled since formation of the union, completion of interconnected power grids between countries has been delayed mainly because of political problems. There is clear agreement, however, that the grids are needed to reduce investment and operating costs and to increase the dependability of supply. Integrated telecommunications networks have also been planned. Another badly needed type of support facility is an increased grain-storage capacity to reduce the serious grain losses and fluctuating supply that have hampered grain-marketing in the Common Market. Foreign loans and grants administered by CABEI have financed a program to construct a system of regional grain-storage silos.

An indirect effect of economic growth in the CACM has been an expansion of the tertiary sector. In the Common Market the increase in commerce, finance, and other services has generally kept up with the rapid rate of the GDP. Once more the exception is Honduras, where the services have lagged far behind those of the Central American bloc.

trade effects of union

One of the most important tests of the success of an experiment in integration such as this is the degree and nature of the changes it has made in the trade patterns of member countries. The first trade goal of the CACM has been to improve the allocation of Central American resources through trade creation, especially where this creation results in increased intraregional trade rather than trade with more powerful nonmembers. A second major purpose is to manage external trade to provide increased support for growth and development. This is to be accomplished through a diversification of linkages with foreign suppliers and markets generally and a reduced dependence upon heartland countries in particular. A third objective is to diversify the commodity structure of exports—to reduce dependence upon a narrow range of primary exports.

The pursuit of these aims raises a number of fundamental questions that have caused much argument. One of these is whether the overall effect of integration has been to create more trade than it has diverted (see Chapter 11). Theoretically, it is desirable to maximize trade creation and to minimize diversion; that is, to shift each country's foreign purchases to the most efficient supplier and avoid a shift to the more inefficient supplier. Considering the production problems of underdeveloped countries, a certain amount of diversion is an unavoidable result of union; however, the long-term advantages of economic growth generated by integration should more than compensate for the temporary losses from this inefficiency. After weighing all these considerations, what evidence can we find in the changing volume, structure, and spatial pattern of CACM trade to confirm that the group has achieved any of its integration goals?

The period since integration has seen a remarkable growth in the CACM's trade. Exports of the group multiplied 2.5 times between 1960 and 1971, twice the rate at which their GDP grew. Although the Central American countries were already exporting 16 percent of their GDP in 1960, by 1971 they exported nearly 22 percent of their total output. Meanwhile, imports grew even more rapidly than exports causing Central America's balance of payments to worsen. Exports could not rise fast enough to cover expanding import needs for development purposes and to accommodate the demand generated by rising incomes.

The members of CACM shared unequally in trade growth. The CACM's principal exporter in 1960, El Salvador had by 1971 surrendered this lead to her larger neighbor, Guatemala, whose rate of trade participation had risen more rapidly. The highest rate of trade growth following union, however, was attained by Nicaragua, followed closely by Honduras and Costa Rica. Honduras, whose exports were 30 percent of gross output in 1971, had become unusually dependent upon trade, although her economy was so small that this constituted only 16 percent of the CACM total.

How much of this trade increase can be attributed to integration? The changing composition and increased diversity of CACM trade provides a partial answer. Manufactured products had contributed only 3.3 percent of Central America's exports in 1960, but they comprised 20 percent of the total by 1970. Although traditional exports still predominated in 1970, substantial increases had taken place in exports of both consumer and producer manufactures by 1970. As in the EEC, the trade of the CACM had begun to show indications of both product differentiation and intraindustry specialization during the eleven years.

No longer are the Central American nations among the world's most specialized exporters. Before union, Guatemala had received more than 99 percent of her export earnings from coffee and bananas; today she is the bloc's least specialized exporter. During the CACM's first decade the bloc's imports changed less in structure than did its exports, an experience typical of developing countries with growing needs for capital goods and industrial raw materials.

Another test of the effectiveness of union is whether it has reduced the dependence upon a limited number of trading partners in the world heartland. Is the United States still so overwhelmingly important as a customer and supplier as it was in 1960? Has formation of a union induced its members to begin trading with one another instead of confining their exchanges to the heartland nations? If both changes have occurred in the direction of CACM trade, have they resulted in trade creation or diversion? One way to answer these questions is to analyze the factors affecting the choice of trading partners, at the time of union and today.

The two most significant influences then and now are distance between trading partners and the size of their GDP (a measure of economic size). When the Central American countries began their experiment, the negative influence of distance on their trade was not so strong as it is today. Meanwhile, GDP, the dominant influence at the time of union, now has no more effect than does distance. This suggests that the Central American countries are no longer so dependent upon remote but rich trading partners in North America and Europe as they used to be; instead they would seem to be turning more to nearby, less well-off countries as customers and suppliers. Among the latter are Mexico and other Caribbean rim countries, but, especially, other members of the CACM.

From the moment that integration took place,

intra-CACM trade commenced to soar. Between 1960 and 1971 the trade among member countries increased 8.5 times; during the first six years it actually grew at an average annual rate of 32.2 percent! Although intrabloc trade had been only 7.4 percent of the total in 1960, by 1971 it had risen to 25 percent, and for certain members it was even higher. Today both Guatemala and El Salvador send more than one-third of their exports to other CACM countries. Among the group the only exception is Honduras, whose shipments to other members have actually declined since 1960. Thus the two main source areas at either end of the five-nation territory provide most of the intra-CACM trade.

Despite these high rates of intrabloc growth, Central America's trade with the rest of the world is still the major part. By 1971 the CACM countries still shipped three-fourths of their exports to destinations outside the group. This external trade was, of course, overwhelmingly important to Honduras, which sent 97 percent of her exports to nonmember nations. Even during the period between 1960 and 1971, when intrabloc trade was rising so rapidly, external shipments continued to grow at an average annual rate of 6.7 percent. Only Guatemala and El Salvador, who were becoming more dependent upon trade with other CACM members, failed to increase their non-CACM sales as rapidly as the group.

One of the most notable changes in the spatial pattern of Central American trade between 1960 and 1971 was the increased diversification of linkages. Although the United States had traditionally dominated the exports and imports of Central America, today the CACM nations are forming new links with a greater variety of heartland countries. They are also acquiring new connections with Mexico, other Latin American Free Trade Association countries, and a number of the African nations. Altogether, by 1969 the CACM had 86 trade linkages of more than $1 million each, by comparison with only 56 such links as recently as 1963.

The kinds of goods that move between CACM members are distinctly different from those shipped to their customers elsewhere. Exports to other members are composed largely of manufactured goods, but exports to nonmember countries still consist mainly of the familiar primary staples. On the other hand, CACM imports from either source are comprised principally of manufactured goods, although there are some foreign purchases of wheat and a few other food items, together with imports of oil and some industrial raw materials.

Despite the continued importance of coffee, bananas, cotton, and sugar for sale in world markets, there are indications that these are beginning to lose some of their overwhelming dominance. These items constituted 74 percent of CACM shipments to all destinations in 1962, but by 1971 they had declined to 56 percent. Guatemala experienced the greatest decrease, while Honduras increased her dependence upon traditional exports.

The size and composition of intra-CACM shipments are of vital concern to the members of this bloc because of the direct impact this trade has upon their incomes. Manufactured goods constituted 76 per[cent of] all intraregional exports in 1971, a proportion that [has] continued to rise in each of the five except Honduras, which has had little success with its industrial exports. More than nine-tenths of CACM's industrial exports go to other member countries.

Do these changes in the volume, composition, and direction of Central America's commerce describe a pattern of trade creation or diversion? Undoubtedly there has been a considerable amount of trade diversion, because many products now manufactured and traded to each other by CACM members could be obtained more cheaply from heartland countries—notably, refined oil products, chemicals, and rubber items. Yet there is also evidence of trade creation, both in CACM's exchanges with nonmember countries and its intraregional commodity flows. The sharp rise in the total volume of CACM exports and imports is far in excess of the increases that might have been expected if integration had not occurred and pre-union trends had continued unchanged. A large part of this excess is attributed to integration, a byproduct of the rising incomes and the new needs and wants it has generated. Import substitution has diverted trade in specific items, but other imports have taken their place; meanwhile, much trade has been created by the general acceleration of international flow of commodities. In some measure, therefore, the CACM has repeated the experience of the EEC.

The CACM seems to have furthered several of its trade goals. Some reallocation of Central American resources has resulted from the increased intrabloc trade, which has had the effect of stimulating industrialization. This has in turn put to work underused domestic resources: labor, entrepreneurial skills, and capital that might otherwise have ended up as Miami bank deposits. The very existence of troublesome disparities in export growth rates among CACM members reflects a reallocation on the basis of relative efficiencies. Poorly endowed Honduras, for example, has grown least.

The group has succeeded in diversifying Central American trade to an encouraging extent. The increased variety of trading partners relieves member countries of at least some of North American dominance of their trade and enables them to deal more effectively with nations at similar levels of development. Although not wholly emancipated from their dependence upon their traditional staple exports, they are now exporting a greater variety of commodities, many of which enjoy more stable demand and prices. No longer are the Central American countries identical in the structure and spatial patterns of their trade; integration has helped each to develop a new individuality.

national programs

Integration has produced some demonstrable benefits to the Central American region and to individual member countries; but formation of the CACM has also had some unfortunate results. One of its less desirable

...tensify regional disparities within ...he gains from integration have ...number of growth centers, mainly ...ng peripheral areas of the union ...before or even adversely affected. Be- ...largest concentrations of population ...egions, the CACM's overall progress mas... ...at integration has contributed little toward reduc...g the proportion of Central Americans living at or near the subsistence level, and it has done even less to improve their circumstances. Preexisting regional differences have thus tended to grow rather than diminish.

the problems of lagging regions

Regional disparities within underdeveloped countries usually replicate in miniature the center-periphery problems between nations. Hampered by inaccessibility and poor communications, the marginal regions of Central America began their development later and lag far behind the national centers of growth. These poorer districts lack the special advantages of the metropolis with its accumulation of infrastructure and facilities, external economies, and capital and its irresistible attractions for decision makers and the more vigorous and better educated members of the population generally. Because of their poverty in these human and man-made resources, peripheral regions are unable to match the primate city's productivity.

To some extent the growth induced by the CACM has caused the gap between growth centers and lagging regions on the margins to widen, not only because of the center's accumulations but also because of the periphery's losses. Unlike sovereign nations with their border controls, these disadvantaged regions lack the means under free market conditions to protect themselves from the unequal competition of the primate city. The outlying regions therefore find their productive resources constantly draining to the center: their most capable workers and the savings of their landed aristocracy. The market mechanism therefore tends to widen the gap by its "backwash" effects, which reduce the marginal regions' capacity to exploit their natural comparative advantages with respect to the center.

Integration has also helped to weaken the ties between the modern and traditional economies of the Central American states. Because of the CACM's emphasis upon those types of import-competing industries that have low levels of labor absorption and high skill requirements, relatively few workers are able to make the transition from subsistence farming to factory employment. At the same time, those people existing in the traditional sector are unable to consume many of the high-priced products of the new industries.

Polarization of this kind is a common problem among countries just beginning to develop. Studies of many countries at various levels of development suggest that regional disparities tend to follow a regular pattern as a nation advances. At first the contrasts between regions increase, but eventually the gap begins to narrow as the economy matures. When the prosperity of the center reaches that point at which it starts to spill over into surrounding regions, peripheral areas become progressively integrated into the national space-economy. This tendency toward ultimate equalization, which is illustrated by the experience of the American South, suggests that regional disparities are self-correcting.

Where the process progresses slowly however, as in the Central American countries, political pressures to relieve the problems of the disadvantaged populations may become irresistible. This popular insistence upon equalization of regions differs little from the doctrine of balanced growth among member countries of the CACM. Some argue that this regional dualism is contrary to the national interest, because it deprives the economy of potential markets required to provide the new industries with adequate economies of scale. They maintain further that the country cannot afford to deprive itself of the underused human and physical resources of undeveloped regions. Finally, they note that the depressed area becomes an increasingly heavy burden on the national economy and a breeding ground for social and political unrest.

A number of countries have attempted to solve this problem by deliberately decentralizing production. One of the technologically advanced nations that has used this approach is the United Kingdom (see Chapter 14); less developed countries that have adopted it include Puerto Rico, India, Chile, Venezuela, Ghana, Tanzania, and Egypt. Although the basis for such a policy is the arguement that "excessive" urbanization is inefficient, the empirical evidence appears to indicate the opposite. There is no proof that cities become more inefficient with increasing size; indeed, a substantial concentration of manufacturing and services is required for a take-off to occur. In Honduras, for example, the lack of such agglomeration advantages has obviously retarded the country's advancement.

There has been a continuing argument in Central America over the relative merits of equity and efficiency. In other words, should growth of a nation's GNP be sacrificed in the interests of regional equality? As in the United Kingdom, Central American solutions to this problem usually take the form of political compromise. This is but one of the planning dilemmas that governmental decision makers must attempt to solve.

difficulties of national planning in Central America

In addition to these disagreements over basic development theory, planners of the CACM's member nations must contend with pressures from special-interest groups whose prerogatives are threatened by change. Chief among these groups in Central America is the landed aristocracy, whose influence is difficult to resist because of their active participation in government and even in the activities of the planning agencies themselves. A further problem is that of defining meaningful, viable planning regions because of the conflicting views and interests of the various government ministries involved. Decision making is hampered by insufficient and inaccurate data and by inadequate analysis of information at hand. Finally, there is the problem of political instability—the plans made by one national administration are cast out by the next. The continuous threat of political takeover in some Central American countries results in a diversion of scarce resources to provide protection for the group in power, and it tends to paralyze decision making by planners, entrepreneurs, and donors of international aid funds.

UNSOLVED PROBLEMS AND UNUSED OPPORTUNITIES

During the 1960s, the CACM countries experienced a remarkable growth and compiled an enviable record of achievement that is often cited as a model for underdeveloped countries who are considering a cooperative approach to modernization. The time for testing the staying powers of their union has arrived. The surge of growth during the early years was followed after 1966 by a slackening of the pace; the ensuing five-year period brought a series of setbacks, both natural and man-made, that have adversely affected the region's production and trade.

Since the watershed year of 1966, the CACM has experienced a deceleration of annual growth rates, figured at constant prices. Before that year the average yearly rate of growth had been 6 percent, but since then the rate has slipped to 5.4 percent and recently, even lower. Meanwhile, Central America's population has continued its rapid and steady climb, causing net per capita growth to decline even more: from 2.6 percent in the 1960–1966 period to only 2.1 percent since. In large measure this change in growth rates following 1966 reflects a drop in gross domestic investment, which affected El Salvador and Nicaragua with a special severity.

The greatest declines in growth among the various sectors of the economy occurred in construction and manufacturing. Before 1966, industrial growth in the CACM proceeded at the unusually high rate of 9.3 percent per year, declining thereafter to 7.9 percent per annum between 1966 and 1971. Growth in construction was severely affected by declining investments and fell from 8.4 percent to 3.4 percent and then to only 2.7 percent between 1969 and 1971.

Some of the most severe changes occurred in the growth rates of Central America's exports, which declined from an annual average of 10.7 percent between 1960 and 1966 to only 3.2 percent during the following five years. Intrabloc and external exports experienced

declining rates of growth, which, in each case, fell more rapidly than did the growth rate of CACM's GDP. More recently, higher coffee prices have substantially raised Central America's export earnings, helping to offset higher prices paid for imported oil.

What were the reasons for these changes in growth rates? A major purpose of the union was to convert a substantial proportion of pre-CACM merchandise imports from nonmembers into flows of investment capital—a substitution of capital for imports. Initially this was very successful; union was immediately followed by a surge of investment by foreign firms wishing to get in under the high CACM tariff. This was to be only a temporary phenomenon, however; the initial spurt was not to be duplicated. The trouble was that CACM industries, both new and old, directed their marketing efforts specifically and exclusively to Central America. As the union's market for these goods became saturated, new opportunities for import-substitution vanished; Central America quickly exhausted its possibilities for "easy" import-substitution, accomplished with little effort in the case of the traditional industries, which merely had to bring into operation the idle capacity of existing facilities or to expand their capacities.

The first of the "new" industries were introduced with relative ease, because they emphasize the last stages of manufacturing—the final mixing, assembling, packaging, or bottling of imported goods—and make little use of Central America's own raw materials. This provided a ready way for foreign investors to gain easy access to the Central American market. It is a common path to industrialization, usually followed in time by gradually adding the earlier stages of manufacturing in a process of backward linkage. In Central America, however, there has been a tendency for this emphasis upon final assembly to be exaggerated and to be perpetuated. It has had the effect of locking the Central American nations into a costly pattern of importing raw materials and partially assembled goods, intensifying an already worrisome balance-of-payments problem. This in turn automatically reduces the scope for further growth.

Another drag on the economy has been the excessively high tariff protection that Central America had provided its import-substituting industries. This comfortable situation tends to perpetuate inefficient manufacturing and to place a high cost burden on the users of the products. We saw the effect of this earlier in the case of Central America's commercial agriculture, which must now pay more for fertilizer and other agricultural chemicals than previously.

A further burden on the Central American economy is the persistence of colonialism in manufacturing, which assumes novel and insidious forms. One of these is the artificially high cost of imported technology. Central American manufacturers, subsidiaries of multinational corporations, and unaffiliated licensees have to pay inflated prices for the licensing of brand names, engineering design, specialized equipment, and technical and management advice. In some cases they must also agree to tie-in sales of parts, raw materials, and equipment from parent firms, a practice usually illegal within the United States. The royalties paid by one American firm to another for the use of its technology is normally about 2 percent of sales, but in Latin America it is commonly 5 to 6 percent and may be as high as 15 percent. Some claim that this is merely an accounting device for heartland firms to repatriate disguised profits and thereby reduce their local taxes. Unfortunately, the technology that is thus expensively purchased is often poorly suited to Central American needs. The net effect is to stifle research and development in the region and to perpetuate its technological dependency. This practice reduces Central American tax revenues because these fees are taken off the top; moreover, it is a serious drain on the balance of payments.

In addition, there are persisting problems that result from the limited scale of operations that the small Central American market is able to offer. Many new industries are able to function only because of the very high tariff protection; thus, further growth is effectively hampered by market size, which will be difficult to increase beyond its present levels. The domestic market can be materially enlarged only by bringing more people into the economy by transforming traditional agriculture or by massive infusions of industrial employment. The foreign markets for Central American manufactures are severely limited because the region's goods are so costly they are noncompetitive outside the union.

The growth problems of Central American industry have been compounded: the disruptions of the Honduran-Salvadorian war and the closing of the Inter-American Highway have reduced the union's market to an even smaller size. Because of the element of uncertainty it introduced, the war severely retarded the influx of foreign private investment throughout the Common Market. Manufacturing and construction have been much affected by this loss of foreign funding. The sharp decline in El Salvador's growth, formerly so promising, can be attributed in large measure to the war. Not only did she lose Honduras as a principal market and source of raw materials, but she was cut off from Nicaragua and Costa Rica by the loss of the overland connection. Many of El Salvador's exports had consisted of manufactured goods sold to other CACM countries. The industrial growth of Guatemala, Costa Rica, and Nicaragua was also severely affected by the war. Honduran manufacturing, on the other hand, had been so poorly developed that the war losses of that combatant nation's industry were minimal. Such industry as Honduras had managed to acquire was sufficient merely to serve the national market. Adding to the damage caused by man-made calamities is that inflicted by such hostile acts of nature as the devastating hurricane of 1974 and the Managua earthquake.

Yet another deterrent to further growth and more effective unification of the Central American nations is the inequality in their levels of development. From the very beginning, the disadvantages of Honduras, with her low per capita GDP and poorly developed industry, have created stresses in the CACM. Honduras' sales to the other members have lagged, especially her manufacturing exports, which have dropped in absolute terms. Since 1960 Honduras has therefore been unable to close the gap between her level of development and that of the group. Her poor infrastructure, shortage of skilled workers, political instability, and lack of the necessary agglomeration requirements for industry have militated against this.

During these years, Honduras and Nicaragua, who was also a lagging member at the outset, have demanded preferential treatment. The doctrine of balanced economic development was therefore formally agreed upon, providing the poorer members with extra loans and special preference in the location of integration industries. In practice, however, the other members have been reluctant to relinquish their advantages within a free market situation; at the same time, industries have been hesitant about locating in Honduras, and foreign governments have not been eager to grant developmental aid to subsidize poor economic locations. Nevertheless, the Central American bank has been working to achieve a balanced growth among the members and has been directing investment funds in such a way as to compensate for disparities. Indeed the record of CABEI loans shows that the two lagging members have been much favored by the bank's policies.

Even with this special help for poorer members, the problem of achieving a balanced development is still a major obstacle. Honduras has been so preoccupied with her intrabloc balance of payments that she has failed to recognize the other benefits that have accrued to her as a result of union: the extra investments, loans, and industries, and a more efficient allocation of her resources.

Because integration is first of all a political exercise, some of the most difficult questions remaining for the future of the CACM are of a political nature. The group must contend with a variety of related political problems, including the quality of national administration, political instability, and excessive nationalism. These affect the growth of individual economies and limit their capacities to work together.

The day-to-day operations of national governments and their various agencies is often subject to crippling inefficiencies because of a chronic shortage of skilled administrators. This compounds the difficulties of decision making and results in the inept implementation of planning programs. Honduras is particularly hampered by the lack of administrative skills, a problem that is worsened by the frequency of *coups d'état*, which produce a complete change in personnel.

Administrative inefficiency is thus a product of political instability, a basic problem in all the Central

American countries but Costa Rica. The region has a long history of violent changes of government, usually palace revolutions in the past; but today there is increasing danger of genuine insurrections by suppressed populations. This presents a problem for development planning because political stability is required to provide private enterprisers with the assurance of continuity and consistency they need in order to risk long-term investments. Even the suggestion of instability has debilitating effects on economic growth, and severe internal strife can be ruinous.

As we have observed in other contexts, excessive nationalism presents a number of obstacles to effective operation of the CACM. The members of this organization have thus far refused to surrender much of their sovereignty to the CACM, even though this is basic to the whole idea of integration. The CACM needs greater authority to make decisions in order to act effectively in the long-term regional interest. Meanwhile, the organization must contend with frequent unilateral interruptions to trade and with national development plans that conflict with integration aims.

Worst of all are national animosities that occasionally arise among members, such as the Soccer War between Honduras and El Salvador, whose disruptive effects we have observed previously. The conflict arose from the circumstances surrounding the overflow of migrants from overcrowded El Salvador into lightly settled Honduras. Of the estimated 300,000 who participated in this movement, many became squatters and occupied land to which they lacked titles. When Honduras expelled those lacking legal claims to their land, the flood of 100,000 refugees intensified El Salvador's already serious population and employment problems.

Feelings between the two countries grew until a riot at a soccer match touched off a bitter war. This illustrates the potentially explosive effects of population pressures and their political implications.

Indeed, many of the obstacles to economic growth are related to Central America's problems of population and society. The specter of explosive population growth overshadows most of the decisions made by the CACM and its members, who must conduct an unending battle to ensure that rates of economic growth outpace population increases. Central Americans are currently losing the fight to maintain satisfactory levels of food supply and dietary adequacy. Meanwhile the subsistence sector lags badly, unemployment rises, education levels are slipping, and illiteracy is growing. All this reduces the effectiveness of the labor force, reduces communication with the populace, retards modernization, and inhibits efforts to integrate the national economies.

Much of the economic lethargy can be attributed also to the obsolete agrarian arrangement described earlier. The land tenure system, which tends to perpetuate dualism in agriculture, is very difficult to change. While large acreages are wasted on the grand estates, subsistence plots are being subdivided until they have become too small for economical operation, and stagnation results at both levels.

The archaic social structure provides little mobility between classes. Divisions along ethnic lines prevent effective communication. Great disparities in income increase political unrest and limit the effective demand for their own goods. But the pressure for change is rising as dissatisfaction continues to feed on the witnessing of affluence amid want.

RECOMMENDED READINGS

Castillo, Carlos, *Growth and Integration in Central America.* New York: Praeger, 1966.

Hansen, Roger D., *Central America: Regional Integration and Economic Development.* National Planning Association Studies in Development Progress No. 1. Washington: National Planning Association, 1967.

James, Preston E., *Latin America.* New York: Odyssey Press, 1969.

Joel, Clark, *Growth Trends in the Central American Common Market (CACM), 1960–1971.* Guatemala City: U.S. AID Regional Office for Central America and Panama, 1972.

new zealand: prosperity and dependence in a remote land

21

New Zealand shares many of the basic traits and inherent problems of other hinterland nations but has managed to avoid the extremes of poverty and social disorder that burden much of Latin America, Africa, and Asia. New Zealand is far away from world markets, has a history of colonialism and dependence, and, as a supplier of primary commodities, is vulnerable to economic and political events in the heartland. Long after attaining political independence, she is still struggling to shed her precarious dependence upon a declining mother country and to form more diverse economic ties without becoming enmeshed in a new kind of colonialism.

Despite these similarities to other hinterland countries, New Zealand has succeeded in providing her citizens with a level of material comfort and social security comparable to that of most Europeans. Although New Zealand's economy is resource-based, the country has followed a different strategy for exploiting those resources than have other hinterland nations that depend upon the land for their support. These tactics have provided the country with a rate of economic growth as steady and rapid as most heartland countries. The task to which New Zealanders have now set themselves with characteristic energy and resourcefulness is to secure and broaden this prosperity in a rapidly changing and increasingly uncertain world.

When viewing the more specific characteristics of New Zealand, one is inevitably reminded of the country's British homeland. Indeed, New Zealand seems in many respects to be a hinterland counterpart of the United Kingdom (see Chapter 16), another small island nation with limited physical assets but with a number of unique human assets. The parallel becomes more interesting when we consider that New Zealand's people are largely a British population transplanted to the Antipodes along with their British economic and political attitudes and practices, democratic institutions, and cultural and social values. Nearly a century and a half after their arrival in this remote land, New Zealanders have continued to preserve their long-range British connection. However, as recent events in the heartland endanger the New Zealand economy and threaten the old special relationship with the United Kingdom, New Zealand's focus is turning in very different directions.

NEW ZEALAND'S ASSETS AND LIABILITIES

How did New Zealand achieve her unique prosperity? What kind of resource endowment underlies the country's comparative advantage in the world economic system? The answer lies partly in the physical qualities of the land and partly in the kind of people living there and the nature of their experience.

physical attributes of the land

Two of New Zealand's most significant physical characteristics are her small size and remote location (Fig. 21.1). The nation occupies two larger islands,

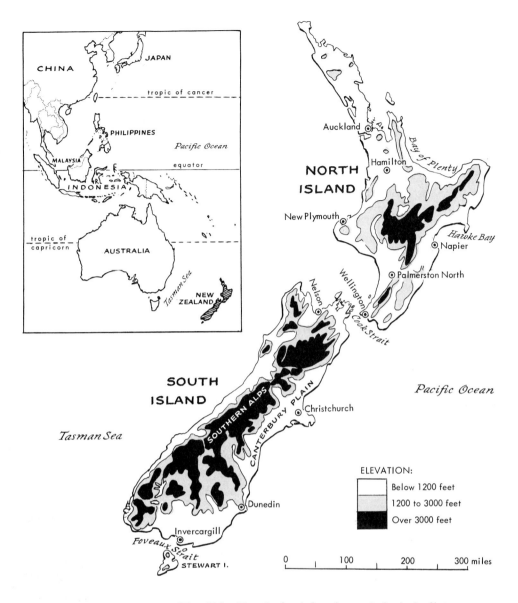

Fig. 21.1 *New Zealand: location and physical relief*

North Island and South Island, several smaller ones nearby, and a number of island territories in the South Pacific. Exclusive of territorial dependencies, the total area is 103,736 square miles, about the size of Colorado and only slightly larger than the United Kingdom. The archipelago is long and narrow: the combined length of the two larger islands is a little over 1,000 miles, and the widest part of the archipelago measures 280 miles. New Zealand is 12,000 miles from the mother country, on almost the exact opposite side of the globe, and far from the nearest large continental land mass. This physical isolation has had many consequences.

New Zealand is a mountainous land like Japan, Indonesia, and Central America. Her two main islands share the same mountain system, which reaches elevations of almost 10,000 feet on North Island and more than 12,000 feet on South Island. On the west coast of South Island the mountains reach the sea, forming ruggedly beautiful fjords. The country reaches from 34°S to 47°S, which is equivalent to the interval be-

tween Athens, Georgia, and Quebec City. This latitudinal extent gives the country a set of climates ranging from subtropical on the Auckland Peninsula of the far north to cool and temperate at the southern tip. The great contrasts in elevation and proximity to the sea affect temperatures and precipitation—a permanent snow cover for the highest peaks, rainfall of more than 100 inches per annum on some of the exposed western slopes, and rain shadows on the leeward eastern sides of the mountains. Yet, because of the maritime influence, annual temperature ranges are not very great. Given these physical conditions, only 4 percent of New Zealand is suitable for field crops, but much of the country provides superb conditions for grasses—one of the best livestock-producing environments in the world.

Before European settlement, much of the country was heavily forested. A dense growth of temperate mixed-evergreen rain forest covered much of North Island and the west coast of South Island, while pure stands of southern beech occupied many of the high mountains. The early colonists cleared and burned most of these forests and sowed the land to grasses. Subsequent overgrazing and erosion destroyed large areas of productive woodland. Although less than one-sixth of the country is forested today, there are remnants of great rain forests in the mountains and west coast of South Island. The rate of tree growth is rapid in this mild, rainy climate, and government reforestation schemes of recent times have revitalized the wood products industry. Another of New Zealand's biotic resources is fish, attracted by rich feeding grounds on the narrow shelf surrounding the islands. Although the potential is limited, catches of snapper, flounder, oysters, crayfish, and many other commercial species supply domestic needs and provide a small surplus for export.

The nature of New Zealand's energy resources has influenced the growth of the country's economy in several respects. Because of an abundance of cheap electric power, per capita energy use is unusually high; indeed, electricity is so plentiful and inexpensive that it is emphasized to the neglect of other forms of energy. Consumption, aided by an excellent distribution system that includes a submarine cable linking the two main islands, is still rising and is expected to grow by another 130 percent during the 1970s. The inexpensive electric power results from the high mountains, heavy rainfall, and abundant falling water. Although hydroelectricity was almost the sole kind of power until recently, geothermal sources are now providing increasing amounts and are drawing upon a large supply of natural steam and hot water in North Island's central volcanic basin. The large potential from this and other forms of thermal power will provide most of the future expansion.

Another source of thermal energy is coal, which occurs in several localities on both islands. The reserves are limited and dwindling, however, and they contain a large percentage of low-grade brown coal. Bituminous coal is present in smaller quantities, but it is costly to mine from the faulted and folded seams.

One of New Zealand's best hopes for sustaining her rapidly growing electricity needs is natural gas, which has been discovered recently in large quantities. In the short term, use of this gas is expected to remain limited because of the country's excessive commitment to electricity. Indeed, much of the gas will be allocated to the generating of electricity, despite the inherent inefficiency of this use of gas. Gas condensates will provide needed feed for the country's petroleum refineries, and some gas will probably go to Japan in liquid form. In the longer term, gas will help to stimulate the country's industrialization, particularly the development of its petrochemical industry.

New Zealand does not appear to be well endowed with other minerals, but minerals played an important role in the country's development—a series of gold rushes between the 1850s and the early part of this century. The most important metallic mineral resource at present is iron ore, which occurs in large deposits of titanium-bearing magnetite in beach sands washed upon the west coasts of North and South Islands. Although the 7 percent titanium content of these ores previously complicated recovery of the iron, new techniques have made the recovery economically feasible and provide the basis for a growing domestic steel industry and a surplus of iron ore concentrates for export. Supplies of other metallic minerals are limited, but such mineral building materials as sand, gravel, and limestone are plentiful.

New Zealand's physical resources alone are not sufficient to account for the country's economic successes. The soils are not particularly fertile, little arable land is available, the native grasses are not very nutritious, and minerals are limited in quantity and variety. Clearly, other explanations are needed.

people

Undoubtedly, New Zealand's most valuable resource, as in the cases of Britain and Japan, is her people. This is the feature that most clearly distinguishes this nation from most hinterland countries.

numbers and distribution

Unlike many countries outside the heartland, New Zealand has relatively few people and these few are concentrated within a small part of the land (Fig. 21.2). Excluding the Pacific island dependencies, New Zealand has approximately 2.9 million people, about the same number as Honduras or in the tenth largest U.S. metropolitan area. They live along the coastal margins of their country and avoid much of the interior, with its rugged mountains, hill country, and swamps. Seventy percent live on North Island, two-thirds in cities and towns, and more than two-fifths in the four largest cities, which are all important seaports. This degree of urbanization, which appears paradoxical in a country whose economy is so firmly rooted in the land, is a measure of the efficiency of the nation's farms and ranches.

ethnic composition

New Zealand is a multiracial society with a modern history of relatively equal treatment. At least nine-tenths of the population is of European descent, mostly British but with some Dutch and others. The nonwhite members of the society include Pacific islanders from New Zealand's dependencies in the Cook, Niue, Tokelous, and Western Samoan Islands; but the largest group of non-British stock are the Maoris, the indigenous inhabitants of New Zealand at the time of European arrival. The Maoris are a brown-skinned Polynesian people, whose skilled navigator ancestors spread from South Asia throughout much of the Pacific centuries ago. A dynamic people, with the highest culture of all the islanders, they quickly assimilated European farming skills but carefully preserved their valued tribal

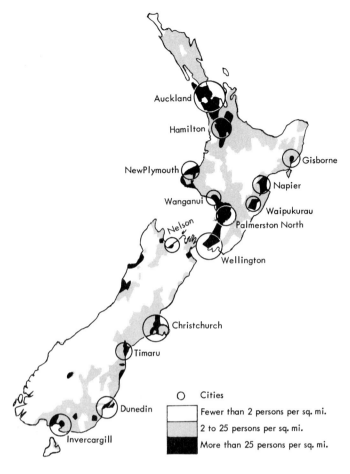

Fig. 21.2 *Distribution of population*

Cities ○
Fewer than 2 persons per sq. mi.
2 to 25 persons per sq. mi.
More than 25 persons per sq. mi.

traditions. Although the proportion steadily diminishes through intermarriage, two-thirds of the present-day Maoris are of unmixed ancestry.

Most Maoris now live in the northern, central, and eastern parts of North Island. Although they formerly occupied a much larger territory, they lost most of the best agricultural lands to the first white settlers. In the past they were mainly a farming folk, but recently increasing numbers of them have been moving to the cities nearest their northern tribal areas. Today the Maoris are almost one-half urban, and more than one-third of the total Maori population now lives in Auckland, New Zealand's largest city. Racial problems are minimal, reflecting attitudes of fairness and an official policy of equality. Maoris have special representation in Parliament and stated rights to lands and fisheries. Amicable relations have been aided by the relatively small size of the minority, but the proportion is now changing.

demography

New Zealand has a history of steady population growth through natural increase and net immigration, but the country has avoided the grave demographic problems of most less developed nations in the world hinterland. Typical of advanced countries, New Zealand has a low death rate and a birth rate that has fluctuated in the modern period, falling during periods of economic depression and rising during good times. The early post–World War II years saw an unusually high rate of population growth, encouraged by the country's national system of "cradle-to-the-grave" social security. More recently the overall growth rate has slackened to only 1.2 percent per annum and is still falling. At the same time, the number of Maoris has continued to increase at a much higher rate than the country as a whole, having reached 8 percent of the total population and still rising.

The country has a long-standing official policy of encouraging and assisting European immigration. There has been a continuing search for special skills from abroad and a hospitable attitude toward refugees and displaced persons. The nation has freely admitted islanders from New Zealand's dependencies in the South Pacific; the number of such immigrants currently runs to 40,000 annually. Meanwhile, there has also been a certain amount of emigration of New Zealanders.

the political economy

The nature of the political and economic organization that has evolved in New Zealand is further evidence of her advancement. Although basically a capitalistic, free enterprise system, it has been so modified that the country may now be classified as a redistributive welfare state, like the United Kingdom (see Chapters 1 and 16). This is not unexpected, considering the fact that New Zealanders have consciously patterned their political and economic institutions closely after those of the mother country. Having been settled by northern European people, who had already experienced the industrial and agricultural revolutions, New Zealand has escaped the problems of dualism that hobble the Central American economies. This is shown by a comparison of the productive efficiency of the two areas. Whereas in 1971 New Zealand's 2.9 million people enjoyed a national income of $5.2 billion, the 15 million people of the CACM countries had a combined national income of only $4.8 billion.

role of government

For a nonsocialist economy, New Zealand has an unusual degree of state ownership and control. The government operates virtually all public utilities—telephone and telegraph, water, gas, electricity, radio and television—and the railways and domestic airlines. The state is involved in coal mining, afforestation and forest products industries, and the financing of land settlement and home construction, including even such related legal services as title searches and transfers.

The government is constantly seeking new measures for overcoming the economic effects of isolation, and it provides much protection to newly established industry through tariffs and other official devices. Indeed, the state extends its protection widely throughout the society. It shields its citizens against many of the uncertainties of life—illness, dependency and other social distress—but without the problems of inefficiency and dishonesty characteristic of public officials in many larger societies who are less directly exposed to the public view.

In addition to these social and economic measures reminiscent of Britain, New Zealand has a borrowed political system. Like the United Kingdom, it is a unitary state with a parliamentary system; its two major parties, at opposite ends of the political spectrum, alternate in office. The country tends to apply similar legislative remedies, often copied intact or modified, to its national problems as do the British. The political and legal institutions have proved so stable that the country has been able to attract capable people to government service and to provide a hospitable environment for foreign capital, despite the continued presence of government in economic affairs.

labor force and entrepreneurship

New Zealand has a literate, skilled, industrious labor force, and has been able to attract from abroad needed skills lacking at home, or, more often, to send New Zealanders to other countries for training. Even though more than nine-tenths of New Zealand's export earnings come from the sale of primary goods, less than one-seventh of the labor force is engaged in primary production. This is a measure of the exceptional productivity of labor in the agricultural and grazing industries. A rising proportion of the work force, more than one-third, is employed in manufacturing, despite the necessity for importing a major part of the country's industrial raw materials. As in other advanced countries, New Zealand now supports an increasing number of its workers in the services, which already employ more than one-half of the total. The efficiency with which the labor force is used and the steady rise in the GNP demonstrates the managerial skills of New Zealand's entrepreneurs.

level of development

By every measure, New Zealand ranks among the world's more advanced nations. Per capita GDP is $2,188 (1970), well above that of the mother country. The proportion of the labor force in primary production, 13 percent, is only slightly more than Canada's. Per capita ownership of motor cars is about equal to that of Canada but substantially higher than in the United Kingdom. Because there is little heavy industry, however, per capita consumption of all forms of energy is not very high for a developed nation, although electricity comprises an unusually large part of the total energy used.

How has New Zealand managed to mobilize her physical and human resources to attain this level of prosperity when other resource-based economies on the periphery have lagged so badly? The evolution of New Zealand's strategy for growth and development in the face of a number of handicaps provides a potentially useful guide to other hinterland countries striving against the same kinds of problems.

ASSUMING A PLACE IN THE WORLD ECONOMIC SYSTEM

In some respects, New Zealand's obstacles to gaining a secure place in the world economy resemble those of Japan. Both are small, remote, mountainous island nations with limited minerals and arable land. On the other hand, New Zealand has a far smaller labor force and a history of colonialism and neocolonialism that Japan has managed to escape. New Zealand has therefore entered into the world commercial economy by a different route, although by a growth strategy that is hardly less radical than Japan's. From the outset, New Zealanders have had to find ways of overcoming the distance barrier and of exploiting a relatively modest natural comparative advantage.

colonization and nationhood

European colonization of New Zealand came in the third phase of British empire building. During the first phase, Britain had founded the American colonies partly in a spirit of pure adventure and partly as a place for the country's dissidents and poor. The second phase, marked by the securing of India and Canada, was part of the political struggle with the French. Neither the first nor second phases gave much economic benefit to the home country at the time, but constituted a financial drain instead.

The third phase of British expansion, which occurred during the nineteenth century, was motivated by economic rather than political or sectarian considerations. It came at the climax of the British Industrial Revolution when both manufacturing output and population were expanding rapidly. Colonialism fulfilled needs for foreign raw materials and markets and a supplementary food supply. Empire building and industrial growth therefore went hand-in-hand. The flow of British trade multiplied many times and the nation's familiar structure of imports and exports evolved at that time. This trade was not a simple bilateral movement; it involved various third parties, especially the United States. From this commerce, Britain gained a substantial balance-of-payments surplus, which she invested in the colonies to generate even greater earnings. The colonial empire thus provided Britain with enlarged market and supply areas and increased capital accumulation through investment earnings.

a transplanted culture

The colonization of New Zealand was delayed by her remoteness; although discovered in 1642 by the Dutch Captain Tasman and subsequently visited and claimed by Captain Cook, the islands did not become a British colony until 1840. Exploitation of the colony then had to await further transport innovations: improved sailing ships and, later, steam propulsion. These events foreshadowed the central role that technological innovation was subsequently to play in New Zealand's progression to prosperity and nationhood.

Unlike most of the British colonies of Africa and Asia, however, New Zealand was not merely exploited but was actively settled by emigrants from the increasingly crowded homeland. Like Australia, New Zealand provided a number of attractive conditions for its settlers. The islands offered an invitingly temperate climate, and they were only thinly populated by the aboriginal Maoris, from whom the European settlers appropriated the best farm lands. Despite the great distance of this colony from the heartland, it was never truly isolated. The constant flood of new immigrants provided a continuing renewal of ideas and a convenient conduit for information from the homeland. Having been settled in the modern age, therefore, New Zealand represented a transplanted technology and culture; the settlers did not so much adapt to new surroundings as change what they found to suit their own concepts and purposes.

political independence and the Commonwealth

Political independence came to the colony only gradually and in a much different manner than it came to the Spanish colonies of Central America (Chapter 20). The first important step was the granting of dominion status in 1907, which provided for internal self-government, including a parliamentary system similar to Britain's, but which left New Zealand still subject to the mother country in foreign affairs. New Zealand, along with the other self-governing dominions—Canada, Australia, and the Union of South Africa—finally gained independence under the Statute of Westminster (1931). This act of the British Parliament granted the dominions autonomy in both domestic and foreign matters but joined them with the United Kingdom in allegiance to the British Crown. At first this association of sovereign countries was termed the British Commonwealth but was later called simply the Commonwealth.

During the depression of the 1930s, the United Kingdom had to abandon her traditional policy of free trade with the world. This meant adopting the kinds of elaborate import controls that became general during that period of national autarky and shrinking world trade. Nevertheless, Britain succeeded in establishing, under the Ottawa Agreements of 1932, a system of imperial preferences encompassing the mother coun-

try and her existing and former colonies. In this manner the Commonwealth became an explicit economic entity.

strategy for growth and development

Early in the colonial period, New Zealand's settlers developed a unique strategy for their growth and development; after they gained independence, they perfected and are still modifying it today. New Zealand's solution to the problems of distance, size, and limited physical resources was to discover the basic comparative advantage of their new land and to develop a planned specialization based upon this advantage. Subsequently, they availed themselves of each new technique for increasing the efficiency of production and transporting their goods and benefited by the existence of a guaranteed market in the home country.

capitalizing on complementarity to the heartland

The comparative advantage that New Zealand's producers recognized was the islands' mild, year-round climate, which, with its abundance of well-distributed rainfall, was well suited for grasses. Because livestock can graze outdoors throughout the year, farmers save on supplementary feeding and avoid the expense of costly shelters and storage facilities. Grazing is also an activity that can productively use land unsuited to arable crops. These excellent conditions for animal production gave New Zealand's farmers a distinct set of advantages over their competitors in other parts of the Commonwealth. Nevertheless, they had to make the most they could of these production advantages if they were to offset the disadvantages of 12,000 miles of ocean transport, small land area, and insufficient agricultural labor.

New Zealand's farmers set about this by first intensifying production to get the most output per acre of scarce land. Although for a time they were able to get sufficient labor through the use of Maoris, the supply of manpower soon proved inadequate to the increasing need and has continued to be a problem since. New Zealand's farmers have therefore sought to economize on labor through mechanization, making use of the latest equipment and adapting it to their particular requirements and relying wherever possible on New Zealand's abundant hydroelectricity. In numerous ways they have applied greater amounts of capital to the land to increase the output per acre, such as replacing poor-quality native grasses with more nutritious imported types, modified to New Zealand's special conditions and made to yield even more heavily by applications of fertilizer. Farmers have introduced superior animal varieties and improved upon them. New Zealand has developed sophisticated agricultural processing industries in order to reduce the bulk and perishability of their commodities and to put them into forms capable of sustaining the cost of long-distance transporting.

The success of New Zealand's highly capitalized farms and processing operations has made it easier to attract capital from abroad. For the most part, however, the country's agricultural sector has managed to generate its developmental capital domestically. Thus New Zealand has used capital-intensive methods to support a dynamic agricultural economy despite persistent shortages of two important factors of production—land and labor.

A second major element in New Zealand's developmental strategy has been to emphasize products that have a high income-elasticity of demand. As their incomes have risen, consumers in the heartland have included larger amounts of animal proteins in their diets (see Chapter 3). New Zealand's specialization in meat animals and dairy products fits well into this changing demand pattern. Because of its fluctuating prices in world markets, wool does not conform so neatly to this plan, although as a joint-product with lamb and mutton it is an unavoidable part of the scheme and provides an important source of income during periods of high wool prices. As a further concession to the rising incomes and increasingly exacting tastes of heartland customers, New Zealand's producers have stressed quality. This emphasis upon commodities for which demand is rising more rapidly than the rate of population growth contrasts with the agricultural specialties of Central America, which have a relatively inelastic world demand. As a consequence, New Zealand is not troubled with deteriorating terms of trade to the same degree as other hinterland nations.

Another essential element in the New Zealand strategy has been its guaranteed market. Since the early days of colonization the country could always depend upon the mother country as an outlet for her products. In latter years New Zealand secured firm commitments from Britain, formalized in bilateral treaties. This has meant not just a preferential tariff but a zero tariff. This longstanding arrangement has led British consumers to acquire a taste for New Zealand's superb agricultural products, especially her "fat" lamb, cheddar cheese, and butter; it has also stimulated New Zealand's producers to engineer their products more closely to the particular preferences of British households. Thus New Zealand became in fact an overseas extension of Britain's domestic agricultural supply area, essentially the outermost Thünen ring in the United Kingdom's agricultural hinterland. The unique feature of this partnership is that it linked countries on directly opposite sides of the globe—an arrangement secured by British command of the seas.

New Zealand is also distinctive among hinterland nations because it was born during an age of change. In their ceaseless efforts to preserve and enlarge their comparative advantage, New Zealanders have been quick to seize new opportunities offered by advancing technology in agricultural production and processing and in transport and communications. It was the barrier of distance that delayed New Zealand's development in the first place, but transportation is perhaps more susceptible to technological change than any other sector of the economy. Once New Zealand had entered the world economic system, transport improvements came quickly. By the 1870s and 1880s sailing ships attained surprising speeds, making the 12,000-mile trip to Britain in as little as 73 days. Nevertheless, it was steam that brought New Zealand the market access she required, both in terms of reduced sailing time and costs. In 1882 the country benefited especially from the introduction of refrigerated shipping, which permitted animal products to be transported in more valuable, higher-quality, and more compact forms. Subsequent improvements in surface transportation continued to reduce time and costs, and the arrival of air transport has greatly increased New Zealand's communications. The country's domestic transport linkages also steadily improved.

New Zealand's producers have eagerly sought new techniques for increasing output, improving product quality, and adapting to the country's specific production conditions and to changing demand conditions abroad. They have carefully studied local variations in soil, climates, and other physical conditions, and have adapted their crops, animals, and farming practices accordingly; they have also made widespread use of fertilizers, insecticides, and herbicides. Continual research and experimentation provide New Zealand's producers with the increases in efficiency that they must have to maintain their competitive effectiveness.

At the same time, New Zealanders have stressed the development of new processing techniques and new products. Not only have they found it necessary to reduce costs by improving their methods of processing meats and dairy products but they have worked to develop new products that are more transportable, less perishable, and acceptable to a wider range of customers. Processing industries are located in each primary producing region and tend to emphasize local product specialties.

role of the state

In New Zealand there is unusual general public awareness of the country's world economic role, hence the public gives political support to the government's efforts to enhance that role. The state participates in the ownership and operation of support facilities required by the export industries, in financing productive enterprises, and in research and the diffusion of information and new techniques. The government carefully controls immigration with an aim toward acquiring the right mix of labor skills, protects export industries from foreign competition, and supplies the stability needed to attract investment. To see how well this strategy has worked, let us look at the way in which each of New Zealand's major primary exports evolved.

New Zealand's primary export industries

Grains, hides, and wool were the original staple exports, because the first settlers found that these products were most capable of bearing high transport costs. When gold was discovered on South Island in 1861, it assumed first place for a time in the colony's exports. The discovery also attracted a flow of immigrants, many of whom remained in New Zealand to become farmers. During this period the colony's dairymen began exporting their surplus milk in its most transportable form cheese. It was refrigerated shipping, however, that gave New Zealand's animal products industries their greatest stimulus, and butter and meat were added to the list of staple exports. With the rapid development of dairying that followed, especially on North Island, the country's export industries began to assume their present form.

meat and wool

Despite New Zealand's large domestic consumption of meat (about twice as much per capita as in Britain), a substantial surplus remains for export and, with wool, is the leading source of foreign income. The country also has increasing numbers of beef cattle and substantial herds of swine. Important byproducts, especially hides and skins, contribute additional foreign earnings. The main sheep-rearing areas are east of the mountains on both North and South Islands, where drier conditions prevail. Cattle predominate on the rainy west coast of South Island and the wetter areas of North Island.

Sheep are economical animals to raise because they eat less in proportion to the meat they give than do cattle or swine. Moreover, the products of sheep can be shipped long distances easily. The main disadvantage of sheep production is that mutton and lamb are important parts of the diet in only a limited number of countries, the most significant of which is the United Kingdom. The early settlers allocated large tracts of land to the pasturing of sheep, which they grew for meat and wool. At the outset, New Zealanders followed the Australian example of stressing wool breeds, especially the merino sheep, which give excellent wool but poor-quality lamb and mutton. Upon the arrival of refrigeration, New Zealand's farmers converted from merinos to high-quality meat animals wherever physical conditions permitted, although merinos continued to occupy the highland pastures on the leeward eastern slopes.

Since the introduction of sheep, New Zealanders have continued to breed better varieties, with a special emphasis on meat-animal strains. New Zealand slaughters a much higher percentage of its animals for meat each year than the Australians do, who keep sheep for several years for their extra wool output. As a result, New Zealand contributes two-thirds of the mutton and lamb that enters world trade. New Zealand's high-quality meat animals—the English Romney Marsh, Romney crosses, and South Downs varieties—require more care and are kept on much smaller farms (except in the highlands) than in Australia. The average sheep farm is only 250 to 400 acres, with the result that many pastures carry as many as six sheep to the acre, an unusually high animal-carrying capacity. The farms are able to maintain high animal densities with the aid of sown and fertilized grasslands and supplementary feeding of root crops and green fodder.

Even though secondary to meat in New Zealand's agricultural scheme, wool can be very profitable when prices are high, as they have been during the recent world shortage of textile fibers. New Zealand is one of the world's leading suppliers and provides about one-seventh of the total. (Australia is first.) At present, about 40 percent of New Zealand's export earnings are from wool.

North Island produces about 55 percent of the country's sheep. In the country as a whole, sheep are produced both in the highlands and lowlands on specialized ranches, on ranches where cattle and sheep are both kept, in mixed-farming areas, and on fat-lamb farms. There is a close adaptation of animal types and practices to local physical conditions. On highland pastures, where sheep graze up to the snow line, poor-quality native grasses and scrub prevail, but ranchers are beginning to upgrade these rough pastures through aerial sowing of clover and top-dressing with chemical fertilizers. Much of New Zealand's wool comes from the merinos and merino crosses pastured in the mountainous areas. The lowland pastures provide the excellent special grasses and clovers required by the meat-animal breeds. In addition to this spatial separation of many highland and lowland grazing operations, there is also a considerable amount of transhumance—seasonal movements of animals from high pastures to low. In addition, the highlands serve as a reservoir for breeding stock for the lowland fat-lamb farms.

The beef cattle industry is an increasingly important part of the domestic economy. In some localities farmers maintain cattle on the same lands as sheep, a type of joint-process operation in which the cattle eat the larger scrub vegetation and the sheep eat the shorter grasses left by the cattle. Four-fifths of the beef cattle are on North Island, especially in the district south of Auckland. South Island's beef cattle ranches are extensive operations occupying tens of thousands of acres in some cases. A transhumance system similar to that in the sheep industry combines extensive pasturing in the highlands with intensive fattening in low areas close to packing plants.

Swine-rearing in New Zealand, as in Denmark,

was traditionally a joint-process operation in connection with dairying. Now that farmers have stopped separating their own cream and no longer have leftover skim milk to feed pigs, joint process swine fattening has largely disappeared. Most of the remaining production takes place on specialized pig farms in remoter areas, where the animals are fattened on grains. Export earnings from the sale of pork to the British have therefore diminished.

dairy farming

Milk products provide the country's other traditional staple export. The nation is the major supplier to the Commonwealth and the world, providing one-fourth of the world's butter exports and the major proportion of the cheese and other milk and cream products. New Zealand has the world's most efficient dairy industry, an accomplishment dictated by the necessity to remain competitive in a distant world market. As in the case of her meat animals, New Zealand has had to stress compact products of uniformly superior quality produced by intensive methods resembling those in Denmark and the Netherlands.

The country's dairymen are skilled managers, who invest much capital to maximize output and continually look for ways to intensify their farming still further. Mainly owner-operated, the farms are small, averaging less than 200 acres, but they support large herds. To increase milk yields farmers sow both their permanent pastures and rotation pastures with nutritious grasses and clovers specially adapted to particular local conditions and liberally fertilized. Dairy farmers also grow hay and fodder for supplementary feeding during dry periods.

New Zealand's dairy industry engages in constant research to improve the quality of its carefully selected milk animals. Artificial insemination and frequent herd testing are general practices. Unlike the dairymen of Anglo-America and Europe's low countries, who prefer Holstein-Frisians for their high output of fluid milk, New Zealand's farmers maintain mostly Jersey cattle for their richer milk. Because of the importance of butterfat yield for New Zealand's traditional dairy exports, the constant aim has been to increase the butterfat as much as possible. Through careful breeding, the industry has, in the past two decades, raised the butterfat per gallon of milk by 5.5 percent and increased the butterfat per cow by 23 percent. Meanwhile, the total number of dairy cows in New Zealand has risen by more than 30 percent. Recent changes in the product mix of the country's dairy exports have altered this situation, however, and have increased the need for milk volume rather than quality. As a result, Frisian cattle are becoming more numerous, a trend reinforced by the rapidly expanding demand for fluid milk in New Zealand's cities. The New Zealand department of agriculture maintains strict quality control over the country's milk industry.

Dairy farmers supplement their incomes with a number of functionally related sidelines, including the keeping of breeding ewes for fat-lamb production. Dairy cows, sheep, and lambs graze the same pastures in a sequence carefully regulated to ensure maximum yield from the forage. Dairymen also obtain income from the sale of field crops grown as part of their regular rotation schemes.

To overcome the persistent labor shortage, dairy farmers employ much mechanical equipment, particularly milking machines and bulk cooling tanks. They have also mechanized the work of tending rotation field crops and hay crops. As a result, New Zealand's labor input per acre is among the world's lowest.

Milk products are efficiently marketed through cooperatives, as in Denmark, with individual farmers sharing in the proceeds in proportion to the butterfat supplied. This cooperative arrangement ensures stability and maximum prices, further aided by government guarantees. The co-ops also make bulk purchases of dairy farm inputs, such as seeds and fertilizer, thereby reducing production costs.

Nine-tenths of the dairy industry is concentrated on North Island, mostly in the southwestern and northern areas of coastal plains, interior valleys, and rolling lower slopes. With their mild temperatures and ample moisture throughout the year, these areas provide outdoor grazing at all seasons. Dairying is less developed on South Island, where conditions are not so ideal. Fluid milk sheds are prominent around the major cities, especially Christchurch and Dunedin, however; and a few other districts produce milk for export. In the southern end of the island colder winters reduce the volume of output.

other crops

Because of the shortage of arable land, other forms of agricultural production are relatively minor. The country has a good wheat climate and exported significant quantities in the 1870s and 1880s, when wheat was produced by extensive methods on the Canterbury Plains of South Island. Wheat farming could not compete for long, however, especially after the arrival of refrigeration made animal production a more attractive alternative. Subsequently, the Canterbury Plains were converted to more intensive forms of land use.

One of these is mixed farming of the English type, which combines arable crops with animals. The principal cash return is from fat lambs, supplemented by income from the sale of grass seed and small grains. Ninety percent of the country's wheat production is on South Island, where very high yields are obtained by fertilization. New Zealand does not grow enough wheat for her own needs, however, and must import sizable quantities.

Fruit orchards and market gardening occur in certain areas where physical conditions are favorable. Apples, grown particularly in the Nelson area, and other temperate fruits provide significant export earnings. In the balmy climate of the Auckland Peninsula in the far north, citrus and other subtropical fruits flourish. Market gardening is increasing in a number of localities to supply the rapidly growing towns and cities.

processing of agricultural commodities

An essential element of New Zealand's developmental strategy has been to increase world competitiveness and maximize the return from the foreign sale of primary goods by processing these to the greatest possible extent, using the most efficient capital-intensive techniques to obtain products of the highest quality in the most transportable form. Considering the specialized nature of the New Zealand economy, it is not surprising that the most important industries on the islands have traditionally been those processing animal products. Meat packing, chilling, freezing, and canning plants and milk processing establishments still contribute more than one-third of the total value of the country's manufacturing.

Of all the milk products that New Zealand produces and exports, the most important is butter, which consumes almost two-thirds of the total butterfat output. Another one-fifth is used for making cheese, while approximately one-tenth is consumed domestically as milk or cream. The remainder goes into a wide variety of other manufactured milk products or is fed to livestock as skim milk or whey.

Milk processing plants are cooperatively owned by the farmers, and these co-ops are usually associated together in large organizations. Many co-ops specialize in a single product, such as butter, cheese, or condensed or powdered milk, and in some instances all the co-ops of a given district emphasize a local specialty. To economize on labor, the dairy plants use superb mechanical equipment, including huge electrically driven churns and automatic buttermaking machines, cheese presses, drying equipment, and automatic wrapping and packing machines. These operations stress economies of scale, which enable New Zealand to compete effectively in foreign markets. The New Zealand Dairy Board, which is the sole purchaser for export, fixes and guarantees prices and does the final marketing.

Milk plants are widely distributed throughout the main dairy farming areas, especially on North Island. Half the country's manufactured dairy products come from the district south of Auckland, where the main emphasis is on butter. On the southwestern side of the island the Taranaki District concentrates principally on cheese making; this was an early center for New Zealand cheddar manufacture. Cheese production also occurs in some of the southernmost districts of South Island.

The largest of New Zealand's industries are the meat-processing firms, whose methods are as modern as those of the dairy industry. Packing plants are located in all the principal towns of the meat-animal areas, where they are coastally situated for ease of exporting. There are special concentrations, however, particularly on the margins of Auckland city, which is one of the main centers for the meat industry. Christchurch, whose local economy is heavily based on mutton and lamb, is a major exporting port for much of the meat-canning industry and also specializes in leather tanning and other byproducts.

rapid economic growth

In serving as an outer Thünen ring for the world heartland, New Zealand has thus focused upon those primary foodstuffs and industrial raw materials that have a high income-elasticity of demand and are most easily shipped. As a result, this country has attained a level of productivity on a par with the heartland, all within the comparatively brief time of little more than a century.

Although the most rapid economic growth occurred during the latter part of the nineteenth century and the first half of this one, GDP has continued to rise at a rate approaching 4 percent per annum in the decade of the 1960s and has more recently reached 4.5 percent or more. Even though its population was growing during much of this time, New Zealand's per capita income rose by 40 percent in the last decade.

To a considerable extent, this growth was based on foreign trade. Typical of hinterland nations, New Zealand has a high export dependence, obtaining more than one-fifth of her national product from sales abroad. Although this means that national growth is tied to levels of foreign demand, the country has managed to make a better adaptation to that demand than have other countries outside the heartland. New Zealand's strategy has been successful, thus far, at least, but she has paid a price for it.

THE PRICE OF GROWTH

New Zealand has been spared many of the problems of resource-based lands on the world periphery by her successful production and marketing policy and her avoidance of the demographic, social, and political burdens of the others. Yet New Zealand's escape has not been complete. Despite all the hard work and superior entrepreneurial skills that have brought high incomes to its citizens, the country has become as firmly dependent upon the heartland as any of the less developed lands. The heartland has provided much of the investment capital and technology, and it remains the principal market for the output. The concentration of this dependency upon a single heartland nation, the United Kingdom, further intensifies New Zealand's problem. The bilateral ties of colonial times have survived as an equally restrictive form of neocolonialism, made all the more hazardous by the deteriorating economic position of the mother country (see Chapter 16). At the same time, New Zealand has become dependent on a narrow range of primary staple exports presenting many of the same problems of excessive commodity specialization as those of Central America. New Zealand has not been able to avoid entirely the problems of internal disparities so prevalent in nations of the hinterland.

neocolonialism

Many years after her political independence, New Zealand continues to experience pervasive British influence on her society, economy, and institutions. Just as the Spanish descendents of Central America's first settlers still look to Spain, so the latter-day New Zealanders look to regard Britain as their model. Unlike the earlier British colonies, New Zealand was never cut off from the home country, and its social life did not develop in isolation. With frequent ship arrivals from Britain and a continual flow of British news and information, the colony did not acquire the primitive quality of a frontier land. No new dialects or unique institutions developed nor has there been any peculiarly New Zealand literature, art, or music. Although the British influence continued to flow uninterruptedly into the colony, the information was delayed because it depended upon slow-moving ocean vessels. Consequently, the islanders have always lagged behind their British exemplars. As New Zealand's own social critics often state, the country's society has been fairly sophisticated from the outset but has always been secondhand and out-of-date. British mores are carefully preserved but often in exaggerated form, and they tend to survive long after their disappearance in the United Kingdom.

One important set of institutions derived from the British model is New Zealand's politics and administration. New Zealand has always been considered the "most loyal" colony or Commonwealth member—a reputation gained by the country's ready identification with British causes and her eagerness to follow the British lead in international affairs. She has always been quick to come to the aid of Britian in her colonial wars and in both World Wars, even though most of these conflicts presented no direct threat to a land so thoroughly insulated by distance. It is in the economic sphere, however, that New Zealand's dependence upon the United Kingdom presents the most critical issues today.

British economic hegemony

In many respects New Zealand's dependency relationship to the heartland is as great as that of the Central American countries. Following independence, however, the latter shifted their economic focus away from Spain and to the United States; but New Zealand has continued her economic ties to Britain, unchanged throughout the long period when British political control was being relaxed. Finance was the cementing agent of Britain's empire of the nineteenth century; London's financial role remains the most persistent bond of the Commonwealth today.

The introduction of refrigerated transport, which brought the first influx of foreign capital of any consequence, mainly concentrated in the meat-packing industry. Until recently, direct foreign investment in New Zealand's enterprises came almost solely from Britain or Australia, but most of the Australian money actually originated in London. For a long time Britain was the only source of New Zealand's loan capital.

New Zealand has traditionally run a balance-of-payments deficit, which has kept the country continuously in debt and borrowing to service earlier debts—a characteristic problem of primary exporters. New Zealand pegged her currency to sterling for more than a century and has remained a loyal supporter of sterling to the present. The nation has banked all foreign exchange reserves in London and has made all government financial settlements through British banks. Indeed, New Zealand historically depended upon the United Kingdom for all sorts of services; as late as the fiscal year of 1950–1951 the country made financial transfers to Britain representing 95 percent of her foreign expenditures for transport, 73 percent of interest and dividend payments, 100 percent of the insurance, and 67 percent of the travel.

bipolar trade

Britain's main purpose for developing New Zealand in the first place was to supply British needs. Britain was ready to accept any quantity of the colony's goods at fair prices, and this prompted New Zealanders to design their animal industries precisely to British specifications. In addition, the first settlers brought with them British tastes in manufactured products, which could be satisfied only with British imports. Thus from the outset the country based its development on trade—a British-centered trade. Even though the economy has since matured considerably, a process that usually reduces a country's trade dependence (see Chapter 11), New Zealand continues to rely heavily on foreign commerce.

Although New Zealand is farther away from Britain than any other Commonwealth member is, she has continued to maintain closer trade links with the United Kingdom than have all the others. The advantage of this British connection was demonstrated by her experience during the Great Depression. In the predepression year of 1928, New Zealand made 73 percent of her foreign sales to the United Kingdom. When economic conditions worsened, and Britain, along with most other industrial nations, imposed severe restrictions on her imports, she nevertheless exempted New Zealand from these measures and continued to treat her former colony as a distant extension of her domestic supply area. By 1931, therefore, Britain was taking 88 percent of New Zealand's exports and was still buying 84 percent of the total by 1938, the eve of World War II. During the course of the war, New Zealand made bulk-sale and purchase agreements, covering virtually all her exports and imports, with the United Kingdom. This total reliance upon the British market continued throughout the post-war period, when the United Kingdom was particularly dependent upon New Zealand for food. The agreements were permitted to lapse in 1954, and by 1967 the British share of New Zealand's trade had dwindled to 44 percent —still an uncommonly high dependence. Thus, whenever New Zealand's goods have been shut out of other lands in the past, the United Kingdom has always remained a customer of last resort.

Except during times of war or depression, New Zealand's dependence upon the mother country was greater for some exports than for others. Although she always sent almost all her lamb and dairy products to the United Kingdom, she sold her wool in a wider world market.

So long as Britain prospered economically and politically, this special relationship relieved New Zealand of the necessity to develop other markets; but when the British economy began to deteriorate, New Zealand's position became more tenuous. Questions began to arise regarding Britain's continuing ability to accommodate New Zealand's increasing output. At the same time, New Zealand's faithful adherence to the pound sterling was poorly rewarded by the United Kingdom's currency devaluations.

commodity trade specialization

Another basic trade problem for New Zealand has been her concentration upon only a few exports, a familiar dilemma for hinterland countries. Ninety percent of her export earnings are from animal products, with wool accounting for one-third of the total, meat and dairy products one-fourth each, and hides, skins, and other byproducts another 5 percent. Much of the rest comes from other primary goods, mainly wood products, fish, and seeds.

For a country so dependent upon trade, this kind of commodity specialization has meant fluctuating rates of growth in national income. This is illustrated by the recent history of New Zealand cheese: recurring cycles of global oversupply, saturated markets, and disastrous price drops, followed by production cutbacks and ensuing shortages. World wool prices have followed a similar pattern.

Although New Zealand's specialties enjoy much more favorable long-term price trends than do most agricultural goods supplied by the hinterland, they have some basic weaknesses. Despite the high effective demand for animal products among the prosperous peoples of the heartland, most industrialized countries subsidize and protect their domestic agriculture, especially dairy products. The ill-fed millions in the Third World, on the other hand, badly need these proteins but cannot afford them. As a result, New Zealand's products do not command the prices that the world's actual need for them would seem to justify. Meanwhile, the country's industrial imports from the heartland become more costly year by year. Thus once again we see repeated the common hinterland problem of deteriorating terms of trade.

internal inequalities

Despite short-term fluctuations, and even such long-term worries as unfavorable balances of payments and terms of trade, the country has somehow prospered. But the benefits of that prosperity have not reached some parts of the country and some members of the society. Even New Zealand has distressed regions and socioeconomic problems. The causes and symptoms of these conditions resemble those of other hinterland nations, but the dimensions of New Zealand's internal disparities are not nearly so great as those of Latin America, Africa, or Asia.

New Zealand's spatial structure

The paradox of urban-centered spatial development in a resource-based economy exists in its most extreme form in New Zealand. Eighteen urban areas of 20,000 people or more contain almost two-thirds of the country's population; and the four largest of these areas—Auckland, Wellington-Hutt, Christchurch, and Dunedin—constitute 45 percent of the total. There are at least 100 other places having from 1,000 to 20,000 persons. What is more, the urban population is continuing to grow at an annual rate of 4.5 percent, much greater than the rate of total population increase.

As in most hinterland countries, New Zealand's regional pattern grew out of her colonial experience. Colonial development ordinarily produces a set of port-hinterland regions resting on an economic base of extensive agriculture, grazing, or mining. In most countries the system focuses upon a single primate city, the port used by the colonizing group as a point from which to penetrate the interior and to exercise political and economic control. Because of the character of the physical environment and the late date of settlement, however, New Zealand's space-economy took a different form. The rugged mountains and dense vegetation in the island interiors caused the colony to become compartmentalized into many small districts along the coasts and in the river basins. Every district established its own commercial agriculture and acquired a separate urban system focusing upon its own port city, with its own overseas links to the mother country. There were 26 such ports by the late 1860s.

This is much like the colonial experience of Central America, where early settlement was fragmented by physical isolation. Following independence, Central America's compartmentalization became fossilized into distinct sovereign states; but New Zealand was settled at a later date and the various settlements became linked by rail during the colonial era. New Zealand's transport system focused upon the four major ports that ultimately became the country's leading cities. Within the sphere of influence of each of the four were several smaller ports that served to collect and distribute overseas shipments for the main center. Eventually the four principal ports and their hinterlands were interconnected into a national system by transport and communications networks. Today's regional pattern preserves this early arrangement, which provides both North and South Islands with two large urban centers, each a major overseas port.

The transport system that evolved along with this hierarchy of centers, and provides the essential linkages for them, grew up in three stages. In the first stage, there appeared a few rudimentary roads reaching out into the local rural districts from each of the small early ports having overseas connections. In the second stage, the local road systems became elaborated and rail lines were added. The local networks were also joined together by interregional links built at a high cost because of the many long tunnels, deep cuts, and bridges required to penetrate the islands' internal barriers. In time, the four present major ports dominated their respective systems and served as the major foci for both land and water routes. In the third stage, the major regional networks were joined into a national system. This evolved slowly, however; not until 1910 were Wellington and Auckland linked by the rail line that now carries three-fifths of the total railway traffic of the country. The ferry between North and South Islands across Cook Strait became an essential unit of national surface transportation, and was later supplemented by an interisland air service.

Fig. 21.3 *Railways*

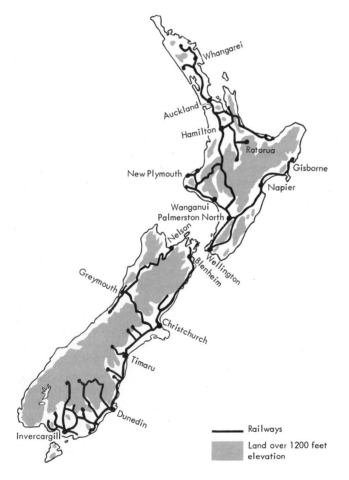

Railways

Land over 1200 feet elevation

The present national railway system has 3,500 miles of track and is mostly state-owned (Fig. 21.3). South Island, with its larger area, has the greater mileage; but more populous and industrialized North Island generates greater rail tonnage and more passenger miles. The country has 60,000 miles of improved roads, many penetrating rugged parts of the interior not reached by rail. Today there are 16 ports serving overseas commerce. Two-thirds of the foreign sailings are through North Island ports, with Wellington and Auckland dwarfing all others in the country. Most of the South Island's foreign trade passes through three centers, each of which is served by an outport: Christchurch (and outport of Lyttleton), Dunedin (Otago), and Invercargill (Bluff). Coastal traffic remains important also, owing to the difficult terrain, the division of the country by Cook Strait, and the dispersed nature of the urban centers, most of which are on the sea. Much of this trade is transshipment trade. Because sea voyages from New Zealand are lengthy, most passenger travel and mail service abroad is by air. Domestic air travel is well developed too, because surface movement is slow and circuitous.

The character and role of the cities in this spatial system have undergone considerable change since early colonial times. Not only has there been much urban growth at the expense of rural areas but there have been important relative changes in the size, importance, and functions of cities. In earlier times, virtually all acted as central places serving adjacent rural territory, and the service function is still the most important role of most urban centers in New Zealand as in other countries that are primary exporters. Manufacturing on the whole plays a lesser part; in most centers it is confined to the processing of locally produced commodities for export and such market-oriented industries as food and beverage preparation. More substantial industrial activity is limited to only a few larger centers and most is of recent development.

One of the reasons New Zealand has lacked a single primate city in the usual sense is that the political capital is separated from the leading commerce and manufacturing center, as it is in the United States. Nevertheless, the nation's urban hierarchy has become increasingly integrated as Auckland continues to gain dominance over its nearest rivals. This city's one-half million people outnumber those of any other in the country. It continues to grow rapidly, adding more people each year than does all South Island.

Auckland's dynamism can be attributed partly to the fact that it has the largest and richest hinterland of all the major centers. The region it serves is the most populous and urbanized part of the country, and contains many lesser centers of considerable size and the most productive farmland. From the local area come 40 percent of New Zealand's dairy products, 50 percent of the pork, and much of the beef, lamb, and wool. From this concentration of people and output Auckland gained its early lead in commerce, which in turn attracted more in-migrants, who then provided the market and labor force for the country's first major industries. Studies have shown that Auckland can supply the national market more cheaply than can any other city.

Auckland has a superior port with two excellent natural harbors, one on each side of the narrow isthmus on which the city stands. It is the first port of call for most vessels serving the country, an important consideration for manufacturing establishments requiring imported raw materials. The manufacturing output of Auckland currently exceeds the total of all the industries on South Island, and this production is also more diverse than that of any other New Zealand city. Auckland is the country's leading processor of agricultural commodities; it has most of those industries requiring economies of scale, especially the one-of-a-kind establishments that serve all New Zealand; and it is the preferred center for manufacturers dependent upon external economies—interfirm linkages, specialized services, and a varied labor force.

If its present growth were to continue, Auckland would soon have half the country's manufacturing establishments. It has been gaining a majority of the industries that are being established, and it is the leading choice for the relocation of plants from other parts of New Zealand, including South Island. Auckland has been the chief beneficiary from the mounting trend toward consolidation of firms.

New Zealand's political capital, Wellington, is its third largest city, with a population of a little more than 150,000. When the adjacent industrial and dormitory satellites are included, however, the metropolitan area totals a quarter million people. Wellington proper performs mainly administrative functions, because its further expansion is restricted on either side by steep slopes. The area's population and economic activities are therefore spreading up the Hutt Valley, where industrial establishments include manufacturers of motor vehicles, textiles and clothing, machinery, furniture and other wood products, electronics, and chemicals.

The leading center of South Island, Christchurch, was originally an Anglican settlement; and, as a university town and cultural center, it still retains a very English air. With more than 220,000 inhabitants, it is New Zealand's second city. Since colonial times its main function has been commerce, which relies upon a large tributary area, including the extensive Canterbury Plains, much of the high country, and part of the Westland area beyond that. Its port functions have always been important, although further growth of its water commerce is hampered by the silting problem in its outport of Lyttleton. There is some local manufacturing, including meat processing, canning, leather tanning, and fertilizer production, and such light industries as food processing, woolen mills, and clothing factories.

The other major center on South Island, Dunedin, is New Zealand's fourth city, with about 105,000 people and a sizable hinterland. The early gold rushes made Dunedin the country's leading port and commercial center for a time. More recently, however, it has declined, first with the decrease in gold output and subsequently with the slow growth of local agriculture and rising competition from Invercargill in the far south.

New Zealand's second- and third-level centers perform mainly service functions, although most have a little manufacturing. The latter consists mainly of low-threshold, market-oriented production and the processing of local agricultural, mineral, or forest products.

spatial problems

Inherent in the spatial system just described are a number of problems: disparities in the growth and progress of regions; dislocations and inequalities among and within cities; and conflicts between urban and rural uses of the land. Regional disparities are of several kinds. There are underdeveloped regions, which are remote from centers of growth, have few resources, are relatively untouched by progress, and whose inhabitants have a relatively low standard of living. Other areas are progressing but lag well behind the nation as a whole in their rate of growth. Then, too, there are depressed areas that were formerly prosperous but are now in decline as a result of the loss or deterioration of old economic bases. As this implies, New Zealand is experiencing some significant regional shifts in production in response to long-term trends that favor certain areas at the expense of others.

The North-South problem is one of New Zealand's national concerns. The two main islands have a history of changing relative economic positions, beginning with North Island's loss of its original lead to South Island. The latter's ascendency came by 1860, when sheep farming began to prosper in the south, the Otago gold rushes were on, and export production of wheat from the virgin lands gained temporary importance. After 1900, however, North Island again surged ahead with its intensive agriculture and growing urban population.

Although it contains 56 percent of the national territory, South Island lags badly today both economically and in population. With 70 percent of the population, North Island has three-quarters of the country's industrial jobs and is gaining new industrial employment at a rate 75 percent above that of the south. South Island has actually lost some industries, has lagged in the development of its services, and has generally become economically stagnant. Even within North Island there is a pronounced northward drift as Auckland and its environs continue to grow more rapidly than the remainder of that island, except for the Wellington-Hutt district.

North Island's growing dominance stems from the natural interplay of important market forces. First, it is more attractive to industries, particularly those of a market-oriented type, because it has twice the population of the south and has the two largest urban concentrations. Second, average incomes are higher, further accentuating the disparity in aggregate buying power between north and south. Third, North Island has much material-oriented production: processing of export staples from the country's most intensive agricultural lands; industries based on such local resources as iron sands, lumber, natural gas, and coal; and those dependent upon imported raw materials entering through the leading ports. Fourth, Auckland has a special dynamism and Wellington has the unique advantage of being the political control center.

By contrast, South Island's growth is hampered by its essentially rural character. In addition to the extensive, less productive nature of agriculture in the south, there is the slow population growth of New Zealand's rural areas generally owing to more capital-intensive farming methods. The south's farming districts are not only losing people to the cities, but to the cities of North Island in particular. And it is the usual selective migration of the young and most enterprising.

Almost all the west coast of South Island is a depressed area, suffering from the decline of its extractive industries. Yet even North Island has its problem areas. The eastern and western extremities of the island are losing out to Auckland and Wellington-Hutt, and the peninsular area of the far north has much rural poverty.

New Zealand has its urban problems, too; one of these is the differential rates of growth among the nation's cities. The northward movement of the country's population is reflected in the relative fortunes of its cities, especially as import-competing industries increasingly shift to the major centers of North Island. The northern cities have greater industrial diversity, and they are gaining most of such high-growth industries as vehicles and chemicals. Half the net gain in industrial employment goes to Auckland alone, and another 40 percent to other northern cities.

The effects of this shift are apparent in the trend of events in the cities of South Island. Dunedin has been losing out in the competition for population and employment and appears to be slipping to a lower level in the country's urban hierarchy. It has experienced no net in-migration in two decades, and its manufacturing has lagged far behind that of the other three major centers of the country. Although Christchurch retains its importance as the main service center of the south, it has had little manufacturing growth. Greymouth is the focus of depressed conditions afflicting the west coast of South Island generally.

The prospering cities of the north are now beginning to feel some of the kinds of urban problems afflicting cities of older heartland countries: the dislocating effects of growth and congestion; decaying neighborhoods and incipient slums; and socioeconomic problems stemming from cultural and ethnic diversity. The slum problem is only a relative one, because New Zealand's cities are not yet as crowded as those of North America and Europe. They also have fewer aging multi-family dwellings and no tenements at all, because New Zealand has more private ownership of housing than do

most countries. Nevertheless, the city's older housing stock is beginning to deteriorate; in a few more years it could become derelict. Crowding also threatens as large numbers of Maoris and Cook Islanders pour into Auckland with large families and communal customs of living. Even so, New Zealand's urban problems are mild compared with most other countries.

A potentially serious problem for land-short New Zealand, however, is the encroachment of cities upon adjacent rural lands. The difficulty is all the worse because of the direct relationships between rural productivity and urban development in an economy based on the products of the land. Auckland already occupies 2 percent of New Zealand's total national territory and it continues to expand outward rapidly.

socioeconomic inequalities

New Zealand does not have the extreme variations in personal incomes characteristic of most hinterland countries. Full employment has been the national norm for a long time, and in some years, labor shortages present more of a problem than unemployment. Although inequities do exist, they are related mainly to spatial inequalities. The major centers of North Island offer rising incomes to their populations, but the less dynamic areas are unable to prevent local incomes from lagging behind the country as a whole.

As yet, New Zealand experiences little discrimination on the basis of ethic background. Nevertheless, some fear that feelings may rise as Maoris and Islanders flow into Auckland, already called "the world's largest Polynesian city." There is an increasing unpopularity of dark-skinned people, whose mores are different from those of the dominant white population. These differences, which went unnoticed so long as Maoris remained in their tribal areas, gain more attention with the closeness of urban contact. Moreover, the minority peoples lack urban and work skills and compete with other unskilled persons for low-paying jobs and cheaper housing.

ATTACKING NEW ZEALAND'S CONTEMPORARY PROBLEMS

How will New Zealanders solve the problems confronting them? What are they doing to reorder their relations with the rest of the world now that their old arrangements can no longer be relied upon? What are they able to do about the internal stresses that are building up?

a new drive for independence

The first task for New Zealand is to shed the accumulated burden of neocolonialism. No one can say how long the country would have remained content with the comfortable old arrangement as Britain's supplier of animal products had it not been for events in the heartland. Forced to reexamine a pattern of dependency dating from the middle of the nineteenth century, New Zealand has been actively putting together a new strategy for survival and growth in a competitive world.

threats to the British market

New Zealand's links to Britain were forged at a time when the latter was approaching the peak of empire. The twentieth century has seen Britain's world leadership dissipate, her empire shrink, and her attentions shift to domestic affairs (see Chapter 16). Yet New Zealand's ties with the mother country survived until economic necessity forced the United Kingdom to apply for membership in the EEC. This suddenly brought into serious question the viability of the partnership between the two countries at a time when New Zealand's need for growth was placed under special pressure by an expanding population and labor force. French President de Gaulle's veto of Britain's first bid for EEC membership gave New Zealand a temporary reprieve, but the success of the United Kingdom's second attempt reopened the issue.

British membership in the Common Market poses a number of serious dangers to New Zealand's economy. Britain's Commonwealth ties have generally been regarded as incompatible with EEC policies, including the EEC's stress on European self-sufficiency in temperate-land foodstuffs. The EEC's methods for promoting this goal, particularly the high levels of protection for dairy products, strike directly at New Zealand's principal agricultural specialties. The EEC's Common Agricultural Policy (CAP) would effectively discriminate against New Zealand's goods by automatically raising their prices to EEC consumers well above those of domestically produced goods. The threat to New Zealand's foreign sales of lamb, mutton, and wool is less severe than it would have been at an earlier date because Europe's per capita consumption of meat is rising more rapidly than are domestic supplies and because textile fibers are generally in short supply in the world at this time. Nevertheless, the danger to New Zealand's crucial dairy exports is grave, and New Zealanders are braced for the probable loss of most British sales for these goods. What they fear most are the effects of being deprived of the British market too abruptly, before they are able to make the necessary complex overhaul of their external relations and product emphasis.

With this in mind, New Zealand conducted an intensive drive to obtain concessions from EEC members, with much lobbying in European capitals and at EEC headquarters. New Zealand's aim, at best, was to obtain a permanent arrangement for favorable access to EEC markets for the country's goods; failing that, the goal was to achieve some compromise or delay. The arguments used in this campaign were, first, that New Zealand's export production has been exactly tailored to the United Kingdom's needs over a very long period, and the sudden loss of that market would mean bankruptcy for New Zealand. The second argument was that

New Zealand is an efficient producer of animal products despite the lack of subsidies, whereas the EEC's output of these same commodities is very inefficient even though sustained by costly subsidies.

The final outcome of these negotiations was more favorable than New Zealanders had expected. The agreement with EEC on dairy products provided for (1) a phased, gradual reduction of guaranteed access for New Zealand's dairy products to a level of 71 percent by 1977, (2) price guarantees for the five-year period, (3) the possibility of special arrangements for butter to be renegotiated later, (4) an effort on the part of EEC to obtain an international accord on dairy products, and (5) an EEC trading policy that is not prejudicial to New Zealand's efforts to diversify her markets (in other words, not to engage in cut-throat competition or dumping of surplus EEC commodities on the world market). This agreement is good only to 1977, and forces New Zealand to a close timetable for diversifying her markets and products.

New Zealanders have had to recognize that British entry into the EEC was not the only threat to their prosperity and growth. It was already becoming apparent that Britain's market would not be able to absorb New Zealand's increasing output in the years ahead in any event. The growing world surplus of dairy products has been another threat to New Zealand's position. Only Japan and the underdeveloped countries have unsatisfied needs; but Japan is developing her own dairy industry (albeit at a high cost) and the underdeveloped lands cannot afford large imports of dairy products.

diversification of trade links

Ever since the United Kingdom's original announcement of her intent to enter the EEC, New Zealand has had an official policy of diversification, which has two related elements: the cultivation of more overseas markets and the development of new and more varied exports.

As New Zealand undertakes a drive for new trading partners, she finds herself exposed for the first time to the full impact of a competitive world economy. Deprived of the British shelter, she is now forced into a lonely search for alternatives. The government, supported by general public recognition of the urgency of the problem, has taken the initiative in this effort. One official measure has been to offer special incentives to exporters: financial aid to firms shipping additional lamb to non-British markets, and a variety of devices to encourage manufacturers to export their products. The government has undertaken a vigorous drive to extend the variety and range of dairy exports by developing new products having a wider demand, including nonfat milk solids and other specialties. Governmentally sponsored trade missions have visited a number of countries, most recently to Latin America. Official agencies have worked to develop and promote transport, innovations to increase the speed and reduce the cost of exporting New Zealand's goods, such new ideas as roll-on, roll-off ferries to Australia and containerships and other facilities for handling containerized freight.

One of the most important of the government initiatives has been the effort to form ties to a variety of countries through special intergovernment trade agreements. Notable among these have been the special arrangements for New Zealand products under the protocol admitting the United Kingdom to the EEC. In addition, New Zealand has been making a concerted effort to promote meat sales to France. Because Europe is a difficult market for ordinary dairy products, New Zealand has emphasized, with some success, such commercial dairy specialties as casein, made from skim milk. Overtures have been made to the Soviet Union also.

Ending her longstanding blindness to trade opportunities closer to home, New Zealand has also begun to focus on markets within the Pacific realm. This initiative is beginning to produce results: 40 percent of New Zealand's exports now go to the United States, Canada, Australia, and Japan. Indeed, the United States has now become New Zealand's second best customer, a development aided by the growing demand for beef, lamb, and wool in the United States. Although dairy products have been heavily protected in the United States by a politically inspired quota system, a worsening milk shortage is causing the bars to imports from New Zealand and other countries to drop.

New Zealand has also gained a new appreciation for the natural complementarity she enjoys with Japan. As a consequence, exports to Japan, which were small in the past, are now expanding rapidly. Japan's rising demand for animal products has helped in this respect; the Japanese market for meat is growing at a rate of 7 percent per annum, its market for butter is rising at a rate of 10.5 percent, and wool demands are growing by 3.3 percent. But New Zealand has found it difficult to break through the protective barrier of Japan's domestic dairy industry.

New Zealand now has rising sales of powdered milk, dry butterfat, and other processed dairy foods to India, Thailand, Taiwan, Singapore, Malaysia, and the Philippines. China has made purchases of wool, fats, hides, and pedigreed cattle. New Zealand's missions to the Pacific rim of Latin America have also produced results: 10 percent of the country's dairy exports now go to South America, especially to Chile and Peru.

New Zealand has always maintained economic links with Australia, including common ownership of manufacturing enterprises and financial institutions; however, trade between the two neighbors has been limited by the competitive nature of their primary staple exports. New Zealand has taken a significant amount of Australia's manufactured exports for some time, but her shipments to Australia were confined mainly to pulp and paper. Britain's overtures to the EEC, however, brought the two Tasmanian Sea countries closer together, formalized in 1966 with the New Zealand–Australia Free Trade Agreement (NAFTA).

Among New Zealand's motives for entering into this limited form of integration were the desire to redress her unfavorable balance of payments with Australia, to gain an assured market for wood products and pulp and paper, and to give New Zealand's manufacturers access to a larger market. The chief aim for both countries, however, was to free up trade on selected items without adversely affecting production in either country.

A major provision of NAFTA called for phasing out, over a period of 8 years, the duties on more than half the items traded between them. The arrangement further contains arrangements to facilitate specific trade deals between Australian and New Zealand companies. Under this agreement the two countries maintain a closely managed trade that is hedged with many exceptions and safeguards. New Zealand's caution is dictated by the knowledge that Australia has four times the population, far more physical resources, and a great deal more industry. Because of these disparities, New Zealand's industries lack many of the locational advantages of Australia's.

As a result of the many controls built into the agreement, therefore, NAFTA has had only limited impact on trade. Even though there has been little substitution of Australian imports for local production, New Zealand has managed to improve her balance of payments through this device. Little noticed also, the two countries have developed considerable intraindustry specialization in the goods exchanged between them; indeed, 30 percent of NAFTA trade is in products of the same industries. One feature of the arrangement is a provision for market-sharing agreements, notably in auto assembly.

At the same time, New Zealand is seeking closer commercial relations with her nearest neighbors—the islands of the South Pacific—with some of whom she already has political ties. These neighbors comprise some 14 small island-nations scattered over 9 million square miles of ocean. Although the New Zealand market is vital to the islanders, they supply only 2 percent of New Zealand's total imports, mainly tropical fruits and minerals. After many years of neglecting this opportunity, New Zealand is at last actively promoting the island trade and is enjoying rapidly rising sales of meat, dairy products, vegetables, and wood products. To stimulate this regional trade, New Zealand and Australia have joined with the islanders in a South Pacific Bureau of Economic Cooperation, conceived as the forerunner of a free trade area.

Despite the difficulties New Zealand has encountered in the effort to diversify her trade connections, she has made some progress. Her dairy sales to the United Kingdom have become a substantially smaller proportion of the total, and her wool is now reaching a wider market. Japan and North America have recently displaced the United Kingdom as principal markets for her mutton, beef, and veal. On the whole, however, the United Kingdom is still New Zealand's leading customer by a considerable margin; much therefore remains to be done.

diversification of production and exports

New Zealand clearly recognizes the need for a more diversified product mix and the need for a greater variety of trading partners. To counter structural deficiencies in her trade, New Zealand has set about (1) to redesign her traditional exports, introducing new types and processing them further, and (2) to accelerate her rate of industrialization, with a view to both the export and home markets.

New Zealand's natural comparative advantage is still valid in the world market, particularly if that market were truly free. If it were not for the myriad of artificial barriers to trade, New Zealand's butter and cheese could easily compete on a basis of price and quality. One solution to this problem is to convert the old products into new types more acceptable to a different set of foreign customers. Therefore, in addition to the famous New Zealand Cheddar favored by the British, the Dairy Research Institute has developed a Colby cheese for the United States market and New Zealand blue, Gouda, Cheshire, Havarti, Danbo, and Gruyère cheeses for specialized European tastes.

The most rapidly growing segment of the country's dairy industry today, however, concentrates upon radically different forms of milk, especially skim milk powder. This product is sold in ever larger quantities to advanced countries, who use it in the manufacture of convenience foods and as livestock feed, and to underdeveloped countries, who make use of milk in this form because it is easily shipped and preserved. Another important new product is recombined milk, which requires no refrigeration and is therefore well suited to tropical markets. One type of recombined milk is yogurt, a product much in demand in the Middle East and parts of Asia. Underdeveloped Asian countries are also taking much of New Zealand's dry butterfat, which is used in making reconstituted milk, and also dry buttermilk, formerly a waste product and stream pollutant in the producing areas. New Zealand now leads the world in the sale of casein, which is second only to powdered milk in its rate of market growth. Casein has an increasing number of such industrial uses as filler for fine papers, buttons, artificial fiber, ice cream, and sausages.

Other primary commodities being redesigned are forest products, whose variety continues to increase. Nearly 13 percent of the country's output is exported, the largest percentage sold abroad of all New Zealand's manufactures. New Zealand's meat industry packages an increasing percentage of its output in prepared forms, and uses operations that raise the labor content and increase the value added.

The second main plank in New Zealand's program for diversification calls for increased emphasis upon manufacturing. At present, only 17 percent of the GNP comes from manufacturing. This is much less than other developed countries, most of whom obtain half or more of their GNP from this source. New Zealand has three kinds of manufacturing: (1) the processing of locally produced primary commodities; (2) import-competing manufacture for the home market; and (3) the production of manufactured goods for export. New Zealand's policy makers are focusing their attention mainly on the second and third types, both of which are hampered by the country's small size. For instance, the fact that New Zealand, like the countries of Central America, lacks many of the raw materials required by industry is itself a function partly of size. The country's population is also too small to provide an adequate labor pool for many types of manufacturing.

Perhaps the severest restriction is market size. Under today's conditions, an increasing number of industries cannot attain optimal scale economies when serving a market of under three million people, nor can they obtain all the specialized services and interfirm linkages they need. New Zealanders are well aware of their scale problems, which was one of their chief reasons for accepting limited integration with Australia.

Domestic production as a replacement for imports is not a wholly new development for New Zealand. A fair amount of such production took place during colonial times, when high transport costs helped protect early industries from foreign competition. Manufacture of food, clothing, tools, and implements prospered until transport improvements permitted cheaper imports to overwhelm many pioneer firms. A number of domestic producers making consumer goods from local raw materials managed to survive, however, especially the manufacturers of woollen textiles and clothing, furniture, and other wood products.

Several newer types of import-competing production appeared during the Great Depression, when the government promoted industrialization as a way of reducing the adverse effects of fluctuating foreign commodity markets on employment and incomes. Following a diversification policy much like that of Britain in that same period, the government actively pushed manufacturing and granted tariff protection to firms that could not otherwise compete against imports in New Zealand's small market. One of the country's assets in this early industrialization program was its abundance of cheap hydroelectricity.

During the 1950s, New Zealand revived and intensified her drive for industrialization, with some success. Among those industries attracted to the country, small establishments engaged in light manufacturing predominate. The fastest growing of these has been the electrical goods industry, followed by manufacturers of household appliances, vehicle parts, rubber products and a variety of such miscellaneous products as sporting goods and other light consumer goods catering to New Zealanders' rising incomes. Some heavier manufactures have also appeared, notably vehicle assembling and metal products. The latter industries export only minute quantities of their products.

The import-substitution program has enjoyed modest but steady progress, as shown by the long-term decline in the import-GDP ratio. Imports represented 27 percent of GDP in 1951–1952, but they have since fallen to less than 18 percent. Aided by the government's protective policies, import-substitution has been the main basis for New Zealand's industrial growth up to the present. As in the CACM, however, it seems probable that the days of simple, easy import-substitution are about to end. The more difficult kinds of import-competing manufacture ahead will require greater infusions of capital for increased imports of raw materials, intermediates, and equipment. They will also need larger markets.

Many believe that New Zealand's future lies in introducing new kinds of industry geared mainly to the export market. Their rationale is that world demand for manufactures is growing more rapidly than for primary goods, thereby offering a solution to New Zealand's balance of payments problem. They point also to the success of another former agricultural specialist of small size, Denmark, which has managed to develop a large and diverse output of manufactured goods for export.

Although New Zealand's manufactured exports have increased at a rapid rate, they are still little more than 3 percent of total manufacturing output (excluding processed agricultural commodities), in spite of the fact that industrial production as a whole has doubled in the last decade. The exports that have increased most during this time have been new types of forest products, especially pulp and paper, whose foreign sales have risen twice as fast as GNP, mainly in response to burgeoning demand in Australia. New Zealand is also finding new markets in Oceania and Southeast Asia for her foods and beverages, textiles and clothing, metals and metal products, machinery, petroleum products, and fertilizer and other chemicals.

The country also hopes for important export earnings from her new steel industry. The deposits of iron sands have proved larger than expected, and the newly discovered Taranaki gas field nearby will provide a much needed energy supply. Despite the complexity of the ore, a sophisticated and intricate new process now makes recovery economically feasible. The use of direct-reduction and continuous casting techniques will reduce labor needs and unit costs in the steelmaking operations. Production should be great enough to make New Zealand self-sufficient in steel and permit sizable exports. Like Norway, New Zealand is also capitalizing on her surplus hydroelectricity by introducing aluminum smelting at a new mill at Invercargill.

Lately, the capital for New Zealand's industrialization has changed in its nature and source. Although the country's financial sector was overwhelmingly British-owned, most of its manufacturing has been, with important exceptions, New Zealand-owned and controlled, even though dependent upon British loans. More recently, direct foreign investment has become more common, a trend that began after World War I but has accelerated since World War II. This shift followed a stiffening of New Zealand's import controls and a consequent entrance of American interests. By the 1960s British direct investment was a little over one-half the total, Australian was one-quarter, and most of the rest was from the United States. The total equity of American firms has been increasing rapidly, partly because of their greater tendency to reinvest profits in New Zealand. Foreign ownership is especially great in meat processing, tobacco manufacturing, baking, distilling, engineering, transport equipment, and soaps.

Despite the substantial role of foreign investment, the government has retained a strong voice in the reordering of New Zealand's export economy. With its policy of import restrictions combined with export incentives, the government has introduced a number of measures affecting the direction of industrial development. Governmental agencies can control investment through their power to grant or withhold approval for overall projects, their authority to license imports of capital equipment and raw materials, and their ability to afford tariff protection to infant industries.

With all their promise, New Zealand's export industries nevertheless confront problems different from those of Denmark and other countries pursuing this strategy. New Zealand's population and labor force are still smaller than Denmark's; and New Zealand is widely separated from her foreign markets, even those in the Pacific basin, whereas Denmark is located in the midst of the world heartland, immediately surrounded by numerous and prosperous customers. Also, New Zealand lacks the large supply of cheap labor that has given Taiwan, Singapore, and Hong Kong their comparative advantage in this type of export production. All such countries have to import costly raw materials.

The prospects for quick diversification of New Zealand's manufacturing exports do not appear great, if only because such radical changes take time. Foreign exchange earnings from the sale of agricultural commodities will be needed for a long while to generate the capital needed for industrialization. Although the country's traditional exports are a slowly diminishing proportion of the total, they still account for more than four-fifths of New Zealand's sales abroad.

reducing disparities

In most respects New Zealanders have worked as hard to correct their domestic inequalities as they have to reorder their economic relations with the outside world. Yet they have not all agreed on the ordering of priorities in their domestic policy, a question that separates the two major political parties. Past governments have concentrated most, and with the best results, on reducing income disparities; they have also had some success with the emerging urban problems. Until very recently, however, the country has put less effort into redressing regional imbalances and resolving the problems of lagging and distressed regions.

income differences

It has been long-standing public policy in New Zealand to eliminate poverty and maintain the general social security of all citizens. For a people who are so conservative in other things, New Zealanders have adopted the methods of British-style welfare statism to an unusual degree. These measures include state assistance for housing (without the requirement of a strict means test); complete medical care; unemployment and disability insurance; and children's, widows', and orphans' benefits. Taken together, these provide a remarkable degree of protection against any social distress that is beyond the control of the individual.

With considerable foresight New Zealand has anticipated the dangers of social disorganization and racial conflict threatened by the influx of Maoris and Islanders into the cities. Parliament expressly forbade discriminatory treatment by the Race Relations Act of 1972, and local governments aid rural in-migrants in their adjustments to urban life. Indeed, New Zealand's success in relieving disparities among individual members of the society may well have delayed the attack on urban and regional disparities.

urban planning

New Zealand's urban programs have been concerned mainly with the rational use of urban space, slum prevention and clearance, and the alleviation of the impact of urban growth on rural lands. Although planning schemes appeared as early as 1926, the first concerted effort came with the Town and Country Planning Act of 1953. Although this legislation mandated planning at both the urban and regional levels, in the end only the urban features of the act were seriously implemented.

By American or European standards, New Zealand has no real slums. Perhaps the country's most effective slum preventative has been the government housing program, which has permitted New Zealand's cities to avert the kinds of housing shortages that produce slums. This is not public housing in the customary American sense; instead it provides public support for the construction of private dwellings, often through a second mortgage held by a government agency. This program is one of the reasons 70 percent of New Zealand's homes are owner-occupied. Another aid to slum prevention is the country's high standards for municipal services, including garbage and refuse removal and street cleaning. The government also requires owners to keep their houses in good repair.

regional development

Projections of present trends indicate that, in the absence of government intervention, the disparities between the north and the south will continue to grow and that the dominance of Auckland will increase further. Because New Zealand takes such good care of individuals in the society, the problems of regions mainly take the form of the waning fortunes of local commerce; inability to attract or hold industry; and out-migration of workers to other, more dynamic areas.

Although New Zealanders have appeared wary of regional planning in the past, the pressures for special help to disadvantaged regions have increased.

The distressed regions, such as the west coast of South Island, have had their local regional planning groups, which have had little authority or government support and have therefore functioned mainly as pressure groups. Aside from this, past support for problem areas has gone mainly to poorer rural regions under the Marginal Lands Act of 1950, which provided developmental aid to lagging rural areas for the purpose of converting idle land to productive agricultural use through clearing, fertilizing, and other reclamation measures.

In summary, the traditional role of government in regional problems has been one of "benign neglect," in contrast to the country's activist approach to other national problems. The conservative government that was in power until recently had opposed direct intervention on the grounds that New Zealand's most pressing need was to maintain and strengthen the national economy during this perilous period when the country's international economic outlook has been changing. It maintained that the disadvantaged regions are too small for self-sustaining growth, that firms choose the economically most efficient locations, and New Zealand's best interests lie in permitting this locational pattern to develop naturally.

THE CURRENT OUTLOOK

As a result of a major electoral upset in November 1972, New Zealand's affairs have taken new political directions. The elections reinstalled the Labour party and brought major policy shifts both in domestic and foreign affairs. The new domestic policy called for tax relief, further expansion of social services, and a major emphasis upon regional development. Foreign policy changes included the ending of participation in the Southeast Asia Treaty Organization (SEATO), withdrawal of military training teams from Vietnam, recognition of Communist China, firmer ties with the Soviet Union, widened representation in Europe, joining the Organization for Economic Co-operation and Development, and sending trade missions to Peru and Chile.

regional development policy

One of the chief differences between the new administration and the old has been their attitudes toward regional development. The Labour party has a program of balanced regional development, which represents an attempt to stem powerful centralizing forces within the national space-economy. Ultimately, it could have important effects on the location of import-competing industries and many kinds of market-oriented production.

One of the questions this new emphasis raises is whether Auckland's rapidly increasing ascendence in the country's economic affairs can be countered, in view of that city's superior accessibility to the national market. Can industries be persuaded to locate in areas that are peripheral to that market? Can investors be led to accept locations that do not offer significant external economies? Can New Zealand afford the economic burden of promoting inherently inefficient lagging regions? Is the nation large enough to support a dispersed space-economy? These are the same questions that the mother country, Britain, is having to ask in dealing with similar but larger-scale problems.

persisting neocolonialism

The people of New Zealand have long debated whether they should encourage or limit direct foreign investment. In their desire to reconcile their need for industrial progress with the perceived disadvantages of foreign ownership, they face the same dilemma that has become a major national issue in Canada (see Chapter 15). Most New Zealanders accept the necessity for foreign capital, which has represented about 13 percent of annual new investment in recent years; but they dread and resent the measure of foreign control this injects into the national economy.

arguments for foreign investment

Those New Zealanders who favor a continuing large role for foreign investment insist that the country's future growth depends upon sizable additions of capital, considering the depleted foreign currency reserves. They maintain that overseas capital makes available resources that otherwise would not become accessible to New Zealand, that it increases the supply of funds for investment by supplementing receipts from exports and domestic savings. They point out that overseas capital has historically played a substantial part in the country's industrialization. By comparison with domestically owned firms, foreign enterprise in New Zealand generally has a larger scale of operation, uses more modern technology and more advanced management practices, is more capital-intensive, and does more exporting.

opposing arguments

Those who fear a foreign "take-over" of the New Zealand economy counter with the argument that capital gains from foreign direct investment are often illusory. They marshall statistics that suggest an actual net outflow resulting from foreign operations, a disparity that appears to increase with time as overseas investors expatriate their profits. Foreign concerns obtain 15 percent of all New Zealand corporate profits from the services, 40 percent of those from mining, and 35 percent from manufacturing as a whole. For specific types of manufacturing the proportion ranges as high as 50 to 67 percent.

It is further maintained that foreign firms do not bring as much capital into the country as usually thought, because so many companies do not invest cash but gain equity in New Zealand firms in return for their technology. In many cases they actually finance all or part of their investments through local borrowing within New Zealand. Multinationals often disguise their cash outflows as royalties or fees paid to the parent concern. These large companies engaged in "tax games," often by overpricing their technical assistance to subsidiaries or by overcharging for the raw materials, parts, and assemblies they supply from abroad (see Chapter 11).

Going one step further, the critics say that alien firms often exert an unwholesome influence on New Zealand's political affairs. The government is moved to accommodate its actions to the needs of foreign investors by the eagerness of officials to attract capital. The net effect, they say, is a strong influence for conservative governmental policies, because voters fear a flight of capital if they elect a liberal government. This situation produces a direct conflict between policies of full employment and a need for international solvency, accompanied by pressures to raise taxes on the one hand and to reduce them on the other.

governmental policy

Confronted with such opposing views, what has been the official stance on these questions? Traditionally, successive administrations have tried to encourage "worthwhile" foreign investment without sacrificing local ownership and control. Among the first significant legislation on this subject, the Overseas Takeover Regulations of 1960 stressed the government's preference for loan capital rather than equity capital. Past administrations generally have not refused foreign direct investment but have instead encouraged New Zealand participation in such ventures. (A minimum local participation of 40 percent is usual.) Earlier governments of New Zealand have had the capability of influencing investment through the control of capital stock issues, controls over foreign exchange, and regulations governing takeovers of domestic concerns by foreigners.

The greatest difference between the new Labour government and its predecessors is in the way it implements and enforces existing regulatory tools. The old government used exchange controls sparingly, rarely invoked takeover regulations, and freely repatriated interest, dividends, and capital; the new government is less reluctant to exercise firm control over foreign investment. The current administration bases its acceptance of new overseas investment on a number of regulations that carefully control the nature of the contribution, attempt to avoid excessive overseas ownership and control, and exclude enterprises that would operate against the country's national interests. The government also prohibits investments for the purpose of land speculation.

challenges to New Zealand's agriculture

With all their attention directed to problems of industrialization, New Zealanders recognize that they must sustain and increase their primary exports, which remain the foundation for their country's industrial growth. In the short term the principal problem is to reorient production toward broader export markets with a wider range of products to compensate for the loss of their special ties to the United Kingdom. In the longer term, however, they must contend with the likelihood that further intensification of agriculture will yield diminishing returns, barring some dramatic advance in technology. It is estimated, for example, that the full potential of the nation's grasslands will be reached within a decade and a half. Another long-term problem is the limited capacity of the country's mere two million acres of arable land. With the population migrating to the cities, farmers are diverting increasing acreages from export production to provide for domestic urban needs.

If ways can be found, perhaps through technological advances, to break these long-range barriers to increased output, New Zealand's agriculture can look to tempting opportunities for expansion to meet the needs of the world's steadily growing population. With a major part of the world's people undernourished or malnourished, the global food supply is increasingly taxed. The most serious deficiency is protein, which is New Zealand's specialty. With FAO forecasting a rising demand for dairy products and meat, New Zealand remains a valuable world food resource area for the future. If the country can continue to increase its agricultural output, its long-term prospects are good.

the continuing question of distance

New Zealand's problem in the 1840s was distance, and even with the accumulated benefits from transport innovation, this old problem refuses to disappear. Just as new developments in transport technology were promising further economies, world energy supplies have suddenly become much costlier. The sharp rise in world oil prices following the 1973 Middle Eastern crisis was a severe blow to New Zealand and other peripheral nations heavily dependent upon fuel to maintain their long transport lines. Will the sudden steep rise in transport costs once again cut off New Zealand from her foreign markets?

Although the evidence is not yet clear, it would seem that higher fuel costs may tend to accelerate certain trends already in motion. For example, these events should intensify still further New Zealand's efforts to increase the transportability of her exports by reducing their bulk and perishability and increasing their unit value, so that they can remain competitive in distant markets. The increased need to minimize her costs for goods that have been obtained overseas should further stimulate New Zealand's drive for import-competing manufactures, which are once again sheltered by distance from foreign competitors. These same considerations should promote more backward integration of industries in order to reduce imports of bulky raw materials and intermediates.

The steepening transport-cost curve should also prompt New Zealand to cultivate closer markets even more assiduously than she has recently been doing. This would mean sharpening her focus on the Pacific basin countries of the Americas and Asia, with a special emphasis upon the countries and territories of Oceania. Although the island territories increased their imports from New Zealand from NZ$9.2 million in 1965 to NZ$40.0 million in 1971, this is still but a small percentage of the country's current sales to the United Kingdom. Regardless of the form that their solutions may take, New Zealand's people can be expected to approach these new problems with the same ingenuity and initiative they used so effectively in overcoming formidable obstacles of the past. These are some of the qualities that cause New Zealand to be unique among nations of the hinterland.

RECOMMENDED READINGS

Cornwall, J. P. M., ed., *Planning and Forecasting in New Zealand*. Wellington: New Zealand Institute of Public Administration, 1965.

Economist Intelligence Unit, *An Economic Geography of the Commonwealth*. London: Blackie & Son, 1957.

Money, D. C., *Australia and New Zealand*. London: University Tutorial Press, 1968.

indonesia: the challenge of size and diversity

22

Indonesia, the world's largest archipelago, faces very different problems from those of New Zealand: great size, physical and cultural diversity, and the consequences of dualism. The archipelago stretches 3,400 miles (more than 5,000 kilometers) from west to east along the equator, a distance equivalent to that from the west coast of Ireland to the Caspian Sea. The largest island, Kalimantan (Indonesian Borneo), is as large as France; the smaller of the more than 3,000 islands are but a few acres in size. The total area of 750,000 square miles (2,000,000 square kilometers) and a population of 120 million make Indonesia the third largest country in Asia after China and India.

Each of the islands, formed by intersecting mountain chains, provides a variety of environments from tropical coastal swamps to alpine mountain heights. The cultures vary from westernized residents of Jakarta and the wet-rice agriculturalists of Indonesia's Javanese heartland to primitive marshland and upland hunters and food gatherers in the country's Outer Island hinterlands. Indeed, Indonesian history, until the Dutch finally linked some 300 separate native states into the Netherlands Indies, was the history of component places and peoples rather than that of a nation. Yet out of this history and the subsequent colonial impact certain common economic and social patterns have emerged, as have a single national language and determination to maintain national political and economic unity while respecting the integrity of local cultural differences.

It is in the economic sphere that traditional organization has been most modified by the colonial experience. Before the arrival of the Europeans, agriculture, supplemented by fishing and hunting, was the means of subsistence of the vast majority of the population. The peasants had little incentive to produce more than they themselves consumed. Exchange of produce and labor was reciprocal rather than commercial. Until 1800 no far-reaching changes had been made, but in the aftermath of the Napoleonic wars the Dutch instituted the "culture system" to force the Javanese to produce an export surplus. The "liberal" and "ethical" policies that followed did not relax Dutch control but, by making it less direct, fostered a degree of regional economic self-determination and helped bring to the isolated, self-sufficient village an understanding of the money-based market. However, these policies also produced all the problems of a dual economy and led a Dutch Indies economist, J. H. Boeke, to develop his theory of economic dualism.

Indonesia emerged from colonial status with its economy still largely agricultural. In 1961 some 70 percent of the total population was employed in farming. Exports were dependent on conditions in world markets, and neither the government nor the businessman had much disposable capital. Dualism had distorted the society and its economy. Years of Dutch rule provided Indonesians with little incentive to formulate their own theories as to how the domestic economy should be run. This was hardly an auspicious beginning for a new nation, especially one which, when created, became the world's largest and most populous unitary (non-federal) state. To make matters worse, years of internal dissension and disorganization followed independence. By 1966 much of the inherited Dutch infrastructure had deteriorated. Yet by 1973, even though inefficiency remains endemic, a semblance of economic and political stability had been achieved by the military government that assumed power in 1966, and in a Second Five-Year Plan scheduled for 1974–1979 a new developmental course has been set, largely planned and directed by the central government but executed by such large-scale autonomous organizations as Pertamina, the state oil monopoly.

PRE–EUROPEAN HEARTLAND-HINTERLAND PATTERNS

Even before the eastward expansion of European powers, there were common patterns in the archipelago that remain significant today. Thousands of small islands or fragments of the larger ones each had its peasantry and local nobility and was organized, for the most part, around agriculture or trade. Thus the early history of Indonesia is largely that of the relations between the many petty kingdoms—their rivalries, their periods of independence and of supremacy over or subjugation by neighboring states. The most stable kingdoms and most developed cultures were found where irrigation made possible wet-rice farming (*sawah*), and the support of fairly dense population in an *Inner Indonesian heartland* consisting of Java, Madura, and Bali (see back endpapers). Central and East Java recurrently experienced the rise and fall of predominantly agricultural states; in most periods they dominated the archipelago politically and culturally. In the *Outer Island hinterlands,* where the people lived largely by practicing shifting cultivation (*ladang*), the dominant ties usually were to clans, and political institutions were much less developed. On the coasts, where, except for Java and Bali, the populations are concentrated, fishing and trade were as important as agriculture. The coasts of all the islands were the homes of small trading kingdoms that became powerful according to the extent of trade open to them at a particular time and to their degree of control over it.

Where larger political structures existed in the islands, they too were based on control of trade in addition to agriculture. The sea routes between the islands—particularly the narrow straits of Sunda and Malacca, through which ships sailing between India and the East must pass, and the sea lanes to the Moluccas (Maluku, or Spice Islands)—were constant sources of rivalry among near and distant powers. Through the contacts arising from trade, political and cultural ideas reached Indonesia and were accepted or rejected, assimilated and diffused in varying degrees throughout the islands. For example, the centuries during which India was the area's major trading partner brought the religions of Hinduism, Buddhism, and Islam and their accompanying political thought and institutions, scripts, and literary traditions.

traditional agricultural differences

Thus, on the eve of the European penetration there was already a heartland-hinterland difference in population densities and the power of petty states that derived from the cultivation of irrigated rice in the lowlands of Inner Indonesia and of dry rice in the upland forests and the Outer Island hinterlands. This difference persists to this day.

physical basis

Sawah can only be established where the soil is naturally fertile and where flatland conditions favor the use of irrigation for the production of *padi* (rice). *Ladang*, the shifting cultivation of rice and a range of other crops relying on natural rainfall, takes place, on the other hand, in temporary clearings in the forested upland zones. Thus, the physical geography of the islands was important in determining the range of alternatives open to farmers. Mountainous spines and swampy coasts limit the agricultural potential of many of the islands, especially Sumatra, Kalimantan, and Sulawesi. The only extensive dry flatlands are found in Java and central Sumatra, where soils are also enriched by volcanic ash. Indonesia is the most highly volcanic region in the world.

Climatic differences were important, too. The Indonesian climate is tropical, moderated only by the islands, being situated between two large continental land masses and by wide differences in elevation.

Rainfall, although naturally influenced by the mountains and increasing with altitude, is never less than 40 inches a year. In the equatorial rain belt, which covers most of Sumatra, Kalimantan, and Sulawesi, 90 to 100 inches annually are regularly recorded. However, there is a progressive lessening of precipitation towards the southern and eastern parts of the archipelago. The climate is drier in Java, Sulawesi, and Nusa Tenggara than in the larger islands of Sumatra and Kalimantan.

The wind pattern and the only two recognizable seasons—wet and dry—are determined by the monsoons. The southeast wind carries dry air from the interior of Australia during the "northern" summer, giving a comparatively dry period of about four months—June to October—to eastern Java and Nusa Tenggara. At the same time, warm, humid air from the Indian Ocean denies relief to Sumatra, western Java, and the islands of the equatorial rain belt. During the "southern" summer the direction of flow is from the Asian mainland, south and then southeast to Australia. This northwest monsoon, which lasts from November to March, brings rain to all parts of the archipelago.

The amount and distribution of rainfall has marked effects on soil and vegetation. In areas of heaviest precipitation soluble soil ingredients are dissolved and carried away. This leaching accounts for the poor nature of many of the soils of Sumatra, Kalimantan, and Sulawesi and is an important contributory factor to the low population density. Conversely, in central and eastern Java, Bali, Lombok, and Nusa Tenggara generally, the dry season gives the soil a respite from the constant leaching. More important still, in areas of volcanic activity the wet-season leaching process is beneficial because it exposes new, fertile volcanic soil.

sawah and ladang contrasted

Because of the physical differences, large sections of the inner Indonesian core of Java were blessed with environments permitting *sawah,* and in these areas elaborate systems of irrigation have been developed to bring water from the rivers and streams to grow wet rice. A little over 40 percent of the cultivated land area in Indonesia is irrigated, and three-fourths of this total is in Java. On this small island every effort has been made to till the last possible square foot of land, and thousands of small *padi* fields extend across the plains and hills and cover the sides of mountains in elaborate terrace fashion.

Sawah is extremely responsive to labor inputs. As population has grown and land holdings have been subdivided, *sawah* has continued to produce substantial returns, especially when the opportunities for double cropping and for interplanting of supplementary crops have been exploited. The result has been what anthropologist Clifford Geertz has called *agricultural involution*—the continuing ability of Javanese agriculture to absorb mounting numbers of people at growing densities and still provide minimal subsistence levels for all within the village communities. (*Adat,* traditional Indonesian law, ensures that through communal sharing of output, none starve.) Indeed, to produce higher yields greater numbers of field hands are essential; reductions in labor-intensity reduce output.

Ladang—"shifting" or "slash-and-burn" agriculture—is more widely practiced in the hilly hinterlands of Outer Indonesia. A plot of virgin forest is cleared by ringing the trees and then by burning them, and the fertile ground is planted, generally with dry upland rice. After a few years the soil becomes depleted, however, and the plot must be abandoned. Large areas can thus support only small populations. Left to itself, *ladang* will be quickly reclaimed by new wild growth, and in about ten years the fertility of the soil will be restored; but unless land is sufficiently abundant so that the former *ladang* can be left until an upper layer of humus can be rebuilt, destructive grasses take root, preventing further cultivation by indigenous methods. In some parts of Sumatra great stretches of land covered with permanent *alang-alang* (savanna) grass attest to a failure to respect the necessary cycle of ten years.

If population pressure increases, shifting cultivation must be abandoned. Only different farming practices and the application of commercial fertilizer will restore the depleted soil and feed the extra mouths.

core-periphery differences within the traditional societies

Perception of the differences between the Javanese core and the Outer Island periphery is relatively recent in Indonesia. However, core-periphery distinctions were significant much earlier in the perception of territoriality by many of Indonesia's cultural groups. For example, the Minangkabao (whose traditional kingdom became the province of West Sumatra) traditionally distinguished between *Darek* and *Rantau. Darek* meant "central homeland," and was the *sawah*-based core of the Minangkabao kingdom. *Rantau* was the "surrounding neighborhood" partially settled by Minangkabao, but in environments that, in contrast to the homeland, supported fewer people on *ladang.* Like the Indonesian core, *Darek* is overpopulated today, while *Rantau* does not suffer from the same population pressure.

The distinction between *sawah* and *ladang* also played an important role in Minangkabao life at the village level and illustrates the complex links between social structure, economic life, and the spatial organization of peasant societies. Minangkabao society was matrilinear. The smallest genealogical unit was the mother and her children, called *samando,* or "one mother." These units were integrated into a living unit called *paruik,* consisting of the mother's sisters and brothers under the lead of mother's mother, occupying one huge domicile, the famous Minangkabao long house. Members of a *paruik* cultivated their land as one operational whole. The men's role in this setting was unique. The husbands were not considered members of the *paruik.* They came to their wives in the evening and left in the morning to return to their mother's *paruik,* where they worked, ate, and fulfilled their social obligations. Therefore the mother's oldest brother was the most important man in the *paruik.* He ran the farm, cared for the children, and represented the *paruik* in public. Several *paruiks* of the same kinship formed a *kampong* (village).

Agricultural production by the *paruik* involved both *sawah* and *ladang.* Each Minangkabau village had its own *sawah* on which rice was cultivated as monoculture. Since the topography of *Darek* required the construction of terraces and the work was done with hand tools, it exceeded the labor potential of a single *paruik.* Thus, the whole *kampong* was mobilized for construction work. The land would then be divided among the *paruiks* and the women had full rights to the *padi* produced. The men would contribute to the heavy work—terracing, plowing, and harvesting—but their property came not from the *sawah* but from shifting cultivation. Forested areas would be cleared by burning, and dry rice would be cultivated along with a variety of other food and, later, cash crops. Traditionally, this meant that the power was held by the women. As commercial activities increased and cash crops became more important, it was the men who came to dominate marketing, however, and gradually the balance of power shifted between the sexes. The long houses have fallen into disuse, and the *paruik* no longer plays its traditional social role.

THE DUTCH EAST INDIA COMPANY AND THE CREATION OF THE INDIES

Europeans entered the trade and politics of Southeast Asia at the beginning of the sixteenth century. Vasco da Gama's establishment of a Portuguese port at Calicut (1498) followed by the conquest of Goa in 1510 marked the end of the earlier Arab monopoly of Indian Ocean trade. The Portuguese were closely followed by the other European powers, and a period of struggle for supremacy lasted from the conquest of Malacca in 1511 until its capture by the Dutch in 1641. The Europeans sought Malacca to control the strait; a strong position in the Moluccas to obtain spices; and contact with Java to obtain a rice supply for Malacca and to prevent serious competition or harassment on the Java Sea. However, none could depend on an overwhelming superiority of force. What was sought was control of the spice trade without territorial involvement; and, dependent on a long and difficult sea route, they sought to defend their position by building fortresses dominating major ports and by taking advantage of the abundant local rivalries to maintain their superiority.

The early Dutch expeditions to the islands were backed by the civic corporations that dominated political life in the Netherlands at that time. Finding that competition with each other was ruinous in the face of foreign competition, the United East India Company (Vereenigde Oost-Indische Compagnie-VOC) was organized in 1602. This was the first step in the welding of the many islands and petty kingdoms into a single colony, and thus in the emergence of Indonesia as a separate state. The VOC was given a government-protected monopoly of commerce in Asia and control of the factories already established by the separate companies.

The decisive struggle for dominance in the archipelago occurred between 1600 and 1640. In 1600 the Portuguese still controlled considerable trade. The Spaniards had established themselves in the Philippines around 1570 and from Manila made recurrent efforts to enter the competition in spices. The British, after a few voyages in the late sixteenth century, entered the contest in earnest with the chartering in 1600 of the British East India Company, which at that time was a smaller organization than the VOC and had less governmental support.

By 1640, the Dutch prevailed over both the European competitors and the local powers and became dominant in the region. Monopoly in the Spice Islands,

near monopoly of the trade of the rest of the archipelago, and supremacy in the trade with China and Japan brought tremendous wealth to the VOC throughout the seventeenth century. Yet despite their continued attempt to avoid territorial commitment, the Dutch found in Java, as in the Spice Islands, that their position had political aspects that drew them further into local affairs. The prosperity of trade depended on peace; in addition, their interests were gradually expanding beyond the more limited role of trade to include supervision of the production of items of trade. During the seventeenth century the VOC depended largely on the monopoly export of spices, especially pepper, and the import of cloth and opium. As they found it necessary to intervene further in Java in order to protect their position, the Dutch obtained a supervisory role over production of pepper, sugar, and cotton, and in the next years new crops were introduced that promised to be equally profitable. Experiments were made with various plants, including the coffee tree. Beginning in 1707, coffee plants were given to district rulers in western Java, and indigo was introduced at about the same time. At first the local rulers made enormous profits on the coffee crop; but since company policy was to prevent the accumulation of great wealth or coffee stocks in the hands of the Javanese rulers, the VOC took drastic steps to reduce the size of the crop.

Gradually it became the practice to require the delivery of stated amounts of various crops from each regency (a local state governed by a regent appointed by the Dutch), according to the system known as *contingents and forced deliveries*. The regents provided required amounts of coffee as tribute (contingents) and for sale at fixed prices (forced deliveries). Supervisors were appointed to see that the specified number of trees were planted and that they were taken care of; at first called coffee sergeants, these foremen were the first Europeans to come into regular and extended contact with the Javanese, and, with the later title of Controller, they remained the important link between the European hierarchy and the local Javanese officials.

Territorial expansion brought hundreds of new problems. Indicative of the new Dutch role in Java was the action taken in 1764 of replacing the many local and foreign coins circulating in Java with a single monetary system using copper coins stamped in Batavia (modern Jakarta). Several guiding principles of later Dutch rule were accepted in the days of the company: for example, that in legal matters each national group should be left under its own law as much as possible; and that, except in matters related to the production and delivery of produce for export, the existing rulers of the people should remain the effective instruments of government.

Despite its role in agricultural production, the VOC was bankrupt at the end of the eighteenth century and was dissolved on January 1, 1800, leaving to the Dutch republic a sizable debt and the responsibility of administering a heterogeneous collection of territories, no two of which had had exactly the same relationship to the company. In Java, Batavia had grown to be a large city of canals and houses in the Dutch style but crowded and unhealthy. Around Batavia were the directly administered lowlands where Dutch- and Chinese-owned plantations produced coffee, sugar, indigo, and cotton for export. Elsewhere in Java, Dutch officials—coffee sergeants and residents attached to local courts at Bantam and the central states—exerted a considerable but uneven influence on Javanese life. Outside Java, the company possessed a series of fortresses in the eastern islands, control of several ports in Sumatra such as Padang, from which they traded for gold with Minangkabao, and control of the trade of south Borneo and some of the Lesser Sundas. Bali and Lombok had seen nothing of Dutch influence, and only Java had felt it reaching into the way of life of the people as a whole. The eastern islands were, by the end of the century, considered of little importance.

THE COLONIAL PERIOD

With the acceptance by the Netherlands government of governing authority over the territories of the company, a century and a half of colonial rule of the Indies began, during which far deeper changes occurred in the archipelago than those brought about by previous European interventions. The major innovations were economic; a period of free trade policies was followed by governmental direction of agriculture under the Culture System and then again by freer trade. Administrative developments were usually designed to facilitate the working of the desired economic system, while political and social changes, when they occurred, were unplanned and, unless of crisis proportions, almost unnoticed. So long as the Dutch were concerned exclusively with obtaining wealth from agriculture, their interest was concentrated upon Java, the most fertile and most densely populated island; their territorial sovereignty was extended only when it seemed absolutely necessary or clearly profitable. Toward the end of the nineteenth century the increasing industrialization of the Netherlands, the new wave of imperialist expansion that engaged all the European powers, and the new spirit of humanitarian concern that changed all their policies combined to bring about a revolution in attitudes toward colonial government, however. This led the Dutch to extend their interest in the Outer Islands, to consolidate their position throughout the archipelago, and to accept a guiding role in political and social as well as economic evolution.

opening the Indies to free trade

During the Napoleonic Wars, new ideas about colonial policy had been discussed, particularly the relative virtues of trade monopoly and of company control as opposed to state control. Suggestions were now put forward that if in Java, as in Europe, the economy were open to private competition, the Javanese would respond by transforming their village economies and that toward this end, land should be privately owned, all services and labor paid, and trade free to all comers. By provisions of an 1804 charter, the Indies were opened to free trade, and the principle of indirect rule by the Batavian governor general through native rulers was confirmed.

In 1811, however, the British arrived to remove the islands from control of the French (who had incorporated the Netherlands and its possessions into the Napoleonic empire). Thomas Stamford Raffles, the British governor general, introduced further changes in Java in an effort to make the island a place of free cultivation and free trade in which taxation could replace tribute as the source of government revenue. He rationalized territorial administration by dividing Java into sixteen residencies, each with its European head of administration, and he sought to strengthen the village (*desa*) as the basic unit of taxation. The village tax was set at the cash value of two-fifths of the crop. Payment could be in kind, but by various means it was made easier to pay this land rent in money in order to spur commercialization.

After the final defeat of Napoleon, Holland was given back its colonies as part of the general European plan to strengthen the countries along French borders. Raffles' system of territorial administration—residency, regency, district, and village—was retained. However, the free trade experiment did not prove financially rewarding. The Javanese did not respond to the possibility of cultivating for export and, in fact, went into debt to the moneylenders to obtain the money for taxes, and a considerable increase in crime was noticed.

mercantilist policies of the culture system

In the critical year of 1830, when Holland itself was threatened with bankruptcy at the outbreak of the Belgian revolt, King William turned to Johannes van den Bosch, who was convinced that through government-organized agriculture the Indies could not only pay their own way but remit profits to the empty Dutch treasury. Van den Bosch, as governor general from 1830–1834 and colonial minister from 1834–1840, created the *cultuur-stelsel,* a system of government-directed agriculture usually translated as the Culture System. His premise was that the Javanese were not ready to respond to the incentive of economic gain; that, left alone, the peasant would cultivate just enough for the needs of his family; and that the peasant must, therefore, be obligated to work until the time when the visible increase in prosperity would itself gradually create incentive for further effort.

Van den Bosch's original instructions provided for the encouragement of both individual and government enterprise in the production of export crops, but government enterprise proved much more successful. Convinced that the districts where coffee already was grown under compulsion provided the greatest revenue to the state and were the best-off areas of Java, he tried to extend the system of revenue in kind rather than in money to all Java. Agreements were made with village headmen concerning production, labor, and transport of crops. At first, villages had the choice of paying the land rent as before or of using one-fifth of village agricultural land for the cultivation of a crop assigned by the government, but within a few years, the Culture System was made compulsory. All villagers were forced to spend some time (theoretically calculated at 66 days per year) in labor concerned with the export crop—cultivating, harvesting, transporting, or processing—but the last could be done by paid labor if necessary. At first, sugar and indigo were the major export crops; later, coffee and several others were added.

Initially the system had the desired results. All crops exported were carried by the Netherlands Trading Company, and Amsterdam prospered. The value of exports increased sixfold from 1830 to 1840, the Indies budget was balanced in 1831, and after that large profits flowed into the Dutch treasury. In the first few years, the system appears to have increased prosperity in Java, too; population and land under cultivation increased, imports increased, and new crops such as tea, tobacco, cassava, and cinchona were successfully introduced.

Gradually, however, the abuses of the system became tremendous. More and more labor was required for the export crops, and, in order to obtain the better roads necessary for transport to the coasts, additional forced labor was levied to build them. Land rights were often ignored in the establishment of plantations, and labor was requisitioned for the sugar mills or roads at times when the peasants' rice fields demanded attention. Land rent seems often to have been required from the same persons who theoretically were paying their taxes in labor. In the 1840s, when famine struck several areas of Java, it was apparent that forced cultivation of export crops had reached the point of taking precedence over the provision of a domestic food supply.

return to liberalism

The response was to return to more liberal policies. The transition took twenty years. The difference was not in the type of economic activity, which remained agricultural production and export, but in ownership. The choice of policies of private investment, free cultivation, and free trade was determined as much by developments in Holland as by pressure in the Indies. The rising middle class gained political power throughout Europe in the revolutions of 1848, and a new Dutch constitution provided for parliamentary government and for legislative control of financial and other important matters in the Indies.

Not least among the factors that made it possible and profitable to open the Indies to private investment were developments in transport and communications.

The increased use of steamships from the 1850s onward began a much larger trade in bulk products. Both local and Chinese traders, dependent on the smaller sailing vessels, were eased out as British and Dutch steamships entered interisland trade. The opening of the Suez Canal in 1869 was the greatest single boon to trade. In the last decades of the century the telegraph, cable, railroad, and a regular postal service revolutionized communications within the Indies and between the islands and Holland. As steamships came into greater use Batavia harbor was rebuilt to accommodate them; the Dutch shipping company, KPM, which virtually monopolized interisland shipping from the early twentieth century until 1957, began operations in 1888.

Growing liberal sentiment was gradually reflected in measures to protect the cultivators from the abuses of the Culture System. The year 1860, when slavery was officially prohibited in territories administered from Batavia, was a turning point; debtor bondage was abolished in Java, and forced cultivation of most crops—but not of the two most important, coffee and sugar—ended. Not even the liberals wanted to end the system completely, for there was no certainty that taxation would immediately provide the same amount of revenue, and neither political party intended to stop the *batig slot*, the remittance of the Indies surplus to the Netherlands treasury. The trend of change had been established, however, and a conservative government in 1870 passed the Agrarian Law, which provided for the gradual cessation of the government's role in sugar cultivation and set the stage for private agricultural interests to develop an export-oriented estate economy. Although government interest in coffee decreased somewhat, the culture system in coffee did not end completely until 1917.

The Agrarian Law, intended in part to safeguard the rights of Indonesians by preventing the alienation of rice lands to foreigners, provided also for the use of "government land," land not under cultivation and land formerly farmed directly under government auspices by private interests. In this way, European planters obtained large blocs of land to produce export crops, largely the sugar, coffee, tea, and tobacco already important under the Culture System. Production of these increased substantially, and new crops such as the oil palm also were introduced, especially in North Sumatra. Estate production became highly efficient and innovative; yields per acre increased as the planters experimented with new varieties and new methods of cultivation.

As a result, the Indies government became less and less a business concern. For the first time, in 1877, more revenue was derived from taxation than from the sale of agricultural produce. At the same time the vastly increased numbers of resident Europeans, the general increase in economic activity, the problems created by the labor needs of the European investors and the resulting Chinese immigration, and the growth of cities required innovations that substantially increased the costs of administration. Although private investors were interested in agriculture and minerals, the government had to undertake the provision of most transport facilities, which it did where commercial traffic warranted them. The Europeans required better health and educational facilities, and by 1870 new central government departments of education, religion, industry, civil public works, finance, justice, and internal affairs had been created. In the 1880s the government began to establish a school system for all European and some Indonesian children, the latter generally the children of regents and local officials who would succeed to positions of authority in local government. Another increasing cost came with the gradual replacement of compulsory labor by paid labor in public works and construction. As a result of liberal economic policies, the farming-out of most taxes and licenses came to an end; some were abolished while others were collected directly by the government. The increased income from taxation and government monopolies on opium, salt, and pawnshops, however, did not make up for the decline in revenue from produce. After 1877 no remittances were made to the Netherlands treasury, and as administrative expenses grew the Indies budget became impossible to balance.

expansion into the outer island hinterlands

For the most part, the Dutch ignored the Outer Islands between 1750 and 1870, but they could claim a vague sovereignty over many of them. For example, in Minangkabao the Dutch succeeded the Portuguese and established their main center at Padang, trading for gold and spices. Padang grew rapidly, for it was the only deep water harbor on the west coast of Sumatra. The company's records mention that between 1800 and 1810 Padang Factory achieved a yearly capital turnover of about 600,000 guilders and made a profit of 400,000 guilders. Later, during the British reign of Dutch India (1808–1818), Raffles fortified Padang. Upon their return, the Dutch penetrated into the homeland of Minangkabao. Within a few years they spread a fortification network over *Darek* and introduced the Culture System. In contrast to the Javanese, however, the Minangkabao turned *Darek* into one of the very few market-oriented peasant agricultures in the Indies. The coffee and spices exported via the factory in Padang made Minangkabao more important for Dutch trade than any other residency in Sumatra until the 1880s and 1890s when agricultural production increased around Medan in North Sumatra owing to the growth of the oil palm and rubber estates.

Outside Sumatra, the first nineteenth-century expansions were for specific purposes—the occupation of Belitung to obtain tin, of the Kutei and Bandjermasin areas to obtain coal supplies for the steamships—and to prevent further British competition after the British occupied North Borneo in the middle of the century. Later, the Dutch also extended real control over the eastern islands. They took Bali and Lombok in the 1890s as the first in a series of steps that led them into the interior of southern Borneo and Celebes by 1910.

Pressure toward economic expansion in the Outer Islands and toward the raising of living levels came primarily from businessmen interested in the Indies as markets and sources of raw materials. Oil was already becoming a major field of investment on Sumatra, and rubber plantations became an important part of the economy in the early years of the century. The major economic changes were in the quantities of crops and minerals produced and exported. Welfare was an avowed goal, but ethical responsibility was incapable of solving the basic problem of the Indies' economic structure-population growth without the development of new sources of income for or by the Indonesians. Although there were few doctors, measures taken in the interests of public health limited epidemics; there were no wars; and famine was prevented. The population of Java and Madura increased from 20 million in 1880 to 30 million in 1905 and 40 million in 1930. Meanwhile, the Outer Islands, newly opened to mining and plantation interests, were relatively underpopulated. Yet professional agents recruited more Chinese than Javanese to work there. A system developed in which Europeans dominated the production of goods for export and the export-import trade. The Chinese provided the majority of wage-laborers needed on plantations and mines and, as entrepreneurs, developed a strong position in retail trade. The Indonesians continued to prefer agriculture of the self-sufficient type over all other occupations except government employment (which was open only to the wellborn) and worked for wages only when driven by necessity to do so. The same divisions were reflected politically in the continued Dutch policy of administration by "like over like" and in representation by communal groups when representative institutions were created. The division was equally strong in social life where differences in attitudes and ways of life tended to become even wider in the dual economy. Indeed, it was a Dutch Indies economist, J. H. Boeke, who coined the term *dual economy* and described it as "the clashing of an imported social system with an indigenous social system of another style."

the rise of nationalism

Dutch plans for further economic development and political progress presumed a long period of peace, of growing prosperity, of careful tutelege and grateful acceptance. For a time this appeared possible; the Indonesians who obtained a Western education pressed only for the extension of opportunity to a greater number. The Indonesian organization generally considered the first of the nationalist groups, the *Budi Utomo* (Pure Endeavor), founded in 1908, announced as its goals the encouragement of Western and traditional education and of economic development; its membership was largely aristocratic and conservative.

The influences that combined to make impracticable the Dutch concept of political progress were varied, but many of them contributed to the growth of a nationalism essentially hostile to the Dutch and to the West. Various internal causes of dissatisfaction were byproducts of the economic and political developments. First among them was the resentment caused by the lack of Indonesian participation in the more profitable sectors of the economy. The Indonesians who adopted Western attitudes found themselves shut out of all but the agricultural sector or the lowest grades of the civil service. There was no promotion from the Indonesian administrative service headed by the regents to the European service, which filled the higher positions.

The twentieth century saw the growth of social barriers and prejudices inherent in the paternalist attitude of all the colonial powers; the Dutch administrative system, paternal even in the heyday of liberalism, became tremendously so when paternalism was in fashion. As the number of Europeans grew and as their families more and more accompanied the men to the islands, European society became closed, carefully graded within itself but united against intrusions from outside. All these things had existed for a long time. They came to be noticed and to cause unrest in direct proportion to the increase in educational opportunities, and the most radical nationalists were those who attended universities in Holland.

External influences also had profound effects on the Indonesian elite as they began to criticize Dutch rule. The Chinese in particular began to adopt nationalist ideas in the first decade of the twentieth century, not in regard to Indonesia but in response to the ideas of Sun Yat-sen. They began to take renewed interest in their own culture and to establish Chinese schools on a much wider scale in order to preserve their Chinese heritage for their children. With the Chinese revolution of 1911–1912 this trend became more pronounced, and, although it led eventually to greater hostility between Chinese and Indonesians, it also provided an example for the Indonesians. Still more impact was made by Japan, whose unexpected and dramatic defeat of Russia in 1905 presented all Asia with a demonstration of the potential of an independent Asian nation; after this, Japan's attempts to industrialize and become a modern state were watched with considerable interest. The ideas of Marxism found ready acceptance among some of the Indonesian elite, especially during the short depression that followed the end of World War I, and the efforts of the new Soviet state appeared to provide a model for social and economic reform. The appearance of communism led to repressive action by the Dutch, particularly after 1926, when the Communists led an abortive rebellion in Java and West Sumatra.

It was World War II that brought a sudden end to the relatively stable political situation of the prewar Indies. The Japanese, who captured the Indies in 1942, made themselves welcome by releasing nationalist leaders from prison, by permitting the previously forbidden use of the nationalist flag and anthem, and by sponsoring nationalist organizations. When defeat seemed imminent, the Japanese discussed independence with Indonesian leaders. Upon the Japanese surrender in 1945, Sukarno proclaimed the existence of the Republic of Indonesia.

the Republic of Indonesia, 1945–1975

From 1945 to 1949 the republic fought for its existence against the Dutch—in battle, in diplomacy, and in the United Nations—and finally Dutch political claims to Indonesia were relinquished. After the transfer of sovereignty, the Indonesian government faced serious problems of recovery and reconstruction. The economy was weighted heavily to the side of agriculture; it was, moreover, oriented to production for export and completely vulnerable to world market conditions. Both the private entrepreneur and the government were short of capital. The labor force lacked the skilled workers and technicians required to develop the economy along better balanced lines. Productivity, already low, was continuing to fall, with much of the nation's economy still firmly controlled by the same foreigners against whom the war for independence had been waged.

There was an immediate attempt to formulate a program of economic development through national planning. Through 1955, the planning was still conducted by foreign experts, however, and only in 1956–1960 did a plan begin to take shape. In 1959, a National Planning Council (DEPERNAS) was established, and an eight-year plan was announced, the intent of which was to mobilize mass support for the Sukarno government's political and ideological goals.

But meanwhile, the government permitted the economy to fall into a vicious pattern of inflation and low productivity from which it could be extricated only through the most basic reorganization. The roots of the problem lay in the low level of income and of productivity, which, in turn, did not provide sufficient tax and foreign exchange revenues to cover the government's expanded domestic and foreign obligations. The resulting budgetary deficit gave rise to inflationary pressures and the eating away of foreign exchange reserves. Inflation intensified the demand for imported goods, added to production costs, and tended to depress the level of exports. The drain on reserves forced the government to curtail imports, further aggravating inflation and limiting government tax revenues and industrial production —both of which depend on high import levels.

The eight-year plan was thus abandoned in 1966 in an atmosphere of neglect, mismanagement, and hyperinflation. The consumer price index for food in Jakarta, set at 100 in 1958, went from 426 in 1961 to 5,272 in 1964, 41,404 in 1965, and from 58,851 in January 1966 to 138,944 in June and 248,521 in December 1966! There was a breakdown of government services and adminis-

Table 22.1   Major Indonesian Economic Indicators:
Annual Average Change (in percent)
1960–1972 at 1960 Prices

	1960–64	1964–68	1968–72
GDP at market prices	2.1%	4.0%	6.8%
Gross domestic investment	3.2	3.9	24.6
Export of goods	1.2	3.0	14.3
Import of goods	1.4	4.8	13.9
GDP price deflator	394.0	–	16.3
Cost of living index*	250.0	–	10.0
Private consumption	2.8	4.6	4.7
Commodity production	1.7	3.8	5.0
Sectoral GDP in:			
Agriculture	1.5	3.4	2.8
Food crops	-0.7	4.9	1.3
Mining	2.0	2.0	10.6
Manufacturing	2.5	3.3	10.5
Construction	-5.0	9.1	24.0
Trade	0.5	3.7	12.7
Services	2.5	2.6	34.0
Transportation and communication	0.5	1.8	9.0

*Jakarta index.

Source: World Bank estimates.

tration, a paralyzed planning apparatus, and cessation of all development activities. An abortive Communist coup led to a military takeover and the ouster of President Sukarno. Members of the left wing and many Chinese were slaughtered. Estimates place the total number of people killed at more than 1 million.

Not until 1969 were conditions stable enough for a new five-year plan (Repelita I) to be put into effect. This plan emphasized both political and economic stabilization, achievement of national unity, rehabilitation of the economic infrastructure, increases in income-producing exports, and meeting the people's basic demands for food and clothing. Its goals have largely been achieved, as the economic indicators presented in Table 22.1 show.

Now, a second five-year plan (Repelita II) has been developed for the period 1974–1979 by the new National Planning Agency (BAPPENAS) focusing upon national and regional growth under new conditions of national unity, internal security, and independent self-determination. It is with Indonesia's aspirations, as expressed in this plan, that we shall conclude this section, after exploring salient features of the country's economic geography in the 1970s.

SALIENT FEATURES OF INDONESIAN ECONOMIC GEOGRAPHY IN THE 1970s

population and labor force

Epidemics, famine, and civil disorders, contributing to high mortality rates and short life expectancy, were the most important factors controlling population growth in the precolonial era. The population of Java numbered only about 3 million during most of the

eighteenth century. When Dutch control in Java began to take effect, the population began to expand rapidly in the Indonesian heartland. By the beginning of the twentieth century, 20 million people were living in Java. In Java and Madura together, according to the official census, there were 47.7 million people in 1930 and 63.0 million in 1961. The numbers increased to 76.1 million in 1971, 64 percent of the country's population. The current rate of growth adds 1.5 million to Java's population each year, on only 6.9 percent of the total land area of the archipelago, so that Javanese population densities are tenfold those in the Outer Islands. This crowding in Inner Indonesia is of major concern to Indonesia's policy makers.

Rapid population growth in the Outer Islands did not begin until the early 1900s when Dutch rule became more firmly established and improved medical and hygienic techniques were introduced. The population of the Outer Islands, estimated at 10 million inhabitants in 1905, increased to 18 million by 1930, to 34 million by 1961, and 43 million by 1971. (See Table 22.2.) Vast areas of the Indonesian hinterlands remain available for settlement expansion.

trends in employment and the economy

As population has grown, there has been a *decline* in the percentage share of employment in agriculture from 71.9 in 1961 to 63.2 in 1971, with corresponding *increases* in the shares of manufacturing, trade, transport, and services. Between 1961 and 1971 employment in agriculture grew at only 0.5 percent a year, compared to increases in manufacturing employment in rural areas averaging 6.8 percent a year. There was an actual 0.3 percent decline in workers employed in urban manufactures.

In these changes, we can see marked regional differentials. Agriculture remains more important as a source of employment in the Outer Islands. The dominant growth sectors—manufacturing, trade and services—are concentrated in Java. Thus, a picture emerges of a high-density inner Indonesian core emphasizing secondary and tertiary activities, and a set of sparsely-populated agriculture-oriented hinterlands. But this spatial organization, despite the seeming similarity, is in fact very different from that obtaining in the West.

First, there is a contrast between sectoral shares of employment and of gross domestic product. The province of Riau has by far the highest regional gross product per capita. This is a typical case of a sectorally led development; in this case, oil. Other resource-oriented provinces with high per capita products are West and South Kalimantan and North Sulawesi, which have grown on the basis of exporting logs, and North and South Sumatra, which have been influenced by oil and estate agriculture. Conversely, Jakarta, the primate city, has a per capita product that is about two and a half times the national average, owing to the great concentration of recent investment and employment in adminis-

Table 22.2 Indonesia's Population in 1930, 1961, and 1971: Average Annual Growth Rate, 1961–1972 and Population Density, by Region & Province (in thousands)

	AREA (IN SQ. KM.)	1930 CENSUS	1961 CENSUS	1971 CENSUS	GROWTH RATE (PERCENT) 1961–71	DENSITY (PERSONS/KM²) 1971
D. C. I. Jakarta	592	811	2,907	4,576	4.6%	7,944
West Java	49,144	10,586	17,615	21,633	2.1	440
Central Java	34,353	13,706	18,407	21,877	1.7	634
D. I Jogjakarta	3,090	1,559	2,241	2,490	1.1	793
East Java	46,865	15,056	21,823	25,527	1.6	539
Total Java, Madura	**134,044**	**41,718**	**62,993**	**76,102 (63.8%)**	**1.9**	**565**
D. I. Aceh	59,904	1,003	1,629	2,009	2.1	34
North Sumatra	71,104	2,541	4,965	6,623	2.9	94
West Sumatra	49,333	1,910	2,319	2,793	1.9	42
Riau	124,084	493	1,235	1,642	3.1	16
Jambi	62,150	245	744	1,006	3.5	51
South Sumatra	104,363	1,378	2,733	3,444	2.2	33
Bengkulu	20,760	323	406	519	2.5	25
Lampung	33,866	361	1,668	2,777	5.2	82
Total Sumatra	**524,097**	**8,255**	**15,739**	**20,813 (17.4%)**	**2.8**	**38**
West Kalimantan	157,066	802	1,581	2,020	2.5	13
Central Kalimantan	156,552	203	497	700	3.5	4
South Kalimantan	33,966	835	1,473	1,699	1.4	49
East Kalimantan	202,619	329	551	734	2.9	4
Total Kalimantan	**550,203**	**2,169**	**4,101**	**5,152 (4.3%)**	**2.3**	**9**
North Sulawesi	24,200	748	1,351	1,718	2.8	71
Central Sulawesi	88,655	390	652	914	2.8	10
South Sulawesi	83,799	2,657	4,517	5,189	1.4	63
Southeast Sulawesi	32,454	436	559	714	2.5	22
Total Sulawesi	**229,108**	**4,232**	**7,079**	**8,535 (7.2%)**	**1.9**	**37**
Bali	5,623	1,101	1,783	2,120	1.8	377
West Nusa Tenggara	21,740	1,016	1,808	2,202	2.0	101
East Nusa Tenggara	48,889	1,343	1,967	2,295	1.6	47
Maluku	83,675	579	790	1,089	2.5	13
West Irian	421,981	179	758	923	2.0	2
Total other islands	**581,908**	**4,218**	**7,314**	**8,529 (7.3%)**	**1.8**	**15**
Total	**2,019,360**	**60,593**	**97,019**	**119,232 (100%)**	**2.26**	**59**

Source: Biro Pusat Statistik, *1971 Census and Statistical Pocketbook of Indonesia* (Jakarta: Directorate of Topography).

trative, transportation, and other services. Indeed, the affluent primate city is apparently but a small island in an impoverished Javanese heartland (Table 22.3).

Regional growth in per capita gross domestic product likewise favors the resource producers. Sulawesi and Kalimantan are growing rapidly largely because of phenomenal growth in forestry; Jakarta and West Java also are growing rapidly, the former largely on the basis of public administration, trade, and services and the latter on the basis of rice, forestry, and large scale manufacturing. The growth of Riau and West Sumatra also has been substantial, as a result of the growth of forestry and the mining sector. In these provinces, the growth of public administration and services also is substantial, implying that the service sectors are catching up to leading productive sectors. Central and East Java are stagnant, as are West and East Nusa Tenggara. Although small handicraft manufacturing is growing in Central and East Java, the stagnation of nonfood agriculture, large-scale manufacturing, and the trade sectors are responsible for the slow growth of these provinces. In both provinces of Nusa Tenggara, slow growth is due to stagnation of agriculture.

In contrast to the Western heartland-hinterland model, then, it is the resource-oriented hinterlands rather than the heartland that, together with the primate city, have the highest income levels, wage rates, and food consumption. Despite the great concentration of Dutch infrastructure on Java, it is the Outer Islands that produce an export surplus, enabling Java to support the needs of its teeming population. Of Indonesia's 1973 exports, oil contributed over one-half, 70 percent going to Japan (Indonesia has 2 percent of the world's known oil reserves). This share will increase as Indonesia takes advantage of the Organization of Petroleum Exporting Countries' (OPEC's) oligopolistic pricing in world markets. Of the balance, less than one-quarter each were earned by rubber and by lumber, and the remainder by a variety of products, including oil palm and kernels, tin, and so forth.

Let us look at each of these sectors—estate agriculture, oil, forestry, and hard minerals production—that

Table 22.3 Per Capita GDP of Selected Provinces, 1969 and 1971

	PER CAPITA GDP IN 1969 PRICES		PERCENTAGE INCREASE OF 1971 OVER 1969
	1969	1971	
D.I. Aceh	22,529	—	—
West Sumatra	22,542	24,474	8.57
Riau	114,334	128,192	12.12
South Sumatra*	42,294†	—	—
D.K.I. Jakarta	51,410	55,845	8.63
West Java	16,363	18,817	14.85
Central Java	17,319	17,938	3.57
D.I. Jogjakarta	17,980	—	—
East Java	20,156	21,279	5.57
West Kalimantan	25,317	27,311	7.88
South Kalimantan	21,692	27,471	26.64
North Sulawesi	26,192	29,578	12.93
Central Sulawesi	11,103	12,116	9.12
Southeast Sulawesi	13,415	—	—
West Nusa Tenggara	14,796	15,271	3.21
East Nusa Tenggara	11,222	11,510	2.57
Maluku	22,434	—	—
Irian Gaya‡	1,296	1,353	4.40

*From Leknas/Kyodai, *The Regional Economic Survey of the Province of South Sumatra*.
†1970 in current prices.
‡In West Irian Rupia.

Source: Biro Pusat Statistik.

contribute to the affluence of the Outer Islands, and then examine the special problems of Java, the growth of Jakarta, and the expansion of rural manufacturing. Some themes will be found to repeat themselves in this discussion:

1. The importance of independent state monopolies in the management and development of each sector.
2. The present government's willingness to attract foreign investment capital and expertise to stimulate the growth rate of earnings-producing activities.
3. The particular development pattern that results: one of export-oriented "development islands" that traditionally have generated few forward- and backward-linkages to the surrounding peasant economies but are now doing so as a result of explicit state policies, namely:
   a. using the state-run estates as sources of expertise and marketing for small-holder production of estate-type crops;
   b. investing in export preprocessing and in the agriculture, oil, forestry, and hard minerals sectors;
   c. a continuing drive to achieve whatever import substitution may be possible.

In addition, for the first time the great labor supplies of Java are being tapped as Japan and other powers are beginning to "export" their labor-intensive textile and electronic assembly plants to areas of West Java surrounding Jakarta.

estate agriculture

The estates were a creation of the Dutch, who, following the Agrarian Law of 1870, developed a European controlled highly organized high-technology agriculture to produce such perennial crops as rubber, cinchona, oil palm, coffee, tea, and cacao. The Law of 1870 enabled the colonists to acquire large tracts of land or to manage land rented from the villages.

Before World War II about 2,400 private estates covered an area of some 7.26 million acres (about 15 percent of the arable land area), largely on Java and Sumatra, and accounted for 60 percent of Indonesia's exports. In Java about 1,200 estates (43 percent of the total), averaging around 2,200 acres each, occupied 7 percent of the arable land area. In Sumatra, where 51 percent of the estates were located, the size averaged more than 5,000 acres. Although estates in the Outer Islands, as in Java, included some of the best land, only about half of the estate area was actually cultivated, the rest being held in reserve or left fallow. On Java they were found in almost every part of the island, and about half of them concentrated upon the production of a single crop. In Sumatra most estates were centered in the East Coast Residency (North Sumatra); and in the Outer Islands in general more than four-fifths of the estates specialized in the cultivation of one crop, such as rubber, coffee, or oil palm.

The postwar period has seen a steady decline in estate culture. Only 1,280 estates, with a total area of around 1.96 million acres, were reported in operation in 1953, and by 1970 the number was 350 publically owned and 693 privately owned, including 139 under foreign ownership by such companies as Goodyear and Uniroyal. Compared with 1938, sugar production had fallen 53 percent by 1963, tea 55 percent, coffee 52 percent, tobacco 86 percent, cocoa 64 percent, and cinchona 78 percent. Rubber, however, continues to make a major contribution to Indonesia's export earnings.

The system of estates was developed because the arrangement of European controlled, highly organized capitalism in the export sector of the economy, and small-scale food crop agriculture, petty trade, and cottage industry in the Indonesian subsistence sector was to have been a flexible way to respond to the vicissitudes of world markets. The subsistence sector was to give up and reabsorb land and labor as world demands increased or declined. However, what actually resulted was a dislocation of the society and its economy. Protective measures could not isolate the villager from the changes taking place around him, yet at the same time they removed from him the means of adjusting freely to those changes. They strengthened the position of the Chinese middleman as the provider of economic services—moneylending and the distribution and collection of goods—that the European would not or could not undertake. Hence, a *plural* society emerged alongside the *dual* economy, in which economic functions were divided according to ethnic groups—European, Chinese, and Indonesian.

Since independence, the Indonesians have sought to combat this dualism. Indonesia now operates the former Dutch estates as public corporations (PNPs). They serve as training grounds for Indonesian personnel, as well as sources of expertise and marketing channels for the many Indonesian smallholders who produce estate-type crops on former estate lands occupied by squatters after the war.

oil

Most of Indonesia's oil production still comes from fields in Central Sumatra developed by Caltex. These were able to increase their output to 1.5 million barrels per day by the end of 1973. However, under a 1971 law, Pertamina, the state oil company, acquired exclusive rights to the exploration of Indonesia's oil and gas resources, to domestic processing, and to sales of petroleum products. Pertamina is playing a leading role in new oilfield developments on Irian Jaya, in West Java, in the Java Sea and offshore East Kalimantan, as well as with exploitation of large natural gas fields in Aceh and Southeast Kalimantan.

Pertamina is an independently run public corporation whose function is to maximize the contribution of the oil resource to the growth of Indonesia's GNP. Thus, it is taking full advantage of OPEC's new pricing policies. However, its independence is a considerable source of tension, for although the government receives 60 percent of Pertamina's earnings, the balance can be used by Pertamina for a variety of ventures other than oil and gas development. Part of Pertamina's earnings is used to subsidize domestic consumption of oil products (especially the kerosene needed by peasant households), to increase domestic refining capacity, to sustain a fleet of aircraft and a tanker fleet, and to supply subsidiary companies, but a substantial share is used for other types of investments (office buildings, golf courses, housing, and recreation facilities) that some feel are not in the nation's best interest. The Indonesian government has been willing to take this risk, however, in order for Pertamina to have maximum flexibility as a large-scale corporate entity competing in a world of multinational giants, just as it has been willing to turn over its other export crop and resource development activities to similar monopolistic corporations to ensure scale and, it is hoped, efficiency in the nation's drive for economic growth.

forestry

Forestry and forest industries also are playing a very significant role in Indonesia's economic development for three main reasons. First, the forestry resource is the largest in Asia. Second, the long-term demand prospects for exports and domestic consumption offer a sound basis for development—exports could reach nearly US$600 million by 1980, an increase of almost sixfold over 1970. Third, the government's policy of attracting foreign capital has led to the granting of 55 forestry concession agreements that have resulted in a large volume of investment. Development of the forestry sector, however, is constrained by a series of problems related to the institutional framework, the exploitation of the Outer Islands, and the situation in Java.

All but 20,000 hectares (1 ha. = 2.471 acres) of the forest land is state-owned and administered by the Directorate General of Forestry of the Ministry of Agriculture. A weak institutional structure, an inadequate supply of properly trained personnel at all levels, a dichotomy between regional forest control and central technical backstopping, and many clear cases of corrupt practices, are some of the problems affecting the forest service, just as they affect many other aspects of Indonesian life.

The Outer Islands contain vast areas of indigenous hardwood forests with high export potential, although the productive forests are probably less extensive and lower in quality than originally thought. Comprehensive inventories do not exist, and only small areas have been surveyed and demarcated. Since 1967, the Government has granted concessions on about 50 percent of the productive forests. This has led to a spectacular increase in log exports and in revenues to the provincial and central governments but has not yet been accompanied by the establishment of wood processing facilities. Wasteful logging methods and poor silvicultural practices are common. Moreover, only 30 percent of the directorate general of forestry staff is assigned to look after the entire Outer Islands forest resources—over 97 percent of the country's total—so supervision is almost nonexistent.

On the other hand, the forests in Java, especially the teak and conifer plantations, have been surveyed and demarcated and are, in general, reasonably well managed. There are areas, however, where population pressure has led to acute overexploitation, causing grave watershed problems and a severe shortage of forest products and fuelwood. Forest industries are obsolete and operate at low levels of efficiency.

Because of these problems, a development strategy for forestry was formulated within the wider national objectives of Repelita I, which were to develop agriculture and infrastructure; to establish natural resource-based industries that contribute strongly to import substitution and export earnings; and to encourage foreign investment as a means of overcoming shortages of capital and skilled manpower. Strategy for the forestry sector aims at several major objectives: self-sufficiency in wood-based panels and paper production; and a major expansion in the export of sawnwood and plywood, with a corresponding steady reduction in the export of logs. These major objectives are being complemented by policy measures aimed at rehabilitation of water catchment areas; the preservation of protected forests and nature reserves; and the management of forests on a sustained yields basis using proven silviculture techniques.

hard minerals

Except for a limited quantity of coal, nearly all Indonesia's hard mineral products are exported. Table 22.4 lists the exports in the last several years. Although they have been rising in an absolute sense, their share in total exports declined to 5 percent in 1972. Tin accounts for about 80 percent of these exports, with production administered by P. N. Timah, the state tin enterprise. Recent activity in the hard mineral sector has concentrated on efforts to restore existing productive capacity, exploration, and exploitation of mineral deposits. Because these efforts require substantial amounts of financing, skills, and new technology, the government has encouraged private participation in each of these activities and allowed the state mining companies to retain almost all their foreign exchange earnings in order to pursue their rehabilitation and expansion programs. Foreign project aid and technical assistance also have played a significant role in these efforts, leading to several major new discoveries, such as the copper resources of West Irian. Since 1967, seventeen foreign companies have signed "contracts of work" with the Indonesian government, and two companies, Freeport Indonesia (copper) and Karimun Granite, are now in production. However, most domestic mining operations remain small.

industry

Manufacturing is still a relatively small sector of the Indonesian economy and accounts for less than 10 percent of the GDP and 7.5 percent of employment, according to the presently available but inadequate statistics. It has grown only moderately faster than the rest of the economy in recent years.

Table 22.4   Exports Receipts From Hard Mineral Products (in millions of U.S. dollars)

	1968	1969	1970	1971	1972*
Tin	$50.6	$55.0	$62.4	$60.7	$71.1
Bauxite	4.0	4.7	6.3	6.3	6.0
Nickel	2.3	2.8	7.4	11.0	11.8
Silver	—	—	—	0.5	0.3
Iron Sand	—	—	—	1.2	1.1
Total	**56.9**	**62.5**	**76.1**	**79.7**	**90.3†**
Percent of total exports	**6.5**	**6.3**	**6.5**	**6.1**	**5.1**

*Note Indonesia's first *copper* exports were made in 1972 from new mines in West Irian. Sales are expected to total 225,000 tons with a value of $76 million in 1973.

†Compare with petroleum exports of $435 million in 1970, $587 million in 1971, and $966 million in 1972.

Source: Department of Mining, Government of Indonesia.

The manufacturing sector in countries at a comparable stage of economic development generally makes a larger contribution to the national product than it does in Indonesia. There are several reasons. Most large- and medium-scale industry is raw-material oriented, thus being tied to a slow-growth sector. The exception is the recent industrial development around Jakarta in West Java, where foreign-financed, labor-oriented factories are now concentrating. Furthermore, relatively little of Indonesia's industrial employment is in large- and medium-scale enterprises. Of the country's total installed capacity of 1.4 million horsepower (which is a good indicator of the modern sector), the provinces of Java accounted for some 82 percent (Jakarta and East Java alone accounting for 31 and 27 percent, respectively). Similarly, of the total labor force of 848,000 employed in these enterprises, Java accounted for 86 percent of the total.

Most industrial workers are employed by small-scale businesses (1.57 out of 2.3 million in Java and Madura) and these are growing in *rural* Java. Indeed, the evidence suggests that the process of "agricultural involution" in which increasing numbers have been employed in over-intensive cultivation of *sawah* lands may have entered a new phase in which the "involution" increasingly involves nonagricultural activities. This development appears to have gone considerably beyond domestic manufacturing activities of the sort characteristic of rural households and villages in a primarily subsistence agricultural economy. In certain parts of Java this seems to be an extension of traditional forms of village specialization in such items as bricks, clay tiles, blacksmithing, gamelan instruments, footwear, baskets, mats, batik, and so forth. But *traditional* is not a wholly descriptive term. A traveler through rural Java cannot fail to be impressed by the amount and range of manufacturing activities in which substantial portions of the population are engaged. Although much is concentrated in the larger rural towns, it is pervasive even in the smallest settlements. Moreover, operations appear to be conducted on a commercial scale oriented to urban markets or larger manufacturers and processors beyond the immediate local area. In some cases, urban wholesalers appear to have been important in initiating production of new types of articles with only minimal modification of traditional techniques and skills and using reprocessed or locally available materials. In one village near Surabaja visited in November 1973, traditionally specializing in blacksmithing, the number of enterprises had increased by over 70 percent in ten years and the inhabitants are now engaged in manufacturing a wide range of metal products—bicycle fenders, metal furniture, lamps, agricultural implements, metal sheathing for electrical cables, and so on. The units were on an extremely small scale, extremely labor intensive, and without power. While apparently quite profitable under present conditions, they were highly dependent upon urban wholesalers both for marketing and credit. They apparently have become an important supplement to rural employment and incomes.

Table 22.5   Population Growth of Cities over 250,000

CITY	LOCATION	POPULATION (IN THOUSANDS)		ANNUAL RATE OF GROWTH (PERCENT)
		1961	1971	
D.K.I. Jakarta	Jakarta	2,971	4,576	4.4%
Surabaya	East Java	1,008	1,556	4.4
Bandung	West Java	973	1,202	2.2
Semarang	Central Java	503	647	2.5
Medan	Sumatra	479	636	2.9
Palembang	Sumatra	474	583	2.1
Ujung Pandang	Sulawesi	384	435	1.3
Malang	East Java	341	422	2.2
Surakarta	Central Java	368	414	1.2
Jogjakarta	D.I. Jogjakarta	313	342	0.9
Banjarmasim	Kalimantan	214	282	2.8

Source: Biro Pusat Statistik

migration

As differential population growth and sectoral shifts in employment have taken place, one accompaniment has been migration, of which there are two streams: to the cities, and *transmigration* (the term the Indonesians use for interisland movements).

urbanization

It was not until the beginning of this century that towns and cities in the modern sense began to emerge in Indonesia. The institution of public services brought to the towns administration buildings, lighting, water supply, and urban transportation; as the roads were paved, European-type buildings rose along the main streets. The inspiration for the transformation came from the foreigners; behind the Westernized facades were congested, unhygienic Indonesian quarters. Until World War II about 80 percent of the 210,000 Dutch, 60 percent of the 1.2 million Chinese, and 75 percent of the other foreign Orientals lived in the cities.

In 1930 only 7.5 percent of the population lived in places vaguely defined as being of a "more or less urban character." Of this urban population of just over 4 million, slightly more than 3 million lived in Java. Six of the seven largest cities were in Java, including the two largest, Jakarta (then Batavia) and Surabaja, which had populations of approximately 350,000 and 340,000. By 1971 the population of Jakarta had grown to 4.6 million, that of Surabaja to slightly over 1.5 million (Table 22.5), and six cities in all exceeded 500,000. Yet Indonesia's degree of urbanization (only 17.4 percent in 1971) remains one of the lowest among the world's developing countries.

The rate of urban growth went up steeply after the Japanese surrender in 1945. The revolution brought chaos and insecurity to both town and country people, but economic necessity (often rural indebtedness) and the threat of starvation or slaughter sent villagers to the cities by the thousands. In 1950 it was estimated that more than one-third of the people living in cities had arrived within the previous four years. Today, however, economic necessity or the hope of improvement in economic status is the primary motivation for moving to the cities, but other factors such as the desire for better educational opportunities for children are now beginning to be influential.

As noted earlier, urban employment grew at the annual rate of 2.8 percent during the period 1961–1971 while rural employment grew at 1.6 percent. The growth of urban employment was largely due to growth in the service sectors, including transportation. Manufacturing employment in urban areas did not grow at all. This is a peculiar characteristic of urbanization in Indonesia. Urbanization is not supported by the growth of manufacturing, but more heavily than in most other countries by the growth of the service sectors, while manufacturing is increasing in rural areas of Java.

Other supplementary sources of rural incomes are provided by a variety of trade and service activities both in the local area and in the larger towns and cities, thus leading to different connections between urban and rural areas than exist elsewhere. Local and village officials have reported that much of the movement to urban areas during slack agricultural periods was for the purpose of engaging in trade as well as seeking employment. It is not clear what the bulk of this trading activity consists of; however, it does not seem to be confined merely to street vending or petty retail operations. The rehabilitation of roads and the availability of imported vehicles has also led to a burgeoning of transport services, typically with small trucks or vans. The numbers directly employed in transport are no doubt relatively small. But increasing availability of transport must be expected to have considerably larger indirect effects on rural employment and incomes by extending access to both urban product and labor markets.

Because of growth of rural employment, the 1971 census statistics show that only Jakarta and Surabaja, the two largest cities in the country, had grown with a substantial amount of net migration among the eleven largest cities. The growth of other large cities was meager. Many had grown more or less in line with the natural rate of growth, and some, such as Ujung Pandang (Makassar), Surakarta, and Jogjakarta had net outmigration from 1961 to 1971.

The growth of any city reflects the growth of the economy in its region. Jakarta grew largely because of the expansion of administrative, trade, and manufacturing activities, and Surabaja because of the growth of manufacturing and trade. Medan grew in response to the rapid growth of North Sumatra, which is based on estate agriculture; Banjarmasin on the phenomenal expansion of forestry extraction in South Kalimantan. The slow growth of cities in the central part of Java, including Bandung, Semarang, Jogjakarta, and Surakarta, results from the stagnation of agriculture and large and medium size manufacturing in that part of Java. In addition, recent development policies for freer trade and international transactions have evidently favored the expansion of cities having direct access to sea and, in particular, those with a favorable port.

growth of Jakarta

Analysis of the 1971 population census shows that nearly 2 million persons migrated to D.K.I. Jakarta during the period of 1961 to 1971 (see Table 22.6). Of these, 43 percent came from West Java and another 36 percent from the rest of Java and Madura. However, when the number of migrants is related to the population at the originating province, the dominant positions of Java and Sumatra are substantially lessened. As shown by the fourth column of Table 22.6, the propensity to migrate to Jakarta (migrants per 1,000 persons of provincial population) is extremely high for West Java, which is explainable by geographical proximity. Jogjakarta and Central Java also have high migration propensities, which are, however, less than that of West Sumatra. The migration propensity of East Java is among the lowest. Some geographically distant areas such as West Nusa Tenggara, Maluku, and North and Central Sulawesi also have relatively high migration propensities. Only short-distance migration is influenced by geographical proximity. Furthermore, high migration propensities from West and Central Java and Jogjakarta are due to a "push factor," the relative poverty of the areas, whereas East Java's relatively low propensity to migrate to Jakarta appears to be due to the presence of another competing growth pole, Surabaja, within it.

Of the migrants to Jakarta, 4 percent came because of a transfer of job, 6 percent to study, and 30 percent in search of employment. Forty-nine percent were dependents, and 11 percent of migrants came for other and

Table 22.6   Origin of Migrants to Jakarta 1961–1971

PROVINCE	POPULATION (IN THOUSANDS) 1961	MIGRANTS INTO JAKARTA 1961–1971 Persons*	MIGRANTS INTO JAKARTA 1961–1971 (Percent)	MIGRANTS PER 1000 PERSONS OF PROVINCIAL POPULATION
DKI Jakarta	2,970	—	—	—
West Java	17,673	816,400	43.04	46.2
Central Java	18,456	487,657	25.71	26.4
DI Jogjakarta	2,247	65,264	3.44	29.0
East Java	21,880	127,112	6.70	5.8
DI Aceh	1,636	9,518	0.50	5.8
North Sumatra	4,984	65,484	3.45	13.1
West Sumatra	2,330	72,873	3.85	31.3
Rian	1,240	14,584	0.76	11.8
Djambi	748	7,594	0.40	10.2
South Sumatra	4,865	57,700	3.04	15.5
Bengkulu		4,773	0.26	
Lampung		12,557	0.66	
West Kalimantan	1,578	23,789	1.25	15.0
Central Kalimantan	499	1,492	0.07	3.0
South Kalimantan	1,479	9,116	0.48	6.2
East Kalimantan	553	5,757	0.30	10.4
North Sulawesi	2,012	16,962	0.89	10.7
Central Sulawesi		4,474	0.23	
South Sulawesi	5,097	32,935	1.73	7.0
South-East Sulawesi		2,843	0.14	
Bali	1,790	5,133	0.27	2.9
West Nusa Tenggara	1,814	23,789	1.25	13.1
East Nusa Tenggara	1,971	5,696	0.31	2.9
Maluku	793	9,499	0.50	12.0
West Irian	761	3,963	0.20	5.2
Abroad		29,919	1.57	—
Total		1,896,703	100.00	

*Suharso, "Cityward Migration and Educational Attainment in Jakarta-Indonesia," *UNESCO/PDEP/7-1* (September 1973).

Source: Biro Pusat Statistik and Suharso.

Table 22.7   Share of Jakarta in Indonesian Economy

INDICATOR		JAKARTA AS PERCENTAGE OF INDONESIA
Population, 1971		3.8
GDP, 1970	Total	8.5
Originating from	Manufacturing	6.5
	Construction	18.1
	Electricity, gas, and water supply	32.8
	Transport and communication	23.0
	Wholesale and retail trade	22.7
	Banking and other financial intermediary	75.8
	Ownership of dwelling	15.6
	Public administration	13.9
	Services	3.4
National government tax revenues 1970–1971		49.8
Domestic investment project, (Rp) 1968–1971		31.7
Foreign investment projects, (Rp) 1967–1971		19.7
Savings in tabanas (small savings) accounts, 1972		37.5
Large manufacturers, 1970		8.3
Government employees, 1970		13.4
Routine expenditures for urban services, 1971–1972		11.3
Development expenditures for urban services, 1971–1972		38.6

Source: For GDP components, Census and Statistical Office, D.K.I. Jakarta, *Regional Income of D.K.I. Jakarta, 1966–1971.*

For others, Planned Community Development Ltd, *Urban Development Study Jakarta,* 1973.

unknown reasons. Therefore, the single most important reason for migration to Jakarta is the expectation of better job opportunities.

A higher proportion of migrants from nearby provinces, West Java and Lampung, were less educated persons, whereas the migration from distant provinces to Jakarta contained higher proportions of highly educated people.

Despite this large amount of migration to Jakarta in search for jobs, the unemployment rate in Jakarta is

not particularly high relative to other urban areas in the country. According to the population census of 1971, the unemployment rate in Jakarta was 5.3 percent and that for all urban areas in the country was 4.8 percent. There were other regions that had higher urban unemployment rates: 5.3 percent in Sumatra and 7.5 percent in Sulawesi. Therefore, it can be concluded that most of the migrants are finding jobs in Jakarta despite their large inflow.

The availability of jobs in Jakarta is a consequence of the concentration of recent investment in the primate city. Jakarta accounts for a major share of many sectors of the Indonesian economy, far beyond its 3.8 percent share of the population (Table 22.7). A high proportion of both foreign and domestic investment projects were approved for location in Jakarta in the period 1968–1972 (Tables 22.8 and 22.9). These investments will substantially increase Jakarta's per capita product, making it increasingly attractive to further streams of migrants. Yet, despite the fact that Jakarta's growth provides opportunities for Indonesians who might otherwise be underemployed elsewhere, many in the Outer Islands feel that the concentration of growth in Jakarta has been too great, and they are calling for a better regional distribution of new investments.

transmigration

The hope of finding better conditions elsewhere has also produced migration from areas where the peasant's dwindling resources were making it impossible for him to support a family. For example, the inability of the infertile island of Madura to support its dense population has for several hundred years caused a steady influx of Madurese into eastern Java both for permanent residence and for seasonal labor. From western Java a steady stream of Bantamese has moved across the Sunda Strait into southern Sumatra. Toward the close of the nineteenth century a decline in the number of imported

Table 22.8   Approved Domestic Investment Projects Located in Jakarta, 1968–1972

SECTOR	NUMBER OF PROJECTS		INTENDED INVESTMENT	
	Number	Jakarta as percent of nation	Rupiah (in millions)	Jakarta as percent of nation
Agriculture	1	3	1,945	31
Estates	—	—	—	—
Forestry	—	—	—	—
Fisheries	1	11	372	14
Livestock	4	50	412	25
Mining	—	—	—	—
Manufacturing	272	41	89,661	33
Transportation	34	76	26,682	90
Public utilities	4	80	2,909	95
Tourism	34	.53	26,831	71
Infrastructure	2	29	178	8
Others	—	—	—	—
Total	**352**	**34**	**148,990**	**32**

Source: DKI Jakarta Investment Office

Table 22.9   Approved Foreign Investment Projects Located in Jakarta, 1967–1972

SECTOR	NUMBER OF PROJECTS		INTENDED INVESTMENT	
	Number	Jakarta as percent of nation	Thousands of US dollars	Jakarta as percent of nation
Basic & heavy industry	33	63	43,802	58
Chemical industry	15	79	25,697	29
Plantation & agriculture	—	—	—	—
Fisheries	1	10	2,700	16
Forestry	—	—	—	—
Hotel	7	78	54,890	81
Infrastructure	16	100	9,841	100
Light industry & handicraft	86	62	101,088	68
Mining	1	6	500	0
Pharmaceutical industry	18	53	21,522	52
Construction	25	86	52,116	48
Textile industry	12	46	46,199	23
Trade	2	18	600	7
Transportation & communication	11	73	9,339	58
Total	227	47	368,330	20

Source: D.K.I. Jakarta Investment Office.

Table 22.10   A Rough Estimate of Net Movements of Population Between Regions, 1961–1971

	ESTIMATED* NATURAL RATE OF POPULATION INCREASE	ACTUAL RATE OF POPULATION INCREASE	IMPLIED NET MOVEMENTS OF POPULATION 1961–1971† (IN THOUSANDS)	
			In	Out
DCI Jakarta	2.1	4.6	996	
West Java	2.2	2.1		269
Central Java	2.1	1.7		785
DI Jogjakarta	1.4	1.1		85
East Java	1.7	1.6		303
Java & Madura (subtotal)	2.0	1.8		446
Sumatra	2.4	2.8	870	
Kalimantan	2.1	2.2	57	
Sulawesi	2.2	1.9		265
Other Islands	2.0	2.0		215
Indonesia	2.0	2.0	0.0	0.0

*Derived from natural rates for 1961 estimated by M. Iskander as reported in IBRD, *Population Projects Report,* No. PP8a, February 28, 1971.

†Assuming no net movements between Indonesia and abroad.

Chinese laborers and the oilfield development in South Sumatra stimulated a more rapid movement from Java, and in 1930 at least half a million Javanese, a large proportion of them contract laborers, were established in the east coast residency of Sumatra. Many of them returned upon completion of their contracts, but newcomers held the Javanese population of the area at a fairly constant level. Altogether, in 1930 there were over 1 million Javanese in Sumatra.

Migration from the Outer Islands to Java and from island to island outside Java has been numerically less. Nevertheless, in 1930, 90,000 Minangkabau were established outside Sumatra, mainly as traders; about 150,000 Bandjarese from southeast Kalimantan were scattered throughout the islands; and a roughly equal number of the seagoing Buginese of southwest Sulawesi had found homes elsewhere. The motivation for migration in these cases, however, was the pursuit of trade and not the necessity of finding an escape from possible starvation, as in transmigration from Java.

Unfortunately, there is distressingly little information about the recent movement of population. Consumption data suggest that there should indeed be rural-to-urban and Java-to-Outer Island movements in search of better opportunities. A crude effort to calculate net movement of population between 1961 and 1971 is presented in Table 22.10. It shows low interregional net migration rates, including a net outflow from Java and a net inflow to Sumatra.

Many of those moving between the islands are "official" transmigrants going to settlement schemes for landless or near landless Javanese farming families, or workers recruited by the estates, forestry enterprises, and mines in the Outer Islands. These activities are organized and/or carried out by a number of private and public institutions, of which presently the most important is the Ministry of Transmigration and Cooperatives (Transkop). This ministry sets up settlement schemes with the help of a number of other government agencies and recruits labor for employment by private or public companies, with the exception of estate labor, for which the Directorate General of Estates in the Ministry of Agriculture is responsible.

The first organized transmigration started in the second half of the last century when the Culture System was abandoned and the possibility was opened for private entrepreneurs to develop estates. With the introduction of estate production on the northeast coast of Sumatra (later elsewhere in Sumatra and on other Outer Islands) the estates became dependent on labor imported from Java and from China, because the new areas were sparsely populated and the local population not interested in estate work. Similarly, before World War II considerable numbers of Javanese went to work in the tin mines of Bangka and Belitung, while others left for other countries (Surinam, for example) to work in estates.

After World War II, the flow of Javanese workers to the estates in the Outer Islands dropped considerably below prewar levels and since 1968, there has been a small net outflow of labor from the estates.

The rapid expansion in logging operations in Kalimantan and Sumatra has, on the other hand, required a growing number of laborers. Data are not available, but an estimate can be made on the basis of output figures. Assuming that one man produces about 400m³/year, logging operations may have attracted an additional 36,000 men, mostly from Java, between 1966 and 1972. To this must be added a considerable number of traders, artisans, and others to provide services to forestry laborers.

Officially sponsored movement of Javanese peasant farmers to unoccupied land in southern Sumatra began in the early part of this century in the attempt to alleviate the population pressure in Java. At the outbreak of World War II, 200,000 people (about 40,000 families) had been resettled. These settlement activities were resumed in 1950. Some 460,000 transmigrants (112,-000 families) have been handled by government agencies over the past two decades. If private organizations are included, the actual figure for 1950–1971 may be close to 150,000 families (600,000 people), not including an unknown number of spontaneous settlers, very few of whom have returned to Java. Although these numbers may seem large, they fall far short of the government's targets. Repelita I called for a program of 100,000 families, but by the end of the plan period less than 30,000 families will have been moved. This is in spite of the fact that at least 200,000 families from Java, Madura, and Bali applied for resettlement. The failure to meet goals is largely due to administrative deficiencies in Transkop, and it means that transmigration policies have had little impact upon overpopulated Inner Indonesia. Indeed, only a massive foreign-directed program of rehabilitation of Java's irrigation network combined with the fruits of the *green revolution*—intensification of rice production, more than doubling yields through a massive injection of fertilizer, improved seed, and pesticides—has averted a Malthusian crisis in the areas with the lowest man/land ratio, lowest incomes, and highest underemployment.

NEW POLICIES EMERGE: REGIONAL DEVELOPMENT OBJECTIVES OF REPELITA II

With the achievement of political and economic stability by a strong central government that emphasized national integration as a goal above all else during Repelita I, a new range of issues is emerging in Indonesia. These issues relate largely to matters of equity—of sharing the benefits of economic progress—and they are producing a new concern for regional planning and development because of the wide disparities in social conditions and economic opportunities that exist in the various parts of the country.

As we have seen, the 3,000 islands of the Indonesian archipelago present regional diversity in the extreme. Not only is there a wide array of physical landscapes but the islands are also inhabited by diverse cultural groups ranging from Stone Age societies in the heart of Irian Jaya to the modern primate city of Jakarta. By the historical accident of Dutch colonialism, scores of traditional kingdoms have been assembled into a single country, maintaining their identity in the provincial and *kabupaten* (regency) levels of government, and producing to this day strong sectional feelings. However, the majority of the island's inhabitants remain peasant agriculturalists striving to maintain subsistence levels by wet-rice cultivation in overpopulated Inner Indonesia and by slash-and-burn cultivation of dry rice and other crops in the uplands and in the Outer Islands. Much of the modern sector consists of export-oriented raw material production undertaken by state monopolies. Few backward or forward linkages take place into peasant society, so that the economic dualism that resulted from Dutch colonial policies remains. Interisland communications by sea and air are of varying quality—good between the major cities on the main islands but making scarcely any impact upon the inaccessibility of outer Indonesia or the many isolated zones existing within the main islands. The administrative hierarchy inherited from the colonial period (nation, province, *kabupaten, kecamaten, desa*) is used by the central government to maintain order, raise taxes, and ensure national unity. However, the traditional independence of the provinces remains a potential source of conflict.

With this diversity, there is little wonder that in Repelita I the government set the achievement of national unity as its prime goal, alongside of securing the availability of the main needs of society and the strengthening of the balance of payments through strategic economic developments likely to raise national income per capita. By and large, these goals were achieved. But the problems of socioeconomic disparities and dualism remain and are of growing concern, for although sociocultural diversity within a unified Indonesian state is welcomed, differential benefits from economic progress are not.

The case for formulation of a regional development policy in Repelita II for the period 1974–1979 rests primarily in the fact that given the scale, differential population geography, and endemic social and economic diversity of Indonesia, equity and social justice will not necessarily flow from national plans that emphasize growth alone. A basic imbalance in population distribution between Inner and Outer Indonesia remains, while paradoxically the Outer Islands are the main source of Indonesia's current and potential wealth in natural resources. Thus, a resource-rich, thinly populated group of Outer Islands keeps afloat an impoverished Indonesian heartland afflicted by serious population pressures. Add to this the fact that a centrist Jakarta-based government until recently did not welcome separate regional initiatives and interests, and there is reason enough for discontent in the outlying provinces. In its brief history, Indonesia has seen all the turbulence of attempted regional separatism. There were twenty-one local rebellions in the country's first twenty years, and these, combined with vivid memories of colonial divide-and-rule policies, led to an overriding concern with national integration in a wholly monistic sense and the creation of the world's largest centralized (nonfederal) state.

Yet with achievement of political and economic stability in the past five years, there is now a searching for a politically viable regional development approach that reflects the pluralistic base of Indonesian society and obviates the need for the totalitarian controls that would otherwise be required to maintain unity in the long run. A whole range of development problems is attracting national and provincial concern: overpopulation on Java alongside labor shortages in the Outer Islands, continuing concentration of investment in and around Jakarta, and the need for greater social justice in the distribution of the benefits of economic progress. Central to each of these concerns is the fundamental problem of regional disparities in social and economic progress. To redress these imbalances, regional and provincial development constitutes a principal thrust of Repelita II.

The principal regional development objectives of Repelita II, formulated in a series of directives by the country's Peoples' Assembly (MPR), are:

1. *To achieve balance between regional and sectoral development.* Here the intent is to include regional goals in the

Fig. 22.1   *Indonesia's development regions*

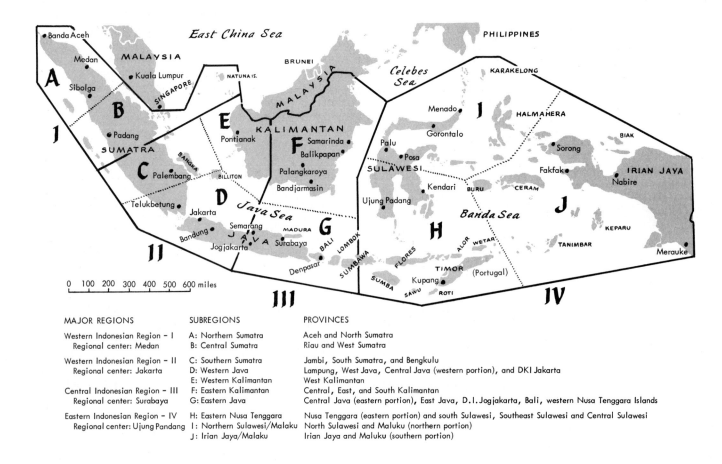

MAJOR REGIONS	SUBREGIONS	PROVINCES
Western Indonesian Region – I Regional center: Medan	A: Northern Sumatra B: Central Sumatra	Aceh and North Sumatra Riau and West Sumatra
Western Indonesian Region – II Regional center: Jakarta	C: Southern Sumatra D: Western Java E: Western Kalimantan	Jambi, South Sumatra, and Bengkulu Lampung, West Java, Central Java (western portion), and DKI Jakarta West Kalimantan
Central Indonesian Region – III Regional center: Surabaya	F: Eastern Kalimantan G: Eastern Java	Central, East, and South Kalimantan Central Java (eastern portion), East Java, D.I. Jogjakarta, Bali, western Nusa Tenggara Islands
Eastern Indonesian Region – IV Regional center: Ujung Pandang	H: Eastern Nusa Tenggara I: Northern Sulawesi/Maluku J: Irian Jaya/Maluku	Nusa Tenggara (eastern portion) and south Sulawesi, Southeast Sulawesi and Central Sulawesi North Sulawesi and Maluku (northern portion) Irian Jaya and Maluku (southern portion)

planning activities of each of the central government's sectoral ministries, thus setting regional equity alongside efficient growth as a national objective.

2. *To reduce inequalities in the rate of development between the provinces.* During the first five-year planning period strictly sectoral planning produced the greatest growth in those provinces already well-endowed with infrastructure. This "parasitic" relationship, which increased rather than decreased disparities, is to be countered in Repelita II by explicitly allocating a proportion of all development activities to the poorest provinces.

3. *To help the provincial governments solve large-scale provincial problems.* Some problems are peculiarly provincial and thus, even though they may be beyond provincial financial capability, never enter into central planning channels; others are provincial, but arise from causes outside the province. It is the explicit concern of Repelita II to provide the provinces with aid to tackle such problems.

4. *To improve the planning, development, and taxing capacities of the provinces.* This involves both efforts to increase the levels of provincial planning skills and the attempt to improve developmental management capacities and resources.

Two key issues are raised by these MRP directives: how to combine national and regional developmental goals in a proper manner, and how to devolve authority without threatening national unity. BAPPENAS, the National Planning Commission, feels that it has a solution to both.

First, for planning purposes, the provinces have been grouped into a hierarchy of four and ten development planning regions, and subdivided into a third level of subregions focusing on ninety urban growth centers. Each of the four highest-level regions has a prospective regional metropolis at its center (Jakarta, Surabaja, Medan, Ujung Pandang). (See Fig. 22.1.) These regions are viewed as providing a means of bringing about greater regional equity in the sectoral plans, providing a complete range of sectoral activities for each region, encouraging specialization and the development of intraregional exchange, and including industrialization and related programs necessary for making the regional metropolitan centers growth centers that develop adequate forward and backward linkages into the regions. Each region and province is also to have its key developmental proposals, emphasizing equitable shares, to be set alongside those of the sectors, emphasizing efficient growth.

Second, to make this possible, each region is also to have its BAPPEDA, or Provincial Planning Unit, adequately staffed and funded, to aid the governors in the new decision-making responsibilities that decentralization of many kinds of development activities will entail. In Repelita I, most of each province's development budget was planned and managed by the central government. In Repelita II this will change as the center substitutes revenue sharing for central control.

Whether these bold ventures succeed in reducing regional inequities while maintaining a rapid rate of economic progress will be a matter of much interest to the developing world's policy makers in the next few years, for with the ouster of President Sukarno in 1966 Indonesia disavowed the radical approach to development and social equity that has been pursued in Maoist China, the topic of the chapter that follows.

RECOMMENDED READINGS

Beers, Howard W., *Indonesia: Resources and Their Technological Development.* Lexington: Kentucky University Press, 1970.

Boeke, J. H., *Economics and Economic Policy of Dual Societies as Exemplified by Indonesia.* New York: Institute of Pacific Relations, 1953.

Glassburner, Bruce, ed., *The Economy of Indonesia: Selected Readings.* Ithaca: Cornell University Press, 1971.

Higgins, Benjamin, and Jean Higgins, *Indonesia: The Crisis of the Millstones.* New York: Van Nostrand Reinhold, 1963.

U.S. Department of the Army, *Area Handbook for Indonesia.* Washington, Department of the Army, September, 1964.

Wertheim, W. F. et al., *Indonesian Economics: The Concept of Dualism in Theory and Policy.* Amsterdam: W. Van Hoeve, 1966.

china: marxist planning in the oriental mode

23

Our last example is a national system with immense problems and unique solutions for those problems. China's program for development prescribes more drastic remedies for the ills of a lagging hinterland economy than do any of the strategies outlined thus far. The Chinese approach to the Marxist-Leninist model differs in many important respects from the Soviet Union's (Chapter 18). Just as the Japanese have modified capitalism to fit their own particular experience and needs (Chapter 17), so have the Chinese adapted Marxism to suit their special circumstances. The unique features of China's developmental strategy stem partly from the peculiar character and ideological bent of the country's leaders—an authoritarian regime that holds a powerful grip on every facet of national life. In large measure, however, this deviation from Western patterns derives from the nation's ancient culture; formed in isolation, it gives a distinct perspective to Chinese life, but at the same time it adds to the country's massive problems.

Indeed, everything about China seems outsize. The country has the world's largest population, the third largest national territory, and perhaps the fifth or sixth largest economy. Nearly one-fourth of the world's people live in China, outnumbering Indonesians by a factor of six and one-half and the citizens of the United States by a factor of four. Although only 6 percent of China's inhabitants are of non–Chinese extraction, these minorities taken together are equal to about twice the population of Canada. The Chinese population is both immense and still growing. Whereas Central America's major demographic problem is the high rate of population growth, China's main concern is that her growth is occurring on top of a population base already too great for the amount of arable land available for its adequate support.

This problem of land scarcity seems paradoxical in a country as large as China. Only two countries have more territory, the Soviet Union and Canada; and the latter is only slightly larger than China. Physically, China is one of the most diverse of countries. It has vast plains and the highest of mountains, areas of plentiful rainfall and some of the driest deserts, great regions with subtropical climates and others with severe continental climates. In this respect, China more nearly resembles the USSR than isthmian Central America or the island nations of Indonesia and New Zealand. With its great territory and contrasting conditions, China is endowed with a large and varied resource base. Although the land has been occupied for millenia, it still contains great stores of untapped minerals whose dimensions are only now becoming apparent. Yet in other ways it has suffered severely from prolonged overuse, especially the biotic resources, which have been substantially modified by long human habitation.

Many of the country's problems are thus attributable to the length of settlement and the intensity with which the land has been used.

Among the burdens of China's past are the accumulated masses of humanity with their deeply imbedded attitudes, customs, and institutions, many of which are inimical to the workings of the contemporary world economic system. As in Central America, these incrustations of the past add to the difficulty of bringing the economy up to modern standards.

China's history has its positive side, however. Unlike most contemporary underdeveloped countries, China looks back to a proud era when her culture led the world. She was a heartland nation when Marco Polo visited in the thirteenth century, a period when Europe was only starting to emerge from the Dark Ages and America remained a primitive wilderness. China's perception of herself as the center of the civilized world persisted through succeeding centuries, during which, closed off behind her wall, she continued to resist Western encroachment. Although she was not wholly able to avoid modern European incursions and the dualistic forms they brought, China did not succumb to these in the degree to which Indonesia or Central America did.

Contrasting with her ancient greatness, twentieth-century China has a backward economy, clearly peripheral to the contemporary world system. Although her total national product is estimated to be as large as that of France, this output must be divided among at least fifteen times as many people as there are in France. Per capita national income is therefore very low, variously reckoned at between $100 and $165 per annum, only slightly more than that of Indonesia and well below Central America. Like Indonesia, China is mainly a nation of farmers, even though her cities are among the world's largest. Typical of underdeveloped lands, China's economy is hobbled by an excess of people, an insufficiency of capital, and an inadequate gross output. Yet, several of the usual problems of underdeveloped countries are missing: China does not, for example, have Central America's exaggerated economic dependence upon the heartland, inadequate market size, dualistic social and economic structures, or a narrow range of physical resources.

Communist China's growth strategy is designed to make radical changes in the national economy's unbalanced factor proportions. The plan is to generate the scarce factors through a forced draft mobilization of the currently plentiful ones, following in the way taken a generation earlier by the Soviet Union but using different methods toward somewhat different ends. More recently, China has sought to reduce her ancient barriers to the West by forming new external links, a move that is as political in its motivations as it is economic.

China's distinctive approach to the problems of growth and development will occupy the remainder of this chapter, together with the salient features of the Chinese national economic system now evolving. Given the magnitude of China's problems and their deep roots in the past, the country has made only a start in solving them. We shall therefore be interested in concluding by reviewing the unfinished tasks that still remain: the need to achieve balance between population and food supply,

to raise the standard of living, to avoid the numerous political hazards threatening from within and without, and to attain a secure and satisfying place in the world economic system.

BEFORE MAO TSE-TUNG

Many of the public episodes in contemporary Communist China that appear so incomprehensible to most Westerners make good sense to those who understand China's beginnings and the continuity of social thought in that ancient land. Because China's past and present are so intimately connected, it is important for us to see how the nation arrived at the state in which the Communist revolutionary leader, Mao Tse-tung, found it upon his assumption of power. Mao's predecessors left him with some valuable national assets but also with a great many liabilities.

China's past

Mobile, restless occidentals cannot readily appreciate the depth of China's roots, reaching back through thousands of years of uninterrupted human occupance. The social and economic systems of pre–Mao China had evolved more than forty centuries ago in virtual isolation from the rest of the world. Only in modern times have Western influences penetrated the Chinese realm to any significant extent; yet when they finally came, these foreign intrusions caused profound political upheaval but surprisingly little basic economic or social change in the country as a whole. In the end, the nation was to be ruled by a political system ostensibly modern but actually shaped by social attitudes as venerable as China's origins.

the cradle of Chinese civilization

Today Mao Tse-tung rules from a capital situated only a few miles from one of Asia's oldest presapiens anthropological finds, Peking man. Although there is no evidence that the modern Chinese descended directly from this early creature, they are clearly related to the primitive, nomadic hunters and gatherers who made this part of China their home in late Neanderthal times. The basins of the Hwang Ho (Yellow River) and its tributary, the Wei Ho, provided these people with a physical environment peculiarly suited to the evolution of a simple agricultural economy and the use of rudimentary tools (see Fig. 23.1). The fine, wind-blown loess and river-deposited alluvial soils of the region were easily worked and the grassland natural vegetation required little clearing. Where sufficient water is available, land of this type is very productive for agriculture.

Adequate moisture was the principal basis on which the primitive economy of China's cradle area became differentiated. A sedentary form of primitive agriculture emphasizing a cereal (millet) developed in the well-watered middle and lower valleys, where the

Fig. 23.1 *Political and physical map of China*

ELEVATION:

- Over 10,000 feet
- 5000 to 10,000 feet
- 2,000 to 5,000 feet
- 1,000 to 2,000 feet
- Below 1,000 feet

farmers easily carved their cave dwellings into the loess of the steep valley sides. In the drier areas farther west and north, a primitive pastoral economy persisted. The division between these two areas subsequently came to be marked by China's famous Great Wall, built for the purpose of protecting one group from the incursions of the other. This economic distinction continues today.

Within the cradle area a distinctive political and social organization evolved, its progress marked by a succession of royal houses or dynasties. The first to leave written records was the Shang (Yin) Dynasty (1523–1030 B.C.). The Shang kings and their successors, the Chou Dynasty (1030–221 B.C.) presided over an agricultural economy advanced for its time. Their subjects introduced irrigation; used money and acquired rudimentary industry and commerce; developed a sophisticated literature and a rich bronze culture; established schools; and adhered to a philosophy based on Confucianism and Taoism. Confucius (551–479 B.C.), whose ideas have con-

tinued to dominate Chinese thought to the present, sought to save society by a return to the past, emphasized ethics and ceremony and promoted the idea of leadership by the educated members of the society.

Under the long rule of the Han Dynasty (206 B.C.–A.D. 220), the nation became consolidated and extended its control over the greater part of the territory now called China. Governing through a civil service recruited by examinations, the Han kings built upon the culture and technology of their predecessors. They acquired an elaborate iron technology well before the birth of Christ, became skillful engineers, and accumulated much scientific knowledge.

It was during the Han reign that China's distinctive social system developed and crystallized. In a land divided into great estates, the Chinese acquired a social structure forming a broad-based pyramid rather like that of Central America. At the top were the land-owning scholar-officials, a small oligarchy who maintained their dominance by controlling education, the only means of entry into their ranks, and by extolling the Confucian virtues of respect, submission, humility, and filial piety. Next came another small group, the merchants, artisans, and handicraftsmen, who, however wealthy they might become, were able to command little social status (which was conferred only by land ownership). At the bottom of the pyramid and supporting the entire structure were the peasants—the great mass of society. These were the mainly subsistence farmers, who owned or rented small plots of land, which they tilled intensively despite the handicaps of primitive tools, poor seeds, and low yields. Because of their combined numbers, however, they were able to provide a sufficient surplus output to supply the non-agricultural members of society. Thus by Han times, contemporary with the rise of the Roman Empire, China's cradle area had developed a cohesive, distinctive society with a high culture based on an intensive hydraulic agriculture.

diffusion of the Han people

Meanwhile, the Hwang, Wei, Ching, and Fen valleys had become densely populated, and the Han people had begun to spill over into neighboring lands. Because the regions to the north and west were too cold and dry for their traditional form of agriculture, and in any event were already controlled by hostile nomads, the Chinese spread gradually southward into areas that presented no physical or human barriers. Before the end of their reign, the Han kings had extended political control over the greater part of South China, leaving their subjects free to move into this lightly occupied region.

Physical conditions in the new land were decidedly different south of the Chinling Mountains, which, although not very high, effectively divide North and South China (Fig. 23.1). In the milder, more humid south, with its long growing season, the Han people adopted the rice-farming economy of the area's previous occupants. In this way arose the basic division of Chinese cereal culture that still obtains: wheat and millet in the drier, cooler north and wet rice in the south.

the Middle Kingdom

So cohesive were the Chinese people by this time that the nearly four centuries of political turmoil following the end of the Han Dynasty failed to shake their cultural unity. Later dynasties were therefore able to continue the development of the Middle Kingdom, as old China was called, as though the interruption had not occurred.

A Mongol invasion during the thirteenth century ended Chinese rule for a time. The Mongol (Yüan) Dynasty (1279–1368) controlled the country for a comparatively brief but active period highlighted by the reign of Kublai Khan, who, from the future site of Peking, ruled all of China, together with a Mongol empire extending to Mesopotamia and Eastern Europe. Kublai completed China's Grand Canal and entertained numerous foreign visitors, including Marco Polo. The Ming Dynasty (1368–1644) reasserted Chinese political control and restored Chinese culture, including superb art and literature, academies, book printing, and libraries.

China's modern period came with an invasion from the northeast by the Manchus. The Manchu (Ching) emperors (1644–1911) adopted the Chinese culture but ruled as foreign conquerors over China proper (the 18 eastern provinces), Mongolia, Tibet, and Formosa, as well as their homeland of Manchuria.

European encroachment

Although there had been occasional contacts with the outside world before the Manchu Empire, China had remained largely isolated behind great mountain ramparts to the west and southwest and the psychological barrier of the Great Wall—a symbol of China's attitude to the rest of the world—on the north. At first, even the sea had served as a buffer, but as foreign pressures intensified, it became a highway instead. The later Manchu rulers were too weak to resist these intrusions, led at the outset by Christian missionaries and later by commercial interests.

By the nineteenth century, European colonialism had become a major force in Chinese affairs. At a time when Western nations were seeking new markets for the products of the Industrial Revolution, their prospering populations were acquiring a growing taste for China's teas, silks, cottons, and other exotic goods. The Chinese, however, felt no serious need for Western goods and were reluctant to admit this alien influence. The Manchu government at first permitted trade only through the single port of Canton and specified that all business be conducted through officially designated Chinese merchants.

The British, who were particularly affronted by this resistance, demanded concessions from the Chinese. Open conflict ultimately resulted from British insistence on the "right" to sell opium to the Chinese, an exceedingly profitable traffic that nicely solved an otherwise unfavorable trade balance for Britain. When the Chinese government attempted to suppress the opium trade, which was demoralizing the population and imposing a heavy financial burden, the British attacked and defeated the Chinese. The resulting treaty of 1842 ceded the island of Hong Kong (near Canton) to the British and opened five ports to foreign residents and to commerce. These first Treaty Ports introduced the extraterritoriality question that was subsequently to create such rancor. Other Western powers quickly took the opportunity to secure similar concessions from the weakened Chinese.

Even these successes failed to satisfy the intruders, who intensified their pressures. Further armed conflicts with the British followed, forcing additional commercial concessions and other special privileges from the

Manchus. Thereupon the Russians demanded, and got, large sections of Chinese territory along their common borders. The Sino–Japanese War of 1894–1895, over control of Korea and Manchuria, signaled a Western scramble for leases, concessions, and privileges, notably Britain's 99–year lease to the New Territories on the Chinese mainland opposite Hong Kong. The Russians, French, and Germans all secured special extraterritorial rights in China and the Western powers joined in delimiting "spheres of interest," which gave them exclusive development rights to particular sections of the country. Only United States insistence in 1899 upon an open-door policy in China prevented Europeans from actually carving up China into separate colonies as they did in Africa. The United States, determined not to lose the country's lucrative China trade, obtained an agreement that the Chinese government should continue to control its collection of customs and retain ultimate control over its trade.

By the latter part of the nineteenth century, Chinese alarm at the threatened dissolution of their country brought forward a number of reformers, who attempted to counter the alien threat by introducing modern industry and commerce into the national economy. Patterned after the successful strategy of Japan's Meiji rulers (see Chapter 17), these reform efforts nevertheless met determined opposition from conservative elements in Chinese society, including some at the weak Manchu court. Certain of these ventures did succeed, however; government-operated arsenals, shipyards, and other military undertakings, and a number of joint-stock companies, including steamship lines, coal and iron mines, iron and steel mills, cotton mills, and banks, came into being. Yet many of China's indigenous undertakings suffered from graft, inefficiency, and political reaction; on the whole, the nation failed to respond adequately to the foreign challenge, unlike vigorous Meiji Japan. Meanwhile, foreign investment, concentrated largely at the Treaty Ports, continued to rise steadily.

nationalism

China was thus progressively reduced to semicolonial status by the Western powers and Japan, who asserted control over most manufacturing, communications, and trade with the rest of the world. Foreign individuals and groups gained privileged positions, including extraterritoriality in legal matters, and virtually exclusive use of sizable pockets of Chinese land. The increasingly ineffectual Manchu monarchy was itself a foreign (non–Chinese) regime. Patriotic Chinese deeply resented all this, and they developed a growing hostility toward the intruders, whose "barbaric" ways and arrogance offended a people with ample reason to be proud of their own ancient and sophisticated culture.

This resentment engendered nationalistic feelings, resulting in such outbursts as the Taiping Rebellion of the 1850s. Only alien military intervention saved

the Manchu throne in that case. After several unsuccessful attempts, the nationalists finally toppled the Manchu throne in 1911 and set up a Chinese Republic, with Dr. Sun Yat Sen as its first president. Shortly thereafter, however, a group of military leaders overthrew Dr. Sun's government and the warlords continued to reign for several chaotic years.

Forced out of power, Dr. Sun and a number of other nationalists organized a political party, the Kuomintang (KMT), which formed a rival government in Canton. Following World War I, Dr. Sun met rebuff from the Western powers in his search for help but was more successful in his appeals to the Communist leaders of the new Soviet Union. After Sun Yat Sen's death in 1925, the KMT and the Chinese Communist Party (CCP) continued to cooperate intermittently for an extended period. In 1926 a nationalist army, built up and led by General Chiang Kai-shek with the aid of Russian advisers, invaded northern China and defeated the warlords. After this victory the irreconcilable philosophical differences separating the nationalists and Communists caused the partnership to split up. Henceforth the KMT and CCP were to remain implacable enemies despite occasional grudging cooperation against common enemies.

the growth of communism

The Chinese Communist party was a product of the informal association of various socialist groups following the 1911 revolution. When it became formally established in 1921, one of the founding members was Mao Tse-tung, who in later years would lead the CCP to ultimate control of the country. The governing body of international communism, the Comintern, directed the new Chinese Communist party to cooperate with the Kuomintang in throwing off the warlords.

Following the Soviet example, the CCP at first focused upon organizing urban factory workers. Mao Tse-tung's insistent opposition to this policy was vindicated when the party failed to incite revolution in the cities. As Mao had predicted, greater success attended the CCP's efforts to propagandize the rural population, who were organized into peasants' unions. The CCP formed soviets that were able to control sizable areas in the mountains of Hunan and Kiangsi provinces in the South. In addition to Mao, leaders of the party during this period included Chou En-lai, Lin Piao, and other famous Communists of more recent times. Between 1928 and 1934, the CCP built up a Peoples' Liberation Army (PLA), and developed military tactics used by Communist guerrillas ever after.

When the rift occurred between the Kuomintang and the CCP following the successful joint northern expedition against the warlords, Chiang Kai-shek set out to destroy the Communist group. In 1934 Chiang finally defeated the PLA, after which the Communist survivors set out under Mao's leadership on the famous and arduous Long March into remote sanctuaries in the far north, proselytizing peasants to communism en route. During the decade that they lived in Shensi province, Mao's followers consolidated their forces, recruited new members, and increased the territory under their control. By 1945 they ruled a region containing 90 million people.

During the war against Japan (1937–1945), the CCP and the KMT uneasily joined once again in a united front against the enemy. Previously (1930) the Japanese had seized Manchuria and proceeded thereafter to grab additional territories. The patriotic fervor this aroused among the Chinese masses contributed to the success of the CCP's guerrilla tactics against the Japanese, enabling the Communists to hold much of the countryside and pen up the enemy in the cities. This strategy gained the CCP the peasants' favor as a patriotic party. Final victory over the Japanese brought renewed rivalry between the CCP and KMT, precipitating a fierce civil war that ended in nationalist defeat. With surprising suddenness, all China fell into Mao's hands.

Mao's inheritance

China's new leaders found themselves in control of a vast and diverse store of resources, both physical and human. In this ancient land it is often difficult to separate these two kinds of resources, so great has been the impact of the one on the other. The social organization of the country, as well as its space-economy, had evolved and fossilized during the course of four millennia. Let us see what Mao's initial inventory must have looked like.

the land

One of the nation's most impressive assets was its great supply of territory—approximately 3.7 million square miles (9.6 square kilometers), slightly more than the total area of the United States. China had the majority of the countries of continental Asia as neighbors: the Soviet Union on the north and west, Outer Mongolia to the north, and North Korea on the northeast; Afghanistan and Pakistan on the southwest; and India, Nepal, Bhutan, Burma, Laos, and North Vietnam on the south (see Fig. 23.1). Across the eastern seas were the Japanese and Philippine archipelagoes and the island of Taiwan. China's latitudinal extent (18°N to 54°N) is comparable to the distance between the southern tip of Hudson's Bay and Puerto Rico (Fig. 23.2). Her east-west expanse (74°E to 135°E) is roughly equivalent to the distance separating the Atlantic and Pacific coasts of the United States.

Despite China's size, the utility of her land is limited by its physical character, the great diversity of its relief, climates, and soils. The greater part of the country consists of mountains, high plateaus, hills, and large deserts. The west is dominated by lofty mountain systems, oriented mostly east and west, and including

Fig. 23.2 *China's area and latitude compared to the United States*

the world's highest range, the Himalayas. Encircled by these mountain chains are great arid basins. The eastern mountains, which are somewhat lower, parallel the Pacific coast in a series extending from southwest to northeast and separated from each other by plains and river basins.

The interior is drained by great rivers and their tributaries, most of which flow eastward into the Pacific. These rivers are important to China not only for irrigated agriculture but also for transportation. Chief among them are the 2700-mile long Heilung Kiang (Amur River), forming part of the boundary with the Soviet Union; the Hwang Ho (Yellow River), a 2900-mile, silt-laden stream, which, with its chief tributary, the Wei Ho, drains the cradle area of North China; and, most important, the Yangtze Kiang, the 3430-mile stream that crosses middle China to reach the sea near Shanghai. There are also many lesser rivers.

Of special importance to an agricultural people are the country's climates, which are shaped by China's location at the eastern end of the world's largest land mass and on the western side of its greatest ocean, and by the elevations and barrier effects of her mountains. The influences of land and sea alternate to produce unusual seasonal extremes. During part of the year, the country is dominated by cold, dry winter air masses that pour from the polar heart of Asia and produce a continentality like that of the Soviet Union; during the remaining months the land is blanketed with warm, moist winds blowing in from the Pacific. Much of the west and northwest are cut off from these moisture-laden maritime breezes by high mountain walls, behind which lie some of the world's driest lands, among them the Tarim Basin and the Gobi and Ordos Deserts (see Fig. 23.1). The Chin Ling Mountains penetrate into

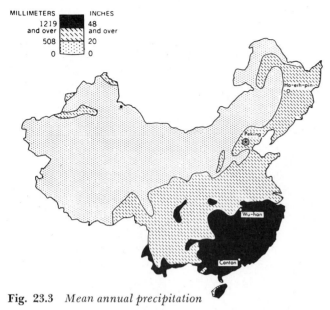

Fig. 23.3 *Mean annual precipitation*

Source: Agriculture in the United States and the People's Republic of China, 1967–1971, *Foreign Agricultural Economic Report No. 94 (Washington: Economic Research Service, U. S. Department of Agriculture, February, 1974), p. 15.*

eastern China, forming a divide between the Hwang Ho and Yangtze basins (Fig. 23.1) and distinctly separating the climates of the northern and southern provinces. In this respect, China differs from the United States, whose south has no such protection from northern cold-air masses. In addition, high elevations produce arctic and subarctic conditions in the Himalayas and other mountains. China's contrasting climatic conditions compare interestingly with their North American equivalents. Southernmost China is tropical like the Caribbean, the southeast resembles Georgia and the Carolinas, the far northeast is similar to Minnesota and Alberta, but the west has climates like those of Wyoming, Montana, Nevada, and Idaho.

In the most populated parts of China, the original natural vegetation has long since disappeared, leaving the country severely short of wood in many places. This does not mean that trees are entirely lacking: South China, with its heavy rainfall (Fig. 23.3) has subtropical forests, and the uplands south of the Yangtze provide suitable conditions for the cultivation of trees for wood. Most of North China's cradle area was originally covered with grass, which disappeared many centuries ago everywhere except in the subhumid northwest. The nearly uninhabited basins of the far northwest have desertic vegetation, but much of Tibet and other mountainous areas are covered with tundra. The soils, formed initially from bedrock and stream- and wind-borne materials and shaped by climate and vegetation, have been much altered by long human occupance.

Reflecting these varied natural and human influences, the potential of China's land for agricultural use is severely circumscribed. Arable land is much reduced in extent by rugged relief, inadequate water, severe cold, and man-induced erosion; in all, only 11 percent of the country is suitable for agriculture. This is a grave handicap for an expanding farm population.

In pre-Communist times, China was generally considered poor in industrial raw materials, a notion based on only meager exploration. Intensive prospecting since has yielded important discoveries, notably a supply of energy resources sufficient to support major industrial development. Coal and hydroelectric reserves appear comparable to those of the United States and the Soviet Union, and petroleum seems to be adequate. China's largest coal deposits are in Shensi and Szechwan, but at least some coal appears in virtually every province. There is a full range of types from lignite to anthracite, but most of it appears to be of only poor to fair quality.

Although the Chinese produced very little petroleum before 1949, they have subsequently found numerous large fields. In earlier years Sinkiang and the northwest were the major source areas but Heilungkiang in the far northeast now leads in output. A significant quantity of oil also comes from oil shale, which was first exploited by the Japanese. Both hydroelectric and thermal generators supply China's electricity, coal and falling water occurring in a neatly complementary fashion. Electricity is produced thermally in the coal-rich north and northeast, which have little hydroelectric potential; it is generated by abundant falling water in the south and southwest, where coal is in short supply.

China seems to be well endowed with most other minerals. Overseas capital financed many of China's earlier mines, mostly near the coastally situated foreign concessions because of difficult transportation into the interior. Although reserves of iron ore are widespread and substantial, known deposits contain mainly lower grades of ore requiring beneficiation. Major deposits of tin are in the southern part of Yunnan province, and copper is widespread in such places as Hopeh, Kansu, and Yunnan. There are also considerable amounts of bauxite, lead, magnesite, manganese, molybdenum, and mercury. China has become a major source of antimony and tungsten, much of the latter coming from the Nan Ling Mountains of west central China. Among other alloying metals are large supplies of chrome, nickel, and cobalt.

the Chinese people

The Communists confronted the same initial problem with their human resources as with their land: a supply large in quantity but low in productivity. There has always been some uncertainty as to how many Chinese there actually are; the 1949 estimate of 475 million was subject to considerable error. More recently (1971) the country's population has been estimated at 787,-176,000, which would give an overall density of 213 persons per square mile. Many parts of the country are known to have much greater densities, however,

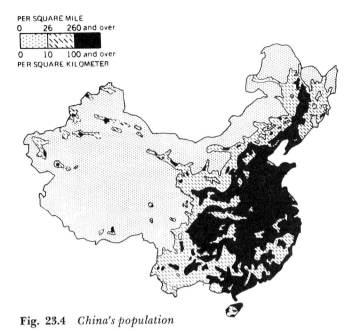

PER SQUARE MILE
0   26   260 and over

0   10   100 and over
PER SQUARE KILOMETER

Fig. 23.4 *China's population*

Source: Agriculture in the United States and the People's Republic of China, 1967–1971, *Foreign Agricultural Economic Report No. 94 (Washington: Economic Research Service, U. S. Department of Agriculture, February, 1974), p. 17.*

because the population distribution in China is closely adjusted to the agricultural potential of the land. In the best areas, high rural densities are made possible by labor-intensive farming techniques. This kind of land use concentrates in alluvial lowlands, lake plains, loess regions, and other well-watered areas with gentle slopes; it is poorly represented in the uplands, which do not fit into the Chinese style of cultivation. For this reason nine-tenths of the Chinese population occupy only one-sixth of the total land area; in those sections, rural densities average nearly 1,200 persons per square mile. (See Fig. 23.4.)

There are four major population regions in China. The North China Plain, an area with loess and alluvial soils and a Kentucky-like climate, has more than one-fourth of the country's people and rural densities that average at least 650 persons per square mile. One fifth of the total is in the middle and lower Yangtze Valley, where rural population densities reach 2500 per square mile in places. South China, consisting of the Canton Delta, the coastal plains of Kwantung and Fukien, and ribbons of farm land along the river valleys, has local densities as high as those of the lower Yangtze. The Red Basin of Szechwan, with one-eighth of the population, has average densities of 500 per square mile but much higher ones in specially favored districts. By contrast, only 5 percent of China's population live in the western half of the country, parts of which are entirely devoid of people.

When the Communists came to power in 1949 only 13 percent of China's people were urban dwellers. Yet even at that time 51 million people lived in cities of more than 20,000 persons, and more than one-fourth

of this urban population were in 9 cities of more than 1 million population. The largest was Shanghai, the nation's leading port and chief industrial and commercial center; Peking, the capital of Communist China, was second. Following these in order were Tientsin, North China's leading port; Shenyang, largest center of Manchuria; Chungking, the wartime capital of the nationalists; Canton, leading port of the south and former capital; Wuhan, a tri-city area at the confluence of the Yangtze and its principal tributary, the Han; Harbin, Manchuria's capital; and Nanking, Chiang Kai-shek's old capital near Shanghai.

In modern times this population pattern had remained unusually stable, partly because of the Chinese attachment to the soil. Also important, however, were cultural and social ties: attachments to family, the village, and the place of one's ancestors. Moreover, each region had its own distinctive dialect, which made communication difficult for newcomers. Finally, there was the barrier of poverty, which denied most Chinese the means to move to other areas.

When Mao Tse-tung assumed control of China the population had been growing at a slow rate throughout most of the modern period. From 1779 to 1850 the population had risen at an annual rate of only 0.63 percent, and between 1850 and 1953 the rate fell to only 0.3 percent per annum. Considering the great size that China's population had already attained by the mid-twentieth century, the absolute numbers of people added to China's population each year were exceedingly large, even at these low rates of increase. This situation well illustrates the Malthusian principle at work in a land occupied continuously for thousands of years by a farming population. At the margin of starvation and with no surplus from one year to the next, the Chinese population was limited by Malthus' positive checks. China's demography had also affected the structure of the country's population. With more than 40 percent of the population under 18 years of age, the country had a level of dependency typical of underdeveloped lands.

Because virtually all Chinese are of Mongoloid stock, the country's ethnic differences are more linguistic than racial. Almost 95 percent of the population are Han Chinese, and the remainder belong to more than 50 other groups officially designated as minority nationalities by the Communist government. In 1949 many of these minority peoples dwelled along the nation's frontiers, across which they had ethnic and religious ties in neighboring lands (Fig. 23.5). China's borders rarely coincide with ethnic divisions.

Two major languages predominate in the country. The Sino-Tibetan group of languages are spoken by the Han Chinese, all of whom use the same written language, Mandarin, regardless of the many spoken dialects in various localities. South of the Yangtze the number of such dialects is especially great. Another branch of the Sino-Tibetan language, called Tibeto-Burman, is the dominant tongue in the southwest. The

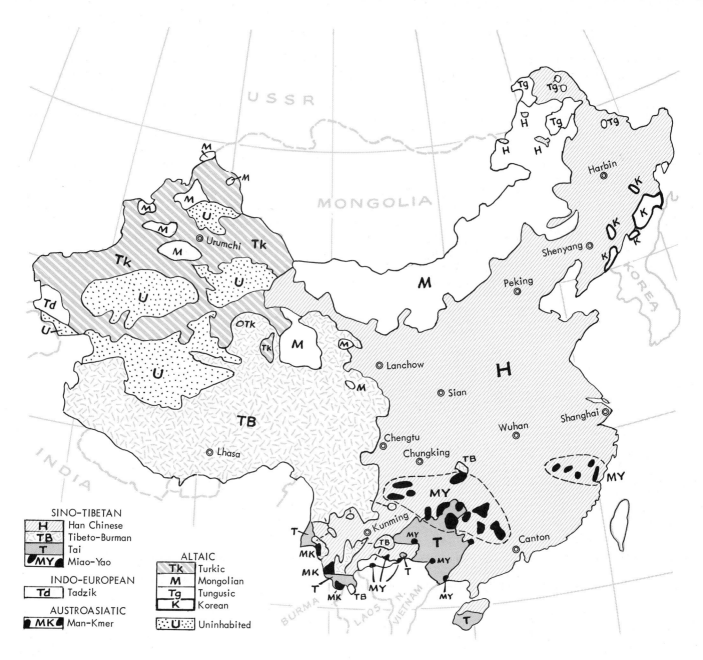

Fig. 23.5 *Major ethnic groups of China*

Legend:

SINO-TIBETAN
H — Han Chinese
TB — Tibeto-Burman
T — Tai
MY — Miao-Yao

INDO-EUROPEAN
Td — Tadzik

AUSTROASIATIC
MK — Man-Kmer

ALTAIC
Tk — Turkic
M — Mongolian
Tg — Tungusic
K — Korean
U — Uninhabited

second major language in China is Altaic, the language of the Mongols, Turkic, and Korean peoples found along the northern margins of the country.

When the Communists assumed power the country still retained its ancient occupational and social structures. Agriculture employed 75 percent of the population but contributed only 40 percent of the GNP. On the other hand, the rural nonfarm population, representing only 10 percent of the labor force, produced 20 percent of the GNP; the urban population, a little more than 15 percent of the labor force, provided 40 percent.

As a good Marxist, Mao attributed China's backward state to its traditional socioeconomic class structure. He described this as having at the top a landlord group numbering 5 percent of the total population.

According to his reckoning, an additional one-fifth of the total comprised the petty bourgeoisie: "owner-peasants," handicraftsmen, intellectuals, professionals, and trades folk. Next came the semi-proletariat—peasants who owned their own land but had an inadequate amount of it for their support. Another 70 percent constituted the poor peasants, mainly tenant farmers. Below these in Mao's classification were the small handicraftsmen, shop assistants, peddlers, and the modern industrial proletariat (factory workers). At the bottom came the laborers in small industries.

Chinese transportation in 1949

As the Revolution ended, production was heavily concentrated in the east. A small number of metropolitan

428

centers in that section of the country provided the main market; the agricultural population, also in the east, had little buying power. The main sources of industrial raw materials were also in the eastern provinces, because little mineral exploration had taken place in other parts of the nation. Altogether, in 1949 five of the seven most developed provinces of China were in the east; the two exceptions were Szechwan and Hupeh.

Concentrated in these same areas was China's pre-revolutionary transport system, which had been built to serve the leading centers of modern production, mostly seaports and river ports (Fig. 23.6). Transportation also focused on the political capital, which shifted between Peking, Nanking, and other centers, depending upon the group currently in power in the country. Although transportation is very important to China's

development, considering the enormous distances to be covered, her transport system in 1949 was merely a series of poorly interconnected links, which left much of the interior lacking modern transport altogether.

One peculiarity of Chinese transportation before 1949, and to some extent even today, was its dual character—the side-by-side existence of traditional and modern forms. The traditional means of moving goods are the junks and sampans, human- and animal-drawn vehicles, and human porters with their carrying poles. These forms appeared very early in China's history and remained essentially unchanged and unchallenged for many centuries until the European intrusions of the nineteenth century. In 1949 the modern types of transportation—inland and coastal waterways, roads, and railways—had barely managed to generate gross

Fig. 23.6   *The Chinese railway system*

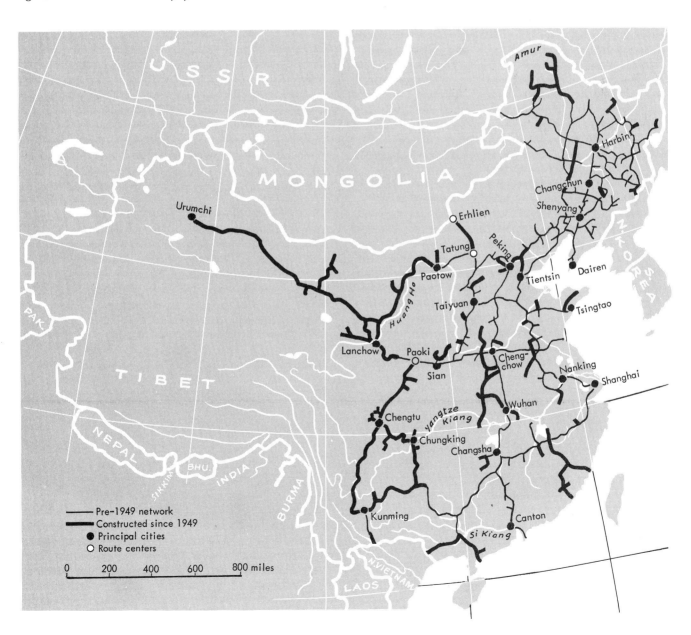

receipts matching the total earned by the traditional forms, despite the inefficiency of the latter, which still employed 88 percent of the total transport work force in that year.

Under the largely primitive economic conditions prevailing in pre-Communist China, water transport was the most important single mode. It was preeminent in central and southern China, where many rivers are navigable for virtually their entire lengths and interconnect with numerous large lakes. Even today, two-thirds of the country's inland waterway network is in the south. Water transport is less important in the north, where, although canals are numerous, the rivers draining the loess regions are badly silted and have seasonal flow.

Canal construction began very early in China's history. By comparison with the canal-building era of Europe, mainly in the late eighteenth and first part of the nineteenth centuries, China was constructing the Tai Hu-Hangchow Canal as early as 506 B.C. Beginning in A.D. 1283, Kublai Khan built the famous Grand Canal, a 1,020-mile waterway linking five major rivers on its way from Hangchow to Peking. Although it had been the country's main north-south transport artery and an integral part of the imperial grain collection system until modern times, the Grand Canal fell into disrepair early in this century.

East-West transportation in China has benefited from navigation on the mainly eastward flowing rivers, especially the Yangtze and its tributaries. This most heavily used Chinese waterway has long been the principal outlet for the mountain-ringed Szechwan basin, a populous and productive region. The Si Kiang is an important waterway of the south, and the Amur and Sungari carry much traffic in the far northeast.

Coastal shipping along the 8,400 miles of Pacific shoreline developed early, especially in the south and southeast, where the deeply indented coast provided many excellent natural harbors. Although the rugged mountains rimming these southern shores have limited the size of the hinterlands served by these ports, this part of the country has an ancient seafaring tradition. The water-borne commerce of the region grew rapidly with the opening of the Treaty Ports during the 1840s.

Before 1949 the chief ports of the country were Shanghai, Taku (outport for Tientsin at that time), Whampoa (port of Canton), and Dairen. Leading them all was Shanghai, then one of the world's great ports and the foreign outlet for a very large hinterland in the Yangtze basin. Its prominence dates from the 1840s, when it was selected by the British as their main base at the end of the Opium wars. By 1863 it had acquired its International Settlement, a foreign enclave with large shipyards and much manufacturing. Its population has continued to grow rapidly ever since, and it is today one of the world's largest cities. By the end of the Revolution, however, China's ports and her water transportation generally were in chaos.

The roads of China have always functioned as a supplement to other forms of transportation, being used mainly for farm-to-market and other short-haul movements. From early Han times until the beginning of this century the country's roads were mere dirt tracks. Between 1930 and 1936, however, the Chiang Kai-shek government undertook a national program of road building, which continued in the west during the Sino-Japanese war. The entire system deteriorated badly during the three years of civil war that ended in 1949, at which time only 50,000 miles out of the previous total of 124,000 miles of roads remained serviceable. Three-fourths of these roads were in the east, especially in the coastal and plains areas.

The principal form of modern transportation in China by 1949 was the railway system, which had been built mainly between 1900 and 1920 by foreign interests. The Japanese invasion terminated a further spate of railway building by the KMT during the 1930s. The 12,000 miles of total trackage still in existence by 1949 had been badly damaged. The system Mao inherited was also poorly distributed and inadequately interconnected. As Figure 23.6 shows, most of this mileage was in the east and northeast, leaving much of southern China without railways and still dependent upon water transportation. The western part of the country was wholly lacking in railways. Meanwhile, China's civil air transport, begun in the early 1930s, had disintegrated entirely by the end of the civil war and its fleet was lost.

prerevolutionary agriculture

Although most Chinese obtain their livelihood directly from the soil, the most characteristic forms of traditional agriculture are those practiced in the east, where 95 percent of the population reside. As we have already noted, China has long suffered from a chronic food supply problem. With a large and growing population on the land, and with only one-ninth of the total area suitable for crops, China's rural land use has necessarily been intensive. This intensity, however, is achieved almost entirely by massive inputs of labor, at least twenty times as many man-hours per acre of wheat as in the United States, for example. Capital inputs, on the other hand, are low; there is no machinery—only crude hand tools and implements. Yields per acre are high, especially in those areas with sufficiently long growing seasons to produce two successive crops per year. Like the Japanese, the farmers of China also do much intercropping; that is, the growing of one crop between the rows of another crop making complementary demands upon the soil.

Traditional Chinese agriculture stresses the production of grains, which provide the country with nine-tenths of her food supply. The Chinese consume the output of the land directly, rather than through the intermediate stage of conversion into animal products. Animal industries are much too inefficient in this land of food scarcity; it is not feasible to divert valuable grain for the feeding of animals or of precious land for pasture. Chinese farms therefore have few animals—only a few pigs and chickens scavenging for household scraps and other refuse. These poor creatures yield only enough meat to serve as seasoning for vegetable and grain dishes. In certain favored areas, fish supplement the generally starchy diet and are obtained locally from coastal waters, rivers, canals, and fish-farming in the rice paddies, ponds, and irrigation ditches. In all, the Chinese earth provides very little animal protein for its people.

Before the Communist takeover, the average size of farms in China was very small. In the south, with its double- and intercropping, two to three acres supported a family, but in the north individual farms ranged up to seven acres. Small as these were, each farm was uneconomically fragmented into scattered, tiny plots. Consequently, the output per person was very low, close to the margin of subsistence. With little or no surplus to carry over from one year to the next, most farm families were pitifully vulnerable to natural calamities.

Although these were the general conditions of agriculture in pre-Communist China, there was much variation then as now in the kinds of crops and agricultural practices from one part of this huge land to another. The clearest distinction is between the wheat and rice regions of eastern China. The boundary separating the two areas follows fairly closely the water shed between the Yangtze and Hwang Rivers, which is marked farther west by the crest of the Chin Ling Mountains. This boundary represents the northern limit of continuous rice culture, although not the absolute limit of rice farming, because some of it is grown on the basis of one crop per season as far north as Manchuria. The south, with its subtropical temperatures, abundant rainfall, and long growing season, is able to produce two rice crops per year and a large total output of this grain, despite the fact that the agricultural land is much interrupted by hills and mountains. The north is drier and cooler and has a shorter growing season, conditions that are more favorable to wheat and certain other grains than for rice. These two major areas are further subdivided, as Figure 23.7 shows.

Rural land use in the west of China is of a very different sort. In 1949, at the start of Communist rule, the grasslands of the far northwest supported a sparse population of mainly nomadic herdsmen living under tribal rule in the primitive fashion of earliest times. In the steppelands of Heilungkiang and eastern Inner Mongolia (Fig. 23.7), the comparatively well-watered mountain slopes support good pastures, whereas farther west the cold and subhumid high plain of Inner Mongolia has pastures of low productivity. Sinkiang province, in the far northwest, offers good grazing on the mountain slopes, which surround basins that are virtually rainless—true deserts incapable of supporting human or animal life except in a few oases. The lofty Tibetan plateau of the southwest is cold and mostly

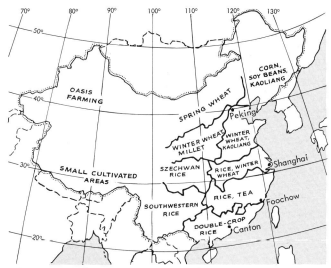

Fig. 23.7 *China's rural land use regions*

Source: Data from Communist China Map Portfolio (U.S. Central Intelligence Agency, 1967).

very dry, offering good pastures only along its eastern margins and near the old capital of Lhasa. Limited areas of arable farming occur in certain favored localities of the west. Ancient oasis settlements in the valleys of rivers issuing from the mountains produce a variety of food grains, cotton, fruits, vegetables, and melons.

industry before Mao

Although some industrialization had taken place under the KMT, this had amounted to very little; at the end of the Revolution, China's manufacturing sector was still underdeveloped. The majority of industries were small-scale, handicraft operations that used little mechanical energy. Some modern industry did exist, but it was highly localized and accounted for only about 6 percent of the GNP. Even this was virtually destroyed by the Sino–Japanese War and the Civil War that followed it; industrial output was almost nil when Mao took over.

Pre-Communist industry focused primarily on consumer goods; textiles, clothing, and food, drink, and tobacco accounted for 72 percent of total factory output in 1933. Nevertheless, there was some heavy industry, concentrated in a few key localities and emphasizing basic metals production. In all, the country depended upon imports for a wide variety of both producer and consumer goods. A major part of the infrastructure was foreign-owned—50 percent of the railways and 57 percent of the utilities, for example—and foreign trade was almost wholly under foreign control. Slightly more than one-third of all factory ownership was in foreign hands, but this proportion was much greater in certain lines. For instance, foreigners owned 40 percent of the textile spindles and 70 percent of the looms in the country.

Modern industrial production before the Communists was concentrated in the coastal areas, except for a few river ports and isolated cities. Eighty percent of the factories and 90 percent of the mechanical energy use was in the coastal provinces. Eight of the largest cities accounted for 97 percent of the motive power used in manufacturing and 92 percent of the industrial employment. In China proper, excluding Manchuria, Shanghai was dominant, with 61 percent of all Chinese factory employment at the end of World War II. Tientsin, the large north-coast port, had another 10 percent, and Tsingtao, Peking, and Nanking followed. Wuhan, the large Yangtze port at the confluence of the Han River, was a major steel-producing center. In addition to these, Manchuria, under Japanese control until the end of World War II, was a large region of heavy industry developed by the occupying power. Foreign-controlled industry in China proper was confined almost entirely to the treaty ports along the Pacific coast and the Yangtze.

dualism

During this period China exhibited the same kinds of contrasts between traditional and modern economies, existing side by side, as Indonesia, Central America, and most other underdeveloped nations. Indigenous economic activities were characterized by hand methods, lack of machinery, lack of division of labor, small-scale operation, and dispersed spatial pattern. Among these industries were handicraft manufactures, primitive mining enterprises, native banks, and transportation by junks, coolie carriers, and human- and animal-drawn conveyances.

When Mao Tse-tung gained power, the indigenous forms of production still predominated. For example, in 1933, just before the long period of warfare, agriculture, providing 60 percent of the GNP, was almost wholly of the traditional type. Mining was the most modern—only 22 percent of the coal production and 23 percent of the iron ore was of the old type. Three-fourths of the manufacturing, on the other hand, was still traditional. Transportation was still 92 percent traditional. Altogether the modern sector of the Chinese economy in the last years of peace under the KMT contributed no more than 13 percent to the national income.

Unlike most underdeveloped nations, China's indigenous economy was not extinguished or even seriously harmed by the intrusion of modern forms. One of the reasons for the resilience of the traditional sector was the unusually small contribution made by modern activities. Moreover, in the face of competition the demand for traditional goods and services remained strong, both from foreign and domestic markets. Chinese handicrafts and agricultural products, particularly silks and teas, were always prized in Western lands. Domestic demand remained steady, fed by a growing population with incomes so low that relatively few could afford factory-made goods, especially when the high costs of

inland transportation were added to their price. Thus the effective competition of modern production was limited. In this manner the traditional sector managed on the whole to survive quite well. Even in Shanghai, center of modern production, large numbers of hand looms operated alongside large, mechanized weaving mills. In view of the low wages and the high price of capital in China, modern technology was unable to gain any cost advantage.

The result was a coexistence between the traditional and the modern and a division of manufacturing output between them. Modern factories concentrated on making products that lay beyond the technical capabilities of native industry, while the latter retained most of what was left. For example, modern looms manufactured the finer cloths demanded by resident foreigners, the more prosperous Chinese, and exporters; the native hand weavers continued making the coarse, durable cloths that were all that the mass market of China could afford.

Yet certain modern products did gain quick acceptance in China at the expense of the native. Kerosene, matches, lamps, needles, and window glass, for instance, largely eclipsed the demand for their traditional counterparts. Even these, however, were quickly imitated wherever possible by native craftsmen. Many traditional activities actually benefited from modern innovations in inland transportation, services, and such aids to native workers as iron hand looms. Thus in the Chinese case the net effects of dualism on the health of the traditional handicraft sector were mixed, at the least.

foreign trade

Despite her resource-based economy, China's foreign trade has always been different from that of other primary-producing, underdeveloped countries. For one thing, trade has been only a small element in the Chinese economy. The peak year was 1928–1929, when the total reached $1.5 billion, after which foreign commerce, like the economy as a whole, declined because of world depression and wars. In 1933, near the end of the KMT's peacetime reign, China's foreign trade was only 3 percent of national income, one of the lowest levels of trade participation of all the underdeveloped nations. One reason for this is the country's huge territory, which makes it easier for the economy to remain relatively self-contained. Foreign trade also suffers from the large proportion of the population living at a bare subsistence level, with little surplus to sell and per capita incomes too low to buy very much abroad. Moreover, the Chinese have always maintained an attitude of aloofness to the world at large, rather like Stalin's USSR. Indeed, the Manchus actually resisted commercial contact with the outside world until literally forced by armed foreign intervention to admit trade.

Another way in which China's trade differs from most underdeveloped nations and a further reason for the low level of trade participation is that foreigners invested comparatively less in the country's export production, even though foreign interests were largely responsible for the conduct of external trade. A third distinguishing characteristic of Chinese trade before Mao's assumption of power was the fairly diverse nature of her exports. Although the country's exports were specialized mainly in tea and silk at the outset, these two commodities declined subsequently because of competition from other producers. Japan, Ceylon, and India captured much of the tea trade, and silk ultimately lost out to synthetics. By 1931 silk represented only 14 percent of the nation's exports, and tea accounted for only 4 percent. Meanwhile, soybeans had risen to 21 percent. Among other exports, none of which represented more than one-tenth of the total, were tung oil, linen, metals and metallic ores, ground nuts (peanuts) and oil, and raw cotton. As often happens with protein-short underdeveloped nations, China also exported a number of animal products, including eggs and egg products (from her flocks of scavenging chickens), and wool, hides, leather, and skins (from the grazing lands of the west).

In a few respects, however, China's trade more closely resembled that of other underdeveloped lands. First, there was the emphasis upon exporting primary commodities, with little if any processing, and importing a variety of manufactured consumer goods. Second, China was a price-taker—she had to accept whatever prices the world market assigned to her exports and imports. As is usually the case, this meant that her international terms of trade were continually deteriorating. China's trade was therefore vulnerable to world economic conditions and suffered from instability of demand and price. Although this instability had little impact on the economy as a whole because trade was such a small part of the total, it severely affected those few regions specifically geared to export production such as the silk districts.

Mao's problems and opportunities

In summary, then, this is what Mao Tse-tung saw before him when he found all China under his control and looking to him for leadership. No doubt the first thing that confronted him was the awesome dimensions of the problems that had to be addressed. As a disciple of Marx, he was especially conscious of the rigidity of long-entrenched social organization and social attitudes, the fatalism, submissiveness, and helplessness before nature and other men.

As a Marxist, however, Mao tended at first to denigrate another problem that was subsequently to prove equally severe: the difficulty of feeding a population whose numbers had long since reached the Malthusian limits. This second major problem was made all the more difficult by a third one: an economy that was not only poorly developed but stagnating after 13 years of turmoil. In addition to their severely limited

supply of arable land, China's peasants remained isolated and helpless before (1) the oppressive demands of a landlord class that monopolized the land and other factors of production; (2) natural calamities that included drought, floods, and animal and insect pests; and (3) innumerable poverty diseases, such as tuberculosis, dysentery, typhus, hookworm, filariasis, malaria, and schistosomiasis. Meanwhile, China's poorly developed industrial sector was characterized by dualism and burdened by inadequate capital and industrial skills. The transport and communication systems, which had always been sparse and poorly interconnected especially in the interior, lay in ruins following more than a dozen years of warfare.

Mao Tse-tung's fourth major challenge was to establish national unity and to assert political control. The country's administrative machinery was yet another casualty of the long conflict. Indeed, China had rarely experienced complete national unity in the past, so poor were her internal communications, so great her territorial extent, and so large her population, including ethnic minorities outside the national economy and polity.

Finally, Mao had to be concerned with grave problems of international relations, both political and economic. His assumption of power aroused hostility and suspicion from the non–Communist world and relied upon an uneasy alliance with uncertain and untried friends of common ideology. Among Mao's oldest political inheritances was a set of unsatisfactory political boundaries. China had bitterly disputed her long borders with the USSR and India, asserted old and unsatisfied claims to a number of Pacific island territories, and endured within her own land several surviving enclaves of extraterritoriality, notably Hong Kong and Macao. China's international economic problems included a poorly developed external trade and severe obstacles to increasing that trade.

Yet, as Mao Tse-tung viewed them, his land offered some tantalizing opportunities. Although it had been little explored for minerals, that land promised to yield a great many such physical resources. And according to Mao's ideology, China's large population should be regarded as a potential asset of importance. The country's numerous minorities represented only a small proportion of the total, and the nation as a whole benefited from an unusual degree of cultural unity, considering her size. Finally, Mao was able to count as one of his major assets the great surge of patriotic feeling that arose among the country's peasantry following the expulsion of the Japanese and the conclusion of the Revolution.

THE CHINESE MARXIST SOLUTION

Among the architects of the new China were several founding members of the Chinese Communist party. Foremost among these, party chairman Mao Tse-tung was the principal theoretician. As a strict Marxist-

Leninist, Mao has adhered to the doctrine of dialectical materialism, maintaining that human existence consists of many contradictions and contending forces. The idea that struggle is basic to life, that it is desirable to be confronted by opposition, conforms with Mao's own personal history. Born in 1893 of a peasant family, he learned firsthand that feeling of constant struggle, which was the Chinese farmer's lot. Although he ran away from home to study at Normal College (Changsha) and Peking University, where he adopted communism, he has never forgotten his peasant beginnings. His writings and policies disclose a faith in the peasant masses that is contrary to the Russian Communists' emphasis upon the industrial proletariat.

As party leader, Mao has stressed the need for actual experience rather than dependence upon doctrine or theory alone. Even while building up the Red Army as an agency for the spread of Communist ideas, he has insisted that theory be tested and applied directly. Mao has always seen himself as engaged in a world mission to liberate all oppressed peoples, expressing complete faith in the ultimate success of this crusade and contending that any firmly held goal is possible of attainment, whatever the obstacles. Notable among the other original CCP members is Chou En-lai, premier of the People's Republic of China. A pragmatic person and a skilled administrator, Chou is more urbane, is more widely traveled, and has a better perception of the world beyond China than does Mao Tse-tung, who has never left the country.

In planning for China's development, the country's Communist leaders have had, from the outset, to contend with one fundamental problem: how to feed and clothe a large and growing population. Hence the broad goal of Chinese Communist planners has been to eradicate poverty through socialism. Although Communist China has passed through a number of episodes since 1949, its history falls into two main phases of contrasting nature. The first of these was the Soviet period (1949 to 1958) during which the new nation relied upon Russian advisers and followed the Soviet Union's planning model. With the Great Leap Forward of 1958 the Chinese Communists began to pull away from their Russian mentors, and they have since abandoned the Soviet model as irrelevant to China's special circumstances and problems.

In its place China's leaders have adopted a peculiarly Chinese approach to development. Acknowledging that capital is severely lacking in China, this new policy seeks to convert the country's superabundant labor into capital. To perform this alchemy, Chinese planners have turned to massive public works projects. Meanwhile, the regime campaigns to glorify the work ethic, preaching a dedication to rigorous toil and exhorting the workers to revolutionary zeal, reinforced by diligent study of the thoughts of Chairman Mao and by relentless group pressures upon the laggards. The system calls for participatory management at the local level, including lengthy discussions that involve all members of the group. This peculiarly Asian approach to conflict resolution and decision making resembles the Japanese practice in some respects (see Chapter 17). In summary, the Chinese strategy is to mobilize the peasantry, decentralize planning and control, and change customary Chinese attitudes and behavior to eradicate traditional thought patterns.

In applying this strategy, Chinese policy makers have followed an erratic course, with violent swings from left to right and frequent changes of direction. Although this results to some degree from the factionalism that infests the CCP, it tends also to conform with Mao's belief in the necessity for alternately creating tensions and relaxing them. Assessing the results of Chinese policy and practice is complicated by severe data problems, because official quantitative information has been sparse and unreliable. Much that we have been able to learn about China's modern experiences has come from foreign analysts, who must painfully piece together any scraps of information they can find.

the Soviet period

The Soviet Union assumed an important role in the initial planning and direction of the Chinese Communist economy. The USSR provided technical assistance, loan capital (but not grants), and capital equipment and helped to direct the course of the new nation along a Stalinist path. During the Soviet era, the Chinese exercised central planning and control over the economy and emphasized the same sectors and employed the same locational principles as had the USSR before them.

following Stalin's lead

China's reconstruction occupied the years from 1949 to 1952, during which the country underwent rehabilitation from the destruction and chaos resulting from 13 years of war and revolution. During this first period China had a mixed economy that combined both privately owned and state-owned enterprises, an arrangement much like the USSR's New Economic Policy of the early 1920s.

The first five-year plan (1953–1957) eliminated private enterprise and placed the entire economy under central planning and control from Peking, with the aim of assuring orderly economic development. Economic planning proceeded, after the Soviet manner, to develop a system of priorities that assigned primary emphasis to manufacturing, especially heavy industries making producer goods by large-scale, capital-intensive methods. The plan deemphasized the manufacture of consumer goods and other light industry. It gave low priority to agriculture, which was almost neglected, except that farms were collectivized and expected to produce a surplus for the support of industrial development, as in the USSR. Planners attempted to minimize investment for social overhead, providing only that which was absolutely necessary for the success of other, high-priority ends. Thus railways were constructed mainly to serve raw material deposits and manufacturing sites. In an effort to force economic development at the fastest possible rate, the plan set high targets for each sector. Administration and investment were centrally controlled, with each branch of the economy under the direction of a ministry in Peking.

The Soviet era of Chinese Communist planning substantially affected the location of production. The first five-year plan stressed development of the backward interior in an effort to redress the heavy imbalance that had hitherto favored the coastal provinces of the east. One of the reasons for the westward shift was the Soviet belief that production should be oriented to domestic raw material sources, reflecting the Stalinist aversion to dependence upon foreign suppliers. Strategic interests also influenced the westward movement, because Chinese memories of Japan's occupation of the east were still fresh. China's dependence upon the USSR during this period likewise favored western locations, which were nearer the source of capital equipment and other needs obtained from the Soviet Union. To ease the supplying of western China from the USSR, the two countries were linked by the new Trans-Mongolian Railway (1955) and the Sinkiang Railway. Despite this attempt at regionally balanced production, the Soviet-influenced plan concentrated investment in a limited number of places. Of 120 cities singled out for such investment, the greater part of it went to only 18 centers.

Because the first five-year plan took effect at a time when the nation's economy was at a low level of production, its reported results were impressive. China's leaders claimed that industrial output had doubled during the period. Agriculture was still in a bad state, however, just as in the case of Russian agriculture during the earliest years of the USSR.

weaknesses of the Soviet model

During the period of Soviet influence there quickly appeared serious problems for which the USSR's experience served as a poor guide. In several important respects China's circumstances were very different from those of the Soviet Union at the time of the latter's Communist takeover. For one thing, the China of 1949 was at a far lower level of development than was the Russia of 1917, whose economy had already entered the takeoff stage. Another difference was the overwhelming preponderance of peasant farmers in the Chinese labor force, which included only a miniscule urban proletariat. Moreover, China was severely short of educated and skilled manpower, which is used extravagantly in the Soviet strategy.

The two countries also differed in their population–resource relationships. With less territory than the USSR, China had three times as great a population, making it exceedingly difficult to generate an agricultural surplus that could be used to pay for the import of capital goods and raw materials. Indeed, China's farm output was actually hampered by the neglect of agriculture under Soviet-style planning. There were also significant cultural and organizational differences between the two countries, particularly China's unique and very ancient civilization with its intrenched attitudes and social organization.

China alone

Feeling uncomfortable in the Soviet mold, China's leaders became increasingly dissatisfied as the first five-year plan proceeded. They were unhappy with progress in areas they deemed important, notably food supply, and they began to assert increased independence from their Soviet advisers. Launching a new crash program on their own initiative, against strenuous objections from the Soviet Union, they failed resoundingly. When the USSR then withdrew its advisers and economic assistance, China's leaders undertook a thorough reassessment. Out of this came a new, wholly Chinese strategy incorporating Chinese goals, attitudes, and methods. This new program's implementation has followed an erratic course, as the utopians and pragmatists among China's top leaders battled over basic policy. The utopians maintain that production should be increased by the exercise of sheer political will, strengthened by a sublime faith in the mythical innate wisdom of the masses. The pragmatists, on the other hand, consider the utopian approach both unproductive and potentially disastrous. These shifts in Chinese policy also conform to Mao's theory of alternating tension and relaxation. Through it all the Chinese people have remained fortunately resilient, insulated as they are by their own self-sufficiency.

the great leap forward

China's Soviet-designed second five-year plan was to have started in 1958, but China's leaders made an abrupt change of course instead. Their Great Leap Forward represented the beginning of China's divergence from the Soviet model, but only part way, because it retained the latter's emphasis upon heavy industry and capital goods. The main difference was in pace and method. This was to be a crash program, which would push the economy to its utmost capacity, with the aim of overtaking the United Kingdom's output within a fifteen-year period.

One of the key elements of the Great Leap Forward was its efforts to mobilize the Chinese masses to hard work and sacrifice by means of ideological exhortations. With massive applications of labor, China's leaders expected to overcome the country's severe shortage of capital. Millions of untrained workers would make up for China's shortage of skills and would literally turn labor into capital. At the same time, this would provide a way of absorbing the excess laborers still on the farms by converting them into industrial workers.

Another significant feature of the scheme was its revival of the familiar Chinese form of dualism, now officially blessed as "walking on two legs." This meant the continuation of large-scale industrial projects previously undertaken, together with a proliferation of myriads of small rural industrial projects typified by the famous "backyard furnaces." At the same time, the leadership decreed that the agricultural collectives formed in the previous period be combined into communes: large, highly ordered, factory-type, farming operations. The Great Leap Forward was thus a hybrid, crossing Soviet priorities with Chinese methods.

The effect of this strenuous drive was greatly to overextend the Chinese economy and resulted in confusion and declining output. Ultimately the program collapsed entirely, although the dimensions of the failure have been obscured by the official blackout of data that ensued. Apparently the Great Leap Forward failed not only because it overtaxed the economy but also because it badly distorted the entire national system. The program interrupted the coordination among sectors of the economy; it overdeveloped some industries and created shortages in others; and it greatly overloaded the country's transport system, especially in the east. Matters worsened when Soviet aid abruptly stopped. In a fit of pique the USSR withdrew funds and advisers, left projects uncompleted, and halted the flow of Russian capital equipment, oil, and raw materials. The final blow was a series of crop failures in China—the result of droughts, floods, and other natural calamities.

a truly Chinese model

Following the collapse of her economy, China entered three years of retrenchment and rebuilding, during the course of which the country's leaders abandoned their schemes for forced-draft industrialization. Instead they undertook a reassessment of their developmental policies in the light of Mao Tse-tung's philosophy, so different from the Soviet outlook. As their overriding objective they chose to attempt to improve the real welfare of the Chinese people, to eradicate poverty and to gain security rather than to seek growth in GNP per se. To accomplish this they determined to change their countrymen's fundamental outlook, to remold the population in a new image by transforming their thought patterns and behavior.

As the basis for their development efforts, China's leaders adopted Mao's concept of the *mass line,* anticipated by their ill-conceived Great Leap Forward. This meant mobilizing China's manpower and engaging the people's native skills and abilities. The greatest departure from previous programs was the new emphasis given to agriculture. Recognizing that most Chinese are farmers, Peking planners set out to increase the country's farm output, with a view not only to

feeding the population better but also providing greater security for the farmers themselves. This contrasts with the Soviet Union's policy of suppressing the farm population and exploiting them for the benefit of industry. Also differing from the Soviet approach was the anti-urban bias built into the program, based on the view that cities are corrupting and dehumanizing and that urban dwellers need frequent contact with the countryside. It was on this foundation that China developed a wholly new developmental strategy stressing balanced growth and greater moderation.

This program incorporated a set of revised priorities more in accord with China's condition. The country's leadership assigned the highest priority to agriculture, but with the stipulation (1) that the nation's farms were to produce a surplus output sufficient to support the nonagricultural sector and (2) that the farms were to use their labor more productively to free workers for nonagricultural employment. Second priority went to those industries serving agriculture and the farm population: enterprises making irrigation pumps and equipment, tractors and farm implements, fertilizers and insecticides, and consumer necessities required by farmers as well as the population generally. The planners assigned the lowest priority to those heavy industries that do not contribute directly to agriculture.

Another sharp break from the early years of Soviet tutelage was the decision to redirect investment away from the west. In a sense this became necessary because of the new emphasis on agriculture and agriculturally oriented manufacturing, which tended to focus industrial production upon those parts of the east where the main population and farm output were centered. This halted, or at least slowed, the raw material-oriented projects previously commenced in the west, including new transport ventures, which had proved too costly for China's capabilities. Accompanying this change of focus was the fortunate discovery of important new petroleum deposits in the east, notably the much heralded Taching oil fields of northern Manchuria. Meanwhile the country's strategic circumstances had changed abruptly. As the threat from the east, especially Japan, abated, there came a renewed cause for concern from the opposite direction, namely the USSR, lately an ally but long before that an enemy of China. Further reversal of the country's orientation occurred as foreign trade shifted from overland exchanges with the USSR to waterborne commerce through east coast ports to Japan, western Europe, and other overseas points.

China's revised policy downgraded the role of cities in the developmental scheme, representing another break with Soviet planning. China resolved to avoid the building of new megalopolises, deciding instead that any increases in population would have to be absorbed by rural areas and smaller centers. Wherever possible, manufacturing should go to the small urban places rather than to the great cities. At the same time, the country's leaders agreed to decentralize planning and control. Planning was to become more flexible, mistakes were to be permitted, and a larger share of the decision making would be assumed by the local party structure relying on the "spontaneous initiative of the masses." In some measure at least the new scheme seemed to work, to the extent that, under operation of the unpublicized second five-year plan, the national economy had by 1965 made a partial recovery to a point above 1957 levels.

the cultural revolution

Just as the economy was gaining momentum, another of the Chinese Communists' recurring ideological upheavals surfaced. The conflict that broke out during the winter of 1965–1966 on the eve of an announced third five-year plan (1966–1970) may well have been precipitated by disagreement over the new plan. Again the dissention pitted utopians against pragmatists, although it also appears to have involved a leadership struggle. Temporarily gaining the upper hand, the utopians initiated what they called the Great Proletarian Cultural Revolution. Their leaders accused the country's professional managers and local officials of emphasizing production to the neglect of the class struggle. The stress should instead be on Mao's "revolutionary initiative of the broad masses," in which they felt the managers had been showing too little faith.

The resulting civil disorders threw local administration into confusion, ripped apart the Communist party apparatus, and undermined the authority of professional managers and local officials. In many cases committees of zealous but inexperienced workers, students, and soldiers replaced trained managers. Before long the Cultural Revolution had produced a substantial reduction in output.

When the extent of the damage became excessive, Chairman Mao finally intervened to end the disorder. The party reestablished local administration in 1967–1968, with revolutionary committees assuming control to get production moving once more. To augment output, the regime again encouraged the establishment of small rural manufacturing ventures, but more carefully planned this time. Among the great number of such undertakings were small plants and workshops making walking tractors, farm implements and parts, and agricultural chemicals. Where possible these ventures were locally self-sufficient, relying on nearby raw materials and markets. This was intended to reduce the burden on the country's weak transport system, help restrain the population flow into the cities, and provide employment for the large numbers of young people entering the labor force.

The fourth five-year plan (1971–1975) appears to introduce a new phase of Chinese development. The mood of this plan is prudence and pragmatism, with orderly progress and balanced development. The ultimate goal is to acquire the full range of heavy industry,

but also implicit in the plan is the need first to lay a firm foundation for this. The plan calls for (1) rapid development of agriculture and light manufacturing, simultaneously fostering both large and small industries (dualism), (2) establishment of self-sufficient farming and industrial communities throughout the country, and (3) continued decentralization of industry and planning, with local enterprises arranging for their own capital, raw materials, and equipment. The peasant is still the chief resource for national development. Among the key features of the current approach is a cost consciousness; to minimize unit costs factories are encouraged to design their own mechanical short cuts. It is intended that these ventures make a profit for the enterprise, although they are not to pay bonuses or overtime to individuals.

Another important policy shift in the 1970s is the Chinese decision to undertake new trade initiatives. By ending the country's traditional aloofness from the world economic system, the regime is consciously making a policy reversal likely to have profound consequences.

population policy

The fundamental challenge to the current regime in Communist China is to achieve a satisfactory balance between numbers of people and output. Although in most basic terms this means ensuring enough food, shelter, and clothing for each citizen, there is a host of other problems associated with excess numbers and overly rapid rates of population growth. We have noted that the Chinese Communists assumed control of the country at a time when its population had long since reached the Malthusian limits but was nevertheless still inclined toward further expansion. With output stagnating, this meant real human misery: poverty and disease, rural underemployment, and mass migrations to cities. Meanwhile dense concentrations of people accumulated in some areas leaving others virtually unpopulated. For a number of reasons the regime was also concerned by the number of minority peoples existing outside the national economy.

Consequently, from the outset there was a crucial need for a coherent policy concerned with the population's growth, spatial distribution, and integration into the economic system. Because of ideological bias, doctrinaire Marxists are ill-equipped to address these questions is a truly practical manner. Yet the problems are of such a nature that they present ready solutions to any totalitarian regime willing to face them squarely and ready to apply methods a democratic society would find too ruthless.

population growth

Although in 1949 China's immense population was still uneasily restrained in its growth by Malthus' positive checks, the early years of Communist control had the effect of relaxing those restraints. The regime had succeeded in providing political stability, more reliable food distribution, and improved public health and medical care. The predictable result was a significant drop in the death rate by 1953. Meanwhile the fertility rate remained as high as ever, an ingrained part of the Chinese culture. With the demographic transition thus set in motion, China became a Type 2 nation according to the UN demographic classification system (see Chapter 2). Moreover, she was in danger of entering the explosive third stage of population growth, threatening the country's development, political stability, and general welfare. This would bring China into the company of the Central American nations and many other rapidly growing underdeveloped lands, except that China's case involves hundreds of millions of people. Those familiar with China's demographic situation found this a frightening prospect.

China's leaders were keenly aware of the country's population size and its enormous potential for growth, but they disagreed on the appropriate solution for the problem. Indeed, some did not even regard it as a problem. The official population policy therefore wavered, depending upon which party faction was in ascendency. The hard-line ideologs took the doctrinaire Marxist and anti–Malthusian view that population size is not a long-run problem, that supporting large numbers of people is merely a matter of mobilizing national resources and distributing the output equitably. To these individuals China's huge population was a source of pride and the main foundation of economic and military strength. This utopian line was the accepted one in the early Chinese Communist period.

In time, as problems mounted, the pragmatists came to prevail in matters of population policy, leading the regime to adopt a birth control program in 1954. This practical outlook experienced a temporary setback during the Great Leap Forward of 1958, when millions were being employed in great construction projects and expansionist ideas were resurfacing. The country's subsequent economic retrenchment, however, brought a return to realism in population policy.

The wisdom of this realistic policy was dramatized by the excesses of the Red Guards during the Cultural Revolution, when masses of these Chinese youth rampaged through the land. Many observers attribute their destructiveness to their frustrations with the inability of China's still underdeveloped economic system to absorb them into roles commensurate with their abilities and training. This episode underscores a serious problem typical of underdeveloped countries where disproportionately large numbers of young persons are entering the labor force at a time of rising expectations.

China's current population policy has as its aim the close control of growth. With birth control the official line, the country is taking strenuous measures resembling those employed earlier by Japan, including all methods for restricting fertility. Every type of contraception is provided; the pill is freely available every-

where, and sterilization and abortion are practiced legally. Malthus would have derived particular satisfaction from the Chinese use of social pressures to postpone marriage—the minimum acceptable ages are 25 for women and 28 for men. More direct still is the official practice of limiting family ration cards to cover only four persons: the father, mother, and two children. As a consequence, China appears to have gained better control over population growth. If this is true, it is a remarkable achievement for a newly developing nation, suggesting that it is possible for a Type 2 country to skip the explosive third period and go directly into the moderating fourth category.

population redistribution

In modern times, China's population pattern has remained remarkably stable. Although the Communist era has produced very large internal migrations of people, these movements have been overwhelmingly of a short-range character. Another characteristic of population movements in Communist China is the strict official control exercised through the government's registration program, in effect since 1958. Indeed, much of China's internal population flow has represented forced migrations in accordance with official programs, which contrast with Indonesia's government-sponsored but voluntary migrations to outlying parts of the country.

Since falling under Communist control, China experienced significant interregional migrations only during the early years when the Soviet influence was strong. It is interesting to note, however, that, although the first five-year plan called for development of the interior, only 1 percent of the population actually went west. There have been no important interprovincial shifts since the Russians departed. Indeed, the largest movements of the Communist era have been urban-rural population transfers, which have produced flows in both directions. A great influx into China's cities occurred at the outset, when Soviet planners were promoting large-scale industrial growth in a limited number of major centers at a time when rural underemployment was worsening.

As in other underdeveloped countries experiencing industrial growth, the flood of rural migrants into the cities caused many problems for the Chinese and conflicted with Mao's bias against urban life. When they reasserted mastery over their own planning operations, the Chinese regime undertook a program of forced deurbanization, partly as a solution to the problem of unemployed educated youth. With 23 million graduating from secondary schools and institutions of higher learning between 1961 and 1966, the urban labor market became saturated. Furthermore, the rising numbers of young people intensified the shortages of consumer goods in urban areas.

Under Mao's "go-to-the-countryside campaign" the government undertook the forced resettlement of educated youth. The program systematically assigned graduates to rural areas, overcoming their reluctance to leave the cities by transferring their household registrations to the new locations, thus depriving them of any way to get ration coupons elsewhere. As its rationale for this arbitrary action the regime observed that the transfer served to close the gap between manual and mental labor and to reduce rural-urban differences. The leadership also reasoned that the educated youth could provide a service to their country by helping to diffuse modern agricultural technology, operating modern farm implements and machinery, taking part in the administration of agricultural producing units, teaching in rural primary and secondary schools and adult literacy programs, and sponsoring cultural activities. After the Cultural Revolution this large-scale transfer of the educated gained momentum, because it provided a means for containing the Red Guards and for isolating youthful obstructionists and other young rebels.

minority policy

An early problem confronting the Chinese Communists was what they term the *great Han chauvinism,* the tendency of Han Chinese to discriminate against minority peoples. Although the latter are a relatively small part of the total population, they occupy large and strategically important border areas. The present regime has developed a policy that proscribes discrimination against minority peoples and seeks to preserve and promote their languages and cultures. To accommodate the largest of these minority groups the government has established five autonomous regions, which, following the Soviet example, are called autonomous republics or ARs.

Communist China's economic growth

Now that China appears to be getting its population increase under control, the total national output of goods and services can be expected to go much farther than it otherwise would. The question that remains is whether the economy has actually experienced any net growth while being administered under the succession of sometimes contradictory and vacillating policies. In attempting to assess China's economic growth, we must remember two things. First, the country has actually had only a few truly normal years during the past two decades, for during most of this period, her economy has had to absorb the shocks of the Korean War, the Great Leap debacle, the Cultural Revolution, and a series of droughts and other natural calamities. These adverse developments have contributed to the erratic growth of the economy during this period when rapid gains alternated with sharp drops.

Second, we should remember that economic growth per se is not the nation's main goal. The Chinese regime is more interested in achieving political stability and strength, eliminating poverty, reforming the economy, and building a cohesive society. For the private citizen

of China the main goals are to gain personal security and freedom from famine, disease, and poverty.

measuring growth

Assessing China's economic growth under the Communists is difficult. Until recently, official data have been skimpy and contradictory; although during earlier years the regime made extravagant claims, it is now more open and frank. China's administered prices have tended to overvalue manufactured goods and to undervalue agricultural commodities. Foreign analysts, *sinologists,* have made numerous attempts to measure China's output, but they differ widely in their estimates.

According to a recent Harvard study, the nation's total output doubled during the recovery period, 1949–1952. Between 1952 and 1972 the economy continued to grow at a more restricted rate, averaging 3.5 percent each year. The main sectors of the economy did not share equally in that growth, however. Between 1952 and 1972 China's agriculture apparently grew at a rate averaging about 2.1 percent per annum, which is about the same as the rate of population growth until recently. During those two decades, industry seems to have grown at an average annual rate of 7.2 percent per year, despite the loss of much output during the Cultural Revolution, when industry became virtually paralyzed. On the other hand, the service sector (including transportation and government) may actually have declined, reflecting wholesale reductions in numbers. It seems likely that the rate of growth in national income has exceeded that of population growth and that per capita incomes must have experienced a gradual rise.

THE EVOLVING SYSTEM

In a land where change once came slowly, if at all, the sudden imposition of a revolutionary new philosophy by a determined group has radically altered the society and economy. In a remarkably short time the new rulers have restructured the economic system and rearranged it spatially. As we turn now to the spatial effects of the events in China since 1949, we are impressed by the inconsistencies in the new directions taken by the regime. Certainly, if China's leaders had continued to follow Soviet advice, the country's internal spatial pattern would have changed drastically; their rejection of that advice has preserved much of the old distribution. Yet, because of China's schismatic leadership, the abrupt change of direction following the departure of the Russians has not been the last such upheaval. The frequent and seemingly quixotic deflections in policy have affected the country's administrative arrangements, agriculture and industry, urban system, and transportation. More recent policy shifts have brought sudden and unexpected realignments in China's external connections, which may yet cause even more sweeping changes in the country's spatial economic system.

administrative organization

Reorganization of the administrative system was one of the first orders of business for the Chinese Communist party. Following a long period of unrest, warlordism, Japanese occupation, and revolution, China's political structure was in shambles. Antiquated regional divisions had caused serious administrative difficulties for the nationalist government, which had lost control of several large regions altogether. The Communists began immediately to reorder the political structure, outlining their basic pattern in the 1954 constitution, which abolished some provinces, reducing the number of first-order administrative units from 35 to 23 and altering the boundaries of others. The most numerous changes of all, however, were at the local levels of administration. Although these revisions affected Old China very little, they substantially modified the peripheral regions. It was largely for reasons of national defense that the Communists gave special attention to outlying areas, especially along the Soviet border, where they revised boundaries and administrative arrangements to strengthen military control from the center. There was also the need to accommodate minority populations, which, although comprising only one-twentieth of the nation's population, occupied 60 percent of the territory, mainly in sensitive border areas. The regime accomplished this by establishing autonomous areas at each level in the hierarchy, depending on the sizes of ethnolinguistic groups.

the administrative hierarchy

Although formally the hierarchy had only two basic levels, an intermediate level has evolved to serve practical needs. The first order includes all those larger or more populous areal units falling directly under national government control: 21 provinces, 5 autonomous regions, and 3 municipalities. Han Chinese are actually numerically superior in all but two of the autonomous regions, Tibet and Sinking, both in the far west. The three municipalities with first-order status in the hierarchy are major cities of special importance because of their size and functions: Peking, the national capital; Tientsin, Peking's outlet to the sea and a major industrial center; and Shanghai, the nation's premier city in population and economic functions.

Next is an intermediate, or subprovincial, level not mentioned in the 1954 constitution but now an integral part of the system. These units, each of which answers directly to the provincial government, are special districts (*ti-ch'ü*), 175 in all; autonomous *chou*, which accommodate smaller groups of minorities than do the autonomous regions, and which are equivalent in size and rank to the special districts; and large cities having populations roughly similar to those of the special districts.

Further down the scale are second-order (county-level) units, which also answer to the provinces. The basic second-order unit is the *hsien*, or county, of which there are about 2,000 in the country as a whole. This same rank in the hierarchy is also given to the autonomous *hsien*, about 70 in all, which accommodate ethno-linguistic minorities having populations roughly equivalent to ordinary counties. In addition, there are about 90 second-order cities, distinquished from intermediate-level centers by their comparative lack of industry and generally smaller populations.

administrative changes

Since the Communist takeover there has been little subsequent change at the provincial level except along the Soviet border. Because of tensions and border incidents between the two countries, the Chinese have altered the boundaries between Inner Mongolia and other provinces, shifting special districts from one to the other as the need arose. Even more numerous have been the changes at lower levels, many of which have resulted from internal political upheavals. The regime discontinued the former local (third-level) units, called *hsiang* (townships), during the Great Leap Forward, at which time the newly forming communes assumed administrative jurisdiction over local rural areas. The Cultural Revolution of the late 1960s also caused some reorganization of lower administrative units.

reorganizing Chinese agriculture

China's development strategy has allocated a key role to agriculture, by contrast with the Soviet Union's neglect of this sector. Since the departure of Soviet advisers, China has not only favored agriculture in its planning but it has emphasized those branches of industry serving agriculture, both in the provision of capital goods and the supplying of consumer goods for the farming population. Among the reasons for this ordering of priorities is the predominance of agriculture in the economy, as the principal contributor to the GNP, the chief source of governmental revenue, and by far the largest employer. Although this might describe the situation in most underdeveloped lands, it is all the more true of China because of the thin margin that separates national food requirements and the available supply.

China's leaders well remember that food shortages have frequently caused civil unrest in the past, and they are conscious of the wretched and precarious state of the farmer throughout modern history. The accelerating population growth that followed the peace of 1949 has further added to the urgency of food shortages. And industrialization is continuing to exact ever greater demands on the farming sector, because it increases the nonagricultural population to be fed, draws upon agriculture for a major source of its developmental capital, and calls for greater amounts of industrial raw materials of agricultural origin. Agriculture is thus the main determinant of China's economic growth. Over and above these urgent economic considerations is Mao Tse-tung's reputed rural bias.

In its efforts to develop China's agriculture, however, the regime confronted a difficult challenge: the shortage of arable land and the meager prospects for significantly increasing that acreage; recurring floods, droughts, and other natural calamities; an entrenched, unwieldy, uneconomic, and unfair land tenure system; and an accumulation of cultural barriers. The Chinese Communist approach to this assortment of problems was, first, to reorganize the farming sector through a wholesale program of land reform and, second, to allocate further resources to agriculture in an effort to expand the output of the land.

socialization of Chinese agriculture

When he came to power, Mao was ready with a program for agrarian reform. He had given considerable study to the national farm problem, as shown by his writings dating to 1926 and 1927; and he had experimented with various solutions during the fugitive period in the Communists' base area in Shensi and Shensi provinces. Despite much forethought on this subject, however, Chinese planning for agriculture since 1949 has vacillated and has fallen victim to a number of serious errors requiring costly correction. First, there was the problem of inadequate financing of agricultural development during the first five-year plan, when the nation's planners still adhered to a Soviet-style stress on heavy industry despite frequent official statements about the importance of agriculture. Only after some disastrous harvests did the planners correct this misallocation of funds. When they got around to reorganizing their agricultural program on a more rational basis, however, their efforts were marred by disruptive and counterproductive schemes, each causing a retrenchment.

The process of socializing Chinese agriculture took place in stages. The immediate aims of land reform were (1) to provide for landless farmers ("land to the tillers") and (2) to destroy the political power of the landlord class, the source of China's prerevolutionary scholar-administrators. To accomplish these ends the Communists first stripped the landlords of all land that they were not themselves actually farming. The regime then divided this surplus, comprising millions of hectares, among the peasants and other landless persons on a per capita, family basis and issued new title deeds. This process engendered intense class hatreds and caused much loss of life. At the end of this phase, completed in 1953, all land was under the control of individual owner-tillers. The results were understandably popular with the impoverished beneficiaries of this redistribution, who were intensely proud of their new land. Because many of these persons were inexperienced managers, however, national farm output fell at a time when the need for more food was becoming still more acute.

In an attempt to solve this managerial problem and also to move subtly closer to socialization, the Communists next instituted *mutual aid teams,* groups of several households working together throughout the season, planting, cultivating, harvesting, and sharing labor, tools and draft animals. The next step was to join together several mutual aid teams on a year-round basis, each group having a leader and an accountant. Although at this point the land was still individually owned, the group made all decisions and accumulated a supply of jointly owned equipment and reclaimed land. Output thereafter began to rise but not fast enough.

Next, the regime introduced *producers' cooperatives,* which were expected to raise production levels and to increase the degree of socialization. The cooperatives evolved in two stages, the first of which appeared in the early 1950s. This elementary stage of agricultural cooperation approached the idea cautiously, stressing the "voluntary" nature of entry into the program or withdrawal from it. Each cooperative joined 20 to 30 households into an economically self-sufficient unit with a central administration that included a chairman, committees, and accountant. Although the members ostensibly made all decisions, party-appointed cadres in fact held firm control. Members contributed land, tools, animals, and their own labor to the enterprise, retaining title to the land ceded to the group and keeping small individual plots for their own use. Production teams of 7 to 10 families performed the work. Cooperatives shared their proceeds among members according to each individual's contributions of land, capital equipment, and labor, the last being reckoned on a basis of "work points."

Agricultural producers' cooperatives, even at this modest scale, offered several advantages. Combining the land of many farmers permitted more economical field sizes and productive units than did the tiny garden-size family units they replaced, making it possible to use better techniques. This organizational arrangement also provided a supply of surplus labor (especially during slack seasons) for such public works as the construction of roads and irrigation systems. The central government in Peking favored this arrangement because it provided the regime with an easier and more direct mechanism for controlling the country's agricultural output. By 1956, 682,000 such cooperatives had formed and national farm production was rising.

Also by that date political pressures were increasing for still more communization of agriculture. Accordingly, a movement began to form *advanced agricultural cooperatives* corresponding to the Soviet Union's collective farms. Each advanced cooperative combined several of the lower-stage cooperatives into units comprising 100 or more households. The collective pooled all this land, abrogated individual titles, and removed the old boundaries, leaving members only small private plots and a few pigs and chickens. Even their tools and draft animals went into the central supply pool.

Members of advanced cooperatives received pay only for their labor, and the amount was determined on the basis of work points; they got nothing for the land they had contributed to the enterprise. Elected chairmen, committees, and other official personnel conducted the collectives' administration; while production brigades, each divided into production teams, carried out the farm work. The collective system provided the Communists with a convenient means for taxation, because each unit was required to contribute 10 percent of its output to the central government in Peking. The regime also instituted a state procurement system under which all surplus produce had to be sold to the government. Despite the bitterness of farmers over the loss of their cherished private ownership of land, the number of such advanced producer collectives grew rapidly, reaching possibly 740,000 by 1957.

Still the Communists were not satisfied, and, incited by the fanaticism of the Great Leap Forward of 1958, they began to form agricultural *communes*. Each commune merged together scores of collectives into *hsiang*-size units (equivalent to a township) consisting of 1,000 to 5,000 households. In agricultural regions the communes assumed total administrative control at the local level: government, agriculture, industry, and commerce, education, military defense, and the construction of large public works. Communes are organized in a hierarchical arrangement, with the production team at the lowest level, the production brigade next, and the commune as a whole at the top. An elected legislative body, the commune delegates conference, makes general policy for the commune, while a commune management committee performs executive functions.

The first communes permitted members to retain only their most personal possessions, discontinuing all private gardening plots. The commune owned all housing, provided free food at communal kitchens, and paid for all work according to the need of the individual. So deep was the resentment of commune members at the loss of their private plots, and so poor was the quality of commune management, that China's agricultural production slumped during this period. In the general reassessment that followed the failure of the Great Leap, communes were reduced in size (usually by subdivision) and farming decisions were allocated to production teams of 20 to 40 neighboring families (88 to 176 people on the average) rather than to the commune as a whole. Communes also restored private plots to their members, who currently produce an estimated one-quarter of the country's agricultural output on these tiny patches of land. For their labor on behalf of the commune, members receive payment based on work points but are mostly paid in kind. Families have also resumed living and eating privately rather than in communal style. In 1971 communes cultivated 92 percent of China's arable land, selling 20 percent of their output to the state and paying taxes generally in kind. China now has 50,000 communes, averaging about 1,900 hectares (4,700 acres) of arable land each.

Throughout this period when cooperatives were evolving into communes, the Communist regime was establishing another form of agricultural unit, the *state farm*. The first few began operations in 1949; today the total has reached more than 2,000, occupying almost 4 percent of China's acreage and employing nearly 2 percent of the rural population. The state farm is the very antithesis of traditional Chinese agriculture: each farm covers an immense acreage, is divided into very large fields, and uses extensive, mechanized farming practices, with an emphasis upon large-scale grain, cotton, or animal production. The state farm is like a factory in the organization of its management and its employment of wage laborers. At the outset state farms provided a way of increasing badly needed output in the shortest time. They have since served a number of other purposes: as demonstration farms to introduce new techniques to communes, as the principal means of reclaiming wasteland, and as a way of resettling populations. State farms are most numerous in the west and in border and coastal areas.

increasing agricultural output

Farm production was at a dangerously low level in 1949 as a result of war destruction of irrigation works, the uprooting of farm populations during the fighting, and the general disruption of farm routines. One of the first orders of business, therefore, was the reconstruction of Chinese agriculture, which again reached prewar levels of production by 1953, when the first five-year plan began. The official agricultural strategy that evolved during the next few years called for more intensive use of land and labor but without the addition of modern capital inputs; in short, it attempted to develop agriculture by exploiting the growth potential of traditional farming. The results of this approach were poor and output barely kept up with population growth. Moreover, by 1957 the potential for growth by traditional means was pretty well exhausted as increased labor inputs gave diminishing returns.

Failure of the Great Leap in 1958 and 1959 forced the Communists to reevaluate their farm policy, especially since agricultural stagnation was beginning to hold back the progress of industrialization. The result of this reassessment was the decision to restructure the allocation of national investment resources. From the early 1960s onward, therefore, the regime channeled increasing amounts of modern capital into agriculture: expanding rural electrification, increasing factory output of modern farm implements, mechanical pumps, chemical fertilizers, and other farm needs, and deploying these throughout the countryside. Let us now look more closely at each of these approaches to increased farm output and see how the country's leaders eventually arrived at their present strategy.

One of the first things the Communists tried during their period of dependence upon traditional methods was to expand the country's arable acreage. In their campaign to reclaim land in areas of marginal agricultural production, they claimed to have effected a 3.6 percent increase in arable acreage during the first five-year plan. In the 18 provinces of Old China the opportunities for reclamation by the usual means were severely limited; indeed, farmers in this part of the country had, in the past, often expanded their arable lands too far. Land more appropriate for forests or grass under existing technology went under the plow, causing wind and water erosion, floods, and stream silting.

New approaches, however, offered more promise for the long-settled lands of Old China. By mobilizing a large work force, the farm population could undertake massive projects beyond the capabilities of farmers working individually. They built large numbers of terraces, so that hill land could be farmed without eroding and so that water runoff could be controlled. They reclaimed wet lands for agricultural use by drainage projects. Lastly, they removed graves from good farmland to wasteland, thus releasing for productive use the almost 2 percent of China's arable acreage that family burial plots formerly occupied. With the accomplishing of these objectives, the farmers of Old China soon exhausted their limited number of opportunities for making new farmland.

It is in the outlying areas, therefore, that China has been able to add most of its new arable acreage. The longstanding problems of the peripheral regions of the northeast, the north, the northwest, and the southwest have been excessive aridity, severe winters, short growing seasons, isolation, and primitive minority populations. In these parts of the country the need was clearly for more capital, in the form of machinery and large irrigation works, and modern agricultural technology.

In the northeast, Manchuria offered wide expanses of virgin steppelands with rich soil. The problems there were the severe winters and strong winds, which made agriculture precarious before the introduction of new fast-maturing crops and techniques for averting wind damage to soils. With the introduction of such innovations as these, this part of the country has made the largest contribution of all, with 27 percent of the nation's reclaimed land appearing in the border province of Heilungkiang alone. Here are many of Communist China's state farms, very large enterprises that grow grains by extensive, mechanized methods like those of North America's western plains and prairies.

Neighboring Inner Mongolia had some of these same problems, in addition to its chronic shortage of moisture. The new regime established agricultural cooperatives and communes, which were supplied with irrigation water from thousands of wells and meltwater from the snowfields of nearby mountains. In this manner China's spring wheat region has been extended outward into the traditional grazing lands of Mongol tribesmen. In harmony with the official policy of agricultural diversification, this area produces not only wheat but other grains, as well as fiber crops, vegetables, and fruits.

Sinkiang province, in the far northwest, contains some of China's driest deserts; but it also has many oases, some dating back more than 2,000 years, along the upper courses of rivers flowing from the mountains. Since 1949 this area of mainly Turkic folk has received a large influx of Han Chinese, part of a government-sponsored migration from the overcrowded east. State farms, operating at a large scale and using mechanized equipment, produce wheat and other grains, along with cotton, sugar beets, and livestock. Similarly, the government has introduced arable farming into some of the more promising valleys of southern Tibet.

Even these lightly populated, remoter parts of the country offer only limited possibilities for increased agricultural use. China's planners therefore realized at an early date that expanding the nation's acreage by reclamation would soon reach a point of diminishing returns, and they have increasingly concentrated their efforts upon getting a greater output from existing land. The official program for agricultural intensification was expressed in an Eight-Point Charter, which instructed all farmers to observe these essentials: water conservation, fertilization, soil conservation, seed selection, dense planting, plant protection, tool improvement, and field management.

At the heart of the water problems of eastern China is the paradoxical alternation of devastating floods with severe droughts, all the more damaging because the country's most productive agriculture is of a hydraulic nature. The Communist regime has therefore stressed water control, promoting both large and small public works programs to contain flood waters, to store them, and to channel them into productive agricultural uses. At the same time they have pushed irrigation projects as a means for extracting more food and fiber from the soil. The chief beneficiary of these programs has been rice culture, although most other crops have also responded favorably. Not only does irrigation increase the output per crop but it often permits the Chinese to harvest two or more crops from the same land in a given year.

All parts of China are participating in the irrigation programs. In the arid lands gravitational methods are most common—the usual canal-channel-sluice gate arrangement—along with the use of electric and diesel pumps to move water directly up from streams into fields or from wells in those places at a distance from rivers. Irrigation of hilly lands often entails construction of retaining ponds at the heads of valleys from which the water descends to one terrace field after another. Today many large reservoirs are being built in the mountains to provide a larger and more dependable supply. The plains areas depend mainly on wells for their irrigation water.

The use of fertilizer is another old method of expanding output that is receiving even greater emphasis today than in the past. The traditional way of maintaining soil fertility was by laboriously collecting, processing, and applying organic materials, especially night soil (human excreta), despite its tendency to breed disease. Other organic fertilizers used by the Chinese are animal manures, particularly from pigs, and composts made of all kinds of organic wastes, mud from ponds, and green manures obtained by plowing under young leguminous plants.

Because these sources of soil enrichment have proved inadequate, the regime has turned more and more to the use of chemical fertilizers. Although manufactured fertilizers were too costly for China's peasants before 1949, the Chinese are today making their own ammonia and urea fertilizers in increasingly large quantities, along with phosphorus fertilizers, especially needed in the warm and humid south. Because of the inadequacy of local transportation in much of China and the overloaded railway system, the government is emphasizing the construction of many small fertilizer plants in each region. Even so, it has been necessary to import large quantities of chemical fertilizers, and the quantity of such foreign purchases continues to grow. In spite of the high priority given to fertilizer use, the country still applies only one-fourth as much as the United States does.

Another program China's leaders are stressing is the development and selection of better seeds. The country now has an estimated 1,700 seed-breeding centers and continues to import new varieties from abroad. Most of this attention goes to five main grain crops— rice, wheat, corn, kaoliang, and millet, especially rice and wheat—which are being bred to mature more quickly in areas of short growing seasons, as in the northeast and southern Tibet.

Although most Chinese still farm with the same tools they have used for two millennia—the hoe, sickle, and iron-tipped plow—the regime is promoting farm mechanization as a way of getting more out of the land. In the early years state farms were the first to receive new machinery, much of it imported from eastern Europe. Communes must still improvise new equipment in their own workshops, pursuing a policy of semi-mechanization based on the expanded output of improved types of traditional hand tools and animal-drawn equipment. Nevertheless, since the Great Leap, the nation's industry has stressed production for the needs of agriculture: pumps, sprayers, combines, plows, carts, seeders and drills, cultivators, and tractors, predominantly garden-size. Progress has been slow, however; the country still has only 1 tractor for about 2,250 acres as opposed to 1 for every 57 acres in the United States.

The Eight-Point Charter emphasizes the use of new farming techniques, including the close planting of crops to get more plants per acre. Although this should theoretically give a larger output, it can do so only if large amounts of fertilizer are applied and the land is plowed deeply. But fertilizer and power equipment needed for pulling plows continue to be in short supply, a problem only partly solved by intercropping.

Finally, the regime has undertaken an agricultural diversification program involving not only new crops and new strains but also a greater variety of production within each area, with the aim of increasing total output and ensuring against crop failures. Rice culture has been expanded into newly irrigated areas; and new strains of wheat, corn, kaoliang, and rice specially adapted to sometimes severe local growing conditions are being introduced in a number of areas that could not grow these crops before. The new irrigation works have also made it possible for the area of cotton culture to expand, along with other commercial fibers, various oilseeds, and sugar beets. The regime has also promoted sugar cane production in the subtropical south and has revived the production of such specialty crops as tea and silk worms in a number of places.

Old China has only limited numbers of farm animals. The main exception is swine, which have become the subject of an organized government program aimed at supplying each household with two or three pigs to provide much needed protein in the diet and manure for the soil. Today official policy calls for reserving a certain amount of grain, oilseed cake and meal, and other feed to supplement the scraps traditionally given to pigs. The government also encourages pig production in a number of other ways. Except for highly efficient meat-converting animals like swine and chickens, the Chinese have done little to develop animal industries in the eastern part of the country, where land is too valuable for use as pasture.

Only in the arid and sparsely settled peripheral regions can the Chinese afford to spare land for grazing. About two-thirds of the national territory is of this type, notably Inner Mongolia, Sinkiang, and Tibet, where nomadic herding has been the main way of life for millennia. This subsistence activity has been the main occupation of minority peoples, who have no link to the national economy, society, or political life. Communist policy, as in the Soviet Union, has been to settle the nomads, bring them into the national economy, and increase their animal output to provide a surplus of food and fiber for the rest of the country.

The official program has succeeded in increasing animal numbers in these regions by increasing the water supply and providing supplementary forage crops, irrigated pastures, winter fodder, animal shelters for the long, cold winters, control of animal diseases, and new, more productive breeds. In Inner Mongolia, for example, the government has drilled deep wells and supplied power pumps to provide drinking water for human beings and animals and irrigation for forage crops; it has also reseeded pastures and introduced fine-wool sheep and promoted cattle breeding. The cattle are improved types that are increasing the output of beef in that region, some of which goes to local canning plants. Dairy herds are also supplying new processing plants that make powdered and condensed milk, butter, and cheese.

Meanwhile, Sinkiang's upland pastures, nourished by snow melt-water and by the natural precipitation that falls on these upper slopes, now carry fine-wool sheep of the better British varieties. These are also good meat animals, which have a high propagation rate and yield five times as much wool as the indigenous types. At lower elevations in Tibet, the land is also used mainly for sheep grazing. Here special crossbreeds have been introduced because of their adaptability to local conditions. Veterinary services are raising the survival rate of lambs, many of which are grown on stock-breeding cooperatives. The increased output of animal products by the pastoralists of the west is providing a surplus for exchange with local farming oases and for shipment to the east. Nomadism is ending in these areas and the tribal people are being settled in houses and provided with education and with medical services. The animal industries of the north and west have not entirely solved their problems, however; the increase in animal numbers, for example, has caused serious overgrazing. Although there is a general shortage of large animals, especially draft animals, in the country as a whole, China is working hard to remedy this.

results of the farm program

An assessment of Communist China's progress in agriculture thus far indicates net gains in arable acreage, yields, and total output; but it also underscores the long way that the country has to go before achieving a truly secure food supply. By placing even greater stress on the old-time practice of multiple-cropping, the Chinese are now sowing 40 percent more land per year than the total of their arable acreage. Although they have only 264 million acres available for crops, they are actually sowing 371 million acres each year. By comparison, the United States, which has one-quarter of its arable land lying fallow, has 386 million acres available but sows only 287 million acres in crops in an average year. Despite the strenuous efforts to increase yields described above, however, China is still unable to achieve more than half the output per acre that the United States averages, mainly because of China's fertilizer shortages.

Although China annually plants a total grain acreage almost twice that of the United States, the two countries harvest about the same amounts in total. China produces mainly *food* grains, using between 80 and 90 percent of the output directly for human consumption, whereas the United States plants mostly *feed* grains for animals. The American people consume only 15 percent of their grain output directly, feeding the rest to livestock or exporting it. China's grain production is inadequate and necessitates massive imports.

The nation's oilseed crop occupies an acreage about 80 percent that of the United States, but total output is less than half of the American amount. China slightly exceeds the United States in production of cottonseed, sunflower seeds, castor beans, peanuts, rapeseed, and sesame seed but obtains only one-fourth as much soybean output as the United States. Cotton output, predominantly short-staple, is four-fifths of United States production and is hardly enough to provide for China's clothing needs. Because the regime assigns a high priority to cotton, second only to grains, production is growing steadily. China produces about four-fifths as much cane sugar as the United States and approximately one-fifth as much beet sugar. The country has only half as many cattle as the United States and uses the majority of them for draft purposes. There are three times as many hogs and sheep in China, however, and their numbers are increasing rapidly. It is estimated that hog numbers rose 4.5 times between 1949 and 1972, while sheep and goats increased 3.5 times and draft animals by 60 percent.

Despite this progress and the intensive efforts to obtain it, China's agricultural output has not grown nearly fast enough. Total farm production apparently grew at about 2.2 percent per annum between 1952 and 1972, about the same as the rate of population growth. This growth fluctuated greatly between the two years, however, rising at a 4.3 percent annual rate up until 1959 but only 1.5 percent each year since. Within the latter period there were temporary setbacks caused by failure of the Great Leap (1959–1960), severe drought (1960–1961), and the Cultural Revolution (1966–1969). Although overall results are therefore not impressive so far, the country has nevertheless had a more equitable distribution of food and at higher per capita consumption levels, thanks to these modest increases in output, accompanied recently by falling population growth rates and very large grain imports.

other rural land uses

Originally most of China proper and the northeast were covered with forests, which were felled at an early date by the Han Chinese to make way for their intensive form of agriculture. Since those early years, growing population pressures have caused even hillsides to be stripped of every bit of vegetation for use as fuel (in a land with great coal reserves). By 1949, only 5 percent of China's national territory was forested and much of this was in inaccessible mountainous areas. Meanwhile the country was starved for fuel and building materials.

The Communist regime has given much attention to afforestation, beginning with an education program for the peasants. In Old China they had to teach farmers about the role of trees in holding moisture and reducing floods, erosion, and droughts; in western China they had to demonstrate the value of trees planted as shelter belts to reduce wind damage and conserve moisture and the ability of grasses and shrubs to contain shifting sands. The government directed communes to undertake tree-planting programs and promoted large-scale afforestation projects among the population as a whole.

The campaign generated an enthusiastic response, especially among the youth, who planted great shelter belts in the uplands of the northeast (Great Green Wall). Peasants planted shelter belts around their villages and set out trees along the dikes and in sandy waste areas of the North China Plain. Tree planting has taken place even in areas not originally forested, such as the loess region of North China and parts of the arid west. State farms of Inner Mongolia and Sinkiang and some oasis settlements have planted shelter belts. Forests destroyed during the war in parts of Szechwan and central China were restored, and many valuable fruit, nut and oil-bearing trees are being planted in the south and along the coast.

The country's wood products industry has already benefited from these programs. Today the northeast is supplying 60 percent of the nation's lumber; and the mountain forests of northern Szechwan, formerly too remote for exploitation, are now able to ship large quantities of wood products over newly constructed rail lines. The campaign to restore China's trees has apparently doubled the amount of forest land, but it has a long way to go before the national need for wood is satisfied.

industrialization

Like the other underdeveloped countries we have examined, China is in great need of industries, if only to provide employment for the massive annual additions to her labor force. There is also a need for import-substituting manufacture, as a way of reducing the drain on foreign reserves caused by unavoidable purchases abroad. Because China, unlike the USSR, has no personal income taxes, she also has to have the additional governmental revenue that taxes on industries provide. Finally, Communist China, with her seige mentality, regards industrialization as an indispensible foundation for military strength.

mobilizing industrial resources

The immediate aim of the new regime was to rebuild the country's war-damaged factories, a task that proceeded so rapidly that 1943 levels of industrial output were exceeded by 1952. The country's stated long-range goals were:

1. to make China an advanced industrial nation within 15 years
2. to redistribute manufacturing in such a way to overcome the heavy imbalance favoring the coastal provinces and port cities
3. to socialize the manufacturing sector.

The Communists achieved their first governmental penetration of the economy between 1949 and 1952, when they seized the banks, took over all wholesaling, and established state trading companies. Socialization of industry accelerated during the first five-year plan to the extent that private control of manufacturing had virtually ended by 1956 and was replaced by direction from ministries in Peking. Meanwhile the regime had converted the many domestic handicraft operations into cooperatives.

One of the main tasks in all this, as in any underdeveloped country, was to mobilize the factors of production. In their energetic search for industrial raw materials, the Chinese were well rewarded by the discovery that their large national territory is much better endowed with minerals than had previously been thought. Looking for developmental capital, the Communists immediately seized all Japanese assets, as well as those belonging to China's indigenous propertied classes. They generated further funds from the profits of state industries and taxes on cooperatives, communes, and other enterprises. The Chinese also borrowed from the Soviet Union, although they obtained only one-thirtieth of their annual needs for developmental capital from this source, which had dried up by 1960. Even though capital was always severely short, the Chinese Communists managed to sustain a relatively high rate of reinvestment.

The one factor of production that was never in short supply, of course, was manpower. China's only labor problem was the scarcity of industrial skills, which had not been a part of traditional Chinese education. To remedy this lack the Chinese established technical colleges and institutes, which have since largely overcome the initial shortage of skills. The Communists ensured high levels of labor productivity by subjecting workers to concentrated political indoctrination and by using strong social pressures to remind laggards of their patriotic duty.

Equally serious was the scarcity of skilled managers, made all the worse by the emigration of experienced entrepreneurs who had been the targets of class warfare. The Communists compounded this problem by undermining professional managers' authority during such ideological upheavals as the Cultural Revolution, anarchical tendencies finally brought into check only by the army's presence. During the past quarter century of Communist control, decision making in the factories has evolved into a system somewhat like Japan's. Although a revolutionary committee composed of elected workers, party members, and army representatives comprises the usual management of a factory, no decision becomes final until all the workers have engaged in group discussions of the problem.

structural and locational shifts

The allocation of resources between industrial sectors and between regions has caused much disagreement among Communist party factions. During the period of Soviet influence, as we have seen, production planning and management resided ultimately in Peking, where each branch of manufacturing fell within the jurisdiction of a particular ministry. Capital goods constituted only 29 percent of pre–Communist industrial output, but under Soviet direction the first five-year plan allocated nine-tenths of total industrial investment to this class of manufacture. During that period the Chinese had a strong incentive for such specialization because heavy industry covers most military production, a major concern at a time when the Korean War was in progress. The national reassessment of development strategies following the Great Leap debacle, which coincided with acute shortages of food and agricultural raw materials, brought a change in industrial priorities. Without sacrificing national military capabilities, manufacturing was to concentrate on making agricultural machinery, fertilizer, and irrigation and drainage equipment.

Views on manufacturing location also changed during this era. Following Soviet theory, China's official policy called for regional specialization of production (to the extent that this did not conflict with national plans for fuels, raw materials, and transportation) together with intraregional self-sufficiency within the broad framework of interregional trade. Industries were also to locate as close as possible to raw materials, fuels, and markets to make full use of local resources, reduce production costs, and minimize transport costs—a Weberian approach to location, despite Marxist contempt for such capitalistic theories. Chinese policy at first insisted on achieving a balance between new and established economic bases by developing remote and backward areas while continuing to strengthen old areas. Finally, planners were to choose locations in accordance with national security considerations.

China's leaders abandoned, or at least deferred, some of these requirements when the Soviet influence waned. They suspended the inland development program, although still regarding it as an ultimate goal, and turned their immediate attention to the established industrial regions, where their limited capital would produce the quickest return. In effect, the Chinese were shortening the time-frame of their planning. Simultaneously, however, they began their efforts to reduce the concentration of industry in the largest centers by promoting small-scale, labor-intensive industries in every locality, each with links to large plants for the exchange of raw materials and technicians. Localities were thus to become relatively self-contained, providing many of their own industrial needs and supplying jobs for the endless stream of young people entering the labor force. The deconcentration program was widely implemented, causing a myriad of local industries to spring up throughout the countryside and in nearly every rural commune. China's revised locational policy also called for a diversification in operations, meaning that each large, modern factory should develop into a comprehensive enterprise making not just one but a wide range of products. Let us now see how these events affected certain key industries.

energy production

China's leaders have given the production of energy a central place in their planning. The country is able to draw upon an ample natural endowment, even though deposits are not always in the most convenient locations. The Communists have made extensive use of the large reserves of coal, which now supply 90 percent of

the nations's primary energy. Industry generally takes 35 percent of the output of coal, the basic fuel for thermal electric generation and for the iron and steel and other metallurgical industries. The railways use nearly one-tenth and households the remaining 50 percent. Although China has invested heavily in modern coal-mining installations, the regime currently encourages the opening of many small mines to provide local self-sufficiency in mechanical energy. Despite severe setbacks caused by the Great Leap and Cultural Revolution, coal production has risen steeply throughout the Communist era, from only 32.4 million metric tons in 1949 to about 300 million tons in 1970. Even so, shortages of coal still persist. The major producing areas today are the northeast, with 30 percent of the total; the north, with 25 percent; and the east, with 20 percent.

Spurred by the importance of oil to modern military machines, the Chinese have made a strenuous effort to find petroleum deposits. During much of the 1950s large new oil fields in the far northwest supplied most of the nation's needs, despite the remoteness of these fields and the high cost of transporting their product to the eastern markets. Large finds in the northeast and east have partially relieved the country of this burden. Shale oil, developed in Manchuria by the Japanese, still provides one-tenth of the total.

By 1952, after having regained prewar levels, China's oil output quadrupled during the next five years, tripled again by 1960, and has continued to climb since. Being a capital-intensive industry, oil production was unaffected by the Great Leap or Cultural Revolution. The country is currently self-sufficient in oil, although total production is still not very great for so large a country—hardly more than the output of Mexico. At present more than half of China's oil comes from the Ta-Ch'ing field, opened in the northeast in 1960. The northeast as a whole supplies two-thirds of the national total, and another one-fourth still comes from the distant western fields. Although refining takes place mainly in the major centers of consumption, especially old coastal sites such as Shanghai, some of it occurs in field refineries and at such transport centers as Lanchou (see Fig. 23.6).

Nine-tenths of the electricity generated in China goes to industry; only modest amounts are consumed by households and other users, despite the fairly widespread availability of installed capacity. Although the water power potential is very great and is well located, China has been slow to develop it because of its large capital requirements. The Chinese have build multipurpose dams on some of the larger streams, but they are also promoting the installation of many small local units. Consequently, there are innumerable miniature generators throughout the countryside, operating irrigation and drainage pumps and providing for other rural power needs. China now manufactures her own generators and other electrical equipment formerly imported from the USSR and eastern Europe.

The country has three major power grids: one

in Manchuria and the northeast, which carries 35 percent of the nation's electric power; another in the Peking-Tientsin region of the north, with 15 percent; and a third in the Shanghai-Nanking region, with 20 percent—as well as a number of lesser systems. China's electric power generation increased tenfold between 1949 and the Great Leap Forward (1958–1960), rose by another third by 1970, and is still climbing.

metal industries

The iron and steel industry is vital to the Chinese, as a basis for defense production and national development generally. The country has a plentiful supply of ore, coal, and ferro-alloys. The problem of quality control, which has plagued the industry in the past, especially in the many small workshops, is now said to have been solved. The larger installations use modern, advanced technology, including oxygen converters.

The country's only integrated iron and steel works in 1949 was at An-shan in Manchuria. It had been started during World War I, further developed by the Japanese in the 1930s, and dismantled by the occupying Russians at the close of World War II. Elsewhere in Nationalist China there had been only a few small, nonintegrated works. The highest output of the prerevolutionary period was a meager 900,000 metric tons. When the Communists assumed control, they rebuilt and expanded the An-shan plants and erected lesser mills in other regions, attaining a total output of 5.4 million tons by 1957.

During the Great Leap Forward, the Communists pushed iron and steel production to the utmost, for their stated aim was to surpass the United Kingdom in steel output within 15 years. They constructed two large new integrated works—Wuhan, upstream on the Yangtze, and Pao-t'ou, Inner Mongolia—integrated the operations at other previously specialized mills, including those at Peking and Shanghai, and established a number of other smaller integrated plants at various places. It was also at this time that the regime promoted primitive handicraft (backyard) furnaces, 2 million in all, in the rural communes. Raw steel output reached 13 million tons during the Great Leap period but dropped to 8 million tons immediately afterwards.

Steel production again reached 13 million tons in 1966, fell during the Cultural Revolution, then rose to 23 million tons in 1972. According to recent estimates, the 1974 production reached 26 million tons, a landmark figure indicating that China has at last attained her interim goal of surpassing the United Kingdom in steel manufacture. In the mid–1970s China's modern steel industry is concentrated in three main areas: the northeast, with 40 percent of the national total; the north (including Inner Mongolia), 25 percent; and the eastern (especially Shanghai) and central regions (mainly Wuhan), 14 percent each.

China also has good supplies of the raw materials for nonferrous metal production. Though hampered by a shortage of electricity for refining, aluminum output grew from 39,000 tons in 1957 to 230,000 tons in 1970, half of this total coming from smelters in the northeast and east. Similarly, copper production rose from 9,300 tons in 1952 to 281,000 tons in 1970. Two-thirds came from the western provinces.

The metal fabricating industries are also vital to the country's developmental strategy and military preparedness. When the Soviet Union cut off China from her previous supply of imported metal products, the nation's planners established self-sufficiency as a critical goal in this industry. China's metalworking industries have had to solve a number of problems: inadequate investment funds (essential for these capital-intensive enterprises), shortages of scientific and engineering manpower, lack of specialized management skills, and insufficient advanced technology.

The manufacture of transport equipment is one fabricating industry in which the Chinese have attained a degree of self-sufficiency. Like the Russians, the Chinese emphasize the manufacture of commercial vehicles —trucks, buses, and tractors. Following the first significant production of trucks in 1957, China's output reached 75,000 units in 1970 and has risen steadily since. Ninety percent of the nation's trucks are manufactured in the northeast and east. Farm tractor production is distributed widely throughout the agricultural regions, and tractors are made in all sizes, although small, garden-sizes predominate. Less important in the national developmental strategy is passenger car manufacture, which has progressed but little. Recently, however, an assembly plant opened at Ch'ang-ch'un, and smaller operations have commenced in both the northeast and the east.

Because of China's dependence upon rail transportation, the manufacture of locomotives and railway cars is an essential industry, concentrated mainly in the heavy-industry centers of the northeast, north, and east. Today, as in the past, Shanghai leads in shipbuilding and repair, followed by Dairen, Canton, and a few other port cities.

Although China made very little machinery before the Revolution, the Communists have given this industry high priority, especially since the departure of the Russians, who had supplied China previously. Output rose from only 28,300 machine tools in 1957 to more than 50,000 in 1970. Like much of China's industry, machinery manufacture is oriented mainly to its sources of raw materials. Three-fourths of the machine output is in the big industrial centers of the northeast and east, especially such steelmaking cities as Mukden (Shen-yang) and An-shan. Harbin (Ha-erh-pin) also makes heavy machinery, as do several other Manchurian cities. Wuhan, the big steel center on the Yangtze, also makes heavy machinery. The manufacture of instruments, precision equipment, bearings, and other highly engineered items appears to be concentrated in centers such as Shanghai, which offer large pools of skilled labor and access to related forms of production.

other heavy industry

The chemical industry began slowly in China, just as it did in the USSR, but it has gained substantially with the increased demand for chemical fertilizers and the growing supply of petroleum. During their occupation of Manchuria the Japanese had started a coal chemical industry based on coke oven byproducts in the steel centers. In the Communist era the main growth of chemical production has come since the early 1960s, when the drive for increased farm output placed heavy pressures on the fertilizer industry.

Although the major coal-chemical and petrochemical plants of China are close to their raw material sources, fertilizer manufacture is more widespread than are most Chinese industries. In addition to the large modern plants making nitrogenous and phosphatic fertilizers, which are often in chemical complexes like those at Kirin, Shanghai, Nanking, and Lan-chow, there are many small and medium-size local plants scattered throughout the main agricultural regions. More than two-fifths of total fertilizer output is said to come from these smaller, market-oriented establishments. Since 1966, China's fertilizer production, along with insecticide, herbicide, and other farm chemical production, has more than doubled.

In recent years, China's main petrochemical industry has expanded, especially in those centers having large refineries, notably Shanghai, Dairen, and Lanchou. The rapidly growing number of chemical products manufactured in China now includes plastics, many kinds of pharmaceuticals, and a wide range of consumer products.

Spurred by a rising demand from the construction industry, China's cement production increased sixfold during the two decades following the start of the first five-year plan (1952), and it has accelerated since. Along with most other modern production, the industry was located mainly in the northeast in 1949 and at least 25 percent of it is still there. Much like the chemical fertilizer industry, however, cement plants are springing up throughout the country. The cheap, bulky raw materials for cement manufacture are not economical to transport over long distances, but they are common and plentiful in most parts of China. As a result, perhaps 40 percent of current cement output comes from small, local establishments.

One industry that is not specifically identified in official communications is defense production. In view of China's uneasy relations with the Soviet Union and past hostility toward much of the non-Communist world, the nation's leaders have pressed the development of war related production. The country's potential for military production is tied closely to her capabilities in ferrous and nonferrous metallurgy and in heavy machinery and machine tool manufacture. China's recent advances in the production of nuclear weapons and military jet aircraft also indicate growing capabilities in the manufacture of precision instruments and electronics.

As evidence of increasing technical sophistication, China now makes digital computers and electron accelerators (both important for the nuclear program), electron microscopes, semiconductors, and a wide range of other advanced electronic equipment. Two sections of the country dominate this kind of production: the east (principally Shanghai and Nanking) and the north (mainly Peking and Tientsin).

consumer products

As a percentage of total industrial output, consumer products have declined considerably during the Communist era. This suggests the low priority given to this kind of production by China's current leaders, who continuously exhort their people to work hard and live ascetically. Planners make an exception to this policy, however, for those consumer goods that are absolutely necessary, particularly staple items of clothing and food. Moreover, the regime is making some effort to improve living standards, which have been exceedingly low, by supplying a greater variety of goods.

Because of the great domestic demand for cotton textiles, from which most of the clothing for the masses is made, the Communists have given a high place in national planning to this commodity. Before 1949 most of the country's modern mills were in the east coast ports of Shanghai, Tientsin, and Tsingtao. In addition there was a widespread cottage industry engaged in the spinning and weaving of cotton. Because this domestic output was still not sufficient to clothe the hundreds of millions of Chinese, the country also had to import both raw cotton and cotton cloth.

Under communism, as we have seen, the cultivated area under cotton has expanded into many new areas, providing a much larger domestic supply of raw cotton fiber. At the same time, the regime has established new cotton textile mills in a number of new localities. Most of these are raw-material oriented. Unlike the United States and other cotton-growing countries that also make cotton cloth, China has built her most recent mills in areas producing the fiber. Meanwhile, the Chinese have had to modernize and enlarge their older coastal mills to accommodate the growing need, with the result that the coastal zone still produces 45 percent of the nation's cloth. Despite a 55 percent increase in total output between 1966 and 1972, cotton cloth is still in short supply. The Chinese make all types of cotton textiles, but they concentrate mainly on the coarser materials used by peasants.

The world monopoly in silk that China once held has long since been lost to competing producers and to synthetics. The present regime is attempting to revive the silk industry, particularly in the old east coast areas of production in Chekiang and Kiangsu provinces. Meanwhile, with the advent of petrochemicals, synthetic fiber manufacture has become established in the country. Shanghai, Peking, and Shenyang are prominent in this fast-growing industry, although it is spreading to other places. A major import point for Australian wool, Shanghai also leads in woolen textile manufacture. A new woolen industry is developing in the far northwest, where domestic breeds of fine-wool sheep are now coming into production.

In a land where the great majority are self-sufficient farmers, food processing exists mainly to supply the 20 percent who live in cities; yet in China even that relatively small group of urban dwellers is equivalent to the entire population of the United States! Like most of China's food industries, sugar refining takes place in the raw material source areas: the sugar beet regions of the north and northeast and the irrigated oases of the far northwest, and the sugar cane districts of the coastal provinces of the south. Two-thirds of the output is from large modern mills, and the remainder is produced in small local operations. Flour milling in Nationalist China began in Harbin and subsequently spread to other parts of the northeast and the east coast, particularly Tientsin and Shanghai, import points for North American wheat. With the increase in domestic wheat output, modern flour mills have appeared throughout China's northern wheat belt. Dairying, which was poorly developed before 1949, has become well established both in the humid south and the irrigated grasslands of the north. Canning is increasing in the meat-producing areas of the north and northwest and the fruit-growing lands of the south.

To serve an increasingly widespread domestic market, China now produces an expanding list of consumer items—such things as sewing machines, watches and clocks, cameras, radios, cosmetics, soaps and detergents, and bicycles. Intended as visible rewards for the population's efforts, even these "luxuries" were campaigned against by the Red Guards during the Cultural Revolution.

results of the drive for industrialization

What has been the net impact of a quarter century of Communist rule upon China's industry? How have Maoist planning and direction of industry affected its output, structure, and spatial pattern, and do the results conform to the planners' intentions? Despite the policy emphasis on agriculture since 1960, manufacturing output has grown much faster than farm production. Between 1952 and 1972, while value added by agriculture was growing at a little more than 2 percent per annum, value added by manufacture was increasing at an annual average of 7.2 percent, despite three years of lost output because of the Cultural Revolution. Thus, while industrialization increased faster than population growth, agriculture barely kept up. Nevertheless, those industries serving agriculture were among the fastest growing, in accordance with national policy. Between 1966 and 1972 steel production grew 92 percent, chemical fertilizer output rose by 105 percent, and farm machinery production went up by a like

amount. At the same time, cotton cloth, though a priority item, went up only 59 percent, and other consumer goods rose by much smaller percentages. The newest industries, such as chemicals, far outpaced growth in the old, established industries.

The impact of Communist China's locational policy is clearly evident in some cases and less so in others. We have seen that, following the Soviet example, China has tied its industries to raw material sources to a degree not usual in nonplanned economies.

The inland development program of the Soviet era had only limited effect on the country's industrial landscape, but some of these effects are important. One example is the industrial concentration at Lan-chou, the transport gateway to the great northwest, with its oil refineries, chemical plants, and nonferrous smelters. Among others are the steel complex at Pao-t'ou, Inner Mongolia, and the industrial developments in Chunking and neighboring cities of Szechwan.

Yet the same seven provinces in eastern China still dominate the country's manufacturing. With its deposits of fossil fuels and other raw materials for industry, and the early start it received during the Japanese occupation, the northeast continues to lead the country in value added by manufacture. It remains the largest concentration of heavy industry—basic metallurgy, chemicals, trucks, freight cars, machinery, and equipment. Still an area of growth, the northeastern industrial district is spreading northward.

Close behind is the east, which includes the major centers of Shanghai, Nanking, Hangchow, and Tsingtao. With a third of the nation's population and an established industrial tradition, these coastal provinces lead in the manufacture of textiles and other consumer goods, as well as in shipbuilding, machine tools, and precision equipment of many kinds. The north, focusing on Peking, Tientsin, and T'ai-yüan, is the third-ranking industrial region. Its factories, most of which have been built since 1949, produce locomotives, tractors, metals, and chemicals. Next in output is the central-south. Loyang, Wuhan, and other central cities concentrate mainly on heavy industry, while farther south, Canton and its neighbors have mainly light industries. This region also supplies important mineral raw materials.

The mountains, basins, and high plateaus of the southwest yield a great many minerals but have little manufacturing except for the heavy industries of the Szechwan basin. Least industrialized of all is the northwest, which had no manufacturing at all before 1949. In addition to the Lan-chou complex, the region has some lesser industrial centers started during the Soviet era.

China's deconcentration program has been only partly successful in moving industry into the countryside. A limited number of industries now obtain a sizable proportion of their national output from widespread small operations, among these being plants that make cement, fertilizer, iron, and innumerable small workshops turning out farm tools and machinery. Otherwise, China's industrial production comes from large, mostly raw-material oriented installations. On the whole, the largest cities still dominate Chinese industry to an unusual degree. Shanghai alone accounts for 30 percent of total industrial output, six times more than the second-ranking center, while the top nine manufacturing cities contribute 60 percent of the national total. In view of the continuing importance of China's cities as centers of manufacturing, what, then, have been the effects of Communist rule upon urban life?

China's cities under communism

Cities played a more important part in the Chinese Communist Revolution than is generally appreciated. Although the Maoist strategy called for winning rural bases first and then taking the cities, the latter were the prime targets. Even before their victory over the Nationalists, the Communists formed urban cadres, who studied urban problems in preparation for establishing law and order, organizing administration, and developing manufacturing, commerce, and finance in those cities to which they would be assigned. Certainly there was much that needed to be done. After years of warfare, China's cities were badly neglected, their local economies in collapse, and their social and political institutions in decay.

Despite their urban-based strategy for controlling the country, the Communists did not intend to favor the city at the expense of the countryside. Mao Tse-tung was determined to avoid the kind of urban exploitation of the rural hinterland usually found in underdeveloped countries. Instead of an urban elite indifferent to the rural masses, Mao's doctrine calls for the city and country to be linked together in a mutually beneficial partnership. He insists on eliminating the distinctions between urban and rural, between mental and physical work, and between urban specialists and peasants and workers. Toward this end, city dwellers of all occupations are to spend part of each year at physical labor in the countryside. This doctrine seeks on the one hand to minimize the "destructive elements" of the cities and on the other to bestow the benefits of industrialization and modernization equally to the urban and rural sectors.

To avoid metropolitanization—the formation of great urban complexes—Mao insists that city size be limited. Although China cannot yet avoid putting part of the country's heavy industry along the coast, investment should, to the extent possible, favor new centers in the interior so that industry can be "rationally" distributed throughout the nation. Nevertheless, Mao acknowledges that urban conditions must be improved. Planning should give priority to urban housing (to be located near places of employment), public health, pollution abatement, control of urban land use, and crime and accident prevention. Education and social welfare should also receive close attention.

growth of urbanism

How well has Mao's urban policy worked? Has it halted the growth of giant cities, provided satisfactory arrangements for urban administration, or solved the internal problems of the cities? Though China's censuses are infrequent, the information we have clearly indicates that city growth has not halted. The official figures for 1958 showed an increase in the number of medium and large cities and a decline in the number of small places since the Communists' first census in 1953. The number of cities having one million or more people increased from seven in 1948 to nine in 1953, and to sixteen in 1958, and additional million-plus cities have appeared since. In 1958 the northeast led in million-plus cities (five), followed by the north and east (three each). There were two in Szechwan on the eastern margins of the southwest region, one in Shensi province, gateway to the northwest, one in the center, and only one in all that large and populous area south of the Yangtze. Meanwhile, there has been a rapid growth in medium-size cities in the inland provinces.

Why has metropolitanization actually accelerated in China, contrary to Maoist theory? At the heart of the dilemma is the fact that the Chinese Communists do not really understand the processes of urban growth. Peking has decried the "blind" influx from the countryside into the cities and has tried everything to control it but has found nothing that works. Urban living has many attractions for the in-migrants. As a natural consequence of forced industrialization, the cities offer better employment opportunities and higher per capita incomes, and higher food and clothing consumption. At the same time, the cities have been able to achieve health standards higher than those of the rural areas. And despite an ideologically supported official policy to the contrary, city dwellers have educational advantages, reinforced by the better performance of the urban bourgeoisie in school entrance examinations. The Communist rulers have repeatedly blundered in their administration of education, which has produced policy shifts so abrupt and frequent that already the country has several distinct generations of educated young, each different in quality of training and outlook.

During the crisis years of the 1960s rural standards of living actually fell, relative to those in the cities. Communist efforts to make the cities self-reliant (each urban area contains within it much agricultural land) have merely exaggerated rural-urban divisions. These distinctions between urban and rural have deeply disturbed Mao, as shown by the frequency with which these form the subjects of his writings and official pronouncements. The Communist party's urban policy dilemma is reflected in its experiments in administering cities.

urban administration

At the beginning, the Communists attempted to assert firm control over urban affairs and to provide uniform solutions to all problems in spite of the wide differences between Chinese cities in their basic character and levels of development. Because uniform policies proved unworkable, the regime permits more local decision making today. The early administrative arrangements, however, left a trilevel hierarchy of urban places. The first order consists of centrally administered municipalities, provincial-level centers that answer only to the national government. These are Peking, Shanghai, and Tientsin—the nation's three largest cities, each with wide range functions: government, finance, commerce, and diversified industry.

Next are the intermediate, or subprovincial level cities—approximately 80 large centers that answer directly to the provincial government. Their rank in the hierarchy is based not only on population size but also on their degree of economic development. Many of the cities in this intermediate rank have jurisdiction over large areas that include several *hsien* (counties). Some 90 other cities are classified in the next lower rank (actually the second order according to the constitution). These cities are under the jurisdiction of either special areas or autonomous *chou* and occupy a level in the hierarchy comparable to the *hsien*. They are less developed than the subprovincial cities, and their populations are smaller.

Finally, there are the *chen* (towns), rural service centers that lack modern industry. Many function as administrative seats of *hsien*. The country has possibly 5,000 *chen*, although the number keeps changing as some become industrialized, causing them to be reclassified as *shih* (cities). Thus there are three levels of *shih* (cities), whose rank depends upon population size, level of industrialization, and types of functions performed, plus the fourth-order *chen* (towns).

The internal administrative arrangements of Chinese cities have changed frequently under Communist rule. The urban cadres placed in charge during the early years managed to become entrenched and formed local bureaucracies. Although these arrangements were supposedly temporary, they tended to crystallize as local cadres developed their own methods, formed their own institutional worlds, acquired perquisites for themselves and families.

More recently the country's leaders have modified the internal administration of cities to provide for increased involvement of the residents. In 1959 this was the rationale for forming urban people's communes, which attempted to integrate manufacturing, commerce, education, household operations, and agriculture into cohesive units. Although 1,064 urban communes had formed by 1960, the experiment was short-lived because it fragmented the city population and increased the separation of city and countryside.

Mao has always distrusted the urban bureaucracy and has called for a mass-based political leadership that would curb the burgeoning power of entrenched bureaucracy. The principal outcome of this Maoist effort was the devastating Cultural Revolution, which had the cities as its prime targets.

urban functions

Aside from their important role as political control centers, China's cities perform the usual central-place, industrial, and transport functions. One of Communist China's unresolved issues is the relationship of the city to the countryside. Mao has recognized that the usual center-periphery arrangement works to the latter's disadvantage and results in a transfer of factors from the periphery to the center. The city gains from the influx of capital and the best labor and entrepreneural skills, which drain from the outlying territory. Given Mao's concern that Chinese cities not be allowed to exploit the countryside in this manner, the Communists have strived to develop a mutually beneficial urban-rural relationship but with little success.

In their industrial role, many of China's cities rank differently than they do on the scale of population size. Although the three province-level municipalities are at or near the top in industrial output, some of the other larger centers manufacture relatively less than their size would suggest, because of their specialization in some other function, such as trade or transportation. It is clear, however, that manufacturing is much more concentrated than the Communists would wish. Continuing a lead first asserted in the nineteenth century, Shanghai dominates the industrial sector with 30 percent of the nation's total value added by manufacture. The next ranking city in industrial output producing only one-sixth as much as Shanghai, is Tientsin, another leading port.

Together, the cities of three provinces—Kiangsu, Hopeh, and Liaoning—contribute half the nation's modern industrial product, just as they did in Nationalist times. The coastal cities, taken as a group, have twice as much manufacturing as all the rest of the country. Much of the remainder, moreover, comes from cities inland from Shanghai on the Yangtze, especially Wu-han, the nation's third ranking industrial center, and Chungking, which is fifth. Aside from these, the interior has a number of industrial centers in the medium-size range. The only southern city that ranks among the leaders in manufacturing is Canton.

transport development

China's leading cities owe much of their dominance to their superior access by water, the principal mode of transport in earlier years. When the Communists assumed control they stressed transport development, especially to the more isolated parts of the interior. Following the Soviet model, they allocated one-fifth of their capital investment in the first five-year plan to railways, roads for motor vehicles, coastal and inland waterways, and airways. At the same time they mobilized the rural labor force to construct local road systems that would provide improved access to market, facilitate procurement of fertilizer, fuel, agricultural chemicals, machine parts, and other agricultural inputs, and would help to diffuse new agricultural technology. Current planning stresses local and regional self-sufficiency, one aim of which is to reduce the transport burden.

In their transport policy the Chinese, like the Russians, have placed most of their reliance upon the railways, with waterways and roads secondary and serving mainly as feeders to the rail lines. Because modern highway transport is costly for the Chinese, they use it mostly for hauls of intermediate length. Most local hauls still rely on such traditional means as junks, animal and cart, and human porters. Thus China still maintains her dual economy in transportation.

railways

The Communists' railway program began by rehabilitating the country's badly war-damaged network. This was accomplished quickly. Because the pre–1949 railway system was largely confined to the northeast and north, serving the rest of China poorly if at all, the program for new rail construction focused upon the west and the south (see Fig. 23.6). The first five-year plan produced a flurry of railway building, which halted after the failure of the Great Leap but resumed once more in the late 1960s. Among the new routes, several were clearly military lines, and others served to solidify central government control. Much of the early construction was intended to further the dispersal of the nation's industrial base and to perform other regional development purposes.

transport planning

Considering its important locational impact, China's transport policy has had a number of internal inconsistencies requiring compromises and causing radical shifts of direction. The stated aim of minimizing transport costs and increasing the efficiency of the system would seem to suggest giving first consideration to improving the poorly connected network already in existence. Under Soviet guidance, however, the planners stressed

1. the construction of wholly new transport facilities to exploit major raw material sites and to contribute to the growth and development of industries
2. expansion of facilities in currently developed areas having inadequate network connectivity
3. over the longer term, extension of lines into inland provinces and less developed regions.

Implementation of these plans immediately encountered the problems of insufficient capital for overly ambitious undertakings and poor coordination between transport and locational policies. The tendency to allocate construction funds to areas lacking immediate productive potential caused a drain on scarce developmental capital. The Chinese paid a heavy price for the policy shifts that became necessary when they abandoned the Soviet model. Soviet-influenced planning, with its stress on heavy industry and development of the interior, required large investments in transportation and made heavy use of transport facilities. Although the Chinese shifted their emphasis to the near-term goal of building up old areas following the departure of the Russians, they had already invested in costly railways to the northwest.

Between 1950 and 1971 China managed to construct 11,000 miles of new railway trackage. The national network now totals 25,000 miles and provides every province and region except Tibet with direct access to a main line. The principal new routes include the Lan-chou Sinkiang (Lan-Sin) Line, built between 1953 and 1963, which was originally intended to link with the Soviet system at Druzhba on the Kazakh-Sinkiang border. It actually terminates at Urumchi, for the remainder of the project was abandoned after the break with the USSR. The main purpose of this line today is to further the development of the northwest and to link the oil fields of that region with the national railway network, and especially to the new refinery and petrochemical complex at Lan-chou. In addition to oil, the new route brings the cotton and animal products of Sinkiang to markets in eastern China. The Pao-t'ou-Lan-chou Line, completed in 1958, also contributes to Lan-chou's emerging function as a major rail hub. It connects with the new iron-steel complex and other regional development projects of Inner Mongolia.

One cooperative venture between the Soviet Union and China that was completed before the rupture is the Chi-ning-Erhlein Line, linking North China with the USSR by way of the Mongolian Republic. This route ties into the Trans-Siberian Railway and cuts 700 miles off the Peking-Moscow run, a service that still operates regularly. Another important contribution to national economic and political unity is the Pao-chi-Ch'eng-to Line, which at last provides dependable access to the rich agriculture and industry of the Szechwan basin over difficult mountainous terrain from the north. To fill gaps in the railway system of the south and to strengthen China's military and political influence in Southeast Asia, new lines were built from the interior to the southern ports and to the North Vietnamese border. A number of new short lines have also been built to improve the connectivity of eastern China's network.

The nation has also undertaken programs for double-tracking main lines burdened by dense traffic. Always heavily used, the Chinese railways were excessively strained during the Great Leap, and contributed to its failure. Rail service was also disrupted during the Cultural Revolution of 1966–1967.

roads

China now has 300,000 miles of roads, half of which are merely dirt tracks. Although only a few thousand of miles have hard surfaces, the system carries only light traffic, mostly commercial vehicles. Trucks are the principal mode of freight haulage in remoter regions, especially Tibet and much of the west, where railways are lacking.

Before 1949 three-fourths of the roads were in the eastern half of the country. The Communists have since constructed new roads into the less developed interior, particularly the southwest but also in border and coastal areas. Military roads, including those extending into Indo-China, have formed an important part of the total. Three-fifths of the country's new roads are in the minority regions of the west. Most of the roads, notably the farm-to-market roads, which now provide access by truck to most communes, are complementary to, rather than competitive with, the railways.

waterways

China's numerous large rivers provide superb, deep-draft connections in an east-west direction. The Yangtze, which today carries 70 percent of the nation's inland waterway tonnage, has been a main artery for inland penetration of industry. Of the water traffic in China, three-fourths now use the inland waterways, and the remainder uses the coastal service. Shanghai is the focus of domestic and foreign waterborne commerce and is the main point for transshipment between Yangtze River traffic and coastal and foreign shipments. Other coastal ports important to domestic water transport are Tsingtao, Tientsin, Lü-ta, and Canton. Two-thirds of the waterway network is in the south.

The national transport policy calls for the waterways to carry mainly bulk cargoes, especially the surplus grain of Szechwan and coal and other bulk commodities to the middle and lower Yangtze. The 100,000 miles of waterways now in use are twice the length of the system in operation in 1949. The dredging and repairing of the Yangtze navigation and the Grand Canal have been among the waterway construction projects of the Communist regime. These and other improvements have substantially increased the length of the waterways, which now totals 25,000 miles, that can be navigated by motorized vessels. The Chinese have constructed new harbor facilities, notably at the major port of Tienstsin, and have installed navigational aids, locks, and other facilities. The nation's many flood control projects have had the further effect of aiding the inland waterways.

airways

As in other newly developing lands, China's airways have a central role in tying together far-flung territory, for much of it is difficult to reach by surface transportation. The domestic system, which carries mainly passengers and mail, focuses on Peking, linking it to Shanghai, Canton, Wuhan, Chungking, Sian, Lan-chou, Urumchi, and other large cities. Formerly, the international service connected principally with the USSR, North Korea, and North Vietnam, but it is now expanding to other countries as China's political and commercial relations with the non-Communist world continue to improve.

expanding horizons

It is somewhat easier to follow the evolution of China's trade pattern because much more information is available, mainly from transactions reported by her trading partners. China's trade is still very small; but the trade she does have is vital. The unique trade policies and practices of the Chinese have been influenced by a variety of both domestic and international political considerations. Yet, in view of her growing material needs, China has never entirely submerged economic considerations in her trading relationships.

Since 1949 China's trade has markedly changed in direction and content, as her relations with other nations have shifted. Substantial fluctuations in trade have also resulted from domestic political and economic events, which have caused the first decade of Communist rule to differ from the second. This second period of important policy reversals has brought sharp changes, and the 1970s promise even greater ones. Indeed, some of the most significant news in world commerce lately has been China's decision to open her doors more widely to expand trade with a large number of countries, especially the United States and Japan.

Communist China's approach to trade

In 1971 China exported only $2.3 billion worth of merchandise—only 2 percent of her GNP. This small trade, about the same amount as Taiwan's, nevertheless satisfied China's crucial developmental needs for producer goods: machinery and other high-technology items required for her expanding industry, as well as many of the raw materials needed to run that industry. The country also requires a number of commodities to compensate for shortfalls in domestic production, especially grains needed to make up farm deficits and fertilizers essential for the long-term effort to expand a domestic food supply under pressure from a growing population. To earn the exchange to pay for these imports, China must obviously find foreign markets for her own products.

At the outset, the official line called for "leaning to one side," meaning that the country should favor trade with the USSR. Because her falling out with the USSR made China uneasy about excessive dependence upon only one or a few trading partners, she has, since 1960, held to a policy of "leaning to all sides"; that is, having a diversity of foreign customers and suppliers.

Under her current policy of selling to anyone willing to buy at a satisfactory price, three-fourths of China's trade is with non-Communist lands. Indeed, her leading partners, Hong Kong and Japan, are blatantly capitalistic. Economic considerations have become increasingly important in China's trading relations; disagreement on ideological matters is no longer a serious obstacle.

Yet it can hardly be said that politics have lost all influence; the diversification policy is itself politically motivated, the outgrowth of an ideological quarrel and the feelings of insecurity it raised. Despite the size of the Soviet economy, China's most important Communist trading partner is not the USSR, or even the Soviet satellites, but the "unorthodox" Communist nations of Albania, North Korea, North Vietnam, Cuba, and Romania. China has also insisted on confining her trade to "friendly" firms, companies that do not do business with her rival, Taiwan; but even here she has been willing to bend the rule when convenient to do so.

Since 1961 China has had a declared policy of self-sufficiency, which would seem to imply a reduction in foreign trade. In practice, however, the policy has had the opposite effect because it has required establishing import-substituting industries. This is necessarily a long-term objective, having the short-run effect of actually increasing import needs for capital goods and industrial raw materials. Moreover, the final attainment of self-sufficiency is an elusive goal that may not be fully attained.

In their trade with other countries the Chinese Communists have established a reputation for impeccable ethics. Despite the excellent credit rating they have acquired, the Chinese have until recently avoided long-term credit, preferring to pay their accounts promptly. They also keep a careful watch on their balance of payments, which is usually in surplus even though their merchandise trade is sometimes in deficit. They more than make up this difference, however, from other foreign exchange earnings, most importantly from the services and supplies they provide to the British colony of Hong Kong, as well as from sales of gold and silver bullion and from remittances sent to private Chinese citizens by their overseas relatives. China's foreign transactions are conducted by officials of state trading monopolies, reputedly hard and astute bargainers who are quick to learn from their mistakes. Twice each year China sponsors the Canton Fair, which foreign traders attend by special invitation only.

the first two decades

The 1950s were a period of rapid trade expansion, with increases averaging 13 to 14 percent per year; indeed, the nation's trade rose much more rapidly than domestic production, faster even than the world's trade as a whole. China's total trade (exports plus imports) grew from $1.9 billion in 1952 to $4.4 billion in 1959, from 2.4 percent of the world total to 3.7 percent. The economic depression following the Great Leap Forward caused a deep slump in Chinese trade, which did not regain 1959 levels until 1971.

The structure and composition of this trade underwent even greater changes than did its growth rates. One large import category, machinery and equipment, has risen and fallen with rates of manufacturing growth. It comprised one-fifth of total imports in 1950, reaching two-fifths by 1959 during the Great Leap, fell to only 6 percent of the total during the succeeding depression, and again reached 20 percent by the end of the 1960s. Meanwhile, the agricultural crisis of the early 1960s caused a sharp rise in imports of grain, which reached one-quarter of the total by 1964 from previously negligible amounts. Fertilizer and other chemicals, only 7 percent of the country's imports in the 1950s, had grown to 15–20 percent by the end of the 1960s. On the other hand, China has managed to reduce her imports of crude oil and petroleum products from nearly one-tenth of the total in the earlier years to almost zero today. Imports of war material have also fallen sharply in recent years from 40 percent of the total in the 1950s as domestic capacity for war production expanded and dependence on the USSR and Eastern Europe ended. At the same time, imports of industrial inputs increased.

These changes in import composition contrast with the remarkable stability of China's exports, which, on the whole, are much the same as they have been for many years. As always, the chief categories are still raw and processed foodstuffs, animal and vegetable raw materials, minerals, and metals. There have been some relative changes, however during this twenty-year period: the decrease in foodstuffs from 50 percent of all exports to 40 percent and metals and minerals exports from 15 percent to 10 percent. In each case the decline is attributable to increased domestic consumption. Meanwhile, textiles have become significant Chinese exports, rising from less than 5 percent to 20 percent. Also entering foreign trade are other Chinese manufactured products, such as bicycles, pens, and handbags, all of which comprise about 8 percent of the total in recent years.

Some of the greatest changes have been in the direction of Chinese trade, which has resulted from shifts in political alignments. In 1954 more than half of China's trade was with the USSR and an additional 20 percent was with other Communist lands, but the proportion has since been reversed. In the mid–1950s, non-Communist Europe eased restrictions on trade with China and subsequently made important gains at the expense of the Communist bloc. Trade with the USSR slumped sharply after the schism in 1960 and now represents only 3 percent of China's total; indeed, only one-fifth of the nation's trade is with Communist lands today. In 1971 China sent 24 percent of her exports to Hong Kong, 14 percent to Japan, and 6 percent to Singapore; she received 27 percent of her imports from Japan, 9 percent from Canada, and 6 percent from

West Germany. A significant amount of trade also took place with the United Kingdom, France, Australia, and Italy.

Although before 1949 much of Nationalist China's trade had been with the United States, the Communist takeover ended commercial and political relations between the countries. China's "lean-to-one-side" policy heavily favored the USSR; and the United States blocked Chinese assets and imposed an embargo that virtually halted all USA–China trade. This economic warfare against the Chinese Communists was militarily ineffectual, of course, because China merely turned to other sources.

new opportunities in the 1970s

The dramatic development of the early 1970s have brought a further realignment of Chinese trade. This has resulted from a diplomatic offensive undertaken by China, beginning with Chinese trade missions and cultural and athletic exchanges, followed by the nation's admittance to the United Nations and a seat on that body's Security Council, events that have signified that her long-sought status as a major world power was achieved. Among the most significant happenings of the period, however, were China's openings to the United States and Japan, which brought a resumption of US–Chinese diplomatic and trade relations and an increase in the already large Sino–Japanese trade.

A necessary precondition for improved relations with the United States was the relaxing of the American threat to Chinese security. Previously, China had felt simultaneously imperiled on two fronts. On her northern and western frontiers is the USSR, with whom a growing ideological rivalry had been transformed into a direct military threat by the Soviet invasion of Czechoslovakia in 1968. The ominous implications of this intervention in the affairs of another Communist nation were reinforced by incidents on the Russo–Chinese border, along which half a million Russian troops were poised. The other menace to Chinese security, the American presence in Indochina, however, receded as the United States took steps to withdraw from Vietnam, leaving China once again insulated from the east by the reassuring expanse of the Pacific. While this was happening, China's national policy had shifted again from the doctrinaire to the pragmatic approach, as the nation's continuing leadership struggle entered a new phase following the Cultural Revolution and the fall of Lin Piao. This combination of circumstances permitted the regime to conceive of détente with the United States as a convenient balance to the Soviet peril.

The drive for détente brought reciprocal overtures from both sides. In April 1971, the United States relaxed its twenty-year embargo on commercial dealings with China, followed by Dr. Kissinger's visit to Chinese Premier Chou En-lai and an invitation for a meeting with President Nixon. One week after a further relaxa-

tion of American trade restrictions, a Nixon-Chou summit conference (February 1972) made possible an agreement to (1) continue official contacts, (2) develop bilateral trade, and (3) begin cultural, scientific, journalistic, and athletic exchanges between the two nations. Subsequently, American business representatives received invitations to the Canton trade fair and were able to make important sales to the Chinese. Foreign ministers of the two countries have held further meetings on the subject of trade expansion and have established "liason" offices in each other's capitals, a first step toward an embassadorial exchange.

One concrete result has been a substantial growth in U.S.–Chinese trade, which rose from virtually nothing in 1971 to $90 million in 1972 and reached $750 million in 1973, the first full year of two-way trade. United States exports to China exceeded $1 billion in 1974. A majority of China's purchases from the United States have been agricultural commodities. The Chinese imported large quantities of grain, apparently to feed the nation's urban population so that farmers could concentrate more upon producing valuable industrial crops and also to reduce the strain on China's overburdened transport system. In addition to wheat, corn, and soybeans, the United States has supplied China with large shipments of cotton. American imports from China have been much smaller, one-third of the total consisting of agricultural commodities, including specialty meats, walnuts, hog bristles, camel hair, anise and cassia oils, and raw silk. China has made up much of the large deficit in her balance of trade with the United States by selling rice at good prices to neighboring lands of Southeast Asia.

China has also imported substantial amounts of industrial products from the United States: transport equipment (including $125 million for Boeing 707 jet aircraft), electronic and communications equipment, drugs, and phosphate rock for fertilizer manufacture. Meanwhile, the United States has purchased Chinese luxury consumer goods (art works, for example), nonferrous and alloying metals, and consumer products high in labor content (shoes and textiles).

The prospect of nearly 800 million customers is almost irresistible to American business leaders. A frequently overlooked problem, however, is that China's total trade (exports plus imports) is still very small— only $4.5 billion. Moreover, there is fierce competition for that market from China's existing trading partners, especially Japan and Western Europe, who are determined to hold on to what they have. There is also the problem of the limited size of the American market for most of China's traditional goods, which are much harder to market in the United States than in Europe or Asia. The opposition of American manufacturers and trade unions to competing imports from China represents a still further obstacle. Finally, there is the special difficulty of doing business with China, which requires individual Western firms to deal with China's state trading monopolies and their ponderous bureaucracies. The United States government provided a tentative solution to this problem by establishing the National Council for United States–China Trade, a quasi-official businessmen's group that serves as a bridge to the Chinese agencies.

Next to Hong Kong, Japan is already China's chief trading partner, despite the lack of formal diplomatic relations until recently. In many respects the Japanese and Chinese economies are complementary in their production, the one being a producer of high-technology manufactured goods and the other a producer of primary commodities. The two nations have the further advantage of being neighbors. Prompted by the success of the Nixon-Chou summit meetings, the Japanese attempted to establish diplomatic relations with China to help preserve their leading trade position. After much hard bargaining, formal diplomatic relations were finally established between the two nations in September 1972.

POTENTIAL HAZARDS AND OPPORTUNITIES

How good are China's prospects for future growth and development? To a great extent the answer depends upon whether or not the Chinese can solve a number of formidable domestic problems having to do with leadership, population, food supply, industrial growth, and urban administration. In addition, they will have to meet some important foreign challenges, both political and commercial.

domestic problems

supporting a growing population

Following earlier vacillation on the question, the Chinese Communists currently appear to be trying hard to control population growth, and they have instituted one of the most effective family-planning programs of any developing nation. Even so, the nation's 2.2 percent annual rate of population increase is difficult to reduce because of the very large proportion who are in the family-forming, childbearing ages. With zero population growth several years away at best, China can continue to expect an additional 15 to 20 million each year, exerting unceasing pressure on the nation's agricultural resources.

Given that China's leaders are firmly committed to keep the population adequately fed, what are the prospects for a sufficient expansion in food output? One continuing problem is the existing organization of Chinese agriculture, which, the Communists are now forced to admit, inhibits growth of farm output. The commune-brigade-production team arrangement has not proved responsive to the nation's needs, at least in part because of the planning difficulties of watching over millions of production teams farming under a great variety of local physical conditions and with a wide range of management and worker skills. Even the policy

of local self-sufficiency, which attempts to deal with this problem, tends to complicate decision making. Chinese agriculture is still suffering from inadequate investment funds, which hamper efforts to increase productivity. Yet the intensification program is already confronted with diminishing returns; barring a technological breakthrough there is no assurance that agriculture can continue to grow at its present rate, which just about matches that of population.

In addition to the various measures described earlier, the official response reportedly includes a reassessment of the current organization of agriculture, although the regime is reluctant to tamper further in a situation that is already in such delicate balance. A more concrete step taken by the government has been to provide more material incentives to farmers: encouragement to make greater use of their private plots, payment for labor according to the amount and quality of work performed, and increased consumer goods to relieve the Spartan quality of rural life. Nevertheless, according to estimates of the United States Department of Agriculture, the best that the Chinese can expect from their farmland, even if their technology should reach North American levels, is an increase in output of two and a half times in the next 50 years. Most population projections, however, anticipate that China's population will *triple* during that period.

prospects for industrial growth

Increased agricultural output is vital to China's development also because it is basic to the entire economy, including industry, for which it is expected to provide both raw materials and investment capital. Moreover, slow growth in the agricultural sector increases the flow of surplus farm workers into the industrial labor market, which cannot readily absorb the number reaching it now. The shortages of raw materials that retard China's industrial growth are further aggravated by a policy of regional self-sufficiency in a land where resources are unevenly distributed spatially. The scarcity of investment capital afflicts industry as well as agriculture, a problem that is worsened by the serious drain upon public funds from the $1 billion allocated each year to the nuclear weapon program and the similar amount going into foreign aid for other underdeveloped nations. Another shortage Chinese industry feels is the inadequate supply of advanced technology, resulting in some measure from a policy of self-reliance. Finally, there are the inefficiencies and high unit costs of the innumerable small local industries scattered about the countryside.

Forecasts of China's industrial growth are hazardous at the least, because they must be based upon a number of assumptions: (1) that the leadership attitudes of prudence and economic rationality will continue, (2) that raw material bottlenecks will be solved, and (3) that good growing weather will prevail generally. Given these conditions, optimistic estimates hold that between now and 1980, the nation's light industry should grow at an annual rate of 6 percent, heavy industry by rates of 11 to 12 percent (giving 36 million tons of steel per annum by 1980), and GNP by 6 to 7 percent. These rates of growth would substantially raise the national standard of living; but they are, however, clearly based upon improbable assumptions.

the urban dilemma

After a quarter century of Communist rule, China's problems of urban administration still remain unsolved. From the outset, city administrators have occupied an uncomfortable middle position between the generalized requirements of the national leadership and the immediate needs of the cities and of their inhabitants. The Cultural Revolution further complicated their work; out of the turmoil of that period came a desirable increase in local autonomy, which, however, was not accompanied by a clearly drawn, practical model for urban management. Mao's prescription for development, which calls for societal routines to be disrupted and local groups pitted against one another, is supposed to yield productive results; in China's cities it has more often bred intergroup strife, rancor, and chaos. The national urban policy currently stresses direct citizen involvement in public affairs, which is intended to foster local self-sufficiency, rural-urban cooperation, and a sense of community. So far the system has failed to achieve this communal spirit, and the trend seems to be more toward increasing urbanization of the countryside than bringing rural values into the city, as Mao would wish.

political uncertainties

Overshadowing all China's many problems today is one of leadership. Those who successfully led the Communist Revolution and have directed the affairs of the party and the nation since, are aging and divided into competing factions. With much maneuvering and bargaining among individuals and cliques, first one group has gained the ascendency and then another, usually in alliance with the army. The abrupt reversals of policy that have resulted have been responsible for strife and confusion of the sort that accompanied the Cultural Revolution, which, typically, was followed by the army's becoming the dominant force under Lin Piao. Mao and Chou finally moved against Lin, who supposedly died in a plane crash, and succeeded in rehabilitating and gaining the much needed services of many of the officials purged during the Cultural Revolution. By 1974, however, an ailing Chou appeared to be losing power as the forces behind the Cultural Revolution began to reassert themselves. Although the excesses of that period are not likely to be repeated, a resurgence of the utopians could alter the direction of the economy and negatively affect the nation's growing commercial relations abroad.

external problems and prospects

external threats

With the United States apparently neutralized and safely back across the Pacific, China's apprehensions focus on other, more immediate, rivals. In each case there is a question of disputed territory. Tensions continue along the Sino–Soviet border and occasionally flare into polemical outbursts and armed border clashes. Although the immediate danger of open warfare appears to be receding, the two Communist powers continue to be openly critical and suspicious of each other, and their negotiations on border issues remain stalemated. As long as the bitter rivalry between them persists, China's incentives for good diplomatic and commercial relations with the United States continue.

An invasion of their homeland is constantly threatened by the Nationalists now living in exile on Taiwan, an island also claimed by the Communists. Although the Nationalists were long supported politically and militarily by the United States, the latter's détente with Communist China has effectively reduced this menace. Optimists speculate that a new generation of leaders in China and Taiwan may reach some kind of accommodation. Also unsettled is China's old border dispute with India, a basis for armed conflict in previous years. Although India also has nuclear warfare capabilities, that country is still not China's equal, so direct armed confrontation does not appear imminent.

economic opportunities from abroad

From what we have seen thus far of China's current production possibilities, it would seem that her need to obtain certain products from abroad will hardly diminish soon. Barring a breakthrough in domestic agriculture, the country's food imports must necessarily rise at an accelerating rate. Furthermore, in order to get the most from her domestic agriculture, China will have to continue to buy large quantities of fertilizer from foreign sources; already she is the world's largest importer of fertilizer and raw materials (mostly phosphate rock). As is true of any developing nation, China must also continue looking to foreign sources for advanced technology, a ready-made asset for development. Included in this category are fertilizer factories, a number of which have been ordered from abroad. To finance this growing volume of imports, the country must expand her exports. To this end she is having to step up production of exportable items and continuously seek new markets for them.

The promise of a fabulous Chinese market for world exporters remains elusive but irresistible. Not only is China's population to reach 1 billion by 1980 but her rulers are determined to raise per capita income. With the population now but little above the subsistence level, any additions to individual incomes will yield more than proportional increases in the country's market potential. But forecasting China's trade is difficult because of unpredictable fluctuations of the economy owing to "politically induced business cycles."

In the case of the United States, trade between the two countries is closely tied to the sum of all Sino-America relations. With the frequency of China's ideological shifts, much diplomatic skill is required to thread the maize of Chinese political hazards. From the Chinese point of view, the chief danger to USA-China trade arises from the leadership struggle, which could give power to the utopians, who are opposed to Chou's policy of détente. For the United States, the main danger is the fear of betrayal of American interests on the part of the political right wing.

Most analysts predict that US-China trade will remain small, at least in comparison with American sales to Japan or Western Europe. Relative to China's small total, however, the amount could be substantial. Furthermore, trade between the two could rise much higher than the forecasts if China's economic growth should begin to exceed population increases. Meanwhile, grains will probably continue to be a major part of United States sales to China, and they could rise steeply if China loses the capacity to feed herself. The United States is the only grain producer to whom China could turn for any massive amounts. This trade would become increasingly unbalanced, forcing China to sell goods to other nations to pay for her American purchases, as, in fact, is now the case.

It is likely that only a few manufacturing firms will gain most of the sales to China. Those few, however, will probably receive very large orders for such things as jet aircraft, mining machinery, oil exploration rigs, complete factory construction, and other high-technology purchases. For many other firms, the China trade will remain an inviting mirage.

Japan will continue to benefit from her locational advantage for trade with China. Japan should offer a growing market for Chinese exports, while the Chinese should find Japan a logical source of imported capital and high-technology manufactured goods. Western Europe should also provide a growing outlet for China's agricultural and mineral products and her labor-intensive manufactured goods. Like the United States, Australia and New Zealand cannot absorb very large quantities of China's exports, but they are already supplying increasing amounts of grain and animal products to the Chinese. Meanwhile, Hong Kong can be depended upon to continue its present unique role as a major outlet for Chinese commodities.

China, therefore, has reason for both apprehension and optimism for the future. At home the vexing and dangerous leadership problem remains to be solved, as does the desperate struggle to feed and employ a huge and growing population. Meanwhile, large military forces of openly hostile neighbors are arrayed along her borders. If she can survive these problems, however, we can expect China to be able to increase per capita income sufficiently to become a substantial economic power. If this is to be accomplished, foreign commerce will play an important part.

HONG KONG: CAPITALISM ON THE DOORSTEP

As an instructive postscript to our review of the Communist Chinese prescription for development, let us examine the contrasting formula given by the paradoxical case of Hong Kong (Fig. 23.8). The paradox lies in Hong Kong's continued existence as a separate entity despite its vulnerability to the neighboring People's Republic of China, to whom this outpost of British capitalism provides a constant, provocative reminder of China's past humiliations. The Treaty of Nanking (1841), following the shameful Opium War, forced imperial China to cede in perpetuity the island of Hong Kong to the British, who wanted it as a base for their commercial operations. In 1861 the British forced China to yield nearby Kowloon Peninsula on the mainland, also in perpetuity, and in 1898, to lease for 99 years an additional piece of land known as the New Territories. This combined land area has remained to the present as the British colony of Hong Kong, ostensibly ruled from London but increasingly exercising local control over economic matters and social welfare.

Another reason Hong Kong constitutes an affront to the Chinese Communists is that the colony continuously flaunts before the Chinese and the world one of

Fig. 23.8 *Hong Kong*

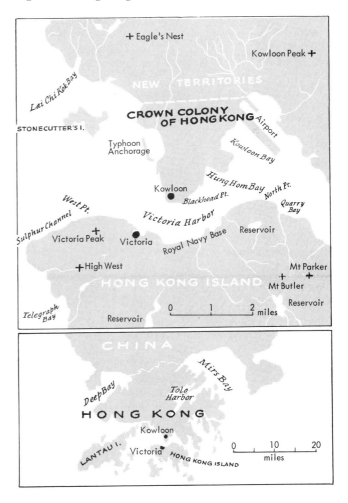

the best examples of free enterprise remaining in the world today. It is an outrageous embodiment of everything Mao denounces: laissez-faire capitalism in its purest, archtypical form. The colony has a uniquely Western economy, operating under the protection of a British-style legal and judicial administrative system. Even worse from Mao's vantage point, the system works: its growing affluence is visible to all. Moreover, Hong Kong serves as a convenient haven for China's refugees, many of them enemies of the Peking regime.

Presumably, however, China could seize militarily weak Hong Kong at any instant she chooses. It is all the more vulnerable because it depends upon China for much of its food and water, which could be cut off at any time, bringing instantaneous paralysis. Certainly there has been no lack of pretexts for Chinese intervention, as, for example, the rioting in Hong Kong's Chinese community during the Cultural Revolution.

Communist China's failure to reclaim Hong Kong is a measure of how useful China finds the present arrangement. She obtains one-third of her foreign exchange earnings from Hong Kong and, at the same time, receives from the city-state some valuable lessons in the modernization process—techniques of development that can, in some cases, be adapted to Chinese needs. Perhaps another reason China has not seized Hong Kong before this is the knowledge that she can retake the colony the instant its usefulness has ended.

from entrepôt to city-state

Since 1841 Hong Kong has earned a distinctive place in the world economic system and in the region it serves. In recent decades the colony has entered into a new era, evolving into a special kind of economic and social entity and following a successful path to development that many emerging nations could usefully imitate. Although in several respects Hong Kong's experience parallels Singapore's, another city-state that developed as a British colony, the growth strategies of the two differ in several significant respects.

service in Britain's China trade

Hong Kong Island, a tiny mountainous area off the south coast of China, had a population of hardly more than 2,000 when the British assumed control. To the 29-square mile area of the island, Kowloon Peninsula adds another 4 square miles and the New Territories 360 square miles. One-third of Hong Kong's land area consists of rugged mountain terrain; the only lowland of any size lies along the Chinese border. This lowland, supplemented by small patches of valley bottom, is the main agricultural supply area. Altogether the colony has only about 50 square miles of arable land (about one-eighth of the total).

Hong Kong owes its existence as a thriving center of commerce to the British, who, in 1841, needed a

protected base that could serve as one anchor for her triangular trade. This involved moving Indian goods (mainly opium) to China, Chinese commodities to Britain, and British products to India. During Hong Kong's first hundred years as a British colony it performed an almost exclusively commercial function, for which it is particularly suited: it is convenient to China, because it lies at the entrance to the Pearl River estuary leading to Canton, China's principal port until recent times; and it lies on major steamer lanes serving the Orient (Fig. 23.8). It also offers safety to shipping with its superb, protected, and very large deep-water anchorage—altogether one of the world's finest (and most scenic) ports.

Thus Hong Kong makes the perfect entrepôt, a center that acts as middleman between its regional hinterland and the world beyond. Performing a wide range of distributive, financial, transport, and communications functions, the entrepôt collects products from the hinterland, and stores, sometimes processes, and reships them to the world market. It also maintains a stock of foreign goods to supply the needs of its regional hinterland and provides for the retailing and service needs of its own residential population.

With its superior advantages, Hong Kong grew during the nineteenth century to become one of the world's leading entrepôts. The prosperity, stability, and security it offered its residents under British rule drew a constant flow of Chinese from the nearby provinces to work as laborers, shopkeepers, and clerks in the city's growing commerce. Its promise of adventure and economic opportunity attracted many Britons to the mercantile and shipping firms operating in this growing colony. As a consequence, Hong Kong's population increased steadily, rising to 19,000 during its first year (1841), and has continued to climb ever since, except during periods of crisis, to reach 1.6 million in 1941. By that time it had also become the base for a variety of British ventures in China: companies financing and managing transport, manufacturing, communications, and utility projects on the mainland. By the eve of World War II, Hong Kong was second only to Shanghai in its volume of foreign business activity.

years of crisis

The Japanese occupation halted all this and caused Hong Kong's population to fall to only 600,000 people. With the end of hostilities, the colony regained its lost population and resumed its familiar routine under British control until events in China and other Asian lands intervened to confront Hong Kong with grave new problems. First, there was the Communist takeover in China, which produced a flood of refugees to Hong Kong and swelled the population to three times its former size. The number of the colony's inhabitants (mainly urban) continues to increase today; the population, crowded into 3 percent of the total area, has become exceedingly dense in some neighborhoods. The next crisis for Hong Kong was the United Nations embargo of China during the Korean War, which shattered the entrepôt trade.

transforming the economy

Hong Kong's business and political leaders responded energetically and imaginatively to these problems. In this they benefited from the fact that among the refugees from communism were some of China's most capable entrepreneurs and skilled workers. There was also an inpouring of Chinese capital fleeing the Communist takeover. Within a short time Hong Kong managed to convert itself from a commercial economy to a mainly industrial one capable of competing aggressively and successfully with a variety of manufactures in world markets. Its renewed prosperity has attracted still other economic activities and even more people and has brought the population to its present 4 million.

conditions for development

Hong Kong has accomplished all this despite a number of disadvantages. Its natural resources are negligible: the colony depends upon neighboring China for much of its food and even some of its fresh water. (New reservoirs and a desalinization plant now under construction should permit eventual self-sufficiency in water.) It lacks a rural hinterland, a territory of its own to serve as a market and supply area; and its residential population is not large enough to provide an adequate base for industrialization. The local economy is vulnerable because of its extreme trade dependence; total trade (exports plus imports) is actually twice the colony's GDP, compared with 4 percent for Communist China. Hong Kong could not survive even briefly without its imports of raw material, food, and fuel, or its exports to the world market.

On the other hand, the colony has a number of advantages, including its superb accessibility and unexcelled natural harbor. Even more important are its people, who represent an accumulation of entrepreneurial, technical, and commercial skills unusual for that part of the world. Another asset that evolved during the years of orderly British colonialism is its political and economic institutions, made all the more effective by the ease of communications among this concentrated urban population. The local economy benefits also from the colony's world perspective, its access to new ideas and advanced technology, and its receptivity to these. The general awareness that the city-state has no alternative to succeeding with its chosen strategy provides strong motivation to its workers and administrators.

the strategy

The developmental path to which Hong Kong is committed places almost total reliance upon private enterprise and free operation of the market. Even so, the city-state's administrators find it necessary (1) to be responsive to the needs of business, supplementing the operation of the free market where necessary, and (2) to remain sensitive to the social welfare of the population. Hong Kong's approach has been described as a median strategy for growth and development.

In its efforts to stimulate the economy, the administration had judiciously developed measures that would foster growth in manufacturing for export and, at the same time, provide full employment, rising incomes, and a higher standard of living for the population. The government has given direct assistance to business by building and renting factories, providing an export-credit insurance plan, and supplying technical assistance to private firms to improve their product design and operating methods. It engages in land reclamation and provides utilities, transport, and communication facilities. It also educates and trains the local population in order to increase the technological input of the colony's exports. The administration manages to keep taxes low, and it follows careful fiscal and monetary policies to minimize inflation. In pursuing this strategy, Hong Kong's administrators have invited participation of the business community in government policy making, an arrangement that is reminiscent of Japan's partnership system (see Chapter 17). The general aim in all this is to help manufacturers diversify their markets, increase their productivity, and raise the level of their technology.

In its program for advancing the social welfare and private rights of its citizens, Hong Kong's government regulates working hours and conditions, especially for women and the young; sets standards for health and safety in all types of undertakings; and protects union rights. The official policy favors passing along the benefits of economic growth to the people in the form of improved services and higher standards of living. In pursuing this objective the government has energetically attacked the housing problem by undertaking extensive construction projects, widespread urban renewal, and the development of new towns.

In guiding the direction of its economic development, Hong Kong has emphasized manufacturing for export. This is contrary to the usual approach of developing nations, which stresses import-substituting production for sale exclusively within the protected home market, a procedure that invariably entails high unit costs and local monopoly. As we saw earlier in the case of the Central American Common Market, this customary strategy quickly exhausts its possibilities for growth. Instead, Hong Kong has determined to compete boldly in the world at large, which requires high standards of quality and low costs, comparable to those of the older, well-established manufacturing nations. To do this in the absence of trade protection, it is necessary to overcome quickly the usual problems of infant industries: low efficiency, high initial operating costs, and lack of experience in production and marketing.

In its successful efforts to break into the world market with its manufactured products, Hong Kong initially relied on a comparative advantage in cheap labor to produce such consumer goods as textiles, clothing, footwear, household furnishings, and utensils, and to assemble such electrical and electronic products as shavers and radios. These are mature industries, which use simple, standard production techniques and rely upon imported raw materials. For marketing expertise in matters of design, style, and seasonality, Hong Kong has been able to draw upon the experience of local mercantile houses—old firms operated under British and Chinese management. The colony's industrialists have also received this type of assistance from large American and European mechandising firms—mail-order houses, discount chains, and department stores in search of low-cost suppliers. Hong Kong's factories started with the latest machinery and production methods, in recognition of the need to begin as efficiently as possible despite the labor-cost advantage. More recently, Hong Kong has entered into the manufacture of high-technology producer goods. American, European, and Japanese manufacturing concerns first introduced this type of production, which was quickly imitated by local Chinese entrepreneurs.

Indeed, much of Hong Kong's export manufacturing takes place in Chinese-owned firms. Their operators are experienced businessmen and managers, many of them refugees from Shanghai's large industrial community—an adaptable, energetic, and knowledgeable group. From Shanghai they brought their long experience in textile spinning and weaving, much of their equipment and machinery, and many of their skilled foremen and workers. As labor costs continue to rise in Hong Kong, the colony's entrepreneurs are having to draw increasingly upon their ability to innovate and adapt. Continual improvements in product design and production techniques are required to overcome competition from abroad, especially from new Asian lands, such as Malaysia and Indonesia, with their even lower wages. Rising tariffs and other trade restrictions in foreign markets add further to the necessity for increasing efficiency. In financing capital improvements, Hong Kong's entrepreneurs rely mainly upon voluntary domestic savings.

The other Asian city-state, Singapore, also ethnically Chinese, has a similar history and current circumstances, except that Singapore is now a sovereign country, wholly independent of Britain, and, at present, its existence is not threatened by any of its neighbors. Economically, the two city-states have followed similar courses, but Singapore's labor government has favored more direct public intervention in business matters. Singapore's administration imposes direction and control over the economy, supplementing the private sector by (1) providing incentives to local and foreign manufacturers, including tariff and quota protection for noncompetitive infant industries; (2) overseeing and guiding business-labor relations; (3) performing central banking functions—managing the money supply

and credit and regulating the city-state's regionally important financial center; and (4) financing development through forced savings and internal borrowing. Singapore relies upon foreign-owned enterprises more than Hong Kong does. The government takes the lead in selecting the foreign firms to be encouraged and actively seeks subsidiaries of multinational corporations because of their experience, which is generally lacking in Singapore's local business community.

progress in development

Hong Kong's developmental strategy has been remarkably successful. Despite its near brush with disaster immediately following World War II and the absence of outside help for development, the local economy has progressed rapidly and steadily, as measured by growth in manufacturing and trade, rising GNP, increased personal incomes, and improvements in private welfare.

At the outset, Hong Kong's industries, which were started in the late forties and early fifties by refugees, have concentrated upon textiles. The manufacturing sector has since diversified, turning first to woolen and synthetic fabrics, clothing, footwear, toys, handbags, luggage, and bazaar goods, then adding such durable consumer goods as electrical appliances, parts and components, electronics, optical and photographic equipment, and finally introducing machinery. The community's industrial sector has benefited increasingly from the external economies that have accompanied this diversification of production and related services. In addition to construction, transport and communications, and utilities, Hong Kong has acquired such tertiary activities as business services, financial institutions, warehousing and wholesaling, regional headquarters of multinational companies, and a large retailing sector. Hong Kong has no central bank like Singapore's, however.

With growth in production has come a correspondingly rapid increase in exports and a shift in their direction and content. Total exports grew from HK$2.5 billion in 1955 to HK$19.4 billion in 1972. During this period, re-exports (the entrepôt trade) diminished relatively, from 85 percent of the total in the late forties to only 20 percent in 1972. The difference represents the rise in exports of Hong Kong's own products. Today 40 percent of Hong Kong's foreign sales are to the United States, 14 percent to the United Kingdom, 10 percent to West Germany, and 3 percent each to Canada and Japan. Another important market is provided by tourists, who have made Hong Kong a prime shopping stop because of its free trade and low taxes. The colony's chief supplier is Japan, which provides 23 percent of total imports, followed by China (18 percent), and Taiwan (6 percent).

Although Hong Kong has long had a balance-of-trade deficit, this has been diminishing; in 1960 exports were only two-thirds of imports, but by 1972 they had risen to nine-tenths. The balance of payments, on the other hand, is in surplus. The difference comes from tourism and net capital inflows. The Hong Kong dollar is one of the soundest currencies, fully backed by reserves; the government budget has a positive balance, invested abroad for extra security.

Although the GDP has risen very fast since the early 1950s, data are available only for the most recent years. Between 1966 and 1972 the GDP rose from HK$10.9 billion to HK$22.9 billion. There is no domestic public debt and very little foreign debt. Taxes are only 15 percent of business profits and a maximum of 15 percent on private income. The colony has no tariffs—only excise taxes on alcoholic beverages, tobacco, vehicles, and automotive fuel. There are moderate taxes on land and inheritances.

Individual private welfare gains have matched those of the economy as a whole. Although there was a worrisome number of unemployed in the early fifties, this labor supply became a prime locational attraction to industry, with the result that the colony has enjoyed full employment since 1960. Despite Hong Kong's laissez-faire capitalism, its social services are unusually good. Out of a governmental budget that has increased three and one-half times during the past decade, 38 percent is allocated to social services: housing, education, health, and public assistance to the needy. The second largest budget category (27 percent) goes for community services including streets and highways, water supply, sanitation, and fire and police protection.

As an indication of rising living standards, real wages increased by 58 percent between 1964 and 1973, the value of savings accounts rose more than 6000 percent between 1955 and 1972, and by the latter year 80 percent of the homes acquired television sets. The government's low-rent housing program, instituted in 1954, has been very successful and has provided homes for 46 percent of the population since that time. The colony guarantees free primary education to all, provides four hospital beds per 1000 population, low-cost medical clinics, and maintains social welfare and public aid to the poor. Hong Kong also sponsors recreational and cultural programs and supports two universities. A new program begun in 1972 announced a ten-year target of low-rent housing for an additional 1.8 million, a tripling of advanced technical education at the new polytechnic institute, an expansion of the universities, and increased welfare. It is interesting to note the unusually close parallel between the wholly free enterprise system of Hong Kong and the socialist-labor program of Singapore in the degree and nature of their progress in developing their manufacturing, services, and economies as a whole and in improving the material well-being of their citizens.

problems and prospects

This record of progress and growing prosperity tends to obscure the fragile nature of Hong Kong's existence in the shadow of Communist China, the awakening giant from whom Hong Kong was taken during an earlier period of Chinese impotence. The colony's prosperity is wholly at the mercy of world economic conditions, which are even now threatened. Hong Kong's continued health also requires a satisfactory solution to a number of persistent domestic social problems.

The number one problem, of course, concerns the colony's future relations with her huge neighbor. Will Communist China permit the continued survival of Hong Kong as a separate entity? At the least, barring prior agreements to the contrary, the New Territories must revert to China on July 1, 1997. China's formal position on this matter, as stated before the UN, is that the entire colony of Hong Kong is an inalienable part of China and represents a problem to "be settled in an appropriate way when the time is ripe."

China's seizure of Hong Kong would be personally disastrous for most of the colony's Chinese inhabitants, mainly refugees and enemies of the regime; and it would be a severe loss for the foreign subsidiaries headquartered there. A Chinese takeover would end the colony's international role unless China decides upon some compromise arrangement. Indeed, many analysts insist that China will never disturb the present status because it is too productive for her. Such predictions, however, assume that China's present policies will continue indefinitely, a poor bet over the long term considering the volatility of Chinese domestic politics. The short term appears somewhat more secure.

Among the external threats to Hong Kong's economy is the rising competition from other developing nations that can attract exporting industries with even lower wages, just as Hong Kong itself undercut previously low-wage Japan. Hong Kong's answer to this threat has paralleled that chosen by the Japanese: to increase productivity through streamlining production methods and to acquire more high-technology production. Another potential hazard is the resurgence of economic nationalism among nations whose balances of payments have suffered from shortages and rising costs of fuel and industrial raw materials. Any increase in import restrictions by such nations would seriously damage Hong Kong's export industries.

Hong Kong also has a number of unsolved social welfare problems. Despite remarkable progress in relieving the wholesale want and misery of the early postwar era, the colony still has a quarter million people living as squatters in tumbledown, makeshift shacks; many existing blocks of apartments are greatly overcrowded and deteriorating; and one-eighth of the population still receives substandard incomes. The administration recognizes that these problems breed social and political unrest (a special danger during times of political ferment in China) and is working hard to solve them.

implications for other developing nations

On the whole, however, Hong Kong's achievements are impressive, rivaling Japan's fabled "miracle" in many respects, especially when one considers the magnitude of the obstacles confronted thus far, the constant uncertainty of the colony's political future, and the virtual lack of external developmental assistance. With a record unsurpassed among developing nations, Hong Kong provides an instructive example of an alternative path to development, one that permits market forces to operate unhindered except for selected governmental measures to assist the local economy.

Among the salient points in Hong Kong's plan for development is official recognition of the unavoidable necessity to remain competitive and to resist the temptation to give excessive shelter to new industries that may never gain sufficient strength to bear the heat of the world market. Hong Kong's strategy permits market forces to guide the direction of economic development, a welcome answer to those developing countries who have become frustrated by unsuccessful official plans; it also offers a more efficient solution to the problem of public and private investment. The strategy calls for sound fiscal and monetary policies, a fundamental necessity for successful participation in world commerce, especially when private domestic savings are the only source of development capital. As in Japan, business leaders participate in the formation of government economic policy. Hong Kong emphasizes export production rather than import substitution and seeks to form functional ties with firms experienced in marketing abroad. Again like Japan, Hong Kong stresses continuous innovation to keep ahead of new competition. Finally, there is the policy of passing the fruits of growth along to the population as a whole in the form of higher standards of living.

Certainly this is only one possible path to development, the route of a socially responsible free enterprise system. It differs in several respects from the guided economy of the other Asian city-state, Singapore, and it contrasts with the politically controlled economy of neighboring Communist China.

RECOMMENDED READINGS

Buchanan, Keith M., *The Transformation of the Chinese Earth*. New York: Praeger, 1970.

Chen, Kuan-I, "The Outlook for China's Economy," *Current History*, 63, No. 373 (Sept., 1972), 103–8, 133.

Chen, Pi-Chao, "The Political Economics of Population Growth: The Case of China," *World Politics*, 23 (1970–71), 245–72.

Cheng, Chu-yuan, "China's Industry: Advances and Dilemma," *Current History*, 61, No. 361 (Sept., 1971), 154–59, 181–82.

Eckstein, Alexander, ed., *China Trade Prospects and U.S. Policy*. New York: Praeger, 1971.

Geiger, Theodore and Frances M., *Tales of Two City-States: The Development Progress of Hong Kong and Singapore*. National Planning Association Studies in Development Progress, No. 3. Washington: National Planning Association, 1973.

Hou, Chi-ming, *Foreign Investment and Economic Development in China, 1840–1937*. Cambridge, Mass.: Harvard University Press, 1965.

Lewis, John Wilson, ed., *The City in Communist China*. Stanford, Calif.: Stanford University Press, 1971.

Prybyla, Jan S., "The China Trade," *Current History*, 63, No. 373 (Sept., 1972), 109–13, 135.

Shabad, Theodore, *China's Changing Map*. New York: Praeger, 1972.

Tregear, T. R., *An Economic Geography of China*. London: Butterworth, 1970.

Wu, Yuan-Li, *The Spatial Economy of Communist China*. New York: Praeger, 1967.

The hinterland countries are attempting, in common, to accelerate their economic growth to raise their living standards. But there is now evidence that growth, especially in its "take off" stages, produces increasing inequality of incomes. When the benefits accruing to some are interpreted as a prospective benefit to all, Albert O. Hirschman says that a positive "tunnel effect" is working. If the pace of progress lags, however (especially in heterogeneous traditional societies where only one group has benefited) the presence of inequality can lead to political disruption or to revolutionary "development disasters." Existing governments can only combat these threats by repression or by policies designed to produce greater equity, a combination of which is in evidence in Indonesia. Where such responses have not been forthcoming, revolutionary forces have prevailed, bringing with them Marxist solutions for the total societal transformation that this philosophy maintains is essential if equitable growth is to be assured. Such is the basis of China's radical approach to development.

In the West, initial growth and inequality appear to have been followed by increasingly equitable spread of the fruits of progress as sustained development took place. To the extent that the tunnel effect persists, the developing countries can hope that they, too, will experience the same development history. If the tunnel effect weakens, however, they must try to achieve growth and equity simultaneously. The problem is that to the extent such a combination is achieved, the efficiency responsible for growth may be sacrificed and the result may be equality at a lower level of achievement than might otherwise have been possible. For those developing countries that seek to maintain democratic forms of government this is an unwelcome conclusion, indeed, and for this reason, democracy is a luxury that many Third World leaders are willing to eschew in the interest of maintaining order while maximizing crude rates of growth, and they tolerate greater inequality in the short run. The Third World democracies, on the other hand, are making real attempts to combat inequality by plans that seek to alter the regional distribution of growth within their countries.

GROWTH AND INCOME INEQUALITY

What exactly is the evidence about the relationships of growth and income inequality? How does the income distribution change during the course of development? Is personal income more equitably distributed in advanced or developing countries? Such were the questions asked by the International Labor Organization's researcher Felix Paukert in a study published in 1973 ("Income Distribution at Different Levels of Development," *International Labor Review*, Nos. 2–3, 1973). In surveying the most recent information he found the following:

hinterland growth problems and their consequences

24

1. Countries with a yearly per capita income under $100 in 1965, including Burma, Chad, Dahomey, Sudan, have a low degree of income inequality.

2. Higher up in the per capita income hierarchy, inequality grows to reach its peak in the $201–300 and $301–500 groups. Among the countries concerned are Brazil, Colombia, Iraq, Jamaica, Lebanon, Mexico, and Peru.

3. The trend then reverses itself and in the $501–1,000 group (Argentina, Greece, Japan, and Venezuela) the general level of inequality corresponds to that of the lowest income group.

4. As one moves further along the development path to countries with gross domestic products per head of over $1,000 (Australia, Denmark, Israel, Italy, Netherlands, Norway, Sweden, United Kingdom, and United States), there is a clear reduction of inequality.

Paukert concluded that "income inequality tends to increase somewhat with economic development, then remains stable, and then decreases." Why should inequality be greater in developing countries? A major reason is, according to Paukert, that the richest 5 percent of the population in developing countries gets a larger national income share than the richest people in advanced countries—28.7 percent as compared with 19.9 percent. This, it might be suggested from the earlier discussion of Indonesia and the CACM, may in turn be due to the pervasive economic dualism that persists in these countries.

Should hinterland countries welcome growing inequality as a sign of development? Will further development reduce the problem in the long run, as in the West? Other studies indicate that a number of factors in today's developing countries are combining to weaken the operation of the diffusion mechanisms that were historically so important in translating an initial impulse into a process of cumulative economic growth in the West and Japan.

These unfavorable factors include the following:

1. *Increase in disparity between traditional and modern technologies.* The relatively narrow gap in the nineteenth century between the new technologies and the skills of blacksmiths, tinkerers, watchmakers, and other traditional artisans meant that local production could be initiated on the basis of imitating a few prototypes with perhaps a modest amount of private "technical assistance." The importance of this factor is attested by the relatively slight importance of machinery imports by late-developing countries of western Europe, and even Japan. Today's more sophisticated technologies, heavily based on modern science, also imply much higher education requirements.

2. *The increase in the amount of investment per worker associated with present-day technologies.* The average capital investment per worker required in the early nineteenth century was equivalent to four months' wages in the U.K. and six to eight months' wages in France. In the U.S., in 1953, the investment per worker represented 29 months' wages, and in a contemporary underdeveloped country the investment requirement per worker is equivalent to some 350 months' wages.

3. *Predominance of large-scale, centralized factories.* The small-scale and decentralized locations of industrial factories in the nineteenth century were much more favorable to the diffusion mechanisms that were critical in launching a cumulative process of economic growth.

4. *Greater difficulty in the recruitment and training of technical workers and entrepreneurs.* Recruitment and training of technical workers and entrepreneurs for an expanding industrial sector were facilitated by the modest technological gap to be bridged and by the widespread distribution of industry, which meant that recruitment of technicians and entrepreneurs for the new tasks of an industrial society could draw from a very broad base.

5. *Reduced natural protection.* The reduction in costs of transportation and the protection that those costs afforded, both internally and internationally, has greatly increased the difficulty of establishing new industries within an underdeveloped country and in various regions within such a country.

6. *Bias toward reliance on agricultural exports.* The reduction in costs of transport has also contributed to an "excessive" development of agricultural exports that has tended to have an adverse effect on the diffusion process, especially when export production was concentrated in foreign-owned plantations: (a) profits were often exported instead of being reinvested in the expansion of local industries, (b) expatriate firms depended upon foreign sources of supply for agricultural equipment, (c) there was a minimum favorable impact on local subsistence agriculture because plantation techniques were often not susceptible to being generalized within the local agricultural economy, and frequently increased demand for food was met by imports, and (d) there was weak incentive for creation of local industries for processing agricultural raw materials or minerals.

regional planning as a response to inequality

The prevailing response throughout the Third World to problems of growing inequality in the face of these difficulties is not to wait for the long run but, recognizing that inequality is becoming increasingly difficult to overcome, is to develop regional planning programs that, as in both the CACM countries and Indonesia, seek to reduce the inequities by achieving greater regional balance in the allocation of developmental investments. CACM's and Indonesia's programs thus are hedges against likely internal disorder.

Of course, not all regional policies involve equity. Brazil's phenomenal growth record of 4.5 percent per year increase in farm output over the past twenty years was largely due to the opening up of one million hectares of new farm land per year. At the same time, agriculture in the older areas continued to become more intensive with shifts to higher value crops and use of modern inputs and better varieties. Brazil is continuing to follow this strategy with its new Plan for National Integration. The new trans–Amazonia highway is linking up the vast land and water resources of the Amazon with the heavily populated and depressed northeast area. The spontaneous movement of people from the drought areas in the northeast to the wetter areas of Maranhao to the north can now move inward onto the better soils along the higher edges of the Amazon Basin where the new road is being built. This type of regional policy is developmental; it produces aggregate growth.

But the more common type of regional policy, responding to the failure of Hirschman's tunnel effect to maintain tolerance to growing inequalities, is to share direct governmental investments equitably among regions, and by various inducements to increase the willingness of private investors to enter low-income regions. Such policies produce industrial locations that are less efficient than they could be if more centrally located in higher income areas. Thus, the policy of redistribution will have the effect of reducing overall growth while sharing the smaller pie more equally among regions. The degree of loss will depend, among other things, upon the initial degree of disparity, differences in production technology used in different regions, and the tools used to redistribute development.

In one study that attempted to measure the extent of likely loss, a Japanese regional economist, Koichi Mera, found that to equalize the per worker incomes among Japan's provinces by redistributing public investments, the national income loss would be 30 percent in the short run, and 12 percent in the longer run as the complex chain of locational shifts produced by the changed patterns of government investment ran their course. Clearly, if Mera's findings are indicative of results that would occur elsewhere, the social and political gains from greater equity will have to be considerable for effective redistributive regional policies to be worthwhile. Yet many of the developing countries' political leaders think that they are, for throughout the world's hinterlands, central governments are attempting as a matter of policy to change their regional economic structure, just as they are now beginning to combine to attempt to shift the international balance of heartland-hinterland power.

THE CHANGING BALANCE OF HEARTLAND-HINTERLAND POWER

Under the impact of colonialism, the hinterland countries emerged as economically dependent suppliers of raw materials and consumers of the finished products of the world's heartland. If changes were taking place in this pattern in the last two decades, they were the consequence of the transformation of the heartland economies, particularly that of the United States, into post–industrial societies—that is, until the emergence of the Arab oil cartel and the energy crisis.

heartland transformations and the multinationals' game plan

This transformation involved a variety of interrelated shifts within the heartlands:

From primary and secondary industries (agriculture/manufacturing) to tertiary and quaternary industries (service/knowledge activities)

From values posited on survival to security, then belongingness and esteem, and ultimately to self-actualization

From goods to services

From goods/services produced by muscle power to those produced by machines and cybernetics

From unassisted brainpower to knowledge assisted and amplified by electronic data processing

From basic necessities to amenities and eventually to a higher order of sensate needs

From physiological to psychological needs

From scientific emphasis based on physical, "hard" sciences to to one based on social, "soft" sciences

From a few innovative technological introductions to vast and varied new inventions

From a few stark choices to a bewildering array of choices

From independence and self-sufficiency to interdependence

From profit-mindedness to balanced consideration of social responsibilities and the public interest

From Puritan work ethic to leisure as a matter of right

From atomistic to large-scale pluralistic institutions

From national to multinational and "one-world" scale operations

From decentralization to centralization and eventual "globalization"

In broad economic terms, this has meant that the United States, in particular, has been moving away from a heavy stress on manufacturing toward an emphasis on service-oriented and high-technology industry. American corporations have, in several ways, been shifting production operations to countries abroad where labor costs are lower and raw materials more accessible. As the process continues, the United States' role increasingly is as the source of capital, management techniques, and high technology. That the United States maintain its superior scientific and technical capabilities is seen as a necessity to American security and economic well-being. Thus, in the future, Route 128 outside Boston and "electronics gulch" on the San Francisco Peninsula will be the equivalent of Detroit in the assembly-line era.

For the United States, the transformation is most marked in such high technology areas as telecommunications, information processing, and the aircraft and pharmaceutical industries. Japan and the industrialized countries of Western Europe also have leap-frogged industrially to the point where they are also investing heavily abroad. For some time the Common Market nations have been importing workers from the less developed countries around the Mediterranean to meet a shortage of labor. And the Japanese and Europeans have also begun to transfer manufacturing operations to what they call the LDCs (less developed countries). The multinational corporation has emerged as the chief midwife of the new system.

There are today about 300 colossal multinational

corporations whose production of goods and services adds up to about $300 billion a year, a figure higher than the gross national product of every country except the United States. If one takes the 100 largest economic units in the world, only 50 of them are nation-states; the other 50 are the largest of these 300 multinational companies.

Of the 300 multinational corporations, 187 are American; half of the remaining third are British and Dutch, and the other half European and Japanese. The majority of the American giants do more than a half-billion dollars in sales a year. General Motors, the largest, has total annual sales of $25 billion, which exceeds the net national income of all but a dozen countries.

It is not size and income alone that are important, but the change in the control pattern of the "product cycle." In the past, countries found that once a new product or technique had been created, its initial advantage was overtaken by other countries, which, with cheaper labor or newer machinery, could turn out the product cheaper and thus undersell the original country. The textiles industry is perhaps the classic case in point. But the multinational corporation not only transfers capital and managerial know-how abroad; it has become an organizational mechanism for the transfer of manufacturing production to low-wage countries and its managerial techniques and technology to the advancing industrial countries while retaining control —and earnings—at both ends. In the five years between 1969 and 1974 overall employment in electronics in the United States declined by some 219,000 jobs as American firms located their new plants in Singapore, Hong Kong, Taiwan, and Mexico. In the nature of this new product cycle, more and more manufacturing of the standardized sort will, in theory, move to the poorer sections of the world while the post-industrial societies concentrate on knowledge-creating and knowledge-processing industries, and while the control of the product, in many industries, will remain with the multinational corporation.

political-economic challenge by the "external proletariat"

The logic of this new type of heartland-hinterland division, with the industrialized countries providing capital, managerial know-how, and a continuing flow of technology and the LDCs contributing labor, raw materials, and new markets is very tidy, but under stress the theory is already showing some flaws. Some time ago, Arnold Toynbee wrote of the likely emergence of an "external proletariat," the poor perimeter of the world encircling the central heartland of the rich. It was a theme sounded ominously in 1965 by Lin Piao, Mao Tse-tung's former number two man, when he warned that the "class struggles" of the end of the twentieth century would be between nations rather than within them. Given the pattern of economic de-

velopment, such a class struggle, if it ever develops, might become a color struggle as well. And a first sign of this new dimension of the global political economy has been signalled by the 1973–1974 Arab oil crisis. The paradox of the spread of a world capitalist economy is that in each nation-state the economic order is becoming more subordinate to the wider context of political decision.

Most obviously, the Arab oil boycott has shown what can happen if the less-developed countries deny essential raw materials to the industrialized nations. The LDCs' new appreciation of the value of nonrenewable resources in pursuing both political and economic ends is likely to be a major factor in heartland-hinterland relations from now on. Oil has a unique potency in the market place because of the oil-based increases in energy-consuming growth throughout the world, but the LDCs' possession of substantial amounts (in some cases amounting to a monopoly) of the finite supplies of important raw materials, will grow more important.

Even before the melodrama of the oil boycott, the LDCs had begun to take united action in their own political and economic interests. At the 1972 Stockholm Conference on the Human Environment, the LDCs collectively made it clear that they were determined not to allow the industrialized countries to promote antipollution measures that would deter industrialization in the LDCs. At the 1973–1974 Law of the Sea Conference, the LDCs demonstrated a similar concern that the industrialized countries may use their superior technology to monopolize the resources of the sea and seabed. Further evidence of the LDCs' sensitivity is to be found in a 1973–1974 United Nations study on the impact of multinational corporations on economic development and international relations and the tempestuous conflicts at the 1974 World Food Conference. It is clear that the world order of heartland-hinterland relations is undergoing rapid and possibly quite revolutionary change. Let us therefore conclude this section of the book by looking more closely at the raw materials vulnerability of the world's heartland countries and at some of the consequences of the Arab nations' exercise of "oil power." We then will turn in Chapter 25 to the more general issues of growth, change, and the environment.

raw materials vulnerability of heartland economies

Interdependence becomes a two-way street if both heartland and hinterland are able to exercise equal and countervailing powers, in contrast to the one-way direction of influence that traditionally obtained. Pessimists argue that the heartland nations' growing dependence on imports for a number of key industrial minerals is making the threat of producer cartels in the hinterlands more and more likely. Others believe that as far as nonfuel minerals are concerned, there is at present no commodity whose producers have the right

Table 24.1   Percentage of U.S. Mineral Requirements Imported During 1972

MINERAL	PERCENTAGE IMPORTED	MAJOR FOREIGN SOURCES
Platinum group metals	100%	U.K., USSR., South Africa, Canada, Japan, Norway
Mica (sheet)	100	India, Brazil, Malagasy
Chromium	100	USSR., South Africa, Turkey
Strontium	100	Mexico, Spain
Cobalt	98	Zaire, Belgium, Luxembourg, Finland, Canada, Norway
Tantalum	97	Nigeria, Canada, Zaire
Aluminum (ores and metal)	96	Jamaica, Surinam, Canada, Australia
Manganese	95	Brazil, Gabon, South Africa, Zaire
Fluorine	87	Mexico, Spain, Italy, South Africa
Titanium (rutile)	86	Australia
Asbestos	85	Canada, South Africa
Tin	77	Malaysia, Thailand, Bolivia
Bismuth	75	Mexico, Japan, Peru, U.K., Korea
Nickel	74	Canada, Norway
Columbium	67	Brazil, Nigeria, Malagasy, Thailand
Antimony	65	South Africa, Mexico, U.K., Bolivia
Gold	61	Canada, Switzerland, USSR.
Potassium	60	Canada
Mercury	58	Canada, Mexico
Zinc	52	Canada, Mexico, Peru
Silver	44	Canada, Peru, Mexico, Honduras, Australia
Barium	43	Peru, Ireland, Mexico, Greece
Gypsum	39	Canada, Mexico, Jamaica
Selenium	37	Canada, Japan, Mexico, U.K.
Tellurium	36	Peru, Canada
Vanadium	32	South Africa, Chile, USSR.
Petroleum (includes liquid natural gas)	29	Central and South America, Canada, Middle East
Iron	28	Canada, Venezuela, Japan, Common Market (EEC)
Lead	26	Canada, Australia, Peru, Mexico
Cadmium	25	Mexico, Australia, Belgium, Luxembourg, Canada, Peru
Copper	18	Canada, Peru, Chile
Titanium (ilmenite)	18	Canada, Australia
Rare earths	14	Australia, Malaysia, India
Pumice	12	Greece, Italy
Salt	7	Canada, Mexico, Bahamas
Cement	5	Canada, Bahamas, Norway
Magnesium (nonmetallic)	8	Greece, Ireland
Natural gas	9	Canada
Rhenium	4	West Germany, France
Stone	2	Canada, Mexico, Italy, Portugal

Source: U.S. Department of the Interior, *Mining and Minerals Policy, 1973.* (Washington, D.C.: U.S. Government Printing Office, 1973.)

combination of economic strength and political hostility to form a cartel except the Arab producers of oil. Whichever view is correct, the heartland nations' position on nonfuel minerals is an intricate amalgam of diplomacy, economics, and technology, whose importance has gone largely unrecognized until recently.

Let us look at the United States in particular. The basic facts of the case are, on the one hand, that the United States is more autonomous in nonfuel minerals than any other country except the Soviet Union and would probably be less affected than any other by an embargo. But, although rich in minerals, America began to be a net importer in the 1920s. According to the Department of the Interior, U.S. imports of all nonfuel minerals cost $6 billion in 1971 and are estimated to rise to $20 billion by 1985 and $52 billion by the turn of the century.

For twenty nonfuel minerals, including such key metals as chromium, aluminum, nickel, and zinc, the United States already derives more than half of its supply from abroad (see Table 24.1), and the extent of this dependence seems certain to increase. Because of the uneven distribution of minerals in the earth's crust, a handful of countries have dominant positions in several metals. Four countries control more than four-fifths of the world's exportable supply of copper. Malaysia, Thailand, and Bolivia together provide 98 percent of U.S. imports of tin.

Even before the oil crisis, people were expressing concern about America's vulnerability to group action by producing countries. Collective bargaining by raw materials producers is already beginning in the cases of bauxite, phosphates, copper, tin, bananas, and coffee. Third World leverage is being exercised against all industrialized countries, or in some cases discriminatorily against the United States, thus benefiting Europe and Japan. The specter of "cannibalistic competition" among the rich for natural resources is a real possibility, which suggests that the owners of those resources have or can develop tremendous clout.

No other attempts at collective bargaining have so far achieved anything like the success of the oil producers' cartel, the Organization of Petroleum Exporting Countries (OPEC), but the International Bauxite Association has obtained a sixfold increase in earnings. The International Tin Council, which includes both producers and the major consumers, has had little effect on prices. But Chile, Peru, Zambia, and Zaire, the members of the Intergovernmental Council of Copper Exporting Countries (CIPEC), have been able to restrict falling copper prices through production cutbacks in Chile. Elsewhere, the coffee producers' organization, Cafe Mundial, has established firm control on the world coffee price.

Producers are more aggressive today than in the past because they now have the example of Arab success to follow. Third World countries expect a rise in their standards of living but, although their per capita gross national product has been increasing in recent years, so has the gap between rich countries and poor. Growth in both affluence and population cannot but intensify the competition between industrial nations for a finite quantity of natural resources. In 1970 the United States possessed 5 percent of the world's population but consumed 27 percent of its raw materials, a share that will be difficult to maintain in an increasingly competitive world. "As countries become increasingly interdependent, we face the prospect of a single global society in which the glaring inequalities of world income distribution may not be sustainable," notes the report of the U.S. National Commission on Materials Policy.

oil power and OPEC

To the extent that raw materials producers begin to exercise countervailing political-economic power, the most likely direction of change in heartland-hinterland relations may be seen by recounting the twentieth-century history of world petroleum pricing up to the formation of the Arab oil cartel OPEC (The Organization of Petroleum Exporting Countries), and then looking at the dramatic consequences of OPEC's first concerted application of political-economic power.

Before 1911, kerosene was the main product of the oil industry. At that time, three changes occurred. Gasoline production exceeded kerosene production for the first time. The Standard Oil Trust was dissolved, which resulted in a new pattern of competition. Oil production in Oklahoma, Texas, and Louisiana began its rapid growth and exceeded California as the first-ranking oil producing region. This placed the Gulf Coast in the dominant export position in relation to markets in northeastern United States and Europe. The opening of the Panama Canal in 1914 gave the Gulf Coast connections with California prices and other prices in the Pacific Ocean área, the Dutch Indies for example.

In countries other than the United States, only a few companies produced, refined, or marketed oil, and little independent price formation took place. As a result, companies, consumers, and governments looked to the United States for information and leadership. This was available in the form of U.S. Gulf prices. As the United States was by then also the world's largest exporter of oil, U.S. Gulf prices became the world's basing prices. To determine the price of oil in any region outside the United States, freight from United States Gulf of Mexico ports was added to the U.S. Gulf price at the time of shipment. This system of pricing, referred to as Gulf-Plus, was applied irrespective of the origin of the oil. Thus the price of Iranian oil delivered from Abadan to the Stockholm region of Sweden, equalled the U.S. Gulf price for the applicable grade of oil at the time of shipment PLUS freight from Gulf of Mexico ports to the Stockholm region. In this way, United States oil companies earned excess profits on Iranian oil in the form of phantom freights.

Except for a few minor fluctuations, the worldwide price structure thus consisted of a single basing point region from which price increased geographically outward with transportation charges to a worldwide price shed (see Fig. 24.1). There was some regional grouping of freight to some ports. For example, all ports in Europe, from Bordeaux to Hamburg, that could accommodate oceangoing tankers were charged the same freight rate; in the United States, all ports north of Cape Hatteras were so grouped.

This pre–World War II price structure encouraged a remarkably successful search for oil in other countries, because of the profit potential of the phantom freights. The first change came when the Allied forces objected to the high prices of petroleum purchased in the Persian Gulf during World War II. As a result, Persian Gulf prices were made to equal U.S. Gulf prices in 1945. This resulted in a price shed in the central Mediterranean.

The second change came after the war when the United States, paying indirectly for most of the oil in Europe, decided that the Persian Gulf f.o.b. prices should equal U.S. Gulf prices PLUS freight from the U.S. Gulf to Great Britain MINUS freight from the Persian Gulf to Great Britain. This method made the Persian Gulf prices lower than U.S. Gulf prices because the freight rate from the United States to Great Britain was $7.65 per ton whereas the rate from the Persian Gulf to Great Britain was $10.20. Later in 1948, the Caribbean (Venezuela) price was substituted for the U.S. Gulf price as the base price. This resulted in a further decrease in the Persian Gulf f.o.b. price. The resulting price shed was in Great Britain.

In 1949 the Western price-shed was deliberately shifted to the eastern United States north of Cape Hatteras to permit Persian Gulf crudes to meet growing demands in eastern North America. The base price continued to be the Caribbean price and freight, but the effect was again to lower prices in the Persian Gulf and the Levant in the interests of heartland consumers. The reduction in delivered prices aided economic recovery, especially in Europe, after World War II.

The first break came in 1959, when Algeria es-

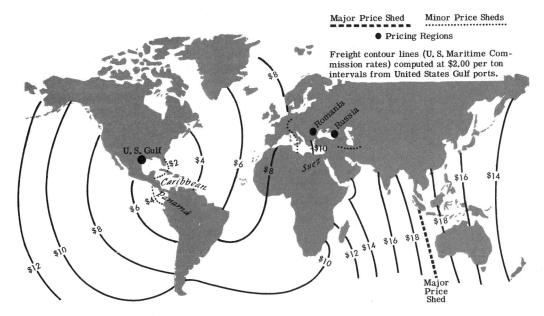

Fig. 24.1 *Pre-World War II world price pattern*

Source: *Adapted from an illustration appearing in Alexander Melamid, "Geography of the World Petroleum Price Structure," Economic Geography, 38 (October, 1962), 289.*

tablished its own basing point, which was consistently quoted about 5 percent below Middle East-Plus (Persian Gulf or Levant) prices. In 1961 Libya announced an even lower price, and others followed suit. The result was a highly competitive multibase pricing structure that further benefited consuming nations.

In response to this competition, the world's major oil producers, the Arab countries, finally determined that only if they acted in unison could they begin to benefit from their control of the world's oil reserves. They formed a producers' cartel, OPEC (The Organization of Petroleum Exporting Countries); transformed a buyers' market into a sellers' market in which they can set the price that heartland countries must pay for their oil; discovered that real political power results from the development and concerted use of a raw materials cartel; and made possible the emergence of a new world power bloc, the oil-rich Third World.

Negotiations with major oil companies had already significantly changed the flows of moneys into the treasuries of the oil-rich states when the Arab-Israeli war broke out in late 1973. For the first time, acting in unison to achieve political ends, oil was denied the heartland countries to ensure that they restrain Israeli forces. Disruptions in heartland economies were immediate and profound; industrial production lagged, unemployment increased, and balance of trade figures went into the red. In the resulting period of uncertainty, OPEC increased the posted price of Arabian light crude oil, which had become the new world base-price, from $US3.07 per barrel in November 1973, to $11.65 in March 1974. Following suit, Indonesia increased her crude oil prices from $2.60 per barrel to

$10.80 per barrel in the same period, thus affecting Japan's economy.

The effects were massive:

1. The oil import bill of the heartland nations was increased by $US53 billion annually for the same quantity of oil as was consumed in 1973. Many of the smaller independent oil companies went out of business. In Japan, the oil companies not affiliated with major multinationals (Maruzen Oil, Kyodo Oil, and Daikyo Oil) were merged by the Ministry of International Trade and Industry to increase international bargaining power.

2. Meanwhile, the oil import bill of the developing countries also increased—by $US10 billion at 1973 levels, wiping out the effects of foreign aid and threatening their development efforts. For example, in India, one effect has been to raise fertilizer prices by $US1 billion. This puts fertilizer out of reach of many peasant farmers and thus is likely to be a severe setback to the "green revolution."

3. $US63 billion extra annually was thereby diverted from other nations to the oil producers' treasuries—half to Saudi Arabia, Kuwait, Qatar, Abu Dhabi, and Libya, with other major beneficiaries, Iran and Indonesia. Iran, in turn, promised to loan the World Bank $1 billion so the bank could make loans to help such lagging heartland economies as Britain solve her balance of payments problems.

the fourth world separates from the third

Consequently, the poorest countries—those with scant resources to finance their imports—have descended into a new category, now referred to in the United Nations as the *Fourth World*. At the 1974 World Food

Conference the concept of *triage* was applied to this group, sorted out as beyond real help. Meanwhile, the old Third World has been transformed into a more exclusive OPEC-led grouping limited to those nations that are exploiting their rich mineral or agricultural resources to speed their development by transferring wealth from the industrial heartlands.

For the Arab nations, the result has been a fantasyland of riches. For example, twenty-five years ago, the tiny Persian Gulf nation of Kuwait was a poor, mud brick sheikhdom with an annual income of $35 per person and no electricity nor paved roads. Today it is the richest country on earth. It has more millionaires per capita than any other nation in the world, and per capita income is approaching $5,000, compared to $4,200 in the United States. It has no taxes, and its 733,000 citizens get free telephone service, medical care, and university education, and interest-free loans for homes and businesses. The New Jersey-sized desert sheikhdom has transformed itself into a complete welfare state, outdistancing even the most paternalistic Scandinavian country.

The problem that the Arab nations face is an enviable one: what to do with their new oil riches. But a plan has been worked out by Arab economists working for the Economic Committee of the Arab League. This plan has two major goals: the political one of progressive erosion of Western support for Israel, and the economic one of rapid industrial development of the Arab world. The strategic plan calls for oil production to be cut back and remain cut back, and for Arab capital to be invested in Arab countries in order to build a strong Arab economy capable of standing firm or plunging into the fatal battle if the cause demands it.

The plan's aims, as outlined in the strategy, is to protect the Arab economic future from the danger that could follow the rapid exhaustion of oil resources. At the same time the intention is to carry Arab states to a level of technology and industrial development that will connect them to the twenty-first century. The plan calls for the development of a petrochemical industry in which the Arabs will use their own oil, and three other major industries: engineering based on supplying engines for ships and turbines, assembly industries for cars and ships, and a selective defense industry.

The essential prerequisite for success is for each Arab state to concentrate on developing a few industries, each on a large-scale for an integrated Arab market. Such a common market, it is contemplated, would propel the Arab Third World to a position of political and economic parity with the heartland. As this is being done, the plan contemplates that funds not needed for domestic investment will be used to acquire strategic investments in major heartland corporations, thus bringing Arab interests to bear on multinational policy-making and economic strategies.

Already the first steps are being taken. Bahrain has a major aluminum plant, and Saudi Arabia is planning the Petroma Steel Complex at a cost of $500 million. This complex will use Saudi oil revenues, Saudi natural gas, and possibly Saudi iron ore to produce semifinished steel for markets in Western Europe and Japan. Its initial capacity is to be 1 million tons of steel products, mainly beginning with oil piping, but with the possibility of rising to 15 million tons annually as the market grows.

The Saudi government has been especially eager to encourage such large industrial complexes to educate Saudis in modern industrial skills and so help the country get away from exclusive dependence on its huge oil resources. The biggest Saudi problems are to train manpower and find productive ways to absorb the world's largest cash surplus, an estimated $177.6 billion in oil revenues for the period 1973–1983.

Similar planning is already well advanced in the non-Arab oil-producing nations as well. Iran, for example, is engaged in a massive modernization program, and Venezuela is acting to secure greater control of petroleum production through nationalization. Indonesia had earlier achieved such control through creation of Pertamina. Venezuela, faced with the embarrassing avalanche of wealth from its oil exports has decided on a major war on poverty to try to solve the nation's staggering social problems. Indonesia's initial actions have been to increase the funding of the growth centers to be developed as part of the regional development strategy of Repelita II. All are attempting to avoid development disasters by sharing the benefits of oil power among their citizens.

retrospect and prospect

Traditionally, heartland countries used their superior political power to impose upon the hinterlands a dependent pattern of economic development. Today, however, control of the world's supplies of essential raw materials places many of the world's hinterlands in strategic positions to begin to exert real influence on the nature and pattern of world growth. No longer, does it seem, will the heartlands be able to continue their accelerated growth and voracious consumption of the world's resources without concern for either the environmental or the global economic consequences of their acts. No longer will some of the hinterlands remain resource-rich but impoverished, although those that are resource-poor, such as Bangladesh, will be hard-pressed to avoid Malthusian calamities.

Of course, heartland responses to reduce sensitivity to global specialization and interdependency also seem likely. On the one hand, approaches are being discussed that will increase national self-sufficiency: improving domestic supplies and recycling and substitution of new energy sources for oil. But with each of these strategies, the room for maneuver appears to be, if anything, shrinking as new constraints emerge such as campaigns for environmental protection and the rising cost of energy from new sources. The second consequence, then, may well have to be a changed lifestyle as the heartlands pay the deferred costs of past consumption and inequities in distribution, and begin to calculate costs of depletion, replacement of renewable resources, and environmental restoration and protection into their future growth equation. It is to these questions of growth and resource use that we turn in the final chapter.

RECOMMENDED READINGS

Alonso, William, "Urban and Regional Imbalances in Economic Development," *Economic Development and Cultural Change*, 17 (1968), 1–14.

Boeke, J. H., *Economics and Economic Policy of Dual Societies as Exemplified by Indonesia*. New York: Institute of Pacific Relations, 1953.

McGee, T. G., *The Southeast Asian City*. New York: Praeger, 1967.

Richardson, Harry W., *Regional Growth Theory*. New York: Halsted, 1973.

Ward, Barbara, *The Widening Gap. Development in the 1970's*. New York: Columbia University Press, 1971.

Williamson, J. G., "Regional Inequality and the Process of National Development," *Economic Development and Cultural Change*, 13 (1965), 3–45.

systems growth and spatial dynamics

eight

Kenneth Boulding, the Anglo-American economist and social philosopher, introduced one of his books with the simple but fundamental insight that *growth creates form but form limits growth*. In the preceding chapters, we have seen many examples of the ways in which growth has produced particular geographies of economic systems and how these systems are now facing limits to growth. The purpose of this chapter is to draw together the insights provided by these examples. First, we present a typology of growth and change. Second, we outline the ways in which growth produces spatial organization. Finally, we discuss the limits to growth and the possible need for major reorganization of world economic geography. The first two sections incorporate ideas derived from General System Theory, including the concept of allometry, and integrate these with insights drawn from theories of diffusion. The final section discusses the Club of Rome's challenging and controversial report *The Limits to Growth* prepared under the direction of Professor Dennis Meadows, and based upon the work of Professor Jay Forrester, the author of an earlier book entitled *World Dynamics*.

TYPES OF GROWTH AND CHANGE

In beginning with types of growth, we are focusing upon different *pathways of change in time*. But we must also admit that there are "no-growth" circumstances in which change still takes place, a possibility that arises because of the importance of distinguishing between a system as a whole, and the parts within a system. *Growth* involves expansion of the system as a whole, through either addition of new parts or the increasing size of existing parts. Growth may produce *change* through substitution of one part of the whole by another or by differential growth of the existing parts. *Development* is a particular kind of change in which there is substantial restructuring of the parts, such as increasing functional specialization or the growth of new types and levels of interaction and organization.

For purposes of the following discussion, it will be useful to distinguish four types of systems on the basis of their growth and change. Obviously there are more such types, but these four are of particular geographic interest. At one extreme is the *closed no-growth system* in which the changes taking place are deterioration and decay. One also can identify *self-maintaining systems* in which neither growth nor change is taking place, but in which a sufficiently high level of interaction and interchange with their environments is maintained to ensure that the existing size, composition and spatial organization of the system is preserved. Next, we can distinguish *growing open systems* in which form may change. This will be the case when the parts must grow at different rates to ensure that the enlarging system remains functional as a whole. Finally, there is the *open developing system* in which growth is accom-

growth
and
its
limits
25

panied by substantial restructuring of both internal organization and the nature of the parts that are so arranged. Often, the developing open system changes by what John Platt has called "hierarchical jumps."

no-growth systems: the geography of decline

In Chapter 13 it was pointed out that the spatial organization of a society is the spatial structure of its interactions, i.e., that spatial organization would disintegrate without the continuing flow of people, ideas, goods, and services. We know from studies of all living systems that growth depends on the ability to interact with the environment both physical and social. A system isolated from its environment, and hence unable to exchange energy or matter with it—a closed system—has an initial energy supply, but once this is consumed, degradation must inevitably set in. The second law of thermodynamics then applies: in a closed system, as available energy is consumed, *entropy* increases to a maximum at which point the system dies.

Entropy is a measure of probability, and so a closed system tends to a state of most probable distribution. The most probable distribution . . . is a state of complete disorder. . . . So the tendency towards maximum entropy or the most probable distribution is the tendency to maximum disorder. (Ludwig von Bertalanffy, *General System Theory*, New York: George Braziller, 1968, p. 39)

Few truly closed systems exist outside of physics. We can, however, identify a variety of the geographical consequences for economic systems of increasing closure due to reductions in the scale or extent of their spatial interactions (such as the consequences for "mini-Britain" of the loss of Empire, discussed earlier).

The most extreme cases are, of course, mining developments. If the resource becomes depleted or demands are diverted elsewhere, the mining settlement declines or dies. Notable examples of such ghost towns resulting from the exhaustion of economically exploitable ores are Virginia City, Nevada, Wabana and Bell Island, Newfoundland.

Another example is the bypassed community. The development of the Interstate Highway System in the United States has led to the decline of many small towns that formerly serviced transcontinental traffic. Similarly, Gander, Newfoundland, and Goose Bay, Labrador, declined as the introduction of long-distance jet passenger aircraft eliminated the need for refueling stops.

There was much interest in the consequences of a stable or declining population in the 1930s which has been aroused once again by the tendency in the more developed countries for growth rates to approach the zero-population growth (ZPG) level, and by the rising role of environmental consequences discussed later in the section on the limits to growth.

There is some disagreement about the precise consequences of a declining population but it is agreed that they are pervasive. The demographic consequences are the most obvious. The total population growth depends on both birth rates and on the number of people reaching childbearing age. Hence the arrival of postwar babies into this age group ensures a substantial growth in population, notwithstanding lower birth rates. Even if family size drops to a two-child average, as in the United States today for example, which is below the replacement level, births would exceed deaths for the rest of the century and produce a population total of 300 million by 2015. But the age structure of the population would change, affecting the mix of goods and services demanded by the population.

A declining population is an aging population, and the increase in the proportion of senior citizens that results from falling birth rates will be augmented by any declines in death rates for older age groups. The burden of providing adequate national pension schemes is increased, particularly if there is a trend to earlier retirement with "30 years and out" becoming the rule and with workers retiring in the 50s age bracket rather than the 60s. Education costs can be held in check with a declining population growth rate, helping to compensate for higher pension costs, but the educational level of the labor force is a major determinant of economic growth and the need for adult education is likely to increase as workers entering the labor force, who typically have above average education levels, become a declining proportion of the total labor force.

A declining population also raises concern about maintaining employment levels. The product mix of consumer demands changes as the population shifts from the Pepsi generation to the Geritol generation and from demanding high chairs to wheel chairs. It is more difficult to adjust production levels to changes in the demand mix if the labor force is aging, and the proportion of new, more mobile workers is falling. Furthermore, if aggregate demand holds steady or even falls so that relative decline for a product becomes an absolute decline, the problems of maintaining employment levels are aggravated. Adjustments to changing demand are further complicated by the implications of a declining population for the ratio of capital equipment to workers, the incentives to investment in new equipment, and the lag in the diffusion of new technology, which in turn have consequences for increasing factor productivity.

Finally there is the impact of a declining population on public opinion and policy making. In the 1930s there was often overreaction to ZPG with extreme anxiety over implications for national prosperity, security, and virility. There was talk of "race suicide" and discussion of ways to encourage higher birth rates (a discussion that is being repeated in Japan today as labor shortages grow). So much attention is given to the public outcry today about the consequences of growth, that we may forget this equally vociferous public reaction to the consequences of decline. And so much attention is being given to the problems of and limits to growth, that we may overlook the problems of a declining population. We must emphasize that these problems are merely signals of needed policy initiatives if birth rates remain below the replacement levels, rather than arguments for encouraging higher birth rates. Economists in the United States and Canada generally believe that the average person will be substantially better off economically if population growth follows a two-child growth projection rather than a three-child one.

self-maintaining systems

A second kind of system is one in which neither growth nor change takes place; rather, the system maintains its size, composition, and interactions through regular *exchange* with other areas. In Chapter 13 we called those interactions "non-innovative." In terms of living system theory they are part of the regular everyday metabolism of the organism, and they have a self-compensating character to maintain the system in balance. For example, we must breathe and eat to maintain our vital body functions. Much of the discussion of spatial interaction (e.g., the gravity model), of trade relations, and of the equilibrating role of prices refers to such self-regulating properties of spatial organization. In general system theory the term *homeostasis* is used to describe this self-regulating, self-maintaining ability.

Of particular interest in self-maintaining systems is the change from one such steady-state equilibrium system to another as a consequence of some major external "shock," as with a thermostat when a different temperature level is set. Figure 25.1 provides an example. World coffee prices maintained themselves at about 56 cents a pound in the period July to November 1953, representing the balance between demand and supply in that period. They then shot up to another equilibrium level close to 90 cents a pound in the period May to July 1954. The external shock was a crop-destroying frost. The pattern has been repeated with the destruction of almost five million bags of Brazil's 1973–1974 coffee crop (a bag is equivalent to 132 pounds of coffee), again changing the supply side of the equation. The result has been another rapid rise in wholesale coffee prices, with the new equilibrium not yet established at the time of writing.

The figure also illustrates other features of equilibrium or steady-state systems:

1. There is a continual fluctuation of prices around the equilibrium level, just as temperature rises and falls in a home around the thermostatic setting. These *oscillations* are the product of action and reaction by the control device as it seeks to maintain the set level.

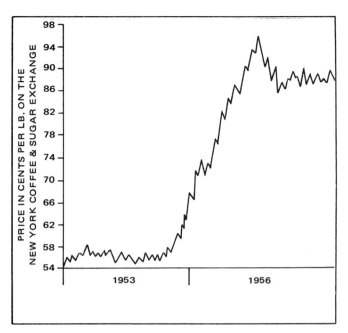

Fig. 25.1 *The jump in coffee prices, 1953–1956. This is what happened in 1953–1954 in the coffee futures market when demand outpaced supply. The price of coffee rose from 50¢ to 90¢ a pound.*

2. The very rapid rise in prices not to, but actually *beyond,* the new equilibrium price level settling back thereafter to the new state of balance. This phenomenon is called *overshoot* and is one of the characteristic reactions of systems to shock.

Both oscillation and the overshoot-and-return phenomena are examples of *negative feedback* at work, the first at the scale of a single steady-state, and the second as one equilibrium position is replaced by another. Negative feedback is the process by which deviations from equilibrium are sensed and corrected to maintain a given equilibrium. Hence the use of the term steady-state for such self-maintaining systems.

growing open systems

There are two possible sources of growth, *external* and *internal* to any system. Externally induced growth involves major shifts in demand and supply, and the development and diffusion of new technologies, about which more will be said later.

Such externally generated changes are important in that they involve interaction beyond the boundaries of the system. Internally generated change takes place as a consequence of causal chains existing within the system. One simple-minded early theory of internally generated change discussed in Chapter 1 was Ellsworth Huntington's global theory of economic growth based upon environmental determinism: climate determines health; health determines efficiency; efficiency produces national growth; climate changes in time; ergo, climate is the "mainspring" factor determining the rise and fall of civilizations.

More modern theories of internally generated change invoke different factors, but use similar self-contained causal chain logic. Frequently the changes arise cumulatively, and should be differentiated from the idea of negative feedback. Negative feedback is a central theme of *cybernetics*, the science of communication and control. The term cybernetics is derived from the Greek word for helmsman or steersman—the person who provides the negative feedback that keeps a ship on course.

The contrasting process involves *positive feedback* in which deviations are amplified, and in which change becomes circular and cumulative. Thus Winslow wrote in *The Cost of Sickness and The Price of Health,*

It was clear . . . that poverty and disease formed a vicious circle. Men and women were sick because they were poor; they become poorer because they were sick, and sicker because they were poorer.

The most important treatise that discusses circular and cumulative causation and its consequences for economic systems is that of Gunnar Myrdal, initially stated in *An American Dilemma* and reiterated on a world scale in *Asian Drama* and *Rich Lands and Poor.* Myrdal said:

There is no such tendency toward automatic self-stabilization in the social system. The system is by itself not moving toward any sort of balance between forces but is constantly on the move away from such a situation. In the normal case a change does not call forth countervailing changes but, instead, supporting changes, which move the system in the same direction as the first change but much further. Because of such circular causation a social process tends to become cumulative and often to gather speed at an accelerating rate. (Gunnar Myrdal, *Rich Lands and Poor,* New York: Harper & Row, 1957, p. 13)

Allan Pred has recently reformulated Mydal's model for urban growth and change. He notes that the most frequently perceived regional problem is the concentration of population and economic functions in large urban complexes. The attendant problems of regional economic inequality and differential rates of city growth are virtually universal. Furthermore, large cities change their population rank only infrequently: population and employment growth concentrate around previous growth foci. It seems clear that the largest cities repeatedly reinforce and renew their advantages after having acquired a dominant position in the urban hierarchy at some relatively early development stage. They do so by the acquisition of growth-inducing innovations which tend to be adopted earliest in large cities because they offer a large local market, because of external economies of scale, which are enhanced where similar industries are competitively spurred to adopt the innovation, and by the "operational" decision-making advantages associated with large cities. Operational decision making includes purchase-source decisions, market investment decisions, private investment decisions, and public organization allocation decisions. Pred believes that in every case the decision-making process tends to stabilize the ranking of large cities according to size as the process of city-system development unfolds. The impacts of interurban diffusion and the accumulation of operational decisions are magnified by nonlocal multiplier effects because cities have open economies; increased economic activity in any city is likely to stimulate economic activity throughout the urban system. Pred then combines these three processes, diffusion, decision making, and multipliers, into a large city-focused model of city-system development which incorporates a circular and cumulative feedback process of urban-size growth for large metropolitan areas.

Is there any way out of the vicious circle described by Myrdal and Pred? Maruyama stresses the importance of "initial kick" in reversing such trends:

Thus in the economically underdeveloped countries, it is necessary not only to plan the economy, but also to give the initial kick and reinforce it for a while in such a direction and with such intensity as to maximize the efficiency of development per initial investment. Once the economy is kicked in a right direction and with a sufficient initial push, the deviation amplifying mutual positive feedbacks takes over the process, and the resulting development will be disproportionately large as compared with initial kick. (Walter Buckley, ed., *Modern Systems Research for the Behavioral Scientist.* Chicago: Aldine, 1968, p. 305)

Most authors who have considered the source of such "kicks" emphasize that the boot must be externally derived; we will return to this source of change later when we discuss diffusion of technology and ideas. However, there is an internally derived "kick" too, that of hierarchical restructuring, an idea that will be developed in the next section.

PATTERNS OF GROWTH

What pathways are followed by open growing systems? Boulding has divided absolute growth into two categories, simple and populational. *Simple growth* occurs in systems that are incapable of accretion through self-reproduction or of depletion through death. *Populational growth* entails a balance between "births" and "deaths" in a population whose growth is related to its age structure. Such growth is multiplicative in the sense that what is produced by growth is itself normally capable of growing and producing growth. Human population growth is the obvious example.

In either case, simple or populational, the growth curve may be approximated by the laws of exponential or logistic growth. The exponential law, sometimes called the *law of natural growth,* applies when growth is unrestricted, unlimited, and accelerating. Logistic growth is found when there are upper limits to growth.

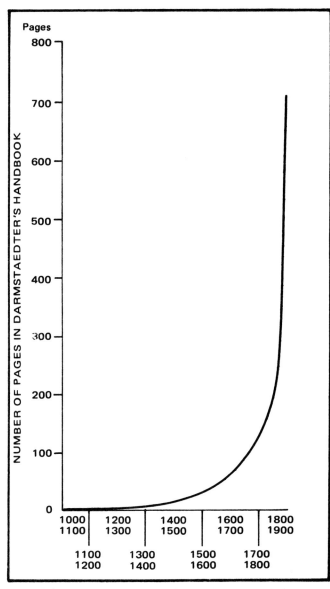

Fig. 25.2 *The growth of human knowledge, 1000–1900*

Source: Alfred J. Lotka, "Population Analysis as a Chapter in the Mathematical Theory of Evolution," in Essays on Growth and Form, *W. E. Le Gros Clark and Peter P. Medawar, eds., 1945, p. 380.*

exponential growth

A prominent example of exponential growth is the growth of human knowledge, which, as Figures 25.2 and 25.3 show, has expanded at a multiplicative rate. Neither graph is completely adequate as a representation of the growth of human knowledge, but together they are probably the best available measurement of the comparative progress of science. The number of discoveries and inventions does not measure quality; most important are those pathfinding achievements that lead to a host of other inventions and discoveries. Inevitably all such enumerations contain systematic bias because of the effacing role of time and distance and the tendency to give greater prominence to the more

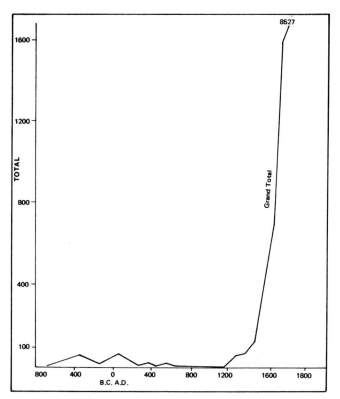

Fig. 25.3 *The total number of scientific inventions and geographic discoveries from 800 B.C. to A.D. 1800, by centuries*

Source: P. A. Sorokin, Social and Cultural Dynamics, II *(New York: Bedminster Press, 1962), 137.*

recent discoveries and inventions of the Western world. Nevertheless, the reality of the unprecedented growth during the past four or five centuries, as well as the existence of secondary peaks in the Graeco-Roman world, must remain unquestioned. A similar picture of accelerating increase emerges for technological invention based on patents issued in Great Britain during the years 1449–1921, and for geography and science. The number of scientific journals has been doubling every fifteen years; the number of geography journals has, in general, followed the trend for the social sciences of doubling every thirty years.

logistic growth

Any detailed analysis of the growth of human knowledge leads one to question whether the impressions of unbounded growth given by such graphs are an adequate representation of the growth trend of human knowledge, or indeed of the growth of any phenomenon. There have been enough fluctuations, including the low rate of European inventiveness between the fourth and twelfth centuries, to raise doubts about steady, unbounded growth. The rate of inventiveness and of patents has decreased; progress in many fields in the natural sciences has slowed from earlier peaks of discovery. It may also be questioned whether world

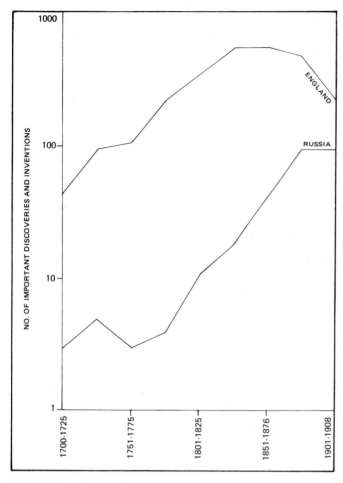

Fig. 25.4 *The number of important discoveries and inventions in England and Russia by 25-year periods, 1701–1908*

Source: Sorokin, Social and Cultural Dynamics.

Fig. 25.5 *The incremental and cumulative number of patents issued for the plow sulky*

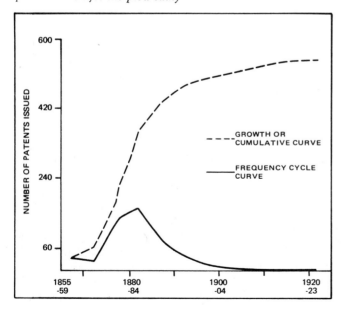

population growth can maintain the present accelerating increase discussed in Chapter 2.

Underlying many of these doubts is the belief that all growing objects must eventually run into conditions that are increasingly unfavorable to growth. Commonly, absolute growth follows a pattern of accelerating growth followed by decelerating growth. When the deceleration is at the reverse rate of the acceleration, the growth curve is logistic. Early growth accelerates because the most favorable and accessible elements are utilized first. Continuing growth entails lower-grade resources, cultivation of more distant areas, and employment of less skilled workers and less productive reserve equipment. Early growth benefits from economies of scale; continued growth encounters diseconomies of scale.

Growth complicates and lengthens feedback, reducing responsiveness to environmental change. In the end all growth must cease. Boulding has noted that if growth did not eventually cease, there would eventually be only one object in the universe and at that point at least, unless the universe itself can grow indefinitely, its growth would have to come to an end.

Referring to the example of human inventiveness, Britain's decline after 1876 becomes clear when the data are graphed (Fig. 25.4). The decline for Russia is less marked and comes later, but this will be shown to fit the European pattern of diffusion of innovation by a process of "lagged emulation." When the development of an individual invention is traced, based on the number of patents issued, the decline is generally even more marked. The cumulative and incremental inventions patented for the plow sulky are shown in Figure 25.5. From 1865 to 1884 there was a yearly increase in the total number of inventions. From 1884 to 1923 there was a steady decline in the yearly number of new inventions added to the original fundamental invention. The incremental curve approximates a bell-shaped or normal curve, and the cumulative curve approximates the logistic. In both, the deceleration of growth is at the reverse of the acceleration.

Population growth, too, may approximate the logistic growth curve rather than the exponential. The transition from a Malthusian-like to a logistic-like age distribution was graphed by Lotka for the United States from 1700 with projections to 2100 (Fig. 25.6). Note that Lotka's forecasts for the year 2100, made in 1920, fall far short of the present-day U.S. population total.

allometric relationships in growing systems

An important concept in unifying the previous sections on growth and change, and providing the links between growth and form, is the *law of allometry*. This law is best illustrated in the case of open developing systems although its greater generality will become clear as the discussion proceeds. The law relates the changes in the proportionality of the parts of any

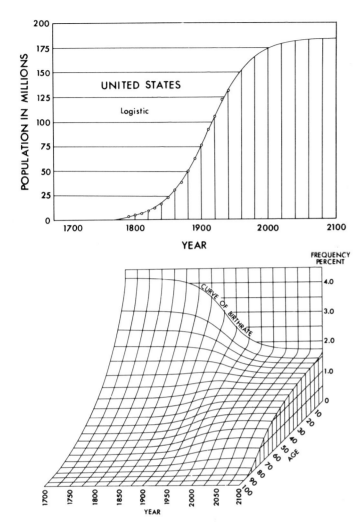

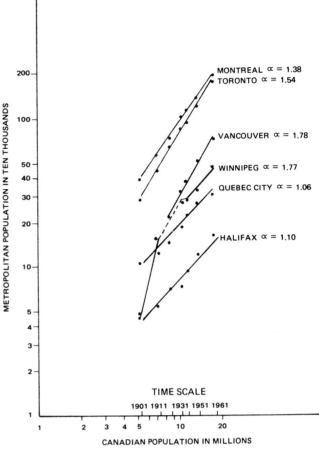

(a) Individual allometries, six selected metropolitan areas

(b) The allometric growth gradient for the Canadian metropolitan areas

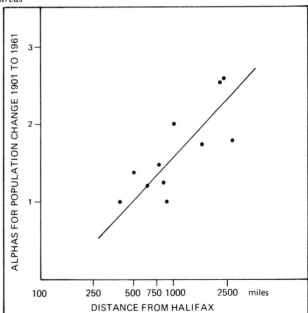

Fig. 25.6 *Logistic growth and changing age composition of the United States population from 1700 projected to 2100. Current population already exceeds this projection for the year 2000. The lower graph shows the changes in age composition that accompany a change from Malthusian to zero population growth.*

Source: Lotka, "Population Analysis."

system to the size of the system as a whole; thus, most broadly, allometry deals with size and its consequences.

Mathematically, when y is the size of a part and x is the size of the whole $y = bx^a$, or $\log y = \log b + \alpha \log x$, and α measures the allometry. Assume that x and y both have the same dimensionality such as population totals or areas of land use. Then, when α is 1.0 the part grows at the same rate as the whole ($y = bx$). When α is less than 1, the part grows more slowly than the whole (for example, if $\alpha = 0.5$, $y = bx^{0.5}$ or $y = b\sqrt{x}$ and the part grows at half the rate of the whole). When α exceeds 1, the part grows more rapidly than the whole (e.g., $y = bx^2$ is a situation in which the part grows at double the rate of the whole).

To illustrate, the population of Canadian cities has grown allometrically in relation to the Canada total from 1901 to 1961 (Fig. 25.7a). Note in this figure that

Fig. 25.7 *Urban allometries in Canada, 1901–1961*

Source: Population data are from Leroy O. Stone, Urban Development in Canada *(Ottawa: Dominion Bureau of Statistics, 1967), pp. 269, 278.*

the allometries increase progressively from east to west (Fig. 25.7b). This gradient reveals both the phenomenon of increasing metropolitan concentration and the westward spread of Canadian growth and development: Vancouver's growth rate was 1.78 times that of Canada, whereas Halifax's was only 1.10.

There is a wide diversity of phenomena whose growth is allometric. For example, allometric relationships are found in central-place systems, in the growth of the world's railway networks (Fig. 25.8), and in the expansion of the settled area of the United States until the early twentieth century (Fig. 25.9).

What is important about the allometry index, α, is that different values of the index reveal different part-whole relationships, and therefore different ways in which the form of the system changes with increasing size. Figure 25.10 shows the effect of the change in alpha in two graphs, one relating log y to log x and the other y to x. Spatial form changes as the size of the whole changes in all systems except for the particular case of a system in which all components have an allometry of 1. If the allometry of the component is greater than 1, the form of the whole must adjust to accommodate the growing share of the part; if less than 1, the form must adjust to a declining share. Thus the form of Quebec cities changes to adjust to the positive allometry of multifamily land use, the isometry of community space, and the negative allometry of commercial space (Fig. 25.11).

hierarchical jumps

Frequently, the stresses generated by the pressure to change form lead to developmental shifts that occur as *hierarchical jumps*—structural transformations that arise because the system is no longer able to function with the changes in proportionalities of parts called for by the earlier allometric relationships. New parts emerge, structured in new patterns with new relationships between them. In essence, one system is replaced by another that is better organized and better able to function at the new scale and complexity. Such is the nature of those internally generated changes that have historically been called revolutions. An example is the early industrial revolution in Britain. The diffusion of this revolution was the external source responsible for growth and change in other areas.

GROWTH AND DEVELOPMENT OF SPATIAL ORGANIZATION: FROM INVENTION TO DIFFUSION

The growth of spatial systems and the development of spatial organization are linked by three interrelated processes: invention, innovation, and diffusion. Invention is central to the internally generated process of structural transformation. Innovation and diffusion involve the transmission of inventions to other places, and the inducement of growth, change, and develop-

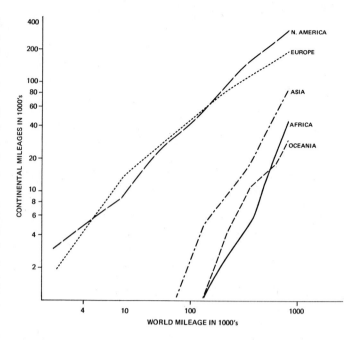

Fig. 25.8 *The growth of continental railroad mileage relative to world railroad mileage, 1840–1950*

Source: Data from W. S. Woytinski and E. S. Woytinski, World Commerce and Governments: Trends and Outlook *(New York: Twentieth Century Fund, 1955), II, 341.*

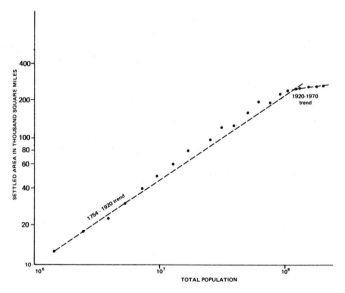

Fig. 25.9 *The growth of population and of the effectively settled area of the United States, 1754–1970. From 1764 to 1920, area grew at the ⅔ power of population. Since 1920, area has ceased to grow.*

Source: Geoffrey H. Dutton, The Shape of Urban Systems: An Allometric Perspective *(Ottawa: Ministry of State for Urban Affairs, Discussion Paper B.73.7, 1973), p. 17.*

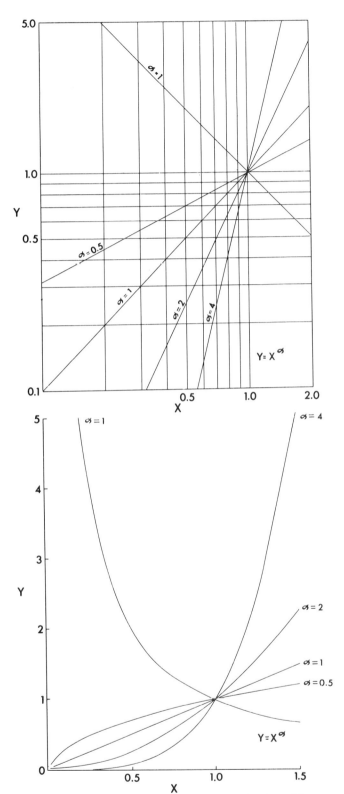

Fig. 25.10 *Relative growth relationships as indicated by α. The upper graph uses a double logarithmic scale; the lower, arithmetic scales.*

Source: D. A. Sholl, "Regularities in Growth Curves, Including Rhythms and Allometry," Dynamics of Growth Processes, *Ed., E. J. Boell (Princeton, N. J.: Princeton University Press, 1954), pp. 224–42.*

invention

Invention is the creative act or process. It involves new ideas, new procedures, new types of organization, new products, and new technologies; it includes *basic* applications of new knowledge and new components— as in the invention of the first radio, jet engine, or computer—and also *elaborations* or *improvements* in later models based on additional experimentation and experience.

One explanation of the inventive act is the transcendental or "heroic" theory, which holds that invention is the inspiration of the occasional genius, and is therefore unpredictable in time and space. The more widely accepted explanation is that an invention is a new combination of a relatively large number of elements, accumulated over long periods of time, with the individual inventor acting merely as an instrument of historical process. For example, in 1858 Darwin and Wallace both presented papers at the same meeting of the Royal Society setting forth the idea of natural selection in the evolutionary formation and change of species. If Darwin had died during his two decades of indecision on whether to publish his results, Wallace would almost certainly be credited with the theory of evolution. If both had died shortly before 1858, the mechanistic view is that in a few years, given the scientific climate of the times, some third man would have documented and presented the theory since conditions were ripe for this interpretive synthesis. Both Darwin and Wallace had been led to their ideas by reading Malthus' work on population, in which he pointed out that population multiplies faster than food. They both concluded that if this is true of animals, then animals must compete to survive.

It is thus evident that invention involves *cumulative synthesis:* successive perceptions of a problem set the stage for invention and lead to a gathering of the necessary facts about the problem and the principles and components that offer a potential solution. Invention is the resolution of the problem. The linkages are diagrammed in Figure 25.12.

Cumulative synthesis leading to invention is an example of positive feedback. It has been characteristic of world history that at any one time there have been relatively few centers in which this cumulative process is taking place. In the centers of invention there is accelerated accumulation; and from them, innovations diffuse, producing change elsewhere (subject to the lags of time and the frictions of space). For those areas beyond the pole of diffusion, there is the problem of not being part of the system within which the process

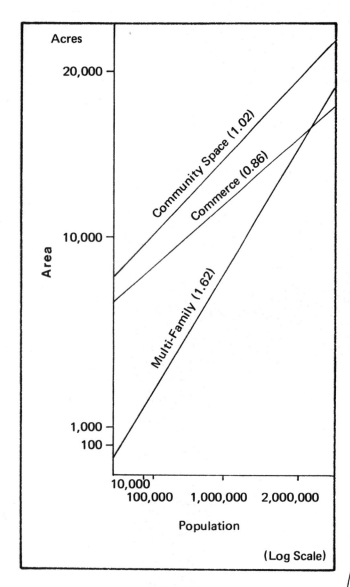

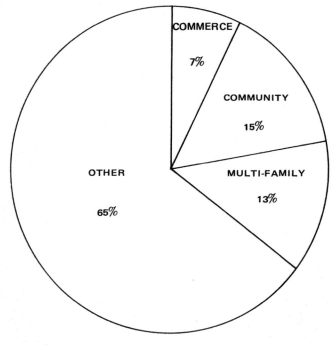

(b) *Land use proportions in commercial, community, and multifamily for Montreal. 1971 population: 2,743,208.*

(a) *The allometry of community, commercial, and multifamily area. Three types of land uses selected illustrate positive allometry (multifamily, α = 1.62), isometry or proportional growth (community, α = 1.02), and negative allometry (commercial, α = 0.86).*

Fig. 25.11 *Differences in urban form at different sizes*

Source: Compiled by Laval Fournier for cities exceeding 20,000 population. The data were taken from the Office de Planifacation et de développement du Québec, Utilisation du sol des 62 principales agglomération du Québec. *Québec City: Gouvernement du Québec, 1971. Multifamily land use includes duplexes, town houses, and apartments. Commercial land use includes tertiary services such as offices, shopping centers, hotels and theaters. Community land uses include churches, parks, schools, recreation centers, and open space.*

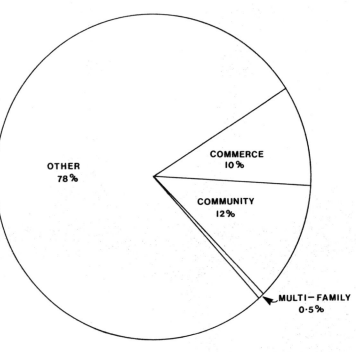

(c) *Land use proportions in commercial, community, and multifamily for Alma. 1971 population: 22,622.*

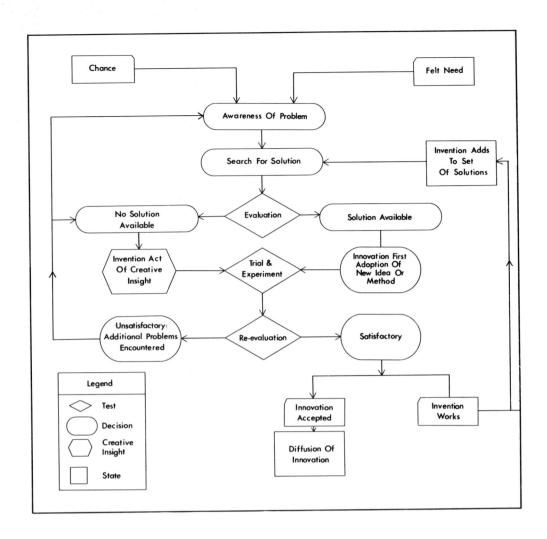

Legend

◇ Test

⬭ Decision

⬡ Creative Insight

▢ State

Fig. 25.12 *A graphical interpretation of the invention and innovation processes. Definitions of invention and innovation differ. This interpretation attempts to incorporate the statements of Vernon W. Ruttan "Usher and Schumpeter on Invention, Innovation and Technological Change,"* Quarterly Journal of Economics, 73 (1954), 596–606; *and Gwyn E. Jones "The Adoption and Innovation of Agricultural Practices,"* World Agricultural Economics and Rural Sociology Abstracts, IX (September 1967), 1–34.

of circular and cumulative causation is taking place. Further, the centers of invention, by virtue of their inventiveness and the rewards that they are thought to offer, continually attract new talent, cementing their advantage by draining from other areas the pool of individuals capable of engaging in the act of creative synthesis.

innovation

Innovation is the acceptance, adoption, and application of inventions. Innovation takes place in areas other than centers of invention after the invention has occurred, so that the time sequence becomes important. Because the most remote areas tend to innovate last

and least, if at all, the spatial sequence of innovation is also important. In short, innovation involves a combined time-space sequence: acceptance over time of some specific idea or practice by individuals, groups, or other adopting units that are linked to specific channels of communication, to a social structure, and to a given system of values or culture. An example of a typical time-space sequence is provided by the diffusion of postage stamps in Europe and North and South America (Fig. 25.13).

The relationships are generalized in Figure 25.14. Many other examples can be given: the Industrial Revolution probably could not have run its course without the parallel spread of railroads. These represented the fastest means of transportation in the century pre-

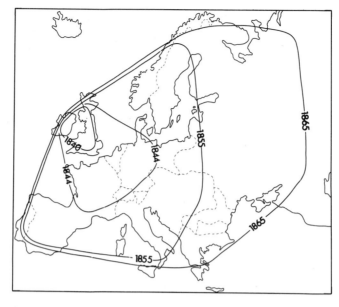

(a) The diffusion of postage stamps in Europe

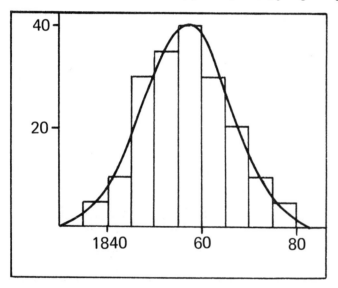

*(b) The distribution of countries in Europe, North and South
America according to date of first postage stamp issue*

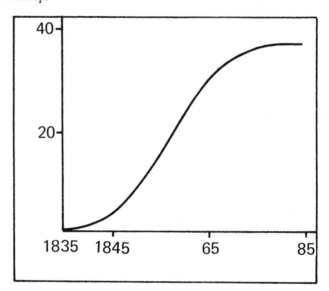

(c) The cumulative distribution of first postage stamps

Fig. 25.13   *Postage stamp distribution*

*Source: H. Earl Pemberton, "The Curve of Culture Diffusion
Rates,"* American Sociological Review, *I (August 1936), 552, 553;
and H. Earl Pemberton, "The Spatial Order of Culture Diffusion,"*
Sociology and Social Research, *XXII (January, February 1938),
No. 3, 248.*

ceding World War I (Fig. 25.15). During the period
that railroads were the best means of transportation
available, railroad mileage grew in a logistic fashion
(Fig. 25.16). This was true· both worldwide and for
individual countries (Fig. 25.17). As in the case of postage stamps, the logistic increase of railroad mileage was
accompanied by a lagged outward spread from the
original center of the innovation, Great Britain and
at an accelerating growth rate (Fig. 25.18).

diffusion

Even in prehistory, there is strong evidence that
innovations diffused outward from certain centers in
a lagged fashion with increasing distance. For example,
Figures 25.19 and 25.20 show the early diffusion of
pottery. Figure 25.21 reproduces Carl Sauer's seminal
diagram of the origins and dispersals of domesticated
plants and animals. In each case, dissemination lagged
with increasing distance.

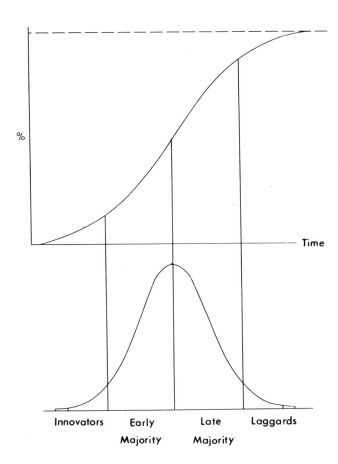

Fig. 25.14 *The distribution of innovation acceptors and the logistic curve of innovation adoption*

Source: Peter Gould, Spatial Diffusion, *Commission on College Geography Resource Paper No. 4 (Washington, D. C.: Association of American Geographers, 1969), p. 19.*

Fig. 25.15 *The accelerating rise in world speed records, 1750–1956*

Source: Hornell Hart, "Acceleration in Social Change," in Francis R. Allen et al. (ed.), Technology and Social Change *(New York: Appleton-Century-Crofts, 1957), pp. 27–71.*

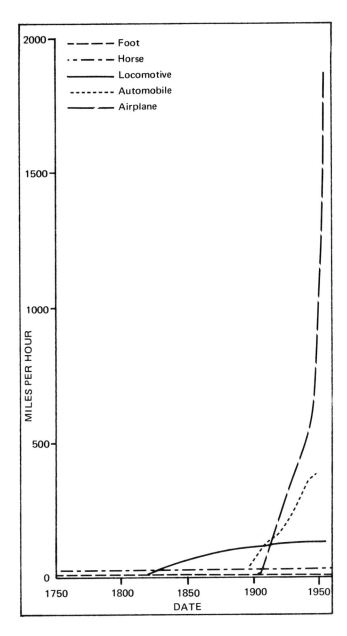

Fig. 25.16 *World railroad building, 1840–1950. Compare this graph with the locomotive and intermodal world speed records. Most railroad mileage was built in the period when railroads enjoyed a speed superiority over other modes.*

Source: Lotka, "Population Analysis," p. 380.

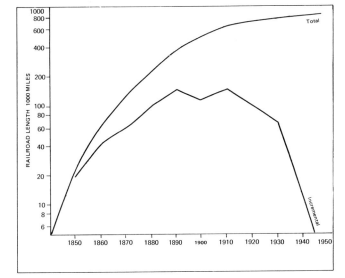

(a)

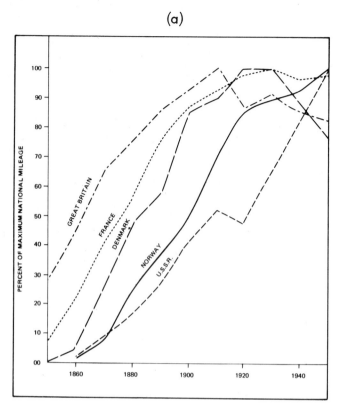

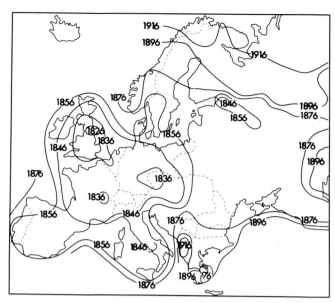

Source: (a) Sven Godlund, "Ein Innovationsverlauf in Europa, dargestellt in einer vorläufigen Untersuchung über die Ausbreitung der Eisenbahninnovation," (Lund, Sweden: Department of Geography, Royal University of Lund, Series B in Geography, Human Geography No. 6, 1952).

(b)

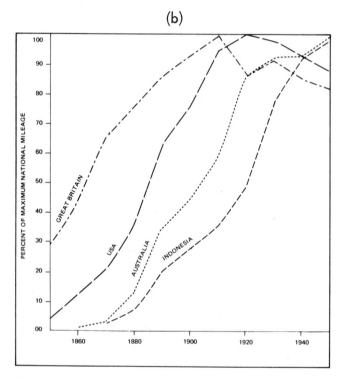

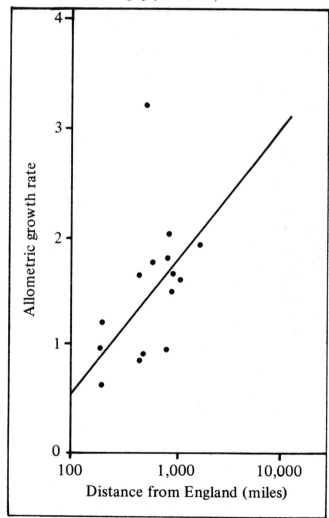

Fig. 25.17 *The logistic curves of railroad building for selected countries (a) Europe, (b) worldwide*

Source: Woytinski and Woytinski, World Commerce.

Fig. 25.18 *The diffusion and growth gradient of railroad building in Europe, 1826–1916*

Source: (b) D. Michael Ray et al., "Functional Prerequisites, Spatial Diffusion, and Allometric Growth," Economic Geography, L, No.p.348.

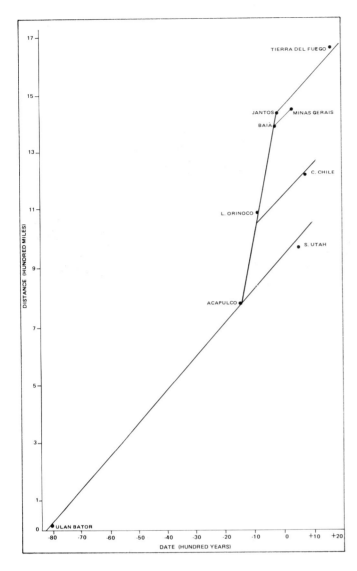

The most significant diffusion for understanding the geography of economic systems in the world today involves that complex set of innovations that comprised the Industrial Revolution. It began with a series of major inventions in Britain, as was noted in Chapter 14. From Britain, use of the new technologies spread across Europe and to the New World. The world's first industrial heartland emerged as other countries came to share in Britain's role as center of innovation and entrepreneurship, and as a reservoir of capital and skilled labor. The heartland-hinterland pattern of world economic organization emerged as the new industrial powers reached overseas for raw materials and markets, fought for colonial empires, and settled the world's mid-latitudes. By the end of the century, increases in the scale, complexity, and organizational and capital requirements of new industry effectively limited its further spread.

However, as we noted in Chapter 12, there are other patterns of diffusion in the world today. Many innovations continue to spread in a heartland-hinterland or core-periphery manner. Accompanying this kind of sequence is often a tendency to move from large cities to small, in a pattern of "hierarchical diffusion." Likewise, there is often a pattern of decreasing dissemination with increasing distance from an urban center within any urban field—a local "spread effect."

Fig. 25.19 *The diffusion of pottery related to location of first innovation. Two slopes are indicated. A land-rate diffusion of 1.1 miles per year and a sea-rate diffusion to key entry ports in Latin America of 8.5 miles per year.*

Source: Munro S. Edmonson, "Neolithic Diffusion Rates," Current Anthropology *(April 1969).*

Fig. 25.20 *Map of pottery diffusion routes*
Source: Edmonson, "Neolithic Diffusion Rates."

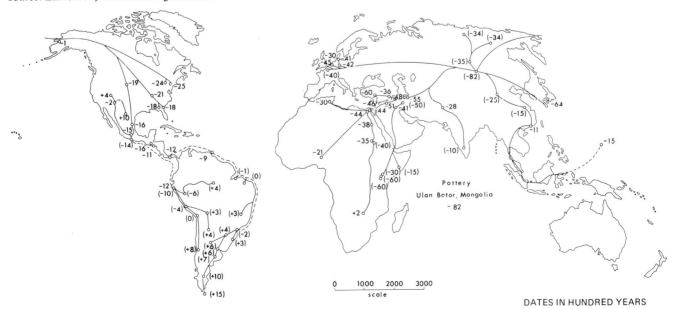

DATES IN HUNDRED YEARS

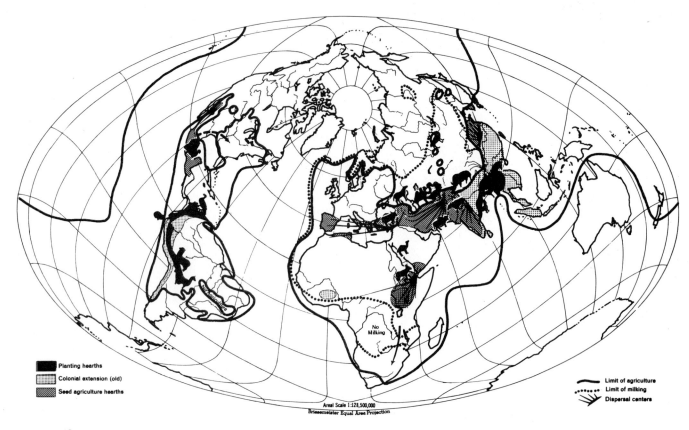

Fig. 25.21 *Hearths of domestication and limits of agriculture and milking about* A.D. *1500*

Source: Carl Sauer, "Agricultural Origins and Dispersals," American Geographical Society Bowman Memorial Lectures, Series No. 2, *PLIV (1952).*

For example, the U.S. television industry grew in the period after 1940 in a logistic fashion, subject to wartime interruptions (Fig. 25.22). The first stations were opened in large metropolitan areas, the last in smaller areas (Fig. 25.23). Closer consumers bought television sets first, and both national heartland-hinterland and local spread effects can be seen in the succession of maps of increasing market penetration (Figs. 25.24–25.26). Importantly, the lagged areas in the sequence are the most backward and conservative, and constitute peripheral pockets of poverty.

THE LIMITS TO GROWTH

The last two centuries have seen accelerated growth of the world's industrial economies, development of worldwide spatial organization, and growing threats of exhaustion of many of the earth's resources. Consequently, many people have now begun to question whether present trends can continue, emphasizing that

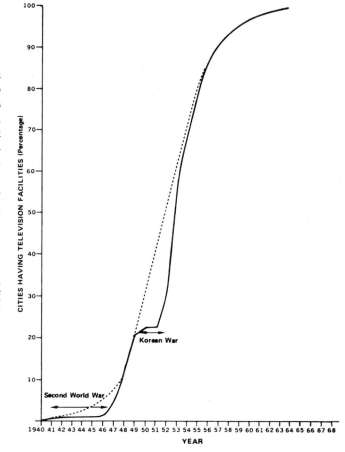

Fig. 25.22 *Growth in number of TV cities, 1940–1968*

Source: Brian J. L. Berry, "The Geography of the United States in the Year 2000," Transactions of the Institute of British Geographers, *LI (November 1970), 21–53.*

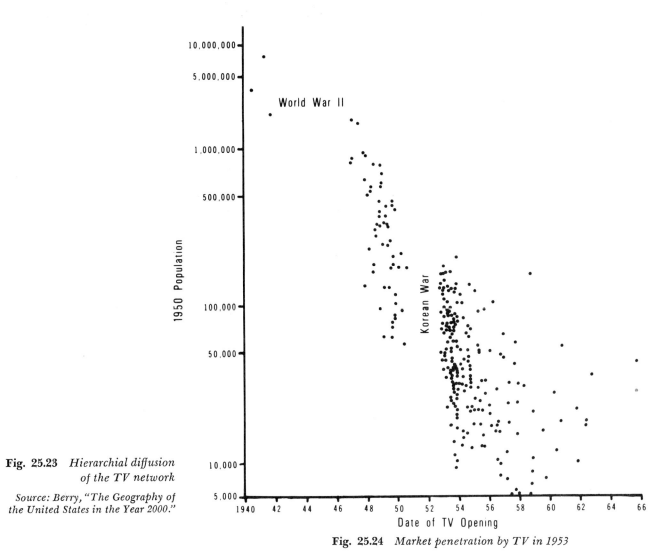

Fig. 25.23 *Hierarchial diffusion of the TV network*

Source: Berry, "The Geography of the United States in the Year 2000."

1950 Population

Date of TV Opening

World War II

Korean War

Fig. 25.24 *Market penetration by TV in 1953*

Source: Berry, "The Geography of the United States in the Year 2000."

Market Penetration: Percentage of Households Having Television Receivers

0%   20%   40%   60%   80%   100%

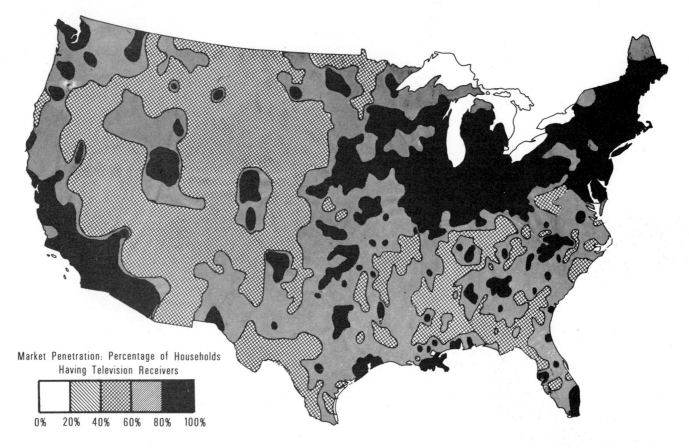

Market Penetration: Percentage of Households
Having Television Receivers

0%   20%   40%   60%   80%   100%

Fig. 25.25 *Market penetration by TV in 1959*

Source: Berry, "The Geography of the United States in the Year 2000."

Fig. 25.26 *Market penetration by TV in 1965*

Source: Berry, "The Geography of the United States in the Year 2000."

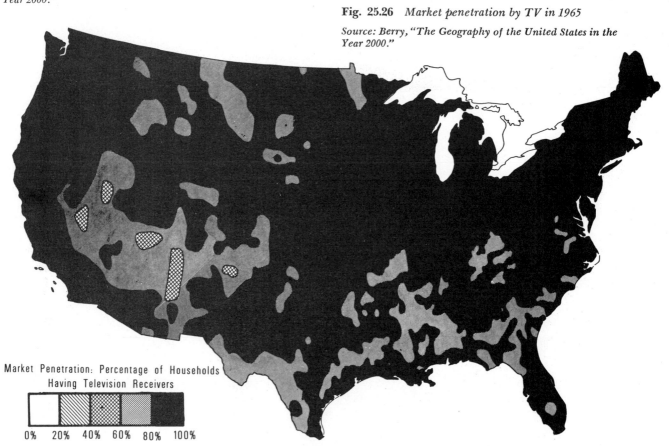

Market Penetration: Percentage of Households
Having Television Receivers

0%   20%   40%   60%   80%   100%

world economic growth trends must be logistic rather than exponential. They point out that the earth is very much an isolated space ship in the universe, and runs the risk of any essentially *closed* system—the rapid approach of entropy—unless a self-maintaining global system can be achieved in which a new balance emerges between man and nature, commensurate with the one external source of life-support on which the earth can rely, the continued input of energy from the sun.

No study has been of greater significance in presenting this challenge to the contemporary pattern of growth in the world and the attitudes that support it than *The Limits to Growth,* a report for the Club of Rome. The Club of Rome was formed in 1968 by Aurelio Peccei and 75 prominant industrialists, scientists, and economists from around the world who were united by an overriding conviction that the major problems facing mankind are of such complexity and are so interrelated that traditional institutions and policies are no longer able to cope with them. A series of early meetings culminated in the decision to initiate the Project on the Predicament of Mankind, which was to concern itself with problems that contain technical, economic, social, and political elements, and that occur to some degree in all societies. Phase One of the Project took shape at meetings held in the summer of 1970 in Bern, Switzerland, and Cambridge, Massachusetts. It was decided to make a systems analysis of the world through the creation of a dynamic world model linking such factors as population, pollution, resources, land, and capital generation. The model is based on the system dynamics model developed by MIT Professor Jay Forrester in his books, *Industrial Dynamics* (1961), *Urban Dynamics* (1970), and *World Dynamics* (1971). It was constructed by a team at MIT under the direction of Professor Dennis Meadows. The results were presented at two international meetings held in the summer of 1971, one in Moscow and the other in Rio de Janeiro.

The Limits to Growth was presented at a press conference held by the MIT group in the Smithsonian Institution on March 2, 1972. Twelve thousand copies of this book were distributed to world leaders, and it was translated into some twenty languages.

The attention that this report has received is due, in part, to the sense of crisis that permeates the study. The authors indicate in their introduction to *The Limits to Growth* that they are concerned with accelerating industrialization, rapid population growth, widespread malnutrition, depletion of nonrenewable resources, and a deteriorating environment, or, in less value-laden terms, with manufacturing, population, agriculture, resources, and environment. They indicate that, to their knowledge, theirs is the only model in existence that is truly global in scope, that has a time horizon longer than 30 years, and that includes a comprehensive set of interacting variables.

The outcome of the analysis is clear and urgent as these quotations illustrate:

We can thus say with some confidence that under the assumption of no major change in the present system, population and industrial growth will certainly stop within the next century, at the latest (p. 126).

The basic behaviour mode of the system is exponential growth of population and capital, followed by collapse (p. 142).

In spite of the preliminary state of our work, we believe it is important to publish the model and our findings now. Decisions are being made every day, in every part of the world, that will affect the physical, economic, and social conditions of the world system for decades to come. These decisions cannot wait for perfect models and total understanding. They will be made on the basis of some model, mental or written, in any case. We feel that the model described here is already sufficiently developed to be of some use to decision-makers. Furthermore, the basic behaviour modes we have already observed in this model appear to be so fundamental and general that we do not expect our broad conclusions to be substantially altered by further revisions (p. 22).

These conclusions are so far-reaching and raise so many questions for further study that we are quite frankly overwhelmed by the enormity of the job that must be done (p. 24).

The implications of these trends raise issues that go far beyond the proper domain of a purely scientific document. They must be debated by a wider community than that of scientists alone. Our purpose here is to open that debate (p. 23).

It is clear that Meadows and his group are deeply concerned with the results that they have obtained, and there is little doubt that the deep apprehension evident throughout this book has struck a responsive chord, especially in North America and Western Europe where the belief is growing that we are in the midst of a profound environmental crisis. There is also increasing doubt whether all the world's population will ultimately enjoy the same standards of living as the United States and whether, even if it could, prosperity would produce social and political harmony.

global overshoot and collapse

The key finding from the system dynamics models about the basic behavior mode of the world is that exponential growth of population, industrial output, and pollution will be followed by global collapse. This conclusion stands whatever variations in their assumptions that they make. Five of the Meadows models illustrate the dilemma.

the world model standard run

This model assumes that there will not be any great future changes in human values or in the functioning of the global population system from the way it has operated for the last 100 years (Fig. 25.27). The computer printout of the results for this, as for other models, shows the change in population, industrial output per capita, food per capita, pollution, nonrenewable resources, crude birth rates, crude death rates, and services per capita from 1900 to 2100. Each variable is plotted on a different vertical scale; the vertical scales are omitted and the horizontal time scales somewhat vague to emphasize general behavior rather than numerical values. The values of these variables from 1900 to 1970 are set to agree with their historical values to the extent that they are known. In the first model, population increases from 1.6 billion in 1900 to 3.5 billion in 1970. Although the birth rate declines gradually, the death rate falls more quickly, especially after 1940, and the population growth rate increases. Industrial output, food, and services per capita increase ex-

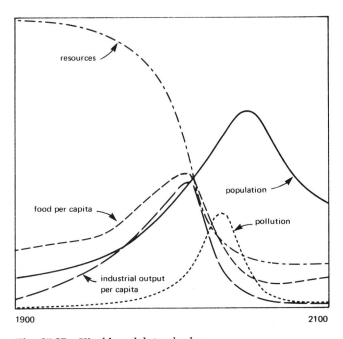

Fig. 25.27   *World model standard run*

Source: Donella Meadows et al., The Limits to Growth *(New York: Universe Books, 1972), p. 97.*

ponentially producing a dramatic decline in the resource base. Finally, food per capita and industrial output per capita decline rapidly paralleling the downward trend of resources as closely as they previously paralleled the upward curve of population. World population continues to climb for a while until finally the birth rate curve intersects the death rate curve and there is a rapid collapse of world population. It is clear in the world model standard run that population collapse occurs because of *nonrenewable resource depletion.*

world model with natural resource reserves doubled

But what if the estimate of the global stock of resources is too low? Assume that new discoveries of advances in technology can double the amount of resources eco-

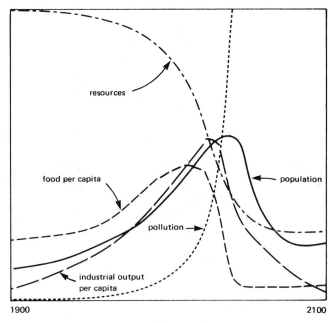

Fig. 25.28   *World model with natural resource reserve doubled*

Source: Meadows et al., The Limits to Growth.

nomically available. Then the scenario is repeated (Fig. 25.28). In this second world model again there is population overshoot and collapse, but this time it is caused by pollution coupled with depletion of nonrenewable resources. Even with resources doubled, they are sufficient for only a few more years of exponential growth.

world model with "unlimited" resources and pollution control

The above results indicate that survival of the world system depends on controlling both the depletion of nonrenewable resources and pollution, and so a further model was attempted with unlimited resources and with strict pollution controls. This model assumed that pollution generation per unit of industrial and agricultural output could be reduced to one-fourth of the 1970 value. Resource policies remained the same, but it was assumed that unlimited nuclear power doubled the reserves that could be exploited and that nuclear energy made extensive pollution-control programs and resource-substitution possible. These changes allowed population and industry to grow until the food-producing limit of arable land was reached (Fig. 25.29). Following this model, food per capita declines and industrial growth is also slowed as capital is diverted to food production. The result is that population and industrial output per person rise well beyond their previous peak values and yet resource depletion and pollution never become acute problems. Nevertheless the system suffers overshoot and collapse. This time it is caused by food shortage.

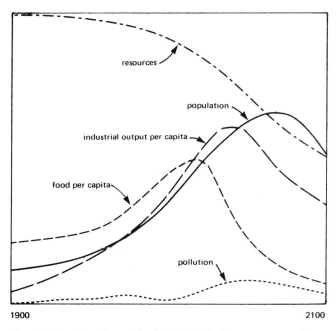

Fig. 25.29 *World model with "unlimited" resources and pollution controls*

Source: Meadows et al., The Limits to Growth.

world model with "unlimited" resources, pollution controls, and increased agricultural productivity

The next Meadows model assumed that the food shortage problem could be solved by increased agricultural productivity in the context of unlimited resources, and effective pollution controls (Fig. 25.30). The combination of these three policies removes so many constraints to growth that population and industry reach very high levels. Although each unit of industrial production generates much less pollution, total production rises enough to create a pollution crisis that overwhelms controls and brings an end to growth. Once again the exponential growth of population exceeds the capacity of the world and there is catastrophic collapse bringing the world back down to 1900 levels.

world model with "unlimited" resources, pollution controls, increased agricultural productivity, and "perfect" birth control

As a final effort, a world model was run with unlimited resources, pollution controls, increased agricultural productivity, and birth control (Fig. 25.31). The model assumed nuclear power; recycling of resources and mining the most remote reserves; withholding as many pollutants as possible; pushing land yields to undreamed-of heights; and birth only of children who were wanted by their parents. The result is still an end to growth before the year 2100. In this case growth is stopped by three simultaneous crises. Overuse of land leads to erosion, and food production drops. Resources

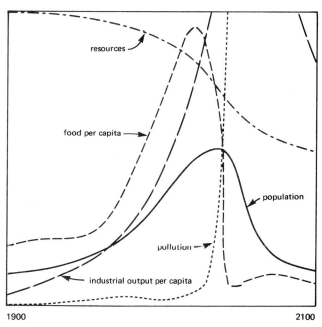

Fig. 25.30 *World model with "unlimited" resources, pollution controls, and increased agricultural productivity*

Source: Meadows et al., The Limits to Growth.

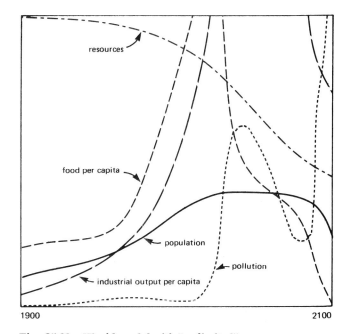

Fig. 25.31 *World model with "unlimited" resources, pollution controls, increased agricultural productivity, and "perfect" birth control*

Source: Meadows et al., The Limits to Growth.

are severely depleted by a prosperous world population. Pollution rises, drops, and rises again dramatically causing a further decrease in food production and a sudden rise in the death rate. The application of technological solutions alone prolongs the period of population and industrial growth but does not remove the ultimate limits to that growth.

The authors of *The Limits to Growth* emphasize that none of these grim results is a prediction of future reality; indeed they would not expect the real world to suffer any of the collapse modes illustrated. Nevertheless, it is clear that there are limits to growth and that we face some critical choices. Fundamentally, the question is whether it is better to try to live within self-imposed limits or to go on growing in the hope that successive technological breakthroughs will overcome the potential natural limits that crop up. For the last several hundred years human society has followed the second course so consistently and successfully that the first choice has been all but forgotten. Moreover, the result has been such a dramatic rise in standard of living for the currently developed countries of the world that the underdeveloped countries cannot be expected to accept limits to growth on the basis of a set of computer results that have in any case been seriously questioned by other scientists. Christopher Freeman, for instance, entitles his lead article "Malthus with a Computer" in a special issue of *Futures*. Given the assumptions, it is argued, the results are inevitable: catastrophe is certain. It is thus critical to examine the assumptions carefully.

assumptions of the limits to growth

The major components of the model are population, capital, food, nonrenewable resources, and pollution. The total model is very complex but some of the basic feedback loops affecting these components will serve to illustrate the strengths and weaknesses of the model (Fig. 25.32). The population is increased by the total number of births and decreased by the total number of deaths. The absolute number of births per year is a function of the average fertility of the population and of the size of the population. Fertility decreases with increasing industrial output and GNP. Deaths are related to population and mortality, and mortality in turn is influenced by food per capita and pollution levels. And this is only the beginning of the complex maze of feedback loops—some positive, some negative.

Professor Jay Forrester emphasizes the difficulty of interpreting and predicting the outcome of system behavior where the systems are complex and contain many such feedback loops. Indeed, Forrester calls the behavior of such systems *counter-intuitive* and says it can only be determined by modeling these systems and simulating their behavior with a computer. Counter-intuitive behavior means that their short-run effects are opposite to their long-run effects so that policy changes based on short-run effects can eventually cause deepening difficulties. The long-run effects of government programs can take an entirely different direction than was originally expected. Supressing one short-run symptom

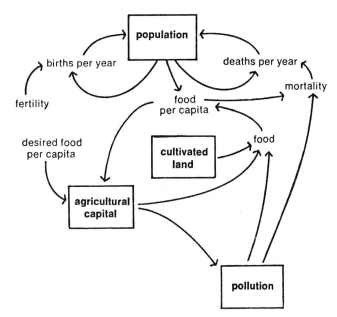

Fig. 25.32 *Some population feedback loops in the world model*

Source: Meadows et al., The Limits to Growth.

only causes other trouble to break out elsewhere later on. Forrester has further argued that we must be cautious about rushing into policy decisions for short-term humanitarian reasons since the eventual results can be antihumanitarian. The similarity of this argument to points raised by the Reverend Thomas Malthus in his "Essay on Population" are quite significant and we return to them later.

The feedback loops shown by arrows in the flow diagrams of *The Limits to Growth* indicate that one variable has some influence on another. The nature and degree of influence are not specified in the diagrams (although they had to be quantified in the model equations). For these purposes the MIT group considered it adequate to use world averages. They explain their purpose with an analogy: if a ball is thrown straight up into the air one can predict with certainty what its general behavior will be and what it will not be. It is this sort of understanding of elemental behavior modes that they are attempting to achieve with their world models. There are, of course, difficulties in using world averages. Increased world economic and population disparities make them less representative, and world averages probably diminish the policy value of the model because only a single set of solutions is suggested that apparently apply to all countries regardless of their particular characteristics. Neither does such a model take into account the problems that are of a local rather than a global nature. But even if world averages could be usefully employed, it is not certain that adequate information was available to the MIT team. Let us therefore examine the assumptions with respect to each model component in turn.

population

The population component is probably one of the more satisfactory parts of the Meadows model. Nevertheless three important points have been raised: the inadequate treatment of factors influencing birth rates; the notorious failure of population projection in the past; and the fact that one model in Forrester's study of world dynamics, where crowding led to a reduction of birth rates and consequently population overshoot and collapse did not occur, is not included in *The Limits to Growth*.

The sole determinants of birth rates in *The Limits to Growth* are the level of industrialization and the food supply. It is assumed on the basis of past experience that birth rates will gradually fall as industrialization proceeds and incomes rise. Otherwise it is assumed that they will not fall unless the food supply becomes inadequate.

In one review of *The Limits to Growth*, Everett C. Hagen points out that this is not good demography. In the West, as death rates fell during the Industrial Revolution so did birth rates, but with a lag of some 75 years. Demographers have long recognized that it may have been the fall in death rates rather than increasing industrialization or the rise in income that produced the decline in birth rates.

This relationship seems to be borne out by current experience in the less developed countries where falling death rates related to the introduction of modern medicine (rather than industrialization) have also been followed by declining birth rates, with a time lag reduced to a quarter century. Birth rates are falling in less developed countries in which there are organized birth control campaigns as well as in countries in which there are not. Hagen notes that of forty-six less developed countries for which fairly complete and reliable birth rates and statistics are available, birth rates have fallen in all but four.

Second, we should recognize that the record in population forecasting is far from impressive and that the science of population forecasting is relatively new. The subject attracted little interest until the turn of the century. The interest in demography grew rapidly during the 1930s and 1940s but population forecasting did not really show marked improvement. Thus population forecasts in the interwar period foresaw declines in the following few decades whereas increases occurred. This is a qualitative error in forecasting the direction of the trend and not simply a quantitative error. It may be concluded that it is impossible to know with certainty and accuracy a country's population over the long-term future. And, of course, the MIT world models should not be seen as attempting to predict future population but to show possible consequences of present trends and relationships continuing without drastic change.

This is not to say that population growth is not of extreme importance or that we should not be concerned with the consequences of continuing rapid population growth. On the contrary, the evidence does suggest that growth is a critical problem.

The population growth rate has been increasing steadily in fact and the doubling time in years has already shortened from 175 in 1800, to 140 by 1900, to 85 by 1950, to 39 in 1960. The evidence is that population growth in the past has tended to be underpredicted rather than overpredicted. But given the difficulties in projecting populations it is unfortunate that the MIT group should have chosen to ignore in their world models one of the assumptions that in earlier studies enabled the world system to remain within its limits.

In *World Dynamics,* the Forrester book that sets forth the basic world simulation model, one model assumes crowding reduces the growth rate to zero before pollution, food shortages, and depletion overtake the planet. But this assumption is never considered in *The Limits to Growth* and instead pollution is less controlled and crowding is not explicitly considered. The effect of crowding on human populations is a topic of rapidly growing interest to sociologists, biologists, and other scientists. At present little is known and the consequences can be deduced only from experiments with animals. As noted earlier, the graphs in *The Limits to Growth* do not indicate the actual populations reached before collapse occurs, but they may well exceed the thresholds at which crowding begins to influence population growth.

nonrenewable resources

It is assumed that nonrenewable resources are used at rates which are growing exponentially, and it is stressed that one of the important characteristics of exponential growth is that it has a *doubling time.* For example, if the use of a resource has a growth rate of 5 percent, the doubling time is 14 years; that is, the amount of the resource needed doubles every 14 years. Hence, after 28 years, 4 times as much is needed and at 42 years, 8 times as much. But in analysis of the reserves of nonrenewable resources, current reserves are generally divided by current rates of use to derive a reserve index that is in reality a static reserves index. Given the exponential growth of resource use, the MIT group argues that what is really needed is an "exponential reserve index" as described in Chapter 3.

Consider chromium, a natural resource with one of the longest static indexes—420 years. However, if we take into account the fact that actual world consumption of chromium is increasing at a rate of 2.6 percent annually, then the exponential reserve index is just 95 years. If we assume that reserves yet undiscovered could increase present known reserves by a factor of five, then this fivefold increase would extend the lifetime of reserves only from 95 to 154 years, and even if it were possible from 1970 onward to recycle all the chromium brought into use so that none of the initial reserves were lost, the demand would still exceed the supply in 235 years.

The results look convincing, but a number of serious objections must be raised. There is a fundamental contrast between the doubling time with exponential growth and doubling the present known reserves or even increasing them fivefold. For example, even increasing chromium reserves to five times the present known world reserves over 154 years is equivalent to an annual rate of increase of less than 2 percent.

Any model that pits exponential growth of demand against a simple multiple of present size on the supply side must lead to overshoot and collapse. Exponential growth continued for long periods is so powerful that it can outstrip the universe, and it was for that reason that Kenneth Boulding was led to conclude that in the end all growth is limited and that exponential growth must become logistic growth. Again, there is a fundamental issue that in permitting resource use to grow exponentially but technology and resources to grow only by simple growth, the MIT group is underestimating the possibilities of continuous technical progress. If a technical progress component is inserted in the MIT model in sectors from which it is omitted, the effect is to indefinitely postpone the catastrophes that the model otherwise predicts. Such continuous technical progress is no less likely than a continuation of present technology. A forecast made in 1870 would have omitted the principal source of energy in 1970, oil, and the fastest growing new source of energy, nuclear power. It would probably have excluded not only all the synthetic materials, fibers, and rubbers but probably also aluminum and other metals. In any case the concept of reserves is a technoeconomic rather than a geophysical problem, as we saw in Chapter 3.

The model assumes that at current usage rates the earth has a 250-year-supply of minerals, and as a concession to optimists takes double and ten times that figure in a sensitivity test. A five-hundred-year supply at current rates will not avert a collapse, but a 2,500-year supply will do so, at least up until the year 2100, which is the horizon for the MIT forecasts. All will agree that the planet's deposits have limits. The question is: How near are we to them? Is 250 years the best figure or is it more like 2,500 years? The earth's crust varies in thickness from around 25 to 40 miles. The depth of present-day mines is measured in hundreds and very occasionally in thousands of feet. Oil wells are among the deepest holes being drilled and the deepest are generally around six or seven miles. What potentially useful minerals lie below this is unknown. And then there is sea water, which has been estimated to contain a one-billion-year supply of sodium chloride, magnesium, and bromine; a hundred-million-year supply of sulfur, borax, and potassium chloride; more than a million-year supply of molybdenum, uranium, tin, and cobalt; and more than a thousand-year

supply of nickel and copper. And then there are other minerals to be found on the seabed.

The immediate limits to the development of nonrenewable resources may come then not from nature but from man's economic and technological ability to exploit these resources. A large proportion of the earth's land mass has hardly been surveyed in any detail, as many recent discoveries of oil and natural gas indicate.

Processing technology too has improved. Veins of gold used to be worked by gravity separation and the waste put on one side. Then a new technology, mercury amalgam, was introduced that was economically capable of removing yet more gold; thus the waste became an ore again, was processed, and went back to being a waste. When another technology, the cyanide process, was developed, the waste once more became an ore.

Or consider the case of copper. In 1880 the lowest grade of copper ore that could be economically handled was around 3 percent. By 1906 it was 2.1 percent and is now almost 0.4 percent. We should remember the lessons learned in Chapter 19 from the Denison model about the important contribution of increasing output per unit of input in national economies as a whole.

pollution

This aspect of the model has drawn very wide attention because of growing concern with pollution and because historically pollution has attracted remedial governmental action only in the face of actual disaster or overwhelming intimation of disaster. A widely quoted example is the British Clean Air Act, which was initiated in the United Kingdom only after some 4,000 deaths were attributed to the London smog in 1952. But there is fear that such remedial action increases the risk of major disaster by removing early danger signals. Such risk is further increased by mankind's growing dependence on a single world technology. Increasing world specialization and interdependence has produced many rewards but carries great dangers, as shown by the lessons of biological evolution. Ecology is displacing economics as the dismal science, and the addition of the environmental component to the already Malthusian MIT world models makes them even more grim than the Malthusian predictions of overpopulation. The feedback loops and assumptions built into the model cause pollution to be the cause of global collapse in several of the model runs.

Let us look at the assumptions of the pollution model. Four main points are stressed by the MIT group:

1. The few kinds of pollution that actually have been measured over time seem to be increasing exponentially.
2. We have almost no knowledge about where the upper limits to these pollution growth curves may be.
3. The presence of natural delays in ecological processes increases the probability of underestimating the control measures necessary and, therefore, of inadvertently reaching those upper limits.

4. Many pollutants are globally distributed; their harmful effects appear long distances from their points of generation.

Data on the exponential increase in pollution are very limited and the MIT group must often be satisfied with data for only ten to twenty years. Even within this period the data are sparse. This reliance on the trends of a few years may not only lead to wrong conclusions but may precipitate hasty reaction—as in the case of substituting NTA for phosphates in detergent—or may generate a counterreaction against concern with pollution, thus discrediting legitimate concerns for resources and the environment. Furthermore, as Professor Forrester himself has stressed, the behavior of complex systems is counterintuitive, with short-run trends often quite different from long-run, so that great caution is needed before any conclusions are drawn and actions taken.

Examples are also restricted to a single class of pollutants in a single locality or region. It is not clear from these examples that one can make any global assumption of exponential growth for the aggregate pollution from all causes. Given our very inadequate knowledge of the rate at which pollution is increasing and of even the levels of pollution themselves, it is clear, as the MIT group themselves admit, that we are ignorant about the limits of the earth's ability to absorb pollution even though we can properly assume that there must exist an upper limit.

How then can this upper limit be set in the model? One answer is to begin by holding pollution levels at their present rate and using the feedback loops to determine the point at which they cause collapse.

Furthermore, the way in which and the rate at which increasing pollution is expected to operate is subject to serious criticism. It has been commented that the short-circuiting of long ecological chains to deduce the impact of increasing pollution on man's life span is an act of heroic extrapolation. The existence of DDT residues has been identified in lower animals and man but no data exist that demonstrate any lethal effects on man.

In summary then, although we cannot dispute the MIT assumption of finite upper limits to the ability of the environment to absorb pollution, we must question the assumption that pollution is directly and linearly associated with increasing industrial output and agriculture and that there is a direct relationship between low degrees of pollution and mortality rates.

Another real problem with the pollution subsystem is the attempt to extrapolate local effects to a global scale. Most disasters caused by material pollutants are likely to be local and to be caused by one pollutant or class of pollutants. Aggregating all pollutants and assuming that they behave in some composite way draws attention away from urgent and still solvable problems and diverts it into speculation about an imaginary race against time between "life" and "global asphyxiation."

food and arable land

Food supply causes collapse in the model of unlimited resources and pollution controls in *The Limits to Growth*. The circumstances are these. It is assumed that unlimited nuclear power will double the resource reserves that can be exploited and make extensive programs of recycling and substitution possible. It is further assumed that pollution generation per unit of industrial and agricultural output can be reduced to one fourth of its 1970 value. These changes allow population and industry to grow until the limit of arable land is reached. Food per capita then declines and industrial growth is also slowed as capital is diverted to food production. But food shortages still trigger collapse. Thus, food is a very serious constraint to growth. Indeed, it is with the example of arable land that the limits to exponential growth are introduced by the MIT group. For even if the total world supply of arable land could be maintained at its present level by compensating for the continual loss of arable land to urban and industrial uses, the agricultural land needed at present productivity level or at any multiple of it would grow exponentially, producing an imbalance between supply and demand of arable land.

The critical assumptions about arable land that trigger collapse are that the amount of potentially arable land is finite and that there are decreasing returns from agricultural inputs. However, more thorough and representative data on land development costs, and on historical trends in both land yields and agricultural inputs are needed to check this assumption. Also, there needs to be a clearer distinction between the physical limits and the political and economic limits to the production and distribution of the world's food. Hence the model could be improved through disaggregation, either between the advanced and the underdeveloped countries of the world, or between those where land is plentiful and those where it is scarce.

exponential versus logistic growth

The MIT approach is Malthusian. The authors write:

We are indeed Malthusians, at least in a broad, total-system sense. The World models express the idea of the earth's limits through four explicit assumptions: there is a finite stock of exploitable, non-renewable resources, there is a finite capacity for the environment to absorb pollutants, there is a finite amount of arable land, and there is a finite yield of food obtainable from each sector of arable land. ("A Response to Sussex," *Futures*, V, No. 1, 1973, 142)

While few would argue with the existence of such limits, the fundamental issue is the distinction between the exponential growth inherent in population and capital systems versus the incremental, nonexponential growth assumed for knowledge, technology, and resources. Here, the argument of the MIT group may sound persuasive.

Population and material capital grow exponentially by the very nature of the reproductive and productive processes. This is not an arbitrary assumption or merely an elegant mathematical invention, it is a fact that is amply demonstrated both by empirical evidence and by knowledge of underlying causes. New people can only be produced by other people, and machines and factories are needed to generate other machines and factories. Whenever the change in a quantity depends on the quantity itself, the change tends to be exponential in form. (*Futures,* V, 142)

No one should argue with this definitional quality of exponential growth, although a great deal depends on the actual exponents that are fitted to the growth trends and on whether one single exponent can be fitted for the whole world rather than applying distinct exponents for different world regions. The point at issue is whether it is reasonable to simulate global growth models applying exponential growth to population, to the demand for arable land, and to the demand for nonrenewable resources on the one hand while employing incremental, nonexponential growth for those processes and subsystems that must meet these growing world demands on the other hand.

The MIT group sees no inconsistency in these assumptions even though knowledge can lead to the accumulation of more knowledge.

It does not follow that any given technological application of that knowledge is inherently exponential. Discovery of oil is not in the long run made easier by the fact that certain fields of oil have already been discovered. The next increment of pollution abatement is not directly facilitated by the increment that went before. One doubling of land yield does not enhance the possibilities for the next doubling. (*Futures,* V, 142)

Here we observe the MIT group's fundamental belief in the law of entropy, which is similar in its effects (from their standpoint) to the law of diminishing returns. Fundamentally they discount the value of human ingenuity and human ability to innovate. They simply do not believe that the experience gained in the successful search for oil provides important geological clues that can directly facilitate the search for new oil fields. Nor do they believe that a technological breakthrough in one specific problem area leads to new applications in other areas. In essence, then, they are siding with the heroic view of development and innovation rather than the cumulative view.

Perhaps taken in isolation without significant regard to historical experience, their assumptions may seem as valid as any other. But historical experience suggests that exponential growth tends to become logistic growth. And there are biologists and social scientists who do believe that world population growth is better

explained as a sequence of logistic curves with each period of accelerating population growth triggered by some fundamental revolution in agriculture, industry, or science, rather than as a single exponential curve applying to all places at all times (as we noted in the discussion on the nature of the population growth curve in Chapter 2). A case *can* be made for alternative assumptions and if they are built into the model, quite different results are obtained.

alternative assumptions and different results

Professor Robert Boyd, a zoologist at the University of California, has shown how sensitive *The Limits to Growth* simulation models are to the assumptions by rerunning the models with a new set of assumptions that reflect the technological-optimist view. This involves adding a new variable—technology—and multipliers to express the effect of technology on other variables. Two birth rate multipliers in the original model also are altered. The new technology assumptions that Boyd makes are: increasing capital investment accelerates technological growth to an asymptote (Fig. 25.33a); if the quality of life declines, society will increase investment in technology (Fig. 25.33b); a sixfold increase in technology over the 1970 level increases the food ratio by a factor of eight (Fig. 25.33c); and a fourfold increase in technology over the 1970 level decreases to zero both natural resource input and pollution output per unit of material standard of living (Fig. 25.33d). Boyd also changes the birth rate multiplier with increasing standard of living from 0.7 to 0.4 and with increasing food supply from a doubling of birth rates with a fourfold increase in food supply to no change.

The results of the new assumptions are that technology increases productivity, which, in turn, increases the standard of living. This eventually drives birth rates down to a "Utopian" steady state (Fig. 25.34).

Boyd concludes:

Forrester's model fails the test. It is completely unable to resolve the technological optimist-Malthusian controversy. In fact the output of the model under each of the different sets of assumptions is the same as was reached without the use of a computer. Thus, the world dynamics simulation is far from useful as a policy tool and, even within his own framework, Forrester was unjustified in making such strong policy recommendations. ("World Dynamics: A Note," *Science,* 177, August 11, 1972, 518)

policy implications of growth analysis

Analysis of world population and resources inevitably carries with it sociopolitical policy implications. Malthus, for example, was driven by his predictions to conclude that it would be of little value to achieve a more equal distribution of production. He felt that the benefits accruing to a society in which a privileged

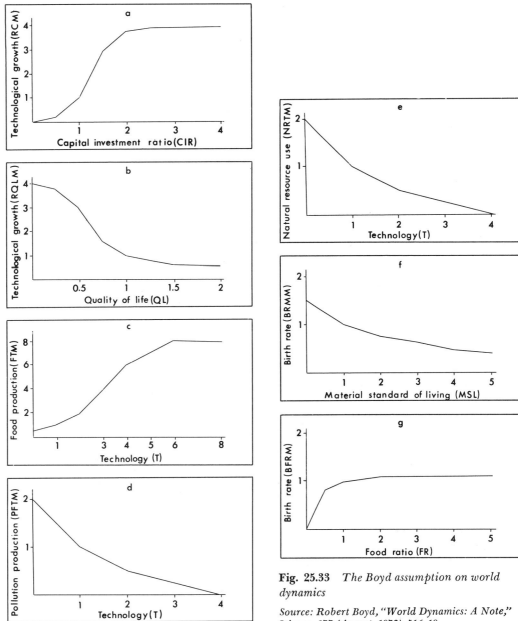

Fig. 25.33 *The Boyd assumption on world dynamics*

Source: *Robert Boyd, "World Dynamics: A Note,"* Science, *177 (August, 1972), 516–19.*

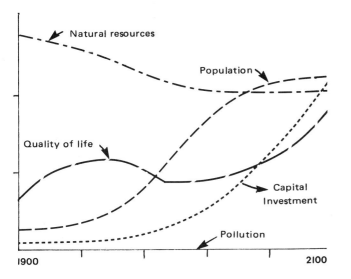

few had the necessary leisure to accomplish progress in the arts and sciences outweighed the disadvantage to the underprivileged many. Malthus was therefore opposed to income maintenance of the poor because it would increase the pressure of population. According to Beales:

The Essay on Population was a godsend to the conservative and frightened people who feared the spread in England of French revolutionary ideas and behaviour. . . . He had driven such proposals as that of Whitbred (1796) for a national minimum wage out of the arena of significant discus-

Fig. 25.34 *Boyd's technological-optimist world model. A new variable, technology, is added and two of the birth rate multipliers are changed from the MIT World Models.*

Source: *Boyd, "World Dynamics."*

sion; he had made impossible such safety-valve flirtations with sentimentalism as Pitt's Poor Law reform project (1796). (Quoted in K. L. R. Pavitt, "Malthus and Other Economists," *Futures*, V, No. 2, April 1973, 162–163)

Some may draw similar conclusions about the wisdom of narrowing the income gap between the rich and poor countries from reading *The Limits to Growth*. Other conclusions, also damaging to the economic development of poor countries, may also be drawn from this study. For example, the MIT group notes that at the present time only the developed nations of the world are seriously concerned about pollution but that many types of pollution eventually became widely distributed around the world. The implication is that heartland countries must try to control pollution in the world hinterland. Already the concern for the environment in the rich countries has resulted in restrictions on the kind of technology supplied to less developed countries. There are reports that United States aid agencies will bar shipments of pesticides that are subject to domestic regulations in the USA. It may become difficult to obtain DDT even where there is no better alternative. It may justify similar restrictions on some imports from low-income countries. In 1969, the Peruvian and Philippine tuna fishing industries were struck crippling blows by the revision of United States standards on mercury content of tuna fish. And it may lead to the reduction of foreign aid because it will be argued that given physical limits, aid is useless and that the money could be better spent cleaning up the environment at home.

Thus the establishment of what Peccei, founder of the Club of Rome, calls a World Forum of experts (representing the United States, Europe, the Soviet Union, and Japan) to serve as a guidance mechanism for central planetary management raises a fundamentally important issue for the future of world order. Can the technologically advanced "few" of this world develop viable and just community relationships with the technologically less advanced "many"? As Wilfred Beckerman has warned:

If we are concerned with the population as a whole, we need to be sure that we are not attributing to the population as a whole a system of preferences that is, in fact, owned only by a minority. *(Futures, V, 1974).*

Thus the underdeveloped countries may believe that increased pollution, particularly in the short run, is a price worth paying for accelerated economic development. From their standpoint, the Club of Rome has failed to distinguish between the general interests of the bulk of the world's population and the narrower interests of a specific, materially well-off group. Thus, at a time when the underdeveloped countries are struggling to free themselves from economic colonialism, they see a threat from the world heartland countries of ecological colonialism. Coupled with this is a danger

that the debate about world resources, limits to growth, and pollution may displace discussion about the economic, political, and moral problems of distributing the world's resources in a more equitable way. It therefore seems unlikely that any "world forum" created and run by the heartland countries would take proper account of the differences between the problems of the rich countries and the poor; nor would it attempt to change the present global heartland-hinterland dependencies and accompanying disparities or accept that the underdeveloped countries should follow their separate pathways of growth free from external political, economic, or ecological controls.

It is not clear that *The Limits to Growth* has adequately encompassed other problems and questions that should be of central concern to any world forum for the management of global developments. Among these are the maldistribution of the resources devoted to research and development. Half the world's research and development activities are devoted to military and prestige objectives. Less than 2 percent of this effort is devoted to the urgent agricultural, environmental, and industrial problems of the developing countries. We need to allocate more of our research and development funds to discover how to increase food production progressively while preventing the runoff of chemical fertilizers from the soil into our bodies of water. We must learn how to recycle our waste products more efficiently and more completely. We need to learn how to utilize solar energy—the ultimate source of all energy on the earth—more efficiently and cheaply. We need to learn how to cope with the disposal of radioactive nuclear wastes and how to solve the problems of heat accumulation caused by the use of energy. We also must learn how to reduce birth rates. The questions that we must ask then are: How can economic resources, at present being mobilized in rich countries for armaments, be diverted to the problems of the underdeveloped countries? Will a natural resource shortage (real or imagined) increase the temptation for more imperialism or even for war? If the shortage is real, will the rich countries use up the cheap, available stocks and make the problems of the underdeveloped countries that much more difficult? If the shortage is imaginary, will the advanced countries nevertheless accelerate recycling and substitution technologies and thereby turn the terms of trade even more against the poor countries? And if the Club of Rome's proposal for a World Forum is not acceptable, how can the divergent sociopolitical forms that control modern economic systems be welded into a global management system that takes fuller account of the diversity of the world's hopes and aspirations for growth and development, and of the risks and opportunities of our uncertain environment? The challenge is imposing, and it is unlikely to be met unless we take full account of the present spatial organization and geographical problems of the world's economic systems.

RECOMMENDED READINGS

Bertalanffy, Ludwig von, *General System Theory: Foundations, Development, Applications.* New York: Braziller, 1968.

Boulding, Kenneth E., "Toward a General Theory of Growth," *General Systems,* 1 (1956), 66-75.

Clark, W. E. Le Gros, and P. B. Medawar, *Essays on Growth and Form Presented to D'Arcy Wentworth Thompson.* Oxford: Clarendon, 1945.

Freeman, Christopher, "Malthus with a Computer," *Futures,* V, No. 1 (February 1973, Special Issue: "The Limits to Growth Controversy").

Gould, Stephen Jay, "Allometry and Size in Ontogeny and Phylogeny," *Biological Reviews,* 41 (1966), 587-640.

Harvey, David, *Explanation in Geography.* New York: St. Martin's, 1969. See Chapter 23, "Systems," pp. 447–80.

Jahoda, Marie et al., eds., *Thinking about the Future: A Critique of Limits to Growth.* London: Chato & Windus, Ltd., 1973.

Meadows, Donella H., Dennis L. Meadows, Jørgen Randers, and William W. Behrens III, *The Limits to Growth: A Report for the Club of Rome's Project on the Predicament of Mankind.* New York: Universe Books, 1972.

Miller, James C., *The Nature of Living Systems and Living Systems: The Organization.* Reprinted in modified form from *Behavioural Science,* 16, No. 1 (January 1972), 1-182.

Myrdal, Gunnar, *Rich Lands and Poor: The Road to World Prosperity.* New York: Harper, 1957.

Naroll, Raoul S., and Ludwig von Bertalanffy, "The Principle of Allometry in Biology and Social Sciences," *General Systems,* 6 (1956), 76-89.

index